Economics for Eastern Africa

STUDIES IN THE ECONOMICS OF AFRICA

Economics for Eastern Africa

I. LIVINGSTONE

Professor of Development Economics,
University of East Anglia

H. W. ORD

Formerly Senior Lecturer in Economics,
Centre of African Studies University of Edinburgh

HEINEMANN

NAIROBI   LONDON

Heinemann Educational Books (East Africa) Ltd
4th Floor, International House, Mama Ngina Street
P.O. Box 45314, Nairobi, Kenya

Heinemann Educational Books Ltd
22 Bedford Square, London WC1B 3HH

EDINBURGH MELBOURNE AUCKLAND HONG KONG
SINGAPORE KUALA LUMPUR NEW DELHI IBADAN
KINGSTON PORT OF SPAIN

Heinemann Educational Books Inc.
4 Front Street, Exeter, New Hampshire 03833, USA

ISBN 0 435 97400 9

First published 1968
Revised and Enlarged Edition first published 1980

Set in 10/11 pt Monophoto Times by Interprint Limited, Malta
Printed in Great Britain by Spottiswoode Ballantyne Ltd, Colchester and London

To the Memory of Henry W. Ord

Summary Contents

Detailed Table of Contents

More advanced sections are marked by an asterisk in the table of contents and are indicated in the text by a line down the left- or right-hand margin.

List of Tables

List of Figures

Preface to First Edition

This note is addressed primarily to the teachers who will make use of this book. The present text aims at providing a basis for a two-year course leading to the GCE 'A-level' in Economics or for a first-year university course. A large proportion of students following either of these courses will not subsequently be pursuing the subject; for others such a course must provide a foundation, a jumping-off point, for further specialization in the field. Fortunately the requirements of the two groups would seem to coincide. They each can do with a basic knowledge of the structure of the East African economy in which they live, seen as a whole, and its various sectors, including a fairly comprehensive coverage of the important economic institutions within it, such as marketing boards, trade unions, cooperatives, central banks, and, of course, government.

And, in order to understand broadly how these function, students need to be equipped with elementary economic theory. In this area we have tried to be as economical as possible, and have thought a great deal about the problem of which aspects of economic theory are most useful in the context of the East African situation. This means we have selected our concepts and have sought modifications of standard textbook theory where necessary. For example, the concepts of opportunity-cost and time preference are given stress, keeping in mind their importance in planning and allocation of resources in a developing country.

In the field of international trade the orthodox comparative cost theory is presented, but there is discussion of its appropriateness in relation to developing countries. Keynesian multiplier analysis is modified to apply outside the underemployment situation. In the theory of the firm, dynamic aspects relating to growth and development of firms have been brought out, and less emphasis has been given to the static pricing problem under monopoly and competition. The problem of developing countries is not only to make existing firms work more effectively but also to encourage more firms to supply more capital and enterprise.

The basic approach followed has been one involving as close an integration of theoretical and applied economics as we could get, the theory being applied in doses as it became needed. In the applied sections we have tried where possible first to present economic facts, in statistical form, and then to analyse and explain them: an ancient, but sometimes lost, tradition.

It might be questioned whether the same volume can be useful at two levels, in school and at university. This is a problem facing all Economics books pitched at this level, since it is only comparatively recently that Economics has been taught as a school subject on any scale, so that the question of overlap is new. It should be remembered, however, that 'A-level' students will have two years in which to cover the contents, and more intensive tuition. We are aware that the text is highly condensed, particularly in its theoretical parts, and that it will require some effort on the part of school teachers to guide their students through it.

The authors are responsible for a companion volume to this one, *An Introduction to Economics for West Africa* (forthcoming) which has the same structure but includes instead applied material relating especially to the economies of Nigeria, Ghana, and Sierra Leone.

August 1967

H. W. Ord
I. Livingstone

Preface to Second Edition

Economics for Eastern Africa, like a number of other introductory texts, is designed to serve a double role as an 'A-level' text and, used more intensively, as the basis of a first-year university course. With its appropriately agricultural flavour, it has also been widely used for the teaching of Economics in agricultural faculties and institutes.

This second edition is considerably larger than the first, and not only because it has been expanded to incorporate material relating to additional countries in Eastern Africa. The volume now covers the whole of the new 'A-level' syllabus prescribed by the East African Examinations Council, incorporating a considerable amount of elementary development economics as well as the economic theory.

While the first edition was produced within the strait-jacket of a syllabus set in the United Kingdom, in the new edition the authors have felt themselves free to choose and organize material which they themselves think can and should be taught within a first-year university course. As before we recognize that the average 'A-level' candidate will not be able to reach the analytical depth that can be expected of a good first-year university student. Accordingly sections which require this depth of analysis or thought are marked by a line down the left-hand margin, as shown alongside the present paragraph, indicating that they may be omitted by schools. The whole of Chapter 10 is made optional. In addition some purely descriptive sections have been marked as optional, where the amount of detailed information provided may exceed the requirements of some readers. Further selection from among the more advanced sections, some of which may be considered specialized, may be made, but this is left to the discretion of individual teachers. Readers primarily interested in the applied economics of Eastern Africa may omit Parts II, IV, V, and part of VII.

Teachers who are used to Western textbooks such as Samuelson, Hanson, or Lipsey will be struck by the re-ordering of the topics in the present text. We have again introduced the economic theory in doses, and have moved to applications of the theory as soon as enough has been covered to deal adequately with an applied topic. Part III, Agriculture and Marketing, applies the analysis of Demand, Supply, and Price in Part II. Discussion of issues in industrial development policy follows the analysis of the operation of the international economic system and international trade in Part V. The section on the decisions of the firm (Part IV) is not given the same prominence as in the ordinary Western text, since these appear not quite as important alongside a discussion of broad issues of development policy.

It may also be questioned whether this amount of development economics is appropriately taught in the first year of an Economics course. However in our view the widespread practice in African universities of teaching a standard 'Lipsey' type of course in Year 1 and a Development Economics course in Year 2 is wrong. Development Economics, or analysis of factors affecting the economic progress of nations, must be introduced right away if African students are to be made to feel immediately that the subject deals directly with the main problems of their own economies. If some of economic theory is not dealt with in sufficient depth in this text this can be reinforced by hard teaching in Economic Theory in Year 2. Having received a broad introduction to the problems of developing countries in Year 1, students will be more able to see how the additional economic theory which they receive subsequently applies to these problems. The text does in fact cover most of the analytical 'tools' in Samuelson or Lipsey which are deemed appropriate, but in seeking relevance throughout we have always preferred to apply a technique to a live issue in developing countries or in Eastern Africa specifically rather than to adopt the applications more usual in Western texts. For example the analysis of isoquants leads to discussion of choice of technique and 'appropriate' technology.

The new edition should be even more suited to use as an Economics text for agricultural students, having now five full chapters allocated to the discussion of agriculture and marketing in Eastern Africa. Chapter 9 includes analysis of the economics of subsistence agriculture and of economies of scale in farming, while Chapter 10 discusses in some detail specialist agricultural topics such as the supply responses of peasant farmers, rural stratification and land tenure, agricultural extension, the economics of agricultural mechanization, cooperative and state farming, and the economics of pastoral societies. In addition the theory of decision-making in the firm is treated with the farm as the 'firm', using an elementary linear programming approach.

Finally, for students not planning to pursue their study of economics beyond the level of this text it is hoped this volume will cover, at an introductory level, as much analysis of the structure and development of their economies as they can expect to have in one year at university or over a two-year 'A-level' course.

It should be noted that the percentages in the many statistical tables will frequently not add up exactly to 100 due to rounding.

Our thanks for the patient and efficient typing of a substantial part of the greatly expanded manuscript of this second edition go to Mrs Lynda Morgan of the Economics Department at the University of Newcastle upon Tyne.

I. Livingstone
H. W. Ord

Part I Income and how it is obtained

1 National Income and the Standard of Living

Introduction: what economics is about

Economics deals with the material well-being of people. People derive this material well-being from the flow of goods and services available for their use, which are produced in the country during the year. It is this flow, which we can call the national income or output, that economists are interested in increasing.

It does not follow that economists are materialists! There are many other things, certainly more important than material goods, that contribute to human welfare, but there are other experts who study these. Moreover, many of these other aspects of life cannot be enjoyed without a basic level of material well-being. In the poor countries of the world large numbers of the population suffer from malnutrition or are afflicted by disease; a relatively small proportion have been able to receive basic education, and death rates are so high that people may not expect to live more than half the normal life span in the developed economies. Even in developed countries there remains considerable poverty among large sections of the population: here also it is still important to raise the level of incomes.

Apart from the level of national income, economists are interested in its distribution among the citizens of the country. Some countries may reveal a high average income per head if we divide aggregate national income by the total population, but if a large share of total income is distributed to a small fraction of the population then the actual standard of living available to the great mass of the people may be much lower.

Economists are also interested in the distribution of income over time. Peasant farmers may do very well for several years and yet be threatened with famine and starvation the following year. Highly skilled workers in industrial societies earning high incomes may suddenly find themselves unemployed if the country is struck by economic depression. Material well-being is clearly enhanced if output and incomes can be stabilized at least so that the most extreme variations are eliminated.

Economics is therefore concerned with the production of income in the form of goods and services, with its distribution among individuals, groups, or countries, with the stability of production, and with a whole range of diverse factors and influences that impinge directly on these things. These include for example the banking system and the system of taxation; but all kinds of social and political factors, even religious attitudes, influence economic life. It is difficult to say where the economist's interest may end and therefore difficult to define the subject matter of economics more precisely than we have already done. Since it may be a good thing anyway not to divide knowledge into compartments, this will not be a serious matter.

The definition of national income

The outcome of the productive process of the country, and of the varied economic activities that go on, is a *flow* of goods and services. Broadly speaking, this flow is the national income of the country. Now if economics is concerned with the production, distribution, and stability of national income, we can only assess the effectiveness of economic policy if we know what is happening to national income, that is, if we can measure it. That will be the first problem for us to consider.

We can note first of all that national income, a flow, is measured per unit of time, usually one year.

Secondly the flow of real income includes services, as well as goods. Services, whether the services of clerks, of hairdressers, or of singers, may give satisfaction to consumers just as much as physical commodities.

Thirdly, although money value is the only common denominator which enables us to add up the diverse collection of goods and services which go to make up income—bowls of rice, tins of milk, rides in taxis—our concern is with the 'real' things: what money will buy, not with money itself. Thus national income is a measure of the money value of goods and services which arise from the productive activities of the nation in any one year. Since it is not possible to measure the satisfaction of wants directly, the prices buyers are willing to pay and the amounts purchased have to be taken to measure real income.

We should note, fourthly, that national income, the flow of produce available, is the same thing as national product, the flow produced. If we think of one man alone on a desert island as a nation, as Robinson Crusoe was (before Man Friday appeared), it is clear that he can only consume as income what he has himself produced. Similarly the point is clear in respect of subsistence output in developing countries, that is, output which is directly consumed by those who produce it, and which may form 30 or 40 per cent, or even more, of total output. Clearly, however, nothing has changed if a group of people, even a nation, produce different things and exchange them among themselves. Whatever they have produced, and no more, will be available to them as a group as income.

Lastly, we must take account of *depreciation*, the 'wear and tear' in capital equipment used to produce the output. If no steps are taken to maintain intact the productive capacity of the nation's *stock* of capital equipment, the flow of goods and services will eventually decline. Thus the true net income or product does not include all final goods and services made available during the year but only that part which is net of depreciation. As it happens, there are tremendous difficulties in estimating the value of capital stock at one point of time, let alone the change in that value over one year due to depreciation or 'consumption of capital', as it is sometimes called. Therefore, though a figure for depreciation is generally calculated, it is more common, especially in less developed countries, to use gross national product or income rather than the net national income, the amount one should deduct for depreciation being very uncertain.

Three approaches to measurement

Each time something is produced and sold we can say:

(1) Its value is equal to purchasers' expenditure on it.

(2) The same sum will be received as income by the various people who contributed at some stage to its production.

(3) The value of the item which is sold will have come about as a result of the 'value added' to the product by successive stages of production: for example, farmers may produce grain, millers will turn it into flour, merchants and transporters will bring it to the consumers. The millers 'add value' to the grain produced by the farmers and the merchants and transporters add value to the flour by bringing it to the reach of consumers.

If, therefore, we wish to calculate the total money value of goods and services produced and sold during the year, in theory, we can do it in any one of three ways:

(1) We can add up market expenditure by final consumers, including purchase of capital goods by firms.

(2) We can add up all the incomes received by the different individuals who have contributed to output.

(3) We can find out the value of each firm's contribution to output, the 'value added' or net output of that firm, and sum for all firms.

The expenditure method, income method, and net output method are three ways of deriving the same total. We can therefore say that national product or output, national income, and national expenditure are necessarily equal, in that they refer to the same total. They are not equal in the sense of algebra, *they are the same thing.* We can express this as

$$O \equiv Y \equiv E$$

where '$\equiv$' is not an ordinary equality sign but is an identity sign meaning that O is Y is E, the different names relating merely to the way in which the data are collected.

The circular flow of income and expenditure

To understand this clearly it is useful to see income and expenditure as a circular flow. This is illustrated in Figure 1.1 which represents a simple economy in which there are only households or 'consuming units' on the one hand, and firms or 'producing units' on the other. The 'household sector' and the 'production sector' are indicated by two boxes: the interrelationships between them are shown by arrows. The dotted lines represent flows of output and of factor services. Thus households supply factor services to firms (arrow 3) and consume the output of goods and services supplied by firms (arrow 2).

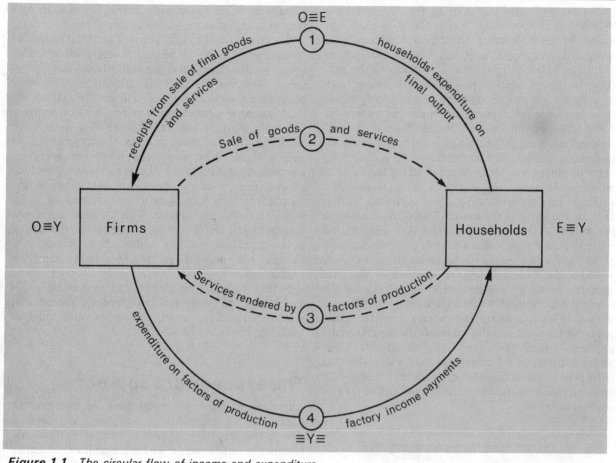

Figure 1.1 *The circular flow of income and expenditure.*

The other lines represent the financial flows corresponding to this exchange. Arrow 1 indicates that receipts by firms from the sale of goods and services sold to households are equal to what households spend on them. The value of the goods and services supplied can be called the value of the 'national product', O, and, being given by firms' receipts (=output sold *times* average price), equals households' expenditure, E. Thus $O \equiv E$.

In producing these goods and services firms employ the services of factors of production. Whatever they spend on factor services goes to the owners of factors of production (households) as wages, interest, rent, and profits: this flow, factor income payments, is denoted as Y. The whole of the receipts of firms must go out again as factor income payments, since whatever is not paid out as wages, interest, or rent must count as profits (even retained profits of firms which are not distributed to individuals may be considered to 'belong' to someone and thus to be a factor income payment). Thus, as indicated on the left-hand side of the diagram, $O \equiv Y$.

Finally, *if we assume households do not save out of their incomes,*[1] then expenditures by households (whether they receive their incomes as wages or profits or whatever) equals what they obtain as factor income payments, that is, $E = Y$. It follows, therefore, that $E \equiv Y \equiv O$.

Where would 'subsistence production' fit into this circular flow? In this case the same family is the producing unit and the consuming unit. They will appear both in the households' box and in the firms' box. They can therefore be regarded from the expenditure point of view as 'spending' on their own output and from the income point of view as receiving income from themselves as a 'firm' for supplying factor services used in producing this output.

The product (net output) approach

The most direct method of calculating the value of national output is, of course, to add together the values of the contributions of all the individual enterprises in the economy. 'Value added' is the value added by each industry to the raw materials or processed products that it has bought from other industries before passing on the products to the next stage in the production process. For example, suppose we have a simple economy in which only maize flour is consumed: farmers sell maize to millers for 1,000 shillings; millers sell maize flour to trader-transporters for 1,300 shillings; and traders sell flour to final consumers for 1,500 shillings. To get the total value of output we cannot simply add up the value of all these transactions to obtain a total of 3,800 shillings: this would involve *double-counting*. This is because the value of the maize (1,000/-) is included in the value of the maize flour (1,300/-) delivered to traders, and in the value of retail sales maize flow (1,500/-). We can regard the maize as an *intermediate product* which contributes to the value of the final product. Since we are interested in calculating the total of final output we should count only the *net* output of each industry subtracting from the gross value of production the cost of the intermediate products which have gone into making it. Value added is therefore a firm's total revenue less what has been paid to other firms for commodities supplied or services rendered. In our example the net output of each industry is:

industry of origin	net output
farming	1,000
milling	300
trading	200
national output	1,500 shillings

This is the total of final products. Final products will include capital goods as well as consumer goods since, while intermediate goods are used up during the period in producing other goods, capital goods are not used up (apart from 'wear and tear' or depreciation) during the period, and may be thought of as consumer goods 'stored up' for future periods. Final output will include *subsistence output*, which is simply the output produced and consumed by households themselves. One difficulty is to find prices at which to value this output. The amounts above were all at market prices: but subsistence output is not sold on the market. There are different prices at which it might be valued. Should we value maize consumed by the farmers at the price at which they could sell it (to millers)? Or at the price at which other final consumers buy it, including the cost of

transport? Some assumption has to be made to deal with this, but it is inevitably rather arbitrary.

We must also take into account the final output of government, which provides services such as education, medical care, and general administrative services. However, since state education and other government services are not sold on the market, we shall not have market prices at which to value them. The only obvious means of doing this is to value public services at what it costs the government to supply them, that is, by the wage bill spent on teachers, doctors, and the like (we should not include expenditure on school books or medicines, as the output of these will already be counted as value added in other industries). This is also rather unsatisfactory: if teachers' salaries are raised, the output of the education 'industry' will be shown to rise, even though the number of teachers and pupils is unchanged.

Finally we must remember that part of output is exported, to be consumed by consumers abroad: that is also part of the country's output, and must be included.

The expenditure approach

Alternatively the same total may be obtained by adding up all expenditures on goods and services during the year. This approach centres on the components of final demand which generates production. As a first step we can represent this by the identity,

$$E \equiv C + G + I + X$$

the right-hand side implying that nationals may receive their income through expenditure by private consumers (C), through expenditure by firms on capital goods produced (investment, I), through expenditure by the government (government consumption, G) and through the expenditure of overseas buyers (exports, X).

If we return to our maize example, we said the total value of all the transactions was 3,800 shillings. This however does *not* measure the value of goods which the economy is producing: all that emerges from the productive process is 1,500 shillings' worth of maize flour which consumers can purchase. The maize is an intermediate output already 'embodied' in the maize flour, and must not be counted twice. It follows that in our expenditure approach we must count only *expenditure on final product*: the expenditure on all goods and services which are not used up in the production of some other good or service. We must also count as part of consumption a farmer's 'expenditure' on his own output (subsistence output), even if he does not actually pay himself any money.

G refers to what is called *public consumption* expenditure, though strictly speaking, the government is the producer, not the consumer of these goods and services, which are consumed by the public. The major items are health, education, general administration, law and order, and defence, which the government makes available to the public. In providing these services the government spends its income (mainly tax revenues) on the wages of doctors, teachers, policemen, and others, as well as on various goods. These expenditures are taken to measure the value of the services provided by the central or local governments and other public authorities.[2] Expenditure by the government on capital goods such as roads and buildings is usually included under 'I'.

International trade complicates the calculation. Obviously we must include exports, since these are part of the economy's output and provide producers with income. But if exports create income at home, imports create income in a similar way for overseas suppliers, not residents of the home country. It follows that in the equation above either C, I, or G must be restricted to expenditure on *home-produced goods*: for instance, C would exclude expenditure on *imported* consumer goods and I would exclude purchases of machinery from abroad; or if C, G, and I are used to refer to total consumption expenditure, and so on, then we should write

$$Y \equiv (C + G + I + X) - M$$

or, as total final expenditure less imports,

$$Y \equiv E - M$$

We can explain this another way. If exports exceed imports in a particular year, the country will earn more foreign currency than it spends: it will be accumulating claims against foreign countries. These claims could be used to acquire consumption goods in the future. An export surplus is therefore a form of *investment*. We could thus distinguish I_h, investment *at home*, i.e. *domestic* capital formation, and $I_f (= X - M)$, foreign investment abroad. Our identity then becomes

$$Y \equiv C + G + I_h + (X - M)$$
$$Y \equiv C + G + I_h + I_f.$$

It may be noted again that X is not part of expenditure by residents of the country concerned, though it is expenditure (by foreigners) on national production. National production is what the nation produces, and equals expenditure on national production, *not* expenditure by nationals.

Expenditures which should not be included in our summation are expenditures on second-hand goods and expenditures on financial assets such as the purchase of bonds and shares. In both cases no fresh output is involved. If, for instance, X sells his second-hand car to Y, the same consumer durable is simply transferred from the ownership of one person to that of another. If X sells his shares in a particular company, and Y buys them, only a financial asset changes hands, a title to part-ownership of the company's physical assets: there will be no change in the latter.

The income approach

As we said above, each time something is produced and sold, someone obtains income from producing it. More precisely, each unit of expenditure will find its way partly into wages and salaries, and partly into profits, interest, or rents. It follows that if we add up all incomes we should get the value of total expenditure, or output.

One important qualification must be made. While we have said that services, like those of musicians, may be just as important in consumers' eyes as physical goods like bread, some people receive incomes without supplying either goods or services in the course of the year: these include the unemployed, who may receive benefits under a state insurance scheme; the sick, who may get sick benefits; old age pensioners; recipients of famine relief; and students who obtain grants. These payments are known as transfer income or *transfer payments*. Clearly these must be excluded from the calculation of the national income by the income approach, or there would be double-counting. Incomes are taken from those who can afford it, through taxation, and 'transferred' to the recipients; but they can be spent only once. We have, in fact, only a *transfer of purchasing power*.

Since we are calculating the value of output, we must only count incomes received by providing output. The test for inclusion in the national income calculation is therefore that there should be a 'quid pro quo', that the money should have been paid *against the exchange of a good or service*. Alternatively we can say that there should be a 'real' flow in the opposite direction to the money flow. If there is no quid pro quo it is an unrequited gift or transfer payment and should not be included. This is in part a question of what is defined as being output, which may be arbitrary. For example, students may study hard, but this is usually not regarded as part of the nation's output by national income statisticians. Accordingly, the grant they receive is regarded as a transfer payment. Yet it can be argued that training of students who will as a result become doctors, architects, or engineers, say, is an important act of *investment* by the nation, and that this work should therefore be counted. Transfer payments, since they are not the counterpart of some addition to current output, are in effect *transfers of purchasing power*. To take another example: suppose a schoolmaster earns 30,000 shillings, pays a domestic servant 4,000 shillings, and gives his mother an allowance of 2,000 shillings. The income of the household which must be taken for the purposes of assessing national income is 34,000 shillings: the schoolmaster contributes 30,000 from his work as a teacher, while 4,000 represents the work done by a domestic servant. The allowance of 2,000 shillings is received by the mother as a gift, not for any services rendered. Suppose however the schoolmaster dismisses the domestic servant and does his own housework, while his mother takes charge of the cooking: national income would fall by 4,000 shillings, simply because work done for oneself or a relative in the home is excluded from the national output total (though not necessarily subsistence output, as we have seen!).

Transfer payments have their counterpart on the expenditure side. We must not count the schoolteacher's expenditure on his mother's allowance, and in calculating G, public consumption expenditure, for instance, we count only *income-generating* expenditures by the government: not expenditures, for example, on students' bursaries, which are simply transfers of purchasing power through the tax system or, similarly, interest on the Public Debt.

As with the product and expenditure approaches we must include income 'obtained' from subsistence output. This is the opposite case from transfer payments since there is a flow of real goods and services, but no corresponding *money* flow. It becomes necessary to 'impute' values for the income received which is of course the same problem as finding appropriate prices at which such output should be valued. Similarly workers may, in addition to cash income, receive income in kind: if employees are provided with rent-free housing, the rent which they would have to pay for these houses on the open market should in principle be imputed as part of their income from employment.

The incomes we have referred to so far have been the *personal incomes* of individuals only: but not all incomes created during the year may accrue to persons or households. Business enterprises generally retain part of their profits to meet future commitments, including investment, rather than distribute them to shareholders as dividends. These profits 'belong' to shareholders, the owners of the company, even though they cannot actually get their hands on them. Publicly owned enterprises may also make such profits or surpluses: we should include as income profits of electricity undertakings, surpluses of marketing boards, and also rents obtained from land and buildings owned by public authorities. Wages of employees in nationalized undertakings or in the civil service will of course already have been counted under income of private individuals.

If we ignore taxation and other transfer payments between the private sector and public authorities, we can define *public income* as the retained profits of publicly owned enterprises and the property income (rents and interest) of the government (central and local authorities). All other income received by either (a) persons or households from employment (wages and salaries) or from property (rents, interest, and dividends) which together comprise *personal income*, or by (b) privately owned business enterprises, in the form of *retained* earnings, is *private income*. However, just as the consumer outlays of an individual need not be matched by his income if he receives gifts from relatives, so the total *personal consumption* of all households and the total *public consumption* of all public authorities need not be balanced by personal and public income. Households receive transfer payment, which are very substantial in developed countries with old age pensions and other state social security schemes.

However, in looking at the distribution of total national income, these transfer payments are excluded: they are 'netted out' to a zero sum. The main distinction is between 'wages and salaries', the remuneration or 'compensation', as it is called, of employees, and the 'gross operating surplus' (from which rents, interest, and dividends will be paid and profits retained for depreciation and net saving) earned by all kinds of enterprise and property-owners, including self-employed workers and public authorities. Tanzania distinguishes between 'compensation of employees' (3,574 million shillings in 1972) and 'operating surplus including income of self-employed' (5,854 million shillings in 1972), yielding a national income, net of depreciation, of 9,428 million shillings[3] divided into what may be called 'wages' and 'profits'.

When we switch from looking at the contribution to output made by the two broad categories of 'labour' and 'business enterprise' to what determines the level of different kinds of spending, then we must take account of transfer payments, however. Consumer spending depends on *personal disposable income*, which is what people actually 'have to spend': personal income *plus* transfers from the government *less* direct taxation. *Government disposable income* is equal to any property income and total tax revenue less transfers paid out. This leaves the rest of national income to be disposed of as *gross business saving* (*after tax*), including the retained profits of publicly owned enterprises. In other words personal disposable income is national income *less* taxes and *less* gross business saving but *plus* transfer payments. We shall see in a later chapter that the level of national income depends on these spending decisions.

The algebraic equivalence of the three methods

The three approaches, as we have said, must yield in principle the same results. This can also be shown algebraically. Firms' sales receipts (R) can be broken down into expenditures on final output (E_f) and expenditures on intermediate output (E_m)—expenditures on services and processed or unprocessed materials supplied by other firms for use in production. Thus

$$R \equiv E_f + E_m \qquad (1.1)$$

These receipts are used by firms partly to pay for intermediate inputs used and partly to pay for factor services rendered, so that

$$R \equiv E_m + w + i + r + p \qquad (1.2)$$

where w, i, r, p represent wages, interest, rent, and profits respectively (p may be negative).

Suppose some particular firm, Firm 1, has receipts equal to R_1 and spends E_{m1} on intermediate product. The 'value added' by the firm will be $(R_1 - E_{m1})$. That for Firm 2 could be denoted as $(R_2 - E_{m2})$ and so on. For any Firm i it would be $(R_i - E_{mi})$ where i goes from 1 to n if there are, say, n firms in all in the economy. We can then write

$$R - E_m = \sum_{i=1}^{n} (R_i - E_{mi}) \qquad (1.3)$$

where Σ is the Greek letter 'sigma' and is used to mean 'the sum of' the items from 1 to n. Thus (1.3) tells us that total value added in the economy is the sum of the values added by all the individual firms. This equals the value of the national output or income, Y. Rearranging the terms in (1.1), (1.2), and (1.3) we have

$$Y = R - E_m = E_f \text{ (the expenditure method)}$$
$$= w + i + r + p \text{ (the income method)}$$
$$= \sum_{i=1}^{n} (R_i - E_{mi}) \text{ (the net output method)}$$

Indirect taxes and subsidies

Whether we use the income, expenditure, or product approach, we should reach the same total. The calculation is complicated, however, by the existence of indirect taxes and subsidies. The total of incomes obtained under the income approach represented payments to factors of production for goods and services supplied, payments 'in exchange for the national output'. This total is therefore referred to as *national income at factor cost*. But people's expenditure on a commodity need not all go to suppliers:

where consumers buy cigarettes or other taxed goods, for example, a proportion of the sales proceeds goes to the government as customs and excise revenue. If we simply sum expenditures, without taking account of this, we shall obtain *national expenditure at market prices*. This would not measure any additional flow of output however. Suppose, for instance, in our example, the government imposed a tax of 10 per cent on maize flour sold to final consumers, and that traders passed on the whole of this tax to consumers by raising their prices by 10 per cent. Final expenditure at market prices would increase from 1,500 shillings to 1,650 shillings. But factors of production would still only receive 1,500 shs (150 shs would go to the government in tax); and real output would not have changed.

Alternatively the government may subsidize some commodities, paying producers a subsidy proportional to the value of sales or number of units sold. This is equivalent to negative indirect taxes, and will mean that market prices are lower than the *factor cost* of the goods and that factors of production receive incomes from the sale of the goods *in excess of* consumers' expenditure on them. We can therefore combine indirect taxes and subsidies to obtain net indirect taxes and, if these are positive, national expenditure at market prices will exceed national income at factor cost by this amount. If we wish to obtain national income at factor cost directly using the expenditure method, we should exclude net indirect taxes (including customs duties) from the values of C, G, I, and X−M. If we are calculating the total by the net output method, we should calculate value added in each industry without reference to taxes and subsidies. Indirect taxes can in fact be regarded as a form of transfer payment, in which the firms in the enterprise sector are acting as a tax-collecting agent for the government; while subsidies are transfers made to firms analogous to grants to persons. We therefore have the following relationship:

National expenditure at market prices *minus* indirect taxes *plus* subsidies = national income at factor cost.

Net factor income from abroad

The definition of national income or product can be stated as the income received by normal residents of the country from productive activity. This tells us that we should include in national income any income from productive activity *even if it is earned abroad*, so long as it accrues to residents. At the same time some of the earnings made within the domestic economy will accrue to non-residents and should be excluded from national income: this results from the fact that local production may be carried out with the help of capital assets that belong to residents of other countries (who have made loans or own shares in various enterprises). We should therefore distinguish *domestic production* within the geographical boundaries of a country, on 'domestic territory', and *national production*, production for which residents of the country are responsible. For instance, in 1972 Tanzania made 'factor income payments to the rest of the world' of 84 million shillings, and Tanzania residents obtained factor income from the rest of the world of 42 million shillings. Accordingly *net* factor income from abroad was *minus* 42 m shs. This accounted for the difference between gross *national* product at factor cost of shs 9,994 m and gross *domestic* product at factor cost of shs 10,036 m.

The difference between these two totals will be greater in countries where foreign investment is more important, and a larger part of the capital employed is owned by foreigners. Thus we see from Table 1.1 that in 1970 net payments abroad of dividends and interest on government loans and private capital (shown as 'property and entrepreneurial income') took 3.3 per cent of Zambia's gross domestic product at factor cost.

For most countries factor income receipts or payments abroad comprise profits and interest on investments made by non-residents, and this is in fact true of most Eastern African countries also. Malawi and Zambia in Central Africa are unusual, however, in having respectively, a relatively large income from nationals employed abroad and a relatively large outflow of the earnings of expatriates working in the country. In 1972, for instance, Malawian workers abroad remitted savings from wages which amounted to almost as much as the total outflow of factor income paid to foreign investors or as pensions and gratuities to expatriates formerly working in the

country. Thus the figure of gross national income was virtually the same as the figure for domestic income.

In principle all incomes accruing to foreigners should be deducted from domestic production, and all incomes earned by 'national' factors of production should be added, to arrive at a measure of national income. In practice, however, the adjustment is often limited to 'investment income' earned by the factors capital and enterprise in the forms of rents, interest, and dividends. Income from employment of labour abroad is either excluded altogether, because data are difficult to collect, particularly from emigrants who may never return to their country of origin, or only that part of income which is actually remitted abroad is included as a *factor* income flow from one country to another. Most developed countries, as well as many African countries where labour remittances are relatively unimportant (or difficult to record accurately) adopt the practice of treating remittances as transfer payments and not as factor payments, this emphasizing the voluntary nature of the gift, there being no 'quid pro quo' in the form of a current service rendered by the country of origin.

While it would make little difference to the figure of national income for the UK or the USA how migrants' employment income is treated, it does make a great deal of difference in labour-exporting countries such as the small Caribbean islands or Southern Africa. Malawi adopts the wider definition of 'factor income from abroad', because her receipts of labour remittances are relatively important components of what people have to spend and of the foreign exchange at her disposal. Neither the government nor the local communities which supply migrant labourers for contract work in neighbouring countries regard their remittances as mere donations: they are the returns on the nation's human capital, matured and often educated for work abroad.

Table 1.1 *Gross domestic income and national disposable income in Zambia and Malawi*

		Zambia in 1970 (m kwacha)	(%)	Malawi in 1972 (m kwacha)	(%)
	Gross domestic product at factor cost	1,004.4	100.0	350.3	100.0
	Property and entrepreneurial income from abroad (net)	−33.4	−3.3	−10.8	−3.1
	Employment income from abroad (net)			+8.7	+2.5
plus	Total net factor income from abroad	−33.4	−3.3	−2.1	−0.6
equals	GNP at factor cost	971.0	96.7	348.2	99.4
plus	Gifts and transfers from abroad (net)	−104.5	−10.7	+10.8	+3.1
equals	National disposable income (f.c.)	866.5	86.0	359.0	102.5

SOURCE: *Statistical Abstracts* and *Economic Reports*

Zambia, which is in the reverse position with expatriate residents employed in the mines and public services making substantial remittances abroad, treats these differently as 'unrequited' transfers from temporary residents who have managed to save part of their contribution to Zambia's national output. The difference in treatment does lead to inconsistency, it may be noted, in direct comparisons of the national income of Zambia and Malawi. Malawi's workers abroad are regarded as producing an invisible service export and not simply the source of gifts.

The concept of national disposable income

Where a country receives substantial transfers from abroad, either to individual residents or to government, or where residents send out substantial remittances, the alternative aggregate of *national disposable income* becomes useful. The latter is equal to national income plus or minus all net transfer receipts or payments, and it is this concept which measures the aggregate resources available to a nation for consumption or saving. In Malawi's case, as shown in Table 1.1, in addition to receiving in remittances from that part of her labour force working abroad a net sum representing 2.5 per cent of her domestic product, she received official aid from abroad (and private donations to missions) sufficient to raise her national disposable income by as much as

3 per cent of GDP. The case of Zambia is striking however. In addition to interest and dividends paid abroad, equal to 3.3 per cent of GDP, expatriate workers' savings transferred abroad produced a further net outflow of 10.7 per cent, making a total outflow of 14 per cent and reducing total income available for spending and saving within Zambia to only 86 per cent of GDP, the income actually earned by production there.

The relationship between various income aggregates

Finally, various national product totals may be given 'gross' or 'net' of depreciation or 'capital consumption'. As mentioned earlier, accurate estimates of the depreciation of fixed capital assets are not readily available in Eastern Africa: in fact Tanzania is rather exceptional in publishing official estimates of net as well as gross product. The relationship between eight alternative concepts of aggregate income is given in Figure 1.2, where the data refer to mainland Tanzania in 1972.[4]

In fact for most countries the difference between the national and domestic concepts is quite small, something like 1 or 2 per cent of total domestic product of less developed countries accruing to foreigners in the main capital-exporting countries like the USA or UK, whose national income is about 1 per cent *larger* than their domestic income. Depreciation of fixed

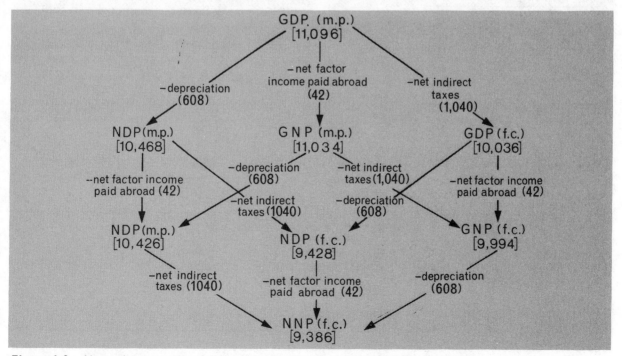

Figure 1.2 Alternative concepts of national income for Tanzania, 1972 (in shs million).

capital constitutes a larger share of current product, about 10 per cent of gross domestic product (GDP) in rich countries, rather less in developing countries with a relatively smaller, and younger, stock of fixed capital. In most countries, rich and poor, it is net indirect taxes which represent the largest difference between GDP at market prices and NNP at factor cost, some 10 per cent or more. The relationships for Tanzania shown in

Figure 1.2 can be summarized in the following adjustments, given in Table 1.2, as we move from the largest aggregate, GDP, at market prices, to the smallest, net national income at factor cost (NNP).

The composition of these aggregates is revealed in Figure 1.3. Aggregate expenditure on GDP at market prices, or 'in purchasers' values' as the United Nations' New System of National Accounts now

Table 1.2   Steps in adjustment from gross domestic product to net national income for Tanzania, 1972

		shs million	%
	Gross domestic product at market prices (GDP)	11,076	100.0
	less net indirect taxes	−1,040	9.4
equals	Gross domestic product at factor cost	10,036	90.6
	less depreciation (of fixed capital assets)	−608	5.5
equals	Net domestic product at factor cost	9,428	85.1
	less net factor incomes paid abroad	−42	0.4
equals	Net national income (product) at factor cost (NNP)	9,386	84.7

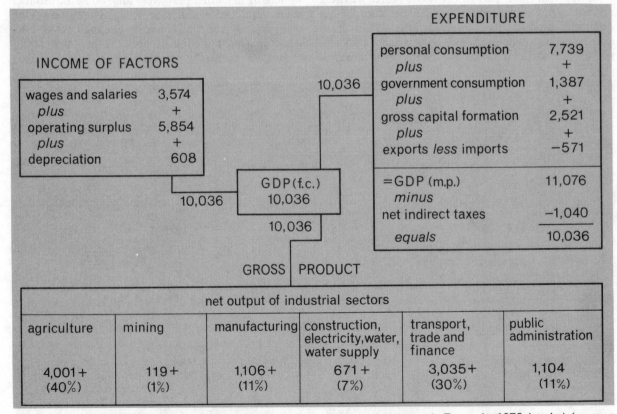

Figure 1.3   Composition of gross domestic income, expenditure, and outcome in Tanzania, 1972 (m shs) (SOURCE: National Accounts of Tanzania, 1964–72, Bureau of Statistics, Dar es Salaam, 1974).

defines it, is shown in the table on the right-hand side of Figure 1.3. Personal consumption, including non-marketed subsistence,[5] accounted for the largest (70 per cent) share of the 'national cake'. And since government consumption and gross capital formation absorbed another 36 per cent, the gap of 6 per cent between total domestic expenditure and GDP was filled by an excess of imports over exports. After deducting net indirect taxes, a figure of shs 10,036 millions is obtained for GDP at factor cost. The left-hand table in Figure 1.3 shows the distribution of this income: about 36 per cent as wages and 64 per cent as *gross* operating surplus which included the 6 per cent for depreciation and also subsistence incomes. The value added by the different economic activities or industrial sectors is shown in the lower table of the figure: agriculture, including forestry and fishing and subsistence activities, was the main source of livelihood, providing 40 per cent of total GDP, and followed by transport and trading services with 30 per cent.

The measurement of East African incomes

In developed countries all three methods may be used to calculate comprehensive national income tables. However in Eastern Africa the Product Method is the main one used in the absence of detailed information on (a) incomes earned in small businesses and by self-employed workers (for the Income Method) or on (b) private consumers' expenditure. As a result of relying on one method mainly, there are fewer checks on the accuracy of the estimates; and, indeed, a combination of approaches is required to complete even a product table because data on some sectors are not readily available. In Tanzania, for instance, the output of agriculture, mining, and manufacturing is estimated by the product method, deriving the value added by deducting purchases of intermediate products from the total value of turnovers. But for other industries the income method is used, adding together wages and other emoluments of employees, and various estimates of operating surplus. Within the category 'manufacturing and handicrafts', the output of 'modern' manufacturing is obtained from surveys of industrial production (product method), while the output of handicrafts is obtained from the number of persons engaged in such industries (estimated from the last census) multiplied by an estimate of average earnings from each activity (income method). The expenditures of government, on capital formation, exports, and imports are calculated directly; private consumption is then deduced as a residual item from $Y \equiv E \equiv O$.

The special problem of measuring non-marketed subsistence output

One particular problem in making calculations of national income is that money is not always used as a medium of exchange in the buying and selling of output. In African countries, in particular, peasant farmers may build their own huts, grow their own food, and provide altogether quite a large part of their total requirements without recourse to the market at all. Such production is often referred to as 'subsistence output', but a better expression is 'non-monetary output', since we are referring here simply to output produced for domestic use and not exchanged against money.

In developed countries the proportion of production which is outside the exchange economy is a great deal smaller, in relation to total output, *and is relatively stable from one year to another*. This last point is an extremely important one. In Eastern Africa annual fluctuations in home-grown food supply, causing famine and even deaths, can have disproportionately great effects on welfare. It would be useful to have these reflected in statistics, and also to be able to gauge the long-term trend in subsistence food production in order to assess, for instance, whether the country is making progress towards self-sufficiency in particular staple foodstuffs.

The first difficulty is the obvious one that much of this output—food production, building of huts, grain milling, collection of firewood and water—goes unrecorded, and can only be roughly estimated. This includes output which is actually sold, in local markets. In fact national income statisticians have to resort for some or all of their estimates of subsistence output to the assumption that this output varies in proportion to population. This may, of course, be highly inaccurate—certainly in respect of year-to-year fluctuations—because of variations in subsistence food production per head *and* because of uncertainty regarding the actual population size. In Eastern Africa subsistence output is mainly estimated by 'raising' estimates of production or consumption per head by total rural population numbers, and unreliable population figures mean very unreliable total product estimates. It omits all year-to-year fluctuations in average output per head. It also makes estimates of personal consumption much more unreliable than other components of expenditure which can be calculated directly through the expenditure approach, as it is found as a residual, subtracting the other figures from the aggregate obtained by the product approach. Thus the one figure which could tell us most about *immediate* welfare standards, average consumption per head, is in fact a very rough 'guesstimate'.

A related difficulty in measuring the output of subsistence activities is that there may be differences between countries as to which activities are included and which are omitted from the calculation. This is a general problem of defining the *boundary of production* and is not limited to calculating the subsistence output in less developed countries. For instance, national income statisticians in developed countries generally exclude services of housewives in shopping, cooking, cleaning, and washing clothes. These activities, on which housewives spend very long hours, are left outside the production 'boundary'. As we have seen already, there is some inconsistency here in that if the same tasks were done by a paid housekeeper, they would be counted. A leading statistician once estimated that if housewives' services were valued at market prices and included in national income, they would in the case of the United States account for around 25 per cent of the total! Since housewives in rich countries have bigger houses to look after and a greater variety of domestic tasks to perform usually, the amount omitted on this score will be much greater than in poor countries: this would make a big difference therefore to comparisons between rich and poor countries, the omission involving an *underestimate* of the gap between them. Practice varies in drawing the boundary of production for non-monetary output in less developed countries. Tanzania has since the late 1950s had a very broad definition, including craft industries and rural construction, which were previously excluded from the Kenya and Uganda estimates of domestic product. All three East African countries and Malawi now have a much broader coverage of non-marketed production, including building, some handicrafts, imputed rents of owner-occupied dwellings in the rural as well as urban areas and, in the case of Kenya, even an estimate of rural water supply collected by households.

After deciding what output to include, the next difficulty is to decide how to value it. If goods are sold on the market, it seems reasonable to take market price as measuring the value of the goods to the consumer. When goods are not sold on the market, we have to 'impute' values by asking what the consumer would be paying if he bought the same item 'on the market'. For instance, we should impute a rent for owner-occupied houses: we can assume that if the owner of the house were not staying in the house himself he would be able to let it out to someone else at a rent equal to that prevailing for similar houses in the neighbourhood which *are* rented. If we did not do this, suppose a large proportion of people in the country decided to buy the houses which they had previously been renting; the national income would appear to decrease! With farmers' output which is self-consumed, there is a rather different problem: should we value the products at the prices the farmers could get if they sold them (ex-farm prices) or at the prices they would need to pay if they had bought the products rather than producing them themselves (that is, at local market prices). The latter prices will generally be much higher, of course, due to the cost of marketing the produce.

We can indicate how important these problems can be, and how shaky resulting statistical estimates may become, by looking at the way in which series have sometimes been revised. Up to 1964 statistics for Malawi were compiled by the Central Statistical Office in Salisbury. When the National Statistical Office was set up within Malawi itself, a fresh approach was embarked upon, resulting in a new series from 1964. The figure for subsistence production in 1964 was revised upwards from £23.1 m to £38.1 m, an increase of 65 per cent. The reasons related partly to the boundary of production—the old series *excluded* any estimate for 'household services'—and partly to the method of valuation—the new series valued output of crops, livestock, firewood and dwellings at *retail* prices rather than at producer prices.[6] The old figure for *monetary* GDP at factor cost was also lower: £27.5 m compared to £34.2 m, the reason for this being that the old series, relying mainly on income tax data, underestimated the output of small enterprises (which often escape payment of income tax). This illustrates the fact that even monetary output may be difficult to record in developing countries, since small-scale manufacturing, transport, or trading enterprises may be important. Altogether GDP in 1964 was increased by 43 per cent by the revisions, nearly one-half!

Nor is this a unique case: in Tanzania the Bureau of Statistics published a new series for GDP in 1970 based on a different methodology and concepts. The new series increased the estimate for GDP for 1968 by 28 per cent. The increase in value of output (at constant prices) between 1966 and 1968 was now shown as 11.1 per cent instead of 4.5 per cent: an annual growth rate of 5.5 per cent compared to 2.25 per cent. We can conclude either that Tanzania's economic performance was much better than she imagined earlier or that we should take calculations of growth rate from national income statistics with a pinch of salt!

The standard of living

By this time it will be realized that calculating a yearly figure for the national income is a major statistical exercise. What is it all for? Five main purposes of national income statistics may be distinguished.

(1) To measure the size of the 'national cake' of goods and services available for the competing uses of private consumers, government, capital formation, and exports (less imports). (For this we need an *expenditure table*.)

(2) To identify the main kinds of economic activity, and their relative importance in producing output. For this we need a *product table*. Accurate and up-to-date 'maps' detailing the economic structure of the nation are needed for short-term budgeting or longer-term planning. We discuss economic policy and development planning towards the end of the book.

(3) To analyse the distribution of incomes between factors of production, or between geographical areas or social groups. (For this we need an *income table* as well as supplementary information obtained from surveys of household income and expenditures or tax returns if available.)

(4) To measure changes in the level of activity and the rate of economic growth and development of the country over time.

(5) To indicate the standard of living in the country compared with that elsewhere in the world at some point in time.

Let us consider the usefulness of national income statistics in measuring people's material well-being or 'standard of living', which is what we set out to examine. The concept of 'standard of living' is widely—but loosely—used by the general public: in fact, however, it is extremely difficult to specify. The most obvious measure is *real income per head*, total 'real' income divided by the number of population. This tells us the value of goods and services received by the 'average man'. Such figures are published annually by the United Nations statisticians for almost all countries.

Problems of measurement

But there are major problems in using real income per head to measure the standard of living in different countries. First, there is a whole set of *statistical problems*. And secondly there are a number of difficult *conceptual problems*, or problems of interpretation.

Inaccurate estimates of population

The first statistical problem in calculating income per head in less developed countries, and especially those in tropical Africa, is that we do not have very accurate population figures with which to divide total national income. For example, in Ghana at the time of the 1960 census it was thought that the population was around 5 millions; the census revealed it to be some 6.7 millions, or one-third larger. The recent 1970 census was nearer the figure estimated on the 1960 basis, however, 8.6 millions compared with a projected 8.9 millions. In Uganda the 1959 census produced a figure for the African population of 6.3 millions, some 10 per cent greater than the number projected from the earlier 1948 census. The 1969 census reported a total population of 9.5 millions, an apparent increase in population of 46 per cent since 1959—nearly one-half in ten years—and implying a very high compound growth rate of 3.8 per cent. However allowing for net immigration and undercounting at the 1959 census, it is now considered that the natural increase in population was around 3.0 per cent. In Nigeria, of course, disputes over regional population figures have led to serious political troubles. The total population of this large country in 1963 might have been as high as the official census figure of 55.7 millions or, as some experts believe, only about 45 millions—a difference of 9.3 millions. The 1973 census reported a provisional figure of 76.8 millions, which exceeded the United Nations' estimate of 56.4 millions by a much larger margin of 20.4 million people! The United Nations Yearbook of National Accounts Statistics for 1972, which provides international estimates of income per head, shows a figure of US$99 for Nigeria in 1969, derived from an aggregate estimate of GDP of US$5,310 millions and a figure for population of some 54 millions, this in turn based on *their* end-1963 estimate of 46.3 millions projected forward at a compound rate of increase of 2.5 per cent per annum. If we used an estimate for population in 1969 but derived from the 1973 census of, say, 68 millions (equal to the 1973 figure of 76.8 millions reduced backwards at the rate of 3.2 per cent per annum, the growth rate for 1969–73) we should obtain an income per head figure for 1969 of US$78, instead of US$99.[7]

Specific items which are difficult to estimate

Another data problem, as already mentioned, is that data for *depreciation* and for *net factor income from abroad* are generally unreliable. Hence although we should prefer figures for 'the' national income, we are likely to fall back on GDP, which is a much less meaningful figure for measuring income per head. *Inventory investment* and *work in progress* are also difficult items to calculate. Part of the output produced by firms in the period may not be sold immediately but added to the stocks or inventories of the commodity which firms usually hold in reserve. Any net increase in stocks in the economy during the period, since it makes possible increased consumption in the future, is a form of investment. In addition there may be 'work in progress' such as half-completed houses or ships, which in some industries could be quite important relative to total annual output. For the economy as a whole the value of physical changes in stocks and work in progress may represent 2 or 3 per cent of final output, or about 10–15 per cent of gross domestic capital formation. In developing countries particularly, where most small enterprises practise only rudimentary commercial accounting and millions of small farmers hold small stocks, particularly for their own use, it is very difficult to measure accurately inventory investment.

Non-marketed subsistence output and output of government

We have already dealt with the problems of measuring subsistence output. Other 'output' which is not sold on the market is the output of government. This, as we have said, is usually measured by taking government expenditure on factor services (teachers, clerks, etc.) as the value of the services in turn provided by the government. This means that the value of the output is measured by taking the cost of the *inputs*. In one country, however, salary of doctors for instance, might be high and their quality low compared to another country: although the medical wage-bill will be higher, the real 'consumption' of medical care in the former might be lower. Since 'public consumption' is an important element in national income, this could affect comparisons considerably.

Changes in the price level over time

As stated at the beginning we are interested in *real* income per head in a country. If over time the average price level changes, we should adjust the level of money income to take account of this. We need to know income 'at constant prices', the value of income if the price level had *not* changed. We deal in a later chapter with the statistical problems of measuring changes in the value of money. But it is clear that if money income remains constant, but all prices rise, people will obtain less real income. In 'open' economies like Eastern Africa which import many of their consumption goods, a similar thing will happen if the relative price of imports goes up compared to exports: they will find the incomes they obtain from the sales of their exported cotton or coffee, say, fetch less when they buy imported consumer goods.

International comparisons using foreign exchange rates

When we add together all types of output in order to get national income, we must first value them in money terms: in terms of the national currency. In order to make international comparisons, however, we must make the comparison in the same kind of money, that is, in the same currency, whether it be pounds sterling, US dollars, or Kenya shillings. To compare, say, Indian and British income, we need to convert Indian rupees into sterling at some suitable rate of exchange between the currencies. If the 'official' exchange rate between, say, the Zambian kwacha and the Malawian kwacha were fixed by the respective governments so that K1 Zambian could be exchanged for K1 Malawian, this would be used to standardize the valuation of national incomes. The difficulty is that these values may not be equivalent *in terms of the goods they buy in their respective countries*. This is because the domestic price levels may be different in each country. Even if K1 Zambian can be exchanged for K1 Malawian, it may not enable us to buy in Zambia the same basket of goods as K1 Malawian does in Malawi, if these goods are more expensive in Zambia.

Different price structures

Quite apart from a difference between the *average* price levels of two countries, differences in price *structures* make comparisons difficult. In poor countries domestic servants are usually extremely cheap, while in advanced countries they are so expensive that they are now rarely used. In Kenya meat, fruit, and vegetables are cheap and manufactured goods expensive, while the opposite is true in the United Kingdom. Differences in the relative prices of different kinds of goods, due to differences in their availability, mean that people can increase their welfare if they are willing to alter their consumption in the direction of cheaper goods. People in poor countries probably are not nearly as badly off as national income statistics would suggest, because the basic foodstuffs which form an important part of their total consumption are actually priced very low.

Income in relation to effort

These are all serious statistical problems. There are also a number of major conceptual problems. Instead of considering simply income per head, it may be argued that we should look at the goods and services produced in relation to the human effort that has gone into producing them. Obviously if people work harder, they will be able to get more goods: but they may prefer the extra leisure. And who is to say they are not 'better off' in choosing the leisure? Indeed, the amount of leisure that people want depends in part on their level of income. As people's incomes in Europe and the USA have increased, they have demanded shorter working days, longer holidays, and expect to enjoy a longer period of retirement rather than continue working all their lives. Thus the working day in manufacturing has decreased steadily over the years and is now shortest in the USA, which is the wealthiest country. Strictly, therefore, we should take income *per unit of labour applied*. It is largely because this would be statistically awkward that economists prefer to take real income per head.

The possibility of transport bias

A problem which is both conceptual and statistical is due to the transport factor. We use market prices to value goods and services, because these can be considered to reflect consumers' valuation of the goods: what they are prepared to pay. But if in one country a commodity has to be transported a long way its market price will be inflated by transport cost. In another country, where it is produced on the spot, it may be much cheaper. Even if the amounts consumed per head in the two countries are identical, the value recorded could be higher in the former. In part this is simply the problem of relative price structure, with some goods dearer and some goods cheaper, in the two countries. But there could be a substantial bias due to the transport element if this does not average out. For example, the whole of subsistence production is free of transport element since it is produced *and* consumed on the farm: this is in large part why the prices of basic foodstuffs in developing countries are generally so low when they are valued at rural markets.

Differences in tastes

Another formidable difficulty is that tastes are not the same in all countries. Britons spend their higher incomes on processed foods like cornflakes or marmalade which most Eastern Africans cannot afford: but if Eastern Africans do not particularly like these things, they will not necessarily be worse off. The point is particularly that tastes are such that while in one country tastes are in the direction of things which are relatively expensive, in another people may consume and prefer goods which are cheaper. Thus Italians eat spaghetti, Indians rice, Eastern Africans maize or matoke, all relatively cheap, while Americans eat larger quantities of steak, which is an expensive commodity! Different tastes in food, however, form part of a much wider problem: in different countries the society and culture may be so completely different that comparisons of material welfare may bear little or no relationship to general welfare in two countries. Religion affects the way of life in India in a way that it does not in Western Europe, for instance; in Africa enjoyment of material comforts is not independent of the strong tribal

communities which exist, and so on. But even between Britain and France, separated by only twenty miles of water, cultural differences produce barriers of communication which extend well beyond the language problem! It has also been argued that tastes, particularly expensive tastes, have in part been induced by the large-scale persuasive advertising which is undertaken in the advanced capitalist countries. It is felt by some that these requirements are to this extent artificial and that their absence in poor countries need not mean a corresponding lack of welfare. Tastes also differ as regards the emphasis on leisure as against the enjoyment of the fruits of labour: if in some societies people prefer leisure and contemplation, who is to say this reduces their welfare as compared to those involved in the hurly-burly of life and labour in modern industry?

Differences in requirements

Apart from tastes, *requirements* may be very different in different parts of the world. Climatic conditions may require more substantial houses and the wearing of warm clothing, these needs being reflected in the structure of production and in national income. The additional expenditure on homes, heating, and the rest is, in comparison with warmer countries, not so much part of income, but a *cost* imposed by the cold climate. Similarly expenditure on roads in a large country like Tanzania compared to a more geographically compact country like Uganda, is in part a cost necessitated by the vast distances that need to be traversed in the former.[8] This does not apply to a comparison of the *same* country at two points of time: if Tanzania spends more one year on transport than in another, it means it has made a greater contribution towards solving its own peculiar transport problem.

Income per head as index of economic welfare

We should remember also that real income per head is only an *index* of economic welfare or material well-being. By this we mean that if income per head increases, material welfare will increase; but we cannot say *by how much* it has increased, and certainly that it has increased in proportion. We cannot, in other words, measure material welfare on an arithmetic scale in the same way as we can measure real income per head. Estimated income per head in Tanzania is about one-twentieth of that in the United Kingdom: but we cannot say that the average Tanzanian enjoys only one-twentieth of the economic welfare of the average Briton. For if the ratio had been 1:100 instead of 1:20, to take an extreme case, the average Tanzanian would enjoy nothing, for he would have starved to death! The point is, of course, that at low levels of income the more basic needs are satisfied, particularly those of food and shelter. The difference in the value of real income per head recorded is due to the fact that in Africa income is largely devoted to consumer goods, especially foodstuffs, which have a low money value, whereas in Europe additional income is available for goods and services with high prices.

Effect of the distribution of income

A crucial factor to bear in mind also is the distribution of income. Comparisons of *average* income mean little if there is a wide spread of incomes: for if income is distributed very unequally the great mass of people may have extremely low living standards despite a high average income. Moreover, low income countries tend to exhibit *greater* inequality in personal incomes, although between low income countries there may be very different patterns of income distribution. Tanzania, for example, has a much more even distribution of income than, say, South Africa. The classic post-war case of a country with a very high average income and an extremely unequal distribution of income is, of course, the oil-rich Sheikhdom of Kuwait in the Persian Gulf. With a small population and a very high income from petroleum, the average income per head of nearly 4,000 US dollars in 1970 was one of the very highest in the world, substantially greater than that of France or West Germany. This meant little when so much of the oil royalties were paid to the Sheikh! In other countries also, exploitation of natural resources has raised average *domestic* income per head, but payment of property income to foreign investors, as well as the internal distribution of wealth and hence *national* income, leave the bulk of the inhabitants with standards of living close to those in neighbouring countries. Zambia, Zaire, Liberia, and some of the Latin American republics are examples.

The problems referred to are obviously more serious in trying to compare economic welfare in two countries than in trying to assess the improvement over time in the situation in any *one* country. We have already mentioned that 'costs' like heating and transportation will be constant in the case of a single country; the price structures will also be fairly constant; and the social, historical, and cultural basis of the society will change only slowly. And of course the statistical coverage will be more uniform.

Questions on Chapter 1

1. What is national income? How is it measured in Eastern Africa?
2. Why do countries estimate the annual value of their aggregate income?
3. Compare the three approaches to national income measurement.
4. What are the main components of total income and total expenditure in any Eastern African country?
5. Why does $O \equiv Y \equiv E$?
6. Explain in detail the derivation of the identity:

$$Y \equiv C + G + I + X - M$$

7. Distinguish between personal income, private income, and national income as used in national income accounts.
8. What is the difference between the foreign trade balance $(X-M)$, and 'net factor income from abroad'?
9. Discuss the relation between each of the following:

$$GNP(m.p.); \ GNP(f.c) \ GDP(f.c.); \ NNP(f.c.)$$

Which is *the* 'national income', and why?

10. Discuss the various kinds of non-marketed output which might enter into the national income total, and how these are dealt with in national income calculations.
11. Why is the boundary of production often difficult to define in estimating the national income of a less developed country?
12. How far do estimates of gross domestic product per head measure accurately differences in material living standards between widely separated countries?
13. Why do you think comparisons of standard of living will be easier:
    (a) for one country over time than for two different countries at one point in time,
    (b) between two developed countries than between one developed and one less developed country, and
    (c) in any one country over a short time interval rather than over a long period of years?
14. Explain the following terms: value added, public consumption, transfer payments, public income, intermediate products, government disposable income, inventory investment, national disposable income.

Notes

[1] The effect of savings on the circular flow of income is discussed in Chapter 28.

[2] Expenditure on goods and services which are sold, e.g. school fees, hospital charges, is not *public* consumption but part of *private* expenditure by households or firms.

[3] This amount is strictly speaking equal to Net Domestic Product at Factor Cost, as defined below.

[4] This layout is borrowed from W. Beckerman, who borrowed it from one of his first-year students at Oxford. See his *An Introduction to National Income Analysis*, Weidenfeld & Nicolson, 1968.

[5] To be defined in the next section but one.

[6] H. W. Ord initiated the practice of valuing subsistence or non-monetary production at local (mainly regional urban) retail prices. The objective was not primarily to value household services as such but to put a money value on the saving of transport and trading margins which own-consumption allows. Thus subsistence output of food and housing was valued at producer ('farm-gate') prices in the product table and at retail market prices in the expenditure table. The difference, amounting to almost a 100 per cent mark-up on producer prices, was shown separately as the product of a non-monetary 'services' sector. The main purpose of this valuation was to permit a better welfare comparison between rural and urban households and, since the former make up 95 per cent of the population, between real income in Malawi and elsewhere. Recently the statisticians in Malawi have reverted to the use of producer prices but now attempt to measure also a wider range of non-monetary or small-scale activity such as grain milling, handicrafts, crop storage, and impute the rental income of home owner-occupiers. The effect of this has been to retain the broader valuation of subsistence.

[7] In fact, as we noted above, the figure for subsistence output is generally increased in proportion to population: so an increase in the population figure (denominator) would lead to an increase also in the output figure (numerator). The income per head figure would therefore not fall as much.

[8] This could, of course, be compensated by adjusting for price levels, if transport costs raise the general price level in Tanzania. This is, however, not reflected in official exchange rates.

2 The Means of Production and Economic Development

The problem of underdevelopment

The difference between rich and poor nations and the wide discrepancies in the standard of living between individuals and social groups within particular countries have always engaged the attention of economists. Adam Smith's famous book of 1776 was called *An Inquiry into the Nature and Causes of the Wealth of Nations*. If we follow our discussion of the previous chapter and use as an index of welfare real income per head, we find that the disparity in levels of income in different countries is today alarmingly great. Table 2.1 gives figures of income per head for selected countries, valued in US dollars. This comparison would indicate for instance that income per head in the USA was some forty times that in Tanzania (not that 'economic welfare' was in the same ratio); that on the other hand income per head in the UK was about half that in the USA; that even income per head in Ghana was three or four times that in Malawi or Ethiopia.

While, as we have warned, very great care must be exercised in using national income statistics for international comparisons, United Nations statistics suggest that something like two-thirds of the world's population share between them less than 20 per cent of the world's income. In 1974 the latter figure was estimated at around 14 per cent. If the world's income had been shared out equally among the world's population, this figure would have been nearly 70 per cent, five times greater.

Moreover there is evidence that the gap between incomes in different countries has been widening rather than closing, and that it is likely to continue to do so. That this is so in absolute terms can be seen from a simple arithmetic calculation. Table 2.1 gives income per head in 1974 as $6,670 for the USA and $160 for Tanzania: a difference of $6,510. Suppose in the next year they had each achieved a 5 per cent rate of increase in income per head. The absolute growth would be $333 in the USA but only $8 in Tanzania. The gap would actually *widen* by $325, from $6,510 to $6,835. Even if Tanzania achieved a 10 per cent rate of increase, double that for the USA, this would raise the average level of income by only $16, and the gap would still increase by $317, almost an identical result. This does not mean that the gap in 'welfare' has widened correspondingly, but that in order that the difference should *not* increase, the extra $16 in Tanzania would need to raise welfare as much as the extra $333 in the USA.

Table 2.2 shows the actual experience of two other countries between 1960 and 1974, a 14-year period including what the United Nations called the 'First Development Decade' (1960–70) during which an international effort was made to start closing the 'gap'. Although the compound growth in GNP per head for Kenya was 3.2 per cent per annum, substantially higher than the 2.3 per cent estimated for the UK, the gap still grew at an average of 2.2 per cent per year. In absolute terms this meant that the gap widened from $2,480 to $3,390, a cumulative increase of about 37 per cent.

To take another example, it is estimated that even

Table 2.1 *Gross national product per head in selected countries in 1974 (in US$)*

Ruanda	80	Kenya	200	Malaysia	680	USSR	2,380
Burundi	90	Sudan	230	Taiwan	810	Saudi Arabia	2,820
Somalia	90	Uganda	240	Brazil	920	Israel	3,460
Ethiopia	100	Cameroon	250	South Africa	1,210	UK	3,590
Guinea	120	Egypt	280	Iran	1,250	Japan	4,070
Malawi	130	Nigeria	280	Argentina	1,520	Libya	4,440
India	140	China	300	Portugal	1,630	West Germany	6,260
Zaire	150	Liberia	390	Trinidad	1,700	Denmark	6,430
Tanzania	160	Ghana	430	Puerto Rico	2,230	USA	6,670
The Gambia	170	Zambia	520	Singapore	2,240	Kuwait	10,030
Sierra Leone	190	Mauritius	580				

SOURCE: World Bank, *Atlas, 1976*

Table 2.2 *The widening gap between rich and poor countries*

	(1) UK $	(2) Kenya $	(3) Difference $	(4) Ratio (1):(2)
1960	2,610	130	2,480	20:1
1974	3,590	200	3,390	18:1
Percentage growth 1960–70	% 37.5	% 55.5	% 36.7	
Annual rate	2.3	3.2	2.2	

(Gross national product per head at constant (1974) market prices expressed in US dollars)

SOURCE: World Bank, *Atlas, 1976*

Zambia, which can start with an income per head in 1974 estimated at more than twice the Kenyan and over three times that of Tanzania, would need an annual growth in real income per head of more than 10 per cent per annum (even 3 per cent can be considered a good performance in per capita terms) to catch up with the 1974 level of income per head in the USA by the year 2000. If the USA maintains its recent (1960–74) annual growth of around 2.9 per cent in average real income, Zambia's income per head would need to increase by nearly 40 per cent each year just to stop the gap widening absolutely!

Despite this apparently depressing situation, some countries have made astonishing 'breakthroughs': among large countries, Japan has for the past two decades or so achieved easily the highest rates of growth in the world, and become one of the world's leading industrial nations. During the 1960s it averaged a rate of growth in real gross domestic product of over 10 per cent, yielding a 9 per cent increase in product per head in real terms. While China, her neighbour, remains relatively poor, it also has made impressive strides in both agriculture and industry. Remarkably impressive rates of growth have been achieved in some other parts of Asia: Taiwan, Hong Kong, Korea, and Singapore. Israel, in the Middle East, and Puerto Rico, in the Caribbean, have also shown noteworthy economic development, and other Middle East economies, based on oil, have shown impressive growth rates in total product. The question arises, therefore, whether more countries could make a 'breakthrough' in development. An attempt to answer this question is part of the objectives of 'Development Economics'. This field is closely linked with Economic History as well as with Economic Theory, since the comparative experience of other countries is worth studying in attempting to analyse the economic development of any particular country. This volume does not venture far into this wide and complex field, but readers will find an increasing literature available now on the recent economic history of African countries.

The factors of production

Before we discuss what determines economic growth, or the expansion of output, we should first see how output comes about. Output is the result of productive processes involving the use of land, labour, and capital. These are usually referred to as the agents of production or more commonly as the *factors of production* or simply as *inputs*. Reproducible capital (machines, buildings, roads, and the like), land, and labour are also sometimes referred to as *physical inputs* in order to distinguish them from *non-physical* inputs. Among non-physical inputs we can distinguish *knowledge* or technology (knowledge regarding the art of production); education and *skills* (as opposed to 'physical' labour); and *enterprise*. Knowledge, skills, and enterprise are all human qualities, since knowledge can be said to have been created by generations of man and to 'belong' to man. Accordingly they may be bracketed together and labelled *human resources*. The factors of production would then consist of land, capital, and human resources. Alternatively we could distinguish five factors of production: land, capital, labour, enterprise, and knowledge.

There is clearly room for different definitions of the factors of production. In order to forestall any argument over what should be classified as 'land', 'labour', or 'capital' we should state clearly that definitions in economics are not ends in themselves, but the means to an end. They are useful if they permit us to identify a problem or permit consistent analysis of a problem. Thus we should feel free to make a different definition if we are tackling a different problem or different aspect of a problem.

Capital as a factor of production

In the case of capital, we must immediately distinguish between *real capital* and *money or loan capital*. By real capital we mean a stock of physical assets capable of providing services: machines, factories, houses, stocks of consumer goods or raw materials, as well as roads, railways, harbours, or public buildings owned by government. We can distinguish here between private capital, physical assets owned by private individuals, and *social capital* which is owned by the state on behalf of citizens. In socialist countries in particular the state may own and operate factories or farms: but even in the most capitalistic economy there will be social capital in the form of *infrastructure*: roads, water supplies, public buildings, and the like, which can be said to form the basic foundations of the economy but contribute only *indirectly* to output.

The primary significance of capital is that with it we can obtain a much larger output: man with machines is much more productive than man without. Secondly, the acquisition of capital goods involves the sacrifice of present enjoyment. At any time the resources of an economy are limited: hence if a country devotes a larger proportion of its resources to building up private and social capital, less will be available for making consumer goods. In other words the extent of sacrifice of present enjoyment in an economy is given by the relative size of the 'capital goods sector' and the 'consumer goods sector' or the level of capital formation relative to national income, I/Y. For example, in Russia it has been deliberate policy since 1917 to maintain a very high level of capital formation while keeping consumption in check, in order to expand productive capacity.

We can now see the basic distinction between capital and land, or natural resources. By devoting more resources to the capital goods industries, we can increase the stock of physical assets in the country; and in principle this stock could be increased indefinitely. It is *reproducible* capital. On the other hand, this cannot be achieved without sacrifice: more production of capital goods means less production of consumer goods in the same period, the expansion of production of the latter coming only in later periods. The basic reason for this sacrifice is that capital is man-made: land is not made by man and involves no sacrifice—nor can it be increased. An alternative name for capital is therefore *man-made resources*.

Natural resources ('land')

In contrast with capital and labour, land cannot be increased. Its supply is fixed, and it is this characteristic which economists find the most interesting. The reader will be quick to point out that the effective supply of land can be increased by reclaiming it from the sea or by draining marshlands; land can be reclaimed from the desert by irrigation; and the existing land can be made to produce more by the addition of fertilizers. But all these things require the application of labour and capital, they involve sacrifice of resources. Building irrigation channels is costly, as is building machines, though they both increase output. It is costly in the sense that if irrigation channels are not built, *other* things can be built.

The important distinction is between what is provided by nature and what is not—that which is man-made. We should therefore talk about 'natural resources' rather than 'land'. Three types of natural resources may be distinguished: mineral resources; agricultural resources, which will include climate as well as soils and forests; and water resources, which will include rivers which lend themselves to the production of electric power or irrigation. All these have the same basic characteristic that their supply is fixed.

We shall discuss the relationship between natural resources and development presently. Meanwhile we may note that one of the main applications of our concept is in the theory of rent. If land, for instance, is privately owned, the owners will be in a monopolistic position, since supply cannot be increased. Any increase in demand will allow them to charge increased rents. This applies equally to any natural resource, for the same reason of fixed supply: thus if anyone were fortunate enough to own the only oil well in the world, he would be in a position to charge more or less 'any price he liked' without fear of competition. We shall return to this point in Chapter 8.

Labour (human resources)

It is fairly obvious why labour is distinguished as a factor of production. Labour has a will of its own: it may organize itself into trade unions, decide to work long or short hours, or not at all. It is certainly a different factor of production from 'land', since it is not a perfect substitute for land: in overpopulated countries labour is an 'abundant' factor while land is scarce.

A moment's thought however will tell us that we should distinguish between various categories of labour or 'manpower'. In particular, if we are discussing the problems of less developed countries, especially, we should distinguish between physical or unskilled labour and *skilled* labour: because while such countries often have an abundance of unskilled labour they have an acute *shortage* of skilled labour of all types, and this in fact could be a major constraint on their economic development.

Secondly we should distinguish between all kinds of hired labour and *enterprise*. The individual providing the enterprise is referred to as the 'entrepreneur', since he undertakes the task of organizing the other factors of production. There is a great deal of vagueness as to the essential qualities needed in an 'entrepreneur', and as regards his real function. In hiring the other factors, he does of course coordinate their activities and can therefore be described as a *coordinator* or simply as a *manager*. Being the person who hires the other factors, he undertakes responsibility for the fortunes of the firm, which may mean that he undertakes risk, and is essentially a risk-taker.[1] Alternatively the entrepreneur may be seen as being linked with economic progress, as the person who directs the factors of production into new kinds of enterprise, associated with new products or new ways of making products. He thus appears above all as an *innovator*. What is common to all these qualities is that the entrepreneur is a *high-level decision-taker*. This implies that his work may not be so very different from other kinds of labour, for decisions of some kind have to be taken at all levels of work, and all levels involve some responsibility and even qualities of leadership, as in the case of a foreman in charge of a group of fellow-workers. Enterprise or 'entrepreneurship' thus appears as a special kind of labour or human resource.

The 'entrepreneur' is often thought of as an individual. This is because the term originated in connection with the nineteenth-century enterprise in the Western capitalist economies, where firms were usually 'run' by one man or as a family enterprise. This is no longer very appropriate in the days of the large joint stock company where important decisions are taken by a large group of directors; where there is a well-developed managerial organization; and where 'innovation' may be the outcome of work done in a huge research department comprising several laboratories or technical units. Nor is 'entrepreneurship' as defined above the exclusive property of capitalism. Socialist economies and enterprises are equally dependent on management and on innovation. Indeed some African countries have found some of the technology developed for instance in China to be more appropriate to their requirements than that available in the West. What is certain is that while in developing countries there is plenty of labour, especially unskilled manpower, there is a distinct shortage of entrepreneurial ability, and for this reason it needs to be distinguished as a factor of production.

Knowledge or technology is not completely independent from entrepreneurship, as the innovator may add to knowledge in the course of introducing new methods or products. However since the stock of accumulated knowledge is available for developed *and* less developed countries to draw on, irrespective of whether they are well supplied with or short of entrepreneurship, we can perhaps consider this a separate constraint on production. Rather than a separate factor of production we should perhaps consider knowledge as a *conditioning* factor affecting production. As far as labour in general is concerned we should note that it is very much conditioned also by the *social environment* existing in a particular country. We shall see that this can affect the quantity and nature of available labour and enterprise of all kinds, and the extent to which existing labour skills are directed into productive channels.

Natural resources and economic development[2]

The ingredients of output and of the growth of output are therefore natural resources, man-made resources, and human resources, these conditioned by the state of knowledge and by social and cultural factors. An interesting question is whether any one of the three or four (if we separate enterprise) factors of production is the *crucial* one in determining whether economic growth starts or proceeds. This question has occupied the time of a great many economists.

As far as natural resources are concerned there is a tendency to take one of two extreme views. What might be termed the 'geographical approach' is to explain economic activity as a direct function of the resources available in a region. This approach ignores, first, the fact that countries, including Japan, Israel, and Puerto Rico, which were mentioned above, have developed rapidly without any obvious natural resource endowment. Japan in particular has had the most striking economic growth in the world since the war, and yet has to import many of its raw materials, and all its oil. Secondly this ignores the fact that the exploitation of a major natural resource, like copper in Zambia, may fail to generate economic activity throughout the economy, something which we shall explore in the next chapter.

Sometimes, on the other hand, there is a tendency to regard development as inevitable, irrespective of the resource base. For example, the very term 'underdeveloped' implies the existence of untapped potential; while the term 'developing' country implies that it will inevitably develop. It is worth pointing out, in this respect, that there are in fact *two* possibilities for raising people's standards of living: the one is to develop resources where people are, and the second is to move people to where there are resources. It is sometimes forgotten how important the latter method has been in the economic development of the world, as instanced by the growth of the United States, of Australia, and of many other countries. Within Africa today migration of labour is a major economic phenomenon: ironically some of the most important migration is towards Southern Africa where some of the continent's richest natural resources are under the control of White regimes.

If we accept that natural resources are an important element in growth, the implication is that we will not always be able to compare the development process in the different countries, for resources in each country will vary. The study of economic growth in the United States, or Russia, or the oil kingdoms of the Middle East, may provide hints for African economic development, but not the whole lesson.

The existence or otherwise of natural resources within a country is a matter of luck. The discovery and exploitation of minerals is another matter. Unfortunately, so far as mineral deposits are concerned, with the exception of Zambia, the countries of Eastern Africa, from Sudan down to Malawi, appear relatively unlucky, though we need to bear in mind that Eastern Africa has not yet been adequately explored. The experience of West Africa offers some encouragement here, since the same thing might have been said there until quite recently. It was only after the last war that vast iron ore deposits were found in Liberia, and these have made a substantial contribution to economic development in that country since. On a larger scale, the exploitation of Nigeria's petroleum and natural gas deposits, which began only in the 1960s, offers Nigerians a rate of social and economic progress well in excess of what could have been expected earlier.

Capital and economic development

On the other hand, the accumulation of capital is often held to be the real basis of economic development. A simple comparison of the landscape in developed and less developed countries focuses attention on the vast stock of capital, private and social, which the advanced countries have been able to accumulate over many decades, even centuries, and it is easy to ascribe the great disparity in standards of living to this difference. It is also true that in countries exhibiting a very rapid rate of growth the rate of saving and investment has been very high: for instance in 1970 Japan was saving 40 per cent of gross domestic product compared to 21 per cent for Kenya, and 15 per cent for India.[3]

When Western economists first paid serious attention to the problems of underdeveloped countries towards the end of the last World War, they saw the problem especially as one of lack of capital.[4] The problem was not simply a matter of the 'lead' gained by the advanced countries in the accumulation of capital, however: it was claimed that there existed a 'vicious circle of poverty', preventing underdeveloped countries from getting started at all. At low levels of income savings are low; a low level of savings implies a shortage of loanable funds for investment, and low investment; a low level of investment prevents rapid increase of the capital stock and the capacity to produce; and this keeps income low. If K represents the capital stock we can represent this diagrammatically as:

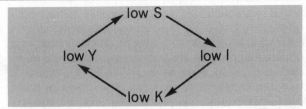

Another reason for stressing capital is that in most developing countries at the time there was a serious shortage of social capital or infrastructure—particularly transport systems—to provide the foundations for economic growth. It seemed reasonable to suppose therefore that in the early stages of development, capital investment of this type would be very important.

In recent years however the importance of capital has been increasingly questioned. In the first place while progress may be *associated* with capital accumulation, this is not the same thing as saying that capital is the direct *cause* of economic progress. In contrast with the philosophy of the 'vicious circle', it has been suggested that if there are entrepreneurs able to search out investment opportunities they will also find ways of securing finance or accumulating savings themselves out of their own profits. Therefore incomes and savings are both low *because of the absence of entrepreneurs*. When an entrepreneurial class is developed, on the other hand, it accumulates savings, in the form of profits, *and* income expands as these are invested. The 'vicious circle' does not really exist!

Another reason for the reduced emphasis on capital is the experience of investment in developing countries since the war. It was at one time thought that the transfer of capital funds from the rich countries in the form of foreign aid would permit the poor countries to break through the circle, raising incomes quickly to the point where domestic savings would be high enough subsequently for 'self-sustained growth'. Evidence of some failures among projects financed by foreign aid, and some waste of aid, as well as failure to achieve the rather unrealistic expectations of producing self-sustained growth in a short period of time, has caused a lot of disillusionment about the role of capital. In addition attempts to provide finance domestically to African businessmen over the years through various loans schemes have encountered many difficulties. George Bosa, a Ugandan economist, has described these problems in Uganda.[5] In Nigeria examination of the history of such schemes led an American economist to conclude that capital shortage in the developing countries was an 'illusion' and that the capacity to absorb capital was the problem.[6] As a warning to those who think that lack of infrastructure is the main constraint one might cite again the experience of Uganda: in the early 1950s it was hoped that the provision of social capital built around the Owen Falls hydro-electric scheme would provide the impetus for major industrial development: but despite some limited development, this impetus proved quite inadequate.

Further doubt stems from consideration of the rapidity with which the European countries, Western Germany in particular, were able to restore the gap left by the ravages of the war. The apparent conclusion would be that if the know-how is 'right', technical skills are available, and the cultural framework appropriate, a deficit in the stock of capital can be made up quite quickly.

More recently there have, been a number of careful statistical studies of the relation between the expansion of capital and output. These have proceeded by measuring the amount of physical capital and other physical inputs such as labour and land, over a period of time. It has been found that output has been increasing much more than in proportion to the physical inputs used. Specifically it was calculated that in the advanced countries the growth of capital stock accounts for *less than a quarter* of the total growth of gross national product.[7] If only part of the increase in output is due to an increase in physical inputs, it is argued, the rest must be due to other factors, such as an improvement in the quality of the labour force (skills) due to education and training or increase in technical knowledge. These other elements have together been described as the 'residual factor' in economic growth.

Having said all this, if the problem of how to 'inject' capital into developing countries can be overcome, we should recognize that developing countries may be in a different position from the advanced countries as regards the effect of capital. The latter already have large quantities of capital per head: labour in the less developed countries works with very little capital and this factor must *in part* explain the very low productivity of labour. The contribution of capital to growth may be very much more important the smaller the initial capital stock of a country. What we can say, perhaps, is that the provision of capital *by itself* will not produce development.

Technical progress (knowledge) and development

Cairncross some time ago pointed out[8] that there have been cases where periods of growth in output have been much more rapid than could be explained by the corresponding increase in the capital stock over the same period, referring especially to economic growth in the UK and USA during the interwar period, 1918–39. He deduced that if the quantity of capital had not increased in proportion to output, there must have been an improvement in the old capital stock to account for the difference. This is possible since, as old machines wear out, they can be replaced by *new kinds* of machines which can produce more, without an increase in the stock of machines. Thus technical progress does not need to wait for net investment: so long as there is 'gross investment' productivity can increase, as new machines replace old. Cairncross therefore considered technical progress to be the driving force behind economic growth, rather than the accumulation of capital as such.

According to this view, the crucial difference between developed and less developed countries lies in the 'capacity to create wealth', rather than, say, a stock of accumulated capital. Thus, it is suggested, it was inventiveness which permitted Britain at one time to be 'the workshop of the world', and inventiveness in particular which is behind the rise of Japan as a leading industrial nation. Singer[9] has estimated that developed countries spend as much as 1.5 or 2 per cent of their national incomes on research and development: but that this research spending creates new investment opportunities permitting capital accumulation of up to ten times this amount.

However, problems arise when we relate this to economic development in the underdeveloped countries. For these would appear to have ready access to a whole stock of technical knowledge already accumulated in other countries. Certainly the technical problems facing these countries are not identical, particularly in tropical agriculture. But in manufacturing industry production processes do not appear to require much adaptation and a cotton textile factory in, say, Jinja, is pretty much the same as any in the world. And if the underdeveloped countries do have access to ready-made technical knowledge, it becomes necessary to explain why its application is not more rapid.

The explanation may be that to become effective technical progress requires also accumulated capital *or* entrepreneurship *or* a stock of educated manpower—or even, perhaps, all of these together. In fact a large proportion of technical research is carried out by industrial enterprises themselves. It is because developed countries have a lot of capital locked up in various industries that the vast proportion of research is carried out in those countries and *applied* in those countries.

Human resources and development: enterprise

Technical progress consists of a series of *technical*

innovations, which Cairncross describes simply as 'the introduction of new and cheaper ways of doing things'. Technical progress thus involves *two* stages: research and invention, the creation of knowledge; and innovation, the introduction and application of new knowledge in any sector of the economy. Now if technical progress consists of the 'introduction of new ways of doing things,' the rate of technical progress will clearly depend on the number and vigour of the businessmen introducing them, on the supply of enterprise. Without a class of innovators or entrepreneurs, technical progress will be slow.

Schumpeter, more than any other economist, made the entrepreneur the basis of a general theory of development in capitalist societies.[10] The essential function of the entrepreneur, moreover, was innovation. The key of development, Schumpeter argued, was the *innovating* entrepreneur, not the inventor or the supplier of capital: it was he who directed the use of capital resources.

A common characteristic of less developed countries in Latin America, much of Asia, and even more of Africa, is the relative scarcity of indigenous entrepreneurs. However, as suggested earlier, 'entrepreneurship' has never been clearly defined, and appears to cover a wide range of skilled decision-taking, including administration and coordination, risk-taking, and innovation. We cannot go into a detailed discussion of the nature of entrepreneurship here, but would disagree with the tendency in many textbooks to treat entrepreneurship as a single category. We should argue first that 'entrepreneurship' ought properly to be divided into subcategories according to level; and secondly that different activities require different kinds of enterprise. The types of entrepreneurship required in peasant agriculture, in retail trading, and large-scale manufacturing are likely to be very different.

In most of the Eastern African countries until recently the retail and wholesale trades have been dominated by members of the minority Asian community, which has always specialized in commerce. This specialization can be explained partly by lack of opportunities in other fields, especially agriculture, in which on the whole they have not been permitted to participate, and partly by a social and cultural bias which gives the Asian in Eastern Africa a business orientation from a very early age. Nevertheless, although a few Asians have been able to develop large-scale industrial enterprise in Eastern Africa, the majority tend to be confined to trade and small-scale industry. This has in the past left the field to expatriate enterprise, and large-scale manufacturing enterprises have tended to be branches of companies with their headquarters in overseas countries. The managerial expertise required in such companies, in running a textile factory or mining company for example, is probably very different in nature from that required in much of commerce.

In contrast to the Asian in Eastern Africa, the African tradition has been in agriculture, and while there is plenty of evidence of good economic response in this field, Africans have not been so far very successful in trading and have made little or no impact, as private capitalists, in industry. Only in Kenya so far is there a clear sign of change in this respect. One reason is that compared with the salaries and allowances of senior civil servants and executives of public enterprises, the attractions of starting a new business or even entering an existing one as a partner or manager appear small for the successful African graduate or skilled artisan. Nevertheless the contrast between African and Asian entrepreneurship in Eastern Africa clearly indicates that we should be prepared to examine social factors in producing or inhibiting enterprise and effort.

Geography, culture, and social organization

An important question to ask, therefore, is what *determines* whether a country develops an energetic entrepreneurial class. Economists and, even more, other social scientists have suggested that it is in fact the energies of the people as a whole which determine how fast a country progresses. They sometimes allege that the invigorating temperate climate in North America and Europe explains their advantage over the tropical countries, where climate is not conducive to hard work. This theory shows a poor knowledge of geography: many so-called 'underdeveloped' countries have excellent climates, including Kenya and Ethiopia; while other countries have progressed without this benefit. Another theory is that there are racial differences affecting rates of economic progress: this shows a poor knowledge of history, since before their decline and before their classification as countries in need of development, countries like Greece, Egypt, and China were ancient centres of civilization, long before Western Europe.

What these facts suggest is that the cultural framework or social system may be the dominating factor. Here we should perhaps distinguish between *social organization*, such as the land tenure system or the class structure, and the *traits of character* of the people, as determined by various social factors. As regards the former there is no doubt that in Africa the traditional system of leaving much of the responsibility for food farming to wives and children has had an inhibiting effect on the emergence of progressive, modern-minded farmers. The traditional communalism of African society, with its preference for cooperation rather than competition among neighbours and kinsmen, may well work against initiative and enterprise (we consider in a later chapter how it may be used progressively). Indeed any system which penalizes the unorthodox may be unhelpful: in African society jealousy of the successful may manifest itself in burning down his hut and slashing his crops! Economic progress may be seen as the outcome of the efforts of hundreds of individuals: hence if a class structure exists, or a system of racial segregation, entire segments of society may be held back, at the cost of progress in the society as a whole. The caste system in India is frequently cited as an example, and in a much milder way, the 'class system' in Britain. Overlooking the problem of racial segregation, the dynamic growth of the United States is sometimes ascribed in part to the essentially open, friction-free American society in which, it is claimed, any individual with sufficient drive may reach the top.

Turning to factors conditioning character and attitudes, religion is one important aspect of society which may hinder or foster economic progress. An American economist, E. E. Hagen,[11] has put forward the theory that the fundamental and *ultimate* reason for economic development lies in the character of the people as determined by the social environment, in particular the way in which they are brought up. He considers that children must be 'indoctrinated' with ambition and the desire to succeed from an early age, either financially or in a similarly progressive way, and must continue to receive encouragement in advancing themselves as they grow older. Childhood upbringing is important also because in developed countries children obtain much of their education, in the wide sense, from their home: in contrast, children in traditional Africa tend to be left very much on their own, and in any case their main contact will be mostly with their mothers, who are still largely uneducated. This leads one inevitably to consider the role of education in economic development.

Human resources and development: education and skills

Technical progress involves improvements in the quality of the capital stock with which labour works, as well as to some extent improvement in the quality of organization, how factors of production are used. An alternative explanation of differences in productivity and growth has been popular among economists, particularly since the publication in 1961 of an article by the American economist, T.W. Schultz,

called 'Investment in Human Capital':[12] This involves an improvement instead in *the quality of the labour force*, as a result of *education and training*. For instance a recent statement by Maddison goes as far as saying:[13] 'Rich countries have a much higher stock of education and skilled people than poor countries, and it is clear that most of their productive achievements depend on the availability of these skills.' If, for instance, we consider the stock of people with high level skills, it has been estimated that while in developed countries some 4 or 5 per cent of the labour force have these skills, the figure for less developed countries is just 1 per cent, a ratio of 5 to 1.

According to this new wisdom, we can talk about 'investment in human capital' first because this is a *stock* of skills, just as accumulated capital is a stock. The contribution of the educational system to output is *indirect*: the output of the system is in fact a 'stock' of skills which are *then* employed directly to yield output. Secondly the acquisition of this stock involves current *sacrifice* for the sake of extra future output, i.e. investment: we can spend more now on education rather than consumption goods or more on other forms of investment such as building factories; but later on when the extra educated manpower becomes available, output will go up. Thirdly, this investment will *take time* to yield a return in extra output: it can take twenty years of education, for instance, to produce a fully qualified engineer. And since an important part of education is actually obtained *in the home*, the children of educated people have been observed to have a tremendous advantage over those of uneducated parents: hence educational expenditure can continue to have effects on output several generations later. Investment in human capital has so many of the features of ordinary capital investment that capital is sometimes defined broadly to include both forms, physical and human.

An efficient educational system has also been classified as part of a country's *infrastructure*, being considered by some as a *precondition* of a high level of output. Maddison has also suggested that educational programmes played a major role in the economic transformation of the USSR and Japan.

If the stock of skills is a major constraint on economic development, this must be considered serious; and particularly serious for Africa. For there is very great variation in the size of this stock, not only between the developed and less developed countries, but also among the less developed countries themselves. Some indication of this is given in Table 2.3 which gives the ratio of selected types of 'high-level manpower' to total labour force in different countries. The professions listed in the table account for something like half of all high-level manpower in the country. From the last column we see that the 'developed countries' have a ratio of around 2 or 3 per cent in the professions listed (around 25 per 1,000). Unfortunately information is given regarding only two African countries, Guinea (0.025 per cent or 1 out of 4,000) and Nigeria (0.07 per cent or less than 1 per 1,000): but since Guinea is one of the worst-off African countries and Nigeria one of the better-off in terms of trained manpower, we can assume that most of the Eastern African countries will have ratios somewhere in between these two. The developed country ratios are thus about *a hundred times* that for Guinea and *35 times*, say, that for Nigeria. Even India's ratio is 6.5 times that for Nigeria, and Brazil's ratio is 10 times the Nigerian and 28 times the Guinean. In general we can say that within the 'Third World' the African countries have only a fraction of the supply of local skilled manpower which the Asian countries have, while the Latin American countries are even further ahead.

In interpreting these figures, we must remember that they relate only to high-level manpower: they give only an indication of what the situation might be regarding the total stock of skilled manpower. The position with respect to middle- and lower-level (including manual) skills, may be even more important, particularly for industrialization. The *type* of skills is obviously important, and the table shows that the distribution is different for each type of manpower. While India and Iran are equally well off taking the three categories together, Iran has three times the ratio of scientists and engineers. The developed countries have something like 120 times the number

Table 2.3　*The ratio of selected types of skilled manpower to the labour force, 1959*

	Scientists and engineers	Doctors, dentists, pharmacists, and veterinarians	Secondary and higher teachers	Sum of three columns
Developed countries				
France	0.8	0.4	0.6	1.8
Italy	0.9	0.6	1.0	2.5
UK	1.0	0.3	0.7	2.0
USA	1.7	0.7	1.0	3.4
Canada	1.3	0.5	0.9	2.7
USSR	1.2	0.4		
Developing Europe				
Greece	0.4	0.5	0.4	1.3
Spain	0.3	0.6	0.3	1.2
Turkey	0.2	0.1	0.2	0.5
Yugoslavia	0.5	0.2	0.3	1.0
Latin America				
Argentina	0.2[1]	0.4[2]		
Brazil	0.1[1]	0.2	0.4	0.7
Columbia		0.1	0.5	
Peru		0.2	0.6	
Mexico		0.2	0.4	
Asia				
India	0.05	0.1	0.3	0.45
Iran	0.16	0.1	0.2	0.46
Pakistan	0.05	0.03	0.2	0.28
Philippines	0.24	0.42		
Taiwan	0.1	0.2	0.6	0.9
Thailand	0.01	0.03	0.1	0.14
Africa				
Guinea	0.002[1]	0.007	0.016	0.025
Nigeria	0.01	0.01	0.05	0.07

SOURCE: Maddison, op. cit.

NOTES: [1] engineers only;
　　　　[2] doctors and dentists only

of scientists and engineers per 1,000 that Nigeria has (compared with 30 times for the three categories together).

While investment in human capital, through education and training, seems to be an important source of economic growth it is not clear that all kinds of education and training bring economic returns or which types and level of education bring the highest returns. Indeed some education seems to have brought more dissatisfaction and social problems. Thus primary or secondary school leavers have drifted from the rural areas to the towns where they have been left unemployed: education has left them unwilling to remain in the rural areas, without qualifying them for jobs in town. In some developing countries, particularly India and Pakistan, overproduction of low-quality graduates, especially though not exclusively on the Arts side, has brought about the phenomenon of graduate unemployment.

Clearly the type and level of education provided are important. Should educational investment be in primary education or secondary education, or in university? Should it be in technical subjects or in general education? Lewis has argued that returns in primary education should be high, since it will help to change attitudes from those of a traditional social system to those required in a modern economy.[14] G. K. Helleiner has argued, in contrast, that primary and technical education should be concentrated on the adult population which is actively employed—and this is mainly in peasant agriculture. 'The highest returns from educational inputs,' he says, 'undoubtedly come from adult education—where it is effectively offered.'[15]

A general review

Since interest in the problem of developing countries increased after the war, emphasis has been put in succession on different elements. At first the greatest emphasis was on lack of capital, and later on lack of entrepreneurship and on social factors. More recently it has been on the lack of education and skills. The search has been for a single missing ingredient or missing factor towards which corrective action could be directed. The underlying analyses have been described as *single-barrier theories* of development,[16] in that they imply that if one barrier could be surmounted—whether capital shortage or lack of

educated manpower—everything would then proceed smoothly. Attempts to take corrective action on these lines have brought a series of disappointments, perhaps for two reasons. First, it may be that developing countries today are expecting results too rapidly: they would like the amount of development in 25 years which the present advanced countries achieved in 200 years. Any attempt to 'concertina' the process of development in this way is bound to involve some disappointments. Secondly, it may be that the 'single barrier' approach is the wrong one. The factors affecting development may be interdependent and complementary—for instance, as we have said, technical progress may be fastest where there is already a stock of capital, where there is an innovative entrepreneurial class, and where there is a stock of educated and skilled manpower. It may therefore be necessary to operate on all these things *simultaneously*.

An alternative explanation of underdevelopment: the international economic order

These theories, however, all emphasize *internal* factors within the country retarding development. A different view altogether puts the blame on *external factors*, specifically the international economic system.[17] It is argued that international trade favours the present developed countries. The exports of the developing countries face much fiercer competition from advanced countries than these countries did when they themselves were developing. Expansion of these exports is further handicapped by policies of protection pursued by the rich countries. Economic development in some poor countries is dominated by multinational companies with headquarters overseas, who are mainly interested in short-term profits and not in the long-term development of the countries concerned, and who have regarded the underdeveloped countries especially as a source of raw materials for sale in the metropolitan industrial centres. These factors, particularly access to markets, are undoubtedly very important, and a proper explanation of development and underdevelopment must involve a number of internal factors and these external factors. We shall look at the international economic system in more detail in Chapter 19.

Questions on Chapter 2

1. How does 'capital' differ from 'natural resources'?
2. Can the supply of 'land' be increased?
3. What is 'entrepreneurship'? Does it exist in a socialist system?
4. In what sense is 'human capital' capital?
5. How important are natural resources in economic development?
6. Is capital accumulation the cause or the effect of economic development?
7. Discuss the view that economic growth depends on 'inventiveness'.
8. Why is technical progress possible when net investment is zero or even negative?
9. How important do you think the 'cultural framework' is in producing underdevelopment?
10. What is 'education'? Can education by itself bring development?
11. What do you understand by 'single-barrier' theories of development? What is wrong with them?
12. Compare the importance of 'internal' and 'external' factors in holding back development. What effect would an improvement in the external trading position of less developed countries have on the *internal* factors?

Notes

[1] Although anyone lending money to the owner of the enterprise may take more risks.

[2] The remainder of this chapter will repay a rereading after the reader has completed the text as far as Part VIII.

[3] These figures are given more fully in Chapter 37, where they are further discussed. It should be noted here that for a country 'saving' and 'investment' come to the same thing. In order to 'save' and have more consumption goods available in the future a country has to expand its productive capacity or stock of capital goods. An act of 'investment' means adding to this stock of capital goods, which is therefore also an act of 'saving'.

[4] The most influential writers at the time were P.N. Rosenstein-Rodan ('Problems of Industrialization of Eastern and South-Eastern Europe'. *Economic Journal*, June 1943); and R. Nurkse (*Problems of Capital Formation in Underdeveloped Countries*, Oxford University Press, 1953); the latter also stressed the lack of internal markets.

[5] G. R. Bosa, *The Financing of Small-Scale Enterprises in Uganda*, Oxford University Press, 1969.

[6] Sayre P. Schatz, 'The "Capital Shortage" Illusion: Government Lending in Nigeria', *Oxford Economic Papers*, Vol. 17, 2, 1965. This analyses attempts by the Federal Loans Board in Nigeria to find enterprises which might make profitable use of loans.

[7] See particularly E. F. Denison, *Why Growth Rates Differ*, Allen & Unwin, 1968, and H. B. Chenery, 'Targets for Development', in Barbara Ward *et al.*, eds. *The Widening Gap: Development in the 1970s*, Columbia University Press, 1971.

[8] A. K. Cairncross, *Factors in Economic Development*, Unwin University Books, 1962, Chapter 4.

[9] H. W. Singer, 'Education and Economic Development', in H. W. Singer, *International Development: Growth and Change*, McGraw-Hill, 1964.

[10] J. A. Schumpeter, *The Theory of Economic Development*, Harvard University Press, 1934.

[11] E. E. Hagen, *On the Theory of Social Change: How Economic Growth Begins*, Dorsey Press, 1962.

[12] T. W. Schultz, 'Investment in Human Capital', *American Economic Review*, 1961.

[13] A. Maddison, *Foreign Skills and Technical Assistance in Economic Development*, OECD, Paris, 1965.

[14] W. A. Lewis, *Development Planning*, Allen & Unwin, 1966, p. 101.

[15] G. K. Helleiner, 'Structural Change in Africa,' in Barbara Ward *et al.*, eds, *The Widening Gap*, Columbia University Press, 1971, p. 101.

[16] P. Streeten, 'Single Barrier Theories of Development', *The Frontiers of Development Studies*, Macmillan, 1972.

[17] See for example, P. Baran, *The Political Economy of Growth*, New York, 1962; C. Furtado, *Development and Underdevelopment*, University of California Press, 1971; T. Szentes, *The Political Economy of Underdevelopment*, Alcademiai Kiado, Budapest, 1971; Richard Harris, ed., *Political Economy of Africa*, Schenkman. Cambridge, Mass., 1975.

3 Population and Economic Development

The discussion in the previous chapter was entirely in terms of absolute quantities of the factors: but the relative amounts are also important, that is to say, the proportions in which they exist. The reason for this is simply that the factors of production are not perfect substitutes for one another. For example, if we have lots of labour, as in India, we can use it instead of land or capital only to a limited extent. This means that there will be too many workers for what is a fixed amount of land, so that the extra workers do not add much to the total product. Overpopulation is in part, therefore, a problem of balance between the quantities of factors of production.

The balance between the factors of production: the population problem

The problem of excess population may be a serious obstacle to development. From our earlier discussion it might appear that, given the appropriate conditions, sufficient foreign capital and technical assistance, the poor countries could move along the same path of economic progress as the developed nations. Often, however, this is frustrated by growth of population which means that the expansion of output is outstripped by increased need. This is aggravated by the fact that poor people tend to have large families, rather than the other way round, so that countries whose poverty is increased by population pressure are the very ones which find it difficult to limit family size. While improvements in medical knowledge and increased application of that knowledge have been able to produce dramatic reductions in death rates, so that the average life expectancy in Asia may well have been doubled over the past half-century, application of the improvements in technical knowledge has not been able to produce equally dramatic changes in the supply of food.

T. R. Malthus, an English clergyman interested in economics, or 'Political Economy' as it was then called, was concerned with this problem of population pressure at the end of the eighteenth century. The basis of Malthus' theory, outlined in his *Essay on the Principles of Population* (1798), was that whereas population tended to grow at a geometric rate (by a constant percentage each period, as, for example, 4, 8, 16, 32, 64, 128, ...) the food supply could only be expected to grow at an arithmetic rate (by a constant amount each period, as, for example 8, 16, 24, 32, 40, 48 ...). With a higher rate of growth for population than for food, the former must inevitably outstrip the latter at some point; and population would continue to grow until the food available was only sufficient to provide basic subsistence to the people. Population would then be checked at this level, since births in excess of this would be offset by the tendency for deaths to increase through lack of food; thereafter population would grow only as the supply of food expanded.

The theory is illustrated in Figure 3.1 using the series quoted. The line ABC represents the growth of population in millions, in the absence of checks. The line DBE represents the hypothetical increase in the maximum numbers of population that the available food supply can support. The actual growth of population will therefore be given by the line ABE.

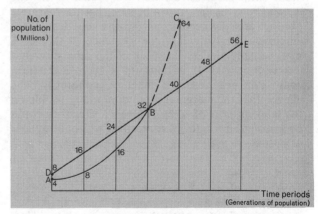

Figure 3.1 *The Malthusian theory of population.*

The Law of Diminishing Returns (Variable Proportions)

Another English 'classical' economist, John Stuart Mill, later developed and refined the 'Malthusian' theory in order to generalize the relationship between the supply of labour (population) and the supply of food from land. This generalization is known as the *Law of Diminishing Returns*, sometimes called the *Law of Variable Factor Proportions*. This can be simply stated as follows.

As successive units of a variable factor are added to a given quantity of a fixed factor *after a certain stage* additional units will increase output by successively smaller amounts.

Let us illustrate this 'Law' by a hypothetical numerical example in which labour is the only variable factor, being applied to a fixed area of land, to produce maize. Column 1 indicates that the number of hectares is fixed at one throughout, column 2 giving the number of workers applied to it, and column 3 the total product resulting. The marginal product of a factor of production is defined to be the extra product due to the employment of one more unit of the factor, the amounts of the other factors being held constant. This is given in column 4. For example when 5 men are employed, 60 bags of maize are produced and when 6 men are employed, 66 bags. The 'marginal product' of the sixth man is therefore 6 bags of maize. The rest of column 4 may be calculated in the same way. The data are illustrated in Figure 3.2, where the vertical rectangles represent the marginal products and the total product, being the sum of the contributions of all the workers, is represented by the total area. It can be seen that the marginal product first of all rises, reaches a maximum of 18 when 3 men are employed, and then diminishes progressively in accordance with the 'Law'. From the data it will be seen that the marginal product actually becomes negative when 10 men are employed, implying that the existence of the tenth man actually hinders the work of the others, so that less is produced. It is doubtful if such a situation could ever exist, but a number of economists have alleged that the marginal product of many people on the land in parts of India is zero, in that they could be transferred to other occupations without any loss of output.

Table 3.1 *The law of diminishing returns (variable proportions)*

Column 1 Fixed factor (no. of hectares)	Column 2 Variable factor (no. of men)	Column 3 Total product (bags of maize)	Column 4 Marginal product (bags of maize)	Column 5 Average product (bags of maize)
1	0	0	—	—
1	1	10	10	10
1	2	24	14	12
1	3	42	18	14
1	4	52	10	13
1	5	60	8	12
1	6	66	6	11
1	7	70	4	10
1	8	72	2	9
1	9	72	0	8
1	10	70	−2	7

Column 5 in Table 3.1 gives values for the average product of labour. This is defined simply as the total product divided by the number of workers employed. This also increases at first, up to 14, and then falls progressively. This is a result of this same 'Law' and indeed the law could be expressed in terms of either the average or the marginal product, since there is a necessary relationship between these two, as we shall see later.

An alternative name for the 'Law' is the Law of Variable Proportions. This designation emphasizes that this is a matter of the proportions in which the factors are applied. Thus corresponding to the phase of decreasing returns we have a phase of increasing returns: one man, for instance, cannot cope with one hectare of land, that is to say, there is too much land in relation to labour to start with. Also since diminishing returns are caused by the variable factor being an imperfect substitute for the other, the speed at which the marginal product declines obviously depends on how imperfect the factors are as substitutes.

The following conditions must be noted with respect to the operation of our 'Law'.

First, it assumes that only one of the two factors is variable and that other things remain the same, including the state of technical knowledge. An increase in the quantity of a third factor or a series of new inventions could lift the whole curve bodily upwards as in Figure 3.3. This in no way invalidates the 'Law'.

Second, the 'Law' assumes that all units of the variable factor are equally efficient. Output per man is less when nine men are employed than when five are, but in each case each man contributes the same proportion of total output as his fellows. It is like asking two men to share a hoe: each man is as

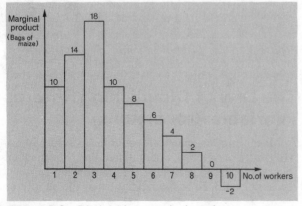

Figure 3.2 *Diminishing marginal products.*

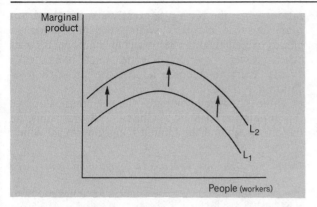

Figure 3.3 *Effect of changes in the quantity of a third factor.*

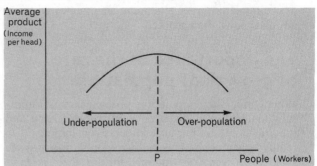

Figure 3.4 *The 'optimum' population.*

efficient as the other, but each is less efficient than if he had a hoe to himself.

Third, while the fall in output per man implies increasing cost of output, the law is independent of any change in factor prices: for example, a rise in the wage rate as more men are employed. It will operate even if labour is available in indefinite amount at the going wage rate. It may happen that wage rates rise as more men are employed, either because of the need to attract men from other industries, or the need to offer more incentive to train for a particular type of job, or the need to persuade the existing work-force to work overtime; but these are additional reasons for increasing costs.

The concept of an 'optimum population'

Some economists have talked about an 'optimum' population for a country, implying that the population can be either too small or too large in relation to its other resources. 'Underpopulation' arises because a thinly distributed population means relatively high transport costs. This in turn has two effects. First, trade and exchange are made more difficult: hence there is less specialization and more inclination to undertake subsistence production in agriculture, and less specialized industry because of a smaller market. Secondly, the amount of social capital required per head of population is increased, so that it may not be worth building roads, dams, bridges, or even schools and hospitals, or spending money on general administration for the small number of people in each area. It is argued that if 'underpopulation' and 'overpopulation' can exist, somewhere in between there must be an 'optimum' or best size of population. This will be at the point, illustrated in Figure 3.4 as point P, where the average product is at a maximum and where the standard of living each person could enjoy is greatest, if the product were shared equally.

As it turns out, the concept has rather a shaky basis. As we saw earlier, the Law of Diminishing Returns assumes that other things remain the same. But in some countries technical progress and the application of new methods of production has been shown to be capable of increasing output potential tremendously. Malthus' own fears were proved unwarranted by the social and economic transformation which accompanied the Industrial Revolution in Britain, already under way at the end of the eighteenth century. Secondly, although land is in fixed supply another factor of production, capital, can be increased and is in fact a good 'substitute' for land even in agriculture (where intensive improvements in methods of production such as the use of fertilizers can greatly increase yields) but more especially in the manufacturing industry. Thirdly, even if possibilities for food production are limited, as in Britain, opportunities for trade may be developed whereby food is obtained from overseas in exchange for manufactured goods.

Thus we would agree that while there is sense in talking about 'overpopulation' and 'underpopulation' it does not follow that some size of population must be the 'optimum'. In the first place there is a wide area of flexibility where the size of the population is probably not important. Secondly the argument, if sensible in a static context, is less meaningful in the dynamic context of growth. However an excess population may make it extremely difficult for a country to 'get started' on the path towards economic growth. Because of excess population, there is poverty; because of poverty, people find it difficult to save and acquire capital equipment; therefore agriculture stagnates, education is limited, and health poor; the lack of capital and technical progress keeps incomes low and, as we pointed out earlier, poor people tend to have large families, making the population problem worse. We have a 'vicious circle'. If, on the other hand, the circle can be broken by finding some means to control population, the country may make a start in economic development, and as economic progress gets under way more and more population will be absorbed.

The importance of the rate of growth of population

When discussing population problems, it is important to distinguish between population *density* and the *growth rate* of population. Here it is important to realize what constitutes a high population growth rate: 3 per cent per annum, for instance, is *high*, and very different from a rate of 1 per cent. A 1 per cent per annum growth rate will, due to the effect of 'compound interest', double population in 70 years; a 2 per cent rate will double it in 35 years; and a 3 per cent rate in $23\frac{1}{2}$ years.[1]

This means that even if population densities in a country are not very high *now*, with a 3 per cent per annum rate it could soon experience such densities.

Secondly, a high population growth rate means that a much higher rate of growth in national income than otherwise will be needed to raise income per head and the standard of living. Suppose, for example, a country succeeded in increasing output by 50 per cent over 25 years, but at the same time its population grew at 3 per cent per annum. We can refer to output (income) at the start as Y_0, and to the initial population as P_0. Initially, then, income per head would be (Y_0/P_0). At 3 per cent per annum population would double in 25 years (slightly less in fact), to $2P_0$. If in the same time output has increased by 50 per cent, this would now equal $\frac{3}{2}Y_0$. Income per head after 25 years would then equal $(\frac{3}{2}Y_0)/(2P_0)$. This is equal to $\frac{3}{4}(Y_0/P_0)$. Thus income per head would be only three-quarters of the original level, and the standard of living would have *fallen* by one-quarter.

This example is a *bit* misleading. Obviously with double the number of people, in the second situation a lot of additional labour would be available with which to increase output. On the other hand, if there is a shortage of land, or lack of capital, or limited export markets, it may be difficult for this extra population to make a very effective contribution to output.

The structure of the population

The third point about a high population growth rate is that it will affect the *age structure* of the population. A high birth rate means that there will be a relatively high proportion of children to adults in the population. This arises because a high population growth rate occurs (excluding the effects of mig-

ration) when the birth rate greatly exceeds the death rate: thus the numbers joining the population as babies exceed the numbers leaving the population as deaths. Over a period of time, since babies take twenty years to become adults, the proportion of children will increase. This relationship can be seen in Table 3.2, which compares the age composition of the population in Kenya, Ghana, and Mauritius, on the one hand, and the United Kingdom on the other.

Table 3.2 *The age structure of population in selected countries*

Age group (years)	Kenya 1969 (%)		Ghana 1970 (%)		Mauritius 1971 (%)		UK 1971 (%)	
0–14	48	58	47	56	40	52	24	31
15–19	10		9		12		7	
20–59	37	39	38	40	42	44	50	56
60–64	2		2		2		6	
65 and over	3		4		4		13	

SOURCE: *UN Demographic Yearbook*, 1975

The composition of the population is of economic significance because not all individuals in the population contribute equally to production. Given the numbers of the population, the supply of labour depends upon the proportion of people who are members of the work-force. The size of the *economically active* population is determined especially by the age structure; the ratio of men to women; the average working day put in; and the efficiency or quality of the labour effort. The proportion of the population in the work-force is a matter of the proportion of old people and the retiring age or, in the case of African farmers, the age at which they cease to contribute much to agricultural output; the proportion of children in the population; and the proportion of women participating in work outside the home.

In developed countries, government or private insurance schemes are increasingly operating to ensure that through old age pensions a person continues after retirement to enjoy at least a minimum standard of living, if not a standard equal to that enjoyed during his working life. Social security is comparatively undeveloped in Africa in the modern sense of the word but is, of course, a feature of traditional life, where old people are by custom looked after by their families or local communities. As we have stated previously, old age pensions constitute a transfer payment: that is to say, a claim against the flow of goods and services produced by the current work-force. Clearly the number of retired people in the work-force determines the extent of this burden.

Like old people, children contribute little to output, even if employed to some extent on African farms. And while their direct consumption of goods and services is relatively low, they also 'consume' the resources spent by the government on education, health, and other services. Children and old people are referred to as 'dependants' in that they consume goods and services produced by the work-force without *at the moment* producing goods themselves. To that extent, their consumption also constitutes a 'burden' on the work-force, even if one that the work-force are very happy to bear.

Table 3.2 shows that 58 per cent of the population in Kenya and 56 per cent in Ghana were estimated to be below the age of 20, presumably not contributing a great deal to output, with a figure for Mauritius of 52 per cent. In contrast, the figure for the United Kingdom was 31, just about *half* the Kenya figure. The exact definition of the work-force is somewhat arbitrary, and the economically active age groups may well differ between Kenya, Ghana, and the United Kingdom, for instance. However, if we take the age groups 20–64 years to constitute the bulk of the work-force in all three cases, this accounts for 56 per cent of the population in the United Kingdom, compared to 44 per cent in Mauritius and only 39–40 per cent in Kenya and Ghana. The ratio of dependants to work-force, *the dependency ratio*, thus comes out on this definition as $44/56 = 0.8$ for the United Kingdom, $56/44 = 1.3$ for Mauritius, and $61/39 = 1.6$ for Kenya. The relative numbers of dependants for Kenya and other less developed countries may be even higher, since poor health may reduce the effective contribution to output of people above, say, the age of 50; and fewer young people in the 15–19 age group may be able to find productive employment.

Another important feature of the structure of population is the ratio of women to men, since women tend to stay at home as housewives or, if they work, tend to be limited in the range of jobs which they can do or are permitted to do. In Africa, of course, wives constitute an important part of farm labour, quite apart from engaging in such activities as hut building or grain pounding. It is significant, however, that they tend to be restricted to the sort of work in which they are obviously most handicapped, namely, physical labour.

An interesting and unusual exception to the generally low participation of women and children in the labour force is, however, found in the Sudan. In the 1955/56 census as much as 48 per cent of the total population of just over 10 millions reported themselves as having at least a subsidiary occupation, and of these 4.9 million workers, 1.2 million were adult women, and nearly 1 million children between the ages of 5 years and puberty. The explanation for the high participation rate of young boys, especially, is partly to be found in the traditions of pastoral and agrarian societies and partly in the shortage of school places. Although the Sudan is a predominantly Arab country, female farm labour is important in the southern and western regions. If social and religious restrictions on the female Arab population were relaxed, it is believed that the Sudan's participation rate could be increased still more. Here and elsewhere female labour constitutes a 'reserve army' of labour which could greatly reduce the dependence of households on male workers.

The case for controlling population

When we look around at the many seriously overpopulated countries in the world, the case for these countries controlling population seems obvious. In fact the economists' case for population control is more complicated, and needs to be considered rather carefully.

We can consider this case the other way round, by looking at what the effects would be of *not* controlling population. Here we need to consider separately (1) the effects of increasing population *densities*; and (2) the effects of a higher population growth rate.

The effects of increasing population densities

The main analysis here has been done above. In general terms, the expansion of population increases the size of the labour force, and if the amount of land is limited, the labour/land ratio will eventually rise, producing diminishing returns to labour. The average product of labour, and thus income per head, will fall. In terms of the family, food and other output will not increase in proportion to the size of the household, and each member of the household will be able to consume less. Over the long period, if land becomes scarce, the family plot of land will have to be split up among several sons or daughters, yielding a lower income per head to the newer generation.

Alternatively, there may be a second effect of increasing population densities, the creation of open unemployment as numbers of the population are driven off the land altogether. The cause of this is basically the same as that producing reduced income per head, or underemployment, in the countryside; but open unemployment is apparently more effective in drawing the attention of the government towards the dangers of uncontrolled population growth.

The third effect of increasing population density may be to increase social inequality. For income per head will not necessarily be reduced evenly for all members as population increases. As the ratio of labour to land increases, land will become increasingly scarce, and rents per acre will go up. If land is held by a few large landowners, these will become relatively *richer*. This will not apply to a significant extent when the land is owned by large numbers of small peasant farmers, or when it is owned communally under, for instance, traditional African custom. But in many less developed countries, land-ownership is very unequal, and population growth can benefit the rich landowners. Owners of capital, also, may benefit. And not only will the rent of land go up but, because of expansion in the number of labourers, wages will go down. A well-known British economist, James Meade, has suggested this might be one result of population expansion in Mauritius, and similar economies.[2]

The effects of a high population growth rate

Even if the country is not presently overpopulated, there could be important benefits from restricting population expansion. In the previous chapter we saw that output depends on land, labour, *and* capital. If the number of workers expands, the amount of capital should expand in the same proportion: otherwise the extra workers would be less well equipped with machinery, tools, and others forms of capital, and output per worker would fall. If we are to *avoid* a fall in income per head as population grows, we must expand the capital stock: which means raising the level of investment. Thus expanding population (even from a low level) means that a higher rate of investment (and saving) is needed, simply to avoid a fall in income per head, in the standard of living.

We can put this argument in more precise terms. Suppose the capital stock of a country is valued at $4,000 million, and that annual output (income) is $1,000 million. The capital–output ratio is then said to be 4:1. Suppose further that the population is growing at 3 per cent per annum. Income per head will be constant if output also increases by 3 per cent, that is, by $30 million during the year. Assuming that to produce this extra output requires the corresponding amount of capital, in the ratio 4:1, the capital stock will need to be increased by $120 million. Thus, out of the annual output of $1,000 million, $120 million must go towards producing the new capital goods with which to equip the extra workers. This is 12 per cent of total output. Hence 12 per cent of income must be saved, and allocated to investment,

just to maintain the same output per head. To *increase* the standard of living would mean raising the rate of investment *above* 12 per cent.

The second effect of population growth arises out of its effect on the dependency ratio. A high population growth rate, we said, produces a high ratio of children in the population. Children may be described as 'pure consumers' for the first 14 or so years of their lives. Not only do they consume food, clothing, and the like provided by their parents, but they require school, medical facilities, and other services generally provided by the state, all of which consumes resources.

Although when they grow up they will contribute to output, this will not happen for 14 years or more. If, on the other hand, children are not born, because of a family planning campaign, the most immediate effect is that resources which would have been used up over the next 14 years for their consumption are saved. There is *released consumption* due to these 'avoided births'. This output, which would have gone into consumption, could instead go into investment. Controlling the birth rate could, therefore, mean a higher rate of investment, and thus *a higher rate of growth of national income*. The value of this would increase over time since, as income increases, it will be easier to invest still more.

At the same time, if population growth continues to be restricted, there will be an increase in income per head, Y/P, for two reasons: the increased income means a larger *numerator*, and the reduced population means a smaller *denominator*.

Finally, we should note that a reduced population growth rate will delay the time when population densities will reach a critical level, bringing into play the effects mentioned. As pointed out earlier, a 3 per cent rate of growth can double the population in what is, historically, a very short space of time, about 23 years.

The possibility of beneficial effects from population increase

A number of influential economists have argued that population growth may either be harmless as far as real income growth is considered, or even beneficial. It is said, first, that the expansion of population may stimulate demand, and in particular may give a useful stimulus to investment. This argument may have some validity for the rich industrialized nations which are prone to periodic lack of effective demand, causing resources to fall idle: but the less developed countries suffer from lack of resources, capital or skilled labour, for instance, affecting the supply of output, rather than lack of demand.

Secondly, it has been argued that pressure on standards of living due to land shortage may produce the necessary 'shock' to the system, leading peasant cultivators, for example, to look for new ways of increasing productivity. Once new methods have been adopted to stop income per head from *falling*, there might be continued interest in innovations for the purpose of *raising* incomes. The difficulty with this argument is, first, that in all the less developed economies there is *already* enough poverty, if poverty is all that is required to stimulate change; and, second, that there are many countries and parts of countries suffering from severe land pressure which have *not* shown this desirable response.

Finally, it has been pointed out that many countries have shown high rates of economic growth *despite* high population growth, and that high population growth is generally not correlated with low income growth. Our argument, however, is not that high population growth makes income growth impossible, only that it may make it considerably more difficult, *especially* when other factors exist to prevent the ready expansion of output. Indeed those countries which face the most serious obstacles to growth *apart from* population growth are those which can least afford unrestricted population increase.

Population in Africa

Is there a population problem in Eastern Africa? The East Africa Royal Commission was set up in 1953 in order 'to examine all possible measures to achieve improved standards of living, having regard to possible increase in the population and to the present congestion of African population in certain areas'. Although this Commission reported in 1955 that there was no serious overall population problem 'provided that obstacles to the development of a modern exchange economy are overcome', subsequent evidence of a more rapid increase in population has worried many observers, and the International Labour Organization (ILO) Mission on employment in Kenya,[3] reporting in 1972, laid great stress on the need for a policy to control population if the problems of unemployment were to be kept in check.

Yet, if we look at Table 3.3, which compares total population *with total land area* for a number of countries, we find that population in mainland Tanzania, the Sudan, and Zambia, for example, appears positively *sparse* in relation to countries with well-known population problems, like India and the Caribbean countries. Tanzania mainland has only 16 persons per square kilometre, on average, and Zambia just 7 persons. Only Mauritius and Zanzibar within Eastern Africa can rank alongside these, although Burundi and Ruanda, on the border with Uganda and Tanzania, also have population densities of near-comparable proportions.

In fact, the answer lies partly in the statistics as they have been presented. In the first place it is not *total* land area which is relevant, strictly, but the amount of *cultivable* land. Problems may exist in areas

Table 3.3 Population densities in selected countries, 1975

Estimated population per square kilometre in 1975					
World	29	Africa	13	Asia	82
				Latin America	16
Eastern Africa	18	Western Africa	19	North America	11
		Liberia	15		
Tanzania (Mainland)	16	Ghana	41	USSR	11
Kenya	23	Nigeria	68	Europe (exc. USSR)	96
Uganda	49	Sierra Leone	38		
Zambia	7	Rwanda	148	UK	229
Malawi	43	Burundi	159	Japan	298
Sudan	7	Zanzibar	171	India	182
Ethiopia	23	Mauritius	440	Caribbean	113

SOURCE: *UN Demographic Yearbook*, 1975

Table 3.4 Population densities for selected regions or provinces within Kenya, Uganda, Tanzania, and Malawi (persons per square kilometre)

Country	Province/Region	Population density
Kenya (1969)	Nyanza	169
	Western	162
	Central	127
	North-eastern	11
Tanzania (1967)	Zanzibar & Pemba	134
	Mwanza	54
	Kilimanjaro	49
	West Lake	23
	Coast	15
	Tabora	5
Uganda (1969)	Buganda	71
	Eastern	51
	Northern	30
Malawi (1966)	Southern	65
	Central	42
	Northern	18

SOURCE: *Population Census Reports*

with very low densities if the food supply is inefficient to sustain even a thinly scattered population.

Secondly, the figures given are averages, which may hide very high densities in some areas. Table 3.4 gives population densities for some of the provinces within the Eastern African countries. This reveals that we have an imminent population problem in Nyanza and Western Provinces of Kenya, and possibly in the Central Province, despite the higher productivity of land there. The high densities of Buganda and Eastern Regions of Uganda and of the Mwanza Region of Tanzania reflect similar geographical locations around Lake Victoria as Nyanza.

In Malawi over half the population is concentrated in the Southern Region which has only one-third of the country's land area, and even here the average density of 65 persons per square kilometre understates the density in particular districts like Chiradzulu which has 185 persons to the square kilometre.

However it is not so much existing densities of population in Africa which cause concern, but the *rate of growth* of population. Table 3.5 gives *very rough* estimates of births and deaths for different parts of the world, and the rates of increase of population which can result from them, together with any net migration. It will be seen that the birth rate in Western and Eastern Africa is nearly *three times*

the European rate, while that for Africa as a whole is now higher than that for South Asia. To take one country, Kenya, it has been estimated that in 1969 (the Census Year) the rate of natural increase was 3.3 per cent compared to less than 3 per cent in 1962. This would indicate that not only is the rate of increase high, but there is even an *acceleration*. It is thought that the rate could move up still further to 4 per cent. At 4 per cent, the population of Kenya would double in 18 years! And if this is true of Kenya, the position in other countries in Eastern Africa will not be too different.

It should also be stressed that rates of growth of population even of 2 or 3 per cent are something quite different from those experienced historically in Europe. The average annual growth rate in Europe was only 0.682 per cent over the earlier period of the Industrial Revolution, 1770–1800, and did not reach 1 per cent until the decade 1900–10, when it was 1.1, after which it began to fall. The current high rates are not, therefore, simply a phase through which Europe has already passed. If we look back to our discussion of Malthus' theory, we see that Malthus was concerned with the *growth* of population compared to the likely growth of the food supply. His theory could be very relevant to Kenya, and to other parts of Africa.

Table 3.5 *Estimated numbers, birth, death, and net rates of increase in population for the world and for selected regions, 1965–74*

	Population 1974 mid-year (in millions)	Births per 1,000 of population (BR)	Deaths per 1,000 of population (DR)	Annual rate population increase (%) (BR−DR+Net Migration)
World	3,967	32	13	1.9
Europe (exc. USSR)	473	16	10	0.6
USSR	255	18	8	1.0
North America	237	17	9	1.0
Latin America	324	38	9	2.7
South Asia (inc. India)	1,250	42	17	2.5
East Asia (inc. China+Japan)	1,006	27	10	1.6
Africa	401	47	20	2.7
Western	115	49	24	2.5
Eastern	114	48	21	2.7
Ethiopia	28	49	26	2.6
Sudan	18	48	18	2.5
Tanzania	15	47	22	2.7
Kenya	13	49	16	3.6
Uganda	12	45	16	3.3
Malawi	5	50	26	2.6
Zambia	5	51	20	3.2
Mauritius	1	25	8	1.5

SOURCE: *UN Demographic Yearbook*, 1975.

What determines the population growth rate?

The *natural rate increase* of population is the difference between the number of live births per thousand of the population and the number of deaths per thousand. For example, if the birth rate is 40 per thousand and the death rate 15 per thousand, the natural rate of increase will be $(40-15)/1,000 = 25$ per thousand or 2.5 per cent per annum. The actual growth of population, however, will depend on the natural rate of increase and *net migration*, the numbers of people entering the country to take up residence less those leaving.

Ignoring migration, the population growth rate depends on the birth rate and the death rate. An increase in the population growth rate may be due *either* to a rise in the birth rate *or* to a fall in the death rate. This may be seen from Figure 3.5, which gives birth and death rates for a hypothetical country over time. This illustrates the fact that in recent decades it has been especially the dramatic fall in the death rate in less developed countries, due to the introduction of public health measures, including vaccination campaigns, rather than an increase in the birth rate, which has caused an upsurge in the population growth rate.

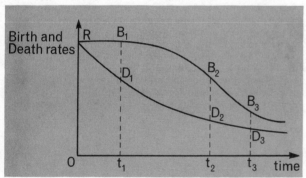

Figure 3.5 *The effect of changing birth and death rates on the natural rate of increase.*

Initially, as at R in Figure 3.5, the population growth rate is low, because though the birth rate is high, this is offset by an equally high death rate: there is a population 'balance' between births and deaths. Now suppose the death rate falls rapidly until at time t_1, it is equal to D_1t_1. With the same birth rate, the natural rate of increase jumps from zero to B_1D_1. In fact, a high death rate may *cause* a high birth rate. This is because if parents think there is a high risk of losing some of their children through illness, they will be encouraged to have large families: only if the death rate (especially infantile mortality) is low, as at t_3, will the birth rate fall.

The evidence is also that when the country is economically developed, and standards of living are high, there is a tendency (it is not uniformly true) for parents to have smaller families so that they can be in a position to offer their children more education and other comforts. The position t_3 may be held to represent, therefore, the position in a rich country where there is again some sort of population balance, but with both birth and death rates *low*, and the population growth rate also low.

It may usefully be noticed, in addition, that if there are two countries, one at t_1 and one at t_2, although the natural rates of increase are the same $(B_1 - D_1 = B_2 - D_2)$, the second is in the better position in that it can expect that the growth rate will fall in the future, whereas the former can expect it to increase rapidly. Thus, going back to Table 3.5, though the natural rate of increase in Latin America is 27 per thousand, as high as the average for Africa, we could judge the former to be in the better position since its death rate is down to 9, somewhere near the 'minimum' reached in developed countries. In tropical Africa the death rate could easily be reduced in the relatively near future (and it would of course be highly desirable to reduce it), to the same figure, which would raise the natural rate of increase fairly quickly to 38 per thousand. The other data we have referred to indicate that this has already been happening.

To give a concrete illustration of this arithmetic we

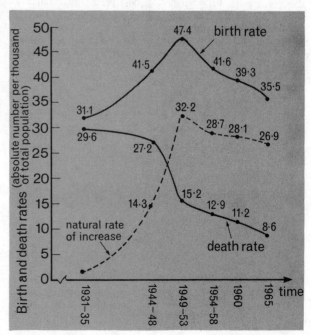

Figure 3.6 *Birth and death rates in Mauritius* (SOURCE: *J. E. Meade, loc. cit.*).

can consider some figures for Mauritius, which we have already described as having a 'classical' population problem (Figure 3.6). This shows a low natural rate of increase of population in 1931–5 with both birth and death rates high (around 30 per thousand). The rapid fall in the death rate, due to improvements in medical science and public health, is shown to occur after 1944–8. In the case of Mauritius, however, the rapid rise in population growth is due to a sharp rise in birth rate during the period 1931–43: when the birth rate falls after about 1951, the death rate is by then already falling, to offset this, so that population growth remains at the very high level of 30 per thousand (3 per cent per annum).

Questions on Chapter 3

1. Describe the Law of Diminishing Returns (Variable Proportions). What assumptions are needed for this 'Law' to operate?
2. Why would the Reverend T. R. Malthus, if he were alive today, consider his population theory applicable to Kenya?
3. What do you understand by the concept of an optimum population? Is it a useful concept in studying population problems in your country today?
4. What is the significance of the age structure of population for economic growth?
5. How might population growth affect (a) the supply of savings, and (b) the need for investment?
6. In what senses are (a) a large population and (b) a rapidly increasing population a 'burden' on less developed countries?
7. 'It is not population density on land which matters in Africa but population density on capital.' Discuss.
8. Discuss the case for controlling the size of the population.
9. Does Africa have a population problem?
10. How might population expansion affect the inequality of incomes?
11. In what circumstances do you consider an expansion in the population would be beneficial?

Notes

[1] Some readers may need to be reminded how compound interest works. Suppose the population is initially P and grows at the rate of 2 per cent per annum. After one year it will equal $P(1+2/100)$; after two years $P(1+2/100)(1+2/200)=P(1+2/100)^2$; after n years, $P(1+2/100)^n$. At the rate of g per cent per annum it would equal $P(1+g/100)^n$ after n years.

Suppose population is growing at this rate g, and we wish to know how many years it will take to double. This will happen when $P(1+g/100)^n=2P$, when n is the number of years. Cancelling the Ps on both sides, and taking logarithms, the number of years is given by

$$\left(\frac{1+g}{100}\right)^n = 2$$

$$n \log\left(\frac{1+g}{100}\right) = \log 2$$

$$n = \log 2 / \log\left(\frac{1+g}{100}\right)$$

A useful rule for calculating the number of years required to double any figure growing at any compound rate, g, is simply to divide g into the number 72. If g is 1 per cent, it takes 72 years to double population or any other variable; some $28\frac{1}{2}$ years if g is 2.5 per cent; $14\frac{1}{2}$ years, if 5 per cent; and so on.

[2] J. E. Meade, 'Population Explosion, the Standard of Living and Social Conflict', *Economic Journal*, June 1967.

[3] *Employment, Incomes and Equality: A Strategy for Increasing Productive Employment in Kenya*, International Labour Office, Geneva, 1972.

4 The Structure of the Eastern African Economies

Having examined in some detail the factors determining the standard of living in different countries, let us look now at the economies of Eastern Africa. How do the people in this part of the world earn their living? What are the basic features of the Eastern African economies?

The dominance of agriculture

The majority of people in Eastern Africa, as in West Africa, are farmers. Mostly they are 'peasant' farmers, which implies that they are self-employed, operating on a small scale with mainly family rather than hired labour, and producing their own food and other subsistence requirements, as well as cash crops for the market. Thus agriculture is the dominant 'industry' in Eastern Africa in terms of the numbers of people it employs and the value of output produced. Moreover in addition to direct output and employment provided by the agricultural sector, there is indirect output and employment created by it in other sectors, such as agricultural crop processing in the manufacturing sector and marketing activities in the services sector.

Apart from the vast numbers of peasant farmers, agriculture is important in terms of providing *paid* or wage employment—Table 4.1 gives the distribution of paid employment by sector in the Eastern African

countries. Thus in Kenya and Tanzania (despite a drastic fall in employment on sisal estates in Tanzania in recent years) something like one in every three or four paid workers was employed in agriculture, presumably on large farms and estates. The ratio was similar in Malawi, where tea and tobacco estates are important employers, and lower in Uganda where estates are less important relative to peasant farming. In Zambia, where commercial agriculture is so much less important than mining, less than one in ten hired workers was employed in agriculture. It should be noted, however, that in all cases a substantial amount of hired labour is used even on small farms, but that these employees are not 'reported' for statistical purposes and are therefore excluded from the statistics. The statistics are in fact collected from larger employers only or from 'formally' recognized establishments subject to employment regulations, including government inspection and taxation. In addition to 'informally' organized activities by self-employed workers, very small private enterprises with fewer than, say, ten workers, are usually not covered in the figures reported. The figures for agriculture are thus probably substantial *under*estimates of actual paid agricultural employment.

Mauritius provides an interesting contrast to most African countries in having a largely monetized economy, with negligible subsistence production. The

Table 4.1 *Sectoral distribution of reported employees in Eastern Africa, 1970*

Sector	Kenya (×1,000)	%	Uganda (×1,000)	%	Tanzania (×1,000)	%	Zambia (×1,000)	%	Malawi (×1,000)	%	Mauritius (×1,000)	%
Agriculture	204	32	55	18	107	29	33	10	54	34	59	47
Mining	3	0.5	8	3	6	2	56	16	1	1	—	—
Manufacturing	87	13	52	17	47	13	41	12	21	13	9	7
Construction	31	5	48	15	57	15	69	20	18	11	2	2
Commerce	43	7	15	5	21	6	33	10	13	8	4	3
Transport	45	7	13	4	34	9	20	6	8	5	6	5
Other private services	75	12	44	14	22	6	25	7	10	6	4	3
Public services	157	24	78	25	77	21	67	19	35	22	42	33
Total	645	100	313	100	371	100	344	100	160	100	126	100

SOURCE: *Statistical Abstracts*

NOTE: Percentages in this table, and in tables throughout the text, may not add up to 100 due to rounding.

highly capitalized plantation sugar industry alone accounted for 55,000 workers in reported employment in 1969—93 per cent of agricultural employment and 44 per cent of total employment. The small proportion of the paid labour force in manufacturing, commerce, and other private services reflected the prevalence of small-scale employers (with fewer than ten workers) excluded from the coverage; while the rather large public service sector resulted from the need to use government relief works for about 10 per cent of all reported workers.

A further measure of the predominance of agriculture is given by its contribution to the total product of the country, indicated in Table 4.2. This table shows, for instance, that agricultural output is valued at four or five times that of manufacturing in most of these countries. Manufacturing provides only about 10 or 12 per cent of total output. Even in Kenya, where manufacturing is more developed, the output of agriculture is still estimated at nearly three times as much.[1] Moreover in all countries the value of subsistence agricultural output may be substantially undervalued, so that the figures for agriculture are probably underestimates of its true importance.

Only in Zambia do we find the contribution of agriculture to be relatively unimportant in value terms, a mere 7 per cent. This is because the copper produced there is such a valuable item, so that mining accounts for 37 per cent of GDP. At the same time agriculture in Zambia, though it is still the main user of labour, lacks valuable cash crops like the other countries and therefore does not produce very much in value terms. Mineral extraction and agricultural output both represent *primary production* in any case: output based on the exploitation of a natural resource (land in the case of agriculture). Hence these are all 'primary producing countries'. The table shows also that, with the notable exception of Zambia, the countries of Eastern Africa have generally not been very successful so far in discovering and exploiting minerals as compared to South Africa, Central (Zaire and Angola), West (Nigeria, Sierra Leone) and North Africa (Algeria, Libya).

Another indicator of the importance of a sector is how much it contributes to earning foreign exchange, which a country needs to buy goods and services from abroad: that is to say, the share of exports produced by the sector. This is indicated in Table 4.3. In all cases, except one, 75, 80 or 90 per cent or more of exports are agricultural. The exception is Zambia, where only 1 per cent of exports is agricultural and copper output alone accounts for 95 per cent of exports, and all minerals 98.5 per cent. Primary product exports account for the bulk of domestic exports in all cases.

The occupational distribution of the labour force

It is common to distinguish between three categories, *primary* production activities, *secondary* activities, and *tertiary* activities. As just mentioned, primary production activities are those based directly on the exploitation of natural resources, including agriculture, based on arable or grazing land, mining, forestry, and fisheries. Secondary activities comprise manufacturing and construction, while tertiary activities comprise services such as distribution and commerce, transportation, banking and insurance, rec-

Table 4.2 *Gross domestic product at factor cost by industrial origin, 1970*

	Kenya %	Uganda %	Tanzania %	Zambia %	Malawi %	Ethiopia %	Sudan %	Mauritius %
Agriculture, non-monetary	20	29	21	5	84	—	25	—
Agriculture, monetary	16	26	20	2	14	—	11	23
Agriculture, total	36	55	41	7	48	55	36	23
Mining	—	2	1	37	—	—	—	—
Manufacturing	14	10	11	12	17	11	12	18
Construction	6	2	5	7	5	6	4	6
Commerce	11	11	13	8	10	8	23	10
Transport	8	3	9	4	4	4	9	11
Private services	13	8	6	25	25	16	16	32
Public services	12	9	12					
Total	100	100	100	100	100	100	100	100

SOURCE: *Statistical Abstracts*

Table 4.3 *Domestic exports of principal commodities from Eastern Africa, 1970*

	E.A.C.[1] %	Kenya[2] %	Uganda[2] %	Tanzania[2] %	Zambia %	Malawi %	Ethiopia %	Sudan %	Mauritius %
Coffee	36½	31	58	18½	—	—	61		
Cotton	13	1½	20	14½	—	7		64	
Tea	8	18	5½	2½	—	27			4
Sisal	4½	2½	—	10	—	—			
Confectionery nuts	3½	2	—	8	—	10½			
Cloves	2½	—	—	6½	—	—			
Tobacco	1	—	½	2½	½	41			
Sugar/molasses	—	—	—	—	—	—			94
Other agricultural	14	21	6	16½	½	11½	32	32	
All agricultural	83	76	90	79	1	97	93	96	98
Copper	3	—	8½	—	95	—	—	—	— —
Diamonds	3½	—	—	9½	—	1	—	—	—
Other minerals	½	2½	—	—	3½	—	—	—	—
All minerals	7	2½	8½	9½	98½	1	0	—	—
Petroleum products[3]	6	11½	—	6½	—	—	—	—	—
Other manufactures	3	10	1½	5	½	3	7	3	2
All manufactures	9	21½	1½	11½	½	3	7	3	2
Total	100	100	100	100	100	100	100	100	100

SOURCE: *Statistical Abstracts*

[1] EAC=East African Community, consisting of Kenya, Uganda, and Tanzania and excluding interstate exports between these three countries

[2] External exports of domestic produce to countries outside EAC

[3] Refined products based on *imported* crude oil

reation and domestic services, public administration, and defence.

We have seen already that in the Eastern African countries the majority of the 'economically active' population is engaged in agriculture. There is evidence that the proportion of the total labour force engaged in primary production as a whole is closely associated with the level of economic development, as measured approximately by average income per head. This tendency can be observed in Table 4.4. At higher income levels manufacturing among the secondary industries and the provision of services other than commerce among the tertiary activities become relatively more important. It is worth noting that even Denmark, which is specifically known for the importance of its agricultural exports, does not deviate from this general pattern, only about one-tenth of the labour force being engaged in agriculture compared, for example, with about two-thirds in Zambia and as much as three-quarters or more in the less developed economies of Ethiopia and Malawi.

This pattern can be explained by two factors. On the supply side we may note that higher incomes are brought about by a general increase in productivity. In the case of agriculture this means that the number of workers required to satisfy essential demands for staple foodstuffs or basic raw materials tends to fall, both absolutely and relatively, as farmers adopt improved methods of production and become better provided with cooperant factors, better tools, more skilled labour, fertilizers, and the like. Thus, as the economy develops, it is possible for agriculture to 'release' labour to other occupations. Secondly, on the demand side, we can say that food, basic shelter, and to some extent clothing, represent the first needs to be satisfied: at low levels of income, demand has to concentrate on these items of consumption and agriculture, which supplies them, will be the dominant activity. As incomes rise, demand will be increasingly for manufactured products and services.

It should be observed that it is the percentage of the labour force engaged in services *other than commerce* which increases as levels of income rise. This is because commerce includes people engaged in petty trading which is commonly an important source of livelihood in poor countries. It is, for instance, a notable feature of the economy of India, and, within Africa, of West Africa, where specialist trading creates jobs for people who lack the capital and skills to enter other industries, including small-scale farming. In Eastern Africa, on the other hand, much of the local trading in staple foods is carried out by farming families themselves, so that a separate category of people engaged in low-level commerce has not developed to the same extent. However, as we shall see, even in Eastern Africa there are expanding job opportunities for small-scale traders and craftsmen which have been created by rising consumer incomes in the more 'formal' employment sectors, in commercial agriculture, factories, and the public service.

The statements above must be qualified in one important way, however. In a subsistence economy many of the secondary activities—maize pounding for instance—or tertiary services such as laundry, which in a developed economy would be done commercially, are carried out entirely within the household. To this extent the pattern revealed by the statistics reflects a more advanced level of specialization and exchange, with services appearing as separate full-time occupations, compared to 'subsistence' service activities, rather than any change in the relative volume of such activities. Moreover the value of such services may be either omitted in the statistics of national income, or lumped in with agriculture as a 'primary' activity.

Table 4.4 *Occupational distribution of the labour force in relation to economic development*

| | Primary | | Secondary including power and construction | Tertiary | | GDP per head 1970 (US$) |
| | Agriculture | Mining | | Commerce | Other services | |
	%	%	%	%	%	
Malawi	90	—	3	1	6	72
Sudan	86	—	6	2	6	100
Mauritius	40	—	26	10	24	233
Ghana	58	2	12	14	14	262
Zambia	67	6	12	4	12	417
Japan	19	—	34	22	25	1,911
UK	3	—	47	16	34	2,128
Denmark	11	—	37	16	37	3,141
USA	4	—	32	24	39	4,734

Dual economies and the informal sector

A number of writers have asserted that the less developed countries exhibit a specific type of economic structure: that of a *dual economy*. A dual economy is one in which there is a *traditional* or *pre-capitalistic* sector on the one hand, and a capitalistic or *modern* sector on the other. The former consists mostly of peasant farmers using simple methods of cultivation, while the modern sector comprises mines, large-scale manufacturing concerns, plantations, and large export-import trading companies as well as all the public services operated or controlled by the central government.

The 'gap' between the traditional and modern sectors exists on a sociological and on an economic level. On the social side it has been argued[2] that the two sectors have quite separate *social systems*: in the rural traditional sector the indigenous culture, beliefs, and religions will dominate, while in the urban, modern sector Western and expatriate values will be introduced. The different social systems will, secondly, produce different attitudes: whereas the modern sector is dominated by the profit motive, the pre-capitalistic sector is supposed to comprise peasants with communal rather than individualistic profit-making interest. With 'limited needs' in terms of material goods, and perhaps a fatalistic attitude that, given the harsh natural conditions in which they find themselves, they cannot expect to improve their lot, traditional producers hence lack the initiative to seek out or adopt possible innovations. In addition to this *social dualism* on the more narrowly economic side it is argued that there exists a technological difference between the two sectors, producing *technological dualism*. There are a number of related elements on the economic side, which distinguish the modern sector from the traditional, according to this theory.[3] While the traditional sector uses small-scale labour-intensive methods, with little capital, the modern sector uses capital-intensive methods and operates on a large scale. Secondly, while the modern sector enterprises, whether mining companies, factories, or plantations, are involved in commercial production, farmers in the traditional sector are concerned primarily, so it is said, with subsistence food production. Thirdly, whereas the traditional sector is populated by indigenous farmers, the modern sector is dominated by foreign capital brought in by expatriate-run firms, generally based overseas and operating in several countries: 'multinational' companies. Fourthly, it is suggested, while the traditional sector is concerned with subsistence production for its own use, the modern sector is 'export-oriented', primarily concerned with exporting raw materials

and other primary products. Finally, and this is the crucial point, it is argued that the economic links between the modern sector and the traditional sector are minimal. The modern sector does not buy things from the traditional sector or sell things to the traditional sector: hence it could expand without affecting the latter very much. And since the modern sector is relatively small, it could expand without bringing about the general development of the country, doing little more than provide a supply of raw materials for the industrial countries and profits for the international companies involved.

Professor Ann Seidman has argued strongly[4] that the model of a dual economy applies with special force in East Africa and in West African countries like Ghana. For her the modern sector is an 'export enclave', by which she means that it lacks economic links with the traditional sector, called the 'hinterland'. She states that

> The export enclave is characterised by the production and export of a few raw materials for processing in the factories of developed industrial countries; and the import of manufactured consumer goods with a significant share of the foreign exchange earned.

In contrast,

> The majority of the population lives and works in the traditional agrarian economy, using age-old simple productive techniques geared to survival in the face of the uncertainty of a harsh nature. There may be some trade in local produce which may even extend across national borders, but most of the peasants in the traditional sector produce the bulk of their own needs.... The traditional sector contributes one important factor to the export enclave: cheap unskilled migrant labour, workers willing to work for wages which barely cover subsistence.

In a number of ways, however, this model of a dual economy presents an inaccurate and to some extent misleading picture. First, most African peasant producers, while certainly still bound by tradition, are no longer as described above. They produce cash crops as well as their own food crops, and produce these for the international market: cocoa, coffee, cotton, oilseeds, and many other crops. In producing these, they have shown great interest in seeking out profit opportunities and responding to cash incentives, as we shall see in Chapter 10. Nor can we make a strict division between 'subsistence' food production and cash crop production: many food crops are sold on the market, and farmers do vary the amount of food crops and cash crops they produce to take into account relative profitability. Thus we do not have simply a traditional pre-capitalistic sector concerned with subsistence: the activities of peasant farmers are part of the money economy, they sell through intermediaries on world markets, and operate as small 'capitalists' with an eye to cash returns. Most of the agricultural exports listed in Table 4.3 are grown by peasant farmers, although tea, sisal, sugar, and some tobacco are still largely estate crops.

Secondly, whereas mines and factories do use highly capital-intensive methods, employing less labour, this is not so true of large farms and plantations: these are substantial employers of labour. To take an example, in Tanzania in 1964, just before the fall in the price of sisal led to a drastic reduction of employment on the sisal estates, the latter employed more than 100,000 workers, nearly half of the total number of paid employees in the country.

Thirdly, it has fairly recently been stressed in East Africa that there exists a sector intermediate between the traditional farming sector and the 'formal' or modern sector: this has been termed by the 1972 ILO Mission to Kenya the *informal sector*. This consists of petty traders and hawkers, tailors, carpenters, taxi-drivers, small-scale metal-workers, motor car and machine repairers and mechanics, brewers making 'local' alcoholic beverages, and some small-scale industries such as sawmilling and posho (maize-flour) mills. The ILO Mission, examining data for 1969, made rough estimates according to which such non-farming activities accounted for 28–33 per cent of African *urban* employment in Kenya and 37–39 per cent of *total* African adult employment excluding farming. There are, therefore, a substantial number of people who work neither in the traditional rural sector, nor in the formal sector. One rough estimate for 1969 suggested that about 72 per cent of employment in Kenya was in the traditional sector, 9 per cent in the informal sector, and 19–20 per cent in the formal sector.[5]

Despite these important qualifications, there remains a good deal of meaning in the concept of a dual economy, though it applies more clearly in some African countries than in others. Zambia is an extreme case of the phenomenon, whereby 'too many' workers are employed in agriculture and 'too few' in secondary industries. Table 4.5 shows that although 67 per cent of the total labour force is engaged in agriculture, the sector produces as little as 7 per cent of gross domestic product (though this value may be an underestimate for reasons given in Chapter 1). At the same time a mere 6 per cent of the work-force in mining provides as much as 37 per cent of output.

Zambia is in fact a classic example of the 'dual economy'. The modern mining sector shows a high value of output per worker because it uses highly capital-intensive techniques, with a lot of capital per worker, and secondly, because it involves the exploitation of an internationally valuable natural resource: copper. In contrast Zambia's rural sector is particularly backward, lacks a valuable cash crop, and

Table 4.5 *Employment and output by sector, Zambia, 1970*

Sector	Labour force		GDP	
	Thousands	%	Million Kwacha	%
Agriculture:				
subsistence	565	62	64	5
marketed	35	4	21	2
total	600	66	85	7
Mining	57	6	437	37
Secondary	110	12	225	19
Tertiary	148	16	438	37
Total	915	100	1,185	100

consists of peasants very much reduced to subsistence food production, under quite arduous and uncertain conditions, and employing traditionally simple techniques. There is thus an exceptionally big gulf between formal and traditional sectors in Zambia. Moreover the copper is all exported, and we have a clearly defined 'export enclave', since the mining industry has fewer linkages with the rest of the economy than even formal sector manufacturing would have. Finally the difference in social systems between this enclave and the hinterland is magnified by the narrow geographical form of the copperbelt, and the alien culture of the European miners who work along with Zambians in the mines. This difference in ways of living is accentuated by the relatively very high wages that mine workers and others employed in the formal sector are able to earn, compared to the subsistence income earned by the vast majority of the rural population. Thus in 1970 the average subsistence income of the two million rural population was only K30 per annum per head compared to average earnings from wages and salaries in the formal sector of around K930 per African employee, representing perhaps K150 per head for the other half of Zambia's population. Before deduction of taxes or remittances to rural dependents, the average Zambian living and working in the modern sector was some six times better off in terms of money income than the average rural Zambian relying on subsistence farming.

External economic dependence

Developing countries are frequently referred to as 'dependent' economies and in recent years African countries which already have political independence have been talking of the need to obtain also 'economic independence'. Very often, however, different things are meant by 'economic dependence', and it is necessary to sort these out carefully in order to see what the real problems are. We may distinguish *trade dependence*, the extent to which a country depends for income on selling goods and services in foreign markets or to which it has to rely on imports from abroad to satisfy local requirements; *external resource dependence*, the continued reliance on foreign capital, enterprise, or technical skills to supplement the domestic supply of productive resources; and *direct economic dependence*, where key positions in the economy are controlled by foreign capitalists and multinational companies, so that economic decision-making is not entirely or mainly in the hands of citizens and their representatives.

Trade dependence

Even trade dependence, however, has several aspects, which are frequently confused. The first aspect is where *the ratio of exports to national income is high*. Table 4.6 shows that export sales to foreign markets generate about 25 per cent of the gross domestic products of Uganda, Tanzania, and Kenya, for example. However we observe that the UK and West Germany were also 'dependent' in this sense, to the same extent of 20–25 per cent, while the USA, the world's richest economy, and India, one of the world's poorest, were unusual in having a relatively small dependence on foreign trade. The United Kingdom is much more dependent in this sense than Ethiopia. In general dependence on trade is not related to the stage of development or income per head of the country. Trade, in fact, permits specialization, which we have already said should mean increased output and incomes. Traditional subsistence economies with no specialization and exchange

are likely to be poorer as a result. Geographical size is also a factor: a large country can develop an extensive system of specialization and exchange within its own borders without need for foreign trade, exchange *across* borders; small countries are more likely to specialize narrowly and exchange with other countries' products as in the case of Mauritius and other sugar islands or the Gambia with groundnuts.

Contrary to the impression given by many observers, less developed countries are *not* as a group more dependent on trade than developed countries as a group. This false impression may derive from the fact that the majority of developing countries are dependent *for their exports* on just one or two commodities. Or it may derive from a tendency to relate these exports to *monetary output* rather than to the whole of national income including subsistence output. Table 4.7 shows that in Tanzania and Kenya income from exports represents over 40 per cent of monetary sector activity, a very high degree of dependence of the monetary economy on exports; but when account is taken of unrecorded or subsistence activities the degree of export dependence of the whole economy is reduced to around 30–33 per cent in these two countries, and to only 22 per cent in Malawi and Uganda where subsistence activities are relatively more important. Zambia differs in continuing to show an extremely high degree of dependence on exports of both monetary and total income: as can be seen, this arises from the relative unimportance of subsistence primary production *as measured by the national income statisticians in Zambia*. This is partly due to the very narrow definition of the production boundary used and to the low prices assigned to subsistence food output. Most important, however, is the contrast between the high-value copper exports and the output of the relatively undeveloped subsistence agriculture sector.

Dependence is used sometimes to mean *dependence on primary products*. Thus whether *or not* the ratio of exports is high, it is considered a disadvantage if these exports comprise only primary products, while all manufactured goods are imported. Table 4.3 shows that the Eastern African countries export primary products, either agricultural or mineral. Manufactured goods exports are negligible, particularly if we take into account that petroleum products comprise commodities which are re-exported after refining of imported crude oil. Concern about this dependence on primary product exports arises because primary product prices are thought to be declining over time relative to the prices of the (imported) manufactured goods, that is, that the 'terms of trade' of primary products are declining (the evidence on the movement in relative prices over the long term is in fact unclear). Or, alternatively, it is that the *value* of such exports (price times quantity)

Table 4.6 *Dependence on foreign trade, selected countries, 1970*

	Exports and imports as Percentage of GDP		GDP per head
	Exports	Imports	(US$)
Ethiopia	11	12	65
Malawi	21	34	72
India	4	5	91
Tanzania	23	28	99
Sudan	16	19	100
Uganda	24	23	131
Kenya	28	32	140
Mauritius	49	49	233
Ghana	18	17	262
Japan	11	10	1,911
UK	23	22	2,128
W. Germany	22	20	3,034
Denmark	29	32	3,141
USA	6	6	4,734

SOURCE: *UN Statistical Yearbook*, 1971

Table 4.7 *Relative share of subsistence activity and exports as percentages of GDP (factor cost), 1970–2*

	Zambia %	Kenya %	Tanzania %	Uganda %	Malawi %
Subsistence sector	6	22	29	33	37
Monetary sector	94	78	71	67	63
Total GDP	100	100	100	100	100
Exports as % monetary GDP	55	42	42	33	35
Exports as % total GDP	52	33	30	22	22

SOURCE: *Statistical Abstracts*

will increase much more slowly than that of manufactured goods: so that incomes of countries dependent on these exports will also grow relatively more slowly. Some evidence is shown in Table 4.8.

This shows the distribution of international trade both within and between the three main trading areas as defined by the General Agreement on Tariffs and Trade (GATT), i.e. industrial areas, developing areas, and the Eastern trading area which comprises the planned economies of the USSR, Eastern Europe, and China. The figures refer to the percentage share of world exports originating in the three areas, this reflecting the concentration of world *production* in the former areas. The significant fact, however, is that the share of the industrial areas has been actually increasing, up to 67 per cent in 1970, while the share of developing areas *declined* from 25 to 19 per cent. This was not due to a fall in absolute terms, since the total value of world trade almost doubled: the reason was that while the value of exports from developing areas increased by about two-thirds, around 66 per cent, that of industrial areas increased by as much as 145 per cent over only eight years, 1962–70. Moreover much of this increase was trade between the industrial countries themselves, this trade increasing by 160 per cent compared with a growth in trade with developing areas of less than half as much, 70 per cent. For various reasons, therefore, industrial output is increasing at a faster rate than demand for and output of primary products: hence the desire to be less dependent on primary production.

Moreover developing country exports include not only agricultural commodities but also minerals and *some* manufactured goods; and over the same period agricultural product exports have declined in relative importance. Petroleum, especially, has accounted for an increasing proportion of exports from developing countries, accounting in 1970 for 33 per cent of the total, this largely from the Middle East. Manufactured goods exports, accounting for 25 per cent, had also increased, but were mainly from Asian countries such as India and Hong Kong. Since African countries depend much more on non-oil primary product exports, their position is rather worse.

Apart from being dependent on imports of manufactured goods, developing countries are dependent specifically *on imported capital goods*. Table 4.9 shows the kinds of goods Eastern Africa obtains in exchange for the primary products exported overseas.

Table 4.8 *Trade within and between main trading areas as percentage of world exports in 1962 and 1970*

Origin \ Destination	Year	Industrial areas	Developing areas	Eastern trading area	Total world
Industrial areas	1962	44	17	2	64
	1970	52	13	3	69
Developing areas	1962	17	6	1	24
	1970	13	4	1	18
Eastern trading area	1962	2	2	8	12
	1970	2	2	6	10
World Total	1962	63	25	11	100
	1970	67	19	10	100

SOURCE: GATT, *International Trade*, 1971, Geveva, 1972

Table 4.9 End-use of imported commodities retained in Eastern Africa, 1970 (per cent)

	EAC	Zambia	Malawi	Ethiopia
Machinery and transport equipment	36	39	27	50
Mineral fuels	8	10	8	8
Manufactures and materials	35	31	28	
Food, drink, tobacco	5	9	14	8
Other	16	11	23	
TOTAL	100	100	100	100
of which: Producer capital goods	33	n.a.	23	33
Producer materials (excluding fuel)	37	n.a.	47	20

SOURCE: *Statistical Abstracts*

It will be noted that in 1970 the category 'Machinery and transport equipment' headed the list, not only for EAC but for the others, especially Ethiopia. Manufactures and materials (the latter largely chemicals and other producer materials) followed in importance. Unlike some developing countries, Eastern Africa is not very dependent on imported 'Food, drink, and tobacco', although at present the absence of exploitable deposits of fossil fuels (coal and petroleum) involves imports of 'Mineral fuels' which accounted for about 10 per cent of total imports in 1970.[6] If these retained imports are analysed by end-use, for EAC, something like 30 per cent, only, represented goods for consumption (including private cars and 30 per cent of the import bill for mineral fuels); 37 per cent were producer materials, including fuels, fertilizers, and building materials; and 33 per cent was capital equipment. Analysis of Malawi's

imports in 1970 revealed a somewhat similar pattern: 30 per cent represented consumer goods, 47 per cent producer materials, and 23 per cent capital equipment. The significance of dependence on imported capital equipment, which has been increasingly criticized, is that the machinery will incorporate technology more suitable to advanced economies: in particular it will be capital-intensive rather than labour-intensive, whereas the less developed economies would prefer production techniques which use as much cheap labour as possible, and so increase employment.

Dissatisfaction is also expressed occasionally with dependence on particular export markets, with what is referred to as the *geographical concentration of trade*. Table 4.10 analyses the markets for domestic exports of Eastern African countries on a similar basis as that adopted in Table 4.8. This shows that 73

Table 4.10 Destination of exports from developing areas and Eastern Africa, 1970 (per cent)

Origin \ Destination	Industrial areas %	Developing areas %	Eastern Trading areas %	Other areas %
Developing areas				
(1) exports of petroleum included	73	20	1	6
(2) exports of petroleum excluded	70	19	8	3
East African Community	60	32	5	3
Kenya	56 (41)	40 (57)	3 (2)	1 (1)
Uganda	64 (57)	26 (35)	8 (7)	2 (2)
Tanzania	54 (50)	39 (45)	5 (4)	2 (2)
Zambia	77	22	1	—
Malawi	84	14	1	1
Ethiopia	46	46	—	8

SOURCE: *Statistical Abstracts*
NOTE: Figures in brackets include interstate trade in the EAC in the figures for developing areas, thereby lowering the market shares (percentages of exports) to industrial areas especially.

per cent of developing countries' exports went to the 'Western' industrial areas, only 20 per cent to other developing countries, and a mere 1 per cent to the Eastern trading areas. Exports from Zambia and Malawi fit with this general pattern, though we find the East African Community countries actually a good bit *less* dependent on exports to industrial countries than less developed countries as a whole. In particular Kenya, if exports to its two EAC partners are included, falls to 41 per cent, with markets in Africa and other developing countries as important as 57 per cent. This figure, amounting to more than one-half of total exports, is in striking contrast to those for most other developing countries, in Africa especially, and represents a promising aspect of Kenyan economic growth. Tanzania also enjoys fairly diversified markets, with 45 per cent of exports directed to developing areas, including 20 per cent to Asia and 17 per cent to African countries.

Geographical concentration of exports occurs where an exporting country exports mainly to one or a few countries only. Table 4.11 gives a more detailed breakdown by country of the destination of exports for the three EAC countries. Kenya's special interest in both the East African common market (EAC) and the European common market (EEC) is clearly illustrated in this table. Kenya imports especially from the EEC, USA, and Japan. Tanzania has gone furthest in diversifying its sources of imports and has continued this since 1970. The figures in brackets for the UK give the corresponding percentages for 1960: it can be seen that since independence the EAC countries have found it profitable to reduce the relative amounts imported from the former colonial power.

Critics of dependence on foreign trade have very often had in mind, not dependence on trade as such,

but rather dependence on exports of a limited range of commodities: that is, the *commodity concentration of exports*. We have seen that developing countries are frequently *not* more dependent on trade than industrialized countries. What certainly *is* true is that their exports are frequently concentrated on just two or three products. Table 4.12 shows that more than thirty of the forty countries depend on three major exports or less, and a dozen rely heavily on just one export. Some extreme cases are Libya, with petroleum virtually the *only* export, Zambia, for which copper accounts for 95.7 per cent and Mauritius, 91 per cent accounted for by sugar. Table 4.13 gives similar information on a regional basis. Figures for other developing countries in Asia and elsewhere would tell a similar story.

The difficulty with depending on just one or two primary exports is that instability of export earnings may result due perhaps to climatic factors affecting the *quantity* produced in some years or to fluctuations in the world market *price* of the commodities concerned. This could cause extreme hardship in bad years for peasant farmers producing cash crops for export, and it will certainly be inconvenient for them not to be able to expect roughly the same incomes each year. Since the government in this situation usually relies heavily upon revenue obtained by taxing such exports, government revenue will also fluctuate, making government year-to-year budgeting difficult, and long-range planning problematic.

It is wrong to think, though, that *all* countries which rely on one or two exports all suffer from export instability. Mineral production is not usually affected by weather conditions and some agricultural products have very stable prices—bananas for example—while others have had their prices stabil-

Table 4.11   *Main trading partners of EAC countries, exports and imports, 1970 (per cent)*

	Kenya Exports	Kenya Imports	Uganda Exports	Uganda Imports	Tanzania Exports	Tanzania Imports
Kenya	—	—	10 ⎱ 12	28 ⎱ 30	6½ ⎱ 8	13 ⎱ 15
Uganda	16 ⎱ 30	7 ⎱ 11			1½ ⎰	2 ⎰
Tanzania	14 ⎰	4 ⎰	2 ⎰	2 ⎰	—	—
UK	(25)15	(44)27	(16)19	(19)22	(32)20	(27)18
W. Germany	6½ ⎱ 29	7 ⎱ 45	4 ⎱ 26	6 ⎱ 38	3½ ⎱ 36	8 ⎱ 36
Other EEC	7 ⎰ ⎱ 37	11 ⎰ ⎱ 63	3 ⎰ ⎱ 55	10 ⎰ ⎱ 50	12 ⎰ ⎱ 49	10 ⎰ ⎱ 50
USA	6½	7½	19	4	8½	7
Japan	1	10	10	8	4½	6½
Zambia	3	—	—	—	6	—
All other	30	26	33	20	38	35
Total	100	100	100	100	100	100

SOURCE: *Economic and Statistical Review, 1971* (EASD)

NOTE: Figures in brackets for the UK are corresponding figures for 1960

Table 4.12 Countries dependent on one, two, or three major export commodities, Africa, 1971

One major export		%
1. Libya	Crude petroleum	99.4
2. Zambia[1,2]	Copper	95.5
3. Mauritius[1]	Cane sugar	88.3
4. Reunion	Cane sugar	82.8
5. Mauritania	Iron ore	79.6
6. Nigeria[1]	Crude petroleum	74.4
7. Liberia[1]	Iron ore	72.2
8. Zaire[1,2]	Copper	67.1
9. Algeria[2]	Crude petroleum	66.0
10. Chad	Raw cotton	65.5
11. Ghana	Cocoa	64.3

Two major exports			%
12. The Gambia[1]	Groundnuts	Groundnut oil	88.2
13. Uganda[1,3]	Coffee	Cotton	79.8
14. The Sudan[1]	Cotton	Oilseeds	77.6
15. Somalia	Animals	Bananas	76.0
16. Sierra Leone[1]	Diamonds	Iron ore	74.8
17. Rwanda	Coffee	Tin ores	69.5
18. Egypt	Raw cotton	Textiles	68.3
19. Gabon[4,7]	Petroleum	Wood	67.7
20. Ethiopia[1]	Coffee	Oilseeds	67.0
21. Malawi	Tobacco	Tea	65.8

Three major exports				%
22. Central African Republic[7]	Diamonds	Coffee	Cotton	82.4
23. Ivory Coast	Coffee	Cocoa	Wood	78.8
24. Upper Volta	Animals	Oil seeds	Cotton	77.2
25. Togo	Phosphates	Cocoa	Coffee	73.3
26. Congo Republic[7]	Wood	Fertilizer	Veneers	73.3
27. Mali	Animals	Cotton	Oilseeds	67.7
28. Niger	Groundnuts	Metal ores	Cattle	69.1
29. Morocco	Citrus fruit and vegetables	Phosphates	Fish	65.5
30. Cameroon	Cocoa	Coffee	Wood	64.1
31. Angola	Coffee	Petroleum	Diamonds	63.3

Other countries: most important exports		%
32. Dahomey	Food, palm kernel oil, oilseeds, cotton	
33. Kenya[1,3]	Coffee, tea, petroleum products	
34. Madagascar	Coffee, spices, rice	
35. Mozambique[2,4]	Cotton, cashew nuts, sugar	
36. Rhodesia[1,5]	Tobacco, food, asbestos, machinery	
37. Senegal	Groundnut products, phosphates, fish	
38. South Africa[6]	Gold, food, diamonds, wool, copper	
39. Tanzania[1,3]	Coffee, cotton, diamonds, sisal	
40. Tunisia	Petroleum, olive oil, phosphates, fertilizers, fruit and vegetables	

SOURCE: United Nations, *Yearbook of International Trade Statistics*, 1972–3
NOTE: Figures give the percentage of total export earnings accounted for in 1971
(except where otherwise stated) by one, two, or three major export commodities

[1] Excluding re-exports
[2] 1970
[3] Excluding intertrade between Kenya, Tanzania, and Uganda in local produce and locally manufactured goods
[4] Excluding exports of gold
[5] 1965
[6] Including Botswana, Lesotho, Swaziland, and South West Africa (Namibia)
[7] Excluding intertrade with Customs and Economic Union of Central Africa

Table 4.13 *Percentage share of major commodities in total commodity export earnings, Eastern Africa, 1971*

Ethiopia[1]			Somalia	
Coffee	56.6		Live animals	50.1
Oil seeds	10.4		Bananas and plantains	25.9
Other	33.0		Other	24.0
Kenya[1,3]			Sudan[1]	
Coffee	26.7		Raw cotton	57.8
Tea	16.2		Oilseeds, oil, and cake	24.3
Petroleum products	14.5		Gum Arabic	10.1
Other	42.6		Other	7.8
Madagascar			Tanzania[1,3]	
Coffee	26.5		Raw cotton	14.1
Spices	14.1		Coffee	13.2
Other	59.4		Diamonds	12.0
			Sisal, etc.	9.6
Malawi[1]			Other	51.1
Tobacco	45.7			
Tea	20.1		Uganda[1,3]	
Groundnuts	9.9		Coffee	58.7
Other	24.3		Raw cotton	21.0
			Other	20.2
Mauritius[1]				
Cane sugar	88.3		Zambia[1]	
Other	11.7		Copper	95.5
			Other	4.5
Mozambique[4]				
Fruit and vegetables	21.2			
Raw cotton	16.4			
Raw sugar	12.8			
Other	49.5			

SOURCE: United Nations, *Yearbook of International Trade Statistics, 1972 3*
For NOTES, see Table 4.12

ized through commodity agreements, as explained in Chapter 12. Indeed it is not certain that the export earnings of developing countries are *on average* more unstable than those of industrialized countries. There are great differences in experience, with some countries' exports being very unstable, and others very stable. It should be noted that the petroleum-exporting countries, though dependent on one commodity, have been able to derive high, stable, and, recently, expanding export earnings from this oil. There is, however, a second major disadvantage of relying on a single export commodity. This is the disadvantage of 'having all one's eggs in one basket': the commodity may, for instance, be replaced by a synthetic product and its market disappear almost 'overnight'. Thus exports of Tanzania sisal, used for fibre and cord, were hit by the introduction of nylon rope and other products, and fell from shs 437 millions in 1964 to shs 201 millions in 1967, a fall of 54 per cent in three years. The price per tonne of sisal fell by about the same percentage from £105 to £50 over the same period.

External resource dependence

The above are various aspects of trade dependence. Clearly it is important to distinguish them: dependence on trade, dependence on primary product exports, dependence on imported capital goods, geographical concentration of trade, commodity concentration of exports, dependence on particularly unstable exports.

We may, however, distinguish separately external resource dependence, or dependence on external factor services, particularly capital, in the form of investable funds; skilled manpower in the form of managers, engineers, technicians, teachers, and others; and technical knowledge, for which the developed world may hold patents or other forms of control. Capital funds may be imported in the form *either* of private foreign investment in the country *or* through foreign aid, technical assistance, loans and grants supplied by international organizations or foreign governments. Foreign investment may itself result in increased reliance on foreign technology, and it is a current criticism that foreign firms are more likely to use the techniques of production which they use at home, rather than technology appropriate to a developing country. Foreign investment may also imply greater dependence on imported manpower than necessary, if the firm lacks a proper programme for training local personnel. Against this, of course, foreign investment may be said to have the special *advantage* that it brings with it much needed resources of capital, skilled manpower, and technical knowledge. It must be realized at the same time that these resources are not supplied free: foreign investors will only invest because they expect to make profits and expatriates will expect higher salaries than they can earn in their home lands. Foreign investment thus involves costs, particularly in the form of profits remitted to the metropolitan country. National governments will wish to see that the export of this 'economic surplus' is not excessive.

Direct economic dependence

Another aspect of foreign investment which must be mentioned is that it may result in much of the important economic decision-making in the economy being made by other than nationals, and particularly if the modern sector is dominated by large multi-national companies, either in mining, manufacturing, plantation agriculture, or trading, then even the government may have limited powers to effect decisions regarding the economy. Economic independence here would therefore imply local participation in the supply of capital, either by local capitalists or by the state, and local participation in management and decision-making. It was these sorts of consideration which prompted the 'Arusha Declaration' in 1967 in Tanzania, aimed at bringing the 'commanding heights' of the economy, the most important sectors, under management of the state.

Finally, we may mention *financial dependence*, reliance on a financial system dominated by expatriate banks. Various forms of government intervention in this sector have occurred in the Eastern African countries, including complete nationalization in Tanzania. This is discussed in Chapter 27.

East African economic integration

We cannot leave this discussion of the economic structure of the Eastern African countries without noting that the East African Community countries, Kenya, Uganda, and Tanzania, have economies which, as a result of the long-established common market between them, developed specially close links, so that their economies are interdependent or integrated in a way that the others are not. This is reflected in the pattern of trade of the three countries as given in Table 4.14. The table shows that Kenya was making the greatest use of the common market as an export outlet. Over 30 per cent of the total value of her domestic exports were to Uganda (16 per cent) and Tanzania (14 per cent), exceeding in value sales to her four largest overseas customers, the UK, the USA, Japan, and West Germany, taken together. These exports represented Kenya's lead in the manufacturing field and greater capacity to produce and process temperate foodstuffs like wheat and dairy produce. It is the inability of the other two countries to match the value of Kenya's interstate exports which is behind periodic discussion on the future of the East African common market. This we shall discuss more fully in Chapter 24.

The characteristics of underdevelopment

We can now ask ourselves whether there are any general characteristics of underdeveloped countries, and how far and in what respects the Eastern African

Table 4.14 *Importance of interstate trade in total trade of EAC Partners, 1970*

	Domestic exports to			Retained imports from		
	(a) Other EAC	(b) All countries	(c) (a) as % of (b)	(a) Other EAC	(b) All countries	(c) (a) as % of (b)
	m shs	m shs		m shs	m shs	
Kenya	628	2,061	30.5	320	2,724	10.5
Uganda	240	1,981	12.1	363	852	29.8
Tanzania	148	1,835	8.1	335	1,924	14.8

SOURCE: *Economic and Statistical Review* (EAC)

countries fall into this category. We can divide the main features of underdevelopment into various aspects of *poverty*, characteristics of *economic structure*, *demographic features*, and finally *social and political characteristics*. The first characteristic of a less developed country is obviously that it is poor—income per head is low—relative to the developed countries. Associated with this poverty are such things as poor health and access to medical care, high mortality rates (particularly for infants), a high level of illiteracy and acute shortage of trained manpower, and poor housing. From the various tables we have already given incorporating figures for income per head, it will be seen that *most of the African countries are among the very poorest in the world*. More than that, it can be seen that the income 'gap' between many of the African countries and some Asian countries, and between many of the Asian countries and some of the Latin American ones, is as significant as that between 'developed' and 'undeveloped' countries. The differences in nutrition levels, say, or literacy levels in Africa and Latin America are indeed perhaps greater than those between Latin America and some parts of Europe. Even *within* Africa, important differences exist: thus if all African countries were to be brought up to the level of the best-off, this would represent a major increase in economic welfare.

The characteristics of the economic structure which we have mentioned in different places and can now summarize are: a large non-monetary sector and a less extensive system of specialization and exchange; associated with this, and with the absence of developed financial institutions, a low degree of monetization of the economy and incomplete use of money as a medium of exchange; an economy which is not fully integrated internally, as a result of inadequate transport, concentration on subsistence, and lack of specialization; the dominance of the agricultural sector in employment; economic dependence of various forms, particularly reliance for exports on a few commodities, and these mostly primary ones, external resource dependence, the continued reliance on foreign capital, enterprise or technical skills, and direct economic dependence associated with the dominant position in trade or industry of expatriate enterprises; a small domestic market, in terms of purchasing power; a dual economy, in many cases, with a high-productivity 'formal' sector; a structure of industry biased towards consumer goods production and lacking any substantial capital goods sector; a low level of capitalization, particularly in agriculture; a relatively low rate of capital formation, and the absence of the 'automatic' process of invest-

ment and growth characteristic of countries in the post-'take off' stages; backward technology in agriculture and the absence of domestically developed technological change in other sectors. All these features will be recognizable from our description of the economies in Eastern Africa.

Turning to demographic features, the mistake should *not* be made of classifying all developing countries as overpopulated, though most have a population *problem*. Indeed we may distinguish between the 'Asian model' of an underdeveloped country, suffering from land shortage as a result of serious overpopulation, and the 'African model' in which labour, not land, is the limiting factor in agriculture, and current population density is low. All countries may have a population problem in that the annual rate of population growth is as high as 2 or 3 per cent: we have seen that this applies in Africa, Asia, *and* Latin America.

The social and political characteristics are perhaps most difficult to generalize about: cultural patterns are very different in Asia, Africa, and Latin America, and in different parts of each continent, and the precise effect of these on economic growth is not certain. Within peasant agriculture, despite evidence of good economic responses, there remains an element of traditionally determined behaviour preventing the emergence of a fully progressive agriculture. Just as the economy is not fully 'integrated', the society may be divided by tribe or caste. The political frontiers drawn up in colonial times have also left many of the developing countries as small nations, aggravating the problem of small markets: this is particularly true in Africa, less so apart from Central America in the other continents. An important political and social feature is the lack of a middle class. The dominance of peasant agriculture and the late development of education, particularly in Africa, again, has created a dangerous gap between the mass of peasants, generally with little political control or influence, and an educated elite or landed aristocracy with disproportionate political influence and economic power. The potential clash of interests has created difficult political problems in many countries.

Some of the characteristics described above are causes of underdevelopment—traditional behaviour perhaps—some are effects, and some, like high population growth, are both cause and effect. Nevertheless the above list probably paints a fair picture of countries in the situation of underdevelopment, so long as we remember the great differences which exist in different parts of the Third World.

Questions on Chapter 4

1. In what ways could we measure the dominance of agriculture in the economies of Eastern Africa?
2. How would you expect the occupational distribution of the labour force in a country to vary with the level of income per head? For what reasons?
3. What do you understand by a 'dual economy'? For what reasons would you say that Zambia conforms more closely than Kenya to this concept?
4. What economic activities go on in the 'informal sector'? What features distinguish this from the formal sector?
5. Distinguish between trade dependence, external resource dependence, and direct economic dependence.
6. How far does trade dependence depend on the level of economic development?
7. Why do very large countries trade less?
8. What are the disadvantages of dependence on primary products?
9. What are the main features of the geographical concentration of trade of the Eastern African countries?
10. Why do Eastern African countries trade mainly with rich industrial countries rather than with each other? Describe the main changes in the distribution of world trade between developing countries and industrialized countries since around 1960 and give reasons for any noticeable changes.
11. What are the disadvantages of dependence on a limited range of exports?
12. Discuss the advantages and disadvantages of external resource dependence.

Notes

[1] The relatively largely manufacturing sector in Malawi, at 17 per cent of GDP in 1970, reflects the inclusion of tea manufacturing which in other Eastern African countries is included with commercial agriculture, as well as the special importance of tobacco handling as a factory process before shipment as the leading export commodity.

[2] See especially J. H. Boeke, *Economics and Economic Policy of Dual Societies*, Institute of Pacific Relations, New York, 1953.

[3] See, for example, B. Higgins, *Economic Development*, Norton, 1959.

[4] A. Seidman, *Comparative Development Strategies in East Africa*, East African Publishing House, 1972.

[5] Frank C. Child, 'Employment, technology and growth—role of the intermediate sector', in F. C. Child and M. E. Kempe, eds, *Small Scale Enterprise*, Institute for Development Studies, Nairobi, 1973.

[6] Since 1973 the sharp increase in the price of petroleum and petroleum-based goods like some fertilizers and synthetic textiles has forced non-oil-producing countries to spend twice as much or more on such imports, and caused very serious problems of foreign exchange.

Part II The allocation of resources

5 The Economic System

It is frequently stated that the fundamental problem of economics relates to scarcity and, through scarcity, choice or the taking of the right decision. This refers to the fact that the resources available in the economy at any moment of time are strictly limited, so that if they are devoted to given uses they will not be available for others. Because of this scarcity of resources a choice must be made as to how resources are to be employed and which commodities therefore are to be produced. While the amount of consumer goods and services that consumers are willing to use is indefinite, the means to satisfy these wants are limited. This must be true, we should stress, whatever the form of economic system prevailing, whether capitalist, socialist, or communist, or whether we are talking about a purely subsistence producer in a 'one man economy'.

Choice in the subsistence economy

It is easiest if we examine first the problem of choice which a subsistence producer would face. By definition, he does not trade with anyone. He has to make the best he can of his own resources: his plot of land, any capital goods he has previously managed to make, and his own labour. For the sake of simplicity, let us leave out of account his need for clothing and shelter, and assume that all he is interested in acquiring is food. The first choice our producer must make is how hard to work. This depends on whether he prefers food or leisure. If he sacrifices leisure he can have more food; if he works less hard he can have more leisure but will have less food.

Suppose the possibilities are as in Table 5.1. Since there are just 24 hours in one day, the most leisure our producer can enjoy is 24: in this situation, however, he would do no work and therefore have no food. This is the position in the first row of the table, with no hours worked, 24 hours of leisure, and a

Table 5.1 *Choice between income and leisure*

Hours worked	Hours of leisure	Total product (units of food)	Marginal product (units of food)
0	24	0	—
1	23	22	22
2	22	40	18
3	21	54	14
4	20	62	8
5	19	68	6
6	18	72	4
7	17	75	3
8	16	77	2
9	15	79	2
10	14	80	1
11	13	81	1
—	—	—	—
—	—	—	—
23	1	$99\frac{3}{4}$	?
24	0	100	$\frac{1}{4}$

total product of zero. The next row indicates that if he works one hour he will have 23 hours' leisure and 22 units of food, and so on. The final column gives the marginal product of labour, the addition to the total product when one more unit of labour is applied. In this example we assume diminishing returns to labour, so that the marginal product declines continuously. The middle two columns give the combinations of leisure and food which our producer can obtain: we plot these in Figure 5.1, measuring hours of leisure and units of food on the horizontal and vertical axes respectively, and obtain the line AB. We can call this line a *production possibility curve* or the producer's transformation curve, since it gives the rate at which he can 'transform' leisure into food. The segment OAB gives us the combinations of food and leisure within his reach, given his productivity. If we assume he does not care to waste either food or leisure he will select a combination on the boundary AB; Q, perhaps, if he is a lazy man (working 4 hours) or P (working 8 hours) if he values leisure less highly.

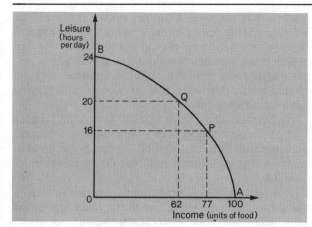

Figure 5.1 *Choice between income and leisure.*

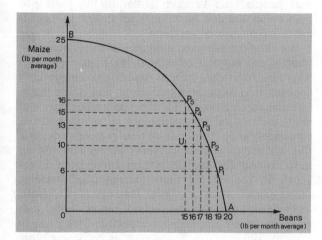

Figure 5.2 *Choice of products.*

The second choice which would face our producer, having decided how much time he will devote to food production, is what combination of products to produce. Suppose he is able to produce either maize or beans or a combination of both. His production possibilities are illustrated in Figure 5.2.

Again AB is a transformation curve, giving the rate at which he can 'transform' beans into maize, or vice versa. If he devotes all his time to producing beans he can obtain a monthly average production of 20 lb of beans, but no maize; alternatively, devoting all his time to maize production yields 25 lb of maize and zero beans.

If he devotes rather less time to bean production and produces maize in the remaining time he can produce 6 lb of maize and 19 lb of beans, or 10 lb of maize and 18 lb of beans, and so on. Conversely, starting at, say, P_5, to get an extra pound of beans the producer would have to sacrifice 1 lb of maize; at P_4, 2 lb of maize; at P_3, 3 lb and so on. These amounts are increasing, implying diminishing returns as more resources are devoted to beans rather than

maize. The same will hold for movement in the opposite direction. The effect is to make the transformation curve concave to the origin. The combination he finally selects will reflect his tastes as between maize and beans.

We can say that the maize which has to be sacrificed for the extra pound of beans is the opportunity-cost of the beans: the opportunity-cost is thus successively 1 lb, 2 lb, and 3 lb of maize. This is an extremely important concept in economics, and we must distinguish it very carefully from money costs. Opportunity-cost refers to the opportunities forgone, or the sacrificed alternative in deciding to do one thing and not another. In just the same way, in Figure 5.1, the opportunity-cost of extra food was the leisure forgone in acquiring it.

Of course, it is always possible to make 'less than best' or *sub-optimum* choices within the producer's transformation curve. For instance, at a point like U in Figure 5.2, a production choice of 10 lb of maize and 15 lb of beans indicates some unemployment or underemployment of available resources, since 18 lb of beans could be produced without sacrificing any of the 10 lb of maize at P_2: the extra 3 lb of beans have a zero opportunity-cost. Any point like U within the production possibilities curve or 'frontier' represents a feasible but wasteful choice. Only points *beyond* the frontier are infeasible, given the available supply of productive resources and techniques of production.

A third major choice facing our subsistence producer stems from the fact that he can increase his rate of output if he can acquire capital equipment. For example, if he spent some time building a rudimentary plough, he might be able to increase his output of food in future seasons, although for the time being he will have less time to devote to current production, part of which he will have to sacrifice to find the time to build the plough. The possibilities are shown in Figure 5.3.

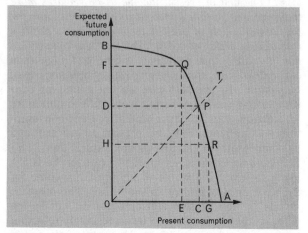

Figure 5.3 *Choice between present and future consumption.*

AB is again a transformation curve, this time giving the combinations of 'food now' (present consumption) and 'food tomorrow' (future consumption). If he spends less time producing 'food now', he can acquire additional tools and produce more 'food tomorrow', and vice versa.

If he does the former, we can say he is 'saving' or 'investing' for the future period. Not being in a money economy, the only way he can 'save' is to expand his productivity capacity (assuming food is perishable and cannot be stored): only then will he be able to consume more in the future period. Let us draw a line OT to bisect the angle BOA. P is on OT, and we have OC=OD. Thus, a choice of P and AB would imply a decision to save (invest) nothing, for the producer would expect to have the same consumption in the two periods. He would simply be maintaining his productive capacity at the same level. If he chose combination Q he would be consuming OE and 'investing' the difference EC: as a result he could look forward to the higher consumption OF in the future period. A choice of combination R would give him more food 'now' but only at the expense of failing to maintain his capital equipment and reducing his expectation of food 'tomorrow': he would actually be disinvesting.

Our producer's actual choice will depend on how thrifty he is. We can measure this 'thriftiness' by introducing the important concept of *time preference*. 'Time preference' refers to the relative value that a person attaches to having income now and having income in the future. A person who seldom thinks about the future, letting it 'take care of itself', will have a high rate of time preference, much preferring to have income now. A person who worries more about having income available in the future will have a lower rate of time preference. *We can measure time preference by considering the amount of future income that a person would need to compensate him for the loss of one unit of present income. If he requires more than one unit of future income to compensate him for the loss of a unit of present income he has a positive rate of time preference; if just one unit will compensate him, his rate of time preference is zero; and if less than one unit will compensate him his rate of time preference is negative.* In this last case an extra unit of consumption in the future period would afford him more satisfaction than an extra unit of present consumption, so that more than one 'present' unit is required to compensate for the loss of one 'future' unit.

Even if a person is very thrifty, however, he is not likely to invest the whole of his present income for the sake of high returns in the future. The more he invests the less present consumption he will be left with, so that he is likely to be increasingly reluctant to sacrifice additional units. His rate of time pre-ference will increase, in other words, the more he invests, and the more future consumption he expects to have in relation to present consumption. We can therefore distinguish two separate reasons why a person may have positive time preference, why he should prefer an extra unit of income now to the same unit in the future:

(1) because he is 'short-sighted' about the future;

(2) because he expects to have greater income and consumption in the future than he has in the present, making an additional unit in the present more valuable.[1]

It is because it is difficult to imagine one's needs in the future, in ten, twenty, or thirty years' time, that one may give less than equal weight to them. Evidence of this short-sightedness is given by the fact that people tend to save harder in the years just before they are due to retire, when their future needs are more obviously apparent.

We should have clear evidence of the existence of 'short-sightedness' if even at point P in Figure 5.3 where the individual expects exactly the same level of consumption in present and future, and where therefore the second reason for time preference does not exist, the rate of time preference were still positive. Conversely if at P the rate of time preference is zero, this will imply absence of 'short-sightedness'. As we move round the transformation curve from P towards B, the rate of time preference will become increasingly positive, not because of short-sightedness, but for the second reason only, that more future consumption is expected in relation to present consumption. 'Food now' is becoming more and more short and 'food tomorrow' more and more plentiful.[2]

Returning to Figure 5.3, if our producer is rational, as he invests he will first of all select the most productive way of investing and then, if he still wishes to invest, select the second best, and so on. As he moves upwards along AB, the extra amount of future food he can obtain from investing an additional unit will diminish steadily as the best investment opportunities are used up. To start with, at P, the extra amount of future food he can get by investing a unit might exceed the extra amount he needs to compensate for the loss of this unit of present food. Eventually he will arrive at a point, let us say Q, where the extra product is just equal to the extra amount he needs to compensate him and no more: this will give the amount he is willing to save or invest. If we define the 'marginal product of capital' to be the extra product arising when one unit is invested, it follows that the amount he saves is given by the point where the marginal product of capital is equal to his rate of time preference.

We do not need to worry about what our

producer's rate of time preference might be for all combinations of present and future income. The segment OAB contains all the choices open to him: assuming he is rational and consistent, if he then chooses combination Q where, say, the marginal product of capital is two (one unit of 'food now' yields three of 'food tomorrow') this will 'reveal' that his rate of time preference is also two.

We have seen, then, that even the subsistence producer is faced with at least three important choices: *how much* to produce, *what products* to produce and consume, and how much to *save or invest*. In the course of these we have introduced the fundamental concepts of *opportunity-cost* and *time preference* which underlie the choices. These are difficult concepts, but extremely useful if they can be grasped.

Subsistence production and the advantages of specialization and exchange

The amount of product that the subsistence producer, in Africa and elsewhere, manages to produce is, however, very low. What is the explanation? In part it is due to his failure to take advantage of the benefits of specialization and exchange. Specialization and exchange go hand in hand. If a producer makes small amounts of everything he needs, he will have no need to exchange with others. If he concentrates on producing just one item, say, catching fish, he will have more fish than he needs but less of his other requirements: by exchanging his fish for what others have produced, however, he can satisfy the full range of his needs within the limits of his income.

It would clearly be inefficient for each individual to cater for the whole range of his own requirements, and not to specialize. In the first place a great deal of time would be lost in switching from one job to another.

Secondly, the plots of land owned by different individuals, if they own land, may have different qualities: some land for example may be quite unsuitable for cultivation but may be good for raising sheep or goats. By specializing in the product for which each plot is best suited, the total product can be increased.

Thirdly, just as land may have varying attributes, so may human beings: some people may have a natural ability which makes them good doctors, artists, shopkeepers, carpenters, shoemakers, or whatever it may be. By allowing people to specialize in the field in which they are most gifted, the quality and quantity of all goods and services can be increased.

Fourthly, by specializing, people can develop skills for the job: if they know they are going to concentrate on a particular trade they can, in the first place, take steps to obtain special training or technical education: but, more important, the experience of repeating the same job over and over again has a profound effect on their efficiency and skill. Businessmen in Africa are well aware of this fact: if they employ new workers coming direct from the countryside who are quite strange and unused to factory conditions, there follows a difficult learning period before these recruits attain the same efficiency or productivity as experienced workers. That factory labour in Africa still has a proportion of such recruits is an important factor in raising labour costs, as we shall see again in Chapter 31.

Lastly, and perhaps most important, specialization facilitates the use of machinery. Machines today have taken over a great many of the tasks that used to be done manually. But in comparison to human labour, machines tend to be limited in two important ways. First they can only be substituted for men when tasks can be broken down into a finite number of simple repetitive operations, with separate machines or parts of a single machine carrying out each process. Secondly, machines are usually specific, that is to say, they cannot be applied to more than the specific task for which they have been designed. Within these limits, however, machines are capable of a much larger output than man. The combined effect of this is that machines must also specialize, and in specializing produce a large quantity of one or a few products. Given the cost of machines, it will therefore not be worthwhile employing a machine unless the excess product can be disposed of through exchange; and an exchange economy, by enabling machinery to be widely used, can produce a much greater total output.

These, then, are the advantages of 'the division of labour'. Specialization of labour and the use of specialized machinery will not be worthwhile except if the scale of output is large. Conversely, if the scale of output is large, the product can be made in most cases incomparably more cheaply as a result of these advantages. The phenomenon can thus be described as producing economies of large-scale production or simply, *economies of scale*. The effect of economies of scale is therefore that average costs of production will decrease as the scale or volume of output produced per period increases, other things being the same.

Specialization and economic progress

Specialization, we said, implies that each person produces a surplus of one or a few items in which he has specialized: these surpluses make exchange necessary between individuals, regions, and countries of the world. Because of this, specialization and exchange go hand in hand. The snag is that an individual cannot specialize unless he can dispose of the surplus product he produces.

Hence we arrive at the famous dictum of Adam Smith[3] that 'the division of labour is limited by the extent of the market'. In this statement the word 'market' is used in the economist's way to refer not to an actual market *place*, but to *market demand*. By market demand we mean not just the desire for the goods but demand backed by the ability and willingness to buy, alternatively known as the level of *effective demand*.

This is partly why underdeveloped countries generally appear to find it difficult to make a real start in economic growth. Because specialization has not developed far, productivity is low; because productivity is low, real incomes are low, and therefore market demand is small; and this limits specialization. We have a 'vicious circle' keeping back growth, lack of specialization restricting market demand, and market demand preventing the development of specialization. If only the circle can be broken, however, the same mechanism can work to the advantage of the country by accelerating economic growth; if something can be done to increase productivity in a significant way, incomes and therefore market demand will expand and this will in turn permit further specialization, raising productivity again, and so on. This process has undoubtedly been a major force in the historical development of both capitalist and planned economies from simple to complex economies. Economic progress has thus been associated with increasing returns and the tapping of a progressively wider range of economies of scale. Part of this process has been progressive specialization by industry: as markets expand it becomes possible for different parts of an industry to split off from the parent industry and operate as separate branches on a bigger scale either supplying parts to the parent industry or making use of by-products of the parent. Greater specialization is not of course the only cause of economic progress: the accumulation of capital, the invention and application of new ideas for new methods or new products, and the improvement of human capital through the general and technical education of citizens all have fundamental roles to play in the achievement of economic growth. But all of these are nevertheless linked with specialization, which gives them the necessary scope to operate.

The value of subsistence output

While we have extolled the advantages of specialization and exchange, this should not be taken to mean that so-called 'subsistence output' is unimportant or to be despised. As indicated in Chapter 1, subsistence production is better referred to as 'non-marketed output', or 'household own-account production'. Most rural households in Africa produce output for their own consumption as well as, generally, for the market. It *may* be better to specialize in a cash crop for the market, using the cash received to buy other goods which the household is not well fitted to produce, manufactured goods especially. But it is also important that the rural household is able to produce a number of goods and services for itself, including much of its own food supply. There can be as much variation in the richness of subsistence production in different countries in Africa, and in different regions within one country, as there is in the value of marketed output. While farmers in regions with good soils and abundant rainfall can practically 'live off the land,' without too much effort on their part, others in semi-arid areas may put in a great deal of labour effort in obtaining a bare minimum of food supply amounting to no more than a survival diet. Thus the level of economic welfare in different parts of Africa is determined to an important degree by the quantity and quality of non-marketed production or 'subsistence output'. Hence efforts at increasing economic welfare should incorporate efforts at raising productivity in non-marketed production as well as increasing cash incomes from marketed surpluses.

It may be stressed that in many cases the crops involved are the same, staple food crops such as maize, rice, or oilseeds being consumed domestically and only the surplus sold for cash. Here it is clear that there is no firm line between 'subsistence' production and production for the market: but even where the crops are different and the so-called 'cash crop' is entirely produced for sale, farmers must make a definite choice of food/cash crop combination just as when they select an optimum combination of cash crops.

Because of the *physical risks* of food failures—leading to starvation—as well as the *economic risks* involved in market price fluctuations, poor farmers will, normally, assign a higher 'implicit' price to some minimum output of food crops for their own consumption than the 'explicit' market price of the same goods. Only when they have ensured their own survival will they choose to produce for the market. The agricultural development programmes of most Eastern African countries now recognize the need to improve yields of maize and other 'subsistence crops' as a necessary first step before peasant farmers can be induced to expand production of more specialized cash crops.

A major advantage of own-account production over production for the market is that no transport or marketing costs are incurred between the producer and the final consumer, who become one and the same in this case. Costs are saved in two directions as compared to marketed output, from the producer to the produce-collecting centre and from this to the consumer, together with handling costs for produce buying, wholesaling, and produce distribution. Finally, we may note that it will be valuable to encourage specialization and trade between regions within a country (and between countries) where natural conditions differ, producing variations in comparative advantage. But in countries such as Tanzania, for instance, there are also many regions capable of growing the same range of food crops: where this is so, it may be worth encouraging regional self-sufficiency in this range, in order to reduce costs of internal transport, although this does not mean that each farming household need be completely self-sufficient.

The price mechanism and the allocation of resources

Specialization requires exchange. But exchange can take place in different ways. If, say, a fisherman exchanges some of the fish he has caught for some maize grown by the farmer, we have *barter*—the direct exchange of physical goods or services. At a very early stage of economic development, however, it is common to use a medium of exchange, money, in preference to bartering: the fisherman would sell his fish on the market, obtain money and use this to buy whatever maize he wanted from the farmer, or from a middleman. Where exchange is organized in this way through the market, so that prices are determined on the market by supply and demand, and consumers base their expenditure plans and producers their production plans on market prices, we can say that exchange is carried out through the *price mechanism*.

In the course of exchange the price mechanism determines the allocation of resources in the market economy, and indeed under competitive conditions it is claimed to produce an 'ideal' allocation of resources. Competitive conditions arise among other things from the following sequence of events:

(1) Consumers buy from the cheapest source. If some firms are more efficient and have lower costs than others, they will be in a position to charge lower prices. Inefficient firms will thus not be able to obtain the higher prices necessary to cover their higher costs and will sooner or later go out of business.

(2) There is a plentiful supply of would-be businessmen who will be attracted into an industry if they observe that they could earn revenue in excess of their costs.

If these conditions hold, we can proceed as follows. Consumers, on the one hand, have only limited incomes and can be assumed to aim at maximizing the satisfaction they can get with them; producers, on the other hand, are interested in making profits and can be assumed to try to maximize profits. The expenditure of consumers forms the receipts of producers. Thus each time a consumer spends money on a particular good, he is, as it were, 'casting a vote' for its production rather than another by providing an incentive to the producers of that particular good to supply it. Suppose we start with a situation where consumers are spending their incomes on a wide range of products; and the producers of each product are earning just sufficient to cover their costs, and no more.

Now suppose consumers' tastes change: they buy more of commodity A, say, and less of commodity B. The revenue of the producers of commodity B falls. Assuming their costs are unchanged, revenue will no longer cover costs for producers of B, and some of these will go out of business. This will leave resources—capital, labour, and raw materials—unemployed in industry B. However, demand and profits in industry A will have increased, new producers are attracted there, and the resources released in industry B will thus be switched to the production of A. The composition of output has therefore been remoulded to suit the tastes of consumers through profit incentives to producers. Thus, without need for any overall planning, the allocation of resources is automatically determined by the 'price mechanism' through appeals to the self-interest of consumers and producers. Adam Smith called this the 'invisible hand' of the market, and said it should ensure that the selfish interest of entrepreneurs in pursuing profits would lead to the right commodities being produced in the relative quantities desired by consumers.

The concept of opportunity-cost can be seen to operate here just as it did with our subsistence producer, where consumer and producer were one and the same. The existing supply of resources determines the total amount of output and consequently total income. Thus consumers have limited incomes: by spending more on product A, they can encourage producers to supply more of A, but only by diverting resources from the production of B. The opportunity-cost of the extra supply of A is the decline in the amount of B.

Consumers can also abstain from spending and save money incomes for a future date: in so doing they release real resources which would otherwise have been attracted towards producing consumer goods to satisfy their demands. Instead, these savings can be channelled through the 'capital market' and made available for producers to borrow in order to purchase capital goods. Hence the reluctance or otherwise of consumers to save will determine the supply of savings which can be directed into investment. As in the case of the subsistence producer, productive effort can be directed towards producing consumer goods or capital goods. In the case of the complex market economy the choice is given by the relative sizes of the consumer goods industries and capital goods industries: the way in which the choice between the present and future is made, however, is complicated by the fact that the consumers who do not spend all their incomes on consumer goods and the producers who are thus enabled to purchase capital goods are not necessarily the same people. The decisions to save and to invest are brought into line through the complex machinery of the capital market, which we shall be examining in later chapters.

Defects of the price mechanism

The price mechanism can therefore operate to allocate resources between different uses in the present and between the present (represented by consumer goods industries as a whole) and the future (represented by the capital goods industries). In practice, however, things do not work out so smoothly. There are a number of generally recognized defects in the operation of the price mechanism which we can discuss under the following headings.

Distribution of income

We stated above that when consumers spend money on particular commodities they are in effect 'casting their votes' for the production of those commodities rather than others: in a competitive system, there will be a tendency for producers to supply output according to 'votes cast'. The defect lies in the inequality of incomes: some people have more 'votes' than others! That is to say rich men have more money to spend and thus can attract relatively more resources producing the sort of goods they buy, like fine houses, large motor cars, and other luxuries. In fact the problem goes beyond this, for rich men will have the means to offer their children special advantages in education and training, later enabling them to secure the best jobs; in addition a son may be able to inherit a business or a large amount of wealth on his father's death. There is thus a danger of inequality of incomes generating *inequality of opportunity* causing incomes to become progressively more unequal as time goes on. Inequality of incomes tends to be even greater in the early stages of economic development when educational facilities are generally lacking and access to them is a matter of good luck and good connections!

Monopoly

The second major criticism of the operation of the price mechanism is that in practice it will not operate freely, due to the existence of monopoly. Monopoly implies that one firm has control over a substantial part of the supply of a particular product, and power to restrict entry of other firms which might wish to compete in its production. The effect is that where consumer preferences would require that more resources be moved into the production of a particular commodity the holding of a monopoly position might prevent this. Insufficient resources would be devoted to producing the monopolized product and too many resources to other products, as compared to the allocation conforming to consumer wishes. Thus the allocation of resources is disturbed. Apart from this misallocation, by restricting the supply of a product, the monopolist can raise its price and reap monopoly profits, as we shall see in detail in Chapter 17. Monopoly incomes may in this way be a major source of income inequality, so that this reinforces our first point.

As we shall see later, an important factor permitting the holding of monopoly positions in a capitalist economy is the fact that not all firms or would-be capitalists can obtain the necessary finance to set up in business: thus large corporations who have over a long period acquired large reserves of money capital are to a great extent shielded from competition. In other words, the market for finance or money capital does not operate so effectively that when consumer demand requires an increase in the supply of a product more firms can secure the finance necessary to enter the industry and thus produce the increased output.

Consumer ignorance

We stated above that under competition inefficient firms will be driven out of business, since consumers will prefer to buy from efficient low-cost producers who are able to ask lower prices for the same goods. This assumes however that consumers know what prices are being charged by all firms in the market and that they know precisely the content and value of the goods they are buying. Unfortunately, this is often not the case and consumers are probably to an important degree ignorant of their full market opportunities. This is particularly likely to be true where the goods are of some technical complexity as in the case of electrical equipment, say, or medical supplies. But this is not simply because the consumers have poor or inadequate information: modern business enterprises use advanced advertising techniques deliberately aimed at persuading consumers to buy their products in preference to others. They direct their persuasive force not only by advertising through posters, newspapers, cinemas, or other media, but by trying to make their products appear to differ from others, if only by means of attractive wrappings, even if no fundamental difference or basis for preference exists. Thus advertising is not only *informative* but also *persuasive*. The result, it is often claimed, is that the final composition of output does not conform to genuine consumer tastes, but is in part determined by the business world itself.

Divergence between social and private advantages

Another part of our argument above was that if consumers spent more on a particular good, profits in the production of that good would go up, and this would induce new firms to enter the industry, thus increasing the supply. Profits provide the incentive inducing businessmen to supply the output desired by consumers. In fact, however, we can cite many situations where profits—and we are not referring to monopoly profits here—might prove an imperfect guide as to the goods which it is to the advantage of society to produce. There may, in other words, be a divergence between *private benefit*, to the businessman, and *social benefit*, to the community. For example, left to themselves, private fishermen might fish a lake so heavily that the fish were unable to replace themselves and future supplies were therefore endangered: the government might then be justified in licensing fishermen in order to restrict the total amount of fish landed each year. Likewise cattle traders might be in a position to make profits by travelling vast distances to reach more lucrative markets: this might, however, involve costs to others in that the movement of cattle might bring an increased risk of cattle disease to herds in the regions through which they pass, and again some restrictions might be called for in keeping the interests of all

producers in mind. Again, the concentration of industries in towns might be advantageous to the firms who were setting up there, but might eventually produce social problems which cost the government a great deal to cure. There are many such cases where the operation of one enterprise involves costs to other enterprises or more directly to the community: *social costs* which are not included in their calculations of profits but which must ultimately be met by the consumer. On the other hand, a benefit may accrue to other enterprises or to the community from the actions of a private business: for example, in developing countries many new lines of activity have to be embarked upon by 'pioneering' firms, who cannot draw upon the experience of other firms who have successfully operated similar businesses under the particular local conditions of the region. Even if these 'pioneers' fail, their experience may help their future successors to make good, to avoid the mistakes they themselves made and the pitfalls they encountered. When the profit calculations of private firms exclude such benefits accruing to or costs imposed upon other firms or upon the community directly, we have what may be termed *external economies* or *external diseconomies*, since these are benefits and costs which affect people outside the firms responsible for them.

Instability and unemployment

A major defect in the competitive market system which economists have observed and investigated now for centuries is the tendency of the system towards instability and crisis. This instability may be local, affecting one industry: we shall analyse presently why prices and incomes in agriculture in particular show a tendency to fluctuate under free competition. On the other hand, the instability may affect employment and incomes right across the country and may even spread from one country to another, causing many millions of workers to be unemployed. Fortunately economists now have a fairly good idea of the reason why capitalist economies are liable to such complete breakdown and have devised remedial measures to tackle unemployment and reduce its incidence, even if it remains a serious problem in many countries.

Inability to cope with rapid structural changes

Lastly, many consider that if a drastic structural transformation of the economy is required, the price mechanism is either an ineffective means or a painful means of effecting the changes required. It is generally acknowledged, for instance, that in time of war, though the government may still make widespread use of price and profit incentives, it will have to assume a major responsibility for the mobilization of resources with the war effort as the overriding aim. Even in peace time, the invention of new products or changes in demand may require a drastic cutting-back in a particular industry: the post-war reduction in the Lancashire cotton industry in Britain necessitated by severe competition from foreign producers and by the development of artificial fibres provides a good example. The government might in such a case feel bound to moderate and plan the change to avoid excessive hardship to workers who are laid off from the declining industry but are reluctant or unable to abandon their homes and other links with the region to find alternative employment elsewhere.

The most obvious case where drastic and accelerated transformation of the economy might be involved is where the economy is in the early stages of economic development: here it is argued that the price mechanism reflects the economy broadly as it is in the present, rather than as it might be in the future. To *transform* the economy and set it on the path towards more rapid economic growth requires deliberate government strategy. Exactly how far government action should supplement market forces as an engine of development is a matter which requires careful analysis, as we shall see later on, but it seems to be hardly disputable that the state bears special responsibility in a developing country.

Planning versus the price mechanism

If the price mechanism does in fact suffer from the defects listed above, why do so many people have such faith in its operation? The first reason is that they feel that once defects are identified, they can be corrected to an important degree and the price mechanism made to work better. It is argued, for instance, that the inequality of incomes and opportunity can be remedied through the medium of taxation of income and wealth without necessarily abandoning the basic system of free enterprise. Monopoly can be tackled specifically by anti-monopoly legislation and the supply of finance to small firms supplemented by government loan schemes, if this is likely to be productive. Consumer ignorance can be reduced by encouraging consumers' associations to carry out objective tests on the relative merits of the different goods on the market and thus counter the most misleading advertising. Where private and social costs and benefits diverge, the government can bring them into line by demanding

an equivalent tax from private firms who are imposing costs on the community, or conversely by granting a subsidy to them if they are producing benefits to the community as a whole; or, as in our fishing and cattle-trading examples, the government can use licensing to prevent the divergence occurring. Instability and unemployment, again, can be tackled directly by monetary and fiscal policy to stimulate or restrain demand, and so on.

The second reason put forward by adherents of the price mechanism is the belief that human nature is such that it requires incentives to efficiency and penalties for inefficiency, that it is simply not realistic to expect a sufficient response from general appeals to work hard for the common good; and that even if factors of production including labour were responsive to organization by an all-powerful planning body, the sheer complexity of the organization problem would engulf the planning authority and produce unwieldiness, inflexibility, errors, and other inefficiencies.

Apart from the fact that the issues involved are highly emotional, it would clearly require a vast amount of evidence supporting or contradicting the above claims to resolve them. The evidence can certainly not be produced within the pages of an introductory textbook such as this, and the authors will be satisfied if they can persuade readers that they need to read more widely to discover the answers.

The allocation of resources in centrally planned economies

The basic economic problem of scarcity and choice, and therefore of allocating resources in some 'optimum' way, still exists in the centrally planned economy. The difference lies in the way in which this allocation is made. This will not be the result of hundreds of separate decisions by producers and consumers made compatible by the 'invisible hand' of the market, but ultimately by a central planning committee of some sort. This committee would make decisions of exactly the same type as our subsistence producer: how much of each kind of product to produce (choice of products), how much to produce altogether by setting production targets (though incentives are often offered to workers to work hard enough to achieve these), and what proportion should consist of capital goods (how much to invest).

The committee, or rather the planners operating at different levels—decisions will of course be delegated downwards, and regionally through the planning apparatus—will, in making a choice of products, still be confronted in effect by a transformation curve, such as in Figure 5.2, marking the limit of the resources available. They will know that every commodity produced will have an *opportunity-cost* in terms of alternative goods or services which could have been supplied from the same sources.

In Figure 5.2 the point on the transformation curve chosen by the subsistence producer depended on his own scale of preferences as between maize and beans. While a planning committee could not afford to ignore consumers' preferences—for instance by setting production targets for a commodity well in excess of what consumers want, and are willing to buy—they would be in a strong position to influence consumption in any direction. If production was entirely in the hands of the state it could, for a commodity of which a relatively great amount had been produced, set the price low compared to alternative products, to ensure sufficient purchases.

Likewise the planners will need to determine the proportions of national resources to be devoted to producing consumer goods and investment goods: that is, to make the choice between more income now and more income in the future. The analysis relating to Figure 5.3 can thus be applied directly to such planning decisions. Different plans, embracing different combinations of projects, some with immediate, some with delayed returns, will produce different 'income streams' or, if we continue with our simple two-periods case, different combinations of present and future income. The choice between them, however, will depend on the rate of time preference *which the planners consider appropriate*. In Russia, after 1917, the government adopted a policy of maintaining for several decades a very high rate of investment at the expense of consumption, preferring to increase the output of machinery to provide the basis for industrial expansion to expanding agricultural output of food for consumption purposes. This was successful in building up the USSR as one of the foremost industrial nations of the world, eventually to have a high standard of living, but only at the cost of a considerable sacrifice on the part of the earlier generations. The post-1917 government in effect applied a low rate of time preference in its investment decision, not particularly favourable to the generation of the day, but to the benefit of later generations. China, in her development since 1948, has adopted a contrasting policy emphasizing agriculture and implying a desire to expand food production, though not of course neglecting industrial growth.

What time preference the state should adopt is difficult to say. We may note, however, that any element of 'short-sightedness' as discussed above should be absent. The state ought to be rational where individuals may be irrational in neglecting their old age, and it will also have to safeguard the interests of the yet unborn citizens of future generations, interests which might otherwise be neglected. There is, though, a valid reason for the state to adopt a positive rate of time preference. Given a reasonably high rate of net investment, income per head will be increasing over time (unless population is also expanding rapidly), and it can then be argued that an increment of income will be worth more to the present generation than the same income offered to the (richer) future generation. In terms of Figure 5.3 as the volume of investment in the Plan increases, the ratio of expected future income to the present income of the society will increase, and the higher this ratio, the higher will be the appropriate rate of time preference. As with our subsistence producer, the optimum amount of investment will be given by the point at which the extra output from an extra unit of investment (marginal product of capital) is only *just* equal to the extra output which the planners think sufficient to compensate for the present consumption forgone (its rate of time preference).

Economic systems: capitalist, socialist, and traditional

The problem of scarcity and choice is common to any economy and economic system. Our discussion of specialization, the use of capital, and economies of scale also applies to an advanced socialist economy as to a capitalist one: the economy of such a state is equally *complex*, involving the division of labour, as the developed capitalist economy. It is equally dependent on exchange in order to tap these advantages, and it uses money to facilitate exchange as in the capitalist economy. On the other hand, it can equally be limited 'by the extent of the market' for this is just a matter of a low level of real income. If real incomes are low in a socialist state, it will still not make economic sense to devote scarce resources to a large-scale motor car factory, say, when the people want food and clothing rather than cheap motor cars. The traditional African economic system was *not* based on specialization and the division of labour—though some wants were provided collectively, the individual household by and large provided itself with all its requirements—and thus the productivity of this system has in the past been low.

We may ask ourselves therefore, in what essential ways the capitalist and socialist systems differ. Four main aspects may be compared: (1) the ownership of factors of production, especially land and capital, which we may call *property*; (2) the control of business decisions (including the degree of workers' participation) and the motives underlying them; (3) the determination of incomes and their classification; and (4) the class system and status of wage earners.

(1) The centre-point of the capitalist system is private property, comprising both land (and other natural resources) and capital. Land is a marketable commodity, which can be bought and sold, while capital may also be accumulated by individual entrepreneurs or private companies. In contrast a socialist system is characterized by state ownership of property, including the capital incorporated in factories, farms, and other productive establishments.

(2) While under capitalism business decisions in respect of investment and the running of firms are in the hands of private businessmen pursuing the profit motive through the price mechanism, a socialist economy will comprise mainly state-run enterprises, at least in the large-scale sectors, which will be run by the state with the object, ideally, of maximizing the 'social dividend': obtaining the level and composition of output which best satisfies the wants of the population. Decisions will be made and coordinated by planners and bureaucrats rather than by the 'invisible hand' of the price mechanism. Workers' participation may be encouraged so that workers share in decisions at the factory level.

(3) In the capitalist system the distribution of income is determined by the sale of factors of production in the factor 'markets': land is sold or leased for the payment of *rent*, to the highest bidder; funds accumulated by individuals and companies may be loaned in return for the payment of *interest*; labour is purchased in return for *wages*, the rate of wages being determined in the labour market or by free 'collective bargaining' between trade unions and employers; and capitalists who bring together these factors of production to form an enterprise earn *profits* on their operation, the level of which is determined by the degree of competition.

In a socialist system, rent will not exist as a payment for the lease of land, since state-owned land will simply be made available to any use as decided by the planners: planners will on the other hand need to take account of the alternative uses of any piece of land, and consider the scarcity of particular types of land. Interest will not exist, either, as payments to private accumulators of capital; though, as we have seen, something equivalent to interest will be required for accounting purposes in order to compare the values of present and future income: this will not be determined by market forces, however, but as an accounting tool.

It would be disputed by Soviet economists whether interest exists at all in a socialist system, or profits. The important fact however is that interest does not exist as payment to private accumulators of capital. There are no private capital markets where owners of wealth may trade in titles to land, buildings, or shares in productive enterprises. However, some non-marketable government debt, like National Savings Certificates, or savings deposits in State Banks may earn interest the main function of which is to reward holders for *not* spending. Various kinds of 'implicit' rates of interest exist whenever discounts for 'cash' payments and surcharges for deferred payments exist; these exist in Soviet countries, as they do in African villages where shopkeepers charge more to their customers who cannot pay in ready cash.

Profits would only exist as temporary surpluses (negative profits as deficits) of the receipts over the payments of an enterprise, and would not accrue to capitalists. Price and output would be fixed in such a way as to equalize receipts and payments over a period of time: except that a surplus of total output over consumption would be used by the state for investment. With this qualification, all income in a socialist state would thus accrue as wages and salaries to labour of different kinds, whether manual, technical, or managerial. Underlying this is the *labour theory of value*, which states that all goods derive their value from the labour which has gone into producing them. Thus capital goods are a means of *storing up* labour to provide a greater supply of consumer goods in the future.

(4) While in a socialist system there are in theory only various kinds of labour, a distinguishing feature of capitalism, lastly, is a division into socio-economic classes, in particular landowners, employers (capitalists), and employees (workers). Divergence of interest between the two groups, employers aiming at maximum profits and minimum labour costs, and employees at increasing their wages, may produce conflict or even *class warfare*, as it has been called. We mentioned above that the operation of the price mechanism may be inhibited by the existence of monopoly. If monopoly is widespread, with concentration of 'economic power' in the hands of monopolists, there is an obvious danger that this economic power will bring with it a concentration of political power, with rich capitalists or property-owners being able to wield considerable political influence as compared to those with the status of wage earners and labourers. There would then exist the opposition of classes on the social and political level as well as the economic one.

These are two contrasting pictures. The reality of today is rather different. No *fully* planned economy exists, just as no purely 'laissez-faire' or unplanned capitalist economy exists. The Western capitalist economies are now generally described as *mixed economies*, since many important industries are run as state enterprises and there is often a substantial state sector providing social services, particularly medicine and education. For instance in Britain post and telecommunications; gas, electricity, and water supplies; coalmining; steel production; and the railways and some roads, ports and air transportation are organized by the state, and further state participation is planned. A National Health Service provides medical services, though some private medicine also exists; and one-third of the population rent their homes from local government authorities. In France, a major motor car firm is state-run. While workers' participation in decision-making is not usually far advanced, there are generally various forms of consultation between management, unions, and workers. The distribution of income in capitalist countries is probably more equal than it was—inequality may be much greater in some developing countries, particularly in the ownership of land—and has been modified substantially by the tax system, on the one hand, and the provision of social services, including national insurance and pensions, through the 'welfare state', on the other. Greater equality of opportunity through the expansion of education has moderated the extent of class conflict.

At the same time there have been changes within socialist countries in Eastern Europe towards making more use of the price system as a guide towards consumer tastes, permitting more 'consumer sovereignty' as a test of managerial efficiency at the factory level, and in the use of wage incentives to labour. There is more explicit use of what is in effect a rate of interest ('discount factor') in planning output. It should be noted also that inequality of incomes has by no means been eliminated in such countries, there being a relatively well-to-do managerial class there also. Equality of income opportunity and status has gone much further in China, for example, than in the Soviet Union.

The traditional system and 'African Socialism'

We shall refer to the 'traditional system' as being that which generally existed throughout Africa at the beginning of the century prior to the development of the money economy and of cash crops, a system which remains intact in a few areas today. The position regarding property in this system is somewhat ambiguous. Land was, and generally still is, regarded as belonging to the community or to the tribe: it would not be bought or sold or, specifically, sold outside the tribe. On the other hand individual rights were recognized in that particular pieces of land were regularly farmed by one family, who would have effective security of tenure. This apparent conflict is reconciled to some extent by the fact that a family's 'title' to the land depended on the family's

using it: if the family left the area the plot would revert to the community or to any individual who took over the plot. The basic factors of production were land and labour, so the accumulation of much capital was generally absent.

Production was organized on the basis of the family farm, though some special tasks might be done collectively or on a neighbourly basis of mutual assistance. The aim of production was not profit, but to provide for the subsistence requirements, including housing, of the family unit. The introduction of cash crops has brought the profit motive into African farming, but on the whole it has been possible to adopt these without any fundamental alteration of the system of communal land tenure.

A labour theory of value might also be said to apply in that output was the direct product of a family's labour. Income distribution was egalitarian because each family was assigned a similar means of livelihood: a piece of land. This was supported by a system of 'mutual social responsibility', as it has been called, or the 'extended family', whereby members of the same community would help each other, particularly in times of food shortage, during sickness, or in old age. This historical system of allocation of land in Africa has resulted on the whole in a very equal distribution of land throughout the continent—with the obvious exception of South Africa and Rhodesia particularly, and other areas of present or former white settlement in the Kenya Highlands and in former Portuguese Africa. On the whole Africa has avoided the problem of a landed aristocracy as it exists in Asia and Latin America, though some of this did exist for instance in Buganda and in Ethiopia, or could emerge with the 'localization' of former expatriate estates.

Finally it may be noted that the problem of class structure was absent in most African societies— though there were chiefs wielding a varying degree of feudal power and authority. The Kenya Government's Sessional Paper No. 10 of 1965 on 'African Socialism and its application to planning in Kenya' stated that:

The sharp class divisions that once existed in Europe have no place in African Socialism and no parallel in African society. No class problem arose in the traditional African society and none exists today among Africans. The class problem in Africa, therefore, is largely one of prevention, in particular ... to plan development so as to prevent the emergence of antagonistic classes. (p. 12)

There was certainly no class of proletarians, hired workers without land of their own and dependent on farmer-entrepreneurs for employment. With low population density land was sufficiently plentiful for each family to be self-sufficient in most parts of Eastern Africa before the colonial period.

The traditional system thus appears, in many ways, to have been the ideal one! Its weakness lies in the extremely low labour productivity that has been associated with it. As we have pointed out, it is a system in which specialization and the division of labour are largely absent, and in which little capital is employed to raise labour's productivity. Political leaders and theorists in several African countries have, on the other hand, contended that the traditional system could form the basis of a *modernized* African Socialism. Two questions therefore arise.

(1) Can the system be modernized, without losing its traditional virtues?

(2) Can it really provide the basis for an African Socialism in a modernized economy?

Two governments in East Africa, those of Kenya and Tanzania, have at various times adopted African Socialism as their objective, and attempted to define the term[4]—though the former cannot be said to have pursued this interest very far.

The Kenya government paper referred to above states:

> There are two African traditions which form an essential basis for African Socialism—political democracy and mutual social responsibility .... Mutual social responsibility is an extension of the African family spirit to the nation as a whole, with the hope that ultimately the same spirit can be extended to larger areas .... The state has an obligation to ensure equal opportunities to all its citizens, eliminate exploitation and discrimination, and provide needed social services such as education, medical care and social security.

This is strikingly similar to a statement by President Nyerere:

> The foundation, and the objective, of African Socialism, is the extended family .... We, in Africa, have no more need of being 'converted' to socialism than we have of being 'taught' democracy. Both are rooted in our own past—in the traditional society which produced us. Modern African socialism can draw from its traditional heritage the recognition of 'society' as an extension of the basic family unit.

This also stresses political democracy in African society as the opposite of class warfare. Elsewhere, in respect of the ujamaa (cooperative) village programme, Nyerere stresses cooperative production as a means specifically of avoiding peasant capitalism, involving eventually a class of hired farm labourers.

We shall examine the progress of the ujamaa village programme in a later chapter. The reader meanwhile may think more about his own experience and ask such questions as: how effective is the extended family in providing mutual support? How far has such cooperation stood the test of time with the development of the economy? How would it operate in the industrial sector? How does it compare with socialism as generally defined?

The business enterprise

The 'actors' within any economic system, like the actors on a stage, comprise the hundreds of firms or business enterprises in the economy: the units in which output is organized. Theoretical analysis of decision-making within these separate units is an important part of economics, and is known as *microeconomic analysis*, in contrast with analysis of the broad development of the economy and its main aggregates (consumption, saving, investment, exports, and the like), known as *macroeconomic analysis*. Microeconomic analysis is simply analysis of the individual producing unit, and is just as important in a socialist or mixed economy as in a capitalist economy.

Theoretical analysis of the decisions of the individual producing unit is also referred to as the 'theory of the firm'. What is important to note here is that 'the firm' may refer to very different kinds of enterprises: to peasant farmers, for example, pursuing a way of life aimed at subsistence and based on a system of communalism rather than on the profit motive; or to family retail businesses which again may offer the family a way of life, but less income than the family could separately earn as wage earners; or to millers, transporters, taxi-drivers, watch-repairers, and other small capitalists—even shoe-shine boys; or to joint-stock companies run by salaried managers, but owned by hundreds of small or large shareholders. Or finally the firm may be a huge multinational company with branches in a large number of countries and with profits or 'turnover') annual sales) greater than the revenue of many governments or the total national income of small countries. These types of firm may differ considerably in their organization; in their methods of financing (as we shall see in a later chapter); in the motives underlying decisions; and as already mentioned, in the kinds of entrepreneurial capacity they require.

Questions on Chapter 5

1. Define the following: opportunity-cost, time preference, transformation curve.
2. How will diminishing returns affect a subsistence producer's choice between work and leisure?
3. Discuss the shape of a hypothetical peasant producer's transformation curve between two products.
4. For what reasons may an individual have 'positive time preference'?
5. How is an individual's rate of time preference revealed by his behaviour?
6. Use a diagram to illustrate a peasant producer's decision regarding how much to invest.
7. 'The division of labour is limited by the extent of the market.' Discuss.
8. Compare the advantages of producing for domestic consumption and producing for the market.
9. What is meant by the 'invisible hand' of the market? How effective is it (a) in a developed economy and (b) in an underdeveloped economy?
10. Give examples of external economies and diseconomies.
11. Distinguish between social and private costs. How may they diverge?
12. On what bases would you distinguish between socialist, capitalist, and 'traditional' systems?
13. Does 'interest' exist in a socialist state?
14. What use, if any, do Soviet planners make of the rate of interest in planning investment?
15. How are resources allocated in centrally planned economies?
16. On what basis is income distributed in (i) a capitalist economy, (ii) a centrally planned economy, and (iii) a traditional African economy?
17. What is the labour theory of value? Is it relevant to an understanding of a traditional African economy?
18. What do you understand by 'African Socialism'? How strong a basis do you think traditional communalism provides for a modern society?
19. Is the 'extended family' in traditional society an adequate substitute for the welfare state?
20. What is 'the firm'? Are all types of firm equally motivated by the pursuit of profits?

Notes

[1] We are ignoring here the possibility that the individual's needs may be different in present and future: our producer might, for instance, expect to marry later and raise a large family, increasing the household's requirements of food, etc.

[2] In our discussion we have assumed for the sake of simplicity that if our producer undertakes no saving (zero net investment) he will expect to enjoy the same level of consumption in present and future periods. But apart from his own investment efforts there may be other reasons why he can expect more or less future than present income. Our producer might expect to inherit more land from his father in the future, for instance. Wage and salary earners in a money economy tend to earn progressively higher incomes as time passes and as they gain more skill, wisdom, or experience in their jobs. We have also mentioned people who expect shortly to retire and to have considerably reduced incomes.

[3] We referred earlier, in Chapter 2, to Adam Smith, Professor of Moral Philosophy at the University of Glasgow, who wrote *The Wealth of Nations*, published in 1776, and is widely regarded as the 'father' of Economics.

[4] Readers are referred to *Kenya Sessional Paper No. 10*, *op. cit.*, and J. K. Nyerere, 'Ujamaa—The Basis of African Socialism', in his *Ujamaa—Essays on Socialism*, Oxford University Press, 1968.

6 The Demand for a Commodity

In the previous chapter we outlined in an extremely sketchy way the manner in which the price mechanism operates to allocate resources in a free market economy. Increased demand by consumers for a commodity results in an increase in price, which acts as a signal for producers to produce more of it. Price is the intermediary, as it were, between demand by consumers and the willingness and ability of producers to supply the commodity: and in turn, the forces of demand, on the one hand, and of supply, on the other, together influence and determine the level of price. It is now necessary to examine this process of price determination more carefully, and we shall start by looking more closely at the factors affecting the demand for a commodity.

The factors determining the amount demanded by an individual

First of all the amount that an individual wishes to buy of a commodity depends on his tastes or preferences. In the extreme case, if he dislikes the commodity altogether he will not buy any at all. Each person is likely to have his own individual tastes, influenced by all sorts of factors such as age, sex, education, or religion. For example, a Muslim may not purchase pig meat or wine, while a scholar may prefer a good book to a cheap thriller!

Secondly, the amount he buys will depend on its price. If the good is very expensive he may buy very little of it, and in general we should expect him to buy more as the good becomes cheaper—although in fact there may be exceptions to this rule.

Thirdly, how much he buys will be affected by the availability of other goods. For example, if one kind of meat falls in price, and if he decides to buy more of this kind, he is likely to buy less of another kind the price of which has not fallen.

Lastly, the size of his money income will affect the amount that he buys of a commodity. If his income increases, he will be able to buy more of various commodities as he chooses, including the one under consideration.

Altogether, then, we can say that the amount a person buys of a commodity depends upon:

(1) his tastes,
(2) the price of the commodity,
(3) the prices of other goods, and
(4) his money income.

Thus if any one of these four determinants changes, the amounts demanded by a person would be expected to change. In the real world these are constantly changing, and changing simultaneously. For purposes of analysis, however, we can *assume* first of all, (1), (3), and (4) of the determinants constant, and consider the relationship between the price of the commodity and the amount of the commodity which would be bought. Later we shall suppose (1), (2), and (4) constant, and discuss the possible relationship between the amount bought of the commodity and the prices of other goods, and finally, with (1), (2), and (3) constant, between money income and the amount bought. This assumption of 'other things being the same', that is to say, of other factors supposed constant, is a common device in economics for helping us to unravel complex relationships.

The relationship between price and the amount demanded

Let us suppose then that the tastes and money income of the individual and the price of other commodities do not change. Table 6.1 shows the amounts, D_x, of a good X that the individual would be willing to buy at different possible prices of the good, P_x. Such a table is referred to as a demand *schedule*. If we plot the data on a graph, then this *graph* is referred to as a demand curve. Thus, the demand curve is simply a visual representation of the data embodied in the

Table 6.1 A hypothetical individual's demand for good X at various prices

P_x (shillings)	D_x (kg)
1.60	50
1.50	55
1.40	60
1.30	65
1.20	70

demand schedule. It is customary to plot price on the vertical axis and quantity on the horizontal axis, as in Figure 6.1. The demand curve here slopes down from left to right, reflecting the fact that the individual buys more X when P_x falls.

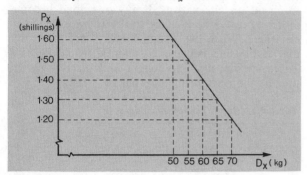

Figure 6.1   *An individual's demand curve.*

Movements along the demand curve versus shifts in the demand curve

We must now remind ourselves that this demand curve was drawn up on the assumption of given tastes, money income, and prices of other goods. For a different combination of these we should in general expect to have a new demand schedule and therefore a new demand curve. If money income increases, for example, the individual would most likely be willing to buy more *at each price* than he was before. Table 6.2 gives the amounts that he is willing to buy for different combinations of P_x and money income, M. Thus at $P_x = 1.60$ and M = 1,000, the amount bought is 50 kg. Again of course the example is fictitious. We can now observe that Table 6.1 is obtained from Table 6.2 by taking the first two columns only. Thus the demand curve we drew assumed that money income, M, was 1,000 shillings. The curve is plotted again in Figure 6.2, this time labelled M = 1,000.

The figures in the *next* column of Table 6.2 assume that the individual has a money income of 1,100 shillings per annum. This demand curve is also plotted in Figure 6.2 and labelled M = 1,100. *The effect of the change in money income can be seen to be a shift of the entire demand curve to the right in this instance.*

It is extremely important not to confuse a movement along a *given* demand curve with a shift of the curve, as we shall see when we come to make use of this analysis later on. We can see that it is a matter of *which determinant changes.* If P_x changes, we move *along* the curve; but if tastes change, money income changes, or the prices of other goods change, the effect, if any, would be to alter the position of the whole curve.

Table 6.2   *Amounts bought (in kg) for combinations of price and money income*

P_x	Monthly money income (shillings			
	1,000	1,100	1,200	1,300
1.60	50	55	58	60
1.50	55	60	63	65
1.40	60	65	68	70
1.30	65	70	73	75
1.20	70	75	78	80

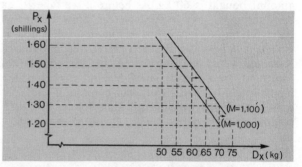

Figure 6.2   *A shift in the individual's demand curve due to an increase in income.*

An expression which produces a great deal of confusion is that of 'an increase in demand'. Sometimes this expression is used with reference to a movement along the curve, and sometimes to a shift of the curve. To avoid confusion, we shall say that when price falls, and more is bought as a result, there has been an increase *in the amount demanded.* When one of the other three factors changes, and the demand curve is shifted to the right, we shall say that there has been a change in the *state* of demand, or simply *an increase in demand.* Conversely a decrease in demand involves a shift of the curve to the left.

Effect of changes in the price of substitutes and complements

The demand for a good X may also be affected by the price of certain other goods. If two goods, X and Y, say, are used together, then a fall in the price of Y will encourage the consumer to buy more Y, and this in turn may also induce him to buy more of X, if X is used in conjunction with Y. For example, if bicycles become cheaper, more people will acquire bicycles, and it may be expected that the demand for bicycle *tyres* will increase. Table 6.3 gives the amount of X demanded, D_x, for different combinations of P_x and

Table 6.3 *Amounts bought (in kg) for combinations of P_x and P_y*

P_x (cents) \ P_y (shillings)	0.90	0.80	0.70	0.60	0.50
1.60	60	65	70	75	80
1.50	70	75	80	85	90
1.40	80	85	90	95	100
1.30	90	95	100	105	110
1.20	100	105	110	115	120

P_y. For example, if $P_x = 1.60$ and $P_y = 0.90$, then the amount bought is 60 kg. As before if we take P_y as constant, equal, say to 0.90, we can draw a demand curve relating P_x and D_x as in Figure 6.3, labelling it $P_y = 0.90$. If, however, P_y stood at 0.80, the amounts of X bought would be those given in the second column. Plotting these we get the new demand curve labelled $P_y = 0.80$ in Figure 6.3. Thus each column of Table 6.4 represents a new demand schedule for X. The next column gives the curve labelled $P_y = 0.70$ and so on.

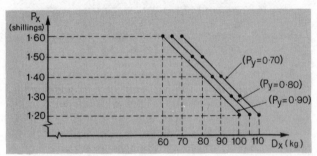

Figure 6.3 *A shift in the individual's demand curve due to a change in the price of another good.*

If we follow a particular *row* in the table, we have the amount of X demanded as P_y varies, *the price of X remaining* constant. For instance, if $P_x = 1.60$, we have

Table 6.4 *Goods X and Y complementary*

P_y (shillings)	0.90	0.80	0.70	0.60	0.50
D_x (kg)	60	65	70	75	80

When a fall in the price of Y increases the demand for X, as in this case, X and Y are said to be *complementary goods*.

The more usual case however is where the two goods are *substitutes*. Rice and potatoes, for example, may be substitutes, in the sense that if rice becomes relatively expensive, consumers may reduce the

amount of rice they buy in favour of potatoes, and vice versa. Dried fish can be considered a substitute for fresh fish, and so on. But this applies not only to close substitutes: if a consumer has a limited income, whatever he spends on one good will not be available to spend on alternatives. If any one good becomes more expensive he is likely to divert his expenditure elsewhere. When two goods X and Y are substitutes the relationship between P_y and D_x would be as in Table 6.5, the amount bought of X *decreasing* this time as the price of the alternative Y falls.

Table 6.5 *Goods X and Y substitutes*

P_y (shillings)	0.90	0.80	0.70	0.60	0.50
D_x (kg)	45	41	38	36	35

Effect of a change in money-income

Equally, we may be interested in seeing how the amount of X bought varies when the individual's money income varies, assuming that P_x and other prices, as well as his tastes, remain unchanged. For instance, reading along the first row of Table 6.2 above, we obtain, for $P_x = 1.60$ constant, the data of Table 6.6. These data are plotted in Figure 6.4. We may call this an income-consumption curve, since it tells us the relation between the consumer's income and the amount consumed. For the present we are still discussing the income-consumption re-

Table 6.6 *The relationship between an individual's money income and the amount bought*

Y (cents)	1,000	1,100	1,200	1,300
D_x (kg)	50	55	58	60

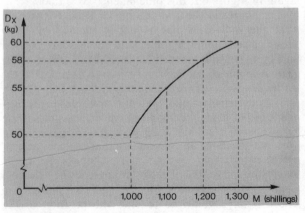

Figure 6.4 *The income-consumption curve.*

lationship for one individual. Figure 6.4 depicts what we should expect to be the usual relationship between money income and the amount bought. Since more is bought when money income is increased, the curve slopes upwards from the left.

However, this need not always be true. In Figure 6.5 OD_1 represents what we have suggested will be the 'usual' form of relationship: but OD_2 can be seen to flatten out after a certain point, no more of the commodity being bought despite an increase of money income. This might be true of the demand for salt for example: the amount of salt a family uses is probably fixed within very narrow limits. Even if the family becomes better off it will not put a lot more salt on its food, and the number of meals it has per day using salt is not likely to change, even if the quality of what is eaten improves. But there are probably many goods which tend eventually to reach a saturation level, though not as quickly as in the case of salt. Such a commodity, the consumption of which tends to a fixed amount independently of the level of income, is sometimes referred to as a 'necessity'.

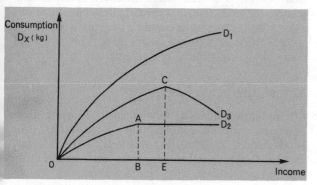

Figure 6.5 *Income-consumption curves.*

The curve OD_3 illustrates a case where as income increases beyond the level OE the amount of X bought actually decreases. This case might occur when, as a person becomes better off, he abandons in part the consumption of a particular commodity in favour of another which he now feels he can afford. In Africa it is possible that rather less of the less exciting rootcrops like cassava, say, might be eaten and a more varied diet with rice, vegetables, and the like adopted if an individual became better off.

A good, the consumption of which actually declines when income increases, is referred to as an 'inferior good', implying that a preferred good is substituted for it. The word 'inferior' here is of course used only in a relative sense, and is defined strictly in terms of the observed relationship between income and the amount demanded. The term 'necessity' is also a relative term: there are areas of Africa for

example where salt is short and where more would be bought if incomes increased. In this sense a commodity may be an 'inferior good' or a 'necessity' at one level of income but not at another. Figure 6.5 depicts Good 3 as 'inferior' over the range of income beyond OE and Good 2 as a 'necessity' beyond income OB only. At lower levels of income the relationship between income and the amount bought is 'normal'.

Aggregate demand functions

So far we have been dealing with the amount bought by one consumer at different prices and incomes. But this was to enable us to understand factors affecting *total* demand in the market from all consumers. It is in fact very easy to obtain a market demand curve simply by summing the demand schedules of the individual consumers or, in terms of graphs, *by adding horizontally* the individual demand curves. Let us make things easy by imagining there are just *two* individuals in the market, John and Shona, with individual demand schedules as in Table 6.7.

In this table total demand at each price is obtained simply by adding the amounts that John and Shona would each buy at that price. The corresponding demand curves are shown in Figure 6.6.

The derivation of the total market demand curve is not so easily derived in all cases. Supposing we were interested in the market demand for portable radios in Eastern Africa. There are two points to be made here. First of all, most people have no use for more than one portable radio! If the price of radios falls, we must not talk of the previous buyers buying additional radios; it will be largely people *previously without radios* who are now persuaded to acquire one. Secondly, to the extent this is true, as soon as people have a radio, they will disappear from the potential market, at least until their radios begin to wear out. For by demand we mean the amount people are willing to buy *per period of time*, and this is what we measure on the X-axis. The demand curve relates to potential sales in the current period and not to *past* sales. This must be borne in mind when

Table 6.7 *Deriving an aggregate demand schedule*

P_x (shillings)	Amount demanded at each price by		Total demand
	John	Shona	(kg)
16	50	0	50
15	55	5	60
14	60	15	75
13	65	25	90
12	70	35	105

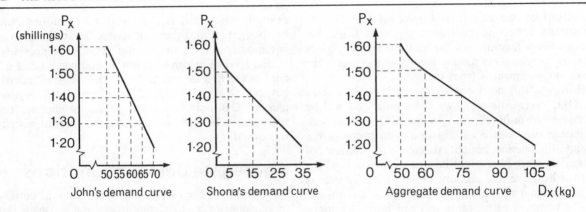

Figure 6.6   *Deriving an aggregate (market) demand curve.*

considering market demand for the whole range of *consumer durables*, like radios, refrigerators, bicycles, and so on.

We can also derive an aggregate income-consumption curve. This tells us the total amount demanded by all individuals in the community for each level of their total money income. It is not so easily obtained as the market demand curve however. When aggregate income goes up, the total amount of commodity bought will probably increase. But by how much it increases will depend on *who gets* the increase in income. If most of the increase goes to people whose demand is responsive to an increase in income, there will be a significant increase in the amount bought, while if it goes to people whose demands are not responsive to an increase in income, there may be little effect.

Suppose there are just two individuals again, John and Shona, and they each have the same individual income-consumption relationships, given in Table 6.8:

Table 6.8   *Income-consumption relationships for John and Shona*

Money income (shillings)	Amount bought (kg)
400	20
500	28
600	30

If John and Shona each have an income of 500 s, aggregate money income is 1,000 s, and the amount bought 56 kg ($=2 \times 28$ kg). But if John had 400 s and Shona 600 s aggregate income would still be 1,000 s, while the amount bought would be only 50 kg ($=20+30$ kg). *The amount bought thus depends not only on the level of aggregate money income, but also on its distribution.* Similarly for *increments* in income:

if John and Shona each have 400 s to start with, an increment in total income of 200 s will increase the total amount demanded from 40 kg to 56 kg ($=28+28$ kg) if John and Shona each get half the total increase, but only to 50 kg ($=20+30$ kg) if one of them gets the whole of the increase and the other none. Thus only if we make some assumption about what happens to the distribution of incomes (e.g. relative incomes remain approximately constant) can we get an aggregate income-consumption curve by adding those of separate individuals. This is one of many similar 'problems of aggregation'.

Actual aggregate functions

Attempts have already been made to estimate some aggregate income-consumption relationships for West Africa. In 1960, for example, I. G. Stewart carried out a small-scale survey into expenditure patterns in Ibadan. This relates income per household to the expenditure on food.

The result is summarized in Figure 6.7.[1]

It is interesting to compare this curve with the theoretical ones we drew in Figure 6.5.[2] Expenditure on food shows the 'normal' response up to an income of around £12–£16 per month, after which it increases much more slowly as income increases, look-

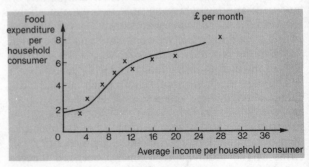

Figure 6.7   *An income-consumption curve for food in Ibadan, Nigeria, 1960.*

ing more like the curve drawn earlier to represent 'necessities'.

The degree of responsiveness of demand to changes in price or income

So far we have suggested that in the usual case the amount demanded will increase when the price of a commodity falls or money incomes increase. What is also important, however, is by *how much* the amount demanded increases when prices or incomes change. How responsive, in other words, is the amount demanded? The most convenient measure in the case of a change in price is the *elasticity of demand*. The elasticity of demand for commodity X is defined as:

$$E_D = \frac{proportionate \text{ change in amount of X demanded}}{proportionate \text{ change in price of X}}$$

$$= \frac{\triangle D_x / D_x}{\triangle P_x / P_x}, \text{ where } \triangle \text{ means 'the increment in'.}$$

For example, in Table 6.1, when the price, P_x falls from 1.60 to 1.50, the amount demanded by the individual, D_x, increases from 50 kg to 55 kg. Hence we have:

the initial quantity $D_x = 50$ kg
the change in quantity $\triangle D_x = 55 - 50 = 5$ kg
the initial price $P_x = 1.60$
the change in price $\triangle P_x = 1.60 - 1.50 = 0.10$ s

$$\text{and } E_D = \frac{5/50}{0.10/1.60} = 1.6$$

The larger this value, the more *'elastic'* is demand said to be, that is, the more *responsive* to changes in price. If E_D equals one, demand is said to be of *unit elasticity*. There is no particular significance surrounding this value, except that if $E_D = 1$, then a small price change *leaves total expenditure* (or from the point of view of suppliers, total revenue) *unchanged*. This is easy to see. If the proportionate change in price and in the amount demanded were each, say, 5 per cent, then elasticity would be unity. A 5 per cent cut in price with quantity unchanged would *decrease* expenditure by 5 per cent; and a 5 per cent increase in quantity with price unchanged would increase expenditure by 5 per cent. Hence a simultaneous 5 per cent cut in price leading to a 5 per cent increase in quantity would leave expenditure unaffected.[3]

From our discussions of substitutes and complements, we saw that the amount demanded of one good may be responsive to a change in the price of another good. This responsiveness is measured by the *cross-elasticity of demand* E_C, defined as:

$$E_C = \frac{proportionate \text{ change in amount of X demanded}}{proportionate \text{ change in price of Y}}$$

$$= \frac{\triangle D_x / D_x}{\triangle P_y / P_y}$$

For example, in Table 6.5, when the price of Y, P_y, falls from 0.90 to 0.80 s, the amount of X demanded by the individual, D_x, decreases from 45 kg to 41 kg. Hence we have:

the initial quantity $D_x = 45$ kg
the change in quantity $\triangle D_x = 45 - 41 = 4$ kg
the initial price of Y, $P_y = 0.90$
the change in price $\triangle P_y = 0.90 - 0.80 = 0.10$ s

$$\text{and } E_C = \frac{4/45}{0.10/0.90} = 0.8$$

In Table 6.4, the amount of X *increases*, from 60 to 65 kg, when the price of Y falls from 0.90 to 0.80 s indicating that X and Y are complementary goods. To distinguish between substitutes and complements, cross-elasticity is taken to be positive in the more common case of substitutes, and negative in the case of complements. Hence we have in this case:

$$E_C = -\frac{5/60}{0.10/0.90} = -0.75$$

To measure the responsiveness of the amount demanded to changes in money income, we can employ the term *income-elasticity of demand*, defined as:

$$E_M = \frac{proportionate \text{ change in quantity of X demanded}}{proportionate \text{ change in money income}}$$

$$= \frac{\triangle D_x / D_x}{\triangle M / M}$$

In Table 6.6, when income increases from 1,000 s to 1,100 s, the amount demanded increases from 50 to 55 kg, so that

$$E_y = \frac{5/50}{100/1,000} = 1$$

It may be wondered why we have introduced this concept of elasticity at all. Could we not tell simply from the slope of the demand curve whether it represents an inelastic or an elastic demand? If the demand curve slopes down steeply, this will indicate that the amount demanded changes very little even when price falls considerably, so that demand is *unresponsive* to price changes. A gently sloping or near-horizontal demand curve would indicate a responsive or highly elastic demand. In fact this is inadequate. First of all, just by changing the horizontal scale, without any change of data, the demand

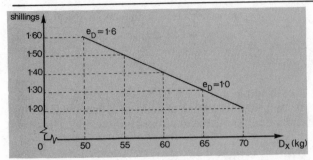

Figure 6.8 *The slope of a demand curve does not indicate elasticity.*

curve can be made to appear as gently sloping as we like. For example, in Figure 6.1, $\frac{1}{4}''$ on the horizontal axis was taken to represent 5 kg. If instead we take $\frac{1}{2}''$ to represent 5 kg, we obtain the gently sloping curve in Figure 6.8. Yet the price–quantity relationship is as before.

Even if the scale is fixed, the slope is not an accurate guide to the responsiveness of demand to price. For in Figure 6.8 the slope is constant all the way down the demand curve, but the elasticity varies.

At $P_x = 1.60$, $E_D = 1.6$; at $P_x = 1.30$, $E_D = \dfrac{5/65}{0.10/1.30} = 1.0$;

while at intermediate prices elasticity is falling steadily from 1.6 towards 1.0. The reason is simply that although the absolute increase in the amount demanded is 5 kg each time, this increase is less important in percentage terms.

What determines the value of price-elasticity of demand for particular goods? The main part of the answer lies in the *availability and prices of close substitutes* for the commodity. If *in the eyes of consumers* commodity X and commodity Y are very similar, a rise in the price of X would induce them to switch to commodity Y, so that the existence of Y makes the demand for commodity X 'elastic' with respect to its price. In part, of course, the value of elasticity we have depends on how broadly we define the commodity. The demand for a particular grade of rice is likely to be elastic, because consumers can easily switch to other grades; but the demand for rice as a whole will be less elastic since potatoes, maize, millet, etc., are likely to be less effective substitutes; the demand for foodstuffs as a whole may change very little if the price of foodstuffs rises in comparison to the prices of goods *other* than foodstuffs, and so on.

The slope of the individual demand curve

We suggested above that an individual's 'demand curve' will slope down from left to right, implying an inverse relationship between price and the amount an individual buys of a commodity, that is, that he will buy more the cheaper the commodity. That this is generally so appeals to common sense; but in fact some cases have been observed which appear to contradict this, where *less* is bought when the price falls. It is therefore worthwhile examining more closely the proposition that as a *general rule* the demand curve will slope down.

We find that we can in fact distinguish *two* reasons why we can expect this form of relationship. Since we are assuming 'other things the same' including the prices of other goods, a fall in the price of a particular good implies a fall in relation to the prices of goods for which it is a substitute. The consumer is therefore likely to 'substitute' this good for the others and buy more of this good and less of the others as a result of the price fall. This we can call the '*substitution effect*' of the price change.

But this is not all: as well as the prices of other goods being held constant, the consumer's money income is assumed not to have changed. He is therefore better off and we can say that his 'real income' has increased, since with the same *money* income he can buy a greater 'basket of goods' than before. What effect will this increase in real income have on the amount he buys of the good? We stated the three possibilities above: in the case of most goods we should expect that more would be bought, but it is *possible* that the amount either decreases or remains unchanged. If then we refer to the change in the amount demanded when real income increases, after a price fall, as the '*income effect*' of the change in price, this income effect may be positive *or* negative, although in most cases we should expect it to be positive.

Analysis of income and substitution effects

It is possible to make the argument more precise by means of a diagram. In Figure 6.9 the amount of rice bought by a particular consumer is measured along the horizontal axis in kilogrammes weight per month; his monthly expenditure on other foodstuffs, in cents, is measured on the vertical axis. Let us ignore, for the sake for simplicity, his expenditure on goods other than foodstuffs and assume our consumer has a fixed amount of money to be allocated between rice and other foodstuffs, and that this fixed amount is precisely 48 shillings.

Suppose the price of rice initially is 0.80s per kilo: if he buys no rice at all, he will spend OA (=48s) on other foodstuffs, assuming he does not save; if he bought 5 kg of rice, he would spend 44s (=48−5×0.80s) on other foodstuffs; if he bought 10

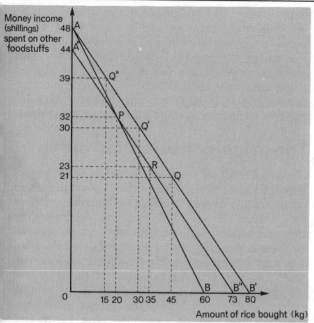

Figure 6.9 *Income and substitution effects of a price change.*

kg of rice, 40 s on other foodstuffs, and so on; until if he spent nothing on other foodstuffs he could buy OB (= 60 kg) of rice. Thus the line AB represents the combination of rice and other foodstuffs which the consumer can obtain with the limited money income OA. He cannot buy combinations above and to the right of the line AB, for these would exceed his limited 'budget'. We can therefore call AB his *budget line*.

Assuming he spends all his income, the consumer will choose a combination somewhere along the line AB. The exact combination will depend on his preferences as between rice and other foodstuffs: let us suppose he chooses combination P, buying 20 kg of rice and spending 32 s on other foodstuffs. Suppose the price of rice then falls to 0.60 s: the consumer's budget line becomes AB', with a more gentle slope corresponding to the lower price, 0.60 s, of rice. The consumer might now buy a combination Q on AB', including 45 kg of rice. The effect of the change in price in this case has thus been to increase the amount of rice bought by the consumer from 20 to 45 kg. We can thus describe this increase of 25 kg as the *price effect*. The question is, how much of this is 'income effect', and how much 'substitution effect'?

To help us here, we draw a line A″PB″ through P parallel to the line AB'. This represents a situation where (a) the relative prices of rice and of other foodstuffs are as in the new situation, since the slopes of the price lines A″PB″ and AQB' are the same but (b) the consumer's real income is what it was *before* the price change, since the previous combination P could still just be obtained. Since income is un-

changed, and the only change is in relative prices, there will be no income effect, and any change in the amounts bought will be entirely *substitution* effect. Suppose in *this* hypothetical situation the consumer would select a combination R, buying 35 kg of rice. This 15 kg increase in the amount bought, from 20 to 35 kg, is thus a substitution effect.

We are, however, interested in analysing the effect of a shift in the price line from AB to AB'. Clearly this can be separated, conceptually, into a change in relative prices at a given level of real income, represented by the slope of P swivelling from APB to A″PB″, *and* an increase in money income, represented by a shift outwards in parallel fashion from A″PB″ to AQB'. The latter implies an increase of money income from OA″ to OA, that is, of A″A. A simple calculation reveals that A″ corresponds to 44 s on the vertical axis: so that A″A is 4 s. The effect of this increase in money income can be considered as being a move from R to Q, or an increase from 35 to 45 kg of rice bought. This difference, 10 kg, is thus the income effect of the price change. The price effect of 25 kg therefore consists of substitution effect, 15 kg, and income effect, 10 kg.

The direction of the substitution effect

From our previous analysis of the income-consumption relation we know that the income effect may be positive, zero or negative. We can now show more precisely that the substitution effect *must* always be zero or positive, never negative. We assume simply that the consumer makes his choice in a rational and consistent way. If, therefore, he chooses combination P when he could have obtained some alternative combination with the same income, we suppose that he *prefers* P. In Figure 6.10, with

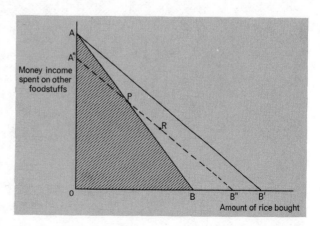

Figure 6.10 *The substitution effect is always positive (or zero).*

money income OA, the consumer could have purchased any combination of rice and other foodstuffs
within the shaded triangle OAB: P therefore represents the most favoured of all these combinations. If,
then, we consider a change in relative prices without
any change in real income, represented by the new
budget line A″PB″ in Figure 6.10, we should expect a
new favoured combination, R, somewhere along
A″PB″. But on our assumption, R cannot lie in the
range A″P, for all these combinations have already
been revealed less favourable than P, given the
consumer's tastes: if the consumer is consistent, and
his tastes have not changed, he cannot now choose
one of these in preference to P. Thus R *must* be in the
range PB″: it must be either at P or to the right of P,
that is, in the positive direction. But the movement
from P to R is the substitution effect described above:
this must therefore be zero or positive.

We can now examine again the total effect of a
price change on the amount bought. We can see that
it is *possible* for the amount bought actually to
decrease when the price falls, since the income effect
can be negative. If the new choice, in Figure 6.9, had
been Q′ instead of Q, the price effect would still be
positive, equal in fact to 10 kg, being the sum of a
substitution effect of plus 15 kg (35−20 = +15 kg)
and an income effect of minus 5 kg (30−35 = −5).
On the other hand, if the choice had been Q″, with
the same substitution effect of 15 kg and an income
effect of minus 20 kg (15−35 = −20 kg), the price
effect would be negative, equal to −5 kg (−20+15 =
−5 kg). Thus for the price effect to be negative it is
necessary not only for the income effect to be negative, but also sufficiently large to offset the sub-

stitution effect which is pulling in the other direction.
We should not therefore expect many cases where
this is so, though whether or not cases can be found
is a matter for empirical confirmation. We should
certainly *expect* that a fall in the price of a good
would cause the amount bought by a consumer to
increase. On this basis we can draw the demand
curve for a commodity sloping down from left to right.

The price-consumption curve

Figure 6.9 analysed the effect of a single price change,
from 0.80 s to 0.60 s per kg of rice. The price lines in
Figure 6.11 (a) represent a series of possible prices of
0.90, 0.80, 0.70 and 0.60 with the corresponding
amounts bought. Suppose the combinations selected
for these prices are given by P_1, P_2, P_3, and P_4. If we
join such points we get, for continuous variation in
price, the curve labelled PCC, that is, the *price-consumption curve*. This corresponds to the individual
demand curve since it tells us the amount of the commodity bought for each consecutive price. Figure 6.11
(b) gives the same information in a more conventional
way, with price represented by a distance on the vertical
axis rather than by the slope of the budget line.

Additional notes on the concept of elasticity

When we talk about demand for, say, cigarettes being
'inelastic' or for motor cars being 'elastic', we imply
that the respective demand curves are inelastic, or
elastic, throughout their whole length. In fact a de-

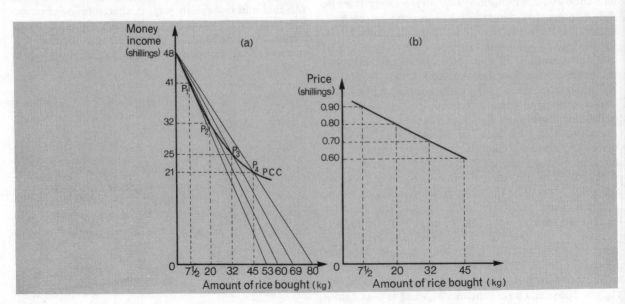

Figure 6.11　(a) A price-consumption curve. (b) The corresponding industrial demand curve.

mand curve may be elastic over one price range and inelastic over another and, as we saw above, elasticity is likely to vary along the curve. It is necessary, therefore, to be somewhat more precise and talk about elasticity at some *point* on the demand curve.

Point elasticity

At a point, we can talk about the ratio of an infinitesimally small proportionate change in quantity to an infinitesimally small proportionate change in price. This we can refer to as *point elasticity*.

Suppose we have a demand curve such as DD in Figure 6.12, and we wish to calculate elasticity at some point T. If we draw a tangent at T intercepting the two axes at A and B, it can be shown that the elasticity at T, e_D, equals TA/TB.

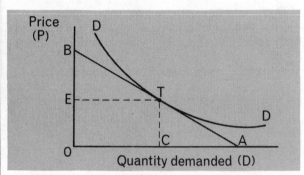

Figure 6.12   *Calculation of point elasticity.*

The slope of the demand curve at T is $\dfrac{\triangle P}{\triangle D}$ and is equal to the slope of tangent AB. The slope of AB is given by $\dfrac{OB}{OA}$, or $\dfrac{TC}{CA}$. Hence we have $\dfrac{\triangle P}{\triangle D}$ equals $\dfrac{TC}{CA}$, while the reciprocal of this, $\dfrac{\triangle D}{\triangle P}$, equals $\dfrac{CA}{TC}$. The elasticity at point T is defined as $e_D = \dfrac{\triangle D}{D} \Big/ \dfrac{\triangle P}{P} = \dfrac{P}{D}\left(\dfrac{\triangle D}{\triangle P}\right)$. But at T we have P equal to TC and D equal to OC, so that:

$$e_D = \frac{TC}{OC}\left(\frac{CA}{TC}\right) = \frac{CA}{OC}$$

However consider the triangles $\triangle TCA$ and $\triangle BOA$. These are similar triangles. It follows that the ratio $\dfrac{CA}{OC}$, along AO, equals the ratio $\dfrac{TA}{TB}$ along AB. Hence

$$e_D = \frac{TA}{TB}$$

This result can be used for rough estimation of elasticity. Suppose T can be seen to be roughly halfway along the tangent between A and B, so that TA equals TB. Elasticity will equal one.

Arc elasticity

If we wish to estimate elasticity from some actual data, point elasticity is an ambitious measure, since it assumes we know more or less the exact shape of the demand curve. In fact we may have just a few price–quantity observations suggesting what the amounts demanded might be at a few different prices. In this situation *arc elasticity* is a useful measure to use. This is a measure of average elasticity over a portion or segment of the demand curve.

Consider the demand curve DD in Figure 6.13. It is estimated that at a price of shs 100 six units would be demanded and at shs 80 ten units would be demanded. We thus have a fair idea of how the amount demanded varies when price falls from shs 100 to shs 80; but this is rather a wide price range.

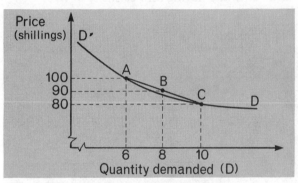

Figure 6.13   *Calculation of arc elasticity.*

Because it is a wide price range rather than a point, elasticity measured from A for a downward price change differs from the value measured from C. Thus elasticity at A for a downward movement along DD is $\dfrac{100 \times 4}{6 \times 20} = \dfrac{10}{3} = 3.3$; whereas elasticity at C for an upward movement along DD is $\dfrac{80 \times 4}{10 \times 20} = 1.6$. To calculate arc elasticity we calculate changes from the midpoint B halfway along the line ABC joining A and C. At B price and quantity are each intermediate between values at A and C. Thus we can write elasticity as:

$$e_D = \frac{\triangle D}{\frac{1}{2}(D_1 + D_2)} \Big/ \frac{\triangle P}{\frac{1}{2}(P_1 + P_2)}$$

For *either* a fall in price (from B to C) *or* a rise in price (from B to A), elasticity is now:

$$e_D = \frac{2}{8} \Big/ \frac{10}{90}$$

$$= \frac{9}{4}$$

$$= 2.25$$

While it is convenient to indicate inelastic demand with a steeply sloping demand curve and an elastic demand with a gently sloping one, it should not be thought that slope measures elasticity or indicates it in any precise way. Thus the elasticity along a straight line will definitely not be constant, although the slope remains the same. Suppose along the demand curve AB in Figure 6.14 T_1, T_2, and T_3 are at equal intervals, that is, one-quarter, one-half, and three-quarters of the way along from A. Since point elasticity is given by $e_D = \dfrac{TA}{TB}$, elasticity at the three points will be respectively $\frac{1}{3}$, 1, and 3, ranging from very inelastic to very elastic, and being infinitely elastic at B and having zero elasticity at A.

This result is not surprising: slope is given by $\dfrac{\triangle D}{\triangle P}$ and elasticity by $\dfrac{P}{D}\left(\dfrac{\triangle D}{\triangle P}\right)$, or $\dfrac{P}{D}$ *times* the slope. In addition *any* curve can be given a gentle or steep slope by altering the scale of the diagram changing the units of measurement along the two axes, without affecting elasticity.

Similarly two lines with the same slope will not have the same elasticities at corresponding prices. Suppose in Figure 6.15 the demand curve shifts to the right from D_1 to D_2, retaining the same slope, so that D_1 and D_2 are parallel. At point T_1 on D_1 elasticity is $e_{D_1} = \left(\dfrac{P}{D}\dfrac{\triangle D}{\triangle P}\right) = \dfrac{5}{4}$ times slope of D_1. At T_2 on D_2 elasticity is $e_{D_2} = \dfrac{P}{D}\left(\dfrac{\triangle D}{\triangle P}\right) = \dfrac{5}{8}$ times slope of D_2.

Since the slopes are equal, $e_{D_1} = 2e_{D_2}$. The underlying reason for this is the same as for the previous result that elasticity calculates increments in price or quantity *as a proportion* of some initial amounts.

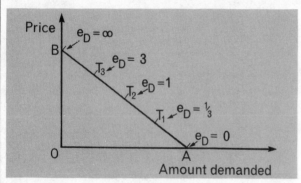

Figure 6.14   *Constant slope but varying elasticity.*

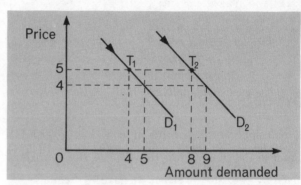

Figure 6.15   *Two curves with same slope but different elasticity.*

Questions on Chapter 6

1. Give definitions of: an inferior good, complementary goods, income-elasticity of demand, cross-elasticity of demand.
2. Use a diagram with numbered scales along the horizontal and vertical axes to calculate numerical values for the income and substitution effects of a change in the price of a good.
3. Prove that the substitution effect of a change in the price of a good must always be non-negative.
4. Distinguish between 'point' elasticity and 'arc' elasticity, and show how these are derived.

Notes

[1] Reproduced from I. G. Stewart, 'Consumer Demand in Nigeria', in *African Studies in Income and Wealth*, ed. L. H. Samuels, 1963, p. 317.
[2] Notice that here *expenditure* is measured on the vertical axis, rather than the amount bought, and that we are considering not a single commodity, but a group of commodities, namely, food.

[3] This is strictly true only for infinitesimal changes of price. If price decreases from 100 s to 95 s, and quantity increases from 100 to 105 (5 per cent change in each case), expenditure would change from 10,000 s to 9,975; for 1 per cent changes, expenditure would alter to 9,999 s. The discrepancy thus approaches zero as smaller increments are considered.

7 Demand, Supply, and Price

In discussing how the price mechanism operates to allocate resources we deliberately left the supply relationship extremely vague: increased demand raised the price of the product, and the increased price encouraged producers to supply more. Having examined the demand side in some detail we need to elaborate on the factors affecting the amount supplied.

Factors affecting the amount supplied

First, the amount supplied depends on the price of the commodity. This relationship, however, is not direct: increased demand and price affect revenue; revenue *and costs* together determine profits, *and it is on the level of profits at different levels of output that the amount produced and supplied depends.* Thus increased demand for maize means that the previous amount can be sold at a higher price, or that more maize can be sold at the same price, or that to some extent both price and quantity of maize sold can increase, in all cases increasing revenue. Even if potential revenue increases, however, not much more may be supplied if the cost of increasing maize output is very great, because, say, most of the land in the area suitable for maize growing has already been taken up.

Secondly, the amount supplied of a particular commodity depends on the prices of other commodities that could be produced instead of the commodity in question. If the price of, say, millet or cassava increases, farmers might be induced to switch their farms over to millet or cassava production from maize, the relative profitability of the former having increased. This is because maize and millet are to some extent alternatives or *substitutes in production.* The degree to which products are substitutes in production depends, of course, on how far the resources in the production of one can be diverted to the production of the other. Thus coffee and sisal are not close substitutes in production because the land suitable for sisal production cannot be used for coffee growing (although the other factors, labour and capital, may be 'mobile' as between the two commodities). In

such a case a fall in the price of sisal would hardly affect the amount of coffee supplied. Commodities might, of course, be *complements* in production. It might be sensible to combine the production of maize and root crops in a farm rotation designed to preserve the fertility of the soil. In such a case a rise in the price of maize might increase the amount of root crops produced, and vice versa.

Thirdly, the amount of the product supplied may change if the availability and/or price of the factors used in its production alter. If the wage rate to be paid to farm workers increases, the farmer may be forced to hire fewer workers and to restrict his output. *How important this effect will be depends on the share in total costs of production* of the factor concerned. Thus if a farmer uses relatively few simple tools and equipment but depends largely on hiring cheap labour, a rise in the price of tools might have little effect on his output, whereas an increase in the wage rate could lead him to contract output drastically.

Fourthly, the amount supplied may alter as a result of improved technology. Improved methods of production on farms or in factories may increase productivity, and thus reduce average costs of output. Alternatively improvement in transport facilities, reducing the cost of carrying produce from farm or factory to consumers, may increase supply.

Quite apart from profitability, people's willingness to pursue a particular occupation may depend on the pleasantness or unpleasantness of an occupation, or on other non-pecuniary factors such as the prestige attached to the job. Hence peasant farmers may continue to earn low levels of income on small plots of land rather than sacrifice their independence and their social contacts in the village in order to seek higher cash incomes as labourers in the towns; or people may prefer to have the prestige, as clerks, of working in an office even if they receive less pay than they might be able to earn as skilled agricultural workers. On the other hand they may not be willing to work in mines, with the difficult conditions and the risk that this involves, except at higher rates of pay. Hence, *lastly, a change in the non-pecuniary advantages or disadvantages of working in an industry will affect the supply of output of that industry.*

As in the case of demand, we can obtain a supply schedule, relating the supply of the commodity to its price, by assuming all other factors affecting supply to be constant, namely,

(1) prices of other goods;
(2) prices of the factors used in its production;
(3) technology;
(4) non-pecuniary advantages and disadvantages of the industry.

As with demand we should refer to 'an increase in the *amount* supplied' when a change in the price of the commodity leads to a movement *along* the supply curve, and to 'a change in the supply position', or simply 'an increase in supply' when a change in factors (1), (2), (3), or (4) results in a shift of the entire supply curve, implying that *at every price* producers are willing to supply more than previously.

An increase in the amount supplied of any product in response to a change in price may come about in several ways. Most firms keep stocks of commodities in reserve in order to be able to satisfy a temporary or unexpected increase in demand, so that some increase in supply is possible very quickly by running down stocks; given more time, however, increased supply is possible through increased utilization of existing equipment by producers already in the industry; in the longer run, sufficiently high prices could persuade existing producers to expand their capacity by enlarging their factories, or farms, and encourage entirely new firms to enter the industry. Thus the responsiveness of supply to price will be a function of time, as illustrated in Figure 7.1. In this figure S_1S_1 might refer to the supply curve when changes in supply can only come from running down or adding to stocks, and S_2S_2, S_3S_3, and S_4S_4 to the supply curves when firms can raise, respectively, output from existing equipment, from enlarged capacity, or from new factories altogether. An increase in price from P_0 to P_1 would therefore bring forth an increase in the amount supplied of Q_0Q_1. Q_0Q_2,

Q_0Q_3, or Q_0Q_4 according to the time allowed for adjustments to take place.

The importance of time in determining the supply response may be increased by the influence of expectations. Firms may hesitate to invest in enlarged capacity or to enter an industry until they are assured that an increase in price is not just a temporary one.

The degree of responsiveness of supply to changes in price

As in the case of demand the concept of elasticity may be used to measure the degree of responsiveness of supply to price. In this case the *elasticity of supply* of a good X is defined as

$$E_S = \frac{\text{the } \textit{proportionate} \text{ change in the amount supplied}}{\text{the } \textit{proportionate} \text{ change in the price of X}}$$

$$= \frac{\triangle S_x / S_x}{\triangle P_x / P_x},$$

where S_x is the amount supplied and P_x the price offered. This measures how far producers are induced to increase the total supply on the market when the price of the commodity rises. The elasticity of supply will depend on how easily resources can be switched from one activity to another, for example, how easily land can be converted to other uses, or how easily people, skilled personnel especially, can be persuaded to change occupations. Elasticity thus depends on how *specific* the resources used in the industry are. As we noted also in the previous paragraph, elasticity of supply will also depend on the time allowed for adjustment, so that in Figure 7.1 the 'short-run' supply curve S_1S_1 is inelastic compared to S_4S_4, the 'long-run' supply curve.

The concept of a 'market'

Having explored in some detail the influences behind both demand and supply, we can now turn to the question of how the price of a commodity is determined. We should generally expect a 'scarce' commodity to have a high price and a commodity in plentiful supply a low one. How 'scarce' a commodity is can be determined by the *relationship of supply to demand*: the physical quantity of the good available may be very small, but if there is little or no demand it will nevertheless not be 'scarce'. Price is thus the result of the interaction of two sets of forces, supply *and* demand.

We should be clear, however, about *which* demand and supply we are referring to. Although the supplies and demands for different goods are related, it is

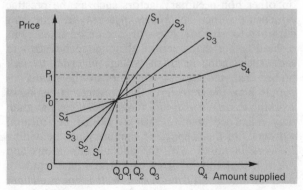

Figure 7.1   *The response of supply to an increase in price.*

common to isolate the market for one commodity, and talk about 'the market for rice' or 'the market for meat', and so on. Here we do not refer to the physical site of a market but *to a particular set of consumers*, and to the people who supply them. We might, for instance, talk of the 'world' market for rice, or of the 'Eastern African' market for rice. It is possible to distinguish the latter because it is to some extent isolated from the world market due especially to high costs of transport and to lack of contact between Eastern African buyers and sellers of rice and others.

This suggests the meaning of the term 'market' as a group of buyers and sellers of a commodity in close touch with one another. We shall therefore use the term 'perfect market' to imply

(1) a homogeneous product;
(2) perfect knowledge by buyers and sellers;
(3) absence of transport costs;
(4) large numbers of buyers and sellers.

The last of these serves to ensure that no single buyer or seller can influence the price of the commodity by varying the amount he buys or sells.

Geographically, the market is best identified by consumers, since the supply may originate from outside the consumers' locality and even from overseas. The retailers who supply consumers directly need not be the 'suppliers' in question and may simply 'pass on' the product after adding a retail margin to the price. Thus if we referred to the 'Dar es Salaam market for foodstuffs' the supply of foodstuffs will originate from the hinterland of Dar es Salaam, especially, from other parts of Eastern Africa, and from imports, and the supply schedule will refer to these various sources.

The determination of equilibrium price

Suppose the supply and demand schedules for rice in

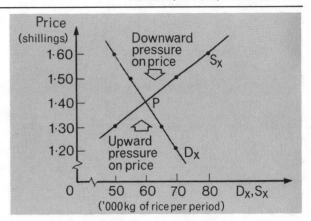

Figure 7.2 *Supply and demand curves.*

a particular market are as in Table 7.1. We can plot the data to form demand and supply curves in Figure 7.2. It will be observed that at a price of 1.60, while suppliers are willing to supply a regular amount of 80,000 kg, consumers are only willing to buy 50,000 kg per period. If the price remains at 1.60 suppliers will be left with unsold stocks of 30,000 kg which by definition they are anxious to sell at that price rather than retain. In such a situation it is plausible to suppose that suppliers will be induced to accept lower prices and that therefore prices will ease downward under pressure of excess supply. Likewise at a price of 1.20 demand will exceed the amount suppliers are willing to put on the market by 30,000 kg, and this time one would expect that consumers will 'bid up' the price of the commodity on the one hand, and that, on the other, as suppliers run out of supplies they will perceive that they can increase profits by raising their price. In this case there will be *upward* pressure on price, tending to the level P, again, at which price the amount supplied and demanded will be equal.

This price is generally referred to as an *equilibrium* price, and the amounts supplied and demanded at this price as equilibrium quantities. This is to signify first that P_x, D_x, and S_x show no tendency to change at point P, that they are in a 'state of rest' or equilibrium position; and secondly that if for any reason price were temporarily displaced, there would be pressure for it to revert to position P (1.40). This second aspect is said to make the equilibrium *stable*.

The argument can be restated entirely in terms of *excess demand*, defined as the excess of the amount demanded over the amount supplied at each price. We can thus write:

$$D_x - S_x \equiv E_x = f(P_x)$$

indicating that E_x is a function of price. This is obvious from Table 7.1, in which the fourth column is obtained by subtracting S_x from D_x at each price. It will be noted that, where the value of S_x exceeds

Table 7.1 *Supply and demand schedules*

P_x (shillings)	D_x (×1,000 kg of rice per period)	S_x (×1,000 kg of rice per period)	$E_x (=D_x-S_x)$ (×1,000 kg of rice per period)
1.60	50	80	−30
1.50	55	70	−15
1.40	60	60	0
1.30	65	50	+15
1.20	70	40	+30

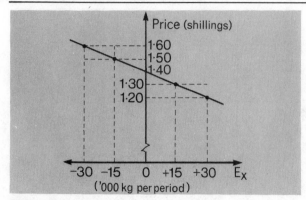

Figure 7.3   *Excess demand as a function of price.*

that of D_x, E_x is negative, and vice versa. E_x is plotted against P_x in Figure 7.3. Equilibrium price is given by the price at which 'the market is cleared', meaning that excess demand is zero and all consumers looking for purchases at the price can find a seller, i.e. supply equals demand.

The effect of shifts in supply and demand

We can now see the effect on price of a change in the state of demand, or in conditions of supply. Suppose, for any one of the reasons suggested in the previous

Table 7.2   *Effect of a change in demand*

P_x (shillings)	D_x (×1,000 kg)	D'_x (×1,000 kg)	S_x (×1,000 kg)	SS_x (×1,000 kg)
1.60	50	65	80	65
1.50	55	70	70	62
1.40	60	75	60	60
1.30	65	80	50	58

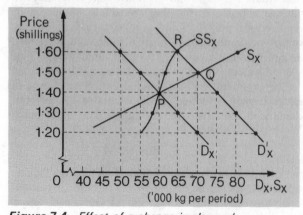

Figure 7.4   *Effect of a change in demand.*

chapter, that the state of demand alters, so that increased amounts are demanded at each price. In Table 7.2 the old amounts are given in the second column, headed D_x, and the new amounts in the column headed D'_x. If we plot these two, and the supply column S_x, in Figure 7.4, we observe that the change appears graphically as a shift in the demand curve, with the effect of raising the equilibrium price from 1.40 to 1.50, the equilibrium point shifting from P to Q.

It is also possible to see that the amount of the rise in price due to a given change in demand will vary with the elasticity of supply. In Table 7.2 the last column is added to represent possible supply *in the short run*. The corresponding graph is labelled SS_x in Figure 7.4. Assuming, in this case, that we start with an amount supplied of 60,000 kg per period, then SS_x indicates how much suppliers are able and willing to put on the market in the short run. Thus at a price of 1.50, suppliers, given time, are willing to supply 70,000 kg, compared to 60,000 kg at 1.40. This gives a long-run elasticity of supply, E_{LS}, as

$$E_{LS} = \frac{10/60}{10/140} = \frac{14}{6} = 2\tfrac{1}{3} \text{ or } 2.33.$$

In the short run, however, as implied by curve SS_x, suppliers are willing to put only an additional 2,000 kg on the market at a price of 1.50, perhaps running down stocks to this extent, and this will not satisfy demand. At a *higher* price of 1.60, however, suppliers are willing to put on the market a total of 65,000 kg, perhaps by running stocks down still further. Point R in Figure 7.4 thus represents the short-run equilibrium position. We can therefore say that the *short-run* elasticity of supply, E_{ss}, at point P, is

$$E_{ss} = \frac{2/60}{10/140} = \frac{28}{60} = 0.467$$

referring to the immediate effects of a rise in price from 1.40 to 1.50 (one unit). This value is very much lower than that for 'long-run' elasticity.

The effect of a sales tax

The effect of a change in the conditions of supply can be worked out in a similar way. To see how a shift in the supply schedule affects price, we can consider the imposition of a sales tax. We may note first that a specific tax is one of a fixed amount per unit, which amount is independent of the level of the price of the commodity. In contrast an *ad valorem* tax is fixed as a *percentage* of the commodity, its absolute amount therefore increasing when price increases.

Suppose in our example a specific tax of 30 cents per kg were imposed. Such a tax is generally col-

Table 7.3 *Effect of a specific tax*

Column 1	Column 2	Column 3	Column 4	Column 5
P_x (shillings)	S_x (×1,000 kg)	D_x (×1,000 kg)	P'_x (shillings)	S'_x (×1,000 kg)
1.60	80	50	1.30	50
1.50	70	55	1.20	40
1.40	60	60	1.60	30
1.30	50	65	1.00	20
1.20	40	70	0.90	10

lected from the supplier, so that if he sold, say, 200 kg, he would pay $\dfrac{200 \times 3}{10} = 60$ altogether. The effect of the tax is a divergence between the buyer's price (the market price) and the seller's price (the price net of tax): if, for example, the market price is 1.60, the seller will receive only 1.30 per kg. Table 7.3 summarizes the position. Column 1 gives the market (buyer's) price and columns 2 and 3 the amounts supplied and demanded for each price, in the absence of a tax. To obtain the seller's price we simply deduct 30 cents from the market price and get P'_x in column 4. Column 5 gives the amounts supplied once a tax is imposed, the amounts each corresponding to combinations of P_x (market price) and P'_x (net price paid to sellers). Now column 2 tells us, for instance, that if sellers are paid 1.30 per kg, they will put 50,000 kg on the market. Hence if the market price is 1.60 and the net price to sellers 1.30, the amount supplied will again be 50,000 kg; if $P_x = 1.50$, then $P'_x = 1.20$, and supply 40,000 kg and so on. This gives us the figures in column 5.

The three demand and supply schedules are plotted in Figure 7.5. It will be seen that the effect of the tax is to shift *the supply curve* to the left, and alter the equilibrium from P to Q. The equilibrium price will increase, in this example, from 1.40 to 1.60, that is, by 20 cents, although the tax imposed is 30 cents per kg. The whole of the tax has not been passed on to consumers: part of it is absorbed by suppliers who obtained a net price of 1.40 before the imposition of the tax (the full market price) and obtain only 1.30 after tax. The amount of rise in price this time depends on the elasticity of demand (and the extent of the shift in the supply curve). Had demand been given by the more elastic curve D'_x in Figure 7.5, equilibrium would have been at Q', buyers paying 10 cents more (1.50) and sellers receiving 20 cents less (1.20); and had the demand curve been the completely horizontal one D''_x, equilibrium would have been at Q'', buyers paying *no more than before*, per unit, and the sellers' price being reduced by the full amount of the tax, from 1.40 to 1.10. We can therefore say (1) that the rise in the market price due to the tax depends on the elasticity of demand, and (2) that the extent to which buyers have to pay a higher price and the sellers have to accept a lower price, the 'incidence' of the tax as between buyers and sellers, also depends on the elasticity of demand.

The effect of demand and supply elasticities on the incidence of a tax can be spelled out more fully with the aid of Figure 7.6(a) to (d). In Figure 7.6(a), demand is perfectly inelastic as in the case of a 'necessary' good. The market price is increased from P_x to P'_x by the full amount of the tax, the whole of which may be said to have been shifted *forwards* to the buyer. In Figure 7.6(b), a tax is imposed on a commodity the *supply* of which is completely in-

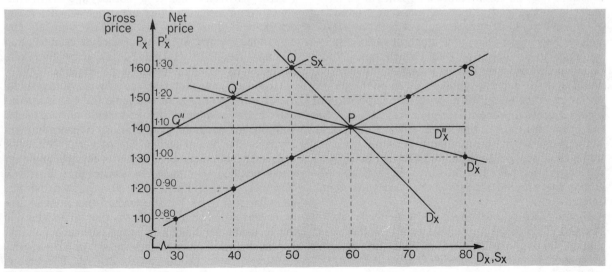

Figure 7.5 *Effect of a specific tax.*

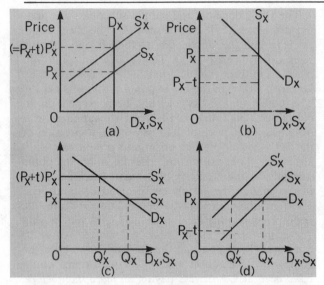

Figure 7.6   *(a) Inelastic demand: complete shift of tax forwards. (b) Inelastic supply: complete shift of tax backwards. (c) Perfectly elastic supply: complete shift of tax forwards. (d) Perfectly elastic demands: complete shift of tax backwards.*

elastic. It can be assumed that demand conditions are the same before and after the imposition of the tax (not the amount demanded, which depends on price as well as the state of demand), and since supply is completely inelastic the amount supplied remains the same at every price, i.e. the supply curve does not move after the tax is imposed. Thus the gross market price remains the same, at P_x, but suppliers receive the net price, $P_x - t$: the whole of the tax is shifted backwards to suppliers. This could illustrate the case of a land tax, the commodity being land, in perfectly inelastic supply, and price being the rent of land.

Figure 7.6(c) illustrates the case of perfectly elastic supply. This might relate to a situation where a tax is imposed on an imported good which has a local substitute. If the home market is small relative to the world market for the good, any amount can be imported at the going world price. The imposition of a tax means that domestic consumers have to pay the old price plus the tax (the world price being given), but can again obtain any quantity at this price. In terms of price, the tax is shifted forward entirely to the consumers who will, however, be able to substitute the domestically produced variety to some extent.

Figure 7.6(d) shows the case of perfectly elastic demand. This might apply to demand on the world market for an export from a small country, for example, cotton from Uganda. The small country is in effect a price-taker here, and can sell any quantity on the world market at the given price. The imposition of any export duty will shift the supply curve to the left, without changing the world price, P_x, but reducing the price payable to producers to $(P_x - t)$. Thus the tax here is shifted backwards to the seller.

Partial and general equilibrium analysis

Most of the foregoing analysis was in terms of a 'market for rice' and treated this market in isolation. It may be asked whether such a procedure is valid. After all, the price of rice in Eastern Africa may be affected to a varying degree by its price in Burma, or India, or the Middle East, or any other place where rice is produced or consumed. Moreover if the price of rice is affected by the price of substitute commodities, what goes on in the 'rice market' depends on what is happening in all these other markets. And this includes factor markets; for example, a fall in the price of coffee in East Africa will affect the incomes of independent coffee growers and of hired labour used in coffee production, and changes in these incomes could affect the demand and hence price of rice. What we really have, therefore, is a series of interconnected markets in which an initial change in one market can have effects on other markets and these in turn affect the original market, and so on. These repercussions may be transmitted via changes in prices *or* by changes in factor incomes, or by both.

When economists try to explain how an entire 'system' involving several or many markets settles down to a state of rest, this is referred to as 'general equilibrium analysis' which, as the term suggests, is the analysis of how a 'general' equilibrium, involving several *particular* markets, comes about. In this equilibrium, instead of just one price, say P_1, being determined along with the amounts supplied and demanded, S_1 and D_1, 'n' prices are determined, and 'n' quantities, S_1 to S_n ($= D_1$ to D_n respectively), 'n' being the hypothetical numbers of markets.

However, it is not easy to say anything useful about so many things at the same time! It is for this reason that economists tend to single out particular markets for separate examination, a procedure referred to as '*partial equilibrium analysis*'. But while this is an extremely productive approach and very often justified, we must be aware that it is not obviously or *always* justified. Figure 7.7 (more or less identical to Figure 1.1, illustrating the circular flow of income in the economy) shows that all 'markets' in the economy are linked, however indirectly.

The diagram distinguishes betweeen 'consumers', in Box A, and 'producers' in Box E. The arrows labelled B and D indicate that consumers' expendi-

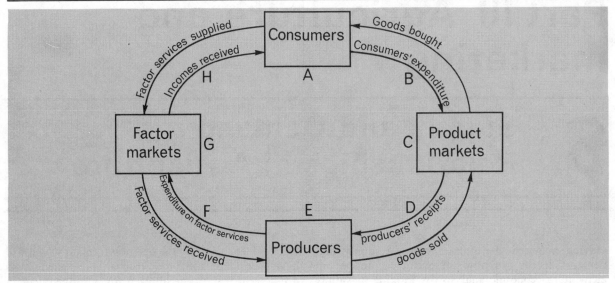

Figure 7.7 *The circular flow of the economy.*

ture goes to producers, becoming producers' receipts, and that a flow of consumer goods passes in the opposite direction from producers to consumers. These 'demands' and 'supplies' meet in the various product markets, Box C. Arrows F and H indicate that incomes received by consumers derive from expenditure by producers on factor services supplied by the consumers. These demands and supplies, this time for factor services, meet in the various factor markets, Box G, where the prices of these services are determined. This shows again the double circular flow in the economy: in the clockwise direction the diagram shows a *money flow* of income and expenditure, and in the opposite, anti-clockwise direction, a *real flow*, 'real' in the sense that it consists of physical goods and services exchanged for money.

Thus a change in a particular product market X could not only have an effect 'horizontally' on other product markets but also 'vertically' round the circle, via the factor markets, that is, through prices or incomes. Fortunately, for a very large number of interesting problems, these interrelationships are not so important as to prevent 'partial' analysis. However, partial analysis of market X independently

of other markets is invalidated when: (1) a change in market X has an important repercussion on the 'other markets', and (2) the resulting change in 'other markets' has an important *further* repercussion on market X. If this is so, any temporary equilibrium in market X, following some change, is upset subsequently by the repercussion via the 'other markets' resulting from that change. Equilibrium analysis must in such a situation involve a 'state of rest' simultaneously in both markets.

If in just *one* direction, however, the repercussion is small or negligible, partial analysis is validated. Thus in East Africa a change in the price of coffee will affect incomes significantly and thus the demand for rice; but a change in the price of rice in East Africa will not have an effect on the price of coffee, which is determined in the world market in which East Africa's supply is a small part of the total. The East African rice market can therefore be examined separately, with incomes of coffee producers regarded as an 'outside' or 'exogenous' factor which may produce shifts in the demand curve for rice, as in the analysis of this chapter.

Questions on Chapter 7

1. Discuss the factors affecting the amount of a commodity supplied to a market.
2. What is meant by an 'equilibrium' price?
3. Discuss the incidence of a sales tax on a commodity as between buyers and sellers (a) when demand is perfectly inelastic, (b) when supply is perfectly inelastic, (c) when supply is perfectly elastic, and (d) when demand is perfectly elastic, the other curve being normally sloped.
4. Distinguish between 'partial' and 'general' equilibrium analysis. In what circumstances is partial equilibrium analysis invalid?

Part III Agriculture and marketing

8 Supply and Demand Relationships in Agriculture

Having acquired the simple tools of supply and demand, let us see how these can be applied in elementary economic analysis, by looking at supply and demand relationships in agriculture.

The instability of agricultural prices

One of the main problems facing the agricultural industry is the instability of the prices of agricultural products, which fluctuate more widely than the prices of industrial products. There are, of course, plenty of agricultural products which are relatively stable in price and industrial products which are not. But nevertheless one can distinguish certain factors at work which are likely to support this generalization.

(1) The supply of agricultural products is more directly affected by natural factors such as the weather, disease, or pests than is the supply of industrial products. In agriculture, there is a divergence between planned and *actual* output, whereas in industry the output, especially when highly mechanized, is in contrast relatively predictable. The effect is a *shift* in the short-run supply curve. The position of this curve will depend on whether the harvest is good or bad and it will tend to be inelastic, since the amount put on the market will depend largely on the size of the harvest rather than price.

(2) Secondly, the short-run elasticity of supply is low, since once a given amount of the crop has been planted it is comparatively difficult to increase or decrease the resulting output. Hence high prices are likely to persist in the short run, before additional supply can be made available. There will, of course, be some variability: for example, in the case of cotton, while prices are high it may be worthwhile for the farmers to pick over the crop twice or even three times, which they may not bother to do when prices are lower. Broadly, however, the amount harvested

will be determined by the decision to plant which will have been taken some time before. This inelasticity is a function of the time allowed for an adjustment in the amount supplied and the *gestation period* for additional output to be forthcoming. In the case of some crops, like maize, which in Africa can yield more than one crop per year, a high price would be likely to induce further planting and increased supply within a relatively short period. Others, especially tree crops like rubber and coffee, do not produce an increased supply for some *years* after planting: the 'gestation period' is longer and supply inelastic over a longer period. The same applies to certain livestock products: an increase in the production of bacon, for instance, requires the breeding of pigs, which takes time. In contrast, industrial products do not in general have such lengthy gestation periods or such rigidly determined ones. If the increased supply requires the establishment of additional machines or factories, this may take longer, but existing machines can generally be worked more intensively, workers can be asked to work overtime, or additional shifts can be introduced. Thus increased output in the short run is mainly a matter of hiring additional labour and raw materials, and is not to any great extent subject to limitations of nature.

The above points are illustrated graphically in Figure 8.1. DD is the demand curve, and LS the 'long-run supply curve' giving the amounts that producers would plan to supply at each price. Thus OQ_0 and OP_0 would be equilibrium quantity and price respectively if actual production were equal to that planned. In fact, due to uncertainties of weather and other natural factors, the actual amount harvested might turn out to be, say, OQ_1. If this amount were absolutely fixed, the 'short-run' supply curve would be the vertical line S_1 and the price therefore OP_1 at which this supply equals demand. If the harvest had exceeded expectations, on the other hand, and the amount produced were OQ_2, price would fall to

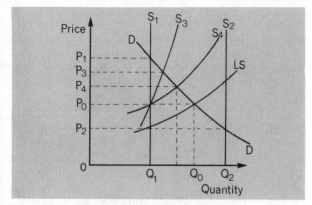

Figure 8.1   *The effect of (1) fluctuations in supply and (2) inelastic short-run supply.*

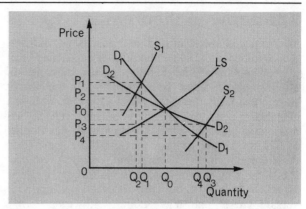

Figure 8.2   *Inelastic demand increases price instability.*

OP_2. Thus fluctuations in the amount supplied, due to uncontrollable factors, can produce wide fluctuations in price. If the short-run supply curve had not been completely inelastic, say S_3 instead of S_1, the rise in price, in the first instance, would have been to OP_3 instead of OP_1 and if it had been the still more elastic curve S_4, the rise in price would have been still less, to OP_4. Thus the more inelastic the short-run supply curve the greater the fluctuation in price produced by a given change in output.

(3) The effect of fluctuations in the amount supplied is aggravated in the case of agricultural products in that the demand, for foodstuffs especially, tends to be inelastic. This is because of the difficulty of substituting one product for another. Industrial products provide for an immense range of needs, and if one type of need becomes expensive to fulfil, consumers can often divert their expenditure in other directions and vice versa. In contrast, an increased supply of a specific category of foodstuffs is probably absorbed only with difficulty even at significantly lower prices. Suppose in Figure 8.2, the initial equilibrium price is again OP_0. Again there is a divergence between planned and unplanned supply, so that short-run supply is given by the curve S_1 (assuming once more some flexibility even in the short run).

If the demand curve had been the relatively inelastic curve D_1D_1, as before, price would rise sharply to OP_1. On the other hand, had demand been given by the more elastic curve, D_2D_2, the rise in price would have been the more moderate one to OP_2: if demand was more elastic a relatively small increase in price would be sufficient to choke off demand until the amount demanded at the going price equalled the diminished supply. Likewise if actual supply had exceeded that planned, so that the short-run supply curve S_2 was obtained, a relatively moderate fall in price to P_3 would have been sufficient to encourage consumers to absorb the unexpectedly large supply. If

the more inelastic demand curve had been obtained, price would have been forced down to the lower level OP_4.

(4) Price fluctuations also depend on the degree to which it is possible to store the product. Producers need not put their output directly on to the market, and firms generally retain stocks so that they can quickly supply the market from them if demand increases beyond the level expected. The effect is to increase the short-run elasticity of supply. A very sharp increase in price as described in (2) could be prevented by sales from stocks, and conversely by adding to stocks in periods of glut. How far this is possible, however, depends on how easily the product can be stored, and agricultural products are often perishable, like fruit or milk, or too bulky, like wheat. Industrial products tend, on the other hand, to be much less perishable (though metal does go rusty!) and thus not to have such problems of storage. The difference is reflected in the wide seasonal variation in prices exhibited by many agricultural products. Prices tend to be lowest immediately after harvest, rising later. This implies that additions to and reductions in stocks only partially offset seasonal variation in supply.

(5) Another factor is that agricultural products are sometimes only inputs used in the production of another product and form only a small part of the total cost of that product. Thus the most important demand for rubber is from the motor car industry for tyres. Tyres, however, form a relatively small part of the total cost of a motor car. It is thus possible for the price of rubber and of tyres to go up substantially without substantially affecting the total cost of the car. Thus the price of rubber could rise considerably without causing any substantial reduction in the demand for rubber. The demand therefore is inelastic, and as we pointed out under (3) above, inelastic demand will aggravate fluctuations in price due to change in supply.

The cobweb theorem

(6) We noted above in (2) that prices of agricultural commodities can fluctuate because of unplanned variations in supply and because of the difficulty of altering this supply in the short period. In the case of certain products, this difficulty of adjusting supply to demand appears capable of producing *cyclical fluctuations* in price. We can illustrate how this can occur as follows. Let us suppose that producers base their decisions on how much to 'plant' on the price currently reigning in the market. If the present price is high, they will be encouraged to plant more, and vice versa. These plantings cannot, however, come straight on to the market, but become available only at the end of the period needed for growth, after the crop has been harvested and transported to the market.

We can assume that this takes a given amount of time which we can call one 'period'. Thus the price reigning in a given period will not affect the amount supplied in *that* period but in the next period. If S_t represents the amount supplied in period 't', then

$$S_t = S(P_{t-1})$$

denotes that the value S_t depends on the price reigning in period '$t-1$' just preceding it. The demand curve, on the other hand, is specified in the normal way, the amount bought depending on whatever the current price is, so that

$$D_t = D(P_t)$$

Equilibrium would be given where the amount currently put on the market equals the amount demanded:

$$S_t = D_t$$

Suppose however that the market is not in equilibrium to start with after, say, an unplanned variation in supply. Supply in period 1 might be OQ_1 in Figure 8.3, which quantity producers find that they can sell at the price OP_1. If producers then base their plans for period 2 on the expectation that this price will continue, they will plan to supply the larger amount OQ_2 in the second period. The demand curve tells us, however, that consumers will only absorb this amount at a price of OP_2. Producers would be disappointed to find, therefore, that they could only sell this amount by bringing down the price to OP_2. If they then based their plantings for period 3 on an expectation of price remaining as low as OP_2, planting would only provide a supply OQ_3 in this period, and price would rise again to OP_3, and so the process would continue. The right-hand part of Figure 8.3 shows the price ruling in successive periods. Time is plotted on the x-axis and the same vertical scale is used, so that the prices can be obtained by horizontal extension from the left-hand diagram. This fluctuation in price is referred to as the 'cobweb cycle' due to the appearance of Figure 8.3 from which it is derived. The fluctuations can be seen to be *convergent*, steadily approaching the price at which D_t and S_t are equal. This result turns out to depend on the relative slopes of the supply and demand curves. We can see this by imagining a similar sequence in Figure 8.4. Here the demand curve is given the same slope as in Figure 8.3 but the supply curve is drawn with a more gentle slope (though in the opposite direction) than the demand curve. If we now plot the sequence of prices in the right-hand diagram we find price fluctuations becoming wider over successive periods, and moving away from P_e, the price at which D_t and S_t would be equal. This is referred to as the *divergent case*. Readers can experiment for themselves to show that if the supply and demand curves had identical slopes the cycle would be completely regular and price would alter-

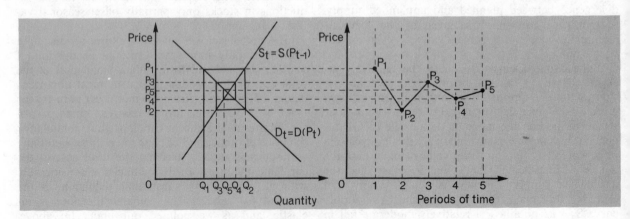

Figure 8.3 *The cobweb cycle: convergent oscillation of price and quantity.*

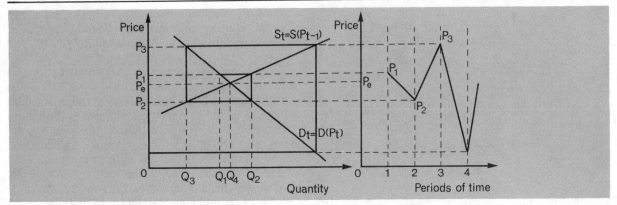

Figure 8.4 *The cobweb cycle: divergent oscillation.*

nate on either side of P_e without converging or diverging. It is worth recalling our statement in Chapter 7 that price would *tend* to the equilibrium level at which the amounts supplied and demanded were equal. We can see now that this is based on special assumptions, and not inherently true. With the assumptions made above regarding the behaviour of producers and their *lagged response* to price, we were able to show that the 'equilibrium' level of price in this sense might not be attained at all!

The assumptions in our 'cobweb model' are of course not completely realistic. We assume that though producers are continually disappointed, they never become wiser as a result and thus anticipate the price movements; and that stocks of the commodity are not stored by producers or middlemen in periods of low prices to be resold in periods of otherwise high prices, thus ironing out the unevenness of supply and price. Yet statistics from many countries show that at various times, markets for a considerable number of agricultural products have exhibited fluctuations of the same sort, even if the fluctuations are not as regular as those in the model. The 'pig cycle' is a well-known example, as a result of the clearly defined gestation period in breeding pigs for market and the difficulty which large numbers of relatively small pig producers find in basing their individual and uncoordinated plans on other than the ruling market price. Where such instability in price and output exists, there is a strong argument for a marketing board or some other form of control to coordinate production plans. This is more likely to be the case in agriculture where activities are often carried on by large numbers of small productive units than in industry, which has shown a greater tendency to concentration. The 'cobweb model' is therefore a useful illustration of the potential instability which may affect agricultural producers who operate under 'competitive market' conditions.

Government action to stabilize prices

Because of the inherent tendency of agricultural products to fluctuate in price, governments have frequently taken measures aimed at stabilization. There has sometimes been confusion, however, as to whether the proper aim should be to stabilize *prices* or to stabilize *incomes* of producers: for these are not the same thing. Suppose the demand schedule for a particular crop were as in Table 8.1. The second column represents the amounts demanded at the various prices. Ignoring costs of marketing and assuming that the whole of the consumers' expenditure accrues directly to growers, the third column, calculated as price *times* quantity, represents the gross incomes of growers. In such a case, if supply turned out to be 12,000 tons, price would be £12 and incomes of growers £144,000. If supply were bigger, say 18,000 tons, price would fall to £8 per ton, but incomes would remain at £144,000. Thus fluctuations in price occur here without any change in the incomes of growers: if income stabilization were the aim no action would be necessary at all.

This demand schedule is plotted in Figure 8.5 as curve D_1D_1. The area of the rectangles, subtending the curve at various points, equals the product of their length times breadth, that is, price times quan-

Table 8.1 *Unit elasticity of demand*

Price (£ per ton)	Quantity (×1,000 tons)	Revenue (£×1,000)
24	6	144
18	8	144
12	12	144
8	18	144
6	24	144

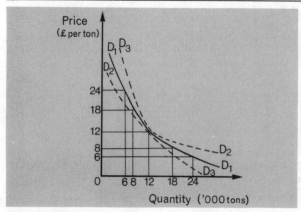

Figure 8.5   *Unit elasticity of demand.*

tity bought (and sold). Simple inspection shows that all such rectangles which we can draw beneath D_1D_1 are equal in area. A curve with this property is referred to as being a *rectangular hyperbola*. It will have an elasticity of demand throughout its length of unity: a small proportionate fall in price will produce an equal proportionate rise in quantity such that the *value* remains constant.

Suppose, however, that the demand curve had been the more elastic one D_2D_2. For outputs less than 12,000 tons, incomes (represented by the rectangle under the curve) are obviously smaller, and for outputs greater than this obviously bigger, than with D_1D_1. On the other hand, with the less elastic curve D_3D_3 smaller outputs would *increase* incomes of producers and bigger outputs would *decrease* them.

Buffer stocks and stabilization funds

One method that governments have used in order to stabilize incomes and prices is the operation of 'buffer stocks'. Governments buy up part of the supply when output is excessive, store this surplus, and re-sell it to consumers in times of shortage or reduced supply. Assuming that the government wishes to stabilize incomes of producers, how should it determine its purchases and sales? Again ignoring costs of marketing, suppose, in Figure 8.6, DD is the demand curve and LS is the long-run (planned) supply curve for a commodity, then OQ_0 would be the normal amount supplied, OP_0 the price, and $OQ_0R_0P_0$ gross incomes of producers.

Suppose, however, that actual output is unpredictable, due to weather and other hazards, and output fluctuates on either side of OQ_0. The fluctuation in output will cause fluctuations in price and in producers' incomes. Thus with an output OQ_1, price will

rise to OP_1 and incomes to $OQ_1T_1P_1$ (an increase in incomes resulting from inelastic demand in this case); and with an output of OQ_3 price will fall to OP_3 and incomes to $OQ_3T_3P_3$.

To see how the government ought to operate in order to stabilize incomes, we draw curve RH, which is a rectangular hyperbola passing through R_0. This curve tells us the combinations of price and quantity sold which would give producers the same gross incomes as $OQ_0R_0P_0$. If the amount producers can put on the market is OQ_1, the government will need to ensure a price of OP_2: the rectangle $OQ_1R_1P_2$ touches the rectangular hyperbola at R_1. At price OP_2, however, demand is OQ_2: to maintain that price therefore the government will need to supplement the amount OQ_1, forthcoming from producers, by the amount Q_1Q_2 out of its 'buffer stock'. Likewise in a period of 'glut', if output is, say, OQ_3, the government will need to intervene to raise the price to OP_4, the rectangle $OQ_3R_3P_4$ touching RH at R_3. But since at this price consumers are only willing to buy the amount OQ_4, the government will need to buy up the difference Q_4Q_3.

If output fluctuates on either side of the 'normal' or planned level OQ_0, the amounts that the government buys up and the amounts it sells out of stocks should roughly cancel each other out over time. Similarly the *expenditure* by the government in buying up stocks (e.g. $Q_4Q_3R_3T_4$) and its receipts from sales out of stocks (e.g. $Q_1Q_2T_2R_1$) will allow the government to 'balance its books', hopefully, over a period. It will be noticed, however, that the amounts that the government has to sell or buy, Q_1Q_2 and Q_4Q_3, depend on how far apart the two curves DD and RH are, that is, on how different the elasticity of demand is from unit elasticity. *The amounts that the govern-*

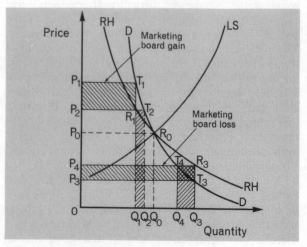

Figure 8.6   *Stabilization in the face of unplanned variations in supply.*

ment must buy or sell to stabilize incomes will therefore depend on the elasticity of demand.

Instead of actually dealing in the commodity, the government could, of course, stabilize incomes directly by operating a fund from which it could make direct payments to growers when incomes fell below 'normal'. This normally operates through a marketing board controlling the industry, with monopoly powers to fix prices to producers. The Board will usually guarantee a minimum price for the commodity and may make an initial payment to the grower followed by an additional payment if sales by the Board subsequently realize a price in excess of the minimum. Producers of the crop are thus encouraged by the knowledge that any decreases in price during the season will be moderated by government action. The government 'cushions' growers against fluctuations in receipts by varying the price it pays independently of the free market price. In Figure 8.6, if output were OQ_1, price OP_1, and receipts $OQ_1T_1P_1$ the government would buy up the output at price OP_2 (still selling it at price OP_1 to consumers) and thus add the value $P_1T_1R_1P_2$ to its 'marketing board reserves'. If output were OQ_3, price OP_3 and receipts $OQ_3T_3P_3$ the government would buy from growers at price OP_4 and sell at OP_3, thus making a loss of P_3P_4 per unit, altogether a loss of $P_3T_3R_3P_4$, financed from accumulated reserves such as $P_1T_1R_1P_2$.

In our example the need for stabilizing action arose from unplanned variation in the amount supplied: equally, this need might arise from short-run fluctuations in the level of demand above and below DD. The action required to stabilize price in these circumstances is illustrated in Figure 8.7. Let us assume that producers have in fact produced the amount OQ_0 which they would have been able to sell at price OP_0 had demand remained at the level given by DD. If demand is temporarily higher, at D'D', this amount could fetch a price of OP_1, bringing more than the 'normal' level of receipts; and if demand is temporarily low, as given by D''D'', a lower price of OP_2 would bring down receipts below the normal level. When demand at price OP_0 exceeds the amount supplied, by using a buffer stock, the government could sell stocks equal to Q_0Q_1 and thus keep the price at OP_0 and producers' incomes at $OQ_0R_0P_0$. When the demand falls short of OQ_0 at price OP_0, the government would need to buy up the difference Q_2Q_0 and thus maintain incomes of producers at the same level with a price of OP_0. Alternatively, the government could fix incomes at $OQ_0R_0P_0$ by retaining amounts like $P_0R_0T_1P_1$ when demand is high, and subsidizing the price to producers when demand is low, paying out amounts like $P_0R_0T_2P_2$. This would be a simple stabilization fund without a buffer stock.

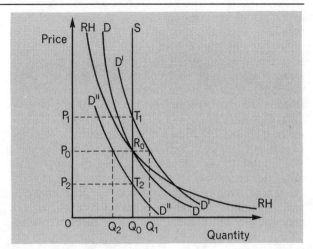

Figure 8.7 *Stabilization in the face of changes in demand.*

In practice, buffer stocks or stabilization funds are not as easy to operate as these illustrations might suggest. In particular it will be difficult to separate 'planned' from 'unplanned' outout, or 'normal' demand from temporary demand, and therefore to distinguish 'normal' or average price and incomes—more so because the average may be itself changing over time due to changes in the long-run situation of demand or supply.

Each of the two methods of stabilization, by buffer stock and by stabilization fund, has its advantages and disadvantages, besides those just mentioned involved in guessing at the desirable 'target' level of incomes. The buffer-stock method has the disadvantage of forcing the government, through a marketing agency, to involve itself directly in storing the commodity as well as making decisions to buy and sell. In contrast, by using the stabilization fund method the government could in theory stabilize incomes of producers without physically dealing in the commodity. The *dis*advantage is on the side of consumers. Although their expenditure in money terms on the commodity is stabilized, nothing is done through the stabilization method to stabilize the physical volume of the commodity becoming available to consumers. If the commodity is a basic foodstuff on which large numbers of poor families are dependent, its physical availability to consumers may be as important, or more so, than the revenue accruing to producers, in terms of general welfare.

The case for diversification

It has already been mentioned that many developing countries depend for their exports on only one or two crops, and that fluctuations in the output or price of these may cause considerable instability of exports and incomes in those countries. Such instability affects the economy as a whole, particular regions within the economy, and individual farmers. It is worth emphasizing that even if a country has quite varied and diversified exports, as does Tanzania, such diversification may not exist at the regional level: individual regions may still be largely monocultures, as in the case of Tanzania's Sukumuland, based on cotton, and Kilimanjaro Region, based on coffee. Because farmers are generally immobile, and attached to land in one region only, and because developing economies are not fully integrated, with variations in income and employment spreading through the economy as a whole, it is necessary to consider the number of crops available within each region, and to individual farmers within these regions.

To reduce the effects of dependence on one or two crops, the case is frequently made for diversification, through the addition of an extra crop or crops. The need to diversify arises out of two kinds of uncertainty associated with dependence on a restricted number of crops, as mentioned in Chapter 4. Fluctuations in the price or quantity of a major crop result in an uncertain livelihood for the farmer. This *may* be reduced by the addition of a supplementary crop, if fluctuations in income obtained from different crops tend to cancel out.[1] Secondly, dependence on one crop, involving 'putting all one's eggs in one basket',[2] may mean a danger of loss of livelihood altogether, if the market for the product were to disappear. Zanzibar has run this risk in being so dependent on the export of cloves, while on a regional level, the substantial fall in world demand for sisal, as a result of the development of synthetic substitutes, caused a permanent reduction in incomes and employment within the sisal-producing areas of Tanzania.

Thus interest in diversification may arise out of a desire to stabilize incomes (and perhaps to spread the receipt of income more evenly over the year). Or it may be desired as insurance against the loss of livelihood. Alternatively, people referring to the need for diversification may have in mind the need to find additional means of earning income. Thus in the case of the coffee-growing areas of East Africa, the problem may not be so much that of instability, which has been reduced through various international agreements, as the fact that the *quantity* of coffee which can be put on the market under international agreement is limited, leading to a need to find alternative commodities to maintain the expansion of farm incomes.

In pressing for diversification, however, the difficulties and costs of diversification are frequently underestimated. The predominant cash crop often carries a substantially higher rate of return than any feasible alternative, so that reduced specialization in favour of an alternative involves a heavy opportunity cost. There are usually, in fact, strong technical, ecological, as well as economic, reasons for a region or country's having a monoculture. Finding additional crops with a satisfactory return may be extremely difficult.

Economic rent and land rent

Another important application of simple supply and demand analysis relating to agriculture (although not exclusively to agriculture) is in the theory of rent of land. In order to stress the fact that this theory relates to any factor of production and not simply to land, we may start by considering, say, the supply and demand for a particular kind of labour on a large plantation, as illustrated in Figure 8.8. SS is an ordinary supply curve telling us the 'supply prices' of different quantities of labour. The 'supply price' is simply *the price that must be paid to secure the services of a particular unit of the factor*, or *the minimum level of earnings the factor must be paid to retain it in a particular use or occupation*. Since Figure 8.8 tells us that at a wage of 140s per month exactly 100 workers would be 'supplied' to the plantation, and no more, we can say that the 'supply price' of the hundredth worker will be 140s. Similarly the supply price of the two-hundredth worker will be 145s, and of the three-hundredth 150s, and so on. There may be a number of reasons why the supply prices of additional workers increase. They may have to be persuaded to come from homes further and further away, involving increased inconvenience or transport cost; or they may have to be persuaded to leave their own farms, which they are increasingly reluctant to do; or they may be

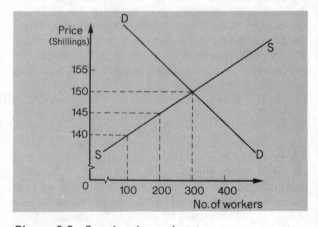

Figure 8.8 *Supply price and rent.*

recruited from other industries which are increasingly reluctant to allow their labour force to be reduced, and so on. An alternative term sometimes used instead of 'supply price' is *'transfer earnings'*. This implies directly that if the supply price of a factor is not paid, it will be 'transferred' to some other occupation. Supply price is therefore determined by what the factor can earn in its 'next best' possible use.

We can now define what we mean by 'economic rent': *economic rent is simply the excess that a unit of the factor earns over its supply price.* Thus if the wage rate of the workers referred to were determined in a free market by the intersection of the supply and demand curves as 150s, the hundredth worker would earn a 'rent' of 10s: whereas he would personally have been willing to work for 140s, he will be paid, like the other workers employed, 150s. Similarly the two-hundredth worker, who also earns 150s and who would have been willing to work for 145s, will earn a 'rent' of 5s. The three-hundredth worker, who as the last man employed may be described as the 'marginal worker', earns precisely his minimum supply price and therefore earns no rent. This is a general result: *the marginal unit of a factor of production earns no rent.* Rent is only earned by units 'inside' the margin, which may be described as the *intramarginal* units.

It is obvious that in our example the gap between the supply price of 140s for the hundredth worker and the 150s market price which he receives depends on how 'steep' the supply curve is, that is, on the elasticity of supply. Had the supply been *less* elastic and the curve steeper, the gap representing the amount of 'economic rent' would have been correspondingly greater. Two limiting cases may be distinguished: that in which the supply curve is horizontal (supply 'completely' elastic) and that in which it is vertical ('completely' inelastic). The former case is illustrated in Figure 8.9. Since the supply curve is horizontal at the level OP, the supply price of all units of the factor coincide at the price OP. This being also the market price at which supply equals demand, market price and supply price are equal for *every* unit and no unit earns rent. The whole of the payment to the factor, OQRP, consists of transfer earnings necessary to ensure its availability.

In Figure 8.10 the supply curve is vertical, implying that the amount OQ would be available not only at the market price OP but at any price whether OP_1, OP_2, or even zero. The supply price of every unit is therefore zero, and the whole of the market price is rent, in the sense of not being a necessary payment to ensure the supply of each unit of OQ. We can conclude, therefore, that with completely elastic supply no rent is earned, but with completely inelastic supply, the whole of earnings constitute rent, and that *in between these two limiting cases earnings*

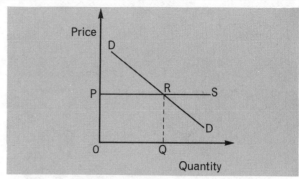

Figure 8.9 *Supply completely elastic: no rent.*

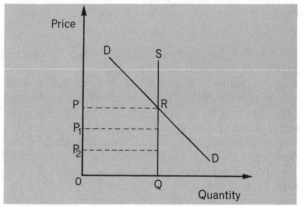

Figure 8.10 *Supply completely inelastic: all earnings rent.*

are divided between transfer earnings and economic rent in a proportion determined by the elasticity of supply.

Although our analysis has not been specifically in terms of land, we can now see its particular application to that factor of production. It follows from our definition of natural resources in Chapter 2 that if we consider the supply of natural resources to an economy, this supply corresponds to one of our limiting cases in which the whole of earnings is rent. Since man plays no part in the provision of natural resources, the supply is independent of man. All resources will be there whether used or not 'or whether discovered or not). The supply price (opportunity-cost) of the resources is therefore zero. This is why the famous economist Ricardo originally described rent as being the amount paid to a landlord for the use of the 'original and indestructible powers of the soil'.

Figure 8.11 shows the effect of an increase in demand for the factor on the level of rent employed by the factor. Taking supply as given, the increase in demand will raise the market price: in our diagram from 150s to 155s. As the supply curve remains where it is, the supply price of the hundredth worker is still

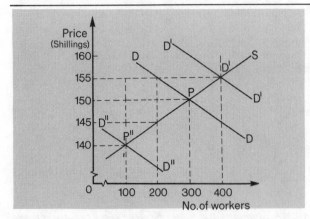

Figure 8.11 *Effect of an increase in demand on rent.*

140s, so that he enjoys an increased rent, now equal to 15s. This applies to all previously intramarginal units. In addition, the three-hundredth worker, who was previously 'marginal' and earned no rent, now earns a rent of 5s. An additional hundred workers are employed, and the four-hundredth worker is now the 'marginal' worker. Thus when demand increases, intramarginal units earn increased rent, and units previously beyond the margin will be employed and earn rent. If the level of demand fell to D″D″ the reverse would happen: in the case of the hundredth worker he would earn only his supply price and no rent. It follows that *the level of rent is a function of demand.*

It is often alleged that landlords are responsible for the high price of foodstuffs, say, because they are charging excessive rents for the land on which the food is produced. We can now see that this allegation is misplaced. Demand for land is a *derived* demand and depends on the demand for foodstuffs: if demand for foodstuffs is high in relation to supply, the prices of foodstuffs will be high, and it is this which *permits* landlords to charge high rents for scarce land to be used in the production of food. The rent of land, and any economic rent, is *price-determined*, we may say, and not *price-determining*. Thus increased demand for maize will increase the price of land suitable for growing maize if this 'maize-land' is in short supply. We cannot ascribe high rents merely to the acquisitiveness of landlords: for we assume they will charge as much as they can even if rents are low due to lack of demand. Indeed the concept of economic rent will still apply even where there are no landlords and tenants as such: if all maize-land, say, were owned by peasant producers, an increase in demand for maize would raise the value of maize-land (even in the absence of a market for land) and benefit those producers who for any reason were lucky enough to own the largest plots.

The whole of the foregoing analysis has been in terms of 'homogeneous' units of the factor: the workers we discussed were all of the same quality, as were the units of maize-land. Land, in particular, may not be homogeneous: some pieces of land may be less fertile than others, or less favourably situated. In such a case the 'marginal' unit of land will be the least fertile of the units used: it will be the plot which is *just* worth using in that the value of the product which it yields is just enough to cover the cost of the other factors used with the land: labour and capital. This unit will earn no rent. The value of intramarginal units of land, units of superior quality, will be in direct proportion to the extra net revenue they can yield. Thus if one piece of land can produce twice the value of another, after deducting the cost of cooperating factors, its value, or market price if there is a market, will be double the other. Therefore any unit of land more fertile than the marginal unit will earn a *differential rent* in proportion to its extra productivity, the rent accruing to whoever owns the plot. As in the general case of *scarcity rent*, an increase in demand for foodstuffs will make it worthwhile to use land that was previously idle; the 'margin' will shift outwards, and the value of rents earned will increase. There is no real difference between scarcity rent enjoyed by homogeneous units of a factor and differential rent. One is due to limited supply of units all of the same quality, the other to the limited supply of good quality units.

Differences in the usefulness of land may arise not because of intrinsic differences in quality, but simply because they are located in different places. Land in the centre of Accra or Nairobi fetches a high price in relation to that in the surrounding areas simply because demand for it is high, and because land in the surrounding area is a very imperfect substitute for it. This is again differential rent, or we may call it *site rent*.

The concept of rent as we have defined it, however, is ambiguous: rent is the excess of a factor's earnings over its supply price, or transfer earnings: but supply to what? The answer is that how much of a factor's earnings is transfer earnings and how much is economic rent depends entirely on what sort of transfer we are considering. The total supply of agricultural land in a region may be quite inelastic, but the supply to one particular agricultural use, maize growing perhaps, may be very elastic: land may be switched out of maize production into producing millet, say, or vice versa.

It follows from our definition of economic rent that it can be taxed away by the government without affecting the supply of the factor in question. If earnings are composed of supply price plus economic rent, and the whole of the latter is taxed away, we are left with the supply price: but by definition this is sufficient to ensure the unchanged supply of the factor. The taxation of economic rent will leave the allocation of resources untouched, a fact which has not escaped the notice of tax-collectors. In practice, of course, it is not easy to identify precisely either the supply price or the economic rent, particularly as the demand for the factor, and therefore the amount of rent, may fluctuate greatly from period to period.

It will be clear by this time that our concept of economic rent has little to do with *commercial rent*, the everyday meaning of the word rent. In this latter sense rent is the price paid for the hire of a durable asset, whether a piece of land, or a house, or even a small article such as a radio. In a free market, the rent of a house would be determined by supply and demand, and the commercial rent paid would equal the market price. This is clearly different from *economic* rent which is the *excess* of the market price over the supply price. For the 'marginal' house, economic rent is zero, and for the other houses supplied the supply prices would need to be deducted from the actual commercial rent charged to give economic rent.

Share-cropping and its effects

Rent need not be paid in the form of money; sometimes it is paid in the form of produce, as when the tenant undertakes to give a certain proportion of the output he derives from the land to the landlord; or labour, as when in exchange for the use of a piece of land, he undertakes to devote a certain proportion of his labour time to work on the landlord's holding. Clearly there is no important difference between the last two since receipt of produce is equivalent to receiving the benefit of given amounts of land and labour.

An arrangement whereby the product of a piece of land is divided between tenant and landlord on the basis of a fixed proportion is referred to as *share-cropping*. Very often the proportion paid over is fixed by custom rather than any formal contract. Payment is generally in kind rather than cash, but it is the payment of a fixed proportion of the value of output rather than a fixed rent which is important, not whether the payment is in kind. A share-cropping system prevailed in Japan and Taiwan before the reforms of the 1950s, and this form of land tenure arrangement is still very common in much of South-East Asia, and in many other parts of the world. In Egypt it used to be very important before land reforms there. In tropical Africa it has not been usual, but it was the most common form of tenure arrangement in Ethiopia, where it was a serious problem until the 1974–5 reforms.

Share-cropping will have an effect on the distribution of income and wealth in the country, as does any system of land-ownership and property rights, but in addition may have serious effects on incentives and output.

(1) First of all it may affect the supply of labour effort by the tenant, as shown in Figure 8.12. Under share-cropping the gross output is divided between landlord and tenant in a fixed proportion. Gross output is given in Figure 8.12 by the area under the marginal product of labour curve, GA, marked MPL. If, say, 50 per cent of each successive increment of product has to be paid to the landlord, the marginal *net* product of labour curve, for product retained by the tenant, will be HA, marked MNPL, lying below MPL such that, for example, GH = HO and RS = SD. The upward-sloping curve MVL represents the tenant's marginal valuation of leisure, which will increase the more hours per day he puts in. If he were an owner-cultivator, paying no rent, he would work OB hours, given by the point of intersection P where the marginal product of labour just equals his marginal valuation of leisure. A share-cropper, however, would only work OC hours, given by point of intersection Q where his marginal *net* product of labour, the extra product accruing to him, just equals his marginal valuation of leisure.[3] It may be observed that this effect on labour effort is due entirely to the share-cropping arrangement. If the rent to be paid were a fixed amount, say GRDO, after which all additional output accrued to the tenant, then there would be no reason for the tenant to work less than the full amount OB which he would work as an owner-cultivator.

We may note here one advantage of share-cropping over fixed-rent payment, however. This is that the risks of output variation due to climatic and

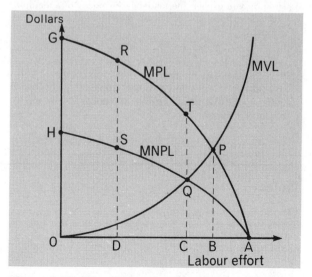

Figure 8.12 *The effects of share-cropping on tenant's labour effort.*

similar factors are assumed jointly by landlord and tenant, so that when gross output falls, for reasons beyond the tenant's control, his liability for rent also falls. This is a major reason for the widespread prevalence of crop-sharing tenancy arrangements in developing countries where natural hazards create uncertainty.

(2) A share-cropping arrangement will also weaken the tenant's incentive to invest in the land or to undertake output-increasing innovations such as using improved seeds or applying fertilizers. It is normal, of course, for the landlord to provide the land and some of the fixed capital (in farm buildings, fencing, water, etc.) while the tenant provides other factors, working capital, labour and other inputs. Again, this can be shown by comparing tenant with owner-cultivator. Table 8.2 shows that an improvement which would yield a high rate of return over cost to an owner-cultivator might offer zero return to a tenant and would thus most likely not be undertaken. In general, the smaller the tenant's share of gross output, the greater the disincentive to adopt improvements the cost of which in cash or effort falls on the tenant. This effect is greatly increased if the tenant also lacks security of tenure: if he is evicted after investing in the land he will fail even to recoup his investment, so that the rate of return over cost will be negative! This applies to any land tenure arrangement, of course, and provides the main economic case for granting security of tenure.

Table 8.2 The effects of share-cropping on the incentive to invest

	Tenant	Owner-cultivator
Cost of improvement	$30	$30
Value of resulting increase in output	$60	$60
Tenant's share at 50%	$30	—
Net return over cost	Nil	$30
Rate of return over cost	Zero	100%

It may be noted also that high rents, under whatever tenure arrangement they are levied, will by impoverishing tenants reduce their *capacity* to invest in the land, as well as the incentive to do so as described above.

(3) A subsidiary effect is that share-cropping may distort the allocation of resources between different activities. This occurs if the tenant produces several crops while the landlord exacts his 'share' on the basis of only one of the crops: the latter may, for instance, find it easier to collect a share of the main cash crop, leaving the producer free to consume his own food crops. In these circumstances, tenants will tend to avoid 'work for the landlord', using more land and labour on their 'own' crops, livestock, or non-farm jobs than would otherwise be desirable; an example of this type of effect, in Sudan's Gezira scheme, is given in Chapter 10.

Questions on Chapter 8

1. How do you explain the tendency for prices of agricultural products to fluctuate more widely than those of manufactured goods?

2. Examine the conditions under which a 'cobweb cycle' may produce convergent and divergent price fluctuations. Discuss the implications for the theory of perfect competition.

3. Use diagrams to show how a marketing board should operate a buffer stock if it wishes to stabilize (a) producer prices, and (b) producer incomes.

4. Discuss the advantages and disadvantages of operating (a) a buffer stock, and (b) a stabilization fund.

5. Discuss the benefits and difficulties associated with encouraging diversification of agricultural production in developing countries.

6. 'The rent of land is price-determined, not price-determining.' Discuss.

7. Discuss the usefulness of the concept of 'economic rent' for taxation policy.

8. What is share-cropping? Discuss its possible effects on output and investment.

Notes

[1] There could, on the other hand, be an increase in uncertainty if income from the new crop is much less stable than that from the old.

[2] See Chapter 4.

[3] It follows that it will not always pay the landlord to extract the largest possible percentage share. If he extracted 100 per cent of the product it would not pay the tenant to work at all, and the landlord would be paid nothing. He ought to maximize the area GTQH, the output paid over to him.

9 The Structure of Agriculture in Eastern Africa

The dominant position of agriculture within the various economies of Eastern Africa has already been stressed, in Chapter 4. The next two chapters will look in more detail at the development of the agricultural sector, the main basis of nearly all these economies.

The characteristics and types of African agriculture

In discussing African agriculture, we should first of all distinguish different types of farming, which includes livestock production as well as the cultivation of crops. There are, first, the pastoral areas, now often described as 'ranchlands' but supporting mainly pastoral peoples using livestock largely for subsistence purposes. Secondly, there are the plantations, which are important in a number of African countries. These are generally based on a single cash crop for export, such as tea, rubber, or sisal, but may produce crops like sugar and tobacco for local consumption also. Whether particular crops are grown on plantations or on smaller farms will depend on whether there are economies of scale in cultivation (from mechanical cultivation or perhaps in irrigation provision) or in processing and marketing. The need to process the crop does not always require large-scale production as raw cotton, for instance, is frequently carried from smallholdings to ginneries some distance away: but where processing is a difficult process, as in the case of tea and tobacco curing, or the raw material is expensive or difficult to transport, cultivation and processing are often done together in one place on a plantation basis, as in the case of sisal or rubber. A third type of farming area is the tree crop area where smallholders rely on tree crops for their cash return, supplemented by food production. The characteristic of such tree crops is that, like coffee and cocoa, they involve a long period of waiting after the initial investment in clearing land and planting, and then an annual yield over a long period. These areas generally concentrate on one particular crop. Lastly, we have the ordinary mixed farming areas in which a mixture of crop and livestock activities are undertaken, on either a small or large scale.

African agriculture may be described by the following set of characteristics.

(1) Productivity is often, though not invariably, low. Agriculture is in many areas on a very extensive and apparently inefficient basis with considerable use of shifting cultivation, although in part the use of shifting cultivation represents a sensible economic response to a plentiful supply of land; while the failure to use fertilizers to raise productivity, which is a general characteristic, is frequently (but not always) due to poor soils which offer only low returns to fertilizer application. Table 9.1 shows how minute the use of fertilizers is in Africa, however, and how low it is relative even to other developing areas.

Table 9.1 *The use of fertilizers in Africa and elsewhere, 1969–70*

	Consumption per hectare of arable land (kg)
Europe (excluding USSR)	158
North and Central America	66
USSR	34
Oceania	33
Asia (excluding China)	20
South America	14
Africa	7
World total (excluding China)	45

SOURCE: FAO, Annual Fertilizer Review, 1970, Table 12

(2) There is a low level of application of capital inputs generally. Apart from fertilizers and insecticides, which are also little used, there is limited use of either tractor or animal power for cultivation. While tractors are frequently uneconomic in African situations, even ox-ploughs are not widely used, compared to developing countries elsewhere. An overall comparison is given in Table 9.2.

(3) In contrast with Asia, population is spread very thinly across Africa, except for particular areas of dense population. Land is generally plentiful and labour, not land, is the limiting constraint in agriculture. Farms are frequently limited to their own family labour. The lack of mechanization means that seasonal bottlenecks occur, in planting, weeding, or

Table 9.2   *The use of animal and tractor power in Africa and elsewhere*

Regions and countries	Power units per 1,000 of agricultural population
Africa	21
Far East	53
Near East	64
Latin America	133
Morocco	59
India	76
Japan	104
USA	2,864

NOTE: Tractor power is expressed as mechanical horsepower divided by five; animal power is converted to horse equivalents

SOURCE: FAO, *The State of Food and Agriculture*, Rome, 1969

harvesting, restricting the acreage which can be cultivated by a family.

(4) The family labour force is often not well integrated. Instead of working together, women are customarily left the responsibility for food production while men concentrate on cash crops.

(5) Subsistence production continues to provide the foundation for agriculture. It is estimated that as much as 70 per cent of the land and 60 per cent of the labour are devoted to subsistence production.[1] A major factor here is the poor internal transport across the vast distance of the African continent. As transport facilities improve, production for the market can be expected to increase relatively in importance.

(6) The backbone of agricultural production has undoubtedly been the peasant producer or smallholder rather than estates and plantations. The economic development of many African countries is largely the story of the introduction of cash crops and their production for export by peasant farmers who responded eagerly to new opportunities to earn cash incomes. An important fact here, as explained in more detail below, with respect to Uganda, was that the new cash crops like coffee, cotton, or cocoa, could be produced by African smallholders, using much the same simple agricultural techniques as they had always used for the cultivation of food crops.

(7) Very often African countries introducing export crops have found themselves heavily dependent on one or two major crops, as already discussed in Chapter 5, leaving themselves open to export instability and uncertainty regarding export proceeds. Even where, as in Tanzania, total exports have been more diversified, particular regions within the country may be heavily specialized in producing one crop.

(8) The uneven distribution of the cash crops introduced has brought with it considerable *regional* inequality, as we discuss again below.

Variations in relief, rainfall, and soils also result in very great differences in the quantity, quality, and variety of food crops produced in different regions. The two factors together result in considerable regional differences in real income and standard of living, fertile regions often lying adjacent to others where the environment is extremely harsh.

(9) In particular there are in Africa extensive areas of semi-arid land. These substantial pastoral areas or 'ranchlands' within the agricultural economy constitute a special development problem.

(10) Within the arable and mixed farming areas, livestock activities are generally poorly integrated with the rest, and the quality of animals and animal husbandry is generally poor. A notable exception is the Central Highlands of Kenya, where the introduction of grade cows has eventually been very successful, leading to rapidly expanding production of milk and dairy products by African smallholders, both for the market and for their own consumption.

(11) One problem which fortunately does not bedevil African agriculture in the way that it does the agricultural sectors in Asia and Latin America is huge inequalities in land-holdings. By comparison, land is distributed fairly evenly, although there is some concern about the extent of rural stratification in many countries and the possibility that differences in access to land might widen over time.

(12) A basic feature of African agriculture is the system of land-holding on which it is based, incorporating traditional communal rights to land. The general absence of the European and North American concept of freehold title to land on an individual basis has restricted the emergence of a commercial market for agricultural land.

The peasant farmer and vent-for-surplus expansion in Uganda

As stated above, the economic development of many African countries has been bound up with the introduction of cash crops for export, as these have been taken up by peasant producers. Uganda is a good example. Two crops, cotton and coffee, have formed the basis of Ugandan economic development to date.

An important feature of this development, and here Uganda contrasts with Kenya, was the relatively unimportant role played by non-African producers. The production of cash crops for export in Uganda has been largely the work of African smallholders, and we can say that the peasant farmer has been the backbone of economic development in Uganda, as indeed has been the case in other countries, in West Africa especially.

Table 9.3 summarizes the development. The percentages give the value of cotton and coffee exports separately in relation to their *combined* value and not to the value of exports as a whole. There were other agricultural exports, notably sugar (mainly to Kenya), tea, hides and skins, and cottonseed oil and cake (for animal feed), an important by-product of the cotton ginning and processing industry. These other agricultural exports, however valuable, still accounted for just 19 per cent of agricultural exports (coffee and cotton thus amounting to 81 per cent) and 17 per cent of total domestic exports in 1969.

From Table 9.3 it can be seen that in 1906 Uganda must have been very largely a subsistence economy. From that time until the beginning of the 1950s the story is essentially one of the extension of cotton acreage and output. The volume figures, which give the best indication of effort put into export production, show a steady rather than spectacular development until the early 1930s, when output nearly doubled in the space of five years. After the war the volume of cotton exports became stabilized: indeed the average for 1962–4 was less than that in the immediate *pre-war* period, 1936–8. This is explained partially by the expansion of coffee production as an alternative high-priced crop (the other reason is examined presently). If output did not increase, however, value did, so that value of cotton exports in 1950–2 was seven times more than that in 1936–8, due almost entirely to higher prices. Cotton therefore still played a key role in the rapid economic expansion of the period.

Although coffee was already established in 1930–2 as a useful supplement to cotton exports, accounting for a tenth of their combined value, it still provided only one-fifth of the combined value after the war in 1947–9. Uganda therefore had a 'cotton-dominated' export economy right up to 1950. In the very early 1950s coffee exports increased in value very quickly and for the remainder of the decade there was a two-crop export sector, with exports of the two commodities roughly equal in value. During this period, however, the *volume* of coffee production increased spectacularly.

The 1950s, in fact, represented a period of very rapid economic development, and the combined value of cotton and coffee exports serve as a good indicator of this development. The main jump, however, was at the beginning of the decade when the Korean War raised world commodity prices, helping Uganda's cotton and coffee exports to increase in value from shs 262 millions, the annual average in 1947–9, to an annual average of shs 730 millions in 1950–2. The combined value of the two exports remained fairly steady during the rest of the decade, the expansion of output being offset by lower prices. From 1962, however, there was a further move ahead, due entirely to an increase in both the price and output of coffee. The effect was that in the early 1960s the export sector became 'coffee-dominated', with coffee accounting for nearly 70 per cent of the combined value, though, of course, by that time other exports, excluded from the table, were of some importance.

Table 9.3 *The development of cotton and coffee exports from Uganda*

Year	Cotton exports (raw lint)		Coffee exports[†] (unroasted beans)		Share in combined cotton–coffee export value	
	average annual		average annual		cotton	coffee
	volume (m kg)	value (m shs)	value (m shs)	volume (m kg)	%	%
1906	0.04	0.02	—	—	100	—
1911	2.4	3.3	—	—	100	—
1921–3	13	28	0.18*	0.15	99.5	0.5
1930–2	32	32	3.6	4	90	10
1936–8	63	74	7.4	13	91	9
1947–9	49	212	50	28	81	19
1950–2	65	502	228	39	69	31
1953–5	62	360	302	49	54.5	45.5
1956–8	67	366	388	76	48.5	51.5
1959–61	63	314	332	105	45	55
1962–4	53	256	552	140	32	68
1965–7	70	315	665	162	32	68
1968–70	64	299	836	175	26	74
1971–3	66	352	1,178	205	23	77

* rough estimate   [†] including estate coffee
SOURCE: *Statistical Abstracts*

The rapid increase in agricultural export production by peasant farmers needs some explaining. Why, if soils and climate were excellent for cotton and coffee production, could not this output have been produced earlier? An explanation has been put forward in terms of the 'vent-for-surplus' theory. This suggests that until Ugandan peasant farmers were given the opportunity to grow export crops, through the construction of a railway to the coast,[2] and the opening up of overseas markets, they were forced to concentrate on producing only their own limited subsistence food requirements, which would not fully employ available family resources of land and labour. With access to export markets, a 'vent' or outlet for these surplus resources, it was possible for peasant farmers to increase export crop production very rapidly. Once these surplus resources were fully used, however, further expansion would occur much more slowly and depend on increases in productivity per acre. Thus cotton production has not continued to expand, partly because of substitution by coffee, and partly because the 'slack' in readily available resources became fully taken up. We examine this 'vent-for-surplus' theory in more detail in Chapter 19.

The economics of subsistence agriculture[3]

A tendency exists to underestimate the importance of non-marketed food production in African agriculture, and to overemphasize that of cash crops. S. M. Makings has said, for instance, that 'Generally ... both planners and governments tend to lose sight of the importance of subsistence production in their preoccupation with marketed outputs, perhaps because it is taken for granted.'[4] The striking rate of expansion in cash cropping for export which we have just described in our Ugandan example may be the main reason, combined with the fact that governments are able to tax export crops much more easily than food crops which are used for household own consumption or sold internally.

Governments may also tend to assume either that subsistence output is adequate or that little scope exists for raising productivity in subsistence food production. In fact the provision of food for families' own consumption is frequently inadequate, and insufficient to prevent widespread malnutrition: here increasing the quantity and variety of food produced is important. The assumption that little can be done to increase productivity is also inaccurate, since new varieties of maize, wheat, rice, and other crops, which have contributed towards a 'Green Revolution' in other developing countries, have begun to make some impact in parts of Africa also, showing that

scientific research on food crops may have a high return. Thus it is frequently not true that efforts to promote food crop production are unnecessary or unrewarding.

In any case non-marketed production and food crop production are not the same thing. Very often a staple food crop, such as rice in South-East Asia, is also a major export or, as in the case of maize in Eastern Africa, a crop with an important local and regional market.

Increases in food production may permit increases in cash crop production or permit the benefit from export crops to be realized. If a country's food production is inadequate to feed its population scarce foreign exchange may have to be used to import food from abroad, perhaps very expensively, rather than being available for the purchase of other consumer or capital goods. Secondly, increased productivity in food production will release resources, land, and labour, to produce cash crops. In fact, farm households will generally only be willing to produce for the market after they have catered for their own basic requirements, so that the expansion of cash production is not possible *until* 'subsistence' production has reached an adequate level. This is particularly true because non-marketed food production absorbs a large proportion of family labour and land, and thus accounts for a large part of the total agricultural effort. Thus in Kenya, which is considered to have a highly commercialized agricultural sector in comparison with many other African countries, the Agricultural Census of 1969–70 revealed that some three-quarters (76 per cent) of all cultivated land was given over to food crops, as shown in Table 9.4. Most of the 81 per cent of land cultivated on small farms and settlement schemes (SF) was still needed to feed the rural population itself; and even the fully commercialized large farms (LF) devoted more than half their arable land (58 per cent) to wheat, maize, and other food crops for the local rather than the overseas market. It follows that food crop production, whether for own consumption or local sales, generally involves an opportunity-cost in terms of each output;[5] and improvements in productivity in food production may release substantial amounts of labour and land for alternative uses.

Thus it is important to avoid putting 'subsistence' food production and cash crop production into two separate compartments. The African farmer must choose an optimum combination of crops, as we shall see in Chapter 13, whether these be food crops for his own household consumption or crops for the market. A situation where compartmentalization is valid, however, is where the rural household can more than adequately supply itself with food, but has only a limited and low-priced local market for any

Table 9.4 *Cultivated areas under food and export crops in Kenya, 1969–70*

	Area (×1,000 hectares)			Percentage of total area under crops		
	SF	LF	Total	SF	LF	Total
Area under food crops (cereals, pulses, vegetables, root crops)	1,252	271	1,523	81	58	76
Area under export and other crops (sisal, tea, coffee, sugar, coconuts, cashews)	295	192	487	19	42	24
Aggregate area under crops 1969–70	1,547	463	2,010	100	100	100

SOURCE: *Statistical Abstracts*, 1975

surplus.[6] It is then that production for export markets will have a low opportunity-cost and provide a 'vent' (outlet) for surplus resources.

Peasant farmers in Eastern Africa have sometimes been criticized for not growing enough food crops, and sometimes for growing too little compared to cash crops. Thus colonial administrations have sometimes required that each farmer should grow at least one acre, say, of a famine reserve crop, such as cassava: implying that peasant producers were short-sightedly failing to take account of the risks of crop failure. Such regulations have generally been ignored or resisted by farmers who preferred their own combinations of food and cash crops.

Sometimes they have been criticized for being 'subsistence producers' who fail to take full advantage of market opportunities for cash crops. There may, however, be good reasons for concentration on food crops. First, there is the advantage that producing directly for own-account consumption saves transport costs and marketing charges. This is particularly true when a farmer has to choose between selling a food crop such as maize for cash or consuming it at home. The more remote the farmer is from markets, and the higher the transport charges incurred to reach a market, the lower the ex-farm price that the farmer will receive and the greater the incentive for him merely to provide for his own family with the resources at his disposal. Secondly, if his real income is low because, say, his land is infertile and yields a low output, he will be concerned first to satisfy basic requirements rather than to seek cash to purchase 'luxury' goods. At low levels of income, the demand for food, which the farmer produces himself, is income-elastic. Finally, at low levels of income and in a harsh environment where rainfall is erratic, as in some parts of Eastern Africa, the farmer may prefer to follow a 'survival algorithm'[7] rather than to maximize his profits: that is, to ensure survival of his family, having little or no reserve of income or wealth to fall back upon, he must aim at planting sufficient food crops every year, even at the expense of produc-

ing for cash, to be able to survive even the worst years of drought.

Peasants versus large farms in Kenya

The development of agriculture in Uganda was comparatively simple to describe: the rapid adoption by peasant farmers of cash crops, first cotton and then coffee, readily incorporated into the traditional system of farming. Kenyan agriculture and its development are much more complex, particularly because of the past dominance of European farming in the so-called 'White Highlands' of Kenya. In order to justify the cost of building the Uganda Railway, over a 600-mile stretch linking Lake Victoria to the coast, it was felt necessary to encourage settlement by European farmers in the temperate highlands of Kenya. European and Asian settlers were originally granted tenure on the basis of 99-year leases, by a 1902 Ordinance, but given the opportunity in 1915 of taking out 999-year leases, which the majority did. Although the 'Scheduled Areas' reserved for European farming were extended from over two million hectares in 1915 to just over three millions by 1923, the number of occupiers and their cultivation were always insufficient to justify alienation of as much as 20 per cent of Kenya's usable land. The number of European farmers increased from 800 in 1908 to about 1,000 in 1914, and barely exceeded 2,000 during the inter-war years. The number of occupiers actually declined from a peak of 2,097 to 1,819 in 1938 because of the world economic depression. After 1945 a European Settlement Board settled 493 British ex-servicemen as tenants or assisted owners, raising the total of occupiers from some 2,800 in 1948 to 3,600 by 1960. Unlike many of the wealthier early settlers who developed large plantations and extensive ranches, the post-1945 settlers developed smaller, more intensive mixed farms producing temperate foodstuffs for the East African market rather than tropical export products. With independence this process of European settlement had to be set in reverse through various programmes of land transfer, starting with the mixed farms rather than the more highly capitalized plantations and specialized ranches (which by 1960 were mainly in the hands of companies which could continue to attract capital and managerial skills from abroad). However, the historical background of Kenyan agriculture, with the dominance of a large expatriate farm and plantation sector during the first half of the twentieth century, when Uganda and most of West Africa were developing on the basis of African peasant production, has had a profound effect, which is likely to continue, on subsequent development.[8]

The effects of the large-scale non-African sector

The effects of European farming may be divided into (a) its positive contribution to the general economy of Kenya; (b) positive effects on African farming; and (c) negative effects on African farming. In 1956, for example, 84 per cent of gross cash revenue to producers came from large non-African farms. And in 1961 the 3,624 European and Asian holdings yielded about 78 per cent of gross revenue compared to 12 per cent from an estimated 950,000 African holdings although, of course, the latter also produced a substantial non-marketed output. Thus the non-African sector produced valuable export earnings, substantial tax revenue, very substantial agricultural employment (around 250,000 or one-third of total formal employment during the period 1955–64), and was a major source of food supply through the production of maize. It led to the creation of a more diversified agriculture and secured substantial agricultural development earlier, perhaps, than would otherwise have been achieved. It had some beneficial effects on African agriculture, by expanding the stock of agricultural knowledge, through the agricultural research which was established in support of the large-farm sector particularly, and by a demonstration effect, for example in demonstrating to African smallholders the value of fertilizers and pesticides and, in the Central Highlands, the superiority of grade cattle. In a number of other ways, however, European agriculture had negative effects, first, by taking some of the best land (although a considerable proportion of what a World Bank report classified as 'high potential land' was in the 'non-scheduled' or African areas);[9] second, by leading to the imposition of restrictions on the type and quantity of crops which Africans were allowed to grow (imposed to safeguard quality of product and for fear of the spread of pests and disease); third, by offering a precedent for large-

scale farming which has had a permanent mark on the land tenure position and policy; and last by diverting attention and resulting in the neglect of African agriculture.

The impact of the Swynnerton Plan

Thus by the early 1950s African agriculture in Kenya was still relatively underdeveloped. From 1956 onwards, however, expansion was impressive. This owed much to the introduction in 1954 of the 'Swynnerton Plan' to intensify the production of cash crops in African areas.[10] It is perhaps misleading to call this a 'plan': what was introduced, after years of comparative neglect, was a new and wide-ranging *policy* aimed at developing the African sector on more modern lines. Increased emphasis was put on cash crops, and specialization, in contrast to the previous tendency to stress food production and the dangers of famine. It involved the consolidation and enclosure of land to provide more economic sizes of holding, and the granting of land titles to individual farmers, to provide greater incentive for investment and development. Direct technical and financial assistance was given on a bigger scale than had been given previously, including investment in roads, water supplies, and cooperative processing and marketing organizations. Between 1954 and 1960 shs 218 million was spent on 'Swynnerton Plan' schemes.

While the Swynnerton Plan involved an important change of attitude on the part of the colonial Kenya government, however, its role in stimulating agricultural expansion has sometimes been exaggerated. Table 9.5 shows how commercial production in the small farming areas of Kenya expanded over the whole period 1945–74.[11] This shows that African production had started expanding *prior* to the introduction of the Plan and was actually expanding faster *before* the introduction of the Plan (86 per cent during the period 1949–53) and *after* the Plan (81 per cent increase during 1962–6) than during the implementation of the Plan (27 per cent during the period 1954–8 or 28–36 per cent from 1958 to 1962).[12] Secondly, although cash production had been expanding fairly steadily from 1945 to the time of independence, starting from the incredibly low figure of £1 million in all in 1945, it was still at a low absolute level in 1962 just before independence: whereas from 1962 to 1974 cash crop production increased four-fold, from £18 millions to £75 millions. It is in *this* period that Kenya may be said to have become a 'cash economy' with the bulk of its farmers selling for the market as well as producing for their own consumption. Thirdly, it was also the case that under the Swynnerton Plan the expansion of African

Table 9.5   *Value of gross marketed output from small farms in Kenya, 1945–74*

Old series			New series			
Year	£m	Four-year % increase	Year	£m	Four-year % increase	Small farms' % of share of total marketed output
1945	1.0	—				
1949	1.8	78				
1953	3.4	86				
1954	6.0	—				
1958	7.6	27	1958	(13.3)	—	(30.3)
1962	10.6	28	1962	(18.1)	36	(34.4)
			1966	32.8	81	47.5
			1970	44.2	35	51.7
			1974	74.6	70	50.9

NOTE: The two series of data are calculated on different bases and cannot be directly compared
SOURCE: J. Heyer *et al.*, loc. cit.

cash cropping was strictly controlled. In many cases, the planting of cash crops was only allowed on holdings that showed what was considered a minimum level of management, and then limited in amount to what the Agricultural Department thought could be effectively supervised by small farmers. In the case of coffee new growers were limited to 100 trees, this limit being raised to 280 only in 1958, and in consolidated areas.[13]

Despite these initial controls on expansion, smallholders in Kenya, particularly in Central Province, responded impressively to the opportunities presented to grow cash crops previously grown mainly on a large scale on non-African estates although, as shown by Table 9.6, much of this expansion occurred well after the Swynnerton Plan period.

The relative efficiency of large and small farms

At independence it was obvious that substantial tracts of land in the 'White Highlands' should be transferred to African hands. Two apparently con-

flicting objectives appeared. Population pressure in the more heavily populated parts of Kenya suggested a policy of settling as many farm families as possible, on smallholdings. Economic considerations or rather a belief in the existence of various types of economies of scale, first, and second, a belief in the efficiency of 'modern' or 'scientific' agricultural methods, suggested that the advantages of large-scale farming should be preserved during the course of land transfer. These considerations affected the rate at which land was transferred from European ownership, and also the nature of the settlement schemes that were implemented. Thus the Million Acre Scheme, started in 1961 and continuing to 1971, was divided into a high-density scheme of one million acres and a low-density scheme, with larger farm units, of 0.2 million acres. By 1971 some 35,000 families had been resettled on 1,161,000 acres, an average of around 33 acres each. Under the Shirika Programme, started in 1971, the aim was to retain large farms intact by transferring them as single units to individuals, partnerships or cooperative groups. By 1975, 76 farms transferred on this basis had an average size of 2,675

Table 9.6   *Expansion of smallholder tea and coffee production in Kenya*

Tea production				Coffee production			
Year	Metric tons (×1,000)	Hectares (×1,000)	Growers (×1,000)	Year	Metric tons (×1,000)	Hectares (×1,000)	Growers (×1,000)
				1954	1	2	19
1960–1	—	1	9	1957	2	7	62
1965–6	2	6	30	1961	7	18	141
1971–2	13	26	67	1964	17	51	236
1974–5	16	37	97	1974	39	54	

SOURCE: *Economic Survey*

acres, giving the 4,521 settlers involved an average of 45 acres each.[14]

The question of economies of scale in agriculture, and the relative efficiency of large and small farms, is therefore a significant one for Kenyan agricultural development policy and indeed for agricultural policy in a great many developing countries. Economies of scale were briefly referred to in Chapter 5 and are discussed in detail in Chapter 16 on The Size of the Firm. We said in Chapter 5 that economies of scale would be reflected in falling average costs of production as the scale or volume of output produced per period increases, other things being the same. Statistical data on this question are scarce, but Tables 9.7 and 9.8 give some indication. Table 9.7 does not refer to smallholders generally, but only to

smallholdings on settlement schemes. Table 9.8 refers to large farms in Trans Nzoia, one District of Kenya. However, we see that gross output *per acre* is much the highest (K shs 635) on small farms of less than 10 acres, and that gross output on small settlement farms generally (K shs 156) is higher than on large farms (K shs 117). Gross output per acre does not, of course, refer to the farmer's net earnings from the farm: gross output could be high but net earnings low, because of heavy expenditure on inputs. The figures do imply however that as far as making the most of the scarce land resource is concerned, small farms are superior. This has not been achieved by the application of more capital (as can be seen, small farms use very little capital per acre), but by the application of much more labour, particularly on

Table 9.7 Farm size, output, and inputs on Kenyan settlement schemes, 1967–8

Farm size group (acres)	Average farm size (acres)	Gross output (K sh per acre)	Labour (no. of family & regular labourers per 100 acres)	Expenditure on machinery cultivation (K sh per crop acre)	Proportion of land under crops (%)
less than 10	7.3	635	808	6	45
10 and under 20	13.8	250	399	11	30
20 and under 30	23.5	156	234	9	24
30 and under 40	34.7	161	159	28	16
40 and under 50	44.4	113	124	21	14
50 and under 60	52.3	98	111	19	13
60 and under 70	64.5	98	109	12	19
70 or more	124.8	111	70	10	14
All farms	30.5	156	190	14	19

SOURCE: Kenya, *Statistical Digest*, March 1972

Table 9.8 Farm size, output, and inputs on large farms in Trans Nzoia, 1970–1

Farm size group (acres)	Average farm size (acres)	Gross output (K sh) per acre	Labour (no. of family & regular labourers per 100 acres)	Expenditure on machinery cultivation (K sh per crop acre)	Proportion of land under crops (%)
Less than 250	183	248	93	135	46
250 and under 500	326	161	62	140	21
500 and under 950	546	133	43	136	24
750 to 1,000	816	113	44	146	19
1,000 to 1,250	1,012	89	34	119	13
1,250 and 1,500	1,194	149	46	167	18
1,500 to 2,000	1,502	128	28	155	10
2,000 or more	2,979	65	14	131	9
All farms	890	117	36	143	16

SOURCE: Kenya, *Statistical Digest*, March 1972

very small farms of less than 20 acres, and more intensive use of the land. Moreover, since the proportion of land under crops is not very different as between small settlement farms and large farms, 19 per cent compared to 16 per cent (though within each category the proportion cultivated decreases with size), the productivity *per acre cultivated* must have been higher on small farms.[15]

Large farms may nevertheless be technically more efficient by economizing labour: on average they used only one-fifth of the labour force, while very small settlement farms used 10–20 times that number of labourers. Which is *economically* the most efficient will depend on the cost of labour, and we cannot answer this without calculating what the opportunity cost of labour is in the Kenyan economy. In the overpopulated parts of Kenya, the opportunity-cost of labour will be low. And since the Kenya government has been seriously concerned with the problem of unemployment, it can be seen that small farms are effective in providing employment opportunities of some kind.

If we look at the figures for different sizes of large farm, it is again difficult to find evidence of economies of scale. While the smallest farm category has the highest gross output per acre, and the largest farm category has the lowest, the intermediate categories from 250 acres up to 1,500 acres show no relationship between farm size and gross output, or between farm size and inputs, the number of labourers per acre and expenditure on machinery per acre being fairly constant.

In conclusion, we can say that small farms *are* able to secure a higher output per acre and are important for absorbing labour and creating employment. The tendency to assume that large farms in all circumstances provide economies of scale is not justified, though these economies will exist in particular types of farm activity and for particular crops. It is not necessarily true, certainly, that scale economies extend over the whole range of farm size, e.g. over 500 acres, which exists in Kenya.

The size distribution of large farms in Kenya

Despite this apparent lack of scale economies and the existence of a settlement programme for relieving pressure in the overpopulated areas, the official statistics show surprisingly little change in ownership structure within the large-farm sector.[16] Table 9.9 compares the size distribution of farm holdings within the large-farm sector in 1963 and 1973. According to these figures, the number of large farms enumerated has not decreased significantly. The main change, through the settlement programme, appears to have been an increase in the number of farms at the very bottom end of the scale, below 100 acres, where the percentage has increased from 25 to 34 per cent. But the middle grouping of holdings, between 100 and 500, accounted for almost the same percentage, 37 compared to 38, and the large proportion of extremely large holdings has fallen only from 36 per cent to 29 per cent.

It must be said that the official statistics disguise a substantial part of the change which has been effected under the settlement programme, since many farms counted in Table 9.9 as large single units were in fact already being shared among a large number of settlers:

Table 9.9 *The size distribution of large farm holdings in Kenya, 1963 and 1973*

Size of holding in acres	1963			1973		
	Number		Percentage	Number		Percentage
0 and under 20	293			429		
20 and under 50	285	847	25.1	338	1,065	34.0
50 and under 100	269			298		
100 and under 200	363			380		
200 and under 300	368			337		
300 and under 400	288	1,295	38.3	259	1,178	37.3
400 and under 500	276			202		
500 and under 1,000	625			489		
1,000 and under 2,000	313			210		
2,000 and under 4,000	148	1,226	36.4	107	922	29.1
4,000 and under 20,000	126			102		
20,000 and over	14			14		
	3,368		100	3,165		100

SOURCE: Kenya, *Statistical Abstracts*

accurate up-to-date figures simply do not exist. Nevertheless, the pace of change would not appear to have been very great given the extent of land hunger in Kenya.

A number of factors have probably contributed to the maintenance of the status quo. The high capital costs of buying out large farmers made transfer difficult. There were difficulties in organizing settlement schemes to permit the subdivision of large units among new settlers. There has remained a belief in government circles and among influential advisers in the superior efficiency of large farms. But in addition the lack of change reflects the tendency mentioned for the colonial structure of land ownership to maintain itself in the absence of very determined attempts at achieving equality in the ownership of land.

Structural features of Kenyan agriculture

From what has been said already, it is clear that Kenyan agriculture exhibits a number of structural features which distinguish it from those of many other African countries.

(1) The division between the small-farm sector and the large-farm sector is a special feature. Although many countries have significant sectors of plantation agriculture, they are generally much more dependent on the small farmer or peasant producer.

(2) Agricultural wage employment is especially important in Kenya.

(3) Because of the reservation of the so-called 'White Highlands' up to independence, and the need to relieve population pressure in different parts of Kenya, the settlement programme has been an especially important element in agricultural development policy in Kenya.

(4) Peasant producers have shown the same responsiveness to market opportunities in Kenya as in other countries, although this response was, for historical reasons, delayed.

(5) The domestic and East African market has

Table 9.10   *The diversity of marketed agricultural production in Kenya: gross farm revenue by commodity, 1974*

	Value (K£ million)	Percentage
Cereals		
Maize	8.5	5.8
Wheat	7.0	4.8
Other (barley, rice, etc.)	2.3	1.5
Total, cereals	17.8	12.1
Temporary industrial crops		
Sugar cane	5.9	4.0
Pyrethrum	4.2	2.9
Other (oilseeds, pineapples, etc.)	2.1	1.4
Total	12.2	8.3
Other temporary crops (vegetables)	4.5	3.1
Permanent crops		
Coffee	34.5	23.5
Tea	19.3	13.2
Sisal	18.4	12.5
Other (cashewnuts, coconuts, wattle, etc.)	3.0	2.1
Total	75.1	51.3
Total, all crops	109.6	74.8
Livestock and products		
Cattle and calves	17.6	12.0
Dairy products	10.1	6.9
Other	4.7	3.2
Total	32.4	22.1
Unrecorded marketed production	4.6	3.1
Total: Gross farm revenue	146.7	100.0

SOURCE: Republic of Kenya, *Economic Survey*, 1975

provided an important outlet for Kenyan agricultural produce, both crops and livestock products, so that Kenyan agriculture has been much less dependent on primary product exports than other African countries.

(6) The wide variations within Kenya in climate and soils have, together with the additional factors of a large-farm sector and a domestic market for foodstuffs, produced a very diverse pattern of agriculture.

The diversity of Kenyan agricultural production is shown in Table 9.10. Smallholder export crops, like coffee and cotton, so dominant in commercial farm revenue in Uganda, for instance, do not figure so prominently. The important domestic market for foodstuffs (including the large Nairobi market) is reflected in the 12 per cent of gross farm revenue contributed by maize, wheat, and other cereals, and also by the 22 per cent share of livestock and livestock products, including dairy products, which more than anything else contributes to a diversified agriculture. Permanent crops such as coffee, tea, and sisal contributed only just over half (51.3 per cent) of total farm revenue, and a substantial share of this, in the Kenya case, is contributed by large farms. The most valuable single crop produced for cash is coffee, accounting for just 23.5 per cent of revenue in 1974. If due weight is given to production for own-account consumption, however, cereals, particularly maize and millet, become very much more important.

Cash crops and regional inequalities

The expansion of cash crop production for export in East Africa has been the basis for the rapid economic development which has taken place since the time when East African countries were primarily subsistence economies. However, the opportunities to earn cash incomes have not been spread evenly, and as areas suitable for cash crops have forged ahead, some other areas have remained largely outside the cash economy. Thus in Uganda, development was concentrated in the rich coffee- and cotton-growing areas, especially Buganda in the south and Bugisu in the east, while the northern region in particular lagged behind. In Tanzania economic development was concentrated in 'islands' of development, in the Bukoba area (coffee), in Kilimanjaro Region (coffee), in the Southern Highlands (coffee and tea), all well-defined areas with rich soils and abundant rainfall, together with Sukumuland, in a rich cotton-growing belt below Lake Victoria. Thus the expansion of cash crop production has been associated with major *regional inequalities* which today constitute major problems for regional planning and income distribution in East Africa.

Table 9.11 illustrates the process as it has occurred in Kenya. The final column shows the aggregate value of marketed output from small (African) farms for the five provinces mentioned up to 1962. It may be observed that marketed output in 1938 was minimal, only one-twentieth of that for 1960, measured in current prices:[17] African production was largely for subsistence, although the seeds of subsequent cash crop expansion in Central and Nyanza Provinces had been sown. Subsequently expansion proceeded mainly in these two provinces, with Nyanza Province, due to the expansion of cotton production around the Lake, being the furthest advanced by 1955. While the value of marketed output in Nyanza rose only slowly after 1955, and was actually lower in 1962 than 1960, expansion of cash production increased sharply in Central Province, mainly due to the acceleration of African smallholder production of coffee after 1957. Thus while marketed output in Central Province was only 23 per cent greater than in Nyanza in 1960, in 1962 it was 90 per cent greater, and the economic dominance of the Central Province was established as far as African production is concerned. Of course European pro-

Table 9.11   *Regional differences in the value of output marketed from small farms in Kenya (in K£ thousands).*

	Central and Southern Provinces	Central Province	Southern Province	Nyanza Province	Coast Province	Rift Valley Province	Total five provinces
1938	205	(153)	(52)	221	—	—	426
1945	525	(411)	(114)	438	80	—	1,043
1950	1,358	(1,062)	(296)	1,411	268	—	3,037
1955	1,869	1,462	407	2,500	208	—	4,577
1960	3,972	3,259	713	2,654	1,133	713	8,472
1962	5,035	4,018	1,017	2,191	751	650	8,627

SOURCE: J. Heyer *et al.*, loc. cit.
(As Southern Province was part of Central until 1953, their respective shares in the combined figures for 1938, 1945, and 1950 are assumed on the basis of the 1955 figures, this being the earliest date for which a breakdown is available)

duction in the 'White Highlands' was dominant until after independence was established. By that time the Southern, Coast, and Rift Valley Provinces were well behind, *together* accounting for no more than around 30 per cent of the value of marketed output for small farms in 1962.[18]

Of course these regional comparisons focus on different rates of growth of total *marketable* surpluses, and do not take account of differences in the size of the population or the availability of cultivable land. If, as was in fact the case, the Southern, Coast, and Rift Valley Provinces were less densely populated and their rural inhabitants had greater access to wage employment on large farms, then their lagging behind might not raise serious inequalities in average *family* incomes. We should therefore examine more closely differences in the marketed output *per head* of

the population in those areas which depend on peasant farming for the great bulk of their livelihood. Table 9.12 provides some of the details for 1969, after a further seven years of greatly accelerated agricultural development for African farming had elapsed.

It is clear from the second column of the table that the economic dominance of Central Province in cash crop production continued after 1962. The Districts of Central Province, plus Embu and Meru, which were part of Central Province in 1962, accounted for 49 per cent of all marketed output of small farming Districts by 1969, compared with 45 per cent in 1962 and 38 per cent in 1955. The last two columns, however, show in detail the variation in cash incomes brought about by the development of cash cropping. If the average marketed output per head over all these Districts, which was £3.08 in 1969, is taken as

Table 9.12   *Population, marketed output, and marketed output per head in Kenya's smallholder farming districts, 1969*

Province/ District	Population (thousands)	Marketed output (£ thousands)	Marketed output per head (£)	Marketed output per head (Index)
Western	1,328	2,247	1.69	55
Kakamega	783	1,039	1.32	43
Bungoma	345	877	2.48	81
Busia	200	331	1.66	54
Nyanza	2,122	3,952	1.86	60
Kisumu	401	579	0.74	24
Siaya	383	n.a.	n.a.	n.a.
S. Nyanza	663	1,291	1.95	63
Kisii	675	2,082	3.08	100
Central	1,676	9,003	5.37	174
Kiambu	476	2,500	5.25	171
Murang'a	445	1,436	3.20	104
Nyeri	361	1,907	5.28	172
Kirinyaga	217	1,160	5.34	173
Nyandarua	177	2,000	11.30	367
Rift	847	2,165	2.57	83
Kericho	479	930	1.94	63
Nandi	209	1,165	5.58	181
Elgeyo	159	70	0.44	14
Eastern	1,826	6,682	3.66	119
Embu	179	978	5.46	177
Meru	597	2,664	4.46	145
Machakos	707	2,783	3.93	128
Kitui	343	257	0.74	24
Coast	625	1,826	2.29	95
Kilifi	308	945	3.07	100
Kwale	206	396	1.93	63
Taita	111	485	4.37	142
Total above	8,424	25,875	3.08	100

SOURCE: J. Heyer *et al.*, loc. cit.

100, that in Central Province was 174 per cent, compared to 60 per cent in Nyanza and 55 per cent in Western Provinces, where expanding numbers of population also reduced sizes of land-holding and therefore marketed output per family. Thus marketed output per head in the Western Province was only one-third that in Central Province. Even within Provinces there were great differences, for instance between Murang'a (104 per cent) and Nyandarua (367) in Central Province, and between Kwale (63) and Taita (142) in Coast Province. Inequalities between Districts in different Provinces, between Kakamega (43), say, and Embu (177), are even greater.

Questions on Chapter 9

1. Discuss the main characteristics of agriculture in Africa.
2. In what way can the economic development of Uganda be described as typical 'vent-for-surplus' expansion?
3. Compare the advantages of producing for the household's own consumption and producing for the market.
4. Assess the impact of the Swynnerton Plan on the development of Kenyan agriculture.
5. How far do you think the maintenance of a large-farm sector in Kenyan agriculture is justified by economies of scale?
6. Discuss the way in which the expansion of cash cropping in East Africa has produced regional inequalities in development. How easy do you think this would be to correct?

Notes

[1] J. C. de Wilde, *Experiences with Agricultural Development in Tropical Africa*, Vols. I and II, Johns Hopkins University Press, 1967, p. 21.

[2] The Uganda Railway, opened in 1901 (from Mombasa to Kisumu), reduced the cost of transporting goods from as much as £300 per ton for porterage to a mere 48 *shillings* per ton.

[3] This section should be read in conjunction with that on 'The Value of Subsistence Output', in Chapter 5.

[4] S. M. Makings, *Agricultural Problems of Developing Countries in Africa*, Oxford University Press, 1967, p. 64.

[5] This opportunity-cost may be even greater if food crops and cash crops have labour peaks which clash with each other at a particular time of year.

[6] The main reason why the market is limited will be that other rural households are growing the same crops and supplying their own needs. There may however be a large and expanding urban market for foodstuffs to which farmers can 'export' their produce.

[7] See M. Lipton, 'The Theory of the Optimising Peasant', *Journal of Development Studies*, April 1968.

[8] For further details, see R.S. Odingo, *The Kenya Highlands: Land Use and Agricultural Development*, East African Publishing House, Nairobi, 1971. In 1960 there were 3,609 large, mainly European, farms occupying 3,130,000 hectares and comprising some 2,500 mixed farms with rather less than half the area; 590 plantations with some 150,000 hectares and 390 ranches with the remaining area. Even in 1960 before subsequent amalgamation of some smaller estates into companies, 71 per cent of the large-farm coffee acreage was controlled by 294 companies and 92 per cent of the sisal and tea on large farms was owned by 52 and 74 companies respectively.

[9] IBRD, *The Economic Development of Kenya*, Johns Hopkins University Press, 1963, p. 72.

[10] R. J. M. Swynnerton, *A Plan to Intensify the Development of African Agriculture in Kenya*, Government Printer, Nairobi, 1954.

[11] See J. Heyer, J. K. Maitha, and W. M. Senga, *Agricultural Development in Kenya: An Economic Assessment*, Oxford University Press, Nairobi, 1976.

[12] The second of these periods allows for more of the gestation period involved with tree crops and inevitable planning implementation delays, as well as the impact of the State of Emergency, 1952–8.

[13] J. Heyer *et al.*, *loc. cit.* From 1964 the International Coffee Agreement restricted the expansion in coffee planting, as can be seen in Table 9.6.

[14] This would not necessarily be a large amount if it comprised very dry ranchland capable of maintaining only a low density of livestock.

[15] However, this will partly reflect the better average quality of the land on small settlement farms, since such land will have been carefully selected to provide at least a minimum level of income to settlers.

[16] Except of course, the transfer of holdings from non-African to African ownership since 1963.

[17] However, if account is taken of the four-fold increase in the price of maize and other crops between 1938 and 1960, the marketed output in 1938 was probably only about one-fifth that in 1960. The authors estimate that non-marketed output in 1938 had a current (1938) market price of £2.3 millions, more than five times as much as the marketed output from African farms. Even by 1962 non-marketed output was about four times greater, and still as much as marketed output in the early 1970s.

[18] Partly, of course, this was due to the greater relative importance of extensive large-farm production in those provinces, and of pastoral areas.

10 Topics in Agricultural Development

In this chapter we shall deal with a number of advanced topics in the area of agricultural development. Readers wishing to avoid this more advanced and specialized discussion may proceed directly to Chapter 11.

The supply response of peasant producers

A great deal of discussion has taken place regarding the 'supply responsiveness' of peasant producers. It has been argued that peasant producers are 'irrational' in that they do not respond in the 'normal' way to price incentives. This has been applied not merely to African peasant farmers, but throughout the developing world. For instance, J. H. Boeke was referring to small-scale producers in Indonesia when he stated:

When the price of rice or coconuts is high, the chances are that less of these commodities will be offered for sale; when wages are raised, the manager of the estate risks that less work will be done ... only when rubber prices fall does the owner of a grove begin to tap more intensively, whereas high prices mean that he will leave a larger or smaller portion of his tappable trees untapped.[1]

It will be noticed that there are two elements here. The first is that the supply curve for the producers 'slopes the wrong way', implying that producers

supply *more* of the commodity when the price is low than when the price is high. Figure 10.1(a) illustrates what is regarded as a 'normal' or 'positive' supply response, and Figure 10.1(b) a 'perverse' or 'negative' supply response causing the supply curve to slope 'backwards', that is, to slope up from right to left, over part of its length (S_1 to S_2).

The second element in the quotation implies one possible reason for the 'perverse' response, which is that producers are only willing to work or 'supply effort' up to a certain level because, presumably, they have a limited demand for income. This might be because, in a rural society, they have relatively limited wants and cash needs. Thus when wages go up, estate workers can earn their 'target' level of income without working quite so many hours as before,[2] and owners of small groves of rubber trees work less hard to extract the maximum possible amount of rubber.

Allegations that peasant producers are *irrational* and insufficiently influenced by the profit motive are often combined with related charges that they are *inefficient* or simply *conservative*.

A rational, efficient producer would:

(1) show a positive supply response, supplying more to the market when a commodity's price increased, by (a) *switching* a given amount of labour and cooperating factors to the higher-priced product, in *substitution* for less attractive crops, now relatively less profitable, and/or by (b) *increasing his labour*

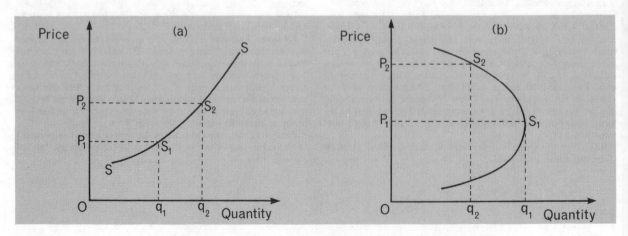

Figure 10.1 (a) A 'normal' supply response. (b) A 'backward-sloping' supply curve.

effort and possibly the employment of other inputs, to take account of a more profitable market for his output as a whole. Only the second of these two responses to a price change necessarily involves an increase in the supply of effort;

(2) combine his cropping and other activities in the most profitable way, using the most efficient (least-cost) methods of production; and

(3) respond to opportunities to innovate by introducing new crops, and also new techniques which over the longer run could reduce the cost of producing a larger output.

In contrast with this ideal, it has frequently been alleged, peasant producers (1) show perverse supply responses; (2) have a high preference for leisure or inelastic 'supply of effort'; and (3) are inefficient in a number of ways, specifically (a) using 'sub-optimal' combinations of products, (b) being poor farmers at the technical level, using poor agricultural techniques, failing to use fertilizers, pesticides, and the like, causing very low productivity, and (c) being conservative and unresponsive to change, or to the advice of agricultural extension officers.

As regards the slope of the supply function, numerous statistical studies in Africa alone, excluding those in other parts of the world, have revealed a positive slope, or normal responsiveness to price among peasant producers. To take just two examples, Dean,[3] using figures for tobacco supply in Malawi from 1926 to 1960, estimated the relationship between price and quantity supplied, and found tobacco growers in Malawi quite responsive to price incentives. Maitha[4] estimated statistically the supply responses for coffee producers in Kenya from 1946 to 1964 and found that smallholders, who were mainly African, showed a higher response, if anything, than estate farmers, who were mainly European.

Thus there is not much evidence of a 'backward-sloping' supply curve among African smallholders. It is worth pointing out, however, two cases where a backward-sloping supply response could exist *and yet be quite consistent with rational behaviour.* The first situation is where the product in question is the marketable surplus of a staple food commodity, a part of the output of which the farmer and his family consume themselves. Suppose the farmer, in an over-populated area, has only a small plot of land on which to maintain his family, or alternatively has access only to infertile or arid land which, even with maximum effort from the family, yields a low total output. Suppose further that the farm is suited to the production of only one major crop. The farmer relies on part of his crop to satisfy his family's food requirement and sells the rest for cash, to satisfy his needs for purchased goods. If his output is low, he will be forced to sell some output for cash even though his food requirements are not fully satisfied. The higher the price of the good the more easily he will be able to satisfy his most urgent needs for purchased goods. At a high price, therefore, he might feel that he can afford to retain a higher proportion of his crop, to feed his family better, and sell a *lower* quantity. At a low price, he will have to sell more to obtain the same cash income as before, and the same quantity of purchased goods (or to find the cash required to pay taxes, rent to the landlord, or school fees). Thus the size of the marketable surplus (the quantity put on the market after own-account consumption) may be greater the *lower* the price, implying a downward-sloping market supply curve.

The second case relates again to a situation where there is one major crop, produced this time entirely for cash. Since all or most of the farmer's effort goes into the production of this crop, increasing supply when the price goes up means increasing the supply of effort, exchanging leisure for more income. In these circumstances it is possible to visualize a situation where a fall in price would lead to an increase in the quantity supplied:[5] this would be because of an increase in effort made by growers in order to counteract the downward pressure on cash incomes and in order to maintain a certain standard of living. Thus in Figure 10.1(b), price might initially be at Op_2 with revenue to farmers equal to $Oq_2s_2p_2$. If price falls to Op_1 and growers supply the same quantity (or less), revenue to growers clearly falls: to maintain incomes at the same level growers would need to increase the quantity marketed to Oq_1 where $Oq_1s_1p_1 = Oq_2s_2p_2$, sacrificing leisure, working harder, and producing a larger quantity.

Consideration of this case leads on to the question of the supply of effort by peasant producers. Are the latter as interested in earning cash incomes as Western producers or do they suffer from excessive 'leisure preference'? This is different from the previous question, since it is quite possible for the supply curve to be normal (upward-sloping) when the total effort is relatively low. Evidence on this point is contradictory. In some cases idleness simply reflects seasonal unemployment, periods in the year when, in an agricultural economy, work is not required. If we consider an example, Norman[6] calculated labour inputs by male adults in three villages in Zaria, Northern Nigeria, to be as in Table 10.1. This shows that on average males worked only 13 days during March (only four of these on farm work), and less than three hours per day. That this largely reflected enforced seasonal unemployment is indicated by the fact that the same group worked approximately 23 days, and five hours per day, during June, more than three times the number of hours per month. To test

Table 10.1   Labour effort on family farms in three Zaria villages, North-Central State of Nigeria, April 1966 to March 1967

	March (low peak)		June (high peak)	
	No. of days worked monthly	Average no. of hours worked per day	No. of days worked monthly	Average no. of hours worked per day
Farm work	4.4	—	16.9	—
Other work	8.7	—	6.0	—
Total work	13.1	2.7	22.9	4.9

SOURCE: D. W. Norman, loc. cit.
NOTE: data refers to work done by male adults.

leisure preference we need to examine the number of hours worked in June, the month of peak labour demand, when plenty of work was available. Here these data show that there was still plenty of scope for increased effort, particularly in terms of the number of hours worked per day. On the other hand poor health might provide an alternative explanation of the relatively low number of hours worked.

If we turn, thirdly, to the issue of the technical and economic efficiency of peasant farmers, it is even more difficult to reach a conclusion. Very often attempts by agricultural officers to transplant the technically superior methods employed on agricultural research stations to peasant farms fail because these more advanced methods require capital inputs which the peasant farmer lacks or which are not economic on a small scale and with the factors of production available to the peasant farmer. A number of researchers in Asia, Latin America, and Africa have claimed that the peasant farmers studied by them were 'poor but efficient', making the most of very limited resources and a harsh environment.[7] However variations in productivity between one farmer and another suggest that many farmers are *not* operating in the most efficient way, and that considerable increase in productivity and output would occur if the mass of farmers could be brought up to the level of the most efficient. Thus in a study of

cotton farmers in Sukumuland, Tanzania, Shapiro[8] found that the farmers obtained very different efficiency scores, measured on a scale which he had devised. His results are summarized in Table 10.2. The score measures actual output obtained against potential output from the inputs used, assuming maximum efficiency. The mean score was 0.663 or two-thirds, implying that if all farmers operated at maximum efficiency, increasing their scores on average from 0.663 to 1.00, output could be increased by 50 per cent, without increase in the inputs used!

Income distribution and rural stratification

The objectives of economic development are not limited to increases in aggregate income and output, economic growth in the narrowest sense: but must include the equitable distribution of income and employment, such that all, or most of the population can participate and share in the benefits of economic growth. Rural development is currently emphasized largely because it provides the means for broad participation by the people in development.

However, in many parts of the Third World, Latin America and Asia in particular, there has been considerable *in*equality in the rural sector arising out of the huge estates and land-holdings of the large landowners. One of the main objectives of land reform in Latin America has been to replace or reduce the *latifundia* system, where much of the land is owned and farmed by big landowners, frequently only farming a portion of the estate, in favour of small family farms, referred to as *minifundia*, cultivated on an intensive basis.

In Africa the distribution of land-holding has been much more even. Nevertheless there are signs that inequality could develop over time, that considerable inequality already exists, in relative terms, and that government policies to assist farmers often have the effect of increasing rather than decreasing inequality.

Table 10.2   Distribution of technical efficiency scores among cotton farmers in Sukumuland, Tanzania

Score	No. of farms
0.231 to 0.385	3
0.385 to 0.539	12
0.539 to 0.693	6
0.693 to 0.847	6
0.847 to 1.000	10
Average score: 0.663	37 Total

SOURCE: K. H. Shapiro, loc. cit.

Unequal incomes may be associated with *rural strati-fication*, the formation of different classes or strata within rural society, contributing to the problems of *class formation* within the country as a whole.

We may take several examples of this from different Eastern African countries. A detailed investigation into the distribution of wealth in rural households in Mbere, Eastern Kenya,[9] revealed the following wide variations in wealth, given in Table 10.3. We see that the top (richest) 10 per cent of the population owned 43 per cent of the wealth[10] and the top 20 per cent (one-fifth) of the population owned 63.6 per cent (practically two-thirds) of the

Table 10.3 *Distribution of wealth in Mbere, Kenya*

(1) Household groups	(2) Value of household assets, including livestock as % of total for all households	(3) Cumulative % of households	(4) Cumulative % of wealth
1st 10%	0.0	10	0.0
2nd 10%	0.3	20	0.3
3rd 10%	0.9	30	1.2
4th 10%	1.9	40	3.1
5th 10%	4.0	50	7.1
6th 10%	6.7	60	13.8
7th 10%	9.6	70	23.4
8th 10%	13.0	80	36.4
9th 10%	20.4	90	56.8
Top 10%	43.2	100	100
	100.0		

% of households with assets below the mean: 66.0

SOURCE: D. Hunt, loc. cit., p. 20

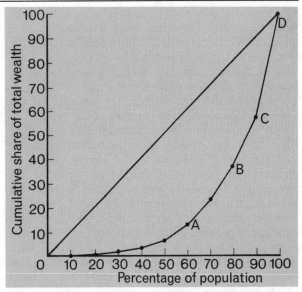

Figure 10.2 *A Lorenz curve for the distribution of wealth in Mbere, Kenya (SOURCE: D. Hunt, loc. cit.).*

wealth. The cumulative figures are given in columns (3) and (4), which show also that the lowest 50 per cent (half the population) owned only 7 per cent of the wealth, and the lowest 70 per cent only 23 per cent of the wealth. The cumulative figures are plotted in Figure 10.2 to give a *Lorenz curve*. Lorenz curves are used to give a visual impression of how even or uneven a distribution is. Thus if wealth here were distributed completely equally, 10 per cent of the population would own 10 per cent of the wealth, 50 per cent of the population 50 per cent of the wealth, and so on. If we plot the cumulative proportion of wealth against the cumulative proportion of the po-

Table 10.4 *Distribution of small-scale farms by size in selected districts of Kenya, 1969*

District	% of farms with less than 2 acres	% of acreage in farms with less than 2 acres	% of farms with 5 acres	% of acreage in farms with 5 acres or more	% of farms with 10 acres or more	% of acreage in farms with 10 acres or more
Kiambu	57	21	8.6	27.4	1.4	17
Murang'a	78	47	3.6	17	0.7	5.7
Nyeri	68	39	4	17	0.5	3.5
Kisumu	76	40	3.6	22	1	9
Siaya	62	15	16	66	8	50
Kisii	56	24	10	35	2	14
S. Nyanza	31	4.6	42	82	25	63
Kakamega	55	22	13	40	1.8	9
Bungoma	11	3.5	46	73	9	30
Taita	63	12	22	80	20	77
Embu	51	28	5.3	20	1.3	8

SOURCE: *Statistical Abstracts*

pulation, we should then obtain the straight line OD. With less evenly distributed wealth, we shall have a curve of the form OABCD. The more unequal the distribution, the more this will bulge out away from OD. In this case the two diverge considerably, indicating an unequal distribution. Point A indicates, for example, that the bottom 60 per cent of the population own about 14 per cent of the wealth.

Further evidence of rural differentiation is given in Table 10.4. This relates to the size distribution of *small* farms in selected districts of Kenya, that is, to variations in the size of small farms only: if the considerable large-farm and plantation sector were included, the full variation could be appreciated. However even here we see that in South Nyanza, for instance, 25 per cent of the farms (those of 10 acres or more) accounted for 63 per cent of the small farm acreage; in Bungoma District 9 per cent of the farms accounted for 30 per cent of the acreage; and in Taita 20 per cent of the farms accounted for nearly 80 per cent of the acreage. At the same time, at the bottom end, in Taita 63 per cent of the farms shared only 12 per cent of the acreage; in Kiambu 57 per cent shared 21 per cent of the acreage: and in Siaya District 62 per cent of the farms shared just 15 per cent of the acreage.

Even in a country aiming at an egalitarian socialist society like Tanzania, although the vast mass of households belong to smallholders, there is significant differentiation among them. In Lushoto, two-thirds of the land was reported in 1968 as being owned by one-third of the families.[11] The coffee-growers in Kilimanjaro are by no means a homogeneous group: holdings were said in 1961 to range from 1 to 9 acres.[12] In one Tukuyu village in Southern Tanzania one rich farmer owned as much acreage as that owned by 44 per cent of the poorest families taken together.[13] At Ibala, nearby in Rungwe, looking at income obtained from the main cash crop, pyrethrum, over a one-and-a-half year period, 75 per cent of the farmers obtained only about 40 per cent of the income, and the richest 9 per cent of farmers secured 27 per cent of the income approximately.[14]

Taking next a Ugandan example, a German researcher, Volker Weyel investigating landownership in Nyakmengo, Ruzhumbura,[15] in North Kigezi District of south-west Uganda, decided that five 'classes' could be discerned, based on the number of acres owned, as in Table 10.5, corresponding to a well-known classification by Professor Dumont,[16] and concluded that 'class differentiation was more manifest than just emergent'. Here again one-fifth of the landowners owned more than half the land in private ownership, while the poorest 10 per cent of 'landowners' held less than 1 per cent of the total, and the poorest 20 per cent held less than 3 per cent. There was thus a large percentage of virtually landless people, which Weyel described as a 'rural semi-proletariat' who, having lost the means of maintaining their families on independent holdings, would be bound to look for employment with more fortunate farmers, as 'landless labourers'. The group of farmers with 20–50 acres were described as 'kulaks', meaning larger, commercialized farmers, using their farms as commercial enterprises, hiring labour and selling a substantial part of their output. These 'kulaks' owned holdings of 2–4½ times the size of the average farm holding in the area of 11.5 acres. However, larger still, and according to Weyel meriting the title of 'landed proprietor' (by comparison with the rural proletariat), were owners of over 50 acres, including one holding of 70 acres. The figures indicate not only the emergence of 'kulaks' but, in an overpopulated area with serious land pressure, the appearance of a landless class of labourers seeking work with larger farmers.

There is, therefore, considerable *relative* inequality within rural areas in Eastern African countries. How serious a problem, if at all, is this? Many economists

Table 10.5   *Rural differentiation in Kigezi District, Uganda*

Class	No. of acres owned	No. of households	Percentage of total households
Rural semi-proletariat	under 2	60	12.0
Bakopi	2 and under 8	191	38.2
Peasants	8 and under 20	158	31.6
Kulaks	20 and under 50	85	17.0
Landed proprietors	50 and over	6	1.2
Average size of holding: 11.5 acres		500	100.0

SOURCE: Volker Weyel, loc. cit.

argue that it is not serious at all, that it is inevitable and that it may in fact be a sign of progress. The emergence of business-minded farmers is part of the commercialization of agriculture, considered necessary for development. The rise of 'kulaks' represents the development of an entrepreneurial class. Inequality of income will lead to an increase in the level of saving, leading on to more investment and growth. An argument that we have already examined is that there are economies of scale in farming, so that efficient output requires larger farms. Further, increased efficiency and productivity require richer farmers who can afford the additional inputs required, or who can save up to buy them. At the same time, the existence of larger farmers is due to their superior efficiency, being the result of their greater responsiveness to economic opportunity, and is thus to a large extent inevitable. It is argued, also, that the superior farm holdings and the success of the kulak group will have a demonstration effect on others who will wish to emulate them. Finally, and more generally, it is said that we 'must first create wealth, and then distribute it': that inequality may increase during the initial process of growth but that this will diminish once a degree of transformation into a modern economy has been achieved.

Other economists dispute these arguments. It is argued that in developing countries, with relatively small industrial sectors, the amount of land possessed by an individual determines the level of earnings, and that lack of access to land can mean extreme poverty: hence an inegalitarian distribution of land-holding means much more than simply an unfair distribution of welfare. Secondly, and related to this, large land-holdings reduce employment opportunities compared to smallholdings, which absorb larger numbers of self-employed farmers on the land. It is also disputed whether larger holdings are necessarily more efficient from an economic point of view, if land is the scarce factor: the greater density of settlement on smallhold-ings may increase productivity *per acre*, since it implies more intensive cultivation. Finally, it is suggested that inequalities are more likely to be self-reinforcing than to diminish, as entrepreneurs or kulaks will progressively increase their economic power by buying up more land (increasing the numbers of landless) and by accumulating capital with which they can hire more workers. Kulaks and large land owners will also be able to widen their political influence in order to make their position more secure, and the class structure will become established.

These are difficult questions, on which it is not easy to come to a firm conclusion. We can say, however, that the development of the agricultural sector involves major issues of equity and efficiency, affecting the whole economy.

Land tenure and land reform in Eastern Africa

Underlying agricultural production in any given area is a system of *land tenure*. A land tenure system can be said to refer to the system of rights regarding land ownership *or* use of land, including for instance arrangements governing the relationship between landlords and tenants. *Land reform* refers to a deliberate change in the system of land tenure involving *either* (a) a redistribution of land-ownership, particularly the break-up or state/cooperative take-over of large estates; *or* (b) a change in the legal and contractual arrangements affecting the land, which could be aimed at any of the following:

(i) the level of rents paid to landlords or the manner of their assessment;

(ii) security of tenure, which could relate *either* to a change in the powers of landlords to evict tenants through, say, the granting of longer leases, *or* to a change from communal to individualized rights over land;

(iii) the right to sell land, which is different from the right to use it;

(iv) consolidation of small, scattered plots into single, larger plots.

The land tenure position in tropical Africa may be said to have three distinctive features compared to that in other continents.

(1) The distribution of land is comparatively egalitarian. Although there *is* a degree of rural stratification, which may be increasing in some areas, as we saw in the last section, there are very few huge landowners as there are in Asia and especially Latin America.

(2) There is generally speaking no landlord class, although a classical alliance of landlords and the ruling class did exist in Ethiopia up to the 1974–5 land reforms. Some localized situations do exist where 'feudal' land-ownership situations exist, in the former Buganda Province of Uganda for example, and the 'nyarubanja' system remaining in the Bukoba District of Tanzania. The position contrasts with that in Asian countries where landlords own much of the land, farmed by share-croppers and tenants in small independent operating units, in what has been called the 'rent collection system' of Asian peasant agriculture.[17]

(3) Customary land tenure is widespread. Ownership of the land is vested in the community or tribe. Although individual families have rights of use of parcels of land, they have no legal title to land, which cannot be sold or mortgaged. The situation in Africa again contrasts with that in Asia where, al-

though there are some areas of tribal lands and customary tenures, this is not the predominating and prevailing feature.

Land reform (changes in the land tenure system) in Africa may similarly be discussed under these three heads, namely, (1) redistribution of land-holdings; (2) abolition of established landlord/tenant relationships; and (3) individualization of communal land tenure.

(1) The main ways in which land has been redistributed have been (a) redistribution of land purchased from expatriates by independent farmers as individuals or as members of settlement schemes, principally in Kenya, (b) nationalization of former expatriate companies' estates and some individual expatriate family farms, principally in Tanzania; (c) nationalization, by confiscation without compensation, of land and other properties formerly owned by indigenous ruling groups; particularly the expropriation of land and other feudal rights possessed by the royal family and aristocracy of Ethiopia in 1974–5. Finally, a less obvious change of land rights is involved in the establishment of state farms and cooperative/settlement farming schemes on unused communal or Trust (state-owned) land.

(2) The problem of landlords in tropical Africa has been confined largely to Ethiopia. Before the nationalization of rural land in 1974–5 agricultural productivity was kept low by a complex and archaic system of land tenure which prevented the majority of peasants from owning their own farms or receiving adequate incentives for improvements. The effect of share-cropping on tenants' supply of labour effort and incentive to invest was analysed theoretically in Chapter 8. In many districts in Ethiopia the ruling feudal classes owned the majority of land which was farmed by tenants who lacked long-term security and frequently paid more than half their crop to landowners as rent or so-called taxes. Land tenure reform was therefore seen by many agricultural economists as a necessary precondition before extension services, credit facilities, and other incentives to greater productivity could be expected to become effective. In 1975 the new republican government proclaimed:

  (a) the annulment of all tenant debts;
  (b) nationalization of all rural land, and redistribution of holdings above a maximum of 10 hectares;
  (c) transfer of large-scale farms to the state;
  (d) establishment of peasant associations as a first step towards the eventual aim of group farming by producer cooperatives within a planned socialist economy.

The long-term objective thus appears to be closer to Tanzania's socialist rural development programme than to the establishment of a private property-owning peasantry.

(3) Communal land tenure has frequently been criticized by economists who advocate instead the individualization of tenure. The latter is said (a) to offer security of tenure, considered necessary to provide incentives for investment and improvement; (b) to facilitate the development of a market in land; (c) to permit the use of land as collateral for loans; and (d) to be related to the consolidation of small plots into convenient-sized farm units. A market in land is facilitated because the granting of land titles to individuals implies the *right of sale* as well as the right of use. A market in land is considered necessary for the development of competitive, capitalist agriculture which allows more efficient farmers, those who are capable of making the best use of the land, to buy out the less efficient. The more efficient farmers can also expand by buying up unused land. The ability to use land as security for loans, to be used for investment, is also considered to be important for the development of capitalist agriculture.

The *East Africa Royal Commission 1953–1955 Report*, on land and population, published in 1955, made a strong argument for furthering agricultural development through the granting of individual freehold title to land. Following the security offered by such land titles, the Commission argued, 'new genius would be released'. It was further argued that 'to the extent that barriers to free land exchange are not removed, the prosperity of the peoples of East Africa will be retarded'. The arguments for individual titles and encouragements of a land market were echoed six years later in the World Bank report of 1961, *The Economic Development of Uganda*, which stated (pp. 188–9) that:

land need should be the criterion for land rights and the market should be the arbiter of those rights. However, if there is to be a market for land, there will have to be individualization of title and tenure and this will require a survey, adjudication of rights and registration of title.

After adjudication and issue of titles:

Land would have a market value determined by its productive capacity in a market-oriented society. Land would thus be used in line with market forces, rather than being the pivotal factor in providing subsistence or near subsistence in a narrowly based economy. (p. 190)

In fact the differences which are considered to exist between customary and individual land tenure are not as great as often supposed, and the advantages of conversion to individual land titles less great also.[18] In addition customary tenure does avoid a number of disadvantages which may spring from individualized tenure:

(a) Legal ownership may be unnecessary if an individual's right to *use* the land is unchallenged. Issue of formal land title would then scarcely offer additional incentive. Thus in large parts of Africa lack of titles to land has in no way prevented producers from planting tree crops, which represent investments with very lengthy gestation periods: a coffee tree, for instance, takes four or five years before yielding its first crop.

Some evidence of this is available from Uganda. Following acceptance by the Uganda Protectorate Government of the main land tenure proposals in the Royal Commission Report, pilot land adjudication schemes were instituted, from 1958, in Kigezi and Ankole. However the Commissioner of Lands and Surveys in Uganda reported that adjudication and granting of title 'had been followed by no perceptible agricultural development, as far as members of his department could judge', and that they 'had not led to the release and encouragement of new genius and to new experiment'. Moreover in the Ruzhumbura pilot scheme in Kigezi, where 6,400 plots had been demarcated and surveyed by April 1968, only 28 per cent of the titles had been taken up and paid for.

(b) The right of sale has its dangers where opportunities for employment outside agriculture are limited, so that for many, land offers the only means of livelihood. A communal system offers *some* guarantee of access to land, and a means of livelihood for all. It should be noted that if land is not scarce, a market in land would be pointless. If land is scarce, an increase in the land-holdings of some at the expense of others will force some to seek employment as wage labourers or else become unemployed.

(c) Individualization of tenure does not in fact guarantee full use of the land. Under this system abandoned land would no longer revert to the community for reallocation, but could be hoarded. Thus in Uganda, where in the past large holdings of *mailo* land with individual titles were created, large tracts of good arable land have been left undeveloped. More significant is the Latin American example where the estates of large landowners (the 'latifundia') have been under-utilized at the same time as there has been serious overcrowding among smallholders occupying the 'minifundia'.

(d) Land titles will not be effective as collateral for securing loans unless it is possible for creditors actually to take possession of the land in the event of failure to repay: but it would in fact be politically and practically difficult for a commercial bank, say, to do this. If it *were* possible, there would be an obvious danger of substantial numbers of smallholders losing their plots. In any case the best security and guarantee of repayment occurs when the farmer's crop is sold through a cooperative or statutory marketing authority which can deduct instalments from the annual proceeds due to the farmer. Thus loans to smallholders are better made through such a cooperative organization rather than through a bank.

(e) Finally it should be pointed out that in the pastoral areas the case may be quite different. Whereas in arable areas individual rights of *use* exist, in pastoral areas there are generally only communal rights of use. In arable areas also it is necessary to consider how individualization of tenure would affect grazing rights.

Having said this there may be advantages in the issue of individual land titles (a) as an adjunct to consolidation and rationalization of small plots; (b) to safeguard the position of the local community if land has become short; (c) to clarify the position for passing land on to heirs; and (d) to settle or avoid demarcation disputes. All of these things only become important once land has become scarce. Where land is still plentiful, the process of survey and issue of legal title is likely to impose considerable cost without any necessary benefit.

In Eastern Africa policies for the individualization of land tenure have been carried furthest in Kenya where spectacular increases in agricultural production were said to have followed on land reform, including consolidation as well as the issue of land titles, in Kikuyuland. The difficulty here is to distinguish between the effects of changes in tenure and a whole package of measures which went along with them, including agricultural extension and credit and particularly the removal of previous legal prohibitions on the cultivation by Africans of high-value cash crops, as noted in the previous chapter.

'Transformation' versus 'improvement' strategies for agricultural development

A distinction is frequently made between the 'transformation' and the 'improvement' strategies for agricultural development. The improvement approach relies heavily on agricultural extension, the provision of technical and economic advice to the farmer, supplemented by efforts to improve the existing situation by removing specific bottlenecks, perhaps by the construction of feeder roads, or improvements in marketing facilities, or the provision of credit. The transformation approach aims at a much more drastic reshaping of the conditions of agricultural production, and may involve the introduction of capital equipment, particularly tractors, the extension of the public sector into agriculture, through large-scale state farms, the organization of major resettlement schemes involving the movement of population, or the establishment of cooperative forms of production, either among new settlers or within existing villages.

The anxiety of governments and development agencies to make more rapid progress away from underdevelopment has naturally inclined them towards the transformation approach. 'Transformation' is one of the many terms in the vocabulary of development economists, like 'take-off' and 'balanced growth', which appear desirable almost by definition. In fact, as we shall see presently, mechanization has generally not proved economic in African agriculture, and needs to be applied judiciously; state farms have often proved to be expensive ventures or even outright failures; and settlement schemes have been beset with problems. As a result a more cautious and selective approach to transformation schemes has been adopted in Africa in recent years. At the same time, as we saw in our discussion of Uganda, quite rapid rates of growth have been possible with simple peasant cultivation of cash crops, leading to what amounts to the transformation of previously subsistence economies. This suggests the need 'to make haste slowly' and to undertake large-scale schemes when these have been worked out very carefully, and conditions appear especially favourable. We examine various kinds of transformation scheme presently, and turn first to a discussion of agricultural extension, under the 'improvement' approach.

Approaches to agricultural extension

Extension services include the education of farmers and the offer of advice to farmers regarding agricultural methods; the communication of research results and news regarding innovations, such as the discovery of new crop varieties; and, possibly, the supply of free or subsidized inputs such as new seeds, fertilizers, or insecticides. This last is included because extension advice is not infrequently given along with a 'package' of inputs which are required for the implementation of the improvement proposed. However, as Makings has said,[19] 'it is an important attribute of extension that it provides a means of increasing production very largely without quantitative change in the basic factors of land, labour and capital'. The term 'extension' implies that assistance is extended to individuals or groups at their farms, or in the areas in which they farm. Thus extension may comprise farm visits by agricultural assistants, village meetings, courses at nearby farm institutes or farmers' training centres, or agricultural propaganda in magazines or by the radio, which may reach the farmer in his own location.

The important questions that may be asked about agricultural extension are: how good are the economic returns derived from expenditure on extension compared to other forms of social or development expenditure? How can extension best be organized to maximize these returns? To whom should extension be directed? And what extension *strategy* should be adopted?

Even if the offer of extension advice is not accompanied by inputs, extension is not costless: the apparatus of agricultural officers and assistants, through which extension advice is passed, involves heavy expenditure on salaries and other items, particularly in relation to the incomes of the farmers receiving the advice. And since the service is free, it involves a subsidy to the farmer. Such expenditures have a high opportunity cost, and it is essential that they should bring concrete economic returns if they are to justify themselves. The effects of extension are, however, either immeasurable or difficult to measure with any accuracy, although some attempts have been made to apply cost-benefit analysis to extension programmes in Africa. Nevertheless there are plenty of separate pieces of evidence to show that the effectiveness of extension is highly variable. Some of the problems have been:

(1) Agricultural assistants, who frequently lack even a bicycle for transport, fail to visit many farmers. Partly as a matter of policy, but also for reasons of convenience, they frequently pay a disproportionate number of visits to the larger and better-known farmers. Such farmers are manageable in number, too influential, perhaps, to be ignored, and much more easy to demonstrate positive results with.

(2) The advice being offered may be either (a) out-of-date; (b) not applicable to the particular locality (blanket recommendations regarding cultivation techniques are often made for a large region or the entire country, whereas variable ecological conditions would require differences in practice in different areas); (c) more applicable to government research stations and demonstration farms than to smallholders with limited land, capital, and family labour;[20] or (d) just wrong. For example, in Uganda, several commentators have noted that cotton production was being encouraged in the 1960s and 1970s even in areas where far better returns to labour were obtainable from other crops like coffee and bananas.[21] In this last case, returns from extension will actually be negative!

Where returns from extension may be very high, however, is where it really has something valuable to offer, such as information regarding cultivation methods for a new cash crop which large numbers of farmers are anxious to take up. Here a quite modest input of time may have important and continuing effects on farm earnings.

The most debated aspect of extension policy, however, relates to its focus: should it focus on individual farmers or groups of farmers and, a related question, should it focus on so-called 'progressive' farmers or on the mass of average farmers or even the poorest part of the farming community?

The strategy of concentrating on individual, progressive or 'master' farmers was widely adopted in British colonial territories in the 1950s and is still employed in a number of countries, but has come in for heavy criticism in recent years. In Uganda the policy is described as being 'officially discredited'.[22] Malawi, however, puts strong emphasis on the individual farmer through its 'Achikumbe' (progressive farmers) programme whereby smallholders who persistently achieve certain high standards of husbandry and market orientation receive an Achikumbe certificate signed by the President, and other more tangible benefits such as priority in marketing of crops through the state Agricultural Development and Marketing Corporation (ADMARC) and permission to take certain crops such as tobacco straight to the auction floor like the estates, rather than having to sell to ADMARC at prices perhaps only a quarter or one-third of the auction price.[23]

The most important argument for concentrating on the more progressive farmers is that, assuming a general difficulty in securing response from the mass of farmers, adoption of improvements by the more progressive farmers scattered throughout the country will have a 'demonstration effect' on other farmers which may eventually spread through the farming community. This is supported, secondly, by the fact that funds may be inadequate to permit the extension effort to be spread more widely without loss of effectiveness. The idea that extension effort had to be highly concentrated in order to make a significant impact was, for instance, behind the Buganda 'Saturation Extension Project' conducted in Uganda. Thirdly, if the aim is to increase output rapidly, the greatest immediate returns to expenditure on extension, at lowest cost, will be obtained by concentrating on the most responsive farmers. By the same argument, fourthly, returns to extension will be greatest if most attention is paid to farmers in the high-potential areas. A further point is that the rich, more progressive farmers will be more likely to repay loans made to them to permit improvements, allowing such funds to become available to other farmers. Finally, as a more general consideration in Malawi, 'it appears that lack of entrepreneurs is considered a key constraint and thus individuals thought to have potential entrepreneurial ability are encouraged to set up businesses and in the agricultural sector great encouragement is given to individual farmers who have proved themselves responsive to economic opportunities.'[24] There is thus a short-run objective of increasing output quickly, and a long-term objective

of establishing a 'dynamic forward-looking entrepreneurial class' that will be beneficial for the economy in the longer run.

The first criticism which may be made of these arguments is that the 'demonstration effect', or spread effect, may not operate because the progressive farmer is not typical of the community and not operating under the same conditions as most farmers. Other farmers may not be *able* to copy an innovation by a progressive farmer, either because the innovation is relatively sophisticated or, especially, because it requires additional capital or other inputs to which they do not have access; or *unwilling* to copy the progressive farmer either because, considering him to be in a different category, they do not identify themselves with him or because they cannot afford to take the same *risks* as he can. The traditional farmer's resistance to change may be quite rational if he and his family obtain only a minimum subsistence food supply and little cash income, such that failure in experimentation may be disastrous. This suggests a need not only to gear extension to average farmers, but also to select *types* of innovation which do not require much more capital or entail greatly increased risk, as, for instance, the introduction of improved seed.

This also affects the claim of the 'progressive farmer' approach to greater economic efficiency, since the latter must depend on two things, success in *introducing* innovations and improved practices, and success in promoting the spread or *diffusion* of such innovations. While individual progressive farmers may be induced to increase output rapidly, the effect on aggregate output may not be large, since their numbers are relatively small, if the demonstration effect on other farmers is limited. Differences in efficiency may also arise because economies of scale exist in marketing, so expansion of transport or marketing facilities is only worthwhile if the large mass of farmers is able to increase output. Economies of scale may also exist because of the dangers of spread of pests and disease: thus the introduction of grade cattle into African smallholdings in Central Kenya only proved successful after they were taken up by a larger proportion of the farmers, since it was then in the interest of all to check the diseases to which grade cattle are so prone.

While returns to extension may be highest in the high-potential areas, such as the Central Highlands of Kenya, this need not mean a progressive farmer strategy, since even in such areas (perhaps more so) there is a wide gap between the most progressive (and rich) farmers and the majority.

While the Malawian policy hoped to create 'entrepreneurs', the approach has been explicitly rejected in Tanzania because it tends 'to promote capitalism and individualism'.[25] In addition there is the basic objection that the 'master farmer' approach accentuates or creates inequality, and subsidizes richer farmers. Moreover it does not deal directly with the problem of extreme poverty and malnutrition, which is serious in many African countries, this possibly requiring an emphasis not even on the average farmer but on the poorest segment of the farming community and on the types of innovation which can help it most.

The alternative approach to that focusing on the progressive farmer may combine two elements, (a) communicating with groups of farmers, rather than individuals, and (b) gearing extension advice and the promotion of innovations to the average or poorer farmer. Experiments with various approaches of this type were conducted under Kenya's Special Rural Development Programme in the early 1970s. In Migori, in south-west Kenya, an experiment in the promotion of soya bean production compared a control group of 12 individual farmers, given traditional extension assistance, with eight groups of 10 or 11 farmers (94 farmers in all). Although the ratio of extension officers to farmers in the control group was three times as high, 40 per cent (5 out of 12 farmers) failed with their soya bean crop, compared to none within the eight groups, while only 17 per cent (2 out of 12) secured yields of over 7 bags per hectare, compared to 50 per cent for the groups.[26] The feature of the groups was that they included *all* the farmers at a particular location and that farmers were allowed considerable freedom in selecting their groups.

In Tanzania the settlement of scattered population into 'ujamaa' villages, with elected village committees, was aimed in part at facilitating extension by making it easier to reach all farmers and to engage the support of the entire village in attempts to raise productivity. Another aspect of social organization in Tanzania which is potentially helpful to extension is the system of 'ten-cell leaders', spokesmen elected for each group of ten households in the country. The help of ten-cell leaders may be enlisted in securing the adoption of agricultural improvements, as well as in other aspects of the government's social policy.

Thus very different policies may be pursued in agricultural extension. Experimentation continues in finding the best approach, as well as increasing the efficiency of the service.

The economics of mechanization[27]

The simple nature of African agriculture, with its shifting cultivation and primitive hand tools, requiring hours of backbreaking labour, has frequently been described as 'backward' and 'inefficient'. Both colonial and independent administrations have from time to time attempted to transform the traditional agricultural system by the introduction of mechanization, specifically of tractors for ploughing. As we shall see presently, the history of these attempts has been quite dismal. It is clear that the success of mechanization depends on a number of complicated factors and is assured only if 'the conditions are right'. It is because governments have attempted or encouraged mechanization *regardless* of these conditions, and without sufficient analysis of the conditions of each particular case, that failure has been so frequent. Let us examine, therefore, the factors which will determine whether or not mechanization can be successful or 'economic'.

Conditions affecting the profitability of mechanization

(1) A precondition of mechanization is that the physical conditions should permit the use of tractors. If the ground is excessively hard, stony or under thick bush as in many parts of Africa, tractors may not be efficient or their use may involve costly breakages in ploughing, let alone clearing bush.[28] In hilly areas tractors will be difficult to use. The type of crop is important. Tree crops do not permit the use of tractors directly. On the other hand crops like wheat produced under extensive cultivation on open plains on which tractors can secure long runs are particularly favourable. Given suitable physical conditions, whether the purchase or hire of a tractor is worthwhile will depend on its cost compared to the benefit derived from it, which may be *either* in terms of increased output *or* in terms of reduced costs of other factors of production, in particular labour.

(2) Mechanization can increase output *either* by increasing yields (output per acre) *or* by increasing the number of acres cultivated. Yields may be increased either by better seed-bed preparation (especially where the crop requires good planting or where the soils are very heavy, making hand-planting difficult and inefficient) or by better timing of operations. Because hand-planting is slower, it may not be possible to seed the entire acreage at the best time. Thus in the case of cotton growing in Uganda it is said that tractor-ploughing, by making it possible to plant in early May instead of early June, when hand-digging is used, will increase yields by 25 per cent: however it is uncertain how far *in general* mechanization can by itself, without improved seeds, extra fertilizer and the like which are often employed at the same time, increase yields.[29]

Acreage can be increased, again, because hand-digging is very slow compared to a tractor. For this reason, where the number of family or hired workers is limited, labour may be a constraint on the number of acres which can be planted. We should point out here that labour demands in farming are not constant during the year: most of the work on a crop will come at certain times, planting and harvesting periods especially, with weeding or spraying to be done at other times. Although a suitable combination of crops can help to even out labour requirements over the year to some extent, any profitable combination is likely to involve 'peak' labour demands at particular times of the year, when labour becomes a bottleneck or limiting factor restricting the expansion of output. In northern Ghana, for example, the labour constraint arises principally during the early part of the single rainy season when maximum physical activity to plant and weed, unfortunately, coincides with the worst of the 'hungry gap' in family food stocks when nutrition is at its lowest. This shortage of food, 'human fuel' for manual effort, restricts the expansion in acreage and hence food supply. By easing this constraint, mechanization can permit acreage to be increased. Against this it will, of course, not be effective to reduce labour demands at planting time by the use of a tractor if the *main* labour peak is at harvest time, for which a tractor is of no service: acreage would still not expand, because of harvest labour shortage.

Thus mechanization may, in principle, increase output either by increasing yields or by increasing the number of acres cultivated, or both. Whether mechanization is worthwhile, however, depends on the *value* of this increased output. An increase in the output of a *low-priced* crop may be insufficient to cover the extra costs of ploughing by tractor. Thus many African cooperative tractor schemes have been based on low-value food crops, rather than cash crops, and have not been financially successful for this reason. A basic reason behind the most spectacular failure of an agricultural development scheme, the so-called 'Groundnut Scheme' in Tanganyika, in the immediate post-war period, was that it was located in marginal lands, where output per acre ploughed was certain not to be very high, and relied on groundnuts, a not particularly remunerative crop.

It should be mentioned here that it is not necessary for tractorization to be applied to a high-priced cash crop *directly*. If a basic subsistence food crop is absorbing a large proportion of total farm labour, or if its labour demands at a particular time of year clash with those of a cash crop, the use of a tractor on the food crop could release labour to work on the cash crop. It is necessary to look at the impact of mechanization on the entire farm system and combination of crops.

(3) Apart from producing more output, mechanization could save costs by producing the *same* output more efficiently, using a superior 'capital-intensive' technique: that is, by substituting capital for labour. Here we need to compare costs using the capital-intensive method with those using the labour-intensive method. This will depend entirely on the real cost or *opportunity-cost* (we call this the 'shadow price' of labour in Chapter 15). If there is a labour surplus, with a great deal of unemployed or under-employed labour, then the real cost of labour will be low. In this case even if the mechanized method is *technically* more efficient, doing the job much more quickly and saving a large number of man-hours, it may not be *economically* efficient or worthwhile: although traditional hand-digging uses a large amount of labour, this labour may otherwise be left idle. This difference between economic efficiency and technical efficiency is examined in detail in Chapter 13. If the labour released by mechanization is, on the other hand, peak labour which can be put to work on high-priced cash crops, then the opportunity-cost of labour will be high, and the probability of the capital-intensive method being economic will be greater.

We can therefore make a general statement about the kinds of situations and economies in which mechanization is likely to be successful or unsuccessful, and why. There are two especially favourable conditions for success: *labour should be scarce* and, in order that mechanization can lead to increased acreage and output, *land should be plentiful*. Mechanization should therefore be considered especially in labour-scarce/land-abundant economies. In contrast, in land-scarce economies, returns to mechanization will be less because it will be difficult to increase the size of farms.

(4) Finally, we come to the cost of the tractor itself. We have already noted that in assessing the cost of labour used up by a labour-intensive method we need to estimate the real scarcity value or opportunity-cost of labour. In assessing the cost of machinery we should take account the fact that such machinery is often imported, in developing countries. Unlike a labour-intensive method, therefore, this may use scarce foreign exchange: hence its cost will depend on the scarcity value attached to foreign exchange.

Apart from this factor, the costs of motorized methods may be divided into overhead costs, maintenance, and running costs. As we shall see presently, even if running costs are not high, tractors may not pay because overhead or fixed costs are too high. In Africa, and in developing countries elsewhere, maintenance costs have often been a problem: because of poor management and lack of experience with tractors and other mechanical equipment, these have not been properly maintained, so that they have become inefficient or unusable, at enormous cost. And rough usage by inexperienced drivers has frequently resulted in expensive breakages.

Overheads, or fixed costs, are those which do not vary with the level of output: in this case with the number of acres ploughed. To bring these (average fixed costs) down, it is necessary to 'spread' the overheads over a large enough output. It will not pay to buy a tractor to plough a three-acre farm, as the cost of the tractor would be large in relation to the number of acres ploughed. Figure 10.3 represents a hypothetical case illustrating this point. Suppose the purchase price of a tractor (fixed cost) is $3,000 and that ploughing costs an additional $40 per hectare (variable costs). The sum of these, total costs, is given in Figure 10.3 (a) by the line TC intersecting the y-axis at a level of $3,000 (indicating that when no hectares are ploughed costs are $3,000) and with a constant slope (such that total costs increase steadily at a rate of $40 per hectare). Let us assume also that each hectare ploughed by tractor increases net revenue by $160, partly by increasing output and partly by saving labour costs, net revenue here excluding the costs associated with the tractor. Figure 10.3 (a) is an example of what is known as a *break-even chart*. Such a chart is always drawn under the sim- plifying assumption of constant variable costs, as in this case. This tells us that at the 'break-even point' B, corresponding to 25 hectares, the extra revenues from mechanization just balance the extra costs: beyond 25 hectares mechanization becomes increasingly worthwhile, but *below* 25 *hectares mechanization does not pay.*

The reason for this is emphasized in Figure 10.3(b). Average costs AC fall steadily, mainly because the purchase price of the tractor, $3,000, is spread over a larger number of hectares. Thus when 5 hectares are ploughed total costs are $3,000 plus variable costs of $200, giving average costs of $640 per hectare, which fall to only $100 when 50 hectares are ploughed (at a total cost of $3,000 + (50 × 40). This is an example of technical *economies of scale*, which we discuss more fully in Chapter 16.

A realistic example of costs under hand labour and mechanization, relating to coffee farms in Uganda in the 1950s, is given in Figure 10.4. Line A gives average costs under hand labour (here the cost per acre is the same no matter how many acres are prepared). Line B shows the cost of ploughing plots of different sizes by standard tractor and harrow (costing shs 17,400), and line C the cost of ploughing with a small tractor and harrow (costing shs 12,000). The last two exhibit the same shape as the average cost curve in Figure 10.3(b). The diagram indicates that hand labour is the cheapest method for plots of up to 5 acres. Subsequently the small tractor and harrow is cheaper up to at least 40 acres, when the standard tractor becomes worthwhile. (Detailed assumptions underlying the estimates are given in Joy, op. cit.)

One way of overcoming the disadvantage of small size of plot and obtaining the economies of scale to be derived from mechanization is to combine plots

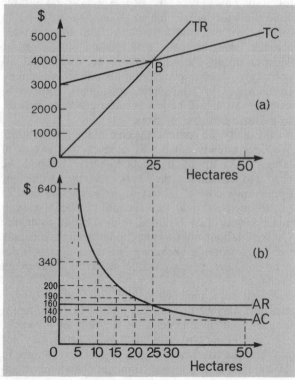

Figure 10.3 *Costs and ervenues associated with mechanization: (a) a break-even chart; and (b) effect of spreading overhead costs.*

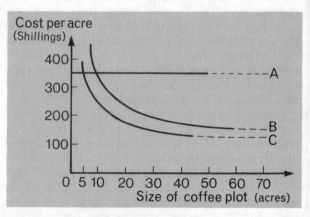

Figure 10.4 *Comparative costs of using hand labour and field machinery: a Ugandan example (SOURCE: L. Joy (ed.), Symposium on Mechanical Cultivation in Uganda, Kampala, 1960).*

and operate them collectively, on socialist lines: this underlies many of the socialist schemes which have been attempted. Another way is to encourage large landowners within a capitalist framework or to operate large state farms within a socialist economy. Tractors can also be shared, however, among smallholders: either one farmer who has a tractor can sell tractor services to his neighbours, or a businessman can establish a commercial tractor hire service; or more commonly in Africa the *government* can operate tractor hire services, so that each tractor can be fully utilized. In practice, the under-utilization of tractors and other equipment, with tractors idle for long periods at time, has been a major source of failure among transformation schemes based on mechanization, and of weakness in tractor hire services, as we shall see presently.

Mechanization and employment

The decision of a government to encourage or discourage mechanization may not be based entirely on costs and revenues, that is, on profitability. If there is widespread unemployment or underemployment in the country, one of the goals of government may be to increase employment as well as increasing incomes: particularly if population growth is expected to aggravate the position in the future. But mechanization may displace labour and *increase* the amount of unemployment. In this situation labour used up should not be considered as a cost, but as a *benefit* from labour-intensive methods, just as increased value of output is a benefit of mechanized methods.

Quite a different question is whether mechanization *does* displace labour. In many cases mechanization will be employment-*creating*, rather than employment-*destroying*. This is possible because farming consists of several operations—planting, weeding, harvesting etc.—and usually covers a number of crops. Thus the use of machinery to eliminate a labour peak in, say, planting could permit increased acreage, requiring more labour; or increased yields could require more labour for harvesting; or the release of labour at planting time for other crops could expand the demand for labour at weeding times or harvest times for these other crops, increasing labour demands for the year taken as a whole. Increased output may also increase employment in marketing. To take an example of cotton farming in the Lango District of Uganda, it was suggested in 1966 that mechanization there had a beneficial effect on employment in that labour normally used on cotton was released to cultivate more millet, bringing more employment and cash from beer-brewing, which cash could be used in part to hire more labour to harvest an increased cotton crop.[30]

The East African experience of mechanization

Some successful applications of mechanized farming outside the large estates can be mentioned, but as noted above, attempts at introducing tractors within the small-farm sector in East Africa have been singularly unsuccessful.

In Uganda an early scheme which ran in South Busoga from 1950 to 1954 was based on housing tractors in Central Government farms surrounded by tenant smallholdings. Though this reached an area of 750 acres, it was abandoned in 1954 as uneconomic, the returns in the area apparently being insufficient to cover the fixed costs of the tractors. A large-scale mechanized farming scheme to open up new land for tenant farmers, run by the Bunyoro Agricultural Co. and sponsored jointly by the government and some commercial firms was abandoned in 1956, two years after inception. Though social factors affecting the success of the scheme had not been properly considered, the main factor was apparently that crop revenues were too low in comparison with the costs of mechanization.

Attempts at transformation through mechanization, however, despite these early failures, came in the 1960s, partly through the group farm programme, and partly through a major expansion of the government tractor hire service. The group farm programme under the Second Five Year Plan, 'Work for Progress' (1966–71), was for cooperative farming but with the primary aim of permitting economies of scale from mechanization to be reaped. Table 10.6 shows the expansion of the Uganda Tractor Hire Service from humble beginnings in 1948, together with a summary of the financial results.

This shows that right from the beginning the service was subsidized and a significant deficit on operations was being incurred. Nevertheless a major expansion was planned under the First Five Year Plan 1961/2–1965/6, this resulting first in a big jump in the number of tractors in 1964, when 200 new tractors arrived, and a steady increase subsequently. Further intensification was planned under the Second Plan, despite the increasing deficit, and 30 per cent of the total development expenditure on agriculture under the Plan (U£5.8 millions out of U£19.6 millions) was allocated to mechanization. With the failure of the group farming programme during the Plan period, tractors were switched to the Tractor Hire Service, further expanding it, along with imported tractors. As the deficit increased, imports of tractors were fairly quickly discontinued. By then, in 1966–7, the Hire Service made a loss of nearly half a million pounds on the operation of some 650 tractors.

We can observe that mechanization in Uganda

Table 10.6 *The expansion of the Uganda Government Tractor Hire Service and financial results*

Year	No. of tractors	Revenue (U£×1,000)	Expenditure (U£×1,000)	Deficit (U£×1,000)	Years
1948	1				
		3.5	19.9	16.4	1947–53
1950	17				
1953	45				
		15.2	34.4	19.1	1954–63
1963	44				
		73.0	130.6	57.6	1963–4
1964	245				
		101.4	305.9	204.3	1964–5
1965	341				
		150.3	470.9	320.6	1965–6
1966	489				
		190.0	675.0	485.0	1966–7
1967	651				

SOURCE: E. S. Clayton, loc. cit.

was not applied selectively. It continued to be pressed by government despite persistently unfavourable results within smallholder agriculture. It was in fact uneconomic without subsidy. It was used mainly by a minority of richer farmers. It was not taken up in imitation by other farmers impressed with the financial benefits.

We have already mentioned mechanization in Tanzania under the Groundnut Scheme. During the 1950s a tractor hire service of a similar sort to that in Uganda proved a financial failure, more than half the total costs not being recovered. Nevertheless the First Five Year Plan 1964–9 adopted a transformation approach with a heavy emphasis on mechanization, to be introduced through the medium of cooperative village settlements. This programme failed for a variety of reasons, the fact that tractors were introduced without attention to the particular circumstances being an important one. The programme was modified in 1966 to de-emphasize the role of tractors. At the same time tractor hire services were greatly expanded under a scheme to purchase and distribute tractor services through the marketing cooperatives. In 1963–5, 673 tractors were distributed. Apart from the question of economics, the marketing unions, though competent to market the main cash crops, were not experienced in or suited to organizing technical services of this sort: of shs 18 millions loaned out, little more than one-third was repaid. Also in this Plan period 1964–9 mechanized block cultivation schemes, based on the same principles as the group farms in Uganda, were organized in the cotton-growing area of Sukumuland, below Lake Victoria. Here the 158 tractors still owned by the

Victoria Federation of Cooperative Unions were to be utilized by amalgamating cotton fields into optimum-sized 300-acre plots or 'blocks' suitable for tractor ploughing. The plan was to establish 150 such blocks, each to comprise 75 families holding four acres each. Fifty blocks were initiated, though with a lower average size of 153 acres, but the scheme was eventually abandoned as a financial failure. A number of factors were involved here, but indications are that tractors were clearly less economic than ox-ploughing. A much later estimate of comparative costs in Tanzania put the cost of ploughing by tractor as shs 40 an acre and that of ploughing by oxen at only shs 7 an acre, though ploughing by tractor was five times as quick.[31]

There had in fact been previous attempts at promoting the use of ox-ploughs in various parts of Tanzania, but particularly Sukumuland, where their introduction had permitted a considerable expansion of acreage under cotton. After the negative experiences with tractors just mentioned, the Second Five Year Plan stated that 'tractors and other expensive forms of mechanization will be introduced in carefully selected areas, after study has proved their viability'.[32] This statement could usefully be adopted by African countries in general as an appropriate basis for policy, if they resist political pressures to attempt to 'transform' agricultural methods overnight by inappropriate technology. Tanzania is now encouraging ox-plough cultivation, and has established training centres for this purpose. Kenya has a similar centre in Kisii. In Tanzania small farmers were estimated to have bought more than 8,000 ox-ploughs during 1967 and the numbers purchased annually were expected to have risen to 15,000 by 1974.[33]

Policy towards mechanization has always been more cautious and selective in Kenya, where there has been little emphasis on mechanization within the small-farm sector. This was despite extensive use of tractors within the large-farm sector (6,400 tractors in 1960 and 1,050 combine harvesters, dropping only slightly to 6,000 tractors and 780 harvesters in 1969). Under the 'Million Acre Scheme', whereby Africans were brought in as settlers on formerly expatriate-owned land, settlers were helped in their first year by mechanical land preparation, on a loan basis, after which large numbers of settlers continued to use tractor services on a hire basis. The fact that settlers here were taking over established farms, albeit now subdivided, previously under mechanization, appears to have been of considerable assistance, and a number of farms settled on this basis have carried on established methods of production. Mechanization has been successful in the wheat-growing areas, for reasons already mentioned. Another special case is mechanization in relation to irrigation schemes, particularly those at Mwea and Perkerra. The favourable factors at Mwea, in line with our general analysis, are first of all a substantial increase in yields bought about by the use of tractors, a relatively high (if protected) price for the product, rice, and relatively high annual operating hours, spreading overhead costs. This also provides a good example of employment-*creating* mechanization. Since rice cultivation includes several other stages, besides ploughing, which are highly labour-intensive, the additional production of rice due to mechanization requires more labour: thus as many as 2,800 persons per hectare were employed at Mwea.

Settlement schemes

There have been a wide range of settlement schemes throughout Africa, aimed at agricultural transformation on a larger or smaller scale. The basic feature of a settlement scheme is that it should involve the planned relocation of population, in other words, settlers. But there are many different types of scheme, and we may subdivide them:

(1) according to whether they concern arable farming or livestock. The latter usually relate to a quite different environment and involve different considerations. Many schemes in the pastoral areas have as a major objective the sedentarization of nomadic peoples. Commercial ranching schemes involving the transfer of settlers have also been attempted outside the pastoral areas, for instance in Uganda.

(2) according to whether they involve heavy infrastructural investment, as in the case of irrigation schemes and, in particular, whether mechanization and heavy equipment are employed.

(3) according to the type of settlers involved, particularly (a) whether they are farmers transferred from other rural areas suffering from overpopulation, (b) whether the scheme caters for some of the urban unemployed, or (c) whether it provides employment for school leavers.

(a) The purpose of the Kenya settlement schemes was to relieve population pressure in overcrowded African smallholder areas as well as to take the opportunity provided by the availability nearby of vacated or under-utilized land in the former 'White Highlands', a programme involving the transfer of population on a substantial scale. Under the Million Acre Scheme, launched in 1961, over a million acres of land were apportioned between 34,000 African households. The main constraint here was the administrative one of organizing a smooth transfer at a rapid rate, and the maintenance of efficient farming with high yields per acre after the switch from large-scale commercial farmers to small-scale peasant producers. The planned level of income was modest, about £25–70 per annum, and realistic in relation to the rest of the economy, unlike the West Nigerian schemes discussed below.

(b) In Tanzania some World Food Programme Assisted schemes, Tanu Youth League and Administration schemes in the 1960s were aimed at relieving urban unemployment. Here it was found that 'such urban elements have usually already rejected rural life and are the least likely material out of which to build pioneer rural settlements. On the other hand, the victims of overpopulation in rural areas, for example among the Chagga, the Nyakusa, and the Sukuma, often make the best settlers, for they must succeed, since they have nowhere else to go.'[34]

(c) One of the aims of the group farms established in Western Nigeria during the early 1960s was to find a livelihood for school leavers. It was hoped to emulate the success of the *moshavim* of Israel, individually owned farms with cooperative central services, but the possibility of doing this within a different social structure was not adequately considered. The cost of establishing one settler was planned at the fantastically high level of £4,000 (income per head in Nigeria then being around £25). By the end of 1966 some 1,200 settlers had been installed on 19 settlements at a cost of £7 million, equivalent to £4,000–5,000 per family.[35] The costs included generous allowances to settlers over a long period before tree crops matured, not to mention two years' training at a farm institute. Not surprisingly school leavers were found not to be motivated towards an arduous farming life, particularly after having been subsidized for so long. More success was achieved with school leavers in the Nyakashaka Scheme in Western

Uganda. Started in 1963, it aimed to transfer some 200 school leavers from the overpopulated district of Ankole to the neighbouring district of Bunyoro. Factors behind the success here were that the scheme was based around a high-priced cash crop; suitable tea land having first been identified, mechanization was not used, and excessive managerial overheads were avoided.

(4) according to the supervising agency. In particular we may distinguish here schemes supervised by agriculture corporations and those by large commercial companies. Thus in Tanzania the Tanganyika Agricultural Corporation, set up in 1953 to administer the three major development areas occupied by the defunct Groundnuts Scheme, started 9 small schemes for cattle, tobacco, and groundnuts before handing over to the Village Settlement Agency in 1964. Examples of company-assisted schemes are the various licensed-producer tobacco schemes set up in different African countries by the British and American Tobacco Company (BAT), the Mumias Sugar Development Scheme in Kenya, set up with the assistance of the Booker Group, and various outgrower tea schemes in Eastern Africa. Vital factors in the success of these kinds of schemes have been the foundation provided by a high-valued cash crop, the importance of technical supervision where quality is important, as in the case of tobacco, and the need for access to central processing facilities as in the case of tea and sugar.

(5) according to whether the scheme is a strongly supervised scheme or a cooperative one. Cooperative schemes are discussed more fully in a subsequent section. Schemes may, of course, combine some of the characteristics above, so that the mechanized block cotton cultivation schemes in Tanzania, to take an example, combined mechanical cultivation with a cooperative element.

A review of rural development schemes over the years in Tanzania shows the widest spectrum of types of scheme. The post-1945 history of agricultural schemes in Tanzania may be said to have consisted of the following sequence: (a) the Groundnut Scheme, a mammoth development corporation-sponsored transformation scheme based on mechanized, large-scale methods; (b) the residual Tanganyika Agricultural Corporation (TAC) schemes, 1953–64, comprising remnants of the old Groundnut scheme (together with commercially sponsored licensed-producer tobacco schemes); (c) schemes developed under the Village Settlement Agency, 1963–6; (d) schemes to resettle urban unemployed (the World Food Programme Assisted Schemes and some TANU Youth League and Administration schemes); (e) some earlier cooperative schemes, particularly the cotton block cultivation schemes, based on mechanization; and (f) the later cooperative or ujamaa village programme from 1967, which eschewed mechanization, leading on to (g) the compulsory villagization policy, dating from the start of 1974. The greatest contrast is between the TAC schemes, mainly before independence, and the mass ujamaa village movement. The former aimed at promoting 'a healthy, prosperous yeoman farmer class (i.e. progressive farmers), firmly established on the land, appreciative of its fruits, jealous of its inherent wealth, and dedicated to maintaining the family unit on it'.[36]

Ujamaa villages are discussed in a later section. The other schemes, and the experience with them, are summarized in Table 10.7. By and large the results, like those in most African countries, are depressing, and point to the difficulties inherent in sponsored agricultural development.

The Village Settlement Agency experience is worth somewhat closer examination. The Village Settlement Agency programme was set up in the early 1960s following the recommendation in the World Bank Report of 1961 of a transformation approach in agriculture, based on a pessimistic view of possibilities for agricultural improvement within the existing peasant farming areas. The aim was to transfer settlers to newly cleared areas and to make use of more modern methods of cultivation, including mechanization, than in the traditional farming areas. The VSA took up a very large percentage of the resources devoted to rural development during the country's First Five-Year Plan, 1964–9 ($13\frac{1}{2}$ per cent of the total development budget), proposing to settle about 500,000 people on 70 schemes, costing over £12 million. The expected cost of each scheme embracing 250 families was thus shs 3 million, or shs 12,000 per family. Each family was expected to earn revenue of shs 3,000, some 4 or 5 times the national average. To take an example, 'in June, 1965, one Pilot Scheme had four bulldozers, two tractors, a field car, seven lorries, a workshop and two stump pluckers to clear the site, seven tractors implements, a maize mill, water pump, land-rover and an electric generator as permanent equipment. On the management side, it had a manager, assistant manager, clerical officer, survey assistant, chief mechanical supervisor, 'jack-of-all-trades' volunteer, three drivers, two junior clerks, a mechanic, storeman, plumber-fitter and three survey assistants....' In addition 'schools, dispensaries, roads and piped water were supplied as a matter of course, generally on a subsidized basis.'[37]

This story, summarized in Table 10.7, underlines three common weaknesses in settlement schemes:

(a) they are frequently over-capitalized and rely on mechanization even where this is uneconomic;

(b) they are frequently over-managed, burdening the schemes with heavy managerial overhead costs;

(c) preferential treatment is frequently offered to

Table 10.7 *The major agricultural settlement programmes in Tanzania 1958–66*

Programme	Purpose	Initiating/managing agency	Scope (at peak)	Fate
A. Supervised settlement schemes				
(1) Tang. Agriculture Corp. (TAC) settlements	Creating modern yeoman farmers under supervision on old sites of groundnuts	TAC (Public Corporation under colonial Govt.).	9 schemes 1,600 settlers	Most still continue
(2) Licensed-producer schemes	Controlled production of high-priced cash crops	British–American Tobacco (BAT), Govt., Tea Cos. etc.	10? 1,000+	Continuing
(3) Village settlement pilot schemes	'Transformation' schemes in selected, non-settled areas	Village Settlement Agency (Govt. statutory body)	10 schemes (64 planned) 1,500 families	Programme discontinued 1966; best converted into ujamaa
(4) World Food Programme (and other VSA Assisted) schemes	Settlement of urban unemployed	Regional Administration and Min. of Agriculture (WFP Finance from UN)	10? 1,000+	Most schemes closed down
Programme	Main purpose	Initiative	Scope	Fate
B. Cooperative farming settlements				
(1) Cattle & coconut schemes	Rationalize and integrate cattle herding and coconut growing	Min. of Agriculture through elected committees	34 schemes 1,500 (?) members	Almost all closed
(2) Cooperative sisal farms	Africanization of sisal industry by teams of small producers	Min. of Agriculture	350 5,000 members	Most closed down
(3) Ruvuma and other ujamaa settlements	Pioneering Socialist path of development	Spontaneous	15 RDA 5–10 others	Continuing
(4) Other TYL and spontaneous settlements	'Building the Nation'	Local leadership; community	500+schemes ?	Almost all closed
(5) Agridev/schemes	Modern irrigated farming under 'expert' management	Agridev (Israeli co.) with Israeli Govt. loan	3 200 settlers	Closed down
(6) Cotton block farms	Mechanized, block production of cotton	Min. of Agriculture, Reg. Administration, Victoria Fed. Coop. Unions	5,000 farmers	Most closed

SOURCE: L. Cliffe and G. Cunningham, loc. cit.

settlers in other ways, whether social services or extension services. Thus the Sukumuland block cultivation schemes were said to have drawn upon 60 per cent of the extension staff in the Tanzanian Lake area for less than 5 per cent of the cotton crop.[38] In addition they showed very poor results, at the same time as agricultural output in the traditional area, about which a pessimistic view had been taken, increased substantially, suggesting greater scope for an 'improvement' approach.

Irrigation schemes: the example of the Gezira

A particular type of agricultural development scheme involving settlement is that based on irrigation. Water storage, requiring the building of a dam and large irrigation works, may or may not be involved. Where it is, heavy capital costs will be involved. If the scheme is to be successful, therefore, it will have to supply a very large number of farmer/settlers, usually, and must be based on at least one high-valued cash crop. State intervention is thus required for the provision of costly infrastructure and for the recruitment of a large number of settlers and subsequent management of the scheme.

The Gezira Scheme, started in the 1920s, is still reckoned among the most successful agricultural development projects attempted in Africa. Water supply is mainly by gravity irrigation from the Blue Nile, and partly by pumping. The scheme operates on a partnership basis, combining elements of private property and individual farm management with substantial physical and managerial inputs by government. Thus the government controls the use but is not the owner of all the land in the scheme. More than half the land in the original scheme area (one million feddans) is still owned by the original owners who are paid rental fees in addition to what they earn as tenant farmers. Tenants, numbering about 96,000 in recent years, are responsible for their own plots and are free to hire labour: some 400,000 casual local and migrant labourers work for them in addition to some 140,000 tenant family workers, making about 540,000 in all (in 1973/4). A prescribed rotation assigns about one-third of the land to cotton each year, but on the rest of the land tenants are free to grow wheat, groundnuts, and other food or fodder crops which they can dispose of at will.

The government provides water and the rest of the land, while management is provided by the Sudan Gezira Board (SGB), a public authority, which took over responsibility after the concession of the original management, a British-owned company, expired in 1950. The SGB carries out research, allocates tenancies, provides technical supervision and credit, mechanically cultivates the land, supplies seed and fertilizer, carries out pest control, and transports, gins, and markets the cotton on behalf of the tenant producers. Labour is provided by the tenants and their employees. Tenants are paid according to the quantity and quality of cotton delivered to the Board. The distribution of cotton revenue in recent years has been some 50 per cent to the tenants, in addition to a full, tax-free right to other crops, 36 per cent to the government as payment for land and water supplied, 10 per cent to the SGB for administration, technical services and marketing, 2 per cent to a Social Development Fund, and about 2 per cent to local governments as tax.

As was mentioned in Chapter 8, in the section on share-cropping, this difference between the way in which cotton revenue is treated as compared to revenue and direct benefits from other crops may well have a distorting effect on the allocation of resources between the two. The ILO Report on employment in the Sudan[39] mentions that tenants on the Gezira and most other irrigation schemes in the country are given an incentive to concentrate on crops which they do not have to 'share' (in the manner of share-croppers) with their other partners in the schemes, management and government. This arises because, although cotton accounts for only about one-third of the total Gezira acreage, all costs of common services including water, ploughing, and scheme management overheads are paid for by a charge on cotton revenue alone, tenants receiving 49 per cent of this and the other 'partners' 51 per cent. The ILO Mission recommended the sharing of net revenue after charging costs to *all* crops, not just cotton, as well as shifting some of the scheme's other costs from cotton revenue to specific land rent and water consumption charges where tenants would pay for land and water used whether for cotton or other crops.

The scheme, together with the substantial Managil extension carried out by the Sudan after independence, now covers over two million feddans (acres). Tenants have made incomes of around 500 dollars a year,[40] which is a great deal for farmers in a poor country. Jobs have been created for nearly 100,000 tenants, 450,000 casual labourers hired by them, and some 10,000 workers employed by the Board mainly in cotton ginneries. The employment created is as much as or more than total paid employment in some countries of Africa such as Uganda or Ghana. The distribution of income under the scheme as between relatively privileged tenants, on 30-acre farm units, and their labourers can however be criticized.[41]

The Gezira Scheme has been copied in other parts of the Sudan and elsewhere, notably on the Niger in West Africa. Most large irrigation schemes require at least some element of public ownership and control of the use of land, if only because the provision and maintenance of water supplies are expensive. In the Gezira a flexible approach was followed which permitted in addition the harnessing of the enterprise and labour of small farmers responding to price incentives and security of tenure, on a partnership basis.

Other ingredients in the successful implementation of the Gezira Scheme, which are still relevant for further irrigation projects in the Sudan and elsewhere, have been:

(a) careful pre-investment 'feasibility studies', in this case the cotton-growing trials on irrigated plots organized by the commercial promoters, the Sudan Experimental Plantation Syndicate, as early as 1911;

(b) the availability of cheap casual labour for seasonal cotton picking from traditional dry-farming areas of the Sudan and abroad (including, initially, the overland pilgrims to Mecca from Chad and Nigeria). Voluntary migration, often over long distances, and private contracting arrangements avoided reliance on central direction or compulsory recruitment measures;

(d) initial specialization in a relatively high-value export crop, long-staple cotton;

(e) availability of natural resources, land and water, suitable for alternative and increasingly profitable food crops for local and export markets.

Socialist transformation schemes:
state farms and
cooperative production

A great number of African countries have experimented at one time or another with socialist schemes of different kinds. Two different kinds of motivation were behind these. For some, the main aim has been to raise productivity to new levels through mechanization: it was considered necessary, in order to tap economies of scale from mechanization, to work the land in large units, either through state farms or through collective or group farms, rather than through individual African smallholders. For others mechanization has not been the main aim, but rather the socialization of agriculture as such: the ujamaa village programme of Tanzania, described in detail presently, is the best and most current example. This is aimed at reducing inequalities in the rural sector, avoiding the development of a rural wage-earning proletariat which could be 'exploited' by large farmers, and deliberately organizing social as well as economic life on a communal rather than competitive basis. Mechanization was to play a minimal

part is this programme since, as already mentioned, Tanzania had had previous disillusioning experiences in this direction.

The main African countries to experiment with state farms have been Guinea and Ghana. Apart from the ideological attractiveness of state organization *per se*, the motivation has been a feeling of impatience with tradition-bound peasant farming as compared to modern and supposedly high-productivity methods. Thus in Ghana the state farms were expected 'to show the advantages of large-scale mechanized socialist farming over small-scale peasant farming'.[42]

Farms were established in Ghana from 1962 to 1966 under the Ghana State Farms Corporation. The programme was launched in an incautious manner, the number of farms increasing from 26 in 1962 to 107 in 1963, rising to 135 farms with 20,800 workers in February 1966, at the end of the Nkrumah period. A number of basic errors were made in addition to the speed with which the programme was embarked upon. Peasants were antagonized by the brutal manner in which their land was seized without compensation to be turned over to state farming. There was gross over-ordering and misuse of tractors and other expensive equipment, which were not properly maintained. The farms were not well managed, with over-centralization of decisions in Accra. Finally, the land probably did not have such a high potential yield as to cover high running costs easily. The cost of maintaining the labour force often greatly exceeded the value of the crop, even in an established state farm, before taking into account machinery costs.[43]

State farms were also launched on a wide scale in Guinea, and these too failed badly. Again poor management and failure to cover heavy costs of mechanization were to blame. In Ghana state farms were reactivated under a new Food Production Corporation as part of an 'Operation Feed Yourself' aimed at eliminating expensive food imports which had aggravated serious balance of payments problems. The experience of these new state farms is not fully documented, but their continued inefficiency has apparently been criticized.[44]

Ironically, there were great similarities in the motivation behind these socialistic projects and the large-scale transformation schemes of the colonial period, such as the Tanganyika Groundnut Scheme of 1946–51. In both cases a pessimistic view was taken of the possibilities for progress through conservative or 'backward' peasant farmers, there was impatience with attempts to cajole small farmers, through agricultural extension, to higher levels of productivity, and a desire to take a short-cut through direct state action. As in the case of the Groundnut Scheme, this impatience has arisen particularly out of a food crisis.[45] Not only was the reactivation of state farms in Ghana in 1972 a response to this, but the original programme coincided with a switch of attention from cocoa to food production for domestic consumption.[46] The failure of state farms so far has been for the same kind of reasons also: inadequate technical/economic preparation; incautiously rapid rates of implementation; and lack of consideration of the human factor involved in labour supply or settler participation.

Experience of state farms in Eastern Africa has been much more limited. Tanzania has adopted a rather careful and selective approach towards state farms during the 1970s, again with a view to dealing with a problem of food supplies, but concentrating on activities such as irrigated rice, wheat production, and cattle ranching, where economies of scale were thought to exist. Even so, a consultant 'was able to find little evidence of efficient production, acceptable husbandry standards, effective utilization and maintenance of agricultural machinery or even knowledge of essential farm management techniques on some 10 state and parastatal farms visited in 1975'. 'With one exception all these farms were overstaffed, over-mechanised and under maintained.... On many farms planting dates were months late, missing the best of the rains. Harvesting very often extended over three months, even to the point of harvesting the second generation rice crop at the same time as the first.'[47]

As with transformation schemes in general, this experience does not prove state or parastatal farms to be inherently unworkable. For instance the Mbarali State Rice Farm in Southern Tanzania has, after a lengthy learning process, attained an extremely high level of technical efficiency and obtained some of the highest rice yields per acre in the world. Much more important as an example of a state-organized scheme is the Gezira cotton scheme in the Sudan, discussed earlier. And it should be remembered that estate agriculture, which is similarly organized, has proved highly successful in many parts of Africa. Clearly, a careful and selective approach is required. If high capital costs are to be recovered, a high-priced cash crop is needed. If the aim is food crop production, the domestic price of the food crop should be high enough to offer a good rate of return on the investment made.

A more appealing form of socialist production for many African countries, however, has been communal farming by cooperative groups. Hopes for this form of development have been raised by the existence of traditional forms of cooperation of African society, particularly communal ownership of land, and communal grazing on the production side, and the extended family on the side of distribution of

benefits. Moreover, cooperatives have been extremely successful in Africa at the marketing level, which is held to indicate possibilities for extension of cooperation into production.

How strong a basis traditional cooperation can provide for cooperative production in a modernized economy is uncertain. Even if individual land titles do not exist, land in Africa has largely been worked on an individual basis, and it has been pointed out[48] that 'even within African polygamous families it seems so necessary to get direct responsibilities and incentives for labour that usually each wife has her separate plots'. The most fundamental problem in cooperative production is, of course, that of incentives, together with the peasant's desire for security associated with having his own piece of land (among pastoralists, his own livestock). This is the reason, no doubt, that although a number of countries in each of East, West, and North Africa have experimented with group farming, the results to date have been uniformly disappointing, with very few exceptions.

In West Africa the Mali government has encouraged farmers to move in the direction of cooperative production by forming groups to work common fields, or *champs collectifs* as they were called, in addition to their own individual holdings. As in the Tanzanian case, less attention was given by farmers to these communal fields than to their own holdings, and there has been no apparent interest in expanding the size of the cooperative fields relative to individual holdings. In North Africa the Tunisian government made a major effort in the early 1970s to transform the basis of agriculture in the direction of cooperative production. This programme ran into major difficulties however.

Cooperative enterprise appears to have been introduced with successful results in Dahomey, in the form of rural development cooperatives, starting in the early 1960s. By 1971 nearly 40 cooperatives were in operation mostly based on oil palm production, with rice or other crops in other areas. Work teams are organized from among the participants with various specialized tasks, daily labour records being kept of work put in by all participants. A particular feature of the cooperatives is that revenue is distributed in the form of interest on shares, shares being allocated to an individual on the basis of the land he contributes initially and the labour contributed subsequently. Individual claims to land are verified and registered before the scheme is launched.[49]

An early example in Eastern Africa were the group cotton farms of Central Nyanza, in Kenya. These farms apparently grew up quite spontaneously, based on an aspect of traditional society, the kinship group known as *jokokwaro*.[50] There were about 90 such farms in 1964. They appear to have been quite viable and to have been successful in improving methods of cultivation to some extent. Whether they still exist is uncertain.

Although earlier attempts at cooperative farms in Uganda in the 1950s had come to nothing, a major programme for group farms was launched in 1963. These had no strong ideological motivation and were essentially schemes for mechanization. As an official statement at the time said, the scheme 'was designed to enable modern machinery to be applied in cotton production'. Land was to be cultivated on a 'block' basis, with each member allocated a different piece within the block each year. A central area was provided for settlement and food crop production.

The first 3 group farms were established in 1963, and 20 more added in 1964. The Second Five-year Plan, 1966–71, gave a major role within the agricultural sector to an expanded programme of group farms. A number of factors contributed to what was eventually the disintegration of the programme. The most fundamental one lay in the economics of mechanization where, despite research and earlier negative experience demonstrating the costs of tractors, the costs were higher than expected. In addition there was poor settlement planning, giving rise to a reluctance to live on the site and incomplete commitment to the group farm. There were also management problems, managerial responsibility for the group farm not always being clearly specified. Where a manager was provided, he was generally a very junior and inexperienced expatriate who had problems of communication with farmers.

Cooperative production and villagization in Tanzania

The most interesting, and certainly the most thorough-going attempt in Africa to transform rural organization along cooperative lines has been pursued in Tanzania, since its Arusha Declaration in 1967. Up to the end of 1973 the main objective was to foster communal production into 'ujamaa' or socialist villages. Subsequently the emphasis has been on villagization, gathering people together in villages rather than scattered settlements, with less emphasis on communal production.

The ujamaa village programme may be said to have had the following general and specific objectives.

(1) First of all, among general objectives, was the desire to move away from capitalist agriculture. As stated in the Second Five Year Plan,[51] the aim was 'to create a society based on cooperation and mutual respect and responsibility, in which all members have equal rights and opportunities'. This included the abolition of wage earnings, whereby some individuals depend on others for employment, and of rural stratification and unequal ownership of land. Wage earning in the agricultural sector itself depends on unequal land-ownership, since in particular it is the landless who are forced to seek wage employment while owners of very large holdings must hire labour if their land is to be worked.

(2) The second objective was to build upon traditional African cooperation, taking advantage of these traditions and putting them to productive use. The word 'ujamaa' means 'familyhood', here to be used as the basis for bringing villagers as a whole together into communal production with shared benefits.

(3) Thirdly, the objective was to launch a frontal approach to rural transformation. While the earlier village settlement schemes in Tanzania were transformation schemes in so far as they implied a drastic change in the method of agriculture rather than an attempt at improvement through ordinary extension methods, they also represented a selective and limited programme, their costliness in particular limiting the number of villages and villagers involved. The ujamaa village programme was intended as a mass movement and, unlike extension methods focusing on progressive farmers, was in principle directed at *all* farmers in Tanzania. Some movement of population was involved in the concentration of people into villages. In a number of cases there was even a specific settlement objective involving the physical transfer of people. In Handeni there was a movement of villagers to improved sites. In Bukoba District landless labourers previously working under the feudal 'byarubanja' system were resettled, while it was a response to overpopulation pressures which led the authorities to assist in 1969 in the transfer of 900 farmers from Kilimanjaro to a new village in the Mwese Highlands of Mpanda District and of Wanyakyusa from Rungwe District in the Southern Highlands to tobacco-growing villages further north in Chunya District. But in general the aim was to transform production in villages throughout Tanzania rather than to secure limited resettlement objectives.[52]

(4) Finally, and related to this, the objective was to secure increases in labour productivity in the rural areas through the efforts of peasants *without* any substantial injection of capital.

If these were the broad objectives, we can also distinguish three specific ways in which improvement was to be obtained from the ujamaa village programme.

(a) First, communal work would bring economies of scale in field operations such as land clearing, ploughing, and harvesting, and in marketing, as well as permitting specialization of function and division of labour within the village work-force.

(b) Secondly, by concentrating people from scattered settlements into villages, it would be possible for agricultural extension services to reach them more easily, and with greater effect, while village reorganization would itself help to break down conservative attitudes among farmers.

(c) Thirdly, concentration would permit economies of scale to be reaped in the provision of social infrastructure, making it possible to provide schools, medical facilities, water supplies, road communications, and the like more cheaply and to a greater proportion of the population.

At the same time an essential feature of the ujamaa programme was to be its voluntary nature: ujamaa villages were to be formed by the people themselves without coercion by the authorities and without persuasion by the 'bribe' of securing preference over others in the provision of social services.

The greatest problems met with in attempting to establish ujamaa villages across the country occurred in three types of areas.

(a) It proved extremely difficult to promote them within the tree crop areas, particularly the rich coffee-growing areas around Kilimanjaro and Bukoba. Coffee trees are in effect 'capital goods' yielding a return over a long period of time to their individual owners who were reluctant to hand them over in this case to communal ownership. It is doubtful also whether there would be substantial economies of scale, either, sufficient to offset the advantages of careful individual cultivation.

(b) Secondly, promotion of ujamaa villages proved difficult in other cash crop areas where private farming was well established. One reason here was inequality in land-holding, particularly where there were economies of scale in production, such as among commercial maize farmers in Ismani, Iringa Region, or wheat growers in Mbulu District. Thus in a representative sample of 9 out of 28 ujamaa villages in Ismani it was found that 9 per cent of the households together accounted for 88 per cent of the purchased land, 53 per cent of cultivated land, 96 per cent of capital equipment owned, 47 per cent of the cattle, and 51 per cent of the sheep and goats. In this situation wealthier members of the community will obviously be reluctant to sacrifice their position in order to move towards one of communal ownership of village resources. A second reason, related to unequal ownership of land, was the already developed use of hired labour. Thus in the cotton-growing region of Sukumuland, a region which showed particular resistance to efforts to promote socialist organization, it is reported that in 1970 nearly 80 per cent of all farmers used hired labour. Dependence on hired labour was said to be common in all the major cash-crop growing areas of Tanzania.[53] In some of these areas it was found specifically that attendance at the communal farm was affected by farmers' absenting themselves on communal work days in order to work as hired labourers, for larger farmers.

(c) The third type of area which raises special problems for villagization is that comprising the nomadic pastoral areas. Here settlement in villages is often not compatible with the necessity of movement in search of grazing. Individual ownership of cattle among pastoralists, sometimes highly unequal ownership, is also a problem. At the same time there was a failure among officials to recognize that pastoral society was already the most cooperative and socialized in Eastern Africa, with the strongest element of traditional ujamaa.

Despite these obstacles the number of ujamaa villages expanded rapidly following the Arusha Declaration and in particular a statement by President Nyerere in 1967 on 'Socialism and Rural Development'.[54] The number of registered ujamaa villages increased from 180 at the end of 1968, containing at that time 58,500 people or less than 1 per cent of the population, to 809 villages in 1969, and 5,628 villages by the end of May 1973. By that time over two million people, or 15 per cent of the total population, were living in ujamaa villages, as shown in Table 10.8.

Table 10.8 also shows, however, that this development was very uneven between regions. In Mtwara Region nearly two-thirds of the population were in registered ujamaa villages. Mtwara Region was one of the first to develop ujamaa villages, demonstrated by the fact that earlier, in 1969, it actually contained 400 out of 650 ujamaa villages in the country. This reflected a quite special factor operating along the border with Mozambique, the need to settle in villages for purposes of defence and security. Secondly, Dodoma Region stands out as having almost half its population in ujamaa villages. The proportion here was boosted by the rapid movement, following a severe drought in 1971, of some 100,000 people in Dodoma into 80 new ujamaa villages. In general, however, it can be said that a large proportion of ujamaa villages were established in the economically less developed parts of the country (e.g. Coast, Lindi, Dodoma, Singida), where cash cropping was less advanced and land was plentiful. While therefore ujamaa villages were more readily accepted in these areas, the economic basis of the villages was less strong. Table 10.8 demonstrates the relative lack of success in such cash crop areas in Kilimanjaro (coffee) and Shinyanga (cotton) in each of which regions only 1 per cent of the population were in registered ujamaa villages in 1973.

Table 10.8   Regional distribution of ujamaa villages in Tanzania, 31 May 1973

Region	No. of villages	Population in villages	Percentage of total population in villages	No. of villages registered as multi-purpose cooperatives
Arusha	95	20,100	3	8
Coast	188	115,400	21	55
Dodoma	336	378,900	47	66
Iringa	659	243,500	29	80
Kigoma	129	114,400	22	1
Kilimanjaro	24	4,900	1	3
Mara	271	108,100	16	34
Mbeya	715	103,700	9	7
Morogoro	118	19,700	3	1
Lindi	589	169,100	36	2
Mtwara	1,103	466,100	64	9
Mwanza	284	49,800	4	14
Ruvuma	242	42,400	9	3
Shinyanga	108	12,100	1	9
Singida	263	59,400	12	5
Tabora	174	29,300	5	14
Tanga	245	78,000	7	13
West Lake	85	13,300	2	18
Total	5,628	2,028,200	15	342

SOURCE: Peter E. Temu, 'The Ujamaa Experiment', in *Ceres*, July August, 1973
NOTE: Final column refers to March 1973

Progress towards rural socialism cannot be measured simply by the numbers of ujamaa villages registered, however, particularly as officials frequently registered villages as having adopted the ujamaa form once a declaration of intent had been made, even where no progress towards socialist organization nor indeed any noticeable change had taken place. While the ultimate objective was that the villages would progress into multi-purpose cooperatives doing their own joint production, marketing, and purchasing, the final column shows that only a small percentage had even been registered as such in early 1973. Moreover the villages registered as cooperative societies, which registration was meant to be a final stage after successful establishment of cooperative production, were often less advanced in the latter respect than those in earlier 'stages'.[55]

The most difficult problem in giving socialist content to the villages was in establishing communal production. The overwhelming weight of evidence shows that there was low attendance on days set aside for collective work on the communal plot. Sometimes the work carried out on this plot was done by women and occasionally even outsiders were employed to do this work. In many villages farmers had, by 1973, reverted to doing their own private cultivation only.[56] Neither was communal self-help action to make use of surplus labour in off-peak periods in order to build common amenities as great as it might have been.

A number of criticisms have been levelled at the ujamaa village programme:

(1) As just indicated, greater success was obtained in increasing the numbers of registered ujamaa villages than in giving them content in terms of communal production. In many cases, especially under the more recent villagization policy, several neighbouring smaller settlements were simply relabelled ujamaa villages. This might or might not make possible economies of scale in the provision of social services and infrastructure. It has been referred to as 'ujamaa through sign painting'.[57] This was much the easiest way for regional officials to achieve targets required of them for progress towards ujamaa and, of course, it is statistically easier to measure numbers of villages than the extent of communal production and cooperation.

(2) Contrary to the original objective of a voluntary movement towards cooperation, there appears to have been an excessive degree of persuasion and even coercion by officials in order to secure the establishment of villages. Thus ujamaa villages could be said to have been initiated by the authorities rather than by the villagers themselves. This became commonplace under the subsequent villagization policy.

(3) Another criticism is that ujamaa villages were excessively favoured in the allocation of social benefits, this allocation being used to persuade farmers to move into villages. This has been referred to as 'villagization through material inducement':[58] 500 million shillings were invested in ujamaa villages during the period of the Five Year Plan 1969–74. Ujamaa villages received a significant part of an expensive rural water supply programme and of allocations for rural health centres and primary schools, and were assisted through the grant of tractors, pesticides, fertilizers and other farm inputs. Government-owned equipment was sometimes used to clear land or to plough communal land. Such favoured treatment could not only be inequitable, but act as a deterrent to self-help effort by the villagers themselves.

(4) There was a lack of detailed planning with regard to sites, so that sites were sometimes chosen where there was a danger of floods or, more frequently, where there was an inadequate supply of fertile land for the number of people that had been brought together. A fundamental question here is how far the underlying assumption behind villagization was correct, that people were unnecessarily widely distributed into scattered settlements. It was estimated that before villagization there were some 500 traditional 'gathered' settlements while nearly nine million of the population lived in scattered settlements.[59] It is likely that this dispersal was not entirely unnecessary and that concentration of people into villages has put pressure on the carrying capacity of the land around the villages in some cases. In particular it may make it more difficult to practise the traditional form of shifting cultivation and crop rotations which help to maintain the fertility of the soil.

At the end of 1973, as the government became impatient at the speed of the response to its call to form ujamaa villages, the emphasis changed from the more socialistic aspects of 'ujamaa' to one of villagization per se. On 6 November 1973, a new 'villagization policy' was introduced when it was announced that 'to live in villages is an order', and one to be fully implemented by the end of 1976. Within a year three million out of fourteen million inhabitants were moved into what were now called 'planned' or 'development' villages. The minimum size of such villages was to be 250 families, with the same aim in mind as previously of concentrating the supply of social services and facilitating extension and development advice. The policy was to be extended to the pastoral areas with the establishment of 'livestock development villages'. With the abolition of cooperative marketing societies in Tanzania in 1976 the villages will become key organizational units, since they will *have* to be developed as multi-purpose cooperative units responsible for marketing village production.

The main problem in the short run has been the lack of sufficient planning capacity at the local level for detailed implementation of the policy. While the long-run benefits could be substantial, it will not be possible for some time to assess fully the effects of a major attempt at rural transformation.

The economics of pastoralism and pastoral areas

So far we have discussed agricultural development in Eastern Africa as if this were confined to growing crops. In fact livestock activities may be just as important, or more so. In Europe some of the richest farms are based on *mixed farming*, which combines crop and livestock activities. Australian sheep farms constitute an example of pure livestock activity yielding high profits. In Africa, and this is often forgotten, large areas are pastoral and a substantial number of the people derive their livelihood from *pastoralism*.

These areas, and their peoples, are often considered backward, by other Eastern Africans as well as expatriate observers, and most Eastern African governments have neglected them as being 'problematic', concentrating their development efforts elsewhere. Without saying that there is no justification at all for this, a large part of this attitude stems from a fundamental misunderstanding of the pastoral economy.

Pastoral peoples may be considered less 'developed' than cultivators for a number of reasons: (1) because they are nomadic (i.e roamers from pasture to pasture); (2) because of their lack of commercialization and reluctance to sell cattle for cash; (3) because of their poverty; (4) because they do not cultivate; (5) because of their lack of interest in education; (6) because of their so-called 'cattle complex' and obsession with livestock; and (7) because of their alleged poor herd management and overgrazing of pastures.

In fact there is evidence that pastoral peoples in many cases do not *choose* to be nomadic and that groups such as the Maasai prefer to move within a limited radius where the availability of pasture permits this, and have sometimes lived in permanent settlements of some size. Thus nomadism has been forced upon them by the circumstances of ecology, the search for the two basic ingredients of pasture and water for their cattle. Where the grass cover is very thin, and the carrying capacity of the land very low (carrying capacity is measured by the number of acres needed to support one adult animal, often 10 or 15 to one in the range areas of Eastern Africa), then cattle-keepers must wander over a wide area if they are to obtain enough grass. This need is increased as a result of the unpredictability of rainfall in the range areas: for grass grows where rain has fallen, making the distribution of the grass cover dependent upon the incidence of rainfall. This means that pastoralists cannot *afford* to remain in one place: they appear in fact to be quite knowledgeable about the probable availability of pasture over vast areas.

In contrast government ranching schemes for pastoral groups have often neglected this and tried to confine movement to areas which are too small to guarantee the availability of water and pasture somewhere within the ranch boundary each year. We may refer to this as an *economy of scale*: unreliability of rainfall means that cattle-keepers must be prepared to operate over a wide area if they are to be certain that they will always find pasture and water supplies *somewhere* within their area of operation. We may note in passing that even cultivators do not necessarily stay in one place either, and that shifting cultivation may be economic in areas of land surplus.

The reluctance of pastoralists to sell cattle is sometimes exaggerated. Substantial sales are in fact made, though not always large in relation to the number of cattle owned. And frequently sales are not made because the cattle-owner cannot *afford* to sell. A point of great importance is that a family subsisting on milk, blood, and meat will require a substantial number of animals if they are to be adequately nourished; and since the milk yield per beast will be lower in areas of poor pasture, the number of animals required per family will increase, the lower the quality of the pasture. Thus in many range areas of Eastern Africa as many as 10 or 15 animals are required to feed adequately one person, and several times that number to sustain a family: more than the family may own. In these circumstances a reluctance to sell is understandable and is due simply to the lack of a *marketable surplus* over and above subsistence requirements.

While many pastoral groups *are* very poor, where grazing is inadequate, they are often in a better condition as regards health and nutrition than neighbouring cultivators (not necessarily cultivators in other areas with richer soils and more plentiful rainfall) and may even hire people from nearby cultivating areas as part-time herders. Local cultivators often themselves recognize the pastoralists as being the richer group.

It is not generally true that pastoralists do not cultivate: many or most of them grow small quantities of food crops for their own consumption although, equally, it may often be more sensible for them to obtain most such requirements by exchange for cash or by barter of livestock products, in which they have a comparative advantage. The importance of cultivation among cattle-keepers varies and some groups have been labelled 'cultivating pastoralists', to distinguish them from 'pure' cattle-keepers.

As regards education, it is true that there has been a reluctance by pastoralists to send their children to school, although poor school attendance is not confined to pastoral areas. However this is due partly to the pastoralists' non-sedentary existence, which makes regular attendance in one place difficult or impossible. And, not surprisingly, pastoralists have not found formal education very relevant as a preparation for lives as cattle-keepers: in this respect knowledge passed down from generation to generation has been more valuable.

The term 'cattle complex' implies an 'irrational' interest in cattle for their own sake, rather than as a source of food for domestic consumption or as a means of obtaining income. The idea that pastoralists suffer from a cattle 'complex' appears to derive from two things: first, the fact that cattle perform a wide variety of functions within the pastoral society, serving as money (as a unit of account and store of value) and such social functions as bridewealth; secondly, that cattle play a dominant role in legend and story-telling and in daily conversation.

However, the use of livestock as money seems only sensible in remote, largely subsistence economies where people lack cash or access to banks nearby. The bridewealth custom has many disadvantages, but is not confined to pastoralists; and it is part of a way of life which is different from Western industrial society, but not necessarily inferior. That cattle feature so largely in story-telling and conversation is not altogether surprising among households forced to depend for livelihood almost exclusively on livestock activity. Most significant, however, is the fact that most pastoralists keep just as many sheep and goats as cattle, so that this concern is not limited to cattle or other large stock like camels.

The most important criticism of pastoralists from an economic point of view, however, is of poor herd management, in particular the retention of excess numbers of livestock, to the point of overgrazing, permanently damaging the grass cover and reducing in the long run the carrying capacity of the land area. While, however, this may appear to be irrational, or inefficient, there may in fact be valid reasons for such behaviour.

First, the retention of excessive numbers of livestock may result from a divergence between private and social interests, arising out of the system of property rights. If the available pasture is owned communally,[60] it will not pay an individual to restrict his personal holding of cattle, if others do not do the same. He would lose personally, while no significant impact would be made on the preservation of the grass cover: on the contrary, it would pay a rational stock-owner to maximize his own stock numbers. The remedy here would be either division of the communal pasture into individually owned units, to eliminate the divergence between private and social interests, or agreement among members of the group to restrict total livestock numbers, together with some allocation of grazing rights (permitted numbers of cattle) among themselves.

Secondly, cattle numbers *may* be excessive in relation to the carrying capacity of the land, but not in relation to the subsistence needs of the resident population. We stated earlier that a certain minimum number of livestock are needed to supply the subsistence needs of a pastoral family unit. Thus the livestock-to-land ratio may be too high, while the livestock-to-*people* ratio is too *low*. In such a situation, it is difficult to ask owners to de-stock, even if this is to their long-run advantage, since it means in the short run reducing their consumption below an already low level. The basic problem here is excessive numbers of people in relation to the quantity (and quality) of land. Historically this has arisen much less through expansion of population than through progressive reduction of the land areas open to the pastoral groups, as cultivating tribes, communal ranches or estates, and state-run schemes have encroached on areas over which they have traditionally grazed.[61]

Just as we rejected the notion that peasant farmers exhibit 'irrational' supply responses, therefore, we must guard against assuming that pastoralists and cattle-keepers are necessarily irrational in their behaviour and unable to make the best use of their environment.

This does not mean that range management in the pastoral areas cannot be improved. The system of common property rights has produced serious overgrazing in many areas. Pastoral groups have seldom been able to agree on a sensible system of rotational grazing in order to preserve their pastures, although where this has been tried (sometimes, unfortunately, through compulsion), it has proved highly beneficial. When grazing is in short supply, judicious investment in water supplies, through bore-holes or earth dams, may expand the supply by making available grazing which was previously unusable due to its remoteness from water.

Finally, the level of technical efficiency in herd management is still very low among pastoralists, reducing the annual rate of off-take of mature cattle for sale (as a ratio of the size of herd) and the average value of each beast (mainly because of small size and poor quality). As a result the available pasture and water resource inputs do not maximize output, and governments are thus pressed to replace traditional pastoralism with ranching schemes and commercial ranches.

Questions on Chapter 10

1. Discuss the view sometimes expressed that peasant producers are generally irrational, inefficient, and unresponsive to change.

2. What evidence exists of rural inequality and class formation within the rural sector in Eastern African countries? Is this inequality good or bad, or just inevitable?

3. What are the main differences between the system of land tenure in Africa and those in other parts of the developing world? How would this affect the direction of land reform in the different continents?

4. Compare the advantages of communal and individualized systems of land tenure.

5. Compare the two basic approaches to agricultural extension, and their relative advantages. Why is it difficult to compare their results?

6. Discuss in detail the conditions affecting the profitability of mechanized farming.

7. Discuss the usefulness of a 'break-even chart'. On what assumptions is it drawn?

8. Distinguish between 'fixed' and 'variable' costs. How do these affect the economics of mechanized farming?

9. Discuss how 'labour peaks' may arise in agriculture. What measures can be adopted to reduce their effect?

10. Why is mechanization less likely to be economic (a) in land-scarce/labour-abundant economies; (b) in subsistence food-producing areas?

11. In what way can mechanization be employment-creating?

12. How would you set about deciding whether tractors or ox-ploughs were the more economic in any situation?

13. Why do you think the experience of mechanization in Eastern Africa has generally been unfavourable?

14. Discuss the various kinds of settlement schemes that have been set up in Africa. Why do you think so many have failed?

15. Why has the Gezira cotton scheme in the Sudan been held up as a 'model' for large-scale irrigation projects? What ingredients in its operation do you think underlie its success?

16. Discuss the main lessons to be learned from the experience of state farms in Ghana.

17. What were the main objectives of Tanzania's 'ujamaa village' programme? Discuss the problems faced by the programme and the progress achieved by it. Compare with the subsequent villagization policy.

18. What economic basis exists for 'pastoralism' and what limitations exist in the traditional system?

Notes

[1] J. H. Boeke, *Economics and Economic Policy of Dual Societies*, Institute of Pacific Relations, New York, 1953, p. 33.

[2] The possibility of a 'backward-sloping' supply curve for wage earners is analysed theoretically in Chapter 31.

[3] Edwin Dean, *The Supply Response of African Farmers: Theory and Measurement in Malawi*, North-Holland Publishing Co., Amsterdam, 1966.

[4] J. Maitha, 'A Supply Function for Kenya Coffee', *Eastern African Economic Review*, Vol. 1, No. 1, June 1969.

[5] An African study in Malawi, however, showed a highly positive response in *total* cash crop sales, implying an increase in effort, to real producer price: P. Minford and P. Ohs, 'Supply Responses of Malawi Labour', *East African Economic Review*, Vol. 8, No. 1, June 1976.

[6] D. W. Norman, 'Labour Inputs of Farmers: A Case Study of the Zaria Province of the North-Central State of Nigeria', *Nigerian Journal of Social and Economic Studies*, March 1969.

[7] Two such classic studies by Sol. Tax of a Guatamalan (Central American) community and by David Hopper of a village in North Central India, are discussed in T. W. Schultz, *Transforming Traditional Agriculture*, Yale University Press, 1964.

[8] Kenneth H. Shapiro, 'Efficiency Differentials in Peasant Agriculture and their Implications for Development Policies', Centre for Research on Economic Development, *Discussion Paper No. 52*, University of Michigan, June 1976.

[9] D. Hunt, *Growth versus Equity, an Examination of the Distribution of Economic Status and Opportunity in Mbere, Eastern Kenya*, Institute for Development Studies, University of Nairobi, 1975.

[10] Wealth was measured by a selective list of items, excluding land, but including for instance doors and mbati roofing, as well as livestock in addition to ordinary household items such as tables, beds, lamps, blankets, and the like.

[11] M. Attems, 'Permanent Cropping in the Usambaras', in H. Ruthenberg (ed.), *Small-holder Farming and Small-holder Development in Tanzania*, Munich, 1968.

[12] S. Beck, *An Economic Study of Coffee-Banana Farms in Machame Central Area, Kilimanjaro District*, Ministry of Agricultue, Dar es Salaam, 1961.

[13] N. van Hekken and H. Thoden van Velzen, *Relative Land Scarcity and Rural Inequality*, Africa-Studiecentrum, Leiden, 1970.

[14] Estimated from figures by van Hekken and van Velzen, op. cit., p. 22.

[15] Volker Weyel, 'Land Ownership in Nyakmengo, Ruzhumbura (North Kigezi), A Preliminary Survey', in *Research Abstracts and Newsletter, A Journal of Policy Communication*, Vol. 1, No. 3, 1973, Makerere Institute of Social Research, Kampala.

[16] R. Dumont, *Types of Rural Economy*, Methuen, London, 1957.

[17] E. J. Long, 'The family farm in foreign land tenure policy', *Journal of Farm Economics*, Vol. 44, 1962.

[18] See Beverley Brock, 'Customary land tenure, individualization and agricultural development in Uganda', *East African Journal of Rural Development*, Vol. 2, 1969.

[19] S. M. Makings, *Agricultural Problems of Developing Countries in Africa*, Oxford University Press, London, 1967, p. 62.

[20] Researchers at Makerere University in Uganda set up a series of smallholdings designed to adapt developments on the 500-acre University Farm to suit the 5-acre farmer with family labour and very limited capital, and found that comparatively few of the innovations could be reproduced because of the capital and labour involved. See E. Ronald Watts, 'Reaching East Africa's Farmers', *Journal of Administration Overseas*, Vol. XLI, No. 2, April 1973.

[21] E. R. Watts, loc. cit., p. 112.

[22] E. R. Watts, 'Agricultural Extension Services in Uganda', *Uganda Agricultural Journal*, Vol. 2, No. 2.

[23] D. H. Humphrey, 'Malawi's Economic Progress and Prospects', *Eastern African Economic Review*, Vol. 5, No. 2, December 1973, p. 74.

[24] D. H. Humphrey, op. cit., p. 74, referring to the Malawi Government Economic Planning Division's *Statement of Development Policies, 1971–1980*, Zomba, December 1971.

[25] President Nyerere, interviewed by G. Githii, *Daily Nation*, 6 August 1968.

[26] See 'Agricultural Extension and Farmers' Training: Results of SRDP Experimentation in Agricultural Extension', in *SRDP Second Overall Evaluation of the Special Rural Development Programme*. Institute of Development Studies, Occasional Paper No. 12, Nairobi, 1975.

[27] This section has benefited especially from review articles by E. S. Clayton, 'Mechanization and Employment in East African Agriculture', *International Labour Review*, Vol. 105, No. 4, April 1972; M. Hall, 'Mechanization in East African Agriculture in G. K. Helleiner (ed.), *Agricultural Planning in East Africa*, East African Publishing House, 1968; and the ILO Employment Mission, *Growth, employment and equity: A comprehensive strategy for the Sudan*, ILO, Geneva, 1975.

[28] For a detailed account of the problems of large-scale bush clearing and crop cultivation using machinery, see Alan Wood, *The Groundnut Affair*, The Bodley Head, London, 1950.

[29] E. S. Clayton, loc. cit., p. 310.

[30] D. Forbes Watt, E.D.R.P. Paper No. 104, Makerere University, Kampala, 1966.

[31] *Report of Second Five Year Plan Working Party No. 12 on Agricultural Mechanization*, Appendix 3, Dar es Salaam, 1968.

[32] The United Republic of Tanzania, *Second Five Year Plan for Economic and Social Development*, 1969, p. 39.

[33] *Second Five Year Plan*, p. 38.

[34] L. Cliffe and G. L. Cunningham, Ideology, Organisation and the Settlement Experience in Tanzania', in L. Cliffe and J. S. Saul, *Socialism in Tanzania*, Vol. 2, East African Publishing House, 1973, p. 135.

[35] J. C. de Wilde, *Experiences with Agricultural Development in Tropical Africa*, Vols I and II, Johns Hopkins University Press, 1967.

[36] Overseas Food Corporation, *Report and Accounts for 1954–55*, London, HMSO, quoted by Cliffe and Cunningham.

[37] Cliffe and G. Cunningham, op. cit., p. 135.

[38] P. W. Landell-Mills, 'On the Economic Appraisal of Agricultural Development Projects: the Tanzania Village Settlement Schemes', *Agricultural Economic Bulletin for Africa*, No. 8, 1966.

[39] ILO, *Growth, employment and equity: A comprehensive strategy for the Sudan*, Geneva, 1975, pp. 48–52, 255–65.

[40] The SGB estimated from a survey in 1974/5 (a good year) that 20-feddan tenants earned incomes of about £S350 and 40-feddan tenants some £S700. Their seasonal labour earned some £S515 per month during the cotton-picking season (which is concentrated in some ten weeks from January to March, and takes up rather more than half the annual labour requirements).

[41] The ILO (1975) Mission Report, however, stressed the unemployment and loss of cash incomes that could result from mechanized harvesting of grains and groundnuts, induced by higher money wages from seasonal labour accelerating a shift from labour-intensive cotton picking to other crops.

[42] First Biennial Report, State Farms Corporation, Ghana.

[43] For a fuller account of state farms in Ghana, see J. Gordon, 'State Farms in Ghana', in A. H. Bunting (ed.), *Change in Agriculture*, Duckworth, 1970, and M. P. Miracle and Ann Seidman, *State Farms in Ghana*, Land Tenure Centre, Madison, 1968.

[44] B. Beckman, 'State intervention in agriculture: Ghana, 1951–76', paper given to the conference on Agricultural Change in Africa, Durham, 1976.

[45] However, whereas Ghana State Farms set up by the Nkrumah government in the early 1960s were instruments of socialist policy and a radical transformation of the economy, the Tanganyika Groundnuts Scheme in the late 1940s aimed to meet Britain's import demand for oilseeds; indeed, the administration in Dar es Salaam was hardly responsible, and warned of the many obstacles facing such a short-cut venture.

[46] B. Beckman, loc. cit.

[47] J. M. Beeny, *Agricultural Mechanization Study*, UNDP Report to the United Republic of Tanzania, FAO, October 1975.

[48] J. R. Raeburn, 'Some economic aspects of African agriculture', *East African Economic Review* (Old Series), January 1959.

[49] P. Dorner, *Land Reform and Economic Development*, Penguin, 1972, p. 58.

[50] See J. C. de Wilde, *Experiences with Agricultural Development in Tropical Africa*, op. cit.

[51] United Republic of Tanzania, *Second Five Year Plan for Economic and Social Development*, 1 July 1969–June 1974, Vol I, p. 26.

[52] For a discussion of different motives behind the establishment of ujamaa villages, see A. Q. Ellman, 'Progress, Problems and Prospects in Ujamaa Development in Tanzania', ERB Paper 70.18, Economic Research Bureau, Dar es Salaam, 1970.

[53] G. Hyden, 'Ujamaa, Villagisation and Rural Development in Tanzania', *Overseas Development Review*, 1, 1975.

[54] President J. K. Nyerere, *Socialism and Rural Development*, Government Printer, Dar es Salaam, 1967.

[55] Three stages were distinguished: (1) concentration of people into a designated village; (2) establishment of communal production; (3) registration as a cooperative society to market surplus production.

[56] See Hyden, loc. cit.

[57] P. Raikes, 'Ujamaa and Rural Socialism', *Review of African Political Economy*, No. 3, 1975.

[58] ibid.

[59] N. Georgulas, 'Settlement Patterns and Rural Development in Tanganyika', *Ekistics*, Vol. 24.

[60] The problem described here is known as the 'common property problem', and can also apply to hunting, fishing, and the collection of forest products including the cutting of timber.

[61] There may be some additional reasons for holding cattle beyond the maximum set by carrying capacity. For example a greater number of animals may reduce the danger of an individual's losing his entire holding of cattle through disease or theft.

11 Marketing and Distribution in Eastern Africa

Whereas the value of agricultural producers and factory workers is readily appreciated, there is often misunderstanding of the role of traders and middlemen, and of the functions of the marketing system generally.

Local, internal, and external trade in Africa

Before looking at the functions of the marketing system, it is worth noting the different patterns of trade in Africa. Broadly speaking, there are two patterns of trade, superimposed on one another. The dominant one is the export-import trade, in Eastern Africa funnelling on Mombasa and Dar es Salaam and other ports, with internal centres such as Nairobi and Kampala acting as entrepôts in Kenya and Uganda; the West African export trade, passing through major ports like Lagos and Accra was the subject of a classic study by P. T. Bauer.[1] The export trade has concentrated on primary products, particularly cash crops like cocoa, coffee, and cotton grown by African peasant farmers, together with mineral exports such as copper and, more recently, Nigerian petroleum.

In addition to this export trade, an important interregional trade in foodstuffs exists within each country and from time to time between countries, although this international trade in foodstuffs between African countries has been hampered by restriction and not developed as much as it might have. The trade in foodstuffs between surplus and deficit areas each season within each country may be carried on over vast distances and despite difficult transport conditions. This trade is greatest in West Africa because of the vast distances possible, for example, within Nigeria and the different agriculture in North and South Nigeria (or Ghana), providing possibilities for interregional exchange of different commodities. Figure 11.1 shows as an example the supply areas for rice and cowpeas for the town of Ibadan in Nigeria, showing how far these commodities travel. The long-distance trade in livestock and kola nuts in West Africa is also well known.[2] Apart from this substantial trade between regions it is important not to neglect trade in foodstuffs within the local farming community, where farmers place on the market any small surplus which they have. Although very local, this is still of considerable significance as an extension of subsistence or own-account farm production.

A major criticism of the marketing system made frequently in the past was that it was geared particularly to the requirements of the export-import trade or the 'metropolitan trade', as it was called, supplying the needs of metropolitan countries in Europe and North America for supplies of primary products and for markets. Thus transport facilities, road, rail, and harbour investments, and the organizational system of wholesaling and export-import companies, and even of marketing boards, all catered for the needs of this trade rather than facilitating internal exchange within African countries.

The functions of the marketing system

Elsewhere we have already lauded the benefits arising out of specialization and the division of labour. But

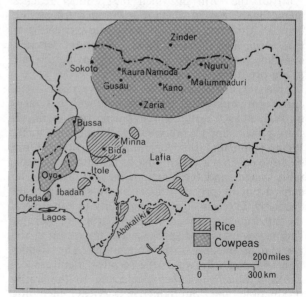

Figure 11.1 *Supply areas for rice and cowpeas for Ibadan, Nigeria (SOURCE: A. R. Thodey, Marketing of Staple Food in Western Nigeria, Stanford Research Institute, 1968, Map 1.1, pp. 1–6).*

specialization requires exchange. And exchange is effected through the network of markets which form the system of marketing or distribution. In a subsistence economy, we may note, marketing services will not be required.

Specialization may take place among people in one area, that is, between occupations, or between regions or countries. Whereas transportation will be involved in the latter exchange, transport services will not be a major part of middlemen's activity in the former case.

The aim of production, of course, is nothing other than the satisfaction of consumers' wants, the provision of utility to consumers. The marketing system must therefore in the first place transmit information regarding the wants of consumers back to producers, and ensure that producers can respond to these wants by supplying consumers, through various intermediaries. It is not enough that the commodities in demand are produced: they must be provided *where* and *when* and *in the form that* the consumers want them. Consumers are thus willing to pay:

(1) for the intrinsic qualities of the product;

(2) for the place at which it is available, that is, for having the product brought to somewhere near their homes;

(3) for the time at which it is available; for instance, consumers will probably want to purchase small quantities of the commodity throughout the year rather than having to purchase all their monthly or annual requirements at the same time;

(4) for the form in which the product reaches them: for the way in which it is wrapped, for buying it in an attractive shop, for being allowed credit at that shop, and so on, that is, for certain services, including processing perhaps, accompanying the sale of the product.

Thus the marketing system may give place, time, and form utility to the commodities that pass through it as a result of (1) transporting them, (2) storing them, and (3) processing and packaging them. We may note that these functions are carried out in a socialist economic system just as much as in a capitalist system, and the functions may in principle be carried out by private traders or by state agencies. Secondly, in terms of supplying utility to consumers, the subsequent activities of transportation, storage, and processing would appear just as important as the original production of the commodity. The distinction sometimes drawn in the socialist literature between 'productive services', referring to the initial production, and 'unproductive services', including marketing and other direct services to consumers, is thus rather artificial.[3]

Processing, as well as the provision of the raw commodity, may be carried out by the producer himself, but usually processing, sorting, grading, and packing of commodities are carried out by middlemen. The middlemen's basic functions are perhaps transporting and storing: the first involving the movement of commodities over space, one might say, and the second movement 'over time'.

In the physical movement of commodities the major cost is of course transport, and this is especially true in Africa where the required distances are often vast and communications poor. But much more than transportation is involved, because this movement requires organization. Obviously it would not be economic to move thousands of small bundles of produce separately over long distances: the commodity must first be assembled at a number of central points and then moved in bulk consignments. In Africa farmers generally take their produce to the local market (or cooperative society) or local shop ('duka' in East Africa), and these form the primary buying points. In the case of export produce (the sequence for foodstuffs for domestic consumption is more complicated), an agent or small trader will purchase at the local market for transfer to a large merchant in a major township (or to the local marketing board store), who will in turn move the produce in large lots to an export-import company (or marketing board again) at the port. This process, illustrated in Figure 11.2, is referred to as *bulk-building*. Corresponding to this on the side of distribution we have *bulk-breaking*, the breaking-up of large consignments into smaller lots for distribution over a wider area.

Involved in the collection and distribution of produce will be not only labour and transport, but also

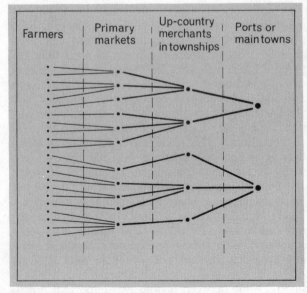

Figure 11.2   The process of bulk-building.

management and book-keeping. The more widely scattered are the producers, and the lower the production or consumption per head, the greater will be the costs, including transport costs, in relation to the value of the product.

Time is involved in marketing in two ways: in the first place, time is involved in the ordinary process of collection, transportation, and distribution, causing a time lag between a merchant's paying out money for produce and his being recompensed for its resale. Secondly, this lag may be appreciably widened because the market is unfavourable at a particular time for the disposal of the commodity, because supply and demand are not 'in step'. Seasonal variations in supply and demand are just one example of this. The commodity needs to be stored until a time suitable for its disposal on the market.

Because time is involved, the middleman requires capital to finance the holding of stocks and to pay for storage accommodation. He also has to face certain risks: that the produce he has bought may be already spoiled, or become spoiled before he is able to sell it, but more important the risk that the price of the commodity which he holds may fall while the commodity is in his possession.

Summarizing, therefore, we can say that the functions of the middleman and the costs of marketing include:

(1) Transportation
(2) Management and book-keeping
(3) Labour
(4) Finance of stock-holding
(5) Provision of storage accommodation
(6) Risk-bearing
(7) Market assessment and communication of market intelligence.

This last item requires further explanation. We said above that the marketing system transmits information or market 'signals' regarding the wants of consumers and the production possibilities of producers. This operates through individual traders who have to assess the terms on which producers and earlier middlemen in the marketing chain are willing to provide the commodity, on the supply side, and how much consumers are willing to pay, on the demand side. 'Assessing the market' is thus an important part of a trader's function.

Middlemen and the stability of prices

By carrying out movement of commodities over space and time, middlemen help to stabilize prices. For they can only make profits by 'buying low' and 'selling high'. If meat, say, is in abundant supply in Region A and in short supply in Region B, prices will be low in A and high in B: traders will thus be encouraged to move cattle from Region A to Region B, where meat is in short supply. Supplies in A will be decreased, and in B increased, so that prices in the two regions are brought closer together. In fact, if cattle can be moved freely from the first region to the other, the price differential should be progressively narrowed down until it only just covers the full costs of transferring cattle between the regions.

Middlemen transfer supplies from one period of time to another in much the same way, the transfer being effected by buying the product in periods of relative abundance and storing it for resale in periods of expected shortage when prices will be higher. Seasonal variation in the prices of agricultural commodities, for instance, generally arises because, while demand remains more or less steady during the year, supplies vary with the season: hence prices tend to fall immediately after harvest and to rise between harvest as stocks are used up.

Seasonal fluctuations in the prices of agricultural products can be very wide. If the commodity is a staple food for a large majority of the population, this can be a major inconvenience and even cause extreme hardship. The expected effect of middlemen's operations, however, will be to reduce the amplitude of such fluctuations. If again they buy when prices are low and sell when they are high, they will be buying (increasing demand) when supply is great and selling (increasing supply) when supply is short. This will benefit producers as well as consumers, since producers will be less affected by selling 'at the wrong time'.

Prices will not become completely equal as between seasons as a result of this activity. This is because there are costs associated with transferring commodities through time, costs of storage in particular. The seasonal rise in price of the stored commodity should in fact approximate to the cost of storage. For this reason, goods that are costly to store because they are bulky or especially because of perishability, and storage losses, will tend to show wider seasonal fluctuations.

This is borne out in Table 11.1, which is taken from a study of the marketing of staple food crops in Africa by William O. Jones.[4] In this table the seasonal index referred to is given by the ratio, as a percentage, of the price in a particular season to the trend value, these percentages being averaged for the corresponding month, over a period of years. Thus if the seasonal index for yams were 135 per cent in June and 65 per cent in November this would mean that June prices tended to be on average 35 per cent above the level they would have been in the absence of seasonal fluctuation, and November prices 35 per cent

Table 11.1   *Seasonal movement in prices of food commodities at Ibadan, Nigeria, 1952–3 to 1965–6*

Commodity	High month	Low month	Range of seasonal index*
Rice	August	February	8
Gari (cassava meal)	June	December	15
Cowpeas	October	January	24
Maize	May	September	29
Yams	June	November	70

SOURCE: W. O. Jones, op. cit., Table 15, p. 26

*Seasonal indexes are simple averages of the ratio of reported prices to a twelve-month centred moving average

below the level they would have been. The range of the seasonal index is from 65 to 135 per cent, or 70 per cent.

It can be seen that the seasonal fluctuation is markedly higher for yams than for the other commodities, which might be expected from the fact that yams are much more difficult and costly to store. In contrast, gari (cassava meal) which is easily stored, simply by leaving it in the ground, shows much greater seasonal price stability. Despite this, gari prices show *some* seasonal price variation apparently because the hardness of the ground at a particular time of year makes harvesting cassava roots more difficult but especially because the possibility of substitution between gari and other foodstuffs such as yams makes the demand for gari vary with the supply and price of these alternatives. Thus the highest prices of gari occur during April to July when yams are least available, and demand is diverted to gari.[5]

Despite what we said previously, it is quite possible for the action of middlemen to operate in a contrary manner to *destabilize* prices. Suppose, due to a minor shortage, there is a small rise in the price of the commodity. Traders *might* be led to take this as an indication that the price is likely to rise still further. Instead of selling their stocks, therefore, they might decide to *add* to them, with a view to reselling later at still higher prices. Instead of increasing supply when prices rise, they increase demand. This increase in demand will tend to raise the price. Traders, seeing that the price has actually risen, might feel justified in their previous expectation and expect the price rise to continue, they might buy up still more stock, and so on. In the end, where the original shortage was quite minor, there might be a genuine shortage due to the increased demand by such traders. People who speculate on the possibility of a rise in the price of a commodity, and who buy up stocks of the commodity in the hope of making a profit out of the change in price of the stocks they own, are referred to as *speculators*.

It is interesting to note that in this process prices may rise because people *think* they will rise. The process may also work in reverse: traders expecting a fall in price sell their stocks to avoid being 'caught' with them when they fall in value. If a sufficient number of traders think in this way, supply on the market will be increased substantially from stocks and the price *will* fall. Traders may speculate in this way without physically moving stocks from their warehouse: middlemen can buy and sell pieces of paper giving them *ownership* of the goods without actually seeing the goods themselves. In this way the goods may change hands fifteen or twenty times without ever leaving the warehouse, all the time, however, fluctuating in value. Thus the activities of middlemen, while perhaps being expected to reduce fluctuations in price, sometimes aggravate such fluctuations.

The division of labour as applied to marketing

From the outline of marketing functions given above it is easy to see that the reason why middlemen exist is associated with the division of labour: there is a division of labour between those who actually produce the raw product and those who process and distribute it.

The principle of division of labour accounts also for much of the detailed structure of marketing. It is responsible for the specialization between *concentrating middlemen*, who are engaged in bulk-building activities, and *dispersing middlemen*, who are engaged in bulk-breaking, that is, in distribution. There is in addition specialization between buyers and sellers operating at export-import level, at the wholesale, and at the retail or primary level: in other words there is *vertical* specialization between different *levels* of marketing. Besides this there is *horizontal* specialization according to the type of product. This occurs where there is a large volume of a single crop to be handled, as in the case of coffee, or where the handling of a particular crop involves individual difficulties, as in the case of hides and skins, which require specialist knowledge, or in the case of perishable commodities such as fish or matoke (plantains). For similar reasons specialist functions like transportation, warehousing, and insurance are often undertaken separately: thus independent road hauliers are part of the distribution and marketing system also.

On the other hand specialization is seldom complete. In the first place farmers themselves will be undertaking part of the marketing function if they take produce from the farm to the nearest market, and so will the consumer when he travels to a shop to make his purchases instead of accepting delivery at home.

In the case of certain industrial products, manufacturers often prefer to develop their own retail outlets, and this practice seems to be increasing in many countries. Specialization between concentrating and dispersing middlemen is very often only partial, and this is generally the case in Africa, where there is considerable integration between the produce-buying trade and wholesale/retail distribution, due to the economies this can bring in entrepreneurship (since produce-buying is seasonal, the businessman is unoccupied part of the year), in the use of finance and credit (cash earned in retailing can be used to finance produce-buying, since it is usually easier to obtain trade credit for retailing than for the riskier business of produce-buying), and in the use of storage accommodation. The extent of specialization here as elsewhere will depend on the 'size of the market': a retailer, for instance, servicing a small local market is more likely to combine the two sides of marketing than a large firm operating at the exporting or importing level.

The application of division of labour among different levels of marketing means that there may be several successive intermediaries, or middlemen, through whose hands the product passes. It is worth noting this in relation to the common criticism that an excessive number of middlemen will raise the price to the consumer and lower that to the producer. In fact the presumption following our analysis is that if an intermediary is able to survive, he must be doing a given task as cheaply as anyone else could do it: if for instance secondary-stage buyers could do the primary buying in addition to the second stage more cheaply than the primary buyers, they could put the latter out of business by offering producers a better price. Thus the 'number of stages' in marketing will also be a function of the advantages of the division of labour. This is not to say that a given number of middlemen will always be necessary. There have been important changes in the organization of marketing and distribution which have involved the cutting out of certain intermediaries. In other words, it does not mean than a new organization, like a cooperative, may not be developed which eliminates the need for as many intermediaries.

Criticisms of marketing in Africa

Partly because of misunderstanding of the functions of marketing, and of middlemen, however, marketing and distribution tend to be a criticized sector of the economy, and their efficiency in less developed coun-

tries has been particularly criticized. Let us see why the marketing sector in Africa and other developing areas might be less efficient, and give brief consideration to the arguments.

(1) Efficiency in transportation depends not only on the efficiency of transporters but on the adequacy of infrastructural provision: the availability and quality of roads and railways. William O. Jones has asserted that inadequate physical facilities have not restricted marketing in two countries examined by him, Nigeria and Kenya, while admitting that in Sierra Leone 'the skeletal road and rail network and frequent interruption of road transport by rain and flooding makes it much more difficult to establish regular market connections throughout the country'.[6] The position in Southern Nigeria and Kenya he regards as more typical, however, and here he considers that transportation 'permits regular movement of produce throughout the economy at what appears to be reasonable cost'.[6]

It is difficult to generalize about communications in tropical Africa, but one can perhaps make the following assertions:

(a) while many areas are made remote by lack of major transport links, the system of trunk roads, supplemented by railways, is relatively good;

(b) in the more populated regions, especially, internal communications are often quite good and despite the low level of economic development it is unsafe to conclude that inadequate infrastructure is necessarily holding back development;

(c) on the other hand, local feeder roads to support the system of trunk roads are often lacking;

(d) and, as discussed earlier, the main transport links of road and rail are generally oriented to supporting the export-import trade rather than facilitating the internal circulation of commodities between regions within the country.

(2) Given reasonable communications, if the marketing system, and the traders within it, are working efficiently, prices for the same goods in neighbouring markets should move up and down together, differing only by the cost of moving supplies between them. In this respect the performance of African marketing systems does not appear good. Thus Whetham states that 'the evidence suggests that there may be considerable differences in prices for common foods between adjacent markets at the same time'.[7] and Jones finds similarly that 'the general low correlation of prices must be accepted as evidence that allocation of commodities among markets is considerably less than optimum'.[8] More specifically Whetham found this to be the case for food crops in both Eastern and Western Nigeria although the towns there are linked by good roads through densely populated areas; M. G. Smith some time ago re-

corded considerable differences in market prices between Zaria and Giwa, which are only 20 miles apart in Northern Nigeria;[9] and Anne Martin found that prices in Kampala and Jinja in Uganda, though separated by only 50 miles of good tarmac road, could differ by wide margins.[10]

We should expect, of course, that if prices for the same commodity in adjacent markets differed by more than the cost of transport, traders would be able to make a profit by shifting supplies from the cheap market to the dear market, and would continue to do so until the price difference was just equal to the transport cost. Since the problem of communications is not the explanation, one needs to consider whether market information is adequate or whether perhaps traders lack capital for effective operation or whether the organization of the trade is lacking.

One particular problem which arises is where a major market may receive supplies from a number of very separate source regions. It then becomes extremely difficult to coordinate deliveries to the market, where prices fluctuate in irregular fashion. Mbilinyi and Mascarenhas have remarked upon this in respect of the prices of cooking bananas delivered to the Dar es Salaam urban market,[11] while Jones comments with respect to Nigeria that 'week-to-week price changes showed signs of serious random disturbances consistent with the hypothesis that traders were poorly informed about episodic changes in the conditions of supply and transport'.[12]

(3) How effective the marketing system in Africa is in providing 'movement over time' through storage of commodities is subject to debate. Thodey[13] has calculated that the rise in prices in most seasons was barely adequate to cover the costs of storing maize, when account was taken of the high rate of loss in the humid climate of Western Nigeria, and Jones in his book concludes that in Nigeria seasonal increases in prices are in line with rough estimates of the cost of storage, suggesting that traders are effectively performing the storage function.

On the other hand it is widely considered that there are heavy losses through spoilage at the farm level, because farmers lack good facilities to store basic foodstuffs. Thus in Tanzania investigations have been going on for sometime into the feasibility of improved maize storage bins for distribution throughout the country. According to the FAO, lack of farm storage facilities together with 'the ever-prevailing need for cash among farmers' has been responsible for farm surpluses being sold off immediately after harvest, causing prices to fall more sharply than necessary.[14]

(4) If the efficiency of the marketing system is measured by the spread between the price received by the producer and the price paid at the other end by the ultimate consumer, or by what one might call 'the farmer's share of the consumer's dollar' then, excluding the transport element, one might ask first, how long is the buying chain of middlemen between producer and consumer and, secondly, are such middlemen extracting excessive profit margins? A very frequent complaint about middlemen in developing and even in developed countries is that there are too many of them, that in effect the 'marketing chain' is too long. As already stated above, this is a dubious argument from a purely theoretical point of view since if an intermediary is able to survive in the face of competition it must be because he is doing a particular task as cheaply as anyone else would find it possible.

Table 11.2   *Average number of transactions between producer and consumer, selected commodities, Kenya and Western Nigeria*

Commodity	Kenya	Commodity	Western Nigeria
Maize	2.63	Maize	3.40
Beans	2.55	Gari (cassava meal)	2.91
Potatoes	2.52	Yams	3.85
Bananas	2.36		

SOURCE: W. O. Jones, op. cit., p. 215

Table 11.2 gives the average number of times various commodities were calculated to change hands in Kenya and Western Nigeria in going from producer to consumer. This appears quite short, particularly in the case of Kenya, though these are average figures, and the fact that substantial sales were effected direct from producer to consumer (giving a figure of 1.0) would bring down the average. The higher figures for Western Nigeria probably reflect longer distances involved, as well as the type of commodity.

(5) While good incomes can often be obtained in retailing in Africa, it is unlikely that margins generally are excessive. For the most part there is ease of entry into retailing in Eastern *and* West Africa, and retailing is highly competitive. This is not the case at the wholesale level, whether in produce-buying or on the side of distribution. The main requirement for participation here is working capital to finance the movement of commodities, much more substantial at the wholesale level. It was found some time ago in Eastern Africa that it was 'largely through their control over the supply of credit that the large merchants maintain their control over purchases of produce', while the distributive trade appears to rely even more heavily on credit than the produce-buying trade from the importer through to the small

dealer.[15] Thus it is only at the wholesale level (often combined with processing) and the export-import level that monopolistic margins are likely to exist.

(6) This point is significant with respect to another major criticism of the marketing system in Eastern Africa. Before independence, and for some time after that, it was often remarked that trade was 'in the hands of Asians'. However it was never true that Asians had a 'monopoly of trade' in the technical sense, in that no other traders existed. In the first place, trade in local foodstuffs and handicrafts was largely confined to unspecialized or informally organized African suppliers. Even within the 'formal' sector of licensed traders, the majority, whether itinerant traders or static shopkeepers, have been African. As far back as 1952–3 an enquiry into the distribution of imported manufactured and processed consumer goods for African consumers in Malawi and Tanzania estimated that some 70 per cent of all static retail shops were in the hands of Africans in both countries, although about a quarter of the 200 non-African retailers in Malawi and the same share of the 11,000 Arab and Indian retailers in Tanzania were concentrated, conspicuously, to give the impression of greater numbers, in the two capital cities.[16] Table 11.3 shows that in 1960–1 over 70 per cent of licensed traders in Tanganyika were Africans. Over 80 per cent of retailers were African. On the other hand, at the *wholesale* level only a handful of African traders participated; and as we have said, it is at this level that competition was less intense and profit levels substantially higher. Thus only at this level can we talk of any monopoly power being exerted.

Nevertheless ethnic and tribal groupings have been of considerable significance in commerce. Thus in Uganda and Tanzania some 45 or 50 per cent of

gainfully occupied Asians were engaged in trade. In Kenya the proportion was rather less, with more Asians being engaged in manufacturing and other source activities as well as commerce. It is quite usual for immigrant minority groups such as the Asians in Eastern Africa, the Chinese in Malaysia, and the Levantines in West Africa, to enter trade, partly because they are excluded from or at a disadvantage in other sectors such as agriculture or the civil service, and may lack the capital for entry into large-scale manufacturing. Once the tradition of commerce has been established within such a minority group, new generations are taught business skills, and acquire ambitions for business, from an early age.

Tradition had also been behind the association of certain tribal groups with particular trades. Thus tribal networks have dominated the long-distance trade in cattle and kola nuts in West Africa, while Somalis have been predominant in the cattle trade in Eastern Africa.

Apart from tradition and the occupational barriers mentioned, these patterns have been reinforced in many cases by very effective systems of mutual help in terms of market information, business contact, and granting of loans and trade credit. Given the reluctance of banks and other financial institutions to lend to Africans and others operating on a small scale and lacking security to bolster their creditworthiness, mutual help, particularly credit, within racial or tribal groups, has been of great importance. This, more than anything else, has been responsible for resentment among indigenous groups who have felt excluded from trade.

As a result positive steps have been taken in a number of countries since independence to promote indigenous traders. In Nigeria there have been efforts to promote non-Ibo traders. In Uganda there was adopted a policy of rapid expropriation of Asian traders, citizens as well as non-citizens, who were forced to leave the country in 1972, leaving their businesses for distribution among favoured Africans, often with no previous experience in this case. In the case of Kenya the policy has been one of very gradual expropriation or forced sale through the withdrawal of trading licences to non-citizens, combined with strong efforts to promote African traders. Whereas in Kenya a successful policy of *localization* of commerce organized on a *capitalist* basis was adopted, which has resulted in the almost complete replacement of Asians by Africans in the smaller towns, in Tanzania the aim has been the *socialization* of the commercial sector, particularly at the export-import and wholesaling levels, and Asians have remained as employees of state trading organizations and as independent small-scale retail or combined wholesale/retail operators.

Table 11.3 *Trading licence holders in Tanganyika, 1960–1*

	Dar es Salaam No.	Tanganyika No.	% of total
Wholesalers	1,250	3,890	8
Non-African retailers	1,480	10,090	21
Wholesalers plus non-African retailers	2,730	13,980	29
African retailers	230	34,850	71
Total traders (excluding itinerant)	2,960	48,830	100
Itinerant	50	11,580	—

SOURCE: H. C. G. Hawkins, *Wholesale and Retail Trade in Tanganyika*, Praeger, 1961, pp. 34–5

Cooperative marketing in Eastern Africa

An alternative form of marketing organization to the private trader and trading company, and one which has played a major role in the marketing system of Eastern Africa, is the cooperative.

Types of cooperative

The most common types of cooperative organization, corresponding to different types of economic activity are: (1) farm production cooperatives; (2) cooperative marketing societies for the collection and processing of farm produce; (3) consumer (retail) societies on the side of distribution; (4) credit societies and savings clubs; and (5) trades and craft societies such as those in handicrafts, building, and construction. A special type of production cooperative, mentioned below in relation to the Sudan, is one based on the joint purchase and use of expensive capital equipment, such as pumping equipment for irrigation.

Cooperative agricultural production was discussed in the previous chapter. In Eastern Africa the main form of cooperative has been the cooperative marketing society, where marketing here refers to the collection of produce from the grower, and subsequent stages of bulk-building, rather than to the distribution of goods to the consumer, though in the case of basic foodstuffs the cooperative chain may reach from the producer to the consumer. Primary cooperative marketing societies are often associated with a secondary cooperative union covering particular districts or regions. Unions in turn may be affiliated under a nation-wide 'Apex' organization.

Generally speaking, attempts at establishing consumer retail societies for distribution have not met with much success in Africa. Credit societies and savings clubs have a long and relatively successful history in Nigeria, but have not until recently been much in evidence in Eastern Africa. Kenya, Zambia, and Zimbabwe (Rhodesia) are countries where they are to be considered part of the financial system rather than the marketing system, however, since they deal with the mobilization of savings and the distribution of loanable funds, and not with the distribution of goods. In Mauritius, however, cooperative credit societies of small sugar growers are the backbone of a movement of great variety, including consumer (retail), housing, thrift, and transport societies. The earliest cooperatives date from 1913.

Reasons for promoting cooperatives

Cooperative marketing societies have been pro-moted, in Africa and elsewhere, for both economic and political reasons. On the economic side, cooperatives may succeed in increasing the prices received by growers in a given demand situation in a number of ways.

(1) Cooperatives may in favourable circumstances reduce the costs of marketing by doing the job better than the private traders they replace. This might be where the small primary traders lack the finance and the storage facilities to enable them to carry out effectively the middleman's functions described earlier. A large group of producers, by paying comparatively small financial contributions into a central pool, may be able to raise more capital. They may also, by pooling their labour, be able to build storage or processing plant within closer proximity of their farms.

(2) Cooperatives may provide a useful channel for propagating ideas for the improvement of methods of cultivation to their membership of peasant farmers. They may also help to improve the product marketed by encouraging the production of a more standardized product or more effective grading of the product. They may also be a useful channel through which loans to farmers may be made.

(3) If the middlemen they replace had been enjoying profits in excess of the competitive level, due to a monopoly position, cooperatives can absorb part or all of these excess profits by improving the bargaining position of growers.

(4) Where cooperatives are linked to a marketing board set up for the sake of marketing a product overseas, it may be possible to raise prices obtained from overseas consumers to the benefit of growers by taking advantage of any monopolistic position in world markets and restricting supply.

However, political considerations have also lain behind the encouragement of cooperatives.

(1) Fitting in with ideas of traditional African forms of cooperation, marketing cooperatives have been seen by African governments as a way of realizing 'African Socialism'.[17] Just as African Socialism was intended to be something different from the full-bloodied Marxist version, so these cooperatives could be supported as a form of socialism not requiring direct state participation in marketing and having a strong democratic element. Since the cooperative structure of produce-buying and marketing could be applied within a generally capitalist system based on the price mechanism, just as much as in a socialist one, the political leadership could accept cooperatives within the marketing sector without committing themselves to one political system or another.

(2) A second reason which could be termed political was the desire to promote indigenous African enterprises and to replace non-African middlemen,

in Eastern Africa particularly. This was certainly the predominant motive behind the encouragement of cooperatives by the colonial governments who, adopting a paternal attitude towards the encouragement of African enterprise, found themselves generally more successful with these than with the promotion of individual African entrepreneurs. This was also the chief motive, of course, of the African producers themselves, who saw collective action through the cooperative movement as their best chance of getting a better deal for their produce and of actually taking over trading from the financially more powerful non-indigenous traders.

The importance of cooperatives in Africa

Table 11.4 gives some idea of the importance of cooperatives in different African countries, particularly the last column, which shows the number of registered members. This shows clearly the dominance of the East African countries as far as cooperative development is concerned, Uganda, Tanzania, and Kenya together having easily the highest membership in the years concerned.

A feature of the cooperative movement in Africa which is not too easy to explain is its much greater importance in Eastern Africa compared to West Africa. In Eastern Africa, as we shall see, cooperatives have developed most strongly in areas where there was a single high-priced cash crop being produced for export, as in the case of the coffee- and cotton-marketing societies in Uganda and Tanzania. Yet export crops such as cocoa were important in Nigeria and Ghana without providing the same foundation for cooperative development. The difference is probably in part, at least, explained by the earlier rise of indigenous African entrepreneur/traders in West Africa, and the much less dominating position in up-country marketing held in West Africa by expatriate traders, compared to the Asian trading community in Eastern Africa. This itself would reduce the interest of the colonial governments in promoting cooperatives as a form of indigenous African enterprise; but secondly it is likely that the colonial governments in Eastern Africa happened in general to pursue more paternalistic policies of encouraging cooperatives than those in West Africa.[18]

A better measure of the importance of cooperatives within the system of marketing than the number of membership of societies, as given in Table 11.4, is, however, the proportion of the value of all agricultural goods marketed cooperatively. In 1967 this was 90 per cent in Tanzania, 75 per cent in Uganda, and 25 per cent in Kenya. These countries have been described as the 'cooperative giants' of the African continent,[19] though we see from these figures that cooperatives were much more important in Tanzania and Uganda than in Kenya. Three factors help to explain the much lower percentage in the case of Kenya: the importance of the large-farm sector, which markets a substantial amount of high-valued produce directly, without use of cooperatives; the existence of tea, sold directly to the Tea Board, and other plantation and estate commodities, sold directly to commodity boards; and the much greater importance of private traders. As we shall see, on the other hand, there is a greater diversity in the Kenyan cooperative movement, with a much greater variety of produce handled.

Common problems of cooperatives

In practice cooperatives the world over have faced certain common problems.[20] First, cooperatives probably have an inherent weakness in management. There can be no one person who as a result of investing large sums of money in the concern has a compelling interest to pursue its financial success. Inevitably, since produce marketing cooperatives bring together farmers, and not traders, there will be a lack of business management experience and a lack of accounting expertise since full-time farmers will find it difficult to spare the time for the acquisition of these skills. At the same time, there is often unwillingness to pay a sufficiently high salary to attract a really competent manager who might be able to overcome these deficiencies.

Secondly, the reluctance of members to pay very

Table 11.4 The importance of cooperative societies in different African countries in the late 1960s

	Year to which data refers	No. of societies	No. of members (×1,000)
Uganda	1967	1824	521.2
Tanzania	1967	1399	500.0
Kenya	1967	1783	500.0
Nigeria	1965	5516	328.7
Ghana	1967	1382	201.0
Tunisia	1966	13	120.0
Sudan	1966	976	100.0
Western Nigeria	1967	2112	84.3
Sierra Leone	1968	929	46.3
Zambia	1970	1098	43.7

SOURCE: G. Hyden, 'Can cooperatives make it in Africa?', *Africa Report*, December, 1970, p. 13; and *Year Book of Agricultural Co-operation*, 1971, Basil Blackwell, 1971

high subscriptions, and their reluctance to pay well in advance, means that cooperatives are in fact often at a disadvantage with the traders they are competing with through 'lack of capital'. It is important to remember that the main aim in developing marketing cooperatives at all is not the pursuit of the 'cooperative spirit' but the belief that cooperatives may be turned into viable business enterprises capable of carrying out necessary marketing functions more effectively than alternative forms of enterprise. If they are inherently weak, therefore, in two major ingredients of business activity, namely, enterprise and capital, this must be a serious obstacle.

A third problem of cooperative enterprise is to maintain loyalty among its members. Once the cooperative is well established and flourishing, of course, this is unlikely to be a source of difficulty, since producers will benefit from 'keeping in line'. But in fact it may require some considerable time, due in part to the problems already mentioned, to build up an effective organization, a sufficient membership, and a large volume of business in order to achieve this comfortable state. This is connected in part with our second point since, particularly in the initial stages, cooperatives are likely to be short of capital and may not be able to pay cash in full to growers until after they have in turn resold the product. In contrast, traders are likely to be in a position to pay cash immediately on receipt of produce, or even before producers have the commodity available. It is in this period that there must be sufficient enthusiasm for cooperation and sufficient patience to wait for benefits which will be obtained only at a later stage, so that members do not prefer immediate opportunities for profit by selling outside the cooperative to traders.

How have these general difficulties of cooperative enterprises affected the development of cooperatives in Africa? The management problem in Africa is aggravated by the widespread illiteracy among producers and often the difficulty of finding among their members someone with even a minimum education, let alone training in book-keeping. For a variety of social reasons, particularly in certain regions, there has been a general lack of the business and commercial sense which might have compensated for this. Management problems have been a major cause of the high rate of failure, particularly among societies handling perishable products. The educational gap between the secretary/treasurer and other members of the society results in the former being tempted to mishandle finances, and societies have sometimes been subject to frauds or embezzlement; this has had an adverse effect on morale and on loyalty. It cannot be said, finally, that *up to now* cooperative societies have been particularly successful in transmitting

knowledge of improved methods of cultivation and similar improvements back to growers, although they have often proved a useful channel for enforcing the regulations of marketing boards or passing on the advice of agricultural extension officers, especially in the case of export crops such as coffee.

Cooperatives in Africa have also been handicapped vis-à-vis the trader by the inability to pay growers fully in cash on receipt of produce. This is a more severe handicap where producers at low levels of income are particularly impatient to obtain payment. This has been a major cause of disloyalty, particularly in some areas outside the main cash crop areas, and has significantly retarded the growth of cooperatives. On the other hand, the strong tribal loyalties and traditional African community sense have operated in the opposite direction and have provided cohesiveness.

Features of cooperative development in the East African countries

These difficulties help to explain the main feature in the development of the cooperative movement in East Africa, namely, the outstanding success of cooperatives in the main cash crop areas, especially those which handle coffee and cotton, as compared to cooperatives handling food crops for internal East African consumption. The reasons for this are:

(1) In a region based heavily on one crop, economies of scale in marketing including the cost of transportation, storage, and accounting can be obtained by dealing in large consignments of a single commodity. In contrast small quantities of varied produce will be difficult to handle.

(2) This is particularly true when the produce is perishable, as in the case of most food crops. Perishability increases management problems considerably, even if suitable storage accommodation is available.

(3) Funds are more easily built up when the region has a major high-priced cash crop.

(4) The road and rail transport network, and the corresponding marketing structure, have always been geared in colonial and post-colonial times to the export of produce. Moreover, the export-import trade has always been relatively concentrated, with a comparatively small number of large companies dominating the trade. The collection of goods for export has thus always been a much simpler matter than the handling of goods destined for internal distribution within East Africa.

(5) As compared to the handling of a few major cash crops for sale on an organized international

market, the handling of more varied produce for local consumption requires much more information on prices and markets, with correspondingly more risks.

(6) The operation of marketing boards for the main cash crops, with their policies of fixed prices, have undoubtedly shielded cooperatives from competition with traders and from entrepreneurial risks. Not surprisingly, therefore, it has been remarked that the handling of a few main cash crops for an export market and under the 'umbrella' of marketing boards 'is not really trading at all'!

Tables 11.5 and 11.6 illustrate the importance of cash crops in the early development of cooperatives in mainland Tanzania. The Kilimanjaro Native Cooperative Union (KNCU) is justly famous in the history of cooperative development in Africa, having

Table 11.5 *Mainland Tanzania: value of products handled by cooperatives (per cent)*

	1956	1958	1960
Coffee	95	63	48
Seed cotton	2	34	48
Other	3	3	4
Total	100	100	100

Table 11.6 *Value of gross proceeds of cooperatives by product and region, Tanganyika, 1960 (in £ × 1,000)*

Northern Province	Coffee	3,700	
	Cotton	78	3,782
	Other	4	
Southern Province	Coffee	267	
	Tobacco	75	378
	Other	36	
Southern Highlands Province	Coffee	473	
	Rice	156	667
	Other	38	
West Lake Province	Coffee	1,657	1,657
Lake Province	Seed cotton	6,188	6,207
	Other	19	
Eastern Province	Seed cotton	26	
	Rice	55	147
	Other	66	
Tanga Province	Coffee	145	
	Seed cotton	8	193
	Rice	29	
	Other	11	
Western Province	Coffee	8	8
		Total	13,039

started as far back as 1925. It was centred upon the small-scale coffee growers around Kilimanjaro. Table 11.5 shows that as late as 1956 coffee accounted for 95 per cent of the value of produce handled by cooperatives. The position had changed rapidly by 1960, but only through the development of cooperative marketing of a second cash crop, cotton, the turnover of which equalled coffee in value by 1960.

Table 11.6 illustrates the comparative difficulty in developing a cooperative movement faced by regions lacking a major cash crop. The provinces which stand out in the table are the Northern Province (nearly all coffee produced by the Chagga in the Kilimanjaro area), the West Lake Province (coffee produced in the Bukoba area) and, especially, the Lake Province (cotton). The contrast with the remaining provinces is striking.

Subsequently there was a much wider development of cooperation in Tanzania, particularly after the National Agricultural Products Board was established to handle basic food crops as well as minor crops, and was able to act as an 'umbrella' for cooperatives handling a much greater range of commodities. Weakness in the handling by cooperatives of food crops and perishable produce for domestic consumption remained, however, and may well have contributed substantially to the serious problems among societies and unions, which came to a head in the mid-1960s.

The cooperative movement in Uganda is very similarly based to that of Tanzania, on coffee and cotton. The Buganda Growers' Association was set up as long ago as 1920, based on cotton, and in 1935 cotton farmers from all over Buganda founded the 'Uganda Growers' Cooperative Union'. As coffee developed as a second cash crop in the post-war period so the cooperative movement extended its focus to cover this also. Among the coffee-growing farms of Mount Elgon, in Eastern Uganda, the Bugisu Cooperative Union, the BCU, was explicitly modelled upon the KNCU in Tanzania. By 1967 there were as many as 1,970 societies in Uganda, and 31 unions. These societies were engaged overwhelmingly in the marketing of crops, as shown in Table 11.7 (95 per cent were crop marketing societies) and these concentrated on coffee and cotton. The small but significant development of thrift and loan societies is worth noting and comparing with similar developments in other African countries.

The pattern of development in Kenya has been rather different. Table 11.8 gives the turnover of cooperative societies and unions in Kenya in 1969. We do see again the features of development remarked upon with respect to Tanzania: 57 per cent of turnover was accounted for by coffee, supported by some additional export crops like pyrethrum; secondly the most important 'cooperative' provinces, Central and Eastern Provinces, owe their predominant position entirely to the cooperative marketing of coffee. At the same time, however, there is here still a substantial spread of cooperation into diverse other activities, as seen more clearly in Table 11.9. This shows that there were, for example, 156 societies engaged in marketing grains and cereals, just about the same number as were marketing coffee. These were mainly maize societies, and their success probably owes a great deal to the encouragement and protection offered by maize and other produce mar-

keting boards, an indication of the role that such boards can perform as an 'umbrella' under the shelter of which cooperatives can develop. Apart from this, however, there was a remarkable development of cooperative dairies, numbering 108 in 1966, with a significant number of cooperatives dealing in eggs and poultry, and others dealing in pigs, in addition. Also interesting is the spread of cooperative activity outside crops and livestock: particularly the significant development of credit and savings societies (118 of these), of consumer societies (69 of these), and a large number of farm purchase societies, but also including cooperatives for housing, building and construction, charcoal, timber, transport, butcheries, fisheries, and craftsmen. The wide spread of activities covered itself suggests the considerable scope which exists for cooperatives within the small-scale sector of the economy, based especially on the benefits from pooling capital where this is scarce.

Table 11.7 *Activities of Uganda cooperative societies in 1967*

	Societies	Unions
Crop marketing	1,863	29
Cattle and livestock	15	2
Farming	12	—
Dairy	9	—
Hides and skins	9	—
Fishing	8	—
Transport	4	—
Handicrafts	4	—
Traders	1	—
Housing	2	—
Consumers	8	—
Thrift and loan	35	—
TOTAL	1,970	31

SOURCE: O. Okereke, *The Economic Impact of Uganda Cooperatives*, East African Literature Bureau, 1974, Table 1, p. 26

Crisis in the East African cooperative movement

During the 1960s the type of problems described above as commonly associated with cooperatives became more serious in East Africa until something of a crisis was reached in the mid-1960s in both Tanzania and Uganda. In both cases the problems may be said to be the result of (a) an overambitious rate of expansion of the movement as a whole, as a result of 'forced' growth of cooperation as government policy, and (b) an overambitious spread of

Table 11.8 *Turnover of cooperative societies and unions in Kenya, 1969, by activity and province (shs million)[1]*

Province	Activity											
	Provincial total	Coffee	Dairies	Pyrethrum	Sugar cane	Livestock, pigs, wool, eggs and poultry	Cereals, vegetables	Cotton	Tobacco	Fish	Farm purchase societies	Distribution and services
Central Province	85.4	69.6	12.8	1.6	—	1.5	—	—	—	—	—	—
Eastern Province	49.7	47.4	1.4	0.2	—	—	0.4	—	0.4	—	—	—
Nyanza Province	37.5	14.7	1.2	15.6	3.8	—	—	1.8	—	0.4	—	—
Western Province	11.0	4.4	0.4	—	0.3	—	2.0	2.9	—	0.1	—	1.1
Rift Valley Province	17.4	0.2	3.3	0.9	3.1	—	1.9	—	—	0.9	3.4	3.7
Coast Province	9.2	0.2	3.0	—	—	—	3.7	—	—	0.3	—	2.1
Settlement cooperatives	21.7	0.04	8.8	5.4	4.9	1.2	1.1	—	—	—	—	0.3
Nairobi area	8.8	—	—	—	—	4.3	—	—	—	—	—	4.5
National total	240.7	136.4	30.8	23.6	12.0	7.0	9.1	4.7	0.4	1.6	3.4	11.6

SOURCE: G. Hyden, op. cit., Table 7

[1] Excludes country-wide cooperative organizations

Table 11.9 *Numbers of cooperative societies and unions in Kenya at the end of 1966, by activity and province*

		CROPS AND LIVESTOCK																OTHER ACTIVITIES										
	Provincial total	Coffee	Grains and cereal	Cotton	Pyrethrum	Sugar	Fruit and vegetables	Other crops	Sisal	Dairies	Eggs and poultry	Pigs	Ranching and livestock	Other animals	Multi-product	Farm purchase	Credit and savings	Consumer societies	Housing	Building and construction	Charcoal	Timber	Transport	Butcher and meat supply	Fisheries	Craftsmen	Miscellaneous	Unions	Country-wide Apex organisation
Nairobi	123	—	—	—	—	—	—	1	—	2	3	—	—	—	—	19	44	25	8	3	—	—	—	2	—	4	4	2	6
Central Province	377	40	7	1	14	—	9	2	1	27	13	20	2	1	53	139	17	14	1	—	1	1	—	1	—	5	2	6	—
Coast Province	94	2	14	—	—	1	6	14	1	7	2	—	4	—	4	—	20	7	1	—	—	—	—	—	4	2	4	1	—
Eastern Province	158	45	33	1	1	—	1	4	2	12	9	—	16	—	18	2	5	1	1	—	—	—	1	1	—	1	—	4	—
Rift Valley Province	307	5	5	—	5	2	—	3	1	21	1	—	7	1	56	157	12	19	—	—	1	—	2	—	3	—	2	4	—
Western Province	165	26	81	17	1	1	—	2	—	5	5	—	1	—	5	3	9	—	—	—	—	—	1	—	1	1	—	6	—
Nyanza Province	221	39	16	17	23	28	—	17	—	34	1	—	1	—	13	4	11	2	—	—	—	—	—	—	4	—	1	10	—
North Eastern Province	1	—	—	—	—	—	—	—	—	—	—	—	—	1	—	—	—	—	—	—	—	—	—	—	—	—	—	—	—
Total, all Provinces	1,446	157	156	36	44	32	16	43	5	108	34	20	31	3	149	324	118	68	11	3	2	1	4	4	12	13	13	33	6

SOURCE: G. Hyden, op. cit., Table 4, Appendix III

cooperative activity beyond the simpler functions of marketing export crops, also as government policy.

In Tanzania there was a government decision following independence to make cooperatives the sole marketing agencies of agricultural produce, replacing private traders. A 1962 Act[21] gave the Minister of Agriculture powers to establish marketing boards which would have exclusive rights to market scheduled crops and rights to appoint agents. The establishment of the National Agricultural Products Board (NAPB) in 1963 handling maize, cashew nuts, paddy, groundnuts, sunflower seed, simsim, cassava, and a few other crops, greatly widened the range of crops passing through marketing boards and, before that, through societies, and also widened the geographical area encompassed by the cooperative movement. A directive compelling everyone in the rural areas to market their produce through co-operative societies also forced an acceleration of expansion in those regions where societies did not previously exist in any number, in the period 1961–5, especially Dodoma, Singida, Kigoma, Mtwara, Coast, and Morogoro Regions. Thus in Tanzania the number of societies grew from 691 in 1960 to 1,533 in April 1966, more than doubling in five years, while the number of unions increased from 7 in 1956 to 33 in 1966.

The sheer pace of expansion would itself have been expected to give rise to problems. However it may also be noticed that the developments ran to some extent counter to the spontaneous or natural development of marketing societies and unions for the main export crops. Many of the products handled by the NAPB and thus by cooperatives were low-valued crops, as well as being in some cases foodstuffs for domestic consumption within Tanzania and therefore more difficult to market compared to export crops. Many were crops previously only handled by private traders. And many of the new societies were developed in regions where, in the absence of lucrative export crops, cooperative development had been slow or non-existent.

A second factor leading up to the crisis is said[22] to have been the government policy 'to transform existing marketing societies into multi-purpose or multi-functional units, dealing with retailing, savings and credit, provision of agricultural inputs and other services to the farmers. The unions have been encouraged to engage in wholesale trade, transport and other essential commercial and productive activities,' one judgement on this being that 'in view of the scarcity of socialist leaders and technically qualified manpower, it is somewhat premature'.[23]

In 1966, following numerous complaints by farmers of inefficiency in management, cases of misuse of funds, and corrupt practices, and direct evidence that the price paid to farmers for their produce had in many cases fallen drastically, the President set up a Special Committee of Enquiry into the Cooperative Movement and Marketing Boards in Tanzania. The Committee found that the general structure of the agricultural cooperative movement was sound, and that the defects were problems of growth. Five basic defects were listed, (1) uninformed membership, (2) shortage of appropriate manpower and, related to this, (3) lack of skilled people in the movement with specialist knowledge, (4) lack of democracy at union level, and (5) susceptibility of the movement to political interference.

As regards the first, it was stated that:

> There are a great many societies whose members are uninformed about the nature of co-operatives, how they are supposed to function, the duties of the Committee of the society and the powers and responsibilities of the members assembled in the general meeting. Even less is understood about the relation between the Union and the various marketing boards. The whole structure thus rests, in many places, on a weak foundation: without an informed membership co-operatives cannot function soundly.

This no doubt relects the lack of spontaneity in the movement where its growth has depended upon government pressure, as does the lack of democracy at union level where it was said that:

> In a great many instances the farmer does not regard the union as belonging to him. Often it is thought of as an arm of the government.

As regards the second defect it was stated that:

> There are two aspects of the shortage of appropriate manpower, although they are interrelated: dishonest employees and inadequately trained employees. The common thread in the manpower situation is the fact that the employees of co-operatives do not adequately regard themselves as a professional group, with ethical standards to live up to, with career possibilities and with opportunities for growth into situations of greater responsibility.

Partly because of the manpower situation, especially in the regions where cooperatives were developing for the first time, leadership of the societies and unions often fell into the hands of large farmers ('kulaks') and petty African traders in produce (the 'walanguzi' in Kiswahili) who were acceptable as committee members and not considered 'exploiters' in comparison with the richer Asian produce merchants for whom they may previously have acted as buying agents. The 'susceptibility to political interference' refers in part to the participation of these traders in the movement and its effects.

There was particular dissatisfaction with the contribution of the cooperative unions, and in 1966, the Minister used his powers to dissolve the committees of 16 of the weakest unions. Dissatisfaction with the efficiency of the movement continued, however, long after the 1966 Enquiry, and in 1976 all existing cooperative societies and unions in Tanzania were abolished, to be replaced by direct marketing board collection of produce, with marketing at the primary level to be carried out through multi-purpose village societies. Whether this radical change will bring the required improvement remains to be seen: it is to be hoped, however, that the benefits of well-run cooperative societies will not be lost in the process of eradicating the deficiencies which have developed in the movement.

In Uganda, similarly, there was a series of enquiries into the affairs of the cooperative movement in the 1960s, leading up to the Report of the Committee of Enquiry into the Affairs of All Cooperative Unions in Uganda, in 1967.[24] The 1967 Report criticized the premature promotion of untrained managers and technical staff, especially in processing, again reflecting the manpower problem, and found that 'large unions have fared worse than small unions due to the degree of management and accounting required.... There is need to split some large unions into smaller ones.'[25] Related to the size of unions was the range of activities engaged in. According to a West African economist, O. Okereke, who carried out a study of the Ugandan cooperative movement, this was a major cause of the problems. He mentions for example that the Bugisu Cooperative Union, specializing in the local arabica coffee crop, had proposals to erect a two-storey block of flats to rent, a bag factory to replace bag imports from Kenya, block-making, and an extension of the present workshop garage, while the Masaka District Growers' Cooperative Union, one of the largest robusta coffee unions, was thinking of a ranching scheme, a consumer shop, and entering the produce trade.[26] The Report on the Busoga Growers' Cooperative Union, the largest cotton trader, criticized the 'spate of buying and building by the Busoga Committee'. A particular feature of the Ugandan cooperative movement as noted by Okereke was the eventual 100 per cent take-over of the cotton-ginning industry; and the efficiency of operation of these ginneries has been the object of concern on several occasions.

Thus Whetham concludes in her review of agricultural marketing in Africa[27] that:

> To embark on the further stages in the marketing of produce—cotton ginning, coffee hulling, the manufacture of dairy products or of palm oil—requires a considerable investment of capital, which must usually be borrowed; and a trained manager is also needed ... [farmer/mem-

bers] cannot easily judge the efficiency of management of an enterprise which is outside the scope of their own experience.

> In African countries, co-operative societies have been most successful where they have confined themselves at first to a simple function of importance to all members, such as the collection and transport of crops to an assembly point for later export....

Cooperatives in Zambia[28]

Although the first cooperative society in Zambia was registered in 1914, until 1948 practically the only cooperatives in existence were those formed by European farmers for agricultural purposes. The movement only got under way in 1948, after the establishment of a Department of Cooperatives, the passing of a Cooperative Societies Ordinance, and the appointment of the first Registrar for Cooperatives. The movement expanded quite rapidly until 1960, after which, as Table 11.10 shows, it has tended to stagnate, measured in terms of size of membership and value of share capital. In particular the value of the share capital of cooperative societies was substantially less in 1970 than in 1960.

Table 11.10 The development of the cooperative movement in Zambia

Year	No. of societies	Membership (×1,000)	Paid-up share capital (K×1,000)	Turnover (K millions)
1949	69	10.8	458	1.6
1960	239	33.8	1,082	13.9
1962	227	35.6	1,160	14.4
1964	220	43.7	1,678	11.5
1966	601	44.3	1,248	9.9
1968	1,091	52.7	1,222	11.2
1970	1,098	43.7	712	7.8

SOURCE: *Statistical Year Book, 1971*

At the end of 1970 the structure of cooperation in Zambia was as in Table 11.11. About two-thirds of the largest category in the table, producer/marketing and farm settlements, were in fact farm production cooperatives mainly concerned with producing maize. These have generally not functioned well, as discussed already in the last chapter. In general we can say that the movement has not been strong in Zambia, probably because of the absence of a good cash crop around which to build cooperatives and, due to the low level of productivity in agriculture and the lack of substantial marketable surpluses of maize from smallholders.

At the same time there are a number of other interesting developments in the field of cooperation, even if not all are very successful. From about 1965 a

Table 11.11   *Types of cooperative society in Zambia at the end of 1970*

Type of society	Membership (×1,000)	No. of societies No.	(%)	Share capital (%)	Turnover (%)
Producer/marketing and farm settlements	23.2	778	71	18	54
Traders	5.2	190	17	6	32
Consumer and supply societies	3.4	34	3	3	4
Thrift and thrift/loan building societies	5.5	22	2	62	—
Credit and savings societies	1.1	13	1	6	—
Other	5.4	61	5.5	5	10
Total	43.8	1,098	100	100	100

SOURCE: *Statistical Year Book, 1971*

number of building and brick-making cooperatives grew up, until in 1970 128 societies had some 3,000 members. Despite government loans of nearly K2 million by 1971 the cooperatives lacked good organization and often failed to finish or simply abandoned jobs which they had started. These have since been acknowledged as failures.

The consumer and supply cooperatives which grew up quite early on (there were 26 societies in 1950) to cater for urban Africans and Europeans have also not been very successful, suffering from lack of capital and entrepreneurship. Similarly the thrift and loans societies, which served mainly Africans, especially civil servants, in the urban areas, struggled to some extent, particularly because of competition from alternative financial institutions, the post office, building societies, and the banks.

Thus, despite the lack of a high-value cash crop to support the marketing societies, it is these societies which have 'formed the backbone' of the movement in Zambia as in the East African countries. These societies, operating under a well-established structure of provincial and regional marketing unions, have been able to deal with a wide range of crops, including maize, groundnuts, millet, beans, cowpeas, rice, tobacco, cotton, and fish, while the unions were undertaking up to 1970 crop financing, marketing, transport, and bulk supply of seed and other inputs.

Although there was already a considerable element of government participation and supervision of the five marketing unions, it was decided at the end of 1970 that these would be in future mainly involved in primary marketing up to National Agricultural Marketing Board (NAMB) collecting centres, while responsibility for subsequent secondary marketing would be assigned to this and other statutory boards. Thus the NAMB has acted as a strong 'umbrella' covering the marketing cooperative societies since that time.

Cooperatives in the Sudan

In the Sudan, again, British officials attempted to act as 'benevolent colonialists' by encouraging peasant farmers to set up credit cooperatives in the Tokar Delta in the Eastern Sudan as long ago as 1921.

Using a well-worn phrase among dedicated cooperative department officials it was said that 'farmers showed little understanding of the principles of cooperation' and the experiments failed. However in the 1930s a further attempt was made with the establishment of cooperative agricultural companies the sole purpose of which was the purchase and operation of pumping equipment and the maintenance of irrigation canals.

Although the cooperative movement accelerated only after 1947, when a Registrar was appointed, and 1948, when a Cooperative Societies Ordinance was passed, these early pump schemes were of great significance, pump schemes and other similar schemes now constituting the distinguishing feature of the structure of cooperatives in the Sudan.[29] This structure is summarized in Table 11.12. In 1967–8 pump-scheme cooperatives in the Sudan, of which there were about 150, had nearly 40,000 members and very substantial share capital.

A glance at the table is sufficient to see that the cooperative movement in the Sudan is very different in nature from those of the East African countries. Marketing societies are much less important relative to the total, the groundnut marketing societies being the major ones. Here it should be realized that the major cash crop, cotton, is marketed through Gezira Board arrangements. The pump-scheme cooperatives have no parallel elsewhere and reflect the importance of irrigation in the country. Irrigation provides a ready-made situation for cooperation, since a large number of farmers generally have to share an irrigation furrow and must have some agreement about the allocation of scarce water such that some better-situated farmers do not take a disproportionate share. A water users' association may be established for this purpose and may easily be developed into a cooperative for other purposes. In this case, where pumping of water is needed, costly pumping equipment can conveniently be shared among a group of

Table 11.12 Cooperatives in the Sudan 1967–8

Cooperative societies	No. of societies or unions[1]	No. of members[2]	Share capital (£×1,000)	Reserve (£×1,000)
Pump scheme cooperatives	149	39,800	787	105
Mechanized crop production cooperatives	62	2,600	144	47
Combine harvester cooperatives	44	22,600	68	15
Total, equipment cooperatives	255	65,000	999	167
Flour mill cooperatives	208	41,500	234	38
Groundnut marketing cooperatives	54[3]	14,300	35	6
Milk producers' cooperatives	5	90	—	—
Multi-purpose cooperatives	99	,23,200	238	52
Consumers' cooperative societies	179	31,700	228	118
Other cooperatives	129	5,400	193	25
Total, all societies	929	181,190	1,927	406
El Khaudag Cooperative Union	1	65	27.5	1.5
Mechanized Harvesters Unions (Hassakeisa)	1	26	24.1	10.8
Mechanized Harvesters Union (S. Gezira)	1	7	5.7	3.6
Groundnut Marketing Union	1	54	0.5	0.9
Wholesale Cooperative Society	1	40	1.2	11.0
Wholesale Society Altbara	1	16	3.6	—
Central Cooperative Union	1	14	10.0	—

SOURCE: Bardeleben, op. cit., Table 24, p. 66
[1] Unions in operation
[2] In the case of unions, no. of societies
[3] 27 societies were in operation at this time

users, in addition to the water, to their mutual benefit. The mechanized crop production cooperatives and the combine harvesters cooperatives are in the same category, since they also involve the sharing of mechanical equipment. All three groups are production cooperatives, even if cooperating with respect only to one of the production processes, being aimed at pooling capital and obtaining economies of scale associated with the use of large equipment. The flour mill cooperatives are in this sense closely related. The importance of consumers' cooperative societies, with 32,000 members, is to be noted also, given the failure of efforts to promote these in East Africa.

State trading

The criticisms of a private marketing system made earlier have played a part in persuading governments in many African countries, not only to encourage cooperative marketing, but also to take over some of the marketing functions themselves through state marketing agencies. The most important of these are the marketing boards discussed in the next chapter, which have dealt especially with export crops. The substantial import trade has more often been left alone, but in Tanzania this was wholly taken over in 1967 by a State Trading Corporation (STC). Subsequently it was felt that the handling of the entire import trade of Tanzania through one organization was unmanageable, particularly where some items are very specialized, such as the import of motor cars, and the STC was split up into smaller organizations, with the same objectives in mind. After initial problems, the functioning of this import business has improved. Efforts in Tanzania at takeover of wholesaling and retailing, also on the side of distribution, have been more problematic.

Questions on Chapter 11

1. Discuss the services provided by middlemen and how these are related to the costs of marketing commodities.
2. Show how the activities of middlemen might (a) help to stabilize prices and (b) increase price instability.
3. How far can the principle of division of labour be used to explain the existence and structure of the system of marketing and distribution in Africa?
4. Discuss the criticisms that have been made of the free marketing system in Africa and assess their validity.
5. Why is it surprising to find lack of price correlation between adjacent markets in many parts of Africa? What explanation would you offer?
6. Did the Asians ever have a 'monopoly' of trade in Eastern Africa?
7. Compare the structure of the cooperative movement in any two out of (a) Uganda or Tanzania (b) Kenya (c) Sudan (d) Zambia.
8. For what economic and political advantages have cooperative marketing societies been promoted in East Africa?
9. How do you account for the greater development of cooperative marketing societies in East compared to West Africa?
10. Discuss the most common problems associated with cooperative enterprise in marketing. How far do you think these can be overcome?
11. What factors do you think contributed to the 'crisis' in the East African cooperative movement during the mid-1960s?

Notes

[1] P. T. Bauer, *West African Trade*, Cambridge University Press, 1954.
[2] See Polly Hill, 'Landlords and Brokers', in *Markets and Marketing in West Africa*, ed. H. W. Ord *et al.*, Edinburgh University Centre of African Studies, 1966; Abner Cohen, 'Politics of the Kola trade', *Africa*, January 1966; and A. G. Hopkins, *An Economic History of West Africa*, Longmans, 1973, pp. 246–9.
[3] The distinction between primary and secondary production and service activities, and the relative numbers employed in each, may be useful for certain analytical purposes, however.
[4] William O. Jones, *Marketing Staple Foods Crops in Tropical Africa*, Cornell University Press, 1972.
[5] ibid., p. 123.
[6] ibid., p. 247.
[7] Edith H. Whetham, *Agricultural Marketing in Africa*, Oxford University Press, 1972, p. 52.
[8] W. O. Jones, op. cit., p. 158.
[9] M. G. Smith, 'Exchange and Marketing among the Hausa', in P. Bohannan and G. Dalton (eds), *Markets in Africa*, North-Western University Press, 1965.
[10] Anne Martin, *The Marketing of Minor Crops in Uganda*, HMSO, London, 1963.
[11] S. Mbilinyi and A. C. Mascarenhas, 'Sources and Marketing of Cooking Bananas', *Economic Research Bureau Paper, No. 69*, University of Dar es Salaam, 1969.
[12] W. O. Jones, op. cit.
[13] A. R. Thodey, *Marketing of Staple Foods in Western Nigeria*, Draft Report, Stanford University for USAID, 1968.
[14] *Agricultural Development in Nigeria, 1965–1980*, FAO, Rome, 1966, pp. 352–3.
[15] I. Livingstone, 'The marketing of crops in Uganda and Tanganyika', in I. G. Stewart and H. W. Ord (eds), *African Primary Products and International Trade*, Edinburgh University Press, 1965.
[16] F. Chalmers Wright, *African Consumers in Nyasaland and Tanganyika: An Enquiry into the Distribution and Consumption of Commodities among Africans carried out in 1952–3*, HMSO, London, 1955.
[17] G. Hyden, *Efficiency versus Distribution in East African Co-operatives*, East African Literature Bureau, Nairobi, 1973.
[18] The first Cooperative Society Ordinance allowing for cooperatives among smallholder peasants in British Africa was passed in Tanganyika in March 1932, after the government had asked Mr C. R. Strickland, a former Registrar of Cooperatives in the Punjab State of India, to advise on the setting up of a cooperative movement in the country. An Ordinance of 1913, also modelled on Indian legislation, established Cooperative Credit Societies for small planters in Mauritius.
[19] G. Hyden, op. cit.
[20] The points we are making here with reference to Eastern Africa are similar to those made for example, by Clark and Weld with special reference to the USA in their book *Marketing Agricultural Products*, published in 1932.
[21] The Agricultural Products (Control and Marketing) Act.
[22] G. Hyden *et al.*, *Co-operatives in Tanzania, Problems of Organization*, Tanzania Publishing House, 1976, p. 18.
[23] See G. Hyden *et al.*, op. cit., p. 12.
[24] For example, the Report of the Committee of Enquiry into the Cotton Growing Industry of Uganda, in 1962, and the Report of the Committee of Enquiry into the Affairs of the Busoga Growers' Cooperative Union, Ltd, 1965.
[25] Summary of Recommendations, paras 19–53.
[26] O. Okereke, op. cit., p. 118.
[27] E. Whetham, op. cit., p. 94.
[28] See C. Stephen Lombard, *The Growth of Co-operatives in Zambia, 1914–71*, University of Zambia, Institute for African Studies, 1971.
[29] See Manfred Bardeleben. *The Co-operative System in the Sudan*, Weltforum-Verlag, Munich, 1973.

12 Marketing Boards and Commodity Schemes

An important part of the marketed surplus of agricultural producers in tropical Africa is handled by marketing boards, which are trading agencies established by governments to control the marketing (and in some cases production) of primary and processed agricultural commodities.

Main types of marketing boards

The two main types of marketing board are (1) *export* produce marketing boards such as those established in Nigeria, Ghana, Uganda, and Malawi to handle export crops grown by peasant farmers and (2) 'statutory' boards concerned with the marketing of staple foodstuffs like maize or paddy for *domestic* consumption, as developed especially in Kenya and Tanzania. In addition, often overlapping with the second category, (3) there have been a number of *general* produce boards, handling a wide variety of commodities, including minor crops and a mixture of crops for domestic and export markets: the Provincial Marketing Boards in Kenya and the National Agricultural Products Board in Tanzania are examples.

Objectives of the export marketing boards

A number of separate objectives lay behind the establishment of export marketing boards in tropical Africa.

(1) A much-publicized objective of the export marketing boards has been price and income stabilization (particularly income stabilization in the case of export commodity boards, price stabilization in the case of statutory boards). Thus it was considered that 'the remedy for many of the evils afflicting the West African cocoa industry lies in imposing a buffer between the producer and the international market which will protect him from short-term fluctuations of world prices and allow him a greater stability of income'.[1] The possible conflict between price and income stabilization, in the face of supply variations, was examined in Chapter 8. Intraseasonal price stabilization, that is, guaranteeing a minimum price for the

season at the beginning of the season (and undertaking to absorb the entire supply at that price) was an objective in many cases, the purpose being to reduce the uncertainty faced by small farmers.

(2) A second aim was the general one of encouraging production. This general objective was usually written in the declared policy of the boards as being 'to develop the industry and the growing areas', or some similar statement. Encouragement of production might relate to either the quantity or quality of output. Price stabilization, guaranteeing at least a minimum price at the start of the season, would itself encourage output, and might be especially effective in persuading farmers in more remote areas to undertake otherwise risky cash crop production over and above subsistence farming. Secondly, the boards financed research into the conditions of production, into such things as plant breeding, improved husbandry, and pest control. Thirdly, the boards have sometimes undertaken, directly or via cooperative societies, to supply farmers with inputs such as fertilizers and insecticides and credit, against crop deliveries, to finance working capital.

In addition to these there have been measures to safeguard or improve the quality of production, and thus to enhance the reputation of the country's exports in world markets. In Nigeria, especially, there was the introduction of price differentials for superior grades and restriction of exports of 'substandard' production. In Ghana and Nigeria, also, the boards financed control campaigns to reduce swollen shoot disease and capsid infection of cocoa trees.

(3) The most obvious aim of marketing boards, of course, was to improve marketing. Despite the criticisms made presently of the functioning of the marketing boards, it must be remembered that the pre-war system of private trading which the marketing boards replaced was a far from perfect market situation. A small number of large buyers of produce were in a dominant bargaining position as compared to the large number of small unorganized peasant producers from whom (via small traders and agents) they were buying. Bauer, in particular, has documented the way in which a small number of large, expatriate export-import firms dominated the produce-buying trade in West Africa.[2]

Secondly, the marketing boards provided a medium for channelling investment into marketing whether in the form of storage facilities, transport, processing, or crop finance. It was argued that the small traders acting as intermediaries between the large exporters and the producers lacked the finance to be fully effective as primary buyers of produce.

Thirdly, the marketing boards could act as 'umbrellas', sheltering cooperatives in their early stages before they became fully viable, by simplifying the process of marketing. If efficiently run, cooperation can bring many advantages, as we saw in the last chapter. Cooperative unions may also take over the processing of major agricultural commodities from private firms.

(4) Marketing boards may be used to exercise control over output and therefore over price in international markets. In the absence of international commodity agreements or export restriction schemes organized by a majority of world producing countries, the scope for raising the export price will be very limited, since most individual countries are 'price-takers' in export markets. In Tanzania, however, the Sisal Board was instrumental in cutting down output in line with reduced world demand for sisal.

(5) As we shall see in more detail presently, the marketing boards acquired important tax or fiscal objectives. A substantial part of marketing board reserves and revenue in East and West Africa was diverted towards financing infrastructural and other development projects, so that the boards acted as very effective 'tax-gatherers' for government.

Secondly, there was the objective here of macroeconomic stabilization; apart from stabilizing prices and the incomes of growers, the boards performed the additional function of stabilizers of the economy as a whole. In West Africa, for example, it was suggested that if people had been permitted to spend the high incomes they were earning in the early post-war period, this would have resulted in inflation, since both local and imported commodities for consumption were in short supply. This is strictly speaking an argument for a policy of heavy taxation at this time rather than for marketing board organization as such, although it may be said that the existence of marketing boards provided a more flexible mechanism for stabilization policy than export duty, which is less easily varied than the prices which the marketing boards pay to growers.

The origins of export marketing boards in Africa

The circumstances in which the export marketing boards were established in Eastern and West Africa were much the same, the boards emerging from the wartime period of commodity control. Prior to the introduction in the early 1940s of wartime commodity control schemes, the marketing of export crops in tropical Africa was undertaken by private traders. Large enterprises like the United Africa Company (general merchants) and more specialized dealers and processing manufacturers such as the British Cotton Growers' Association (cotton ginners) and Cadbury Bros (cocoa manufacturers) maintained extensive buying stations in West Africa, using local middlemen to 'bulk-build'. Much of this produce-buying was integrated with the internal distribution of imported goods, which had evolved over a long period. During the war the West African Produce Control Board, which brought or stored the crops on behalf of the Ministry of Food in London, had a monopoly of exports. The Board kept producer prices down to levels not much greater than those of 1939, despite wartime inflation, and retained the surplus. This meant that by 1949 the Control Board had accumulated some £22 million from the sale of cocoa, £11 million from palm produce, and £10 million from groundnuts. These reserves were then transferred to form the basis of separate marketing boards, four in Nigeria (for cocoa, oil palm products, groundnuts, and cotton), two in Ghana, one in Sierra Leone (the Sierra Leone Produce Marketing Board) and one in the Gambia. A major reorganization took place in Nigeria in 1954, resulting in the establishment of Regional Marketing Boards: the Northern Region Marketing Board assumed control of most of the marketing of cotton and groundnuts; the Eastern Region Marketing Board inherited most of the former Nigerian Oil Palm Produce Marketing Board, while the Western Region took over the bulk of Nigeria's cocoa crop, as well as oil palm products and other export crops produced in the Region. A fourth marketing board established for the new Mid-West Region was concerned mainly with rubber.

The sequence in Uganda was similar. During the war most export crops as well as marketable surpluses of staple commodities were subject to various kinds of bulk-buying arrangements. The wartime schemes for cotton and coffee required government intervention, including the introduction of guaranteed prices for these important crops. After the war, in 1948, the government established two separate Price Assistance Funds for cotton and coffee, into which were placed the reserves or profits accumulated during the war and early post-war period, when payments to growers were kept below export proceeds. The Lint Marketing Board and Coffee Industry Board were established simultaneously to handle the marketing of seed cotton and peasant-grown robusta coffee respectively. These funds were the instrument of stabilization policy in Uganda, as we shall see presently, until the mid-1960s, and were run down over the five-year period 1961–6 from a surplus of £135 million in 1961 to a deficit of £2 million by 1966–7, after which the stabilization aim had to be abandoned in Uganda.

The Farmers' Marketing Board in Malawi was established considerably later, in 1956, as the statutory marketing board for African smallholder cash crops, particularly tobacco, cotton, maize, and groundnuts: though tobacco (from 1926) and cotton (from 1951) had previously been marketed by separate boards. The primary objective of the FMB was its marketing function, to provide guaranteed markets at its own buying stations and depots for all scheduled crops at fixed prices usually pre-announced for each season. It was the only legal buyer of the main smallholder export crops, tobacco and seed cotton, but competed with private traders for marketable surpluses of other produce, of which groundnuts were usually the most important by value for the export trade. Like the boards already discussed, it maintained price support reserves to stabilize prices within each season and to provide some longer-term stability of prices and incomes.

The FMB stabilization functions were badly interrupted in 1967 by a huge deficit, incurred after unprofitable purchases of poor quality tobacco. This also interrupted the FMB's role as a supplier of development funds for the government's other parastatal bodies. A new *direct* development function was initiated in the early 1970s with a change of name to the Agricultural Development and Marketing Corporation (ADMARC). In effect the 'Board' was to become an agricultural development corporation[3] providing funds from its trading profits for direct investment in large-scale estates, mainly tobacco, and often as joint ventures with private African planters. In addition, ADMARC invested in the loan or equity capital of agro-industries such as grain milling and fruit canning, and in road transport and distribution. While it borrowed long-term loans for some of these investments, a principal source has been the 'forced saving' of smallholders, part of whose potential income may be withheld from them and diverted to wider development purposes, in a more direct way through this medium than occurred in other countries, as discussed presently.

Functioning of the export marketing boards

These marketing boards functioned in much the same way in both East and West Africa. We examine first the experience of the Ugandan marketing boards.

Export marketing boards in Uganda

During the earlier years of their operation, the export marketing boards in Uganda accumulated large reserves by fixing producer prices well below export prices. The sharp increase in primary product prices associated with the Korean war period of 1950–1 resulted in large 'windfall profits' which could be added to reserves without reducing the net price to the producer. A subsequent boom in beverage products, tea, cocoa, and coffee, in 1953–5, further increased marketing board reserves, as well as government export tax revenue. From the producer's point of view, of course, these net trading surpluses of the boards were no different from export taxes in operating as deductions from current potential income. While initially the desire was to use part of the accumulated funds for infrastructural and development expenditures related to the expansion and improvement of cotton and coffee production, the wish to accelerate general economic development in Uganda led to much greater diversion of funds to public development projects outside the cotton and coffee industries and growing areas. The marketing boards thus played a major role as 'tax-gatherers' for the government, as mentioned already, in addition to the stabilization objective.

The results of the policy pursued by the marketing boards, or in effect by the government, are shown in Table 12.1. Column 1 gives total export proceeds. If marketing costs, indicated in column 2, are deducted, we obtain, in column 3, growers' potential income, the amount that *could* have been paid to producers had it not been desired to withhold some of their earnings, for whatever reason. Columns 4 and 5 give the amounts deducted in export taxes and for adding to board reserves, respectively, the sum of the two deductions being given in column 6 as 'total withdrawals'. Deducting these from potential income in column 3 gives the actual payment to growers in column 7.

The upper part of the table compares 1951, a year of high world prices, with 1960, when prices had fallen back to much lower levels. In 1951, because of high prices, gross export proceeds were as great as £40 millions, while these were as low as £28 millions in 1960. The lower part of the table compares the results for cotton and coffee combined as annual averages for the three periods 1948–54, 1955–62, and 1962–6.

The marketing boards can be seen to have been so effective as tax-gatherers that growers received only 37 per cent of potential income in 1951, and 52 per cent over the seven-year period, 1948–54. The question is what effect such a punitive rate of taxation would have on the incentives of peasants to work,

Table 12.1   *Division of Uganda Marketing Board proceeds in 1951, 1960, and 1948–66*

Crop year ending 31 October	(1) Total export proceeds (£m)	(2) Marketing and processing costs (£m)	(3) Growers' potential income (1)−(2) (£m)	(4) Export duties (£m)	(5) Net surplus of boards (£m)	(6) Total withdrawals (4)+(5) (£m)	(6) (% of potential income)	(7) Actual net payment to growers (3)−(6) (£m)	(7) (% of potential income)
1951									
Cotton	29.3	2.3	27.0	5.9	10.4	16.3	60.4	10.7	39.6
Coffee	10.7	0.9	9.8	1.9	4.9	6.8	69.4	3.0	30.6
Total	40.0	3.2	36.8	7.8	15.3	23.1	62.8	13.7	37.2
1960									
Cotton	18.3	4.2	14.2	2.3	1.0	3.3	23.2	10.9	76.8
Coffee	9.9	2.8	7.1	0.5	−4.3	−3.8	−53.5	10.9	153.5
Total	28.2	7.0	21.3	2.8	−3.3	−0.5	−2.3	21.8	102.3
Cotton and coffee *Annual averages*									
1948–54 (7 years)	26.7	3.5	23.2	4.8	6.4	11.2	48.3	12.0	51.7
1955–62 (8 years)	29.1	6.1	23.1	4.0	−2.0	2.0	8.7	21.1	91.3
1962–6 (5 years)*	40.0	10.0	30.0	5.3	−3.4	1.9	6.8	28.1	93.4

SOURCE: *Uganda Statistical Abstracts* and Marketing Board *Annual Reports*

*Coverage includes robusta coffee marketed outside Board's control; export proceeds valued f.o.b. Mombasa, thereby raising marketing costs

and to expand production. As we saw earlier in Chapter 9 (Table 9.3), cotton did decline in importance, partly the result of its having been overtaxed in the earlier years of the Board. Moreover the reduction of cash incomes in the hands of growers over such an extended period would have curtailed their ability to accumulate funds and no doubt affected capital investment in land clearing, and the like, on peasant farms, again restricting the expansion of cultivation.

In relation to stabilization, we have already distinguished between intra-seasonal stabilization, short-term stabilization over a period of a few years, and longer-term stabilization. Table 12.1 does not suggest that short-term stabilization of incomes was actively pursued: since average withdrawals over the period 1948–54 equalled 48 per cent of potential income, variations in the rate of withdrawal above and below 48 would not have had a substantial effect in comparison with the rate at which incomes were 'creamed off' in withdrawals.

Longer-term stabilization *might* be said to have been pursued to some extent. Taking cotton and coffee growers together, growers' potential income fell from £37 million in 1951 to £21 million in 1960, as a result of a fall in world prices: but the payment to growers actually increased (in money terms) by over 50 per cent from £14 million to £22 million, as a

result of a balancing reduction in the rate of withdrawals from 63 per cent of potential income in 1951 to *minus* 2.3 per cent in 1960.

On the other hand, further scrutiny of the table shows that policy over long periods in particular could be considered *de*stabilizing. Again taking cotton and coffee together, average potential income in 1948–54 and 1955–62 was about the same (£23.2 million and £23.1 million respectively) but in the former period £12 million was paid out compared to £21 million, 75 per cent more in money terms, in 1955–62: withdrawals of 52 per cent and 91 per cent being clearly destabilizing in this case. Further, when average potential income increased by £7 million between 1955–62 and 1962–6 payment to growers was increased by the same amount, percentage withdrawals staying at much the same levels rather than moving in a balancing direction.

It is somewhat misleading to take cotton and coffee proceeds together, however, since in Uganda, although the production areas for cotton and coffee overlap, there are also substantially separate regions of cotton growing and coffee growing. To see how far the money incomes of farmers in these areas were stabilized it is necessary to consider the two crops separately. We find that coffee growers received only £3 million in 1951, compared to £11 million in 1960, more than $3\frac{1}{2}$ times as much, although potential income was greater in 1951. Payment to growers was 31 per cent of potential income in 1951 and 153 per cent in 1960, an immense variation, but not one justified by differences in potential income.

Finally we may note that even within a season price stability was not adhered to: in the late 1950s persistently falling prices of coffee, together with increased output, involved periodic revision of published prices within a given season.

We may detect also from Table 12.1 adverse effects on the allocation of resources and on the distribution of income. If the policies of two or more export commodity boards are not in step, there may result a misallocation of resources as between the two commodities, or inequitable distribution of income as between the producers of the two commodities. Where cotton and coffee can be grown by the same producers as alternatives, divergent commodity policies alter the relative net prices paid to producers and thus the allocation of resources between them; where they are grown in different areas by distinct groups of producers, divergent policies will affect income distribution between two groups, if withdrawals are uneven and if public expenditure beneficial to both is financed especially by one group.

Table 12.1 shows that in 1951 withdrawals were relatively more severe on coffee (without as we have seen achieving any stabilization objective), but that in 1960 (and generally in the late 1950s), when world coffee prices were falling, coffee producers received substantial subsidies, obtaining 53 per cent above potential income when cotton producers still suffered 23 per cent withdrawals. This provided substantial incentive for the substitution of coffee for cotton production although long-run prospects for selling increased quantities of coffee, given international quotas for coffee, were much poorer than for cotton, for which world demand is much more price-elastic.

The relative impact of marketing board and export tax policy on the two commodities over the decade 1950–60 is shown in more detail in Table 12.2.

Cotton growers paid not only *absolutely* more towards the government's current budget or to development funds through either export taxes or withholdings through board surpluses, but they paid *relatively* more, obtaining only 62 per cent of their potential income, against 73 per cent paid out to coffee growers, *who generally were a richer group*. Moreover, whereas no cotton grower could escape these compulsory taxes (except by smuggling his seed cotton across a border), a declining proportion of robusta coffee growers marketed through their board, thereby reducing the average 'tax' on the industry as a whole.

The experience of the Nigerian marketing boards

The experience of the Nigerian marketing boards is very similar to those in Uganda. Once again reserves were accumulated in the early years, but the boards acted more as tax-gatherers than stabilizers. The course pursued by the boards is indicated in Table 12.3. This distinguishes between the first seven crop years, when export markets were generally buoyant, and the subsequent period when export prices were on the decline. This division also coincides with the replacement of nation-wide commodity boards, each handling one major commodity, by multi-commodity regional marketing boards. For purposes of comparison the trading activities of the Regional Marketing Boards established in 1955 have in Table 12.3 been allocated under the main commodities.

The table covers five major products: cocoa, palm kernels, palm oil, groundnuts, and cotton. Slightly different periods of operation are covered in each case, but approximately the two periods are 1947–53 and 1954–61. The first column gives 'potential producer income', that is the amount that could have been paid out to producers had it not been desired to withhold part of their earnings in the form of taxes or

Table 12.2 *Division of potential income to cotton and coffee growers in Uganda, 1950–60*

	Cotton (£m)	Cotton (%)	Coffee (£m)	Coffee (%)	Total (£m)	Total (%)
(1) Payment to growers	135	62	97	73	232	66
(2) Increase in price assistance funds*	16	7	10	8	25	7
(3) Contribution to development funds	24	11	1	1	25	7
(4) Export tax proceeds: development fund	12 ⎱ 20		7 ⎱ 19		19 ⎱ 19	
(5) Export tax proceeds: current budget	31 ⎰		18 ⎰		49 ⎰	
(6) Total potential income to growers	219	100	132	100	351	100

SOURCE: D. A. Lury, 'Cotton and Coffee Growers and Government Development Finance in Uganda,' *East African Economic Review* (Old Series), Vol. 10, No. 1, 1963
*Includes small provision for depreciation

Table 12.3   *Division of Nigerian marketing board proceeds, 1947 61*

Main crops and crop year periods	(1) Potential producer income (£m)	(2) Export duties and produce purchase taxes (£m) (as % of (1))		(3) Marketing board trading surplus (£m) (as % of (1))		(4) Total withdrawals (2)+(3) (£m) (as % of (1))		(5) Payments to growers (1)−(4) (£m) (as % of (1))	
Cocoa									
1947/8–1953/4	157	28	18	34	22	62	39	95	61
1954/5–1961/2	206	41	20	13	6	54	26	152	74
Total	363	69	19	47	13	116	32	247	68
Palm kernels									
1947–54	126	12	9	25	20	37	29	90	71
1955–61	117	19	17	12	10	31	27	85	73
Total	243	31	13	37	15	68	28	175	72
Palm oil									
1947–54	82	7	9	7	8	14	17	68	83
1955–61	72	14	20	4	6	18	26	54	75
Total	154	22	14	11	7	32	21	122	79
Groundnuts									
1947/8–1953/4	99	12	12	28	28	40	41	59	60
1954/5–1960/1	150	24	16	−2	−1	22	15	127	85
Total	249	36	15	26	10	62	25	186	75
Cotton									
1949/50–1953/4	23	3	12	7	30	10	42	13	58
1954/5–1960/1	43	7	15	−2	−4	5	11	38	89
Total	66	10	15	5	8	15	22	51	78

SOURCE: G. K. Helleiner, 'The Fiscal Role of the Marketing Boards in Nigerian Economic Development, 1947 1961', *Economic Journal*, September 1964

marketing board surpluses. This potential income is less than the full value of export proceeds, since there are unavoidable costs of marketing which must be covered. Columns (2) and (3) respectively show the amounts deducted for tax and for addition to marketing board reserves, in each case given in value terms and as a percentage of potential income. The sum of these two items gives 'total withdrawals' in column (4). Subtracting these from column (1) gives the actual payments made to producers, shown in the final column.

The table shows that in the early period comparatively high shares were added to marketing board reserves: in the case of cocoa, 22 per cent; palm kernels, 20 per cent; groundnuts, 28 per cent; cotton, 30 per cent (heavy deductions were not made in the case of palm oil). In combination with the taxes levied through the boards, this meant that producers received 61 per cent, 60 per cent, and 58 per cent of

potential income from cocoa, groundnuts, and cotton respectively, though they received larger proportions in the case of palm kernels and especially palm oil.

In the subsequent period of decline in prices, the continued expansion of output nevertheless increased the value of export proceeds. To avoid an excessive fall in prices paid to growers, however, the percentages subtracted for addition to reserves were reduced substantially, being only 6 per cent in the case of cocoa and 10 per cent for palm kernels, while the prices of groundnuts and cotton were actually subsidized by payments out of reserves. It is worth noting that, overall, the marketing boards continued to make net deductions during the later period. Over the whole period under review in fact the boards withheld 12 per cent of potential income, on top of the 15 per cent deducted for taxation, leaving producers with just 73 per cent of potential income. Since part of these funds was spent on development projects the boards were in effect making tax deductions beyond that officially designated as export duties and produce purchase taxes.

Tax policy did not operate in the same way, overall taxation increasing in percentage terms over the period. This somewhat reduced the cushioning effect of the reduced level of marketing board surpluses in the later period. At the same time actual earnings of producers increased substantially in most cases, due to the expansion of output despite increased taxation.

The combined result was that in the later period producers of cocoa, groundnuts, and cotton were allowed to retain substantially higher proportions of potential income, the percentages being 74, 85, and 89 respectively, compared to 61, 60, and 58 in the earlier years of 1947–54. In the case of palm kernels the percentages were much the same in both periods, while the percentage actually fell in the case of palm oil over the two periods. The Northern Nigerian Marketing Board, dealing especially with cotton and groundnuts, pursued the most 'interventionist' policy which was aimed at stabilization.

Helleiner calculated measures of instability of prices and incomes for major Nigerian marketing board exports up to 1961. The first two columns of Table 12.4 show that considerable success was achieved in stabilizing producer prices in Nigeria, as compared to world prices. The other three columns, however, show that the boards were relatively ineffective in their objective of stabilizing producer incomes (whether in money or real terms), palm kernels representing the only clear 'success'. In the case of cocoa and cotton the intervention of the boards appears to have been clearly destabilizing. In these cases it is likely that price stabilization contributed directly to income *des*tabilization.[4]

The Nigerian marketing boards made greater efforts to use their monopolistic powers of pricing to attempt to induce growers to raise the quality of their produce. There has been criticism, however, to the effect that the price differentials offered for superior grades of groundnuts, say, or palm oil, were excessive and arose from a confusion between technical efficiency (obtaining the best grade irrespective of the demand for quality) and economic efficiency (obtaining the grade which will over the long period maximize the earnings of producers). In Uganda there has been little criticism of the premium paid for 'good' as opposed to 'stained' seed cotton; in the case of coffee it was the absence of a price differential which might have been criticized in view of the need to improve quality in order to maintain exports in the face of a world coffee surplus.

In Nigeria, where the policy of paying producers large premiums or 'bonuses' for the highest grades of cocoa, palm oil, and groundnuts has succeeded in raising the average quality of export produce quite rapidly, the criticism has perhaps more weight. Professor P. T. Bauer and other critics have argued that, first, the fact that overseas buyers generally offered lower price premiums for the highest grades (i.e. the 'differentials' between grades were narrower) indicated that too much emphasis could be placed on technical standards and that the additional export income received by the boards might fall short of the extra costs of sorting and grading. Secondly, the power of the boards to frustrate exports of 'sub-

Table 12.4 *Average annual changes in prices and incomes for major Nigerian marketing board exports up to 1961*

Commodity	Prices		Incomes		
	World price (%)	Producers' money price (%)	Producers' potential money income (%)	Producers' actual money income (%)	Producers' actual real income (%)
Cocoa (1947/8–1961/2)	22.5	14.2	18.9	23.1	21.7
Groundnuts (1941/50–1960/1)	20.6	7.6	27.8	29.9	31.1
Palm oil (1949–61)	12.7	7.9	13.4	11.6	15.9
Palm kernels (1949–61)	12.4	4.2	15.9	8.8	13.0
Cotton (1949–1960/1)	10.6	3.8	22.6	26.3	32.2

SOURCE: G. K. Helleiner, 'Marketing Boards and Domestic Stabilization in Nigeria', *Review of Economics and Statistics*, Vol. 48, No. 1, 1966

standard' produce was a serious objection to their monopoly of export marketing: it deprived the poorer farmers of opportunities for earning cash income (for instance those without the labour or capital necessary for sorting or processing to the higher grades), and deflected their activities to less profitable outlets, for example, local markets for groundnuts or palm oil, or to more subsistence forms of production.

Table 12.5 illustrates the pronounced effect of price differentials on the quality of produce purchased and sold by Nigerian marketing boards. In the case of cocoa and oil palm the lowest grades were abolished by 1951, thereby excluding 'substandard' grades from the export market. Since 1950/1 over 90 per cent of cocoa purchases has been in the highest grade, compared with less than 50 per cent in 1947/8 when the premium for Grade 1 cocoa was only £2 over Grade 2. A Special Grade for palm oil, introduced in 1951, accounted for over 60 per cent of marketing board purchases by 1954. In the case of groundnuts purchased by the Northern Nigerian Marketing Board a similar trend is apparent: in 1954/5, before the introduction of a Special Grade, only 7 per cent of the volume of purchases was of that high quality; by

1958/9 a widening differential had led to the virtual disappearance of Standard Grade deliveries, and this grade was subsequently abolished.

Experience suggests that on balance the Nigerian boards were probably quite wise to encourage quality improvements by price differentials. Consumers in export markets have paid a premium for the high average quality of Nigerian cocoa, while competition from animal fats and synthetic substitutes have reduced the profitability of lower-grade groundnuts and technical grades of palm oil. Moreover, the loss of export markets for 'substandard' oils and fats may not have had a very serious impact on poorer producers who have supplied local markets; certainly local consumers may have benefited from a supply at subsidized prices.

The Ghana Cocoa Marketing Board

Ghana's Cocoa Marketing Board is one of the largest single-commodity marketing boards in tropical Africa. Table 12.6 gives information similar to the previous tables, but this time gives more detail re-

Table 12.5   *The effect of price differentials on quality (grade of produce)*

Crop season	Price by grade (£ per ton)						Percentage of purchases (quantity) by grade					
Nigerian Cocoa Marketing Board: Cocoa												
	I	II	III	IV				I	II	III	IV	
1947/48	62	60	57	48				47	25	21	7	
1948/49	120	115	105	90				76	21	2	1	
1949/50	100	95	75	—				89	10	1	—	
1950/51	120	110	—	—				95	5	—	—	
1951/52	170	115	—	—				96	4	—	—	
1952/53	170	115	—	—				95	5	—	—	
1953/54	170	115	—	—				98	2	—	—	
Nigerian Oil Palm Marketing Board: Palm Oil												
	Special	I	II	III	IV	V	Special	I	II	III	IV	V
1949	—	43	37	33	30	36	—	66	14	13	6	*
1950	53	43	37	33	30	26	—	60	18	14	9	*
1951	71	55	43	34	30	—	6	71	11	8	4	—
1952	80	61	47	35	30	—	30	56	7	5	2	—
1953	76	58	45	34	—	—	50	38	7	4	—	—
1954	65	50	38	33	—	—	61	30	4	5	—	—
Northern Nigerian Marketing Board: Groundnuts												
	Special		Standard				Special		Standard			
1954/55	—		45.7				7		93			
1955/56	46.9		45.4				6		94			
1956/57	46.0		42.4				38		62			
1957/58	47.5		42.5				95		5			
1958/59	43.3		38.3				100		*			
1959/60	45.2		—				100		—			

NOTE: —indicates price for grade not in operation or abolished with purchases not accepted

* means less than one per cent; producer price at port for cocoa and groundnuts; basic producer price at bulk oil plant for palm oil before £4 Produce Purchase Tax introduced from 1953

Table 12.6 *Ghana cocoa marketing board: prices and proceeds, 1947–62*

Cocoa crop year (1 Oct. to 31 Sept.)	(1) Average export price, f.o.b. (£ per ton)	(% change)	(2) Net producer price (£ per ton)	(% change)	(3) Quantity purchased by CMB (× 1,000 tons)	(4) Total sales proceeds, f.o.b. (£ per ton)	(% change)	(5) Net producer payments (£ per ton)	(% change)
1947-8	201	—	75	—	208	41.5	—	15.4	—
1948-9	138	−31	121	+61	278	37.5	−10	33.7	+119
1949-50	178	+29	84	−31	248	45.1	+20	21.2	−37
1950-1	269	+51	131	+55	262	70.3	+56	34.2	+61
1951-2	245	−9	149	+14	211	51.6	−27	31.4	−8
1952-3	231	−6	131	−12	247	57.1	+11	32.5	+4
1953-4	358	+55	134	+2	211	74.7	+31	28.0	−14
1954-5	353	−1	134	—	220	77.5	+4	29.5	+5
1955-6	222	−37	149	+11	229	52.3	−33	35.0	+19
1956-7	189	−15	149	—	263	50.7	−3	39.9	+14
1957-8	304	+61	134	−10	206	62.9	+24	27.7	−31
1958-9	280	−8	134	—	255	70.9	+13	33.4	+21
1959-60	226	−19	112	−16	317	69.9	−1	34.8	+4
1960-1	175	−23	112	—	432	71.6	+2	48.3	+39
1961-2	164	−6	112 } 101*	−10	409	69.0	−4	52.6 } 41.3*	−14
Annual average	235.5	25.1	123	15.9	—	60.2	17.1	32.4	29.9
Fluctuations exceeding 10%	9		7			8		10	
Fluctuations exceeding 20%	7		3			5		6	

SOURCE: Ghana Cocoa Marketing Board, *Annual Reports*
*Producer price and payments received *net* of 'voluntary contribution to the Development Plan'—actually a compulsory levy of tax. Latter figure used in calculations

garding the movement of prices and production from 1947–8 to 1961–2. The first column shows the average price per long ton received by the Board for exports or deliveries to local mills. The product of this price and the volume sold appears as total proceeds in column (4), while net producer payments shown in column (5) are obtained by multiplying the producer price in column (2) by the quantity purchased in column (3).

The first two columns show the average export price and the price actually paid to producers, the difference being the marketing and other running expenses of the CMB as well as the withdrawals in export duties and profits retained. These columns also give the percentage change from year to year in the export and net producer prices, as well as the *average* of these annual fluctuations over the 14 years reviewed and the number of years in which the change exceeded 10 per cent and 20 per cent. These calculations indicate that the CMB did manage to insulate producers from the larger and more numerous fluctuations in world cocoa prices: the 14-year average of annual changes being about 25 per cent and 16 per cent respectively; and in only 3 of the 14 years did the producer price change exceed 20 per cent against 7 of these years for the world price. It is also clear why the CMB could achieve this aim: by stabilizing the producer price at around only one-half the export price from 1949 and lowering this fixed price in line with the falling world price in the later years.

In Chapter 8 we showed that price stabilization would also stabilize incomes if the quantity supplied was also relatively constant. By comparison with many other crops handled by export marketing boards, the quantity of cocoa purchased by the CMB was fairly stable; and also there was no marked trend until the extra output from new plantings in the mid-1950s appeared from 1960. However a comparison of the annual fluctuations in total sales proceeds obtained by the CMB with the net producer payments, shown in columns (4) and (5), respectively, indicates that producers' incomes were rather more unstable than the Board's. The 14-year average of annual fluctuations was around 17 per cent for the CMB (and the economy as a whole) but about 30 per cent for cocoa producers. The latter's income varied by more than 10 per cent per annum in 10 of the years, compared with only 8 years for the CMB proceeds. Moreover, although fluctuations exceeded 20 per cent in only 5 or 6 years for both, the size of these wider variations was much greater for producers. In fact the money incomes of producers were really only effectively insulated from fluctuations in export earnings during the mid-1950s when both producer prices and the volume of purchases were fairly constant, or,

as in 1951–2, a change in the producer price was compensated by an inverse shift in the quantity purchased. By contrast, when an unusually low volume was purchased in 1957–8 at a producer price fixed at the perceived long-term level of £134 per ton but sold at the relatively high world price of £304, producers suffered a 31 per cent fall in income to the lowest level since 1949/50 at the same time as the CMB increased its sales proceeds by 24 per cent. This decline in producers' incomes had a marked deflationary effect on the economy as a whole, with less private expenditure injected.

The somewhat greater relative stability of cocoa export earnings by the CMB reflected Ghana's dominant position as largest world exporter, with export price movements compensating in part for changes in the volumes sold. Under these circumstances producers' incomes would have been more stable if producer prices could have been fixed as a *proportion* of the export price rather than set at a particular level.

Although nominal producer prices were stabilized, this did not necessarily mean stable *real* prices. Cocoa farmers suffered from inflation in the Ghana economy along with others, inflation raising the cost of production inputs, including wages, as well as of consumer goods purchased by farmers. In real terms the incomes received by farmers in 1960–1 were probably no higher than those of the early 1950s and the producer purchasing power of a load of cocoa was possibly only half that at the beginning of the period.

Table 12.7 shows that the marketing board in Ghana followed a very similar policy to those in Nigeria and Uganda in 'taxing' growers. Nigerian policy was actually milder than in Ghana or Uganda in the sense of making less drastic deductions from potential income. In the first period Nigerian producers received 67 per cent of this income, compared to 52 per cent in Ghana and 53 per cent in Uganda. In the second period of declining prices Ghana made

Table 12.7 Actual producer payments as per cent of potential income available to export marketing boards in Nigeria, Ghana, and Uganda

		1947–54 %	1955–61 %	1947–61 %
Nigeria:	five commodities[1]	67	79	73
	cocoa only	61	86	67
Ghana:	cocoa only[2]	52	66	59
Uganda:	cotton and coffee[3]	53	89	72

[1] Covers a 15-year period for cocoa only
[2] Covers a 15-year period
[3] Covers the 14 crop years 1948–61

Table 12.8 The Malawi Farmers Marketing Board: fluctuations in proceeds, 1956–67

Year	Stabilization reserve (£m)	Tobacco				Groundnuts				Cotton			
		Marketing board receipts* (£×1,000)	(% change)	Farmer receipts (£×1,000)	(% change)	Marketing board receipts (£×1,000)	(% change)	Farmer receipts (£×1,000)	(% change)	Marketing board receipts (£×1,000)	(% change)	Farmer receipts (£×1,000)	(% change)
1956	1.40	1,557	—	864	—	—	—	—	—	233	—	104	—
1957	1.80	1,748	+12	1,020	+18	808	—	460	—	294	+26	181	+74
1958	1.60	1,734	−1	1,283	+26	631	−22	426	−7	369	+13	243	+34
1959	1.30	1,093	−37	928	−28	708	+12	428	+0.5	640	+73	466	+92
1960	1.67	1,375	+26	673	−28	1,237	+75	858	+100	828	+29	569	+22
1961	1.85	1,167	−15	578	−14	1,375	+11	1,049	+22	816	−1.5	538	−5.5
1962	1.74	1,884	+61	1,150	+99	1,762	+28	1,504	+43	1,311	+61	914	+70
1963	1.80	2,347	+25	1,437	+25	1,552	−12	1,062	−29	807	−38	510	−44
1964	2.16	1,812	−23	768	−47	1,259	−19	768	−28	1,010	+25	763	−50
1965	2.55	3,106	+71	1,925	+151	1,942	+54	1,050	+37	1,556	+54	1,126	+48
1966	2.50	2,412	−22	1,422	−26	2,971	+53	2,260	+115	947	−39	631	−44
1967	0.69	1,798	−26	1,601	+13	2,896	−2.5	2,360	+4	949	0	534	−15
Average year-to-year variation %		33.6		50.2		31.9		47.7		31.1		37.3	
Number of fluctuations exceeding 20%		8		8		5		7		8		9	

SOURCE: C. P. Brown, loc. cit.

* Marketing board receipts adjusted for stock changes, throughout

use of accumulated reserves to support producer prices, but after taking account of export taxes, payments were only 66 per cent of potential income, compared to 86 per cent in the case of Nigerian cocoa, and 79 per cent for Nigerian boards taken together. Uganda pursued the most marked stabilization policy, with the greatest difference in percentage withdrawals between the two periods although, as we have seen, this policy was scarcely successful.

Malawi's agricultural and development marketing corporation

C. P. Brown has shown[5] how the Farmers' Marketing Board (later ADMARC) in Malawi in the late 1950s and 1960s actually aggravated the instability of producer incomes, as well as involving the FMB and the country as a whole in financial losses. Table 12.8 shows the percentage change from one year to the next in marketing board receipts and farmers' receipts for tobacco, groundnuts, and cotton, as well as the *average* year-to-year change over the whole period 1956–67. First, we may observe that the stabilization reserve, which should have fluctuated in size if used seriously to offset variations in export receipts, showed only minor changes between 1956 and 1963, then increased substantially over two or three years to £2.50 million, before being run down drastically in one year to £0.69 million in 1967, as the reserve funds were used to meet trading losses on tobacco and maize purchases, and therefore no longer available for stabilization in subsequent years.

The table shows that the average size of fluctuations for each crop (particularly tobacco) were larger for farmer receipts than for Board receipts from sales. Thus income would have been *more* stable if the Board had not intervened, but simply passed on fluctuations in its own selling prices to the farmers. The Board's operations in particular accentuated the peaks of the fluctuations: increasing a 61

per cent change in 1962 to 99 per cent, and a 71 per cent in 1965 to 151 per cent in the case of tobacco; pushing up a 75 per cent rise to 100 per cent in 1960, and a 53 per cent in 1966 to 115 per cent in the case of groundnuts; and raising a 73 per cent increase in 1959 to 92 per cent, and a 61 per cent in 1962 to 70 per cent in the case of cotton.

Table 12.9, referring to the more recent period, gives the division of Marketing Board revenue from 1964 to 1975. The table shows that up to 1967 the FMB operated rather like other export marketing boards, accumulating some net profits for stabilization reserves, as given in Table 12.8. Payments to growers (and traders who handle maize) accounted for 67 per cent of revenue from sale of produce in the three years, 1964–6. Other expenses of marketing absorbed 28 per cent, so that only 5 per cent of total FMB revenue was retained, representing a withdrawal of potential producer income of about 7 per cent (as there were no export duties on these crops). The details for 1967 and 1968 show, respectively, the large trading deficit mentioned earlier and the subsequent need to reduce producer prices and purchases of unprofitable crops to restore the board's financial solvency. Thereafter the Board as ADMARC became increasingly concerned with retaining a larger proportion of revenue and potential producer income to finance its growing function as an agricultural development corporation. Fortunately the buoyant export market for tobacco permitted higher prices to be paid for the main export crop. The need for incentives to producers thus involved less emphasis on price and income stabilization.

Criticisms of the export marketing boards

It will already be apparent that the boards in all tropical African countries have been subject to a

Table 12.9 *Division of Malawi Marketing Board revenue, 1964–75*

Annual average	1964–6 (m kw)	(%)	1967 (m kw)	(%)	1968 (m kw)	(%)	1969–71* (m kw)	(%)	1972–5* (m kw)	(%)
Revenue	14.4	100	16.4	100	13.2	100	20.1	100	34.0	100
Purchase of crops (payment to growers)	9.6	67	13.5	82	7.4	56	11.7	58	16.5	49
Other expenses	4.1	28	5.5	34	5.6	42	5.1	25	8.8	26
Net profit before tax	0.7	5	−2.6	−16	0.2	2	3.3	16	8.7	26

SOURCE: *Economic Report* and *Public Sector Financial Statistics.*

*Years beginning 1st April

great deal of criticism, which we may summarize here.

(1) Although some success has been achieved in respect of the stabilization objective, more often, perhaps, destabilization has followed from intervention.

One difficulty, which has already been mentioned, is that stabilizing prices is easier than stabilizing incomes: and indeed the stabilization of prices may *increase* the instability of incomes, if higher prices would have compensated smaller quantities, and vice versa. In the second place price does not fluctuate about a constant level, usually, but about either an upward or a downward trend. The problem therefore arises of separating the trend from temporary variations. If, for example, the world price falls for two years in succession, this could be part of a downward trend (outside the scope of short-term stabilization policy and therefore requiring a downward revision of the producer price) or part of a temporary downward movement later to be reversed (requiring the producer price to be temporarily subsidized out of reserves). If the fall in price is part of a trend, subsidizing out of reserves may mean that later, when the price has fallen still further and subsidy is much more needed, the stabilization fund is exhausted, as happened in the case of Uganda.

(2) A side-effect of the application of different price and stabilization policies to different crops has been a misallocation of resources. This has also in some cases had an adverse effect on the distribution of income between regions and groups of farmers.

It has also been argued that stabilization affected the allocation of resources in a second way, by delaying farmers' adjustment of production towards the commodity currently most favourably priced on the world market, reducing the country's total earnings. This applies more to the case where one commodity shows a trend, up or down, which is not seen to be such, or treated as such. If a *permanent* increase in price is not immediately passed on in full to producers, they will have correspondingly less incentive to divert resources towards this high-priced crop, even though stabilization policy is only appropriate to smooth out temporary fluctuations. Conversely, if a commodity shows a downward trend in price the temporary maintenance of a subsidized price above the free market level will delay a switch of resources towards alternative crops.

(3) As we have seen, the boards were more effective as instruments of taxation than of stabilization. It has been argued that total withdrawals, including marketing board surpluses, amounted to punitive taxation of the peasant farmer, affecting welfare and creating a disincentive to production. Even where boards were able to build up their initial reserves in periods of buoyant prices, it could be said that low-income producers, presumably with high 'time preference' rates, were forced to save and cut down consumption more severely than they should have been—especially as the benefits from the development expenditure only accrue after a delay of many years and to some extent will be enjoyed by a later generation of Ugandans, or Ghanaians, than those who are forced to save. It is important to recognize that the funds diverted from peasant growers by the marketing boards were not simply lost: they provided benefits in social capital or infrastructure such as roads, schools, agricultural research stations, and so on, or contributed directly to national development plans. The criticism should not be that growers were taxed, but that they were taxed excessively.

(4) On the other hand, there is some criticism of marketing board surpluses as a form of taxation. It might be said that the surpluses represent in part a more acceptable form of taxation, more acceptable in so far as the growers expect to be repaid the amounts deducted. Because the amounts deducted by the board are not regarded as lost income entirely, this method of taxation will not have the same disincentive effect on production. Against this, it could be argued that this confusion of functions is undesirable, and that it is more democratic for taxpayers to be aware of what taxes they are paying and, as far as possible, what they are getting in return. Another criticism is that the surpluses constitute a proportional tax, levied at a constant proportional rate instead of being more than proportional in its incidence on rich farmers' incomes: this, however, would apply equally to an export duty, which presumably is the form of taxation that would have been adopted in the absence of marketing boards. Finally, although the surpluses are paid by the rural sector of the economy, urban dwellers, including higher income groups such as civil servants and traders, have in the past benefited greatly from general expenditure financed by these surpluses.

(5) The diversion of funds away from growers towards public development agencies has been criticized in some quarters as favouring public over private enterprise. Also, if incomes are permitted to fluctuate, producers may be induced to save more. Whereas peasant farmers receiving a stable, but low, level of income are likely to adjust their spending on consumption up to this level, if they are subject to good and bad years they are more likely to save part of peak incomes in unusually good years, and use these savings to invest in improving their land or equipment. Thus, quite apart from diversion of income, its stabilization may reduce the level of private saving.

(6) In similar vein it has been suggested[6] that a

system of isolating producers from world price fluctuations provides a poor 'school' for entrepreneurs, who learn better by having to deal with market uncertainty; and that it is such a class of enterprising producers which developing countries need most.

(7) While the promotion of the long-run growth of the industry through the encouragement of improvement in quality was mentioned earlier among board objectives, there has been frequent criticism in the case of West Africa that the price differentials offered for superior grades of groundnuts, say, or palm oil, were excessive and arose from a confusion between technical efficiency (obtaining the best grade irrespective of the demand for quality) and economic efficiency (obtaining the grade which will over the long period maximize the earnings of producers). In Uganda there has been little criticism of the premium paid for 'good' as opposed to 'stained' seed cotton, while in the case of coffee it is possible that the introduction of a premium would have been beneficial as a means of improving quality in order to maintain export earnings despite a world coffee surplus in the 1960s.

(8) Although economists have generally focused their analysis on the stabilization and fiscal objectives of the boards, there is a tendency to ignore their most immediate function, which is the organization of marketing, particularly at the final stages. While one of the reasons for the establishment of boards was to counter the monopolistic position of the large export-import firms, the monopolistic position of the boards themselves has been criticised,[7] and it has been argued that take-over by a board tends to 'freeze' a previously competitive situation among traders and processors who subsequently become little more than agents with guaranteed positions and paid, usually, on a 'cost-plus' basis rather than competing in bidding up the price to growers.

Controlled marketing in Kenya and Tanzania

Whereas in Nigeria, Ghana, and Uganda, in particular, marketing boards are associated mainly with income stabilization policies for major export crops, these have not been important in Kenya and Tanzania, where the dominant marketing boards have been concerned with the regulation of marketing of staple foodstuffs for domestic consumption, leading to comprehensive controlled marketing systems covering most cash and food crops.

Free versus controlled marketing in Kenya

The interesting feature of marketing in Kenya is that,

despite the strong settler influence on the colonial government, before independence, and the private enterprise orientation of the government since, a comprehensive system of controlled marketing of agricultural commodities should have evolved much earlier than that in the more socialist Tanzania.

Historical background

Thus the law providing for the establishment of marketing boards for agricultural produce in Kenya is the Agricultural Production Marketing Act of 1936, introduced at a time of falling prices and economic uncertainty. There followed the introduction of Maize and Produce Control established during the war, and carried on into the post-war period. By 1945, boards had been established to handle maize, coffee, sisal, pyrethrum, passion-fruit, flax, dairy products, pork products, legumes, and oilseeds. The establishment of the Maize Marketing Board in 1959 confirmed the permanency of the organized system of maize marketing, its functions being 'to regulate, control and improve the collection, storage, marketing, distribution and supply of maize and maize products'. At the same time many of the administrative functions previously centralized in Nairobi under the Maize and Produce Control became decentralized under Provincial Marketing Boards dealing with many other commodities besides maize. Thus the Nyanza Province Marketing Board established earlier in fact, in 1955, handled a large number of crops, (1) operating as an agent for the Maize Marketing Board in the case of maize, for the Kenya Farmers' Association (KFA) in the case of wheat, and directly for the government in the case of rice, all purchased at a guaranteed price fixed by the government; (2) buying other scheduled crops for which the government operated a support price (beans, millet, sorghum, njahi, sunflower); dealing in other regulated produce for which no support price was maintained by government (grains, peas, groundnuts, simsim, cassava, ghee, eggs, poultry); trading to some extent in other commodities not regulated at all (vegetables, fruit, jaggery, castor seed). This Board later extended its activities into the Rift Valley Province, while the Central Province Marketing Board, established in 1959, expanded its operations into the Southern Province. In 1964 a new West Kenya Marketing Board took over the activities of the Nyanza Province Marketing Board in the Nyanza and Rift Valley Provinces, while a new Kenya Agricultural Produce Marketing Board was set up. A general rationalization of the marketing structure for maize and general produce took place in 1966, as all these were merged into a single Maize and General Produce Board.

Thus it can be said that after 1955 there was a progressive extension of the marketing board structure, both geographically and in terms of coverage of crops, particularly in the direction of covering the general produce of the small African farmer. There were in addition export commodity boards, but the Cotton Lint and Seed Marketing Board was the only one organized on a similar basis to the Uganda Boards. The Tea, Coffee, Sisal and Pyrethrum Boards, dealing in commodities where large-scale estate production was much more important, were in part 'producer boards' with membership made up partly of estate farmers elected to represent their fellows, as well as having general supervisory and research functions. Finally, reflecting the more diversified nature of Kenyan agriculture, compared to other East African countries, there are specialized industry boards, particularly the well-established Kenya Meat Commission, the Dairy Board, the Pig Industry Board, and the Canning Crops Board.

The most obvious features of the marketing boards in Kenya were therefore:

(1) The large number of boards, and their diversity. Even in 1960, the MacGillivray Committee on the organization of Kenyan agriculture found 27 boards in existence.

(2) These boards added up to a comprehensive system of control over the marketing of agricultural and livestock products, with the widest possible coverage in terms of major and minor crops, and emerging very much earlier—before independence in fact—than the Tanzanian system.

(3) Unlike West Africa, the marketing board system in Kenya has always centred on control over the marketing of the main foodstuff, maize, and the export commodity boards have been of very much less importance. These latter boards have also not been concerned with income stabilization for small farmers as was the case in West Africa and Uganda.

(4) Some of the major commodity boards have been in part 'producer boards' with representation of large farmers and cooperatives. A distinction can in fact be drawn between 'producer organizations', being boards under the direct control of producers, through their elected members, even if generally with government advice and representation, and 'control organizations' whose primary function is to control the industry under varying degrees of government direction. The Cereal Producers' Board was a good example of the former, being a 'representative' body of 10 elected producers, plus two directors of the KFA, with the chairman also taken from this same cooperative organization for large *general* farmers. To some extent this distinction corresponds to the division between large-scale, including European, farmers and small-scale peasant producers.

Reasons for the establishment of maize and produce control

(1) The primary purpose of maize control and organization in Kenya has been to stabilize the flow of essential foodstuffs to the consumer. Thus in addition to the fixing of a maize price there is control over *quantity*, through a system of regional maize quotas. The amount of maize required to satisfy internal demand is estimated, and regional quotas allocated. Surpluses can be absorbed into buffer stocks by the Board or exported, and deficits made up correspondingly by Board imports or releases from stock.

(2) A related purpose has been the protection of farmers' incomes. In Kenya this was centred not on income stabilization for peasant producers—cotton incomes for example—but on incomes of large-scale commercial, usually *European* farmers. Thus an official publication[8] in 1958 stated that:

> In order to feed the Colony's African labour force together with their families, especially in the two major towns ... it would be imprudent to rely solely on deliveries by peasant growers whether in Kenya or in neighbouring territories. While Africans in certain areas, especially Nyanza, have come to rely on maize to a considerable extent as their main cash crop, it still remains true that the majority of the 6,000,000 African farmers in Kenya plant maize primarily for African subsistence and only secondarily for cash.

Thus one object was to ensure basic food supplies by guaranteeing adequate returns[9] and reasonably stable prices to large-scale commercialized farmers, with the Board exporting any surplus to domestic requirements, selling this usually at very much lower prices. The Board's monopoly over exports and imports was therefore not merely a direct means of ensuring that domestic requirements were met, but also a means of maintaining a sufficiently high and stable domestic price.

(3) A third factor was the feeling that private traders in East Africa, as in many developing countries, exploited monopolistic positions, especially at the wholesale marketing level, while at the primary level the large number of small traders were often considered to lack the capital to perform the middleman functions effectively. These considerations, in part, lay behind arrangements for the licensing of traders as agents of the Boards, and the desire to extend coverage of the Boards' marketing activities to include a wide range of minor crops, which cannot be considered to be staple foodstuffs and are not grown by large farmers.

(4) This wide range of activity also reflected the desire to offer small farmers known prices ahead of the planting season, the object here being to reduce uncertainty rather than to guarantee incomes, as in the previous case.

Looking at the position with respect to maize and other major foodstuffs in Kenya in the 1970s we may note that the same mixture of economic and political factors enter into the determination of prices. As we saw in Chapter 9, although the large-farm sector has been localized to a considerable extent, it remains substantially intact. Since a higher producer price for maize and other major farm commodities is likely to benefit large farmers proportionately more than peasant producers, for whom marketable surpluses constitute a smaller proportion of output, there are necessarily strong vested interests in the direction of higher producer prices. On the other hand, secondly, just as the colonial government was concerned to ensure supplies of basic foodstuffs to urban, as well as rural areas, so there is today strong political pressure on the authorities to keep down the prices of those basic commodities which determine the cost of living of the urban wage earner.

Criticisms of the Kenyan maize marketing system

The main features of the operation of maize marketing are (1) first, the monopolistic position of the Board: under the Maize Marketing Act the Board acquires ownership of all maize in Kenya as soon as it is harvested, except for the maize consumed by growers and their families or employees. All maize has then to be sold to the Board, through traders who are appointed as agents. (2) Related to this is the monopolistic determination of prices: these are set for every level of the system with sales at prices higher than these rendering buyers and sellers subject to fines. The Board also uses its monopolistic position to fix different prices in the domestic and export markets,[10] paying producers an average price which reflects losses made from exports (or imports).[11] (3) There is regional estimation and determination of quantities and, in order to enforce monopolistic organization of marketing, strict control over movement of maize between Districts. Amounts of 1,000 lb or less can be transported within a District for the exclusive consumption of the owner and his family and amounts of 60 lb or less, only, outside the District if accompanied by the owner.

Despite the laudable aims of the system of securing a stable maize industry capable of providing regular supplies of a basic foodstuff at steady prices, the system of controlled marketing has been periodically criticized. In large part the debate has been the old conflict between 'free enterprise' and planning, centring this time specifically on maize production and marketing. As early as 1955, the East Africa Royal Commission Report[12] severely criticized the system of 'state-regulated monopolies', and subsequently a number of different academic economists have made similar criticisms and argued the advantage of reversion to a freer system of marketing.[13]

The most thoroughgoing criticism of the established system, however, was in the Report of a Working Party set up by the Ministry of Agriculture itself, in 1966.[14] Among the detailed criticisms which have been made are the following:

(1) Whereas costs of production for maize vary greatly from area to area within Kenya, the system of pricing under the policy of regional self-sufficiency means that farmers in the best maize-producing districts face a considerably lower price than farmers in poor maize-producing districts in which there are shortages. As a result specialization between Districts is not made on the basis of real costs, and an inefficient pattern of production is encouraged.

(2) Board distribution of maize between Districts is faulty, with shortages of milled maize occurring in some Districts at times when there is plenty of milled maize in the country. Often the unofficial market price in a District exceeds the official Board selling price, implying a failure by the Board to supply sufficient quantities at the official price. Cases are quoted of lorries having to wait as much as three days to unload at Board stores, leading to a shortage of lorries for collection from farmers.[15]

(3) Excessive overhead costs, resulting in a large gap between the Board's buying and selling prices are said to have encouraged substantial 'black market' sales with so-called 'smuggling' of maize across District boundaries. The advantage to the grower from this is that he obtains a price somewhat higher than that offered by the Board, while the miller or trader obtains supplies at a rather lower price, with possible additional savings in transport costs. The Working Party estimated that in years of normal harvest the Board handled no more than 10 per cent of the total maize crop. Given that an efficient system of organized marketing would offer no incentives for smuggling and black marketing (supplies would already be getting shifted efficiently from excess supply to excess demand areas), this measures the extent of inefficiency which had entered the system. In addition, the benefit yielded from having a licence for shipment of maize across a District boundary offers great scope for corruption and creates privilege in that farmers able to secure such licences are invariably able to obtain a better price and a higher rate of return. Finally, constant checks on lorry traffic in an effort to stem illegal marketing imposes additional costs on the general taxpayers and on transport users.

(4) The offer of fixed prices throughout the season has been criticized for not holding out to private individuals any incentive to build additional storage,

since costs of storage are not compensated by a higher price later in the year.

(5) Stability of prices is also thought to have contributed to instability of *incomes*, due to the unavoidable variability of maize output from year to year.

The Working Party made radical proposals for the overhaul of the system which, however, have yet to be taken up. Pointing to the fact that in many African countries, such as Nigeria, essential foodstuffs were efficiently marketed over long distances by private traders, it recommended a free market system for internal distribution, with the Board retaining responsibility for a strategic reserve, operating a buffer stock (and thus setting floor and ceiling prices for maize), and continuing its monopoly of export sales and imports. Another recommendation was that producer prices should be allowed to fluctuate within a limited range of, say, 35–40 shillings a bag, to help stabilize incomes in the face of quantity variations, and to encourage consumption in periods of surplus maize and vice versa. Finally it was recommended that different prices be paid for maize delivered to each Board railhead store, to reflect the actual real costs of transporting maize by rail from each alternative source, to the market.

Tanzania: marketing boards into development authorities

Whereas the colonial Kenya government developed a sophisticated system of internal marketing of staple foods, subsequently developing this into an extensive network of commodity boards, government regulation of agricultural marketing in Tanzania, just before independence, was much less extensive.

The grain storage department

As in Kenya, food marketing was controlled during the war years, and when the wartime emergency regulations were abandoned in 1949, the Grain Storage Department (GSD) was set up. As the name suggests, this was established with the aim of ensuring a sufficient supply of basic foodstuffs in the face of periodic droughts and famine, and was a buffer stock rather than a marketing board, although it was authorized to control the marketing of a scheduled list of 'controlled' produce covering the main foodstuffs, maize, millet, wheat, paddy, cassava, and mixed beans. Its purpose was to accumulate stocks for distribution in times of shortage and to import supplementary supplies when necessary. The GSD fairly quickly found itself in serious financial difficulties

and was wound up over the period 1953–7, after which a system of largely free marketing obtained.

The establishment of the NAPB

A reversal occurred in 1963 with the establishment of the National Agricultural Products Board (NAPB) to control the marketing of maize, paddy, oilseeds and, anomalously, one important export commodity, cashew nuts. This was intended to operate in conjunction with cooperative unions and societies in a system of single-channel marketing. The NAPB appointed the cooperative unions as its main agents, while the societies received the exclusive privilege of purchasing maize from farmers (with farmers being obliged, equally, to deliver all commercial quantities of maize to the societies). Thus by 1965–6 virtually all purchases of maize were in principle to be sold to the NAPB through the cooperative movement.[16] This dependence on the cooperative movement constituted an important difference between the NAPB and the Maize and General Produce Board of Kenya. The system of pricing for maize was similar, however, with the NAPB fixing an 'into-store' price from which union marketing costs (plus any local produce cess) were deducted to give the price payable to the union. Substantial differences in price could thus be paid to unions in different parts of the country with, however, uniform prices among all societies and farmers serving one union. Similarly the consumer price for maize flour was equalized throughout the country.

Criticisms of the NAPB

A number of criticisms of the NAPB have been made:

(1) Its buffer stock policy, like that of the GSD before it, was relatively unsuccessful. Livingstone[17] pointed out that there were two kinds of contingencies in the supply of maize against which a buffer stock might offer protection: relatively small year-to-year variations in output, and major shortfalls in drought years which might only occur once in seven or eight years. In attempting to cater for the latter, the NAPB expensively accumulated very large famine stocks, much greater than would have been required for year-to-year stabilization purposes, but might eventually finish up selling off substantial quantities on the export market at disastrously low prices, only to be forced to import expensive new supplies if subsequently a major drought occurred.

(2) Although this has not been closely documented, it was not particularly efficient in distributing maize between surplus and deficit regions within the

country, so that shortfalls and surpluses persisted simultaneously.

(3) The inclusion of cashew nuts, a high-priced export commodity for the Southern Region, with staple foodstuffs for domestic consumption, led to cashew producers in effect subsidizing maize, by contributing more to NAPB overheads than warranted by actual costs of handling compared to the bulky, low-value foodstuffs requiring internal distribution.[18]

(4) Most seriously, there is evidence of substantially increased costs of marketing resulting from the intervention of the Board and its appointed agents, the cooperatives.

Kriesel demonstrates this[19] by comparing producer prices and retail prices for maize at Iringa. Table 12.10 shows that total marketing costs nearly tripled in money terms over a decade up to 1969. In 1969 the producer price of maize was just 3 per cent higher than the average for 1956–60, the retail price up by 55 per cent, and marketing costs up by 187 per cent: implying a very substantial increase in real terms as well as money terms. The data are clearly illustrated in Figure 12.1 which shows a marked increase in marketing charges from 1963, the year that the NAPB took over responsibility for maize.

Part of the reason for increased marketing charges was the inefficiency of many of the cooperative societies and unions which had been hastily formed under the policy of aggressive promotion of the movement following independence, despite problems of obtaining trained and experienced staff. But secondly there were substantial additional charges obtaining from the intervention of the top-heavy NAPB bureaucracy. Figure 12.2 compares marketing costs for maize movement between Iringa and Dar es Salaam in 1957–8 and 1967–8, and is likely to reflect the same factors as in the previous comparison. Since transport costs (shaded) between Iringa and Dar es Salaam were equal at shs 80 per ton in the two years, responsibility for the almost 100 per cent increase in marketing costs (from shs 130 to shs 258.6 per ton) can be seen to be divided between societies, or union (60 per cent) and NAPB (40 per cent).

The effect of the increase in marketing charges was, naturally, to raise consumer prices for maize, affecting the urban wage earner, and to reduce producer prices, affecting the return to the farmer. In the case of export commodities such as cashew nuts and oilseeds, Kriesel estimated that returns to farmers were 15–20 per cent lower than they would have been under the previous marketing institutions and their margins.[20]

The development of a 'black market'

The operations of the NAPB stimulated the development of a 'black market' or 'unofficial market' in maize in two ways. Local sales within each Region of Tanzania were perfectly legal outside the marketing board. But for trade between Regions, given the

Table 12.10 Producer and retail prices for maize at Iringa, Tanzania, and implied marketing charges, 1956–69 (shs/kg)

Calendar year	Producer price		Estimated marketing charges*		Estimated retail price	
	(shs)	Index (%)	(shs)	Index (%)	(shs)	Index (%)
Average, 1956–60	0.243	100	0.094	100	0.335	100
1956	0.290	119	0.090	96	0.380	113
1957	0.250	103	0.090	96	0.340	101
1958	0.270	111	0.090	96	0.360	107
1959	0.230	95	0.090	96	0.320	96
1960	0.170	70	0.110	117	0.290	84
1961	0.330	136	0.100	106	0.430	128
1962	0.350	144	0.110	117	0.460	137
1963	0.345	142	0.155	165	0.500	149
1964	0.277	114	0.253	269	0.530	158
1965	0.338	139	0.182	194	0.520	155
1966	0.270	111	0.250	266	0.520	155
1967	0.300	123	0.220	234	0.520	155
1968	0.300	123	0.220	234	0.520	155
1969	0.250	103	0.270	287	0.520	155

SOURCE: Kriesel et al., op. cit., Table 22, p. 38
*Marketing charges are those implied by the difference between purchase price and retail selling price at Iringa

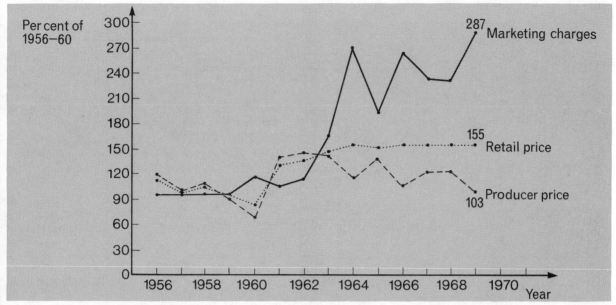

Figure 12.1   *Variation in producer and retail prices at Iringa, Tanzania, and implied marketing charges, 1956–69 (SOURCE: Kriesel et al., op. cit., Figure 14, p. 37).*

spread between the price paid to farmers by the Board and the retail price fixed to permit the Board and its agents to cover their costs, it paid farmers to 'short-circuit' the system by selling to traders who could market 'unofficially' direct to wholesalers and retailers in the consuming areas. Secondly, the failure of the Board to move produce efficiently between surplus and deficit regions further stimulated illegal trading. According to Kriesel no more than 10 or 20 per cent of maize was being marketed through the Board in 1970.[21] The attempted prevention of illegal trading nevertheless involved the maintenance of a 'large cadre' of surveillance and inspection forces, including the police and occasionally even the defence forces, adding further to the cost of the system.

The structure of marketing in 1970 and 1974

Although we have concentrated so far on the NAPB, handling maize, paddy, oilseeds, and one import-export crop, cashew nuts, there were in fact *nine* commodity boards on Tanzania mainland in 1970, most of which had been in existence since before independence: these covered, apart from an embryonic Dairy Board, the most important export crops, cotton, coffee, sisal, tobacco, pyrethrum, and tea, and the valuable domestic cash crop, sugar.

These were not marketing boards as such, in most cases, however, and the degree of their involvement in marketing varied. The most important Board was the Lint and Seed Marketing Board for cotton, set

up in 1952 on similar lines to those in Kenya and Uganda, which licensed buyers of lint and seed, and in particular bought from the ginneries all cotton lint produced in Tanzania for export. The LSMB made recommendations of prices to be paid for seed cotton to the Ministry of Agriculture, which would announce a uniform price payable to farmers for given grades of seed cotton in advance of the planting season. This remains the basic system for cotton.

The Coffee Board licensed handlers and buyers and ran auctions at which the coffee could be purchased for export. The Sisal Marketing Board had been established in 1965, and while having wide powers to control the production (through quotas to sisal plantations) and marketing of sisal, operated by appointing licensed sisal agents to market and export sisal. The functions of other boards such as the Tanganyika Tobacco Board, the Tanganyika Pyrethrum Board, the Tanzanian Tea Authority, and the National Sugar Board, were similar, involving licensing, regulation, advisory work, and research.

Subsequent changes, mainly in 1973 and 1974, produced a drastic restructuring and extension of the commodity system, as can be seen from Figure 12.22. Although the Coffee and Pyrethrum Boards are referred to here as marketing boards, their functions remained as just described above. The rest comprises four corporations and six crop and livestock 'Development Authorities'. These were in fact agricultural parastatals controlling subsidiary and associated companies.[23]

The NAPB, which previously had made use of milling facilities at the National Milling Corporation

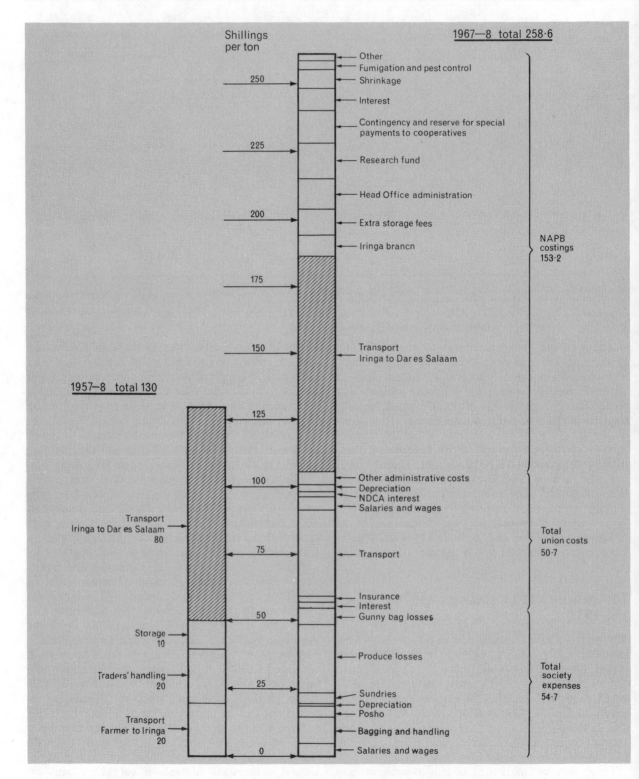

Figure 12.2 Marketing costs for maize between Iringa and Dar es Salaam, 1957–8 and 1967–8 (shs/ton) (SOURCE: Kriesel et al., op. cit., Figure 11, p. 30).

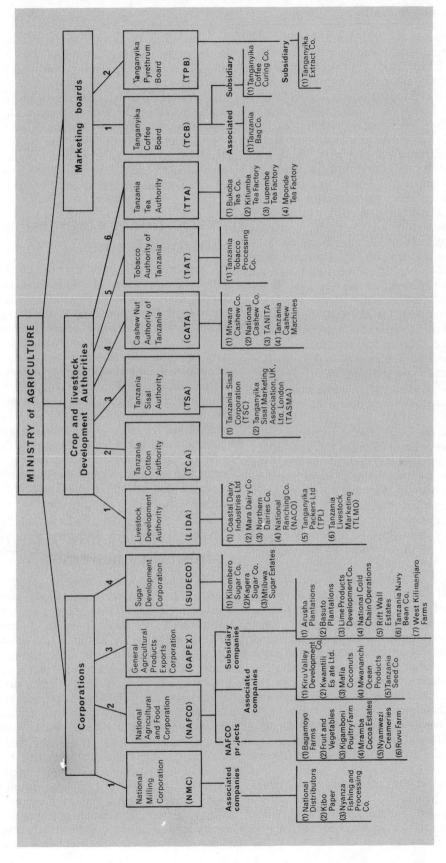

Figure 12.3 Agricultural parastatals and marketing boards in Tanzania: structure at the end of 1974 (SOURCE: Marketing Development Bureau, op. cit.).

(NMC), was abolished in 1973, its marketing and other responsibilities being taken over by the NMC, with cashew nuts being hived off to the Cashew Nut Authority of Tanzania, and oilseeds to a new General Agricultural Products Export Corporation (GAPEX).

The Crop and Livestock Development Authorities (as well as the Coffee and Pyrethrum Boards, which were similar in scope) combined the former function of regulating the industry as a whole, with direct involvement in production through subsidiary and associated companies. There was, therefore, 'backward integration' from the marketing level into production. In the case of sisal, this was achieved directly by nationalization of some major existing plantations in 1967. In 1973, the Tanzania Sisal Corporation, a subsidiary of the Tanzania Sisal Authority, controlled over 50 per cent of Tanzanian output, a figure which was increased in 1974 by the nationalization of 20 more estates.

This is in contrast with, for example, the National Agricultural and Food Corporation (NAFCO, set up in 1969), which is concerned with production rather than marketing and particularly with the initiation of new agricultural ventures. In 1974, NAFCO owned seven subsidiary companies, was a shareholder in five others, and operated a number of other specific projects.

Like the Tanzania Sisal Authority, the Sugar Development Corporation (SUDECO) was established in 1974 'with the general mandate to accelerate the development of the sugar industry in Tanzania by consolidating into one organization the functions of production, procurement, storage, distribution and sale of sugar',[24] combining the responsibility of the old Sugar Board for importing and distributing sugar with the take-over of sugar-producing estates from NAFCO.

The broad scope of responsibility given to the Crop Development Authorities is illustrated by the functions specified for the Tanzania Cotton Authority under the 1973 Cotton Industry Act, which were to: '(a) promote the development and improvement of the cotton industry in the country; (b) participate by itself or in company with others in the production, ginning of raw cotton and in the processing and manufacturing of cotton seed and products derived therefrom; (c) regulate, control and secure the most favourable arrangements for the marketing and export of cotton lint; (d) advise the Government on all matters affecting the cotton industry.'

The main features of the commodity board structure in 1974 were therefore:

(1) organization on a separate commodity-by-commodity basis, and extension to all major crops;

(2) merging of marketing functions into broad Development Authorities responsible for the regulation of separate agricultural industries through all their stages;

(3) operation as parastatals, with vertical integration backward to the production stage, in most cases, through subsidiary and associated companies.

The changes amounted to the establishment of a largely controlled or socialized system of management of marketing, covering all major commodities for domestic consumption and for export.

International commodity control schemes

In Chapter 8 we discussed the use of buffer stocks for stabilizing the prices of staple foodstuffs within a country, and above we analysed efforts made by export marketing boards operating at the national level to stabilize prices and incomes derived from major export crops. The price of major internationally traded primary commodities are determined on the world market, however, and elimination or reduction of price fluctuations requires coordinated action at the *international* level. National export marketing boards can only attempt to offset the effects of external fluctuations, for instance, by allowing tax revenue to fluctuate (upsetting public expenditure programmes) in order to stabilize private incomes. Efforts have long been made through international commodity schemes to reduce fluctuations in the world prices of major commodities.

Objectives of international commodity schemes

In fact international commodity schemes have had either of two separate aims which may, however, overlap: price stabilization, on the one hand, and the maintenance or raising of prices and earnings through collective restriction of output on the other. Just as in the case of a national commodity stabilization scheme, stabilization may be achieved internationally by the holding of buffer stocks in specific commodities. The best example of an international buffer stock is that of tin. By accumulating and decumulating the buffer stock, market supply can be regulated and price stabilized. As in the national case, the main problems have been those of financing the stock and also of forecasting world supply and demand, in particular distinguishing between temporary and cyclical movements and the underlying trend. The problems are multiplied in the international case by the difficulty of obtaining agreement among all the countries involved on a future supply and demand forecast, and on the appropriate range over which world prices should be allowed to fluctuate. If finance runs out as world prices fall, preventing further additions to stock, prices have to be allowed to fall below the agreed minimum, destroying the basis of the agreement. Alternatively, if finance has been sufficient for only a modest buffer stock prices may have to be allowed to rise beyond the agreed 'ceiling' once the buffer stock is exhausted, again destroying the basis of the agreement. In contrast with the national situation, abandonment of floor or ceiling prices may be quite serious, as agreements may be renewed only with difficulty.

An alternative to a buffer stock, which stabilizes real flows of the commodity on to the world market, is *compensatory financing*. This works in a similar way to variations in marketing board receipts in stabilizing incomes, but involves compensating financial payments at the international level. The difficulty is that since this represents a form of international aid, the amounts available for such compensation may be inadequate. Secondly, stabilization of cash earnings of primary producing countries without stabilization of the real flows will not help the consumers of the primary products, the industries which require a steady supply of raw materials. A major advantage of compensatory financing, however, is that it can be directed towards a country's *total* export earnings, and its entire macroeconomic position, rather than simply earnings from one commodity.

The second objective, of actually raising prices and earnings obtained, can be achieved through collective action by the countries producing a primary product to restrict world supply. Just as a single monopoly producer can obtain a monopoly price by restricting output, so a group of firms or, in this case, countries, can come together to achieve the same objective. This is described in more detail in Chapter 17 under the title of *collective monopoly*. A detailed agreement by producers to restrict output in this way generally involves agreement of *quotas*, the shares of the agreed output to be allocated to individual producers. When the arrangement extends to determination of specific quotas and openly agreed prices, the collective monopoly may be described as a *cartel*.

When it comes to commodity agreements, however, we may distinguish those which aim at preventing overproduction or the removal of excess supply, such as the coffee, or pre-war rubber or tea agreements, and those which attempt to increase earnings through positive price increases, such as those of oil achieved by the Organization of Petroleum Exporting Countries (OPEC) from 1973. The former category again may involve either of two situations, one where shifts in supply or demand are only temporary or cyclical, and one where prices are falling due to a secular decline in demand, and where the aim is to adjust in an orderly way to a new long-term equilibrium at a lower level of demand and output.

Problems of securing and maintaining agreement

Some commodity agreements, those relating to tin and cocoa for example, involve both producing *and* main consuming countries. Since there is usually an obvious conflict of interest between producers seeking higher prices and consumers desiring low prices, international agreements involving both producing and consuming countries include an element of bilateral bargaining between groups and have been more difficult to achieve and sustain. Failure of producer and consumer interests to agree on new prices for coffee in 1972 and for sugar in 1973 led, for instance, to the break-up of those agreements.

For agreements among producing countries only, the main problems are in achieving comprehensiveness, that is, coverage of the main producing countries, and secondly of allocating output quotas among participating countries. If participating countries together accounted for only 40 per cent of world output, say, restrictive action by them might be insufficient to raise prices appreciably, particularly if excluded countries seize the opportunity to expand their own sales. It is essential, therefore, that all major export producers of the commodity, at least, are persuaded to join the agreement. Thus the so-called Stevenson rubber restriction scheme in the 1920s which involved export quotas among British-owned estates in Malaya and Ceylon collapsed because smallholders in Dutch Indonesia and Thailand in particular could not be controlled and many rubber manufacturing interests, notably US tyre companies, such as Firestone in Liberia, developed new acreages.

As regards market shares, there may be a conflict between countries who have historically had a larger share of the world market, which they wish to retain, who have already achieved a high proportion of actual to potential output, and who, being more developed, have higher wage levels and are relatively high-cost producers, on the one hand; and, on the other, small suppliers who have taken up production more recently, and who therefore have low market shares which they wish to increase, who could in a free market do so, given their low costs of production, and who are currently producing low outputs compared to potential. The clearest example of this is in coffee, the world market for which is dominated by Brazilian and other Latin American production, and where African countries were expanding exports rapidly at relatively low costs before running into market restrictions.

In addition to this direct conflict of interest, the fact that the relative importance of different sources of supply may change rapidly within a few years may soon make a scheme of quotas out of date and thus undermine agreement.

Gwyer has suggested that commodity agreements tend to favour large producing countries, such as Brazil in the case of coffee, over small.[25] If large producers do not join a commodity agreement, such an agreement would not be viable: large countries therefore have a choice between being party to an agreement or a situation of no agreement. If small countries do not like the terms of a proposed agreement, however, the choice open to them is that of membership or non-membership, even if a situation of no agreement—a free market situation—would have been preferable to either. Particularly if the main consuming countries (on which small producers are dependent for markets) are also members of an agreement, the large producing countries can force a not particularly favourable agreement on their smaller partners.

Many attempts have been made over the past 50 years or so to reduce the price instability of primary commodities in international markets, and in particular to raise the price level when this has been very depressed, as in the 1930s, sometimes through formal agreements betwen governments, and sometimes through less formal agreements between leading international companies or private producers' associations. For the reasons mentioned above, these have generally been very difficult to achieve and sustain. Sooner or later one side becomes dissatisfied with price levels or trading restrictions involved in the agreement, and important groups of producers or consumers withdraw from it; or, as already mentioned, where a buffer stock is involved, either the stock is exhausted or finance for accumulation of further stock runs out, leading to the abandonment of agreed ceiling and floor prices.

Examples of particular commodity schemes

The first International Coffee Agreement (ICA) in 1963 was not based on the buffer-stock mechanism but relied on export quotas to maintain a minimum price at the 1962 level: a level which was high enough to allow Brazil, the largest exporter, to supply profitably more than her quota. The agreement, involving 41 exporting and 20 importing countries, specified basic quotas for exporters on the basis of past sales, while importers similarly agreed to limit imports

from non-member countries to past levels. Members can also make sales over and above their quotas, to non-quota markets where prices, however, are significantly lower.

One effect of export quotas is to freeze the existing pattern of world production, retarding the expansion of low-cost producing areas like Eastern Africa and delaying the diversification of high-cost producers like Brazil into other activities. This may be both unfair to recent producing countries who have to sacrifice a larger proportion of potential production and income, and inefficient, in that a more competitive situation would have led to expansion of production in low-cost countries at the expense of high-cost producers. This problem of rigidity and inefficiency in allocation is a general feature of cartels in whatever field.

Even between countries in a similar historical position, issues of equity may arise. Thus the 1963 ICA basic export quotas for the forthcoming period 1963-8 were based on actual exports over the period 1959-62. As Table 12.11 shows, in the decade or so leading up to the Agreement the coffee industries of Kenya and Uganda had been expanding much more rapidly than the Tanzanian one, putting them in a position in 1962-3 where they could claim more generous quotas. Subsequently they could afford only modest rates of expansion while Tanzania still needed to step up the rate of growth of its coffee industry, being forced to accept a much larger share, 25.1 per cent, of sales in non-quota markets, while Kenya could within the Agreement make all but 8.4 per cent of sales in the more profitable quota markets.

Table 12.11 Some effects of the 1963 International Coffee Agreement on the East African countries

| | Annual production growth rates (%) | | Non-quota exports as % of total exports, 1963-4 to 1968-9, average |
	Before Agreement 1950-62	During Agreement[*] 1960-1 to 1969-70	
Kenya	10.2	5.1	8.4
Uganda	14.3	4.8	20.6
Tanzania	4.1	10.8	25.1

SOURCE: G. Gwyer, op. cit.
[*] Actual period of the agreement was 1963-9

From 1966 the African countries pressed for higher quotas and a new ICA in 1968 provided for a general increase in basic quotas. A special feature of the Agreement was the establishment of a diversification fund to be used to assist high-cost producers to change over to other crops in order to permit increased exports from countries with lower costs or no reasonably economic alternatives.

The general position with regard to *tea* is similar to that for coffee, the world market being dominated by India and Sri Lanka, while African countries such as Kenya have expanded much more recently and represent low-cost producers anxious to increase their share of the market. Producing countries have discussed export restrictions since the late 1960s, and measures for diversification into other activities.

In the case of *cocoa*, the major world suppliers are West African countries who together account for about 70 per cent of world production, mainly Ghana, Nigeria, and the Ivory Coast. Compared to many other primary commodities, the world demand for cocoa is relatively price-elastic, but considerable price instability exists for supply reasons. As African production is concentrated mainly in the same West African region subject to the same climatic and disease risks, there is little compensating variation in world supply between the main exporters, so that these factors can produce shifts of an inelastic supply curve. As in the case of coffee, cocoa is a tree crop, with a considerable lag in supply response, in this case the result of a seven-year gestation period. Concentration of production within the same region and among closely connected countries should have facilitated international agreement, but efforts in this direction have not been particularly successful. Attempts to implement an agreement during the 1960s foundered on the failure of the main consuming countries like the USA to agree the 'ceiling' and 'floor' prices at the higher levels requested by producing countries. As in the case of the International Tin Agreement control over world prices has lapsed as buffer stocks have been exhausted, as in the 1970s, or as finance has proved insufficient to limit downward price movements. A new agreement for cocoa was launched in 1973.

The problem of instability is illustrated again in the case of *tin*, the price of which fluctuated between £570 and £1,600, for example, during the period 1955–64. The case of tin illustrates in particular the problems of running an international buffer stock, a buffer-stock manager having been employed by the International Tin Council (ITC) from an early date. Accumulated stocks ran out in 1961 and 1963–4, while finance for purchases of stock was exhausted in 1956 and 1958, for example. Nevertheless this is one of the few international organizations which has operated buffer stocks for any length of time. Two advantages in the case of tin are that as a commodity it is relatively cheap to store, and that it is mainly exported by only a few countries, Malaysia, especially, Thailand, Indonesia, and Bolivia. However it was releases from the US strategic stockpile and exports from the USSR, rather than buffer-stock intervention, which kept fluctuations from being still greater than they were during the late 1950s and 1960s.

Copper is normally the most valuable primary commodity, other than petroleum, entering world trade. The main exporting countries have experienced great instability in export prices and earnings, particularly acute for a single-commodity exporter like Zambia. A buffer-stock scheme seems particularly appropriate, as in the case of tin, to even out price fluctuations, the 'stock' comprising a non-perishable high-value metal already traded in organized commodity markets, notably the London Metal Exchange. The Inter-Governmental Council of Copper Exporting Countries (CIPEC) has not worked very well, however, often failing to agree common action to tackle depressed prices, such as export restrictions and possibly closing mines. Several factors may explain this. Although the number of Third World exporting countries is small, Chile, Peru, Zambia, and Zaire do not form a politically cohesive group as the Arab oil countries do. Moreover, since developed countries can supply a large part of their market from among themselves, by domestic production or refining scrap, CIPEC's effectiveness as a cartel is weakened. Its position is further weakened by the longer-term fear of substitution from aluminium and plastics if prices are held too high.

Reference may be made only briefly to other commodities for which agreements have at various times been made or are being sought. Reference has already been made to the Stevenson *rubber* restriction schemes of the 1920s. Natural rubber is a commodity affected strongly in the past by synthetics. During the 1960s the expansion of synthetic production in fact helped to stabilize natural rubber prices, but at a lower level. Now the increase in petroleum prices has made synthetics a less competitive substitute. A major advantage is that natural rubber exports are dominated by just two countries, Malaysia and Indonesia (producing with Thailand 86 per cent of world output in 1975), adjacent to each other, making it easier to establish an Asian Rubber Producer's Association and in 1976 to set up a producer's buffer stock of 100,000 tons, to stabilize prices.

The position regarding *cane sugar* is complicated by two factors. Throughout the post-war period most of the world's cane sugar has been sold through various preferential trade arrangements organized by the main consuming countries for their colonial or ex-colonial suppliers: the Commonwealth Sugar Agreement, the US system of sugar import quotas for its economic dependencies, and the French colonial system merged into the EEC Yaoundé Agreement. The second factor is the existence of beet sugar as a substitute, and the desire of major consuming countries to protect their domestic beet industries. The EEC itself is largely self-sufficient from beet without imports of cane sugar. Japan and Canada are now the only two major industrial importers.

Cotton also faces synthetic substitution and is also produced in developed countries, notably the USA. A buffer stock is generally regarded as too complex in the case of cotton, but other measures to extend the market and increase price levels are thought desirable. Like cotton, *raw jute and hard fibres*, particularly sisal, are subject to substitution by synthetics or other natural fibres. Exporters are therefore in a weak bargaining position.

The striking success of OPEC in raising the price of oil in 1973–4 has given fresh impetus to the search for commodity agreements. Morocco, the world's largest supplier of *natural phosphate*, raised the price of its phosphate rock by 300 per cent in 1973, a price rise which was followed by Tunisia and Senegal. These three, together with Algeria and Togo, established the World Institute of Phosphates in 1975. In respect of *bauxite*, ten countries have formed the International Bauxite Association, with Jamaica, the major supplier to the USA, in a leading role. *Tropical timber* interests in Indonesia, Malaysia, and the Philippines have formed the South East Asian Lumber Producers' Association, following a recession in the market, while ten African countries began to form their own timber organization in 1975–6. A dozen exporting countries led by Venezuela were investigating the possibilities in respect of *iron* in 1975. While for *bananas*, Colombia, Costa Rica, Guatemala, Honduras, and Panama in Central America formed a Banana Exporting Countries' Union in 1974 in order to 'defend the product'.

The new impetus given by OPEC

The Organization of Petroleum Exporting Countries, OPEC, represents the clearest example of an output restriction scheme or collective monopoly aimed at increasing prices and earnings. Formed by 11 oil-exporting countries in 1971, OPEC demonstrated its monopoly power dramatically by raising petroleum prices five-fold between October and December, 1973, bringing a very substantial increase in revenue to participating countries. A special feature of the organization is that it covers a large number of countries, located in different continents, including not only the Middle East countries but also Nigeria in West Africa and Venezuela in Central America. Its core membership, however, comprises the Arab countries and it is this which explains the degree of

solidarity achieved in particular because the immediate stimulus to agreement and its bold use of monopoly power was the resentment felt against the Western consuming countries following Israeli successes in the Middle East fighting of 1973. This exercise of monopoly power was strikingly successful because of the inelasticity of demand for oil, due to the absence of energy substitutes except at much higher prices.

The Arab action has clearly been important. How far has it been a good thing? Although monopolistic action has its dangers, when it is taken by low-income countries against much richer countries it may be said to produce a 'benign' or favourable income redistribution. It may also be said to offset other factors working in the opposite direction, such as declining terms of trade and more powerful trade union pressure to maintain incomes in the rich countries. While the income distribution effect may be less favourable in the case of oil, the success of OPEC may, as indicated above, have an important demonstration effect for other commodities and be a stimulus for international action as a whole.

Against this, it should be noted that the sharp rise in the price of petroleum had a serious effect on the balance of payments of many 'non-oil' developing countries and also involved a transfer of income from much poorer countries to the oil producers. Secondly, it should be noted that while such commodity agreements raise earnings of the exporting countries they do not involve any increase in total world activity and output as would expansion of incomes through increased productivity in farming, or say, industrialization. What is involved is a transfer of incomes through the extraction of monopoly or economic rent at the expense of other producers.

Optimal conditions for a producers' alliance

A feature of commodity agreements in the past, however, has been their *fragility*. For example, of the four agreements in existence in 1969 (coffee, sugar, wheat, and tin), only tin was still fully in operation in 1975. The optimal conditions for a producers' alliance might be said to be:

(1) world demand for the product should be price-*inelastic*;

(2) there should be a limited number of countries involved, so that it is relatively easy to secure monopoly control over the bulk of world exported production;

(3) the main producing and exporting countries should all be developing countries with close common interests;

(4) related to the first condition: there should not be strong present or potential competition from substitutes of the raw material;

(5) none of the countries should be single-commodity exporters, like Zambia, for example, since this makes agreement to restrict output more difficult;

(6) the commodity should be easy to store, permitting it to be withheld from the market at a particular time.

UNCTAD IV and the Common Fund

In addition to alliances established by exporting countries themselves, there have been a number of recent international measures aimed at stabilization of the export earnings of developing countries. The fourth Nairobi meeting in May 1976, of the United Nations Conference on Trade and Development, UNCTAD IV, resolved to establish a Common Fund to finance stabilization schemes for 18 primary commodities of interest to developing countries. 10 'core' commodities singled out for priority in negotiating buffer-stock schemes to be financed by the Common Fund are listed in Table 12.12. A further 8 commodities[26] were also included in the UNCTAD IV resolution, bringing the total coverage of the 18 commodities to about three-quarters of the value of all non-oil commodity exports from developing

countries in the mid-1970s. Of these the 10 'core' commodities represent well over one-half, and are of particular interest to tropical African countries.

Table 12.12 shows in addition (a) the share of all developing countries in the total value of world exports of each primary commodity and (b) the share of African developing countries, both percentages referring to the average which was obtained in the years 1972–4. The third column, (c), provides instability indicators, showing the extent of fluctuations in (i) the world price and (ii) total export earnings from these commodities during the period, 1953–64, *after* the Korean War price boom but before the currency and commodity instability period of the later 1960s and 1970s. Finally column (d) shows the international commodity agreements in existence in 1976.

It is clear from the table that, as a group, less developed countries dominate world trade in the three tropical beverages, in *natural* rubber, *cane* sugar, tin, and some natural fibres other than cotton. Tropical African countries, again as a group, dominate the world's cocoa market and, within hard fibres, the supply of sisal; they contribute about one-half of all copper and of cotton exported by developing countries and, because of its high value, are very concerned about coffee prospects even if they contribute only about 40 per cent of world exports.

The UNCTAD IV proposals envisaged a Common Fund of some $6,000 millions to finance the 10 'core' commodity schemes, of which one-half

Table 12.12 *UNCTAD IV's ten 'core' commodities: share of world trade, instability and international commodity agreements.*

Commodity	Share of total world exports, 1972–4		Instability indices (1953–64)		Existing agreement
	All LDCs % (a)	African LDCs % (b)	Unit variance (c) (i)	Total value (c) (ii)	(d)
Cocoa	90	70	20	14	International Cocoa
Coffee	95	40	12	8	Organization ICO*
Copper	42	24	14	13	International Coffee
Cotton	68	30	5	9	Council of Copper
Hard fibres	66	27	16	16	Exporting Countries,
Jute, raw	96	—	17	7	CIPOC
Rubber	97 (73)	3	16	17	Association of
Sugar	85 (67)	5	13	11	Natural Rubber
Tin	80	4	10	20	Producers
Tea	85	16	9	7	International Tin Council, ITC*

SOURCE: *UN Yearbook of International Trade Statistics*; Proceedings of UNCTAD

NOTES: *Refers to agreements between producing *and* consuming countries, the remainder being agreements of producers only. Figures in brackets are LDC shares in total exports of natural *and* synthetic rubber and total raw sugar including beet

might be needed to establish the Fund and the rest available on call to meet net additions to the value of stocks. A figure of $3,000 millions represents only about one-seventh of the total net flow of official aid from developed market economies to developing countries in 1975 or 1976. However, such a resource contribution need not be at the expense of alternative methods of international aid, since developed countries and some of the Arab oil exports could finance a Common Fund of physical commodities as part of their foreign exchange reserves as an alternative to holding financial assets in US dollars or gold. Nevertheless, the Common Fund is likely to benefit the richer developing countries which export 'core' commodities rather than some of the very poorest which, unlike Malaysia or Zambia, are not endowed with high-value exports such as rubber, tin, or copper. Because of the high value of such commodities, and the relative difficulty and cost of stocking more perishable commodities such as oilseeds and vegetable oils, the bulk of the Common Fund is likely to be used to finance commodities which are already traded in organized international commodity markets, like the London Metal Exchange for copper and tin.

Compensatory financing for commodity exporters

In the mid-1970s there were two compensatory finance schemes in operation to assist developing countries subject to severe fluctuations in their export earnings. Unlike buffer stock and export quota schemes with the major objective of stabilizing or improving permanently the level of primary commodity *prices*, these were concerned with export *income* stability.

The International Monetary Fund (IMF),[27] concerned with countries' balance of payments, provided its primary exporting members between 1963 and 1973 with some US $1,000 million to compensate for shortfalls of actual export earnings from a hypothetical normal level. Borrowers must demonstrate that the balance of payments difficulties arising from short-term export shortfalls were beyond their control, and must repay the IMF loans within three to five years. This is therefore a self-financing scheme, and covers instability in earnings from *all* exports of a primary producer, that is, it is directed towards the overall macroeconomic position of the assisted country rather that its earnings from a specific commodity.

The European Economic Community (EEC) has operated a commodity export income stabilization scheme, STABEX, since the Lomé Convention was agreed with 46 African, Caribbean, and Pacific (ACP) countries in 1975. Under STABEX, earnings from exports of 12 main groups of primary products from those ACP countries associated with the EEC are to be stabilized. Compensation for shortfalls in the earnings of individual commodities exported to the EEC below their average value in the previous four years is financed by the European Development Fund. STABEX compensation payments are outright grants for many ACP countries, specifically those 24 classified as 'least developed', 'landlocked', or island economies. Others are required to repay the compensation over five years if the volume of their exports is equal to or above the reference level and the prices are above the reference level. However, since the size of the annual compensation fund is fixed, and most financial allocations will not be repaid, the compensation available to meet large shortfalls is rather limited.

The scheme covers cocoa, coffee, tea, cotton, sisal, skins and leather, wood products (except plywood), iron ore, bananas, groundnuts, oil palm products, and coconut products. These commodities are basic raw materials traditionally imported by EEC countries and not directly competitive with many European-produced products. They are, however, generally less suited for international buffer-stock schemes (except for the first three) and constitute a large share of the total export earnings of some of the small island or 'landlocked' economies like Burundi (with 95 per cent earnings from coffee) or the oilseed and vegetable oil exporters in West Africa.

The EEC duty-free import preferences apply to these and some other non-STABEX primary products and to some fully manufactured or processed products. Special arrangements have also been made for sugar, for an indefinite period, in contrast to the five-year duration of the Lomé Agreement. The price to be paid for ACP cane sugar is tied to the EEC's support price for European-grown beet sugar, and also covers exports from India, not one of the ACP countries. However quotas have been agreed limiting each country's exports, so that the large ACP sugar exporters will still be concerned to obtain high and stable prices from any wider international sugar scheme.

Questions on Chapter 12

1. Compare and contrast African export commodity marketing boards and boards concerned with staple foodstuffs marketing. To what extent did they pursue similar objectives?
2. How successful were export marketing boards in tropical Africa in stabilizing prices and the incomes of peasant producers?
3. In what way did the operations of marketing boards in Uganda affect the allocation of resources in agriculture, and the distribution of incomes?
4. How true is it that the intervention of the Malawi's Farmers' Marketing Board actually aggravated the instability of producer incomes in the period 1956–7?
5. Review the criticisms made of the operation of export marketing boards in tropical Africa.
6. Discuss the main features of the marketing board system in Kenya.
7. Discuss the advantages and disadvantages of the system of controlled marketing in Kenya.
8. Discuss the criticisms made of Tanzania's National Agricultural Products Board.
9. What is meant by a 'black market'? Under what sort of circumstances may a black market arise? Give examples.
10. Comment on the changes that have taken place in Tanzania's commodity board structure since 1970.
11. Discuss the different objectives behind international commodity schemes and the difficulties they face in achieving them.
12. Discuss the conditions most favourable for the formation and maintenance of an international commodity agreement, and examine the conditions which exist in respect of a sample of actual commodities.
13. How far can UNCTAD IV's Common Fund and the Lomé Convention's STABEX schemes be expected to improve the position of primary producing countries?

Notes

[1] *Statement on the Future Marketing of West African Cocoa*, Cmd 6950, HMSO, London, 1946.
[2] P. T. Bauer, *West African Trade*, Cambridge University Press, 1954.
[3] Compare the developments in Tanzania, discussed presently.
[4] In the case of cocoa this was to some extent inevitable, since fluctuations in the size of the West African crop are bound to produce compensating price movements to help stabilize export proceeds.
[5] C. P. Brown, 'The Malawi Farmers Marketing Board', *Eastern African Economic Review*, Vol. 2, No. 1, 1970.
[6] D. Walker and C. Ehrlich, 'Stabilisation and Development Policy in Uganda: An Appraisal', *Kyklos*, 1959, Fasc. 3.
[7] See for example E. Whetham, *Agricultural Marketing in Africa*, Oxford University Press, 1972, Chapter 7.
[8] Sessional Paper No. 6 of 1957–8, *The Maize Industry*, 1958.
[9] Large farmers enjoyed a system of 'Guaranteed Minimum Returns' ensuring cash payment for acreage planted under the main cereal crops, maize, wheat, barley, and sorghum, in the event of the *physical* risk of crop failures being experienced due to weather or pest damage.
[10] This is known as 'price discrimination', which is analysed in Chapter 17.
[11] Regions with the greatest maize surpluses are adjudged to make the greatest contribution to export losses, and have correspondingly greater deductions made to arrive at the regional price.
[12] *East Africa Royal Commission 1953–1955 Report*, Cmd 9475, HMSO, London, 1955, p. 65.
[13] In particular, M. P. Miracle, 'An Economic Appraisal of Kenya's Maize Control', *East African Economic Review*, Vol. 6,

No. 2, December 1959; H. Karani, 'Kenya's Maize Muddle', *East African Social Science Conference*, 1966; W. O. Jones, *Marketing Staple Food Crops in Tropical Africa*, Cornell University Press, 1972, Chapter 8; and E. Whetham, op. cit., Chapter 7.
[14] Report of the Maize Commission of Enquiry, Government Printer, Nairobi, 1966.
[15] ibid.
[16] The Tanganyika Farmers' Association (TFA) which sold direct to the NAPB, was not officially registered as a cooperative.
[17] Ian Livingstone, 'Production, Price and Marketing Policy for Staple Foodstuffs in Tanzania', in V. F. Amman (ed.), *Agricultural Policy Issues in East Africa*, Makerere University Press, 1973.
[18] H. C. Kriesel *et al.*, *Agricultural Marketing in Tanzania—Background Research and Policy Proposals*, Michigan State University, 1970.
[19] Kriesel *et al.*, op. cit.
[20] Kriesel *et al.*, op. cit., p. 1.
[21] Kriesel *et al.*, op. cit., p. 40.
[22] *Marketing Development Bureau, Profiles of Major Ministry of Agriculture Parastatals*, Ministry of Agriculture, Dar es Salaam, 1974.
[23] These complement the parastatals in manufacturing and other sectors of the economy described in Chapter 18.
[24] *Marketing Development Bureau*, op. cit., p. 48.
[25] G. D. Gwyer, 'East Africa and Three International Commodity Agreements: the Lessons of Experience', *Discussion Paper No. 129*, Institute of Development Studies, February 1972.
[26] Bananas, bauxite, iron ore, manganese, meat, phosphates, tropical timber, vegetable oils.
[27] See Chapter 30 for fuller discussion of the workings of the IMF.

Part IV The decisions of the firm

13 Economics of the Firm

We saw in Chapter 5 that there are several different types of firm or business enterprise, ranging from the cooperative society to the multinational corporation. In this section we try to analyse in theoretical terms various aspects of the behaviour and operations of such enterprises. The first decision a firm must make is whether or not to 'enter' an industry or to invest in it. Apart from this basic decision to invest, the main decisions that a firm takes are (1) what to produce—the choice of products; (2) how to produce them—the choice of processes or choice of technique; (3) how much to produce of each kind of output; (4) how much of each input or factor of production to employ (which will obviously be determined by the choice of technique and level of output selected); (5) what price to charge (which decision will have to be taken together with (3), since the amount of output consumers are willing to buy depends on the price of the product).

In this chapter we deal with the first of these decisions, the choice of products available to the most typical firm found in Africa, the African smallholder or peasant farmer. We have deliberately centred our attention on the farmer because it allows us to see clearly how he performs the two main functions of an entrepreneur which are (a) to manage the resources available for production and (b) to cope with risk and uncertainty. The usual textbook approach is to adopt as the 'typical' firm an industrial enterprise such as a textile factory producing a single product and purchasing its inputs in various factor markets. In Africa, however, the typical firm is a small farmer supplying all or most of his own factor inputs and producing a variety of products. Because there is this variety of product mix, and different resources available to produce them, agricultural economists have for long used the techniques of linear programming as a method for advising farmers on what to produce. This has become an essential tool of farm management and agricultural extension services in African countries today, and we shall

therefore use it to explain how our entrepreneur might endeavour to allocate given resources to produce the optimum (or best) combination of crops.

This approach is called 'programming' because it indicates the best way of planning or programming activities and the use of resources; and it is called 'linear' because for simplicity it assumes only 'straight-line' functional relationships rather than curves. For example the relationship between maize output O and the labour and capital inputs used, L and K, might be given by

$$L = a.O \qquad \text{and} \qquad K = b.O$$

where a and b are constants. This implies that one unit of output requires (a) units of labour and (b) units of capital; two units of output will require 2a units of labour and 2b units of capital; and so on. Thus output increases in direct proportion to the amounts of the two inputs used. Since a and b are constants, and there are no elements such as L^2, LK^3, or $\sqrt{K}$ in the equation for the production relationship, this functional relationship is said to be linear.

The choice of products: a linear programming example

The decisions taken by the firm will depend first on the *goals and objectives* of the firm, as specified in what we may call an 'objective function'. Secondly it will depend on its *production possibilities*. In the analysis of the capitalist enterprise the most usual assumption made regarding objectives is that firms will seek to maximize their profits. We shall start with this, noting, however, that this is not the only possible assumption, and later we can examine the effect of taking other objectives into account.

The objective function

Let us assume a peasant farmer can grow maize or beans, in various proportions. In growing each of these he has some direct costs, perhaps for fertilizer or to hire labour to assist in weeding or harvesting: but after subtracting these costs he obtains a net revenue or profit per unit of 1 shilling per kilogramme of beans and 2 shillings per kilogramme of maize. We can assume that these unit net revenues remain constant irrespective of the amount of each commodity he produces, so that he could for instance, sell all of his modest output at the going market prices. Let these amounts be x_1, for the amount of beans produced, in kilogrammes, and x_2 for the amount of maize. If he attempts to maximize profits, or total net revenue, it is obvious that the objective function can be written as

$$\text{Max } Z = 1x_1 + 2x_2$$

where Z is total net revenue in shillings. The coefficients in this objective function tell us that an extra kilogramme of beans will increase net revenue by 1 shilling and an extra kilogramme of maize by 2 shillings. We can measure these quantities on a diagram as in Figure 13.1. At point $r_1(300,0)$ the farmer would produce 300 kg of beans and no maize, and would obtain a net revenue of 300 shillings, since

$$Z = 1(300) + 2(0) = 300$$

The same revenue would be obtained at $r'_1(0, 150)$ since

$$Z = 1(0) + 2(150) = 300$$

Obviously any point along the line $r_1r'_1$ would give the same revenue as r_1 and r'_1. However any combination which has more of beans *and* maize than any one of the points on $r_1r'_1$ would represent a higher level of profit. We can draw lines such as $Z = x_1 + 2x_2 = 450$, labelled $r_2r'_2$ in the diagram, and $Z = x_1 + 2x_2 = 600$, labelled $r_3r'_3$. Thus there exists a whole family of such lines, and the farmer's objective would be to reach the highest line or level of profits that he can. Each line refers to a given level of profits.

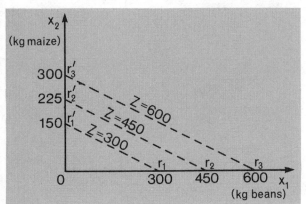

Figure 13.1 *Graphical representation of the objective function.*

Since along any one such line profits will be constant, we can refer to the lines as *iso-profit lines,* or iso-revenue lines. Profit maximization implies that the farmer will attempt to move to the highest iso-profit line possible.

Constraints on output

But in doing so he will be limited by his production possibilities. A little thought here will suggest that how much he can produce will depend on the amount of inputs he has at his disposal, land and labour for example, which we might call his resource availabilities; and secondly on the rates at which these inputs can be converted into outputs of maize and beans, which we might call the *technical relations of production* (input–output relations) or, more generally, the *production function.*

Suppose the resources available to our farmer consist of 4 acres of land and 100 hours per month of family labour. The technical relations of production are such that the production of 1 kilogramme of beans requires $\frac{1}{200}$ of an acre of land (1 acre of land yields 200 kg of beans) and $\frac{1}{5}$ of an hour of labour monthly (1 hour of labour yields 5 kg of beans), while the production of 1 kilogramms of maize requires $\frac{1}{50}$ of an acre of land and $\frac{1}{5}$ of an hour of labour. The limits or *constraints* on output are the amounts of land and labour available.

If x_1 is the number of kg of beans produced, and x_2 the number of kg of maize, then the amount of land used up will be $1/200\, x_1$ (for beans) plus $1/50\, x_2$ (for maize). This sum cannot exceed the amount of land available to the farmer. We can therefore write

$$1/200\ x_1 + 1/50\ x_2 \leqq 4$$

as the land constraint, and

$$1/5\ x_1 + 1/5\ x_2 \leqq 100$$

as the labour constraint. These constraints are represented graphically in Figure 13.2. This indicates that combinations of maize and beans to the right of the line CC′ will not be feasible, as they would require more *land* than is available. Combinations to the right of the line AA′ will not be feasible, since they would require more *labour* than is available. The only combinations which are feasible, for which both land *and* labour are sufficient, are those falling within the area OABC. This can be described, therefore, as the *feasible region* of production possibilities.

Maximization

If we put Figures 13.1 and 13.2 together, combining the objective function with the production possibilities, we have a graphical representation of the farmer's problem, which can be written as

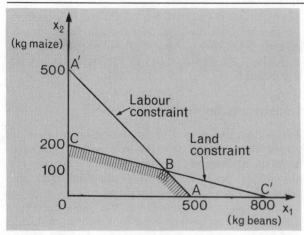

Figure 13.2 *Feasible region of production possibilities.*

$$\text{Max } Z = 1x_1 + 2x_2 \quad \text{(objective function)}$$

subject to

$$\frac{1}{200} x_1 + \frac{1}{50} x_2 \leqq \quad 4$$
$$\frac{1}{5} x_1 + \frac{1}{5} x_2 \leqq 100 \quad \text{(constraint functions)}$$

and

$$x_1, x_2 \geqq 0. \quad \text{(non-negativity requirements)}$$

The last condition tells us simply that the amounts of beans and maize produced can be positive or zero, but not negative, which obviously would make no sense. Figure 13.3 shows that the maximum net revenue which can be attained is at B, where $Z = 600$ shs. The farmer should therefore produce 400 kg of beans and 100 kg of maize. This will use up all his land and labour: 2 acres of land will be used for beans, and 2 acres for maize, while 80 hours of labour

will be used for beans, and 20 hours allocated to maize. The coefficients in the constraint functions indicate that beans are a relatively labour-intensive crop and maize a relatively land-intensive crop.

Effect of a change in the objective function

We can now see that the choice of products will depend on the coefficients in the objective function. If the price of beans goes up, increasing their net revenue per unit relative to maize, the objective function might be of the form:

$$Z = 2x_1 + x_2$$

If we plot a new family of iso-profit lines, we shall obtain a new solution, given in Figure 13.4 at A (500, 0). The farmer now finds it profitable to grow only beans, and abandons the production of maize altogether.

Opportunity-costs and marginal products

We may now explain a little more precisely why in Figure 13.3 point B should represent the 'optimum' combination of maize and beans for the farmer to produce. Why, for instance, would it not suit him to produce 110 kg of maize, instead of 100? The answer lies in the land constraint: the constraint function for land, with $x_2 = 110$, will become

$$\frac{1}{200} x_1 + \frac{110}{50} \geqq \quad 4$$

which gives $x_1 \leqq 360$

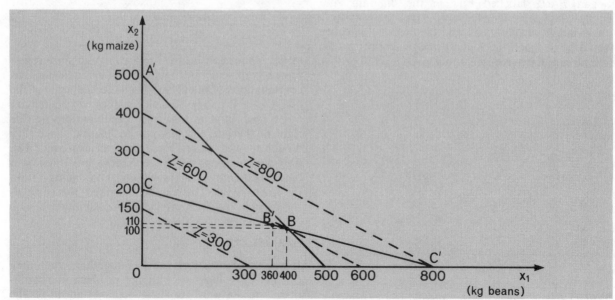

Figure 13.3 *The optimum choice of products.*

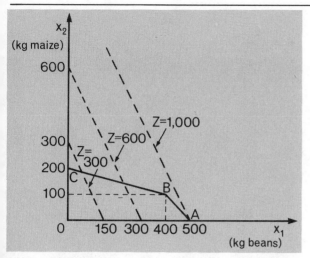

Figure 13.4 *Effect of a change in the objective function.*

that is, the amount of beans produced could not now exceed 360 kg. This is the position of B′ (360, 110) in Figure 13.3. In order to produce an extra 10 kg of maize, the farmer would need to sacrifice 40 kg of beans. The real or opportunity-cost of the extra maize is thus 40 kg of beans. But from the objective function, $Z = 1x_1 + 2x_2$, we can see that the reduced output of beans will reduce revenue by 40 shs while the increased revenue from maize will come to only 20 shs, not enough to compensate. Thus the marginal value of the extra maize is less than its opportunity-cost, so that the move from B to B′ is not worthwhile.

In Figure 13.4 with the objective function $Z = 2x_1 + x_2$, the optimum combination was at A (500, 0). In general we should expect the combination to change if the quantities of the inputs available were to change. Suppose, for instance, the amount of family labour available were to increase from 100 hours a month to 110 hours. The effect would be to shift the labour constraint outwards as shown in Figure 13.5 from AE to A′E′. The new feasible region would be the area OA′B′C, giving a new optimum at A′ (550, 0), with $Z = 1,100$ shs. The level of profits, Z, is increased by 100 shs. Since the increment in labour hours was 10 hours, the marginal product of an hour's labour was 10 shs.

If instead, keeping the original amount of labour, we explore the effect of increasing the quantity of land by a marginal amount, say 0.5 acres, this will shift the land constraint outwards from CF to C′F′, the feasible region becoming OAB″C′. The optimum combination would this time still be at A (500, 0) and $Z = 1,000$. Since the level of profits is unchanged, the marginal product of land, per unit, is zero. The reason for this is fairly clear. At A, the original optimum, the amount of land used was $500 \times 1/200 = 2.5$ acres for beans, and none for maize (not produced), a total of 2.5 acres. There was thus a residual

of 1.5 acres unused, so that adding to the amount of land available would not permit any increase in output. Land was thus *a non-limiting factor* at A, and by the same token, labour was a limiting factor.

In this example, and from the graph, it is only too obvious which is the limiting factor. But the usual problem will be much more complex with a large number of products and inputs; one of the most important tasks for the farmer or the agricultural planner will be to find *which* factors are limiting, which are the bottlenecks preventing the expansion of output. Once these are identified an attempt may be made to remove or slacken constraints. For example, the provision of a tractor hire service could remove a labour constraint in planting, a harvesting machine could eliminate a labour bottleneck in harvesting, or credit facilities might prevent a financial constraint on certain activities. Limiting factors will be indicated by positive marginal products, and the 'most limiting' by the highest of the marginal products.

The marginal product of a factor or input is the increase in the value of Z (revenue or whatever else is being maximized) when the amount of input is increased by one unit; it may be written $\Delta Z / \Delta F$, where ΔZ is the marginal increase in the value (in this case marginal revenue) and ΔF the marginal increase in the factor. Alternatively we could consider the value of Z which would be lost if the input were *decreased* by one unit: this would indicate the value of a marginal unit of the factor, usually called the *shadow price* of the factor. For small changes, the values will generally be the same whether we increase the input by one, or decrease it by one, so that the marginal product of the factor will be the same as its shadow price, both measuring the value of a marginal unit.

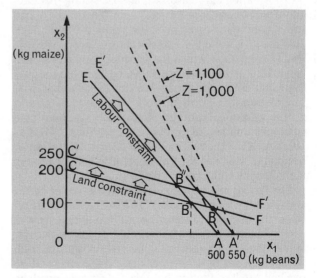

Figure 13.5 *Effect of relaxing resource constraints: labour and land.*

The reader may wish to check that at the point B in Figure 13.3 the shadow price of land is $66\frac{2}{3}$ shillings per acre, and the shadow price of labour $\frac{10}{3}$ shillings per hour.

We repeat the procedures used in Figures 13.4 and 13.5 to obtain marginal revenue products. If land is increased from 4 to 5 acres, affecting the first constraint, the optimum point is shifted from B (400, 100) where Z = 600 shs to the new point $\left(\frac{1,000}{3}, \frac{500}{3}\right)$ where $Z = \frac{2,000}{3}$. The increase in revenue is $\Delta Z = \frac{200}{3}$ per acre. Alternatively if the available labour is increased, say, from 100 to 110 hours, the optimum point is shifted to $\left(\frac{1,400}{3}, \frac{250}{3}\right)$ where $Z = \frac{1,900}{3}$. The increase in revenue is $\Delta Z = \frac{100}{3}$ for $\Delta L = 10$ hours, so that the marginal revenue product of labour is shs 10/3.

The objective, Z, need not be cash or revenue. The farmer could be a purely subsistence farmer selling nothing on the market. Z might then be taken to be the units of *satisfaction* or *utility* obtained by his family from the consumption of maize and beans.[1]

A general condition of equilibrium for choice of products

The feasible region of production possibilities in the preceding example was bounded by angled straight lines, rather than being curved. The production possibilities may, however, be given by a continuous transformation curve as in Figure 5.2. Along this line, the opportunity-cost of beans in terms of maize varies continuously, as we show again in Figure 13.6. The curve is called a transformation curve since it tells us the rate at which the producer can 'transform' beans into maize, and vice versa, by switching inputs from one use to the other. We can call the marginal rate of transformation between two products x_1 and x_2 the additional output of product x_2 obtainable when one unit less of product x_1 is produced. Thus at point A (20, 0) the marginal rate of transformation of beans into maize is 6 kg of maize (for 1 kg of beans), the adjacent point being (19, 6).

The farmer can produce any combination of beans and maize within the area OAB. Any combination *inside* the line AB, however, would imply that he was not producing as much as he could of the two crops, that is, that he was not using his resources to the full: by moving out in a north-easterly direction until he reached the 'production boundary' he could produce more of both maize and beans.

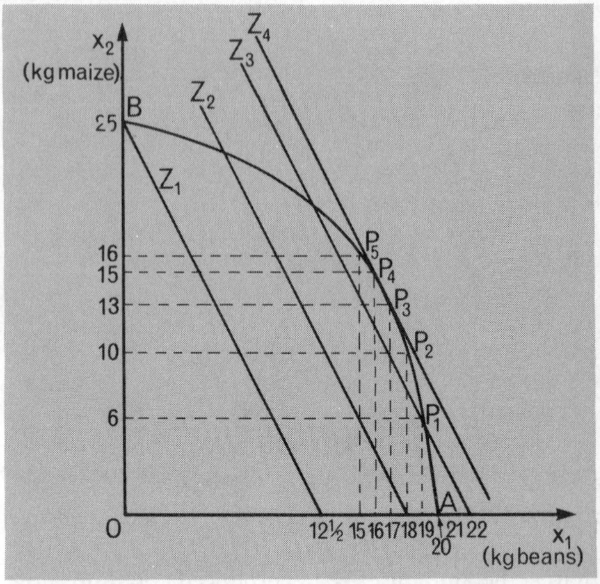

Figure 13.6 *Tangency between the transformation curve and an iso-profit line.*

The problem for the profit-maximizing farmer is the same as depicted in Figures 13.3 and 13.4. He will wish to reach the highest iso-profit line possible while remaining within the feasible region. Simply by inspection we can see that he should move out to the iso-profit line Z_4 which is tangential to the production boundary. This can be explained more precisely however.

Suppose he were producing the combination $P_1(19, 6)$ where relative prices are such that $Z = 2x_1 + x_2$. Since $Z = 2(19) + 1(6) = 44$, the iso-profit line Z_3 passing through P_1 is that for 44 shillings. But P_1 is *not* the best combination for the farmer. For by producing one less unit of beans (losing 2 shillings of profit) he can produce 4 more kg of maize (gaining 4 shillings of profit) a net gain of 2 shillings. Only between P_3 and P_4 is he not able to improve his position by moving to another point. At P_3 the marginal rate of transformation is equal to 2. Thus moving from $P_3(17, 13)$ to $P_4(16, 15)$, the farmer sacrifices one kg of beans (loss, 2 shs) but gains 2 kg of maize (gain, 2 shs), leaving himself no better off. This is true because the marginal rate of transformation is equal to the price ratio (or unit profit ratio) of 2. Thus the best position for the farmer (or any firm) is given by the condition that *the marginal rate of transformation between the products should equal the ratio of their prices*. For any two products, x_1 and x_2, this may be written

$$\text{MRT}_{x_1 x_2} = P_{x_1}/P_{x_2}$$

The marginal rate of transformation is equal to the slope of the transformation curve; and the ratio of the prices, or unit profits, is equal to the slope of the iso-profit lines. The condition is therefore that the slopes should be equal, or that the transformation curve should be *tangential* to an iso-profit line. As just observed, this will be true at the highest iso-profit line which can be reached without leaving the feasibility region OAB.

The effect of risk and uncertainty

Production is generally carried out under conditions of uncertainty. In agriculture—as well as in the construction industry for example—climate may cause fluctuations in output. In all industries prices fluctuate, so that unit profits are uncertain. Costs of production are frequently not known for certain beforehand, and may vary with output, also affecting unit profits. When new processes are introduced, especially, there may be uncertainty regarding the technological relationships between inputs and outputs. Rational producers must take uncertainty into account.

Suppose our farmer is once again in the situation depicted in Figure 13.4, with the objective function given by $Z = 2x_1 + x_2$ in shillings. Suppose however, that x_1 and x_2 are the *expected* amounts of beans and maize obtained, averages taking one year with another; but that the output of beans is subject to climatic uncertainty and the incidence of pests.

We could analyse the possible reaction of the farmer to this uncertainty in either of two ways. One supposition might be that the satisfaction which a farmer obtains from the prospect of given earnings from beans is reduced by the uncertainty attached to those earnings. We could then say that the farmer will 'discount' the unit revenue or price of beans, discounting it more the more he dislikes uncertainty. If he applies a 50 per cent discount, the objective function would become instead

$$Z = x_1 + x_2$$

In Figure 13.4, the selected crop combination would thus change from A (500, 0) to B (400,100), the farmer responding by producing relatively more of the less uncertain crop, maize. Our general condition for equilibrium would thus be that the marginal rate of transformation should equal the ratio of the *discounted* prices of the products.

This response is shown again in Figure 13.7. Suppose here that in the absence of uncertainty the farmer would select the point P_1 at the point of tangency with the profit line Z_2. If the output or price of beans were relatively uncertain he might apply a discount which would have the effect of rotating this line to the position Z_2', and similarly for the line Z_1 and the whole family of iso-profit lines. The

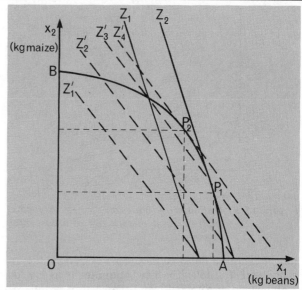

Figure 13.7 The effect of discounting for risk and uncertainty on production: choice of products.

discounted iso-profit line now passing through P_1 is no longer tangential to the transformation curve. The tangent occurs at P_2 with the line Z_4'. P_2 is the selected position, showing some substitution away from the riskier crop, beans.

An alternative possibility is that the farmer simply safeguards his position by planting a minimum amount of the safer crop, or of a reserve crop. In Eastern Africa governments have from time to time *ordered* farmers to plant a minimum acreage of a reserve crop, usually cassava, in order to minimize the risk of famine. Suppose in our example (Figure 13.4) the farmer reacts to uncertainty simply by planting a minimum acreage of maize: in other words, so long as he is assured of a minimum supply of food, he is prepared to take the risk of a poor bean crop. If this minimum is sufficient to yield 150 kg of maize, we could incorporate this requirement into our calculation by adding the requirement

$$x_2 \geqq 150$$

that is, the output of maize should be at least 150 kg. Our linear programming problem becomes

$$\text{Max } Z = 2x_1 + x_2$$

subject to
$$1/200 x_1 + 1/50 x_2 \leqq 4$$
$$1/5\ x_1 + 1/5\ x_2 \leqq 100$$
$$x_2 \geqq 150$$

and

$$x_1,\ x_2 \geqq 0.$$

This is illustrated in Figure 13.8. The feasible region is reduced to the area DEC. Points A and B are no

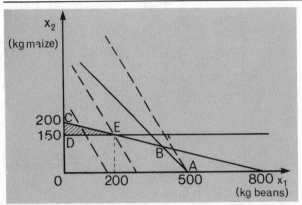

Figure 13.8   *Optimizing production strategy in face of high risk and uncertainty of a cash crop (beans).*

longer 'feasible' in that they do not satisfy the requirement $x_1 \geq 150$. The new optimum is at E (200, 150) instead of A (500, 0), and the level of profits 550 shs instead of 1000 shs; this reduction in profits measures the cost of 'playing safe' in the face of uncertainty.

In 'marginal' farming areas the main preoccupation of peasant farmers may in fact not be maximizing profits from cash crops or achieving a high level of satisfaction from a plentiful and varied food supply, but simply minimizing the risk of famine and thus keeping themselves and their families alive. Lipton has suggested that this preoccupation determines the behaviour of peasant farmers in many parts of India and elsewhere, calling these objectives a 'survival algorithm,'[2] or procedure for surviving. The farmers here take into account from past experience the various 'tricks' which nature can be expected to play and adopt strategies aimed at avoiding the most disastrous possibilities.

Non-economic factors

We have already seen that in deciding what farmers, or firms, are likely to do or 'ought' to do, we can take into account differing objectives. Even if the main objective of a farmer is economic, to maximize his profits, we can also see how his production plans could be modified to take into account other non-economic objectives or how non-economic factors could affect these plans. Suppose that of the 100 hours of labour in the preceding example 40 hours is the farmer's own labour and 60 hours is female labour: those of his wives. Moreover, according to tradition the farmer expects to concern himself only with cash crop production (beans), leaving all work on food crops (maize) to his wives. There would be an additional constraint to take account of the fact that the farmer's own labour could not be freely deployed as between beans and maize. The con-

straints would be:

(1) $\qquad 1/5\ x_2 \leq 80$

that is, the labour used up on maize production should not exceed the amount of female labour available. Secondly,

$$1/5\ x_1 < 40 + (60 - 1/5\ x_2)$$

the labour used on bean production should not exceed 40, the amount of farmer's labour, plus $(60 - 1/5\ x_2)$, the amount of female labour left over after producing the maize. If, for example, 300 kg of maize were produced, no female labour would be left over, and bean production would depend only on the farmer's labour available, that is, $1/5\ x_1 \leq 40$. This second constraint is equivalent to

(2) $\qquad 1/5\ x_1 + 1/5\ x_2 \leq 100$

If we assume this time there is no shortage of land, and if now $Z = 1x_1 + 2x_2$ (measured in units of 'satisfaction' obtained from maize or from the income derived from beans), the problem would be written

$$\text{Max } Z = 1x_1 + 2x_2$$

subject to (1) $\qquad 1/5\ x_2 \leq 60$

(2) $\qquad 1/5x_1 + 1/5\ x_2 \leq 100$

and $\qquad\qquad x_1, x_2 \geq 0.$

But for the first constraint, the feasible region would be OAB in Figure 13.9 and B would be selected, with 500 kg of maize produced, and $Z = 1,000$ units of 'satisfaction'. The additional constraint on the deployment of labour has the effect of reducing the feasible region to OACD. The combination selected is instead C (200, 300) with $Z = 800$ units of satisfaction. The tradition of the farmer's not working on the food crop thus 'costs' the

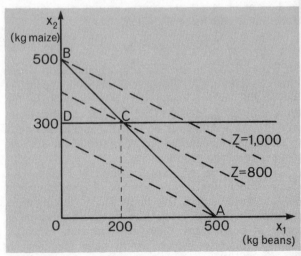

Figure 13.9   *Effect of a constraint on the deployment of labour.*

household 200 units of 'satisfaction' from the consumption or sale of maize and beans.

This is not, of course, a very realistic example. But it illustrates how we may take account of non-economic factors in our analysis, and how these could reduce the efficiency of the allocation of resources on the farm. We have also indicated how risk and uncertainty could affect a firm's decision-making. We have said that profit maximization is the most usual assumption taken in analysing firm's behaviour, on the grounds that firms are, by and large, in business in order to make profits (and also on grounds that in a highly competitive industry firms failing to make profits would go to the wall). It has however, been suggested by some economists who have observed business behaviour closely that big firms, such as the modern corporation, maximize sales (subject to a minimum level of profit) rather than profits. Why this should be, and what effect it would have, we leave to a later chapter, noting here only that different 'objective functions' may be appropriate in different situations for purposes of analysis. Presently we shall go on to consider another set of decisions the firm must take: what method of production or choice of technique to employ, and how much of each input to use.

Entrepreneurs and profit maximization

We began this chapter by listing the main decisions facing the firm, and went on to examine the production possibilities open to a small firm employing two inputs, land and labour, to produce various combinations of a two-product 'mix' of maize and beans, assuming he wished to maximize net revenue. We showed that the optimum combination of products would depend on the relative prices or net revenues of the products. A rise in the relative price of one product should lead the farmer to 'substitute' this to some determinable extent for the other. We also showed that the choice made would depend on the quantity of various resources available to him. It was possible to calculate the benefit, that is, the marginal product, to the farmer from having made available an increased quantity of a factor. Some factors might not be 'limiting' and have zero marginal products. We also examined the effect of risk and uncertainty on choice, and looked briefly at non-economic constraints which may, for instance, inhibit efforts to expand smallholders' production. In this kind of analysis, we said, it was possible to specify different objective functions, either profit maximization or, for instance, in the case of a purely subsistence farmer, levels of satisfaction obtained from consumption of his own output.

There may, however, be some inconsistency between maximizing profits and maximizing satisfaction, whether we are talking about a small farmer or a large corporation. Consider Figure 13.10, which gives total cost, TC, and total revenue, TR, as a function of the firm's output.[3] If we assume that the entrepreneur can sell any amount of output at the going market price, total revenue will increase steadily in proportion to output, that is, it will be a straight line such as TR. Why the total cost curve should have the precise shape depicted we can leave to a later chapter, noting here only that problems of managing very large outputs might be expected to lead to steeply rising costs once a 'manageable' level of output is passed: hence the total cost curve TC rises sharply after a point. Net revenue or profits is given by the difference $(TR - TC)$. The level of output for which net revenue is a maximum is given by the point where the gap between the two curves is widest, that is, by the longest of the distances such as ab or ef. These distances are plotted in the lower part of the graph, giving the line PQ which indicates the level of net revenue or profits for different outputs. Maximum profits are obviously gh, at output Oh.

It is reasonable to suppose, however, that the larger the operations of the firm, as measured by output, the harder will the entrepreneur have to work. Let us therefore measure two things along the x-axis, output and 'entrepreneurial activity', which can be taken to vary in proportion to output (output thus being an 'indicator' of entrepreneurial activity). It is clearly not obvious that the 'rational' entrepreneur should select point g on PQ, giving maximum profits, rather than, say, point c. At point c he obtains a lower net income but works less hard: this choice may therefore give him more satisfaction by

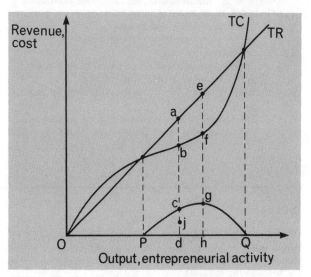

Figure 13.10 *Maximization of entrepreneurial satisfaction.*

saving him extra effort and anxiety. One would expect the businessman to find the 'trade-off' between extra income and extra relaxation which suits him best: which would take him to some point between P and g. He would, of course, never choose a point between g and Q, as this would mean both *more* work and *less* income.

An alternative explanation of the above is this. Net revenue or profits as shown in Figure 13.10 actually include an element of cost not included in the line TC: the cost of the entrepreneur's own labour. This cost will depend on how much the entrepreneur values the leisure which he will have to give up in supplying more entrepreneurial effort for the sake of increasing net revenue. Od might indicate therefore the output at which net revenue is at a maximum *after* taking into account other costs *and* the cost of entrepreneurial activity.

We can be more specific about this element of cost. The owner of a firm can either carry out the management of the enterprise himself or he can recruit a hired manager and pay him a salary, which will be counted as cost. If he does the work himself, the income he receives will include these 'earnings of management' in addition to genuine profits over and above all costs. If he is competent as a manager he will also have the choice of managing his own enterprise or becoming a hired manager himself elsewhere. And if he is not able to earn as much in his own business it would be sensible to 'transfer' himself to someone else's enterprise. What he can earn elsewhere as a manager thus constitutes his supply price or transfer earnings in his own enterprise. Out of his net income cd an amount, jd, might therefore measure this supply price or earnings of management. Unless he receives at least the amount jd he will choose point O supplying *no* entrepreneurial activity but in fact abandoning output altogether and going to work elsewhere. If he is able to earn more than this supply price, his net income dc can be divided into earnings of management dj and 'genuine' profits jc.

An independent smallholder (or small retailer or taxi-driver) also puts in his own labour and managerial effort into his business, and could equally find employment elsewhere as a farmworker. We should therefore here again take into account the cost of sacrificing leisure in determining the 'best' output and income; and in calculating his 'profit', the cost of his own labour and management.

Questions on Chapter 13

1. A farmer has 6 acres of land, 80 hours of family labour, and 600 shillings of capital, with which he plans to grow maize and/or pyrethrum. An acre of land yields $2\frac{1}{2}$ units of maize or 5 units of pyrethrum. Maize requires 2 hours of labour per unit and 20 shs of capital; pyrethrum requires 4 hours of labour and 30 shs of capital per unit. Net revenue is 4 shillings from maize and 3 shillings from pyrethrum, per unit.
   (a)   State the problem algebraically.
   (b)   Solve, using graphical methods, for the optimum combination of crops.
   (c)   What do you observe about the labour constraint?
   (d)   Which factor(s) is (are) limiting?
   (e)   What is the marginal (revenue) product of capital, land?
   (f)   The farmer, to ensure minimum food supply, is unwilling to plant less than 10 units of maize in any

circumstances. Restate the algebraic problem. Find the new feasible region and solution. What is the effect on revenue?

2. Discuss the basis for the criterion for the optimum choice of products that the marginal rate of transformation should equal the ratio of the prices.
3. Demonstrate, using a diagram, the possible inconsistency for an entrepreneur of profit maximization and satisfaction maximization.
4. Discuss the influence of non-economic factors on the production plans of small farmers or traders.
5. Why is the technique of linear programming a useful method for advising African farmers about what to produce?
6. Explain how linear programming solves the problem of finding (a) the best or 'optimum' combination of products to produce and (b) the most profitable use for the scarcest inputs.

Notes

[1] To apply the linear programming technique directly, however, we should need to assume that utility obtained varies in direct proportion to the amount of maize consumed, according to the coefficient in the objective function, and similarly for beans. This excludes 'diminishing marginal utility'. It is possible to modify the technique to take this into account.

[2] M. Lipton, 'The Theory of the Optimising Peasant', *Journal of Development Studies*, April 1968.
[3] The analysis from here on is based on T. Scitovsky, 'A Note on Profit Maximization and its Implications', *Review of Economic Studies*, Vol. XI, 1943, reproduced in *Readings in Price Theory*, Allen & Unwin, London, 1953, pp. 352–8.

14 The Choice of Technique

Having decided to produce a particular commodity, a firm must decide *how* to produce, what technique of production to employ.

Production processes

This choice exists because there are usually several ways to produce a particular product or carry out a particular economic task. Each method of producing the product may be described as a *production process*. Each process is characterized by the proportions of the different factors of production which it uses.[1] One which uses a lot of capital relative to labour, for a given quantity of output, is known as a capital-intensive process, or capital-using method; other processes may be more or less labour-intensive. For instance, lawns may be cut by large numbers of men armed with slashers or by a single man driving an expensive motor mower. Farmers may clear new land by mechanical methods, using a tractor, or by employing many labour-hours and quite simple hand-tools; and so on.

We can represent the possibilities diagrammatically. In Figure 14.1 the two 'rays' projected from the origin represent two alternative processes open to a farmer for clearing land. We can take as output the number of acres cleared. On the Y-axis we measure the capital used in production, in physical units: it should be seen as the capital *used up* in the process, that is, depreciation during the period of use. If, for

instance, the former were hiring the equipment on a competitive market, the hire charge would cover the cost of such depreciation.

Suppose, using a tractor, the farmer can clear 1 acre using up 2 man-days of labour and 4 physical units of capital. This may be represented by point a_1 on OA. It seems plausible that the farmer could therefore clear 2 acres using 4 man-days of labour and 8 physical units of capital (point a_2), and 6 acres using 12 man-days of labour and 24 units of physical capital, point a_6. Thus the ray OA represents a single process or method of clearing land. Along OB, point b_1 represents 1 acre cleared with 6 man-days of labour and 2 units of capital; b_2 represents 2 acres cleared with 12 man-days of labour and 4 units of capital, and so on. This is the more labour-intensive method. We are, of course, assuming that processes are 'divisible': what can be done in respect of 6 acres can be carried out for 2 acres at proportionately reduced cost, for example.

Since the processes are assumed to be divisible, the farmer could also clear 6 acres by using the first method on half the area (using 6 man-days and 12 units of capital) and the second method on the other half (using 18 man-days and 6 units of capital). The combined 'output' of 6 acres would then have been produced with 24 man-days of labour and 18 units of capital. By observation from the graph this combined output, represented by the point $(a_3 + b_3)$, is actually the midpoint of the line joining a_6 and b_6.[2] In the same way, however, any point on this line will represent some combination of the two processes, points nearer to a_6 including a higher 'mix' of process 1, and vice versa. For example, point $(a_5 + b_1)$ represents 6 acres cleared, 5 by process 1 and 1 by process 2. It may be observed, however, that all possible such combinations will lie along this line between OA and OB: there is no way of combining processes to obtain a point to the left of OA or to the right of OB.

Equal product curves

If, however, we have a number of alternative processes available, the range of possible combinations will be wider. Thus in Figure 14.2 six possible processes exist and any point along the bent line $a_6 f_6$ represents an alternative method of clearing 6 acres. Since the

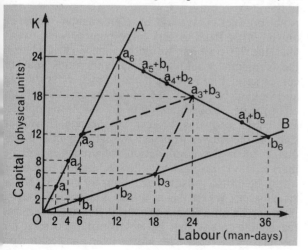

Figure 14.1 Two production processes.

output or product along this line is everywhere the same, it may be referred to as an *equal product line* or *isoquant* (iso meaning 'the same' quantity). The line a_3f_3 represents the 3-acre isoquant, and so on. Thus we shall have a whole 'family' of equal product lines like a_3f_3 and a_6f_6 in Figure 14.3. Together they form what is called an *equal product map* or *isoquant map*, as shown in Figure 14.3. Along each 'isoquant' the output is the

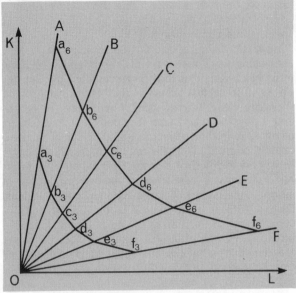

Figure 14.2 *Equal product curves.*

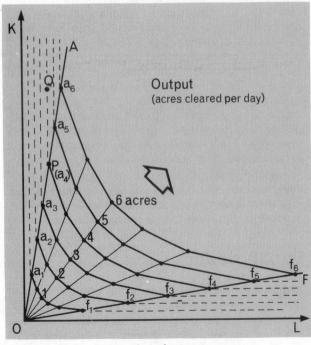

Figure 14.3 *An equal product map.*

same. Movement to a higher isoquant represents an increased level of output. Figure 14.3 assumes that combinations of labour and capital outside the range AOF are not feasible. We might, however, say that the farmer is free to purchase the factors represented by combination Q outside AOF, but that he would still manage to clear only 4 acres as at P, so that the extra capital PQ would be wasted. Nevertheless, we could extend the 4-acre isoquant a_4f_4 up from P to Q, but since points like Q would never be chosen, they do not represent an actual combination of processes. Extensions of the isoquants outside the range AOF can, therefore, be drawn as dotted lines.

The production function

The isoquant map tells us all the alternative processes and combinations of processes that are available: and for any combination of inputs it tells us the level of output. It therefore gives *the state of technology* or *technical relations* within the industry. It is thus simply a graphical expression of the *production function* for the industry. The production function is a statement of the technical relation between inputs and outputs in an industry. We might symbolize it as

$$O = f(L, K)$$

This is merely an algebraic way of saying 'output is a function of the amounts of labour and capital used'. As we have seen, the production function relates not only to the total quantity of factors used—movement outwards to higher isoquants—but also to the *proportions* in which the factors are used—movement along an isoquant.

Smooth equal product curves

If there exist only a few alternative processes, the equal product curves will have an angular shape. If, on the other hand, a very large number were available, the flat portions would become very small and the isoquants would look like continuous smooth curves as in Figure 14.4. If the farmer moves along an isoquant in Figure 14.4 he will be switching from one process (or combination of processes) to another. We could call this *process substitution*. However since, as he moves from left to right down the isoquant, successive combinations of processes will be marked by progressively lower capital-to-labour ratios, he is also substituting labour for capital, *factor substitution*. When the isoquant is a smooth curve, implying an infinite number of possible processes, it is reasonable to say that he is substituting capital for labour, or vice versa, if he 'moves' from one position on a given isoquant to another.

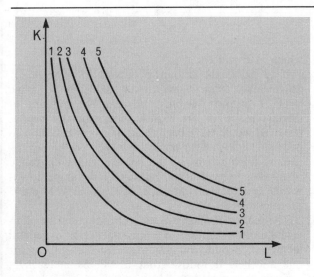

Figure 14.4 *'Smooth' equal product curves.*

The shape of equal product curves

Why do we give equal product curves the shapes above? Since the smooth isoquant is only the limiting case of the 'bent' one we should consider first the latter.

Let us first make the simple assumption that in producing any output an efficient producer will not use more inputs than he needs. Suppose two alternative processes exist for producing a particular quantity of output. If one process uses *more* of some inputs and *not less* of all other inputs, it will be clearly inferior to the other and would never be used by an efficient producer. It would represent inferior technology, and can be defined therefore as *technically inefficient*.

From this definition we can deduce a number of properties of equal product curves.

(1) *An isoquant must slope down from left to right.*

Suppose in Figure 14.5(a), a_1 on OA and b_1' on OB lay on the same isoquant. The isoquant would be upward-sloping in the range $a_1 b_1'$. But b_1' produces the same output as a_1 with more of *both* inputs. Process OB would therefore be technically inefficient and would not be used. In effect it may be omitted from the available set of processes. The same would apply if the isoquant travelled horizontally to b_1'', since the process would then use more of input L and not less of input K. If process OB is among the efficient processes available then the isoquant joining the two processes must slope down, e.g. to b_1'''. Thus if an isoquant describes technically efficient processes which are available it must slope down from left to right. It could be, of course, that no technically efficient process exists *at all* to the right of OA, in which case the isoquant would terminate at OA.

(2) *An isoquant is convex to the origin.* If a curve 'bulges out' towards the origin, it is said to be convex. If it bulges in the opposite direction it is said to be 'concave to the origin': as for instance the isoquant $a_1 b_1 c_1$ in Figure 14.5(b). This isoquant, it will be noticed, does slope down from left to right throughout its length, and therefore satisfies our first property of isoquants. However, if a_1 and c_1 yield the same output it follows from our previous discussion that this output can also be obtained by any combination of processes OA and OC given by points along the connecting line $a_1 c_1$ including, for instance, d_1 on OB. But d_1 is technically superior to b_1, and it would always be better to use some combination of the other two processes rather than process OB. This must be true so long as the isoquant is concave. If it is convex, on the other hand, such connecting lines would always lie above the isoquant, implying that any combination of other processes would yield *less good* results than the intervening process. Isoquants from efficient processes only *must* be non-concave, i.e. convex.

(3) *No two isoquants may intersect.* In Figure 14.5(c) the isoquant for 10 units of output is drawn to intersect with that for 20 units. If we look along

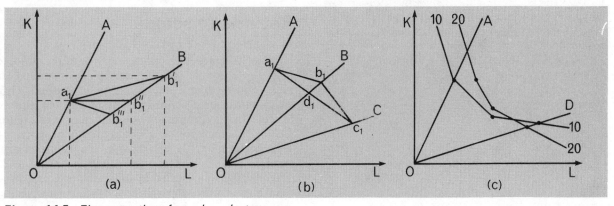

Figure 14.5 *The properties of equal product curves.*

process ray OD this is shown to be inconsistent with the definition of a process. Along OD output ought to increase steadily as more of both inputs are employed using the same method of production.

The 'Law of Diminishing Marginal Rate of Substitution'

The same properties hold true of smooth isoquants, since they can be thought of as derived from an infinitely large number of separate processes packed closely together. For instance in Figure 14.6 vectors OA, OB, OC, and OD are close to one another, and movement along the smooth isoquant PQ from a to d may be considered equivalent to substituting process OB for OA, OC for OB, and OD for OC (process substitution) or simply as substituting labour for capital (factor substitution).

Inset in the diagram is the arc abcd, magnified. This shows that in moving from a to b we substitute $\triangle L_1 (=3)$ of labour for $\triangle K_1 (=5)$ of capital. The rate of substitution of labour for capital is the amount of labour needed to offset the loss of *one* unit of capital—in this case, at point a, 3/5—in order to remain on the same isoquant. More generally we can write

$$MRS_{lk} = \frac{\triangle L}{\triangle K}$$

Since we are talking about marginal changes, we can refer to this as *the marginal rate of substitution of labour for capital*. Since we can move along the isoquant in either direction, if we substitute capital for labour in the reverse direction, we have

$$MRS_{kl} = \frac{\triangle K}{\triangle L}$$

which at b will equal 5/3.

If we reduce the amount of capital (move vertically downwards), then if we are to maintain the same level of output we must *increase* the amount of labour (move to the right): otherwise the capital removed would have been making no contribution to output. Thus *so long as the marginal product of the reduced input is positive* (i.e. we are within the range of efficient processes) the isoquant must slope downwards and to the right: our first property of equal product curves.

The second property of equal product curves, convexity, reflects another economic 'fact': that in general factors of production are imperfect substitutes for one another. It follows that it will be increasingly difficult to compensate for decreases in one factor by increases in the other. The amount required to compensate for given decreases will therefore steadily increase. Thus at point b $\frac{\triangle L}{\triangle K} = 1$, compared to 3/5 at a and 5/3 at c. This property is often put in terms of the reduced input. As we move down PQ over the same range the marginal rate of substitution of capital for labour, $\frac{\triangle K}{\triangle L}$ is successively 5/3, 1, and 3/5. This decline is referred to as the '*Law of Diminishing Marginal Rate of Substitution*'.

The more 'imperfect' the factors are as substitutes, the more rapidly will the amount of one factor need to increase in order to compensate for increases in the other, and the more convex the equal product curves will be. The reason for this convexity—for diminishing marginal rate of substitution—is, we said, the difficulty of substituting one factor for another, that is, of varying the proportion in which the factor is employed. This is nothing other than our old 'law of variable proportions', otherwise known as the 'law of diminishing returns'!

Returns to scale

In Figures 14.1 and 14.2 we assumed complete 'divisibility' of the processes: along *any one* of the process rays, if we double the amounts of both inputs we must obtain double the quantity of output. This situation can be described as one of *constant returns to scale*. In the continuous isoquant case, as in Figure 14.7(a), the same property would hold of proportionality between inputs and output along any vector (straight line) from the origin, such as OA or OB. The effect geometrically is that all the equal product curves will be parallel; and along any vector the spacing will be equal so that, for instance

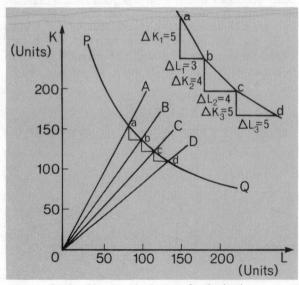

Figure 14.6   *The marginal rate of substitution.*

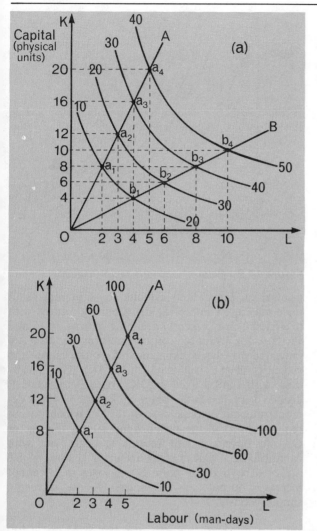

Figure 14.7 (a) Constant and (b) increasing returns to scale.

$a_1a_2 = a_2a_3 = a_3a_4$. Figure 14.7(b), by contrast, shows *increasing returns to scale:* output increases *more than in proportion* to the physical quantity of inputs. Thus at a_3 the quantity of *each* factor is doubled compared to a_1, but output is increased sixfold. Just as the relationship in Figure 14.1 was described as one of divisibility of the factors, this one reflects *indivisibility:* if the quantity of factors at a_3 is halved, the quantity of output is *not* simply reduced in proportion. The process is not equally 'efficient' on a reduced scale. Finally, if along OA, or any other vector, output increased *less* than in proportion to the quantity of inputs, we should have *decreasing returns to scale.*

Returns to scale and economies of scale

A firm may be said to enjoy 'economies of scale' if unit or average costs fall as output is increased, that is, when it operates 'on a larger scale'. It will be seen that the physical relations specified in Figure 14.7(b) would produce this result. Suppose a physical unit of capital was valued at 20 shs per unit, while labour costs 10 shs per man-day. Then costs at a_1 would be 180 shs or 18 shs per unit; and at a_2, a_3, and a_4, 9 shs, 6 shs, and 4.50 shs per unit respectively. In Figure 14.7(a) costs at a_1, a_2, a_3, and a_4 would be constant at 9 shs. *If* these processes were selected as the best way of producing the various levels of output (how processes should be selected we shall see presently), then costs would be as illustrated in Figure 14.8(a) and (b) below.

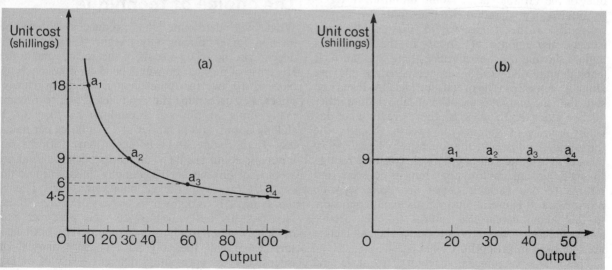

Figure 14.8 (a) Increasing returns to scale yielding decreasing costs; (b) constant returns to scale yielding constant costs.

It follows that the technical relations of production, if they exhibit increasing returns to scale, would produce economies of scale, while decreasing returns to scale would yield *dis*economies of scale and rising unit costs. However these technical relations are not the *only* possible source of economies of scale. For example, if a firm is operating on a large scale, and purchasing raw material inputs in bulk from other firms, it may be able to obtain these at a lower price. This could be for either of two reasons: either because as a big firm it is a monopolistic position as a buyer of materials;[3] or because supplying firms can obtain economies of scale as a result of bulk orders and pass on the cost savings to the purchaser by lowering price. In the latter case the economies are really *external* to the producing firm; but they do permit it to operate at lower costs at increased outputs. Any advantage derived from market power would not, however, be classified as economies of scale.

Returns to scale and diminishing returns

In the preceding discussion we have been considering the effect on output as *all inputs are increased in proportion*. We can also see what happens to output when one input is kept *fixed*, and another is varied. We shall then be considering *returns to one variable factor*, as opposed to returns to scale. This situation was examined in Chapter 3, dealing with population, when labour was the variable factor and land was fixed. This led us to *the Law of Diminishing Returns*, stating that after a certain point the marginal product of the variable factor would diminish. In terms of our isoquant diagram, we can hold, say, capital constant on the Y-axis, as in Figure 14.9, and increase the amount of labour. In the figure this implies moving out horizontally along the line K_0L (capital employed $= OK_0$), as compared to moving along a vector from the origin, such as OA. It may be seen that the marginal product of labour diminishes further along K_0L_1, that of the eleventh man-day being 4 units of output; the twelfth, 3 units; the thirteenth, 2 units; and the fourteenth, 1 unit. Since this result is quite compatible with constant returns to scale, we can confirm that returns to scale and returns to one variable factor are quite separate phenomena. It is useful, in order to avoid confusion, to talk about *diminishing* returns to one variable factor and *decreasing* returns to scale when all factors are increased in proportion.

These two phenomena, of returns to scale and returns to one variable factor, constitute the basic properties of a production function. The two are quite independent. For example, a production func-

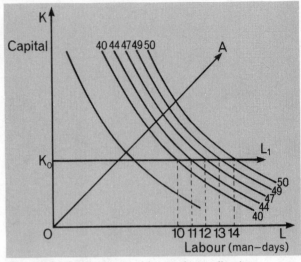

Figure 14.9 *Returns with one factor fixed.*

tion which everywhere exhibits constant returns to scale may show either rapidly declining returns with one fixed factor or gently declining returns. In Figure 14.10(a), for instance, constant returns to scale are indicated by the equidistance of points along any vector from the origin. Along the line K_0ST, however, with capital fixed at OK_0, returns to factor L decline very fast after point S. Figure 14.10(b) demonstrates an extreme case of this, in which output requires fixed factor proportions. Along the vector OA we have constant returns to scale, but with capital fixed at OK_0 returns to factor L along K_0ST are zero beyond the point S: increases in L cannot increase output at all unless K is increased simultaneously.

The choice of technique

What will determine the producer's choice of method for producing any output? Clearly it will depend on the relative costs of the various methods. His costs of production will depend on how much he buys of the two (or more) inputs, and their relative prices. Let us assume the producer is free to buy as many units of physical capital as he likes at 1 shilling a unit, and of labour at 15 shillings per man-day. If in Figure 14.11 he spent, say, 180 shs on inputs he could use $I'_1I'_2$—180 units of capital and no labour, for instance, or 12 man-days of labour and no capital. Since any of the combinations along $I'_1I'_2$ cost the same, $I'_1I'_2$ is known as an *isocost curve*. If he increases his outlay on inputs, the producer can obviously purchase a greater quantity of both factors: there will therefore be an entire 'family' of isocost curves representing different levels of outlay on inputs. The slope of the isocost curves will be the same within the 'family', but the family's slope will depend on the relative prices of capital and labour.

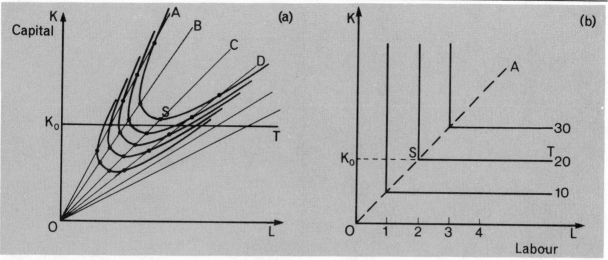

Figure 14.10 *(a) Constant returns to scale but sharply diminishing returns to a fixed factor. (b) Constant returns to scale with fixed factor proportions.*

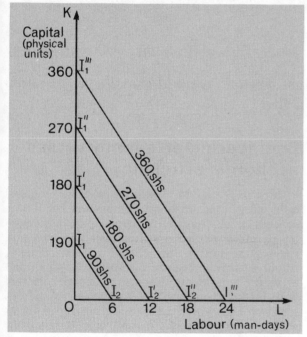

Figure 14.11 *A 'family' of isocost curves.*

In Figure 14.12(a) we impose the same family of isocost curves on an isoquant diagram which again assumes available a finite number of alternative processes, OA, OB, OC, and OD. Suppose our producer desires the output given by isoquant PQRS. What combination of the four processes should he choose in order to produce this output? Obviously he should try to reach the *lowest* isocost curve which is compatible with his remaining on PQRS. This is satisfied at point Q. He therefore selects process B, which is a relatively capital-intensive one, having a capital-to-labour ratio of 180 units of capital to 6 man-days of labour (30 to 1 in terms of these units).

Suppose the wage rate were very much lower: say $1\frac{2}{3}$ shillings per man-day (5 man-days for 3 shillings). The isocost curves would have a slope as in Figure 14.12(b), and the lowest isocost curve passing through PQRS would be that for 120 shs passing through S: process D would be selected, a relatively labour-intensive one, with the capital-to-labour ratio of 120 units of capital to 28 man-days of labour (30 to 7 in terms of these same units). We might conclude that, other things remaining the same, a fall in the relative price of labour compared to capital should induce the adoption of more labour-intensive processes. Secondly, in countries in which labour is 'cheap' and capital dear, or scarce, labour-intensive methods of production will, other things being the same, be less expensive for any output or yield more output for given expenditure on inputs.

The least-cost combination of factors

We can repeat the analysis for the continuous substitution case. The aim of the producer would again be to produce any given output at the least possible cost: geometrically, to reach the point on any particular isoquant that is on the lowest possible isocost curve. If we consider the isoquant PQRS in Figure 14.13, and the relative prices of the two factors such as to generate the family of isocost curves shown, the *lowest* isocost curve attainable—without leaving the isoquant—is obviously the one which is tangential at Q. The optimum factor proportions—those which minimize costs for this output—are equal to $\dfrac{L_1Q}{OL_1}$, equal to the slope of OA, the vector through Q.

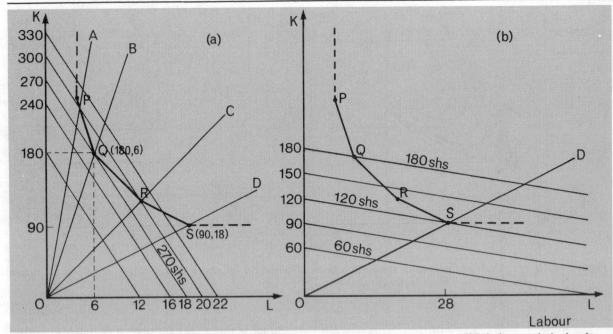

Figure 14.12 *(a) Capital relatively cheap: choice of a capital-intensive technique. (b) Labour relatively cheap: choice of a labour-intensive technique.*

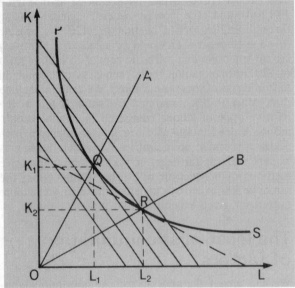

Figure 14.13 *The least-cost combination of factors.*

If relative prices of the inputs changed, so that, for example, the isocosts had the slope shown by the dotted line in the diagram, optimum factor proportions would be equal instead to $\dfrac{L_2R}{OL_2}$, given by the point of tangency this time at R.

The *condition* for the least-cost combination (for any output) is therefore that the slope of the isoquant should equal the slope of the isocost curves. The former slope, we saw earlier, is equal to the ratio of the prices of the two factors, P_k/P_l. *The condition for* the least-cost combination of the two factors is therefore:

$$MRS_{kl} = P_k/P_l$$

Engineering efficiency versus economic efficiency

Figures 14.12 and 14.13 indicate that the economically efficient or least-cost combination of factors depends entirely on relative factor prices. In developing countries, particularly those with very excessive supplies of labour, we should expect relatively labour-intensive processes to be more economic, that is, to be 'appropriate' from an economic point of view. Indeed where urban unemployment is a serious social problem governments may consider it worthwhile adopting processes that are even *more* labour-intensive than is economic in the least-cost sense.

We should distinguish between *engineering efficiency* and *economic efficiency*. The engineer, naturally enough, is concerned first and foremost with obtaining the best technical results. For instance the most efficient way of laying a road will be that which will complete the road in the shortest possible time, and which will produce the best quality of road. Engineering efficiency may thus combine two elements, efficiency in execution of an operation, and quality of the final product. In contrast a road may be built by large road-gangs—even under self-help by villagers—with minimal assistance from road machinery. The engineer may consider this operation 'messy', because of the difficulties of organization, and inefficient due to the time taken on the one hand and because of the poorer quality road which results, on the other. Despite this, particularly if the opportunity-cost of labour is very low, this method may be economically the most efficient—more so if what the country needs most is a large number of additional roads, of reasonable quality, rather than one or two high-quality stretches of 'tarmac'.

Engineering efficiency and economic efficiency have frequently been confused by planners in the less developed countries. The most obvious example is in agricultural mechanization. While tractors are economic in favourable circumstances they have often been used in Africa in preference to simpler ox-ploughs, or even the hoe, where these are much more economic. The results have often been disastrous: indeed the failure of many agricultural transformation schemes in Africa has been associated with an uneconomic agricultural mechanization component.[4] The tractor is efficient in engineering terms,[5] in that it can plough an acre in much less time than can the alternative methods: but time may be cheap!

Capital-intensive methods are attractive to planners and politicians *either* because of impressive technical results of this sort *or* because the machinery employed appears modern, and development is linked with the use of the most modern techniques. Politicians like to be able to point to impressive-looking factories as evidence of their achievement! This could, indeed, be a major reason for the frequent neglect of small-scale industry and a willingness to gamble large resources in highly capital-intensive industries.

Appropriate technology and appropriate products

A further reason for adopting capital-using technologies—a much more fundamental reason in fact—is that less developed countries are forced to rely to a considerable extent on borrowed technology from the advanced industrialized nations. The problem arises because this technology will have been developed in response to relative factor prices *which obtain in the industrially advanced countries*. Since wages there are relatively high and capital comparatively abundant (the situation depicted in Figure 14.12(a) rather than Figure 14.12(b)), such technology will tend to be labour-saving rather than labour-intensive as would be suitable for countries with cheap labour. Since machinery is mainly produced in the advanced countries for their own markets—the less developed countries generally lack capital goods or machine-making industries—more labour-intensive machinery will simply not be available for purchase. It

has been argued therefore that less developed countries should attempt to develop their own technology which would be appropriate to their own factor availabilities and factor price ratios: what is referred to as *appropriate technology*. This has been used to press the case for the less developed countries' developing their own capital goods industries, or at least machine-making industries of some sort.

We could extend the word 'appropriate' to cover *appropriate products*. As we said above, the best quality of road *may* not be the most sensible from the economic point of view. Governments in less developed countries frequently impose building standards for private dwellings *and* for public buildings which are quite *in*appropriate to the economic circumstances of the country, though more attention is now being given in most countries to devising housing programmes that will provide simple dwellings on a large scale at a cost *within* the very low price range that the ordinary low income citizen can afford.

We might mention that the 'informal sector' provides all sorts of services to the ordinary low income citizen and constitutes 'appropriate technology' in the services sector: within the category of transport services, squeezing twelve people into a taxi is a popular form of appropriate technology in Africa! The 1972 ILO Mission to Kenya recommended that government 'harassment' of the informal sector through attempts at slum clearance of ramshackle business premises or the control of hawkers should be discontinued, on grounds of the 'appropriateness' of the informal economic activities being carried on.

How much choice exists?

It should not be concluded that labour-intensive techniques are *always* appropriate in less developed countries, or appropriate in any industry. In copper-mining, for example, the *only* technically efficient methods are capital-intensive. In order to facilitate comparison with the other situations discussed, we may illustrate this in Figure 14.14. The available combinations of efficient processes lie within the narrow range AOB, very capital-intensive, and the isoquants would be of the form PQRS.[6] Even though the isocost curves indicate labour as very cheap, relatively, the optimal process, given by tangency at R, is still the highly capital-intensive one OB. Possible methods of extracting copper might exist outside the range AOB, for instance OC, but these would be technically inefficient. Thus to produce the same output of copper as at R with this method, it might be necessary to use inputs corresponding to C_2 on OC. Thus it is technically inefficient compared to R, which yields the same output with less labour *and* capital.

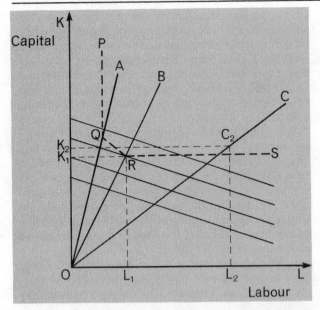

Figure 14.14　*Only capital-using processes efficient.*

The example of copper-mining is however only an extreme case. Many observers are of the opinion that the number of efficient processes available in most industries is actually quite small. Even if research into appropriate technology could bring fruits, moreover, the present choice is largely from among existing techniques. But not enough research has been done to determine the full extent of choice available, so that the evidence is as yet inconclusive. In Eastern Africa a certain amount of research has been carried out in Kenya. Howard Pack collected evidence which suggested that in some Kenyan industries the labour–capital ratio is higher than in the same industry in the advanced countries and that this reflects a response to relative factor prices.[7] He also found that although the basic technical process in a particular industry might be rigidly determined, there was room for substituting labour for capital in the other operations surrounding the basic process, such as handling of materials and packaging of products, so that in terms of the *total* operations of the firm, the labour–capital ratio could be raised. Two Kenyan economists, J. K. Maitha and Leopold Mureithi, have also found evidence of factor substitution possibilities in Kenyan manufacturing.[8] The latter has claimed that 'the so-called factor proportions problem is not a major stumbling block in Kenya'. More research is needed, however, before any firm conclusions can be drawn.

Questions on Chapter 14

1. Show how equal product curves for a firm or industry can be derived from a finite set of production 'processes'.
2. Discuss the properties of equal product curves. What is 'the law of diminishing marginal rate of substitution', and how does this relate to these properties?
3. What is the difference between 'returns to scale' and 'diminishing returns'?
4. Distinguish between 'technically efficient' and 'technically inefficient' processes; and between 'engineering efficiency' and 'economic efficiency'. Could technically inefficient processes be economically efficient?
5. Why does economic theory suggest that developing countries should be interested in 'appropriate' technology? Give examples of what might be appropriate technology in less developed countries.

Notes

[1] As we shall see presently if two different methods used the same factor proportions but produced different outputs one would be technically inefficient and would never be used.

[2] It is easy to prove this result. Draw a line from a_3 to the midpoint $(a_3 + b_3)$ parallel to OB. Movement from O to a_3 represents the clearing of 3 acres by process 1. Movement from a_3 to $(a_3 + b_3)$ represents exactly the same displacement in terms of capital and labour as a movement from O to b_3 (being opposite sides of a parallelogram), that is, it represents 3 acres cleared by process 2. The midpoint $(a_3 + b_3)$ thus represents 6 acres cleared by an equal combination of the two methods.

[3] The term 'monopsonistic' is generally used here, to refer to 'monopoly power in buying'.

[4] Very often there have also been technical and other problems in the use of tractors: poor results have not exclusively been due to bad economics and neglect of factor prices.

[5] We might have said it is 'technically efficient', but we have already used that term in another context.

[6] In mining our assumption of 'divisibility' will certainly not hold, however, because of the 'lumpiness' of the investment required in mining: the processes OA and OB would not be reproducible on a smaller scale.

[7] H. Pack, 'Employment and Productivity in Kenya Manufacturing', *Eastern African Economic Review*, Vol. 4, No. 2, December 1972.

[8] J. K. Maitha, 'Capital-Labour Substitution in Manufacturing in a Developing Economy: the Case of Kenya', *Eastern African Economic Review*, Vol. 5, No. 2, December 1973. L. P. Mureithi, *A Production Function Analysis of Different Firm Sizes in Kenya*, Institute of Development Studies, Working Paper No. 183, 1974, p. 15.

15 The Decision to Invest

Whether a firm is a manufacturing concern or an agricultural enterprise, it has a great many decisions to make: what size of plant to adopt, what method of production to use, what output to produce, what price to charge, and so on. The most crucial decision however may be the decision to invest. By *investment* we mean here the *purchase of a durable producer good*. The feature of a durable producer good is that it produces a series of marketable outputs over a period of time. If a businessman buys a machine, for instance, that machine may have a working life of 5, 10, 15, or more years before it has to be scrapped or becomes out-of-date. It may be possible for the businessman to resell the machine, of course, but in general he is taking on a business commitment of some years' duration.

There are many different kinds of decision to invest: the decision to enter an industry in the first place; the decision to expand an existing plant; the decision to replace old machinery by new; or the decision to introduce a more capital-intensive method of production. All these have in common the fact that there is in each case a net expenditure on a durable producer good which contributes to output over a period of time. We can interpret the term 'producer good' very widely: producer goods employed by a farmer, for instance, include not merely agricultural machinery and farm buildings, but also planted crops themselves. A farmer planting coffee trees will have some three to four years to wait after his initial expense before obtaining his first crop, but subsequently will get a crop almost indefinitely. A businessman who buys a shop from another will pay out a capital sum covering the value of the physical premises and stocks of goods in the shop and of 'goodwill', that is, the reputation the shop has acquired and the number of regular customers it has. Having paid out this capital sum, the new shop-owner can then look forward to returns over an extended period of time.

Business decisions

What, then, determines the decision to invest? We can throw some light on this question if we take a simple theoretical case. Suppose a businessman is contemplating buying a machine which yields an output over a period of five years only, before it has to be scrapped. We can say that

$$Q_1, Q_2, Q_3, Q_4, \text{ and } Q_5$$

together constitute the *prospective yield* of the machine, where Q_1 is the value of total proceeds from the sale of output in the first year minus any labour and raw material costs, that is, total proceeds minus all but the costs of buying the machine. Q_2 will be net proceeds from the machine in the second year after investment, Q_3 those in the third, and so on. The prospective yield is therefore the extra net revenue due to his having the machine, and is spread over the five years. The value of this prospective yield is obviously one of the main factors which will decide whether the machine is worth buying, but we can see that this is only part of it.

It is also a matter of how much the machine costs. The businessman must somehow balance the cost of the machine against the extra proceeds that it brings in. But this calculation is not as straightforward as it sounds. Suppose the machine costs \$100 and brings in \$25 each year for five years. Total proceeds over five years could be \$125, exceeding the outlay of \$100: yet it may not pay the businessman to make the investment, for the following reason. If he borrows the \$100 for the machine, he will have to pay a rate of interest on this sum; or if he uses his own money to buy the machine he has to forgo the interest on this sum which he could have earned by lending his \$100 to someone else. Clearly it is necessary for the proceeds from the machine to cover both the outlay on the machine *and* the interest in either case. If he can lend his \$100 at a rate of interest of 5 per cent per annum, for example, the \$100 will be worth \$100 $(1+.05) = \$105$ in one year's time; if this is reinvested it will be worth \$100 $(1+.05)^2$ in two years' time, \$100 $(1+.05)^3$ after three years, and \$100 $(1+.05)^5$ after five years, assuming that compound interest is paid.

This means that \$100 now is worth more than \$100 in a future period, because it can 'earn interest'. It means, conversely, that \$100 in a future period will be worth less than \$100 in the present. If \$100 can 'grow' into \$125 in a future period by accumulating interest, then $100 'now' can be said to be worth $100 $(\frac{5}{4})=\$125$ in the future period. What is $100 in the future period worth in the present? We can find this from the following equation:

$$\$100 \text{ in the present} = \$100 \left(\tfrac{5}{4}\right) \text{ in the future } (=\$125)$$

This is an equation stating the relative values of income in present and future. Dividing both sides by $(\frac{5}{4})$, we have $\$100/(\frac{5}{4})$ ($=\$80$) in the present $=\$100$ in the future.

In the earlier example, with a compound interest rate of 5 per cent, we obtained the following relationships:

$$\$100 \text{ now} = \$100(1+.05) \text{ in year } 1 = \$105.0$$
$$\$100 \text{ now} = \$100(1+.05)^2 \text{ in year } 2 = \$110.25$$
$$\$100 \text{ now} = \$100(1+.05)^3 \text{ in year } 3 = \$115.76$$
$$\$100 \text{ now} = \$100(1+.05)^4 \text{ in year } 4 = \$121.55$$
$$\$100 \text{ now} = \$100(1+.05)^5 \text{ in year } 5 = \$127.63$$

Dividing by the bracket on the right-hand side, in each case, we have

$$\$100 \text{ in year } 1 = \$100/(1+.05) \text{ now} = \$95.24 \text{ now}$$
$$\$100 \text{ in year } 2 = \$100/(1+.05)^2 \text{ now} = \$90.70 \text{ now}$$
$$\$100 \text{ in year } 3 = \$100/(1+.05)^3 \text{ now} = \$86.39 \text{ now}$$

and so on.

Thus $100 deferred one year is worth $95.24 now, deferred two years is worth $90.70 now; deferred three years, $86.39, and so on.

Looking at these equations the other way round, $95 now is worth $100 after one year because if $95 is invested now at 5 per cent interest it will 'grow' into $100 in one year; $91 now would 'grow' into $100 after two years. Had the interest rate been different, say, 'i' instead of (.05), we should have had

$$\$100 \text{ in year } 1 = \$100/(1+i) \text{ now.}$$
$$\$100 \text{ in year } 2 = \$100/(1+i)^2 \text{ now, and so on.}$$

We can say that in order to find the present value of $100 in a future year we must 'discount' it by dividing by $(1+i)$, $(1+i)^2$, $(1+i)^3$, and so on according to how many years distant the $100 is.

This enables us to see under what circumstances it would pay the businessman to buy the machine rather than lend his money (or borrow money to buy the machine). The machine yields the net amounts over and above variable costs of Q_1, Q_2, Q_3, Q_4, and Q_5 over the five years. To find the present value of these amounts we must 'discount' them at the market rate of interest as we did earlier: the present value of Q_1 is $Q_1/(1+i)$ and so on. If we call the present value of the complete 'stream' of net proceeds derived from the machine V, then

$$V = \frac{Q_1}{1+i} + \frac{Q_2}{(1+i)^2} + \frac{Q_3}{(1+i)^3} + \frac{Q_4}{(1+i)^4} + \frac{Q_5}{(1+i)^5}$$

It pays to make the investment if the value of the net proceeds exceeds the cost of the machine. If the cost of the machine is C, then it will be worth making the investment, if the market rate of interest is 'i', so long as V exceeds C.

We can put this another way, which comes to the same thing. Given C and the value of the Qs, there must be some value of 'i' which is sufficient to reduce V until it is just equal to C. In other words, *no matter how high the proceeds from the investment, there must be some rate of interest at which the investment is only marginally worthwhile*. If that value is 'r', then 'r' can be described as the rate of return on the investment. So long as 'r' exceeds 'i', it will pay to make the investment: for more can then be earned by spending the initial amount on the machine than by lending it; or if the businessman has no finance of his own, it will be possible for him to repay the amount of a loan, plus interest, and have something left over. If the market rate of interest, 'i', exactly equals the rate of return on the investment, 'r', the businessman will be able to get the same return from lending his money as from purchasing the machine and operating it.

An arithmetic illustration

It may be helpful to illustrate this arithmetically. In evaluating a project the best procedure is to write down the outlays and revenues associated with the project over the period of the project, that is, the *cash flow* for the project. To make cash and revenues comparable these must all be converted into present values to obtain the *discounted cash flow* (DCF). Table 15.1 is useful in making conversions; it indicates that the present value of any sum of money is lower the higher the rate of discount and the longer it is 'deferred', that is, the longer the recipient has to

Table 15.1   *Present value of $100 deferred one to ten years at various rates of discount*

Rate of discount Year	5	7	10	12	15
1	95.2	93.5	90.9	89.3	87.0
2	90.7	87.3	82.6	79.7	75.6
3	86.4	81.6	75.1	71.2	65.8
4	82.3	76.3	68.3	63.6	57.2
5	78.4	71.3	62.1	56.7	49.7
6	74.6	66.6	56.4	50.7	43.2
7	71.1	62.3	51.3	45.2	37.6
8	67.7	58.2	46.7	40.4	32.7
9	64.5	54.4	42.4	36.1	28.4
10	61.4	50.8	38.6	32.2	24.7

Table 15.2 *Comparison of projects with different profiles of net proceeds*

		Project A					Project B	
Year	Outlays	Proceeds	Net proceeds	Present values (i=5)	Present values (i=10)	Present values (i=7)	Net proceeds	Present values (i=10)
	(1)	(2)	(3)	(4)	(5)	(6)	(7)	(8)
0	(100)	—	(−100)	(−100)	(−100)	(−100)	(−100)	(−100)
1	40	10	−30	−28.56	−27.27	−28.05	46	−41.81
2	40	60	20	18.14	16.52	17.46	70	57.82
3	40	70	30	25.92	22.53	24.48	30	22.53
4	40	110	70	56.61	47.81	53.41	20	13.66
5	40	86	46	36.06	28.57	32.80	−30	−18.63
Total, excluding initial outlay (=V):				108.17	88.16	100.00		117.19
Net total=net present value (=V−C):				+8.17	−11.84	+0.10		+17.19

wait for it. For instance, at a 15 per cent rate of discount, $100 is worth less than a quarter, $24.7, after 10 years.

Suppose an investment of $100 in a particular project A yields a return spread over a period of five years, as in Table 15.2. Column (3) shows the net proceeds over the five years of the project as the difference between proceeds and outlays (costs). Assuming the businessman borrows his capital at a rate of 5 per cent (i=5), the present values of net proceeds in each year are given in column (4). The total, excluding the initial outlays of $100 in year 0, is shown to be $108.17: the present value of the prospective yield, V. Since this exceeds the capital cost C (=$100), the project is worthwhile at a rate of interest of 5 per cent. Alternatively, including row 0, we can find the discounted cash flow from years 0–5 as the *net present value*, V − C = $8.17. If the rate of interest were 10 per cent, however, the project would not be worthwhile, for the net present value would be negative, equal to *minus* $11.84.

Column (6) shows that at a rate of interest of 7 per cent the net present value is approximately zero, with V = C. This is the rate of interest which would make the project only marginally worthwhile; *that is, the rate of return, r, on Project A is 7 per cent.* We can put the previous statements in terms of the rate of return and the interest rate: if the rate of interest is 5 per cent, then r = 7 > i = 5, and the project is worthwhile. If the rate of interest is 10 per cent, then r = 7 < i = 10, and the project is not worthwhile.

The last two columns refer to a different project B. It may be noticed however that the undiscounted figures of net proceeds in column (7) are the same as for Project A, but occur in the reverse order through years 1–5: but while Project A was not viable at a rate of discount of 10 per cent, Project B is, having a

net present value of $17.19. The reason is obviously that the higher figures for net proceeds such as the $70 and $46 are discounted less heavily in column (8) than in column (5). Thus even if the net proceeds of a project are given, the rate of return will be higher if these occur earlier rather than later. And the longer a project takes to 'yield', the higher will the proceeds need to be if the project is to be worthwhile.

In conclusion we can say that if we are choosing between two projects of the same duration we shall select that with the highest net present value, or rate of return. And in determining the size of our investment programme we should include all projects for which the net present value is positive.[1]

The effect of riskiness

We must make one very important qualification however: the values of the Qs referred to, the net proceeds in each year from the investment, are only estimates or guesses made by the businessman, and subject to a great deal of uncertainty. They may turn out less than those estimated either because there is an unexpected fall in demand for the product, or because of increased competition by business rivals, or because new methods of production are invented which make this particular machine obsolescent, or because the businessman has made a serious miscalculation of costs, or for various other reasons. Because of this the investment may carry, in the businessman's opinion, a greater or lesser degree of risk. Obviously the greater the businessman estimates the risk to be, the more reluctant he will be to make the investment; secondly, the more cautious the businessman is in his attitude towards risk, the more reluctant he will be. Thus if the market rate of interest, i, is, say, 4 per cent, to persuade him to make the investment, it might require an expected rate of return on the investment, r, of, say, 7 per cent if he is very cautious towards uncertain propositions, or 6 or 5 per cent if he is less cautious. In other words to overcome the reluctance of the businessman to bear risks, a *risk premium* is required, the size of which will depend on what the risks are estimated to be and on the willingness to accept risky, though possibly lucrative, ventures. Suppose all businessmen were equally cautious in their attitudes to risk and made the same assessment of the risks attached to a particular investment. If they each required a 2 per cent risk premium and *expected* the rate of return to be 7 per cent, then this 7 per cent would be equivalent to a 5 per cent rate of return after allowance for the riskiness of the project. This 5 per cent rate of return can be described as the *risk-discounted rate of return on the investment*, and it is this which would be compared with the market rate of interest to decide whether or not to make the investment. To calculate this risk-discounted rate of return, however, it is better to reduce the individual Qs by an amount which reflects the businessman's uncertainty regarding them, since he may be more confident in estimating some values than others. In particular he may have a clear idea of Q_1, the profits in the first year, but be extremely hazy about the values of the later Qs due to the difficulty of foreseeing more distant events.

This analysis has been rather complicated but it has allowed us to pick out the general factors which will determine whether or not a decision to invest is taken. These factors are:

(1) the cost of investible funds, as represented by the rate of interest, i;

(2) the level of expected proceeds over the lifetime of the investment, as represented by the size of the Qs;

(3) the distribution of these proceeds over time, that is, how soon the investment brings in profits. Mathematically this is presented by the fact that the more distant in time the profit the more heavily it is discounted: Q_1 is only divided by $(1+i)$, whereas Q_4, say, is divided by $(1+i)^4$ and Q_{10} by $(1+i)^{10}$. Perhaps more important is that the amount by which Q_{10} will be reduced on account of uncertainty will be greater than the reduction in the value of Q_1.

Investment, actual depreciation, and depreciation allowances

If the present value, V, of a series of net proceeds just equals the initial amount invested, C, the project has just paid its way. The rate of return, r, has just covered the rate of interest payable on the funds invested. The business has been able to repay the principal with interest but has no net surplus available for reinvestment in a new machine. Repayment of the principal, C, has come from the income stream of net proceeds, Q_1, Q_2, and so on, over the physical life of the machine. The amounts put aside to repay the principal can therefore be regarded as provision for 'writing off' the machine as well as its loan cost. We therefore calculate the prospective yield of net proceeds *without* considering the physical depreciation of the machine, these proceeds being still 'gross' of any depreciation allowance to replace the machine with an identical one at the end of its life.

However, if the project has a positive rate of return, r, exceeding i, the present value, V, will cover the initial cost of the investment, C, plus some additional net profit, making the investment worthwhile for the businessman. Whether the business uses its own funds or borrowed funds, it must ensure that the capital invested in machines remains 'intact'. Otherwise the businessman will be 'living off capital', and this will mean that there will be insufficient funds to replace the machine when it wears out.

As businessmen do not in general wish to 'eat into' their capital they will usually put aside part of their current proceeds from the investment so that they can at the end replace the machine. The amounts put aside for this purpose are referred to as *depreciation allowances*. It should be stressed that this refers to a cash value, which ultimately provides the finance for a renewal of the investment. A common business practice is to allow a fixed sum each year for this purpose, say, in the case of a £100 investment, £20 annually for five years, if that is the life of the project. The practice is referred to as *straight-line depreciation*, because the initial cost of the machine is 'written off' by a constant amount each year. Another method of calculating depreciation is the *'declining balance' method* in which a fixed percentage of balance is written off each year.

Two points should be noted here. First of all machines do not usually 'depreciate', that is, become less efficient, at a steady rate. Over the first two or three years, when they are relatively new, there may be very little change in efficiency, after which there may be a fairly steady deterioration until eventually the machine moves fairly rapidly towards the end of its life. This may well be the pattern of deterioration for a motor car, for example. In other words, actual depreciation, or loss of efficiency, may not correspond to the depreciation allowances made for the same period. The depreciation allowance made will depend on which accounting practice is followed.

Secondly, depreciation allowances need not in fact be used ultimately for purchasing the same machine: the finance could equally be used to purchase a new model on a larger or smaller scale, or could be applied in a quite different line of industry. Depreciation allowances constitute an important and flexible part of the total supply of finance. In practice there is little real distinction between this and retained profits as a source of funds: depreciation allowances are simply the share of gross profits put aside for the replacement of equipment. But the whole of gross profits could be applied in a new venture.

The decision to invest by a subsistence producer

In Chapter 5 we outlined the process of investment choice for a subsistence producer assuming simply two periods, the 'present' and the 'future'. In this case the rate of return on present income invested was defined as

$$\frac{\text{extra future consumption obtained}}{\text{present consumption sacrificed (amount of income invested)}}$$

If this were extended to several periods, say, five, we could obtain the rate of return on the project by finding the value of i for which

$$\frac{Q_1}{(1+i)} + \frac{Q_2}{(1+i)^2} + \frac{Q_3}{(1+i)^3} + \frac{Q_4}{(1+i)^4} + \frac{Q_5}{(1+i)^5} = C$$

the amount of present consumption given up, assuming the rate of time preference is constant from one year to another. The rate of time preference performs the same role as the rate of interest did in the previous calculation. No matter how high the prospective yield of the project in the future there must be some rate of time preference on the part of the producer at which he would hesitate to sacrifice his present consumption. If this rate is the value r, r must be compared with the actual rate of time preference, i, felt by the producer. If r exceeds i then the investment will increase satisfaction and vice versa.

It is easy to see that, basically, the previous equation comes to the same thing as we derived in Chapter 5. If we consider only two periods, the present (period 0) and future (period 1), the equation reduces to

$$\frac{Q_1}{(1+r)} = C$$

from which we get

$$\Gamma = \frac{Q_1}{C} - 1 = \frac{Q_1 - C}{C}$$

Since C is the amount of present consumption given up (to acquire the 'machine'), and Q_1 the amount of income and therefore consumption obtained in the future year 1, this implies

$$r = \frac{\text{extra future consumption obtained, as before}}{\text{present consumption sacrificed}}$$

As was also explained in Chapter 5, the analysis of the decisions in a socialist economy by a central planning committee would be similar, where i now would be the 'social' or society's rate of time preference as viewed by the planning committee.

The investment function

We have seen that an individual businessman may be willing to invest in a project at one rate of interest, but not at a higher one. In the economy as a whole, also, the amount of investment may depend on the rate of interest.

If we consider all the investment opportunities available in the economy at a point in time, and rank these in order of their rates of return, r, we shall have an 'investment demand function' of the general form of MEI in Figure 15.1. This curve is generally referred to as the *marginal efficiency of investment schedule. It represents the rates of return obtaining on the set of new investment opportunities existing in an economy.*

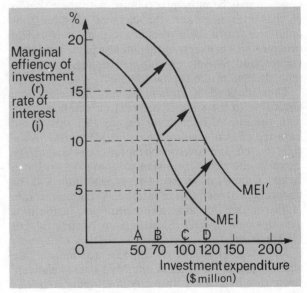

Figure 15.1 *Investment expenditure depends on its marginal efficiency and the rate of interest.*

If entrepreneurs in the economy are free to invest in any sector and are profit maximizers, they will first of all select the most profitable investments, and then the not-quite-so-profitable, moving down the curve. If the rate of interest were, say, 15 per cent in Figure 15.1, they would be willing to invest $50 millions in the next period: they would invest up to the point A where the marginal efficiency of investment (the rate of return on the next best investment opportunity available) is equal to the rate of interest. Businessmen would not invest in projects to the right of A, since for these the rate of return would be less than the rate of interest paid on capital employed. On the other hand, if the rate of interest fell, say to 5 per cent, previously sub-marginal investments would become viable, and investment expenditure would increase to OC, equal to $100 millions in the next period.

The curve MEI thus tells us the amounts that businessmen are willing to invest at various rates of interest, that is, the investment demand as a function of the rate of interest, which we might write as

$$I = I(i)$$

It has been questioned, however, whether businessmen's investment plans are very sensitive to the rate of interest. In the first place investible funds are not allocated automatically to all those willing to pay the 'market' rate of interest, but are 'rationed out' among customers according to their degree of 'credit-worthiness'. Large firms may have access to adequate capital, including their own retained profits, at relatively low rates of interest. Secondly, businessmen may be more preoccupied with the riskiness of the investment and the chances of success or failure: so that if the project is successful it will yield proceeds well in excess of the interest paid; and if it is unsuccessful the interest due will be less important than the loss of the capital invested.

Thus the level of investment may fluctuate more according to the state of business expectations than with the rate of interest. In Figure 15.1 this would have the effect of shifting the entire MEI curve to the right or left. Improved expectations would shift the curve to the right, for instance to MEI'—so that a larger volume of investment expenditure will be undertaken at each rate of interest. At an interest rate of 10 per cent, for example, expenditure in the next period would be OD ($120 millions) instead of OB ($70 millions).

The effect of a lack of response to interest rate changes would be to make the MEI curve relatively steep, that is, inelastic. In many developing countries the number of obviously profitable investment opportunities available at any one time may be quite limited, and in this case certainly interest-elasticity of demand for investment would be low.

Social cost-benefit analysis

Under a capitalist system, when a private businessman contemplates an investment, he will, if he is attempting to maximize profits, only be interested in comparing *his own* costs and *his own* revenues. Whatever he pays out in taxation, for example, is a cost. Suppose there was a heavy import duty on machinery: he might prefer to adopt a labour-intensive method of production as a means of avoiding the tax; or he might decide the tax raises his costs to the point where it is not worth his while investing at all. Alternatively, suppose there were considerable excess supplies of labour in the country, so that the opportunity-cost of labour, some of which is completely unemployed, is very low; but that at the same time minimum wage legislation imposed a relatively high wage at which labour could be hired. The businessman would not concern himself with the real costs or opportunity-costs of labour, but with his own wage-bill, with what he personally will have to pay for labour.

When the *government* contemplates an investment project, it cannot simply calculate how much profit it will make: if it were investing in an industry in which it had a monopoly, for example, it could probably make even a poor project pay, by raising product prices. What it must do instead is to calculate what the net benefit to *society* would be: balancing income created for society against costs to society. If taxes are levied on the product of a state-run enterprise, this should not be considered as a cost, since it represents only a transfer of income *to society* out of the surplus yielded by the project. If wage costs of the project are inflated by the government's own minimum wage legislation, this really only reflects its own decision to pay 'transfer income' to the employees concerned, and might even reduce the amount it would otherwise have paid out in unemployment benefit. Obviously the government should only calculate *real* costs of labour. It is fairly clear, therefore, that public or social cost-benefit calculations may not be made on the same basis as private cost-benefit calculations, which are calculations of private profit: what is cost and what is benefit is likely to differ in the two cases.

There is a second reason for the difference, however. Within the area of public investment there is a special category of what are known as 'public goods'.[2] These are goods which in 'any' economy have to be, by their nature, at least partially provided by the state, and financed on a collective basis out of taxation. These are 'goods' such as defence, public health facilities, education, roads, bridges, or airports. The common feature of projects in these areas is that they are not sold 'on the market', and that benefits are difficult to measure, and to value. The calculation of costs and benefits to society arising out of a project, private or public, which the government is considering supporting in some way can be an extremely complicated one, theoretically and practically. The subject is referred to as *cost-benefit analysis*.

Valuation of benefits and costs to society at large

In calculating these costs and benefits, there are first of all two problems of valuation. These are related to (a) the imposition of indirect taxes and subsidies, which respectively raise or lower market prices above or below factor costs, and (b) the tendency for both imports and exports to be undervalued as a result of 'overvalued' exchange rates and related controls on foreign trade.

Indirect taxation

In order to find the real benefits and costs arising out of an investment project we must calculate the value of outputs and inputs net of indirect taxes, whether customs duties or excise and similar taxes on purchases of local output, and net of subsidies which reduce the market price below the factor cost of producing a commodity. In African economies direct subsidies are not usual except for price stabilization schemes which may involve payments to farmers in unfavourable periods (but more often are taxes in favourable periods). There may be indirect subsidies, however, as for instance transport charges on certain routes, if a manufacturer is not charged the full real cost of the transport facilities enjoyed by his product. For project appraisal purposes, market prices charged to transport users should be adjusted to reflect actual transport costs, again net of indirect taxes.

The most important form of indirect subsidy, however, is through the imposition of protective quotas or import duties. These permit the manufacturer to raise his price, and his profits, above the level he could expect in the absence of protection from imports. By granting a manufacturer protection, assuming the manufacturer does not become any less efficient, the government is directly increasing the manufacturer's profits. Clearly the inflated prices are not directly related to the real value of the goods or to the costs of producing them. These subsidies can be substantial, and widespread: indeed in some developing countries a major part of the manufacturing sector, which would otherwise not be economic, is subsidized by tariff protection. Moreover manufacturers contemplating the setting up of a new industry are particularly likely to request the government to grant protection to them as 'infant industries':[3] in considering how much protective subsidy to give, and for how long, the government should obviously evaluate the costs and benefits to be obtained from the project, in the same way as if it were itself making the investment.

One way which has been suggested to obtain the real value to the economy of the goods produced is to calculate what it would cost to import the good. Since the goods would presumably be imported from the cheapest alternative source in the world, this is in effect the 'world price' of the good. Specifically we should take the 'border' price: the value c.i.f. (i.e., cost, insurance, and freight to the port) of imports at the point of entry before, of course, any import duty is paid. For if the good is produced domestically instead of being imported, this will be the value saved. Exported goods can also be valued 'at world prices', by valuing them f.o.b. (free on board ship or rail at the border): this is the amount of foreign exchange they earn (consumers in the importing countries will have to pay more than this f.o.b. price, since their payment will also have to cover insurance and freight charges to the country concerned—but that is another matter) and which the country can then 'spend' on goods available in the world market. The value of the exported goods is clearly measured by what they can 'buy' in this market.

The foreign exchange element

We discuss the importance of foreign exchange more fully in a later chapter. However it will already be clear that a country's exports earn foreign currency which can then be spent on imported goods. Thus it would not be possible for a country's importers to go on for very long buying foreign goods in excess of what its exporters were earning abroad, without causing a critical shortage of foreign exchange.

If the foreign exchange rate is left free to fluctuate, the market rate will reflect supply and demand for the home currency as against foreign. More usually the government fixes an 'official' rate of exchange however: and this may not measure at all closely the scarcity of foreign exchange at any moment of time. In this situation foreign exchange is usually 'rationed out' through a system of exchange control; or an illegal free market exchange rate may develop which more accurately measures this scarcity.

Why do we need to know all this? Because the selection or encouragement of a particular project can affect the foreign exchange position in various ways, and it may be necessary to choose between two projects with quite different effects. When a new manufacturing project is established, the machinery required will often have to be imported, though not always. On the other hand, part of the resultant output may be exported and earn foreign exchange. The most frequent pattern would be for a project to impose foreign exchange costs (a net increase in demand for foreign exchange) in the first years of its life, and foreign exchange benefits (if any) in later periods: but this will vary.

If the foreign exchange rate accurately measures

the relative value (purchasing power) of the currency, then all inputs and outputs can be measured on a common basis using this rate. If not, it becomes necessary to use a 'shadow price' of foreign exchange which, it is estimated, roughly corresponds to its real value to the economy, that is, its opportunity-cost. Some planners have used the illegal free market premium enjoyed by foreign currencies as a measure of overvaluation. A better alternative, involving some research, would be to compare the domestic prices (net of indirect taxes) of a wide selection of goods with the border prices of the corresponding imported commodities, and then calculate the 'average' difference in prices. At this stage we can skip over the difficulties in this exercise, and note merely that all inputs and outputs of alternative projects need to be converted in terms of the same currency. If the procedure mentioned previously is being used, of measuring the value of goods in terms of border prices (the cost of the imported good), it turns out to be convenient to convert all values in foreign currency terms.

Calculation of costs: the shadow price of labour

As we indicated above, when we come to calculate costs, 'social' prices, reflecting real opportunity-costs to the national economy, will replace the market prices of inputs which are used in private investment decisions.

The essential nature of shadow-pricing is seen most clearly in the case of unskilled labour. The typical market situation in developing countries is one of actual unemployment or at least underemployment in rural and urban areas, and of urban wage rates set well above the equilibrium level by minimum wage legislation, trade union pressure, or other factors. The real cost to the economy of any labour employed in a new project is what that labour would have produced in the absence of the project. If the labour would have been unemployed, the opportunity-cost would be zero; if underemployed, or employed in low-productivity activities, such as shoe-shining or petty trading, some low but positive value. The money cost of labour to the employer in the new project could be much higher, since he would need to pay at least any official minimum wage.

A major difficulty arises, however, in calculating the opportunity-cost of labour, because it has generally proved very difficult to establish what the true extent of underemployment in a country *is* or even if it exists at all in many cases. There is no figure one can take, therefore, to represent unambiguously the shadow price.

There is another complication also. Even if the transferred labour was not contributing to agricultural output, so that no production is lost, there may be an effect on *consumption* as a result of the project. The labour might previously have been sharing out the work on the family farm (so that all are less than fully employed) and also sharing the consumption of the product as a family. When some labour is taken away for work on the project, the remaining household is able to maintain its output, using its labour more fully, but will of course take the opportunity to consume whatever it produces, as before. Since the project labour will also spend its money wage on consumption, there will be a net increase in consumption in the economy as a whole. Since the supply of savings may be a constraint on the growth of output in the economy, this extra consumption, reducing, as it must, the amount of savings available, will have a cost in terms of investment and the larger future income forgone. Some economists have argued that the shadow wage or social cost of labour on the project should be taken as equal to this extra consumption plus any net loss of output in alternative employment such as agriculture. Again estimation is difficult.

The shadow price of land and natural resources

The social cost of idle, uncultivated land is zero. However, if these fixed resources are in short supply and have alternative uses, outputs forgone must be costed. This will be true particularly of agricultural schemes—where the opportunity-cost might be very substantial—since the setting up of a factory uses comparatively little land. In some cases some other natural resource may be used up as an input, such as forests or water resources, involving society in additional costs of replacement or alternative income forgone, in which case these also should be charged to the project.

The shadow price of capital and choice of discount rate

In our calculations of the businessman's return on an investment, we used the market rate of interest, i, to find V, the present value of proceeds obtained from the project in future periods. This rate i measures the cost of capital resources in the economy since, as the 'going' rate in the market, it will represent a rate which other viable projects, and borrowers, can afford to pay.

This description of a competitive market for capital, however, is more appropriate to a developed than a less developed country. In the latter a well-organized market for investment funds and the associated financial institutions will generally be lacking. Small local businesses may, for instance, have much poorer access to finance than large expatriate firms which can obtain capital cheaply via parent companies abroad.

Secondly, the interest rates actually paid by many enterprises may not reflect the real scarcity of capital in the economy. Farmers participating in special schemes may benefit from cheap credit arrangements as may local small businessmen. Industrial Development Banks may offer longer-term loans even to large concerns in order to stimulate and encourage investment in a particular sector. Even in the case of commercial banks, the lending rate to larger 'creditworthy' customers rarely exceeds 10 per cent per annum in Eastern Africa, while small-scale enterprises, and farmers find it difficult to obtain credit on any terms, for lack of what is considered adequate security. How low actual money rates of interest may be is shown in Table 15.3, which gives some of the going lending rates of interest in Tanzania at the end of 1969 and in mid-1973. Not only are most of the rates much lower than in developed countries but they are also very stable—unchanged over four years or more.

Table 15.3 *Interest rates in Tanzania, 31 December 1969 and 30 June 1973*

	December 1969 %	June 1973 %
Bank of Tanzania		
Re-discount and advances		
Commercial bills		
Crop: 90 days	5.00	5.00
91–180 days	5.50	5.50
Other*: 90 days	5.25–6.00	5.25–6.00
91–180 days	5.75–6.50	5.75–6.50
Commercial banks		
Savings deposits	3.50	4.00
Lending rate	6.50–10.00	5.00–10.00
Permanent Housing Finance		
Company lending rate	8.50–9.50	8.50–9.50
Rural Development Bank		
Short-term lending rate	8.50	8.50
Long-term lending rate	7.50	7.50
Post Office Savings Bank Deposits	2.50	3.00

SOURCE: Bank of Tanzania, *Economic and Operations Report*, June 1973

* Rate depends on the purpose for which the bill was drawn

Outside the favoured sectors, and enterprises, *effective* rates of interest may be extremely high. For example, a trader may arrange to buy a small farmer's crop a few months in advance, at a relatively low price, meanwhile offering him equipment or con-

sumption goods 'on credit'. By accepting a lower price for his crop, the farmer is in effect paying interest on his loan. If the period of the advances is three months, say, we need to multiply the percentage 'interest' paid over the three months by four to get the equivalent annual rate of interest. This type of 'hidden' interest rate can range as high as 100 per cent! The interest rates that people are willing to pay in such situations reflect (apart from ignorance in many cases) very high rates of time preference held by the borrowers. Given this, it is frequently held that effective interest rates of as high as 25 per cent should be used to measure the price of capital in evaluating projects.

Certainly, there is a case for using a rate of, say, 15 per cent. The effect of *not* doing so would be (1) to give insufficient weight to projects which yield output *quickly*; (2) to favour the use of more capital-intensive techniques than is strictly justified; and (3) to lead planners to accept more projects than can meet the criterion of positive net present value when discounted at the rate of interest which measures the true cost of capital and the society's rate of time preference, so that the society might be forced to save (invest) more than it really wished.

It is important, therefore, to select an appropriate *social* rate of discount, or interest, to substitute as i in our formula, previously referring to the actual market rate of interest facing the private firm. A high social rate of discount will weed out projects which show a rate of return, r, below this discount rate, i. The function of the social discount rate is therefore to act as a rationing device, allocating funds to the most socially profitable projects; and also to indicate how far to go in investing at the expense of consumption. It will thus affect both the *composition* of the investment programme (the ranking of projects) and the *size* of the investment programme. An increase in the social rate of discount, due for instance to a greater shortage of funds, would lead planners (1) to reduce the scale of the investment programme (some projects for which previously r exceeded i would become sub-marginal); (2) to favour even more strongly than before short-life projects with a low ratio of early (overhead) costs and a relatively short 'gestation period' (the time lag before they yield benefits); (3) to favour those projects which economize on capital, that is, projects within relatively labour-intensive industries and, within any one industry, techniques which are more labour-intensive.

From what we have said elsewhere, however, in a planned socialist economy (and to some extent in any developing economy with substantial public investment) the planners may wish to apply a social rate of discount which reflects less the rate of time preference of individuals in the community than their own judgement as to what sacrifice should be made by this present generation for the sake of economic growth yielding benefits particularly to future generations.

Calculation of benefits: the social welfare function

A private entrepreneur can reasonably be assumed to be interested only in investment projects which yield profit (a positive rate of return) and to select that project which yields the *highest* rate of return—though circumstances may certainly exist where this is not pursued completely. We have already indicated that planners will not wish to maximize only profits from a given investment, necessarily, but all social benefits.

This leads to the question of what *is* the social benefit, how is it to be judged, and who is to judge it. We have already noted that benefit may accrue to the present generation or to a future generation. The choice of project may also affect the distribution of income in the country; for example the encouragement of a capital-intensive project (or technique) will do less to give employment and incomes to the low paid, and may benefit more the suppliers of risk capital; whereas the adoption of a labour-intensive investment programme as a whole might boost the wages of skilled and unskilled workers.

Planners may also be concerned with regional income distribution, and may thus wish to weight more heavily benefits from projects which could be located in needy regions: in effect accepting a lower rate of return in these regions than for projects elsewhere.

Since the unemployed, or poor, may resort to crime, or create other social problems, as well as prove an embarrassment to politicians, planners may wish to give some weight to employment as an objective of investment, *independently of the output objectives*. In developed countries such as Britain, the employment objective and the regional objective may be combined, since unemployment has tended to occur particularly in certain stagnating regions. Reduction of regional unemployment has been the objective of special financial and other incentives (such as a wage subsidy to stimulate regional employment in Britain) offered to entrepreneurs setting up business in these regions. Governments neglecting the overall level or regional distribution of unemployment would certainly risk unpopularity.

A separate objective may be *self-reliance*. This would tend to direct investment away from capital-intensive sectors or techniques where this would involve increased dependence on private foreign investors or foreign aid. This might lead, for instance, to the favouring of labour-using agricultural projects over more capital-intensive investment in manufacturing, or to self-help projects in agriculture, road-building, or other community development. Self-reliance has been an important objective in Tanzania since the Arusha Declaration of 1967. It was a major factor in the decision to emphasize rural development and, within a rural development strategy, the policy of 'ujamaa', as opposed to mechanized agricultural transformation schemes.

Thus in selecting projects several social objectives may be pursued—maximum output, maximum growth rate, income distribution, employment, regional impact, self-reliance. Since these goals may conflict, they must somehow be given weights. This implies some kind of 'social welfare function' which tell us how to combine these separate aspects.

Economic planners can try to estimate the size of these various effects. They cannot, as professional economists, say which should be emphasized and which neglected: for that is a matter of individual opinion and conscience. Planners are responsible to politicians, who will make the choice and decide what the 'social welfare function' ought to be. In an authoritarian regime, the ruling group will make the choice; in a democratic society the politicians will, in order to remain in power, seek to determine the 'mood of the people'.[4]

The external effects of a project

Not all the benefits and costs flowing from a project accrue to it. While a private investor will only be concerned with his own costs and returns, in public and assisted projects the government will need to concern itself with *all* the effects of the project on the economy.

Two kinds of external effects arising out of a project may be distinguished: external economies (and diseconomies) of scale; and multiplier effects.

External economies and diseconomies

External economies and diseconomies arise when an investment, by increasing capacity and the scale of production, reduces the price of an industry's product or raises the prices of factors used by it, respectively. The investment may benefit other enterprises by increasing the availability of an input used by other firms or by reducing its price; or by providing an additional market for the main product, or by-products, of other firms. Alternatively, if lower prices benefit final consumers, increasing their consumers' surplus, this should be measured as a tangible benefit.

In developing countries where the number and scale of established manufacturing and other activities is limited, the setting up of a new enterprise may lead very directly to 'linked' industries which were not viable before or were working below full capacity. When an industry provides a raw material or intermediate good which can be used as the basis of a further industry—fruit growing leading to the establishment of a canning factory, for example— this is known as a *forward linkage*. And when a new industry creates a demand for an intermediate good— an example would be a cigarette factory creating a demand for tobacco—this is referred to as a *backward linkage*. These are both examples of external economies.

External economies of scale may also be of a much more indirect, less tangible kind, as when additional investment contributes towards increasing the pool of skilled labour or business ability, spreads the costs of infrastructural projects such as roads or dams, or even contributes to an optimistic 'investment climate'. Equally, an investment project may have external *dis*economies by bidding up the price of skilled labour, or using up part of a limited supply of some natural resources such as fresh water, or contributing to urban congestion.

Multiplier effects

Multiplier effects are frequently attributed to investment projects. For instance, when a dam is constructed, employing a large number of workers, the expenditure on the dam is an addition to national income (except to the extent that part of the expenditure is on imported inputs). But the incomes earned by the construction workers and others contributing to the production of the dam will be re-spent in large part on food and other consumption goods, generating another 'round' of income and output in food and other production, and so on. The operation of this expenditure 'multiplier' is discussed in a later chapter: the question to be raised here is how far these secondary effects of an investment project should be added to the benefit side of our cost-benefit sum.

For reasons explained later, this process is likely to be limited in Africa and other developing countries, and may be greatest in small-scale, labour-intensive rural development projects where additional income generated is likely to be paid to low-income workers more inclined to re-spend on local products.

The difficulty with including external economies and multiplier effects in a cost-benefit calculation is that they are hard to estimate, particularly in the case of very indirect externalities. Fortunately, if the problem is simply to choose between two alternative projects, the two projects may be judged to have substantially equivalent external economies and multiplier effects: in this case their omission from the calculation would not affect the choice. External economies and linkages may be more important in relation to determining the scale of investment— particularly the scale of the industrialization effort— and the strategy adopted for industrialization. Within the guidelines of any adopted strategy, however, it may be possible to choose among projects without this complication.

The problem of measuring benefits

As mentioned previously, social cost-benefit analysis is increasingly being applied to the appraisal of public good projects, such as roads, education, agricultural extension schemes, and medical facilities. There are particularly great difficulties of measurement here because, quite apart from linkages or multiplier effects, the 'output' resulting from such investments is not always or is only partly something which is sold on the market and can be valued at market prices. For instance the 'output' of a new bridge across a river may simply be reduced congestion on an existing bridge, and thus a saving of time by those regularly using the route. How is this time to be valued? Clearly there are major difficulties here, but, by making some fairly brave assumptions, a cost-benefit approach has frequently brought useful results in dealing even with apparently intractable problems.

The problem of risk and uncertainty

Just as a business investment is fraught with uncertainty, there may be uncertainty regarding the costs and benefits of a public sector project, particularly, as we have seen, in the case of public goods. Such uncertainty will make a project less attractive and it will be wise to 'discount' for risk in this case also. The appropriate treatment of risk and uncertainty may differ in the case of public projects, however, in two ways.

Businessmen generally have much more limited financial resources behind them, and the consequences of failure of the investment may be very serious, even leading to bankruptcy: a businessman may therefore take a very cautious approach and prefer a safe, if not very lucrative investment to an exciting and potentially much more profitable project which does, however, carry a slight risk of a disastrous result. A state enterprise might be in a much better position to carry this risk and thus to discard the 'safety-first' approach.

Secondly, the government may have experience

with a large number of similar projects in different parts of the country or over a period of years. Thus it may be able to apply the 'law of large numbers': while it may not be able to forecast with accuracy which *particular* projects will work out, it may be able to tell with *certainty* that 7 out of 10 projects, say, will succeed. The failed projects can then simply be counted as 'costs', borne by the successful proportion of projects, which can be calculated fairly closely.

Conclusion

Social cost-benefit analysis is required first because the market prices of products and factors may not reflect their real value or cost to society. Prices may be inflated by indirect taxes. The official exchange rate may not reflect the true purchasing power of domestic and foreign currencies. Wages may not reflect the true opportunity-cost of labour, or money rates of interest the true scarcity of capital. Thus shadow prices of labour, capital, and foreign exchange, rather than market prices, may be used. Secondly there may be benefits and costs external to the project which should be taken into account and 'internalized' in the case of public investment choices. Thirdly, the objectives in public investment may be much broader, and conflicting objectives may need to be given appropriate weights. However there are great difficulties in finding what the true shadow prices are and in estimating various costs and benefits: even in the state-run development corporations of East Africa the principles expounded above are a long way from being put into practice or systematically followed.

However, this does not mean that social cost-benefit analysis is not used in evaluating investment projects in Eastern Africa. The various international aid agencies insist on quite thorough project appraisals before they will finance investments involving both marketable output like electricity generation or smallholder tea growing or the provision of 'public goods' like roads or education. The Eastern African governments also maintain staffs of project evaluation specialists who examine not only public investment projects but also many of the large private sector projects, since they too involve wider social costs and benefits affecting the national economy which are not borne or obtained entirely by the project itself.

Some examples of project appraisal in Eastern Africa

The various uses of cost-benefit analysis may be illustrated briefly in four different areas of application.

Electricity generation and distribution

Before advancing finance for a hydro-electric scheme to a state-owned electricity undertaking in Malawi, a major international aid donor insisted on (1) *commercial* viability of project, i.e. a satisfactory private rate of return ensured by appropriate electricity prices being charged to consumers, (2) adequate safeguards that the national economy and its external balance of payments would, on balance, improve as the result of the project, i.e. a comprehensive social cost-benefit appraisal, and (3) that at least some non-economic effects would be allowed for, notably by the construction of dams to control the discharge of water used by fishermen and farmers also, and the use of non-inflammable structures to reduce fire hazards to distribution systems.

Smallholder tea growing in Kenya

Smallholder tea schemes have developed rapidly, in Kenya especially. Each major extension is subject to investment appraisal involving both social and private (commercial) criteria. One thorough appraisal applied the methods developed by the Oxford Professors I. M. D. Little and J. A. Mirrlees, valuing all inputs and outputs in terms of foreign exchange, and pricing farm labour in terms of the opportunity-cost in other activities and the social value of its additional consumption and employment in tea growing.[5] Both the private and social evaluations indicated that this particular project (involving the planting of 35,000 acres in four years) should be highly profitable, i.e. there were considerable net benefits to both the growers and the nation—the latter's benefit being measured not only by the overall increases in income, exports, and employment but also by the discounted value of the future stream of income available to society for reinvestment.[6]

Investment in road improvements

Figure 16.1, concerned with road transport costs, illustrates another aspect of cost-benefit analysis of projects involving non-marketed public goods. The costs per ton mile were *economic* costs of operating various-sized lorries on bitumen roads, i.e. these costs represented real opportunity-costs of resources to the nation, not the private costs actually incurred by the road users. They excluded indirect taxes on vehicles, fuel, tyres, and licences, etc., and, in principle, would have 'corrected' the market price of these and other inputs for price distortions arising from an overvalued exchange rate or wage rates fixed above the free market equilibrium by legislation or other institutional factors. In practice the project planners in Malawi would not make these adjustments for a road project since they consider the exchange rate to be around a free market level (in an open economy with liberal trade and payments arrangements) while lorry drivers and other road transport workers are scarce skilled workers paid market rates which correspond with their real supply price. Road projects are usually evaluated by the criteria of the reduction in users' economic costs arising from the improvement—a better road surface, realignment, extra traffic lanes, and so on. In Figure 16.1 the costs of using lorries on bitumen roads are shown; had the same vehicles and mileages per annum been shown for gravel roads they would have been considerably higher. Thus a road project is evaluated in Eastern Africa mainly by the reduction of, say, X cents per ton mile in economic costs of road users, multiplied by the annual volume of traffic and miles of improved road. Against this annual benefit, discounted to a present value over an estimated 'life' for the road, say 20 years, there are compared initial and recurrent costs, also discounted.

Investment in education

Educational planners and manpower specialists can justify public expenditure on different types of post-primary education, including adult-literacy and rural extension programmes, in terms of the net benefits obtained by society. If we restrict the coverage of social benefits to the present value of the additional income earned by recipients of this education over their working lives, and social costs to the present value of the additional expenditure on education (plus the loss of earnings by students who might have contributed more output instead of being educated), a fairly straightforward cost-benefit appraisal can be attempted. In other cases where the government has decided the planning objective, such as doubling the number of 'A' levels in Science subjects, or eradicating malaria from particular areas, the project evaluation may take the form of a *cost-effectiveness study*. Which of the alternative means available will produce the planned objective most economically? By valuing costs and benefits along the lines discussed above, the real cost of the project in terms of alternatives forgone can be presented to the government.

Questions on Chapter 15

1. Define precisely: investment; prospective yield; rate of return on a project; net present value; straight-line and declining-balance depreciation; marginal efficiency of investment; border prices; backward and forward linkages.
2. Discuss the most important factors affecting a businessman's decision whether or not to make a particular investment.
3. Discuss the factors affecting the interest-elasticity of demand for investment in an economy.
4. What complications are created for public project appraisal by the existence of indirect taxes on outputs and inputs?
5. Why is it necessary to calculate a shadow price of labour in public project appraisal? On what basis might this be calculated?
6. What do you understand by a 'social rate of discount'?

7. Why may it differ from the market rate of interest?
7. What is meant by a 'hidden' interest rate? Give examples.
8. Discuss the consequences for a public investment programme of selecting too low a social rate of discount.
9. Explain what is meant by a 'social welfare function', and how this could affect project planning. How far do you think this function may differ as between 'democratic' and 'authoritarian' regimes, and why?
10. Discuss the problem of measurement in cost-benefit analysis.
11. Discuss the possible effects of uncertainty and risk on (a) private investment decisions and (b) public investment decisions.
12. What are the main differences in approach between private and public investment appraisal?

Notes

[1] There may, however, be projects which are 'mutually exclusive': a farmer with limited land may, for instance, have to choose between investing in coffee or in dairy cows. If a businessman has only capital enough for one project, and cannot borrow more, all projects will be mutually exclusive.
[2] These are discussed in more detail in Chapter 18.
[3] This term is explained in Chapter 20.
[4] Most so-called democratic societies are not so democratic as they claim, and decisions may reflect not so much the majority view as

those of various influential groups or classes in the society.
[5] For details of this project appraisal, see N. H. Stern, 'Experience with the Use of Little/Mirrlees Method for an Appraisal of Small-holder Tea in Kenya', *Bulletin of the Oxford Institute of Economics and Statistics*, February 1972.
[6] For details of other applications to projects in Kenya of the Little–Mirrlees method of social cost-benefit analysis, see M. F. G. Scott, John MacArthur, and D. Newbery, *Project Appraisal in Practice*, Heinemann Educational Books, London, 1976.

16 The Size and Development of the Firm

The individual enterprise within an industry is known as a 'firm'. A firm is simply a business unit under one control. Agricultural enterprises and purely commercial or transport enterprises are, of course, just as much 'firms' as a firm owning factories or mines. There is an important difference between the 'firm' and the 'establishment'. A productive establishment is defined *physically* as a single 'plant' or factory, or farm, in the agricultural case, while the firm is defined *legally* in terms of ownership and control. One firm may own and control several factories.

Economists, particularly since the great Alfred Marshall, have been interested in the *structure* of industry, by which is meant especially the composition of the industry in terms of the number and size of firms which constitute it. They have therefore tried to analyse the factors affecting the size of the firm. When we do this we must be careful always to distinguish between factors affecting the best size of the *establishment* and factors affecting the size of the *firm*.

Economies of scale

We referred in Chapter 5 to the advantages of large-scale production. Economies are of various types, which we may note briefly, with examples.

Technical economies

These may arise because of indivisibilities in capital equipment, as for example a blast furnace, which cannot be reproduced on a small scale while retaining its efficiency. Alternatively, the product may be produced through a series of processes, each of which does not itself require very heavy equipment, but which taken together involve a large capital investment. Large multi-process firms thus derive 'economies of linked processes'. Shoe production and cigarette production are Eastern African examples.

Technical economies however mainly affect the size of plant, rather than the size of firm. If a technical process requires a large indivisible piece of equipment, the firm will need to be at least as large as can sustain the piece of equipment: but the firm could be much larger. For instance the size of the market in Malawi, say, might be adequate to sustain only one large cigarette factory, given economies of scale in manufacturing cigarettes: but this factory could be

one of many in different countries owned and managed by the same expatriate firm. The size of the firm would therefore be determined by considerations, including other types of scale economies, other than technical economies of scale.

Nevertheless we might give one specific example of technical scale economies. Figure 16.1 shows the economic costs per ton mile estimated for small transporters using lorries of different sizes in Malawi. The data given are for lorries operating at 50 per cent load factor on bitumen (tarmac) at 10,000 miles per annum and 40,000 miles per annum. The cost per ton mile for lorries doing the lower mileage is estimated at 6.6 pence for 7-ton lorries and 3.3 pence for 28-ton lorry trailers: costs of shipment fall *by half* due to economies of scale reaped by the larger lorries which can carry so much more at a time. For lorries doing the longer mileage exactly the same pattern of costs is shown, with costs falling by more than half in this instance because the fixed costs are spread over a larger mileage. The fall in costs for each given annual mileage illustrates technical *economies arising from large dimensions*, i.e. a 28-ton lorry carries four times the load of a 7-tonner but need not cost four times as much to operate.

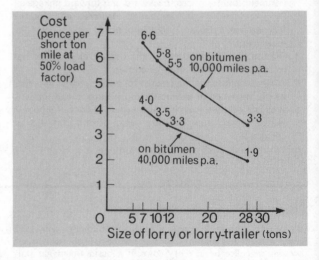

Figure 16.1 *Technical economies of scale: small transporters in Malawi (SOURCE: Economist Intelligence Unit, Malawi Road Transport Regulation Study, 1970, Vol. IV, p. 24).*

Managerial economies

Large-scale production permits the division of labour within management. The task of management can be split up into separate departments, with each departmental head concentrating on one activity and gaining efficiency through specialization. Also, only when operations are on a large scale would it be worth hiring trained specialists such as production engineers, accountants, personnel managers, and the like.

Marketing economies

Large firms may obtain discount from other firms by buying their raw materials in bulk. Economies are also obtainable in bulk selling, since larger sales do not require proportionately higher costs in salesmen's salaries, packing, invoicing, and advertising. A striking illustration of the effect of economies of scale in marketing is shown in Figure 16.2 which gives average or unit costs per ton for cooperative marketing societies handling maize in Central Tanzania. This shows that the smaller societies handling only 200 or 300 tons of product had unit costs *four or five times* as high as those with a larger turnover of 1,200 tons or more. The fitted line shows the general or 'average' relationship between

the size of the society (measured by annual tonnage handled) and unit costs. On the basis of this line we can estimate the 'expected' or average level of cost for a society of any particular size. This is given in Table 16.1. The last column shows that unit costs fall very rapidly at first, before levelling out. Thus it would appear that, other things being the same, a cooperative society of size below 1,000 tons would be uneconomic, with the most economic (in terms of society costs only) being something over 1,600 tons per annum. If unit costs are further analysed it turns

Table 16.1 Schedule of unit costs: maize marketing societies

Volume handled (tons)	Cost per ton (shs)	Percentage decrease from previous volume (%)
200	73	—
400	47	36
600	33	30
800	27	18
1,000	22.5	17
1,200	19	16
1,400	17	11
1,600	16	6
1,800	15	6
2,000	14.5	3

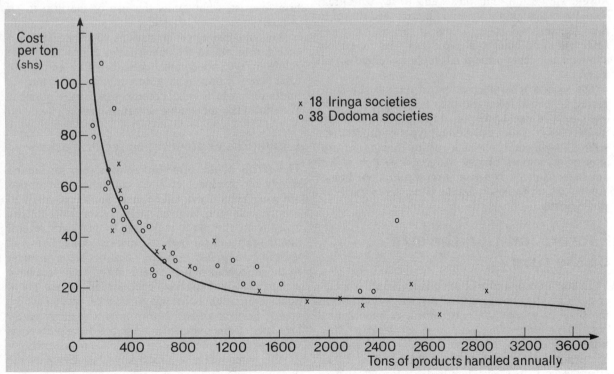

Figure 16.2 Economies of scale in marketing: maize cooperative societies in Central Tanzania (SOURCE: H. Kriesel et al., Agricultural Marketing in Tanzania, Background Research and Policy Proposals, Tanzania Government and USAID, 1970. NOTE: one Iringa society handled 4,500 tons at a cost of shs 14 per ton; 4 Dodoma societies had costs outside the range shown).

out that the main reason for the high costs at low levels of turnover is the cost of salaries and wages: the cost of personnel cannot be reduced in proportion to the rate of turnover but constitutes an 'indivisibility' similar to the indivisibilities in capital equipment mentioned under technical economies of scale.

Financial economies

Large firms can usually raise capital more cheaply since they can offer better security to lenders, as their assets are worth more. Also the costs of lending on a large scale may be less, since a large number of small loans are more difficult and costly to supervise, so that a bank, say, could afford to charge less to a large borrower.

Risk-bearing economies

These may occur in two ways. There are benefits to be derived, first, from the *pooling of similar risks*. This is because the 'law of large numbers' converts risk into certainty. For example, if a bank makes similar loans to a large number of small shopkeepers, it may be able to predict with great accuracy that, say, 1 per cent of loans will be defaulted during the year. The bank may not be able to say *which* borrowers will default, but will be able to say with great confidence that about one in a hundred will do so. In this case this will mean a loss of just £1 for every £100 lent. The bank can avoid any loss by simply adding 1 per cent to the total interest charged on all loans.

The second type of economy is obtained by combining *dissimilar* risks, and thus avoiding 'putting all one's eggs in one basket'. A large firm can diversify its interests by producing several types of product, by selling in different markets, or by having several alternative sources of raw materials, so that it will not suffer as much as a small firm would if one line of activity ceases to be profitable, either temporarily or permanently.

Factors limiting the size of the firm

The effect of economies of scale is to reduce average costs of production (total cost divided by output) as the scale of production is extended. A hypothetical cost curve embodying economies of scale is illustrated in Figure 16.3. In this example a hundred units of output can be produced at a total cost of 1,000s (average cost 10s); two hundred at a total cost of 1,200s (average cost 6s); and four hundred at a total cost of 1,600s (average cost 4s).

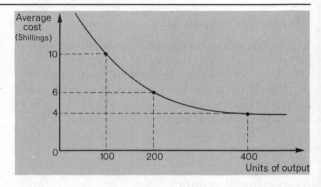

Figure 16.3 *A hypothetical cost curve embodying economies of scale.*

Suppose all the firms in an industry had this identical cost curve. It would mean that the industry was capable of supplying, for example, 400 units through four firms, each producing 100 units, at an average cost of 10s; or through two firms, each producing 200 units, at an average cost of 6s; or through a single firm producing all 400 units at an average cost of 4s. The obvious question arises: if a large firm could always produce more cheaply, why do we not have bigger and bigger firms, until just one firm, a monopolist, produces the whole of the industry's output? Since it is unusual for only one firm to exist, what limits the size of the firm in an industry?

We can consider (1) limitations which exist even if each firm is free to sell any amount of product at the ruling market price, and free to buy any amount of each factor it uses as its ruling market price, and (2) limitations which exist because this is not possible. We shall take the second situation first.

Limitations of product and factor markets

The extent of the firm's operations may be limited simply by transport costs. If consumers are spread out geographically it will be more and more costly to supply them from a given plant (factory) the further away from the plant they are. If there are several plants scattered through the market, consumers will tend to be supplied from the plant or factory nearest to them. Instead of one large market we in fact have a number of sub-markets each served by one plant. Such a situation is known as one of '*spatial monopolies*', because *within its own area* a plant is partly protected from competition by the transport costs which plants further away would need to incur to sell in the same area: a monopoly due to space or distance. For example, a large town may have only one or two butcher's shops in each suburb, which tend to supply those customers who reside in the locality, and which are partly protected from competition from shops in other suburbs by the extra cost of delivery or the inconvenience to customers of having to travel further to get their supplies.

As it turns out, however, this is not so much a limitation on the size of *firm*, but on the size of *plant*. As we stated above, a plant is a producing establishment, like a textile factory or a shop; a firm is a business unit under one management, and one management may control *several* factories. In our example, even if it is economic to have separate butcher's shops in each suburb, it is quite possible for one firm to own the entire string of shops.

Another limit to expansion applies more directly to the size of the business unit. Consumers are not entirely rational in their discrimination between the products of two firms even if the products are identical in quality and price. Many customers deal with a particular shop out of habit, if they have been buying there for some time, because they have come to know the owner personally, or perhaps because they are prejudiced against his competitors. The result is a situation similar to spatial monopoly in that groups of customers are tied to particular firms: in this case they are tied, not by distance, but by their own habits and prejudices.

Moreover, firms deliberately set out to *differentiate* their product from similar articles by persuasive advertising appeals, slight variations of style, differences in packaging, and so on, aimed at getting together a 'clientele' of people accustomed to buying their products in preference to the similar ones of competing firms. While a firm will thus obtain a degree of protection from competition, it will in turn find it difficult to expand its sales at the expense of others. The effect is to impose a limit on the expansion of sales and to restrict the size of the business unit.

The two limitations considered so far are obstacles to expansion on the sales side. But firms may also be restricted in size because of difficulty in finding the additional factors of production, labour, land, and capital, for expansion. Labour is generally mobile between firms, even if it is immobile between geographical areas. However it is possible that, if each factory draws its labour from its local area, its growth is restricted by a shortage of the necessary labour. Again this restricts the size of the plant rather than the business unit. Land is generally less crucial in industry, as factories do not usually require a great deal of space in relation to the value of their production. In agriculture, however, it is a fundamental factor of production. In Africa the market for land is particularly imperfect in the sense that land is not freely bought and sold. The ownership of land is often highly uncertain, even where the same farmer has cultivated a particular piece of land for years,

and his father before him. Even if additional plots of land *can* be purchased, it will be very difficult for a progressive farmer to buy up *adjacent* plots to make up a single large farm. Hence economies of scale in farming will still not be tapped, and the incentive to build up larger efficient holdings is diminished.

However, the most critical restriction probably lies in the third factor, capital. We shall examine the sources of finance available to a firm in detail presently. The capital market does not operate so perfectly that any firm with good economic potential has appropriate access to finance: indeed the market for capital is probably highly *im*perfect in this respect, though more so in the developing countries. Small firms may find it difficult to grow even when directed by the most able entrepreneur, who is capable of organizing a much larger concern, or when they are launching a potentially popular product. Instead large firms find it easier to raise additional finance simply because they have assets to offer as security to lenders: whereas they may be *less* able to turn this finance to productive uses.

Diseconomies of scale

Thus firms may be limited in size due to difficulty in selling a larger output, or due to difficulties in acquiring the extra factors, land, labour, or capital, in order to increase output: limitations imposed either by the product market or by the factor markets. Does this mean that if these limitations were absent there would be *no* limit to the size of the firm? Economists have generally argued that this is not the case: they have argued that one major factor would limit the size of the firm *even* when it was free to sell as much product as it liked at the market price *and* to hire whatever quantities of the factors it required at going market rates. The reason is that as the firm grows in size the problem of managing it becomes more and more complex.

It is recognized, of course, that firms can bring in additional managers, breaking the work of management up into separate departments, as well as bringing in additional supervision at lower levels. In other words management can be extended, as it were, horizontally and vertically. But the work of these departments must be coordinated. And as management is extended vertically it will be more difficult for the director to transmit his decisions and plans downwards through his assistant managers and other supervisors to the workers who are actually doing the job, or to remain fully aware of the detailed problems and performance of his employees. The problem of communication between management and workers which is necessary for maximum efficiency will thus become more acute. The efficiency of a business enterprise also depends on its being possible to take decisions rapidly: in a large organization, where more people need to be consulted before a decision can be taken, this is likely to be more difficult to achieve. It is argued, therefore, that as the firm grows in size loss of efficiency will arise as a result of unwieldiness, inflexibility, and lack of communication, so that costs per unit of output rise. These costs are referred to as *diseconomies of scale*.

As these multiply the downward slope of the cost curve illustrated in Figure 16.3 will eventually be reversed and the curve begin to rise. The curve will therefore be U-shaped, as in Figure 16.4 where costs are a minimum at output OA. It must be stressed that diseconomies of scale do not start at output OA: they operate to some extent as soon as any output is produced at all. Nor do economies of scale necessarily cease to operate at output OA. The cost curve begins to rise because most of the important economies of scale have already been tapped, so that additional economies are less significant, *or* because problems of management result in *increasing* diseconomies of scale or both, in such a way that beyond output OA additional diseconomies outweigh additional economies.

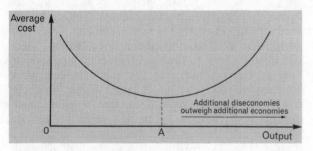

Figure 16.4   *The effect of diseconomies of scale on the cost curve.*

The relation between average and marginal values

Given the relationship between cost and output, we can proceed to analyse which scale of operations (output) will be selected. In this analysis we shall make use of both average and marginal values of variables and it is necessary first to clarify the relationship between them. The relationship is very simple, but it will be most useful to us.

Suppose we take two 'bundles' of some commodity, weighing 6 kg each. The average weight is $\frac{6+6}{2}=6$ kg. If we add a third or *marginal* bundle also

weighing 6 kg, the average weight is still $\frac{6+6+6}{3}=6$ kg. If we had added a third bundle weighing 9 kg, the average would increase to $\frac{6+6+9}{3}=7$ kg; while if we added one weighing 3 kg, the average would decrease to $\frac{6+6+3}{3}=5$ kg. The example is quite general.

It follows that *if the extra or marginal value exceeds the average, the average must increase; if it equals the average, the average is constant; and if it is less than the average, the average will decrease.* In our example, if, as we add an extra bundle, the average weight goes up, it must be because the marginal bundle was heavier than the average. Our statement therefore holds in reverse. *If the average value is increasing, it must be because the marginal value exceeds the average; if the average is constant, the marginal and average values are equal; and if the average is decreasing, the marginal is less than the average value.*

The conditions for perfect competition

We can now go ahead with our problem, that of seeing what output a firm will select if it has the production opportunities implied in the U-shaped cost curve described, and operates without limitations of product and factor markets. To do this we may assume the following conditions.

(1) There are a large number of firms in the industry.

(2) There is free entry into the industry.

(3) All firms are producing an identical product.

(4) There is perfect knowledge in the market, so that all firms know the details of their cost curves, and all consumers know the price being charged by each firm in the industry.

(5) There are no transport costs, as though all firms and consumers were located at one spot.

Together, these conditions are said to constitute a situation of '*perfect competition*'. It is easy to see why it is described thus.

In the first place conditions (3), (4), and (5) mean that all the firms must charge the same price. Since all firms are producing the same product, and all consumers know this and the price each firm is charging, any firm trying to charge a higher price than the others will make no sales: for consumers will hardly pay more for the same product which they can get elsewhere, and without having to incur additional transport costs to get it. Nor could any firm charge less than the others, for then no consumer would buy from the other firms, and this would force the other firms to reduce their prices to the same level, just as the first firm found it could not charge a higher price.

Condition (1) means that each firm will face a completely elastic demand for its own output. This is due to the fact that, since there is a large number of firms, all producing the same product, each firm will be producing a tiny fraction of the total supply of that product. Suppose, for example, there were 10,000 cocoa farmers in the world, each producing 10 tons per annum; annual production would be 100,000 tons. Suppose, further, that the elasticity of demand for cocoa happened to be exactly one (to simplify our theorizing!). This would mean that a 1 per cent fall in price would increase the amount demanded by 1 per cent, or alternatively that if the amount supplied increased by 1 per cent (in this case by 1,000 tons), consumers could be persuaded to buy this additional amount so long as price fell by 1 per cent. Such a fall in price could hardly come about through the actions of one producer however. This would require an increase in his output from 10 to 1,000 tons, an increase of nearly 10,000 per cent! If a farmer managed to increase his output by 10 per cent to 11 tons, or even by 100 per cent to 20, total world supply would increase by a negligible amount (if 1,000 tons are needed to produce a 1 per cent fall) and *price would therefore not be affected*. To all intents and purposes the individual producer is free to put as much output as he can on the market at the ruling price.

Figure 16.5(a) relates to *world* supply and demand, the amounts being measured in thousand tons. The equilibrium price is OP. At point A on the demand curve elasticity of demand was 1 per cent, in our example. The analysis is not affected, of course, if the elasticity has any other realistic value. Referring to Figure 16.5(b) we see that the price to the individual farmer is the same whether he sells 10, 11, or 20 tons. His *individual* demand curve is horizontal, indicating a completely elastic demand.

To make the distinction clear we can refer to the *market* elasticity of demand and to the producer's *own elasticity of demand*. The latter can be high even if the former is quite low. Since the producer in this situation has no control over the market price, which is determined by *total* supply and demand, he may be described as a *price-taker*. Since the same price is charged for each unit of output, price is the same as average revenue (revenue divided by number of units): the demand curve in Figure 16.5(b) is accordingly labelled AR, since it gives average revenue, equal to price, at each level of output.

The scale of output under competition

Since supply conditions are given by the AC curve and demand by the AR curve, the situation facing the firm is fully represented, and we can determine the scale of output that will be selected, if the firm maximizes profits. We can most easily do this by introducing the *marginal* curves corresponding to average revenue and cost. We can define *marginal revenue as the extra revenue obtained when one more unit of output is produced and sold. Marginal cost is the extra cost due to the production of one more unit of output. It follows that if the firm wishes to maximize profits it will produce at the point where marginal revenue equals marginal cost.* For if the two were not equal, say, marginal revenue exceeded marginal cost, our definitions imply that an extra unit of output would bring in more revenue than it would add to costs: that is, total profits would increase as a result of increasing output by at least one unit. On the other hand, if the marginal cost of the last unit produced exceeded its marginal revenue, reduction of output by this unit would reduce costs by more than it would reduce revenue, and *net* revenue, or profits, would increase. Where the two were exactly equal, a change of output in *either* direction would decrease net revenue, indicating that this was the *equilibrium* output.

The cost and revenue situation of Figure 16.5(b) is reproduced in Figure 16.6. Since average revenue is constant for all outputs, average and marginal values must be equal throughout: it follows that the marginal revenue curve coincides with the AR curve. The average cost curve is U-shaped, decreasing at first, reaching a minimum at point C, and then increasing. Before C, marginal values are less than the average value for each output, so that the marginal cost curve lies *below* the average cost curve. After C, marginal values exceed the average, since the average is increasing, so the marginal cost curve lies above the average cost curve. At point C, average cost is con-

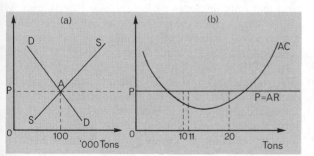

Figure 16.5   *The relation between world supply and demand and the individual firm's supply and demand: (a) world supply and demand, (b) individual supply and demand.*

stant, neither decreasing nor increasing, so marginal and average cost coincide: *the marginal cost curve therefore intersects the average cost curve at its minimum point C.*

Since the marginal cost and marginal revenue curves intersect in our diagram at point D, the output selected will be OB. It might be wondered whether the output selected could not equally be OE, since the two marginal curves also intersect at point F. It can be seen however that an increase in output at this point would increase profits, because marginal revenues exceed marginal costs for outputs greater than OE. This is because, although MC = MR at OE, MC is decreasing at this point while MR is constant. We actually need a *second* condition for equilibrium output: this is that, besides having MC = MR, marginal cost must be increasing faster or decreasing less fast than marginal revenue.[1]

Even this, however, is not sufficient to ensure complete 'equilibrium', for condition (2) in the conditions for perfect competition given on page 222 was that there should be freedom of entry into the industry. If profits were high enough, therefore, new firms would come in, total supply would increase, the market price would fall, and the position of the AR = MR curve in our diagram would change. We need therefore to add something about the level of profits in the industry.

Let us define *normal profits* as that level of profits which is *just sufficient to induce existing firms to remain in the industry without inducing new firms to enter.* Profits in excess of this can be described as *supernormal.* If less than normal profits were being earned, we should say that the level of profits was sub-normal. Normal profits are therefore the profits the entrepreneur must expect to get[2] if he is to carry on in the industry, rather than transferring to some other industry, or even ceasing to be an 'entrepreneur' at all; or if he were not present in the industry, the minimum that would attract him to come in.

We assume here that there are a large number of entrepreneurs who could operate in the industry,

some inside and some out, with identical qualities, and that there is a perfect market for their services, as well as for other inputs and outputs. This assumption implies that entrepreneurs are 'mobile' between industries in the long run, and also 'non-specific', in that they are capable of pursuing other occupations. 'Normal profits' therefore represent the cost of their services, as determined by the market, in the same way that wages represent the cost of more general forms of labour. Since they are a 'cost', it is convenient to consider them as being included in the average cost curve.

Figure 16.7(b) substantially reproduces the situation of Figure 16.6. If the market price is at OP to start with, the output of the typical firm as represented in Figure 16.7(b) will be OB, with marginal cost and revenue each equal to BD. Average revenue at this output is also BD, but average cost only BE. The difference ED is the average profit, over and above normal profits, made on each unit of output. Since EF (= OB) units are produced, supernormal profits are made, equal to ED times EF, represented in the diagram by the shaded rectangle PDEF.

The existence of such supernormal profits would, however, attract new firms into the industry. The resulting increase in output would shift the market supply curve to the right and the price would fall in the direction of OP'. Correspondingly, the level of the revenue curve in Figure 16.7(b) would fall, reducing the amount of supernormal profit. But by definition *any* excess over normal profit brings in new firms. Hence firms must *continue* to enter so long as any supernormal profit remains. The price must therefore fall all the way to the level OP' in Figure 16.7(b) as a result of the shift in the supply curve from SS to S'S' indicated in Figure 16.7(a).

Under our assumptions, if the market price were initially *below* the level affording normal profits, the process would work in reverse, as shown in Figure 16.8. Price is determined initially as OP in Figure 16.8(a). Taking this price as given, the 'typical' firm can only *minimize its losses* since throughout its entire length its average revenue curve lies below average cost. Minimization is again where marginal cost and marginal revenue curves intersect, at D, with output OB. At this output average revenue is equal to BD, and average cost to BE, so that a loss is made on each unit of DE. Since FE units are produced (= OB), losses are given by the shaded rectangle PDEF. In the long run these losses would drive firms out of the industry, causing the supply curve in Figure 16.8(a) to move to the left, until the market price has risen sufficiently to permit the remaining firms to make normal profits. The firm would then be in equilibrium, as before, with an output of OA, and price of OP' (= AR' = MR').

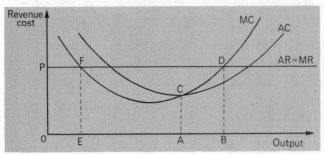

Figure 16.6 *The marginal cost and revenue curves.*

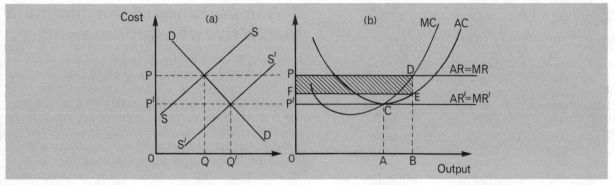

Figure 16.7   *The effect of entry by new firms: (a) market supply and demand, (b) individual demand and output.*

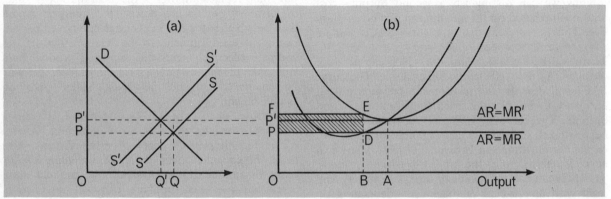

Figure 16.8   *Sub-normal profits with firms leaving the industry: (a) market supply and demand, (b) individual demand and output.*

It will be observed that this equilibrium output is that *for which the firm's average costs are a minimum.* It is for this reason that perfect competition is said to result in an 'optimum' allocation of resources, with each firm of the 'optimum' size.

In any given industry the optimum size will depend on the particular balance between economies and diseconomies of scale in that industry. Thus in Figure 16.9 a cost situation like that represented by average cost AC_1 would optimally result in the setting up of small-scale establishments, each designed to produce output OA_1, while cost situation AC_3 would result in large-scale establishments being typical, and AC_2 in medium-size establishments.

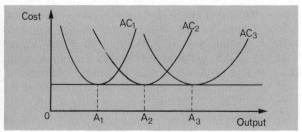

Figure 16.9   *Circumstances giving rise to small- or large-scale industry.*

The relation between 'long-run' and 'short-run' cost curves

This result must be interpreted rather carefully. Given any one of the cost situations above, minimum average costs are attainable with one size of plant only. Thus in Figure 16.10 if LAC represents the cost situation in the industry there will be a certain size of establishment which, *if producing output OA_1*, will have average costs OC_1. If the *same* plant were used to produce *more* output, costs would rise more sharply than suggested by the curve LAC, which assumes larger-sized plants better designed for accommodating large outputs. If output OA_2 were produced, for example, with a plant designed to produce OA_1, costs would rise to OC_3, rather than to OC_2, the costs associated with a large plant. The rise in costs would be explained by the *Law of Variable Proportions.* Capital, embodied in the given plant, is a fixed factor, and as variable factors, labour and raw materials, are applied to it, diminishing returns will set in. The same will apply for production of smaller outputs with the same plant: a progressively smaller labour force will be less and less efficient in operating the plant, the 'proportion' of capital to labour being progressively too large.

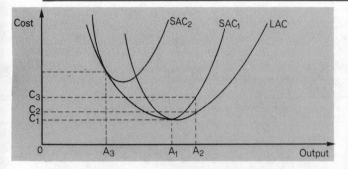

Figure 16.10   *Cost variation with different-size plants and with a given plant.*

Thus we can distinguish a second output—cost relationship based on the assumption of a given plant size. This is represented by the curve SAC_1. *But we can repeat this procedure for every point on LAC.* There will be a certain plant size which can produce output OA_3 most efficiently, for example. The curve SAC_2 will describe the relationship between output and cost if *this* plant is used to produce different outputs. The curve LAC is said to be an *envelope* curve since it embraces a large number of plant cost curves, as illustrated in Figure 16.11. The plant cost curve is referred to as the firm's *short-run cost curve.* This is because at any point of time, a firm may find itself with any size of establishment, depending on historical circumstances. If it wishes to expand output quickly it can 'in the short run' only do so by using this given plant more intensively. In the long run, of course, the firm will be free to select the most efficient size of plant for the output it wishes to produce. As we have seen, under competitive conditions this will be given by the minimum point on the envelope curve. Accordingly this curve is referred to as the *long-run cost curve,* or occasionally the *planning curve,* implying that the firm is free to plan which plant size it wishes to establish out of the whole range of technical possibilities.

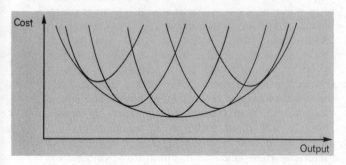

Figure 16.11   *The long-run curve as an 'envelope' of short-run cost curves.*

The importance of the minimum viable size of establishment

The competitive conditions we have described are far from universal, especially in undeveloped countries. In these countries no kind of economic policy will stimulate much competition simply because the market will often be too small to support many firms. Indeed there will often be *no* local firm producing a product, so that the product will instead have to be imported. The government might then wish to promote industrialization through *import substitution,* that is, the encouragement of local firms whose output could replace imports. If the local market is small in terms of purchasing power, the question might then be whether the market is large enough to permit *one* local establishment to be 'viable', that is, to compete effectively with the imported product and still make profits. In such a case the government will be interested in the *minimum* viable size of establishment.

Suppose, in Figure 16.12, that the LAC curve represents the average costs of production in Eastern Africa for all possible sizes of establishment. The price of the product overseas is OX, but since it costs an extra amount XS to transport the product from 'overseas', overseas suppliers can sell in Eastern Africa only at the price OS. They can, however, supply 'any amount' at this price, since Eastern Africa forms a relatively small part of the world market. The supply curve of imports is therefore the horizontal one SS at the price OS. Any Eastern African firm would need to take this price as given.

The most efficient size of establishment which could be set up in Eastern Africa would be that given by the minimum point on LAC, producing OA_4. Unfortunately if Eastern African demand were, say, at the level of D_1D_1, the firm could not sell this amount: the maximum it can sell at the market price of OS is OA_3. If however the best size of establishment for *this* output were established, given by SAC_1, profits could be made, since average cost at this output *is* less than average revenue ($=OS$). The *minimum* viable size of establishment is given by the curve SAC_2 producing output OA_2, and is viable even if demand is at the lower level D_2D_2. For at this output average costs with this plant are just equal to average revenue OS. If demand is at a still lower level, say, D_3D_3, demand at price OS is no more than OA_1: *no* size of establishment is capable of covering costs, given the market price, at this level of output. This is indicated by the fact that at output OA_1 the LAC curve lies above SS.

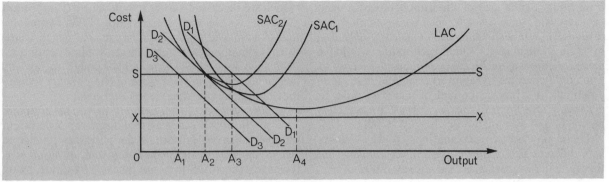

Figure 16.12   *The minimum viable size of establishment.*

The sizes of some manufacturing establishments in Tanzania

Let us now examine some East African data to see what sizes of firm are typical in various East African industries. These data refer to establishments rather than firms (one firm may own several establishments, but in East Africa this is less common). We can use different 'indexes' of the size of an establishment. Thus we might say that an establishment is 'small' if the value of its annual 'net' output is small; or if it employs very few people; or if the value of its real capital—buildings, machinery, vehicles, and so on—is small. It should be remembered that an establishment may not employ such a large number of workers even though it uses a vast amount of capital, simply because the industry is capital-intensive. We must not *only* look at the numbers employed per establishment in order to decide whether the industry should be described as 'large-scale'.

Classification is difficult for another reason, which is that some categories given in the table combine two or more very different kinds of activities. For instance 'meat canning and dairy products' is actually two separate industries and includes one very large meat canning establishment (Tanganyika Packers) and a number of rather small dairy establishments. Had we had available separate statistics for meat canning, this would have been classified under 'large establishments'.

Since absolute distinctions are difficult to make, the table is divided into 'large', 'medium-to-large', 'small-to-medium', and 'very small' categories.

Different firm sizes within one industry

The last two columns of Table 16.2 show clear differences in the size of establishments in different industries. In terms of net value added, the average figure in the first category is about 20 times that of the last; in terms of employment about 16 times.

This comparison is, however, somewhat misleading. This is because, as with most statistical data, it is wise to look at the 'spread' of the values, as well as their average. It is important therefore to look at the central part of the table, which gives the *size distribution* of establishments in Tanzania, in terms of employees. In some industries the 'usual' size of establishments is fairly clear: 6 out of 8 establishments engaged in the spinning and weaving of textiles employ 500 persons or more; 18 out of 20 cotton ginneries employ 100–499 persons; 8 out of 9 cordage, rope, and twine establishments are of this size. At the other end of the scale, 29 out of 35 furniture establishments employ fewer than 50 persons, as do 28 out of 33 printing works, and 18 out of 22 bakeries.

But there is in many industries a surprising variation in the sizes of establishments which exist and appear to survive in competition with one another. Particularly in the 'medium' ranges, among sugar factories, tea processing establishments, in grain milling, edible oil milling, and saw-milling, there is a very even spread of establishments among various sizes.

It is true that our data refer to the size of establishments, rather than to the size of firms. However in Tanzania the number of firms operating several establishments is comparatively small, so that the data roughly represent the size distribution of firms also. In any case, the effect of taking multi-establishment units is to widen the dispersion of units, increasing the gap between the small single-establishment unit and the large multi-establishment unit. Hence the size distribution of firms will be much wider in Europe or the USA, where multi-establishment concerns are common.

These facts suggest that in most industries there is scope for considerable expansion in the size of establishments. Moreover in relation to the size of the firm, limits to the size of the establishment are not very relevant, since a single business unit could operate several establishments, each efficiently organized by a local manager. While each plant would separately enjoy any technical economies to be had, the firm could continue to tap marketing and managerial potentials, or other economies of scale. It could, for instance, raise finance cheaply for all its establishments, or buy raw materials cheaply in bulk.

There may be two explanations of why firms of very different sizes may 'co-exist' in an industry. The first is that the economies and diseconomies of scale which we discussed earlier may not be too important after all. As we shall see presently, firms can evolve more advanced managerial structures which allow them to manage larger and larger volumes of output. Hence so long as the firm is big enough to tap any important economies of scale in the industry, it may not matter much what size it is.

In the second place our analysis of the optimum size of the firms assumes that firms, or a sufficient number of firms, can obtain the necessary finance to set themselves up immediately at the optimum size, or at least to reach that size quickly. However, as we

Table 16.2   Sizes of establishments in some Tanzanian industries, 1970

Industry	Total no. of estab- lishments	No. of establishments by no. employed					No. employed per est- ablishment	Net value added per establish- ment ($\times 1,000$ shs)
		10–19	20–49	50–99	100–499	500+		
Large establishments								
Breweries	3	—	—	2	1	—	117	14,102
Tobacco	4	—	1	—	1	2	618	11,461
Spinning & weaving	8	—	—	—	2	6	1,172	7,648
Basic industrial chemicals & petroleum refineries	4	—	—	2	2	—	153	6,555
Medium/large establishments								
Meat canning & dairy products	6	1	3	1	—	1	2,920	1,095
Sugar factories	14	2	6	1	3	2	322	2,012
Tea processing	20	1	5	4	9	1	141	900
Cotton ginning	20	1	—	1	18	—	160	624
Cordage, rope, & twine	9	1	—	—	8	—	170	1,761
Small/medium establishments								
Grain milling	27	10	8	3	6	—	61	929
Wearing apparel & other made-up textiles	18	—	8	7	3	—	72	479
Paints	3	—	2	1	—	—	47	1,245
Saw-milling & plywood	25	3	11	8	3	—	64	397
Edible oil milling	22	5	6	6	5	—	56	256
Very small establishments								
Furniture	35	14	15	5	1	—	34	751
Printing & publishing	33	13	15	3	2	—	39	568
Bakery products	22	11	7	4	—	—	29	207

SOURCE: Bureau of Statistics, Dar es Salaam, *Survey of Industrial Production, 1970*

shall also see presently, the amount of finance that the firm can raise in any period, by the various means at its disposal, appears to be strictly limited. As a result, in order to finance its growth, the firm depends considerably on its profits, which it can 'plough back' into the business over a period of time. Accordingly at any time we should expect to find firms at different stages of growth, and therefore of different sizes.

Both these observations suggest that we need to look at the process of growth of a firm. Specifically, this requires the study of the different types of firm and an examination of the sources of finance available to these different types, and also the study of the evolution of the managerial organization.

Types of firm and the development of the managerial organization

A great many firms are started as single proprietorships, owned by one person, or as family businesses. Alternatively there may be a partnership of a few individuals who come together to launch the enterprise. The advantage of the latter is that the individuals can 'pool' their capital where an individual might find that he lacks the minimum amount necessary to get started on a sound financial basis. Another possibility is that one person has the entrepreneurial ability and ideas for launching the firm, or perhaps has invested in a new product or method of production, but lacks the capital for launching the firm; to get under way he must therefore persuade one or more partners who have the capital to invest in a joint venture with him. Or again the firm may start as a single proprietorship and be converted into a partnership by the owner inviting others willing to provide either finance or managerial qualities to join him once he finds himself lacking funds for expansion or time to manage a larger volume of business single-handed.

An important feature of the joint stock company, or incorporated enterprise, is the divorce of ownership and control. The owners of an enterprise are those who provide the finance, in this case the shareholders. In this sense every shareholder is legally an 'owner' of the firm, even if he possesses only one out of 100,000 shares. But he may have little or no influence on policy decisions undertaken within the firm. He may, of course, attend annual shareholders' meetings and voice his opinions there, but he will not usually be sufficiently acquainted with the detailed operation of the company for these opinions to be very informed. In any case, since the composition of shareholders is constantly changing as people buy and sell shares, shareholders as a body will not have the organization to be able to exercise a controlling influence. Instead, control will rest with the chairman and board of directors of the company, who may in fact have few or no shares and be little or no more than (well-paid) salaried employees.

The advantage of the joint stock company is, first, that it brings together the professional manager, who may not have capital of his own, with small suppliers of capital who may have little or no business competence, thus combining capital with managerial expertise. Thus the firm need not be dependent on the organizing capacity of the originator. It also means that the firm need not lose its efficiency when the original entrepreneur retires from active life: the firm therefore has more time to grow to a larger size. Joint stock organization facilitates the extension of management both horizontally and vertically: horizontally in the sense that the work can be split into specialized departments such as production, sales, labour relations, and finance, with a head of department or director for each section; and vertically, in that additional supervisors and foremen can be recruited to serve below each head. Finally, as mentioned earlier, management can be extended by setting up new establishments, each with a local manager. Large-scale organization also permits experts in a variety of fields to be recruited, such as engineers, accountants, or research teams. Thus more extensive and better management can be introduced into the firm. It may, of course, be possible to introduce these without joint stock organization, but this would be comparatively difficult.

To achieve such expansion will, however, take time. Wholesale changes in the structure of the firm clearly cannot be introduced overnight. New men will need experience 'on the job' and the firm will only be capable of absorbing them at a certain rate. There will therefore be a limit to the rate of expansion of the firm. Thus while diseconomies of scale may limit output in any one period, it may be possible to 'push back' these diseconomies progressively by introducing new management and organization. This could be represented as in Figure 16.13. This phenomenon has been called the 'receding managerial limit'.[3]

The growth of the firm is therefore likely to be associated with changing managerial structure. A critical point in this growth will be the stage where the firm adopts the joint stock form of organization with professional managers divorced from the control of owners. For at this point the firm will no longer depend entirely on the ability and 'drive' of the individual owner-entrepreneur, and can be self-sustaining.

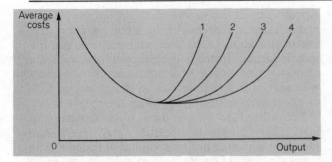

Figure 16.13   *The receding managerial limit.*

Limited liability

The main advantage of joint stock companies, however, over single proprietorships or unincorporated partnerships is that they have limited liability. With unlimited liability, every owner is liable for all the debts of the firm. Even if a partner with little active interest in the firm has invested as little as, say, £100, if the firm goes bankrupt with debts of £100,000, and if his partners have no money or possessions to make any payment, he can be liable for the whole amount; and he can be made to sell any personal possessions he has in order to realize this cash, no matter how unrelated these possessions are to the business enterprise concerned. This legal position will also make it tempting for the partners deliberately to misappropriate the profits of the firm and create bankruptcy in order to benefit in this way from partnership with a richer colleague. Without limited liability, therefore, partners need to be able to trust each other very much indeed before coming together. Both of these effects are likely to reduce the flow of investment and the growth of firms, with adverse economic results.

The prime feature of a limited (joint stock) company is that it has a legal entity separate from the individuals who own it. The company, as opposed to the individuals composing it, can incur debts and, just as any individual, can be sued for breach of contract. The maximum amount the partner referred to earlier can lose in the event of bankruptcy will be the £100 that he put in. Any personal property or any investment in other enterprises will not be liable.

An associated advantage that a limited company may have is that of free transferability of shares, so that one person can sell his shares freely to anyone else who is willing to buy them. This can increase the supply of available finance very greatly since a large amount of money may be supplied by a floating body of small shareholders, none of whom would be able to lend for long periods, and who would be precluded from lending at all in the absence of such arrangements.

Limited liability and free transferability of shares need not go together. To obtain the benefits of limited liability a partnership of as few as two persons can form a private company with limited liability.

A private company cannot offer shares to the general public, and in most Commonwealth countries cannot have more than fifty members. Permission of the company's directors must be obtained before shares are sold, since in most cases private companies are controlled by, say, one or two families or business associates. In Eastern Africa they are either local private companies, owned and controlled by non-Africans in the main until very recently, or subsidiaries of foreign-based companies. A *public limited company* must have at least seven shareholders but there is usually no upper limit to membership. Thus well-known multinational companies like the Royal Dutch-Shell petroleum group or Imperial Chemical Industries have each over 400,000 different shareholders or 'owners'. Public companies can offer shares to the general public which are freely transferable either on organized stock exchanges or by direct transfer through the company's registration office or agent.

Characteristics of the firm's main sources of finance

Let us now examine the main sources of finance available to the firm. These include:

(1) Personal savings
(2) Bank loans and advances
(3) Trade credit and hire-purchase credit
(4) Trade bills
(5) Retained profits
(6) Bonds (debentures)
(7) Shares (preference or ordinary shares).

An individual or family business may be started on the basis of the proprietor's own accumulated *savings*, earned by him as an employee elsewhere, or perhaps obtained as an inheritance. These funds will then most likely be supplemented by *bank loans*. The businessman cannot, however, borrow as much as he likes at the market rate of interest. For the bank will be concerned with the risk of non-repayment due either to the failure of the concern or deliberate default by the borrower. Normally a maximum amount of loan is set based on the estimated 'reliability' of the customer. The level of this maximum will vary according to the bank manager's personal knowledge of the customer and of the risks of the venture.

Since this knowledge will generally be very limited, the amount of loan offered will tend to correspond roughly with the value of the firm's existing assets, since these provide security or 'collateral'. The greater the value of these assets, the 'net worth' of the firm, the greater the chances of the bank's being repaid a loan in the event of bankruptcy. It has been said that to obtain a loan one has to prove that one does not need it! It is, of course an exaggeration, but it is certainly true that no matter how promising a businessman an individual may be, he will find it difficult to convince bank managers of the fact if he is completely lacking in financial assets.

While bank loans may be crucial to the entrepreneur, particularly in the early stages of expansion, they will not form a large part of the total capital employed in a large enterprise. On the other hand, once having fixed a maximum loan, the practice is for banks to allow borrowing more or less automatically within this range. This flexibility means that bank loans are more important as a source of *short-term* finance, acting as a cushion of liquidity.

Trade credit consists of goods made available by one firm to another without immediate cash payment being required. Not only are consumer goods supplied on credit by manufacturers and wholesalers to retailers, but all kinds of manufacturing enterprises may buy raw material from others without making immediate payment. Eastern African retailers are particularly dependent on this form of finance, obtaining retail goods usually on three months' credit, since they frequently lack sufficient capital of their own. Moreover, since cash is received at a steady rate as the goods are sold, and payment to the wholesaler or other supplier need not be made immediately, this cash may also be used to finance other trade like the purchase and resale of produce from farmers.

Trade credit is, of course, the equivalent of a cash loan, since in its absence cash would be required to purchase the goods and would be 'locked up' in the form of goods until they came to be sold. Since trade credit is automatically renewable, it amounts to a permanent loan. On the other hand, since the amount is strictly limited by the current level of the firm's trade, it represents a short-term and inelastic source of finance. It can, however, be especially critical in the early stages of development when the firm is starting up in business. Differential access to trade credit was probably a major factor in holding up the development of African-owned business in Eastern Africa.

Hire-purchase credit is another source of finance which does not involve a direct loan of money. However if a firm buys a machine costing, say, shs 5,000 on hire-purchase terms over three years, it is exactly the same as borrowing from a bank to buy the machine for cash: and the period of the loan is longer than in the case of trade credit. For the smaller firm, which might have difficulty in obtaining a three-year bank loan, hire-purchase credit provided by a specialized finance house may enable it to equip a factory or farm in advance of acquiring its own savings out of profits. It may also be mentioned that instead of actually buying machines over a period of, say, three years these may in fact be leased or rented. Tractor-hire schemes exist for small farmers, but industrial plant and buildings may also be leased.

A development of trade credit is the *trade bill*. Essentially this consists of a post-dated cheque, cashable either three or six months after the supply of goods. The supplier does not, however, have to wait three months for payment, but can sell the bill for cash to a bank or to a discount house, although at a discount if before the date of maturity of the bill. The trade bill has often been an important source of credit in many African countries because of their dependence on foreign trade. Importers, especially, obtain goods on 90-day credit, usually, from their overseas suppliers, normally sufficient time to cover shipment and delivery to the main ports but usually not enough to allow them to sell to other wholesalers or retailers. Importers therefore discount the bills with the banks who take over the loan from the supplier, so that 'trade credit' now becomes bank credit. There are also 'internal' bills financing local production before export or final sales to local consumers. In 1972, for example, about 10 per cent of total commercial bank lending in Kenya to private firms took the form of discounting foreign or East African bills rather than the more usual commercial bank loans and advances.

Since, as we have indicated, a small firm may find great difficulty in finding the outside funds required for expansion, *retained profits* may be a crucial element in financing its growth at this stage. When an enterprise becomes a public company, however, retained profits gain a new significance. We suggested above that 'ownership' of the firm by shareholders is likely to be largely nominal, since decision-taking and control will be in the hands of the board of directors who generally aim at the progressive expansion of the firms. This may be partly because they measure their 'success' in their job not only by the salaries they receive but by the increasing sales achieved; but also in the long run an increase in the size of the firm should result in an upward revision of their salaries. The majority of shareholders have no long-term interest in the success of the firm since within a year, say, they may have sold their shares: their aim will be to maximize the return on their investments during the period in which they own their shares, irrespective of the firm's long-run position.

It follows that the amount paid out as dividends will tend to the minimum required to safeguard future subscriptions of money capital from the public. A firm not giving dividends at all, of course, will eventually find that it cannot raise further capital by the sale of shares, as the public will not buy. In a public company, therefore, reinvested profits become a major source of funds and of course represent *long-term* finance. We may say that firms are to an important extent internally financed.

Change-over to the basis of a public company also means that the firm can go to the capital market. There are two main types of security which it may offer. First, it may sell *bonds* or *debentures*. In this case the firm in effect sells to the public a promise to repay the amount lent at some future date, say, in five or ten years' time, depending on the date of maturity of the bond, and also to pay a fixed rate of interest annually, *irrespective of profits made during the year*. It follows that the sale of bonds is very much like obtaining a bank loan, except that the lender in this case is a member of the general public. Bond-holders are therefore *creditors* of the company and in the event of failure to make payment could force the firm into bankruptcy: they are not in any sense part-owners of the concern.

The difficulty of financing itself in this way is that the firm is saddling itself with an obligation to pay irrespective of its financial situation at the time. It puts itself into an inflexible situation where a temporary crisis could force it into bankruptcy, if its debenture obligations are too large.

For that reason the company will also issue *shares*, which give it more flexibility. Shareholders are the owners of the concern and, unlike creditors, earn income only if the firm is doing reasonably well. Thus they receive dividends only if profits remain after creditors, including bond-holders, have been paid, and then only at the discretion of the board of directors. It is for this reason that shares are a more 'risky' investment for the buyer than bonds. The same also applies in the event of the firm having to be liquidated, in which case it is not only current income which is in danger but the original capital invested.

Two kinds of such risk capital stock may be distinguished, *preference shares* (preferred stock) and *ordinary shares* (common stock). The latter are commonly referred to as *equities*. If there are profits for distribution, preference shareholders will be paid next after the debenture bond-holders, but at a specific rate of dividend, say, 7 per cent of the nominal value of their preferred shareholding.[4] Ordinary shares have no such upper limit and dividends can be increased if the firm is doing well. On the other hand, ordinary shareholders are residual claimants,

the last in the 'queue': they get what is left for distribution after, first, the creditors, including the debenture bond-holders, and, second, the preference shareholders. The fixed dividends paid to preference shareholders are normally higher than the interest rate offered on debenture bonds but lower than the average yield on ordinary shares, as befits their intermediate position as far as risk of loss of income and capital is concerned. Equities carry the greatest risk of going empty-handed if profits are low, and stand the best chance of high remuneration if profits are good. Thus ordinary shares are more risky than preference shares, and preference shares are more risky than bonds. The more risky the security, however, the higher the expected remuneration if the general public are to purchase them. The issue for sale of new ordinary stock will normally be a more expensive means of finance, since it carries a higher yield. The advantage to the board of directors is that it offers flexibility and passes over to the subscribers to the new shares a share of the risk of the enterprise.

The directors will therefore need to weigh cheapness against flexibility in deciding on the ratio of share capital and loan capital to be raised by the firm. This ratio, in turn, affects the degree of risk attached to the purchase of equities in a company. Suppose two companies, A and B, have raised the same amount of capital, A selling relatively more debentures and preference shares and B more ordinary shares. The position might be as follows:

	A	B
Debenture stocks	50	10
Preference shares	30	20
Ordinary shares	20	70
	100	100

The units represent thousands of pounds of securities issued. If the two firms do equally well, ordinary shareholders will be better off in Company A if profits are high and in Company B if profits are low. This is because if profits are high, the majority of security holders in A will still earn only fixed interest or a limited rate of dividend, leaving the bulk of distributed profits to be shared out among £20,000 worth of equities. Each ordinary share will therefore carry high earnings. If profits are low, on the other hand, the probability is that in Company A they will be fully absorbed in payments to debenture and preference shareholders who have first claim. In Company B, however, where there are only £30,000 worth of such claimants altogether, the chances of there remaining some profits for distribution among the equity-holders are much greater. Company A, with a high ratio of 'prior-charge' securities (debentures and preference shares) to equities, is said to be *highly geared* and Company B, with a low ratio, to be *low-geared.* Thus for any given level of expected profits, ordinary shares are more risky in a highly geared company, but also carry a better chance of high remuneration, than ordinary shares in a low-geared company.

The amount of finance that the firm can raise through the capital market will be strictly limited: that is to say, the firm will not be able to sell any volume of securities. This is because people buy shares in order to earn dividends, and the level of dividends in the near future will be closely related to the earning power of the firm; this earning power will, in turn, be related to the existing stock of assets owned by the firm. Moreover, if borrowing by the sale of securities is considered excessive, confidence in the company may be reduced; since the public is in effect lending to the company, it will also require that the company possesses realizable assets as 'collateral' against the sums it borrows. ·

Finance and the growth of the firm

Together with retained profits, shares and debentures have the major advantage that they represent *long-term finance.* Trade credit, trade bills, and bank loans are all essentially short-term. The distinction is fundamental, since the two types of finance may not be able to serve the same functions: while short-term finance will tend to be limited in usefulness to covering the cost of *working* capital, financing turnover, long-term finance can permit 'fixed' investment, including physical expansion of machines and buildings. The possibility of switching from purely short-term financing to long-term funds therefore represents a critical point in the development of the firm. This 'gap' in the availability of finance is particularly important in underdeveloped countries, where the capital market is not fully developed. It helps to explain the difficulty of developing indigenous firms, and the tendency for expatriate firms to predominate, since they are capable of deriving part of their finance from outside the country. It partly explains why governments have felt a greater need in these countries to supplement the flow of private capital investment by public enterprise and investment. This is due to the fact that the lack of local finance means that local firms tend to be restricted to activities involving less capital, such as retailing and road transport, rather than to enter mining or large-scale manufacturing. In some East African countries, Uganda and Tanzania in particular, the injection of capital into industrial enterprises by the government, through the medium of a national development corporation, has been the main force in the expansion of the manufacturing sector.

If we return now to our discussion of the size of the firm, we see that all the main sources of finance for the firm are strictly finite in any given period, including bank credit, retained profits, and funds raised through the sale of securities on the capital market. On the other hand, firms will be able to grow, 'ploughing back' retained profits, especially as retained profits add to the 'worth' of the firm and make it easier to obtain further credit from the banks or capital market. We can therefore distinguish two elements in the growth of the firm, the development of the managerial structure, and the accumulation of finance. Since firms will be in different stages of growth, the size of firms may vary considerably at any moment of time. This suggests also that, particularly in developing countries, development will come not only through increase in the number of firms of a given size, but through the growth of existing firms.

Growth of firms by merger and take-over

The process of growth of a firm can be, and often is, rapidly accelerated by 'amalgamation' (merger) with another firm or the 'take-over' of another firm. Whether firms amalgamate or merge to form an entirely new enterprise or one firm takes over by purchase of the capital assets of others, the result is usually a larger-sized business unit or firm, but not necessarily any change in the number and size of establishments in the industry, which may actually be reduced. The number of *business units* in the industry may well be reduced by a series of mergers or take-overs, of course, resulting in a reduction in the degree of competition and increased monopoly power. The motives for amalgamation may in fact be *either* (1) increased monopoly power (advantages of market domination) *or* (2) real economies of scale.

Since monopoly power is discussed more fully in the next chapter, we may say a little more here on the real economies to be achieved through mergers. Growth by amalgamation may involve either (1) vertical integration or (2) horizontal integration or (3) diversification, all yielding some form of economies of scale.

Vertical integration refers to mergers between firms in different stages of the production process. *Backward* integration may be undertaken to ensure a firm's supply of raw materials or other inputs, as when a large tyre manufacturer like Firestone, say, acquires rubber plantations or a firm with an agricultural processing factory or cannery purchases sugar or wattle plantations or pineapple estates to secure a more even and larger throughput of produce. *Forward* integration takes place when the movement is towards the market: when, for example, petroleum companies or breweries take over petrol stations or hotels, or a manufacturing company takes over wholesale and retail firms. We might mention here that, apart from the motives of ensuring the volume or quality of supplies or market outlets (real economies), vertical integration may be undertaken in order to *increase* competition: thus in Kenya, especially, the long-established producer cooperative associations have been under regular pressure from their members, originally European farmers, to eliminate 'middlemen' or control the prices and profit margins of retailers. Some of the largest 'firms' in Kenya are in fact the vertically integrated processing–marketing cooperatives covering saw-milling, dairy produce, coffee, or pig meat.

Horizontal integration between firms in the same stage of production is much more likely to be directly motivated by the desire to buy out competition in the same line of business, but may also aim at securing real economies. If there is 'excess capacity' in an industry, which is frequently the case in various kinds of retailing, road transport, and some service trades such as garages or hotels, a merger may enable a larger firm to close down and sell off part of the 'plant', operating the remainder to full capacity and thus reducing costs, a process generally referred to as 'rationalization' of capacity. Some of the largest private firms in East Africa have developed through horizontal integration. In Kenya the most notable examples are perhaps East African Breweries Ltd, the largest local public company in terms of capital employed, which amalgamated with its main competitor in the early 1960s, and Mackenzie-Dalgety Ltd, the import-export merchants.

The difference between diversification and horizontal or vertical integration is that the firms taken over or amalgamating may be in different and even unrelated lines of business. This may occur without any real advantages, if large firms have substantial profits which they wish to reinvest in industry or commerce, in any suitable and profitable line of activity; or it may be aimed at spreading the risks associated with investment, a genuine economy of scale, by having interests in a number of lines which are not likely all to be depressed at the same time. A highly diversified 'conglomerate' with widely spread interests is often centred on an investment holding company which has a controlling interest in other firms which continue to operate as individual enterprises with some 'outside' shareholders.

Such conglomerate enterprises may expand so that they have interests not only in widely separated industries but also in a large number of different countries, becoming in effect 'multinational' companies. These draw their capital and management from a variety of nations and move in and out of firms and countries as trading and financial circumstances dictate. Many of these operate in a number of African countries under a regional East or West African directorate, but with links with parent boards of directors in Europe, North America, or Asia. The implications of the existence of very large, multinational companies are discussed in the next chapter.

Capital shortages for indigenous firms

We have seen above how firms can obtain capital for their own growth and expansion. Existing firms have a distinct advantage over new entrants to an industry in raising both long-term and short-term finance, in that they possess real capital assets which can be used as security for new loans, as well as being able to plough back their own profits. In Africa this advantage is reinforced by the imperfect nature of the local capital markets, since businesses operating in the 'modern' sectors have access to banks and other financial institutions which are prepared to supply finance at rates of interest considerably lower than those charged to small indigenous firms, including peasant farmers. 'Modern sector' rates of interest are often kept down by government policy, either because of the desire to finance public sector borrowing as cheaply as possible for budgetary reasons or because it is considered necessary to foster a larger volume of development projects. There is normally little connection between the 'modern' and 'indigenous' capital markets, so that quite distinct levels of interest rate can be perpetuated. Even within the modern sector the large well-established business, often foreign-owned, can borrow much more easily and at the lowest interest rates because it is a 'good risk', while smaller firms find it much more difficult, as well as more expensive, to obtain finance. Most important, however, is the ability of foreign-owned firms to obtain funds from abroad either directly from or through their own parent companies. This 'dichotomy' or division in the capital market, giving indigenous firms poorer access to finance, is bound to affect their growth, and leave the field of large-scale enterprise to large international concerns, keeping the firms small in size and restricting their operations to activities suited to small-scale enterprise.

In West Africa, especially, the indigenous businessmen have long criticized the expatriate banks and foreign suppliers of credit for not helping them enough. At the same time a study of Nigerian government loan schemes for local businessmen suggested that much of this 'capital shortage' is an illusion: that in fact there is really a shortage of viable private investment projects which would benefit from public loan funds.[5] While Nigeria may now have passed this early development phase, this indicates the importance of relating any firm's capital requirements to its other available resources, particularly its management skills and technical expertise, as well as the general business environment in which the firm operates.

Horizontal integration between firms in the same stage of production is much more likely to be directly motivated by the desire to buy out competition in the same line of business, but may also aim at securing real economies.

The capital market and the stock market

Although stocks and bonds represent long-term finance from the point of view of the firm receiving the funds, they need not mean a long-term investment by individual members of the public who acquire them. The reason is that stocks and bonds can be freely traded among members of the public *after issue by the firm*. The 'market' in which existing stocks and bonds are exchanged is referred to as the stock market. This is in contrast to the *capital market in which new capital is raised*, that is to say, new stocks and bonds are sold.

As far as bonds are concerned, a person buying a bond receives a promise of repayment by the firm at the maturity date, and not before. He can, however, obtain cash by selling it to another member of the public who is willing to 'take over' the loan to the firm. A shareholder can similarly sell his shares to someone else. In either case, however, the holder must accept the price he can get, that is, the market price. The price of a share will depend on the purchaser's assessment of the prospects—the future earning power of the company—since this determines how much it will be able to hand out as dividends. Opinions as to these prospects will fluctuate and so, consequently, will the market price, the latter taking a low value if there is lack of confidence in the firm's prospects, and vice versa. Since the market price of stock fluctuates, a shareholder may make a *capital gain* in addition to receiving dividends if he buys a share cheaply before it increases in value. Equally, of course, he may make a capital loss. The *effective* rate of return on a share should therefore be taken as:

$$\frac{\text{dividend received plus change in market value during year}}{\text{amount paid for stock}}$$

It is the *expected* value of this ratio which will determine whether or not the potential buyer 'lends' his money to the firm. The expression 'capital market' suggests the place where money capital is traded, where borrowers are willing to lend at a price. This is

the origin of the loanable funds theory of the rate of interest, in which the rate of interest is determined by the supply of and demand for loanable funds.

Types of business organization in Eastern Africa

Since both the managerial structure and the supply of finance are closely bound up with the type of business organization, let us look briefly at the main types of business operating in Eastern Africa. It hardly needs emphasizing that the most common type of business unit is the *single proprietorship* of the small farmer or other self-employed worker, but only a tiny minority of such proprietorships are included in the registers of business names kept by the public authorities. For instance at the end of 1972 in Kenya there were only 51,737 business names on the Registrar-General's register of single proprietors and unincorporated partnerships, so that practically all small rural enterprises, including traders as well as small farmers, though probably exceeding 2 millions in number, were not registered. In addition there were 9,277 limited companies registered, making a total of around 60,000 or so firms actively engaged in the 'modern' sector. Of this total only about 15 per cent, therefore, enjoyed the advantages of limited liability. An even smaller percentage, about 1 per cent, were public companies, numbering some 600 firms. Only about 60 of these had ordinary or preference shares quoted on the Nairobi Stock Exchange. A mere handful, therefore, of Kenya's private firms had direct access to finance by public issue of shares.

It is not difficult to see why this should be so. On the supply side, the volume of private savings available for investment in the stocks and shares of local companies is limited by the low level of income. Only a minority of the population, until recently mainly non-African, could afford to hold financial assets at all, and of these the Asian community were mainly concerned in direct investment in their own private companies or unincorporated businesses. The European residents, moreover, being much less settled in the country, tended to hold financial assets abroad, investing their savings through London or other overseas stock markets.

Secondly, on the demand side, the structure of the Eastern African economies as they stood, being largely based on agriculture and service activities, did not require many large joint stock enterprises where ownership could be divorced from management. Agriculture and trading are typically small-scale industries in most countries, particularly in countries like Uganda or Ghana where labour-intensive techniques are suitable for growing cotton, coffee, or cocoa, and where markets are dispersed.

A third factor was the availability of foreign capital to finance large-scale enterprises, whether tea or sisal estates, mining, manufacturing, or export-import businesses. Among the 9,277 limited companies on the Kenya register in 1972, and normally much the larger by average size, were some 500 foreign-owned *private* companies. Access to foreign capital markets permitted risk capital to be invested by foreign firms in local subsidiary private companies. Many of these are much larger than local public companies, since they include the subsidiaries of foreign banks, petroleum and chemical companies, some of the large-scale estates and processing factories, some of the large engineering and metal product firms, and civil engineering contractors. Of the 605 establishments covered by the 1967 Kenya Census of Industrial Production (excluding very small firms) only 39 were registered public companies, with mainly local residents' capital, compared with 316 private companies, which included the bulk of the 433 establishment mainly or wholly owned by non-citizens.

In other Eastern African countries the injection of capital into manufacturing industries has depended heavily on government intervention through the medium of national development corporations in Uganda, Tanzania, and Zambia. A quite different structure of the 'firm' is evolving in the latter two as the state, through its development corporations, takes over the functions of management, in part, as well as the supply of finance. In Chapter 18 we shall consider further the state's role in developing and controlling business enterprises.

Questions on Chapter 16

1. Distinguish the various categories of 'scale economies'. Give examples of each.
2. What factors limit the size of the establishment? What factors limit the size of the firm?
3. List the conditions required for perfect competition and discuss the significance of each for the competitive equilibrium model.
4. Why is it only in the 'long run' that perfect competition yields an 'optimum allocation of resources'? What happens in the short term?
5. Why is it appropriate to call the long-run average cost curve a 'planning curve'?
6. How do (a) the Law of Variable Proportions, and (b) increasing and decreasing returns to scale, affect the firm's cost curves?
7. What is the significance of the 'minimum viable' size of establishment for developing countries?
8. Use data for your own country to distinguish industries which

are predominantly large-, medium-, and small-scale.

9. Why do you think it is possible to have establishments of very different sizes within the same industry?
10. What is 'the receding managerial limit'? Discuss its significance.
11. Discuss the importance of limited liability.
12. What are the main sources of finance for the firm? Why are these sources of supply of funds not unlimited?
13. What is 'gearing'? What kinds of industry permit highly geared corporate structures?
14. What is the difference between the 'capital market' and the 'stock market'?
15. What determines the price of a share?
16. Describe the main types of business organization found in your country, and account for their relative importance in (a) agricultural, (b) mining and manufacturing, and (c) distribution activities.

Notes

[1] Mathematically we can write this as follows:

Total revenue, R, is a function of output, Q, as is total cost, C. Profits equal P, the difference:

$$P = R - C = R(Q) - C(Q).$$

Differentiating with respect to Q, we have

$$\frac{dP}{dQ} = \frac{dR}{dQ} - \frac{dC}{dQ} = 0 \text{ at a maximum,}$$

that is, (1) $\dfrac{dR}{dQ} = \dfrac{dC}{dQ}$,

or, marginal revenue = marginal cost.

Differentiating again with respect to Q

$$\frac{d^2P}{dQ^2} = \frac{d^2R}{dQ^2} - \frac{d^2C}{dQ^2} < 0 \text{ for a maximum,}$$

that is, (2) $\dfrac{d^2R}{dQ^2} < \dfrac{d^2C}{dQ^2}$,

or marginal cost increases faster than marginal revenue as output, Q, increases.

Conditions (1) and (2) are referred to respectively as the first and second order conditions for a maximum.

[2] If there is 'perfect knowledge', as under perfect competition, these expectations will necessarily be fulfilled since the entrepreneur will make no mistakes.

[3] E. T. Penrose, *The Theory of the Growth of the Firm*, Blackwell, 1959.

[4] Some preference shares rank higher than others for payment of fixed dividends. Cumulative preference shares of, say, 8 per cent, provide for a deferment of all or part of the dividend if profits are too low, provided the deficiency is made up later to maintain the 'cumulative' rate averaging 8 per cent.

[5] S. P. Schatz, 'The Capital Shortage Illusion: Government Lending in Nigeria', *Oxford Economic Papers*, Vol. 17, No. 2, 1965.

The behaviour of firms, the various decisions they have to take, are very much affected by the market situation in which they find themselves. We shall therefore examine now the effects of monopoly on the firm's output and price, compared to the competitive situation.

Single-firm monopoly

The essence of monopoly power is the ability to limit the supply of a product and thus to control its price. The firm is no longer simply a price-taker, as under competition, but is also a price-*maker*.

This power comes from producing a substantial share of the output of one product. When we discussed the market demand curve for a product, we found that it would generally be downward-sloping. That is to say, consumers will require the inducement of a lower price if they are to accept increasing quantities of the product. But if there is only *one* firm producing the product, the firm's demand curve will be identical with market demand, and will slope down. Suppose, for example, a single firm controls all commercial production of cotton dresses within a region: the demand curve for the firm's dresses might be as in Figure 17.1.

In such a situation the monopolist can obviously raise the market price (his price) by restricting the amount he produces. But how far it pays him to restrict supply will depend on the elasticity of demand. Suppose, for the sake of illustration, the monopolist has no costs, so that the whole of revenue

is profit. *So long as elasticity of demand is less than one* he can increase total revenue by reducing output. It would not pay him to reduce output beyond the point where elasticity is one: since total revenue is constant at that point, marginal revenue is zero. If the monopolist's demand curve is very elastic this point will be reached very quickly. The important thing is therefore not the existence of some control over price, but the *degree* of monopoly control. And this will depend entirely on how inelastic demand is.

This elasticity, as we noted in Chapter 6, depends on the available substitutes for the product. In our example, even if the firm in question is the only commercial producer of cotton dresses in the region, dresses made in other fabrics might be available; or cotton dresses imported from abroad; or women could make their own at home; or they could make the dresses they buy last longer and buy less frequently—thus spending their money on completely different things, such as going to the cinema!

Moreover, whether a firm is the 'sole producer' of a product, of course, depends entirely on how we define the product. Thus Ford Company are the only producers of Ford cars, but they are not the sole producers of cars. How important the 'monopoly' of Ford cars is to them clearly depends on how distinct, in the eyes of consumers, Ford cars are from all the other available makes. We should therefore stress, again, that what is important is the elasticity of demand for the firm's product.

Monopoly price and output

A businessman will tend to select the level of output which gives him maximum profits. This is true whether he finds himself in a monopolistic position or in a competitive one. After all, he is presumably *in* business for the sake of earning income. Businessmen will not all, of course, pursue the goal of 'profit maximization' with the same energy. Some will spend less time working out carefully the best output to produce or price to charge in order to have more time to play golf or to spend in the company of their families. It seems reasonable to assume, however, that businessmen try to maximize profits, even if this is only a statement of tendency.

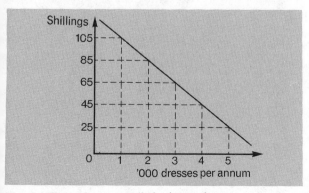

Figure 17.1 A monopolist's demand curve.

Which output and price a businessman selects will be determined jointly by his costs at different levels of output and the demand for his product. Suppose the relationships between costs and output are given in Columns 1 to 4 in Table 17.1 and the demand position is given in Column 5 which states the price at which consumers are willing to buy the full amounts produced. Column 3 (average costs) is obtained simply by dividing Column 2 (total costs) by Column 1 (output). Column 4 (marginal costs) is obtained from Column 2 by comparing total costs for successive levels of output. Thus since total costs are 50,000 shillings when one thousand dresses are produced and rise to 80,000 shillings when two thousand dresses are produced, the marginal cost of the second thousand dresses is 30,000 shillings. It will be noticed that marginal and average cost are equal at 30 shillings, for an output of 6,000 dresses per annum, and that average cost reaches a minimum at this point. This accords with the assertion earlier in our discussion of the firm, that marginal and average values are equal when the average has a minimum value.

Column 5 indicates that the businessman is in a monopolistic position and 'has a downward-sloping demand curve'. In order to sell increasing outputs, he has to reduce his price; conversely by restricting his output, he can keep the price of his product up. Multiplying the number of dresses sold by the price obtained, we get total revenue in Column 6. Thus if 3,000 dresses are sold, the price is 65s and total revenue 195,000 shillings. Marginal revenue (Column 7) is then obtained from total revenue in the usual way.

Profits will be maximized when marginal cost and marginal revenue are equal. Comparing Columns 4 and 7, we see that marginal cost and revenue are each equal to 25s when output is 3,000. At this level of output, profits are 90,000 shillings, as shown in Column 8. Column 8 is obtained by subtracting total cost (Column 2) from total revenue (Column 6). Alternatively since average cost at this level of output is 35s and average revenue (price) 65s, profit per unit is 30s, and since 3,000 dresses are produced, total profits are 90,000 shillings.

Figure 17.2 illustrates the position in terms of total cost and revenue. So long as the TR curve lies above TC, profits are being made.

Profits are measured in this diagram by the *vertical distance* between the two curves. Once the TC curve lies above the TR curve, losses are being made. Where they intersect, at an output of 4,750, the firm is just 'breaking even'. The excess of TR over TC can be seen to be at a maximum at an output of 3,000.

However, since it is not always easy to pick out from this diagram just where the vertical distance between the two curves is greatest (indeed the distance happens to be equally great at output 2,000 in this example), equilibrium is more easily shown in a diagram such as Figure 17.3, incorporating marginal curves.

In this diagram the profit-maximizing output is indicated unambiguously by the intersection of the marginal curve (MR) and the marginal cost curve (MC), when output is OS($=3,000$). At this level of output, price (average revenue) is equal to PS, P being on the demand curve, and average cost is QS, Q being on the average cost curve. The difference PQ is therefore the profit per unit ($=30$s), and since MP ($=$OS) units are produced, total profits are given by the area of the rectangle MPQN ($=30 \times 3,000 = 90,000$s).

Table 17.1 *Determination of price and output by a monopolist*

Column 1	Column 2	Column 3	Column 4	Column 5	Column 6	Column 7	Column 8
Output (×1,000 dresses)	Total costs (×1,000 shs)	Average costs (shs)	Marginal costs (shs)	Price obtainable (shs)	Total revenue (×1,000 shs)	Marginal revenue (shs)	Profits (×1,000 shs)
0	0	—	—	—	0	—	0
1	50	50	50	105	105	105	55
2	80	40	30	85	170	65	90
3	105	35	25	65	195	25	90
4	126	31.5	21	45	180	−15	54
5	150	30	24	27	135	−45	−15
6	180	30	30	7	42	−93	−138
7	220	31.5	40	—	—	—	—
8	280	35	60	—	—	—	—
9	370	41	90	—	—	—	—
10	520	52	150	—	—	—	—

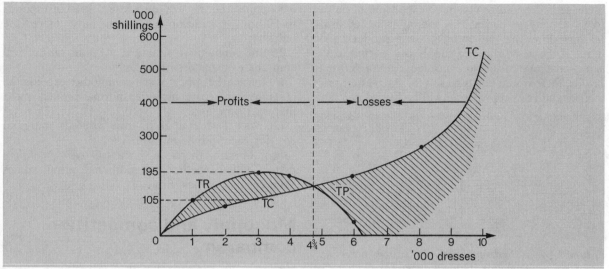

Figure 17.2   *Total cost and revenue.*

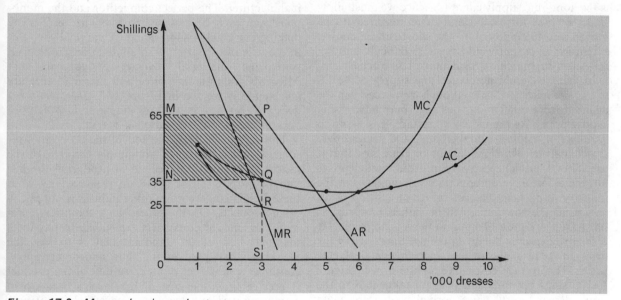

Figure 17.3   *Monopoly price and output.*

Supply under competition

Before making some comparisons with the situation in a competitive industry let us examine more closely the conditions of supply in such an industry. Under competition price is determined by supply and demand, the supply coming from a large number of firms. The actual number of firms will depend on the 'optimum' or most economic size of firm relative to the volume of market demand.

An increase in demand for the commodity in question will result in more resources, labour, land, and capital, being diverted into that industry from other parts of the economy. This diversion will take the form of more firms *of the same size* entering the industry: there is no reason for the economic size of firm to change as the industry expands. If the additional firms could come into the industry with the same operating costs as existing firms the supply curve would be horizontal, implying completely elastic supply, as shown in Figure 17.4. Figure 17.4(a) shows the cost situation for an individual firm, the optimum size of firm being one which produces 50 units of output per period. Since output for the industry, shown in Figure 17.4(b), is initially 5,000 units, we started with 100 firms in the industry. An increase in demand results in an expansion of output to 8,000 units per period, this coming from 160 firms, 60 new firms having entered, each producing 50 units. If the new firms can supply this output at the same cost and also earn no more than 'normal' profits, there would be no reason for the market price to rise, and the supply curve will be horizontal. This

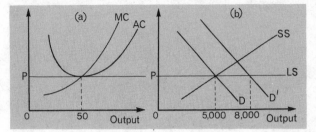

Figure 17.4 *A horizontal industry supply curve: (a) individual firm's supply, (b) competitive industry's supply.*

is the 'long-run' supply curve LS, since we must allow sufficient time for capital and other resources to be moved into the industry. In the short run, of course, expansion of output would be more difficult, and the short-run supply curve SS is made less elastic.

In fact we should not expect the supply curve LS to be completely elastic: though resources can be diverted from other industries they may have rising supply prices. As the industry expands it is likely to find labour, capital, and perhaps land increasingly scarce, particularly if the labour or land, say, that it uses is of a specialized type. Since the market prices for these factors of production will go up for the industry *as a whole* the cost curves of existing firms, as well as the new firms, will be shifted upwards, as illustrated in Figure 17.5. Again there is no particular reason to expect a change in the optimum size of the firm, unless it is due to a change in relative factor prices. The average cost curve for the firm in Figure 17.5(a) shifts upwards and is again tangential to the firm's demand curve since normal profits are again earned. The equilibrium price shown in Figure 17.5(b) is higher.[1] Since output for the industry is

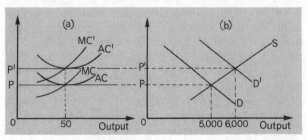

Figure 17.5 *A rising industry supply curve: (a) increase in costs of firm, (b) competitive industry's supply.*

6,000 units and the size of each firm still corresponds to 50 units, an additional 20 firms have entered the industry.

In this competitive situation, we note, output will continue to expand so long as:

(1) the market price of the commodity exceeds the costs (average costs, including normal profits) of the marginal firm, and

(2) price (=marginal revenue) exceeds marginal cost for each individual firm.

In equilibrium, therefore, *price will equal marginal cost of output* whether the additional output comes from existing or new firms.

Monopoly and competition compared

Let us compare this result with the position in Figure 17.3, depicting the activities of our monopolist dress manufacturer. The perfect competitor and the monopolist can each be assumed to maximize profits, by making marginal revenue equal to marginal cost. But in the case of the latter, with a falling demand curve, price and marginal revenue diverge, so that MR = MC implies that price and marginal cost are *not* equal, as we see in Figure 17.3. *The monopolist does not therefore expand his output so long as price exceeds the cost of the marginal output.*

This implies a misallocation of the economy's resources. 'Marginal costs' are simply the cost of the factors of production used up in producing the last unit of output. These costs are measured by what these factors could earn in other industries, supplying other products. On the other hand, the price represents the amount consumers are willing to pay for a marginal unit of the product, that is to say, the valuation they put on it. Thus under monopoly, consumer's valuation of an extra unit of the product is greater than the cost of the factors used up in producing it. The extra unit is nevertheless not produced because it pays the monopolist not to produce it. Under competition no such discrepancy results, and price equals marginal cost. *This condition, price equal to marginal cost, is in fact the condition for the 'optimum' allocation of resources within the economy.* Under monopoly, therefore, too little of the product is produced and insufficient resources are allocated to producing it. Correspondingly, these resources are diverted to producing other products which are produced in 'too great' quantities.

Apart from this, supernormal profits are made, equal to the rectangle MPQN in Figure 17.3. But normal profits measure the market valuation of the entrepreneur's services, the price of these services in a free market. Supernormal profits are for this reason said to produce an unfair, as well as unequal, distribution of income. Moreover, since these profits may be 'ploughed back' into the firm, they may give the monopoly firm an advantage in the supply of finance, permitting it subsequently to gain an even greater monopoly advantage. As we shall see in the next section the earning of supernormal profits depends on there being obstacles to prevent other firms from entering the industry.

It follows also from the fact that 'too little' of the monopolized commodity is produced that, given the demand, its price will be higher than it otherwise would be. However there is no particular significance in this, since it is a direct consequence of 'too little' output, which is the basic deficiency.

Looking back to Figure 17.3 again we note that the monopolist will not produce at the minimum point on his average cost curve, but will produce a smaller output than that which minimizes his average costs of production. This result is often misinterpreted: the firm is alleged to operate with 'excess capacity', with the 'wrong' output for the size of plant, which is underutilized. The error here is that the statement is based on an interpretation of the firm's cost curve as a *short-run* (plant) cost curve. To make the most meaningful comparison between competition and monopoly, however, we need to consider the long-run position. In the first place if there were a misallocation of resources in the short run, this might not be serious if it were corrected in a longer period; and, secondly, monopolies are not temporary, but tend to persist, in the absence of government intervention.

The average cost curve in question should therefore be interpreted as the long-run curve, such as discussed on page 226 in Chapter 16. Since the monopolist may be assumed to be keen to maximize his monopolist's profits there is no reason to think he will unnecessarily 'waste' capacity. The monopolist will restrict his output, certainly, but will select the best size of plant for the smaller output. By producing that output in the cheapest way possible he will be maximizing his profits. Here again, therefore, the basic point is that output is restricted, and resources are not allocated optimally.

Another way of comparing competition and monopoly, a more direct one, is to imagine a competitive industry, comprising a large number of small single-plant firms, being taken over by one company. For the sake of simplicity it can be assumed that costs are unaffected by the take-over, there being no opportunities for rationalization of production among the plants, nor any additional costs due to increased managerial burdens from centralized direction of the industry.

The cost position of the monopolist would be given by the competitive supply curve derived as before from average plant costs at different levels of output for the industry: the industry's output now being also the monopolist's output. Since the demand curve for the industry is also the firm's demand curve, and slopes down, the marginal revenue curve will lie below it. Similarly, since the average cost curve slopes up, there will be a corresponding marginal cost curve lying above it. Marginal cost will exceed average here because the monopolist will expand output by bringing additional plants into operation. Although each plant he uses will have the same costs, and although he will continue to employ the same plants of optimum size as under competition, as output expands the average costs of all plants will increase due to rising supply prices of factors. Hence when an additional plant is brought into use not only will its costs be greater, but the average costs of plants *already in use* will increase.

Equilibrium output for the monopolist will be given by the intersection of the MC and MR curves. This is illustrated in Figure 17.6(b), in which the competitive supply curve, S_c, is equated with the monopolist's average cost curve AC_m, and the demand curve for the industry, D_c, is also the monopolist's demand curve, D_m. The features of this equilibrium are that output is less than in the competitive case; monopoly price, P_m, is greater than the competitive price, P_c, given by the intersection of supply and demand curves; and supernormal profits are earned (shaded), since price exceeds average costs. As before the monopolist will try to produce his output in the cheapest way possible; but output will be less than in the competitive case. This point is emphasized in Figure 17.6(a), which shows the level of average costs for an individual plant. The level of production in each plant is as in the competitive case: but the number of plants in operation will be fewer,[2] producing an aggregate Q_m instead of the competitive industry's output, Q_c, in Figure 17.6(b).

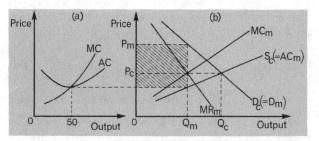

Figure 17.6 *The effect of monopolistic take-over in a competitive industry: (a) average plant costs, (b) price and output comparison for industry.*

Elasticity of demand and the degree of monopoly power

A monopolist is able to raise the price of his product by restricting output. How far restriction of output is successful in raising price obviously depends on the elasticity of demand for the product. If in Figure 17.3, we drew very much less steep MR and AR curves, we should derive a much lower monopoly price and *more significantly a narrower gap between price and marginal cost* at the monopoly output. Since slope is not a good measure of elasticity, however, it is better to derive this result directly in terms of elasticity.

It can be shown without too much difficulty[3] that marginal revenue, price, and elasticity are related as follows:

$$\frac{\Delta R}{\Delta q} = P(1 - 1/e_D)$$

If we denote total costs by C, and marginal cost by $\frac{\Delta C}{\Delta q}$, the profit-maximizing monopolist would put marginal cost equal to marginal revenue:

$$\frac{\Delta C}{\Delta q} = \frac{\Delta R}{\Delta q}$$

This would give:

$$(1) \quad \frac{\Delta C}{\Delta q} = P(1 - 1/e_D)$$

implying

$$(2) \quad P \left/ \frac{\Delta C}{\Delta q} \right. = \frac{1}{1 - 1/e_D}$$

or

$$(3) \quad P = \frac{e_D}{e_D - 1} \cdot \frac{\Delta C}{\Delta q}$$

Under perfect competition, e_D would be infinity, so that $1/e_D$ is zero, and from (1), price equals marginal cost, confirming the result we obtained graphically. From (3) it can be seen for example that if $e_D = \frac{5}{4}$, $P = 5\frac{\Delta C}{\Delta Q}$; if $e_D = 2$, $P = 2\frac{\Delta C}{\Delta q}$; if $e_D = 6$, $P = 1.2\frac{\Delta C}{\Delta q}$; and if $e_D = 21$, $P = 1.05\frac{\Delta C}{\Delta q}$. Thus *as the elasticity of demand increases in value, price approaches the value of marginal cost; the lower the value of elasticity, the greater the divergence between price and marginal cost, and therefore the greater the degree of misallocation of resources caused by the monopoly.*

We may, in passing, comment on some impli-cations of the relationship $\frac{\Delta R}{\Delta q} = P(1 - \frac{1}{e_D})$. If $e_D = 1$, then $\frac{\Delta R}{\Delta q} = 0$. But if marginal revenue is nought, then total revenue must be constant. Hence if the elasticity of demand is unity, total revenue (consumer outlay) is constant.

Secondly, if e_D is less than one, $\frac{\Delta R}{\Delta q}$ will be negative. It follows that *a monopolist will never produce at levels of output where the elasticity of demand is less than one.* This is because while we can assume marginal cost is *always* positive, marginal revenue would be negative and hence less than marginal cost: output should be reduced.

Monopoly and incentive

The absence of free entry under monopoly has provoked some further criticisms. It is sometimes alleged that, whereas under competition a firm will be forced to maintain its efficiency if it is to survive at all, under monopoly the ease with which supernormal profits, let alone normal profits, can be made will encourage the entrepreneur to relax. The resulting inefficiency will mean higher costs of operation and therefore waste of resources.

Secondly, it is pointed out that under competition the application of more modern and more efficient methods of production by one firm will soon need to be followed by the other firms, if they are to survive. If the monopolist is already making good profits, on the other hand, he may have less incentive to invent or apply new methods of production. This will also mean that costs will remain at higher levels than is necessary.

Monopolistic competition

The making of supernormal profits under monopoly is dependent on the assumption of restricted entry into the industry. Even if the firm's demand curve is downward-sloping, however, it does not follow that there are significant obstacles to entry. In small-scale industries, especially, each firm may collect together a group of customers who prefer its product to others, as in the case of retailing, say, or motor-repair garages. These firms could vary their prices without immediately losing all their customers, as would happen under perfect competition. Yet entry into the industry is free, and it is comparatively easy to find the finance required to open a shop or start a motor-repair business.

Suppose, in Figure 17.7(a), SS and DD refer to the market supply of and demand for 'retail goods' respectively. The price of retail goods would be OP.

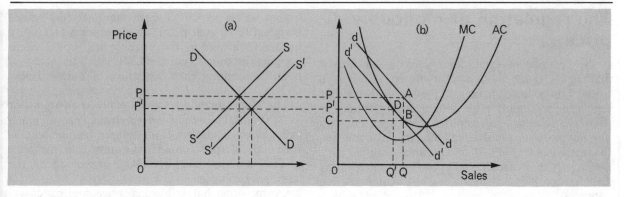

Figure 17.7 *Monopolistic competition with free entry: (a) market supply and demand, (b) individual supply and demand.*

Suppose initially the number of firms in the industry was such that the demand for a particular retailer's goods was given by the curve dd in Figure 17.7(b). By producing output OQ, the retailer could make a profit per unit of AB, and total supernormal profits of PABC. With free entry, however, these profits would attract more people into retailing, the supply of retail goods in Figure 17.7(a) would shift to S'S', causing the price to fall to OP'. At this price individual retailers could just make normal profits by producing output OQ' in Figure 17.7(b), average cost and average revenue each being equal to DQ' at this output. If normal profits were being earned, entry would cease.

This type of market situation is known as *monopolistic competition.* This is because it combines elements of competition (free entry) and of monopoly (especially the downward-sloping demand curve). Indeed monopolistic competition is often criticized just *because* it combines the disadvantages of both types of market structure. Like monopoly, the individual firm's output is restricted by its downward-sloping demand curve, so that price is kept above marginal cost, as shown in Figure 17.7(b). As we have already seen, this implies a misallocation of resources. Price does not equal marginal cost because the firm's output is restricted, each firm producing on a smaller than the optimum scale, which would be given by the minimum point on the average cost curve. At the same time, because of free entry, there are a lot of firms operating on this restricted scale. Although there are no excess profits, therefore, there is 'wasteful competition', with too many firms, each operating below the optimum size. Not only will this waste capital, but it will be wasteful of business management itself, with 'too many' people engaged in barely profitable activities like retailing.

A basic feature of monopolistic competition which permits this inefficiency is some form of *product differentiation*, creating a gap in the perfect substitutability of competitors' output. It is only because consumers perceive, or believe they perceive, differences between rival products, that product demand curves slope down at all under monopolistic competition, and the slope depends on the extent of the perceived differences. Without these, the slopes would be horizontal, and we should have perfect competition. Product differentiation results from the deliberate action of the individual producer to widen existing or contrive non-existing differences between his output and those of close competitors. This is achieved especially by registering and advertising *brand names* for the products or simply advertising the 'superior' quality of the goods and services available from specific suppliers. Advertising has been categorized as being of either the *informative* or the *persuasive* type. Informative advertising can improve the allocation of resources and increase economic efficiency: perfect competition, for instance, assumes perfect knowledge, so that improving consumer knowledge implies a step in the direction of perfect competition. Persuasive advertising, however, may imply a further waste of resources under monopolistic competition, in the following ways. First, if two or more firms spend money on advertising their products, their advertising campaigns may in large part cancel each other out, without any beneficial effect. Secondly, if the advertising is misleading it is likely to divert consumers from one producer to another without good reason, affecting the costs of output. One particular problem in developing countries is that consumers often prefer well-known brands of imported goods to a locally manufactured product, even where the latter is as good, or nearly so. Moreover large international firms are in a much better position to finance advertising campaigns to maintain hold of their markets.

The regulation of monopoly price

If the government thinks that a particular firm is making 'too much' profit or charging excessively high prices, it may decide to control monopoly directly by regulating monopoly price, setting an upper limit to the price charged. The imposition of price controls has not been uncommon in East African countries, frequently, as in 1967–71 in Tanzania, with the aim, not merely of controlling inflation, but of preventing 'exploitation' by traders or by manufacturing concerns.

In Figure 17.8, in the absence of intervention, the monopoly price would be fixed at the level OP_M and output restricted to OQ_M. If the government fixes a price ceiling, say OP_R, the former monopoly price is no longer feasible. At this price the monopolist can sell any amount he chooses up to OQ_R, the limit set by demand: but he cannot charge higher prices. His demand curve is therefore the 'bent' line P_RaD. Since the demand (average revenue) curve is horizontal up to point a, over this range marginal revenue and average revenue coincide: beyond this the 'old' demand curve aD and the corresponding marginal revenue curve bMR apply. The new marginal revenue curve thus becomes the 'kinked' one, P_RabMR. Equilibrium is where this marginal revenue equals marginal cost, at output OQ_R. It can be seen that price regulation has been highly successful: it has not only brought down the price, but *increased output*, from OQ_M to OQ_R. Since monopoly profits were at a maximum at OQ_M, it has also reduced these. And it has improved allocative efficiency by reducing average costs per unit of output.

It can be seen that price regulation could increase

output as far as OP'_R, where marginal cost equals marginal revenue at point c, and output is OQ'_R. Any further reduction in the price ceiling would cause marginal revenue to cut the LMC curve to the *left* of point c, resulting in a reduction of output below OQ'_R.

This analysis could be seen equally as an argument for a state take-over of the enterprise, just as much as for price regulation of an independent concern. A state-run enterprise could, for example, fix the price at OP'_R and sell quantity OQ'_R, improving on the monopoly solution.

On the other hand, 'blanket' price controls covering a wide range of commodities, as have been used in Tanzania, are likely to have rather haphazard effects, beneficial in some cases, and harmful perhaps in others. Before imposing price ceilings (except to combat cost-push inflation) it is necessary to know if competition is in fact absent, whether more than very moderate profits are being made, and the shape and position of the demand curve for the product involved.

Sales maximization

It has been questioned whether in fact large firms behave as restrictively as the theory of monopoly or principle of profit maximization suggest they would. The alternative hypothesis of sales maximization, subject to some minimum acceptable level of profits, has been put forward.[4]

Several reasons have been given for firms adopting such a policy. First of all long-run profit considerations might persuade firms to keep sales as large as possible. In this way the popularity of the product is maintained and the number of wholesalers and retailers handling it remains large. Alternatively it may be simply that the managers and local executives of large concerns gauge their own success in their jobs by how far they are able to expand sales, and the size of the firm. Again, given the divorce of ownership (by shareholders) and control (by executives) in large joint stock companies, the managers may have less to gain from maximizing profits and thus dividends to shareholders, than from maximizing turnover and the size of the firm; for the larger the firm the higher their own salaries are likely to be.

Clearly, however, profits cannot be ignored. These must be sufficient to pay at least a satisfactory rate of dividend to shareholders, to provide for reinvestment and growth, and to retain confidence in the financial viability of the enterprise. For this reason it was argued that sales would be maximized subject to some minimum acceptable level of profits being attained. Figure 17.9 demonstrates how this might affect business behaviour. In the upper diagram,

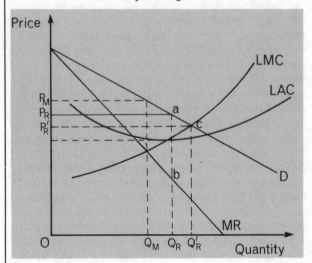

Figure 17.8 *The effect of regulation on monopoly price and output.*

profits at different levels of output are given by the vertical distance between the total revenue (TR) and total cost (TC) curves. The level of profits is further indicated by the curve PcQ, where cA equals ab, gC equals ef, and so on. The monopolist would maximize profits by selecting output OA with profits equal to cA. This differs from the output which would maximize revenue, OB. The lower diagram illustrates the monopoly equilibrium in terms of the marginal curves, and profit-maximizing output OA is that for which marginal cost equals marginal revenue (in addition AR=AC at the same output OQ as TR=TC).

Suppose, however, that the management wish to maximize sales (the *volume* of output) subject to a minimum level of profits, Oh in Figure 17.9(a). Output would be increased to OC where profits, gC, equal the minimum acceptable level. The lower diagram shows the consequences of this in terms of our criticisms of monopoly pricing. Compared to output OA, the level of output is increased, price is reduced, and profits reduced; allocative efficiency is increased in that (a) average costs are brought down towards the minimum point on the average cost curve and (b) the gap between price and marginal costs is sub-

stantially reduced (and in our illustration virtually disappears). The position in Figure 17.9(b) can be seen to be very close in appearance to our picture of a regulated monopoly in Figure 17.8. Indeed sales maximization works in much the same way, except that management now *chooses* to keep its price low and to expand its sales. How general such behaviour is, and how strong the expansionary effect is, is not yet established.

Some arguments in defence of monopoly

The main 'charges' made against monopoly were outlined above. Against these, monopoly, or large size at least, may offer certain advantages.

(1) It may be argued, first of all, that the perfectly competitive model is unrealistic, in particular its assumption of a completely elastic supply of capital. Firms become what they are only as a result of a continuous process of investment and growth of the sort described in Chapter 16. A proper comparison would involve a 'dynamic' approach involving the growth of the firm over time.

(2) A related, but more specific argument is that large firms are more likely to be able to finance expensive research, which in the end may lower costs in the industry (and therefore prices charged to the consumer) by yielding improved methods of production, or which could yield new products altogether. Competitive firms will not make sufficient profits to afford such research, and will not feel sufficiently secure in the industry to wish to make long-term and risky investment in research.

This argument involves two elements, the need for a degree of security, and the advantage of size, that is, economies of scale, in supporting research and innovation. The patent law, which has been generally adopted throughout the world, recognizes the security element and thus the necessity of offering inventors and innovators a guarantee of at least minimum profits for their inventions. A patent prevents others from imitating the product or method of production during the limited period before the patent expires. A patent therefore affords the holder a *temporary* monopoly. In the absence of this law, it might be more profitable to wait for someone *else* to introduce something new, and then to imitate it, than to spend time and money on research. Clearly, if everyone waited in this fashion, no inventions would be forthcoming. The position of a 'pioneer' firm in a developing country is not unlike that of an inventor, in that it faces special risks from being the first in the field: there may be special technical problems in operating in the tropics, or labour supply may be uncertain, or the market may need to be investigated

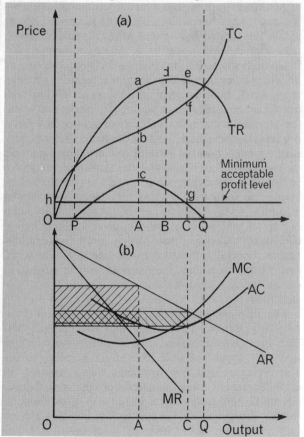

Figure 17.9 *Price and output under sales maximization.*

and developed. Perfect competition assumes, for instance, that the 'market' is given. It may be desirable, therefore, to offer pioneering firms special incentives, including freedom from competition, for a limited period, in order to guarantee a minimum degree of security and level of profitability during this time.

(3) *Research* is just one example of economies of scale which have become more important as the modern firm has developed. It has been argued that the modern firm operates in a different 'economic epoch' from those of earlier periods, and that the distinguishing feature of the modern economic epoch is 'the extended application of science to problems of economic production'.[5] Thus the *technological complexity* of modern industry has considerably expanded the scope and extent of economies of scale—even raising chickens has become technologically more complex, for instance, as a result of the battery farm! It has been suggested that the change in the nature of the firm from the small family enterprise or private company to the modern corporation has in part been associated with these technological changes: large size is more suited to modern technology.[6] As a result of these changes, the firm needs not only more capital, but more technical expertise (scientists, engineers, and other technologists) and more advanced management (involving business executives of various types). Finally, it has been suggested that economies of scale in *marketing* are more important than is often realized, and that multinational companies, with operations spread throughout the world, have significant advantages in this regard.[7] There may be economies of scale in the marketing organization itself when organized on a global basis, and there may result important advantages in the *knowledge* of markets (both for the sale of products and for the purchase of materials) and how these are progressing throughout the world.

Thus large firms, even or perhaps especially multinational concerns, although they may possess monopoly power, may also provide considerable economies and advantages of scale. The difficulty is to identify these and to separate *real economies of scale* from what may be called *advantages of domination* arising out of large size.[8]

(4) Quite a different argument is that large joint stock corporations are typically not 'restrictionist' at all, but that the first aim of these companies is growth. We have seen above that sales maximization, said by some economists to be closer to actual business objectives than profit maximization, may produce a price/output solution much nearer to the competitive one. This expansion might, of course, only be sacrificing short-term profits for longer-run advantages of domination and thus eventually of increased monopoly profits.

Large firms and the control of industry

The preceding comparison of monopoly and competition is useful, but up to a point only. In two important ways it paints a somewhat misleading picture.

First of all, it suggests that the position would be more satisfactory if firms obtained only a 'competitive' level of profits, referred to as 'normal' profits.[9] But 'normal profits' is a rather artificial concept. The 'normal profits' and other earnings of a large British or American company will be sufficient to cover the high standards of living of perhaps hundreds of business executives, as well as remunerating shareholders. This will be very different from the competitive level of 'profits' obtained by African peasant farmers. For example, in 1967 the sixteen directors of Associated Portland Cement Manufacturers Limited (a large London-based company with 43 subsidiaries and associated companies and extensive interests in Africa, including Eastern Africa) alone earned UK £250,000 (an average of about £15,000 each, just from this company), while the chairman received £42,000.[10] Average earnings of African entrepreneurs in, say, Uganda coffee growing might have been, say, £20, in the same year. Even *within* the United States and other developed countries very different rates of profit are earned in different industries, for instance as between the major oil companies, or leading manufacturers, and farmers, small building firms, or retailers. Within less developed countries there will be a difference between the 'normal' or 'acceptable' level of profits (the 'supply price') for small- and large-scale farmers, for shoe repairers and the Bata Shoe Company, for local small-scale industrialists and the large multinational companies. The explanation for this is probably that large-scale industries require very large investments of capital, so that only owners of substantial amounts of capital may enter certain industries, others being effectively excluded. Accordingly very large companies, especially, are to some degree insulated from competitive forces, and can themselves determine to a major extent what salaries they should pay to executives.

The second unrealistic element in the monopoly/competition analysis is the assumption that each firm owns one plant in one industry, in which it may or may not be able to exert monopoly power. The reality is that one firm may own a *number* of establishments, often situated in many different countries, and *spanning a variety of more or less related industries*. As we saw in Chapter 16, a firm may grow over time either by investing directly in additional plants, or even more rapidly by 'take-overs' and 'mergers' with other already established firms. It may establish subsidiary or associated companies (in which it has a shareholding) in related industries and in other countries. As a consequence of this process the term *multinational company* has been coined to refer to a company whose interests are so spread throughout the world that it cannot be said to be heavily based in any one country. Apart from this geographical spread of activities, the profits from one industry or group of industries may be reinvested in further industries to continually expand the range of activities in which the firm, or 'group' of associated firms, is interested. Very often these are related industries secured by *backward linkages*—as for instance when a hotel group enters farming, in order to secure a reliable and cheaper supply of food (Block Hotels in Kenya have done this) or *forward linkages*, as when a firm establishes itself in another industry which uses its products, (as did Madhavani Industries, owning sugar plantations in Uganda, by establishing a sweet factory). To take another example, we should have forward linkage if a timber company established a furniture factory to utilize some of its timber, or backward linkage if an already established furniture factory purchased timber plantations to secure the supply of its main raw material. However, in a great many cases firms have expanded the scope of their interests far beyond such backward or forward linkages to much less directly related activities with only a very tenuous connection. 'Because the potentialities for the growth of the firm tend to exceed the growth of demand for a given product after a point,' it is said, 'the aggressive enterprise will be for ever seeking new fields of activity, devising new products and developing new markets.'[11]

We can illustrate these points with just two or three examples of firms operating in Eastern Africa. A fuller and very useful description of the ownership structure of firms operating in one Eastern African country, Kenya, in 1965–7 exists,[12] but such accounts are rare. The British-American Tobacco Company (BAT) which has established cigarette factories in many African countries has in fact over 100 such factories in more than 50 countries. Among British firms in 1967 it was fifth in size, as measured by capital employed, valued at UK £461 millions, yielding a profit, before interest and tax, of £103 millions.

Still bigger—and the second largest United Kingdom company after Imperial Chemical Industries (ICI) and the international oil companies—is Unilever, which included 400 associated companies and enjoyed world-wide sales in 1967 of UK £1,893 millions. Its main African interests are in West Africa and Zaire, but it had in 1967 a variety of interests in Eastern Africa, including Gailey and

Roberts Ltd and eight associated companies engaged in diverse activities including the sale of machinery and equipment, insurance, construction, and metal furniture manufactures. Unilever controls East African Industries Ltd, described as 'one of the largest producers of consumer goods in East Africa',[13] making margarine, soap, detergents, toothpaste, and other products.

Lonrho is another example of a company which has diversified its interests both geographically and sectorally. This old British company[14] only began developing its African operations outside Rhodesia in 1961 but expanded rapidly, and by only 1967 embraced 67 subsidiary and associated companies, 14 of these in Rhodesia, 13 in Zambia, 12 in Malawi, 9 in South Africa, 4 in Tanzania, and 1 in Mozambique. In 1968 it purchased the UK £5.7 million textile firm of David Whitehead and Sons Ltd with branches in Nigeria, Malawi, Rhodesia, and South Africa, having previously acquired control of John Holt, one of the largest trading firms in West Africa. It went on to purchase the Ashanti Goldfields in Ghana for £15 millions and to obtain a controlling 51 per cent interest in the Belgian investment company, the Société Commerciale et Minière du Congo, with holdings in timber plantations, transport, power distribution, insurance, and automobiles.[15] Since the above list of Lonrho's African interests was compiled in 1967, this multinational investment company has extended its activities in Eastern Africa. In Kenya it has done so mainly by buying either a controlling majority shareholding in existing companies owned already by other British-based investment companies or by locally based European family-controlled companies in Kenya. In 1967 it took over control of Tancot Ltd, itself a large holding company with plantation, manufacturing, and merchanting business in the three East African companies; in the same year it bought a majority holding in Consolidated Holdings Ltd, the East African Standard newspapers holding company, and in the Express Transport Company, the road haulage concern, 'Etco'. It also controls Bruce Ltd and Motor Mart and Exchange Ltd, the main General Motors distributors in East Africa. In Zambia it also controlled a major road haulage concern and newspapers as well as joint ventures with the respective Zambian, Tanzanian, and Malawian governments in brewing and marketing the opaque maize beer, 'Chibuku'. For a time it even owned a majority shareholding in Malawi's railway, as well as a large slice of that country's tea plantations and its newly developed sugar estate. Lonrho has been particularly successful in establishing new sugar growing and refining industries in Swaziland and Malawi and by 1975 was negotiating a major sugar scheme in the

Sudan in a joint venture with the government with capital provided by Arab interests (which have a substantial holding in the group's equity). Clearly shrewd business dealing and the access to capital explain such rapid and wide expansion, rather than any obvious economies of scale.

As a final case, we may cite the merger in 1965 of two leading East African trading companies, Smith Mackenzie and Co. (a subsidiary of Inchcape and Co., of London, a group with wide shipping and other international interests) and Dalgety (East Africa) Ltd (a subsidiary of Dalgety and New Zealand Loan Ltd, of London) to form Mackenzie-Dalgety Ltd, owning assets of Kenya £7.2 million in March 1966. This offers an East African illustration of the way in which mergers may further reduce the numbers of competing firms, already small, in an industry: in this case the lucrative export-import trade, historically dominated here, as in West Africa, by a small number of major firms.

Given that a firm or a 'group' of associated firms may have interests spread throughout a number of industries, it is useful to distinguish between monopoly power, defined in relation to one industry and to the price of particular products,[16] and the *control of industry*, which may relate to influence in several industries, to a major sector of industry, as part of the economy, or even to a particular sector in several economies. Once a firm constitutes a large independent pool of capital, technological expertise, and management within the economy, *even if it did not exert its power in any exploitative way, it would be in a position to exercise 'control'*, for instance, of important investment decisions affecting the growth not only of itself, but of the economy. In fact major companies, and leading industrialists as a group, may exercise considerable political influence in a country, at both local and national levels, just as do, of course, the major trade unions.

Monopoly power and monopoly policy in less developed countries

Most Western countries have definite policies aimed at the control of monopolies. Britain, for instance, has a Monopolies and Mergers Commission which can investigate the consequences of market structure and market policies in any industry, or report any proposed mergers. The United States has the most comprehensive body of Anti-trust Law, which has a considerable history. In less developed countries, however, there is usually no clear policy, let alone formal legislation, relating to monopoly. It is pertinent to ask why this should be so.

One reason is perhaps that even with only one firm in the industry, the size of the market for the product may be so limited, by low purchasing power, that the firm is only just viable, and not making excessive profits. Secondly, even if considerable monopoly profits are being made in quite a number of particular sectors and situations, governments may feel that the still small size of the 'modern' sector makes an active or formal monopoly policy premature, and something to be considered only after a more advanced stage of development is reached. Thirdly, it is likely that the desire to attract foreign investment has overridden concern over monopoly: thus companies are given tax 'holidays' or other inducements to set up establishments in the country. With different developing countries to some extent competing with each other to attract foreign companies in this way, it may be thought that a 'tough' monopoly policy might act as a deterrent to potential investors. Fourthly, a conventional monopoly policy may in any case be much more difficult to apply in developing countries where many local firms are only subsidiaries of overseas companies. The domestic government is in a relatively weak position vis-à-vis foreign companies and, as we shall see presently, the monopoly situation in developing countries is in many important respects a different one from those of the Western industrialized nations. Lastly, partly as a result of the weaker position mentioned, and these differences, there has generally been a preference for alternative forms of control, in some cases outright nationalization, but more often control exercised through the framework of a national development corporation involving joint ventures between the state and foreign and local capitalists. Such control and 'cooperation' has clearly been a direct substitute for monopoly policy in many cases.

We might mention three distinguishing features of the monopoly situation in less developed countries. The first is that the domestic market for many products is small, in relation to the minimum viable size of the firm, so that in many cases the market can only support one or a few firms, creating a monopoly or oligopoly situation.[17] Thus the incidence of monopoly power will be widespread. While this power will be limited in effectiveness by the limited size of the market, and by the potential entry of new firms if prices are raised too high, the limited market will itself discourage potential competitors, leaving the incumbent considerable freedom.

A second factor is that capital markets in developing countries are usually highly imperfect, giving opportunities to those with access to capital to exploit monopoly situations in manufacturing, trade, transport, or other activities. The special access to capital from parent companies abroad by foreign firms is only one example of the operation of an imperfect capital market.

The most significant feature of the situation, however, stems from the importance of foreign and multinational companies. Many of the larger firms in a typical developing country will not be indigenous, but represent merely the 'tail' of the system of monopoly capitalism centred on the industrialized countries. Thus the less developed countries are to a great extent dependent upon the monopoly policies adopted in metropolitan countries: for example, prevention by a host government of a merger between two large local subsidiaries, such as the Mackenzie-Dalgety merger referred to above, would scarcely be effective if the parent companies abroad merged, or agreed to set up a separate holding company with controlling interests in both the local subsidiaries.

Foreign companies may wield disproportionate economic power (a) vis-à-vis smaller, local companies, and (b) vis-à-vis the host government itself. In relation to local firms, multinational companies will have enormous advantages in access to capital, to technology developed elsewhere, to established brand names and so forth. The foreign company may also indulge in 'local price-cutting'—fixing prices in a local area below cost for long enough to drive local competitors, who lack the assets to withstand a prolonged price war, out of business. Even without such 'unfair competition', the advantages just mentioned may provide such strong competition that local firms are eliminated or discouraged from entry. Thus while 'the arrival of the American subsidiary in Western Europe has often shaken up a sleepy entrepreneurial clique ..., in underdeveloped countries the bracing effect of the cold wind of competition may be so harsh as to kill or prevent indigenous growth'.[18]

Even governments may be in a weak position in dealing with large multinational companies. This may relate to monopoly power over prices and profits, or more broadly to the control of industry as defined above. The position here has been described as follows:

> Today, a handful of powerful, large companies confront a host of small, competing, weak and not always singleminded governments. The large and powerful multinational producing enterprise can draw on a pool of skilled and experienced manpower, and on occasion, on the support of the government of the parent company. The officials of the host government, by contrast, are typically inexperienced. The foreign firm will tend to demand privileges with regard to taxation, relief from duties on imported goods necessary for its investment and production, low bank interest rates, and protection against foreign competition.[19]

Thus the company can bargain effectively with the government for various benefits which will all increase their (monopoly) profits and also increase the proportion of those profits repatriated to the metropolitan country, decreasing the benefit of their operations to the domestic economy. If the host country wishes to raise taxes to much higher levels to finance development, the company may be able to reduce its *nominal* profits in that country by 'buying' inputs at artificially high prices from its parent company or an overseas associate, or 'selling' (transferring) products at artificially low prices to them.

Secondly the multinational company can increase the *overall* monopoly profits of all its branches by specifying which markets each branch should supply and avoiding competition among its subsidiaries in the same market, especially competition by overseas subsidiaries in the market of the parent company itself. Thus where independent establishments in various locations might have engaged in healthy competition with each other, the subsidiaries of a single multinational company might be designed to operate as local monopolists in separated smaller markets.

Apart from the question of prices and profits, large expatriate companies may be able to exercise considerable positive control over industry or, negatively, may make it difficult for the government to implement particular policies. This arises first out of their control over the supply of crucial factors of production (capital, management, skilled manpower, and technical knowledge) necessary for the establishment of new enterprises and the implementation of development projects. Secondly, the fact that the centre of decision-making is located in the metropolitan country, in the head offices of parent companies, will make the firms less responsive to influence and specific requests by the government. The management of local subsidiaries will lack the authority to respond, in many cases, and are likely to be only carrying out an overall company strategy determined elsewhere, covering for instance the introduction of new products, the decision to expand or to undertake riskier ventures, to choose particular techniques, or to pursue export markets. Both because the head offices are remote, and because the company can choose to move elsewhere, it will be especially difficult for the government to influence the export of 'investible surpluses', profits which might have been reinvested in the host country.

Finally, the large expatriate company with its relative wealth may be able to wield much wider indirect influence in the domestic economy, because of the number of salaried jobs it can offer to the local 'élite', because of the relatively high wages it can afford to pay to workers, and in some cases because of influence with government officials.

Oligopoly, or 'collective monopoly'

A more usual market situation, probably the *most* common, is one where there is not a single seller, but a small number of large competing firms, each with a substantial share of the market. This market structure, dominated by a few large firms, is referred to as *oligopoly*, and the firms as *oligopolists*.

The analysis of 'competition among the few' is more difficult, and it becomes very difficult to predict an 'equilibrium' price and output as in the case of perfect competition on the one hand, or monopoly on the other. For present purposes it is sufficient to assume that a small group of firms are likely to come together in some way to restrict output and raise prices. If a number of firms come together to act in this way the situation may be described as *collective monopoly*, or alternatively as 'collusive monopoly', since there is collusion among the firms to achieve the effect of monopoly.

Usually this collusion will take the form of a very informal agreement, perhaps reached without actual contact between the firms, not to pursue 'aggressive' competitive policies. However formal agreements to restrict output, in which agreements are written down and made binding on members, also occur, though they are generally prohibited in more recent times. Such formal arrangements are known as a 'cartel'. In an advanced form this may entail a system of pooling profits, with the firms who came off best as a result of the agreement making regular cash payments to the others. More common is for firms to agree on *quotas* fixing the maximum amount each may put on the market. Quotas are fixed sufficiently low to ensure high prices.

Collusive monopoly is sometimes said to have 'all the disadvantages and none of the advantages of single-firm monopoly'. This statement is referring to the fact that output is restricted, prices raised, and supernormal profits made, so that misallocation of resources results. Moreover, resources are inefficiently allocated even within the industry: for cartel arrangements are usually such that all firms at present in the industry can remain in it, earning at least normal profits, no matter how inefficient. Any efficient firm which could expand output, while maintaining lower costs per unit than the inefficient firms, is prevented from so doing by its quota. Since quotas can only be altered with great difficulty, progressive firms will also fail to obtain maximum rewards from any improved methods which they may introduce, as they are prevented from expanding their sales at the expense of other cartel members. The incentive to make improvements within the firm is correspondingly reduced. Nor does this permit the tapping of economies of scale as may be the case with single-firm monopoly. As we have just seen, the more efficient progressive firms may actually be prevented from obtaining economies of scale.

For these reasons, anti-trust law has in many countries discouraged in various ways, or actually prohibited, the formation of cartels in industry. However excellent examples of collective monopolies are provided by the international commodity agreements already described in Chapter 12. These demonstrate in a very clear way the main elements of 'collective monopoly'. They attempt to raise price by restricting output, using monopoly power; output is restricted on the basis of a system of quotas; agreements are reached only with difficulty, and are difficult to maintain, because of the problem of agreeing on 'fair shares' of the market; inefficiency in the world allocation of resources has been introduced where efficient low-cost producers have been unable to expand their output due to quota restrictions. One difference between these agreements and other forms of monopoly, however, is that, to the extent that they are successful, they would benefit the relatively poor at the expense of the relatively rich in the industrialized countries.[20]

In national markets formal cartels are relatively unusual. But oligopolists can tacitly agree to keep prices up (and output restricted). Such a 'tacit agreement' need not involve rival firms contacting each other directly. Each rival firm is likely to decide by itself not to adopt an 'aggressive' policy of price cutting, knowing that this would probably provoke a reaction by other firms, also cutting their prices in order to avoid a reduction of their market shares. A succession of price cuts by rival firms competing for the same market is known as a 'price war'. Firms may temporarily reduce prices well below cost in an attempt to drive their rivals out of the market and thus increase their market shares or even attain a monopoly position, from which they could later recoup their temporary losses. Since all the rivals are likely to lose revenue during a price war, firms generally do their utmost to avoid these, and to charge roughly similar prices for their products. Moreover, since any price cut is likely to be misinterpreted by rival firms, where there are only a few competing firms in the market, firms tend to avoid price competition altogether, and try to increase their share of the market more stealthily by advertising, slight improvements in the quality or design of the product, and other forms of non-price competition. Accordingly, a feature of oligopoly is *price rigidity* and a greater emphasis on *non-price competition*.

If, instead of several firms, there were just one firm, a monopolist, then this firm would select the 'monopoly' price and output which maximizes its monopoly profits. With very close understanding, rival oligopolists might succeed in keeping their prices up towards this monopoly level (they would not want a higher price than this, because this would reduce profits), where the aggregate profits distributed among them were close to the maximum given by demand conditions. With only an informal understanding, particularly to avoid major price cuts, it is likely that oligopoly prices will be somewhat lower than the theoretical monopoly level, with output and sales correspondingly greater.

Some obvious examples of oligopoly in Eastern African markets are in the sale of bottled beer, where each country has only two or three brands on the market, such as 'Lion' and 'Castle' beer in Zambia; or petrol distribution, in which competition is between the local subsidiaries of well-known international oil companies such as Shell, Caltex, or Esso. A feature of petrol prices in these markets, as elsewhere, is a tendency for the prices of different petrol brands to be uniform, and for them to change very infrequently. The prices of competitive brands of beer show the same oligopolistic pattern of price uniformity and price rigidity.

Monopsony and oligopsony

A monopolist is a single seller of a product, or one who is a 'price-maker' as a result of producing a substantial share of the output of one product. Influence over price may exist on the side of the buyer, however, and in the buying of inputs, as well as in the selling of outputs. A single buyer with some control over the price of what he buys (the less he buys the lower the price) is known as a *monopsonist* (single-buyer) and the corresponding market situation as one of *monopsony*. Similarly, just as a market dominated by a few sellers is called 'oligopoly', a market structure involving a few *buyers* is referred to as one of *oligopsony*.

An example of a monopsonist would be a marketing board which has been granted an exclusive licence to purchase specific crops from farmers and to sell this produce in domestic or export markets. Because of its position as the sole buyer of the crop, such a board is a 'price-maker' and can fix the price (in consultation with the government) which producers will receive for their produce.

Before the West African export produce marketing boards were established in the late 1940s, three or four oligopsonists dominated the export trade in cocoa, palm oil, and groundnuts.[21] One firm alone was buying from producers nearly 40 per cent of Ghana's cocoa exports and held approximately the same share of Ghana's commercial (non-government) imports of merchandise as late as 1949–50. The same

firm also handled 40 per cent of Nigeria's commercial imports and of her non-mineral exports. It was thus the leading firm among a group of oligopsonists in the purchase of export crops. Substantially the same group of firms were oligopolists in the importation and resale of manufactured and other import goods, while in addition to this export-import trade, they owned the only large department stores and chains of smaller shops, motor distribution outlets, and many processing or larger-scale manufacturing enterprises. Bauer attributed the collective monopoly of these firms in the post-war period to (1) economies of scale in many lines of trade, but also to (2) access to foreign risk capital with which to finance stocks of goods, especially, and to offer trade credit for the distribution of goods. Additional barriers to entry, in the 1930s especially, were the sole agency agreements which gave one firm (or group of firms in association) the 'franchise' or exclusive right to sell particular commodities or brands. Such agreements are still common everywhere in the motor trade, and at one time in West Africa extended to staple exports like sugar and stockfish. Since the 1950s, the predominant position of these firms, and others like them elsewhere in Africa, has been reduced considerably.

While similar European merchant companies operated in Eastern Africa, they did not in general attain the same degree of concentration as in West Africa, since from the earliest colonial period they faced competition from long-established Asian trade and from statutory boards, and in Kenya especially, from some local European businesses.

Short-run pricing under monopoly

We can consider two situations in which the firm might find itself. When it comes into the industry for the first time, it is free to select whichever size of plant it wishes from the full range of technical possibilities. In other words, it is free to vary the amount of capital it uses, as well as the amounts of labour and raw materials. Existing firms also, given sufficient time, could modify or replace existing plants to any desired size. This is the situation we were considering in the early part of this chapter.

On the other hand, if demand changes, as is likely, after the plant has been selected and constructed, it may no longer be the most appropriate size. For some time at least the firm will have to make the best of the plant it happens to have. To give the first situation a name, we can call it 'the long run', and likewise say that 'in the short run' capital is fixed.

The feature of this so-called 'short run', therefore, is the existence of fixed costs. Given more and more time, the entrepreneur will have more and more freedom to modify his plant, expanding or contracting capacity, and a progressively smaller proportion of total costs will be 'fixed'. To define our terms, we can say that *fixed costs* are those which are independent of the level of output in the period considered, while *variable costs* are those that vary directly with the level of output.

Let us suppose a firm has the same variable costs as our dress manufacturer in the previous example (Table 17.1), but also has fixed costs 'in the short

period' of 60,000s. *Total costs* would then be the sum of fixed costs and *total variable costs*. The three are given in columns 2–4 of Table 17.2. If we divide these three totals by the corresponding levels of output (column 1) we obtain in turn average fixed costs, average variable costs, and average total costs in columns 5, 6, and 7, the first two columns adding up to the third.

Before comparing cost and revenue figures, let us examine the cost relationships carefully, with the help of Figure 17.10. Average fixed costs, column 5 of Table 17.2, are steadily declining: this is because a constant is being divided by an increasingly large

Table 17.2   *The effect of fixed costs on equilibrium price and output*

Col. 1	Col. 2	Col. 3	Col. 4	Col. 5	Col. 6	Col. 7	Col. 8	Col. 9	Col. 10	Col. 11	Col. 12
Output (×1,000 dresses)	TFC (×1,000 shs)	TVC (×1,000 shs)	TC (×1,000 shs)	AFC (shs)	AVC (shs)	ATC (shs)	MC (shs)	MR (shs)	AR (shs)	TR (×1,000 shs)	Profit (×1,000 shs)
0	60	—	60	—	—	—	—	—	—	0	−60
1	60	50	110	60	50	110	50	105	105	105	−5
2	60	80	140	30	40	70	30	65	85	170	30
3	60	105	165	20	35	55	25	25	65	195	30
4	60	126	186	15	31.5	46.5	21	−115	45	180	−6
5	60	150	210	12	30	42	24	−55	27	135	−75
6	60	180	240	10	30	40	30	−95	7	40	−200
7	60	220	280	8.5	31.5	40	40	—	—	—	—
8	60	280	340	7.5	35	42.5	60	—	—	—	—
9	60	370	430	6.5	41	47.5	90	—	—	—	—
10	60	520	580	6	52	58	150	—	—	—	—

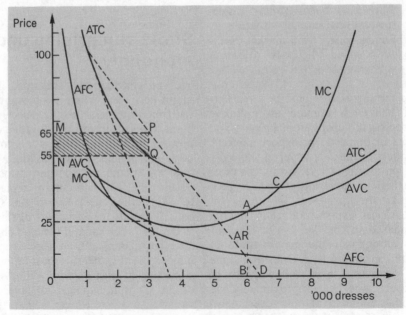

Figure 17.10   *The effect of fixed costs on equilibrium price and output.*

figure. In Figure 17.10 this means that the average fixed cost curve is a rectangular hyperbola. In economic terms, fixed costs or *overheads* are being spread over larger outputs. The ATC curve is obtained as the vertical sum of the AFC and AVC curves. These curves may now all be described as 'short-run curves'. The AVC curve is U-shaped, as explained in Chapter 16, because of the Law of Variable Proportions. Beyond output OB ($=6,000$), the fixed plant is being used with 'too much' labour and materials, and below output OB with 'too little' labour and materials. Maximum output per unit of the variable factors is obtained only at OB, when the proportions between the fixed and variable factors are the 'best'. The ATC curve has the same shape, since it incorporates the AVC curve. It falls faster in its downward-sloping segment, however, since average total costs decrease for *two* reasons. In addition to increasing returns from the application of labour and materials (Law of Variable Proportions, reflected in the AVC curve) overhead costs are spread over larger outputs (reflected in the AFC curve). The rise in the ATC curve is due entirely to the fact that the AVC curve is rising, while the AFC is too small at large outputs to have much effect. This also means that the gap between the AVC and ATC curves narrows progressively as output increases. For example, at an output of 1,000 dresses, average variable and average total costs differ by 60s, at 4,000 by 15s, and at 10,000 by only 6s.

Going back to Table 17.2, we can find marginal costs, given in column 8, *either* from total variable costs (column 3) *or* from total costs (column 4). The existence of fixed costs, therefore, does not affect marginal costs. But since maximum profits are determined only by *marginal* cost and revenue, this means that *the existence or value of fixed costs does not affect equilibrium output or, therefore, the price charged*. This can be verified by checking through Table 17.2 or by an examination of Figure 17.10. From either of these, we can find the data with which to complete Table 17.3. This shows that whether fixed costs are zero or sixty, output and price are unchanged. Unit profits are reduced, however, since average total costs are increased, and total supernormal profits are reduced to 30,000s.

Table 17.3 *Equilibrium with different fixed costs*

	FC=0	FC=60
Output	3,000	3,000
Average total cost	35s	55s
Price	65s	65s
Unit profit	30s	10s
Supernormal profits	90,000s	30,000s

This tells us that once the 'intelligent' businessman has committed himself to a capital outlay, he should not consider overheads in trying to maximize his profits, or minimize his losses. Though his profits are reduced to 30,000s in the second situation, this is still the best he can do. Of course, in both competitive or monopolistic situations, if average total costs exceed average revenue, so that the businessman fails to make 'normal profits', he will eventually abandon the enterprise.

Price discrimination under monopoly

We have seen that the extent of monopoly power, and the ability of the monopolist to raise his price, depend on the elasticity of demand for his product. This elasticity will be low if he is the sole producer of a well-defined product which is quite distinct from others, that is, where similar, competing products are absent. Cases arise where the producer of a good is able to sell it in two distinct and separate markets, in which the demand curves and demand elasticities are different. In this situation it can be shown that the monopolist should charge different prices in each market.

Suppose that the demand conditions in two markets are such that a monopolist's marginal revenues in each market are as in Table 17.4 when different quantities (Q) are sold on those markets. The table also gives the value of marginal cost for different quantities produced. Thus if he produces just one unit, marginal cost is 2 shillings. If he sells this in the first market he will obtain an additional revenue of

Table 17.4 *Allocation of sales between two markets*

(1) Q	(2) MR_1 (shs)	(3) MR_2 (shs)	(4) MC (shs)
1	10 (2)	11 (1)	2
2	8 (5)	10 (3)	2
3	6 (8)	9 (4)	2
4	4 (11)	8 (6)	2
5	2	7 (7)	2
6	0	6 (9)	2
7	—	5 (10)	3
8	—	4 (12)	3
9	—	3	3
10	—	2	3
11	—	1	4
12	—	0	4
13	—	—	5
14	—	—	6
15	—	—	8
16	—	—	12

shs 10 and if he sells it in the second market a marginal revenue of shs 11. Clearly it pays him to produce it, since both marginal revenues exceed marginal cost, and it can be sold most profitably in the second market for 11 shillings. Against the figure 11 in column 3 of the table we mark (1) in brackets, to indicate that if only one unit were to be produced, it should be allocated to the second market. If a second unit were produced, this could be sold in either market, and a third unit disposed of for the same marginal revenue. The fourth unit, produced still at a marginal cost of shs 2, could be disposed of in the second market with a marginal revenue of shs 9. It will clearly be worth increasing output up to the point at which a unit can be disposed of in either market with a marginal revenue greater than or equal to its marginal cost. It can be seen that the eleventh unit, and twelfth, with marginal costs of shs 4, can be disposed of in the first and second markets respectively, each at a marginal revenue of shs 4. The thirteenth unit would *not* be worth producing, since its marginal cost (5) exceeds marginal revenue in market 1 (2) *and* in market 2 (3).

Hence 12 units will be produced, 4 sold in market 1 and 8 sold in market 2. We may note, first, that *the units will be allocated in such a way that marginal revenue is equal in both markets*. It can be seen that this is a *general* condition for 'equilibrium', since if marginal revenues were unequal, it would pay the monopolist to transfer at least one produced unit of output from one market to the other: this would not affect costs, but would yield a net increase in revenue. Secondly, equilibrium output should be such that marginal cost is just equal to the two marginal revenues. The full condition of equilibrium is thus[22]

$$MC = MR_1 = MR_2$$

We have already shown that the relationship between marginal revenue and price in any market is $MR = P(1 - 1/e)$ where e is the elasticity of demand. It follows that our equilibrium condition is equivalent to

$$MC = P_1(1 - 1/e_1) = P_2(1 - 1/e_2)$$

where e_1 and e_2 are the respective elasticities in the two markets and P_1 and P_2 the prices. Hence if the two elasticities were equal ($e_1 = e_2$), the prices fixed should be equal. But in general the prices will differ, in the ratio

$$P_1/P_2 = \frac{1 - 1/e_1}{1 - 1/e_2}$$

For example, if $e_1 = 2$, $e_2 = 4$, then

$$P_1 = \left\{ \frac{1 - 1/e_1}{1 - 1/e_2} \right\} P_2 = \frac{3}{2} P_2$$

If $e_1 = 4$, $e_2 = 2$, then $P_1 = 2/3\ P_2$. That is, if elasticity is lower in the first market, the price there should be higher. Conversely, if the elasticity is higher, the price should be lower. Thus the products should be priced, and the output allocated between the two markets, in such a way that advantage is taken of lower elasticity (greater monopoly power) in either market.

A condition for price discrimination to be possible is that the monopolist must be able to keep the two markets separate. Otherwise people could buy the product in the cheaper market and resell, at a profit, in the dearer till the prices were equalized. One example of price discrimination is where tourist hotels offer a cheaper rate to local residents, and a higher one for tourists, whose demand for 'hotel beds' is less elastic. A similar case could be made for charging higher fees in state hospitals for well-to-do patients and low fees for low income patients: this would increase hospital revenues while having a favourable effect on income distribution. Unfortunately in Africa the practice is frequently the opposite, with higher income groups benefiting from special access to medical services at subsidized rates and poorer groups having to pay, generally for much poorer services.

Some examples of price discrimination

A major example of price discrimination has been that of the Maize Marketing Board in Kenya, which acts officially as a monopsonist in buying and as a monopolist in selling maize. The amount of maize produced in Kenya fluctuates considerably from year to year due to weather conditions. The objective of the Board has been to stabilize producer prices without, presumably, making a loss on its operations. It is able to sell on the Kenyan market, where it is a monopolist, and also on the world market. Since there are large numbers of suppliers to the 'world market', and any maize sold there by Kenya would form only a small fraction of world supplies, the Board can dispose of any amount at the 'export parity price' Ok in Figure 17.11. Hence it faces a horizontal demand curve, D_2, in this market, but a downward-sloping demand curve on the domestic Kenya market. If in a bumper year farmers produce the amount OQ_1, in the absence of intervention the domestic price to producers would fall to the low level Ok, at which OQ_2 would be sold locally, with the surplus Q_2Q_1 exported at the same price. The Board could, however, restrict domestic sales to OQ_3, raising the domestic selling price to Oa and the buying (producer) price to, say, Ob. The surplus could be sold on the world market at a loss to the Board of bK per unit ($= de$), giving a total loss equal

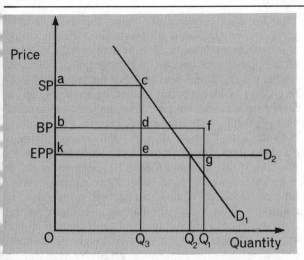

Figure 17.11   *Price discrimination: illustrative diagram of Kenya Marketing Board operations.*

to the area defg. Since on the domestic market the Board is able to make a monopoly profit (abdc), the Board still makes a net profit equal to the difference between the two areas, while in this fashion producer prices are prevented from falling to very low levels. One effect, of course, is to raise the price to Kenyan consumers. Since these include a majority of relatively low-paid urban workers, and the producers who benefit include many well-to-do large-scale farmers, including European farmers, the policy, when it has been employed, is open to question on the grounds of income distribution.

A good example of price discrimination between two or more geographically separated markets is provided by the cement industry in African countries. Here because of high transport costs for cement, and the level of economic development, there usually are just one or two cement factories in each geographical area. At the same time cement is a capital-intensive industry which enjoys important technical economies of scale from full utilization of fixed capacity. A study[23] of one of the two cement works operating in Nigeria in the early 1960s indicated that the fixed costs of plant depreciation and other overhead expenses constituted perhaps as much as 50 per cent of total costs at a capacity of 250,000 tons a year. These high fixed costs form a barrier to entry of additional firms within the same market, quite apart from any industrial licensing which may reinforce this. The cement industry therefore tends to be highly concentrated in a few plants, each enjoying a regional monopoly apart, of course, from competition from imports.

However demand for cement fluctuates widely with building activity, even without the regional monopoly market; and because of the high proportion of fixed costs these large variations in output have a very great impact on profitability. To help stabilize demand at or near full capacity output, therefore, a cement manufacturer is anxious to extend his market to as many locations of building activity as possible (geographical diversification) and to as many potential end-uses as possible (diversification of industrial intermediate demands). In this case price discrimination can be effected by charging a uniform delivered price, instead of charging a *higher* price in more distant markets to cover the extra transport costs. By absorbing transport costs himself, the seller is in effect charging a *lower* price ex-factory gate to more distant buyers. It will pay the seller to do this so long as this lower price covers the marginal costs of the additional output, and any higher price will be a useful contribution to his overhead costs.

Such price discrimination will bring the producer into competition with producers in other areas, on an oligopolistic basis. Generally there will not be deliberate price-*cutting* however. Since cement is a homogeneous or standardized product with little consumer loyalty based on real or apparent quality differences, open price cuts would immediately induce consumers to switch from other suppliers, forcing these to retaliate in order to preserve their market shares. Instead, special discounts may be offered to, say, large building contractors to encourage them to substitute cement for other building materials like bricks, timber, or metal. Of course if the building and construction industries as a whole are depressed, causing considerable excess capacity in the cement industry, the pressure to adopt price-cutting to increase sales will be great and the tendency to maintain sales through price discrimination and 'dumping' in export markets increased.

Price discrimination is also a recognized feature of public utilities like railways, electricity, and telephone undertakings, as well as scheduled airlines.[24] In Eastern Africa, as elsewhere, electricity supply undertakings have a multiple tariff of charges. Thus they generally make an installation charge to connect a customer to the system and then in addition charge a price per unit consumed, as measured by a meter. This helps to cover some of the undertaking's fixed charges even if the consumer does not switch on any power. There may also be a 'two-part' tariff whereby the unit charge is reduced after a certain amount of power is consumed during the month. Thus the price charged to the consumer falls with greater consumption, a form of price discrimination. There may be a further cheap rate for so-called 'off-peak' use, and also a different rate of industrial users as compared to the standard tariff for private households and small commercial premises. Thus discrimination is made between different types of user as well as the same user at different times.

Price discrimination in railway tariffs

It is, however, the African railway undertakings which best illustrate the variety of forms price discrimination may take. Before the development of internal road transport, or pipelines for fuels, the African railways had an effective monopoly of all but the shortest-distance freight traffic. They were, however, subject to government regulations, even if privately owned in a few cases in Central Africa: these regulations covered both control over prices and the obligation to accept all traffic offered ('common carrier' service obligations). Where corporations had to be self-financing, as in the case of the East African Railways Corporation, prices had to be sufficient to cover total costs without a public subsidy. However they were usually encouraged or required by the government to practise price discrimination (a) to utilize capacity more fully and (b) in order to 'cross-subsidize' particular types of traffic. Since we have already dealt with the reasons for increasing utilization of capacity, we can concentrate here on the second aspect, cross-subsidization, that is, making some traffic bear more than its full costs in order to subsidize other traffic.

Arthur Hazlewood has compared the extent to which the East African Railways and Harbours Corporation 'taxed' higher-valued imported manufactured goods in order to subsidize lower-valued bulky exports and local traffic in primary products, construction materials and local producer materials.[25] Table 17.5 summarizes his very detailed analysis of the railway's freight traffic and revenue for 1960. The first column describes the various classes of freight being carried; the second column gives the average revenue per ton mile actually charged in 1960 for each category of freight; the third column gives a rate calculated by Hazlewood which would eliminate cross-subsidization as well as take account of the higher average cost of handling short-distance traffic, which should bear more of the terminal handling costs of loading and unloading than the actual tariff provided for. He calls this rate the 'cost-tapered average tariff', as it would have the effect of lowering the rate of very long-distance traffic and increasing it on short hauls (as for local traffic in basic materials and foodstuffs). Column 5 gives the revenues which it is estimated would have been obtained at the cost-tapered rates, as against the actual rates given in column 4. Subtracting the figures in column 5 from those in column 4 gives an estimate of the amount of subsidy afforded to each class of freight. The direction of cross-subsidization is given by the sign, a negative subsidy implying that the category is actually cross-subsidizing other classes of freight. The final column gives the values of the cross-subsidies in percentage terms, as a percentage of actual revenue obtained from the items.

From this last column we can see that the first two categories were cross-subsidizing the last three by substantial amounts. The first category has been called for simplicity 'manufactured consumer imports', although it actually represents a variety of goods including some locally produced or not fully manufactured: the most important items here are mass consumer goods like cotton textiles, kerosene, and sugar, or producer materials like iron and steel. The second class of item, 'bulk oil', was entirely imported and was the largest single source of 'taxation' used to 'subsidize' the remaining items. Of these, bulky building material like cement and timber, sand and stone, or producer materials like cottonseed (for cottonseed oil manufacture) received

Table 17.5   Rate discrimination between different classes of freight traffic: cross-subsidization by East African Railways in 1960

Class	Average revenue (cents per ton mile)		Total revenue (£m)		Cross-subsidy (£m) (as %)	
	Actual	Cost-tapered	Actual	Cost-tapered		
(1)	(2)	(3)	(4)	(5)	(6)	(7)
Manufactured consumer imports (freight classes 1–8)	24.0	18.8	4.8	3.2	−1.5	−31
Bulk oil	26.7	18.1	3.9	2.6	−1.3	−32
Basic materials (freight classes 9–10)	16.3	23.0	1.7	2.5	+0.7	+43
Exceptional	14.7	21.2	2.1	3.1	+0.9	+43
Export	13.6	18.1	3.3	4.4	+1.1	+32
Total	19.4	19.4	15.8	15.8	±2.7	±17

SOURCE: A. Hazlewood, op. cit., pp. 104–120

about one-quarter (£0.7 millions) of the total 'subsidy', another third went to the so-called 'exceptional traffic', consisting of local traffic in grains and cattle or producer goods like vehicles and fertilizers. Finally there was the export traffic which in 1960 absorbed about 40 per cent of the 'subsidies'. Effectively, therefore, we can say of the East African Railways Tariff in 1960 that imports of manufactured consumer goods and bulk petroleum products were charged more than the *full* cost of their carriage whereas exports, basic materials, and locally produced goods were heavily subsidized, in some cases being charged less than the *direct* costs of carriage, let alone contributing towards the indirect costs of the railway's heavy overhead expenses. Although Hazlewood was not able to identify all the cross-subsidization, he estimated it to be a large element in the railway tariff: taking the last three categories together the total 'subsidy' received in 1960 was £2.7 millions, compared to a total revenue of £15.8 millions, a ratio of 17 per cent.

The traditional policy of the East African governments and the Railway Administration before independence aimed at assisting the region's basic industries, agriculture, mining and manufacturing, by charging them less than average total cost and recouping these subsidies by charging in excess of average total costs on other traffic. The railway was in fact behaving like a discriminating monopolist, 'charging what the traffic will bear' on different kinds of goods. It was possible to charge higher rates for high-value/low-volume imported manufactures and for bulk oil for which transport charges were small compared to the value of the goods and for which the 'elasticity of demand for rail services' was low.

This inelasticity does, however, depend on the absence of competition from other forms of transport, and by 1960 the East African Railway's differential tariff was becoming increasingly vulnerable to road transport competition for its higher-rated traffic. Moreover, road haulage operators could avoid the heavy fixed charges of a permanent way, since the costs of building and maintaining roads were met collectively from taxation. The Railways therefore insisted on government regulation and restrictions on road transport to protect the differential tariff. And if the Railway abandoned the differential tariff to compete freely with road hauliers, the cross-subsidization of agriculture and industry would have to be abandoned.

Similar differential tariffs have been applied by other African railways, but have had to be abandoned or relaxed under pressure from road transport which, with its relatively low fixed costs, has proved an easy industry for entry by small-scale African operators. Nowadays, African railways tend to concentrate on long-distance traffic, which can still include higher-rated imported goods like bulk oil, and high-value exports like copper, particularly for land-locked countries such as Zambia, Malawi, Ethiopia, and the Sudan.

Since 1960, there has been considerable increase in the volume of goods carried by road in East Africa, associated partly with improvements in the road system and partly with increased income and output generally. Table 17.6 gives an indication of this. The interesting question is whether this increased competition faced by the railway has induced the railway to amend its tariff structure, particularly to reduce charges on the items in the first two categories of Table 17.5 which were in 1960 subsidizing the others, and to decrease subsidies in the last three groups.

A strict comparison of rate changes between 1960 and the present time is not possible, because of modifications to the coverage of rate categories, including the introduction of a new class 11. In addition, the comparison in Table 17.7 is between 1960 and 1969, whereas in Kenya, at least, Table 17.6 shows that a significant expansion in road traffic occurred *after* 1969.

However, Table 17.7 shows in the first column a sharp drop in the tonnage of class 9 and 10 and 'exceptional traffic' carried, particularly short-distance traffic for which road haulage is most competitive. This is reflected also in the second column which indicates a quite substantial increase in the average haul (average distance travelled by a load) of these bulky 'basic materials'.[26]

Table 17.6 Growth of road haulage in Kenya and East Africa

	Number of lorries and trucks licensed	
	Kenya (×1,000)	All three East African countries (×1,000)
1952	9.1	20.5
1960	10.3	22.1
1969	13.7	31.5
1972	17.4	35.9

SOURCE: *Economic and Statistical Review*, East Africa

The tariff charged for each class of goods is indicated by the average revenue obtained per ton mile, in column 3. For all categories taken together this was 19.4 cents in 1960. At that time imported manufactured goods (classes 1–8) were being charged 24 per cent above this average rate for all traffic, and bulk oil 38 per cent above; the subsidized categories, basic materials, 'exceptional' traffic, and export commodities were being charged 16, 24, and 30 per cent *below* the average, respectively. The corresponding

Table 17.7   Changes in tariff structure of East African Railways between 1960 and 1969

Class of freight	(1) Tonnage carried				(2) Average haul		(3) Average revenue per ton mile			
	1960		1969		1960	1969	1960		1969	
	(×1,000 tons)	(%)	(×1,000 tons)	(%)	(miles)	(miles)	(cents)	(%)	(cents)	(%)
Classes 1–8	780	19	1,034	19	445	574	24.0	124	24.6	131
Bulk oil	543	13	787	15	534	566	26.7	138	25.3	135
Basic materials	918	22	548	10	235	460	16.3	84	18.3	97
Exceptional	990	24	653	12	295	335	14.7	76	18.1	96
Class 11	—	—	845	16	—	400	—	—	14.3	—
Export (12–15)	906	22	1,465	28	534	373	13.6	70	10.7	56
Total	4,137	100	5,332	100	394	449	19.4	100	18.8	100

SOURCE: For 1960, A. Hazlewood, op. cit., and for 1969, East African Railways, *Annual Report 1969*, statement no. 18

figures for 1969 suggests that this cross-subsidization had virtually ceased for basic materials (3 per cent below the average) and 'exceptional' traffic (4 per cent below). However, the railways had managed to hold on to their most profitable traffic in classes 1–8 and had not then lost a substantial proportion of the Kenya bulk oil traffic. These were still being charged higher rates (31 per cent and 35 per cent above the average) in order now to subsidize the export traffic, for which the tariff had actually fallen from 30 per cent below average to 44 per cent below. Thus the policy of subsidizing export production continued and was even intensified.

We may note that in addition to the use of tariff structure to increase railway competitiveness in cross-subsidized categories, tax policy also affects road–rail competition. Thus commercial road users pay tax in the form of vehicle licences and especially a tax on petrol/diesel oil, as well as import duty on vehicles, all of which are reflected in road freight charges and more than cover their share of road maintenance costs. Moreover by 1969 and in subsequent years the railways were incurring a loss, failing to cover total expenditure with revenue, this constituting a further general subsidy to railway users.

Questions on Chapter 17

1. Explain how (a) the short-run supply curve of a competitive industry and (b) the long-run supply curve are related to the cost curves of an individual firm.
2. How does monopoly bring about a misallocation of national resources?
3. 'Useful statements about the effect of monopoly on economic efficiency can only be made in respect of the long run'. Discuss.
4. (a) Is the number of firms in an industry a good indication of the strength of the producers' monopoly?
   (b) Are profits a good indication. of the strength of monopoly power?
5. Show that the degree of distortion in the allocation of resources caused by monopoly depends on the elasticity of demand.
6. Why will a monopolist never produce at levels of output where the elasticity of demand is less than one?
7. Examine the limits to the exercise of monopoly power.
8. Explain why monopolistic competition may be 'wasteful competition'.
9. What makes the retail trade a good example of monopolistic competition?
10. Compare the economic effects of 'informative' and 'persuasive' advertising.
11. Demonstrate graphically that a government-imposed price ceiling may increase the output of a commodity in a monopoly situation. What limits to such an increase exist?
12. Compare the firm's equilibrium price and output under sales maximization with that under perfect competition. Why might entrepreneurs adopt sales maximization rather than profit maximization? Why would you expect profit-maximizing behaviour under competition?
13. How do you explain the increasing importance of multi-national companies?
14. To what extent or in what ways does the 'monopoly problem' differ in less developed countries?
15. 'Collusive monopoly has all the disadvantages and none of the advantages of single-firm monopoly.' Discuss.
16. Why do oligopolists tend to favour 'non-price competition' to cutting prices?
17. What is a 'discriminating monopolist'? In what circumstances may a monopolist discriminate as a seller?
18. Explain how a marketing board may discriminate between domestic and foreign markets for maize. Suggest how a milk marketing board might adopt price discrimination to get rid of surplus milk.
19. Discuss the reasons why price discrimination is a common practice among cement producers.
20. Explain how a railway may 'cross-subsidize' certain traffic by charging other traffic more than average total cost.
21. Discuss the paradox apparent in the tariff structure of East African Railways when it carried long-distance export freight at only half the rate per ton mile charged for shorter hauls of equally bulky materials like grains for local consumption.

Notes

[1] It is possible that the industry operates more efficiently on a large scale, so that as the industry expands, costs fall. Larger output could then be supplied at a *lower* price, and the industry's supply curve would slope *down*. The lowering of cost for each firm would be said to be due to *external economies of scale*, a concept which is defined in Chapter 23.

[2] We can ignore the indivisibility arising in the case of monopoly output being, say, 5,035 as opposed to 5,000, which could be produced by 100 plants each producing 50 units.

Readers may be puzzled as to why marginal cost in equilibrium should differ between Figure 17.6(a) and Figure 17.6(b). The reason is that the left-hand diagram is drawn on a larger scale than the other. The equilibrium plant output of 50 units is only a small proportion of total output. If there are, say, 25 plants under the monopolist's control, equilibrium industry Q_m in Figure 17.6(b) would be 1,250 units. Marginal cost in Figure 17.6(a) would refer to an increase in plant from, say, 50 to 51 units, and in Figure 17.6(b) from, say, 1,250 to 1,300 units through the bringing into production of *one entire additional plant*. This would have the effect of raising costs for all plants, shifting the average *and* marginal cost curves in Figure 17.6(a) bodily upwards.

[3] We use the rule in calculus for differentiating the product of two terms, u and v, where each is a function of x, viz.

$$\frac{d.(u.v)}{dx} = u\frac{dv}{dx} + v\frac{du}{dx}$$

We apply this to total revenue, equal to price times quantity, where price depends on the quantity sold by the monopolist.

Hence:

$$R = p. q \text{ where } p, q \text{ are both functions of } q; \ p = q(p)$$

$$\frac{dR}{dq} = p.1 + q.\frac{dp}{dq}$$

Elasticity of demand $e_D = -\frac{\Delta q/q}{\Delta p/p} = -\frac{p\Delta q}{q\Delta p}$

(Since q and p will have opposite signs, usually, this will be a positive number.)

Hence

$$\frac{dR}{dq} = p - p\left(-\frac{q}{p}\frac{dp}{dq}\right) = p - p\frac{1}{e_D} = p\left(1 - \frac{1}{e_D}\right)$$

[4] See especially W. J. Baumol, *Business Behaviour, Value and Growth*, Macmillan, 1959.

[5] S. Kuznets, *Modern Economic Growth: Rate, Structure and Spread*, Yale University Press, 1966.

[6] E. T. Penrose, 'The State and Multinational Enterprises in Less-Developed Countries', in John H. Dunning (ed.), *The Multinational Enterprise*, Allen & Unwin, London, 1971, p. 223.

[7] Paul Streeten, 'Costs and Benefits of Multinational Enterprises in Less-developed Countries', in Dunning (ed.), op. cit., and Pierre Uri, 'The Role of the Multinational Corporation', in Helen Hughes (ed.), *Prospects for Partnerships: Industrialization and Trade Policies in the 1970s*, Johns Hopkins University Press, Baltimore, 1973.

[8] This distinction has been stressed by E. K. Schneider.

[9] This need not by itself imply perfect competition or price equal to marginal cost. For instance, we may have a situation of monopolistic competition.

[10] National Christian Council of Kenya, *Who Controls Industry in Kenya?*, East African Publishing House, Nairobi, 1968, p. 52.

[11] E. T. Penrose, in Dunning (ed.), op. cit., p. 223.

[12] *Who Controls Industry in Kenya*, op. cit.

[13] ibid., p. 57.

[14] Incorporated in 1909 as The London and Rhodesian Mining and Land Company Ltd.

[15] See A. Seidman, *Comparative Development Strategies in East Africa*, pp. 49–51.

[16] The multi-product firm, producing and selling a number of products, often a very large number, is a widespread phenomenon. The elasticity of demand, and thus monopoly power, will vary considerably from product to product.

[17] Oligopoly as a market form is discussed later in the chapter.

[18] Streeten, op. cit., p. 254.

[19] ibid., p. 245.

[20] Though the most successful of such agreements, among the oil-producing countries, has also transferred incomes from the poorest of the developing countries, including many African countries, to the relatively rich Arab countries of the Middle East and to the South American countries of Venezuela and Trinidad.

[21] See P. T. Bauer, *West African Trade*, Routledge & Kegan Paul, London, 1963.

[22] This condition can be demonstrated more rigorously using simple calculus (partial differentiation). If q_1 and q_2 are the quantities of a homogeneous product sold by a monopolist in two separate markets, such that his total output equals $q_1 + q_2$, his total profits, π, would be given by

$$\pi = R_1(q_1) + R_2(q_2) - C(q = q_1 + q_2)$$

that is, by the sum of revenues obtained in the two markets less total costs. Profits are affected if the amount sold in market 1 (q_1) is increased or that sold in market 2 (q_2) is increased. Hence, differentiating partially with respect to each of these, we have a maximum π if

$$\partial\pi/\partial q_1 = \partial R_1/\partial q_1 - \partial C/\partial q_1 = 0$$

and

$$\partial\pi/\partial q_2 = \partial R_2/\partial q_2 - \partial C/\partial q_2 = 0$$

Since the marginal cost of producing the output is the same, irrespective of how the output is disposed,

$$\frac{\partial C}{\partial q_1} = \frac{\partial C}{\partial q_2} = \frac{dC}{dq}$$

so that the condition for a maximum is

$$\frac{dC}{dq} = \frac{\partial R_1}{\partial q_1} = \frac{\partial R_2}{\partial q_2}$$

that is, marginal cost is just equal to the marginal revenues in each market.

[23] S. U. Ugoh, 'The Nigerian Cement Industry', *Nigerian Journal of Economic and Social Studies*, Vol. 6, No. 1, March 1964.

[24] The pricing problems of public utilities are examined in more detail in the next chapter.

[25] A. Hazlewood, *Rail and Road in East Africa*, Blackwell, Oxford, 1964.

[26] The fall in the average haul for export traffic does not reflect a loss of short-distance haul to the roads, but mainly an increase in the relative importance of exports from Kenya, which do not involve long hauls to the coast.

18 Public Enterprise

In Chapter 5 it was pointed out that there were no purely 'capitalist' or purely 'socialist' economies. The economies of the so-called 'Western' countries are in fact 'mixed economies', with important industries owned and controlled by the state.

Reasons for state take-over of industries

(1) This arises in the first place because it is generally accepted that there is a minimum number of goods and services which 'have' to be provided by the state. These are goods which are consumed collectively and paid for collectively out of taxation. The feature of these items is that they involve (a) indivisible benefits, and (b) the 'principle of exclusion'. If we consider the sale of bread, for example, those people who do not buy bread get no benefit, while those who buy it obtain a benefit in proportion to their outlay; this is made possible by the fact that the supply of bread is divisible into small units, namely, loaves. In contrast, services like defence, 'law and order', urban sanitation, and so forth, provide indivisible benefits: every citizen benefits from the protection of the Defence Forces and enjoys better health when public health facilities are provided, although it is clearly impossible to discriminate against people not willing to contribute to their cost by 'exposing' them to enemy attack or disease. Since the benefits are enjoyed collectively these services are best organized collectively by the government, made available without charge, and financed out of general taxation to which all contribute. If a good cannot be withheld, thus violating the principle of exclusion, it is a *public* or *collective good*.

Apart from these, however, there are a wide range of goods and services which, even if provided by state enterprise, *could* be charged for on a commercial basis, or which could be left to private enterprise. The costs of a new road or bridge can be recovered, or at least its maintenance costs can be recovered, by charging a fee or 'toll' each time a vehicle makes use of it. This is not usually done for minor roads or roads within towns simply because of administrative costs of paying toll-keepers and the traffic congestion that might be caused; it is a more common practice, however, in the case of ferries, bridges, or 'motorways' linking main cities. Public parks are another example: it is clearly *possible* to charge entrance fees, as some do.[1] There is thus an intermediate category where exclusion is possible, but inconvenient.

(2) There are, secondly, goods which have come to be considered in many countries as 'collective' goods which should be freely available to all (or available at subsidized prices) and financed out of taxation, not so much because they provide 'indivisible' benefits, but for social reasons. Thus medical services could be charged for on a commercial basis, according to the medical costs of the particular treatment required, while costs of schooling could be fully covered by school fees. In Western countries a considerable part of medical and educational services are still provided by private bodies on commercial lines or, if provided by the state, partly financed by fees. More and more, however, these have come to be considered as 'collective' goods, which the state should provide, with social objectives in view: these include health, housing, and education in particular. Interestingly enough, although many people would argue that there is a stronger case for state intervention in industry in less developed countries it is often considered that the state in less developed countries can go *less* far in taking over the supply of goods as social services: thus people generally have to find school fees for their children's schooling, to pay for hospital treatment, to build their own houses and to pay for water or obtain their own supplies.

We can, therefore, make a second distinction, between those forms of enterprise which are conducted, by and large, on commercial lines; and, on the other hand, those which aim basically at providing a social service. The fact that these two categories shade into one another, so that a government housing corporation, for instance, may operate on semi-commercial lines even if the main aim is social provision, does not prevent the distinction being useful. Nor is the distinction invalidated by the fact that charges are often made for social services supplied by the state, as in the case of medical or school fees: in general, revenue from such charges covers only a small proportion of the costs of the service, the bulk of which remains as tax-financed collective consumption of public goods.

(3) Within the category of goods provided on a commercial basis but by public bodies one can distinguish from the rest enterprises which provide *basic* services, such as electricity, water, some forms of transport (urban bus services, railways, airways, harbours, and posts and telephones, generally referred to as 'public utilities'. While some of these are still run by private enterprise in some countries, the state generally takes them over. The reasons for this are first that, because of the scale of investment that public utilities involve, and because of the long-term horizon and planning required, it is not certain that private investment would be adequate in these fields; secondly that, because of economies of scale, there is not likely to be room for more than one or two firms in the industry. This implies that a private firm would be a monopolist, and since demand for basic services is likely to be highly inelastic, the firm will have very considerable monopoly powers; while if two or more firms operate in the industry there is a likelihood of wasteful duplication of facilities, such as two sets of water installation to serve one neighbourhood. Public utilities, in other words, tend to be 'natural monopolies'. Sometimes it is preferred, of course, to allow the industry to continue under private operation, while being subject to close regulation particularly regarding the charges made for its product. How this can be done was discussed in the last chapter.

Governments are likely to be easily persuaded, therefore, to take over industries providing *social* services and those providing *basic* services, the public utilities. There is rather stronger political controversy in Western 'mixed economies' over the question of extending the scope of nationalization beyond this, but arguments are made for and against such an extension. Definitions of what constitutes a 'basic' industry vary; for example, coal-mining has long been accepted in Britain as being in this category, while the steel industry, which also produces a vital input for manufacturing industry, has been the subject of great controversy, first being nationalized, and then denationalized as the political party in power has changed. Other industries may not fit into the category of 'basic' but may still be considered as 'key' industries in the sense of having some special importance. The aircraft industry, quite apart from its military significance, is considered to generate new technology, since aeroplanes involve a wide variety of technical skills and a constantly advancing technology which, after being developed within the aviation industry, may be employed widely outside it. For this reason it may be argued that the government must have responsibility for ensuring a prosperous industry, whether by actual take-over or by lesser forms of control. What is considered 'basic' here is an industry which either because of its size, or its position as a supplier of inputs to other industries, or some other reason, generates external economies. The sort of industries or activities to which this applies in less developed countries may be different. For example the marketing system in developing countries is crucial to the activities of hundreds of small-scale farmers and it is partly for this reason that governments in developing countries have taken over marketing through the agency of marketing boards. The marketing of staple food commodities has also been taken over by statutory bodies in many cases, here in an attempt to safeguard the interests of consumers as well as producers. Banking and insurance may also be considered too essential to leave in the hands of private companies in the case of less developed countries. Major mineral-exploiting industries such as the copper industry in Zambia or diamond-mining in Tanzania may be considered to be so dominant in the economy or so important in generating tax revenue that the governments of the countries concerned have decided to take controlling interests in the industries. Nationalization of industrial and trading enterprises in Tanzania following the Arusha Declaration of 1967 was aimed at bringing the so-called 'commanding heights' of the economy under state or national control. Clearly what is a 'basic' or 'key' industry or what should be considered part of the 'commanding heights' is open to different interpretation: the underlying judgement, however, regards what industry is 'important' in terms of its impact on consumers, on other industries and on the economy as a whole; and, of course, the extent to which this importance justifies intervention or take-over by the state or by a statutory body.

(4) A particular reason for taking over an important industry is if it is considered to be failing in some aspect of its performance; for instance if its export performance is poor or it is not maintaining its share of the world market in the face of competition from corresponding industries in other countries. Recently the take-over of the shipbuilding industry in Britain has been discussed, as this once major industry has fallen behind the industries of Japan, Norway, and other countries. Part of the argument here has been of undercapitalization of private enterprises in these industries. Either private capital was not forthcoming sufficiently to meet the large and long-term capital required to modernize old and 'depressed' industries, like coal-mining, railways, or more recently shipbuilding, or it was beyond the capacity of the private capital market to supply adequate funds for high risk and uncertain ventures like atomic energy, aviation, and aircraft production. Particularly in the new advanced technology industries like atomic energy or aircraft production there are very great economies of

scale arising out of high research and development costs which have to be incurred over a long period before new output is marketed.

In developing countries, again, one reason for intervention in the marketing sector, mentioned above, is dissatisfaction with its efficiency (partly because of monopoly and partly because of undercapitalization of traders). Dissatisfaction with banking arises particularly out of the excessively conservative policies being pursued and neglect of small-scale and other industries where lending is more risky.

(5) Still another case is made sometimes for the nationalization or regulation of a 'distressed' industry, one which has periodically encountered serious economic difficulties: the coal industry in Britain and other countries is in this category, being an industry particularly severely affected in times of economic depression and also having long-term difficulties due to competition from other fuels, such as petroleum, both difficulties being reflected in problems of unemployment. In fact in the face of persistently unprofitable trading conditions, firms may actually approach governments voluntarily to request 'rescue' either by special government loans or by state take-over. Government may also be expected to take a direct role in industry in the 'distressed' or less rapidly developing areas of the country. Thus in Britain there is pressure for the government to provide employment for workers in Scotland or Northern Ireland; it may do this by offering incentives to private industry to move there, or by setting up in partnership of some kind with private industry, or even by establishing industry itself. In these cases the industry itself does not provide a social service, but there is a social objective behind intervention: the protection of those who would otherwise be unemployed. Another example of this is where state enterprises are used to cross-subsidize certain goods and services, making rich consumers pay more than poor customers. Thus poor, rural consumers may be provided with electricity or water below full cost by price discrimination, rich urban consumers paying more than full cost.

(6) It has been argued also that state ownership is the simplest way of controlling monopolies. This applies most directly in the case of 'natural monopolies' inherent in public utilities, but also to the artificial monopolies which have arisen out of monopolistic practices and agreements, take-overs, and mergers. The case here is that if enterprises in a particular industry wield especially large economic power, reflected perhaps in excessive profits, such power should be transferred to state hands in the public interest. Where monopolistic firms are foreign-owned, as is often the case in developing countries, this provides an additional motive separate from the strictly economic one.

(7) The opposite case sometimes made for state intervention is where there is judged to be excessive or 'wasteful' competition in an industry, resulting in excess capacity and duplication of effort. The wastes of imperfect competition are then held to justify a state monopoly aimed at 'rationalizing' the industry. Thus arguments in favour of nationalizing the road haulage industry in Britain were based on the desire to plan and 'organize' *all* the main forms of transportation. In developing countries it is often held that there is wasteful competition and 'too many middlemen' in marketing, and the case is made for a more 'orderly' and 'less chaotic' organized system.

(8) A view held by the nineteenth-century socialists particularly, and frequently reiterated, is that all natural resources are 'gifts of nature' and should be owned collectively through the state rather than exploited for private profit. This has been used especially with respect to land, and recently in industrialized countries with respect to land for urban development. It is pointed out that as a major city grows in size, the surrounding land becomes increasingly valuable and owners of such land will find themselves in the possession of increasingly valuable assets, becoming more wealthy without themselves having contributed to any increased output. If land likely to be required for urban development were owned by a state corporation (and leased to private users who would pay rent to the state as landlord) such benefits, arising out of general and urban growth, could accrue to the people as a whole rather than to particular fortunate individuals. In many developing countries where feudalism or its effects persist land-ownership is extremely unequal, and particular landowning families or groups own a disproportionate share of the basic agricultural resource while the majority live on small plots. In this case again individuals derive wealth from natural resources through the good fortune of inheritance rather than from assets which they themselves have created. In many cases the owners not only do not work the land themselves, but are 'absentee' landlords collecting rents without even supervising the use of the land.

Another example of this is mineral resources which it may again be argued should be considered as 'gifts of nature' to the people living in the country in which they are found, rather than to particular fortunate individuals who happen to have discovered them or to foreign mining companies who happened to be in a position at a particular time to provide capital and mining technology for their exploitation. Where the minerals are extremely rich, private exploitation by mining companies, even though these can be taxed, may be considered not to give the same guarantee as direct state participation or operation of the enterprise that the general public will share in the proceeds.

(9) It may be considered that public enterprise in general, or in particular situations, is a preferable form of organization to private enterprise: this would be a preference for public enterprise per se. However in a less developed country especially, it may be thought simply that the supply of capital, enterprise, and technical skills forthcoming from the private sector is simply not adequate on its own. The state, in supplementing this supply, is 'filling the gap' left by private enterprise: there is not necessarily any preference for public enterprise as such. The aim is not the control or reorganization of existing industries but the expansion of the industrial sector, due to a lack of voluntary activity by private entrepreneurs. Intervention becomes a practical necessity and is not based on any ideology.

There are several reasons why public enterprise may succeed where private enterprise has been unable or unwilling to operate. In developing countries most producers are either small-scale farmers or traders, and most of the supply of manufactured goods has been imported until recently. There is therefore a lack of local experience in large-scale enterprise. Moreover, where so little has been tried on a large scale, where the market as well as production conditions are unknown, there are special risks for the innovator. Elsewhere expectations can be based on the rate of return on investments in similar enterprises, whereas in developing countries such information is seldom available. Given such uncertainty, as well as a general lack of capital, local firms are likely to take a rather short-term view, and to show a preference for small-scale enterprise, often in commerce rather than industry. At the same time it is likely that foreign-based enterprises which could invest in large-scale ventures are just not aware of the opportunities which exist in the country concerned, however good these are. In agriculture, where local enterprise will be particularly small-scale, it is often difficult or impossible for expatriate or immigrant enterprise to enter, and in this sector government intervention may be the only means politically acceptable of securing large-scale commercial enterprise.

Apart from commercially successful state enterprise, however, even unsuccessful ventures may bring benefits. The first in the field can make all the mistakes from which others can learn, and by leading the way, state enterprises can encourage private enterprises to follow. In other words, external economies can in the long run result from short-term financial losses incurred by the government in accepting risks which private enterprise is not, initially, willing to take.

In addition to the state's taking up opportunities to invest where private firms are reluctant to do so, the state may raise the rate of investment by taking over an industry where excessive or high profits are being made but not reinvested locally. In the case of Tanzania and Zambia, for example, it is believed that the state will reinvest more than private businessmen wishing to enjoy high standards of living or to remit profits abroad.

(10) This is an example of a situation where nationalization raises the level of national income, and we could list this separately as a motive for nationalization. Nationalization could in principle raise the level of income accruing nationally first by diverting funds from saving and diverting profits from private consumption to public saving; secondly, by reducing the outflow of dividend incomes remitted abroad to foreign owners; and, thirdly, by accelerating the rate of localization of jobs, thereby reducing the proportion held by foreign workers.

We thus have a number of different possible reasons for state take-over of industries or their establishment as state enterprises. The industries may produce public or collective goods; they may provide social services; they may be basic or 'key' industries of strategic importance within the economy; they may be industries which are considered to be failing in their performance in some way; they may be 'distressed' industries; they may be natural monopolies or industries which have become monopolized; they may be set up to rationalize a situation in which there is 'wasteful' competition; they may be set up in areas or activities in which adequate private investment is not forthcoming; or they may be set up to raise the level of income accruing nationally by investment, balance of payments, or localization effects.

These are all economic reasons. In many developing countries, however, nationalization has been seen as the only effective alternative to continued external resource dependence if not to direct economic dependence in independent nations. The rationale of state take-over has not perhaps been concerned so much with economic questions of resource allocation and efficiency as with political and social questions of ownership and control at least in the first instance. Thus, the desire to take over 'the commanding heights' of the economy in Tanzania and Zambia is partly a general concern to ensure that key economic decisions are taken by Tanzanians or Zambians rather than simply a desire to implement predetermined economic policies affecting the sectors or industries concerned.

Should there be greater state intervention in less developed countries?

It is often said, and accepted even by many who would not be so 'interventionist' elsewhere, that there is a case for greater state intervention in the economy in less developed than in industrialized countries. Some of the reasons are implied in the discussion above. One argument is that sufficient private enterprise will not be forthcoming, either because of the lack of entrepreneurship in an underdeveloped economy, or because of the discouraging effects on private enterprise of special risks encountered in investing in developing countries, or because of a shortage of savings and investible funds. This last argument, for using state enterprise to raise the level of savings and investment, may be based on a 'savings vicious circle' such as was described in Chapter 2.

A second set of arguments relates to economic and political independence. We have indicated above how state take-over of major enterprise can in theory yield important economic benefits. A political desire for localization of decision-making could lead to state direction of enterprises in the absence of a class of indigenous entrepreneurs who could operate them privately.

A third set is based on the assertion that the market mechanism is likely to be much less effective in less developed economies than in developed countries in the efficient allocation of resources, in producing stability and in its effects on the distribution of income. It is argued that because of poor transportation, poor information flows between one part of the country and another, and lack of entrepreneurs, particularly entrepreneurs with sufficient capital, the market mechanism will be inefficient in regulating shortages and surpluses as they arise geographically in different areas within the country or over time, between one season and another. For this reason also the market will be ineffective in ironing out fluctuations of price and quantity. Monopoly is also likely to be greater than in developed countries because of imperfect capital markets and unequal access to capital, dominance of expatriate enterprises, and small markets, particularly for manufactured goods. In less developed countries also, it is likely that those who have inherited wealth, who have obtained monopoly positions, or who have otherwise been able to obtain wealth and power will be able to exploit these positions, so that inequalities will more readily increase.

It is important to consider, however, that underdevelopment will also reduce efficiency in the public sector, as in the private sector, and reduce the capacity for governments to carry out tasks. If there is a shortage of entrepreneurs in the private sector, there is likely to be an equal shortage of good decision-makers in government also. The civil service generally is likely to be much poorer in developing countries. If there are poor information flows, this will affect government and public corporation officials as well. Although a public development corporation

will be able to take risks and to initiate ventures where private companies are reluctant to do so, there is a danger of considerable misinvestment, since individual officials will not suffer from the consequences of wrong decisions and false actions in the way that a private entrepreneur would. If free markets have permitted fluctuations in agricultural prices and incomes, the record of marketing boards in stabilizing them has not been good, and incomes may in many cases have been destabilized as a result of official intervention. Finally, although there may be a strong tendency to the concentration of monopoly power in less developed countries, it is also the case that the concentration of political power, the weakness of parliaments, and the incidence of corruption may mean that the take-over of private monopolies by the state is no guarantee against the concentration of economic power and the growth of inequalities.

The effects of nationalization

We have reviewed above many arguments for setting up state enterprises or for the state's taking over enterprises. Nationalization of industries has become a frequent event in developing countries in recent years, particularly in Africa, and we need to discuss briefly some further aspects of it. *Nationalization refers to the taking over of existing assets of an enterprise by the state, as opposed to the creation of new assets.*

In discussing nationalization, therefore, we can distinguish between the *immediate* effects of the take-over and the *subsequent* effects of operating the concern as a state rather than private enterprise. The subsequent effects depend on how well the enterprise is run under public control as compared to its operation in private hands. From what we have just said it is clear that we cannot make a general statement about this, without examining the records of actual industries in particular situations. And here we must take into account not only the effects of state take-over on managerial efficiency, but more generally on the rate of saving, on the repatriation of profits and on the balance of payments, and so on. We need to take into account also the external effects of the operation of the enterprise on other enterprises and industries, through external economies. And we need to take into account possible external effects on the rate of investment *elsewhere* in the economy and in the long run, as a result of 'scaring off' potential foreign investors.

Since nationalization means the taking over of existing assets, one *immediate* effect of it is to divert scarce financial resources from the finance of *new* enterprises to the take-over of already established enterprises. Not only is there a choice between the use of such funds to promote the establishment of new private firms, but there is a choice between using the same funds to take over existing enterprises or to set up new *state* enterprises. The second point to be made is that the effect on the balance of payments may *in the short run* be negative: this is because although foreign ownership may involve an outflow of foreign exchange through remitted profits in each period, nationalization will require the finding of an immediate substantial sum in foreign exchange to purchase the foreign-owned assets, that is, for the purpose of paying compensation.[2]

Thirdly, the benefit accruing from nationalization will depend on the level at which compensation is fixed, the capital value put on the assets to be nationalized. There are problems in determining an appropriate level of compensation.

In general the value of a capital asset depends directly on the *future* level of net proceeds it is expected to produce, as we discussed in Chapter 15. In the case of privately owned assets their 'net proceeds' will be the profits accruing to the ordinary shareholders or other equity owners after payments of interest and other prior charges on earnings including income taxes. This future income will, of course, be discounted to a 'present value' using a rate of interest which the shareholders might earn with their compensation proceeds. The question is, however, whose expectations of future profits should be taken for valuation purposes, since the present owners will be optimistic while the government more sceptical of these expectations. If the assets are held by a public company whose shares are quoted on a stock exchange, the stock market's valuation may be used. This means that if there are, say, 5 million shares in the company each valued on the market at $2 per share (the nominal or issue price of the share is irrelevant here), then compensation might be fixed at $2 × 5 million or $10 millions. In principle the market valuation takes care of both the estimation of future earnings for shareholders and at the same time the discounting of these to a present worth, since the purchase price of a share is essentially the price paid *now* for a stream of future income (from dividends and any capital appreciation in the assets which investors expect will be realizable in the future). If, however, the assets cannot be valued on a stock market because the shares are unquoted, or compose only a small proportion of the assets of, say, a multinational firm operating in several countries and many industries, alternative valuations will have to be attempted. Normally in developing countries the physical assets and 'goodwill' of the business are 'valued' by firms of accountants representing the two parties and the outcome is either agreed or left to independent arbitration.

If there are excess or monopoly profits being earn-ed, it would not be reasonable to include these in valuing the enterprise. In the case of enterprises based on the exploitation of natural resources—as in the case of farms in the former 'White Highlands' of Kenya or mining companies—part of the profits can be regarded as a 'gift of nature' along the lines already discussed. Finally, in the case of service industries like banking and insurance, for example, the value of the enterprise does not stem so much from the physical assets involved, which may only be office buildings, as from the particular skills and expertise which are not necessarily purchased tog-ether with the physical assets.

Of course any sovereign state may confiscate pri-vate property, be it owned by nationals or foreigners, or pay so little compensation that it amounts to the same thing. Much depends on the demonstration effects of nationalization and the compensation terms: if the country hopes to rely on private capitalists for a major part of its development, it is likely to agree on generous terms so as not to discourage other capitalists including potential foreign investors. If it expects to rely on state enterprises exclusively, it may be less generous, arguing perhaps that the assets taken over have already yielded enough profits to recoup investors for their initial capital outlay and risk-taking.

Types of public enterprise in Eastern Africa

Public enterprises can take a variety of forms, and are often described in Eastern Africa as parastatal or statutory bodies. We can distinguish five different types.

(1) *Government trading departments* are actually government departments, either central or local, but sell certain goods or services either at full cost or at prices subsidized by general taxation. These include 'public works', water supply, and the postal services. Some of these, like the municipal bus services, ferries, and water supply are in fact public utilities; others have been developed by, say, the Ministry of Works or Agriculture to undertake workshop repairs or furniture-making in the absence of private enterprise. It is usual for such commercial activities to be hand-ed over to independent public trading enterprises in due course to free them from civil service 'red tape'.

(2) *Public utilities* supplying water, electricity, tele-phone services, and other 'natural monopolies' often evolved in Eastern Africa, as just mentioned, from being government departments. The 'national' or joint-national airways are also public utilities, al-though sometimes constituted as public companies. Public utilities with private shareholders include the urban bus companies and Kenya's Power and Lighting Company.

(3) *Statutory marketing and production boards* were discussed in Chapter 12. The essential features of agricultural marketing agencies are their stabilization and fiscal functions which distinguish them from other state-owned enterprises supplying services or manufactured goods, such as the various National Trading Corporations which normally compete with privately owned firms in similar lines of business. Sometimes the state has a monopoly of trade in a commodity, such as sugar in the Sudan, and uses the monopoly profits as a source of tax revenue.

(4) *State-owned commercial companies* are those, whether in mining, manufacturing, or commerce (such as the National Trading Corporations), which operate on ordinary commercial lines in industries other than the usual public utilities. The scope and range of such state undertakings, as discussed above, measure most directly the extent to which the economy has moved away from the essentially capitalist or mixed economy towards a socialized or collectivist one.

(5) *Development corporations* are the subject of the next section of this chapter, which will show them to have been a major instrument of industrialization in Uganda and Malawi, while becoming in Zambia and Tanzania promoting and holding companies for the various specialized state enterprises which have now taken over large parts of the modern economy. The relative importance of national or regional development corporations is the most distinctive feature (together with the marketing boards) of economic organization, particularly in the manufacturing sector, in the developing countries of Africa, as compared to the developed capitalist or socialist countries.

Development corporations

Complete take-over of the enterprise and the operation of fully owned state enterprises are not, however, the only alternative available for effecting some state control over particular industries. To restrict monopoly power, for example, as we have already seen, the government could fix maximum prices, or could try to stimulate competition by assisting the development of other firms. Another possibility is for the state to buy only a portion of the shares of an enterprise, thus becoming in effect a part-owner of the company. In Britain the Labour Government of 1965–70 set up the Industrial Reorganization Corporation which was to take shares in strategic or problematic industries, and on its return to power in 1974 revived this in the form of the National Enterprise Board, which can be seen partly as a means for assisting distressed industries or simply as a vehicle for extending state control over industry.

We have already indicated that in a developing country the case for a greater degree of government intervention is widely accepted. This intervention is frequently channelled through a *development corporation* where again only *part* of the capital is held by the state. Let us see why the development corporation has been thought a convenient means of making this intervention.

What are the specific advantages, first of all, as compared to running the enterprise through a government department? It can be argued that the civil service atmosphere of the latter is not best suited for commercial enterprise: civil servants do not make good businessmen. In contrast, a development corporation can more easily acquire the specialized technical and managerial expertise that a particular venture requires, in part by actually recruiting from private firms. A corporation is free to plan independently of periodic government votes and close parliamentary scrutiny and thus to take more flexible and rapid decisions. Nor will it feel bound to stick to previous statements of policy, even when circumstances have changed, as a government department might. The bureaucracy and 'red tape' of a government department are, of course, partly a defence against close public scrutiny: whereas willingness to take risks despite the possibility of mistakes is a necessary ingredient of commercial enterprise.

The basis for a development corporation, however, is that it is an extremely convenient means of combining private with public enterprise and capital. This is especially important in a developing country where of course the finance, enterprise, and technical expertise available *within* the country, whether in the private or public sectors, are simply insufficient, and need to be supplemented by encouraging foreign enterprise to come in. A corporation facilitates joint ventures and a wide range of other forms of joint participation. Different terms of organization may also be appropriate according to the industry, for example as between manufacturing industry, agriculture, and commerce. It may, moreover, be the aim to permit the enterprise to be taken over eventually by private hands, once the venture has been shown to be commercially viable, so that the government can switch its scarce capital and enterprise to yet newer ventures. A corporation in which the government initially holds all or most of the shares can do this simply by selling an increasing proportion of shares to the public, or by selling out to a private firm as soon as a reputable company becomes willing to assume the responsibility.

A development corporation can intervene in commercial enterprise at very different levels. The minimum degree of participation is where it simply engages in research, such as that into the possibilities of introducing new crops or new varieties of crop, or engages in the exploration for minerals. Such activities are preliminary to commercial enterprise, which may then be undertaken by private firms or individuals. Alternatively it may operate as a loan agency, still without itself participating in the organization of enterprises but simply using public funds to make loans to private firms on favourable terms. For more direct participation in economic activity the corporation may set up either subsidiary or associated companies. In the former the corporation provides the bulk of the capital and provides the management, although private capital may also be invested, while in the case of associated companies the corporation operates jointly with a private company, either a local or very often a foreign enterprise, the latter providing management and technical expertise. This is particularly common where the activity requires technical knowledge of a kind which is only possessed by foreign enterprise, as is often the case, for example, in mining. The foreign enterprise generally provides a large part of the risk capital in such a venture, leaving the development corporation to raise the safer debenture capital. The advantage to the private investor is that, although it risks its capital, the company has the assurance of government backing, cooperation, and financial help, while for the government it means that it has attracted additional enterprise and risk capital into the country while retaining a measure of control over the new venture.

A note of caution must be sounded, however, regarding this apparently convenient arrangement. Particularly where the field is a technical one, civil servants, on behalf of the government, may be at a disadvantage in the negotiations with technical and management experts employed by the company over the terms of the 'partnership' arrangement. The foreign or local company may actually be happy to work in collaboration with government as the best means of obtaining security for its capital and various forms of preferential treatment in respect of protection policy or tax policy which reduce its risks and increase its profitability. Where the government provides the bulk of the finance and signs a 'management contract' under which the foreign enterprise will manage the firm on its behalf, the company may be able to negotiate very lucrative terms for its management services leaving the government to provide most of the funds which are at risk. Joint enterprise through a development corporation therefore does not itself provide a guarantee that the maximum domestic benefit from the venture will be secured.

The role of a development corporation

The most obvious role of a development corporation as described above, therefore, is a *controlling role*. This might be described as a form of partial nationalization with the aim of ensuring that the public interest is met. More often, however, development corporations have been set up with a view not of controlling existing private enterprise but of supplementing and expanding the level of investment and enterprise. Here a useful distinction has been drawn[3] between activities in which the corporation plays a *catalyst role* and in which it plays an *injector role*. A catalyst is defined to be 'a substance which produces chemical change without itself changing'. In the present context what is meant is that the government, operating through the development corporation, simply acts as an agent to bring together factors of production from other sources and helps to fuse them into a viable concern, without itself permanently using up its own resources. The purpose in this case is for the government to give the minimum help necessary to get the enterprise established on a sound basis. Once this has been achieved the corporation can re-employ its capital and management resources elsewhere, so that these scarce resources can be made to go as far as possible. If the aim of government is really to 'fill the gap' left by private enterprise, and not public enterprise per se, then its policy will be biased towards this 'catalyst' role, working with private enterprise as much as possible, and handing over substantial responsibility to private enterprise as quickly as possible.

Very often, however, this catalyst role is not considered sufficient and a stronger degree of participation is felt to be necessary. This is especially likely to be the case where the risks are very high and where the immediate commercial viability of the enterprise is less obvious. In such cases private investment is not forthcoming, but possible external economies may make the venture worth undertaking by the government. Alternatively, strong government participation may be needed where there are special difficulties obstructing the entry of new large-scale private enterprise, as is the case very often in agriculture. An example would be the state farms attempted in Ghana and to a much lesser extent in Tanzania, where the objective has been to secure economies of scale in farming without the equity problems involved in handing over large tracts of land to local or foreign private entrepreneurs. In this area it is likely that the government will need to provide the main ingredients of finance and management. Since these ingredients have in this case to be injected by the government itself, we may say that the corporation is engaged in a direct 'injector role' rather than in a catalytic function.

The granting of loans by a development corporation to private enterprise should rightly be considered as part of a catalytic role. The corporation is in a better position to raise loans both from private investors and from international development and financial institutions, which it can then pass on, on favourable terms, to existing and new private concerns within the country. The corporation is acting as a financial intermediary in this case, and is not directly involved in the management of the enterprise.

Loans schemes are in practice often related to developing indigenous business. A major reason for setting up development corporations is in fact to reduce dependence on foreign enterprise and to *localize* industry and commerce. Much of the popular pressure to 'nationalize' private enterprise in Africa and elsewhere is in fact less concerned with public ownership and more with increasing the participation of local citizens in the running of enterprises operating in their countries. Localization refers to both management and finance. This aim is compatible with the catalyst role referred to above when the enterprise can be developed and then handed over to private, but local, and especially African business interests. For example in Nigeria the National Development Plan, 1962–8, stated (on page 362) that 'the primary role of the Development Corporations is to start new industries and to take the initial risks. Once such enterprises have been launched successfully, they will be progressively sold to Nigerian investors in order to raise further capital for accelerated expansion.' In Eastern Africa, due to the lower levels of income and a less well-developed stock exchange, the sale of shares to individual Africans, or the sale to a local company of a majority shareholding, involving control of a corporation enterprise, is more difficult. However another aspect of 'localization' is employment, and even where a foreign company retains control more pressure can be put on it as an associate of the corporation to train local administrative staff to operate the enterprise.

Another question influencing the role of a development corporation concerns how far it should aim at commercial operations since, due to external economies, this aim may not be identical with promoting general economic development within the country. This arises first in the choice of ventures taken up by the corporation. If the aim is to fill the gap left by private enterprise it should attempt especially the riskier projects which private enterprise will not touch on its own. The most adventurous policy, which may involve financial losses or at least less overall profitability, may stimulate the maximum amount of economic development in the long run. Secondly, the corporation can increase its profitability by holding on longer to the financially most successful enterprises under its control, rather than attempting to transfer them or shares in them to private hands at the earliest opportunity. While the success of a development corporation ought not to be viewed in the narrowest financial terms, there is no doubt that among members of the public and among business interests nothing stimulates confidence in the corporation more than good financial results. If, of course, the aim of the development corporation is to pursue a controlling role, the industries and enterprises selected are likely to be the more important and strategic ones, and there would be no question of returning these to private hands.

The Uganda Development Corporation (UDC)

The first major development corporation to be established in Eastern Africa, and one frequently cited as an example to be followed, was the Uganda Development Corporation. The UDC was established in 1952 as an independent corporation, with the Uganda Government as sole shareholder, providing the initial capital of £5 millions. The amount could be made available from the marketing board surpluses acquired in the Korean War period of 1950–1, and it was the existence of these funds which created the opportunity of a plan for industrialization, of which UDC formed part.

Although industrial development was the main objective, agriculture was included in the Ordinance establishing UDC, and Agricultural Enterprises Ltd (AEL) was set up as a UDC subsidiary at an early stage. Later AEL came to have more importance, partly because it was realized that progress in the industrial sector would not be achieved as readily as originally thought, and partly because of the success achieved through AEL in developing tea as an additional export crop for small farmers. The rapid growth in the volume of activity by UDC was accompanied also by an increasing spread of interests, including property, finance and banking, and hotels. Table 18.1 shows the relative importance of investments in the different sectors of the economy. A remarkable feature is the comprehensive scope of UDC activities, illustrated again in Table 18.2 below. Just over half the total accumulated investment in 1970 was in mining and manufacturing, largely the latter, and a quarter in agriculture, mainly tea. Tea and textiles together covered 42 per cent of the gross resources invested, and were the two most important activities measured on this basis, followed by cement production and the tourist (hotel) industry.

Table 18.1   *Development of the UDC's net resources at 31 December 1970*

Activity	U shs (million)	%
Agriculture	72.0	23.8
Agricultural/industrial	2.4	0.1
Textiles	69.5	23.1
Cement	37.9	12.6
Foods and beverages	43.1	14.3
Fertilizers	8.1	2.7
Enamelware	8.2	2.7
Miscellaneous	8.4	2.8
Mining	7.5	2.5
Hotels and tourism	31.9	10.7
Property	16.0	5.3
Finance	32.6	10.9
Total gross resources	337.5	111.7
Less borrowings	35.5	11.7
Total net resources	302.0	100.0

SOURCE: UDC, *Nineteenth Year Annual Report and Accounts*, 1970

The functions of UDC as established were to include:

(1) The direct establishment of enterprises.

(2) The raising of finance by the issue of debentures and the making of loans to both established and new enterprises, as well as the guaranteeing of loans that such businesses might be able to arrange for themselves.

(3) The promotion of new private enterprise.

(4) Research into development possibilities in any field including, if desirable, the setting up of new research institutes.

(5) The development of African commercial enterprise.

The definition of these functions clearly shows no prejudice against either private or public enterprise. This is borne out by an early UDC memorandum which stated the aims of UDC to be:

> To ensure that sound economic development takes place—without participation by UDC capital and organization where possible, but with those things where necessary. Put another way, we are not *primarily* concerned with expanding the UDC balance sheet but rather with increasing the quantum of sound economic activity in the Protectorate which would be reflected ultimately in the national income figures.[4]

Moreover it was the aim to expand the activity of the corporation by constantly ploughing back profits into new enterprise. This would mean that the initial amount of capital provided would limit the possibilities for intervention by the corporation in a direct 'injector' role.

Since we should expect a corporation playing a predominantly 'catalyst' role to operate via a relatively large proportion of associated companies rather than more directly through subsidiaries, let us look at the relative emphasis placed on these two forms of organization within UDC. Table 18.2 gives a comprehensive list of companies for 1970, divided according to these two categories and according to the field activity. In fact we see that subsidiary companies formed the largest proportion by far of UDC companies as far as the number and aggregate size of operations were concerned. It remains true at the same time that some of the associated companies, notably Kilembe Mines, were of considerable importance. The latter were confined by and large to mining and manufacturing. In agriculture we have already suggested that anything but a direct injector role by a corporation is likely to be difficult, which turns out to be the case here: all agricultural activities of UDC have been carried out through subsidiaries of Agricultural Enterprises Ltd, itself a subsidiary of the corporation. Moreover UDC has operated increasingly via subsidiaries as it has broadened its activities to cover other sectors such as tourism, property, and finance, in which it has not made much use of associated companies, and as it has accepted ventures of a more experimental nature, such as the Lango Development Co. Apart from this, there would not appear to have been much attempt to hand over control of viable enterprises to private enterprise, which a strongly catalytic role might favour. In fact quite a number of companies, such as Uganda Meat Packers and Universal Asbestos Co., were taken over as subsidiaries after a period of associateship.

As it turns out, however, the division between subsidiary and associated companies is not an accurate indicator of the relative emphasis placed on the 'injector' and 'catalyst' roles. A wide variety of arrangements for joint participation with private capital and enterprise have been entered into, and have permitted such cooperation in the case of both associated and subsidiary enterprises. These arrangements vary first according to the field of activity, which determines needs. In copper-mining, for example, technical expertise and experience are vital, so that in the case of Kilembe Mines the initial capital was provided jointly by UDC, by the Colonial Development Corporation (CDC), and by a Canadian mining company, Frobisher Ltd, who were brought in to operate the enterprise. In the case of Nyanza Textiles, apart from the technical problems of the factory itself, a vast number of cotton textile operatives, 1,200 to work the first shift alone, had to be trained, where no local experience existed. Though Nyanza Textiles now falls into the class of sub-

Table 18.2 *Subsidiary and associated companies of the UDC, 1970*

Subsidiary	Associated
Manufacturing and processing	
Uganda Metal Products and Enamelware	Steel Corporation of East Africa
Nyanza Textiles (associated till 1958)	Associated Match Co.
Tororo Industrial Chemicals and Fertilizers	Associated Paper Industries
United Garment Industry	Chillington Tool Co.
East African Distilleries	Uganda Fishnet Manufacturers
Solutea Ltd	Uganda Grain Milling Co.
Uganda Meat Packers (associated in 1962–5)	Uganda Millers
Uganda Cement Industry	Uganda Maize Industries
Universal Asbestos Manufacturing Co.	Uganda Feeds
(E.A.) (associated till 1963)	Uganda Bags and Hessian Mills
Uganda Fish Marketing Corporation	Papco Industries
(associated 1958–69; subsidiary till 1958)	African Ceramics
Uganda Spinning Mill	Domestic Appliances
Mining	
Sukulu Mines (associated until 1961)	Kilembe Mines Ltd
	Kilmex
	Wolfram Investments
Agriculture	
Agricultural Enterprises Ltd	
including as subsidiaries:	
Bunyoro Ranching Co.	
Ankole Tea	
Six other tea enterprises	
Lango Development Co.	
Uganda Crane Estates	
Uganda Livestock Industries	
Hotels, tourism and domestic aviation	
Uganda Hotels	
International Hotel, Kampala	
National Park Lodges (Uganda)	
Uganda Wildlife Development	
Uganda Air	
Uganda Aviation Services	
Property	
Uganda Consolidated Properties	
Kulubya Property Co.	
Uganda Properties	
Banking, finance and commerce	
Uganda Bank	Development Finance Co. of Uganda
Uganda Holdings	
Uganda Crane Industries	

sidiary,[5] Calico Printers of Manchester, England, together with the Bleachers' Association, also from England, were originally brought in to provide managerial organization as well as finance. In both these cases foreign enterprises were brought into Eastern Africa; but for the most part joint ventures have been with old-established Eastern African firms already operating in the area or with local firms. Thus the Uganda Grain Milling Co., an associated company of UDC, was in 1970 a joint venture between UDC, and two Kenya companies, Bauman & Co.,who acted as managing agents, dealing with the commercial side only, and Unga Ltd, who were their technical supervisors. In 1970 Uganda's leading local industrialist, Madhvani & Co., was involved in several UDC associated companies, for example, the Associated Match Co. (together with Sikh Sawmills), Associated Paper Industries, and the Steel

Corporation of East Africa, in which Madhvani's were the major shareholders.

In any developing country, as we have already said, it is more difficult to channel private capital into agriculture. Whereas capital in expatriate or immigrant hands is politically tolerable, land is regarded in a somewhat different light. Policy is therefore generally to restrict entry of non-African capital into agriculture. Since management is usually tied to the provision of capital, this has meant that non-African managerial skills have also largely been kept out of this sector. In such circumstances there is a possibility that a development corporation, being a 'parastatal' or semi-government organization, will be more acceptable. Private capital can be employed indirectly if shares can be purchased through the corporation, which then invests such finance in the agricultural sector. UDC has operated in this sector by bringing in local governments, both as shareholders and as directors on executive boards. Thus the Bunyoro Native Government was associated with the Bunyoro Ranching Scheme from the time of its establishment in 1956, while the Ankole Native Government was a joint managing agent with a private company, the Uganda Co., when the Ankole Tea Co. was formed in the same year. This very successful scheme is an important example of the catalyst function that a development corporation can play in bringing together agents of production, even though it is rather exceptional for private capital and management to be brought successfully into the agricultural sector in this way.

It is fair to say therefore that although subsidiary companies have generally been favoured, private capital and enterprise have been encouraged and welcomed whenever they were forthcoming. The approach has essentially been a practical one. It is also fair to say that the bias has been essentially commercial, with an eye to profitability. The Ordinance setting up UDC did require it to aim at breaking even, at least, over the full range of its activity, although individual enterprises might run at a loss; and as we have pointed out UDC has constantly made profits. In later years before the disruption of the Amin period the corporation was in a greater hurry, was willing to be more experimental in many cases, and laid greater stress on the object of increased localization of industry and trade, all perhaps being associated with lower than maximum profitability; but the basic commercial objective remained.

As far as the objective of localizing industry and commerce is concerned, this has always been an important policy in Uganda. Up to 1963 this operated mainly through the African Loans Fund set up to provide loans for small-scale African business. In 1963 African Business Promotions Ltd was created

as a subsidiary of UDC 'to establish and promote our own people in the trade and commerce field generally of the country so that Ugandans may play a reasonable part and hold a reasonable share of the country's commerce'.[6] However, even in small-scale trading and industry these schemes have not so far met with much success and there is a conflict between the desire to establish large-scale industrial and commercial ventures, for maximum development, and the desire to promote African business. In 1970 more direct measures for Africanization of commerce have been taken through the National Trading Corporation which replaced African Business Promotions as the vehicle for such encouragement, and as a result of the departure of non-citizen Asians in 1972.

The Malawi Development Corporation (MDC)

Another development corporation which has played a major role in fostering large-scale industrial and commercial enterprises in a predominantly agricultural economy is the Malawi Development Corporation, established as a wholly government-owned institution in 1964, the year of Malawi's independence. Although it started in a small way as a statutory corporation with a grant of MK 1 million from the UK government as the main source of capital, it subsequently attracted loan funds from the Danish and West German governments, from financial institutions and the Malawi government. In 1968 a major subsidiary was formed to support its industrial promotion activities, the Development Finance Company of Malawi, Ltd (DEFINCO), with 49 per cent of the equity being subscribed mainly by overseas financial institutions. In 1970 the MDC's role as a holding company was formally recognized by its incorporation as a limited liability company with a share capital of MK 2.2 millions, wholly owned by the state.

At the end of 1972 the functional distribution of MDC's investments, amounting to some MK 6 millions, was, approximately, 28 per cent in food and beverages; 16 per cent each in hotels, tourism, and catering and in finance and property; 14 per cent in wholesaling and retailing; 11 per cent in fisheries and farming; 5 per cent in textiles; and 5 per cent in cement and other construction materials. With the exception of some investments in certain trading firms formerly under government control and run as subsidiaries, the bulk of MDC's interests are in a few large enterprises which have been started from scratch since Independence.

In considering the distribution of these interests, however, it should be taken into account that MDC is not the only public enterprise, or necessarily the main institution involved in promoting industry and commerce in Malawi. There are first of all the usual public utility undertakings, in this case covering airways, railways, and lake transport, electricity, urban water supply, broadcasting, and telecommunications.[7] Here we may mention also the New Capital City Development Corporation which was established to look after the new capital at Lilongwe. Another corporation, the Agricultural Development and Marketing Corporation (ADMARC) has expanded public interests into the agricultural sector, although not confined entirely to agriculture in fact. In 1972 ADMARC had MK 23.5 millions in share capital and reserves, making it much the largest public enterprise in which the government has business interest. ADMARC's own investments in subsidiaries, associates, and in loans were at MK 5.5 millions, almost as large as the MK 6.0 millions of MDC. Some of these were in joint ventures with MDC, in grain and oil milling, for example; while others in agricultural estates, canning, and road haulage were of the type which could easily have been undertaken by MDC or in Uganda by UDC. ADMARC has also, as much as MDC itself, supplied loan capital to other parastatal bodies, holding railway stock and investing in the country's first 'national' petroleum distribution company

In addition to MDC, DEFINCO, and ADMARC, the government also continues to hold certain commercial investments directly, in the main road transport firm, for example, where management is relatively straightforward, and is undertaken by the United Transport Group which, incidentally, operates elsewhere in Eastern Africa.

Finally it is important to mention in the case of Malawi a number of private holding companies which have had especially close relationships with some of the public corporations. Most important has been Press Holdings Ltd, which is owned and managed by the country's political leadership. By 1974, this privately owned group had interests especially in distribution, property, finance, road transport, and publishing. The commitment of the political leadership to private enterprise has also been extended to large-scale tobacco farming. This company has therefore been engaged in areas which might otherwise have required the involvement of MDC or ADMARC. There has, moreover, been some mobility of capital between the private holding companies and such institutions as MDC and DEFINCO, acting as an informal stock market for certain kinds of security. Shares, however, have been sold in direct deals between the parties concerned without reference to stock exchange quotations, since no stock exchange exists.

Returning to MDC, we can now consider what kind of role this has played, whether catalyst, injector, or controller. Given the open attitude to private enterprise just mentioned, it is clearly not the last of these. Since as a general rule MDC has limited itself to equity participation in joint ventures with private enterprises and this usually as a *minority* shareholder in *associated* companies, we could consider MDC a clear example of a development corporation attempting to fulfil a 'catalyst' role. At the end of 1971 MDC had investments of MK 5.3 millions in companies with total assets of MK 18.2 millions: in other words, in aggregate terms its holdings in various companies amounted to *less than one-third* of their total assets. This proportion does not change markedly even when the figure is adjusted to take account of MDC's investments channelled through DEFINCO. MDC has succeeded in establishing joint ventures with a number of important foreign manufacturing firms, notably David Whitehead and Co. in cotton textiles, alone comprising assets of about MK 4 millions; Carlsberg, the Danish brewery which has itself 75 per cent of the MK 752,000 equity capital; and a potentially important packaging firm. However it also has minority interests in ventures with (1) old-established local or expatriate-owned companies concerned with construction materials, distribution, and tourism, and (2) the increasingly important Malawian-owned private business enterprise of Press Holdings Ltd mentioned above. We may note, finally, that, also in the 'catalyst' role, MDC is authorized to participate through loans or grants, or in an advisory capacity.

As an 'injector' of capital, using subsidiaries, it has also developed new large-scale trawler fishing and cold-storage industries, expanded hotel facilities for tourists, and fostered a small-scale radio manufacturing firm, started by an enterprising American.

As in Uganda and Kenya, it has been concerned with localization of existing enterprises, particularly in the fields of wholesaling and retailing, banking, insurance, construction, and property development. The wholly MDC-owned Import and Export Company, like other 'national trading corporations', is aimed at securing for Malawians a larger share of the distributive trades, including agency business. MDC also encourages Malawian contractors to tender for building contracts for its estate development company.

Injection and control in Tanzania: NDC, STC, and the DDCs

Although the UDC has undoubtedly been the pioneer of the development corporation as an agency for the acceleration of economic development in Eastern Africa, the *fastest* such development has certainly been that in Tanzania under the National Development Corporation. At the time of independence Tanzania had been the most neglected of the three East African economies and was, in the field of industrialization, especially, starting very much 'from scratch'. In Chapter 23 we review the rapid process of import-substituting industrialization which took place subsequently. The main vehicle for this process was the NDC, established in 1965. From the beginning, and partly because of this particular neglect, Tanzania decided to embark on a distinctly socialist path of development, although this was strongly reinforced in the decisive Arusha Declaration of 1967. This bias can be seen in the financial structure of the NDC, as shown in Table 18.3. The scope of NDC activities has considerably expanded since

Table 18.3 Subsidiary and associated companies of the NDC in Tanzania, mid-1970

Date of incorporation	Subsidiary companies	NDC holding (%)	Associated companies	NDC holding (%)
1965 or before	Salt-mining (1937)	81.3	Diamond-mining (1942)	50
	Meat processing (1947)	51	Metal products (1947)	50
	Plywood (1949)	100	Cement (1959)	50
	Smoking pipes (1955)	56	Blankets (1961)	30
	Brewing (1960)	51	Finance (1962)	25
	Brewing (1961)	60	Pyrethrum processing (1962)	49
	Newspaper (1961)	100	Industrial promotion (1963)	23.7
	Plastics (1962)	100	Cashew processing (1963)	40
	Coffee manufacture (1963)	80	Vehicle assembly (1965)	24.5
	Investment finance (1963)	98		
	(Ocean fishing, 1964)	—		
	Cigarettes (1965)	60		
	Craft industries (1965)	80		
	Footwear (1965)	60		
1966	Textiles	100	Textiles	40
	Diamond polishing	75	Sisal bags	40
	Publishing	60	Invention (of cashew processing machine)	50
	(Steel rolling)	—		
	(Building)	—		
	(Gemstone-mining)	—		
1967	Printing	100		
	Chipboard manufacture	80		
1968	Timber sleepers	75	Cashew processing	50
	Tanning	75		
	Agricultural implements	100		
	(Fertilizers)	—		
1969	(Importation of tyres)	—		
	(Gemstones production)	—		
1970	Textile marketing	100	(Bicycles)	—
	(Cashew processing)	—		
	(Kenaf production)	—		
	(Sawmilling)	—		
	(Fibre board)	—		
	(Paper industries)	—		

SOURCE: *A Short Guide to Investors,* Tanzania, Ministry of Commerce and Industry, Dar es Salaam, 1970
NOTE: Companies given in brackets are those for which financial arrangements were still to be made.

1970, to which this table refers, but it is still possible to identify the approach which is being followed.

The 'injecting' and 'controlling' roles of the Corporation can be seen first of all in the much greater proportion of subsidiary, as opposed to associated, companies. The latter are defined by the NDC as companies in which its financial interest is *not more* than 50 per cent. The proportion of associated, companies is clearly much lower than in the case of the UDC as revealed in Table 18.2. Many of the subsidiary companies are based on a 100 per cent NDC interest. The 'controlling' role is shown particularly in the number of NDC enterprises which were incorporated *before* the establishment of the NDC, that is, in the number of companies which were actually taken over by the Corporation quite soon after Independence. The NDC was thus an instrument for nationalization. It should be added that even in the case of associated companies the NDC often has a 50 per cent holding, quite enough to be able to exert strong influence over the management, and even to represent a 'nationalized' enterprise.

In terms of the value of assets, however, subsidiary companies accounted for only 44 per cent of the total in mid-1970, if companies in process of development are excluded. This is mainly due to the importance of Williamson Diamonds Ltd in terms of asset value, as shown in Table 18.4. The table shows that despite the very large number of NDC subsidiary and associated companies, there is considerable concentration of interests, as measured by the value of assets of the companies concerned. Five activities accounted for 70 per cent of the total. Of these diamond-mining accounted for 30 per cent. Since the corporation is supposed to an important extent to generate its own finance from NDC activities, this indicates the use which has been made of proceeds from diamond-mining to finance industrial diversification. Apart from diamond-mining, however, the important activities are those which are common features of embryonic industrial sectors in developing countries: textiles, cigarettes, beer, and cement. Since 1970, of course, there has been considerable expansion of NDC interests. And towards the end of 1969, these were already sufficient to necessitate a 'hiving off' of NDC's interests in agriculture and processing and in tourism to two new parastatal organizations, the National Agriculture and Food Corporation (NAFCO) and the Tanzania Tourist Corporation (TTC), leaving NDC itself to concentrate on developments in manufacturing, processing, and mining. NAFCO inherited six going concerns and a number of proposed projects in 1969. Set up under the supervision of the Ministry of Agriculture, Food and Cooperatives, it covers direct investments in large-scale agriculture, including sugar, wheat, rice, and coconut production, as well as agriculture-related industries such as maize-milling. We may mention also the Workers' Development Corporation, incorporated in 1964 as a subsidiary of NUTA (the National Union of Tanzania Workers), the aim of which was to mobilize workers' savings for investment, to permit increased participation by workers in development activities, and to make investments specifically in workers' housing. The WDC makes relatively small-scale investments in manufacturing, building, agriculture, and commerce. In addition the National Small Industries Corporation (NSIC) was founded in 1965, starting operations towards the end of 1967. The activities of this corporation (now renamed the Small Industries Development Organization) are reviewed in a later chapter.

Table 18.4 *Relative importance of activities in which the NDC had interests in mid-1970*

Activity	NDC holding in companies involved (%)	Total assets of companies (T shs m)	Proportion total NDC assets (%)
Diamond-mining	50	318	29.5
Textile manufacture and marketing	100, 100, 40	242	22.1
Cigarettes	60	87	8.1
Brewing	51	59	5.5
Cement	50	51	4.7
Other	—	325	30.2
Total	—	1,082	100.0

SOURCE: as Table 18.3

As we have said, the 'controlling' role of the NDC is obvious from the above. More specifically it is stated[8] that 'For those projects which are defined as "major means of production," up to 50 per cent of the equity may be subscribed by private firms and in many cases the partner will also provide technical skills. NDC also participates in enterprises not classed as major means of production in which case there are no restrictions on the proportion of equity which may be held by private interests.' This statement is in line with the desire to control the 'commanding heights' of the economy. At the same time it does not exclude the injector role or the catalyst one, since one function of the NDC is to raise development finance from international institutions and through intergovernment credits (foreign assistance), as well as the Tanzania Treasury, and it welcomes local and foreign financial participation in its projects.

At the same time public control of economic activity is quite comprehensive. The marketing board system covering both export produce and the main foodstuff, maize, has already been reviewed. The State Trading Corporation was established in February 1967, following the Arusha Declaration. In addition to controlling the export-import trade (particularly imports, in view of the importance of marketing boards for exports), the STC was empowered to 'establish branches which would form a distributive network for locally manufactured and imported goods to cover the whole of Tanzania'. Progress in establishing this wholesale trading network has been slow, but the desire has been stated, in principle, to extend state participation to the level of retail trade. Even for the export-import business, however, the STC was found to be unnecessarily large and unwieldy, and it was later decided to split it up into separate organizations dealing in particular import lines. Already in 1970 one of the principal imports, textiles and textile articles, had become the specific responsibility of the National Textile Industries Corporation (NATEX), charged with the task of importing *all* textiles and textile articles which could not be made locally. The nationalization of banking and insurance is discussed elsewhere.

An interesting institutional innovation was made in Tanzania in 1971, when the decision was taken to establish, in every one of the sixty Districts of Tanzania, a District Development Corporation. The purpose was to decentralize the development effort and to encourage local initiative in identifying and establishing local projects. The objective was primarily the 'catalyst' one of securing local initiative to produce new activities: unfortunately in many cases lack of ideas for new activities prompted less development-oriented actions such as the take-over of local stores or petrol stations.

Zambia's progress with nationalization

Since 1968, when the first 'Economic Reforms' were proclaimed at Mulungushi, after the style of the Arusha Declaration in Tanzania, Zambia has moved progressively from acute reliance on foreign private enterprise to a system where almost all the large-scale enterprises in the modern sector are in public ownership. The 1968 measures were aimed at securing Zambian participation by acquiring controlling interests in some major industrial companies. The Industrial Development Corporation, INDECO, was made the holding company for these new subsidiary companies, greatly expanding its activities which till then had involved a number of joint ventures with foreign technical partners and acting as a development bank, providing management guidance and loans on commercial terms to private enterprises. INDECO originated, like several African development corporations, as a capital-injecting loans board in 1951, when the Northern Rhodesia Industrial Loans Board was established, becoming the Industrial Development Corporation in 1960. After Rhodesia's UDI in 1965, INDECO expanded its industrial development responsibilities beyond simple loan injections and catalyst functions to carry out urgent ventures like TAZAMA, the Tanzania–Zambia Pipeline and the Zambia–Tanzania Road Services (ZTRS).

The effect of the 'Mulungushi Reforms', however, was to make INDECO the principal instrument for state equity participation in industry: 23 leading firms were taken over to the extent of at least 51 per cent of their equity; while Zambian entrepreneurs including cooperatives were encouraged to replace non-Zambians (mainly Asians) in the retail and small building industries. Limits were also placed on the overseas repatriation of profits and access to local bank credit for non-Zambians. There was, therefore, the dual aim of 'socialization' and 'localization' in the measures being pursued.

In 1969 the second 'Economic Reforms' involved the 51 per cent nationalization of the two foreign-owned copper-mining groups, this placing the 'commanding heights' of the country's economy in local, public hands. In view of the size of this operation, and the existing size of INDECO, a separate Mining Development Corporation, MINDECO, was formed. In 1970 both INDECO and MINDECO became wholly owned subsidiaries of a new parent company, ZINCO, the Zambia Industrial and Mining Corporation Ltd.

At the end of 1970 in a further set of measures, INDECO was directed to take over some additional companies. Further wholly owned subsidiaries of

ZIMCO were created to hold shares in these new fields of state enterprise. A Finance and Development Corporation (FINDECO) was established to control a wholly state-owned insurance industry (as in Tanzania) and building society, and have a 51 per cent interest in two commercial banks which would replace the existing five banks.[9] A National Hotels Corporation (NHC) was created to develop hotels, and a fifth state corporation, the National Transport Corporation (NTC) to run road haulage and passenger transport companies in which existing private enterprises like United Transport continued as managers and minority shareholders. An innovation of these reforms was the appointment as chairmen of these five corporations of the ministers of the parallel ministries concerned, and of the President of Zambia, as chairman of the ultimate holding company, ZIMCO. In effect, therefore, this pyramid of state enterprises was directly responsible to the Cabinet ministers in their capacity as chairmen of the five main business enterprise sectors in the modern economy: mining, industry and commerce, finance, transport, and hotels.

Table 18.5 illustrates the structure of Zambia's state enterprise sector under the control of ZIMCO and its five group holding companies in 1972. The subordinate holding companies in the INDECO group of companies are also shown, together with their main activities at that date.[10] This structure, extending beyond mining and manufacturing into construction, commerce, property, hotels, transport, banking, and insurance, clearly affords comprehensive control of the national economy on lines very similar to that in Tanzania. The objective is to provide a suitable institutional structure through which Zambia's relative abundance of investible funds derived from copper exports can be channelled to permit the diversification of the economy; and, to the extent that its acute shortage of managerial and technical skills requires heavy reliance on imported skill and enterprise, to permit this without prejudice to national economic independence.

Within this structure it is INDECO which faces the main development task of initiating new industrial ventures. Its performance since the first 'Economic Reforms' were announced in 1968 is impressive in terms of the growth and present size of its annual sales turnover and group assets as can be seen from Table 18.6.

Two related questions arise when a development corporation such as INDECO here, or the UDC in Uganda and NDC in Tanzania, controls a large number of the enterprises within the industrial sector, together perhaps with additional enterprises else-

Table 18.5 The structure of ZIMCO and the INDECO group of companies in 1972

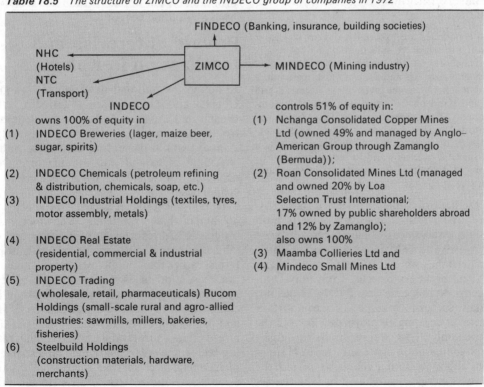

SOURCE: INDECO: *Annual Report, 1972* and ZIMCO: *Enterprise*

Table 18.6 Expansion in the size of the INDECO Group, 1968–72

| | (K million) | | |
	1968	1970	1972
INDECO Group turnover	1.9	123.8	247.1
Group net assets	35.6	119.9	167.9
Group profit before taxation	0.3	11.0	23.5
Group profit after taxation	0.3	9.3	14.3
of which: to INDECO	0.3	6.0	7.1
to outside shareholders	0.1	3.3	7.2
Number of employees (in thousands)	5.6	14.0	21.5

where. The first is how far ordinary commercial objectives of profitability should be pursued, and how far social objectives should be taken into account. The second is how to ensure efficiency in the allocation of funds among existing and new enterprises under the control of the corporation.

In inaugurating the Mulungushi Economic Reforms in 1968, President Kaunda stated that 'Indeco always aims to manage each of these companies in a proper commercial and businesslike way. Of course it keeps the national interest in mind all the time.' And as Chairman of ZIMCO, he subsequently laid down that:

> The Zimco companies are expected to show a greater consideration for social benefit than would normally apply to privately-owned companies. They are nevertheless business organizations and as such must operate in a businesslike manner, become even more efficient and profitable, and stand on their own in a ruthlessly competitive economy. The interest of the State in Zimco will not be protected by the conferment of special and exclusive privileges on Zimco. On the contrary, such action is likely to shelter inefficiency and to breed bureaucratic organizations least equipped to withstand the strenuous demands of a competitive business environment.[11]

Looking at the data of Table 18.6 we see that gross profits before tax have risen as a percentage of both turnover and net assets since the main take-overs were assimilated in 1969 and 1970. However as a return on capital (net assets) they were in 1972 still only 14.0 per cent, lower than might be expected from fully commercial concerns. At the same time INDECO has not been particularly successful in respect of one important social objective, of creating employment. In 1972 the group employed only 21,500 workers in its subsidiary and associated companies, a figure only about $4\frac{1}{2}$ times that in 1968, although during the same period the group's net assets increased sevenfold. In 1972 the net assets per worker amounted to as much as K7,809, a very high capital–labour ratio and a reflection of the high capital intensity of INDECO's main investments in chemicals, properties, and breweries. The only activities with less than K3,000 per worker were found among the smaller-scale rural enterprises, sawmills, grain-milling and fisheries enterprises falling under Rucom Holdings which, with 3,841 workers, employed more people than the much larger Indeco Chemicals Ltd.

The allocation of finance creates a potential problem in maintaining pressures towards efficiency within the group of activities controlled by a national corporation. Even within a so-called 'competitive' economy, the importance of reinvested profits as a source of finance gives large firms a special advantage over others. If a single group of enterprises covers the bulk of the industrial sector or more, as in the case of the UDC, NDC, or INDECO, the group can be more or less independent of the banking system, and new enterprises readily financed out of the aggregate group profits without the need for external assessment of their potential profitability. A project can, moreover, receive an effective subsidy through being allocated funds without paying a 'market' rate of interest or one reflecting the actual scarcity of loan capital in the economy. As in a fully collectivized economy, there is a need for some kind of substitute for the market tests of competition and profitability, but applied within the sector controlled by a monolithic corporation.

Private enterprise and localization in Kenya

Although the national development corporations of Uganda and Malawi have followed a 'catalyst' approach and those in Tanzania and Zambia a 'controlling' approach, all four have also played substantial parts in promoting development through the 'injection' of capital into manufacturing and other neglected sectors of their respective national economies.

Developments in Kenya are in sharp contrast to all four of these experiences. The emphasis has been on gradual Africanization of industry and commerce (and the more rapid phasing out of European large farms) rather than public ownership and control. The first reason for this is of course the different economic and political philosophy which exists in Kenya as compared with Tanzania and Zambia. The second and just as important reason, however, is that Kenya already had a substantial and expanding manufacturing sector and a large commercial sector at the time of independence, so that there was less need for a strong development corporation to 'fill the gap' left by private investment, as in Uganda and Malawi:

rather, the need was seen to be to feed the developing private enterprise sector with loan finance and progressively to restrict trade licences issued to non-citizens in order to Africanize gradually as suitable local entrepreneurs emerged, and without disturbing too much the business confidence of non-citizen and foreign investors. Accordingly we do not find a monolithic development corporation in Kenya but a much greater emphasis on loan assistance and licensing as a means of securing African participation in the manufacturing and commercial sectors which up to Independence had both been mainly in the hands of expatriate or immigrant private enterprises.

Before 1963 a Small Industrial Development Corporation existed which largely confined its limited activities to marginally profitable ventures. In 1963 this was reorganized to become the Industrial and Commercial Development Corporation. Unlike the UDC, however, the ICDC concentrated on relatively small-scale ventures. To cover larger-scale enterprises the government simultaneously established in 1963 the Development Finance Company of Kenya (DFCK) with initial capital equally subscribed by the ICDC itself, the Commonwealth Development Corporation (of the UK) and the (West) German Development Company.[12] Some of the early projects in which the DFCK invested included two sugar mills, three textile factories, and an international hotel. The 'catalyst' function in supporting private enterprise is implicit in its description as a finance company. A similar function is being carried out by a new Industrial Development Bank established in 1973 with equity capital provided by ICDC (51 per cent) and the Ministry of Finance and Planning (49 per cent), but with loan capital borrowed from the World Bank and other financial institutions.

The original aims of the ICDC were given in the 1966–70 Development Plan as: to select projects which would be 'profitable but risky...in which participation by government may be necessary to set in motion profitable enterprises which would otherwise never come about'[13] (the catalytic function) and 'to assist and promote those projects which would be the spearhead of Africanization of the industrial and commercial sectors of the economy' (Africanization). The types of industrial projects envisaged were smaller-scale ones in such areas as food processing, textiles, clothing, leather products, sawmilling, furniture, metal products, and construction, into which African entrepreneurs could most readily move. Assistance in establishment was also given to smaller African enterprises through the medium of industrial estates in the main towns, initially Nairobi, Nakuru, and Kisumu, where the provision of premises and other working facilities reduced overhead costs and

the amount of initial capital needed. This was done through the medium of Kenya Industrial Estates Limited (KIE), established in 1966 as a subsidiary of ICDC. Partly because this was confined to urban areas, and partly because the ICDC found itself giving assistance to larger businesses than the *very* small-scale craft enterprises widely distributed in the towns and throughout the rural areas, the Rural Industries Development Programme was launched in 1971. The scope of this is discussed in Chapter 23.

State intervention in commerce has come about in Kenya through the Kenya National Trading Corporation (KNTC), operating at the wholesale level. However the aim was not so much to 'take over' wholesaling as to be able to assist in the progressive Africanization of retail and wholesale trade, in conjunction with the system of trade licensing. Without any sudden 'expulsion of the Asians' as in Uganda, the number of non-citizens in trade has been steadily reduced until by the early 1970s Africans were running the bulk of the retail businesses in many of the smaller townships, as well as in the rural areas. The process is far advanced even in the capital city of Nairobi, and is being extended to small manufacturing concerns. In addition the National Construction Co. (NCC) has helped to promote African builders, for instance, by awarding subcontracts for building work and providing technical services on a pool basis.

The problem of pricing in public utilities

Before we leave this discussion of public enterprise in Eastern Africa, let us go back to one of the most basic forms of public enterprise, the public utility, to discuss a specific problem which frequently arises. Public utilities, as we stated above, tend to be 'natural monopolies' due to the existence of substantial economies of scale which cause costs to fall over a wide range of output. In other words they often occur in 'decreasing cost industries'. The situation may then arise where the optimum size of the firm is large in relation to demand. In Figure 18.1, for example, minimum average costs of production occur at output OQ_4 whereas even at zero price demand is insufficient to absorb this output.

A monopolist faced with the situation in this diagram would, if he wanted to maximize profits, charge the price OP_1, producing and selling the restricted amount OQ_1. Apart from the high price charged to consumers, as pointed out in Chapter 17, this would represent a misallocation of resources since at this price and output, price would not equal marginal cost. Price measures the urgency of consumers' demand for additional units of the product, being the amount they would be prepared to pay for more; and marginal cost is the opportunity-cost of additional units, since it measures the urgency with which consumers want alternative goods that could be produced instead of the one in question. A divergence between price and marginal cost therefore implies that welfare can be improved by reallocating factors of production in one direction or the other.

If the government took over the industry illustrated in Figure 18.1 from a monopolist, aiming at running the industry in the public interest, it might wish to apply the P = MC criterion. To do this it should charge the price OP_3 given by the intersection of the marginal cost curve and the demand (average revenue) curve. At this price P = MC and also demand is equal to the amount produced, OQ_3. The difficulty is that at this price, average total cost, equal to OC, exceeds price. A loss would therefore be made equal to the rectangle $CDEP_3$. Price would cover marginal costs, but not overhead costs. This implies that the loss would need to be financed from taxation and raises the question of whether it is fair to permit users of this particular commodity to buy it cheaply by being subsidized by the general taxpayer.

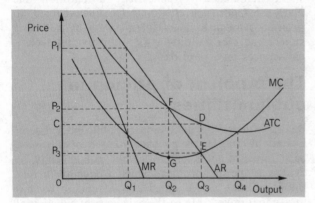

Figure 18.1 *Public utility pricing under decreasing cost.*

The alternative is to charge the price OP_2, given by the intersection of the average revenue and the average total cost curve. The average total cost of OQ_2 units is Q_2F, exactly equal to OP_2, so that no subsidy would be required or excess profit made. The demand curve passes through F, indicating that consumers are willing to buy the amount produced, OQ_2, at this price. This solution implies a divergence between price (equal to Q_2F) and marginal cost (equal to Q_2G). Consumers would be willing to pay more for additional units than their opportunity-cost.

The question of whether public utilities should charge marginal cost or average cost has excited much discussion, and reference is made to the marginal cost pricing controversy. The issue arises in a

wide variety of situations in which a large initial outlay is required and subsequent operating costs are low. For example once a modern road has been built, possibly at great capital cost, the cost of allowing an extra car to use it is negligible. There is a case for paying for the road out of general taxes and allowing cars to use it freely. Making a charge for its use would divert some drivers to alternative roads, implying a loss of benefit to them, without saving any costs elsewhere. Supporters of marginal cost pricing argue that if there are a lot of public enterprise projects of this type, taxpayers will benefit more or less equally. Roads, bridges, and so on, will be distributed fairly evenly throughout the country and each taxpayer will have access to the free benefits from them.

In developing countries, however, it is much less likely that benefits from public utilities and services will be evenly distributed throughout the country. The urban areas are generally much better served than the rural areas, services being especially concentrated in the capital cities. Moreover, the taxpayer includes the peasant farmer, who may be much poorer than, say, the urban consumer of electricity and water whom he is subsidizing. There might on the other hand, be a case for subsidizing industrial consumers of electricity, as an alternative to supporting them through import duties. It might also be considered desirable to subsidize projects in the more remote areas, with a view to stimulating their development.

Not all public utilities operate under the condition of decreasing marginal cost. They may, for example, be engaged in extracting limited natural resources, such as coal or water. In these cases marginal cost pricing is possible without raising any special problem.

Another extreme case of divergence between average and marginal costs in public undertakings, similar to that of the roads, just discussed, is in electricity supply. We may refer to an interesting example of the effects of this which occurred during the late 1950s in East Africa, when the Uganda Electricity Board was willing to sell power to Kenya from the new Owen Falls hydro-electric scheme at a fraction of the average price charged to Uganda consumers. Table 18.7 shows the UEB's sources of revenue in 1960 when, even with the Kenya market, total demand amounted to only about one-half of the installed capacity. The 2.72 cents per kilowatt-hour negotiated with the Kenya Power Company constituted a small but positive contribution to the capital charges of the existing plant over and above actual wear and tear attributable to Kenya's use of the plant. These capital charges, for interest and repayment of the loan finance borrowed to construct

Table 18.7   *Sources of revenue and pricing policy, Uganda Electricity Board, 1960*

	Kilowatt-hours sold		Revenue		Average price per kwh
	(millions)	(%)	(£×1,000)	(%)	(EA cents)
Ordinary consumers	111.3	30.7	1,379	74.7	24.78
Special industrial consumers	91.3	25.1	249	13.5	5.47
Kenya	160.1	44.2	218	11.8	2.72
Total	362.5	100.0	1,846	100.0	10.18

the dam, constituted more than 75 per cent of the cost of generation in 1960. Although the UEB did not obtain a large revenue from Kenya at this time, it was almost completely net revenue. Kenya had, of course, to invest in a large-scale distribution scheme to transmit the power all the way from Owen Falls to Nairobi, some 300 miles away, so that the cost per kilowatt-hour to Kenya was much greater than the 2.72 cents per unit which the UEB received. At the same time this unit charge was only slightly more than *one-tenth* of the price charged to ordinary consumers in Uganda, a striking example of price discrimination between geographically separate markets (where a resale from the cheaper to the dearer market is clearly not possible). While Kenya consumed 44 per cent of the electricity generated, nearly one-half, it contributed only 12 per cent of the revenue obtained by the UEB. The further discrimination in favour of 'special' industrial consumers, part of the effort to promote industrialization through subsidies, is also clearly reflected in the table. The price to ordinary consumers was about $4\frac{1}{2}$ times as high.

Road and rail competition

Another pricing problem arises when a state enterprise operated in part as a public service is in competition with unregulated private entrepreneurs, as when a state-owned railway operates alongside privately owned bus companies and road haulage businesses. As already mentioned in the last chapter, the railway (or public bus or airline) has to provide *scheduled services* along advertised routes at specified times, even when the number of paying passengers is small; while as a *common carrier* it is generally obliged to accept any goods traffic offered to it, whether a profitable long haul of a valuable compact cargo, which can be charged a high price, or unprofitable low-priced cargoes perhaps travelling only a short distance.

In order to 'break even', the public railway would like to charge some average price which would cover the costs of both its profitable and unprofitable services, even though this prevents its charging the lowest possible price for its rewarding operations. If

private businesses are allowed to compete they are likely to concentrate on the busiest routes and on the most profitable types of cargo. By concentrating on these, refusing inconvenient cargoes and avoiding awkward hours, they will be able to reduce their costs and charge lower prices, thus 'creaming off' the most lucrative traffic. Competition from unscheduled transport operators is intensified by ease of entry into the industry: an individual can easily set himself up in business on the best routes with a single taxi or lorry which does not involve much capital expenditure or other heavy overhead expenses of management and control.

We discussed in the last chapter how in response to this situation the railways have often adopted a system of price discrimination. A question of marginal versus average cost pricing of the sort just discussed is also involved. In the case of a railway, once the railway lines and all their associated fixed structures like signals, sidings, and stations have been installed, although overhead costs are high, the marginal cost of carrying goods or passengers along *busy* routes, along which regular trains will be worth running anyway, will be very low. If low rates can be charged for those particular routes or types of traffic, equivalent to marginal cost, the railway should be able to compete with private transporters; but the railway would not then be able to cover its overhead costs, perhaps even on these routes, or its average total costs spread over its entire operations. From a social point of view, once the investment in railway lines and the rest has already been made, it can be said that it is cheaper, in terms of new resources used up, to carry the goods by rail rather than road, and thus socially desirable for prices to be fixed to realize this end. Since the railway would fail to cover average costs overall, however, the railway's financial deficit would need to be made up out of taxation, as in our public utility example. Alternatively, if the railway adopts *average* cost pricing with a uniform average charge per mile, over all its routes, traffic which might have been better carried by rail, at a lower marginal cost, might be diverted to the roads.

An alternative would be to nationalize or otherwise regulate road transport to be able to plan road and rail transportation together, offering road *or* rail services according to which is most economical on each route, and preventing 'unfair competition' and duplication of services. This is in fact the case for nationalization based on 'wasteful competition' which we referred to above.

Problems of road and rail competition have arisen in a great many African countries. In Africa, however, it is very difficult to regulate private road transporters, whether passenger taxi-drivers in competition with both railway and bus services, or lorry-owners, this being an industry with relative ease of entry, offering a relatively good income compared to other opportunities for unskilled or semi-skilled persons in the rural areas. Consequently protection of rail traffic, for example, has depended much more on pricing policy and the physical regulation of road transport by licensing.

Questions on Chapter 18

1. Describe the characteristics of a 'public' or 'collective' good, giving examples.
2. Discuss the main arguments for establishing state-run enterprises, and the types of industries to which each would relate.
3. Why may a public enterprise operate profitably where private enterprise has been unable or unwilling to operate?
4. Discuss the case for nationalizing land.
5. Discuss the possible effects of nationalization on the balance of payments.
6. Discuss the problem of assessing compensation for nationalized assets.
7. Is there a case for greater or less state intervention in less developed as compared to developed economies?
8. Describe the possible objectives of a development corporation, and indicate how important these have been in various development corporations in Eastern Africa.
9. What are the special advantages of a development corporation as a vehicle for state enterprise, as compared to a government department?
10. Compare and contrast the functions of development corporations in any two Eastern African countries.
11. Why do you think Kenya does not have a 'national' development corporation like Tanzania?
12. What is a public utility? What do you understand by the problem of pricing in public utilities?
13. What problems may be posed for a state-run railway by the existence of unregulated road transportation? Why is it more usual to find railways and airways run as state monopolies than road transport activities?

Notes

[1] However, while users of the public park benefit directly from their visits, even those not directly using the facilities gain collectively from living in a city diversified by public parks. To this extent there are indivisible, *as well as* divisible benefits. Users of the park should therefore not be required to cover the full costs of maintenance.

[2] This will not hold true if compensation is paid off in instalments over a period of years. African governments, which have 'taken over' the whole or a 'majority' shareholding in private enterprises (usually foreign-owned), have in fact adopted a variant of the following method: the private enterprise issues the required shareholding to the government in return for interest-earning bonds to be redeemed by the government over a period of years. In effect the government pays for its shareholding, therefore, by borrowing from the former owners at a fixed rate of interest but finances the interest and redemption charges from the dividends received from the shares. Zambia, Sierra Leone, and Ghana have adopted this method in respect of copper and diamond-mining enterprises—and Malawi in respect of state holdings in distribution and banking businesses. Of course in the case of smaller enterprises, the government or its nominee may simply purchase shares through a stock exchange, 'taking over' the firm gradually in the same way as another private buyer may take over a business.

[3] See J. D. Nyhart, 'The Uganda Development Corporation and Agriculture', *East African Economic Review*, December 1959.

[4] ibid.

[5] Although 'Nytil' was only 'associated' with UDC until 1958, the majority shareholding was held up to that time by the Uganda government directly. UDC then acquired the government's $58\frac{1}{2}$ per cent holding.

[6] UDC Annual Report, 1963.

[7] Telecommunications are in fact run by the Malawi Post Office, a government department in name but effectively a public utility enterprise with its own trading accounts.

[8] *A Short Guide to Investors*, National Development Corporation, Tanzania.

[9] In the event, the three expatriate commercial banks were not taken over, but registered as local companies. These compete with FINDECO's wholly owned National Commercial Bank and its 60 per cent owned subsidiary, Commercial Bank of Zambia.

[10] For the most up-to-date details of ZIMCO and the extension of public enterprise in Zambia, readers are referred to Annual Reports of the various group-holding companies and to *Enterprise*, the quarterly journal which describes all the activities of ZIMCO.

[11] Reported in INDECO Limited, *Annual Report and Accounts for Year ended 31st March, 1972*, pp. 7–8.

[12] Development Plan, 1966–70, p. 240.

[13] Development Plan, 1966–70, p. 242.

Part V International trade

19 The Gains from Trade

We discussed in Part IV the various decisions of the firm regarding what to produce, how much to produce, and so on. Let us now widen the discussion considerably to ask what determines what *countries* decide to produce, for domestic consumption and for export, and what goods, conversely, they decide to import: what, in other words, determines the pattern of international trade.

The theory of international trade actually deals with *two* questions:

(1) what determines which goods a country exports and imports?

(2) what determines the gains from such trade as between different countries?

This second question relates to the terms at which goods are bought and sold internationally: the terms of trade. The less developed countries have, increasingly in recent years, expressed considerable dissatisfaction with the existing pattern of world trade, with what they consider the distribution of benefits from trade, and with the terms of trade. Through tariff and other industrial development policies they have sought to change the existing pattern of specialization and trade. In this chapter we shall discuss the so-called 'classical' theory of international trade and its criticisms, before discussing the terms of trade.

The basis of specialization

It should be noted that the classical theory of international trade is a special case of the theory of specialization by individuals and by regions. We have already seen that specialization brings about the more effective use of resources. A doctor may be extremely good at gardening, but will still specialize in medicine and hire a gardener to look after his garden, or a businessman may be able to type faster than his secretary and still find it worthwhile to hire her to do his typing, while he spends his limited time doing other things; and an educated woman may be an extremely able housewife but find it profitable to go out to work as a teacher while hiring domestic help to look after her household. The basis of specialization is that individuals have different capacities or endowments, so that it pays them to specialize in the field in which they have an advantage. Their advantage may be 'natural' or 'acquired': for example the doctor may have natural ability as a doctor which the gardener does not have, but also he has acquired a different capacity as a result of his long training.

Regions also have different endowments. They are characterized by differences in natural resources, human resources, and in the stock of capital and technical knowledge accumulated in the past. And they may possess the factors of production in *different proportions* so that, for example, countries with a plentiful supply of cheap labour might specialize in export products which use a lot of labour. As with individuals, the advantages of particular regions may be natural or acquired: the inhabitants of a region may have acquired superior skills by carrying on a specialized occupation for many years, in the way that Sheffield, in Britain, has made steel cutlery. Or even without possessing skills that are peculiar to one region, an area may have a reputation for a particular product, a particular variety of cheese, for instance, which gives it an advantage over other regions which produce similar products.

In the case of both individuals and regions it will be seen that the important thing is *comparative* advantage. The doctor we mentioned was better at both medicine and gardening than his gardener, but the gap between them was greater in medicine: that is to say, his relative advantage was greater in that field. Similarly the other man's comparative *dis*advantage was less in gardening than in medicine. This is closely related to opportunity-cost: the opportunity-cost to the doctor of one day of the medical work spent in gardening is the amount of medical consulting he could have done in that time. Opportunity-costs, as always, exist because resources are limited, in this case the time available to the doctor. *In contrast absolute cost and absolute advantage are not relevant to specialization.* The labour time put in by the businessman typing a letter is less than that of his secretary: but his time is more valuable. The importance of comparative cost is a fundamental one in the classical theory of trade and has been elevated to the title of the Law of Comparative Costs.

The Law of Comparative Costs: constant costs

Let us elaborate the law in terms of a simple case of just two countries, A and B, each capable of producing just two commodities, cloth and rice. We assume to start with that each commodity is produced under conditions of constant cost in each country. Rice requires relatively more land in its production; cloth is labour-intensive in its production. We can assume that land is relatively plentiful in country A, and labour relatively plentiful in country B, so that country B is relatively more suited to producing the labour-intensive good, cloth, and country A more suited to rice production. However country A, with more resources than B, *could* produce more of both rice and cloth than country B, just as our businessman could be more effective in business affairs and in typing than our secretary.

The production possibilities open to the two countries are illustrated in Figure 19.1. The straight lines are transformation curves, the slope showing the rate at which country A can 'transform' rice into cloth and vice versa, by reallocating its resources, and similarly for country B. Thus if country A devoted all its resources to rice production it could produce 6 units, and if it devoted all its resources to cloth production it could produce 10 units. The corresponding units for country B are 2 and 5. Country A is better endowed, since 1 unit of cloth requires one-tenth of its resources and 1 unit of rice one-sixth of its resources, compared to one-fifth and one-half respectively for country B.

Since the opportunity-cost of 10 units of cloth in country A is 6 units of rice, that of 1 unit of cloth is 6/10 units of rice; the opportunity-cost of 1 unit of rice will be 10/6 units of cloth. Since costs are assumed independent of the scale of production, this will be true irrespective of the amount of resources devoted to the production of the two commodities. In country B, the cost of 1 unit of cloth will be 2/5 units of rice, and the cost of 1 unit of rice 5/2 units of cloth.

It is easy to show that trade can be mutually beneficial if opportunity-costs in the two countries differ. Suppose in this case, starting from any initial position country A switches resources from cloth to rice to produce one less unit of cloth: it will be able to increase rice output by 6/10 of a unit of rice. At the same time country B increases cloth output by 1 unit, 'world' output of cloth will be unchanged. Country B will, on the other hand, have to reduce rice output by 2/5 of a unit of rice ($=4/10$). There will, however, be a net increase in 'world' output of rice by $6/10 - 4/10 = 1/5$. Since there is no change in world cloth output there is an overall gain, from which both countries could gain by trading with each other to exchange rice and cloth. This is obtainable through country A producing relatively more rice, in which its opportunity-cost is lower (and thus comparative advantage greater), equal to 10/6 units of cloth; and through country B producing relatively less rice, in which its opportunity-cost is higher (and comparative disadvantage greater), equal to 10/4 units of cloth.

Thus taking opportunity-costs in the two countries as given, countries should specialize according to opportunity-costs or comparative advantage.

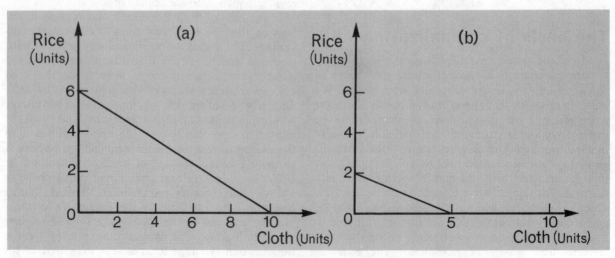

Figure 19.1 *(a) Country A's production possibilities and (b) country B's production possibilities.*

Absolute advantage but uniform opportunity-costs

Only if comparative advantage differs is trade between two countries profitable. Suppose Figure 19.2 depicts the production possibility curves for countries A and B. The outer one is that of A, which is now supposed to have identical resources to those of country B, but due to greater efficiency can produce more of either cloth or rice in total. Since A can produce more cloth or rice per unit of resource used up, it can be said to have an absolute advantage in both commodities.

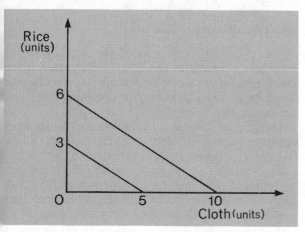

Figure 19.2   *Identical opportunity-costs.*

Specialization and trade, however, will not be beneficial. The opportunity-cost of a unit of rice in A, 10/6 units of cloth, is the same as that in B, 5/3 units. If A produces one more unit of rice and B one less, the world output of cloth will *not* increase (or decrease) this time.

The distribution of gains from trade

If comparative advantages differ, then, a gain from trade is there for the taking. An interesting question is, to whom does this accrue, country A or country B, or if to both, in what proportion? And on what does this proportion depend? We can easily demonstrate that this depends on the world prices of cloth and rice.

Considering again the original set of opportunity-costs, in the absence of trade between A and B, the rate of exchange between cloth and rice, or the 'domestic price' of cloth in terms of rice, must be 6/10 in A. For if the price of cloth were different, say 5/10 units of rice, producers would shift from cloth to rice production. By producing 1 unit less of cloth, they

can produce 6/10 more units of rice, as stated by opportunity-cost: by selling 5/10 of this they can obtain on the market the unit of cloth they would have produced *and still have 1/10 unit of rice left over as profit.* Supply and demand would thus ensure a domestic price of 6/10 in line with relative costs. Similarly in country B the domestic price of cloth will be 2/5.

Only in the absence of trade, however, can the domestic prices of cloth or rice differ in the two countries. If trade is permitted, traders will be able to buy cloth more cheaply in B, at 2/5, and resell in A at 6/10 (= 3/5). They will continue to do so as long as the prices differ. Assuming free competitive trade (and abstracting from transport costs) there will therefore be a single world relative price for rice and cloth.

Let us now use an arithmetic example to show how the distribution of gains from trade depends on this price. In the absence of trade, each country would need to satisfy its own consumption demand for both cloth and rice. The relative amounts produced and consumed would depend on the demand for each. If A devoted three-quarters of its resources to rice production, and the rest to cloth, it would obtain product P_A $(2\frac{1}{2}, 4\frac{1}{2})$ of cloth and rice respectively, and consume the same amounts, C_A $(2\frac{1}{2}, 4\frac{1}{2})$. B might allocate resources equally between cloth and rice, so that it would produce P_B $(2\frac{1}{2}, 1) = C_B$ $(2\frac{1}{2}, 1)$. Total 'world' production would equal P_{A+B} $(5, 5\frac{1}{2})$. This is laid out in the upper half of Table 19.1 which also gives the domestic prices in each country, reflecting domestic opportunity-costs.

If trade were possible, the opportunity-cost of cloth being less in B (2/5 compared to 3/5) and that of rice being less in A (5/3 compared to 5/2), A would specialize in rice and B in cloth. Since the opportunity-cost ratios are constant, this means complete specialization, with A producing 6 units of rice and no cloth, that is, combination $P_A(0, 6)$ and B 5 units of cloth and no rice, combination $P_B(5, 0)$. 'World' production is $P_{A+B}(5, 6)$ compared to $P_{A+B}(5, 5\frac{1}{2})$: production of cloth is unchanged, but there is a net increase of $\frac{1}{2}$ unit of rice. By exchanging cloth and rice, both countries can, as before, consume both commodities. This pattern of production is shown in the lower part of Table 19.1.

This illustrates again the fact that a potential benefit from trade exists for *someone.* The question is, who receives the gain? It is fairly clear that this will depend on the price that A obtains for its rice, in terms of B's cloth, and vice versa: what we may call the 'terms of trade' between rice and cloth.

This price will be determined, as usual, by supply and demand in the world market. It must, however, be between the original domestic prices of cloth of

Table 19.1 The gains from trade

	Price of cloth (in terms of rice)	Production		Consumption		Amounts imported	
		Cloth	Rice	Cloth	Rice	Cloth	Rice
Before trade							
Country A	3/5	$2\frac{1}{2}$	$4\frac{1}{2}$	$2\frac{1}{2}$	$4\frac{1}{2}$	—	—
Country B	2/5	$2\frac{1}{2}$	1	$2\frac{1}{2}$	1	—	—
'World'	—	5	$5\frac{1}{2}$	5	$5\frac{1}{2}$	—	—
After trade							
Country A	3/5	0	6	$2\frac{1}{2}$	$4\frac{1}{2}$	$+2\frac{1}{2}$	$-1\frac{1}{2}$
Country B	3/5	5	0	$2\frac{1}{2}$	$1\frac{1}{2}$	$-2\frac{1}{2}$	$+1\frac{1}{2}$
'World'	3/5	5	6	5	6	—	—

3/5 in country A and 2/5 in B. Suppose demand were such that the world price of cloth settled at 3/5 and at this price A imported $2\frac{1}{2}$ units. To obtain $2\frac{1}{2}$ units of cloth, at 3/5 units of rice per unit, A would need to export $1\frac{1}{2}$ units of rice. A would therefore consume $2\frac{1}{2}$ and $4\frac{1}{2}$ units of cloth and rice respectively, exactly the same as before, and gain nothing; but B would have $2\frac{1}{2}$ units of cloth left (after producing 5) and $1\frac{1}{2}$ units of rice (all imported), a net gain of $\frac{1}{2}$ unit of rice, equal to the total benefit available to the two countries.

If the price of cloth had been 2/5, the entire gain would accrue to A, and B would gain nothing. Suppose at this price country A wished to import $2\frac{1}{2}$ units of cloth, costing $5/2 \times 2/5 = 1$ unit of rice, in order to be able to consume the new combination $C'_A(0 + 2\frac{1}{2} = 2\frac{1}{2},\ 6 - 1 = 5)$, a net gain of $\frac{1}{2}$ unit of rice. Country B would consume combination $C'_B(5 - 2\frac{1}{2} = 2\frac{1}{2},\ 0 + 1 = 1)$, exactly as in the no-trade situation, and gain nothing. This result is given in the upper part of Table 19.2. If the price of cloth were between 2/5 and 3/5, on the other hand, the gain would be divided between the two. For example, at a price of cloth of 5/10, if A imported $2\frac{1}{2}$ units of cloth,

costing $(5/2 \times 5/10 = 1\frac{1}{4})$ units of rice, A and B would each gain 1/4 units of rice. This is illustrated in the lower part of Table 19.2. Clearly the further the world price from a country's domestic price, the greater its gain from trade.

The gain can of course be measured either in terms of rice or in terms of cloth, since the resources going into rice production could alternatively be devoted to cloth. Neither does the principle depend on the precise amount that A wants to import from B, or vice versa. This will obviously depend on the elasticities of demand for cloth in terms of its 'rice' price.

The advantage of small countries

Benefit from trade arises out of specialization. The division of gain depends on the international terms of trade, the 'world price' relative to the domestic prices ruling in the absence of trade. For a large country complete specialization may not be possible: if its total potential output is large relative to total de-

Table 19.2 Distribution of gains for different terms of trade

	Price of cloth (in terms of rice)	Production		Consumption		Amounts imported	
		Cloth	Rice	Cloth	Rice	Cloth	Rice
After trade							
Country A	2/5	0	6	$2\frac{1}{2}$	5	$+2\frac{1}{2}$	-1
Country B	2/5	5	0	$2\frac{1}{2}$	1	$-2\frac{1}{2}$	$+1$
'World'	2/5	5	6	5	6	—	—
After trade							
Country A	5/10	0	6	$2\frac{1}{2}$	$4\frac{3}{4}$	$+2\frac{1}{2}$	$-1\frac{1}{4}$
Country B	5/10	5	0	$2\frac{1}{2}$	$1\frac{1}{4}$	$-2\frac{1}{2}$	$+1\frac{1}{4}$
'World'	5/10	5	6	5	6	—	—

mand in the domestic and export markets, increased output and sales will be possible only if the price falls. But if a small country specializes, the increased output will still be small compared to total world supply, and will not affect the world price. To put this in terms of our examples, we can take B as our small country and A as the rest of the world, considered as one large country. Even if B specializes entirely in cloth production it will still produce only a small part of that produced in A, and the price of cloth will be near to that of A. The benefit will largely accrue to the small country B.

This result is a common feature of world trade. Small countries like Fiji and Mauritius may specialize in sugar production on the basis of a price largely determined by major producers like Cuba. Similarly African coffee producers benefit from a price largely determined by supply from Latin America without even, until comparatively recently, being party to the International Agreement to restrict coffee output. Ghana, on the other hand, suffers a disadvantage in exporting cocoa in that, being the main world producer, it cannot expand exports without affecting the price at which it can sell on the world market.

Limits to specialization: increasing opportunity-costs

The previous examples were unrealistic in assuming that opportunity-costs were constant in both countries, that production, in other words, was not subject to diminishing returns. With diminishing returns in each industry, the production transformation curves

would be convex to the origin as illustrated and as discussed in Chapter 5.

The reason for the convex transformation curve, as stated before, is that if the factors of production are diverted from making one commodity, in this case rice, they become less and less suitable for making the other, cloth. This is because factors are not perfectly substitutable but are to some extent specific to the production of particular commodities or categories of commodity. Thus land suitable for rice production will be only partially usable for producing cotton cloth, and so on. In the constant cost example, trade could take place so long as opportunity-cost ratios were different in the two regions. The difference here is that opportunity-cost ratios now vary depending upon the combination of products produced in the two countries.

Consider the transformation curve AB for country A in Figure 19.3(a). In the absence of trade, the domestic price of cloth (in terms of rice) would again have to be equal to opportunity-costs, that is, to the marginal rate of transformation between rice and cloth. Suppose the domestic price, the market rate of exchange between cloth and rice, were given by the slope of dd, through P. If the economy were *not* producing combination P of cloth and rice, this domestic price could not be maintained. For example if output were given by combination Q it would cost producers ab units of rice to produce an extra Qa of cloth: but the extra Qa of cloth could be sold (d'd' is drawn parallel to dd and represents the same market price), yielding a profit of bc units of rice. It would thus be profitable for suppliers to produce relatively more cloth and less rice which, assuming given demand conditions, would reduce the market price of

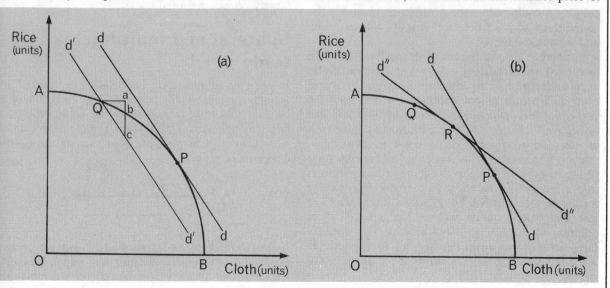

Figure 19.3 No trade: domestic price equal to opportunity-cost.

cloth in terms of rice. The amount of rice to be given up in exchange for cloth would thus fall, and the slope of the market price line dd would be reduced. Equilibrium might be reached at some point like A in Figure 19.3(b) between P and Q where the relative output of cloth has been increased just sufficiently to bring the market price into line with the marginal rate of transformation measuring opportunity-costs.

We can now examine the potential benefits from trade. If the foreign relative price were the same as the domestic, foreign trade would offer no new opportunities, and production/consumption would remain at R. If the foreign price, given by ff in Figure 19.4 (or any line parallel to it, such as f'f'), differed from the domestic price, dd, the position would change.

As we have drawn it, suppliers can get more rice for a unit of cloth on the foreign market (along ff) than they can on the domestic market (along dd). The domestic price would fall into line with the international one, assuming the domestic market is small relative to the world market. If they adopt combination S producing more cloth, and sell this extra amount bS for ba of rice on the world market, country A can have, at point a, the same amount of cloth as at R *and* an extra amount Ra of rice: it *must* therefore be better off. This demonstrates that so long as the foreign price differs from the domestic, there must be gains from trade.

Combination a may not necessarily be the one selected, of course: most likely some of the increased income would be taken by consumers in the form of cloth, as well as rice, at some point between a and S on f'f'. Also, if domestic production is *not* small relative to world production, the export of cloth from country A could reduce the world price, changing the equilibrium combinations of output, consumption, and amounts traded.

Country A's benefit from trade derives from the possibility of specializing to a greater extent in cloth, at S, and exporting its 'surplus' cloth on the world market. Whereas in our constant cost example the two countries *completely* specialized in cloth and rice respectively, the extent of specialization by country A is here limited by increasing costs as cloth production is expanded. This is reflected in the curvature of the transformation curve. The *less* concave this is (the more gentle the effect of increasing costs) the further to the right will be point S. And, as we have just said, specialization will be limited also if, in addition to increasing costs, the exporting country faces an inelastic world demand for its exports. As discussed earlier, a 'small' country is fortunate in not having this problem.

Many goods

No real difference in the analysis would be introduced if we had more than just the two goods, cloth and rice. If there are more, we can suppose that a country begins by specializing in and trading that commodity in which it has the greatest relative advantage. As its production is expanded, however, its costs will increase and at the same time its price in the foreign market will most likely decline due to inelastic demand, until the commodity loses its advantage and the country now finds the export of another commodity profitable in addition to existing exports of the first. It must be noted, however, that in calculating the comparative advantage of the second good, the factors of production used up in existing production of the first will not be available.[1]

Transport costs

In the previous analysis we saw that trade takes place between two countries so long as the domestic prices, reflecting comparative costs, are unequal. If there are costs of transporting the commodities, it will be possible for domestic prices to differ by the amount of these costs. The effect of this is to reduce trade. Goods for which the difference in comparative costs (domestic prices) is less than the transport cost will not be traded at all, and others will be traded to a lesser extent. In those parts of Africa which have poor communications, specialization is limited and subsistence production more important; reduction in transport costs with improvements in roads or rail links brings increased trade and specialization, and an expansion of the monetary economy, often based largely on international trade.

Bilateral and multilateral trade

In our two-country model of trade, the value of A's exports was necessarily equal to those of B. This was because with only two countries we could only have two-way or bilateral trade. This could be represented as follows with arrows, of equal size, indicating the direction of exports:

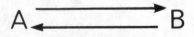

If there are many countries there is no longer any need for the values to balance for individual countries, so long as trade is balanced on a multilateral basis. For example Eastern Africa's exports to the United States generally exceed those of the USA to Eastern Africa. On the other hand those of USA to Europe exceed those from Europe to USA, and those from Europe to Eastern Africa exceed those in the opposite direction. We can illustrate this as follows:

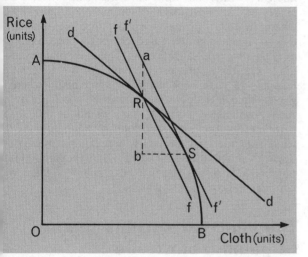

For each pair of countries the arrows in the two directions are of unequal size, indicating trade imbalance; on the other hand, for each country, taking its

two trading partners together, a large and a small arrow for imports is balanced by the same for exports, indicating balance in total transactions. It is evident from this that if trade were restricted to balancing bilateral transactions total world trade would be reduced, with a corresponding loss of gains from trade.

Other sources of gain from trade

So far we have identified the 'classical' theory of international trade with the 'comparative cost' theory, as is commonly done. There are, however, several strands in the classical theory which should be distinguished,[2] and which imply that gains from trade may arise in rather different ways from that just described.

The comparative cost theory assumes costs to be given, and represented by a fixed transformation curve. Specialization in Figures 19.1 and 19.4 did not involve any change in techniques, for instance, but simply a movement along the transformation curve. The increasing cost case is reproduced in Figure 19.5(a). Here specialization is represented by a movement from P to Q, giving a combination which includes more cloth and less rice. The opportunity to export excess production of one commodity at the world price ff permits this specialization, which is obtained by reallocating *existing* resources between rice and cloth. At all points on the transformation curve AB resources are fully employed: the extra cloth can only be obtained by producing less rice.

Figure 19.4 *The gains from trade: increasing costs.*

Figure 19.5 *(a) Movement along a given transformation curve, (b) outward shift of the transformation curve.*

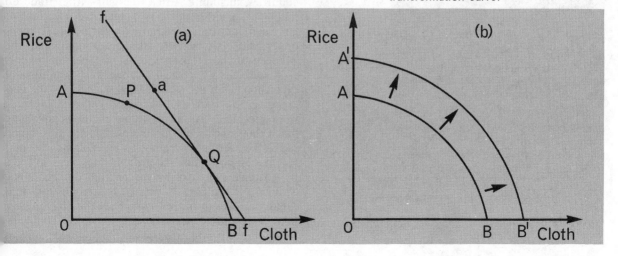

The 'productivity' theory of gains from trade

There are two ways in which this might be said to be an unrealistic theory, or at least an incomplete explanation of the factors behind international trade. In the first place, specialization and large-scale production make possible increased mechanization, as well as technical innovations. New methods can be introduced progressively to increase production, so that with given resources more can be produced. The effect would be as in Figure 19.5(b), in which the transformation curve is shown as shifting outwards. Thus in addition to the 'static' gains from trade obtained by moving along a fixed transformation curve (country A, where land is cheap, producing more rice, which uses a lot of land, and country B, where labour is cheap, producing more labour-intensive cloth) there are 'dynamic' gains, including the introduction of new techniques, due to increasing returns. This has been referred to as the 'productivity theory' of benefits from trade, since specialization and trade are supposed to permit more output from existing resources (though the increase in output means in turn an increase in resources, thus continuously increasing benefits over time).

The effect of specialization may be illustrated in a different way as in Figure 19.6. Suppose in the absence of trade and specialization two countries A and B, producing machinery and chemicals, have the identical production possibilities given by the transformation curve AB. Each country might select some combination like Q, allocating resources fairly equally as between chemicals and machinery. By specializing in chemicals, however, selecting, say, point P,

country A might be able to increase its productivity in this line and push its production boundary outwards from AB to A'P'B. Similarly country B, specializing in machinery at point R, could over time push its boundary out to AR'B'. The combination (P', R') fairly obviously gives a greater 'world' output of chemicals and machinery than Q since extra chemicals output in country A (=aP') exceeds the reduction in country B (=bQ), while the extra machinery produced in B (=bR') exceeds the reduction in A (=aQ).

The argument represented in this diagram is very relevant to the debate on the appropriate trade policy for developing countries. Although comparative advantage might be considered as supporting a policy of developing countries' specializing in primary products, while importing manufactured goods from the industrialized nations, the former have been increasingly dissatisfied with specialization on these lines. The rationale for such dissatisfaction can be expressed in terms of a diagram like Figure 19.6 where, however, primary products are measured on the y-axis and manufactured goods on the x-axis. If, *as is possible*, specialization in primary products cannot yield the same productivity gains—increasing returns—as can specialization in manufactured goods, then less developed countries specializing in such products at point P, say, would be left with substantially the *same* production boundary APB, while the industrial nations would expand their production possibilities to AR'B' and beyond. This possibility is discussed in a later chapter, when we consider industrialization policy.

The vent-for-surplus theory of gains from trade

It has been argued,[3] however, that for developing countries, including Africa, the gains from trade do not all fall in either of the two categories described so far. Such countries are characterized by 'dual' economies with two sectors, the 'traditional' and the 'modern'. It was observed that the peasant export crop sector had historically shown very high rates of expansion, as in the case of Uganda; and yet the new export crops, such as cotton and coffee in Uganda, were produced by fairly simple methods involving much the same techniques as used in the traditional sector. Hence they were not to be explained by new techniques; nor, since the growth rates were so high, by a simple switch of resources from one economic activity to another. It was suggested instead that rapid increases in output have been possible because unused resources were available which could be brought into productive use for the first time: surplus

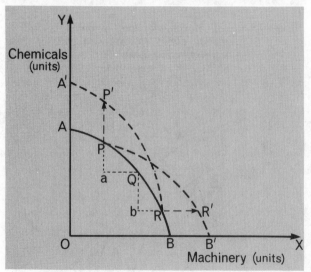

Figure 19.6 Productivity gains through international specialization

land was available in those countries not suffering from overpopulation, and labour was far from being fully occupied.

Why, if incomes are low, should land and labour be idle? Three reasons are given. First, in a traditional society where people are not closely acquainted with 'Western' goods, *there may be a lack of demand* initially for manufactured goods; secondly, there is a limited domestic demand for basic foodstuffs produced locally, such as maize or cassava, while industrial raw materials like copper or rubber are produced only for the export market and are not in demand at home. Thirdly, *resources are specific*: resources (land and labour) not used for providing basic foodstuffs or export crops cannot be used, say, in producing manufactured goods, because cooperating factors, physical capital, technical skills, and so on are not available. It follows that export production can be expanded *in addition to* subsistence food production. Trade does not produce a reallocation of resources between subsistence crops and export crops: it provides a market for export crops, which can be increased without cost simply by using up idle resources. It is obvious that transport, like the Uganda Railway discussed earlier, plays a crucial role in 'connecting up' the developing country with its market. According to this theory, again, the 'gains from trade' take a different form from those under the comparative cost theory: they are *gains from finding a market for the products of surplus resources*, referred to as the 'vent-for-surplus' theory of international trade.

Figure 19.7(a) illustrates this 'vent-for-surplus' theory with U representing a combination of products with underemployed resources available to produce, say, an extra UV of output. Figure 19.7(b) shows the real supply price of potential exports: it is infinitely elastic at a real cost of OC (say leisure forgone), output being limited to OU by the inelastic demand for staple food just discussed. Demand for output can be shifted from dd to d'd' by the opening of an export 'vent', UV. Only when the economy's resources are fully employed will this supply price turn upwards: this point, beyond V in Figure 19.7(b), can be aligned with the shift *along* the transformation curve from V to W. More cotton or oilseeds can be exported only by shifting resources from alternative home consumption goods. Comparative cost theory now 'takes over' from the 'vent-for-surplus' theory.

It is worth noting that this is the opposite, in its implications, of the 'exploitation' theory of international trade, whereby the metropolitan countries 'milk' the less developed countries of essential raw materials.

We have presented here three different explanations of how trade may benefit the participating countries. Together they appear to constitute a strong case for 'free trade'. Matters are not, however, so straightforward, and in the next chapter we shall analyse various arguments which have been made about the possible harmful effects of unrestricted trade on the less developed countries and thus the case for various forms of protection of the domestic economy.

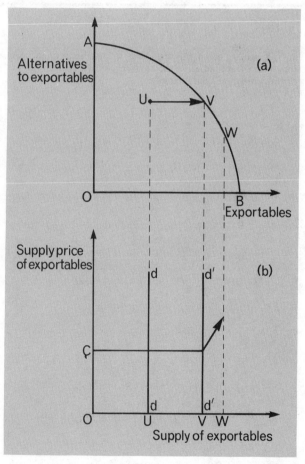

Figure 19.7 (a) 'Vent-for-surplus' theory of trade; with (b) domestic market conditions.

Questions on Chapter 19

1. Absolute cost and absolute advantage are not relevant to specialization.' Discuss.
2. State the Law of Comparative Costs. Explain the argument that countries should specialize in production according to this law, assuming constant costs of production.
3. Show how the distribution of benefits from such specialization will depend on the international price of the goods traded. What will determine this price?
4. Explain the sense in which 'small countries' have an advantage in international trading.
5. Show how the Law of Comparative Costs can be demonstrated in the case of increasing costs. Why is this more realistic than the constant cost example?
6. 'It is unacceptable that Tanzania should continue every year to have a negative trade balance with Japan.' Discuss.
7. Compare the gains from trade obtained according to the 'comparative cost' theory, the 'productivity' theory, and the 'vent-for-surplus' theory.
8. Explain how the productivity theory could be used to support the case for industrialization of less developed countries.
9. How realistic is it to assume, as does the vent-for-surplus theory, that despite being very poor a country does not fully utilize its resources?
10. Explain and illustrate why the comparative cost theory of international trade breaks down in situations of 'idle' or underemployed resources.

Notes

[1] In fact production of the first good will continue to increase along with the second, since the advantage of the second will not remain constant at the initial level.

[2] See H. Myint, 'The "Classical Theory" of International Trade and the Undeveloped Countries', *Economic Journal*, June 1958.
[3] H. Myint, op. cit.

20 Protection and the International Division of Labour

Despite the arguments of the 'classical' theory of trade, restrictions on the freedom of trade are widespread, among both developed and less developed countries. All have adopted, to varying extents, various forms of protection of some of their industries or agriculture.

The forms of protection

There are several forms of protection or ways in which an advantage may be given to home industries. We may distinguish tariffs; physical controls; restrictions associated with foreign exchange; procurement policies; and administrative obstacles.

The most common form of restriction is through the imposition of a tariff: that is, of a tax on each unit imported. The effect of the tax is to raise the price of imported varieties of a product in relation to the domestically produced, so that consumers are discouraged from buying foreign goods by means of the price mechanism. Such a tax may be *ad valorem*, representing a certain percentage of the import price, or *specific*, that is, an absolute charge on the physical amount imported, as, for example, five shillings a ton. Alternatively, an export subsidy may be granted to an industry: as we shall show presently, this is also a form of protection.

The most direct way of offering protection is by limiting the physical quantity of a good which may be imported. This can be done by giving only a limited number of import licences and fixing a *quota* on the total amount which may be brought in during any period. The quota may be imposed in terms of physical quantities or in terms of the value of foreign currency, so that a maximum of so many tons or so many 'dollars-worth' may be imported. There are several ways of giving protection through foreign exchange practices. Exchange controls work much the same way as physical controls. If importers are only allocated a limited amount of foreign exchange, they will only be able to import a limited quantity of foreign goods. Alternatively, the exchange rate may be fixed in such a way as to 'overprice' foreign exchange (compared to what would have been the free market price), so that importers have to pay more for foreign currency (in terms of domestic

currency). This makes *all* imports dearer and thus gives protection 'across the board' to all domestic production for the home market.

Of course instead of deliberately 'depreciating' or devaluing a *single* exchange rate applicable to all foreign-trade goods, a system of *multiple* exchange rates may be established so that importers are allowed foreign currency to buy particular goods and services at one exchange rate, say, one local Rupee = 0.20 foreign dollars, while other items might cost, say, twice as many local currency units: one local Rupee = 0.10 foreign dollars. Usually 'essential' goods with an inelastic domestic demand reflecting little domestic substitution are allowed in at the more favourable exchange rate, while goods with domestic substitutes requiring protection cost more foreign currency. Many Latin American countries have operated multiple exchange rates with one or more rates for exports and one or more dearer foreign currency rates for imports.

The government itself, together with state corporations, is an important purchaser of goods: in its 'procurement' policies, therefore, it can either buy goods from the cheapest source, whether domestic or foreign, or it can give preference to domestic producers. This could amount to a substantial advantage, or protection. Finally, it is possible to place subtle barriers in the way of imports in the form of complicated customs regulations or discriminatory transport charges. For example, the East African Railways normally change higher freight rates on imports than on export goods, and most African railways operate similarly. The term *invisible tariff* has been used to describe the many administrative regulations and other non-pecuniary obstacles placed in the way of importers.

Arguments for protection

Arguments for protection are many and varied. Many are related to development objectives, particularly the case for industrialization (calling for protection of manufacturing as a whole) or particular industrialization strategies (calling, for example, for preference to capital goods industries), or for employment creation (calling perhaps for special protection and encouragement for cottage and other rural small industry). These issues in industrialization are discussed more fully in Chapter 22. The application of tariffs (except revenue tariffs) and other instruments of protection can only be discussed in relation to those policy objectives. The present chapter and Chapter 22 should therefore be read together.

1 Correcting for shadow prices

The theory of comparative costs argues that countries should specialize in production according to comparative costs, that is, 'real' or opportunity-costs. It assumes that domestic prices and money costs will conform to real costs.

In fact in developing countries money wages may differ from the opportunity-cost (shadow price) of labour. Because of overpopulation on the one hand, or simply lack of development to create employment opportunities on the other, there may be a substantial surplus of labour. The real cost of labour may be low. At the same time government wage policies, particularly minimum wage laws, trade union pressures, or simply the desire of big employers to avoid adverse publicity or labour unrest, may raise urban money wages well above the real costs of labour as measured, for instance, by what the labour could produce in agriculture. The need to pay higher wages may thus put the urban manufacturer at a disadvantage compared to agriculture producers. It has been argued that this bias should be eliminated by giving manufacturers a compensating advantage through tariff protection.

Two points may be made here. First of all manufacturers may already be receiving a compensating advantage in the form of cheap capital, through cheap loans for example. Secondly, the argument is really one for removing the imperfection in the labour market rather than for adding another imperfection through the imposition of tariffs. Since, however, changes in the wage structure may be politically impossible, a potentially valid argument for protection remains.

2 Absorbing disguised unemployment

It has been argued that many developing countries suffer from what is known as 'disguised' unemployment, particularly in the rural areas. Rural families, particularly if they have only small plots, may have more family labour than they use: although all members of the family share in the work available, there is some 'disguised' unemployment in that labour time is left unused. Even urban labour may not be fully employed in that people may survive in very low paid occupations, in petty trading or shoe-shining,

for instance, although they would be capable of full-time and more productive employment.

In this situation it could be argued that a tariff could be used to direct demand from foreign goods towards home-produced goods *even if the former could be obtained more cheaply*. Whereas consumers' expenditure on foreign goods creates incomes and employment in those other countries, expenditure on home-produced goods generates income and employment at home. If resources were already fully employed, protection of manufacturing, say, would only divert resources from other industries in which probably they were more efficiently employed: there would be a loss. But if there are *unused* resources, there would be no such diversion and there would be a net increase in employment and especially in income. While consumers could lose something in having to pay higher prices for protected goods, this loss might be much smaller than the gain in income.

This argument is theoretically valid. The question is whether disguised unemployment *is* in fact widespread. And if it exists, the surplus is likely to be of unskilled labour only. There may be an acute shortage of skilled labour or management. Protecting some industries on this basis may therefore divert skilled labour, with adverse effects on production and incomes elsewhere. Finally, other arguments for protecting certain kinds of industry may make this general one, based on using up unskilled labour, redundant.

3 Learning effects and the infant industry, infant economy argument

The major weakness in the theory of comparative advantage is that it does not ask how particular countries came to *acquire* an advantage in a particular line. It is obvious that certain tropical countries have a natural advantage in producing coffee or rubber or bananas. It is less obvious why only temperate countries should have an advantage in producing manufactured goods. Their superiority in this regard is clearly because their industrial progress came earlier than in the present less developed countries and because they were able to *acquire*, over a long period, the necessary skills and experience to produce a wide range of manufactured goods.

Even among more developed countries there may be a case for protecting a newly established industry. This is referred to as the *infant industry argument*. According to this a new industry requires time to 'get on its feet'. It has generally to negotiate some problems early on, collecting together and training a labour force, perhaps, or attracting a steady supply of local raw materials, or organizing production in the most efficient way. It may also have initial problems in developing the most suitable quality of product, and, even if it has a good product, may have to establish a name for itself in the home market as against established foreign products. It might be said that the industry has to pass through a *learning process*. Thus although it may have uneconomically high costs to begin with, it could reduce these costs over time so that *eventually* it will have a comparative advantage. Since industrialists may not be willing to bear the losses in the early years, or may consider delayed returns too risky to rely on, there is a case for the *temporary* imposition of a tariff to last only for the industry's period of 'infancy'.

The danger in the infant industry argument is that the tariff almost inevitably becomes permanent, due to vested interests which make it difficult for the government to remove the tariff once imposed: even an 'infant' which has failed to grow up can appeal loudly and effectively for protection against bankruptcy and loss of jobs, while the general body of consumers who have to pay increased prices suffer in silence.

This 'infant industry' argument can be extended and turned into an 'infant economy' argument in favour of protecting the whole industrial sector of a developing country. As already mentioned, a large part of the advantage of the industrialized countries in this field may have come about merely because they embarked upon industrialization earlier. For this reason this existing industry can provide excessively strong competition for industries newly established in the poor countries unless the latter are protected. Secondly their developed industrial sectors can offer all kinds of advantages or external economies to new types of industry, for instance, through the existence of plentiful skilled labour and managerial expertise or through the ready supply of materials or equipment. A case could be made, therefore, for substantial and extended protection over a long period to the whole industrial sector as a means of industrialization in order (a) to change present comparative advantages, and (b) to develop the industrial foundations which can generate external economies for further industrial growth.

The dangers, as well as potential gains, are however greater than for individual industries, because the costs to consumers of higher prices and industrial inefficiency could be extremely high, and extend over a longer period. Moreover, it will be difficult to check when results are expected only in the long term that the policy is beneficial and that relative inefficiency is decreasing.

4 External economies

If an industry is economically viable, it should not be necessary to protect it, even if it produces external economies of assistance to other industries: for it should already be a sufficiently attractive proposition for private entrepreneurs or for state enterprise. If, on the other hand, the industry would itself make a loss, while generating more than enough advantages elsewhere in the economy to compensate for this, there is a case for protection to ensure that the industry is in fact established and the net gains to the economy therefore obtained. It could also happen that two related industries, such as iron and steel, and coal mining, would each be uneconomic on their own, but economic if undertaken together. Temporary tariff protection leading to the establishment of the first industry would be enough to secure the establishment of the second, so that the protection could later be abandoned. It has also been suggested that individual industries might be uneconomic, because of the small size of the market, especially, but that a whole *set* of industries might be mutually supporting. This argument, for 'balanced growth', is also based on external economies.

If a particular industry offers substantial external economies, even if uneconomic viewed by itself, there is a case for protection. It might, for example, be a 'leading industry' with a variety of linkages with others, either through providing intermediate inputs on which other industries can be based or through providing a market for 'ancillary' industries which supply it with materials or components.

A separate major factor in the industrial dominance of the advanced nations is technical progress. The products of manufacturing industry today are very different from those of fifty years ago, and are continually being modified, improved, or added to. Moreover new products and new varieties are mostly not produced by completely new firms, but by existing manufacturing concerns, which are constantly experimenting and carrying out research. Technical progress brings benefits to the economy as a whole and therefore involves external economies outside the firm responsible for the invention or innovation. Technical progress and innovation are frequently associated with manufacturing industry and it is therefore argued that industry *as a whole* yields external economies which constitute a case for a degree of protection.

5 The terms of trade and division of world trade

The comparative cost theory assumes that after specialization two countries can trade with each other on an equitable basis. In contrast the developing countries have in recent years been increasingly dissatisfied with the terms on which they trade their products (mainly primary products) for manufactured goods. Specialization in primary production according to comparative costs is unsatisfactory, it has been argued, if satisfactory prices for this production are not obtainable. As we shall see in the next chapter, the long-term trend (excluding fluctuations) in the terms of trade between primary products and manufactured goods is far from certain.

What is much more clear is the picture which we described in Table 4.8. This showed that world industrial output is increasing at a faster rate than the demand for and production of primary products. As a result the exports of developing countries have been growing less fast than those of the industrialized countries, and the percentage share of developing countries in world trade has actually been *falling*. This provides an alternative argument for industrialization.

There is another specific terms of trade argument that the imposition of a tariff on a particular imported commodity may directly improve the terms on which it is purchased. If a country is a major buyer of a commodity it may pass on part of the tariff or tax to foreign suppliers if domestic demand is elastic. The USA, for example, constitutes a major part of the total world demand for, say, coffee. The hypothetical position is illustrated in Figure 20.1(a) in which demand is purposely shown as elastic. Since the USA is a major part of the total world market for coffee, producers will find it difficult to find alternative markets, and the supply to the USA will be inelastic, like the curve SS in Figure 20.1(a).

The effect of a customs duty would be to shift the supply curve upwards by the amount of the tax to S'S'. The American price to consumers will go up to OP': but the price paid to coffee exporters will be OP'', the market price in America *minus the tax*. And the tax revenue is retained by the US government for

expenditure within the USA. The quantity of coffee obtained is reduced, to OQ', but the amount paid for it is reduced in greater proportion, to the amount (OP'' × OQ'). The aim is clearly not protection of home industries in this case, since tropical products like coffee cannot be produced in the USA: it is to reduce the price paid to foreigners for an import or imports, in relation to home exports; that is, to improve the terms of trade and to retain as tax revenue a part of what would otherwise be paid to overseas suppliers. Some industrial countries have considered putting a special import duty on oil as a means of countering the effect of the rise in oil prices by the OPEC countries. In Figure 20.2 the demand curve for oil is drawn as inelastic over a wide range, but becoming very much more elastic at very high oil prices where, for instance, consumers may be driven to using smaller cars which use less petrol and industrial users to making serious economies in their use of petroleum products. Let us suppose initially oil producers are supplying oil to this country at the relatively low price OP, at which the amount OQ is purchased: revenue to the oil producers is OQtP. Subsequently these producers discover that the demand for oil is highly inelastic over a wide range: they therefore come together to demand the much higher price OP'. Since demand is inelastic, they are still able to export the quantity OQ' and substantially increase their revenues to OQ'rP'. It may then occur to the importing country to apply a customs duty on imported oil. Suppose for simplicity it applies a tax exactly equal to the previous oil price increase, P'P. If OQ' of oil is still supplied the tax will be rs (=P'P) and price paid to oil producers only sQ'. Revenue to overseas oil producers will be reduced to OQ'sP. If, however, these producers try to offset this tax by raising their prices again, they will this time

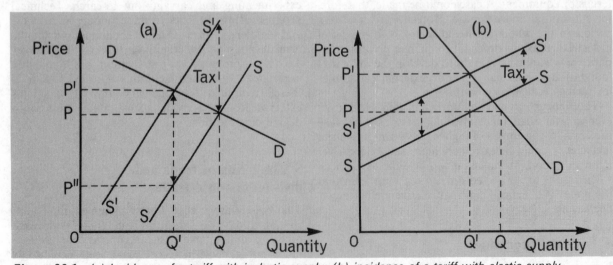

Figure 20.1 (a) Incidence of a tariff with inelastic supply; (b) incidence of a tariff with elastic supply.

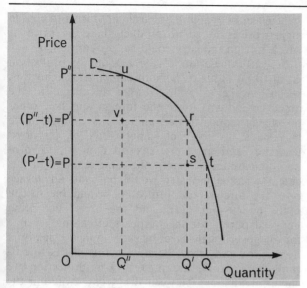

Figure 20.2 *The effects of an oil import tax.*

meet the problem of elastic demand. If, for instance, they raised the price by the same amount of the tax, to $OP''(P'P'' = P'P)$ they could only sell the amount OQ'', and obtain the even smaller revenue $OQ''vP'$.

6 The exploitation argument and international monopolies

Another reason why the less developed countries are concerned as to whether they are receiving an adequate price for their products is that such trade is often conducted by large foreign or multinational concerns, who may be able to exert some monopoly (or rather monopsonistic) influence on prices. This is related to the terms of trade argument above, but provides a case not for a tax but for a state exporting agency, such as that set up for the export of Zambian copper, which might negotiate a better price for the exported commodity.

The complaint that the industrial countries have 'exploited' the less developed countries by 'taking out' minerals and other materials needed for industry is often a misdirected one. But it can be related to that concerned with the decreasing share of the developing countries in world trade. The valid argument is that such countries should be in a position to export other goods *as well as* primary products and that they also should have industries which would consume raw materials.

7 Non-economic arguments for protection

Arguments in favour of tariffs are sometimes made on other than purely economic grounds. These are most frequently made with respect to agriculture, which is often heavily protected in the developed countries. This may be done in order to preserve the countryside (as in Switzerland) or to preserve employment among small farmers (as in France), though such protection may be at the expense of even poorer farmers in the developing countries. Agriculture is often protected for strategic reasons in order to ensure food supplies in the event of a war: such an argument is outdated in the Atomic Age, where warfare is no longer of the type which dislocates maritime transportation. In fact, modern warfare being generally more capital-intensive, using machines rather than large armies of unskilled labour, no longer requires reserve armies comprising agricultural labourers as was the case in the last century when Germany, for instance, protected domestic agriculture in part to maintain a prosperous class of landowners who supplied the Army with officers and men. Indeed, the strategic argument can work in the opposite way since uncultivated land may be used to produce foodcrops for short periods of emergency having lain 'fallow' for decades.

The strongest case depends on the risk factor and the dangers of famine in the event of crop failures in a poor country. This has led to the desire for self-sufficiency in basic foodstuffs among many developing countries. In fact this call for self-sufficiency—which contradicts the law of comparative costs and neglects the possibilities for profitable trade in foodstuffs *between* developing countries—can prove very expensive for them. Since total crop failures are relatively infrequent affairs, famine reserves may have to be stored for very long periods, with substantial storage costs; whereas, given the speed of modern transportation, it should be possible to import supplies occasionally as required, perhaps at much lower costs.

There is *some* sense, however, in the self-sufficiency argument. This is that if the less developed countries have difficulty in efficiently expanding their manufacturing, they may have a better chance, through the introduction of better varieties of crop or improved cultivation practices, of expanding their output of food (especially as within their domestic market this would not meet tariff barriers). However this argument is not for self-sufficiency as such (it would apply also to food production for export) but for expanding production where the returns are higher.

What is left of the comparative cost theory?

We have reviewed an impressive variety of arguments for protection. Does this mean that the law of comparative advantage can be neglected?

Clearly not. The theory of comparative advantage is only an elaboration of opportunity-costs. It may be desirable to work towards changing existing comparative advantage, or opportunity-cost, in the long term. If short-term opportunity-costs are ignored, however, this must reduce output and therefore incomes in the present. And reduced incomes may jeopardize some of the long-term goals, for instance by reducing the size of the market, and the size of government revenues. And if a country is attempting deliberately to foster some new industries through protection it should select those in which it has the best chance of *acquiring* a comparative advantage, and where the costs of protection will be lowest and of the shortest duration, where this is compatible with an overall strategy.

Secondly, many of the benefits from protecting particular industries, and industry as a whole, are highly indeterminate. It is difficult for a government to tell what external economies will actually accrue from an industry or to assess their value. These may, moreover, only accrue in some indefinite future. Governments may therefore prefer to go for more tangible and more quickly realized benefits.

Thirdly, the developing countries are increasingly realizing the dangers of excessive protection. Tariffs may foster inefficient monopolies sheltering behind tariffs which vested interests make it extremely difficult to remove. By raising prices, these tariffs may mean a substantial charge to consumers, as well as a misallocation of resources. If these are industries which supply equipment or intermediate inputs to other firms, this inefficiency and monopoly pricing could adversely affect expansion elsewhere in the economy. Expanding the entire industrial sector through tariff protection, replacing imports with domestically produced goods, is referred to as a policy of *import substitution*. The disadvantages of such a policy are discussed in Chapter 22.

Finally, we may note that many of the export problems of developing countries are due to protection imposed by the rich countries. Removal or reduction of these trade barriers, implying a move towards freer trade on the basis of comparative costs, would substantially benefit the poor countries and lead to a more rational pattern of world trade.

The concept of effective protection

So far when we have talked about protecting an industry we have implied that this would be done simply by imposing a tariff on imports of the commodity: the higher the tariff, the higher the degree of protection. Other forms of protection would have the same effect of enabling domestic producers to charge higher prices for their product than the price at which foreign industry could supply consumers.

In fact calculation of the amount of protection given to an industry is more complicated than this, because while a tariff gives an advantage to the domestic industry over the foreign supplier, other taxes may reduce this advantage. For example there may be a 30 per cent import duty on imported cigarettes and an excise tax on domestically produced cigarettes of exactly the same amount. In this case the home industry would have no advantage over the foreign and protection would be absent, both the customs duty and the excise tax being imposed purely for the purposes of raising revenue for the government. Sales or excise duties levied on a home-produced good therefore act as offsets to customs duty. If we are interested in protection we should distinguish between the 'gross' tariff and the 'net' tariff, the latter being the actual or gross tariff *less* the amount of excise duty on the home-produced good.

The advantage accruing to the home industry from a tariff on an imported good may also be offset or partly offset if it has to pay import duty on imported materials used in producing the good. Suppose the Malawian clothing industry uses imported cotton cloth from India. A tariff on imports of Indian manufactured clothing will give the Malawian clothing industry an advantage over the Indian. But a tariff on imports of *cloth* will give it a *dis*advantage: because while this raises costs in the Malawian industry, Indian garment manufacturers can buy cloth free of duty from Indian cloth manufacturers. If the import duty on cloth is high, the Malawian industry could even be at a net disadvantage compared to the Indian, so that the degree of protection is actually *negative*. It follows that the *nominal tariff*, the actual tariff on the imported good, is itself no clear guide to the degree of protection. What we should be interested in is the degree of *effective protection*, as it has come to be called.

The previous paragraph indicates the crucial element in calculating effective protection, which is that we must distinguish between outputs and inputs, and concentrate on the actual *process* or activity which is being protected. The process here was not so much producing clothing, that is, through all its stages of manufacture, but that of converting cloth into clothing. Similarly, many developing countries talk about having an 'automobile industry' when the automobile parts are almost entirely imported, and merely assembled in the country concerned: the country in effect has only an automobile *assembly* industry. Each process or activity creates some value added, and the output of the industry is really this value added, rather than the final commodity as it appears on the market. In calculating effective protection, therefore, we should focus on the particular process being carried out, and on 'value added' in the industry thus defined. Moreover, if the additional *domestic* 'value added' comprises profits and even wages or salaries accruing to foreign factors of production, as is often the case with much of the manufacturing set up behind protective tariffs, the additional increase in *national* factor income may be very small or even negative.

In the absence of a tariff, assuming the country is relatively small in relation to the world market, the domestic price would equal the world price (including transport costs). Domestic consumers would not pay more for the locally produced good than they had to pay for the imported one; and any amount of this commodity could be imported. The effect of a tariff on the final commodity is to raise the price at which imports can come into the country, and thus to raise the price which local producers are able to charge. The size of this nominal tariff, in percentage terms, is given by

$$\frac{P' - P}{P}$$

where P is the price per unit of output without the tariff (the 'free trade' price) and P′ the price with the tariff. To find effective protection, however, we should take as 'output' of the industry not a unit of final output, but a unit of value added (equal to the value added in a unit of output). Effective protection in any industry j could thus be written as

$$\frac{v'_j - v_j}{v_j}$$

where v_j is the value added in a unit of final output (a unit of value added) without protection (i.e. the 'free trade value added') in industry j; and v'_j the value added per unit of output when there is protection. Protection permits local producers to charge consumers more for the process involved than foreign producers. It need not of course give them more *profits* than foreign producers: they may be so inefficient, with high costs, that *even with this advantage* they cannot break even.

The size of the advantage they have, however, depends on the balance between the import duty on the final commodity and duties on intermediate inputs used in production: this net advantage is reflected in the difference between v'_j and v_j, which measures the extra 'leeway' given to domestic producers in carrying out this process over foreign producers carrying out the same process. The formula

holds for *any* type of protection, not only tariffs: import licensing or foreign exchange controls, for example, also raise the price that a domestic industry can charge for a unit of value added sold, compared to the import price.

There are several points to be noted about effects protection.

(1) *A moderate nominal tariff may yield a very high level of effective protection.* Suppose a country can import radios freely from abroad at the 'world' price of 100 dollars. Of this value, 80 per cent comprises intermediate inputs (radio parts). A developing country can either import the finished radios at 100 dollars or the components, at 80 dollars, for use by a domestic radio assembly industry. In the absence of protection this industry can sell radios at no more than $100, yielding a value added of $20 per radio. If its costs are more than $20 it will make a loss, if less, a profit, but that is another matter.

Suppose now the government imposes a 20 per cent tariff on imported radios, without taxing the import of parts. The domestic price (assuming producers take full advantage of the tariff) will go up to $120, with parts still costing $80 per radio. Value added per unit of output will go up from $20 ($v_j$) to $40 ($v'_j$), an increase of 100 per cent. Effective protection, $(v'_j - v_j)/v_j$, will equal $\frac{40 - 20}{20}$, that is, 100 per cent, compared with the 20 per cent nominal tariff.

(2) *Effective protection depends on the balance between duties on final product and duties on intermediate inputs.* Suppose in the previous example, in addition to the 20 per cent duty on imported radios there was a 10 per cent duty on imported parts. The domestic price of radios would be $120, and the cost of intermediate inputs to domestic producers $88. The new value added (v'_j) would be ($120–88) or $32, compared to $20 in the free trade case. Effective protection would be $\frac{32 - 20}{20}$, or 60 per cent, compared to 100 per cent previously. Thus the effect of the tax on intermediate inputs is to reduce substantially the advantage of domestic radio assemblers.

(3) *Effective protection can be divided into positive and negative parts.* In this example the advantage given to producers through the import duty on radios is $20 compared to a free trade value added of $20, that is, 100 per cent, and the disadvantage due to the tax on imported parts is $8 compared to value added of $20, that is, 40 per cent. The rate of effective protection, 60 per cent, can be seen as the sum of two parts, (+100) and (−40).

(4) *The rate of effective protection varies with the share of value added in product price.* Consider the

original example with a simple 20 per cent duty on imported radios. With a value added by the process of 20 per cent of the finished product, effective protection was 100 per cent. If the domestic industry were responsible for a much larger share of the final product so that the process being compared accounted for, say, 80 per cent of the price, what would be the rate of effective protection? Free trade value added would be $80 per radio and the value of imported parts $20. With a 20 per cent duty, the domestic price of radios would be $120, giving a new value added, v_j', of $(120-20)=100$, and an effective rate of protection of $\dfrac{100-80}{80}=25$ per cent. Thus with the same nominal tariff of 20 per cent, effective protection is 25 per cent when value added is 80 per cent of the final product, and as much as 100 per cent when value added is only 20 per cent. It may be checked that when value added is only 10 per cent of the final product effective protection increases to 200 per cent.[1]

(5) *Effective protection may be negative.* In an earlier example we considered a case in which import duty was 20 per cent on finished radios and 10 per cent on parts. Suppose free trade value added was $20 as before, and the cost of parts $80, but that the import duties on finished product and on parts were 20 per cent and 40 per cent respectively. This would raise the domestic price of radios to $120 and of parts per unit to $112. The new value added v_j' would be $(120-112)=8$, and effective protection $\dfrac{8-20}{20}$ or minus 60 per cent.

The reason for this is that while the tax on final product raises revenue per unit by $20, the tax on radio parts raises costs for the domestic producer by $32, giving the latter a net disadvantage. We can conclude then, that effective protection may be negative. This will occur if, for the local producer, tariffs raise the cost of intermediate inputs by more than they raise the price of the product.

(6) *Export subsidies constitute an alternative form of effective protection.* Putting a tariff on imports will not help an export industry which does not sell on the domestic market. But it can be seen very simply that an export industry may be given protection through an export subsidy in just the same way as an import-substituting industry can be protected by a customs duty.

Suppose a country encourages its pig export industry with an export subsidy of 10 per cent. The world price of pigs is 100 shillings, and pigs each consume 60 shillings of imported feedstuffs, not subject to duty. Free trade value added v_j is therefore 40 shillings. The export subsidy in effect raises the price per pig to the domestic producer to shs 110, of which

value added (v_j') is now shs $(110-60)=50$. Effective protection is therefore $\dfrac{50-40}{40}=25$ per cent.

Assumptions underlying effective protection calculations

In all the above calculations it is assumed that the input–output coefficients of the industry are not affected by the taxes imposed. In fact a tariff on imported materials might persuade the local industry to economize on these and use fewer materials per unit of output or alternatively to substitute other local materials, also affecting the share of value added in the final product.

Secondly it is assumed that imports are available in infinitely elastic supply, so that the domestic price is always equal to the world price plus the tariff. This should be true of small or moderate-sized countries, including all those in Africa in respect of almost all the goods they import. Possible exceptions could be trade in goods supplied on a specialized basis to cater for local tastes such as Dutch wax-print cotton textiles or dark chewing tobacco, where the West African market was dominant, or for particular local production processes, such as imports of sisal decorticating machinery in Eastern Africa, including Mozambique.

An alternative formula for effective protection

An alternative formula may be derived for calculating effective protection which is more useful when there are several intermediate inputs each liable to a different rate of duty. Thus a unit of product in industry j may use a_{1j}, a_{2j}, and a_{3j} (all fractions of 1) of three different inputs. Value added would be $1-(a_{1j}+a_{2j}+a_{3j})$. Using the sign Σ to mean 'the sum of', we have a free trade value added in industry α,

$$v_j = 1 - \sum_{i=1}^{3} a_{ij} \text{ where } i=1, 2, 3$$

Suppose now there is a tariff of t_j on the final product and t_{ij} on each of the inputs. The domestic price of the product would go up to $(1+t_j)$, and the cost of inputs to

$$\{a_{1j}(1+t_{1j})+a_{2j}(1+t_{2j})+a_{3j}(1+t_{3j})\},$$

that is,
$$\sum_{i=1}^{3} a_{ij}(1+t_{ij})$$

The protected value added, v_j', is the difference between these two, that is,

$$v_j' = (1+t_j) - \sum_{i=1}^{3} a_{ij}(1+t_{ij})$$

From this effective protection can be deduced[2] as

$$EP = \frac{t_j - \sum_{i=1}^{3} t_{ij}\, a_{ij}}{1 - \sum_{i=1}^{3} a_{ij}}$$

for three inputs or

$$\frac{t_j - \sum_{i=1}^{n} t_{ij}\, a_{ij}}{1 - \sum_{i=1}^{n} a_{ij}}$$

where n is any number of inputs.

Suppose radios are assembled using two intermediate inputs, radio cases and transistors. The 'world' or free trade prices are \$100 per radio. If we take as a unit the price of one radio the free trade value added is

$$v_j = 1 - \sum_{i=1}^{2} a_{ij}$$
$$= 1 - (a_{1j} + a_{2j})$$
$$= 1 - (0.2 + 0.6)$$
$$= 0.2$$

If duties are imposed of 50 per cent on radios, 20 per cent on cases, and 10 per cent on transistors, the domestic price of radios would increase to $(1+t_j) = 1.5$ and the cost of inputs to $\Sigma a_{ij}(1+t_{ij}) = \{(0.2+0.04)+(0.6+0.06)\} = 0.90$. Hence $v_j' = 1.5 - 0.9 = 0.6$ and effective protection is $\dfrac{v_j' - v_j}{v_j} = \dfrac{0.6 - 0.2}{0.2} = \dfrac{0.4}{0.2}$, or 200 per cent.

Effective protection in Kenya

We can make the following conclusions. First, it is not possible to identify the degree of protection in an industry until we correctly identify the process on which the industry is based: for example, whether it is an automobile industry (converting steel into automobiles) or an automobile-assembly industry (converting automobile parts into automobiles). Secondly, the nominal tariff will provide a very poor guide to the actual degree of protection. Thirdly, a uniform nominal tariff on a wide range of products will mean very different levels of effective protection, possibly forming a far from rational pattern. Thus a developing country might apply the simple rule of a 10 per cent duty on 'essential' consumer goods, 20 per cent on 'ordinary' consumer goods, and 40 per cent on 'luxury' consumer goods: but the effective protection being granted could bear little relation to these administratively convenient figures.

We can see this very well if we look at effective

Table 20.1 Effective protection rates in Kenya, 1967, resulting from the external tariff structure, selected industries

Industry	Nominal tariff (%)	Effective rate[1] of protection (%)
(1) Bakery products, including confectionery	42	769
(2) Leather and leather products	26	421
(3) Spinning, weaving, printing, and dyeing	57	274
(4) Tobacco	309	266
(5) Soap	44	142
(6) Dairy products	12	105
(7) Footwear	33	88
(8) Furniture	22	58
(9) Garment manufacture	45	38
(10) Beer and spirits	103	24
(11) Pulp and paper	9	8
(12) Cotton ginning	0	−6.5
(13) Sawmilling	0	−9
(14) Blanket manufacturing	40	−10
(15) Processing of meat and fish	0	−18
(16) Soft drinks	21	−24
(17) Grain mill products	2	−47

SOURCE: R. Reimer, 'Effective Rates of Protection in East Africa', *Eastern Africa Economic Review*, Vol. 3, No. 3, 1971, Table 1
[1] Based on Reimer's 'modified' method of calculation

protection rates in an actual country. Table 20.1 gives estimates of effective rates for various industries in Kenya based on data for 1967. While a few industrial tariffs have changed since 1967, the picture until the mid-1970s did not differ much from that shown in the table.[3] In addition the 1967 position for Uganda and Tanzania will not differ too much because of the common external tariff and similarity in industrial structures (input–output coefficients), although sales and excise duties, quantitative controls and import regulations, and the imposition of transfer taxes under the Common Market Treaty will by now have changed the position considerably.

As can be seen, the rates vary from very high positive rates (for example, 769 per cent for bakery products) to relatively high negative rates (−47 per cent for grain mill products). Yet the most heavily protected, such as bakery products and soap, are not necessarily 'strategic' industries, or industries likely to have very high external economies.[4]

The lack of correlation between the nominal rate and the effective rates is obvious. For example, the nominal rate for clothing is 45 per cent and the effective rate only 38; for bakery products the nominal rate is 42, and the effective rate 769! The high rate for bakery products reflects the low percentage of value added compared to the tariff (the case discussed in our fourth example) as well as the low tariff (2 per cent) on the major input, grain mill products.

Presumably it is not intended to give negative protection to any industry. The processing of meat and fish, for example, shows negative protection, although agricultural processing, which has linkages with agriculture, and earns foreign exchange, is one of those industries where external economies may be presumed. This illustrates the important point that even uniform effective protection for the home market would affect the allocation of resources as between import-substitution industries and export industries.

In some cases part of the reason for the lack of correspondence between the nominal rate and the effective rate is the effect of excise taxes. There is, for instance, a heavy excise tax on locally produced beer, though in addition one of the major inputs of the brewing industry (and of the soft drinks industry), sugar, is subject to a high tariff. These two factors together make the effective rate, 24 per cent, much less than the high nominal rate, 103 per cent.

The negative protection rate on blanket manufacturing (−10 per cent) and the low rate on garment manufacture (38 per cent), both items which a country producing the basic raw material, cotton and wool, might wish to encourage, illustrate clearly the difficulty faced in fixing tariffs. The low effective rate of protection in this case is due to the relatively high nominal tax (57 per cent) on spinning and weaving. Obviously there is a direct conflict here between protecting the spinning and weaving industry and the garment and blanket industries (as well as other made-up textiles). This illustrates also the danger of protecting an industry which supplies inputs to other industries unless the industry goes through the 'infant' phase within a clearly defined period. In this case protection of spinning implies handicapping the blanket industry, or at least not giving it equal support. Clearly it is not obvious why the effective rates should be in the proportion 274, 38, and −10.

Effects of protection on other industries

We have pointed out that protection of one industry may have adverse effects on the development of other industries. Until very recently the emphasis in most developing countries has been on protecting final consumer goods rather than intermediate producer materials or capital goods. Kenya, in particular, has now recognized that this policy has discouraged the growth of domestic intermediate and capital goods industries, and exports of manufactures generally. In addition small-scale handicraft industries, like small tailors, in fact, have often suffered negative protection as the result of higher tariffs protecting other larger-scale modern manufacturers. There are numerous examples of such negative effects, and other distortions produced by tariff protection. If, for example, a modern metal fabricating industry is protected against imports of hollow-ware and similar galvanized metal goods like bins and 'karai', and at the same time receives an import duty 'drawback' permitting it to claim back the taxes paid on intermediate goods like sheet metal, its competitive position is enhanced in relation not only to imported final goods but also to local substitutes produced by domestic 'informal' artisans which cannot claim 'drawback'. The latter may therefore have to turn to cheaper inputs like scrap metal, old 'debris' and sheets of imported corrugated iron or aluminium. Additional work effort is then expended in converting corrugated sheets into hollow-ware. If, later, extra import duties are levied on the corrugated sheet to protect another local factory turning out asbestos or plastic corrugated roofing, the artisans experience more negative protection. The timber and wood fabricating industries provide other examples of adverse effects: a modern furniture factory may receive tariff protection for its final output and access to duty-free imports of intermediate inputs like plywood, thereby restricting the market for a new local plywood industry; while a high tariff on imported suitcases and travelling trunks may cause valuable local timbers with export potential to be diverted into the making of wooden substitutes.

Questions on Chapter 20

1. Explain the meaning of 'invisible' tariffs, specific tariffs, 'gross' and 'net' tariffs, nominal tariff.
2. How would a divergence between money wages and the real cost of labour affect the application of the law of comparative advantage?
3. Explain clearly the 'employment argument' for tariff protection. Why would this argument point to permanent rather than temporary imposition of a tariff?
4. How might external economy considerations affect tariff policy? Should an industry which generates external economies necessarily be protected?
5. Explain with the use of diagrams the circumstances in which the imposition of a tariff could enable a country to import a particular commodity on more favourable terms.
6. Discuss the case for developing countries' aiming at self-sufficiency in agriculture.
7. Discuss the usefulness as well as the main limitations of the theory of comparative advantage. Which criticisms of the theory do you consider more important and which less important, and why?
8. Why have many African countries adopted systems of import licensing? What are the problems created by these import licensing systems?
9. How can either exchange controls or 'discriminatory' railway freight rates affect the effective rate of protection?
10. Why is the nominal tariff an inadequate guide to the degree of protection being given to an industry?
11. Devise your own arithmetical example to show the effect of the share of value added on effective protection rates.
12. Explain how an export subsidy constitutes effective protection. Devise your own arithmetical example to demonstrate this.
13. There is a 10 per cent excise tax on locally made chocolate and customs duties of 30 per cent, 20 per cent, and 10 per cent on imported chocolate, cocoa, and nuts respectively. Cocoa and nuts constitute 60 per cent and 10 per cent of the value of imported chocolate confectionery. Find the effective rate of protection on chocolate confectionery.
14. Comment on the following data for Tanzania in 1966:

Industry	Nominal tariff rate (%)	Nominal net tariff rate (%)	Effective rate of protection (%)
Tobacco	314	234	538
Matches	174	87	395
Bicycle tyres and tubes	36	36	270
Cosmetics	75	75	265
Radio assembly	50	50	95
Coffee processing	30	10	12
Cashew nut processing	0	10	20
Meat products	37.5	−3	−14
Soft drinks	34	16	−23

Notes

[1] Too much significance should not be placed on these astronomically high rates of effective protection. What this last case means in practice is that whereas the last stage of radio assembly can be carried out abroad at a cost of $10, local firms would be viable so long as they could carry out this process at a cost of $30.

[2]
$$EP = \frac{v'_j - v_j}{v_j} = \frac{\{(1+t_j) - \sum_{i=1}^{3} a_{ij}(1+t_{ij})\} - \{1 - \sum_{i=1}^{3} a_{ij}\}}{\{1 - \sum_{i=1}^{3} a_i\}}$$

$$= \frac{1 + t_j - \sum_{i=1}^{3} a_{ij} - \sum_{i=1}^{3} t_{ij}a_{ij} - 1 + \sum_{i=1}^{3} a_{ij}}{1 - \sum_{i=1}^{3} a_{ij}} = \frac{t_j - \sum_{i=1}^{3} t_{ij}a_{ij}}{1 - \sum_{i=1}^{3} a_{ij}}$$

[3] Since 1973 increasing reliance on the new Sales Tax, more uniform nominal rates of import duty, and a new export subsidy on manufactures have tended to correct the distorted picture somewhat.

[4] However the bakery industry already has complete 'natural' protection from imports, because bread and similar products are perishable. Hence the effective protection rate is of little more than academic interest except in the case of biscuits and confectionery.

21 The Terms of Trade

We have already discussed now in several places why developing countries have for some time been dissatisfied with the prices they obtain for their exports, compared to what they pay for imports, that is, with their 'terms of trade'. In this chapter we look more closely at this concept of the terms of trade.

The concept of terms of trade

The concept of the 'terms of trade' applies not only to trade between nations but also to trade or exchange between individuals or between two sectors within one country. For example if farmers obtain a higher unit price for their maize, they can purchase more cloth, and we can say that the terms of trade between farmers and cloth-makers has changed, becoming more favourable for farmers but 'deteriorating' for cloth-makers whose cloth, per unit, will purchase a smaller volume of maize than before. Governments have considerable influence over the 'terms of trade' between the urban sector, producing manufactured goods, and the rural sector, producing foodstuffs. By raising urban money wages they can cause an increase in the price of manufactured goods relative to agricultural output, whereas by raising the price paid for food crops by the marketing boards they can improve the 'terms of trade' of workers in agriculture. In the USA an index showing the 'farm price parity ratio' is used to measure the current money income required to maintain a farmer's real income, and a system of subsidies and price controls operates to maintain the farmer's terms of trade.

A problem arises when countries export several goods and import, usually, an even greater variety of goods and services. We then need to talk about the 'average price' of exports or of imports, and compile index numbers referring to a 'basket' of exports and a 'basket' of imports in much the same way as a cost-of-living index is calculated to indicate movements in the retail price of a basket of consumer goods. Similar index number problems arise to those involved in measuring changes in the value of money, which we discuss in Chapter 30. In particular the ever-changing commodity composition of both exports and imports makes the task of measuring a country's external terms of trade much more difficult and imprecise compared to, say, the terms of trade of a simple farmer exchanging a single product for a relatively restricted and stable basket of purchases. If we supposed, for instance, that Ethiopia exported a single homogeneous commodity, coffee, its terms of trade would be given by the 'basket' of goods which one unit of coffee, say one tonne, could buy. Since this is similar to the barter of maize and cloth between two individuals, in that it deals with the exchange of real commodities rather than money, this concept of the terms of trade is called the *commodity* or *net barter terms of trade*. With many goods, however, we need to value a country's external terms of trade first in terms of money. If P_x is the 'price' or *unit value* of exports and P_m that of imports, a 5 per cent increase in P_x, with P_m remaining constant, would mean that a unit of exports could buy 5 per cent more imports—an improvement in the 'net barter' terms of trade. If P_x and P_m each increased but at different percentage rates, say 5 per cent and 10 per cent respectively, with P_m increasing faster, there would be a deterioration in the terms as measured by the ratio, P_x/P_m, equal to 105/110 or 95.5, the terms of trade falling by 4.5 per cent.

In this ratio P_x and P_m are both index numbers of prices, and the ratio is subject to the usual limitations of index numbers: in this case the typical 'basket of goods' exported and imported is likely to change in composition from year to year, in less developed economies especially, and for the following reasons.

(1) Since trade encourages specialization, it is to be expected that exports will be less diverse than imports, particularly for small countries. The effect is that the share of different commodities in exports can show pronounced and rapid changes. This can be illustrated by the contribution of raw cotton to the *value* of total domestic exports from Uganda: the share varied from as much as 52 per cent in 1954 to only 22 per cent in 1962. Giving cotton a 'weight' of 52 per cent, based on the 1954 figure, would mean that the fall in the average price of exports would be understated since 1954 if other exports fell significantly in price and cotton did not. A simple *base-weighted* index would give these other exports a weight of only 48 per cent, whereas they did in fact account for 78 per cent of the total value of domestic exports in 1962, because of an expansion in volume.[1]

(2) Apart from merchandise, countries also export

and import services, such as banking or insurance services or tourism, known in the balance of payments as 'invisibles' in contrast to 'visible' goods or merchandise. Since there are additional complications in measuring changes in the 'unit value' and the 'volume' of invisible services, terms of trade indices usually refer only to imports and exports of merchandise. The former is normally in terms of the c.i.f. value, however, and thus includes *some* invisible shipping and insurance services to the ports of entry; while the latter is valued f.o.b. or f.o.r., that is, 'free on board' or 'free on rail' at the points of export from the country. Clearly, for countries with relatively large invisible exports like the UK, or even Kenya, commodity exports do not constitute all sources of export income; and for most developing countries net invisible imports can absorb a relatively large part of commodity export earnings.

(3) Although imports are normally more diversified than exports, developing countries experience marked shifts in the commodity composition of imports. As living standards rise there is, first, an increase in imports of more income-elastic consumer goods. Secondly, increasing incomes are associated with economic development, and economic development with some expansion of domestic manufacturing. This will generally mean greater imports of capital goods for development projects, this itself changing the commodity composition of imports. Finally we may note that in agricultural economies subject to periodic drought and other hazards of nature, there will be years in which the country is forced to spend a large part of its imports bill on importing food, usually produced at home: this will mean that the commodity composition of imports will fluctuate from year to year also.

We will, however, ignore these problems and assume that it is reasonable to talk about a fairly constant 'basket' of imports and of exports. The commodity or 'net barter' terms of trade are not, however, the only indicator of a country's capacity to import. This tells us how much of imports one unit of exports can buy. The actual quantity of imports which can be bought depends not only on the relative prices of exports and imports, but also on the volume of exports produced. Thus a country may experience a decline in its barter terms of trade, but an increase in its ability to import if it can produce more export goods. Indeed if export demand abroad is price-elastic, a country may be able to earn *more* foreign exchange by deliberately cutting its export prices, through devaluation of the exchange rate, in order to increase the quantity of exports. The local import-purchasing power of exports is therefore measured by the *income terms of trade*, which is simply the value of exports divided by the price of imports (in terms of index numbers), giving the quantity of imports which could

be bought. This can be written as

$$\frac{V_x}{P_m} = \frac{P_x \cdot Q_x}{P_m} = \left(\frac{P_x}{P_m}\right) Q_x$$

that is, the barter terms of trade multiplied by the volume of exports, Q_x.

Table 21.1 shows the net barter (commodity) terms of trade and the income terms of trade for Ethiopia. The former are given in column (3) as the ratio P_x/P_m. From 1970 to 1971 there is a deterioration of 15 per cent. This can be seen to be due especially to a fall in the price of exports of 11 per cent. Over the period 1970–3 there is only a slight decline of 6 per cent. This is more than offset by a substantial increase in the quantity of exports by 48 per cent. Multiplying columns (3) and (4) gives the income terms of trade in column 5, which shows a net 39 per cent increase in the purchasing power of exports. The value of exports has increased by 60 per cent over the period (column 6) without increasing purchasing power by 60 per cent since during the same period the price of imports rose by 14 per cent. The income terms of trade can equally be obtained by dividing column 6 (160) by column 1 (114): $\frac{160}{114} = 140$.

Table 21.1 *Commodity and income terms of trade for Ethiopia, 1970–3*

Year	(1) P_x	(2) P_m	(3) $\frac{P_x}{P_m}$	(4) Q_x	(5) $\frac{P_x}{P_m} \cdot Q_x$	(6) V_x
1970	100	100	100	100	100	100
1971	89	105	85	114	97	102
1972	93	108	86	135	116	126
1973	108	114	94	148	139	160

SOURCE: IMF *International Financial Statistics*

Factors affecting the long-run trend in the terms of trade

A number of development economists, notably a Latin American school of economists led by Dr Raoul Prebisch, have argued that the economic development of 'Third World' countries has been held back by a persistent fall in their terms of trade over the long run. There are a number of factors which might contribute to this result.

The income-elasticity of demand for primary products

Basic foodstuffs, especially, may be considered to be 'necessities' on which a decreasing proportion of incomes is likely to be spent as these incomes rise;

nations, like individual households, will devote an increasing proportion of their incomes to manufactured goods and to services. Countries relying on basic foods and other primary product exports may therefore find their exports growing more slowly than those of individual countries exporting manufactured goods. Thus assuming constant for the moment the commodity terms of trade, P_x/P_m, the volume of exports Q_x will grow more slowly for the developing countries than for developed, and thus their income terms of trade, $(P_x/P_m) \cdot Q_x$, likewise.

The discovery of synthetic materials

Over a whole range of items, the substitution of synthetic man-made products has reduced the market for particular primary products. Man-made rubber has substituted for natural rubber for many purposes; nylon and rayon have taken over an important share of the textile materials market and seriously damaged prospects for sisal; plastics have become a major ingredient in a wide range of manufactured goods, and so on. In 1963–5 commodities classified by the UN Conference on Trade and Development as 'facing serious competition from substitutes' accounted for 20 per cent of developing country exports: these comprised raw cotton, natural rubber, raw wool, hard fibres (sisal, etc.), hides and skins, and raw jute.

The long-term trend in the market shares of natural and synthetic products is, moreover, likely to be influenced by a 'ratchet' effect: when prices of natural products are high, due to cyclical fluctuations or temporary shortages, research into possible synthetic substitutes will be encouraged. When prices of natural products revert to more normal levels, these products may have permanently lost a further part of the market.

Raw material-saving innovations

This is likely also to apply to technical change aimed at economizing the use of raw materials in industry. Periodic high prices will stimulate the search for and application of raw material-saving processes. Technical change aimed at a progressive reduction in costs per unit of output will also affect the income-elasticity of output directly by permitting industrial output (and thus income) to expand in greater proportion than the demand for materials.

An important example of raw material saving is the use of tin in cans (metal boxes): in 1938 the amount of tin was seven times as much as that needed by the 1950s. Changes in taste, fashion, and design have also tended to economize the use of many primary products like timber, hides and skins, furs, wool, and tobacco; although in some cases like cotton, for instance, the world market depends increasingly on demand from consumers in developing countries themselves.

Agricultural protection and import-substitution in developed countries

Prebisch and others have also pointed to the protectionist policies within industrial countries which aim to raise the incomes of farmers and other primary producers like fishermen by placing tariffs or quotas on competing imports. As a result, many industrial countries have become almost self-sufficient in producing grains, sugar (from beet), livestock products, and even tobacco and wines. Sometimes the policies have been directed at saving foreign exchange as well as maintaining domestic incomes and employment, and have not only been confined to primary products. Indeed, restrictions on access to markets for manufactured goods by developing countries with large, or potentially large, export industries like India's textiles have forced developing countries to sell *more* primary products instead. Thus even without tariffs or quotas, therefore, the expansion in primary product exports is likely to result in a decline in their commodity terms of trade in the many cases where the *price-elasticity* of demand in industrial countries is very low. When, in addition, these primary products face tariff or quota restrictions, the deterioration in the terms of trade will be greater. We pointed out in the last chapter that one of the economic arguments for protection was the desire to improve the terms of trade, and that large importers like the USA in coffee, for instance, possess this market power. For this reason UNCTAD, under Prebisch as its Director-General, has urged the developed 'Centre' to relax import restrictions on both primary and manufactured exports from the 'Periphery'. In addition most African producers have negotiated 'Free Trade' terms of entry into the European Common Market in order to avoid the high tariffs or quotas imposed by the latter on competing imports like maize, oilseeds, tobacco, fruit, and vegetables.

Against these considerations, there are some factors which should have helped to improve the position of the less developed countries.

Diminishing returns in agriculture and limited natural resources

Whatever the income-elasticity of demand for primary products, continuous expansion of industrial output means a continually increasing requirement of raw materials. If the supply of land suitable for various agricultural products is limited, the law of diminishing returns may apply, leading to increasing scarcity of such products, and a rise in their prices. So far this has not been a major factor, since in particular the opening up of the African continent, somewhat later than Latin America and Asia, has meant a relatively elastic supply. Nevertheless, increasing concern is being voiced regarding the world supply of agricultural and mineral resources, and of the need for conservation.

Technical progress in manufacturing

Prebisch in particular has argued[2] that technical progress in the industrialized countries should, through the market mechanism, have been shared between the industrial producers and the producers of primary products. For technical progress should have continually increased the supply and reduced the prices of manufactured goods relative to primary products, for which methods of production have been relatively constant. The barter terms of trade should in fact have been moving in favour of primary producing countries.

According to Prebisch this desirable development has been frustrated. On the one hand industrial monopolistic practices and trade union action producing cost-push inflation in the developed countries have persistently raised money wages in these countries and, with these, the prices of manufactured goods. In contrast competition among primary producers, and the ineffectiveness of trade unions in the agricultural sectors of these economies, has kept down the prices of raw materials. In fact the benefits of any cost-reducing innovation in these countries is likely to be passed on, as a result of competition, to industrial consumers in the form of reduced prices. The terms of trade between industrial countries (the 'Centre' as Prebisch refers to them) and less developed countries (the 'Periphery'), and between manufactured goods and primary products, thus constitute a crucial ingredient in Prebisch's thesis.

Price-fixing agreements among primary producers

We have already seen the price-raising powers of OPEC, the Organization of Petroleum Exporting Countries. Similar producer organizations are involved in attempts to coordinate the supply and marketing of a wide range of materials and basic foods such as copper, iron, bauxite, phosphates, timber, rubber, tin, coffee, cocoa, sugar, and bananas. Most of these organizations remain relatively weak, but the success of OPEC has indicated clearly to them the possibilities and stimulated their activity.

This factor could eventually reverse the competitive marketing situation as observed by Prebisch however. It depends essentially on joint action to restrict supply to markets where demand is fairly inelastic.

Import restrictions to improve the terms of trade

Prebisch and others have also advocated the raising of tariffs against imports of manufactures from developed industrial countries. Although we noted in the last chapter the weakness of individual countries in this respect, unless they were very large importers like the USA, joint action by all developing countries or regional groupings of them might have more effect in depressing the prices that they have to pay for imports. It is argued that the combined effect of selling fewer primary products and buying fewer manufactured imports would divert exportable resources into the more income-elastic and 'technically progressive' domestic manufacturing sectors growing up behind higher tariffs.

Trends in the terms of trade

There are, then, a number of reasons for thinking that the terms of trade for primary products or for the poorer countries might deteriorate over time. But what are the facts about the trend in the terms of trade?

For a number of reasons they are difficult to establish. One of the earliest historical studies of the terms of trade is for the UK, reproduced in Table 21.2. The series starts in the late 1870s, with average import prices in 1876–80 divided by average export prices as the base, equal to 100, and ends in the immediate post-Second World War years, 1946–7, with an index of 69. This would indicate that in 1946–7 the United Kingdom would be able to buy a given quantity of primary products at about two-thirds of the price (in terms of manufactured goods) which it had to pay in 1876–80.

Table 21.2   Ratio of prices of primary imports to manufactured exports of the United Kingdom, 1876–1947

Year	Index	Year	Index
1876–80	100	1914–18	War
1881–5	102	1921–5	67
1886–90	96	1926–34	73
1891–5	90	1931–5	62
1896–1900	87	1936–8	64
1901–6	85	1939–45	War
1906–10	86	1946–7	69
1911–13	86		

SOURCE: UK Board of Trade, reproduced in G. M. Meier, *Leading Issues in Development Economics*, OUP, New York, 1964, p. 341

Statistical difficulties

(1) The reason for looking at figures of the United Kingdom terms of trade is that, because Britain was a leading commercial nation even in this early period its commercial transactions at that time will have been with a wide variety of nations and over a wide range of products, since it had already a developed industrial sector producing most manufactured goods. Hence Prebisch, for instance, took the reciprocal of these figures to indicate what Latin American countries and other primary exporters would need to pay for manufactured goods (in terms of primary products).

In fact Britain is not entirely typical of all industrial countries for this period. Similar series for the USA and Western Europe show rather different results. Data for the USA for 1879–1960 actually contradict the UK figures. Britain was, for instance, importing a larger proportion of its temperate food supplies from its overseas Empire, Latin America, and the USA itself. It was also in a less competitive situation than other countries in selling its manufactured goods, because of its colonial advantages.

(2) A further problem when we take data from a number of countries to compare relative prices of primary products and manufactures is the changing country composition in the two commodity groups, particularly among the primary producing countries. The pre-1945 series tended to represent high-income primary producers of temperate foodstuffs such as Canada, Australia, and the USA itself, rather than contemporary less developed economies like Eastern Africa, many of which had hardly entered world trade in some of the earlier historical series.

(3) Another complicating factor is the effect of falling transport costs. If transport costs fell (particularly for bulky raw materials and foodstuffs such as Britain was importing), it would be possible for a country such as Britain to pay less for imports without the less developed countries exporting these being paid less. As it happens, the period 1870–1905 was one when large ocean-going steamships and refrigeration for meat and other perishable foodstuffs were introduced and the Suez Canal was opened, resulting in a very substantial fall in freight rates. Thus British import prices (including transport) may have fallen, but not the export prices of LDCs (excluding transport to overseas markets). Against this, of course, we could argue that there is no reason why the industrialized countries should obtain the main benefit from reduced freight rates, and that this itself represents a relative benefit in trading over less developed countries.

This factor would also contribute to a different result for the UK and the USA, as the latter, self-sufficient in the bulkier commodities, would not benefit so much from transport improvements for higher-valued tropical products like coffee or cocoa.

(4) It has been pointed out also that manufactured goods are changing constantly in quality and design, and are likely to incorporate much greater quality improvements than primary products. Imports of cocoa, coffee, copper, and natural rubber are much the same today as they were, say, in 1900, whereas machinery and transport equipment (motor cars) have changed dramatically. New products like aircraft and plastics are included in the later figures, so that the 'basket of goods' imported by less developed countries changes considerably. It is extremely difficult, however, to incorporate all these quality improvements and new products in a price index. Hence part of the prices paid by developing countries might be for better and more costly products.

(5) There are a number of purely statistical difficulties also. Quite different results can be obtained, depending on the statistical index numbers used, even for the same country. For instance, one study of US trade data over a long time span, 1879-1960, using a price series of manufactures imported into the USA, tended to support the Prebisch thesis, whereas a comparison of US exports of manufactures with primary goods tended to show the opposite.

The choice of base period may also affect the results. If prices for primary products in the base year are unusually high, it is only to be expected that prices will fall off subsequently. Thus Prebisch has been criticized for using data for 1950–61 to show deteriorating terms of trade for primary products. The period starts with exceptionally high primary product prices in the Korean War boom (when raw materials were being bought up for stockpiling) and closes with prices depressed by an economic recession in the USA. The results, for any short to medium time span, are thus highly sensitive to the two terminal dates chosen.

The difficulty, in fact, is that if we take a relatively short time span, we could be looking at only the downward part, say, of a cyclical movement, which will be reversed later by the upswing of the cycle. If we take a long-term trend we have greater problems in taking account of such factors as changing quality and transport costs.

(6) Finally, the Middle East War of 1973 leading to the restriction of petroleum exports by the Arab countries has introduced a new element in any discussion of both the balance of payments of *all* countries and their terms of trade. After more than a decade of fairly stable prices, these rose three-fold in the first few months of 1974. The impact on different industrial countries will differ considerably according to their dependence on imported oil: while Japan is

entirely dependent on such supplies, for instance, the UK has access to increasing quantities of North Sea Oil. However the most important consequence is that it will be necessary in future to talk separately of the terms of trade of oil-exporting developing countries and oil-importing developing countries.

Recent trends for the developing countries as a whole

If, therefore, we wish to identify the trend properly, we must be careful to avoid 'exceptional' terminal dates. Table 21.3 shows the trends for the relatively 'normal' period, 1955–70, avoiding the primary product price boom of 1950–1 and 1972–4. The data are rather inconclusive. On the whole, looking at the first two rows, the developed countries seem to have benefited by about 10 per cent and the developing countries suffered by the equivalent amount. On the other hand the third row suggests fluctuating terms for non-oil-exporting countries, rather than any clear trend. And the experience of different groups of developing countries has not been uniform. During the 1960s the oil-exporting countries fared differently (worse in this period) than other developing countries—a situation which has obviously been reversed since. Comparing the last two rows African countries have fared differently from other developing countries, though both series fluctuate.

Data on the income terms of trade $\left(\dfrac{P_x}{P_m}\cdot Q_x\right)$ for the same period are given in Table 21.4. This shows that whether or not the commodity or barter terms of trade have been moving against them in this period the developing countries have been able to improve their income terms of trade, the purchasing power of their exports, during this period. This has been done, of course, by expanding the volume of output exported, as a result of economic expansion.

It should be noticed, however, that in this regard they have still done less well than the developed countries. While the developing countries' income terms of trade improved by just over 100 per cent, those of the developed improved by something approaching 200 per cent, a considerable divergence over a period of only 12 years. The period is too short, however, to put too much emphasis on these precise figures. It is none the less interesting to see that Africa has increased the volume of exports more than other developing areas so that Table 21.4 shows a greater improvement in its income terms of trade despite the larger deterioration in the net barter terms of trade indicated in Table 21.3.

The terms of trade for East Africa

It is worth looking at movements in the terms of trade of the three East African countries over a fairly long period covering the last twenty years. Table 21.5 gives the barter terms of trade (P_x/P_m) for East Africa as a whole. The series is constructed on a different basis from 1966 onwards, but we have 'spliced' together the two periods to give a continuous series. The data are illustrated graphically in Figure 21.1. This shows a fairly clear and continuous decline in the terms of trade over the twenty-year period to 61 per cent in 1972 (there is an improvement in 1973 which may not be permanent) implying a fall of, say, 35–40 per cent in relative prices over the period, about half of this before 1964 and half after 1964. Since import prices were fairly constant up to 1962, most of the earlier decline was due to falling export prices. Subsequently export prices were constant or rising but not rising as fast as import prices (until 1972) so that the terms of trade continue to decline.

Table 21.4 *Changes in the income terms of trade of developed and developing countries, 1958–70*

Areas	1958	1963	1965	1968	1970
Developed countries	100	149	179	234	288
Developing countries	100	128	145	176	208
Africa	100	135	162	224	242

SOURCE: UN *Statistical Yearbook*

Table 21.3 *Indices of net barter (commodity) terms of trade* $\left(\dfrac{P_x}{P_m}\right)$ *1955–70*

Areas	1955	1958	1963	1965	1968	1969	1970
Developed countries	100	104	109	109	110	110	110
Developing countries	100	95	91	91	92	93	92
of which:							
Non-petroleum countries	100	92	91	93	94	97	98
Africa	100	97	87	87	93	96	91

SOURCE: UNCTAD, *Handbook of International Trade and Development Statistics*, 1972

Table 21.5 *East Africa's net barter terms of trade, 1954–73*

	P_x	P_m	P_x/P_m		P_x	P_m	P_x/P_m
1954	100	100	100	1964	88	109	81
1955	94	100	94	1965*	80	110	73
1956	89	103	86	1966	79	111	71
1957	87	103	84	1967	78	113	70
1958	81	101	80	1968	79	118	67
1959	79	101	78	1969	78	118	66
1960	78	105	74	1970	87	121	72
1961	77	99	77	1971	90	134	67
1962	76	97	78	1972	92	150	61
1963	83	107	77	1973	120	166	72

SOURCE: *Economic and Statistical Review*.
*Index constructed on a different basis from 1965 onwards

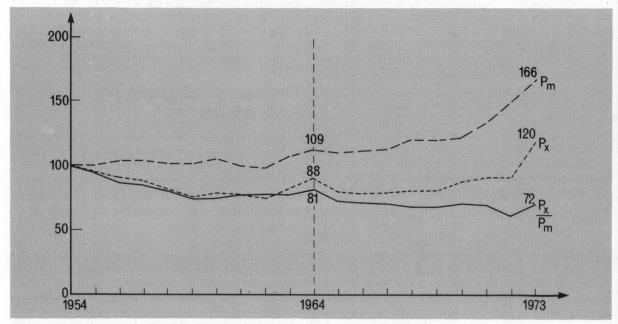

Figure 21.1 *Movements in East Africa's net barter terms of trade, 1954–73.*

Table 21.6 shows separately for the three East African countries the barter and income terms of trade. Tanzania's barter terms of trade were the only ones not to decline seriously up to 1964, but all three declined over the whole period up to 1972 by something like 35–40 per cent. The right-hand side of the table shows that despite this the income terms of trade of all three countries improved considerably. The series fluctuate, but we can obtain a rough idea of the trend by drawing the straight lines which appear best to 'fit' the graphs. On this basis in Figure 21.2 the income terms of trade of Kenya appear to have improved much faster than those of Tanzania, by something like 200 per cent over the period up to 1973 compared to around 110 per cent. The Ugandan terms of trade improved at only around half the rate of Tanzania. Thus Kenya in particular was able to offset much more than the fall in the relative unit price of exports by a very substantial increase in the volume of exports which the other countries, especially Uganda, heavily dependent still on cotton and coffee, have been unable to match. Uganda's dependence on coffee and cotton exports is reflected also in the much greater fluctuations in its income terms of trade.

Thus whatever generalization may be made about the terms of trade of developing countries as a whole, we can say that over the past twenty years there has been a continuous decline in East Africa, amounting to about 35–40 per cent in the barter terms of trade. Though the Kenyan economy particularly has been able to expand despite this handicap, through ex-

Table 21.6 *The net barter and income terms of trade of the East African countries, 1954–73*

Year	Net barter terms of trade			Income terms of trade		
	Kenya	Tanzania	Uganda	Kenya	Tanzania	Uganda
1954	100	100	100	100	100	100
1955	100	101	89	123	103	117
1956	88	93	83	132	128	99
1957	84	92	86	118	114	115
1958	80	85	80	137	121	115
1959	82	90	70	152	133	167
1960	80	90	61	156	152	99
1961	84	91	63	171	142	95
1962	79	97	66	178	157	97
1963	77	101	60	193	176	113
1964	78	94	71	203	179	145
1965	77	80	62	189	154	138
1966	77	80	62	246	196	147
1967	71	74	61	226	182	138
1968	70	79	65	242	191	143
1969	70	76	62	261	195	151
1970	66	78	62	255	201	164
1971	63	75	62	258	197	151
1972	62	66	49	292	184	138
1973	67	72	69	363	172	185

panding the volume of output and exports, *over one-third of the value of these exports has been lost as a result of the decline in the commodity terms of trade.*

Export production and terms of trade of Sudan

In the previous section we explained Uganda's failure to 'make good' the deterioration in the net barter terms of trade by its heavier dependence on just two main export crops, coffee and cotton, which were not only subject to wider short-term fluctuations in price but also revealed a slower growth in volume during the 1960s. Sudan's experience in the late 1960s and early 1970s was rather similar, being dependent on exports of raw cotton for some 50–60 per cent of visible export earnings and having no other important export which was able to enjoy rising prices on world markets. Moreover, Sudan, too, was unable to sustain a rapid expansion in the volume of export production, particularly of cotton, with the result that the deterioration in the barter terms of trade was hardly compensated by a greater volume of exports. Indeed, as Table 21.7 shows, despite the world-wide primary commodity boom in 1973 and 1974, which helped primary exporters to meet the inflationary increases in the price of imports, Sudan's income terms of trade benefited very little because of the failure of export production to expand. In fact in 1974 the quantity of cotton exports was only 28 per cent of the 1970 volume, and it was her other exports which expanded to keep the overall quantum index, Q_x, at 60 per cent of the 1970 level.

Table 21.7 *Movements in external terms of trade for Sudan, 1968–74*

Index Nos. 1968=100		1968	1969	1970	1971	1972	1973	1974
Visible export earnings	V_x	100	106	128	141	154	186	150
Import price index	P_m	100	113	115	123	133	140	149
Income terms of trade	V_x/P_m	100	97	112	116	117	135	101
Export volume index	Q_x	100	96	112	120	121	96	67
Net barter terms of trade	P_x/P_m	100	101	100	96	96	141	150
Export price index	P_x	100	111	115	118	127	133	132

SOURCE: IMF *International Financial Statistics*, June 1975

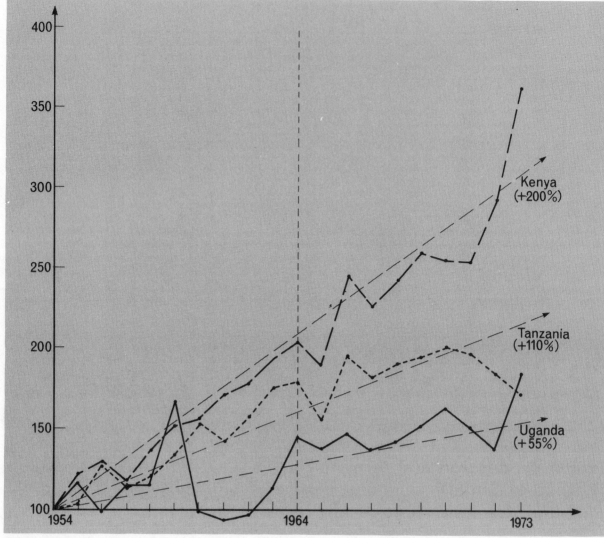

Figure 21.2   *Movements in the income terms of trade, East Africa, 1954–73.*

In Table 21.7 we show, first, V_x, the index for the value of Sudan's total visible exports at current f.o.b. prices, that is, before deflating for changes in price levels. We then deflate this series by the import price index, P_m, to show the import-purchasing power of these exports. As we explained previously, this is in fact the income terms of trade. In the fourth row we see how exports performed in volume terms, Q_x; and by dividing this index into the income terms of trade we can arrive at the net barter terms of trade, P_x/P_m, showing the import-purchasing power of a unit of exports. The last two rows show, respectively, how export prices have behaved in relation to the prices of imports. It will be seen, therefore, that Sudan suffered, in the short period under review, from, first, a deterioration in the barter terms of trade (arising from a more rapidly rising import price level rather than falling export prices) and then, secondly, from a failure of export production just when export prices improved in 1973–4.

Terms of trade in single export economies

Dependence on a single export commodity places a country's whole economy at the mercy of any fluctuations in export production or in export prices *if exports constitute a large part of final demand-generating national income.* Domestic producers often have little control over short-run movements in export production of primary products, since these depend on climatic and other natural hazards; they normally also have little influence on export prices since single countries produce only a small proportion of world output. Nevertheless, single export dependence need not imply any long-run deterioration in the net barter terms of trade, or in the income terms of trade, if the commodity enjoys an income-elastic world market and it is profitable for domestic producers to expand output—which normally implies a price-elastic demand also.

Two of the Eastern African countries are largely single commodity exporters, and it is therefore useful to look at their experiences, to see how far their terms of trade have moved over short- to medium-term periods when world trade has been affected by inflation and commodity speculation. Since during the periods under review (and previously too) sugar accounted for around 90 per cent of the annual value of Mauritian exports and copper represented nearer 95 per cent of Zambian exports by value, we can also avoid some of the index number problems discussed earlier in this chapter if we exclude 'minor' exports from the terms of trade indices. In other words we are approaching nearer to the simple barter exchange between farmers' maize and traders' cloth with which we began the chapter. We can see, therefore, more clearly and precisely how movements in the volume and export price of sugar and copper, respectively, affect the capacity of Mauritius and Zambia to import 'baskets' of foreign goods.

Mauritian terms of trade

In Table 21.8 the various index numbers are arranged in a somewhat different order from that used for the other countries discussed above. Our first concern is to account for the more than four-fold increase in Mauritian export earnings from sugar at current f.o.b. prices over the short period of years 1970–4. This is shown in the top row, followed by the sugar export volume in the next. Clearly the physical expansion in sugar exports is not the main cause of additional export earnings, but rather the rise in world sugar prices, starting in 1972 and reaching a

peak some four times the more stable 1968–70 level in 1974. It is this 'windfall' gain from a world shortage of sugar and speculative trading by commodity dealers which was mainly responsible for the increase in export earnings index, V_x.

While sugar export earnings nearly doubled between 1968 and 1973, however (and more than doubled in the shorter period from 1971 to 1973) the rise in the prices of imports by nearly 50 per cent (also occurring mostly in the latter period) cancelled a substantial part of this, so that the income terms of trade improved by only 36 per cent. Of course the problem for Mauritius, and other export economies heavily dependent on a single primary product like sugar, is that whilst the price increase for the product can be very sharp, it is quite likely also to be very short-lived.

Zambian terms of trade

The statistics for Zambia also show how, in the case of export economies based on the export of one or two commodities, the country's overall terms of trade reflect trends and fluctuations in the price and output of the major export commodity or commodities.

Once again we start in Table 21.9 with an index number series representing the f.o.b. value of exports, and can see the way in which this fluctuated during the period from a low in 1966 to a peak in 1969, falling again to a trough in 1971, and recovering again in 1973. The second and third rows show that these fluctuations reflect cyclical movement in both volume and price. Copper-mining is not so much affected by natural hazards of climatic changes but nevertheless can be disrupted by industrial disputes, by transport bottlenecks, or by unforeseen difficulties in mining operations like explosions or flooding. Thus the reduced output in 1971 was the result of the disastrous explosion at the Mufulira mine. In addition the 'lumpy' nature of large investments in new mines means that their opening up can greatly

Table 21.8 Terms of trade of a sugar exporter: Mauritius, 1968–74

Index Nos. 1968=100		1968	1969	1970	1971	1972	1973	1974
Sugar export earnings	V_x	100	102	106	96	157	195	477
Sugar export volume	Q_x	100	98	94	82	110	117	109
Sugar export price	P_x	100	103	114	118	144	168	439
Import price index	P_m	100	97	96	106	112	145	
Sugar barter terms of trade	P_x/P_m	100	106	118	111	128	115	
Sugar income terms of trade	V_x/P_m	100	104	111	91	142	136	

SOURCE: IMF *International Financial Statistics*, June 1975

change the volume available for export, and even affect the world price. All these problems on the supply side are quite apart from shifts in world demand, since the demand for copper also fluctuates in line with the level of industrial production (the trade cycle) in the main consuming countries.

Because copper accounts for practically all Zambia's exports (minor exports represent only about 5 per cent of the total), we can calculate the 'copper' barter terms of trade for Zambia, and the 'copper' income terms of trade, measuring the purchasing power of copper exports in terms of the amount of imported goods which the foreign exchange obtained can buy. Both of these show the same fluctuations superimposed over a downward trend reflecting especially the steadily rising prices of imports shown in row 4.

Table 21.9 *Terms of trade of a copper exporter: Zambia, 1966–73*

Index Nos. 1970=100		1966	1967	1968	1969	1970	1971	1972	1973
Copper export earnings	V_x	68	64	76	106	100	66	72	103
Copper export volume	Q_x	87	88	94	107	100	93	104	97
Copper export price	P_x	77	72	81	100	100	71	69	106
Import price index	P_m	68	64	91	97	100	106	112	116
Copper barter terms of trade	P_x/P_m	113	112	89	103	100	67	62	91
Copper income terms of trade	V_x/P_m	100	100	84	109	100	62	65	89

SOURCE: IMF *International Financial Statistics*, June 1975, and Bank of Zambia, *Economic and Statistical Review*,

Questions on Chapter 21

1. Explain carefully the distinction between net barter and income terms of trade. Which is more directly related to the economic growth of the country, and why?
2. Discuss the view that the demand for basic foods and for industrial raw materials is likely to be less elastic with respect to (a) income and (b) price, than the demand for manufactured goods.
3. Discuss in general terms the relationship between technical progress and the terms of trade between developed and developing countries.
4. Find data on recent movements in the commodity and income terms of trade of any African country not covered here, and discuss these movements.
5. Discuss the statistical problems in using terms of trade data (a) covering a long time span and (b) covering a short to medium time span.
6. Discuss the special problems of constructing price index numbers of export and import goods (to be attempted after reading Chapter 29).
7. Explain how developing countries as a whole may improve their terms of trade by restricting exports of primary products and imports of manufactures from the industrial 'Centre' countries.
8. Why is it important to take account of changes in a country's terms of trade' when comparing annual estimates of its national income?

Notes

[1] Readers not familiar with the construction of simple index numbers may look ahead to Chapter 29 on pages 421–7 and return later to re-read this section.

[2] R. Prebisch, *The Economic Development of Latin America and its Principal Problems*, ECLA, UN, 1950.

Part VI Industrial development

22 Issues in Industrialization

Before we turn to a detailed examination of industry in Eastern Africa, we need to discuss the role in development that we should like to give to industrialization, and what strategy for industrial development might be adopted. Should industrialization start by focusing on a few 'key' industries or be spread widely? Should capital goods or consumer goods industries be encouraged? Small-scale or large-scale industries? Capital-intensive or labour-intensive activities? Manufacturing for export or for the home market? Let us examine briefly some of these important issues in industrial development.

Agriculture versus industry

The first question is whether the main development effort is to come through industry or through agriculture, and what effort to industrialize should be made.

Interdependence between agriculture and industry

Economists who argue for concentration on the agricultural sector can point to the fact that agricultural development makes easier subsequent industrial growth. Agriculture and industry are thus interdependent. In the first place, in developing countries, where a large proportion of income is earned in agriculture, an increase in agricultural incomes means an increase in effective demand for manufactured goods. Given that in most manufacturing industries there is some minimum viable size of plant, expansion of agricultural incomes may be a prerequisite for establishing efficient industries. Secondly, increased agricultural productivity can, by permitting necessary food supplies to be obtained with less labour, release labour from the land for work in industry. Apart from increasing the supply of labour directly in this way, it may do so indirectly by cheapening the supply of food: this may improve the 'terms of trade' between the industrial and agricultural sectors, and permit employers to pay lower money wages for their hired labour. By reducing wage costs, this will improve the industries' viability in the home market and their competitiveness abroad. Beyond this, increased agricultural incomes are likely to mean increased saving and increased tax revenues for the government, which can then be spent on social overhead capital, this in turn helping industrial development. And if the incomes arise out of increased agricultural exports, the additional foreign exchange earned will permit increased imports of the machinery and intermediate products required by industry and frequently ease a restriction on faster industrial expansion. Finally, agriculture provides raw materials for direct use in industry, and thus offers forward linkages with industry. These may be very important, as in the case of cotton growing, giving rise to ginning and textile manufacture.

However, the fact that agriculture and industry are interdependent in this way—industry perhaps more dependent on agriculture than vice versa in the earlier stages of development—does not mean there is no need to 'choose' betwen agriculture and industry nor that development finance should be allocated, say, on a fifty-fifty basis. Development finance is limited, and a choice must still be made as regards the precise allocation. Thus allocation *must* depend on the rate of return, more precisely the 'marginal efficiency of investment' in the two sectors. The difference is simply that the rate of return should be calculated to include beneficial 'spillover effects' on the other sector.

The predominance of agriculture

Another argument is that since agricultural production accounts for such a large proportion of national output in less developed countries, a high overall rate of growth can only be achieved if the agricultural sector can be made to grow.

Suppose agriculture accounted for 90 per cent of national output, and manufacturing for 10 per cent, also that the two sectors were growing respectively at rates of 2 per cent and 10 per cent per annum.

Despite the good performance of manufacturing, *total* national output would grow only at the rate of $\frac{90.2 + 10.10}{100}$, or 2.8 per cent, due, of course, to the proportion of manufacturing within total output. In contrast if both sectors grew at the same rate of 5 per cent, total output would also grow at 5 per cent per annum, considerably more than in the previous case.

The trouble with this argument is that it is a statement of need, rather than one of possibility. If most of the development finance is allocated to agriculture and still fails to produce a high rate of growth in that sector, overall growth will be even *less* than would have been achieved otherwise. The answer is still that development finance should be allocated where the rates of return are highest, whether that be agriculture or industry.

Labour as the basis of development

President Nyerere, in Tanzania, has persuasively argued, however, that development will not come about by the injection of development finance, so much as by the direct efforts of the people themselves towards increasing output.[1] Since the mass of the population is located in the rural areas in Tanzania, as in all African countries, he concludes that rural development *must* be the main basis for development at this stage.

Clearly this argument bears some resemblance to the previous one based on the predominance of agriculture, and is partly a statement of need: increased output and effort by the mass of the people is needed if there is to be economic development. The important difference in the argument is that labour rather than capital is seen to be the critical resource on which development should be based.

Effect on income distribution

Another reason for the emphasis on rural development in Tanzania, and an important general argument for it, is the stress on an even distribution of the fruits of development. Industrialization, as we note presently, increases employment rather slowly, and therefore brings increased income to only a small minority of the population except in the very long term. By contrast the introduction of a new variety of crop—such as hybrid maize—may bring substantial benefits to a major segment of the population. Income distribution considerations, therefore, strongly favour agriculture.

These are some arguments put forward in favour of an agricultural emphasis. Let us consider some arguments put up in favour of industry.

The problem of employment creation

In countries suffering from excess population and land shortage, particularly, it is often argued first that there simply may not be enough land available for agricultural expansion; and, second, that industrialization will be necessary in order to absorb excess and unemployed labour.

It is often argued that overpopulation results in 'disguised unemployment' in the rural area. Because of overcrowding, the land available is insufficient to keep all of the family's labour fully occupied: accordingly work tends to be 'shared out' among members of the family. As a result, it is said, it should be possible to move many people from the land with little or no loss of output. In the sense that the same output could be produced with fewer people, a proportion of the labour force can be said to be unemployed, though such unemployment is 'disguised' by all members of the household being given some share of the work available (and income resulting).

What the extent of such disguised unemployment actually is, in fact, is open to question, and its existence has been much disputed. Nevertheless in countries faced with serious excess population and land shortage, a policy of industrialization appears to be the only possible option besides, of course, population planning. As mentioned previously, however, we need to distinguish between the typical Asian situation of high population density and that in Africa, where population densities are generally rather low, with land shortage localized only in certain areas.

And, secondly, strong evidence exists for a number of less developed economies showing that in practice manufacturing does *not* absorb workers at a very rapid rate. For example Table 22.1 shows that in Kenya manufacturing industry, while output increased in value (excluding the effect of rising prices) by 43 per cent in four years, employment rose by only 35 per cent. If we measure this in terms of elasticity, the output-elasticity of employment can be defined as $E_N = \frac{\Delta N/N}{\Delta O/O}$, that is, the percentage change in employment divided by the percentage change in gross output in any sector of industry. Since in this case a 35 per cent increase in employment is associated with a 43 per cent increase in gross output, $E_N = \frac{35}{43} = 0.8$. This elasticity is frequently less than unity, and often very much smaller even than this 0.8. Low employment-elasticity is apparently a general phenomenon, with employment growing less rapidly than output, as labour productivity increases. Since in the earlier stages of development the manufacturing sector is relatively small, the rate of growth of the

Table 22.1 *Relative expansion of output and employment in Kenya manufacturing industry, 1968–72*

	Unit	1968	1972
Gross domestic product in manufacturing and repairs (at constant 1964 prices)	K m shs	891	1,273
	% (1968=100)	100	143
Wage employment in manufacturing and repairs	Thousands	70.67	95.27
	%(1968=100)	100	135

SOURCE: *Statistical Abstract*

manufacturing sector would need to be astronomic to make a vast difference to total employment opportunities. Thus wage employment in manufacturing and repairs in 1968 was only about 12 per cent of total wage employment and (although the manufacturing employment figure includes women) only around 4 per cent compared to the total male population of working age.

For the *rapid* absorption of excess labour, agricultural development would seem to be necessary, therefore, where land shortage does not rule this out. The introduction of an additional cash crop, for instance, will provide work for thousands of peasant farmers.

There is much current discussion, as we have seen, about the need to encourage the adoption of more labour-intensive techniques within the manufacturing industry, and to reduce reliance on 'borrowed' technology. But it is probably the case that, whatever the degree of flexibility in manufacturing methods, a relatively small percentage change in the volume or share of agricultural output would have a far greater impact on available employment. In other words, in its effect on employment creation, the agriculture–manufacturing industry choice is likely to dwarf completely the methods-of-production choice within manufacturing.

The case based on labour-absorption or high labour-intensity of agriculture can equally be regarded as one based on low capital intensity and economy in the use of the *scarce* factor, capital. If less developed countries are anxious to economize capital, investment in agriculture may be considerably more effective than attempts to encourage less capital-intensive techniques in manufacturing. It should be admitted that in calculating capital–output ratios in agriculture account ought to be taken of social overhead capital (water supplies, roads, power, and so on), for which the demands of some forms of agriculture, like tea growing and sugar estates, may be much greater than some kinds of industry, like garment making. Part of such investment can, on the other hand, be considered as necessary anyway for the general development of the local region and independent of particular agricultural improvement programmes.

The rate of return in agriculture

A factor which has led many to advocate a policy of industrialization is the belief that agriculture is unresponsive to change, due to social and institutional factors, including feudalistic or unhelpful land tenure systems, on the one side, and the tendency of peasant farmers to cling to traditional farming practices, on the other. As a result, it is felt that investment in agriculture may be very difficult, and wasteful.

We saw in Chapter 10 that there is no simple answer to the question of responsiveness to change in the agricultural sector. Supply responses by African cultivators have been shown to be quite sharp and the value of agricultural output in many African countries has from time to time increased at quite rapid rates, particularly when opportunities for cultivating valuable new cash crops have arisen. At the same time there is also considerable evidence of inefficient methods of cultivation and animal husbandry; of low supply of 'effort' in many areas; and of low response to possibilities of technical innovation. Similarly, while many important agricultural improvements have been carried out, other agricultural schemes have failed.

The 'Green Revolution' which has been under way in Asian countries such as the Philippines, India, Sri Lanka, and Pakistan, has demonstrated that very large increases in the productivity of agriculture can be obtained as a result of scientific research towards producing new strains and varieties of different crops: hybrid varieties of rice, wheat, and maize for instance, may produce as much as ten-fold increases in yields per acre. While, unfortunately, such technical advances are usually not directly transferable to the African situation, there is already evidence that similar advance is possible: in Kenya hybrid varieties of maize capable of eight-fold increases in yield per acre have been developed, and have been increasingly adopted on African farms since the mid-1960s.

The general conclusion to be drawn from our review of Eastern African agricultural development in Chapters 9 and 10 would seem to be that the agricultural sector in Eastern Africa is capable of considerable and even accelerated expansion; but that agricultural improvements are not a straightforward matter, and require careful research and planning.

Increasing returns and external economies

We saw in the last chapter that industry has the tendency to 'polarize' or concentrate itself in particular areas. On a global scale this polarization has meant a tendency for world industry to continue to expand in established industrial countries rather than to spread itself more evenly, except where manufacturing has been deliberately fostered. As a result the problem of international specialization, with less developed countries exporting primary products and importing manufactures, has been perpetuated.

This tendency for industry to 'snowball' depends on increasing returns and external economies, and the case for industrialization has also been put in terms of these phenomena. Thus, while industry exhibits 'increasing returns', agriculture is said to offer, if not diminishing returns, at least only the constant returns obtained by bringing more land into cultivation with more or less given methods of production. In contrast industry offers scope for constantly increasing specialization and division of labour, and the application of machinery, as well as providing greater opportunity for innovation and the introduction of new technology. The argument is that the increasing specialization and division of labour, which Adam Smith said was the basis of economic progress, is a phenomenon associated primarily with *industrial* development.

The concept of external economies is closely related to the increasing returns discussed here. New industry is attracted to established industrial centres in part because of external economies in the form of direct linkages or more general advantages which it hopes to obtain. The social rate of return on investment in industrial projects may thus be higher if they themselves generate external economies in this way. The process of increasing specialization of industry involves linkages and external economies, so that increasing returns and external economies are involved in the cumulative expansion of industry in established centres: together, these make a powerful case for establishing an industrial sector, even on an 'infant industry' or 'infant economy' basis, and attempting to expand this sector steadily, within certain limits of efficiency.

This leaves open the question of what the *pace* of industrialization should be, however: particularly if the domestic market is small, forcing the pace of industrialization could simply mean establishing a large number of inefficient and costly industries. Secondly, it remains possible that efficient industrialization will be obtained *faster* by expanding agriculture *first*, because of external economies obtained by industry from agricultural expansion. In this regard, it is useful to refer to two categories of external economies: (a) the opportunities provided by an industry in supplying products which can form the basis of further industry or in providing a market for the products of other industries—what we have called linkages—and (b) more general advantages obtained as a result of the concentration of industry: better public services, commercial facilities, a favourable climate for investment in centres where industry is already established, and so on. Industry may be more effective in producing linkages, the first category. But in the *earlier* stages of industrial development, in which Africa finds itself at present, such direct linkages may be less important than general factors such as the investment climate, size of the market, or availability of finance. Since a substantial rise in agricultural incomes would increase the size of the market, and indirectly the supply of finance, it is not at all certain that industry would generate far greater external economies than agriculture at this stage.

The promotion of modern technology and social change

We have already discussed the question of whether technological change is more likely to occur in industry or agriculture. In addition manufacturing is sometimes recommended because it 'contributes to an intellectual environment which is less tradition-bound' and is more favourable to the creation of an entrepreneurial class, the expansion of new skills, technical innovations, and the like. There may well be something in this argument. On the other hand, in the short run the numbers employed in the manufacturing sector are not likely to be large, and thus the numbers exposed to this source of social change (though the numbers will be increased through rural–urban migration) not very great.

Agricultural development, on the other hand, will affect more people. Historically the introduction of cash crops has increased commercial-mindedness on a wide scale; and there is evidence in many countries that indigenous entrepreneurs have frequently moved from agriculture into trade, or into small-scale industry, rather than start from scratch. This is particularly so, perhaps, because the supply of finance is critical in the early development of enterprises. Wage employment may generate new skills, but does not on the whole provide finance for new entrepreneurs.

A related argument in favour of encouraging at least a few large modern factory enterprises in a largely agricultural country is the impetus these will give to better methods of business management in the rest of the economy—in small-scale manufacturing, in agriculture, commerce, and the public services. For instance, more complex production and marketing arrangements required to control quality or improve sales can have beneficial effects on other businessmen. They may also begin to apply modern business methods of cost accounting, production control, or communication systems within their own organizations, as well as adopting more effective personnel management and public relations.

The terms of trade

The polarization of the manufacturing industry in the industrialized nations has been associated with a pattern of specialization in trade whereby the less developed countries supply primary products and import manufactured goods. In the post-war period criticisms regarding this situation centred on the *terms of trade* between primary products and manufactured goods, the feeling being that while prices of manufactured goods were stable or rising over time, the long-term trend in primary product prices was downward. The conclusion of a number of observers and governments was that less developed countries should attempt to get away from specialization on primary products, and themselves develop their manufacturing sectors.

As we saw in the last chapter, while these terms of trade fluctuate, it is not at all certain what the long-term trend is. It has become clear now that it is the income terms of trade which should be giving the less developed countries cause for concern. While relative prices of developing country exports and imports may be stable over the long period, it is the failure of developing country exports to expand as rapidly in volume as advanced country exports which is the problem, as we saw in Chapter 21. Various reasons were given for this: but the main factor is that over time world demand for manufactured goods increases faster than world demand for primary products.

This is obviously a potent argument, and while countries should continue to extract the maximum possible income from the sale abroad of primary products (the experience of OPEC suggests that this might be done in part by taking collective action to raise prices even if quantities purchased are increasing only slowly), a strong case can obviously be made for proceeding simultaneously with industrialization at the maximum efficient rate, in order to move towards an eventual restructuring of the economy. For countries lacking natural resources or opportunities for further expansion of primary product exports, the case will be even stronger.

Export instability and diversification

Apart from the long-term trend in primary product prices, their short-term instability has also been a matter of concern. Industrialization has sometimes been recommended as a method of diversifying the economy and reducing its vulnerability to export fluctuations. This particular argument is of dubious value. First of all, as we saw in Chapter 4, the developing countries as a group have been shown to be not significantly more exposed to export fluctuations than the developed countries as a group: and for a large number of developing countries export instability is not a major problem.

Secondly, if we take a country such as Uganda, which is highly dependent on exports of coffee and cotton, the income derived from the two crops is so large, and the number of people obtaining their incomes from manufacturing so small, that manufacturing output would have to be *vastly* increased in amount in order to be able to offset coffee and cotton export fluctuations. Diversification within agriculture by the expansion of other crops is not only an alternative to diversification via industrial development, but may be the only way in the fairly short term of making a quantitatively significant impact on the problem.

Finally, research has tended to show that export instability has not had much effect on economic development anyway, so that it is doubtful if developing countries would be wise to accept *much* loss of real income level for the sake of more stable incomes, following diversification into industry.

The size of the market and economic integration

The main constraint on the rate of expansion of manufacturing is the size of the market, caused partly by the low level of incomes and partly by the geographically small population size of many African countries. The solution may lie either in the expansion of agriculture or, as an alternative, the formation of common markets among neighbouring African countries. But, as we shall see, the problems facing economic integration are greater, and it would be unwise to base industrialization plans on the assumption that an unrealistic degree of economic integration will be achieved.

Balanced versus unbalanced growth

Apart from the debate as between an agricultural and industrial focus, a second major discussion among development economists over the *strategy* for economic growth has been between 'balanced' and 'unbalanced' growth.

Balanced growth and the critical minimum effort

The balanced growth argument combines two elements, one relating to the *composition* of the industrial development programme, and one relating to the *scale* of the industrialization effort. The argument is for simultaneously developing several industries which will complement each other, so that where one industry alone would not be viable, because of the small market, a larger number of industries can help to support each other. For example, there may be insufficient demand, initially, to support one large textile factory, but if many new industries can be set up, income may be raised, and demand increased sufficiently to support the products of the textile and other factories. Different industries might also supply each other with raw materials, or generate other kinds of external economies. The case, therefore, is for simultaneously setting up a large number of mutually supporting industries.

Since this recommends the simultaneous pursuit of development along a wide front, it requires a certain scale of development effort. Thus it has been argued also that there was a *critical minimum effort*, implying that a small effort may fail where a large one would succeed. This view is strengthened if one believes in the existence of 'vicious circles' constraining development, and the difficulty of escaping from these. Thus a modest accumulation of capital may not raise incomes, and hence savings, very much; but if substantial capital accumulation can be achieved early on, incomes will be raised and savings generated to make the process of capital accumulation self-sustaining, thus circumventing the savings vicious circle. Moreover a small increase in aggregate income is likely to be swallowed up by increase in population: a rapid increase in incomes may get over this (the population vicious circle).

This argument has also been referred to as the 'big push', since it advocates intervention on a large scale. Because of this, the policy generally implies a greater degree of state control, and usually a bias towards large-scale industrial projects.

Criticisms of balanced growth

The proponents of balanced growth have been subjected to a great deal of criticism. In respect of the first proposition, whereby mutually supporting industries provide the market demand for each other's products, it is pointed out that the effect on demand would be significant only if a vast number of projects were established simultaneously, particularly since much of the additional incomes created might be diverted to buying imported consumer goods. As far as the 'big push' is concerned, the danger in placing such high 'stakes' is, of course, that failure implies a very heavy loss. It should be remembered that projects in developing countries normally face a specially high degree of uncertainty, since even if similar projects have been successful elsewhere, there are always

local physical and social factors to make the project unique. More important perhaps is that the shortage of skills, trained manpower, and entrepreneurial ability is likely to limit severely the rate of efficient industrialization. It has been pointed out that if a country were in a position to undertake such a programme it would hardly be underdeveloped in the first place. The amount of investment involved does, moreover, imply a very high rate of saving, and sacrifice in terms of current consumption such as the people may not be prepared to tolerate; or alternatively an unrealistic level of reliance on foreign aid. Finally, we may note that a 'big push' in industrialization would be inconsistent with a policy of balanced growth as between industry and agriculture: since the capital available could not cover both a large-scale industrialization programme *and* substantial investment in agriculture. Accordingly the industrial programme would be handicapped by the effects of an underdeveloped agricultural sector, including low rural incomes.

The case for 'unbalanced growth'

As a result almost the opposite policy, of 'unbalanced' growth, was proposed by Professor Hirschman who has made a number of important contributions particularly to the development economics of Latin American countries.[2] He started out from the assumption that capital, managerial ability, and entrepreneurship would all be in short supply in a typical developing country and should be economized. Since sufficient capital would not be available for a 'big push', that which was available should be invested in 'key' industries which would have the maximum effect on the economy through 'linkages' with other potential industries. Where a new industry provides raw materials or intermediate outputs which can be used as inputs in other industries, this is known as a *forward linkage*. Thus a steel-processing plant will have linkages potentially with a range of metal-product or light-engineering industries; a fertilizer plant will have a forward linkage with agriculture. Where the establishment of an industry creates a *demand* for various inputs which can be supplied by other new or existing industries, we have what is called a *backward linkage*. In Hirschman's analysis an industry with a maximum number of backward and forward linkages might be described as a *leading industry* (as in Rostow's 'stages of growth' theory) or *growing point*. Thus instead of investment being made on a broad front as in the balanced growth theory, it would be focused on such 'growing points'.

Hirschman argued that if shortage of entrepreneurship and managerial ability were a feature of less developed economies, this would be true whether the country followed the path of 'free enterprise' or that of planning. Not only did this rule out a 'big push', but it pointed to the need to economize on this factor of production by relying less on state enterprise than on the price mechanism; and secondly to the use of the price mechanism to stimulate increased supplies of 'entrepreneurship'. Thus the establishment of a growing-point industry with backward linkages would create 'shortages' of particular inputs; and these shortages would stimulate entrepreneurs to take advantage of the investment opportunities so created. Equally, with forward linkages, investment openings would be made in industries which could make use of the intermediate outputs resulting. Hirschman went so far as to say that *deliberate* shortages should be created which might elicit a response from potential entrepreneurs.

Criticisms of 'unbalanced growth'

A number of criticisms can also be made of this theory. As far as creating deliberate shortages is concerned, Hirschman does not state clearly what sort of shortages will provide a beneficial stimulus and clearly some shortages which are prevalent in the less developed economies, such as food shortages leading to famines, have *not* been beneficial. While he is right to criticize the 'planners' for assuming there is an infinite amount of planning or managerial talent available to carry out state enterprises, he also assumes that entrepreneurs will be forthcoming in response to the opportunities created. To the extent that he advocates reliance on the price mechanism it may be asked why unbalanced growth left to itself has not already brought development in the countries concerned. Some government initiative to identify and promote key industries would seem to be necessary. Finally we may note that he has little to say about the 'vicious circles', and the problem of small markets for instance, with which the balanced growth theorists were especially concerned.

A compromise between balanced and unbalanced growth?

It is interesting to note that both balanced and unbalanced growth theorists make use of the concept of linkages, or interdependence between industries. The balanced growth or 'big push' theory correctly raises the issue of the scale of the industrialization effort, but in most situations it is probably true to say that the industrialization package will need to be a more modest one. A compromise policy proposal would be to concentrate on a smaller nucleus of interdependent industries acting as a growth point for further industrial development. The balanced

growth thesis would then not be so different from the unbalanced growth policy where such growth points are promoted or 'planned' through government initiatives of one sort or another.

Import substitution versus export promotion

Since World War II a great many of the developing countries, notably in Latin America, have expanded their manufacturing sectors by a process of *import substitution*. Import substitution is the establishment of industries producing for the domestic market manufactured goods which have previously been imported. This method of achieving industrial development has been much criticized in recent years, when many economists have argued that the encouragement of manufacturing for export, or *export promotion*, should be the aim. Let us review some of the general criticisms of import substitution which have been made.

Criticisms of import substitution

Import substitution brings inefficiency

There are a number of reasons for this. First of all import substitution has often occurred without proper planning. In Latin America, for instance, domestic industries were developed first during the war, when imported goods were not readily available, and later, during foreign exchange crises, as a method of saving foreign exchange by cutting down imports.

This itself runs counter to choosing those industries for which the country is particularly suited. However, to the extent that import substitution means producing most of the range of requirements of the domestic market, it runs counter to the theory of comparative advantage, which recommends specialization. Moreover, since the domestic market may be small, another advantage of specialization may be lost, namely, that of economies of scale. This may be reflected in a great many factories suffering from excess capacity, due to inadequate turnover, resulting in high average costs.

Thirdly, import substitution is said to bias industry in the direction of producing consumer goods and non-essential commodities generally, as opposed to capital goods industries or export industries. It is of course consumer goods industries for which a domestic market can be seen to exist and which can be brought into existence with relative ease by offering protection and other subsidies. In contrast capital goods and export good industries are not usually offered so many incentives: yet there may be no particular case for specialization in consumer goods production.

Fourthly, giving tariff and other protection to import-substituting industries may create sheltered monopolies in the local market, giving these industries no spur to remain efficient.

Finally, the *way* in which protection is given may give rise to some inefficiency. If quotas are fixed, for instance, for the maximum quantity of the product which may be imported, then domestic producers will know that the rest of the local market is reserved for them, no matter what the quality of their product or whether their price is competitive. By contrast, with a tariff the domestic price will be the import price plus import tax only, and foreign competition will not be excluded by decree. If an extensive system of tariff protection is used, this often becomes very inflexible, with tariffs on particular products difficult to change even when no longer appropriate, and irrational, with different products receiving either too much or too little protection.

Import substitution may slow down economic growth

Import substitution could affect growth first of all through the types of inefficiency just discussed. This would, by reducing real incomes, reduce the rate of saving and tax revenue.[3] Or the specific bias against export industries could affect its expansion of exports and thus, in the long run, economic growth generally.

It has also been argued that the rate of saving may be affected more directly. To accelerate growth it may well become desirable for the government to take steps to raise the level of investment and saving by discouraging consumption, for instance by imposing heavier taxes- on consumer goods, particularly luxuries. Having encouraged or directly established a wide range of consumer goods industries, however, often with excess capacity already, the government would be in a poor position to take steps to reduce demand for these products. The result would be what has been called *consumption liberalization*, a reluctance to control the rate of spending on consumption.

Import substitution fails to achieve many of its stated aims

Several of the stated objectives of import substitution turn out not to be achieved by the process. For instance, if the aim is to save foreign exchange, experience has in fact been that, because setting up domestic industries requires the import of machinery, and intermediate products, industrialization through import substitution usually means a fairly sharp rise in foreign exchange requirements. If the productivity of the new industries is low, particularly, the foreign exchange saved by producing the consumer goods at home may be less than that required to import the

necessary machines, spare parts, and current inputs, including perhaps skilled labour as well as materials.

If the objective is to reduce the 'vulnerability' of the economy caused by dependence on imports, the result is usually the opposite. The risk involved here is that fluctuations in foreign exchange earnings from exports may result periodically in the country's not having the foreign exchange required to buy 'essential' imports such as food, machinery, or spare parts. But if import substitution has concentrated on less essential consumer goods, leaving capital and intermediate goods to be imported, it will be very difficult to cut back imports during any period of foreign exchange shortage without causing dislocation in domestic industry or severe hardship to consumers: there will be no 'fat' left in the form of luxury consumer goods imports to absorb the effects of the foreign exchange shortage.

If the objective is to create employment, this also does not seem to be achieved. As mentioned earlier, formal sector industry creates employment only very slowly compared to the alternative of agricultural expansion. It is also argued that import substitution, by concentrating on consumer goods industries, usually involves the establishment of subsidiaries of foreign firms, and that these tend to use similar production techniques to those which they are used to using in Europe or North America. Thus borrowed technology is likely to be capital-intensive, aggravating the problem of the slow growth of employment.

Finally, we might note that import-substituting industries may do less to achieve the primary objective, of increasing national output, than might appear. This is because the *value added* by such industries may be quite low. Many industries are in fact only *final-stage* or assembly industries, which simply complete the final stage of production after all the important stages have been carried out abroad. Examples are enamel hollow-ware, radio, bicycle, and motor vehicle assembly. Thus a country may claim to manufacture say, lorries, when all parts are imported and merely put together locally, possibly at great cost. For example, it was estimated for the motor vehicle assembly industry in the United Arab Republic that the cost of local assembly was at one time roughly *four times* that of having the assembly carried out in Italy, due to the small size of the local market.[4]

Import substitution can be of only limited duration

Lastly, the criticism is made that import substitution will come to a 'dead end' once all the obvious consumer goods industries which the local market can support have been set up. This is due not only to the finite size of the market (unlike the open-ended markets for which export industries would cater), but because, being final goods industries, they will not have the same forward linkage effects as capital and intermediate goods industries, or promote technological progress, as capital goods industries might. Moreover inefficient consumer goods producers might oppose giving similar protection to domestic capital and intermediate producers, on grounds that this would raise their costs further: thus the structural bias away from such industries might be extended.

The advantages of manufactured export industries are the opposite of many of the disadvantages listed for import substitution. The extent of such industrialization possibly is not so obviously fixed by the size of the market. Since the industries must compete on the international market they are not likely to suffer from inefficiency due to their sheltered position. If an export subsidy is offered, corresponding to the subsidy of tariff protection for import-substitution industries, this would be in cash, and it would be clear just how much assistance an industry had been receiving, and for how long. The likelihood of almost indefinite protection or assistance would be much less, and firms would have the maximum incentive to learn to 'stand on their own feet' in the shortest possible time. The establishment of export industries fosters international trade rather than reducing it, like import substitution, so it leaves open the maximum scope for international specialization, also promoting efficiency. Specialization for export may be in any branch of industry, not merely in manufactured consumer goods.

Some advantages of import substitution

All this having been said, it remains true that import substitution has some important advantages: indeed, if this were not the case it would scarcely have been pursued by so many countries. First of all, the existence of imports of a particular manufactured good gives a clear indication that a market exists, and the volume of imports indicates precisely the size of this market. Moreover the market will be more or less 'captive' in that the government does have power to reserve this market for domestic producers. In contrast export markets are difficult to break into. Here newly established exporters will have to compete with experienced firms from the industrialized countries. And as we have seen, they are likely to face relatively high barriers erected against manufactured exports from the less developed countries. Indeed it could be argued from the analysis of the previous chapter that import substitution is a less desirable alternative, but one which has been to some extent forced upon less developed countries by the international trade policies of both the old industrial

nations and late-comers within the developing regions themselves.

Secondly, it is quite likely that in many cases an industry catering for the home market will be able to develop export markets later on after it has been able to grow out of the infant industry stage. The Brazilian textile industry, initially an import-substituting industry, began later to export on a substantial scale to neighbouring countries. In East Africa, many or most of the manufacturing industries which are now successfully exporting to countries *outside* the common market, were established on the basis of the Kenyan and East African Community market. In his book *Industrial Development in East Africa* Pearson referred to such industries as 'Janus' industries, after the two-headed Greek god facing in two directions.[5]

Thirdly, *any* industrial development may generate external economies of a general sort through, for instance, the training of an industrial labour force, or the promotion of a favourable 'investment climate'. Thus the substantial industrial sector already established in Kenya is likely to make it an obvious location for further industry looking for an appropriate location from which to supply countries in the Eastern African region as a whole: something which we will consider again when we discuss the economics of the Eastern African Community.

The optimal policy might be a compromise one of *selective* import substitution, combined with the maximum degree of export promotion. This would focus on industries in which the country can be reasonably hopeful of developing a comparative advantage and thus having some export prospects, which would not be confined to consumer goods industries, but which would have some promising 'linkages', and which would not need excessive protection.

Small-scale versus large-scale industries

Another vital decision, regarding the type of industry to be encouraged, is whether to promote large-scale or small-scale industry. This question has been much debated and is one in which the Eastern African governments have in recent years shown increasing interest.

The definition of small-scale industry

There has been a great deal of discussion over how to define small-scale and large-scale industry, and how to measure scale: according to numbers employed, capital employed, value of output (value added), or form of energy used. The most convenient measure is probably the average number of *employees* per establishment, since this gives a good visual impression of the kind of establishment about which we are talking. Thus if a manufacturing industry is characterized by firms employing less than 10 employees, it is likely to be either a handicraft industry producing, for instance, furniture or leather work; or a workshop of some kind employing some skilled labour, such as a tailoring establishment. If a firm employs anywhere between, say, 10 and 100 employees, it is likely to be a small factory using factory or 'production-line' methods on more or less modern lines. Establishments with more than 100 employees can be considered large-scale factories.

There is likely to be a further difference between the three categories on the basis of business organization. Handicraft industries may be carried out in a family's home, perhaps largely with family labour. Small factories will hire more labour but are quite likely to be *owned* as family businesses or as partnerships and private companies. Large-scale factories may well be owned by joint stock companies issuing shares. As it happens, these categories are the most useful for discussing the relative advantages of small and large-scale industries, that is:

(1) craft or household industry employing, say, under 10 employees or family workers in a typical firm or establishment;

(2) 'modern' small-scale industry employing, say, from 10 to 99 employees in a typical firm or establishment;

(3) large-scale industry employing 100 or more employees in firms in *less developed economies* (although clearly in developed industrial economies 'large-scale' usually refers to firms typically employing *thousands* of workers).

Observers have pointed to a variety of advantages which small-scale industries have over large-scale, particularly from the point of view of less developed countries. However the most important question is

obviously which form of industry is the most *efficient*, that is, the most effective in producing output.

The importance of market size

The obvious advantage of small-scale industries here is that many less developed economies offer quite small markets, measured in terms of purchasing power. Large-scale industries will find it difficult to operate economically on the basis of 'narrow' domestic markets and may not have easy access to overseas markets; indeed many of the medium or small-scale establishments already set up in Eastern Africa show excess capacity. This is the most obvious factor militating against the establishment of large-scale iron and steel industries, or motor-car industries, for example, in the majority of less developed economies: although it is also a strong argument for attempting economic integration, establishing common markets to broaden the base of the domestic market.

The survival of small-scale industry

One indication of the efficiency of small-scale industry is the extent to which it has survived in various countries despite competition from large-scale establishments. Table 22.2 gives the percentage share of small-scale industry (establishments employing fewer than 100 persons) in a number of countries, most of which are advanced industrialized economies. What we find is that *even in advanced industrial countries like the USA and West Germany small industry accounts for a quarter or more of output and employment.* If relatively small-scale establishments continue to play a significant role in advanced countries, then we can conclude that they can also play a valuable role in contributing to industrial development in less developed economies. This is reinforced by the evidence presented in Chapter 16 on the size of the firm, suggesting that establishments of very different sizes

Table 22.2   The share in manufacturing of small-scale establishments (employing fewer than 100 persons)

Country	Year	Per cent of all manufacturing establishments	Per cent of all manufacturing employees	Per cent of all manufacturing output
Japan	1952	99	59	37
Australia	1954	97	50	n.a.
United Kingdom	1954	95	33	n.a.
Puerto Rico	1954	91	41	n.a.
USA	1954	91	26	23
West Germany	1953	89	27	23
India	1954	77	11	n.a.

SOURCE: B. F. Hoselitz, *The Role of Small Industry in the Process of Economic Growth,* Mouton, The Hague, 1968

can apparently coexist and compete successfully even within the same industry without the smaller establishments being driven out of business.

The case of Japan seems to offer even greater promise for small-scale industry: here in 1952 *about 60 per cent of employment is accounted for by such establishments*, more than twice the figure for West Germany and the USA. Since Japan has developed dramatically as an industrial nation, this would indicate the possibility of different approaches to industrial development, and that the Western approach, with heavy reliance on large-scale enterprises, is not the only alternative open.

Some qualification is necessary. Table 22.2 classifies as small industry all establishments of fewer than 100 employees. By comparison with many of the manufacturing establishments at present in Eastern Africa this is still quite large. Secondly, the range of establishments up to 100 employees is quite wide and covers different categories of small industry: we need to discuss possibilities for each category separately.

The prospects for household and craft industry

Table 22.3 gives the share of cottage and small-scale industry in manufacturing for the Latin American countries in 1960, these countries being divided into three categories according to their level of development. What is significant is that the percentage share of *cottage industry* declines quite significantly over the three categories from 75 per cent to 54 per cent and then to 41 per cent. In contrast that for 'small-scale factories' (5–99 employees) does *not* decline. This suggests that cottage industry is a much less promising line of development *in the long run*.

This is supported by the data given for Japan in Table 22.4, which shows the same inverse relationship between the level of development and the share of cottage industry, which here declines over time.

The indications are, therefore, that over time a large part of cottage industry will find it difficult to withstand competition from factory production. On the other hand, a number of economists have argued strongly that we should distinguish 'modern' small industry from household or craft industry, and that the prospects for the former are good. Thus 'modern' small-scale industry may, among other things, be more strongly related to large-scale enterprise than to household industry. The latter, it has been suggested,[6] 'cannot be developed into up-to-date industries, since they require different equipment, to a considerable extent different technical knowledge, and special production organization'. Modern small industry may in contrast be directly dependent on large-scale industry, being partly engaged in servicing and repairing machinery for the latter, or in producing components used by large-scale industry. The system of subcontracting such production to small plants is a notable feature of Japanese industrial production, for example, and accounts for the unusually high share of small industry in Japan.

All this does not preclude government assistance and encouragement for the household industry sector, and indeed the data suggest that this might even be emphasized in the African situation. Table 22.3

Table 22.4 The share of household (cottage) industry in manufacturing employment in Japan, 1930–58

Year	Percentage share in manufacturing employment
1930	56
1940	37
1952	34
1958	30

SOURCE: S. Ishikawa, 'Choice of Techniques and Choice of Industries', *Hitotsubashi Journal of Economics*, 1966

Table 22.3 The share of cottage and small-scale industry in manufacturing in Latin America, 1960

	Cottage industry 1–4 employees	Small-scale factories 5–99 employees	Large-scale factories 100+ employees	All factories	Total manufacturing
Most developed countries (Argentina, Brazil, Mexico)	41	24	35	59	100
Middle group (Chile, Colombia, Peru, Uruguay, Venezuela)	54	23	23	46	100
Less developed countries (Bolivia, Central America, Ecuador, Haiti, Panama, Paraguay)	75	16	9	25	100
Latin America, total:	48	23	30	52	100

does show that even in the most developed economies of Latin America in 1960, economies reaching a stage of development well beyond that of the African countries at present, the share of household industry was still extremely large.[7] This is true also of Japan in 1958. In South-East Asia, in countries also enjoying higher standards of living than African countries, in many cases, household and rural industries continue to play a significant role.

The capital and labour intensity of small industry

Small-scale industry is often said to have the great advantage of employing relatively more labour, that is, of having a higher labour intensity of production. In countries where there is a great deal of open or 'disguised' unemployment this could be an important consideration favouring small industry. Alternatively the case can be put in terms of economizing capital: small industry has the advantage of a lower capital intensity, where this is measured by the capital/labour ratio, K/L. The middle part of Table 22.5 gives this ratio for a sample of Japanese industries in 1957 as a function of scale. We see that in all the industries the ratio of capital to labour, as measured by the value of capital equipment employed with each worker, is greater, often much greater, for the large factories than the small, and indeed that the

ratio increases steadily according to the size of the factory.

The right-hand part of the table, however, gives the ratio of capital to *output* for the same industries. Surprisingly, perhaps, we find the capital–output ratio is *larger* for household industry than for small factories, in all four industries. Does this mean household industries use more capital-intensive methods of production? No: the reason is that in these Japanese industries productivity was much lower in handicraft or household production. Although little capital was used, output was very low also, so that the capital–output ratio was *higher* than in small factory industry, where productivity was higher due to the use of more efficient factory methods involving a greater division of labour and the application of machinery. The important thing to note, therefore, is that while capital intensity, K/L, is independent of scale economies, the capital–output ratio, K/Y, takes into account both the method of production (measured by K/L) *and* the effect of economies of scale. On the evidence of Table 22.4, therefore, we might conclude that household industry was not very efficient and, though using a lot of labour, uses more capital per unit of output than small factory industry; small factory industry does, however, use less capital per unit of output than large factories.

This evidence is not enough in itself, however. Table 22.5 gives information on capital–output ratios

Table 22.5 *Capital intensity and capital–output ratios in some Japanese industries, 1957*

Scale (no. of employees)	Capital intensity, K/L (×1,000 yen)				Capital/output ratio, K/Y			
	Textiles	Furniture	Chemicals	Machinery	Textiles	Furniture	Chemicals	Machinery
Household industry								
1–9	85	62	131	69	0.561	0.327	0.438	0.279
Small factories								
10–29	78	48	126	63	0.364	0.192	0.255	0.200
30–49	89	53	186	76	0.353	0.184	0.298	0.177
50–99	114	92	263	103	0.380	0.295	0.365	0.222
Large factories								
100–199	153	78	344	143	0.472	0.203	0.377	0.264
200–299	209	98	370	185	0.601	0.194	0.354	0.321
300–499	218	87	396	213	0.466	0.213	0.252	0.334
500–999	398	70	539	314	0.754	0.176	0.528	0.466
1,000–1,999	414	—	764	371	1.013	—	0.837	0.398
2,000–4,999	404	—	825	362	1.047	—	0.686	0.410
5,000–9,999	523	—	813	362	1.097	—	0.720	—
10,000 and over	537	—	866	—	0.828	—	1.003	—

SOURCE: K. Miyazawa, 'Capital concentration and dual structure', quoted in B. F. Hoselitz, M. Shinohara and D. Fisher, *The Role of Small Industry in the Process of Economic Growth*, Mouton, The Hague, 1968

Table 22.6 Capital–output ratios for small and large factories in Indian manufacturing, 1956

Industry	Small factories (under 50 employees)	Large factories (50 or more employees)	
(1) Fruit and vegetable preservation	4.00	3.33	Lower K/Y ratio in *large* factory
(2) Leather footwear	3.03	1.92	
(3) Cycle tyres and tubes*	2.17	1.64	
(4) Markets	3.45	1.15	
(5) Superphosphate*	3.57	2.22	
(6) Sewing machines*	1.75	1.03	
(7) PVC insulated cables	3.85	1.82	
(8) Bicycles	2.17	1.75	
(9) Steel furniture	1.85	2.08	Similar K/Y ratio in small and large factory
(10) Containers	2.13	2.08	
(11) Bolts and nuts	2.00	2.08	
(12) Storage batteries	1.85	1.75	
(13) Radio sets	1.92	1.79	
(14) Sanitary ware, etc.	1.89	2.86	Lower K/Y ratio in *small* factory
(15) Refrigerators	1.47	3.13	

SOURCE: Derived from P. N. Dhar and H. F. Lydall, *The Role of Small Enterprises in Indian Economic Development*, Asian P. H., 1961, p. 16

NOTE: *Data refer to 3-shift working; remaining data to single-shift working.

in a number of Indian manufacturing industries, divided into small factories (under 50 employees) and large factories (50 or more employees) for 1956. The capital–output ratio here is clearly lower in the case of eight industries for *large* factories, but for small factories in only two cases, with no clear difference in the ratios for another five industries.

We should expect the result to differ from industry to industry since of course economies of scale will vary in importance. Taking into account both Tables 22.5 and 22.6 (and other evidence not presented here) we can perhaps conclude that (1) household or handicraft industry uses a lot of labour but, due to low productivity, may not economize on capital; (2) modern small (factory) industry uses more labour than large factory industry, but it is not clear whether it uses more or less capital per unit of output: this depends in part on the industry in question and the extent of economies of scale. Small industry is not *clearly* inefficient compared to large-scale industry.

Governments may be prepared to sacrifice some efficiency (measured by K/Y) for the sake of creating employment (a higher ratio of K/L), but only to a limited extent. In India where thousands are employed in traditional cottage industry it would be politically difficult if many people were thrown out of employment as a result of too strong competition from modern factory industry, and cottage industry

has been given some protection. In Africa existing commercialized craft industry is not so substantial and there is not the same danger of creating unemployment by establishing modern industries.[8]

Some other possible advantages of small industry

Small industry has been said to have a variety of advantages which might justify some special encouragement.

(1) In different ways it could contribute to the long-run development and growth of the economy. The large number of small establishments, and the ease of entry into the sector, where less capital is required to set up in business, is said to make the small-scale industrial sector a good training ground for entrepreneurs. For similar reasons it may produce more innovations, and it has been suggested that risky new products are best tried out on a small scale in such enterprises. Moreover it has been argued that there is an organic link between small-scale, medium-scale and large-scale forms of organization (we discussed the growth of the firm in Chapter 16), with small firms growing into large firms, benefiting from the ploughing back of profits, the gradual extension of the managerial organization, and a general 'learning process'. Small firms are also thought to help

mobilize savings, since the possibility of 'going into business' is a good incentive to save, as is the need to expand the business once established. This may also be a good way of raising funds specifically for investment in manufacturing. Small firms, with less emphasis on routine production methods and more on crafts, may also contribute more to the training of skilled labour than large establishments, where labour may learn only specialized operations not of much use in other industries. Appropriate technology, suitable for African conditions, is also more likely to be developed in small enterprises, which are more flexible and more often run by indigenous entrepreneurs: large establishments are more likely to use 'borrowed technology' similar to that used abroad. For all these reasons there may be some 'external economies' attached to small-scale industry, which partly compensate for any disadvantages in immediate efficiency.

(2) Another advantage of small-scale establishments is that they may facilitate the *dispersal* of industry as between different townships and into the countryside. In this way employment opportunities will be more evenly spread throughout the country, and a contribution made towards more even distribution of income between regions. This is particularly important if there is immobility between tribal areas, and the existing industrial centres are dominated by one or two particular tribes. By 'taking industry to the people' it may reduce the social costs of urban immigration, another 'external economy'.

(3) There may also be a direct effect on income distribution at the upper end of the scale (assuming successful entrepreneurs are relatively rich) by spreading economic power among a larger number of entrepreneurs.

(4) There may be an important contribution to economic independence, since the lack of local entrepreneurial ability and experience in Africa with which to launch large-scale enterprises may mean increased dependence on expatriate firms. The encouragement of small-scale enterprise may thus be part of a localization programme, as indeed it is in most African countries.

However, this localization, by encouraging individual entrepreneurs, involves the promotion of a capitalist form of development. It could be argued that achievement of economic independence is more quickly achieved through state control and ownership of enterprise, which is more readily obtainable through state intervention in *large* enterprises. Since small-scale enterprise is by its very nature capitalistic, it may be that there is a contradiction in attempts by a socialist country like Tanzania, for instance, to promote craft and other small industries.

The case for large-scale industry

Even if these varied advantages were considered very important, this would not lead to all large-scale industry being given low priority. In individual industries economies of scale may be very important. These may be highly profitable industries, such as, for instance, copper smelting in Zambia: here the technically efficient techniques of production available virtually dictate the existence of large-scale enterprise.

Secondly, the case may be made, not for large-scale industries as such, but for *capital goods* industries, which may in fact require large enterprises. We consider this presently.

Finally we may refer to Hirschman's argument for the selection of 'growing points' or 'leading industries', with the maximum amount of forward and backward linkages. Obviously such an industry is more likely to be a large-scale one (and may be a capital good industry). Indeed it was suggested earlier that the expansion of modern small industry was to some extent dependent upon large-scale industry (that is to say, on leading industries), supplying it with components or intermediate products, or using various products and by-products of large-scale enterprises. To this extent small- and large-scale manufacturing would not be alternatives, but interdependent, though the identification of 'key' large-scale industries would have priority. Against this, important linkages can be described between industries both of which are organized on a small-enterprise basis—sawmilling and furniture works, for instance—and a network of linkages could perhaps be quite effectively developed, without excessive reliance on 'growth poles'.

Capital goods versus consumer goods

A related, but different, choice is that between consumer goods production and capital goods production. Some of the specific disadvantages of exclusive emphasis on consumer goods industries, such as the tendency to produce luxury goods, have already been covered in reviewing the problems of import substitution. Secondly we have already discussed the case for 'growing points' or 'growth points' which may well be based on the production of capital goods, such as machinery, or intermediate goods, such as cement, or chemicals. The case for capital goods here would be based on additional *linkages* as compared to consumer goods, and thus contribution to long-run growth.

A special case for some emphasis on *capital goods* industries has been made by, among others, two Kenya-based economists.[9] This says that technological progress in a country's manufacturing sector, the introduction of new methods and new products, depends upon its having some kind of machine-making, i.e. capital goods, industry. Secondly, and also related to technology, it is argued that the development of appropriate technology—technology suited to the factor availability in the country concerned—will also depend on the existence of machine-making industry. The main obstacle to the establishment of capital goods industries is, of course, the limited size of the domestic market: against this, however, it is said that not all capital goods industries need be large-scale: light engineering and farm-tool establishments, for example.

Choice of techniques

Finally, there is the choice of technique within a particular industry. The case for encouraging labour-intensive techniques, and its limits, has already been discussed in Chapter 14. Many economists now question very seriously the technical possibilities available for producing particular goods by alternative techniques. They argue that the technical choice is very limited, given the *choice of product* demanded by consumers with the present structure of disposable income. What has happened, too often, they contend, is mere import replacement with almost identical local products instead of attempting to satisfy domestic demand with local goods appropriate for populations with low *average* incomes. A small minority of high-income consumers dominate the domestic market for 'Western' type consumer goods which can only be produced using 'Western' technology and 'Western' inputs of capital, 'know-how', and components. What is required, therefore, is a restructuring of consumer demand patterns in favour of local products appropriate to low incomes and local factor endowments. Many of these economists argue that this income redistribution involves a large measure of government control and public ownership of industry, as we discussed in Chapter 18. Others argue for greater reliance on the price system, if it can be freed from the many distortions arising from import protection and official measures which make market wage rates 'too high' and market interest rates 'too low', thus encouraging both products and techniques of production which fail to reflect the 'real' benefits and costs that are the criteria to be considered in deciding socially profitable investments in any industry—the subject of Chapter 15.

Questions on Chapter 22

1. 'Agriculture is the dominant sector of the economy, so it should receive the main emphasis in development.' Discuss.
2. 'From the point of view of labour absorption, the agriculture/industry choice is much more important than the choice of technique.' Discuss.
3. Discuss the external economies you think may arise out of agricultural expansion.
4. Which of the various arguments for emphasizing industrial development do you consider the strongest?
5. Explain the dependence of the 'critical minimum effort' thesis on various types of vicious circle.
6. Discuss the case for and against a 'big push' in industrialization.
7. Discuss the case for a deliberate policy of 'unbalanced growth'.
8. Discuss the possible effects of import substitution on the overall rate of economic growth.
9. Discuss the advantages of a policy of export promotion over one of import-substituting industrialization.
10. Why is it necessary to distinguish between household industry and 'modern' small-scale industry in evaluating the prospects for small industry?
11. How do you account for a significant proportion of small manufacturing establishments in the developed industrial economies?
12. Why is it necessary to take account of the capital output ratio as well as capital intensity in judging the labour-absorptive capacity of small- and large-scale industry?
13. Discuss the case for a country's establishing a domestic capital goods industry.
14. Explain the following: output-elasticity of employment, balanced growth, critical minimum effort, forward and backward linkages, growing points, increasing returns, consumption liberalization, Janus industries, disguised unemployment, capital intensity.
15. How would you explain the apparent paradox that the USA has a relatively larger number of small manufacturing establishments than India, according to Table 22.2?

Notes

[1] Nyerere states 'The development of a country is brought about by people not by money.' 'The Arusha Declaration', in *Ujamaa. Essays on Socialism*, OUP, 1968, p. 28.

[2] A. O. Hirschman, *The Strategy of Economic Development*, Yale University Press, 1957.

[3] Since a large proportion of tax revenue is derived from customs duties levied on imported *consumer* goods, import substitution, which usually starts with mass-consumption goods like textiles, sugar, and alcoholic beverages, tends to reduce the size of the tax base considerably, since the 'prohibitive' tariffs required to protect many of these local substitutes are designed to yield little revenue. This is examined further in Chapter 35.

[4] D. C. Mead, *Growth and Structural Change in the Egyptian Economy*, Richard Irwin, 1967.

[5] D. S. Pearson, *Industrial Development in East Africa*, Oxford University Press, Nairobi, 1969.

[6] G. Cukor, *Strategies of Industrialization in the Developing Countries*, C. Hurst, London, 1974, Akademiar Kiado, Budapest, 1971.

[7] Moreover the definition of cottage industry in Table 22.3 is very narrow: household and craft industry could easily be defined more broadly to comprise establishments with under 10 employees or rather 'persons engaged' since some of the workers will be self-employed proprietors or partners.

[8] Although traditional rural craft industries like beer brewing, grain and oilseed milling and the making of construction materials like clay bricks, whether on a subsistence or commercial basis, are very important and have in fact faced competition from large-scale factories making similar products.

[9] H. Pack and M. P. Todaro, 'Technological Transfer, Labour Absorption, and Economic Development', *Oxford Economic Papers*, November 1969.

23 Industry in Eastern Africa

Having discussed in general terms the main issues and choices in regard to industrial development and the encouragement of manufacturing, we can now turn to examine the nature, extent, and composition of the manufacturing industry in some of the Eastern African countries, and the factors which have determined this. Has industrial development in Eastern Africa been import-substituting or export-oriented? Small-scale or large-scale? Labour-intensive or capital-intensive? Has there been concentration on consumer goods industries or are there some capital goods industries? Have special attempts been made to encourage industries with linkages and external economies?

What sort of industry we have in Eastern Africa at the moment depends *in part* on comparative costs. We can therefore consider the various factors affecting the location of industry in different countries or geographical regions. Why do some industries find it profitable to operate from a location *within* Eastern Africa and others to supply the Eastern African market from locations *outside* Eastern Africa, through exports? This is partly related to the *economic size* of the firm: given the best 'size' of firm for a particular industry, is the Eastern African market sufficiently large to support one firm or more firms of that size? Or alternatively what is the *minimum* economically viable size of firm, and how does the Eastern African market compare? The structure of industry obviously depends also on the stage of development of the country and stage of industrialization. And it depends finally on the industrial policies and incentives to industry which have been and are being used.

The composition and nature of the manufacturing industry in Eastern Africa

The West Indian economist, Arthur Lewis, suggested that a country in the earlier stages of industrial development looking for the industries which it could most easily set up would sensibly examine possibilities within three areas: the processing of primary materials for export; industries producing manufactured goods for the home market; and, for over-populated countries, industries producing manufactured goods for export.[1]

Processing primary materials for export

The first category is the most obvious one for a predominantly agricultural country in the very early stages of industrialization. Usually the main cash crops like sisal, cotton, coffee, tea, or rubber *require* at least some kind of simple processing. Such processing takes place at or near the sources of supply in order to conserve perishable commodities which cannot easily or cheaply be transported in a raw state. In the case of sisal and tea, industrial processing takes place on or near the plantations, and is included in the output of the agricultural sectors in Kenya and Tanzania, where those crops were, until recently, produced mainly by large plantation enterprises with their own manufacturing plants. In the case of cotton ginning, coffee hulling, or tobacco handling, processing is centralized in more specialist factories usually within the growing areas, for cotton, or the main trading and transport assembly points, for coffee and tobacco (Nairobi and Mombasa in the case of Kenya, Blantyre for Malawi's tobacco). In the case of all these crops, *some* curing or refining must take place in the country of origin: seed cotton, green tea leaf, and coffee cherries are not in a physical condition for shipment overseas without processing.

A second advantage from domestic processing is that the industry can be a substantial employer of labour, and one which will derive a comparative advantage from cheap local labour. Hand shelling or sorting of groundnuts and tobacco leaf is much cheaper in Malawi than in overseas consuming countries, and for this reason Malawi has developed a tobacco manufacturing industry which is the largest single employer of wage labour among the country's manufacturing activities.

Apart from perishability and handling problems, and this cheap labour advantage, however, the main reason why processing industries are likely to be located within the country is the great saving in transport costs which can generally be obtained. As Arthur Lewis stated with respect to the Ghanaian economy:

> Since it takes four tons of bauxite to make one ton of aluminium, transport charges are saved if bauxite is turned into aluminium on the spot instead of being transported to the country where the aluminium will be used. Similarly, it is cheaper to transport sawn timber than the equivalent logs, steel than the equivalent iron ore, sugar than the equivalent sugar cane, and so on. It is not, on the other hand, cheaper to export cloth than the equivalent cotton, because very little fibre is lost in the process of manufacture. Neither is it cheaper to transport soap to the consuming market, rather than the equivalent oils, or rubber tyres than the equivalent latex.[2]

This loss of weight factor is obviously the reason for locating the copper-smelting industry in Zambia and, of course, ore crushing to produce diamonds at Mwadui, in Tanzania.

Finally, a particular reason for searching out possibilities for further agricultural processing is that such industries *may* have important backward or forward linkages. Thus there may exist local—or export—markets for the by-products of processing—vegetable oils and cattle cake from cottonseed and oilseed processing, for example, are inputs into the Kenya food and livestock industries (forward linkage), while canning factories for fruit and vegetables of all types in Kenya have helped to make viable a horticultural industry by providing a marketing outlet for what would otherwise be surplus produce (backward linkage). There may also be horizontal linkages from, for example, tea or tobacco processing, arising from the need to purchase inputs from other manufacturing industries producing wooden boxes or supplying electric power. In Malawi these two processing industries, together with, more recently, sugar refining, have provided additional opportunities for sawmilling and paper packaging industries, for plant and vehicle repairs, and for electricity generation.[3]

Tables 23.1 and 23.2 show up the relative importance of the export processing industries in Uganda and Malawi and illustrate some common characteristics which they share with the same industries in other African countries. We comment later on other branches of manufacturing covered by the tables.

In Uganda 251 out of a total of 738 establishments reporting in 1968 were export product processing, more than one-third, reflecting the low level of industrial development and the predominance of agriculture, but important nevertheless. Of total employment in manufacturing 25 per cent was in agricultural export processing and, with copper smelting, more than 20 per cent of value added was in primary processing, agricultural, and mineral.

To check on the labour intensity of the process, we can compare the percentage employed in the industry with the percentage of value added. Thus copper smelting is not at all labour-intensive: it contributes only 1 per cent of the employment, but as much as 10 per cent of value added. This reflects first the trans-

Table 23.1 *The composition of the manufacturing industry in Uganda, 1968*

	No. of known establishments (No.)	Labour employed (%)	Value added (%)	Ratio of value added to gross output
Processing of agricultural exports	251	25	12	0.08
Cotton ginning	57	9	4	0.14
Coffee processing	166	13	6	0.06
Tea processing	28	3	2	0.09
Copper smelting	1	1	10	0.27
Manufacturing and repairs	485	70	63	0.28
Grain mill products	20	2	2	0.12
Sugar and tobacco	47	10	10	0.29
Spirits, beer, soft drinks	9	2	5	0.38
Textiles	9	15	12	0.42
Clothing	29	2	2	0.22
Cement, clay products	19	4	6	0.54
Stone quarrying, salt	8	1	—	0.36
Metal products	51	5	6	0.30
Vehicle repairs	76	5	5	0.31
Other	217	24	15	—
Electricity	1	4	16	0.90
Total	738	100	100	0.24

SOURCE: *Survey of Industrial Products, 1968*

Table 23.2 *The composition of the manufacturing industry in Malawi, 1971*

	No. of establish-ments	Labour employed	Value added	Average size (employees per establishment)	Export sales as % of total sales
	(No.)	(%)	(%)	(No.)	(%)
Processing of agricultural exports	32	38	21	275	84
Grain mill products	5	2	2	106	57
Manufactured tea	18	14	9	186	80
Manufactured tobacco	6	20	9	770	98
Cotton ginning	3	1	1	101	Nil
Consumer goods	114	40	59	82	3
Sugar refining	1	2	} 17	429	7
Beverages, cigarettes	8	4		100	2
Other foods, soap, etc.	19	9	15	110	1
Clothing, footwear	18	7	4	89	9
Printing	12	4	5	80	—
Durable goods	13	4	2	69	1
Vehicle repairs	43	10	16	57	—
Intermediate goods	31	22	20	171	2
Textiles, netting	7	10	12	329	2
Cement	1	4	} 4	878	—
Bricks, concrete	8	2		69	—
Sawmilling, paints, fertilizers, metal products	15	7	5	105	4
Total manufacturing	177	100	100	132	30

SOURCE: *Annual Survey of Economic Activities (Larger Establishments)*

port saving due to weight reduction involved in the process; and secondly the capital intensity of the method. Agricultural export processing is seen to be relatively labour-intensive: for example in coffee processing the production of 12 per cent of the total value added absorbed 25 per cent of the labour (a 1:2 ratio), compared to a ratio of 63 per cent of value added to 70 per cent of labour in manufacturing and repairs.

The table for Malawi shows again the importance of agricultural export processing in terms of employment, here amounting to nearly 40 per cent of labour employed in manufacturing. The export industries listed are all based on processed agricultural commodities, consisting of grain mill products, manufactured tea (of which 80 per cent is exported), and manufactured tobacco (practically all exported). In contrast only about 3 per cent of manufactured intermediate and consumer goods are exported. Cotton ginning is listed among the export industries although in 1971 a surplus of ginned cotton was not available for export, all being absorbed domestically: an example of forward linkage, in this case to David Whitehead's modern textile factory included in 'Clothing, footwear' among the consumer goods industries shown in Table 23.2.

The 1972 Report of the ILO Mission to Kenya makes agricultural product processing an important element in a 'new industrial strategy' which they recommend that Kenya (and presumably other countries in Africa) might adopt. The Mission first suggests the following criteria as a guide to the types of industry that should be favoured:

(1) The industry should if possible use domestic raw materials.

(2) The industry should potentially reflect a comparative advantage internationally, so that it will later, at least, be able to compete effectively in export markets (and thus earn foreign exchange).

(3) The industry should be relatively labour-intensive.

(4) It should be likely to create additional employment through backward linkage effects.

(5) It can be economically located in smaller towns and in the rural areas.

The Mission concludes, and the reader will be able to reach the same conclusion from the information provided above, that agricultural processing industries satisfy these criteria very well.

We should, however, now turn to examine the *limitations* of industry based on agricultural product processing. The first is that, obviously, the scope for such industries is limited by the agricultural products locally available. In Kenya most of the processing industries mentioned by the ILO Mission *already existed*: it is therefore difficult to see how far the list could be extended by adding *new* industries. What we *can* conclude is that a full investigation should be made of all the possibilities which exist for such processing and linked activities: the more difficult question will be, however, what further industries to promote after all opportunities for processing have been exhausted.

Secondly, it must be realized that while gross output in processing may be large, the *net* output or *value added* may be quite small. And it is value added, of course, which measures the contribution of the industry to national income. Thus, Table 23.1 for Uganda shows that processing of agricultural exports actually contributes only *12 per cent* to value added. The contribution to national income of each processing industry also varies greatly, and depends on the nature of the processing. Thus in Uganda, though cotton and coffee are the country's main exports, cotton *ginning* and coffee *processing* together constitute only 10 per cent of value added by manufacturing industry. Copper smelting contributes the same percentage, although copper itself is a very much less significant export.

The last column of the table shows that the ratio of value added to gross output in processing is only 0.08, or 8 per cent. Although the 166 coffee-curing works employed 13 per cent of the labour in manufacturing they together contributed only 6 per cent of value added. Thus gross output (the value of sales and other work done) gives quite a misleading impression of the importance of the industry, since it incorporates the value of the raw agricultural products being processed—the processing industry itself adds only a little more than 8 per cent to the value of this raw material. By comparison the ratio in other kinds of manufacturing is 28 per cent, and for copper smelting 27 per cent.[4] Thus processing of primary materials will be a relatively more important part of manufacturing activities in countries producing commodities which require more complex industrial processing, such as copper in Zambia, or sugar in Mauritius, than in those like Ethiopia, which exports coffee and hides and skins.

It should be noted, finally, that the linkages attaching to processing industries will also vary tremendously. Thus while cotton growing and processing could lead on to textile and clothing industries, tea processing will not have such links. The same is true of copper smelting in Zambia, the absence of linkages being responsible for the economic dualism so clearly a feature there. We might note also that linkages are not necessarily bidirectional. Thus cotton growing must lead on to local cotton ginning, but the establishment of a cotton textile industry will not of itself generate cotton ginning and cotton growing, since cotton lint can be exported, or imported.

Manufacture for export

Arthur Lewis recommended the expansion of *certain kinds* of manufacturing for export, particularly for countries suffering from population pressure and land shortage—countries for which the alternative of agricultural expansion would not be available—but lacking an internal market large enough to sustain manufacturing for the home market. Mauritius would be in this category of Lewis's. Here, even in cases where there has been no advantage from weight-losing raw materials, some countries like Japan, Hong Kong, and Puerto Rico have been able to develop export industries based on *imported* raw materials. For this to be possible, however, two things are needed. First, the raw materials must be light in relation to their value, so that the transport cost of importing them does not add a prohibitive amount to the cost of the final product. If this is the case, the industries involved will not be strongly attached to particular locations. Such industries are sometimes referred to as 'footloose' industries. Secondly, the country must offer some special advantage in order to induce such footloose industries to set up there in preference to the many other suitable locations which they are free to select. In the case of the countries referred to above, this attraction has been the availability of a moderately skilled labour force at relatively low wage rates. This is, of course, an especially great advantage in attracting labour-intensive industry, since the saving in labour costs will be greatest in these. Thus industries making up leather, paper, rubber, or textile fibre have been especially successful. These industries already exist in Kenya, as shown in Table 23.3 below.

Table 4.3 showed that, leaving out of account the export of refined petroleum products by Kenya (mainly to Uganda) and Tanzania (to Zambia), only in Kenya did manufactured goods account for as much as 10 per cent of domestic exports in 1970, and the percentage among the Eastern African countries was often only 2 or 3 per cent. The more detailed Table 23.2 for Malawi confirms this, only 2 and 3 per cent of the production of intermediate and consumer goods being exported. Of particular interest is the growth of manufacturing in Tanzania: Tanzania was a late starter in the field of manufacturing, having very little formal sector industry at the time of independence in 1961, and much less than either Kenya *or* Uganda. Expansion has since then been relatively rapid: the

Table 23.3 *Manufacturing industries in Kenya, 1967.*

Industry reference no.	No. of establishments (No.)	No. of reported employees (×1,000)	No. of persons engaged per establishment (No.)	Gross value added per establishment (K£×1,000)
Processing of agricultural exports				
(1) Cotton ginning	6	0.1	20	22
(2) Pyrethrum extract	1	0.2	204	223
— Coffee processing	n.a.	n.a.	n.a.	n.a.
— Tea processing	n.a.	n.a.	n.a.	n.a.
— Wattle bark extract[1]	5	0.6	116	n.a.
Consumer goods: processed goods				
(3) Meat products	7	2.0	289	120
— Dairy products	24	1.4	—	—
(4) Canned fruit and vegetables	9	1.7	191	28
(5) Grain mill products	40	1.8	46	42
(6) Bakery products	38	1.4	66	29
— Sugar[2]	4	1.7	—	—
— Confectionery	7	0.1	—	—
— Miscellaneous foods	28	1.5	—	—
Consumer goods: other				
— Spirits, beer and malt tobacco	10	3.0	—	—
(7) Soft drinks	16	0.6	38	48
(8) Knitting mills	4	0.8	198	62
(9) Spinning, weaving, finishing of textiles	9	2.8	315	85
(10) Clothing	116	2.6	22	9
(11) Other made-up textiles	5	0.6	116	42
(12) Footwear	29	0.9	32	16
(13) Furniture and fixtures	95	1.7	18	9
(14) Printing and publishing	81	3.4	42	32
(15) Tanning and leather goods	10	0.4	39	17
(16) Fur and leather products	3	0.1	25	9
— Rubber products	14	0.4	—	—
(17) Soap and vegetable oils	19	0.8	44	50
(18) Bicycle repairs	4	0.03	8	4
— Aircraft repairs	2	0.9	—	—
Intermediate goods				
(19) Cordage, rope and twine	8	2.0	254	82
(20) Sawn timber	56	4.5	81	19
— Other wood products	8	0.1	—	—
— Paper and paper products	13	1.0	—	—
(21) Basic industrial chemicals and petroleum	5	0.7	547	132
— Miscellaneous chemicals and products	31	1.2	—	—
(22) Paints	5	0.3	52	55
(23) Clay and glass products	6	0.6	99	110
(24) Cement	2	0.9	473	896
— Other non-metallic mineral products	16	0.5	—	—
— Metal	52	3.1	—	—
— Motor body-building	17	0.9	—	—
(25) Motor repairs	143	4.5	31	22
— Miscellaneous manufactures and repairs	36	1.0	—	—

Table 23.3 *continued*

Industry reference no.	No. of establishments (No.)	No. of reported employees (×1,000)	No. of persons engaged per establishment (No.)	Gross value added per establishment (K£×1,000)
Capital goods				
Non-electrical machinery	50	1.1	—	—
Electrical machinery	22	2.7	—	—
Shipbuilding and repair	10	1.2	—	—
Railway rolling stock	1	6.9	—	—
Total, all manufacturing	*1,062*	*64.2*	—	—
(26) Building and Construction	228	17.1	75	28

SOURCE: *Census of Industrial Production, 1967*

NOTES: [1] Data on wattle bark extract factories for 1972

[2] Numbers employed in sugar industry include plantation labour.

output of manufacturing and handicrafts increased from 394 m shs in 1964, for example, to 687 m shs in 1969, at constant 1966 prices. Thus, excluding the effects of inflation, the value of output increased by about 75 per cent in five years, equivalent to a compound rate of interest of nearly 12 per cent per annum, which is an extremely high rate. Despite this, as just mentioned, exports were relatively small. Industrialization in Tanzania has thus so far been one of the classical import-substituting type, and the figures cited demonstrate the speed at which manufacturing output can expand under import substitution before the 'limit' to import substitution is reached.

It may be asked why the Eastern African countries have made so little headway in this area. Certainly there is no vast excess supply of labour arising out of overpopulation in Eastern Africa, except in Mauritius. But there are substantial 'pools' of unemployed and underemployed in most large towns and, more important, an elastic supply of labour from the rural areas available at a relatively low wage. Thus while there is not the same urgency in developing labour-intensive manufacturing industries geared to the export market, the *possibility* of such industries should exist just as much as in the overpopulated countries.

There is an obviously important factor at work in the landlocked countries—Uganda, Zambia, Malawi, and to an extent in Ethiopia and Sudan—in that export-oriented industry is handicapped to varying extents by transport costs, which at the same time protect certain kinds of import substitution industries for the local market. However, lack of progress in this area might reflect, apart from obstacles to imports from less developed countries raised by developed overseas countries, lack of entrepreneurship and lack of proper incentives offered by the government for such activity.

Kenya has been the most successful in developing external markets for manufactures, mostly within the East African common market. *Some* of these are based on imported materials, particularly refined petroleum products, textiles, and metal products, assisted by Kenya's geographical position and good port facilities at Mombasa. The latter has also permitted Kenya to develop exports of ships' stores, provisions to ships calling at Mombasa; and it should be remembered that tourism is *in effect* an export industry (to the extent that tourists buy goods and services of local rather than foreign origin) in that it earns foreign exchange and is in fact a *major* foreign exchange earner for Kenya. More important than these export goods, however, are exports of goods by industries which rely for the larger part of their sales on the home market: what have been referred to as elsewhere as 'Janus' industries. Compared to some of the other countries where export processing accounts for a large share of manufacturing, Kenya's industrial structure resembles those of developed economies to the extent that only a small part of total output of each commodity is exported, the bulk being absorbed by the domestic market, but where some of the output of a comparatively wide range of manufacturing activities is exported. Kenya's exports of canned foods, dairy produce, beverages and tobacco, petroleum products, cement, textiles, and other items are based in the first place on the home market. Other Eastern African countries sell abroad small quantities on either a regular or an opportunistic basis, out of what is otherwise aimed at domestic consumption and import substitution: for example exports of refined sugar from Malawi to the USA, and exports of sugar and other processed foods from Sudan. In Mauritius where, as indicated earlier, the scope for further import-substituting industries is limited by the size of the market, an attempt is now being made to develop additional export processing industries, arising from agricultural diversification from sugar into tea, tobacco, oilseeds, and fish, and also engineering and other precision industries based on imported material, such as watch jewels.

Manufacturing for the home market

The largest category of the manufacturing industry in Eastern Africa is therefore manufacture for the home market. This can be seen to have come about in the most usual way for developing countries, through import substitution. We may consider first the factors determining why some of the *specific* industries have been established, before going on to discuss the general nature and main categories of manufacture for the home market.

In looking at specific industries we can examine factors operating both on the 'demand side' and on the 'supply side'. For an industry to be established in Eastern Africa it is necessary for the Eastern African market to be sufficient to sustain at least one firm of competitive size. The question is, therefore, what kinds of commodities are in demand at the low levels of income prevailing in Eastern Africa? The most obvious ones are food, giving rise to food processing industries such as grain milling; textiles, clothing, and footwear; and basic housing requirements such as door and window frames, giving rise to woodworking and metal industries. Together these provide food, clothing, and shelter. One might add beer and soft drinks, particularly in a warm climate!

On the supply side, it is a matter of which industries can make the greatest economies in cost by being sited near the market. This is a matter of transport costs; and the principles are much the same as in our discussion of processing industries, except that the market is now in Eastern Africa rather than overseas. There are two kinds of industries which will find it advantageous to locate themselves in Eastern Africa. First, there are those industries which make use of a heavy raw material which is available in Eastern Africa: one might mention cement production, concrete products, bricks and tiles, beer (which uses water), and sawmilling in this category. In these cases transport costs are reduced by using raw materials near the consuming centre. The second variety of industries are distinguished by having products which are more bulky to transport than the raw material. In these cases it would be economic, other things being the same, to develop the industry near the market *even if there were no local supplies of the raw material*. These industries would include the furniture trade, bottle manufacture, shoe production, hollow-ware (pots and pans), and assembly work, such as the putting together of radios, bicycles, and other manufactured goods made up of a large number of components.

If we check down the list of industries for Kenya, the leading Eastern African country in manufacturing, we find our expectations pretty well fulfilled in terms of these kinds of industries. Industries which make use of a heavy perishable local raw material include: meat and dairy products, grain mill products, sugar, beer and tobacco, sawmilling, and cement. Industries which produce goods which are more bulky to transport than their raw material include: footwear, metal products, glass products, electrical appliances, and heavy plant and vehicle repairs, especially railway rolling stock. These are therefore all industries which Lewis would judge to be sound economic activities.

At the same time there are a number of large-scale establishments in Kenya (and elsewhere in Eastern Africa) which do not appear to enjoy clear cost advantages over imported substitutes: textiles, miscellaneous chemicals, including detergents and pharmaceutical goods, paints and rubber tyres, all representing activities which are not based closely on local raw materials, do not economize transport costs, and also usually require much larger markets than those of East Africa to obtain economies of scale. For these reasons such industries have usually needed greater protection from imports by means of import duties and other fiscal incentives to make local manufacture profitable. In these industries there is frequently considerable unused capacity, causing average costs of production to be considerably above the cost of the imported product. Apart from Kenya, many similar industries listed for Tanzania were operating at 50 per cent of capacity in 1970. The position in Ethiopia was very similar. Many of these protected products, like textiles, rubber tyres, and fertilizers, are intermediate goods used as inputs into other industries, in particular the small-scale clothing, road transport, and farming industries respectively, industries whose own output will be affected by the extra costs of import substitution. These facts indicate the difficulties arising out of any attempt to force the pace of industrialization.

The figures in Table 23.3 for Kenya all relate to known employers within Kenya's 'modern' sector, defined to include all establishments. The coverage of the 1967 Census of Industrial Production in Kenya was much wider than the usual Census in covering all establishments with 5 or more employees. It therefore brings out a wider picture of manufacturing activities, including many very small enterprises particularly typical of the clothing, footwear, bakery, furniture, maize milling, printing, hardware, and repair industries. This broader coverage makes comparisons with other countries in Eastern Africa rather misleading, but if we keep this in mind, and the important fact that Kenya's manufacturing sector is the most developed of the Eastern African countries, we can see that the tables given so far for Kenya, Uganda, and Malawi, together with Table 23.4 for Ethiopia and Tanzania (excluding very small handicraft industries in both cases), show a very similar pattern. Table 23.4 shows the *remarkably* similar structure of industry in these two countries, showing that they have followed the same path of import-substituting industrialization. The reported 'formal sector' labour force was, in fact, 49,000 in both cases. The same kinds of industry are revealed, those which satisfy basic consumer demands for food products, beverages (beer and soft drinks), tobacco, textiles, wearing apparel (clothing and footwear), and furniture industries which are likely to be viable on the basis of a comparatively limited consumer market: a market equivalent in terms of purchasing power to that of a single large town in Europe.

If we turn now to the broad categories of industry, we see that in all the countries, even Kenya, there is little or no production of capital goods, though there is *some* small-scale manufacture of machinery and implements in Kenya. In Table 23.2 for Malawi, 59 per cent of value added in manufacturing (and 40 per cent of employment) was in consumer goods productions, compared to 21 per cent in processing. Scarcely any manufactured consumer goods are exported—about 3 per cent—indicating import substitution. No category is given for capital goods production.[5]

While we have described these industries as satisfying 'basic consumer demands', it should be realized that such items as 'European' beer, polished furniture, many kinds of clothing, shoes, and the like, can be seen, in the context of average money income in Eastern Africa, as *luxury consumer goods*, purchased especially (though not exclusively) by the minority of the population based in the urban areas. The ILO

Mission to Kenya in 1972, which was strongly critical of this pattern of import substitution, strongly recommended that, in order to change this industrial structure, an effort should be made in Kenya to alter drastically the income distribution of the country in favour of the poorer section of the community: this would change the pattern of market demand away from luxury consumer goods of the type previously imported towards very simple consumer goods which would be bought by the mass of the population, such as, for example, unsophisticated furniture made by local, including rural, carpenters. The effect would be to encourage the expansion of the 'informal' sector, including rural industry, rather than the formal sector.

One important category of production in Eastern Africa which we have not mentioned is that of intermediate products. These are producers' materials, particularly for the construction industry: cement, clay products (tiles and bricks), stone quarrying, and sawmilling. In Malawi, 20 per cent of the value added in manufacturing is of intermediate production.[6] These do not present a 'radical' industrialization policy as capital goods production might. Building materials in less developed countries may be in demand primarily to construct sumptuous dwellings or 'luxury' hotels, office blocks, and conference centres rather than to build factories or improved housing for the mass of the population.

Scale and factor intensity in Eastern African industry

We discussed in the last chapter some of the advantages of small-scale versus large-scale industries, and also why developing countries may wish to en-

Table 23.4   'Modern' manufacturing in Ethiopia and Tanzania, 1970

Industry	No. of establishments		Average size (no. employed)	
	Ethiopia	Tanzania	Ethiopia	Tanzania
Food products	141	123	58	112
Beverages	38	11	79	80
Tobacco	2	3	216	945
Textiles	50	51	404	322
Clothing, footwear	24	21	90	84
Wood products	73	80	45	43
Printing and paper	29	34	51	39
Chemicals	42	39	67	55
Metals, machines	31	18	59	84
Other	49	39	82	91
Plant and vehicle repairs	—	29	—	52
Total	479	448	102	110

SOURCE: Tanzania, *Economic Survey, 1971–72*, and Ethiopia, *Statistical Abstract*

courage labour-intensive industries. We may now examine briefly the structure of industry in one of the Eastern African countries in order to assess the relative importance of small- and large-scale industries, and the labour or capital intensity of the various industries which make up the sector. Table 23.3 gives two indicators of the average size of establishment in different industries, gross value added per establishment, and the average numbers employed. In Figure 23.1 we measure values of net output (value added) for each industry along the y-axis and values of average numbers employed along the x-axis. Each industry will therefore be located as a point on the graph, and we can tell which industries are small-scale (low value of average value added *and* of ave-

rage numbers employed) and which large-scale; and also which industries are labour-intensive and which are not. Thus if in one industry the average number employed per establishment is low, but value added is high, the industry will be a capital-intensive one (though it could alternatively be based on a rich natural resource). If the average number employed is high, but average value added is low, the industry will be labour-using, or labour-intensive. Particular industries are identified by a number, which corresponds to the industry number in Table 23.3.

The figure shows that a feature of structure of industry in Kenya is the large majority of small-scale and very small-scale industries: there is a concentration of points near the origin in the diagram. The

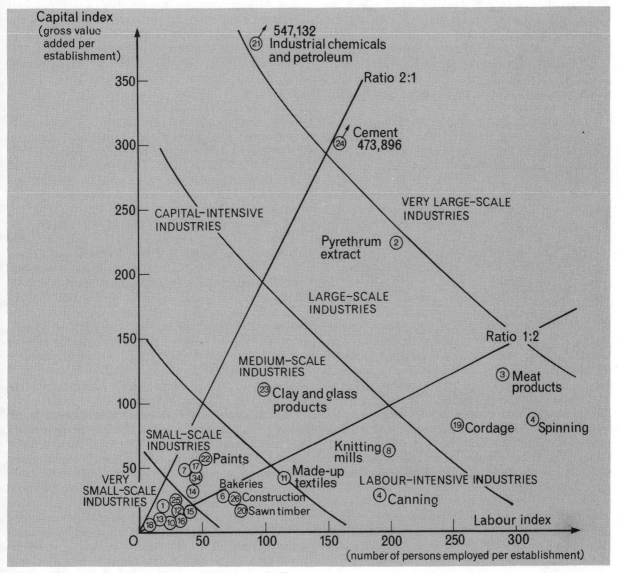

Figure 23.1 An isoquant diagram for industry in Kenya.

number of medium- or large-scale industries, as measured by average numbers employed of 100 or above, is not large: in the diagram are chemicals and petroleum products, cement, pyrethrum extraction, spinning, knitting and made-up textiles, meat products, paint manufacture, and fruit and vegetable canning. Not shown clearly in the statistics are large concerns within dairy production, grain milling (co-existing with small establishments), sugar refining, beer, tobacco and sawmilling, footwear, glass products, and some others. Employment in the formal sector is nevertheless dominated by these larger-scale establishments: 75,189 or 81 per cent of all the 92,609 workers in reported employment in 1972 were employed in 9 per cent of the 4,274 establishments with 50 or more employees. This includes the East African Railways Workshops in Nairobi which alone employs 10,000 workers, and since its establishment more than 50 years ago has been the largest manufacturing establishment in Eastern Africa. We can say, therefore, that while many of the Kenyan industries are small-scale, *employment* in the formal sector is dominated by a finite number of large establishments in a limited range of industries.

In the diagram two lines or 'rays' from the origin are drawn dividing industries into labour-intensive, capital-intensive, and intermediate industries. Along the lower ray the ratio of average value added to average numbers employed is 1:2. Below this the ratio is even more in favour of numbers employed, and we have relatively labour-intensive industries. The upper line plots points where the ratio is 2:1. Above this line would be very capital-intensive industries. These are shown to be very few in Kenya, comprising only industrial chemicals and petroleum products (the Mombasa refinery) and cement (for which the ratio is almost 2:1). Secondly we see that many of the medium- and large-scale industries are in fact labour-intensive ones: meat products, fruit and vegetable canning, paint manufacture, and the spinning, knitting, and made-up textile industries. Thirdly, the large number of small-scale industries are mostly *not* especially labour-intensive, but in the intermediate category: reflecting the point made in the last chapter that because of low productivity and output, small-scale industry may use *more* capital per unit of output than larger-scale industry. On the other hand, some important industries which are organized on the basis of many small establishments, such as sawn timber and building and construction, are shown to be labour-intensive. Since these are industries which are well dispersed throughout all regions of each country (as we shall see presently) they have a double advantage from the policy point of view.

Efforts at small industry development in East Africa

In the last chapter we discussed the need to define 'small industry'. The three categories of industry identified there, in terms of the size of establishments, were:

(1) craft or household industry, with less than 10 employees;

(2) 'modern' small-scale industry, with 10–99 employees; and

(3) medium- and large-scale industry, with 100 employees or more.

Figure 23.1 shows that even in Kenya, where manufacturing is somewhat more developed than in other East African countries, the number of medium- and large-scale industries is not large, and many of the modern manufacturing establishments listed are in the small-scale category of 10–99 employees. It follows that a factory employing, say, 80 persons would in East Africa appear a relatively large concern, even though still in the 'small industry' category. Moreover a small industry programme directed at the 'modern ' small industry sector will be very different from one aimed at promoting craft industry, and the most appropriate methods for promotion will differ. In looking at some of the programmes which have been undertaken in Eastern Africa, therefore, we need to consider action in respect of each of the two categories.

A number of African countries have adopted major promotional programmes in recent years, notably Tanzania and Kenya in Eastern Africa, and Ghana and Nigeria in West Africa. A comparison between the Tanzanian and Kenyan programmes shows some differences and some very clear similarities, the former reflecting in part the different stress laid on the various objectives underlying small industry promotion. The four objectives which may be said to underlie the emphasis placed on small industry appear to be (1) localization and local control of industry, (2) rural development, (3) employment creation, and (4) dispersal of industry.

Localization objectives point towards small industry first because small and medium enterprises are much more 'within reach' of local entrepreneurs than are large-scale enterprises, which require large amounts of capital and, frequently, advanced technology or managerial skills. Thus loans to promote independent African businesses could much more safely be extended to smaller enterprises in these initial stages of localization. For larger enterprises other forms of local control involving cooperation between a state development corporation and larger non-indigenous enterprises were appropriate. Secondly a large proportion of the large numbers of African businesses actually in existence outside farming in East African countries were actually in *craft* industries. Accordingly if assistance were to be given to existing African enterprises, it was likely to be not to small industry in general so much as to the craft industry category. Within Africa, Nigeria, even more than Kenya, has been committed to a programme of 'indigenization' of commerce and industry within the framework of a more private-enterprise based economy than most other African countries. In Kenya this commitment has meant a greater degree of assistance to 'modern' small-scale enterprises using primarily (1) loans offered to 'larger' businesses through the ICDC (Industrial and Commercial Development Corporation), (2) a system of urban industrial estates under KIE (Kenya Industrial Estates Ltd), a subsidiary of ICDC, and (3) progressive restriction of competing non-indigenous enterprise through licensing and forced sale of businesses to local private entrepreneurs. Other African countries which have adopted business promotion programmes for African entrepreneurs are Ghana, Malawi, and Swaziland, though business advice and loan schemes have been directed here mainly at traders and transporters.[7]

The Kenya programme of industrial estates was established in 1966, much earlier than that for developing rural industries, reflecting the greater emphasis on larger enterprises. Five industrial estates were envisaged, originally, to be located at Nairobi, Nakuru, Kisumu, Mombasa, and Eldoret, the five main towns. Only the first two of these were in operation in 1975. The remainder, together with two more at Nyeri and Kakamega, two much smaller townships, were to be completed during the Plan period 1974–8, with estates in other 'growth-potential' towns such as Kisii, Kericho, and Embu coming later. The estates have been criticized, primarily by the ILO Mission, as involving costly subsidization of the favoured enterprises.

In Tanzania, with its socialist programme, there has obviously been less emphasis on loans to private business, except within the framework of the National Development Corporation. In 1965 a National Small Industries Corporation (NSIC) was formed as a subsidiary of the NDC, with an authorized capital of £80,000, of which 80 per cent was held by NDC and 20 per cent by the Workers' Development Corporation (WDC). Subsequently this structure was reorganized and the institution renamed the Rural Industrial Development Organization (RIDO), emphasizing the rural development objective (the first craft industry estate on which its operations were centred had been located

in Dar es Salaam). This objective had been reflected also in the original intention to develop cottage industries through NSIC. Although this may not have been envisaged originally, NSIC came to be concerned almost entirely with craft industry, larger enterprises coming directly under the NDC. Similarly, many of the industries which would form the basis of the 'growth poles' to be developed in nine separate townships under the Second Five-Year Plan (see below) would probably turn out to be factory establishments within the small industry category, but promoted directly by the NDC.

Where the two programmes in Kenya and Tanzania come more closely together is in craft industry promotion. This part of the programmes reflects especially the last two aims of promoting rural development and creating employment. These aims are closely related: employment opportunities created in the rural areas reduce the extent of rural–urban migration and thus the emergence of urban unemployment, as well as reducing rural underemployment directly. Employment considerations have been more important in Kenya, where rural–urban migration and urban unemployment have been much more significant, and where the more recent emphasis on rural development has not had the same ideological basis. Indeed, it was the Kenya government's concern over unemployment which led it to request the ILO to investigate the problem. The ILO Mission, reporting in 1972, laid great emphasis on rural industries, as already mentioned, and on developing the 'informal' craft and very small-scale sector in town *and* country, because of its labour intensity and potential for employment creation.

It is not surprising that major efforts in both countries have been directed towards craft industries. A 1972 report in Kenya by SIDA (the Swedish International Development Agency) estimated the number of informal sector 'industrialists' as numbering 20,000–25,000, and the numbers engaged in the sector as 60,000–70,000. Given the similarity of the economies, it is not surprising that much the same trades are represented in the two craft industry sectors. A survey carried out in Tanzania in 1966–7 by Dr K. Schädler of very small manufacturing establishments in the twenty largest townships of mainland Tanzania produced the numbers of small-scale establishments shown in Table 23.5.

The trades selected to form the basis of the first industrial estate for craft industrialists in Dar es Salaam were woodworking and metal-working. According to the Second Five-Year Plan such estates were to be established in Singida, Tabora, Dar es Salaam, Usangi, Shinyanga or Mwanza, Rungwe, Tanga, Arusha, Songea, and Bukoba, in roughly that order. In practice the programme has not been expanded as rapidly, for various reasons. For a long time the main estate was at Dar es Salaam, with a smaller one at Singida. The Dar es Salaam estate comprised very simple premises capable of housing very small groups of two to three artisans (many of whom had previously been working in the open air) and some common facilities (like machinery available for general use).

Kenya has a similar programme called the Rural Industrial Development Programme (RIDP), which was launched in 1971–2. Four centres were quickly established in the four relatively small townships of Kakamega, Nyeri, Embu, and Machakos. A major programme of expansion of such centres is included in the current plan, as outlined in Table 23.6. The trades assisted have again been especially woodworkers and metal-workers based especially on the provision of common facilities at the centres. The trades assisted are shown in Table 23.7. The first two of these were the most important in practice as common facilities were provided only for these and 'intensive assistance' concentrated on a very much smaller number of clients than the table indicates. Thus both the Kenyan and Tanzania programmes have concentrated in the first place on woodworking and metal-working.

A major difference in approach was, however, adopted in Kenya, reflecting the preference for private enterprise: this was referred to as the 'extension'

Table 23.5 *Number of very small manufacturing establishments in the twenty major townships of mainland Tanzania, 1966–7*

Trade	No. of establishments
Tailors	308
Woodworkers and carpenters	305
Motor mechanics	206
Shoemakers	189
Bakers	106
Barbers	83
Watch repairers	59
Sheet metal workers	46
Letter press printers	39
Soap manufacturers	35
Electricians	35
Other trades	261
Total	1,672

SOURCE: K. Schadler, *Crafts, Small-Scale Industries and Industrial Education in Tanzania*, Ifo-Institut, Munich, 1968, p. 70

Table 23.6 *Proposed RIDP Development Expenditures, Kenya, 1974–8*

Centre	1973–4	1974–5	1975–6	1976–7	1977–8	Total
Capital expenditure:						
(1) Kisii, Malindi, Voi, Meru, Siaya, Kericho	170	100	—	—	—	270
(2) Murang'a	—	200	160	—	—	360
(3) Naivasha, Busia, Bungoma, Kitui	—	—	200	160	—	360
(4) Homa Bay, Kwale, Kapsabet, Garrisa	—	—	—	200	160	360
(5) Kabarnet, Nyahururu, Kerugoya, Kajiado	—	—	—	—	300	300
Subtotal, capital expenditures	170	300	360	360	460	1,650
Operating expenditures	30	60	70	90	100	350
Total expenditure	200	360	430	450	560	2,000

SOURCE: *Development Plan, 1974–78*, Table 12–6, p. 298

Table 23.7 *Clients assisted under Kenya's RIDP 1973, distributed by trades*

Trades	No.	%
Furniture	146	30
Sheet metal-work	53	11
Other metal-working	22	5
Motor and bicycle repair	81	17
Tools and machines	5	1
Sawmilling	41	8
Posho milling	28	6
Other and unknown	109	22
Total	485	100

SOURCE: H. Kristensen, ed., RIDP *Conference Report*, 1974

approach, whereby independent business 'clients' were to be given assistance comprising advice on layout and possible products, skill improvements, and training in book-keeping, in large part *at their own premises*. Only recently has this extension approach been acknowledged to have been expensive, and not very effective, so that in future premises for clients will be provided around the common facility centres, these premises, however, to be privately owned in due course by the clients. The last objective, dispersal of industry, has been an important consideration behind both the Kenyan and Tanzanian programmes. This can be seen from the RIDP centres proposed for Kenya, and in Tanzania's Second Plan. Being concerned only with craft industries, however, such centres can only be a very poor substitute for a location policy relating to medium- and large-scale enterprises, or even small factory industry.

The location of industry within the Eastern African countries

Let us now turn from the discussion of which industries are located in Eastern Africa to this question of *where* industries are located within each country, and to location policy. The size of the national or East African (common) market will not be so important here as in the former case: we can assume that some market for the products considered does exist, and our interest is in determining why the industries are distributed within the market in the way they are.

The problem of location arises simply because the raw materials for the product, the labour supply, the fuel, and the market for the product are not usually located in the same place. If the industry is located near the market, the raw material will need to be transported to the site, and this may be costly. If the industry is located near the supply of raw material, this will not be necessary, but the finished product will then need to be carried to the market. In general, each location will produce for the firm different costs, including transport costs, and different benefits. If a firm is interested in maximizing profits, it will select the location in which net costs are minimized. This location will be the outcome of weighing the conflicting advantages of these different factors.

Location near the raw material

The way in which these factors work to produce a location *within* the country is much the same as in producing a location *between* countries. Once again, where raw material is heavy and bulky *and loses weight in manufacture* the industry will find its most advantageous location near the raw material, for it will be much cheaper to transport the finished product than the raw material.

In general, this can have either of *two* effects on the pattern of location within the country. If the main supply of the raw material is available in a few places, the industry will be similarly concentrated. This is commonly the case with the processing of mineral deposits: here too the raw material undergoes substantial loss of weight, as when mineral ores are crushed and concentrated. Thus diamond ore is crushed in the vicinity of the mines at Mwadui, in Tanzania; the only sodium carbonate plant in Eastern Africa is situated on Lake Magadi in Kenya, adjoining the soda deposits; cement works are located at Tororo in Uganda and at Athi River, near Nairobi, and at other places where the raw material is in good supply; copper smelting is of course, carried on in the copperbelt at various points.[8] A special case of location of industry at the source of the raw material is location at a port where the raw material is imported: thus an important part of the metal products industry in Kenya is located at Mombasa where raw material is imported and from where part of the finished output is also exported (to Tanzania), giving a further transport advantage to Mombasa. Similar considerations placed the petroleum refinery at Changalumi, near Mombasa.

If the raw material is widely dispersed, on the other hand, the effect will be a dispersion of the industry: what may be called a 'dispersed raw material pull'. This situation is common in the processing of agricultural products, which are very often produced over fairly extensive agricultural regions. Thus cotton ginning, maize milling, oilseed crushing, sugar milling and tea processing are dispersed industries. The 28 tea factories operating in Uganda in 1968, for instance, were mostly being operated as estate factories in the main areas of production: 14

were in Mengo District, 7 in Toro District, and 7 in other districts where tea is grown.

Sawmilling is another industry strongly influenced by the distribution of the raw material, since sawn timber is so much more easily transported than logs. This is therefore mainly located in the forest areas. As far as Kenya is concerned, this means a concentration of the industry in the Rift Valley Province, and 64 per cent of persons engaged in the Kenyan sawmilling industry in 1961 were employed in establishments in that Province. In Uganda, as Table 23.9 shows, it meant a rather evenly dispersed industry.

The raw material factor is also important in location when the raw material is *perishable*. Thus dairy creameries are located in the pastoral areas. In Kenya fruit and vegetable canneries are located at Thika near the source of supply. Fish-freezing plants will be at the edge of the productive lakes, like the Tufmac plant on Lake George in Western Uganda. The processing of primary products is often done in the agricultural area, partly because of loss of weight in processing but also because the raw commodity may be spoiled in transit: thus in addition to the tea factories already mentioned in Uganda, in Tanzania there are tea factories in Iringa, cashew nut processing at Mtwara, and pyrethrum processing at Iringa, also. Loss of weight, perishability, and/or local use of some by-products (including waste matter used as fuel or manure) are, of course, relevant in the location of cotton ginneries, sugar mills, and sisal factories in the growing areas of most Eastern African countries.

Location near the market

Industry is attracted to a location near the market if the market exerts a special 'pull' and if the pull of the raw material is not significant. The market exerts a strong pull if the finished product is costly or difficult to transport, either because it is bulky or breakable, as in the case of the furniture and woodworking trades (more precisely if the product adds weight or bulk in the course of manufacture), or because it is perishable, as in the case of bread and other bakery products which are liable to go stale if not delivered quickly to the consumer. A special case of perishability is that of industries providing direct services to the consumer: direct services like haircuts cannot be transported at all! Within 'manufacturing' motor-car repairs are in this category as well as printing newspapers for a localized reading public.

The raw material will not exert an important influence if it does not lose weight in the process of manufacture or if it is generally available throughout the country so that there is access to the material *wherever* the industry is located. Examples of goods which do not lose bulk in the process of manufacture

are bottled drinks, including beer, which besides being fragile are bulkier and more difficult to transport than their ingredients, which mainly consist of water; bread, which is bulkier than flour; and bricks and tiles, which are no less bulky than the clays and sands used in their manufacture. In each case the main ingredients, water, flour, and earths respectively, are generally available throughout the country.

We might note, finally, that the relative importance of market pull and raw material pull depends on the importance of transport costs within total costs. Thus cigarette factories could be located either in the tobacco-growing areas or near the market but are usually located in the urban centres, as they are in Eastern Africa, simply because the cost of transporting either tobacco or cigarettes is small relative to the value of the product.

What effect does 'market pull' have over the pattern of location in the Eastern African countries? Again there are two opposite and contrasting effects depending this time on whether the industry is characterized by large or small firms. If the industry consists of a large number of small firms, as in the case of the furniture trade, these will tend to be scattered throughout the country in rough proportion to the density of population; if the industry is relatively large-scale, market demand may only give scope for one or two factories throughout the whole country. If these are guided by a desire to be near the market they will obviously choose to locate near the main centres of population. Thus beer and cigarette factories, both fairly large-scale, are in the cities, such as Dar es Salaam, Nairobi, or Lusaka.

Location near the source of power

Fuel is simply another raw material, and one which often loses *all* its bulk in the process of production. Thus in the great industrial countries of the world heavy industry became concentrated near the main coalfields, although this pattern is relaxing now as electricity and oil compete with coal as sources of power for industry. In tropical Africa coal is not generally available commercially and has therefore not had any such effect in attracting 'power-oriented' industries. In any case the importance of this factor depends on the share of fuel costs within total costs: this is generally small for light industries such as exist now in most of Africa.

The supply of labour and location

Labour is less important as an original factor determining the location of industry because on the whole it is *mobile*: workers can move to where employment is offered. In general, towns grow up where industrial and commercial opportunities can be exploited. Once a town has developed, however, the supply of labour provided by its population can be an important incentive for *further* industry to locate itself there. In Africa this is particularly important since new firms are anxious to find a supply of labour at least *partially* accustomed to factory conditions, something which the rural population will generally not be. New firms benefit in this way from the fact that other firms have been established before them and have among other things helped to train workers. This benefit is 'external' to the new firms and is an example of *external economies*.

External economies and the location of industry

External economies have been referred to in previous chapters. They are the advantages accruing to one firm from the existence of other firms close by. They may be direct advantages: these establishments might, by being near at hand, be able to supply the firm more cheaply and readily with some of the things it uses, machines, tools, or raw materials; or they might be able to make use of a by-product of the firm's output which it can therefore sell instead of throwing away—for example a meat canning factory might be able to dispose of manufactured bonemeal for use as fertilizer. Or there may be indirect advantages: *because* there is already a concentration of firms in an area, the government will be more willing to develop roads, piped water supplies, and other facilities there, and banking, insurance, and other commercial services will grow up. The effect of these advantages is to reduce costs for new firms which are locating in the region, and the attraction of these reduced costs will tend to produce further concentration.

External economies may, however, be real or 'imagined': it may well be that new firms are attracted to existing industrial centres on the assumption that they will benefit in various ways from this location, whereas in fact costs may be no less than elsewhere or even be higher. It is difficult, of course, to draw a strict line between real and imagined economies since one of the most important 'economies' may be the boost given to the confidence of potential investors by an already thriving concentration of industry.

External economies have played an important part in shaping the distribution of industry in Eastern Africa. This is true between countries as well as within countries, and the dominant position of Kenya, and the Nairobi region in particular, as a supplier of industrial output in Eastern Africa owes something to them: how much, as we shall presently, is disputed.

Non-economic factors affecting location

It should not be deduced from our discussion so far that every firm is located only after a close calculation of the benefits and disadvantages of all possible sites: even major firms and industries have been located as a result of purely random and irrational factors, such as where the entrepreneur happened to live at the time he launched his enterprise—quite apart from the 'imagined' economies mentioned above. This will apply more, of course, to the 'footloose' industries where there is more flexibility in the matter of siting.

One rational, though non-economic, factor in locating expatriate industrial and trading enterprises in Nairobi, historically, was the excellent climate and natural surroundings which senior expatriate business executives would be able to enjoy there.

Patterns of location of industry in East Africa

What general pattern of industrial location in East Africa is produced by all these factors? The most obvious feature is that industry is heavily concentrated in a few main belts: the Nairobi–Thika region in Kenya, the Mombasa and Dar es Salaam 'hinterlands' (the areas immediately behind these ports) and the Kampala–Jinja–Tororo belt in Uganda. This would seem to be strong evidence of the 'pull of the market' on the one hand, and of the effect of external economies on the other. In Uganda in 1968, 85 per cent of industrial establishments and of employees were located in Buganda and the Eastern Region.

The high degree of concentration of industry in Kenya around Nairobi is shown in Table 23.8. This shows that 51 per cent of employment in manufacturing was in Nairobi and 58 per cent of the value added (gross product). This concentration would appear to be *increasing*, moreover, since in 1961 the corresponding figures were 41 and 44 per cent respectively. Thus either the percentage of 'non-market pull' industries has declined or, as the size of the industrial sector has grown, the pull of external economies has increased. The extent of concentration in building and construction is even greater: 87 per cent of the gross product.

For all industry about 60 per cent of employment created and value added was in Nairobi. Mombasa (20 per cent) and hence the Coast Province (21 per

Table 23.8 *Concentration of industry in Kenya, 1967*

Location by main town	Manufacturing and repairs		Building and construction		Location by province	Manufacturing and repairs		All industry	
	No. engaged (%)	Gross product (%)	No. engaged (%)	Gross product (%)		No. engaged (%)	Gross product (%)	No. engaged (%)	Gross product (%)
Nairobi	51	58	84	87	Nairobi	51	58	57	60
Mombasa	15	20	6	6	Coast	16	21	14	19
Nakuru	4	3	3	2	Eastern & North-eastern	4	3	3	2
Thika	5	2	1	1	Central	11	6	9	6
Eldoret	3	2	1	1	Rift Valley	12	8	11	9
Kisumu	3	2	1	1	Nyanza	5	4	5	4
Remaining townships and other areas	20	12	5	3	Western	0.4	0.3	0.3	0.2
Total	100	100	100	100	Total	100	100	100	100

SOURCE: *Census of Industrial Production, 1967*

* All industry includes manufacturing and repairs, mining and quarrying, building and construction, and electricity. Percentages may not add to 100 due to rounding error. Gross product is value added including depreciation.

cent) came out as the secondary centre for manufacturing in terms of output. Together Nairobi (plus Thika) and Mombasa were responsible for 71 per cent of numbers employed in manufacturing and 80 per cent of gross product. The other main towns such as Nakuru, Eldoret, and Kisumu accounted together for only 10 per cent of manufacturing output and employment and 7 per cent of output; while the remaining townships and other areas provided 20 per cent of employment and 12 per cent of output. It will be noted that manufacturing appears as more labour-intensive outside Nairobi and Mombasa.

It should be realized that the table covers only firms included in the census of industrial production, and excludes very small producers in the rural areas and the urban 'informal sector'. Thus construction of huts in the rural areas, if included, would reduce the highly concentrated figure for building and construction. As we saw earlier, also, small-scale industry in the informal sector in Kenya is quite significant and distributed throughout both urban and rural areas.

It is worth asking whether this concentration around Nairobi is a necessary consequence of real locational advantages and subsequently of external economies or whether it results from 'inertia' or imagined advantages. Certainly the Nairobi area has

in the past had certain obvious advantages to offer East African industry. It is centrally situated not only within the most populated areas of Kenya but within the more developed parts of the three East African countries, and is a natural rail and road junction within this developed belt, being also closely linked to the source of imported inputs through Mombasa. It is the natural administrative centre of Kenya. The relatively large and concentrated Asian and European population was useful as a source of technical and commercial personnel and as a market for industrial products, which were mainly manufactured consumer goods. And there was an ample supply of unskilled labour nearby, due to the pressure of population in the surrounding agricultural area. Finally the *increasing* concentration of industry in the area would, as indicated earlier, suggest strongly the importance of external economies. One factor assisting early development in the Nairobi area was provision of an Industrial Area by the City Council in the early post-war period.

The importance of external economies in locating so much of East Africa's industry in Nairobi has however been questioned by F. I. Nixson, who investigated industrial location factors in Kenya and Uganda in the late 1960s.[9] Of 39 firms with manufacturing establishments in Nairobi interviewed by him, 75 per cent stated that 'market pull' was the dominant factor. Only two manufacturing industries, clothing and engineering, stressed the importance of the availability of skilled labour. Pools of skilled labour were less important because most manufacturers undertook on-the-job training, while high-level technicians were in just as short supply as elsewhere. Some Asian entrepreneurs felt that business finance was easier to obtain in Nairobi than elsewhere, but the general view was that financial and business services were not superior in Nairobi to other East African capitals, though superior to those in other Kenyan centres. However, in neither Kenya nor Uganda did Nixson find such commercial facilities a decisive location factor. Nairobi was marginally better off as a stockist of spare parts and replacements. Climate was not a decisive attraction either, and some industrialists stated that they would have located elsewhere if the cost advantage in so doing had been great enough.

In contrast with the elusiveness of the external economies of Nairobi, Nixson found much more conclusive evidence of external diseconomies. The most important was the high cost of land in Nairobi—in 1961 rail-served industrial plots in Nairobi's Industrial Area ranged in capital value from £4,000 to £15,000 per acre, compared with £4,000–£10,000 in Mombasa, £2,000–£3,000 in other main towns, and only £40 at Thika.[10] Thus firms locating in Nairobi were faced with much heavier capital costs for land. A second major external diseconomy (reflecting the higher cost of living in the metropolis) was the higher level of minimum wage rates and other wage differentials, raising labour costs in Nairobi and Mombasa. This was coupled with additional labour costs reported as being increased likelihood of conflict with trade unions, higher housing costs for labour, and longer journeys to work. Finally a third diseconomy which Nixson suggested might become serious was a shortage of water and sewage disposal facilities.

Given the absence of clear-cut external economies and the presence of quite obvious diseconomies, Nixson attributed Nairobi's attractiveness for past, present, and potential industrialists to (a) 'market pull'—the size of the market in Nairobi and its hinterland, and (b) its geographical position offering superior opportunities for supplying the rest of East Africa, particularly Eastern Uganda and the Moshi–Arusha area of Tanzania. Nixson's findings must be treated with a fair degree of caution: his sample of businessmen is small and if he had interviewed a wider range of businessmen he might have obtained a somewhat different response. He does not provide enough detailed data on costs in alternative locations. He probably neglects less tangible external

economies such as proximity to fellow businessmen, as well as non-economic factors such as residential preferences. Nevertheless his study demonstrates the need to sift out possible explanations carefully rather than take them at face value and suggests that, at least in so far as net external economies are concerned, a stronger policy of locating industry in other centres should be possible.

Turning to other features of the location of industry in East Africa, we may note that the main factor which runs counter to this concentration is the importance of processing. In effect there are two patterns superimposed on one another: widely dispersed processing industry scattered through the areas of production of the raw material, and small-scale production of consumer goods which is centred in the towns. The effect of the latter is seen in the fact that in 1967 nearly 80 per cent of manufacturing establishments in Kenya and the same percentage of employees were concentrated in six towns—though we must stress again that this excludes unrecorded employment in 'informal' manufacturing which exists in both urban and rural areas.

The effect of the scale of firms is clearly illustrated in Uganda. Highly capitalized industries with large plants are mainly in Jinja and the Eastern Region, in accordance with long-standing plans to develop an industrial complex there, while the largely unplanned small-scale industry is centred on the main market, Kampala.

The result produced in individual industries by the forces mentioned is illustrated to some extent in Table 23.9, referring to the geographical distribution of certain manufacturing industries in Uganda in 1968. Establishments producing grain mill products are largely located *away from* the big markets in Kampala and Jinja, and situated in the Districts of Buganda and the Eastern Region: reflecting therefore a 'dispersed raw material pull'. The same is true of sawn timber with Kampala and Jinja also exerting some market pull. Cement—comprising the cement factory at Tororo—reflects a 'concentrated raw material pull', reinforced by economies of scale. The bakery, furniture, and motor repairs industries show a dispersal throughout the country, *together with* a concentration in the main urban centres of Kampala and Jinja, obviously this time reflecting a 'dispersed *market* pull', and the absence of important economies of scale. In contrast the clothing, textiles, metal products, and machinery industries are concentrated in Kampala and Jinja. Since these are not tied to a raw material supply in the area of concentration, they are presumably relatively 'footloose' industries which have been attracted to Kampala, the largest market, where they may also benefit from external economies of a general kind, or to the industrial complex and

Table 23.9 *Geographical distribution of selected manufacturing industries in Uganda, 1968 (number of establishments with ten or more employees)*

	Kampala	Jinja	Other areas of Uganda				Total
			Buganda	Eastern region	Northern region	Western region	
Grain mill products	—	3	5	9	1	1	19
Sawmills	3	4	7	4	—	9	27
Cement	—	—	—	1	—	—	1
Bakery products	5	3	4	3	—	4	19
Furniture	23	3	4	5	1	2	38
Repair of motor vehicles	40	7	4	12	3	7	73
Clothing	18	2	2	5	—	—	27
Textiles	1	1	2	1	—	—	5
Metal products and machinery, except electrical	27	10	6	7	—	—	50
All manufacturing except agricultural processing for export	187	61	100	89	7	41	485
Agricultural processing for export	4	—	174	30	14	29	251
Total (no. of establishments)	191	61	274	119	21	70	736
(per cent)	26.2	8.3	37.1	16.1	2.8	9.5	100
Share of population, 1969 (%)	3.5	0.6	24.4	29.0	17.1	25.5	100

SOURCE: *Survey of Industrial Production, 1968*

transport facilities at Jinja. In the case of textiles, economies of scale are evident

Finally, we may examine the aggregates shown towards the bottom of the table. Agricultural processing for export shows dispersed raw material pull, and market pull would not in any case bring these to Kampala and Jinja, which are not the ultimate markets. The row for 'all other manufacturing' shows that Kampala accounts for 187 or 38 per cent of establishments, mostly small-scale enterprises. The concentration of manufacturing in the south and south-east of the country is confirmed, and the Northern and Western Regions together account for less than 10 per cent of manufacturing establishments (excluding processing) and not much more of *all* establishments. The Northern Region has very few, mainly cotton ginneries under 'processing' and some motor repair shops.

Location policy

Since most of the economies of Eastern Africa have only embryonic industrial sectors it is not surprising that governments have been more concerned with expanding industry in the main centres than with location policy and any attempt to spread industrial development among a number of towns. In Kenya, as we have seen, Nairobi has been attracting an *increasing* proportion of industry. The provision of industrial estates in other towns does not appear to have been an effective inducement to new industries. One obvious centre which might have been encouraged through a strong location policy is Kisumu, which is on the railway and well placed on Lake Victoria to export to partner states within the East African Community, and which is in urgent need of employment creation to relieve population pressure in the area. The ICDC (Industrial and Commercial Development Corporation) has promoted industrial estates for small-scale and artisan industry, which we have seen does lend itself to geographical redistribution; but even here the main effort has been made in Nairobi. Following the ILO Mission report in 1972, the government did however intensify efforts to promote rural handicraft industry.

The one country which has strongly emphasized both regional planning and a location policy for industry has been Tanzania. The most unique feature of Tanzania's Second Five-Year Plan, 1969–74, was in fact the proposal to establish 'growth poles' in eight centres outside Dar es Salaam: Tanga, Arusha, Mwanza, Tabora, Dodoma, Morogoro, Mbeya, and Mtwara. As mentioned in the previous chapter, these are sets of complementary or interrelated industries which support each other by buying inputs one from the other and which by generating external economies attract further industry cumulatively to the growth pole. Progress since 1969 in these centres has not been at all rapid, unfortunately, for a number of possible reasons.

(1) The number of growth poles proposed was probably too great, given the limited amount of new industry being created in Tanzania during each period, for each 'pole' to be supplied with even one or two major new industrial establishments. There might in fact be a conflict between the desire to establish a new growth pole away from Dar es Salaam and a policy of dispersing industries widely. This is in direct contradiction to the suggestion of Ann Seidman that 'the important factor in locating poles of growth is to ensure that they *are established in every region* to ensure that all regions take part in the increased specialization and exchange set off by establishment of new manufacturing industries'.[11]

(2) A significant proportion of East African industry, as mentioned previously, consists of small-scale establishments attracted strongly by market pull and not themselves capable of generating major linkages.

(3) The policy might have been more effectively implemented at an *earlier* stage of industrial development when a number of large industries could have been located away from Dar es Salaam. Thus the Chinese-built textile mill, instead of being located outside Dar es Salaam, could have been built in, say, Mwanza or Tabora, which would have provided at once 3,000 jobs (equivalent to about 30 fair-sized factories) in the centre selected, with the possibility of significant linkages. The Tanganyika Packers Meat Factory, again a significant employment creator, could have been located at Arusha (there have been problems of obtaining an adequate supply of cattle in Dar es Salaam), and the cigarette factory in Iringa, near the tobacco-growing area.

(4) A major difficulty in effecting changes in location is that many of the prospective firms are private ones, and frequently expatriate. Even if the enterprise is a joint one with the National Development Corporation, the private firm can ignore government pressure for it to locate away from Dar es Salaam in, say, Dodoma. This is particularly true if the government is anxious to attract firms to Tanzania which might otherwise locate, for example, in Nairobi.

(5) The evidence in East Africa is that a growth pole cannot be initiated except with a substantial amount of new industry and where other conditions—rich agricultural surroundings, perhaps, or good harbour facilities—are favourable. The decision in the 1950s to establish Jinja as an industrial centre based on cheap electricity from the Owen Falls Dam could be described as a 'growth pole' strategy: but despite a few substantial factories being established there, Jinja failed to develop the cumulative growth that Nairobi and Dar es Salaam have shown.

It is likely, therefore, that it will be some years before these designated growth poles become established. Meanwhile the Tanzanian government is attempting to promote rural industry in various ways, including the establishment of District Development Corporations, also with the aim of dispersal of economic activities.

Questions on Chapter 23

1. Describe the composition of manufacturing activities in East African countries, and explain why the size of the market is important in determining the kinds of goods produced.
2. Analyse the main economic factors determining the location of manufacturing industry in your country rather than in some other country.
3. What special advantages does industry based on processing primary materials for export have for a developing country? What are the limitations of industrial expansion based on this?
4. To what extent do you think agricultural processing will have linkages? Give examples.
5. Are transport costs the only economic factor affecting the degree of manufacturing carried out in primary exporting economies?
6. Elaborate Arthur Lewis's argument for countries like Mauritius embarking on a policy of promoting manufacturing export industries.
7. What economic factors limit the development of manufacturing (a) for the home market and (b) for export markets?
8. How do you account for the significant share of the production of intermediate products within manufacturing output in Eastern Africa?
9. Discuss the possible effects of a drastic redistribution of income in your country on the detailed structure of industry.
10. Is small-scale industry labour-intensive, on the whole, or capital-intensive, or neither? Comment with reference to Kenya.
11. What economic factors influence the location of manufacturing industry *within* any East African country?
12. Why are some industries more 'footloose' than others? What factors influence the location of such industries in East African economies?
13. How may the expansion of any one manufacturing industry effect the development of other industries? Illustrate with reference to any industrial activity in East African countries.
14. What are 'external economies'? Illustrate with reference to the location of industry in any East African country.
15. Account for the concentration of manufacturing activity in the main urban areas of Eastern Africa.
16. Discuss the main difficulties likely to arise in implementing Tanzania's 'growth pole' policy.
17. For what reasons might the East African countries wish to adopt a strong location-of-industry policy?
18. Discuss the main objectives in Kenya and Tanzania behind the emphasis placed on small-industry development. How have these objectives affected the form of programme in the two countries?

Notes

[1] W. A. Lewis, *Report on Industrialization and the Gold Coast*, Government Printer, Accra, 1953.

[2] ibid., p. 1.

[3] Industrial consumption of electricity is an important determinant of the scale of the electricity power industry's operations, so that the needs of mineral refining or agricultural processing may dictate the very existence of electricity for other industries or for household consumers outside the main towns, and also its price. This is a very relevant example of an *external economy* rendered by the first or main user of electricity to later or smaller producers and to household consumers.

[4] The ratio of value added in electricity obtained as hydro-electric power is very high, it will be noticed, because the industry uses few current inputs once the fixed capital has been installed.

[5] Although hoes and other implements, vehicle box bodies, small boats, and even fishing nets are produced there, as in most African countries, and are, of course, 'capital goods'.

[6] This includes textiles, which is closely geared to the import substitution policy, textiles being used to make clothing for the home market.

[7] For an interesting study of these programmes, with special reference to Ghana, Kenya, Malawi, and Swaziland, see Bruce Dinwiddy, *Promoting African Enterprise*, Croom Helm in association with the Overseas Development Institute, London, 1974.

[8] Apart from Zambia, the location of Eastern Africa's only copper smelter at Jinja in Uganda, some 250 miles from the Kilembe copper mine at the foot of the Ruwenzori Mountains in the west of Uganda, requires some explanation, since copper concentrates produced at the minehead lose 70 per cent of their weight when smelted to become blister copper. The reasons were (1) the government was anxious to locate a number of industries at Jinja in an attempt to form a 'growing point'; (2) the Owen Falls Dam provided electric power on the spot, avoiding the need to install expensive transmission lines to the copper mine itself; (3) it was hoped that the Jinja smelter would also be able to serve the smaller Macalder copper mine in Nyanza Province of Kenya, too small to have its own smelter (unfortunately this mine later ceased operations); and (4) once the railway to Kasese had been built, the real costs of using it to transport concentrates rather than blister copper were not large, and the railway would have been needed to ship the blister copper and supplies to the mine.

[9] F. I. Nixson, *Economic Integration and Industrial Location*, Longman, 1973, pp. 57–69.

[10] This cost advantage has been an important factor in the growth of industry in Thika and in other satellite industrial areas of Nairobi.

[11] A. Seidman, *Comparative Development Strategies in East Africa*, East African Publishing House, 1972.

24 Economic Integration in East Africa[1]

In Chapter 3 we talked about the 'vicious circle' of small markets which affects developing countries: because countries are poor, purchasing power is low, and the size of the market may be too small to support the minimum viable size of plant in a whole range of manufacturing industries. A large proportion of African countries are also very small in geographical area or in size of population, so that, given low income per head as well, the size of the market provided by such countries, measured in purchasing power, is very small indeed. This can be seen from Table 24.1 which shows that only eleven countries were estimated to have populations of 10 millions or more in 1970, and only five populations exceeding 20 millions, compared, for example, to Britain's population of 56 millions. Many of the countries might be described as 'pocket handkerchief' states, with populations of less than 1 million. These were the national boundaries imposed and left behind by the departing colonial powers, and it has been an unfortunate legacy indeed. It has,

moreover, been made worse in West Africa, particularly, where alternate small states have been left with English and French as imposed languages, making communication and integration between close neighbours still more difficult. The Federal Republic of Cameroon, for instance, is made up of a former French territory and a former British territory. In these circumstances it is not surprising that there has been interest in economic cooperation and integration to counter 'balkanization' in Africa, sponsored in particular by the United Nations Economic Commission for Africa, located in Addis Ababa.

The elements of economic integration

There may be several elements in economic integration. A *free trade area* is the simplest and least onerous in terms of involvement; it exists when a number of countries agree to abolish tariffs, quota,

Table 24.1 *Population size of African states, 1970 (millions)*

Algeria	15.7	Malagasy Rep.	8.8	Spanish Sahara	0.1
Angola	5.5	Malawi	5.1		
Botswana	0.7	Mali	5.7	Sudan	15.6
Burundi	3.7				
Cameroun	7.3	Mauritania	1.3	Swaziland	0.5
CAR	1.8	Mauritius	0.9	Tanzania	14.7
Chad	4.0	Morocco	16.7	Togo	2.2
Congo (Brazzaville)	1.3				
		Mozambique	9.2	Tunisia	5.6
Dahomey	2.7	Namibia	0.9		
Ethiopia	25.0	Niger	4.6	Uganda	11.6
Gabon	0.5				
Gambia	0.5	Nigeria	75.0	United Arab Republic	37.1
Ghana	9.9	Reunion	0.5	Upper Volta	5.9
Guinea	5.5	Rhodesia	6.3	Zaire	24.7
Guinea-Bissau	0.6	Ruanda	4.1	Zambia	4.9
Guinea-Equatorial	0.3	Senegal	5.0		
		Seychelles	0.1	United Kingdom	56.0
Ivory Coast	6.7	Sierra Leone	3.0	W. Germany	61.8
Kenya	13.3	Somalia	3.2		
Lesotho	1.2			Japan	111.0
Liberia	1.5	South Africa	25.5	USA	213.6
Libya	2.4			India	609.6

SOURCE: UN *Demographic Yearbook, 1975* and *UN Statistical Yearbook, 1976* and World Bank, *Atlas, 1976*

and other physical barriers to trade between them, while retaining the right to impose unilaterally their own level of customs duty, etc., on trade with the rest of the world. It may, in fact, be confined to certain trade categories; for example, the original proposal for a European Free Trade Area (EFTA) by the UK in 1957 was to be confined to manufactured goods only. A *customs union* exists where a number of countries decide to permit free trade among themselves without tariff or other trade barriers, while establishing *a common external tariff* against imports from the rest of the world. A *common market* exists when the countries, in addition to forming a customs union, decide to permit factors of production full mobility between them, so that citizens of one country are free to take up employment in the other, and capitalists are free to invest and to move their capital from one country to another. Where the countries set up joint economic institutions, involving a degree of supranational economic decision-making, they may be said to have moved towards *economic union*. In the European Economic Community (EEC), for instance, many decisions affecting the lives of German citizens, or Italian citizens, are taken not in Bonn, or in Rome, but within the Secretariat of the Community located in Brussels. In East Africa there were a number of *common public services* run jointly by the three East African governments, particularly the railways, ports, postal services, airways, and some research organizations. Finally, there may be a *common monetary system*, in which countries share a common currency, or ensure that each rational currency can be exchanged freely at a fixed rate of exchange, and agree to keep any separate monetary policies roughly in line, to make this possible.

The advantages of integration

What are the benefits to be had from close economic integration? By permitting the free movement of goods produced within the area of the cooperating countries, a customs union permits specialization along the lines of comparative advantages, implying in turn more effective use of resources. This is referred to as the 'trade creation' effect of the customs union, since the absence of internal tariffs permits additional specialization and trade.

The extension of the market may also permit *economies of scale* to be tapped where the small size of the national market restricts output below the optimum, as we noted above. One of the features of the East African industrial structure noted already is the preponderance of the small establishment. Because of the small size of market there may be room only for one fertilizer plant, or shoe factory, or textile plant. We should stress again that the 'size of

market' here refers to purchasing power. Though we have mentioned the smallness of many African states, size of market is not directly related to geographical area. Indeed, given the size of population, management of an extensive area increases transport costs in relation to purchasing power and *decreases* the attractiveness of the market, since more of the consumer's money goes to pay for transport than goes to the factory owner. Neither is it related to population size, since the population may be poor. In 1970, the 34 million people living in the East African Community possessed an estimated aggregate *monetary* income of some £1,000 millions. A single reasonably sized city in the United Kingdom of, say, 400,000 inhabitants with average consumer expenditure of around £600 a year per head would provide a consumer market of £240 millions, about the size of that in any one of the East African countries!

A large market is necessary not only for established large factories to be able to operate at efficient levels of output. It may also be necessary for new industry to be attracted to East Africa in the future. In both cases, of course, this is relevant only where the minimum viable or most efficient size of plant is bigger than can be supported by the market of one country by itself. The point remains that the size of the market is important not only in the static sense, in relation to established industry and current resources, but also in dynamic terms, through its effect on the rate of investment and rate of growth of industry.

There is another potential benefit, however, from a larger market, even if the national market is large enough to sustain one plant at full capacity. This is the benefit from increased competition in an enlarged market in which there are two or more competitive plants, assuming that these do actually compete with each other.

There are thus three types of potential benefit within the industrial sector: (1) advantages from specialization on the basis of comparative costs; (2) advantages derived from economies of scale, including fuller utilization of existing plant and increased incentive to invest in new plants which require a market larger than the current national one; and (3) advantages from increased competition within an enlarged market. Where, as in East Africa, industry is not far developed, and where it is not based on specific local resources, the argument based on exploitation of comparative advantage in different industries will be less important. The most important effect will be on the viability of new investments, and the incentive to invest.

Free trade in agricultural produce may also bring important benefits though here, in contrast, economies of scale will not be so important. Where natural and climatic conditions differ between two countries there should be possibilities for trade on the basis of comparative costs. And even if one country is so much more fertile than the other that it could produce more per acre of any agricultural product, opportunity-costs would still apply to make specialization and trade desirable. There may in addition be differences in the seasonal pattern of production: in East Africa for instance it has been suggested that if free trade in foodstuffs were permitted food crops might be exported from south to north in April/May, and from north to south in July/September. Finally, in addition to seasonal variation, periodic surpluses and deficits, due for instance to a drought in one country, could be evened out: the country that is temporarily 'short' can import from one of the others and in turn can export the same commodity when it has a relative surplus.

Another potential advantage of a common market relates to *factor mobility and income redistribution*. The distribution of income may be affected by the movement of both goods and factors within a common market. Free trade permits exports of commodities which are produced cheaply in one country, and thus raises the returns to abundant labour factors used in their production. This will tend to raise the low incomes of what might otherwise be surplus labour. Thus the free export of maize from Uganda to Kenya might in the past have reduced the price of maize in Kenya while increasing the incomes of relatively poor maize producers in Uganda. In the past there were relatively few restrictions on the movement of labour and enterprise in East Africa, though over the years it has been increasingly difficult in any one East African country for nationals of the others to find employment, and instances where they have been made to leave. The movement of labour from one country to another is, of course, possible without there being a common market, and indeed it has been especially small countries with population problems such as Malawi, Burundi, and Ruanda which have exported labour to neighbouring territories.

The advantages of monetary union are synonymous with the disadvantage of separate currencies. Separate currencies carry an increased danger of loss of public confidence in the currency, and uncertainty regarding continued convertibility with other currencies. Assuming that trade between the countries is important, separate currencies may result in balance of payments difficulties in the event of one country pursuing a much more expansionary policy than the others. For these reasons exchange controls may be imposed with the effect of reducing the free movement of capital between the countries involved. None of these effects *need* follow the break-up of a unitary

monetary system, but may do so. Apart from this, there will of course be the extra administrative costs of operating separate systems.

The advantages of operating common services of the type already described are basically those of economies of scale. The railways are more efficiently operated in East Africa, for instance, as a single East African system. Air traffic is insufficient to support more than one Airways Corporation. Research done in one country may be substantially applicable in neighbouring countries, and is more efficiently carried on in larger research institutes rather than in smaller separate units. Large public corporations can attract loan funds more easily and probably more cheaply than small ones.

The problems of integration

It may be asked in view of these advantages why economic integration is generally so difficult to achieve or maintain. There are economic reasons, as well as political ones. These are because economic integration may involve costs as well as benefits for the participating countries, and because the distribution of benefits and costs from integration may be uneven, benefiting some partners more than the others. While we should not want partners to follow too narrow or nationalistic a view, it is also true that governments must pay regard first to the interests of their own citizens and a particular government must try to ensure that its citizens obtain a 'fair' share of the benefits and do not pay too much of the costs of integration.

We should note first that in addition to a trade creation effect, a customs union may have a trade *diversion* effect. Suppose, before a customs union is formed, trade takes place between three countries A, B, and C, specializing on the basis of comparative costs in avocados, beans, and carrots respectively, which are traded between the countries over tariff 'walls'. If A and B form a customs union the tariffs between A and B would be abolished, but A–B together would have a common tariff against C. Even though in terms of real costs C would still be the most efficient producer of carrots, it may now be cheaper for A's consumers to buy carrots from B, since these can be imported free of tariffs, rather than from C, since C's carrots must pay import duty. The effect of the customs union would have been to *divert* trade from the low-cost source outside the union to a higher-cost source inside the union.

When we come to consider developing countries, this may be complicated if *protective* tariffs are being imposed to protect a whole range of 'infant industries' in the growing manufacturing sector. If A and B agree to impose a common external tariff to protect a tyre factory to be established in A, B will find itself importing high-cost tyres from A which it could have imported more cheaply from outside the common market. Frequently, moreover, the products of an infant industry are inferior in quality or reliability of service to the overseas product during the 'learning process' which occurs after a new product is taken up. Finally, it may be remarked that by importing duty-free products from A, B will suffer a loss of customs revenue. If A and B form a customs union with a high protective tariff, therefore, they will need to ensure that the costs of protection are evenly borne, and each country gets its share of protected industries; and also that the loss of customs revenue is taken into account in calculating the distribution of benefits.

The second major problem is that industrial development in a common market, whether assisted by protection or not, tends to be uneven, and frequently tends to concentrate in one of the partner states. In the last chapter we saw for instance how industrial development in East Africa has tended to be polarized around central Kenya, where new industry has been attracted in cumulative fashion by real or imagined 'external economies'. The country which succeeds in attracting the greater share of new activity will also enjoy any expenditure multiplier effects that this generates in incomes and employment in the country. Its government will receive additional tax revenues in proportion to this total activity, though this may be offset to some extent by additional purchases of imports from the other countries as incomes rise. This tendency of industry to polarize and to develop unevenly among partner states makes it more difficult to convince each state that it is benefiting appropriately from the existence of the common market.

The third problem arises where the partner states jointly operate common services, such as railways: this again involves a difficult calculation of benefit and cost. We shall illustrate this presently with reference to East Africa. Since the East African Community, until recent problems, was also one of the most successful examples of economic integration among developing countries, it will pay us to examine in some detail the history of this common market.

The origins of economic cooperation in East Africa

The Common Market in East Africa has an unusually long history, The Congo Basin Treaties drawn up among colonizing powers in 1885 and 1890 specifically prohibited preferential tariffs on imports from metropolitan countries. This facilitated the use of a common external tariff, since it was then only a matter of which goods to charge and at what rate, rather than which countries to charge more or less heavily. Kenya and Uganda each collected their own duties, however, until 1909, when Kenya agreed to collect duty at Mombasa on Uganda's behalf, in effect, by paying over an agreed share of customs revenue. From that time, with only limited exceptions, Kenya and Uganda could be treated as a single import market, though the relationship was not formalized till 1917, when revenue was collected by a joint Customs and Excise Department.

Trade with Tanganyika was not fully integrated till after 1948, when the East Africa High Commission was established. The Tanganyikan Customs and Excise Department was formally amalgamated in 1949. In fact, however, a de facto common market in locally produced goods had existed even during the German rule before 1917. With long land frontiers it would have been impossible to police and regulate inter-territorial trade in local foodstuffs, and wide differences in duties would simply have encouraged smuggling.

A common monetary system came with the establishment in 1919 of the East African Currency Board. Prior to this, however, the German silver rupee circulating in Tanganyika was exchangeable at a fixed rate for the East African rupee. After 1917 the same expatriate banks operated in all East African countries and freedom of capital movements between territories was an integral part of convertibility into sterling at a fixed rate. Local residents and foreign enterprises with branches in more than one East African country had no more difficulty in moving funds between, say, Kampala and Dar es Salaam than between Kampala and Jinja. Later a small East African Stock Exchange centred in Nairobi provided a market in stocks and shares issued by companies operating in one or more East African countries.

Cooperation in the field of public services has also a long history. The Colonial Governors, who always had a major influence on policy-making in the three territories, began to hold annual conferences from 1926. In 1932 these conferences were provided with a permanent secretariat to be used as a medium for the continuous coordination of policy. This was in fact the antecedent of the East African High Commission which was set up in 1948. The Kenya–Uganda Railway was a joint undertaking from the very beginning, although for a time its finances were closely connected with the Kenya Colony Budget. The separate Postal and Telegraph Departments of the three governments had also cooperated, and during the Second World War a number of research and produce-marketing bodies were established under the East African Governors' Conference to cover all three countries.

Nevertheless the establishment in 1948 of the High Commission was a major advance. It was composed of the three Governors together with a Secretariat in Nairobi consisting of the Administrator, Legal and Financial Secretaries, the Postmaster-General, and the Commissioner for Transport. Alongside the High Commission there operated an advisory Central Legislative Assembly through which legislation concerning the Common Services could be passed. The members of the Assembly were in part appointed by the Governors and in part came from the territorial legislatures. The High Commission could be said to have operated to a great extent as a supranational organization, that is to say, as an independent institution rather than a meeting-place at which the separate territorial interests could be discussed and harmonized.

The High Commission controlled a wide range of non-profit-making departments called 'non-self-contained services' such as Customs and Excise, Income Tax, Statistics, Civil Aviation, Meteorology, Agricultural, Forestry, and Veterinary Research. Two 'self-contained' Administrations, independent of the annual contributions from Territorial Budgets, which were the means of financing the rest of the EAHC, were made responsible for Railways and Harbours and for Posts and Telecommunications respectively. These two were financed from their own operating revenue and their own loans, raised under the joint guarantee of their three owners, the East African Governments. East African Railways and Harbours[2] was the largest single employer of labour in East Africa, excluding the Governments themselves. A smaller interterritorial public trading enterprise which is also 'self-financing' was the East African Airways Corporation; it was registered as a public company, even though all its share capital had been subscribed by the three governments.

The balance of trade within East Africa

Even before the three East African countries obtained self-government and then independence in the early 1960s there had been concern over the distribution of benefits from the East African Common Market. This has often been based on a simple examination of the balance of trade surplus which Kenya has had with its two neighbours. Table 24.2 lays out the balance of trade position for the three countries in 1967. Of special significance is the balance of interstate trade in *manufactures* which is given in diagrammatic form in Figure 24.1 for the same year. This shows the exchange of manufactures between each pair of states, as well as the flows between each

state and the other two states taken together. Kenya was exporting manufactures valued at 439 m shillings to the other two states, and importing 201 m shillings worth of manufactures. Uganda had a trade deficit in manufactures of 59 m shillings but Tanzania was easily in the 'worst' position, with a deficit of 179 m shillings.

For a number of reasons, these two tables are a completely inadequate basis for drawing conclusions about the distribution of benefits from the common market. As we have already seen, countries are right in being concerned with the overall balance of trade (more correctly their balance of *payments*) with *all* other countries; but if countries concerned themselves with *bilateral* balance with each individual trading partner the level of world trade would be substantially lower than it is. Moreover, increased

Table 24.2 *Balance of visible trade by each East African country (shs m) in 1967*

	'External'	'Interstate'	Total
Kenya			
Net imports	2,131	270	2,401
Total exports	1,186	528	1,714
Visible balance	−945	+258	−687
Uganda			
Net imports	826	311	1,137
Total exports	1,310	253	1,563
Visible balance	+484	−58	+426
Tanzania (mainland)			
Net imports	1,345	281	1,626
Total exports	1,698	82	1,780
Visible balance	+353	−199	+154

SOURCE: *Economic and Statistical Review* (EASD), June 1969

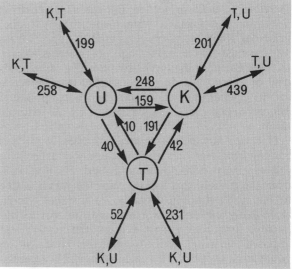

Figure 24.1 *Interstate trade in manufactures, 1967 (shs m).*

incomes in Kenya are much more likely to induce some extra employment and income for her neighbours, so it would be particularly short-sighted to favour overseas countries at the expense of Kenya. This argument needs modification in one respect however: if a country such as Uganda is interested not only in maximizing present income by exporting-primary products but also in making progress in industrial development it might, with some justification, be dissatisfied with a substantial deficit in interstate trade in *manufacturing*, despite an overall trade surplus based on agricultural exports. This indeed is the reason for giving separate figures for interstate trade in manufactures in Figure 24.1.

Secondly, even if Kenya is successful in exporting to her two neighbours, it does not follow that this success is due to the common market as such. It may be due to greater efficiency and enterprise, for instance, and it may be that Kenya can supply many goods more cheaply than Uganda or Tanzania could obtain elsewhere. This may be due also to a transport advantage held by Kenya over foreign imports which have to travel from Europe and elsewhere. Some indication of this competitiveness is given by the fact that some of the internally traded items, such as printing and repair work, do not have an external tariff, and others, notably livestock products, even if they are subject to a tariff, are exported outside East Africa, suggesting that they are quite competitive with potential imports. Another important point is that customs duties in East Africa are a major source of government *revenue* and are more important as revenue duties than as *protective* duties. A *fully* protective duty brings in no revenue, since no goods are imported and no duty paid. Of course revenue duties normally discourage imports to some extent, and are therefore *partially* protective. But the argument that Tanzania and Uganda were made to pay higher prices for Kenya goods as compared to imports from outside East Africa applies only to this partial protective element in the tariff structure. The same holds true, of course, regarding the loss of customs revenue to these countries: it applies to those potential imports which are actually kept out by the external tariff.

One way in which a country can assess what it is gaining from membership of a common market is to calculate what it would lose as a result of withdrawal from the market: this focuses on trade which is due to the customs union. Uganda, for instance, would most likely still find it worthwhile to import manufactures from Kenya even if it left the market and imposed the same duties on Kenyan goods as on goods from overseas. This calculation will not necessarily be the one which a country would make when entering *into* a common market arrangement:

for instance Tanzania and Uganda might feel that, while they each gain by staying in the market, Kenya gains more. In particular they might feel that if a policy of distributing new industry more evenly among the three countries were adopted (for instance by licensing a new industry for a particular country only), external economies would also be distributed, and future industrial development and interstate trade would proceed in more balanced fashion. The question would then be how long the more industrially advanced country would be prepared to 'wait' for the other countries to catch up in developing efficient manufacturing sectors.

East African economic cooperation in the 1960s

After the three East African countries obtained independence in the early 1960s, economic integration in East Africa was subject to increasing strain. National governments bring with them a greater urgency of demand for economic development and a greater concern with the territorial distribution of the gains made. This is particularly so as countries commit themselves to more comprehensive development plans drawn up on a national basis. Moreover, as development takes place, and the pace of industrialization quickens, there is more industry to distribute and more to discuss. Thus difficulties in maintaining and achieving further cooperation need not represent any failure on the part of the governments concerned, but measure the increasing strains which tend naturally to build up.

During the 1960s there were four major landmarks in the area of East African economic integration which we should examine in detail:

(1) the Raisman Commission Report of 1961;[3]

(2) the Kampala Agreement, 1964;

(3) the setting up of independent central banks, 1966;

(4) the Philip Commission Report of 1966, resulting in the subsequent Treaty for East African Co-operation, signed on 6 June 1967.

Developments in the banking system are discussed in Chapter 26 and 27, and we need comment here only on (1), (2), and (4).

The Raisman Commission

The Raisman Commission was a small committee of experts set up to inquire into the distribution of benefits resulting jointly from the East African High Commission Services and from the existence of the Common Market. Although the Raisman Commission was especially concerned with the effects of the Common Market, its proposals greatly strengthened the position of the East African High Commission. It recommended that a fund be set up and maintained by taking a fixed percentage of annual customs and excise revenue (6 per cent) and of income tax on company profits earned in each country (40 per cent), these funds to constitute a 'Distributable Pool'. Half of this amount was to be paid annually to the High Commission thus providing an independent source of revenue in place of annual territorial government grants for the 'non-self-contained services' now called General Fund Services.

The greater certainty of these funds made it easier to plan the activities of the EAHC, and made for more efficient spending of funds, since the High Commission could more easily function as a single authority on an East African basis without too close reference to the allocation of activities among the three territories. This therefore marked a further step in the direction towards an autonomous supranational body.

With Tanganyika's independence in 1961, the High Commission was no longer an appropriate form of organization, and it gave way to the East African Common Services Organization, EACSO. This involved some restructuring, but the new institution operated in much the same way as its predecessor. The executive authority of EACSO consisted of the Chief Ministers of each country, now the three Presidents, but work was carried out through four Ministerial Committees covering Communications, Finance, Commercial and Industrial Coordination, and Social and Research Services. Inevitably the Ministers from each country who formed these committees were very mindful of their own territorial interest, and this must necessarily have influenced EACSO civil servants working under these committees. As compared to the East African High Commission, therefore, there is no doubt that a degree of supranational authority was lost. It remains true, however, that the maintenance of this institution was itself an achievement, and its existence must necessarily stimulate other forms of cooperation. The only danger was that, despite the general acceptance of the desirability of the Common Services, they might be abandoned by one country in retaliation for failure by the others to cooperate in other ways.

The concern of the Raisman Commission was with the distribution of gains arising jointly from the Common Services and from the Common Market. Their conclusion was that though all countries benefited from the customs union, Kenya enjoyed the greatest benefit. Their recommendation of a Distributable Pool to compensate for this was accepted, and went into operation in 1961–2. As we have already mentioned, half of the Pool was to be paid into EAHC/EACSO; the other half was to be allocated equally among the three countries.

Redistribution of income was thus to take two forms. In respect of the financial payment, Kenya was to receive back one-third but actually to pay in more than one-third; in respect of the Common Services Kenya was again to contribute more than one-third and to receive back in the form of services less than one-third, since EACSO services in Tanzania, especially, were subsidized by more economical operations elsewhere. This was due to the fact that the size of Tanzania and the sparseness of population in many areas raised the costs of providing certain public services, especially Revenue Collection and Civil Aviation.

As a result of the Raisman Commission the extra benefit that Kenya was obtaining from the Common Market was not so substantial. In the initial year 1961–2, a comparatively modest redistribution was proposed equivalent to around £600,000, roughly divided between the other two countries; this amount later increased steadily due to increases in customs and company profits tax receipts.

The settlement of 1961–2 did not, however, end discussion, and the strains to which the economic union was subject continued and increased. This was not altogether surprising, since the solution proposed was essentially based on static analysis. Although the other countries were compensated for merely 'supporting' part of Kenya industry, the process of industrialization is cumulative, through external economies in the wide sense, and the other countries were therefore willing to accept merely a redistribution of current benefits, but were anxious to have appropriate shares in development, equated in this case with new industry.

The Kampala Agreement

It was especially the pressure for action regarding the allocation of new industry which led up to the Kampala Agreement, effected at a meeting of Ministers held in April 1964. Under this agreement the imbalance in trade was to be reduced in several ways: by encouraging imports from the deficit countries into Kenya; by persuading existing manufacturers with factories in more than one East African country to expand production in plants outside Kenya; and by applying import quotas for Kenya goods where production in the other countries was capable of expansion. It will be noticed that these measures reflect a preoccupation with the balance of trade, as opposed to the gains from the Common Market.

Moreover, agreement was also reached on the allocation by means of licensing of a short list of six potential industries, three of these being 'awarded' to Tanzania and two to Uganda; a system for inducing and allocating new industries was also to be devised. It was agreed further that an industrial experts committee be set up to draw up a list of potential industries that would require the larger East African market and to examine how these could fairly and rationally be distributed among the three countries. The significance of this is that it might have provided the medium for an extension of the Agreement to cover the long-term situation and thus to have provided an important element of joint planning. Although this redistribution was never implemented it is significant in indicating the direction in which 'planned' industrialization and allocation of industry might have developed within the framework of the Common Market.

Despite the Kampala Agreement, however, dissatisfaction persisted, especially in Tanzania, which had the lowest level of income per head and was particularly anxious to accelerate economic development. Tanzania went on to impose restrictions on a wide range of imports from Kenya, imposing them also on commodities which it was unlikely to be able to produce in the near future. Because of this developing threat to the Common Market, the three countries agreed to set up a full Commission, the Philip Commission, to find a basis under which the Common Market could continue. The lengthy deliberations of the Commission, culminating in the Report, resulted in the signing, in June 1967, of the Treaty which established the East African Community of three states with effect from 1 December 1967.

The treaty for East African cooperation

The most important provisions of the Treaty related to (1) the imposition of transfer taxes, (2) the setting up of an East African Development Bank, (3) the decentralization of the Common Services, and (4) supranational government of the Community.

The system of transfer taxes

The most distinctive feature of the Treaty was the system of transfer taxes which it introduced. Under this sytem the partner states would be permitted to impose transfer taxes or tariffs, against manufactured goods[4] from the other members, but under strict limiting conditions, especially:

(a) Only a country with a balance of trade deficit in its East African trade would be able to impose a transfer tax, and this against a country with which it had a deficit. Since in 1967, at the time of the Treaty, Kenya had a surplus in interstate trade, it would not have been able to impose any transfer taxes.

(b) To impose a transfer tax, a country must either already have the capacity to produce the good in question on a significant scale, or be planning to establish such a capacity.

(c) The number of transfer taxes to be imposed was limited according to the size of the deficit: more precisely taxes could be imposed on imports up to the value of last year's deficit.

(d) The rate of tax could not exceed 50 per cent of the external tariff on the product (equivalent in 1967 to about 15–20 per cent of the import value), so that the level of protection was limited.

(e) No individual tax could be kept on for more than 8 years and the whole system of taxes should end after 15 years. The aim was only to protect 'infant industries' during a transition period, and to protect the 'infant' industrial sectors of Tanzania and Uganda on a temporary basis.

It might be thought that permitting partner states to impose tariffs against each other in this way means the end of a true customs union. But three facts should be kept in mind. First, agreement on transfer taxes permitted the abolition of previous quantitative restrictions on trade, and to that extent meant freer trade. Second, agreement was reached as above, strictly limiting their number (in value terms), and duration. Third, the structure of a customs union, with a common external tariff and free trade except for these limited taxes, was maintained.

The East African Development Bank

To help offset the 'polarization' of industry in the Nairobi area, it was decided to set up a Development Bank which would aim both to raise capital funds for all three countries and to balance up development by investing relatively more in Tanzania and Uganda than in Kenya. In fact just $22\frac{1}{2}$ per cent of total funds was to be invested in Kenya, and $38\frac{3}{4}$ per cent in each of the other two countries. Three question marks were raised against the Bank when it was first set up. Would it succeed in raising finance? Would it succeed in finding enough good commercial projects to invest in (it was not to invest in infrastructural projects)? Would it succeed in finding enough of these in Uganda and Tanzania to operate in the balancing way required?

Some indication of its success is offered in Table 24.3. This shows that while the three countries had agreed to contribute a total of 120 million shillings (40 m shs each) they had been able to attract funds sufficient to approve investments up to 210 m shs. It is possible, of course, that these funds would have been made available anyway as loans to the individual governments if the Bank had not existed; the finance would then have merely been diverted from other channels. Most likely, however, a fair degree of

Table 24.3 The record of the East African Development Bank up to 1973

	Contribution to equity (m shs)	Approved investments (m shs)	Approved investments (%)	Funds disbursed (m shs)	Funds disbursed (%)
Kenya	40.0	—	22	—	36
Uganda	40.0	—	40	—	20
Tanzania	40.0	—	38	—	44
Total	120.0	210.3	100	90.2	100

SOURCE: A Hazlewood, op. cit. Data refer to end February 1973

success can be reported in raising finance. There appears to have been success in finding investments to approve (the difference between approvals and disbursements is due merely to the time required to implement projects). Finally it can be seen that the ratio of projects approved in each country, 22 per cent, for instance, in Kenya, is roughly in line with the policy aim.

The decentralization of the common services

We said earlier that one problem in operating a common market including common services, such as transport, is to see that the costs of and benefits from their operation are fairly distributed among the partner states. Two kinds of benefit are involved. The first is that a service may create employment and incomes. For example the location in Nairobi of the headquarters (including workshops) of the East African Railways and Harbours organization, prior to the Treaty, meant that employment opportunities for Kenyans were created in Nairobi. Wages earned through working for the railways had further 'multiplier' effects on incomes in the area, since they would be spent on other goods supplied locally. The favouring of Kenya in this way was one of the points considered by the Raisman Commission, earlier, in setting up the Distributable Pool. The second benefit is that obtained from the distribution of consumption benefits, that is, benefits derived from the use of the services concerned. For instance Kenya would be reluctant to contribute to the financing of the railways system if the bulk of the traffic carried comprised Tanzanian goods.

The Treaty incorporated a plan to decentralize and relocate the common services organizations as follows. The Railways and Harbours Administration was to be split into two corporate organizations, with the new Ports Corporation Headquarters shifted to Dar es Salaam. East African Posts and Telegraphs would shift from Nairobi to Kampala, which would also receive the new Development Bank. Thus Kenya retained the headquarters of Railways and the East African Airways, which would have been difficult to move; Uganda was allocated Posts and Telegraphs, and the Bank; Tanzania was allocated Ports and, most important, the new capital of the Community at Arusha.

The government of the community

Economic union, as opposed merely to a common market, occurs when to some extent economic decisions are taken jointly, and economic policies pursued jointly. This requires an element at least of joint government, and the establishment of machinery for this was another important part of the Treaty. This was made up of the following components:

(a) the Authority, comprising the Heads of State of the three countries, with full powers to decide issues;

(b) three East African Ministers: instead of the Finance Ministers from the individual governments, these would not represent their national governments, but would act for East Africa irrespective of their country of origin;

(c) three Secretariats, comprising civil servants working under each Minister;

(d) five Councils, covering different aspects of the work of the Community, made up of the three East African Ministers and the Ministers in the appropriate field from the national governments, for the purpose of taking joint decisions;

(e) the East African Legislative Assembly, similar to the old Central Legislative Assembly, comprising 36 members from the three countries, able to debate issues concerning common market affairs, in parliamentary fashion; and

(f) a Common Market Tribunal, a judicial body, which would be able to adjudicate on common market affairs in certain cases in which agreement could not be reached.

Arusha was designated as the 'capital' of the Community, in which these East African 'government' offices would be housed. To have set up this apparatus is itself a considerable achievement, and represented a great commitment to cooperate. On the whole the machinery worked well, if slowly and bureaucratically at times, for some years, though difficulties have multiplied, particularly since the political changes in Uganda in 1971, and her subsequent difficult relations with Tanzania.

Theoretical effects of transfer taxes

It is worth looking more closely at the system of transfer taxes and to consider rather carefully what the effects of such taxes might be. Some thought suggests that, to do this, we should distinguish between 'national' industries, which are viable on the basis of one market, and 'East African' industries which to be economic require free access to the market of two or three of the East African countries.

In the case of national industries, the argument for imposing a transfer tax will be the standard one of protecting an 'infant industry' temporarily, this time against competition from a partner state as well as from overseas. In the case of an East African industry, if the industry already exists in one partner state, this would not apply: since there is already plant capacity in existence capable of supplying the whole East African market, it would hardly pay to set up a second plant and then to protect a national market which is in any case too small (though some duplication of plants has taken place in East Africa nevertheless). Where there is as yet *no* East African plant, however, the system of transfer taxes could bring an advantage to one country through its effects on *locational decisions*. If, for instance, Tanzania has a substantial trade deficit with Kenya, a potential investor would know that by investing in Tanzania he would be free from transfer taxes, since Kenya's trade surplus precludes it from imposing any such taxes: whereas if he sets up his plant in Kenya he may at some future date face a transfer tax on his exports to Tanzania. How important this consideration is, however, is difficult to say: for the investor would know that Tanzania would be prohibited from

imposing this tax until it also establishes a similar plant; and the incentive to do this in respect of an *East African* industry with a plant already in existence would not be great. It is for this reason that the feeling was generally that the transfer tax system would not have a very great impact, during the proposed fifteen years of its life, on industrial development in East Africa.

Trade since the treaty

Did the Treaty strengthen the trading links between the three countries? What happened to trade after the Treaty? Table 24.4 shows that the value of interstate trade in manufactures increased from 690 m shs in 1967 to 855 m shs in 1973. This increase of 24 per cent compares with almost zero per cent between 1964 and 1967, the three years preceding the Treaty. This expansion of trade, it must be stressed again, was not necessarily due to the Treaty or to the customs union, but might have occurred anyway in the course of economic expansion: it was nevertheless a hopeful sign.

The table shows, however, that the balance of interstate trade in manufactures was no less unbalanced overall (keeping in mind, of course, that it is a country's total balance of trade, with all countries, which is more significant): Tanzania's trade balance in manufactures showed roughly the same deficit in 1973 as in 1967, while a small deficit for Uganda had become a substantial one. From Tanzania's point of view, however, there were a number of positive signs: despite industrial expansion in Kenya, Tanzania's deficit had not widened; and the level of Tanzanian exports of manufactures, mainly to Kenya, increased in six years by 130 per cent. The performance of Uganda, on the other hand, was depressing, exports of manufactures having *fallen* by 65 per cent in the same period. Moreover, although the position was aggravated by political events after 1971, a deterioration had already set in before that time. The

Table 24.4 *Interstate trade in manufactures, 1967–73*

		1960	1967	1973
Total interstate trade in manufactures (m shs)		—	690	855
Interstate manufactured exports (m shs):	from Kenya	—	439	670
	from Uganda	—	199	70
	from Tanzania	—	52	115
Balance of trade in manufactures (m shs):	Kenya	—	+238	+503
	Uganda	—	−59	−312
	Tanzania	—	−179	−191
Manufactured exports to other partner states as percentage of imports from other partner states (%):	Uganda	93	77	18
	Tanzania	11	22	38

SOURCE: Hazlewood, op. cit.

balance of trade in manufactures can also be measured in percentage terms, with exports to other partner states as a percentage of imports from the partners: this shows Uganda's position deteriorating from 93 per cent in 1960, to 77 per cent in 1967, and only 18 per cent in 1973; while that for Tanzania increased from a very low 11 per cent in 1960 to 38 per cent in 1973. The 18 per cent for Uganda is an overestimate since there was in 1973 a considerable import trade *into* Uganda, in the form of smuggling, not recorded in the official statistics.

To measure the importance of the trade links between the partner states, however, we really need to compare the volume of interstate trade with that of external trade. Table 24.5 gives this for imports of manufactures (only) and for *all* exports. This shows that Tanzania has been buying an *increasing* proportion of her import requirements of manufactures from her partners (unlike the other countries) and thus has certainly not been taking a specially restrictionist position (though it is possible she could have imported still more from Kenya).The lower part of the table shows, on the other hand, that interstate trade in all products is not very important in Uganda and Tanzania, but substantial (one-quarter) for Kenya. This reflects the dominance of primary product exports in the former countries.

Table 24.5 *Interstate trade as percentage of total trade*

	1960 (%)	1967 (%)	1973 (%)
Imports (manufactures only)			
Kenya	6.5	9	4
Uganda	18	16	9
Tanzania	19	26	37
Exports (all commodities)			
Kenya	28	33	24
Uganda	4	5	7
Tanzania	14	16	4

SOURCE: A. Hazlewood, op. cit.

We can also ask more specifically what have been the effects of the transfer taxes imposed since the Treaty. In 1974 Tanzania levied taxes on about 50 items from Kenya and 30 from Uganda, mostly imposed at the time the Treaty came into effect. In fact it has been calculated that in 1972 Tanzania imposed transfer taxes on only 14 per cent of manufactured goods imports from Kenya and on 3 per cent of those from Uganda; and Tanzanian imports of transfer-taxed goods from Kenya increased at a faster rate after 1967 than did the untaxed ones. Therefore there is no clear evidence that transfer taxes inhibited trade after 1967 to any great extent.

The Common Market and national planning

While the Treaty for East African Cooperation was a historic achievement, it should be appreciated that it fell short of complete economic unification in which planning is carried out on an East African basis rather than a national one. In the former case investment decisions and economic policies would ideally be aimed at maximizing the welfare of all East African citizens, no matter where they were located. The Treaty, however, represented essentially an economic bargain aimed at mutual benefit between three countries still pursuing their own national economic plans.

Moreover the result of the Treaty might be said to be a 'free market' solution in that industries were not allocated directly among the three countries in the way that the Kampala Agreement attempted to do. Firms were quite free otherwise to compete throughout East Africa. There could, of course, be informal agreements, through Arusha, about the allocation of industries.

Monetary and fiscal cooperation in the community

We mentioned above that East Africa had enjoyed a common monetary system since the establishment of the East African Currency Board in 1919 until, in fact, the setting up of three separate central banks in 1966. We shall however postpone to a later chapter a discussion of how far the break-up of this common monetary system represented a set-back to cooperation within the East African Community. It is clear though that the imposition of official restrictions by each of the three governments on the free transfer and exchange of currencies tends to discourage interstate transactions in goods and services as well as the flow of investment funds. If the general public find that it is harder to use, say, the Tanzanian shilling to buy goods in Kenya (because *both* the respective governments prohibit this practice) than to exchange, say, American dollars or sterling pound notes at banks for local currency, then interstate trade is subject to greater difficulty than external trade with non-partner countries. Since the early 1970s importers of goods from partner countries have been subject to increasingly restrictive exchange controls and so have turned to overseas suppliers of goods and services; migrant workers have found it harder to convert their earnings in, say, Uganda shillings, into Tanzania shillings, and even EAC enterprises like

East African Airways refuse to accept local currencies on their flights!

An enlarged East African community

The success of the three East African countries in signing the Treaty for East African Cooperation brought an immediate response from neighbouring countries, so that in November 1968, Burundi, Ethiopia, Somalia, and Zambia all started separate negotiations with the EAC countries for admission to the Common Market. In this they were encouraged also by the UN Economic Commission for Africa who had been pressing for regional economic integration for some years. These applications appear to have come to nothing, eventually, and there have been no formal negotiations at ministerial level since 1970. Nevertheless it is interesting to ask why, and to examine what basis might still exist for some form of regional integration or cooperation in the future. We can consider separately cooperation in industry, agriculture, and transportation, and then additional problems of operating an enlarged community.

Industry

The first point to note is that Burundi and Somalia are in a somewhat different position from Zambia and Ethiopia, being smaller countries and being particularly poor and underdeveloped. However, trade between East Africa and all four applicant countries is insignificant, as shown in Table 24.6.

At present recorded trade is largely confined to exports of manufactured goods and processed foodstuffs from Kenya and Tanzania, with the Zambian market by far the most valuable, taking 4.3 per cent of EAC's external domestic exports in 1970 and accounting for almost 4 per cent of Zambia's total imports. East Africa is also a relatively important supplier of imports to Somalia and Burundi. None of these countries is an important exporter to East Africa, however, and recorded trade with Ethiopia is too small to register in this summary table at all! The level of existing trade reflects the low level of industrial development in these countries (particularly Burundi and Somalia) and secondly the poor communications between them and the EAC countries (particularly Somalia and Ethiopia). The lack of communications means that there exist major *natural* barriers to trade, such that even if the artificial barriers in the form of tariffs were removed trade might not develop. The lack of industrial development means that exports of manufactured goods from the new members to other parts of the enlarged

common market might not develop because these countries lack the productive capacity in manufacturing.

Clearly the present partner states constitute a unified economic region in a way that any enlarged grouping of countries would not. It should be noted that even *within* the three countries of East Africa economic activity is concentrated within a central region embracing south and south-east Uganda, south-west Kenya (from Kisumu to Nairobi) and northern and eastern Tanzania (a more disjointed belt embracing Sukumuland, Arusha, Tanga, and Dar es Salaam). In contrast economic activity in Ethiopia and Somalia is not located in the south of those countries, and is separated from the economically active regions of East Africa by the more remote segments of their own and the East African countries.

Agriculture

In the case of trade and cooperation in agricultural products, it can be argued that there will be more scope in an enlarged community, particularly if communications can be improved. First of all, there will be greater diversity of natural conditions among a larger number of countries, offering a better basis for specialization along the lines of comparative advantage. Secondly, since the number of degrees of latitude from Ethiopia down to Zambia is much greater than that measured by the present partner states, there will at any time be greater seasonal differences between the countries. And thirdly there should be scope for even more cooperation in providing a defence against droughts and famines, since maize could be brought to a disaster area from any one of a number of Eastern African countries, whichever one had a surplus, in order to avoid expensive imports of maize or other foodstuffs from outside the region. Having said that this *potential* for trade exists, however, we must remark that agriculture was the most important area in which cooperation did not develop very far in the *existing* Community, so that, to be realistic, one should not expect much more progress in a wider Community.

Transportation

Thirdly, one may ask to what extent economies of scale or organization might be obtained in operating common transport services on an enlarged basis. For geographical reasons there appears to be little scope here in the case of Ethiopia and Somalia, even after any major transformation of communications in those countries. Burundi at present exports produce through Dar es Salaam, using the East African rail-

Table 24.6 *Visible trade of applicant countries with EAC in 1970*

	(1) Total foreign trade (in US $ m)			(2) Trade with EAC as %			(3) As % of EAC's trade		
	Imports	Exports	Total	Imports	Exports	Total	Imports	Exports	Total
Zambia	502	1,001	1,503	3.8	0.2	1.4	0.2	4.3	2.1
Burundi	22	24	46	6.5	—	3.0	—	0.5	0.2
Somalia	45	31	76	5.0	2.2	4.0	—	0.4	0.2
Ethiopia	172	122	294	—	—	—	—	—	—

SOURCE: *Statistical Abstracts and Economic and Statical Review* (EAC); UN *Statistical Yearbook*, 1971.

way system, and imports goods in the opposite direction: but it might be said to be mainly a 'consumer' of transport services provided by Tanzania rather than a contributor to an enlarged system.

Additional problems

There would be other difficulties involved in expanding membership, though these are not insurmountable ones given a sufficient will to cooperate. First there is the technical one that whereas the existing partner states have had a unified external tariff system for decades as a result of their historical links, the structure of tariffs in the other countries will be rather different. There would be a substantial task of agreeing on an appropriate set of external tariffs for the new customs union, keeping in mind that each tariff may protect an industry in one or two countries in part at the expense of the consumer in the other states. Secondly, it may be noted that the day-to-day running of the Community involved a consider-

able bureaucratic apparatus, with regular and expensive meetings of representatives of the three countries. The *administrative* problem of running an efficient enlarged Community would be great.

The country which could most easily be brought into the Community is, however, Zambia. It is a much richer country, in a position to use its huge foreign exchange earnings from copper to finance an industrial development programme. The Tanzam Railway, linking Lusaka and Dar es Salaam, and the new major road link between the countries, considerably reduce the natural transport barrier to trade between the countries, though certainly do not eliminate it. There should be scope for the export of agricultural products from Tanzania which is agriculturally much more diversified. And there are obvious economies of scale and organization in relation to the operation of the Tanzam Railway. At the same time Zambia will have alternative links to the sea through the independent countries of Angola and Mozambique, which must weaken her interest in looking northwards.

Questions on Chapter 24

1. What is the difference between the following: a customs union; a free trade area; a common market; and an economic union?
2. Explain the meaning of trade creation and trade diversion due to a customs union.
3. What sort of calculations should a developing country make (a) in deciding whether to join a common market, and (b) in deciding whether to leave it? Would the calculations be the same?
4. (a) How may a single country gain from membership of a customs union?
   (b) How may all partners gain from such membership? Illustrate with reference to the customs union between Kenya, Uganda, and Tanzania.
5. What conclusions can be drawn about costs and benefits in a common market from figures of the balance of visible trade?
6. Why should strains have developed in maintaining the East African Common Market *after* the independence of the three member countries?
7. How far did the transfer tax system mean the end of a customs union in East Africa?
8. What indications exist that the East African Development Bank might turn out a successful institution?
9. What theoretical effects would you expect the East African system of transfer taxes to have? What do you think the effects have been so far?
10. Discuss the effects of natural barriers to trade on the operation of a customs union.
11. Discuss the economics of a wider East African Community.

Notes

[1] This chapter draws heavily on A. Hazlewood, *Economic Integration: the East African Experience*, Heinemann Educational Books, 1975.

[2] Since the 1967 Treaty separated into two parastatal enterprises, the East African Railways Corporation and the East African Ports Corporation.

[3] *East Africa, Report of the Economic and Fiscal Commission*, February 1961, London, HMSO, Cmd. 1279.

[4] Interstate trade in some agricultural commodities, notably maize, was also subject to quantitative restrictions.

Part VII Money and aggregate demand

25 Money and Credit

We compared the 'market economy' or 'money economy' with the subsistence economy in Chapter 5. In a subsistence economy people consume what they have themselves produced and exchange nothing. In a market economy exchange may take two forms, direct exchange (barter) or indirect, using a means of payment or 'medium of exchange'. We noted that barter involves such inconvenience that at a comparatively early stage in the development of an economy we should expect a medium of exchange, money, to come into use. Let us examine how money has evolved into its complicated present-day form.

The functions of money

The most important function of money is to act as a *medium of exchange*. In order to perform this function it must be *generally* acceptable as payment: one individual will not accept a form of money as payment unless he is confident that he can in turn dispose of it in payment of his own debts. Money is, in fact, anything that is generally acceptable in settlement of a debt.

However, money also acts as a *standard of value*, that is, as a unit of account for present and future payments. This is because money provides a common basis for calculating rates of exchange between all goods and services. Exchange is thus helped not only by the physical use of money but also by the fact that everything can be given a price in terms of money and its relative value measured to one standard.

Usually the unit of account and unit of exchange are the same. We measure our total income in terms of pounds or dollars instead of in so much corn, meat, clothing, and so on, because we use those currency units and related smaller denominations as means of payment. But this is not always the case. For example, the basic currency unit in Kenya is the shilling, and all bank cheques are drawn in terms of this unit. But since many people think in terms of pounds, larger transactions are often quoted in pounds, not shillings.

The second function of money as a standard of value is its use as a standard of deferred payment. Contracts are made involving payment, either for goods or services to be supplied in the future or in repayment of loans, including interest charges. These are normally stated in money terms. Although some economists distinguish this feature of money as a separate function it is essentially the use of money as a unit of account over time. Money may fulfil this second accounting function less effectively, however, if the value of money changes over time in real terms.

The third function of money is as a *store of value* or wealth, since means of payment may be accumulated for future spending. Money is convenient for this purpose (1) because it is liquid, that is, can readily be transferred into other forms of wealth; (2) because it involves no costs of storage; and (3) because it carries a low risk of physical deterioration although, as we have pointed out, it may change in real value, in terms of purchasing power.

The development of money

We can now see how various forms of money have come to perform these functions. For this, any form of money must not only be generally acceptable but also in order to act as a medium of exchange, it must be transportable; to act as a unit of account, it must be divisible; and to act as a store of value, it must be durable. For the early forms of money the intrinsic value of commodities provided the basis for general acceptability: for instance, corn, salt, tobacco, or cloth were widely used because they had obvious value *in themselves*. We can refer to these as *commodity-money*. Cattle have also long been used as money, and not only in Africa. In fact the Latin word, *pecunia*, meaning money, is derived from the word *pecus* meaning cattle, so the use of cattle to settle debts is not new. Cattle have an obvious advantage in transportability. In Africa they are still used as a unit of account in valuing brides (bride-price) and as a means of payment for them.

A particular type of commodity which has been used from very early times is the various forms of decoration, seashells, beads, but especially precious metal and stones. The latter, being particularly scarce, came to have very high values and therefore to be particularly acceptable as exchange media. Most monetary systems indeed still have some link, however loose, with gold. Gold is particularly durable, much more so than the commodities mentioned above, and, in the form of gold coins especially, is more easily divisible and transportable. As gold and, to a lesser extent, silver became the most general medium of exchange, so the state took over the minting of coins. It was readily apparent, however, that what was important was public confidence in the 'currency' of money, its ability to run from hand to hand and circulate freely, rather than its intrinsic value. As a result, there tended to follow the *debasement* of the coinage, whereby the metallic content of the coins was deliberately reduced below the face value of the coinage. Any person receiving such a coin could afford not to mind, so long as he was confident that anyone to whom he passed on the coin would also 'not mind'. Debasement represents an early form of fiduciary issue, dependent on the 'faith' of the public, since it permitted the extension of the supply of money beyond the available quantities of gold and silver. This faith depended, of course, on the state guaranteeing to limit the supply of coinage thus debased.

If coins are acceptable even when their intrinsic (or alternative use) value does not equal their nominal value, it is an easy step to the acceptability of paper money. For while the good faith of the issuing authority is involved in both cases, paper money is much more transportable, durable (since it can be replaced with little cost if it becomes dirty or tattered), and it can be made as divisible as the issuing authority cares to make it. The important requirement is that the government must, as always, ensure limited availability of supply, first by supervising the banks which issue notes, and secondly by preventing forgeries!

An examination of the way in which paper money has evolved will help us with our main objective, which is to understand the operation of the modern banking system. The development of paper money is closely bound up with the growth of banking in Europe and the Americas since the seventeenth century. Members of the public who owned such valuables as gold coin, plate, and ornaments would deposit these for safe keeping with goldsmiths and other reliable merchants in return for a receipt. The receipts issued by the goldsmiths were, in effect, promises to repay a stated value of gold at such future time as the depositor cared to reclaim it. Since the gold was much less portable than the paper receipt issued by the goldsmith, so long as the reputation of the goldsmith was sufficient to ensure acceptability of his 'promise to pay', it became convenient for the depositor to pass on the goldsmith's receipt if he wished to make payment to a third party. Thus the basic principle underlying the operation of the modern monetary system, the faith of public in the currency, was already invoked.

It was quickly obvious to the goldsmiths that in any period they would only be asked to refund a proportion of the gold deposited with them, and that they could safely issue receipts in excess of their gold deposits. They found, in other words, that a hundred per cent gold backing was not necessary to retain the confidence of the public. They could therefore issue notes to borrowers, who would use them to finance transactions, undertaking to repay the amount borrowed with interest; thus considerably increasing the profitability of the goldsmiths' operations. It is at this stage that the early goldsmith-bankers can be said to have been 'creating money': for the value of receipts in circulation could now exceed the amount of gold 'withdrawn from circulation' by the goldsmiths. The additional receipts issued did, however, mean an increase in the liabilities of the bankers, since they could be presented for repayment at any time. These liabilities were balanced by interest-earning assets: but it was still necessary for liabilities to be 'backed' by a sufficient reserve of gold.

The early merchant banks developed along the lines described above. There were plenty of cases of banks overreaching themselves, backing too high a proportion of notes with risky, if lucrative, loans. But even the most prudent bank could fail if there was a general collapse of confidence in the banks, however unjustified. It is not surprising that governments introduced increasing control over the operations of commercial banks in order to reduce the likelihood of crises of confidence in the banking system. In Britain the Bank Charter Act of 1844 gave the Bank of England the sole right of issue in England and Wales; however, the notes of some Scottish banks remain in circulation even today.

Bank deposits

Bank notes and coin together constitute the *currency* in circulation. But they form only a part of the total money supply today. This is because payments are now widely made by cheque, leaving notes and coin to service mainly smaller day-to-day transactions. The larger part of the money supply in circulation today consists of *bank deposits*. If a commercial bank makes a loan to a customer, for example, the bank simply writes in the stated sum on the credit side of the customer's account and then allows him to write cheques up to this amount. When a cheque is paid in by the recipient the payer's credit at the bank will be reduced and the payee's credit at this or some other bank increased. The bank deposit will thus have been transferred in settlement of debt as a book transaction. If bank deposits are used to effect transactions in this way, they are part of the money supply: for money is simply anything that is generally accepted as a means of payment. Moreover these bank deposits will have been largely *created* by the banks, like part of the goldsmith-bankers' receipts, since only a fraction of total bank deposits need actually be covered by cash holdings.

It should be noted that cheques are *not* money. An individual's cheque is useless, in fact, if that individual has 'nothing in the bank', if, that is, he has no deposits against his name. Nor is a cheque always accepted as a means of payment for the very reason that the recipient cannot be certain that the payer has deposits with which to pay. A cheque is simply an instruction to the bank to transfer deposits from one account to another, or to pay currency to the drawer.

One of the reasons why it is not immediately obvious that bank deposits are money is that they are not *legal tender*. We should therefore specify what is meant by legal tender. Legal tender is money which must by law be accepted in settlement of a debt within the country concerned, and this will normally comprise only the notes and coin issued by the Central Bank or Currency Authority of that country. But legal recognition is not necessary for general acceptability by the public, nor is it always sufficient. Thus the old Maria Theresa dollar circulated freely for over 100 years in the Middle East and with Indian silver rupees in parts of East Africa also before Currency Boards were established. Nowadays the American dollar and other desirable foreign currencies are readily accepted, often illegally, especially when the legal tender is discredited by inflation.

Having established that commercial bank deposits are money, we should note that they are of two kinds: *demand deposits*, corresponding to customers' 'current accounts', and *term deposits*, on which interest is paid because they cannot be withdrawn so easily 'on demand'. Term deposits are usually of two main types, also: *time deposits*, corresponding to customers' 'deposit accounts' and *savings deposits* or 'savings accounts'. Only demand deposits can be freely transferred by cheque or converted into cash on demand 'on sight'; and they earn no interest. Interest is paid on time deposits, varying normally with the time to be deposited and the notice required before withdrawal. In fact most banks will honour cheques so long as a customer has a credit balance in a time deposit account so that these deposits have a claim to be a medium of exchange, part of the money supply. Savings deposits may be similarly regarded as money, because the mainly small depositors can usually obtain cash on presentation of their account book at the banks. Both kinds of term deposit are often referred to as 'near money' or 'quasi money'.

A country's money supply may therefore be defined very narrowly, excluding term deposits, or more broadly. The narrow definition of money comprises:

(a) notes and coins (the currency) held by the general public *outside* the commercial banks; and

(b) *private* demand deposits of commercial banks.

A broader definition of the money supply which is sometimes used includes also in addition to the above:

(c) private term deposits or 'quasi money'.[1]

To distinguish this from the narrow definition of *money supply* comprising currency and demand deposits, the term *volume of money* is often used when private term deposits are added. In Eastern Africa the official definition of 'money supply' comprises items (a) and (b), with 'volume of money' sometimes used, to cover (a), (b), and (c).

The process of credit creation: a single bank model

We stated above that a large proportion of bank deposits were created by banks, in that they were not covered by an equivalent amount of cash held by the banks. We need to look more closely at how money, or bank credit in this case, is created, and especially what limits exist to the process of creating bank deposits. To simplify matters, we shall first take a hypothetical situation, in which a country has only a single banking firm, albeit with numerous branches.

Let us assume that our bank, like the goldsmiths described earlier, has found from experience that it needs only to hold 10 per cent of cash as a proportion of total deposits. This percentage will, in a normal situation, represent the proportion of transactions that customers prefer to settle by means of cash, rather than cheque.

An imaginary balance sheet for the bank is presented in Table 25.1. Deposits are shown as liabilities, since the bank can be called up to repay in cash any amounts credited to customers in this way.

Table 25.1   *Initial position of a single bank*

Liabilities	£×1,000	Assets	£×1,000
Deposits	1,000	Cash	100
		Loans	900
Total	1,000	Total	1,000

Assets consist of cash held by the bank, plus loans, which represent the obligations of borrowers towards the bank. The *cash ratio* is the ratio of cash held (£100,000) to its liabilities (£1,000,000), and is 10 per cent in this case.

Suppose now a customer deposits an additional £20,000 in cash. Deposits go up to £1,020,000, and on the asset side, cash held increases to £120,000. The ratio of cash to total deposits (liabilities) in this initial position will be, as shown in Table 25.2, $\frac{120}{1,020} \times 100$ or 11.8 per cent. This is unnecessarily high, nearly 12 per cent compared to the conventional ratio of 10 per cent. The bank can therefore safely make additional interest-bearing loans. If it lends an extra £180,000, accordingly, deposits will rise from £1,020,000 to £1,200,000, so that the 10 per cent ratio of cash to deposits is restored. The final position is shown in Table 25.3, which indicates that bank deposits have been created to the extent of ten times the new cash deposit.

Table 25.2   *Addition of cash deposit raises cash reserves and cash ratio*

Liabilities	£×1,000	Assets	£×1,000
Deposits	1,020	Cash	120
		Loans	900
Total	1,020	Total	1,020

This is a stable position. Borrowers will make out cheques to other people in payment for goods and services supplied. But these others must be customers of the same bank, since there is only one bank. There will follow no more than a book transaction within one bank, the bank deposits being transferred from one customer to another. Total deposits, total cash, and the cash ratio will not be affected.

Comparing the initial position in Table 25.1 with the final position in Table 25.3, we see that the increase in bank deposits, which we can call ΔD, is 200 and the increase in cash held by the banks, which we can write as ΔC, is 20. Thus ΔD is ten times ΔC, obviously because $\frac{1}{r}$, where r is the cash ratio used, is 10. Thus $\Delta D = \frac{\Delta C}{r}$.

Table 25.3   *Restoration of convential cash ratio by creation of additional bank deposits*

Liabilities	£×1,000	Assets	£×1,000
Deposits	1,200	Cash	120
		Loans	1,080
Total	1,200	Total	1,200

The process of credit creation: many banks

Since the case of a single bank with a 'monopoly' of credit creation is rarely found in the real world, let us now extend our example to take account of a multi-bank system. Suppose the bank receiving the new deposit of £20,000 in cash is now one of several independent banks. This time the bank will not seek immediately to expand deposits to ten times this amount, by extending loans. It will know that the borrowers will use the credit granted to them to pay for goods or services, or to repay debts; and that therefore they will be making cheques out to other individuals *who may now have accounts in other banks*. The bank can thus expect to lose cash to other banks. Either the borrowers will withdraw cash directly, with which to pay individuals who then deposit this cash with other banks; or if they pay by cheque these cheques will be deposited with other banks, and the other banks themselves will present them for cash at the first bank. Only if borrowers make cheques to individuals who have accounts with the *same* bank will there be no drain of cash. Suppose the first bank made the extreme assumption that *none* of the new borrowers' cheques would be paid to its own customers. It will create only a relatively small amount of extra deposits, just sufficient to restore its cash ratio. It will, in fact, make £18,000 worth of additional loans and retain cash of £2,000. That this will restore its cash ratio can be seen from Table 25.4.

However, the £18,000 lost in cash through cheques drawn by borrowers will be received by other banks who in turn will find themselves with excess cash reserves, and in turn create additional loans. There will thus be a second generation of bank deposit creation, each bank again retaining only 10 per cent of the new cash received, and creating loans in the ratio of nine to one. This new drain of cash will generate more deposits, and so on, each new round being nine-tenths of the value of the previous one as follows (in £'000s):

$$20 + 18 + 16.20 + 14.58 + 13.12 + \ldots$$

which can be written as

$$20\left\{1 + \frac{9}{10} + \left(\frac{9}{10}\right)^2 + \left(\frac{9}{10}\right)^3 + \left(\frac{9}{10}\right)^4 + \ldots\right.$$

Each successive round of deposit creation is smaller than the previous one, so that the series *converges*. The mathematicians can tell us that the series will eventually add up or converge to 200. They state that, for any value of Z between 0 and 1 the series

$$1 + Z + Z^2 + Z^3 + \ldots$$

Table 25.4   *Initial round of credit creation by first bank*

	Liabilities (£×1,000)	Assets (£×1,000)		Cash ratio
	Deposits	Cash	Loans	%
Original position	1,000	100	900	10.0
Add cash deposit	+20	+20	—	—
Second position	1,020	120	900	11.8
Increase loans	+18	—	+18	—
Cash drain by cheques	−18	−18	—	—
Final position	1,020	102	918	10.0
Net change	+20	+2	+18	—

tends to the value $\dfrac{1}{1-Z}$.

In our example $Z = \dfrac{9}{10}$, which is between 0 and 1, so the formula applies. Hence

$$20\left\{1 + \frac{9}{10} + \left(\frac{9}{10}\right)^2 + \left(\frac{9}{10}\right)^3 + \ldots\right\} = 20\left\{\frac{1}{1-\frac{9}{10}}\right\} = 200$$

If we use ΔD to refer to the final increase or increment in bank deposits, ΔC to the initial increase in cash received, and 'r' to the cash ratio, then $\Delta D = 200$, $\Delta C = 20$, and $r = \dfrac{1}{10}$. Since $1 - r = 1 - \dfrac{1}{10} = \dfrac{9}{10}$, we have

$$\Delta D = \Delta C\{1 + (1-r) + (1-r)^2 + (1-r)^3 + \ldots\}$$
$$= \frac{\Delta C}{1-(1-r)} = \frac{\Delta C}{r}.$$

Given the increase in cash received, the additional deposits created will depend on the fraction of cash retained as backing. The ratio $\dfrac{\Delta D}{\Delta C}$ of deposits created to increase in cash is referred to as the *bank deposit multiplier*.

The result, of course, is the same as in the case of a single bank. Taken as a whole, they have together received an additional £20,000 in cash and can afford additional loans of £180,000. The credit expansion will be shared among the various banks in proportion to the cash retained by each one out of the additional £20,000. This will roughly correspond to the volume of business handled by each one, smaller banks finding that they retain a correspondingly small proportion of the new cash.

It should be noted that a cash transfer between banks is not necessary each time a customer of, say, Bank A deposits a cheque from another bank, say, B. This is because customers of Bank B will at the same time be depositing cheques from Bank A. A large part of the value of cheques will thus cancel out, and it will only be necessary for the *difference* in the value of cheques presented to be met by a cash transfer. Officials from each bank will thus meet regularly to exchange cheques. In fact, even a cash transfer need not be necessary, since the central bank normally acts as banker to all the commercial banks. The deficit bank can thus write a cheque to the other on its account with the central bank, and a book transfer will take place to settle the debt.

What, if anything, limits the process of bank deposit creation? On the demand side, there may be a lack of demand for loans, or at least a lack of borrowers who are sufficiently credit-worthy. We assumed above that banks receiving an increase in cash have no trouble in finding enough credit-worthy borrowers, and expanding credit and the volume of bank deposits to the extent indicated by the bank deposit multiplier. On the supply side, we must recognize that our example, based on a new cash deposit by a member of the public, was rather artificial. The volume of bank deposits will not in general rise and fall as a result of changes in the amount of cash held or deposited by the public, since the public's currency requirements tend to be fairly stable, and roughly proportional to the volume of transactions. The example does show that the money supply will vary with the amount of cash held by the commercial banks, so long as the latter adopt a constant cash ratio. As we shall see, the government, operating through the central bank, is in a position to control the cash reserves held by the commercial banks. So long, therefore, as the commercial banks stick to a conventional cash ratio, their role will be a passive one, and the money supply will be fully determined by the central bank.

The money supply multiplier

Because bank deposits constitute the larger part of the money supply, we used the *bank deposit multiplier* to explain the process of money creation. Apart from the assumptions already mentioned, we assumed the general public were content to hold the same amount of cash throughout, although bank credit, bank deposits, and general economic activity have expanded. If we assume, more realistically, that the public's demand for currency changes in the same direction and roughly in proportion to the change in bank deposits, then we need to amend the bank deposit multiplier equation, $\Delta D = \dfrac{\Delta C}{r}$. Suppose the public like to keep the ratio of currency with the public, C_p, to deposits, D, at some given level c, where $c = C_p/D$. This time, in addition to the leakage of cash to other banks, there will be an additional leakage of cash to the public as deposits are increased. The equation above will be

$$\Delta D = \Delta C\{1 + (1 - r - c) + (1 - r - c)^2 + \ldots\}$$
$$= \frac{\Delta C}{1 - (1 - r - c)} = \frac{\Delta C}{r + c}$$

where c and r represent respectively the bank's cash ratio and the public's cash ratio. The modified bank deposit multiplier is $\Delta D = \dfrac{\Delta C}{r + c}$, where C represents the total currency issued by the central bank (the 'cash base') and is the sum of holdings by the public, C_p, and by the banks, C_b.

This tells us how the volume of *bank deposits* is affected by an increase in the cash base. But currency can constitute a major component of the money supply, especially in poor countries where a large proportion of the population do not have ready access to banks. Hence it is not sufficient to discuss the volume of bank deposits: we need to discuss the determination of the money supply, including cash. The total increase in the money supply after an increase in the cash base can be taken as the sum of the increase in currency with the public and the increase in bank deposits, that is:

$$\Delta M = \Delta C_p + \Delta D$$

Since $C_p = cD$, $\Delta C_p = c\Delta D$ (the ratio will be held constant as C_p and D increase in proportion). Hence $\Delta M = c\Delta D + \Delta D = (1 + c)\,\Delta D$. From our equation for the modified bank deposit multiplier, this gives

$$\Delta M = \left(\frac{1 + c}{r + c}\right)\Delta C$$

This gives the increase in money supply, comprising both bank deposits and cash with the public, as a multiple of the value of the injection of additional cash, ΔC, assuming a given bank cash ratio, c, and the public's currency to bank deposits ratio, r. ΔM may be termed the *money supply multiplier*. The bank deposit multiplier calculated above is an approximation to this under certain simplifying assumptions.

As just mentioned, the public's cash ratio is likely to be quite high in an underdeveloped country: around 0.4 (40 per cent) in Kenya in recent years, for example, and as much as 1.0 for very underdeveloped monetary and banking systems like Ethiopia's. If we assume typical values of, say, r = 0.1 and c = 0.4, then the modified *deposit multiplier* will be $\dfrac{1}{0.1 + 0.4} = 2.0$, and the total *money supply multiplier* will be $\dfrac{1 + 0.4}{0.1 + 0.4} = 2.8$. Thus the issue of additional currency by the central bank of £20, to take our original example, will involve an expansion of bank deposits of $£\dfrac{20}{0.1 + 0.4} = £40$ with the modified deposit multiplier, and an increase in the public's holding of currency equal to $c\Delta D$ or £(0.4)40 = £16. This £16 of currency with the public must be added to the extra deposits of £40 to arrive at the increase in the total money supply of $£56 = £20\left(\dfrac{1 + 0.4}{0.1 + 0.4}\right)$.

Thus far we have (1) defined the money supply as $M = C_p + D$; (2) defined the currency issued by the central bank, or cash base, as $C = C_p + C_b$, and (3) found that under certain assumptions changes in the money supply will be $\Delta M = \left(\dfrac{1 + c}{r + c}\right)\Delta C$, where r and c are taken to be constant. In fact the latter ratios may not remain constant, at least in the short term. The public's cash ratio may vary, expecially seasonally, as the result of crop payments or in anticipation of holiday spending. Banks may not be able to stick to a rigid cash ratio if there is no unsatisfied demand for credit from acceptable borrowers. The banks may also be able to augment their cash reserves independently of central bank action, so that they do not react completely passively to changes in the cash base. Nevertheless the above analysis provides a necessary step in explaining how the money supply is determined in any monetary system.

Cash ratios and liquidity ratios

In the above analysis the amount of money 'created' by the commercial banks depends on their cash holdings and the cash ratio, r, to which they conform. So long as the commercial banks aim at a fixed cash ratio, the central bank can control the money supply by varying the cash holdings of commercial banks. In addition to cash reserves, holdings of other liquid assets—assets which are 'liquid' in that they can readily be converted into cash—by commercial banks provide another way for the central bank to exercise control.[2] Commercial banks may be required to keep a certain proportion of liquid assets as well as, or instead of, a certain proportion of cash, so that the *liquidity ratio* of banks may be more important than the *cash ratio*. In this case the liquidity ratio would play the sort of role that 'c' plays in the bank deposit multiplier above.

Questions on Chapter 25

1. How would you define money? What are the main functions of money?
2. Distinguish carefully between the following: currency, cheques, bank deposits, the money supply, the volume of money, legal tender, quasi money.
3. How do commercial banks 'create credit'? What are the limits to this credit creation?
4. How does the bank deposit multiplier operate to expand the money supply?
5. Explain the money supply multiplier process. What assumptions have to be made before it can provide a useful explanation of how the money supply is determined in any monetary system?
6. Why is the public's cash ratio generally higher in a less developed country? How will this affect the money supply multiplier? Discuss the significance of this effect.
7. Why do commercial banks compete for customers' deposits as well as for credit-worthy borrowers?

Notes

[1] These are distinguished from government and other public sector deposits of all kinds which are used to effect transactions but not generally included as money.

[2] Apart from notes and coin and balances with the central bank (the cash reserves), the main liquid assets held by banks in Eastern Africa are Treasury bills and balances with other banks. In the case of British commercial banks, as we shall see in the next chapter, the so-called reserve asset ratio, employed since 1971 and equal to $12\frac{1}{2}$ per cent of sterling deposit liabilities, is made up of balances with the Bank of England, Treasury bills, government and local authority stocks redeemable within five years and an important item not found in Eastern Africa, 'money at call' to the discount market.

26 Central Banking and Monetary Policy in Africa

We saw previously that control of the money supply extends back to the central bank or other monetary authority, although this in turn is invariably owned or controlled by the government. There were already thirty central banks in Africa in 1975. Let us examine more closely the functions of central banks in African countries, and the scope of the monetary policy tools which they now have, or could develop, to control the financial systems that are still evolving in the different countries.[1]

Functions of a central bank

The most important functions of a central bank are:

(1) Responsibility for the issue of currency, the nation's legal tender.

(2) (a) Acting as the bankers' bank (i) by accepting deposits from the commercial banks and (ii) standing by as a 'lender of last resort' in the event of their needing additional cash to satisfy their customers or to adhere to any cash or liquidity reserve requirements. This function enables the central bank to control the cash base of the banking system, and thus the money supply.

(b) Supervising the commercial banks and other financial institutions in order to maintain confidence in the country's financial system.

(3) Acting as banker and financial adviser to the government, satisfying the credit needs of the public sector, and managing its Public Debt.

(4) Responsibility for any regulation of, and intervention in, foreign exchange markets, including the administration of exchange controls (major decisions such as that of devaluing the currency must of course lie with the government).

The scope for the exercise of these functions and the institutional structure in which they operate will vary. In Britain, for example, where the Bank of England was originally not only banker to the government but also competed for ordinary customers with other bankers, there are still a few private customers, other than commercial banks, who maintain deposits. Among these are bill-brokers and discount houses, dealers in Treasury bills and trade bills using short-term funds borrowed from

commercial banks and other lenders in the 'discount market'. They are also privileged in being able to resort to the Bank of England for 'loans of last resort' and act as intermediaries in implementing the monetary policies of the Bank. In Australia and Ethiopia, to take two examples, the central banks had commercial offshoots, set up to compete with other commercial banks. In the USA there are actually twelve central banks, each covering a geographical district but together comprising the Federal Reserve System with a Board of Governors, which assumes the regulatory role of a central bank. Not all US commercial banks are members of this System, though 80 per cent of total bank deposits are now with such 'members' banks. The New York Reserve Bank is the largest, with about one-quarter of all the central banks' assets and responsible to the Board for the principal operations in foreign exchange and international financial transactions. The sheer size and variety of the USA is said to require a decentralized central banking system not needed in small compact countries with a single financial centre like the City of London, or Nairobi, where the Governor of the central bank can exercise persuasion over leading members of the financial community over lunch! To take another example, the central bank in Japan enforces its control over commercial banks not so much as 'lender of last resort' on the British model but as an important primary lender or lender of 'first resort'. The Japanese commercial banks are thus very dependent on central bank credit for their own credit creation, and can be squeezed easily not only in respect of overall credit but also in respect of the direction of loans to particular sectors or even enterprises.

In the Commonwealth countries of Africa, new national central banks have only recently inherited the various functions previously performed by Currency Boards and by expatriate banking firms, and it will be some years before they can exercise the same kind of influence over their financial systems as that enjoyed by 'old' central banks. The fundamental constraint on central banking operations is imposed more by the underdeveloped character of the economies with which they are dealing than by their relative recency as institutions. To illustrate the basis of a monetary system it will be useful to examine the situation first in a developed country, and the main methods of monetary management in such a country. After that we can examine how central banking and monetary policy can be made effective in less developed countries such as those in Eastern Africa.

The Bank of England and the 'pyramid' of money

Table 26.1 provides a very simplified picture of the structure of the British monetary system in 1972, to which we shall refer in explaining how monetary policy tools are operated in a developed monetary system. It will also be used to compare with the Eastern African monetary systems as they have evolved.

The upper part of the table shows that *the total money supply*, equal to £26,000 millions, held by the public, *consisted mainly of bank deposits*: only £4,000 millions, or 15 per cent, was currency.

The middle part of the table summarizes the com-

bined balance sheets of all 'credit-creating' commercial banks. Liabilities consisted of bank deposits valued at £22,000 millions. Of these just under 40 per cent were private demand deposits, the rest being mainly private time and savings deposits, but including a small proportion of public sector deposits. The difference between demand and time deposits is not very great. A customer can obtain cash on demand against demand deposits and can make payments by cheque with them, whereas in principle he must give a short period of notice in order to withdraw cash against a time deposit. As discussed in the last chapter, because only demand deposits are subject to cheque, there is a narrower definition of the money supply which comprises only currency and demand deposits, here equal to £13,500 millions. However it is the total of all deposits which is subject to the multiple effects of changes in the banks' reserve assets or reserve asset ratios, so we have adopted the broader definition of money in our table. This is called the *volume of money* in some modern textbooks and central bank reviews.[2]

Table 26.1   *The structure of bank credit and the currency system in the United Kingdom in 1972*

£ millions

VOLUME OF MONEY WITH NON-BANK PUBLIC: UNITED KINGDOM, DEC. 1972
comprising
22,000: BANK DEPOSITS plus CURRENCY: 4,000
is   26,000
of which demand deposits (8,500) and currency (4,000) equals the MONEY SUPPLY
12,500

COMMERCIAL BANKS:

	Liabilities	Assets:		
8,500	Demand deposits	Currency notes and coins (as 'till money')		700
		Cash deposits at Bank of England	220	
		Other reserve assets	2,780	
		Total reserve assets		3,000
13,500	Other deposits	Special deposits		120
		Investments in Government securities	3,880	
		Advances	14,300	
		Total risk assets		18,180
22,000	Total deposits	Total assets		22,000

BANK OF ENGLAND AND ROYAL MINT

		Liabilities	Assets:		
	20	Public deposits	Government securities	490	
	220	Bankers' deposits	Advances and other accounts	40	
	120	Special deposits	Other assets	70	
	240	Other accounts			
600		Total banking liabilities	Banking assets		600
	4,350	Bank of England notes	Government securities	4.250	
	350	Royal Mint coins	Other securities	450	
4,700		Total currency issue	Total currency asset cover		4,700
5,300		Total liabilities	Total assets		5,300

SOURCE: *Bank of England Quarterly Bulletin*

Against these liabilities the banks held a 'portfolio' of assets, seen on the right-hand side of the table. Before 1971 British commercial banks were expected to meet a normal cash reserve ratio of 8 per cent, so that the sum of 'cash deposits at the Bank of England' (considered as good as cash) and currency held as 'till money'[3] would have been roughly equal to 8 per cent of total deposits. In 1965, for instance, these equalled £784 millions compared to total deposits of £10,000 millions, very close to 8 per cent. Now these equal £920 millions, only 4.2 per cent of total deposits, indicating that the cash ratio is no longer considered so important. Since 1971 the commercial banks have been required to maintain 'reserve assets' at a level of $12\frac{1}{2}$ per cent of deposit liabilities. These no longer include 'till money' but include bankers' deposits at the Bank of England and various liquid assets, including short-dated government and other public authority bonds which carry little risk and can be sold for cash quite readily. The ratio of reserve assets to total deposits in 1972 can be calculated to be 13.63 per cent, just over the required $12\frac{1}{2}$ per cent. Once this liquidity requirement is fulfilled, banks are free to invest in longer-dated government securities and to make 'advances' or loans to business firms and other customers at more profitable rates of interest. Thus banks held 'reserve assets' of £3,000 millions and 'risk assets' of £18,180 millions. Banks are, of course, commercial enterprises in a capitalist system, and largely make their profits from the interest on these risk assets. The government, or central bank, controls this urge, through the liquidity ratio, so that public confidence in the banks, and the money supply, is maintained. The reason for the switch of emphasis to liquidity ratios was that it was thought that efforts to squeeze bankers' cash reserves and thus restrict the money supply would not be effective so long as excess liquid assets existed which could be easily converted into cash.

The lower part of Table 26.1 illustrates the key position of the Bank of England. The Royal Mint is in effect performing part of the function of a central bank, responsible for the minting of coins as required, to supplement notes issued by the Bank of England. The bulk of the liabilities of the Bank of England are in fact notes and coins with the public (£4,000 millions) or commercial banks (£700 millions). There were some deposit liabilities in addition, comprising positive balances held by various customers in accounts at the Bank of England. 'Public deposits' represent the working balances of the government, and are usually quite small: £20 millions in this case. 'Bankers' deposits' are the balances held at the Bank by commercial banks, already mentioned among their reserve assets. 'Special deposits' are similar to these, but represent compulsory deposits owned by commercial banks but 'frozen' by the Bank of England to reduce the liquidity of the banks, as we explain presently. The 'other accounts' include balances of non-bank financial institutions and overseas depositors and need not concern us here.

While the bulk of the liabilities of the Bank of England is paper currency, this paper currency has no intrinsic value and, of course, the coinage is debased, no longer containing valuable metals such as gold or silver, so that it also has negligible value in itself. Paper currency and coinage are similar to the receipts issued by our goldsmith-bankers, and together represent the 'currency liabilities' of the state. What assets are held against these? Not gold. Out of the total 'central banking' liability of £5,300 millions, £4,740 millions are 'government securities', that is, *government debt*. Most of the remaining £560 millions also represents government debt in the form of coins issued by the Mint. The total currency issued of £4,700 is a 'fiduciary' issue covered by nothing more than 'good faith' in the government. Any time that there is an increase in the public demand for currency, passed back through withdrawals affecting the cash reserves of the commercial banks and from the commercial banks of the Bank of England, the latter issues more currency as required through its Issue Department, which receives government securities to an equivalent value, to 'balance its books'. Thus the confidence of the public in the £26,000 millions of the money supply is based on commercial bank reserve assets which can readily be converted into currency, as well as the currency issue itself which represents obligations or liabilities of the central bank. These liabilities are covered by government debt. The whole 'pyramid' is founded on the good faith of the government! So long as public confidence in this good faith is not shaken, and governments will be very anxious to see that it is not, the whole system will work.

The instruments of monetary policy

From our analysis so far, it is clear that the government, through the agency of the central bank, can change the supply of money, influence the volume of bank loans, and through this affect investment and consumption spending and the volume of economic activity in the economy as a whole. The deliberate use of the monetary system by the government and the central bank to regulate or influence the economy constitutes *monetary policy*. In developed economies like the UK the monetary authorities[4] have evolved various instruments or 'tools' of monetary policy to control the money supply and volume of credit. The scope for monetary policy in developing countries tends to be more restricted (a) by the less developed monetary and financial system, and (b) by the nature of the economy, including the large subsistence sector and the dominance of exports and imports within the monetized sector. Let us start by describing the general methods of monetary management employed in developed countries before going on to examine central banking and monetary policy in Eastern Africa.

Open market operations

The first method of influencing the money supply is by 'open market operations'. The central bank holds government securities, as we saw in Table 26.1. It can sell some of these, or buy more, on the open market, buying or selling through a stock exchange or money market. When the bank sells securities to be bought by members of the public, the buyers will pay by writing cheques on their accounts with commercial banks. This means a cash drain from these banks to the central bank, represented by a fall in the item 'bankers' deposits' at the central bank, which forms part of the commercial banks' reserve assets. Since the banks maintain a fixed liquidity (or cash) ratio, the loss of these reserves will bring about multiple contraction of bank loans and deposits. By going into the market as a buyer of securities, the central bank can reverse the process, increasing the liquidity of commercial banks, causing them to expand bank credit, always assuming a ready supply of credit-worthy borrowers.

This process can be explained more precisely in terms of Table 26.1. Suppose the initial position were as in that table and that commercial banks were working to a reserve asset ratio of 13.63 per cent. The central bank now sells, say, £100 millions worth of securities. In the central bank's account 'government securities' would fall to 390 and 'bankers' deposits' to 120. In the commercial banks' account 'cash deposits at the Bank of England' would fall to 120 and reserve assets to 2,900. Since customers would have drawn cheques worth 100, to buy the securities, deposit liabilities would fall to 21,900. The reserve asset ratio would fall to $\frac{2,900}{21,900} = 13.24$ per cent. To restore a reserve ratio of 13.63 per cent, banks would need to reduce total deposits to $2900 \times \frac{100}{13.63} = 21,280$, a decrease from the original 22,000 of 720. Bank deposits therefore fall by 7.2 times the reduction in cash reserves of 100. We could, of course, have obtained this result directly: if the ratio of deposits to reserve assets is kept at 100:13.63, a reduction in cash of 100 must mean a reduction in deposits of $\frac{100}{13.63} \times 100 = 720$, approximately. Normally, as we have pointed out, the reserve asset ratio of British commercial banks is $12\frac{1}{2}$ per cent, so that the change in bank deposits will be in the ratio $\frac{100}{12.5}$, or eight times.

Conversely, if the central bank wanted to pursue an expansionary monetary policy by making *more* credit available to the public, it would *buy* bonds from the public. It would pay sellers by cheques drawn on itself, the sellers would then deposit these with commercial banks, who would deposit them again with the central bank, increasing their credit (bankers' deposits) at the central bank. This increase in cash and reserve assets would permit them to carry out a multiple *expansion* of bank deposits, increasing advances and the money supply together.

So far we have been concerned with changes in the quantity of money and volume of credit. Open market operations will also affect interest rates. For if bank loans are restricted, following a reduction in the cash base, assuming demand for loans is as before, the price of loans will tend to rise, loans being granted only to borrowers able and willing to pay the higher rates. Apart from this the sale of securities by the central bank means increased supply of securities and, with demand presumably unchanged, a fall in the price of securities, whether government bonds or Treasury bills. As we shall see presently,[5] this is equivalent to a rise in the effective rate of interest on securities. Moreover in the process of reducing deposits, commercial banks are also likely to sell securities ('investments'), further reducing the price. Since businessmen offering equities have to compete with bonds, which can also be bought by the public, a higher yield on bonds will require a higher yield on equities to attract purchasers, making finance more expensive. The reverse will occur when the central bank *buys* securities, that is, interest rates will tend to fall.

Discount rate (bank rate)

Central banks may also operate more directly on the level and structure of interest rates by changing the official discount rate or 'Minimum Lending Rate', as it is now known in the United Kingdom. This is the rate on central bank advances. When commercial banks find themselves short of cash they may, instead of contracting bank deposits, go to the central bank, which can make additional cash available in its capacity as a 'lender of last resort', to help the banks out of their difficulties. The central bank can make cash available on a short-term basis in either of two ways: by lending cash directly, charging a rate of interest which is referred to as the official 'discount rate', or by buying approved short-term securities from the commercial banks. In contrast with open market operations this cash is made available at the request of the commercial banks, and on their initiative. In the case of open market operations it is the central bank which takes the initiative in buying or selling securities.

The central bank exercises regulatory powers as a lender of last resort by making this help both more expensive to get, and more difficult to get. It can do the former by charging a very high 'penal' rate of interest, well above the other short-term rates ruling in the money market. Similarly, when it makes cash available by buying approved short-term securities, it can charge a high effective rate of interest by buying them at a low price. The effective rate of interest charged when the central bank buys securities (supplying cash) is in fact a re-discount rate, since the bank is buying securities which are already on the market but at a discount. A Treasury bill, for example, is a 'piece of paper', issued by the government, promising to pay cash of £100 in three months from the date of issue. If the central bank buys a new bill for, say, £99 instead of £100, it is in effect making an interest charge of £1 on £100 borrowed by the commercial bank for a three-month period.[6] This is equivalent to a charge of £4 for a twelve-month period, that is, to an annual rate of interest of 4 per cent.

The significance of this rate of interest charged by the central bank in one way or the other to the commercial banks, as a lender of last resort, is that if this rate goes up the commercial banks, who find that their costs of borrowing have increased, are likely to raise the rates of interest on their lending to businessmen and other borrowers. Other interest rates, such as those charged by building societies on house mortgages, are then also likely to be pulled up. Thus to some extent the official discount rate governs the whole system of interest rates, via the rates charged by the commercial banks.

What direct effect changes in the rate have is, however, uncertain. In developed countries a change in the bank rate may act more as a signal than anything else, indicating to the commercial banks that the central bank is anxious to see a restriction of credit. This can have a useful psychological effect since they know that, if they do not respond by raising their own rates of interest, the central bank can step up its open market operations and 'squeeze' their cash still further. In fact open market operations and changes in bank rate are often used together, though commercial banks may react sufficiently quickly to the latter to render open market operations unnecessary.

Variable reserve requirements

Variable cash and liquidity

Open market operations reduce the cash base of commercial bank credit, and thus bring pressure for a reduction of credit. This will be effective, however, only so long as commercial banks do not permit their cash ratios to vary. If the banks happened to start with an excessively high cash ratio, they might well be prepared to allow it to be reduced, without restricting credit. In such a case, an alternative is for the central bank to require commercial banks to keep to a new higher ratio. This method, instead of changing the size of the cash reserve available to banks to support a given volume of lending, increases the size of the reserve needed to support it.

In general, varying the liquidity ratio will be more effective than varying the cash ratio, since an increased cash requirement can be met by the banks by selling other liquid assets for cash, while retaining a sufficient total reserve asset ratio to avoid pressure on advances. Moreover a large change in the cash ratio will affect the profitability of banks by reducing the share of income-earning assets in their portfolios. And in addition, if bank holdings of public securities are large, a switch between these and cash may destabilize interest rates.

In the USA variable reserve requirements have long been used to eliminate excess liquidity of banks, and to discriminate between different types of deposit, being normally higher on demand deposits than on time and savings deposits. By varying these ratios the Federal Reserve Banks can quickly mop up excess reserves and make it clear not only to the banks but to other sectors what policy it is pursuing.

Supplementary reserve requirements

The central bank can in addition require commercial banks to maintain over and above cash or liquid assets some additional reserves in the form of Special Deposits. The commercial banks are asked to maintain additional deposits in their accounts at the central bank, deposits which cease to count among their reserve assets as cover for their liabilities. The effect is similar to varying the liquidity ratio, since these assets are in effect 'frozen' and cease to be available as reserve assets at all: hence this is a form of variable reserve requirement. 'Special deposits' were introduced by the Bank of England in 1958. Banks are simply required to deposit with the Bank of England a specified proportion of their total deposits and are paid the current Treasury bill rate of interest on them. At the end of 1973, for example, 'special deposits' represented as much as 6 per cent of banks' eligible deposits, which is a really massive surcharge on the normal liquidity ratio of $12\frac{1}{2}$ per cent. If we refer back to Table 26.1, at the end of

1971, 'special deposits' were only $\frac{1}{2}$ per cent of the banks' deposits, a mere £120 millions. If they had been 6 per cent *then*, the banks would have had to deposit an *extra* £1,200 millions by contracting their 'investments' in longer-term government securities and, mainly, 'advances' to private borrowers. We see, therefore, that special deposits can be very effective in eliminating excess liquidity. In 1973 the Bank of England introduced *Supplementary Deposits* which are similar, but freeze a proportion of the *growth* in each individual bank's interest-bearing sterling time deposits. Like special deposits these are neither part of the banks' reserve assets nor their risk assets.

Direct control and moral suasion

Without actually using the above weapons, the central bank can attempt simply to use 'moral suasion' to persuade the commercial banks to restrict credit when they wish to limit monetary expansion. This is frequently done in Western countries. In socialist countries where the government and central bank have direct control over the commercial banking system such control is much easier. An example of formal powers of control in Africa is that of Nigeria where in 1964, for example, the central bank imposed a 15 per cent ceiling on the annual rate of commercial bank credit expansion.[7] These powers were given a legal basis in the Nigerian Banking Act of 1968, discussed again below.

Selective credit controls

More common, however, are direct controls on selected *types* of lending. These also can be imposed with the full apparatus of the law or informally using specific instructions to banks and other institutions. To cut down loans for housebuilding, for example, the government could require building societies to grant only 90 per cent or 80 per cent mortgages, so that only those borrowers who were able to find the other 10 or 20 per cent elsewhere would now seek loans. The government could interfere in much the same way in hire-purchase terms to cut down consumer credit for spending on furniture, motor cars, and other consumer durables. Or banks could be instructed to restrict loans to importers to reduce spending on imports. A particularly 'tight' form of credit restriction is requiring importers to make cash deposits to cover all or some proportion of their import bills.

The government and central bank therefore have a number of instruments of monetary control at their disposal in a capitalist economy: open market operations, the official discount rate, variable reserve requirements, and direct controls, both general and selective. A distinction can be made between changes in the discount rate, which try to affect demand for and supply of credit by changing its price (the rate of interest), and open market operations and variable reserve requirements, which operate, through their effects on the liquidity position of commercial banks, on the money supply and volume of credit. Since it is open to doubt whether changes in the rate of interest have any great impact in encouraging or discouraging investment spending, still less consumption spending, monetary policy concentrates more on liquidity and the quantity of money than on the rate of interest. All the methods have in common that they *use the price mechanism*, since when their liquidity is increased or decreased the banks are left to choose which borrowers to select, and will presumably choose those who are willing to pay higher rates of interest or appear to them most credit-worthy when credit is expanded, and vice versa. In a socialist system where capitalist financial institutions and money markets do not exist and where direction of the commercial banking is possible the emphasis will be on direct controls as regards both the overall level of credit and the allocation of credit. The direction of credit will tend to follow some stated priorities rather than narrow financial principles, but will incorporate a more bureaucratic element.

Monetary systems of Eastern Africa

Before we can examine the scope for monetary policy in African conditions, it is necessary to see how African monetary systems differ from those in advanced capitalist countries and, in order to do that, to see how the present African systems have evolved from colonial currency authorities which operated prior to the establishment of independent central banks. We shall take for special study the East African Currency Board and the banking systems of Kenya, Tanzania, and Uganda.

The East African Currency Board was established in 1919, charged with the issue and redemption of a new East African currency. Initially, in 1920, an East African florin (two shillings) was issued to replace the existing silver rupee currency circulating in East Africa; the East African shilling was introduced in 1922. The East African Board was similar to other currency authorities established in other British colonies or groups of colonies, the most important of which were the West African, Southern Rhodesian, and Malayan Currency Areas.

Characteristics of the Currency Board system

Under the Currency Board system Kenya, Uganda, and Tanganyika, and later (in 1935) Zanzibar, had a common currency, the East African shilling. The shilling was freely convertible on demand into sterling at a fixed rate of exchange: twenty East African shillings = £1 sterling. Thus anyone holding East African currency could replace it with sterling any time he liked. Throughout its history the East African Currency Board maintained this rate at par with sterling, charging only a small commission of not more than $\frac{1}{2}$ per cent on transfers between the two currencies. Unlike a central bank, the East African Currency Board had, initially, none of the important banking functions, and did not exercise control over the currency issue. It was essentially a money-changing agency responsible for (1) the physical distribution of currency throughout East Africa, (2) placing orders for the manufacture of currency, and (3) investment of sterling reserves in approved securities in London. Moreover the whole of the East African currency was backed by sterling securities,[8] which could be converted into sterling cash directly, whenever the Board had to convert East African currency. Essentially the Board took out of circulation the sterling currency which might otherwise have circulated and replaced it by East African currency, keeping the equivalent amount of sterling 'on one side'. East Africa was thus an extension of the parent United Kingdom currency area, since it was almost as if sterling currency circulated in East Africa: 'almost', because the East African currency was backed by its *own* sterling assets. Possession of East African currency provided the same opportunities for, and limitations on, convertibility into third currencies, as possession of United Kingdom currency. There was no risk of East African currency losing value in relation to sterling, and therefore it was just as good to hold East African as to hold sterling currency: changes in the rate of exchange had to be approved by the British government, and throughout its history the East African currency was automatically 'pegged' to sterling's rate of exchange vis-à-vis dollars, francs, and all other currencies. Moreover there were no quantitative exchange controls limiting conversion of currency or transfer of bank deposits either between the three East African countries or between East Africa and the United Kingdom (and thereby any other British colonial currency area).

The important question for us to answer is, what determines the supply of currency in circulation in such a situation? It was not the Currency Board, which obviously played a purely passive role. Leaving commercial bank credit out of account for the moment, *the cash base of the money supply is obviously determined, first, by the amount of sterling currency coming into the hands of people resident in East Africa,[9] and secondly, by the proportion of this foreign exchange in sterling which people wished to convert into local currency.*

The sterling was obtained in payment for East African exports. On the other hand sterling, or other foreign currency, was needed to pay for the import of goods and services from overseas. So long as exports were balanced by imports, there would be no net inflow or outflow of sterling, and therefore no change in the amount converted into East African currency (unless for some other reason). If export earnings exceeded the value of imports, there would be a net increase in sterling received, and presumably an increase in the issue of East African currency; the reverse would be true for an excess of imports over exports. *The value of local currency in circulation was thus dependent upon the balance of payments situation.*[10]

It might be noted there that a 'balance of payments crisis' could not arise with this sterling-exchange system. Such a crisis arises if a country is not earning enough foreign exchange through exports to pay for its imports. In effect, the supply of a particular currency on the foreign exchange market (by those who wish to import) exceeds the demand (by those who have something to export) and there is pressure for the price of the local currency to change. Under the Currency Board system the price of local currency always remains at one-to-one to sterling. Any adjustment due to the balance of payments position operates through a change in the money supply.

The relationship between Currency Board and commercial banks

The Currency Board did not directly exchange sterling for local currency and vice versa for the general public. This was one of the functions of the commercial banks who acted as agents for the Board. But the banks also undertook other normal functions of commercial banks, holding demand and savings deposits belonging to the public, and providing credit for local businessmen. From our previous discussion, however, it is clear that the East African Currency Board did not have the controlling relationship with the commercial banks in East Africa that a normal central bank exercises through its control over the cash base.

First, the cash base of the commercial banks was not given by local currency plus deposits with the central bank. The banks held local currency, equivalent however to sterling, plus, instead of deposits at the central bank, 'balances with banks abroad', again consisting of sterling assets. The 'banks abroad' were their own head offices in London. This dependence explains the predominance of expatriate banks in East African commercial banking.

Secondly, the Currency Board did not have the link that a central bank would have via the liquid assets, the short-term securities, held by the commercial banks. The 'balances with banks abroad' were deposits with the head office mostly invested on behalf of the East African branch in 'money on call and short notice' and Treasury bills in the *London* money market. There was no local discount market or stock exchange for government bonds.

Thirdly, although commercial banks created bank deposits on the basis of cash reserves, local credit creation was not limited by cash ratio considerations (indeed there was a very high ratio of cash to local deposits) but by a lack of acceptable borrowers. The limit was thus on the demand side rather than the supply side. It follows that an increase in cash held by commercial banks in East Africa would not necessarily lead to any expansion of local bank deposits, nor would a contraction of bank cash necessarily imply a contraction of deposits.

Fourthly, considerable flexibility was forthcoming from outside East Africa through loans which head offices could readily supply to East African branches. Moreover head offices could easily transfer cash, especially seasonally, from one Currency Board area to another, that is, between West and East Africa,

say, or between Central Africa and the Caribbean, according to the pressure of demand for bank credit.

Finally, the operations of the Currency Board did not need to be backed by East African government securities, nor did the Board need to control the creation of commercial bank credit, as does the normal central bank. The *currency* was fully backed by sterling investments and liquid assets: the Currency Board was a 'money-changer' and supplied no fiduciary issue.

In summary, commercial banks in East Africa did create bank deposits on a cash base, but not in the ratio $\frac{100}{8}$, or any other fixed ratio, and this cash base was *not* controlled by the Currency Board.

These relationships are given in Table 26.2 which is to be compared with the British monetary system in Table 26.1.[11] The upper part of the table shows the composition of the East African money supply in 1955 when the whole of the local currency in circulation was still *by law* covered by external (sterling) assets. Just over one-third (three-ninths) was currency, £42.7 millions. However, by comparison with many African countries in the mid-1950s the share of currency in the money supply was relatively small, a reflection especially of acceptable lending opportunities in Kenya. We should however expect currency to be more widely used in Africa where money

Table 26.2 *East Africa's money supply under the Currency Board system*

£ millions		
MONEY SUPPLY WITH NON-BANKING PUBLIC: EAST AFRICA MID-1955		TOTAL: 123.3
	comprising	
80.6 DEMAND DEPOSITS	*plus* CURRENCY	42.7
COMMERCIAL BANKS create DEPOSITS against ASSETS		
80.6 Demand deposits	Currency as 'till money'	11.0
13.3 Other deposits	Balances with banks abroad (net)	23.6
	Total effective cash reserves	34.6
	Local investments	1.7
	Local loans and advances	51.8
	Local earning or 'risk' assets	53.5
	Other assets (net)	5.8
93.9 TOTAL DEPOSITS	TOTAL ASSETS	93.9
EAST AFRICAN CURRENCY BOARD'S BALANCE SHEET		
Liabilities	*Assets*	
53.7 Estimated currency notes and coin issued in respect of East Africa	Sterling assets cover	53.7
0.4 Reserve Funds	Excess sterling reserves	0.4
EAST AFRICAN CURRENCY ISSUED = 53.7		
Notes 80 per cent approximately		
Coin 20 per cent		

incomes are low, cheques are less generally accepted, and there are fewer bank branches where people can open accounts.

The middle part of the table again shows the combined balance sheet of the commercial banks. Currency (till money) constituted $11\frac{1}{2}$ per cent of total deposits (£11.0 millions compared to £93.9 millions). 'Balances with banks abroad', which replace deposits with the central bank, accounted for a further 25 per cent. From the point of view of the East African branch banks these were as good as cash, bringing the cash ratio to $36\frac{1}{2}$ per cent—a very high one, as stated earlier, and not a constraint on local deposit creation. The small figure of £1.7 million for 'local investments' reflects the absence of opportunities for banks to invest in East African government securities. The limited extent of bank deposit creation is measured by comparing the figure for 'local earning or risk assets' (£53.5 millions) with that for 'total effective cash reserves' (£34.6 millions); or alternatively by the ratio of cash reserves to total deposits (£93.9 millions), which was equal to 39 per cent in 1955.

The lower part of Table 26.2 shows the external assets cover for the currency circulating in East Africa. Against a total outstanding issue of £53.7 millions there were in fact £54.1 millions of sterling assets, the small difference representing the accumulated profits of the Board from the interest-earning sterling investments and commission charged on the exchange of currency. Of the currency issued, £11.0 millions was held by commercial banks and £42.7 millions was in circulation as part of the money supply of the general public.

Evolution of the East African monetary system 1955–66

Between 1955 and the setting-up in 1966 of the new central banks, the Currency Board system underwent important modifications. In fact from 1955 the East African Currency Board came to acquire many of the functions of a central bank, managing an increasingly complex system of currency and credit.

The first important departure took place when the Board was authorized to issue local currency in exchange for *local* securities purchased from East African governments, instead of covering all currency with sterling assets. In other words a fiduciary element, based on the good faith of governments, was introduced. The value of this element was fixed at £10.0 millions in 1955, but was increased in stages to £30.8 millions by 1965. This meant that, had the governments taken up the whole of the fiduciary issue authorized, this element would have comprised just under 50 per cent of the currency in circulation. In fact the amount authorized was not fully taken up, and at the time of dissolution only some £19½ millions of the Board's assets comprised local East African government securities and Treasury bills, and covered just over 30 per cent of the currency, compared to £44 millions or nearly 70 per cent backed by foreign exchange (sterling assets).

The creation of fiduciary currency enabled the Board to develop another central banking function, that of 'lender of last resort' to the commercial banks. This was useful after 1964 when the effective cash reserves of the banks were under considerable strain and when short-term borrowing from head offices was particularly expensive, due to high interest rates in Britain, unrelated to East African circumstances. At the same time uncertainty in the immediate post-Independence period in East Africa caused members of the public to convert a considerable amount of local money into foreign currency, resulting in heavy withdrawals of private deposits. The Currency Board was able to ease the banks' cash position and restrict the rise in interest rates locally by buying ('rediscounting') Treasury bills from the commercial banks, supplying cash in exchange for bills.

The change in the position of the Currency Board in this ten-year period is illustrated in Table 26.3. The middle part, relating to commercial banks, shows several new features. First, there is a noticeable increase in deposits other than demand deposits: this represents mainly savings deposits earning interest, belonging to many 'small' African depositors, reflecting the increasing use of the banks by the African population. Secondly, there appears a new form of commercial bank cash reserve, 'working balances of banks held by the Currency Board', amounting to nearly £1 million, and representing a step in the direction of substituting 'deposits at the central bank' for 'balances with banks abroad'. Thirdly, instead of the East African banks investing in the London money market through their head offices, the table shows branches as net debtors, *borrowing* heavily from their head offices. This meant, in fact, that banks' effective cash ratio was zero, or slightly negative to be precise, a situation which clearly could not be maintained for long. It was sustained by a combination of loans from head offices, 'banks abroad' and by 'loans of last resort' from the Currency Board described above.

The Currency Board's balance sheet, given in the lower part of Table 26.3, now permits us to distinguish both 'currency issue' and embryonic 'banking department' functions, not present in 1955. The 'balances with the East African Currency Board' which appeared as an asset for the commercial banks, appear again, of course, as a liability to the

Table 26.3   *East African money supply: evolution of a fiduciary currency*

£ millions		
MONEY SUPPLY WITH NON-BANKING PUBLIC: 30 JUNE 1965		TOTAL: 144.6
comprising		
94.5 DEMAND DEPOSITS	*plus* CURRENCY	50.1
COMMERCIAL BANKS create DEPOSITS against ASSETS		
94.5 Demand deposits	Currency as 'till money'	4.6
40.5 Other deposits	Balances with E.A. Currency Board	0.9
	Local cash balances	5.5
	Less Balances *due to* banks abroad	−6.4
	Effective cash reserves	−0.9
	Investment (E.A. bonds)	7.5
	Local loans and advances	123.0
	Local earning or 'risk' assets	130.5
	Other assets (net)	5.4
135.0 TOTAL DEPOSITS	TOTAL ASSETS	135.0
EAST AFRICAN CURRENCY BOARD'S BALANCE SHEET (excluding Aden)		
54.7 Currency in circulation	External asset cover	44.0
0.9 Bankers' deposits	E.A. Government securities	18.6
8.1 Reserves and other liabilities	Discounts and advances to bankers	1.0
	Total fiduciary cover	19.6
63.6 TOTAL LIABILITIES	TOTAL ASSETS	63.6
EAST AFRICAN CURRENCY ISSUED = 54.7		

Board. The £8 millions referred to as 'reserves and other liabilities' were various debts to the East African governments, although the Currency Board was never officially recognized as the deposit banker or paying agency for the East African governments: one or other of the commercial banks remained responsible for government deposits until the establishment of the independent central banks. The asset side adds the £44 millions of sterling cover and the £19½ millions of local fiduciary cover mentioned earlier.

Functions of central banks in Africa

The assets and liabilities of the East African Currency Board were shared out in 1966 among three new central banks in Kenya, Tanzania, and Uganda, during a period when new central banks were established in newly independent nations in many parts of Africa. The first task was to issue new national currencies in exchange for the old Currency Board notes and coin. The new central banks thus took over the currency liabilities of the old board and were allocated sterling assets, pound for pound, as cover, while in addition a share of the sterling reserves in excess of the 100 per cent currency cover was allocated to them on the basis of the value of the (old) currency in circulation in each country. Initially the new national currencies were also backed 100 per cent by sterling, though a fiduciary element was introduced later and the external cover came to include gold and other convertible foreign exchange as well as sterling.

At the same time the new currencies were given a fixed rate of exchange which was registered with the International Monetary Fund, and made equivalent to the former parity with the £ sterling. The exchange reserves controlled by the central banks now 'supported' these exchange rates. Other official exchange reserves were gradually centralized within the central banks' control, namely, the foreign balances and securities of governments and marketing boards, as well as some of the commercial banks' balances with banks abroad. In assuming this responsibility for overseas banking transactions, the central banks gradually succeeded overseas head offices as bankers to the commercial banks operating in East Africa, as did the other central banks elsewhere in Africa. The central banks have also become bankers to governments and other public bodies, although one or more commercial banks are still used as agents in certain areas. Government and other public sector deposits are held partly with central banks and partly with commercial banks, and both may supply credit to the public sector in the form of short-term 'advances' or through the holding of 'investments' in government securities and Treasury bills. However we need to examine in more detail the functions of the now firmly established African central banks in Eastern and West Africa.

1. Responsibility for the currency issue

Once the old Currency Board notes and coin were redeemed for sterling and replaced in local circulation with new national currencies, the new central banks began to widen their functions and cease acting simply as currency authorities. During the first two or three years of their operation the central banks in Nigeria and Ghana had continued to function like national currency boards, and it was some time before a fiduciary element was included in their currency issues. In East Africa, as we have seen, the Currency Board had already begun to assume some central banking functions including the issue of fiduciary currency, as early as 1956, and also acted as a 'lender of last resort' for the Kenya banks in the early 1960s. In Zambia and Malawi, where the new currencies issued in 1965 replaced those of an existing federal central bank, the Bank of Rhodesia and Nyasaland, it was a case of devolving functions that already provided for central bank lending to governments and commercial banks, including limited fiduciary cover of the currency.

The original legislation establishing the new banks had adopted a conservative and cautious approach to the question of currency backing, limiting the proportion of currency which could be issued against local government securities, and also specifying the extent to which the local governments' recurrent budgets could be financed by borrowing from the central banks. It soon became clear, in Ghana, Tanzania, and Malawi especially, that central bank lending would be needed to finance much larger public sector deficits than the original legislation envisaged, and so within a few years of their establishments, most or all of the limitations on fiduciary currency issues were relaxed or abolished.

2. Acting as the bankers' bank and controller of the money and credit supply

Under the East and West African Currency Boards, the commercial banks used their own overseas head offices as 'bankers' banks': they were free to transfer cash balances to accounts with these head offices and, if they were short of liquidity, to obtain 'loans of last resort' from them. In its last years, it was true, the East African Currency Board began to assume some functions as a bankers' bank, being willing to rediscount eligible bills to provide banks with cash. The same facility had been established more formally with the creation of the Federal Bank of Rhodesia and Nyasaland in 1956. However, in both these currency areas the banks remained free to move funds abroad, and continued to regard overseas balances, which earned interest on the London money market, as their main cash reserves. As a result, the power to control effectively the cash base of the money supply was not entirely in the hands of local monetary authorities. The new independent central banks, therefore, centralized the foreign assets of expatriate and local banks in their own hands, providing *local* cash reserves in place of sterling and other foreign currency reserves. This policy was designed: (a) to economize the total resources held in such foreign investments instead of local productive capital; (b) to afford scope for the use of local monetary tools, such as open market operations, reserve requirements, and bank rate; and (c) to redistribute earnings on foreign assets from mainly private expatriate banks to a publicly owned central bank.

To illustrate the development of independent African banking systems, Table 26.4 provides an outline of Kenya's monetary system at the end of 1973. This may be compared with the similar Table 26.1, depicting the UK monetary system, and the structure of the monetary system under the East African Currency Board in 1965, as shown in Table 26.3. In 1965 the effective cash reserves of the East African commercial banks were actually negative, as indicated in Table 26.3, mainly because of a negative balance with banks abroad, reflecting their dependence on head offices rather than on the local monetary authority. In 1973 the commercial banks in Kenya had cash reserves of some £19 millions, or 8.3 per cent of total deposit liabilities of £228 millions. This included significant cash balances with the central bank of £7 millions, compared to balances (by all East African banks) with the Currency Board in 1965 of £0.9 millions. Beyond this, reserve assets amounted to £44 millions, or 19.3 per cent of deposits, mainly due to a substantial increase in the importance of Treasury bills, amounting to £23 millions. The Kenya commercial banks thus held a substantial volume of liquid reserve assets locally and were no longer dependent on the possibility of drawing in funds from abroad. The balance sheet for the commercial banks thus resembles much more that for the UK than that for the old Currency Board system.

We may note in passing that although the cash ratio of the commercial banks was quite high in 1973, it was not policy to maintain a rigid cash ratio. There

Table 26.4 *Monetary system of Kenya, 1973*

K £ millions

VOLUME OF MONEY[1] WITH NON-BANKING PRIVATE SECTOR: 31 DEC. 1973
comprising
198: BANK DEPOSITS plus CURRENCY: 50
is 248
of which private demand deposits 98 and currency 50 equals the MONEY SUPPLY 148

COMMERCIAL BANKS

	Liabilities	Assets	
98	Private demand deposits	Currency as 'till money'	12
100	Private time and savings deposits	Cash balances with central bank	7
30	Public sector deposits	(*Total cash reserves*)	(19)
		Treasury bills	23
		Balances with other banks (net)	2
		Total reserve assets	*44*
		Investments	23
		Loans and advances	161
		Total risk assets	*184*
228	*Total deposits*	*Total assets*	*228*

CENTRAL BANK OF KENYA

	Liabilities	Assets	
17	Government deposits	Foreign exchange	74
11	Kenya bankers' deposits	Government securities	6
3	Other deposits	Treasury bills	3
31	*Total banking liabilities*	Direct advances to Government	10
56	*Currency issued*	Other assets (net)	9
15	Other Liabilities		
102	*Total liabilities*	*Total assets*	*102*

SOURCE: Central Bank of Kenya
[1] The Kenyan definition of the volume of money excludes public sector bank deposits, hence the figure of 248 excludes £30 millions of such deposit liabilities.

was a statutory minimum liquidity ratio (reserve asset ratio) of 15 per cent, which we can see was exceeded by 4.3 per cent in 1973, so that the banking system had 'excess liquidity'.

The monetary system had not changed very much, however, as regards external asset cover. We showed earlier that in a developed monetary system such as that of the UK the money supply consists of paper currency and coins issued by the central bank, together with the bank deposits 'created' by the commercial banks on the strength of liquid reserve assets held by them, including deposits at the central bank. These balances and more important the currency issue are liabilities for the central bank. In a developed monetary system this currency issue is not backed by holdings of gold: only by government securities. It is a 'fiduciary' issue, based on faith in the government of the day. Before the establishment of central banks in Eastern Africa, the currency was not backed by securities issued by the domestic (colonial) government, however, but *by foreign exchange*. In this way faith was required only in these other currencies, largely sterling, issued by long-established central banks located in developed countries. Table 26.4 shows that the central bank's asset cover or support for the money supply was *still* provided by foreign exchange, this providing 73 per cent of total assets in 1973, compared to slightly *less*, 70 per cent for the Currency Board in 1965, as indicated in Table 26.3. Today net claims on the foreign sector (foreign exchange) are still the most important asset backing the currency and deposit liabilities of the central banks in Eastern and West Africa.

3. Acting as banker to the government

The third function of a central bank that we listed was that of banker and financial adviser to the government. We also noted that the East African Currency Board (but not the West African Currency Board) had begun to fulfil this function from the mid-1950s, and that all three governments had borrowed from the Board by issuing securities which the Board could purchase. The increasing demands of expanded public expenditure programmes after political independence therefore involved the new central banks in taking up local issues of government securities, Treasury bills, or the making of direct advances to the governments or other public sector bodies. The counterpart of this central bank lending, in terms of the asset structure of central banks, was an increasing proportion of fiduciary cover and, on the liabilities side, the creation of public sector deposits. The latter, when drawn to meet public expenditure, would, of course, increase the cash base of the commercial banks.

Borrowing to meet public sector deficits will automatically lead to either (a) an increase in the domestic money supply, if it is spent on local goods and services, or (b) a decline in the nation's foreign exchange reserves if it finances imports, causing either inflationary pressure or pressure on the balance of payments. For this reason the central banks have endeavoured to develop local markets for public debt. By selling government securities either to the public or to financial institutions which collect savings from the public, the central bank can transfer its own loan to the government, which implies a net increase in spending, to the general public, which in effect lends to the government out of its *savings*, without the same inflationary effect. Kenya and Nigeria, especially, have endeavoured to foster private financial institutions, including stock exchanges, with the aim of reducing the size of the public sector deficit which has to be financed by the central banks.

African central banks usually have to subscribe for a large proportion of new public debt issues and then persuade the commercial banks and other financial institutions to take up some of the issues as their liquidity allows. They usually offer to repurchase such securities, as well as Treasury bills, at prices which will not involve holders in capital losses. In other words the market in public debt is 'managed' in such a way that financial institutions can regard such assets as liquid. Such a policy involves stabilization of yields and hence of interest rates. It is for this reason that bank rate is rarely changed.

4. Management of foreign exchange

The fourth main function of modern central banks, and a most important one, is their control of the nation's foreign exchange reserves. In most countries these reserves are managed by the central banks and largely held by them. Thus, for example, the *Economic and Financial Review* published by East African central banks shows under its table entitled 'Monetary Survey' the foreign assets of the 'monetary authority' (the government and the central bank) and the commercial banks. At the end of 1972 these

comprised in the case of Kenya some K£72.6 millions, distributed between the central bank (92 per cent), government official balances (4 per cent), the IMF 'Gold Tranche'[12] (6 per cent), and a negative amount (1 per cent) representing net liabilities of commercial banks to foreign banks.

Under the currency board system, as we have seen, the exchange rate was *fixed*: variations in foreign exchange earnings produced changes in the cash base of the monetary system and in the domestic money supply. The fall in the money supply exerted a deflationary pressure on East African activity and prices, so restoring the balance of payments equilibrium. Although the system was usually referred to as a *sterling-exchange standard*, it was in effect a gold standard system as far as sterling currency board countries were concerned, since East African currency could be exchanged, via sterling, for gold or US dollars to meet balance of payments' requirements. The transfer of currency liabilities and sterling assets from the currency boards to new central banking systems in Africa therefore raised the question of the exchange rate for the first time since the currency boards were formed. Initially the new national currencies retained their former parity with sterling, and the corresponding 'par value' in terms of US dollars and gold was registered with the International Monetary Fund, which then in 1966 itself operated a fixed exchange system for all the major currencies in the world. Hence the exchange reserves of the new central banks would have to support the external value of the new currencies. We analyse possible foreign exchange rate policies in Chapter 30, and concentrate here on the scope for effective action by the central banks in respect of *domestic* monetary policies.

The scope for monetary policy in African economies

We described above the main instruments of monetary policy employed in developed capitalist countries: open market operations, official discount rate (bank rate), variable reserve requirements, general and selective credit controls. For a number of reasons these may be less effective in less developed economies, as we can now see.

Open market operations

These are virtually not used in the African situation, as a means of controlling the money supply. The main reason for this is the lack of developed money and capital markets, and the limited quantity and range of financial assets (securities, etc.) held in the country which the monetary authority can buy or sell in order to increase or decrease cash holdings with the public. In the second place, the commercial banks in Africa are less sensitive to changes in their cash base. Partly this is because commercial banks have, since the development of independent monetary systems, found themselves with excess liquidity, due especially to the scarcity of good projects and creditworthy borrowers to whom they could lend. If then commercial banks have a higher level of liquidity than the legal minimum liquidity ratio, a reduction in their reserve assets need bring no response in terms of a reduction of credit, while to bring liquidity down to the level of the prescribed ratio and below would require extremely large sales of securities by the monetary authority. A further reason for insensitivity to changes in the cash base, which we have already mentioned, is where the commercial banks are branches of foreign banks, and can turn to the parent organization abroad for liquid funds in the event of having their base 'squeezed' by the local monetary authorities.

For these reasons, when African central banks buy securities, the aim is not to regulate the money supply: it may be to provide finance to the Treasury; to stabilize interest rates and bond prices with a view to encouraging the public and the banks to buy them, and thus to encourage saving; or to offset a reduction in the cash base due to a loss of foreign exchange associated with an excess of imports over exports (a trade deficit).[13]

One way in which the government itself can achieve the same results as central bank open market purchases is to switch some of its own deposits from the central bank to the commercial banks—to this extent increasing its use of the commercial banks as government bankers, rather than the central bank. This simply involves the central bank's crediting bankers' deposits with the same value as the sum switched into government deposits with the commercial banks. In the absence of extensive security markets in Africa, it has been suggested by some economists that the *deliberate* switching of public sector deposits between the central bank and the commercial banks would be the most effective method of changing the cash reserves of banks, achieving the same results as open market operations, but without involving transactions in securities.

Discount rate (bank rate)

Bank rate is also less effective in less developed countries, for a variety of reasons. The central bank's objective in raising the bank rate in *developed* countries is, apart from generally impressing commercial banks with the need to restrict credit, to influence the whole system of medium and long rates of interest, and thus make credit more expensive. This influence works because an increased yield on one type of financial asset tends to pull up yields on assets which are competing for investible funds. The limited range of liquid financial assets in less developed countries weakens this influence.

Secondly, even if interest rates are successfully raised (or lowered), the effect on investment may be limited. Public sector investment is not likely to be very sensitive to changes in interest rates. For local private entrepreneurs who find it difficult to get access to capital, availability of credit may be more important than its price. Even in developed countries uncertainty and the fear of capital losses is thought to affect investment decisions more than interest rates, making investment interest-inelastic. In less developed countries uncertainties will frequently be greater. Private foreign investment is likely to be even less interest-elastic: foreign investors may be more concerned with the risk of investing in more distant countries compared with economies with which they are more familiar. Tax allowances, tariff protection, and the possibility of remitting profits will be more important to them than the rate of interest. And foreign companies may have their own sources of funds anyway.

Thirdly, the greater emphasis on development is likely to reduce the role played by the rate of interest, which has been kept low and stable by most African countries in order to encourage capital formation (something which was a feature of monetary policy even in the UK for much of the post-war period).[14] Moreover development objectives have generally involved making credit available in a generous way to specific sectors—for example manufacturing concerns, cooperative marketing organizations, and, through rural credit institutions, agricultural smallholders—further reducing the scope for interest rate policy.

Variable reserve requirements

A variable reserve asset ratio is potentially the most effective instrument of monetary control in less developed countries. Whereas open market operations are ineffective in situations of excess banking liquidity, varying the minimum liquidity ratio is the most effective and direct method of absorbing such excess. Moreover, because the method is direct, rather than via sales of securities or holding back loans and advances, the effects are immediate. Thus when the commercial banks of Kenya were found to have ratios in excess of the statutory minimum ratio, this minimum liquidity ratio was simply raised in October 1972, to 15 per cent. The third advantage is that this method does not require the existence of a capital market and a variety of financial assets.

Some disadvantages of the method also exist however. Increased liquidity requirements may still be offset in part if the banks have access to credit from their parent companies. This can be dealt with legally, however, by excluding externally held foreign assets from the portfolio of 'reserve-eligible' assets, as was done in Nigeria in 1966. This forces banks to reduce credit and thus restrict the money supply to some proportion of the *local* cash base, greatly strengthening the control powers of the central bank. A further problem (shared by the device of open market operations) is that a variable reserve asset ratio is likely to be much more useful in *restricting* the expansion of credit and of the money supply than in expanding it: if there is a chronic shortage of credit-worthy borrowers and desirable investment projects, reducing the required liquidity ratio of the banks may simply leave them with surplus liquidity and not cause them to expand credit. Finally, we may note that if the banks have substantial cash reserves the change in the legal ratio required may have to be very large: though we may note that this would be even more true of open market operations.

Special deposits are a variety of variable reserve requirements, and should also be particularly useful in dealing with situations of excess liquidity. They have already been used in a number of countries, including Nigeria, Ghana, Ethiopia, and Kenya. The Central Bank of Kenya first introduced special deposits at the end of 1971, when expansion of bank credit and higher spending on imports were putting severe pressure on the exchange reserves. In response to this situation, banks were required, for two months in 1971–2, to make special deposits representing 5 per cent of their net deposits.

General and selective credit controls

We have already mentioned the use of credit ceilings on the rate of bank credit expansion in Nigeria. Credit ceilings have been one of the Central Bank of Nigeria's main instruments of monetary control since its inauguration. One specific power which the Bank has is to have commercial bank loans above a certain size require prior approval from itself: giving itself very direct control over the total volume of loans as well, of course, as over the direction of loans: the type of loans which can be made.

There is in fact an overlap between direct control of total credit and selective credit controls. The central bank can, for instance, fix ceilings for the total volume of loans and advances and also for different *categories* of loans, as it is empowered to do in Nigeria. Selective controls are especially useful in less developed countries where there may be a need to direct resources and investment away from less important sectors such as the construction of buildings, the commercial sector, or speculative purchase of land, towards more important areas such as manufacturing and rural development. They have also been used as a means of encouraging localization of industry and commerce: thus in Nigeria the central bank has the power to prescribe from time to time a minimum ratio of total advances which should be allocated to indigenous businessmen: In particular, measures may be taken to restrict hire-purchase sales of non-essential consumer goods, as well as to restrict credit to firms involved in their importation. A second advantage of selective controls in less developed countries is that they are comparatively easy to administer since there are not so many financial institutions and, because there are only a few sources of credit, they can less easily be evaded.

There are all sorts of ways in which selective credit controls may be imposed. Ceilings or 'floors' may be set, in the form of a maximum or minimum rate of increase in the volume of certain types of loan. Or a limit to the duration of the loan may be set for some categories of loan, or to the value of loans allowed any individual borrower. As just mentioned, it may be made a requirement to have central bank approval for loans exceeding a certain value.

In general the tendency is for monetary policy in less developed countries to rely somewhat less on the 'market mechanism' approach and somewhat more heavily on direct methods of control, partly because it is easier to do so with the more limited range and number of financial institutions, partly because interest rates and manipulation of the cash base are less effective, and partly because of the emphasis on development and the desire to affect the allocation of credit between different uses and sectors of the economy.

Questions on Chapter 26

1. What are the main functions of central banks?
2. What is meant by the 'pyramid of money', and how does it operate in (a) a developed monetary system and (b) a less developed one?
3. Distinguish between the 'volume of money' and the 'money supply'. What is the significance, if any, of the distinction?
4. What are the main aims of monetary policy? What tools are used to achieve these aims, and how do they work?
5. Describe the evolution of independent monetary systems in East African countries during the last decade under the East African Currency Board, 1955–66.
6. Describe the main features of the operation of the colonial Currency Board system.
7. What changes have taken place in the asset distribution of commercial bank balance sheets since central banks replaced the East African Currency Board?
8. Compare the operations of the new East African central banks with those of the former East African Currency Board.
9. 'The Central Bank of Kenya operates just like the Bank of England.' In what respects and to what extent is this true?
10. How far can 'orthodox' tools of capitalist monetary policy be applied in the African context? Which methods of monetary control work best, and why?

Notes

[1] For a fuller account of central banking and other financial aspects of economic development, see E. F. Furness, *Money and Credit in Developing Africa*, Heinemann Educational Books, London, 1974.

[2] For example, by E. L. Furness, op. cit., p. 108, and by the Central Bank of Kenya.

[3] It should be noted that 'till money', notes and coin kept on bank premises to meet the cash requirements of customers, does not constitute part of the money supply in circulation. So long as this money is retained by banks it is not part of the monetary circulation in use to finance transactions by the general public.

[4] Central banks are agents of the central government in carrying out the tasks of monetary management so that the monetary authorities consist of the central bank and the Treasury (Ministry of Finance). In Eastern Africa the monetary assets and liabilities of the central government and the central bank are often shown in consolidated form under the title of 'Monetary Authority'.

[5] The relationship between the rate of interest and the price of securities is explained in Chapter 29.

[6] A peculiar feature of the British system of monetary control is that the Bank of England does not lend directly to the commercial banks, normally, but through the so-called *Discount Market*, which is made up of a dozen or so discount houses, specialist firms dealing in short-term Treasury and commercial (trade) bills.

[7] See O. Teriba, 'The 1967–69 Banking Amendments in Nigeria—An Appraisal of Financial Adaptation in an Underdeveloped War Economy', *Nigerian Journal of Economics and Social Studies*, March 1969.

[8] To be strictly accurate we should say that until as recently as 1950 the sterling reserves covering the outstanding issue were below 100 per cent and as low as 50 per cent during the 1930s. This shortfall was the result of sterling losses on conversion operations during the early 1920s when the new East African currency replaced a temporarily overvalued silver coinage. However, since the East African governments raised a sterling loan and guaranteed the full discharge of any currency redemption, we can say that the currency was fully backed by sterling.

[9] The Currency Board also served Aden in the Middle East, but we need not introduce this complication.

[10] If East African residents were able to borrow (net) from abroad, they received an additional amount of sterling in the form of a loan, and similarly if grants or gifts were received from abroad. These items are included in the balance of payments as receipts of foreign exchange.

[11] The data in Table 26.2, and in Table 26.3, below, exclude transactions in respect of Aden and other territories outside East Africa but include Zanzibar.

[12] This IMF (International Monetary Fund) Gold Tranche represents a payment made by the government in gold as its membership subscription on joining the International Monetary Fund; its size is determined by the relative importance of the member's share of world trade. Some East African countries include the Gold Tranche under their central bank's foreign assets, along with the Special Drawing Rights which will be discussed in Chapter 30.

[13] If a country has a foreign trade deficit, importers will be buying more foreign currency with their domestic bank deposits or currency than exporters are earning and exchanging for local currency and deposits. The domestic money supply will therefore tend to contract as the cash balances of the commercial banks with the central bank are drawn down at the same rate as their customers exchange deposits for foreign currency. To prevent undue contraction of the cash base, some form of open market purchases may be undertaken. The same sort of 'destruction' of the money supply results from heavy tax payments to the Treasury.

[14] The 'distorting' effects of low interest rates have been discussed already in Chapter 15.

27 Financial Institutions and Credit in Eastern Africa

Having seen how the monetary authorities control the commercial banking system, let us look more closely at what commercial banks do.

The functions of commercial banks

The activities of a bank manager and his staff, and the services provided by them, are many and varied, but we can say that the banks have three *basic* functions:

(1) *to facilitate exchange*, by creating money as bank deposits and providing a ready means of making payments through the use of cheque books;

(2) *to provide facilites for saving* to depositors; and

(3) *to distribute credit* to business enterprises and to some extent to consumers.

These same functions are carried out by banks in a socialist economy as well as in a capitalist one.

The role of financial intermediaries

In carrying out the last two functions commercial banks are acting as *financial intermediaries*, that is, as go-betweens, transferring funds from those who have surplus money balances and current savings to would-be borrowers who wish to use the funds for investment purposes (or possibly for consumption). It is easy to see why there should be a need for financial intermediaries. First, in their absence, each individual saver would have to find a borrower who would borrow funds and repay at a suitable later date. This would be a form of direct barter system, with funds being bartered instead of goods, but direct contact having to be made between the two people involved in the exchange. Financial intermediaries thus act as 'middlemen'.

Secondly, the banks (or other intermediaries) can obtain economies of scale, particularly in the pooling of risks. By handling loans to a large number of borrowers, a bank or other intermediary can determine fairly closely what proportion of losses they will sustain through defaulting. Although it will be difficult to say that one particular borrower will or will not default, it should be possible to say from

experience that, say, 3 per cent of debts will not be repaid. Similarly, because the credit provided by banks (apart from that which they themselves create) is obtained from the deposits of a large number of savers, any one saver can extinguish his 'loan' at any time if he wishes to spend the funds himself.

This is in fact a third reason for having financial intermediaries: to provide the public with more liquid and less risky assets. We may distinguish between *primary securities* which are the claims (acknowledging a debt) offered by the ultimate users of finance, for example, the shares issued by business companies; and *secondary securities*, which are claims on an intermediary. For example, an individual may contribute to a private pensions fund and be assured of a pension without taking risks, while finance accumulated in the pensions fund is invested in a variety of securities of varying risk and earning power. Banks provide the most safe and liquid form of asset, bank deposits, to savers while, as we have seen, investing in securities. Thus financial intermediaries increase the liquidity of the financial system, for borrowers, in fact, as well as lenders.

Finally, and related to this last element, banks and other financial intermediaries, by using their specialist knowledge and experience in investment, as compared to the comparatively ignorant general public of savers, can increase the efficiency of investment.

In these various ways, therefore—(1) putting savers in indirect touch with borrowers, (2) pooling risks and securing economies of scale, (3) increasing the liquidity of the financial system, and (4) applying specialist knowledge of investment—banks and other intermediaries can simultaneously increase security, and earnings for savers, *and* reduce the costs of borrowing for ultimate users of funds. In this way both saving and investment will be encouraged.

Commercial banks as commercial enterprises

If we consider again the balance sheets used in the last chapter to depict the monetary system, we see that commercial banks have liabilities, in the form of deposits, and assets, which are roughly divided into liquid (reserve) assets and risk assets, including loans. Banks are, in a capitalist system, commercial enterprises. They have costs to cover, like other business enterprises: not only the interest they pay on time and savings deposits, but the costs (for large banks with many branches) of thousands of ledger clerks and clerical staff, default on loans, and other miscellaneous items—such as insurance against bank robberies! To cover their costs and make profits, including the payment of dividends to shareholders, banks must earn revenue. This they do out of earnings on their assets, including both interest charged on loans and overdrafts and the yield on marketable securities.

In earning revenue in this way banks are, however, limited by the *need to reconcile risk with liquidity*. Banks have a choice of assets which they can invest in or hold, ranging from cash, which is completely liquid but yields no interest, to private loans and advances, which are the least liquid assets but normally earn the highest rate of return. Since all holders of demand deposits expect to be able to convert into cash on demand, banks cannot afford to have all their assets 'tied up' in less liquid investments or loans: failure to pay cash on demand to depositors would produce a serious crisis of confidence in the bank leading, perhaps, to a disastrous 'run on the bank'. It is to avoid this possibility and ensure continuous public confidence in the commercial banking system that governments actually legislate prescribed minimum liquid asset ratios. Banks would in general prefer not to have liquidity in excess of this 'safe' ratio, as this would mean sacrificing revenue which they could earn on riskier, higher-yielding investments. As we have seen, a shortage of good projects and credit-worthy borrowers may, particularly in less developed countries, prevent banks from expanding credit to the maximum extent.

Criticism of commercial banks and the case for nationalization

Before independence in Africa, commercial banking was largely in the hands of a few overseas banks with head offices in the metropolitan capitals such as London, for the British colonies, or Paris, Lisbon, and Brussels. In Anglophone West and East Africa, two or three British overseas banks accounted for almost all the banking business, both in terms of deposits and also in ownership of local branches. Only in the capital cities or main ports was there competition either from very recently established locally owned banks or from other expatriate banks with head offices in, say, India or the Middle East. In East Africa the big three British overseas banks were part of an international banking system with branches or associated banks elsewhere in Africa, Asia, and the Caribbean. Historically these were established locally to finance external trade rather than develop local activity. However the effect of their establishment was to stimulate at least certain sectors of local enterprise, as traders and settlers deposited the proceeds of exports in local accounts or imported foreign capital. In the absence of central banks the local branches of one or other of these banks acted as banker to the government.

Nevertheless, even before independence, the expatriate banks were subject to considerable criticism. These criticisms have counterparts in arguments for actually *nationalizing* commercial banks, and provided the case, for instance, for the state take-over of commercial banking in Tanzania in 1967. Governments of developing countries may wish to replace private ownership of such a strategic industry as commercial banking with public ownership for essentially political reasons. However some of the following *economic* arguments have been advanced in favour of complete or partial nationalization, not only in developing countries, but also in developed financial systems like that of the United Kingdom.

1. Excessive caution and high liquidity

Before independence and the establishment of central banks, the expatriate banks usually had excess liquidity: they were not fully loaned up by extending local loans up to the limit of a cash reserve ratio. Indeed, there was no formally established cash ratio to maintain, and surplus funds arising from a generally favourable balance of payments position were held as cash balances with their head offices overseas. Table 26.2 on page 379 shows the situation of excess bank liquidity in East Africa in the mid-1950s. This situation arose partly because of a shortage of credit-worthy lending opportunities, restricting the proportion of local risk assets; and partly because of the availability of good investment opportunities abroad for surplus cash. We can see from Table 26.3 on page 381 that the situation had changed markedly by the mid-1960s, with local risk assets expanding considerably in proportion to total deposit liabilities.

Nevertheless critics have argued that the banks were excessively cautious and conservative in their assessment of local investment opportunities and did not make sufficient effort to identify these; and that a nationalized banking system would explore the possibilities more strenuously and adopt a more positive lending policy. In addition, it was argued, expatriate commercial banks being primarily concerned with immediate profit, were more interested in establishing branches in the capital and main townships, and less in the rural areas, particularly the less accessible places: a state-run commercial bank would, in contrast, take long-run development objectives into account and, in order to encourage savings and trade in these areas, be less cautious in locating additional branches and seek a broader geographical coverage.

2. Discrimination in lending

Related to the previous point regarding the low level of local lending, it was specifically argued that the banks discriminated against local borrowers, particularly small-scale African businessmen and farmers, and cooperatives: all of whom were not in a good position to offer collateral in order to obtain loans. It is generally true, in developed countries also, that small businessmen find it harder to obtain credit, whereas large firms with substantial resources of their own have much less difficulty.

It is suggested that a state-run commercial bank ought to discriminate *positively*, in favour of disadvantaged enterprises, particularly small businesses, farmers, and cooperatives. Such a bank could also be used as an instrument to encourage localization of commerce and industry for the long-run benefit of expanding the base of entrepreneurship in the country. It is worth noting here that even colonial governments attempted to discriminate in favour of Africans through special African Loans Funds: the argument here is that ordinary commercial *banks* should be more positive in this direction. A nationalized bank with a monopoly of commercial banking would be in a position to subsidize small borrowers by charging them lower interest rates or granting longer credit terms, making good its overhead expenses, and profits, from more profitable loans to other, richer borrowers, assuming that the latter had no alternative source of bank credit.

3. Lack of competition among the few banking firms

This criticism arises from the oligopolistic structure of banking in many countries, and the consequent absence of price competition among them. Rather than have the market for credit and banking services generally 'dominated' by two or three large banks, it is argued the state should take responsibility for this crucial sector of the economy. A supporting point is that because of the large size of such major banking firms, no local entrepreneurs could enter this industry and, in the absence of state enterprise, the sector would be dominated not only by few firms, but by expatriate firms.

The oligopolistic market structure in banking is likely to bring with it monopoly, or rather oligopoly profits, which in a major sector like this could be substantial. When in addition the banks are expatriate concerns, there will be an outflow of such profits to foreign shareholders. State take-over of banking would eliminate excess profits and permit the retention of earnings from banking business as local income.

4. Wasteful competition and lower efficiency

Although price competition may be absent between oligopolistic banking concerns, there is generally considerable non-price competition, particularly through the opening of numerous branches in the main towns. A common criticism is that such 'service competition' is wasteful of real resources by duplicating branch buildings and expenditure on staffs. It is also suggested that there are economies of scale in the provision of deposit banking facilities because of the large overhead costs of management and fixed assets in the form of branch buildings; and that a single firm would be able to secure decreasing costs of production if the market were not fragmented between a number of separate firms. For these reasons a nationalized commercial bank operating as a single firm might be able to operate much more efficiently.

5. Control over money and credit

We pointed in the last chapter to the difficulties of controlling the money supply and volume of credit in a 'dependent' monetary system in which expatriate commercial banks can rely for liquidity on head offices overseas. Control over the volume of money and credit by a central bank requires that it can control the cash base of the commercial banks. This has to a great extent been achieved now, without nationalization: except for working balances with overseas banks all the commercial banks operating in East Africa hold their cash reserves in the form of deposits with the central banks instead of holding balances with head offices abroad.

Apart from the total volume of credit, however, there is the question of *allocation* of credit. If the government owned the commercial banks it could control *directly* the supply of credit to different individual borrowers, to different sectors of the economy, and to different geographical areas, instead of having to rely on indirect controls and monetary policies implemented at one remove through a central bank.

6. Extension of public control in the economy

A nationalized commercial bank will facilitate the extension of public control to other sectors of the economy, if this is desired.

The case against nationalization

Thus a strong case can be made for nationalization

of commercial banking. What arguments exist against such a move?

(1) There is the general argument that a large state enterprise which is in a monopoly position and free of competition, and which lacks a commercial motive, may become bureaucratic and inefficient.

(2) It can be argued that in banking in particular, where projects must be appraised and the credit-worthiness of would-be borrowers assessed, and where a portfolio of risk assets must be carefully managed, a private firm is more likely to have the commercial talents that are needed.

(3) While private commercial banking may involve a degree of wasteful competition, duplication does offer the consumer a choice as to which bank to use, which is of value in itself. A nationalized banking system would restrict consumer choice of banking services.

(4) The act of nationalization may cause a temporary loss of confidence in the financial system, though this is not likely to be a serious problem where the economy is otherwise sound, as in the case of the Tanzanian nationalization. More significant and permanent may be the 'scaring away' of private foreign investment if nationalization is regarded as preliminary to further nationalization of commercial enterprises. How important this is will depend on the degree of reliance on foreign investment which is anticipated or desired.

(5) Some of the sources of criticism of commercial banking can be dealt with without nationalization. For instance, controls may be imposed on the re-patriation of profits; selective credit controls may be applied to control the allocation of credit; legislation may be passed regarding the 'eligible assets' for in-clusion among the banks' reserve assets for liquidity purposes, in order to strengthen the central bank's control over the volume of bank deposits; the government may set up its own commercial bank *in competition with* established private concerns; special public sector financial institutions can be set up to fill specific 'gaps' in credit provision.

State-controlled commercial banks in Eastern Africa

In Eastern Africa Tanzania has gone furthest in the direction of nationalization. The decision to national-ize all commercial banks in February 1967 to form the National Bank of Commerce (NBC) was made simultaneously with the Arusha Declaration, as part of a policy of placing key sectors of the economy under state control. The main elements of policy since take-over have been: (1) the transfer of responsibility for seasonal financing of crop move-ments to the central Bank of Tanzania; (2) a rational-ization of the system of bank branches, closing down a considerable number of urban branches where these were duplicated (14 out of 60 had been closed by June 1968), opening up new ones in rural areas, and establishing mobile units to widen access to banking services; (3) manpower training through the Institute of Finance Management to provide increas-ing numbers of qualified local staff; and (4) definition of a new lending policy, leading up to the involve-ment of the NBC in increasingly comprehensive fin-ancial planning for the economy as a whole.

Elsewhere governments have not nationalized completely, but have entered the banking industry either by taking a majority holding in an existing bank or establishing a new competitor with sub-stantial state participation. In Kenya a series of mergers and amalgamations reduced the number of expatriate commercial banks, and by 1974 80 per cent of total bank deposits were held in three banks, Barclays Bank International, Standard Bank Ltd, and the Kenya Commercial Bank, of which the third was under substantial government control. Until 1969 National and Grindlays Bank (of London) was the third of the 'big three' British banks in East Africa. Its Kenyan business was then divided up between a commercial bank, the Kenya Commercial Bank, owned 60 per cent by the government and 40 per cent by National and Grindlays, and a specialist merchant bank, Grindlays Bank International (Kenya) Ltd, in which the government took a 40 per cent shareholding. The government also has a ma-jority shareholding in a smaller commercial bank which it established in 1968, the National Bank of Kenya Ltd.

In Uganda, the Uganda Commercial Bank, for-merly the Uganda Credit and Savings Bank, was actually one of the pioneers in Africa of this ap-proach of establishing a state-run commercial bank in competition with private expatriate banks, and in this case was established from scratch rather than by take-over.[1] The Uganda Credit Savings Bank (UCSB) was established in 1950 not with the aim of taking over the banking industry but for the specific purposes of mobilizing small savings, particularly among Africans, and of supplying loans to small-scale African entrepreneurs in commerce, industry, and agriculture. Later it operated alongside another source of financing of small business, the Small Industries Development Fund (SIDF), set up in 1955 as a subsidiary of the Uganda Development Cor-poration. Much later, in 1965, the UCSB was reorganized into a fully-fledged commercial bank controlled by government, the Uganda Commercial Bank, still operating alongside expatriate commercial banks.

Non-bank intermediaries and specialized financial institutions

Commercial banks are not the only financial intermediaries involved in finance and the distribution of credit. There is also a whole range of 'non-bank' financial intermediaries.

(1) First of all, there are other institutions involved in the collection of savings. The best known of these is the *Post Office Savings Bank*, now usually called the National Savings Bank. This caters primarily for small savers with relatively low incomes who wish to save and secure small amounts of money and may not have ready access to savings accounts in commercial banks. Post Offices in Africa (and elsewhere) have had problems in competing with commercial banks for savings deposits partly because of the high cost (relative to value of depositors' balances) of operating large numbers of small accounts, and partly because their investment income is earned from government securities rather than the higher interest rates on commercial bank loans to private borrowers. Their survival is possible because they already have a widely distributed network of branches for the purpose of collecting and distributing mail: savings bank activities are supplementary to this and permit the Post Office to spread its overhead costs. Where it finds difficulty in breaking even, there is a case for some degree of subsidization of its activities because of its value in collecting savings in the rural areas and in assisting the development of a cash economy.

Building societies[2] are also of growing importance in Africa and elsewhere in collecting the savings of mainly middle-income households, whose share capital and deposits are repayable at a fixed nominal monetary value at short notice and even on demand. Building societies in Eastern Africa are, however, still very small by comparison with commercial banks; whereas in Britain for example, the assets of building societies now exceed those of all commercial banks put together.

(2) Another category of financial intermediary mobilizing savings is represented by *insurance companies and pension funds*. The distinctive feature of these is the accumulation of *long-term* savings of individuals, who wish to provide for their families on death or retirement. Pension funds for the employees of large firms are mainly managed by insurance companies in Africa, but often by the firms themselves in developed countries. In addition there are state-run social security systems, which are an integral part of the 'welfare state' in social democratic countries in Western Europe, and increasingly being established in developing countries in Africa, the Caribbean, and South-East Asia. In Kenya the National Social Security Fund (NSSF) was established in 1965 and mobilizes long-term *compulsory* savings of lower-paid wage earners and their employers' contributions for investment in government securities. It is important to realize just how important such funds are quantitatively (a) as part of total savings in the country and (b) as a source of investment. Because life assurance and pension funds are very long-term savings, they can be invested in higher-yielding risk assets such as equity shares, mortgages, and property developments. Since they account for a large part of long-term savings undertaken by the personal sector, the governments of most African countries have tapped these savings by insisting on local investment of these funds and have also entered the business themselves. In Tanzania the entire insurance business has been nationalized, partly for this reason, under the National Insurance Corporation (NIC). In Kenya this has not happened, but there has been since 1964 a National Assurance Company, in which the government has a majority of shares, providing life assurance and group pension facilities tailored to African lives. Today the Kenyan NSSF, and some of its counterparts in other countries, are the largest holder of local Public Debt, in other words, the largest source of finance, from local private incomes, for financing the government's development programmes.

(3) A third category is of specialist investment companies of a type common in developed capitalist countries. We can refer again to *building societies* which use the funds they collect to specialize in lending for house purchases, taking a mortgage on the property as security until the loan is repaid over, say, 10–25 years. The Housing Finance Company of Kenya (HFCK) was established with capital provided by the government and the Commonwealth Development Corporation (CDC) but operates like a private building society, accepting savings deposits from the public to finance private house mortgage loans. In Tanzania there has been, from 1968, the Permanent Housing Finance Company of Tanzania (PHFCT), similarly funded by the government and the CDC. In 1972 this was replaced by the Tanzania Housing Bank (THB) with similar functions, but a stronger directive to finance *low-cost* housing and to concentrate less on urban areas to benefit a wider range of people. It has continued to accept deposits and to serve as a savings bank.

Another specialist institution is the *hire-purchase finance house* which makes loans over fixed periods of one or two years, for the purchase of large durable consumer goods, such as motor cars, to consumers, and producers' goods, such as vehicles and machinery for business enterprises. These have sometimes been set up by governments in African countries, as in the case of Karadha, in Tanzania, while in Uganda the government-sponsored African Business Promotions Ltd (ABP) operated a Hire Purchase Guarantee scheme to assist African businessmen.

(4) *Merchant banks or new issue houses* are another specialist institution which use commercial bank loans and their own capital to finance the expansion of private enterprises by purchasing part of their share capital.

(5) Another category is of institutions, generally in the public sector, which attempt to 'fill the gaps' in the provision of credit left by the ordinary commercial banking system and which occur particularly in less developed countries. We may mention here special efforts to provide credit to indigenous entrepreneurs who, due to lack of assets to offer as security, have found it difficult to obtain credit from commercial banks. Before independence *African Productivity Loans Funds* existed in all three East African countries, designed to assist small-scale African entrepreneurs in any commercial activity, who were not otherwise sufficiently 'credit-worthy'.

There were, and are, millions of African entrepreneurs in East Africa in the form of peasant farmers, or small traders, and the major gap in the provision of credit by the expatriate banking system was in supplying credit to the rural sector. To fill this gap most African countries have established special *rural credit institutions*. In East Africa, the provision of rural credit has included *credit for cooperative marketing societies*, partly because cooperative marketing has been of special importance and specially encouraged in East Africa, and partly because the cooperatives have been used as a vehicle for the distribution of credit among individual African smallholders.

Tanzania has perhaps the fullest history of rural credit institutions.[1] The local Development Loan Fund, established in 1947, provided loans to 'Native Authorities' which were intended for the benefit of farmers and rural areas in general. The Land Bank of Tanganyika, established in 1948, offered long-term loans of 15–30 years' duration, and continued until 1961, when it was replaced by the Agricultural Credit Agency (ACA), which also took over the Local Development Loan Fund and the African Productivity Loan Fund in order to coordinate credit provision to the rural areas. It was able to offer short-, medium- or long-term loans of up to 25 years. Like the African Productivity Loan Fund, the Agency experienced a high rate of default and in an effort to reduce this began to work through the co-operative movement. This relationship was strength-ened in the reorganization which took place in 1964, when share capital subscribed by the cooperative movement itself was used to establish the National Cooperative Bank (NCB) and the National Development Credit Agency (NDCA). The former served as banker to the cooperative societies from 1964 to 1970, concentrating for most of that time on supplying crop finance, as required to facilitate the marketing of the major cash crops. Later on it was felt that the commercial bank, now firmly established under state control as the National Bank of Commerce, was in a position to undertake the activities of the Cooperative Bank, so that the latter was absorbed into the NBC in 1970.

The policy of the NDCA was to make loans entirely through the cooperative movement rather than directly to individual farmers. This permitted a closer assessment of the farmer's credit-worthiness, probably exerted greater social pressure on the farmer to repay, and thus succeeded in reducing to some extent the previously high rate of default, although these problems remained.

In 1971, as the rural development programme in Tanzania was intensified, the NDCA was replaced by the Tanzania Rural Development Bank (TRDB) which was to have broader responsibilities than the NDCA, including the supply of credit to rural industries and to ujamaa villages, and the provision of assistance to customers in identifying possible investment opportunities. In these connections close contact was to be established with ujamaa villages, District Development Corporations, and Regional and District Planning Committees. It was thus to be more of an instrument for planned rural development than an agency for the supply of loans to small-scale entrepreneurs and smallholders. For this purpose branches were to be established in every region, and the capital at its disposal considerably expanded.

A different kind of 'gap' in available credit in Tanzania was for *medium- and long-term funds for development projects* which cannot be expected to repay their investments quickly. Since agricultural projects would be covered by the TRDB, the Tanzania Industrial Bank (TIB) was set up in late 1970, mainly for the financing of public and parastatal industrial projects. The main shareholders were the government (60 per cent) and the National Bank of Commerce (30 per cent) with the state-run National Insurance Corporation accounting for the rest. Table 27.1 shows that loans made were directed predominantly towards the public and semi-public sector of industry.

(6) The next type of financial intermediary may be described as *development finance companies*, the purpose of which is to raise additional external finance for development projects. Thus the Tanganyika

Table 27.1 Loans granted by the Tanzania Investment Bank up to June 1972, by ownership of borrowing firms

Ownership	No. of loans	m shs
Wholly public	8	20.2
50% public or more	7	17.9
51% private or more	0	0
Wholly private	3	4.0
	18	42.1

SOURCE: C. Caselli, op. cit.

Development Finance Company Limited (TDFL), established in December 1962, was a precursor of TIB. Though the initial capital, shs 10 m from each donor, was subscribed by the CDC, the Federal Republic of Germany and the Tanganyika government, the objective was for the TDFL to operate as a development bank by attracting additional finance, using the bank as a medium for investment in Tanzania. The Development Finance Company of Kenya (DFCK) is similar to the TDFL, financed in equal portions by the Kenya government, ICDC, the British CDC, and the German and Dutch counterpart overseas finance institutions. The DFCK has a 'catalyst' role, promoting joint ventures with foreign capital in larger projects such as hotels, sugar mills, and textiles. Such companies are similar to development banks, like the African Development Bank, in that they attempt to raise capital internationally for development projects, except that they operate on a smaller scale and within national borders.

(7) Finally, we may mention *development corporations*, in so far as these function as financial institutions. The range of interests of Tanzania's National Development Corporation, for example, has already been shown in Table 18.3. Table 27.2 gives the distribution of NDC investments by recipient sectors at the end of 1970. This indicates that the NDC, operating as a holding company, with a wide range of investments in many sectors of the economy, is in effect a form of development bank, even if its interest in its associated and subsidiary companies goes beyond the mere supply of finance. The difficulty of drawing a line between a vast holding company like this and a development bank may be appreciated from a comparison of the shs 1,453 millions shown in Table 27.2 as invested by the NDC with the shs 42 millions invested through the Tanzania Industrial Bank up to 1972, given in Table 27.1, particularly as both of these are investing in the public or semi-public sector. The NDC is a major continuing source of credit to members of its group and at an early stage set up its own internal bank with which subsidiary companies could obtain credit or deposit surplus funds. The NDC could thus act as a financial intermediary not only by raising finance for the group from outside, but also for the transfer of funds between subsidiary companies. Interest rates were actually fixed for these funds, albeit low rates, as for any bank.

The capital involved makes the NDC a significant financial institution, even alongside the National Bank of Commerce (whose total bank lending in March 1973 was by chance shs 1,454 million, about the same figure as that just quoted for NDC), which raises a number of problems. A substantial amount of the country's flow of funds was passing outside the recognized financial system, giving NDC companies

Table 27.2 Tanzania's National Development Corporation: distribution of investment by recipient sectors, December 1970

Sector	No. of projects	Investments (shs m)	Distribution (% of total)
Food, beverages, and tobacco	9	171	12
Textiles and leather	6	253	17
Wood	6	50	3
Printing and paper	5	406	28
Chemicals	5	225	16
Minerals	9	91	6
Other industries	6	11	1
Commerce and finance companies	4	109	8
Mining	3	137	9
Total	53	1453	100

SOURCE: NDC Sixth Annual Report, 1970

preferential access to capital, obtained at a much lower interest rate, without the same *external* checks on the value of a project which would be involved if a company were forced to seek finance independently. The low rates of interest charged also raised the problem of 'unfair competition' for the National Bank of Commerce to which it was an alternative source of finance. And of course it raises questions for *monetary policy* when a substantial flow of funds exists outside the control of the commercial banking system. For these reasons new annual Finance and Credit Plans were introduced in Tanzania in 1971, and intercompany lending has been regulated and made subject to authority. The same issues of principle arise in respect of the allocation of funds within the other major national development corporations described in Chapter 18, such as Uganda's UDC, and those in Zambia, Kenya, and Malawi.

Capitalist financial systems

Let us now take an overview of the previous discussion and make some general points about financial systems as a whole. In such a system financial intermediaries collect savings and distribute credit. In addition the liabilities of commercial banks[4] (bank deposits) serve as money and facilitate exchange in the money economy. A variety of *non-bank* intermediaries also collect savings and/or distribute credit, although they differ from banks in that they do not create money through their liabilities. There is considerable specialization and division of labour among financial intermediaries. Some, like the Post Office Savings Bank, concentrate on collecting very small savings. Others, like building societies, concentrate on a particular type of investment, in this case long-term mortgage loans to finance housing for owner-occupiers.

The financial system not only permits businessmen and dis-savers (those who spend in excess of their incomes) to use the surplus money balances and savings of other groups in the economy, but *provides liquidity* by widening the choice of assets and liabilities open to both lenders and borrowers. Thus small savers can retain as assets highly liquid bank deposits or deposits with building societies which bear little risk of loss and can be used as cash or converted to cash at any time, while the banks or building societies make riskier or longer-term loans and investments. Similarly business firms can hold a variety of liquid and less liquid assets as cover for their operations and may, for example, be more or less highly 'geared'.

Liquidity can be provided directly by financial intermediaries as above but in particular is provided by the existence of *financial markets*. The existence of a stock exchange, for instance, permits individuals as well as institutions to invest in primary securities (shares and loan stocks) for limited periods and then liquidate even irredeemable securities by selling to other holders. Linked to this organized market in long-term securities are, often, various short-term money markets, a foreign exchange market, and perhaps organized markets for internationally traded commodities like coffee and cotton, and real estate markets for land and property. Alongside the stocks and shares of private firms, financial markets exist in developed market economies for both short-term (Treasury bills) and long-term debt issued by governments. Historically the needs of the state for loan finance were associated with financing wars by issuing public debt to banks and individuals, and the recent development of the Nigerian Stock Exchange was stimulated by the need to finance military expenditure by a rapid expansion of Public Debt which could be issued to the non-bank sector. The Nigerian and Nairobi Stock Exchanges are still small, in terms of the list of stocks and shares in companies quoted, but operate on standard lines. Specialized financial middlemen, called 'stockbrokers', 'bid' to buy, or offer for sale, securities for their clients, taking a commission for their work. The stock exchange is basically a market in 'second-hand' securities so that its main function is to provide liquidity to holders, or potential holders, of primary securities. Because securities quoted for trading on a stock exchange have greater liquidity than unquoted stocks, the stock exchange reduces the cost of new capital for companies as well.

Socialist financial systems

The same functions of collecting savings and allocating credit, as well as creating money, have to be carried out in socialist systems. Forms of control over the total volume of credit and the money supply, and over the allocation of credit are, however, much more direct. Since the commercial banks are state-owned and open to directives from the government or monetary authority, it is not necessary to induce them to vary the volume of credit through indirect methods such as a variation in its cash base. Indeed, since the central bank and a single commercial bank are both under direct government control it becomes hardly necessary for them to operate as separate institutions at all: it is in fact common in socialist countries in Eastern Europe to have a single 'mono-bank' which combines the functions of a central bank and commercial bank, issuing currency, determining both the volume and allocation of credit, guaranteeing the money supply, and acting as banker to the government.

Given the extent of direct control, the question

arises of the criteria for allocation of credit in a socialist system. The basic motivation of capitalist bankers will be profit maximization: which borrowers can pay the highest rates of interest while providing adequate security. Socialist bankers and financial intermediaries must also take into account (social) rates of return and the opportunity-costs of allocating credit to one use rather than another: but their motivation will not be profit maximization. In allocating credit they will need to take account of social priorities and the desirability of various projects as seen by the government. Given government priorities, bankers will have much less discretion in granting credits.

At the aggregate level, in order to avoid over-allocation of funds by allocating more than the 'available' amount of finance, some form of *financial plan* will be essential, to replace the indirect control applied through the cash base of a capitalist system. As indicated above, a special problem exists in a less developed country with a substantial parastatal sector dominated by a major development corporation operating as a holding company and supported by a range of other parastatals. In Tanzania rules for the allocation of funds within the NDC and among parastatals were introduced along with an annual Financial and Credit Plan in 1971. The Annual Financial Plan, worked out by the National Bank of Commerce and Ministry of Finance, now covers all major sectors of the economy, and in a less detailed way the other sectors,[5] and follows guidelines for priority sectors laid down by the central bank in consultation with the government. Financial projections are made for the different sectors within which more detailed allocations can be carried out. Through increasingly comprehensive financial planning and allocation of credit, Tanzania has moved considerably in the direction of a socialist banking system.

The allocation of credit in most African economies, however, reflects their status as 'mixed' economies combining private and public enterprise. They possess a combination of private and public financial institutions and intermediaries, with the latter established particularly to 'fill the gaps' left in the provision of credit by the private system.

Questions on Chapter 27

1. What are the main functions of commercial banks?
2. What are 'financial intermediaries' and how do they contribute to the efficiency of the financial system?
3. How far can banks in a capitalist system be described as commercial enterprises? What limits their ability to earn revenue?
4. Discuss the case for and against nationalization of commercial banking in African countries.
5. How have 'specialization and the division of labour' affected the development of financial systems?
6. Discuss the case for subsidizing the operations of the National (or Post Office) Savings Bank in a developing country.
7. What 'gaps' in the provision of credit tend to occur in the financial systems of less developed countries, and why?
8. In what way may a national development corporation take on the functions of a development bank? What difficulties, if any, are associated with this?
9. What are the main differences which exist between a capitalist and a socialist financial system?

Notes

[1] See G. R. Bosa, *The Financing of Small-scale Enterprises in Uganda*, MISR Occasional Paper No. 3, Oxford University Press, 1969.

[2] Called 'Savings and Loan Associations' in America, these institutions, like cooperative societies, are owned jointly by their 'members': the individuals who subscribe shares.

[3] A fuller account is given in C. Caselli, *The Banking System of Tanzania*, Cassa di Risparmio delle Provincie Lombarde, Milan, 1974. A useful short survey of agricultural credit in Kenya is given in the Central Bank of Kenya's *Economic and Financial Review*, Vol. VIII, No. 11, October–December 1975.

[4] Together with currency issued by the central bank and held *outside* banks.

[5] See A. J. Nsekela, 'The Role of Commercial Banking in Building a Socialist Tanzania', *The African Review*, Vol. 4, No. 1, 1974.

28 Income Determination

In the early part of this book we discussed what we meant by the national income of a country and factors affecting the level of national income and its rate of growth. We suggested that economic growth was synonymous with increases in the *capacity to produce* of the economy, that is, the *aggregate supply* of goods and services forthcoming. As the capacity to produce was expanded, so the national output or income grew. In fact the national outputs of countries, developed or underdeveloped, have by no means exhibited steady growth over time: they have fluctuated, and often the fluctuations have been severe. Thus economies have been subject to 'boom' and 'slump' from time to time. At one time it was considered that the alternation of boom and slump, the *'trade cycle'*, was an inherent part of the capitalist economy, largely beyond the control of policy-makers. Economists now hold the more optimistic belief that economic fluctuations can be controlled and kept within limits. Since such fluctuations appear to be produced in part by changes in *aggregate demand* for goods and services, it is high time we turned to the factors determining total demand in the economy as a whole.

The concept of equilibrium income

It will be recalled that national income was defined as the value of the flow of goods and services in the economy during the year. Furthermore national income is necessarily equal to national expenditure since it is actually derived from this income. Apart from transfer incomes people can only receive incomes as a result of expenditure by others on the goods and services which they provide. There is thus a circular flow of income and expenditure, with expenditure generating income and income permitting expenditure. It follows that if income is to be maintained at a given level through successive periods then expenditure out of the income must be maintained at the same level. If income is self-maintaining in this way we can appropriately refer to it as an *equilibrium level of income*, in that it will show no tendency to alter. What conditions are necessary for such a state of equilibrium?

We note first of all that when an individual receives income, he may either spend it on consumption goods or save it: but whereas the consumption expenditure generates further income, the saving does not. Saving constitutes a loss out of the circular flow of income, or what we may suitably call a 'leakage' from that flow. What compensates for this leakage is investment expenditure undertaken separately by businessmen, which has to be added to consumption expenditure. The position is illustrated in Figure 28.1.

Thus if people wish to save 10 units out of a total income of 100, investment will have to equal 10 if that level of income is to be maintained. If businessmen only wish to invest 5 units, however, aggregate expenditure or aggregate money demand will be equal to 95 only, and incomes in the succeeding period will be correspondingly reduced. The level of income will thus vary with aggregate money demand, $C+I$. Income will be in equilibrium on the other hand, and show no tendency to change, if saving and investment are exactly equal. We can take this equality between what people want to save and what businessmen want to invest, that is, between *desired* saving and *desired* investment, as the condition necessary for income to be in equilibrium.

The way in which the equilibrium level of money income is determined is further demonstrated in Figure 28.2. This represents a water tank in which the water level gives the level of money income. Leakages leave the tank at point B and injections into the circular flow of money income enter through the tap at point A. If the outflow from the tank

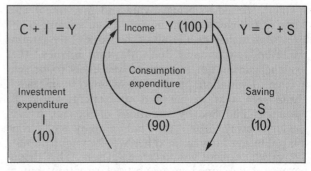

Figure 28.1 *The circular flow of income.*

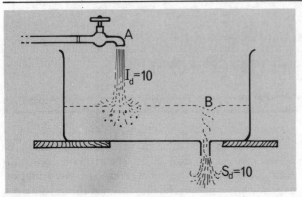

Figure 28.2 *Leakages and equilibrium level of money income.*

through B is greater than the inflow through A, the level of water in the tank (money income) will fall; if the inflow (injections) exceeds the rate of outflow (leakages), the water level must rise. Equilibrium is where the water level is constant, and this will occur when inflow and outflow balance: in the example shown, when desired saving equals the inflow, desired investment, both equal to 10.

Taking the stock of capital and the supply of labour in the economy as given, we may say that *full employment income* is being produced when all those persons who wish to be employed are in fact in employment. As far as our analysis has gone, therefore, we see that there is no reason why equilibrium income and full employment income should coincide: *for how much people will wish to save out of full employment income will have little to do with the amount of investment expenditure businessmen might wish to make.* The latter will be determined especially by investment opportunities, resulting in part from long-term plans, or new products, or new processes invented, and by business confidence. And business confidence is notoriously unsteady. Saving and investment are thus undertaken by two distinct groups of people and for quite distinct motives: they cannot be expected to coincide automatically.

At one time it was thought that the rate of interest would operate to bring saving and investment into line at full employment income. Later it came to be realized, mainly as a result of the work of the famous Cambridge economist, John Maynard Keynes,[1] that neither saving nor investment was likely to be sensitive to variations in the rate of interest: instead it was seen that saving and investment would be brought into line by variations in income, if necessary away from the full employment level. Equilibrium income, in other words, might be at a level where there was *underemployment*. This theory was not developed in an abstract situation, but in response to a real and critical problem; for example

in 1932 as many as 22 per cent of the insured labour force of the United Kingdom were unemployed, not because of the absence of factories or mines where they could work, but because of the lack of effective demand following a collapse of business confidence, and the economic processes which we shall now describe.

The consumption function

The basis of this 'Keynesian' theory of employment and income determination is that the amount the community consumes depends on the income it receives in aggregate. Thus since we have the equation

$$C+I=Y$$

telling us how income is obtained from the two elements of expenditure, and

$$C=c(Y)$$

asserting that consumption is a function of income, it follows that a change in investment, which we may call ΔI, meaning an increment in I, will increase Y by more than ΔI. For while the initial increase in Y, ΔY, will be equal to ΔI, this change in Y will itself produce a change in C, which will increase Y still further. The final increase in income thus exceeds the initial increase in investment expenditure, which is therefore magnified or 'multiplied'. This process is in fact referred to as the *multiplier process*. To understand it, we must look more closely at the *consumption function*, as the relation between consumption and income is called.

Readers will recall that this function has already been discussed in Chapter 6. The first two columns of Table 28.1 give hypothetical figures for money income, in million pounds, and corresponding levels of consumption expenditure. The third column gives saving as the difference between money income and consumption $(Y-C)$. The next three columns give the increments in Y, C, and S, obtained in the usual way. The final two columns give the ratios of the increments in consumption and saving to the incre-

Table 28.1 *Aggregate consumption and saving at different levels of income*

Y	C	S	ΔY	ΔC	ΔS	$\Delta C/\Delta Y$	$\Delta S/\Delta Y$
60	60	0	—	—	—	—	—
70	70	0	10	10	0	1.0	0.0
80	79	1	10	9	1	0.9	0.1
90	87	3	10	8	2	0.8	0.2
100	94	6	10	7	3	0.7	0.3
110	100	10	10	6	4	0.6	0.4
120	105	15	10	5	5	0.5	0.5

ment in income which brings them about. These ratios are going to be important to our analysis and we therefore give them names. The ratio $\dfrac{\Delta C}{\Delta Y}$, which tells us the rate at which consumption increases as income increases, we shall call the *marginal propensity to consume*; the ratio $\dfrac{\Delta S}{\Delta Y}$, which tells us the rate at which saving increases as income increases, we shall call the *marginal propensity to save*. Since an increment in income will either be spent on consumption or saved,

$$\Delta Y = \Delta C + \Delta S$$

Dividing by ΔY, it follows that

$$1 = \frac{\Delta C}{\Delta Y} + \frac{\Delta S}{\Delta Y}$$

The sum of the marginal propensities to consume and save equals 1, as can be checked numerically in Table 28.1.

The data from Table 28.1 are plotted in Figure 28.3, showing that both the consumption function and the 'savings function' are curves. In what follows, however, it will simplify matters if we assume these to be straight-line functions. The rates at which consumption and saving increase, the marginal propensities, will thus be constant. As we shall see now, these marginal propensities are fundamental to the multiplier process.

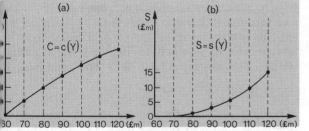

Figure 28.3   The consumption and savings function: (a) the consumption function, (b) the savings function.

The operation of the 'multiplier'

Suppose the increase in investment comes about as a result of decisions by businessmen in the construction industry to increase the rate of housebuilding by, say, 100 houses, each costing £1,000 to build. Investment will increase by £100,000. Now this will be paid out as income to workers of all kinds in the building industry, to workers in industries which

Table 28.2   The multiplier process

Round of spending	Increase in Y	Cumulative increase in Y
1	100	100
2	60	160
3	36	196
4	21.6	217.6
5	12.96	230.56
6	7.78	238.34
7	4.67	243.01
8	2.80	245.81
9	1.68	247.49
10	1.00	248.49

supply materials to the building industry, and others who contribute labour or capital or enterprise to the building of the houses; these people will in turn wish to spend these incomes on a wide range of consumer goods, generating further incomes among those responsible for the supply of consumer goods, and so on. There will thus be a series of further rounds of expenditure, or *secondary spending*, in addition to the initial or *primary spending*. The obvious question is how, and where, does this multiplier process stop?

The answer to how it stops is given by the fact that each successive round of spending is smaller than the last, because of leakages into saving. Suppose in our example an average of three-fifths of any increases in income is spent by the people receiving it: the marginal propensities to consume and save will be 3/5 and 2/5 respectively. Since $\Delta I = 100$ (thousands of pounds), we shall have the series shown above in Table 28.2.

The figures in the third column are plotted in Figure 28.4. From the graph it is clear that the increase in Y converges to the level of 250. The mathematicians can tell us that this convergence is to be expected: we have already stated, in connection with the bank deposit multiplier of Chapter 25, that, for any value z between 0 and 1, the series

$$1 + z + z^2 + z^3 + \ldots$$

tends to the value $\dfrac{1}{1-z}$. In our example we have the series

$$100 + 60 + 36 + 21.6 + \ldots$$

or,

$$100\left\{1 + \left(\frac{3}{5}\right) + \left(\frac{3}{5}\right)^2 + \left(\frac{3}{5}\right)^3 + \ldots\right\}$$

which thus equals

$$100\left\{\frac{1}{1 - 3/5}\right\} = 100\left\{\frac{1}{2/5}\right\} = 250$$

This result can be generalized, using our notation, as

$$\Delta I \left\{ \frac{1}{1 - \dfrac{\Delta C}{\Delta Y}} \right\} = \Delta I \left\{ \frac{1}{\dfrac{\Delta S}{\Delta Y}} \right\} = \Delta Y$$

Dividing by ΔI, we obtain

$$\frac{\Delta Y}{\Delta I} = \frac{1}{1 - \dfrac{\Delta C}{\Delta Y}} = \frac{1}{\dfrac{\Delta S}{\Delta Y}}$$

The ratio, $\dfrac{\Delta Y}{\Delta I}$, of the total increase in income to the increase in investment which produces it, is known as the multiplier, k. If we write c for $\dfrac{\Delta C}{\Delta Y}$ and s for $\dfrac{\Delta S}{\Delta Y}$, we have

$$k = \frac{\Delta Y}{\Delta I} = \frac{1}{1 - c} = \frac{1}{s}$$

The multiplier is thus the reciprocal of the marginal propensity to save.

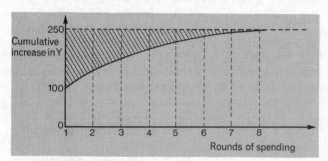

Figure 28.4 The multiplier process.

Let us now attempt a rather different approach which will relate the multiplier more closely to the consumption function and savings function. We stated earlier that income is in equilibrium when desired saving equals desired investment; and that whereas the level of desired saving varies with income, desired investment can be assumed to be independent of income. This situation is illustrated in Figure 28.5.

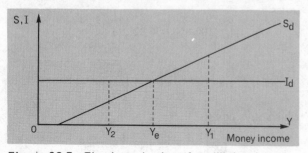

Figure 28.5 The determination of equilibrium income

Desired saving and investment are measured on the vertical axis. It will be noticed that investment always takes the same value irrespective of Y. It is important to look at this diagram in conjunction with Figure 28.1 if its full meaning is to be understood. At income Y_1, the amount of investment is insufficient to absorb the desired level of saving: total expenditure will thus be insufficient to maintain that level of income, which will therefore fall. Similarly at money income Y_2, below Y_e, desired investment expenditure exceeds the leakage into saving, and incomes will therefore rise. At Y_e saving is exactly offset by desired investment and there will be no reason for money incomes to change: Y_e is the equilibrium level of money income.

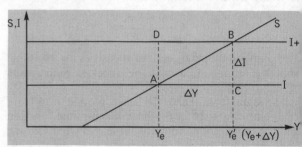

Figure 28.6 Multiplier effects of an autonomous change in investment.

Suppose now there is a change in the level of desired investment, the investment curve shifting upwards as in Figure 28.6. The multiplier process can be seen as an increase in income from Y_e, with saving and investment equal at point A to Y'_e, with saving and investment equal at point B. The increase in investment, ΔI, is equal to BC, and the resulting increase in income, ΔY, to AC. The multiplier k therefore equals the ratio $\dfrac{AC}{BC}$.

We can also see the answer to the question of where the multiplier process must stop. Immediately after the change in investment, desired investment exceeds savings at income Y_e by the amount AD: income then increases to Y'_e where saving equals the new level of investment. In other words *the multiplier operates until the increase in income has generated additional saving equal to the increase in investment.*

Some simple algebra will give us the formula, $k = 1/s$, which we obtained earlier. We are initially in equilibrium at point A with $I = Y - C$ (desired investment equal to saving). If these are to be equal again at point B after an increase in investment, saving must increase by the same amount, that is

$$\Delta(Y - C) = \Delta Y - \Delta C = \Delta I$$

Dividing by ΔY, we get

$$1 - \frac{\Delta C}{\Delta Y} = \frac{\Delta I}{\Delta Y}$$

$$1 - c = s = \frac{1}{k}$$

or $k = \frac{1}{s}$ as before.[2]

The analysis of Figures 28.5 and 28.6 can be carried out algebraically. The diagram indicates that the level of desired investment is constant at some value, say I_0:

$$I_d = I_0 \qquad (28.1)$$

Desired saving is a straight-line function of income;[3]

$$S_d = sY \qquad (28.2)$$

And equilibrium is given by the equality of desired savings and investment:

$$S_d = I_d \qquad (28.3)$$

Putting equations 28.1 and 28.2 into 28.3 gives:

$$sY = I_0$$

or

$$Y_e = \frac{I_0}{s} \qquad (28.4)$$

In equation 28.4 we write Y_e since we are referring to the equilibrium value of income, the particular value of Y which makes $S_d = I_d$. Equation 28.4 states that the equilibrium level of money income will be in a given ratio to the level of investment, I_0, the given ratio being $\frac{1}{s}$ or the reciprocal of the marginal propensity to save.

If we suppose now the level of investment rises to a new higher level, $I_0 + \Delta I$, then the equilibrium level of income will become:

$$Y_e' = \frac{(I_0 + \Delta I)}{s} \qquad (28.5)$$

obtained in exactly the same way as equation 28.4. This can be rewritten as:

$$Y_e' = \frac{I_0}{s} + \frac{\Delta I}{s}$$

or,

$$Y_e' = Y_e + \frac{\Delta I}{s} \qquad (28.6)$$

Hence:

$$Y_e' - Y_e = \frac{\Delta I}{s} \qquad (28.7)$$

But $Y_e' - Y_e$ is the increase in the equilibrium level of income consequent upon the increase in investment, and we may write it as ΔY. Hence:

$$\Delta Y = \frac{\Delta I}{s}$$

or,

$$\Delta Y = k \Delta I$$

The increase in the level of income is the multiplier k times the increase in the level of investment.

Further repercussions: induced investment

In the discussion above an initial or primary increase in spending, say, some additional investment or increase in export sales, produced some further rounds of secondary spending through the multiplier process. However this secondary spending may lead to further *tertiary* spending through its effects on investment.

In order to supply the extra consumer goods and meet the demand involved in the successive rounds of secondary spending, businessmen will need additional capital goods to expand their productive capacity. This involves further spending on investment. Since it is an expansion in demand for and output of consumer goods which calls for and 'induces' the increase in investment spending, the latter is referred to as *induced investment*.

Induced investment is generally explained as a technical or physical relationship. Suppose that there is a given ratio between the level of output Y_t at any time t and the capital stock required to produce it, K_t, and that this ratio is equal to v. Hence:

$$K_t = vY_t \qquad (28.8)$$

If the value of output in the previous period was Y_{t-1}, and the ratio existed in this period also, then in addition:

$$K_{t-1} = v \, Y_{t-1} \qquad (28.9)$$

Subtracting equation 28.9 from 28.8,

$$K_t - K_{t-1} = v(Y_t - Y_{t-1}) \qquad (28.10)$$

The left-hand side of this equation is the increase in the value of capital stock over the period, that is, the value of investment, I_t. The right-hand side is v times the increase in output (equal to money income), ΔY_t. Instead of equation 28.10 we can therefore write:

$$I_t = v \triangle Y_t \qquad (28.11)$$

which says that induced investment equals v times the change in the value of output during the period.

This is referred to as the *acceleration principle* which expresses in money income terms the 'relation' between changes in the level of investment and the change in the level of income or output. The ratio v is known as the acceleration coefficient.

It is doubtful whether even in advanced industrial countries we can assume a fixed capital–output ratio, as required by the acceleration principle, and that therefore there is any very *stable* relation between changes in output and the level of investment. This is true particularly because there are other factors affecting investment, such as business confidence, especially, and the rate of interest and availability of capital. In less developed countries the assumption of a fixed capital–output ratio is less plausible, since the industrial sector is small and likely to concentrate on a limited number of industries, while the agricultural sector is large, with a large share of domestic or subsistence output, and is a sector in which the relation between capital and output is less direct.

An alternative way in which increases in demand and output may be related to investment is through the level of profits. Since a major source of funds for investment is retained profits of firms, an increase in the level of spending on final output, by increasing profits, may 'induce' an increase in the level of investment. According to this hypothesis, which has been referred to as the *profits principle*,[4] the level of induced investment depends upon the *level* of output rather than the *change* in the level of output.

The effect of the level of output on the level of profits may be reinforced by its effect on expectations, also increasing investment, through its effect on business confidence.

It is possible that the profits principle has more applicability in less developed countries than does the acceleration principle. An increase in money incomes in Eastern Africa, for instance, as a result of an increase in export sales will give African farmers more wealth, as well as more incentive, to invest in their farms. In general we can say that in less developed countries an increase in primary spending will produce some secondary spending and expansion of money incomes (limited by leakages abroad), and that this may in turn bring a beneficial tertiary effect on investment, whether by local manufacturing concerns in building up stocks or by farmers in farm improvements: but this effect will be uncertain and not precisely related to the initial change.

Output, employment, and the price level in the Keynesian model

The discussion so far has been entirely in terms of variations in *money income* and expenditure. What is

implied as far as output and employment are concerned? If we start from a position of widespread unemployment, with workers unable to find employment due to the lack of effective demand, though willing to work at the going wage, we shall have in effect a perfectly elastic supply of labour at this wage rate. Secondly, if we make the assumption of constant returns to scale up to the level of full employment, any additional workers employed will produce the same output as the rest. Since each worker produces the same output, and costs the same in wages paid, then obviously each additional unit of output will cost the same to produce. Since costs are constant, prices will be constant; and hence any increase in money income or expenditure will be met by a proportional increase in output and in employment. We may even talk in terms of an *employment multiplier* rather than a real income (output) or money income multiplier: this multiplier will be *the ratio of the eventual total increase in employment to the initial amount of employment created.*

Once we approach the full employment point, where all workers who want employment at the going wage have found it, money income, output, and employment will no longer increase in proportion. The supply of labour will eventually become completely inelastic, and so will output. Any increase in aggregate demand, met with completely inelastic supply of output, will result in higher prices. In this case, since we are talking about output of *all* goods in the economy, this means a rise in the general level: *inflation*. And now instead of output increasing in proportion to expenditure, prices will increase pro-

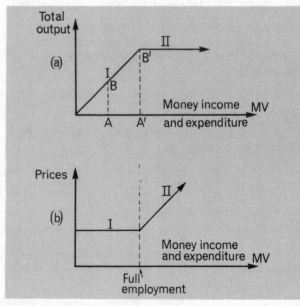

Figure 28.7   *The effect on (a) output, and (b) prices, of changes in aggregate demand.*

portionately. This is illustrated in Figure 28.7.[5] The upper diagram shows how total output varies with money income (expenditure). Up to the full employment level these move in proportion to each other: thus when expenditure doubles from OA to OA′ output doubles from AB to A′B′. The lower diagram shows prices constant up to full employment and then increasing in direct proportion to expenditure.

In fact we should not expect such an immediate switch from constant prices to rising prices. In the first place constant returns are unlikely to hold right up to the full employment point, but will give way to diminishing returns as this point is approached; as this happens costs and prices will begin to rise. This is partly because there will not be any one point at which the supply of labour and output are completely inelastic: there will be a zone over which more labour is obtainable but at higher wages, either through the existing labour force working longer hours or through people who would otherwise stay at home taking up jobs, for instance housewives. Secondly, money wages will rise also because of trade union pressure, as trade unions find it easier to press for wage increases when output and employment are increasing and the pool of unemployed labour is small. Thirdly, full employment output will not be reached at the same time in all industries: shortages or 'bottlenecks' will appear first in one, then in another industry. This depends on factors of production not being completely mobile: resources, including labour, cannot easily be switched from one industry to another where the shortage is acute.

Supply in one industry may therefore be inelastic when supply in another is still quite elastic. Hence prices in some industries begin to rise before those in others. Taking these considerations into account, we have in Figure 28.8 a zone, labelled II, in which output continues to increase, but not in proportion to increased money demand: only when a point of 'absolutely full' employment is reached does output cease to increase and prices rise in proportion to increased expenditure. This point is preceded by what may be described as a 'zone' or range of high employment.

Keynes, however, was primarily concerned with the problem of unemployment, that is, with Zone I in the diagrams. His theory of aggregate income determination was of an essentially short-run nature: *it was concerned with short-run fluctuations in the level of income arising from variations in demand*, and not with the longer-run problems of growth. The nation's stock of capital was taken as given but, due to lack of effective demand, under-utilized: increases in effective demand thus could take up the slack in both labour *and* capital so that output could be assumed to be in perfectly elastic supply. The level of investment spending was the crucial determinant, since money income and consumption spending were determined, via the multiplier process, by investment.

To sustain his theory, Keynes had to deal with two questions. If investment was inadequate to absorb the full employment volume of savings, could the rate of interest not act to bring the two together, a fall in the rate of interest simultaneously stimulating investment and discouraging savings? And if large numbers of workers were unemployed, would competition in the labour market not cause wages to fall and employment to be encouraged? These two 'prices', the rate of interest and the wage rate, were both elements in 'classical economics' which had been employed to secure full employment in the classical model which Keynes criticized.

For Keynes the rate of interest was a 'purely monetary phenomenon', determined by the supply of and demand for money: and increases in the supply of money might simply be absorbed into idle money balances without affecting the rate of interest. Even if the rate of interest were successfully reduced in a depression, it might have little or no effect on investment, which was primarily dependent on business confidence and expectations. As regards wages, money wages were themselves rigid downwards because of institutional factors such as trade unions: but if money wages were cut, the fall in the wage bill would reduce effective demand and prices, so that the *real* wage was not reduced. Hence widespread unemployment could persist as part of an unemployment equilibrium situation caused by lack of effective demand.

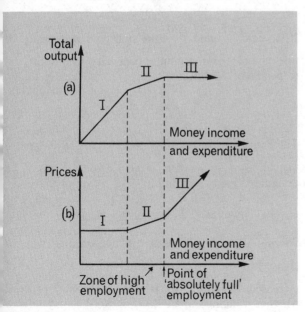

Figure 28.8   A high employment 'zone' with diminishing elasticity of aggregate supply.

The nature of Keynesian unemployment

The feature of this type of 'Keynesian' unemployment is first that it is not only labour which becomes unemployed, but also the cooperating factors of production, particularly capital; and, secondly, this type of unemployment cannot in general be avoided by labour changing occupations or moving to another region, simply because unemployment is widespread, *total* demand in the economy being inadequate.

These factors of production are said to be involuntarily unemployed. *Voluntary unemployment* may be said to exist when a worker is unwilling to work at the going market rate. All workers, for instance, will require *some* leisure hours of 'unemployment' during the day, and people will voluntarily retire from the labour force on reaching a suitable old age. Similarly housewives may choose to stay at home rather than go out to work. In all these cases there is some degree of flexibility in the supply of labour, in the sense that workers may be willing to work overtime, or to retire later, or housewives to accept outside employment, given adequate financial incentives to do so. The feature of *involuntary unemployment* must therefore be that people *who are willing to work at the going market wage* are not able to find jobs. As just mentioned, however, wage cuts would not be effective in increasing job opportunities, and what is required is an increase in the level of effective demand.

The multiplier with government and foreign trade

So far we have assumed that incomes are generated only by consumption expenditure and investment expenditure: we must now incorporate some complications. Government expenditure creates income in the same way, and people can also earn incomes by selling goods abroad, that is, by exports. If we denote these by G and X respectively, the equation

$$C+I+G+X=Y$$

indicates the four kinds of expenditure generating incomes. Since we have brought in the government sector and foreign trade, we must modify our statement as to how individuals may dispose of their incomes: apart from purchasing home-produced consumer goods and saving, they may buy consumer goods made abroad, and they must pay taxes. The last two constitute 'leakages' in the same way as saving, since they do not directly generate incomes: expenditure on foreign goods creates incomes for foreigners but not for residents. The 'income disposal

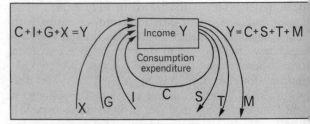

Figure 28.9   *Circular flow of income with government and foreign trade.*

equation' showing what may be done with incomes after they are received becomes:

$$Y=C+S+T+M$$

where T and M refer to taxes paid and to imports respectively. This may be illustrated by the circular flow diagram in Figure 28.9. Income will remain in equilibrium at the level Y so long as the leakages S, T, and M are exactly balanced by the sum of I, G, and X.

Suppose now we wish to trace the effects on income of a change in the value of exports, X. This will also increase incomes through a multiplier process, until the increase in incomes generates additional leakages equal to the increase ΔX, that is, until

$$\Delta Y - \Delta C = \Delta S + \Delta T + \Delta M = \Delta X$$

If we assume investment and government expenditure do not change, so that $\Delta I = \Delta G = 0$, and divide both sides by ΔY, we get

$$1 - \frac{\Delta C}{\Delta Y} = \frac{\Delta S}{\Delta Y} + \frac{\Delta T}{\Delta Y} + \frac{\Delta M}{\Delta Y} = \frac{\Delta X}{\Delta Y}$$

If we call $\frac{\Delta T}{\Delta Y}$ and $\frac{\Delta M}{\Delta Y}$ the marginal propensity to tax, t, and the marginal propensity to import, m, respectively, we have:

$$1 - c = s + t + m = \frac{\Delta X}{\Delta Y}$$

The ratio $\frac{\Delta Y}{\Delta X}$, *the ratio of the increase in income to the increase in exports which causes it*, may be designated the *export multiplier*, k_x. We thus have

$$k_x = \frac{1}{s+t+m}$$

So that if exports increase by ΔX, income will increase by $\frac{1}{s+t+m} \Delta X$. It is immaterial what kind of increased spending starts the multiplier process, whether a change in C, I, G, or X. We may have a 'consumption multiplier',[6] 'investment multiplier',

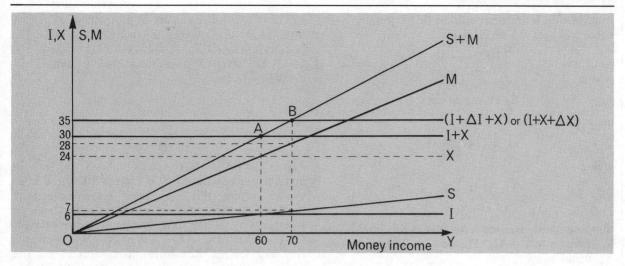

Figure 28.10 *Determination of equilibrium in an open economy.*

'government expenditure multiplier', or 'export multiplier', according to which component of aggregate money demand initiates the multiplier process.

The situation can be depicted in a diagram, Figure 28.10, similar to those of Figures 28.5 and 28.6, in which saving was the only leakage and investment the only category of income-generating expenditure besides consumption. Here we shall neglect the injection of government expenditure and the leakage into tax receipts, and consider the determination of equilibrium income in an open economy with domestic investment and exports as autonomous sources of spending and with two leakages, savings and imports, both functions of income. To take realistic figures for a developing economy, let us assume a marginal propensity to save of 0.1 and a marginal propensity to import of 0.4, so that the combined marginal leakage is 0.5. For simplicity the diagram assumes the propensities to save and to import are both straight lines through the origin.

We assume also that in the initial equilibrium position savings and investment are equal, and imports and exports are equal. The equilibrium condition is given by:

$$I+X=S+M$$

which holds true at A with $Y=60$, investment at 6 and exports at 24, and total 'injections' (over and above consumption spending) at 30.

Suppose now that there is an autonomous increase in the level of investment equal to $5=\Delta I$, so that the line $(I+X)$ shifts upwards to $(I+\Delta I+X)$. A new equilibrium will be given by point B where $Y=70$, $I=6+5=11$, $S=0.1(70)=7$, $X=24$, as before, and $M=0.4(70)=28$. We still have $I+X=S+M$, but I now exceeds S, and M exceeds X. It will be noticed

that since $\Delta I=5$ and $\Delta Y=10$, the multiplier $k=\dfrac{\Delta Y}{\Delta I}=2$; and that this multiplier may be obtained from:

$$k=\frac{1}{s+m}=\frac{1}{0.1+0.4}=2$$

Once again (with the same simplifying assumption regarding the shape of the propensities to consume and import), we could derive the equilibrium level of income by simple algebra. Assume that money income is in equilibrium when aggregate supply, $Y+M$, equals aggregate demand $C+I+X$, so that

$$Y+M=C+I+X \qquad (28.12)$$

and that the propensities to consume and import are:

$$C=cY \qquad (28.13)$$

and

$$M=mY \qquad (28.14)$$

where c, m, are constants. In addition I and X take given values, say, $I=I_0$ and $X=X_0$. Substituting equations 28.13 and 28.14 in 28.12, the equilibrium condition becomes:

$$Y+mY=cY+I_0+X_0$$

or

$$Y_e=\frac{I_0+X_0}{1-c+m}=\frac{I_0+X_0}{s+m} \qquad (28.15)$$

Initially, in the diagram $I_0=6$ and $X_0=24$, so that $Y_e=\dfrac{6+24}{0.1+0.4}=60$. Equally we could derive equilibrium income from the condition that injections $I + X$ equal leakages, $S + M$. This gives:

$$I + X = S + M$$

where

$$S = sY \text{ and } M = mY$$

or

$$I_0 + X_0 = sY + mY$$

giving

$$Y_0 = \frac{I_0 + X_0}{s + m}$$

Suppose money income is initially at this level before I_0 increases to $I_0 + \Delta I_0$. The new equilibrium income Y'_e would equal:

$$Y'_e = \frac{(I_0 + \Delta I_0) + X_0}{s + m}$$

$$= \frac{I_0 + X_0}{s + m} + \frac{\Delta I_0}{s + m}$$

giving

$$Y'_e = Y_e + \frac{\Delta I_0}{s + m}$$

This implies

$$Y'_e - Y_e = \Delta Y = \frac{\Delta I_0}{s + m}$$

so that

$$k = \frac{\Delta Y}{\Delta I} = \frac{1}{s + m}$$

It can be shown quite easily that an increase in exports, with investment constant, will have exactly the same effect on income as we have just calculated for an increase in investment with exports constant. The *export multiplier* would be:

$$k_x = \frac{1}{s + m}$$

In terms of Figure 28.10, the shift from A to B could as easily have been caused by a shift of the curve $(I + X)$ to the position $(I + X + \Delta X)$.

The effect on the *balance of payments*, however, will not be the same. Although the previous analysis implied that the whole of the increased investment spending was on domestically produced capital goods, the gap $(M - X)$ increases from nil to $28 - 24 = 4$. If the autonomous increase of 5 is in export sales instead of investment, the effect on the balance of payments is actually favourable, since $X - M = 29 - 28 = +1$.

The effect on the balance of payments is of general importance for aggregate income analysis. The equilibrium condition $C + I + X = Y + M$ where $Y - C = S$, the level of saving, can also be written, rearranging terms, as

$$I - (Y - C) = M - X$$

or,

$$I - S = M - X$$

Figure 28.10 in fact takes $I + X = S + M$ as the equilibrium condition. If X exceeds M, there is an export surplus: this is in effect foreign investment (lending), since the country is accumulating claims on foreigners by adding to its foreign exchange reserves. On the other hand, if $M - X$ is positive, the country is *receiving* foreign investment from abroad on this account. Where national income is in equilibrium with $I - S = M - X$ both positive, foreigners' savings, $M - X$, are being used to balance the domestic savings gap, $I - S$.

So far we have discussed mainly the multiplier effects of changes in investment or exports. Government spending will have similar effects and, being under the control of government, can be used *deliberately* to increase the level of aggregate demand and take up any slack arising from, say, a deficiency in the level of private investment, or to decrease it in periods of inflationary pressure. Moreover in addition to varying government expenditure, G, the government is in a position to determine the size of T, the tax leakage. Indeed it is the size of the *budget deficit*, $G - T$, or budget surplus, which is used as an instrument of contracyclical policy to stabilize the economy.

The assumption of constant marginal propensities

In deriving formulae such as $k = \frac{1}{s}$ and $k = \frac{1}{s + m}$, we assumed that the marginal propensities were constant: with those assumptions we use the value of the appropriate multiplier to predict the effect of a given increase in autonomous spending on the level of money incomes. This assumption can pass so long as the savings (consumption) function and the import function are reasonably stable: particularly as, in a given situation, we shall always be starting at a given level of income, and point on the curve, and need only calculate the marginal propensity and the multiplier at that point.

However, a number of factors other than income affect savings and changes in these factors could make the savings function shift upwards or downwards: changes in the rate of interest or in the distribution of income are likely to affect saving, as well as expectations of future consumer price rises, which may encourage consumers to spend a larger proportion of their incomes. Keynes, in his *General Theory*, made consumption in *real* terms a function of *real* income and considered that this would be reasonably stable: our analysis above has been in terms of money income, and there is not the same justification for assuming that expenditure in *money* terms is determined by the level of money income, particularly beyond the full employment level when prices are rising, with possible effects on income distribution and on expectations.

Inflation and rising prices are in particular likely to affect the import function, if prices of domestically produced goods rise relative to the prices of imports. This may occur rather unpredictably because of inelastic domestic supply of goods and supply bottlenecks. Most important, sudden serious shortages of basic foodstuffs as a result of drought or other natural conditions can necessitate huge imports of food and affect the entire import function. Fluctuation in the amount of foreign investment or availability of foreign aid may also affect the import propensity.

It may be noted that shifts in these functions will also have multiplier effects on income similar to injections of autonomous demand. In Figure 28.10 a shift in either the savings or import propensity will cause the $S+M$ curve to move, producing a new equilibrium point of intersection with $I+X$, involving an initial change in spending and a multiplier process to reach that equilibrium.

Finally we may note another assumption, that the multiplier process is stable. If in $k = \dfrac{1}{s+m}$, for instance, s and m are both zero (there are no leakages), then $k = $ infinity, and money incomes would rise indefinitely following the smallest initial injection. This certainly would not happen in open economies, since price rises would make imports increasingly attractive and cause m to become positive.

Aggregate demand and the multiplier in less developed economies

The Keynesian theory of income determination was developed to deal with a special situation of industrial depression and unemployment in the mature capitalist economies of Europe and America during the 1930s. As we have already seen, Keynes diagnosed that problem as one of demand deficiency with the level of investment too low, because of lack of

business confidence, to absorb the high level of savings at full employment incomes. The relevance of Keynesian analysis for the understanding of the less developed economies of contemporary Africa has in fact been seriously questioned. Variations in aggregate demand, and the multiplier, will not operate in just the same way and, as we shall see more fully in Chapter 33, the employment problem in Africa is very different in nature. Here we may simply point out the following differences in the operation of the multiplier analysis in the 'poor but open' economies of the less developed world.

(1) *In less developed economies exports, rather than investment, are the key injection of autonomous spending.* Keynes focused on investment as the key variable on the demand side of the income equation because (a) it accounted for a large part of total demand, say, 20 per cent, and (b) it was a particularly unstable component of demand, being largely influenced by the volatile profit expectations of private businessmen, in addition to monetary factors such as the supply and price of investible funds. Magnified by the operation of the multiplier, investment was therefore 'the tail that wagged the dog' of aggregate demand.

The position is different in less developed economies in a number of ways. First of all a substantial portion of investment is carried on within the rural sector outside the cash economy as part of 'non-monetary output'. The key element in the Keynesian theory is, of course, that in a monetized economy with complete division of labour decisions to save and to invest are taken largely by different groups of people and need not be coordinated to ensure equality at the full employment level of income. In the non-monetary sector of less developed economies a single act of investment and saving is carried out by any individual who, say, decides to clear additional land for planting or build himself a house.

Secondly, the volatility or unpredictability of investment which Keynes noted assumes that the demand for capital goods comes mainly from the private sector: whereas in developing countries the government may have a larger say in investment decisions, while investment programmes or expectations may be worked out as part of an overall development plan for the economy.

Thirdly, the key role ascribed to investment assumes the existence of a well-established capital goods industry. In the absence of such, much of the initial investment spending will be on imported equipment and have no domestic impact. The direct import content of investment exceeds half the aggregate value of investment outlays in African countries, though the import content varies widely for investment in different sectors of the economy, ranging from almost 100 per cent on plant and equipment for manufacturing to around one-half on urban construction with imported material, and foreign contractors, and may be as low as 10 per cent or so for land clearance in agriculture or plantation development.

The result is a reduced domestic base for the investment multiplier in less developed economies which does not arise to the same extent when the injection is government expenditure or, especially, exports. Thus in the case of investment a substantial part of what would otherwise have been income-generating expenditure is in effect 'leaked' *before* income generation takes place. In Malawi, to give an example, while the direct import content of investment is around 66 per cent, that for government consumption is only about 20 per cent, and for exports only about 10 per cent, these comprising mainly agricultural products with a high local input of land and labour. In developed countries the import content of personal consumption, public consumption, and investment is, in contrast, fairly uniform, so that the investment and export multipliers have similar effects on domestic income.

The effect on the multiplier is illustrated in the following example. If we take marginal propensities to save and to import of 0.1 and 0.4 respectively, and figures of 0.65 and 0.1 for the direct import content of investment and exports respectively (similar to the rough estimates above for Malawi), we find that an increase in exports of 10 would produce an increase in money income equal to:

$$\Delta Y = \frac{10 - 1}{0.1 + 0.4} = 18$$

implying an export multiplier of $\frac{18}{10}$ or $k_x = 1\frac{4}{5}$. An equal increase of 10 in investment spending, however, would increase money income only by:

$$\Delta Y = \frac{10 - 6.5}{0.1 + 0.4} = 7,$$

implying an investment multiplier of only $\frac{7}{10}$, that is, $k_x = \frac{7}{10}$. In this case the total domestic income expansion resulting from the multiplier is only 7, even less than the gross outlay on investment of 10. The smaller multiplier is due to the fact that only that portion of investment which represents demand for domestic output has multiplier effects on domestic incomes.

The import leakage in the second case consists of two elements, the direct import content of the initial investment plus the induced imports caused by the increase in incomes. These are respectively 6.5 and $m\Delta Y = 0.4(7) = 2.8$. The total increase in imports is therefore 9.3.

Thus for several reasons fluctuations in investment do not play the same role in generating variations in aggregate spending in less developed economies. In contrast the value of exports is more important: while exports may not be, depending on the country, exceptionally large relative to total output including subsistence, they are usually large relative to monetary output which is the relevant component, for example, in generating tax revenue. Moreover exports are even more outside the control of the government than investment, being dependent on external markets and world competition. They are also particularly unpredictable both because of changes in such markets and changes in exportable output as a result of climate or similar factors at home.

(2) In addition *the size of the export multiplier itself will be affected by the economy's dependence on two or three export commodities.* We may note, first, that the value of exports depends not only on their volume, but also on their average price. If the prices of exports fall, there will thus be two effects: first, the deterioration in the terms of trade will reduce the amount of imports that can be purchased with the same volume of exports: but secondly there will be the multiplier effects reducing incomes throughout the country. Thus multiplier effects in a dependent economy may come about through a change in the prices of exports, even if there has been no change in volume. When the economy is heavily dependent on the export of just one or two commodities, as in the case of Zambia or Uganda, *fluctuations in the world price of just a single commodity can have important multiplier effects.*

In this case also the size of the effects will depend on the price of *which* export commodity changes. In a developed economy that has a wide range of exports it is possible to discuss exports in the aggregate: but in the case of Malaysia, for example, exporting mainly the two commodities, tin and rubber, the size of the multiplier will depend on whether the change is in exports of rubber or tin. The rubber industry is a labour-intensive one, using a lot of labour relative to capital, whether the rubber is produced by small farmers or on estates using a large labour force. As a result a large part of an increase in the value of sales will go to fairly poor farmers or workers who will tend to spend most of their income. Tin, on the other hand, is a capital-intensive industry, using heavy machinery, so that a large part of increased proceeds would accrue to suppliers of finance, who would be more likely to save, or would be retained by mining companies as company savings. The marginal propensity to consume would be lower, and in the latter case, the multiplier also. Similarly in African countries increased export incomes from peasant-produced cash crops will have much greater multiplier effects than increased income from the export of, say, copper, oil, or diamonds produced through the large mining companies.

(3) In poor but open economies. *the savings leakage is likely to be very much smaller, and the import leakage much greater than in developed countries.* Savings being an increasing function of income, this leakage is inevitably more important in wealthy countries with high levels of income per head. This is true particularly because saving is generally effected not by the mass of the population, even in rich countries, but largely by those people in the top 10 per cent or so of the income distribution, and by large firms in the form of retained profits, or company savings. In addition countries with large integrated markets of their own, such as the USA, will be less dependent on overseas markets for exports and need to import a smaller proportion of their requirements.

In contrast less developed countries will have high marginal propensities to import. This may be because, even with an increase in effective demand, the local market is still too small to support the industries which could produce the commodities which are in increased demand; or because, although the market is large enough, the factors of production required to launch the industries are lacking: skilled labour, raw materials, capital, and especially enterprise.

The most relevant income multiplier in the poor but open economy case can be written simply as $k_x = \frac{1}{m}$ where k_x is the export multiplier and m is the marginal propensity to import. The change in income will be given by $\Delta Y = \Delta X \frac{1}{m}$, and the equilibrium level of income will be determined by $Y = \frac{X}{m}$ rather than by $Y = \frac{I}{s}$ as in the rich, closed economy model. The first concentrates on m as the most significant leakage, and the second on saving. It is just as realistic to assume saving to be an unimportant leakage in a poor but open economy as to ignore imports in a largely closed economy such as the USA. The relevant equilibrium diagram, corresponding to Figure 28.6 for the closed economy, would be as in Figure 28.11.

For the purpose of aggregate income analysis, in fact, we might define the 'openness' of African economies not so much in terms of the ratio of total imports to total GDP, that is, M/Y, which is the *average* propensity to import, but by their relatively high *marginal* propensity to import, $\Delta M/\Delta Y$, which, when combined with the relatively small marginal propensity to save and to tax, puts a severe constraint on expansionary policies designed to stabilize income in less developed countries. Attempts to stimulate domestic demand by budgeting for a deficit of G over T are likely to have a diminished impact, since much of the additional spending generated through the multiplier will 'leak out' into additional imports.

If we return to the example depicted in Figure 28.10 on page 405, we note that the first effect of a high marginal propensity to import, m, is to produce a low expenditure multiplier. In the example, with m = 0.4 and s = 0.1, we obtained k = 2. Thus the increase in money income (domestic demand) resulting from an increase in investment will be much reduced because increases in spending quickly leak away into imports. As we have seen, this effect is aggravated by the fact that a substantial portion of the initial investment may itself be lost as a result of its high import content. But *in addition* the rise in imports will have serious balance of payments implications. In the diagram, assuming the shift from (I + X) to (I + ΔI + X) is due to an autonomous change in investment, the economy starts from a position of balance of payments equilibrium with X = M at A to one of balance of payments deficit with X = 24 (unchanged) and M = 28 at B. This position would not be tenable indefinitely as it implies a continuous loss of foreign exchange reserves or persistent dependence on foreign aid or capital inflows from abroad.

(4) The last difference, and a fundamental one, is *the difference in less developed countries in the impact of the multiplier on real output, employment, and prices as a result of inelastic supply.* In the earlier analysis of the relationship between aggregate demand and the supply of output in a mature economy we suggested that the supply of output would be completely elastic when unemployment was widespread and then, especially in some industries, inelastic in the zone approaching full employment, and finally completely inelastic, at the point of absolutely full employment. The price level would be constant so long as output was in elastic supply, and would rise to

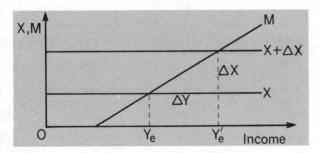

Figure 28.11 *Multiplier effects of an autonomous change in exports in a poor, open economy.*

produce inflation as the supply became inelastic. In a low income country in particular, the higher income-elasticity of demand for food will mean that a large part of the increase in demand will be for food; since however the supply of food is likely to be relatively inelastic, especially in those countries suffering from overpopulation and land shortage, an important part of the increase in money demand may be translated into rising prices rather than increased output. In a closed economy the increased money supply associated with increased money income injections may be absorbed into transactions demand for money at a higher price level. In an open economy the rise in prices of domestically produced goods in inelastic supply will divert demand to relatively cheaper imported goods, this change in relative prices being part of the mechanism producing a high marginal propensity to import.

Lastly it may be noted that in Keynes' model low aggregate demand was associated with unemployment of labour which, because of money wage rigidity, could persist: hence increases in effective demand produced an expansion of employment (employment multiplier) together with an expansion of money income. In less developed economies this wage rigidity does not exist to any great extent, at least in the agricultural sector and informal sector, so that there will be no clear relationship between aggregate demand and the number of jobs, and the concept of an employment multiplier is not valid.

In fact the unemployment and underemployment typical of less developed economies are of a fundamentally different type from what is experienced during depressions in advanced capitalist countries and analysed by Keynes, as we shall see in Chapter 33.

Questions on Chapter 28

1. Define an equilibrium level of national income and explain why such an equilibrium may be below the full employment level of money income.
2. Use both simple algebra and graphs to derive the formula $k_l = \frac{1}{s}$ in a simple model with saving as the only leakage.
3. Compare the 'acceleration principle' and the 'profits principle' as explanations of induced investment.
4. In what way was Keynes's theory one of short-run determination of income and employment? What would the effect of his multiplier process be (a) in conditions of general unemployment and (b) as full employment is approached?
5. Show algebraically how equilibrium income would be determined when investment, exports, and government expenditure are autonomous and s, m, and t are the marginal propensities to save, import, and tax. Find the government expenditure multiplier in terms of s, m, and t.
6. Discuss the main differences in the application of multiplier analysis in developed and less developed economies.
7. Why would you expect the leakage to saving to be smaller, and the leakage to imports to be relatively higher, in an African economy than in a developed economy like the USA?
8. Why is private business investment likely to be more unstable than other components of domestic demand in developed countries? Why is investment likely to be a less important source of income instability in African economies?
9. Discuss the likely effect of a direct import content in investment, government consumption, and exports on the respective multipliers.
10. Discuss the possible effects on the export multiplier of dependence on a limited number of exports.
11. What difficulties may be raised for income stabilization policies by a high marginal propensity to import?

Notes

[1] J. M. Keynes's book, *The General Theory of Employment, Interest and Money*, was published in 1936.

[2] We can also obtain the relationship k = 1/s from Figure 28.6. The slope of the savings function is equal to s. The slope, s, is measured by tan BAC. Thus $s = \tan BAC = \frac{BC}{AC} = \frac{1}{k}$. Hence $k = \frac{1}{s}$.

[3] In order to obtain the simple form of equation 28.2, we assume here that the savings function passes through the origin rather than some way along the x-axis as in Figure 28.5.

[4] See J. Tinbergen, *A Method and Its Application to Investment Activity*, League of Nations, 1939.

[5] It will be obvious presently why the horizontal axis in this diagram has been labelled 'MV'.

[6] Resulting from a *shift* in the consumption function itself, implying a larger (or smaller) propensity to consume at *any* given income level.

29 Inflation and the Value of Money

Let us now examine one of the most serious and universal economic problems which has affected both developed and less developed countries in recent years—inflation. Inflation can be defined as a *persistent rise in the general level of prices* or, alternatively, a persistent fall in the value of money. We shall examine a number of alternative explanations of the origin of inflation, and compare them, discuss some of the consequences of inflation, and go on to discuss the main problems in measuring changes in the price level and value of money.

Inflation and the quantity of money

The earliest theory of any importance regarding the determination of the price level, and changes in the price level is the famous 'Quantity Theory of Money'. This theory, in its rough form, goes back to the sixteenth century, when ships were bringing large amounts of gold and silver back to Europe from the New World. The severe inflation which resulted led people to postulate a direct proportional relationship between the supply of money and the level of prices. If the quantity of money were doubled, prices would double, and so on. Algebraically this could be stated as

$$P = aM$$

where a is a constant, P the price level, and M the supply of money. If the supply of money doubled, to 2M, the new price level P' will equal

$$a(2M) = 2(aM) = 2P$$

that is, double the old price level.

Much later the theory was formulated in a more precise way by Irving Fisher, who took into account the volume of transactions, that is to say, the amount of 'work' that the money supply had to do as a medium of exchange. His theory was based on the following 'Equation of Exchange':

$$M.V \equiv P.T$$

where V is the 'velocity of circulation of money' and T the volume of transactions. It will be observed that instead of the usual equality sign we have the '$\equiv$',

which implies the two sides *are necessarily and inevitably equal*. This is generally referred to as an '*identity*'. M.V and P.T are in fact two ways of looking at the same thing. When a commodity is purchased in a money economy two things happen: the commodity passes from the seller to the buyer and money passes the opposite way, from the buyer to the seller, Obviously to get the total value of transactions made during the year we can trace the movement of commodities or the movement of money. The left-hand side of the identity does the latter. V is the number of times during the period each unit of money passes from hand to hand in order to effect transactions. Thus if the amount of money in the hands of the public during the year was on average one million dollars, and each dollar on average was used five times, the total value of transactions carried out during the year must have been five million dollars. Alternatively, looking at the right-hand side of the identity, if the volume of goods transacted was T, and the average price of these P, then P.T is again the total value of goods transacted during the year. We might say that M.V represents the money paid by consumers and received by producers, while P.T is the value of goods obtained or supplied in exchange during the year.

It has been said that the Equation of Exchange serves no purpose: that because it is a 'truism', inevitably true, it cannot *explain* anything. In fact we might say that if the formula is written not as an identity but as a true equation in the form

$$M.V = P.T$$

then it is useful, if nothing like as useful as Fisher and others thought it was. For it can be interpreted causally. It can tell us that if any of M, V, or T change, then the price level P must change. It can also tell us that if V and T are *fairly* constant, then P will vary in rough proportion with M, as in the form $P = aM$. This is actually how Fisher saw the equation: he thought the velocity of circulation would be dependent largely on the fixed habits of individuals and therefore reasonably constant. There might be seasonal variation with a speeding-up of spending at certain times of the year, but this would be a temporary and unimportant phenomenon. Even if T changed over time, as is to be expected with economic growth, so long as the increase in the volume of output and transactions were steady, we would be in a position to say that prices would rise or fall according to whether the money supply increased faster or slower than the volume of output. This leaves the main burden of the theory intact.

However Keynes, in his *General Theory*, already referred to, showed that it was most unwise to assume that V and T would vary only within narrow limits, or change in steady fashion. In the first place there might be underemployment equilibrium in which transactions, T, remained at a level far below 'full employment', this level varying, possibly rapidly, with the level of effective demand. Secondly the velocity of circulation, V, might fluctuate considerably within a short time because of, say, a loss of confidence, making people hold money idle rather than undertaking business ventures or holding more risky assets.

However, while the theory breaks down seriously in conditions of slump and underemployment, and while fluctuations in V reduce its usefulness in predicting short-run changes, it remains useful in emphasizing the link between the money supply and the price level in conditions of sustained boom and full employment. This is the situation depicted in Phase III of Figure 28.8 in the previous chapter. We may note here that in this figure, M.V, as measured on the x-axis, is simply aggregate money demand (total annual expenditure). Since T is constant beyond the full employment level, $P = \dfrac{M.V}{T}$ tells us that prices vary in direct proportion to M.V.

The Income Equation

We have stated that fluctuations in V may occur because people want to hold more or less money 'idle' than before, because their 'demand to hold money' varies. A modification of the Quantity Theory, known as the Income Equation, stresses this aspect more directly. According to the Income Equation, the amount of money people wish to hold will depend on the level of transactions, which is directly related to the level of final output or real income. The Income Equation is therefore given as

$$M = kPY \text{ or } \frac{M}{P} = kY$$

where Y is real income, and k is a constant indicating the ratio of the value of assets that people wish to hold in the form of money to the value of real income. $\dfrac{M}{P}$ is the amount of money held, in real terms

(money supply divided by the price level), that is to say, 'real' money balances.

We can discuss the effects of an increase in the money supply in terms of these equations. An increase in M will increase the value of $\dfrac{M}{P}$, so long as prices do not change. If Y does not change, holders of money will now have excess real balances in relation to Y: they will therefore reduce them, either spending on consumer goods or on investment goods. Aggregate money demand will therefore increase. The effects will be as described in Figure 28.8 (page 403), a roughly proportionate rise in Y without change in P when there is widespread unemployment, or a change in both Y and P in the zone of 'high' employment. In Zone III, when supply is completely inelastic so that Y cannot increase, prices will go up in proportion to the increase in M, restoring $\dfrac{M}{P}$ to its former value, unless of course there is a change in the ratio k.

The equation $M = kPY$ is similar but not identical to the previous equation $MV = PT$. V is obviously related to the value $\dfrac{1}{k}$, and T is related to Y. However Y refers to *final* output only, whereas T refers to all transactions, including those involving intermediate output. T is therefore greater than Y, since the same commodity may change hands several times in different forms before reaching the final consumer. Y and T ought, however, to move in proportion to each other. V measures the average rate at which a unit of money changes hands in effecting transactions. The higher the velocity of circulation, the shorter the time, on average, that a unit of money 'stays idle', and therefore the smaller the value of k. V and k are therefore *inversely* related, with V proportional to $\dfrac{1}{k}$. But once more V relates to the velocity of circulation of money used in effecting all transactions, the *transactions-velocity of money*, while $\dfrac{1}{k}$ relates to the velocity of circulation of money in effecting transactions of final output only, the *income velocity of money*. V is therefore larger numerically than $\dfrac{1}{k}$.

Just as the Equation of Exchange can be used to predict the effect on P of a change in M so long as V and T are constant, so the Income Equation can be used so long as k and Y are constant. The advantage of the second form, perhaps, is that is focuses on the motives for holding money, and explains the increase in spending due to a change in M as a positive act of choice on the part of those who find themselves with excess balances of real money. The defect of the first Quantity Equation is that it does not specify the *mechanism* which translates an increase in M into an increase in P.

But the Income Equation specifies only one motive for holding money: 'transactions demand' for money, the need to have ready money balances with which to effect day-to-day transactions. Keynes, breaking away from the constraint of the Quantity Theory in his *General Theory of Employment, Interest and Money*, distinguishes additional motives for holding money.

The demand for money: liquidity preference

Basically there are *two* reasons why money is held: first because it is likely to be required in the near future *as a means of payment*, to effect transactions, and secondly because of the demand for money to hold *as an asset* (store of value), this being relevant where money is *not* likely to be required to meet payments for some time.

People hold money for purposes of making transactions because at normal rates of interest, which means rates not exceeding, say, 5 per cent or so, it is not worth their while investing in, say, a government bond for only a short period, due to the costs of investment. This is because there are costs of purchasing and then reselling a bond, notably the fee paid to a broker, but also the inconvenience of buying and then reselling the bond when cash is needed. To make it worthwhile, the bond, or even a savings deposit with a bank, must be held for at least a minimum period of some weeks or months. It follows that this part of the demand for money will be interest-inelastic. Here we mean that it will make little difference whether the rate of interest is, say, 4 per cent or 6 per cent, within the normal range; it *would* presumably make a difference if the rate of interest were 25 per cent! The amount of money held within this category will be related, not to the rate of interest, but to the level of transactions: it will depend on anticipated transactions in the next short period plus a 'precautionary' reserve to cover unanticipated *contingencies* which might arise in the same period.

If the money is not immediately required as a means of payment, it can itself be held as an asset for future consumption, or it can be converted into another asset, any kind of security. We need to explain why money is held rather than these other securities, even though it offers no interest. Obviously in a period of business uncertainty people may be very reluctant to hold commercial stocks and shares,

in spite of the interest they offer, because of the risk of loss of their capital. This hardly applies to government bonds, however, since there is usually no risk of the government defaulting and failing to repay the capital when the bond is due, or to pay the interest. Individuals however cannot usually wait until the maturity date of the bond, since they may require money earlier than that: this means that they will be expecting eventually to resell on the market at whatever the ruling market price happens then to be. They may therefore make a capital loss on the bond.

A fall in the price of bonds can be shown to be identical with a rise in the rate of interest on bonds; this in effect means that people may be reluctant to hold bonds for fear that the rate of interest may go up, and thus bond prices fall. On the other hand, if an individual strongly expects the rate of interest to fall, he will be anxious to hold bonds in the expectation of making a capital gain when their price goes up.

We must clarify this relationship between the price of bonds and the rate of interest on bonds. A bond with a nominal value of £100 is a promise by government to repay £100 at maturity, and interest in the period before maturity. Now the *yield* on a security is the interest paid divided by the amount paid for the security (the amount invested). Thus if a £100 bond which pays £6 per annum (6 per cent) is bought at its nominal value of £100, the yield would be 6 per cent. If it were bought for just £50, the yield would be 12 per cent, since an investment of £50 brings in £6 per annum.

Suppose in Year 1 the rate of interest is 3 per cent, and an individual buys a £100 bond which pays £3 per annum. In Year 2 the rate of interest goes up to 6 per cent. This means the government is selling *new* bonds which offer £6 interest for an outlay of £100. Clearly the old bond will fall in value by half to £50. For no one will buy an old bond for £100 which pays £3 when they can buy Year 2 bonds which earn £6 p.a. for the same outlay. They will, however, be prepared to buy *two* old bonds for £100, yielding £6 together, that is, they will pay £50 for one bond. At this price the yield on old and new bonds is identical.

It follows also that an individual who expects the rate of interest to rise (bond prices to fall) will prefer to hold money and delay his purchase of the bond. If the rate of interest went up by a tenth from 5 per cent in year 1 to $5\frac{1}{2}$ per cent in Year 2, the price of bonds would fall by almost a tenth from £100 to £91. If the bond is held for a year, £5 is made in interest, and £9 is lost due to the fall in price of the bond, a net loss of £4, which would have been avoided if money had been held. Alternatively we could say that by purchasing the bond in Year 2 instead of Year 1 the individual gains £9, getting the bond for £91 instead of £100, though he forgoes £5 of interest during the year, making a net gain of £4.

People may therefore prefer to hold money rather than bonds as an asset for *two* reasons: either (1) because they actually *expect* bond prices to fall, or (2) because, though they have no expectations one way or the other, they feel there is at least a *risk* that bond prices may fall. Those who actually take a view about future prices and interest rates may be described as *speculators*; those who have no expectations either way but avoid risk by holding money may be described as *risk-averters*. However both groups have to make the same choice as to whether to hold assets in the form of money or bonds.

Both these elements in the demand for money will be responsive to the rate of interest. Taking risk-aversion first, different individuals will 'worry' about the risk of a fall in price *to different extents*: those who worry least will be willing to acquire bonds at lower rates of interest than those who are less willing to bear risk and who require higher rates of interest to persuade them to undertake it. It follows that at higher rates of interest more people will be willing to hold bonds rather than money, while at lower rates of interest the demand for money will be greater.

The deliberately speculative element is responsive to the rate of interest in the following way. Monetary authorities do permit the rate of interest to vary but usually within a limited range of up to, say, 8 per cent, so that a rate of 5 per cent is likely to be considered 'normal'.[1] When the rate of interest is below this normal level more people are likely to expect the rate of interest to rise, rather than fall. The demand for money will increase, being greater the further below 'normal' the rate of interest is considered to be, and the greater therefore the expectation of a rise. At very low rates of interest, demand for money will increase rapidly because of the strong conviction that a rise in the rate of interest is likely. The *total* demand for money will therefore consist of two elements: demand for money as a means of payment, which will be interest-inelastic and geared to the level of transactions, and demand for money as an asset (store of value), which will be interest-elastic, especially at very low rates of interest. We could write the total demand for money as L, where

$$L = L(T) + L(i)$$

and where $L(T)$ is that part related to the level of transactions[2] and $L(i)$ that part responsive to the rate of interest. The former may be referred to as *active* money balances, and the latter as *inactive* money balances.

Keynes proposed that the money rate of interest was determined by the demand for money, which he called liquidity preference (money being the most liquid asset), and the supply of money, as determined by central bank policy. His theory, illustrated in Figure 29.1, is referred to as the Liquidity Preference Theory of Interest. The demand for money curve is labelled L, and the supply curve, M. The latter is drawn at a vertical line, since the central bank will determine the stock of money, which will not therefore be a function of the rate of interest. The figure shows that an increase in the quantity of money from M to M', with L given, will reduce the rate of interest from i to i'.

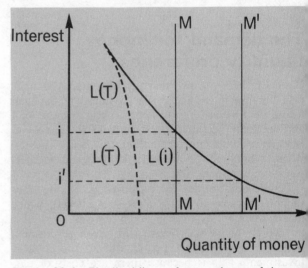

Figure 29.1   *The liquidity preference theory of the rate of interest.*

The relation between the Quantity Theory and the Liquidity Preference Theory

The Income Version of the Quantity Theory shows demand for money balances to be related to the level of transactions, for use as 'active' balances. The Keynesian theory introduced the demand for money as an asset, to be held as 'idle' or inactive balances in preference to other assets. The proportion of inactive balances, moreover, may change rapidly, implying a correspondingly rapid change in the velocity of circulation of money. This means that the level of spending (MV) may fall rapidly in a slump without any change in M: for V will fall if there is an increase in the demand for money as an asset.

It also follows that an increase in MV can occur without any change in M, since V is not always stable, as the quantity theorists assumed. Inactive money can be utilized if there is an increase in business confidence. Moreover, according to the Keynesian theory, this increase in spending is likely to be cumulative: an initial increase in investment following a partial return of business confidence will have multiplier effects, increasing income and hence consumption demand, thus giving cause for confidence picking up still further, and so on. Once full employment is reached, it still remains true that spending, in money terms, can increase without any change in M, but is translated now into rising prices, these being accommodated by activating 'idle' money.

Alternative descriptions of 'excess demand' inflation

A number of explanations of the process of inflation are in terms of excess demand, in which there is 'too much money chasing too few goods', in the popular expression. Although these versions all assume excess demand to be behind the inflationary rise in prices, their descriptions of inflation are not quite the same, and are worth examining separately. We may distinguish:

(1) inflation by 'printing money';
(2) the 'cumulative process' of inflation through bank credit;
(3) the Keynesian explanation of inflation;
(4) the 'modern' Quantity Theory of Chicago.

Inflation by 'printing money' for governments

We saw in the last chapter that government expenditure, like other forms of expenditure, is income-generating. If such expenditure is financed by taxation, or by attracting voluntary savings from the general public, this spending need not be inflationary. However governments may finance spending through a budget deficit, spending more than they receive from the public: either resorting to the printing press to print money with which to pay bills or, what amounts to the same thing, borrowing from the central bank for this purpose. This will mean an increase in the money supply, resulting in inflation if there is full employment.

This explanation is in line with the Quantity Theory and the Equation of Exchange. The difference is that the cause of the inflationary increase in money supply is, specifically, government spending. For this reason this is not a general theory of inflation applicable to all situations. However it has occurred, in less developed countries particularly, that explosive rates of price increase have occurred when governments have financed prolonged budget deficits by borrowing from the central bank. The figures in Table 29.1 relate to the experience of Indonesia in the 1960s,

Table 29.1 *Indonesia's hyperinflation through budget deficit financing*

Year (31 Dec.)	(1) Money supply in old rupiah (m×1,000)	(2) Government budget deficit (m×1,000 old rupiah)	(3) Djakarta price index (1957/8=100)
1956	13	4.6	100
1961	68	25	380
1962	131	50	980
1963	365	180	2,230
1964	615	890	5,320
1965	2,982	1,300	36,350
1966	15,100	12,000	96,030

SOURCE: *Bulletin of Indonesian Economic Studies*, No. 4, 1966

and illustrate an extreme form of inflation, known as *hyperinflation*, when the rate of price increase is exceptionally high and appears out of control. This shows that the level of prices (column 3) increased ten-fold between 1957/8 and 1962, but that thereafter the rate of price increase accelerated sharply, more than doubling each year in 1962, 1963, and 1964, before going up nearly seven-fold in 1965. The immediate cause of the price inflation is seen clearly in the expansion of the money supply (column 1) at the same rate as prices up to 1962. Between 1964 and 1966 prices rose even faster than money supply, implying an increase in the velocity of circulation of money: not surprisingly, since with very rapid increases in prices people would become much more reluctant to hold on to money as the value of idle money balances falls. Column 2 indicates that the expansion of the money supply was in turn associated with the ever increasing budget deficit and the creation of money through government borrowing from the central bank. The process can be viewed as one of competition between the public and private sectors for resources, with the government attempting to maintain its level of real spending by 'printing more money' to permit increased money expenditure as prices rose rather than attempting to reduce private real spending directly through increased taxation. By 1966 the Indonesian economy had broken down completely: the political regime changed, a new currency was introduced, and the rate of inflation moderated.

The cumulative process of inflation through bank credit creation

A more general explanation of the Quantity Theory was offered by the famous Swedish economist, Knut Wicksell, at the end of the last century.[3] His explanation focuses attention on the rate of interest as the instrument through which changes in the money supply can result, not just in a higher price level, but in a cumulative process of persistently rising prices—inflation. The 'neoclassical' (supply and demand) explanation anticipated Keynes' own explanation of the Quantity Theory in terms of the liquidity preference theory of the rate of interest.

In order to discuss Wicksell's theory it is necessary to refer to the 'classical' theory of the rate of interest which is in terms of two factors, productivity and thrift, and a modification of this earlier theory, the *loanable funds theory of the rate of interest* which we shall explain presently. According to the classical theory the rate of interest was a *real* phenomenon, determined by the real forces of thrift (willingness to save out of income) and the productivity of capital (inducing a desire in businessmen to invest). We discussed this theory, in effect, in Chapter 5, in relation to a subsistence producer who has limited resources. Such a producer can devote a greater or smaller proportion of these limited resources to capital goods production, by cutting down on consumption. To persuade him to make the decision to acquire an additional capital good, representing future consumption, the rate of return has to be sufficient to counteract his rate of time preference. This rate of return is thus the 'price' of savings, that is, the rate of interest. The rate of return of the last unit of capital he finds worth acquiring is therefore the *equilibrium* rate of interest. Since we are talking about the allocation of real resources within a purely subsistence economy, in which money is absent, we can refer to this as the 'real' rate of interest, as opposed to a money rate.

But this problem of allocating resources between present and future, and therefore the concept of a 'real' rate of interest, is applicable to any economy. This real rate, which balances the desire or reluctance of consumers to defer consumption with the needs of producers to obtain resources for investment, was referred to by Wicksell as the *natural rate of interest*.

The actual 'market' or 'money' rate of interest need not equal this 'natural' or 'real' rate, however. This is why, in the Keynesian Liquidity Preference Theory discussed above, the rate of interest could be described as a 'purely monetary phenomenon'. To emphasize this, consider first a Keynesian situation of widespread unemployment. Here we can say that a positive real rate of interest would not exist. Since unemployed resources have no opportunity-cost, an increase in capital goods production could take place *without* any cut in present consumption. There would therefore be no time preference to be overcome, and the real rate of interest would be zero. Since the money rate of interest will still be positive, the two rates must diverge.

Wicksell's theory was based on the fact that in a classical full employment situation, also, the rates might diverge. According to the loanable funds theory, the money rate of interest was determined by the supply of and demand for loanable funds. This reflected the forces of productivity and thrift, but involved other factors also. The supply of loanable funds comes from three sources: savings out of current income, new money created by the banking system, and the net dishoarding of 'idle' money balances; while the demand for loanable funds depends on the interest-elastic investment demand of businessmen.

The version of the theory used by Wicksell ignores net dishoarding of idle money (which could be negative) and concentrates on the effect of bank credit creation on the market price of funds for investment. Hence Figure 29.2, which refers to a full employment situation now, assumes that the only source of finance for industry is the savings by consumers out of their money incomes, made available to businessmen for investment through the usual financial intermediaries. If these savings are fully taken up by businessmen, money income, as well as the rate of interest, will be in equilibrium: a portion of money income would simply be diverted from consumption into investment spending, the latter merely filling the 'gap' left by savings. Full employment implies a constant supply of goods, so that constant money income and expenditure would mean a constant price level. In this case the money rate of interest would coincide with the real rate.

In Figure 29.2 the supply and demand curves refer to the supply of investible (loanable) funds from savings and the demand for investible funds, at different rates of interest. The equilibrium rate initially

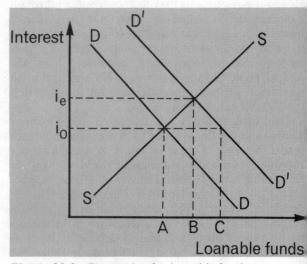

Figure 29.2 *The market for loanable funds.*

is i_0, where the amounts demanded and supplied are each equal to OA. Suppose now the demand for investible funds increases, so that the demand curve in our diagram shifts to the right, to D'D'. If monetary policy continued to be neutral, the rate of interest would rise to i_e. Consumers would then be persuaded by this higher rate to reduce their consumption and save the additional amount AB, which would be diverted to investment spending. Total money expenditure would be unchanged.

Monetary authorities need not act 'neutrally', however. According to the monetary theory of interest, they can maintain the *money* rate of interest at any arbitrary level by increasing or decreasing the available money supply. For example, instead of permitting the rate of interest in Figure 29.2 to rise to i_e, the authorities could maintain the money rate at the original level by creating bank money, in the form of loans to businessmen, amounting to AC. Consumers would then not need to be 'persuaded' by a higher rate of interest to supply the additional savings. What would happen? Assuming that the whole of the additional loans granted to businessmen were spent, there would be a net increase of AC in total spending, MV. Since we are considering a full employment situation this increase in aggregate demand would simply increase prices, output being fixed. Various categories of spenders would find that, with the same level of spending in money terms, they failed to maintain the same level of *real* spending, since goods were more expensive. In the case of consumers, this is referred to as 'forced savings'.

The rate of interest, i_e, in Figure 29.2, which is sufficient to satisfy investment demand by voluntary saving, is Wicksell's 'natural' rate of interest, the rate which would exist with a neutral monetary policy. If a money rate is fixed at a lower level, demand for investible funds will be satisfied partly by forced savings through inflation. To maintain the rate at i_0, the banking system would need to support a 'cumulative process' of inflation since, other things remaining the same, it would need to supply the amount AC *every* period. In each period, therefore, there is an addition to the circular flow of money income, causing prices to rise. Inflation will continue so long as the banks do not allow the money rate of interest to rise to the 'natural' level at which investment demand is matched by voluntary savings.

The reason for the inflation is once again, that at existing prices people (this time, consumers *and* businessmen) want to buy more than the available output. Whereas in the previous explanation of inflation the immediate source of the inflation was deficit financing of government spending (excessive spending in relation to revenue, only), here it is an over-generous credit policy permitting excessive spending by businessmen on investment relative to the amount of voluntary saving.

The Keynesian explanation of inflation

We have in effect described a Keynesian explanation of inflation in the previous chapter, particularly in Figures 28.7 and 28.8. This explanation stresses the level of spending, MV, looked at in its components C, I, G, and X. In this Keynesian theory money plays a largely permissive role: it *permits* rounds of expenditure to generate changes in income by the multiplier process. Moreover the multiplier process can operate in situations of unemployment even without increases in M, since it can be fed by the activation of abundant idle balances and thus an increase in V. Only at full employment does the money supply become important, after excess idle balances have been utilized for transaction purposes and as the multiplier operates on the price level rather than on real income. The stress on MV contrasts with the Quantity Theory, which stresses M: taking the Income Version, in the equation

$$M = kPY$$

k and Y are assumed constant, the latter because of the assumption of full employment, so that changes in M are translated directly into changes in P.

A second important difference, apart from the stress on aggregate money demand, MV, is the dependence on a Keynesian Liquidity Preference Theory of Interest. Changes in M have an effect, in combination with the demand for money, on the rate of interest, and thus on investment, through the marginal efficiency of investment schedule, and on income, through the investment expenditure multiplier. Keynes focused on the underconsumption situation with demand deficiency, but the same general theory would apply in inflationary situations of excess demand.

Like the Quantity Theory, Keynesian analysis suggests that control of money demand, MV, is necessary to limit inflation. The Keynesian solution also envisages some scope for monetary policy but in addition puts more emphasis on fiscal (tax) policy as a means of controlling spending. And the control of spending could be directed at any or all of its components, C, I, or G. Control of the money supply, raising the rate of interest, and decreasing the availability of credit could restrict both consumption and especially investment, this further reducing the level of spending through multiplier effects. Tax policy could be used to reduce *disposable personal incomes*, incomes in the hands of households, and hence consumption expenditure. Taxation can also be used to reduce the retained profits of firms and thus the funds available for new investment. And increasing tax rates, by reducing prospective post-tax rates of return on investment, can be used to restrain investment. Finally direct steps can be taken to reduce government spending, G. In depression, government can spend more than its current revenue from taxation, as a means of raising effective demand: a method referred to as *deficit financing*. Conversely, inflationary conditions can be partially or wholly counteracted by the government's incurring a budget *surplus*, with revenue from taxation exceeding expenditure.

The 'modern' Quantity Theory of Chicago

Since the 1950s, under the influence of Professor Milton Friedman and his colleagues at Chicago University, there has been a revival of belief in the importance of the money supply as a cause of inflation. According to what has come to be known as the 'monetarist view', excessive creation of money is still the fundamental cause of domestic *and* international inflation. However this argument is based on a more sophisticated version of the Quantity Theory which draws on some elements of the Keynesian analysis.

In the Quantity Theory, the Income Equation, $\frac{M}{P} = kY$, stressed the transactions demand for money. $\frac{M}{P}$ is the level of real money balances (the value of M in real terms) and equals Y, real income, times k, the desired ratio of real balances to Y. Since k is assumed stable and Y is constant, assuming full employment, increases in nominal money lead directly to changes in prices. This follows from the fact that the right-hand side of the equation, kY, is constant at full employment, so that the ratio M/P must also remain constant. This implies that increased money incomes are automatically spent on goods, so that their prices increase in proportion to increases in M: substitution occurs between money and goods only.

Keynes introduced the concept of demand for money as an asset, in addition to transactions demand. Thus there could be substitution between money and bonds, and other financial assets, as well as between money and goods. The impact of increased money supply on prices or real output was thus an *indirect* one, involving the demand for money (versus the demand for bonds), the rate of interest, and investment.

In Friedman's theory, individuals may hold any of three kinds of assets: money balances, financial assets, and real assets, which could be either consumer durables or investment goods, which are all alternative forms of wealth. Both financial assets and investment goods offer an explicit rate of return: a yield in the case of securities and a profit in the case of an investment good owned and operated within a business enterprise. Money offers no explicit rate of return but will carry an implicit yield in terms of convenience and security: more cautious individuals, particularly, will prefer to hold money rather than other more risky assets. Holding idle money, however, also has costs: first, the yield which might have been obtained on other assets is sacrificed; second, if there is inflation, a rise in the price level will steadily reduce the real value of money balances, whereas the prices of real assets will tend to go up in line with inflation. In deciding what combination of money balances, financial assets, and physical goods to hold, individuals will take into account the explicit or implicit rate of return, or advantage, to be obtained from each. If an individual holds too much of one type of asset, given the advantages he anticipates from it, he will attempt to substitute other assets for it.

If there is monetary expansion which disturbs the existing balance of asset holdings, increasing the amount of money balances held, excess demand inflation will follow as the public 'work off' their excess balances *on all kinds of transactions and not just on purchases of bonds or other financial securities*. To be more specific, suppose the supply of money is increased through open market operations: the central bank buys bonds, raising the price of bonds and lowering the rate of interest. Sellers of bonds will have substituted money for bonds, in line with Keynesian analysis: but these extra holdings of money may not be retained, but re-spent subsequently on other assets, including real capital or consumer goods. This is likely to occur partly because money balances exceed the level desired in relation to real income and other available forms of wealth and partly because the yield on securities has fallen. The increase in demand for real goods will be met by an increase in their supply, so long as supply is elastic, before full employment, and subsequently by rises in their price: that is, by changes in the price level. Prices will then continue to rise so long as there are excess money balances. The increase in money incomes associated with increases in output and prices will increase the demand for money, for transactions and as an asset. Equilibrium will be restored when the supply of and demand for money are once more in balance. Under full employment increases in money supply will generate roughly proportionate increases in prices.

This theory, unlike the simpler version of the Quantity Theory, accepts that there may be short-run fluctuations in the velocity of circulation of money, V, but argues that there will be a fairly stable *long-run* relationship between M and P: only in times of very rapid inflation will V change as individuals become less willing to hold money compared to other assets.

With appropriate adjustments for the lag in response between changes in the money supply and changes in money income, it is possible to predict the latter using a *money multiplier* instead of a Keynesian multiplier (which specifies particular kinds of autonomous demands, such as an increase in investment, or exports). In the Friedman view, money supply changes can be regarded as autonomous, or independent of, income changes, and so the money multiplier is the more important tool of prediction.

In less developed economies, where the demand for money is determined mainly by the transactions motive, the Friedman version of the Quantity Theory is not materially different from the simple Income Equation. In the absence of extensive markets in bonds and other securities, the choice of assets for people to hold is largely confined to money and physical assets including consumer goods. Bonds cannot therefore be the only really close substitute for money, and thus changes in the money supply cannot have much 'indirect' impact on money income through variations in interest rates. The impact will be more direct as people substitute physical goods for excess money balances, and vice versa. If empirical study indicates a close and stable relationship between money and money income, then control of the money supply can occupy a central position in managing the economy.

In open economies excess money demand induces imports rather than changes in money income, so that the authorities have to pay more attention to the balance of payments effects of monetary expansion than, perhaps, to problems of domestic inflation. If attempts to finance public expenditure by domestic bank credit creation are not accommodated by the domestic public's willingness to hold the additional money balances, the result is likely to be felt by the balance of payments and the foreign exchange reserves. For this reason the International Monetary Fund warns countries to control domestic credit creation rather than the money supply, which will decline as the result of leakage to imports.

Cost-push inflation

The above explanations are all 'excess demand' or *demand-pull* theories. These can be distinguished from *cost-push theories*. Here firms put up the prices of final goods, not because of increases in demand, but because of an increase in their costs. The most common variant of the theory is where wage costs force prices upwards as strong labour unions press for wage increases. In industrial countries wages and salaries represent the largest proportion of total production costs and absorb around two-thirds or so of national income, so that a substantial wage increase can put strong pressure on prices. It has been argued that a *wage–price spiral* could result, wage increases pushing prices up, the rise in prices producing further wage claims, and thus further price rises, and so on. Observers who have viewed the rise in wages as the main cause of the upward spiral have referred to this as *wage inflation*.

It is very difficult to say, in this situation, whether wages put up prices or wage earners seek increases in response to rises in prices. The wage–price spiral must in any case be accommodated by an increase in aggregate money demand, MV, if the volume of output and employment is to be maintained. Hence the wage inflation theory requires at least a *permissive* expansion of the money supply. There is also evidence from industrial countries that a given percentage increase in prices leads to not much more than half this percentage increase in wages.[4] This suggests that a persistent upward spiral would not result from wage claims, although an initial rise in prices due to some exogenous factor could be *magnified* by subsequent wage claims and cost-push effects. In general it is difficult to put down persistent inflation over a long period to cost-push, although this could be important in contributing to inflation in the short run. Other cost-push factors such as increases in import prices or in indirect taxes (particularly on basic items such as petrol) may occur, but their effects tend to be once-and-for-all upward price adjustments to higher levels and it is not easy to explain persistent price increases in these terms.

In Africa and Asia the wage sector of the economy is generally small in relation to the total and unions are very much less strong, so that wage-push is not likely to be a cause of general and prolonged inflation. Some elements of this may be present, however, and governments, in fixing the prices of staple foodstuffs affecting the real income of wage earners, have had to keep in mind possible repercussions on wages. An element of wage-push has also been imported into developing countries through the operations of the local subsidiaries of overseas manufacturing firms, who tend to pay similar wages, or at least award proportionately similar wage increases, to workers in all their plants.

A monetarist model of income determination

We said above that the Keynesian approach to income determination splits up aggregate money demand (total spending) into separate components, C, I, G, and X, and examines the factors affecting each of these. Increasing the money supply need not affect these components of spending, since the extra supply may be absorbed into idle balances: MV may not increase because the increase in M is offset by a decrease in V, the velocity of circulation of money.

According to the monetarist approach of Friedman and others, an increase in money supply is likely to be translated, after a time lag, into rising prices of goods, increasing the value of money income, MV.[5] In the last chapter we showed how a Keynesian model could be used to show the effect of increased spending in an open economy typical of less developed countries. It is also possible to construct a simple monetarist model of income determination in such an economy.[6]

We need to go back first to our discussion of the money supply and how it is determined. The money supply, consisting of currency plus bank deposits, is made up of the liabilities of the banking system. Against these liabilities the banking system, comprising the central bank and commercial banks, holds three kinds of assets or claims: claims against the government (government securities); claims against the private sector (loans and advances); and claims on the foreign sector (holdings of foreign exchange). Expansion in the value of these claims is always balanced by an equivalent increase in bank deposit liabilities, that is, the money supply. Thus an increase in bank lending to government or to the private sector, or a net increase in foreign exchange assets deposited with the bank, will mean an equivalent increase in the money supply.

We can write this as:

$$\Delta MO_t = D_t + \Delta R_t \qquad (29.1)$$

where ΔMO_t is the increase in money supply during any period t, D_t is net domestic credit creation (increase in bank lending) during the period, and ΔR_t is the change in foreign exchange reserves. This equation shows, incidentally, that in an open economy where foreign exchange outflow and inflow in any period are large relative to national money income, and determined by forces largely outside the control of the authorities, the authorities will not be able to determine changes in the money supply very closely simply by controlling bank lending.

ΔR, the net inflow of foreign exchange, will depend only partly on net earnings of foreign exchange during the period, or exports less imports, $X - M$. It will also depend on the size of new capital inflow, private foreign investment or foreign aid, and loans to the public sector. This we can label K, net capital receipts from abroad received by the private and public sectors. Thus we have, for any period t,

$$\Delta R_t = X_t - M_t + K_t \qquad (29.2)$$
$$\Delta MO_t = D_t + X_t + K_t - M_t \qquad (29.3)$$

and we can write aggregate money income or money demand at any time t as

$$Y_t = v MO_t \qquad (29.4)$$

If money income is proportional to the money supply, along monetarist lines, this would hold true for the preceding period, $t - 1$, so that:

$$Y_{t-1} = v MO_{t-1} \qquad (29.5)$$

It follows that $Y_t - Y_{t-1} = v(MO_t - MO_{t-1})$

or

$$\Delta Y_t = v \Delta MO_t \qquad (29.6)$$

the increase in money income is v times the increase in money supply. Substituting equation 29.3 into 29.6, we obtain:

$$\Delta Y_t = v(D_t + X_t + K_t - M_t) \qquad (29.7)$$

This says that the increase in money income depends on the increase in money supply, which depends in turn positively on three sources, bank lending, export earnings, and foreign capital receipts and *negatively* on the level of imports. In addition we assume that the propensity to import function has the simple form:

$$M_t = m Y_t \qquad (29.8)$$

stating that imports in any period, t, equal a given proportion of money income in that period. Substituting equation 29.4 in this gives:

$$M_t = mv MO_t \qquad (29.9)$$

which implies that imports are in a given ratio mv to the money supply. The interesting results are in the three equations:

$$\Delta MO_t = D_t + X_t + K_t - M_t \qquad (29.3)$$
$$M_t = mv MO_t \qquad (29.9)$$
$$\Delta Y_t = v(D_t + X_t + K_t - M_t) \qquad (29.7)$$

These bring out the special features of money supply and money income determination in an open economy in which foreign trade is of major importance. Equation 29.3 shows that money supply is determined not only by bank lending but by the level of export earnings and foreign capital received, and also by the level of import spending which extinguishes foreign reserves. Equation 29.9 permits us to predict the value of the increase in imports following an increase in money supply. Equation 29.7 indicates that money income may increase as the money supply increases, as a result of domestic credit creation, expansion of exports, or foreign capital, and also that *the expansion of money income will be limited in an open economy by increases in imports.*

The consequences of inflation

What are the consequences of inflation, of a persistent decline in the value of money? We can best answer that question by listing again the functions of money, and asking how these various functions might be affected.

Money is first of all a medium of exchange. As such, it is acceptable instead of commodity-money with intrinsic value only so long as people can rely on its not changing value very significantly between the moment they receive it in payment for something they supply and the moment they dispose of it as payment for goods or assets supplied to them. Whether this function is impaired therefore depends on how fast the value of money is changing relative to how fast money changes hands in effecting transactions, the transactions-velocity of money. Most inflations are not so rapid as this would require. But there have been cases of pronounced inflation involving very rapid changes in the value of money, known as *hyperinflations*, in which the legal currency tended to be replaced in circulation by other, foreign, currencies, or by other forms of payment altogether, like, for instance, cigarettes.

One kind of transaction may, however, be significantly affected even by mild inflation. Firms buy inputs and convert them to outputs, which are then sold some considerable time afterwards. A change in the value of money during this time means that in real terms firms obtain inputs, including labour, cheaply and are able to sell their production at a better price. By adding to real profit margins in this way inflation can act as a stimulus to trade. This is sometimes used as an argument for maintaining mild inflation.

Since money is a unit of account most contracts are fixed in money terms. If the value of money changes during the period of the contract the terms of the contract are correspondingly distorted. Retired people who are paid a pension fixed in money terms at the time of their retirement find that the real value of the pension deteriorates: and since the period of their retirement may be a long one, the deterioration in value may be very considerable, causing great hardship. Even if the pension is paid by the state, and revised periodically in money terms, there is invariably a considerable time lag between rises in prices and upward revision of pensions. Similarly holders of securities which pay interest fixed in money terms will lose during inflation. Again, if the value of money falls between the time a lender makes a loan and the time the loan is repaid, the amount repaid, including interest, may actually be worth less in real terms than the original value. The borrower thus gains at the expense of the lender, since money

is no longer an efficient standard of deferred payment. The effect is likely to be to discourage fixed-interest loans for productive purposes.

Money also becomes inefficient as a store of value, since the value of money savings declines during inflation. This is similar to the point made earlier, since savings are held not only in the form of cash but in the form of savings deposits, government bonds, insurance policies, and other contracts to pay amounts fixed in money terms. Moreover it is particularly 'small' savers, who can least afford to lose unfairly in this way, who invest in safe fixed-interest assets. The effect here will be to discourage saving, and encourage consumption, again with adverse effects on productive investment. People will also be encouraged to adopt an alternative store of value to money, and thus speculate in houses, land, or other physical assets which rise in value in step with the inflation. This speculation involves distortion of the price mechanism, since it is not related to productive activity: for instance land which is purchased as a store of value may never be put into productive use, while the price of houses may rise beyond the means of low-income households.

These remarks are sufficient to show that strong inflation, particularly, has a number of undesirable social and economic consequences. Nor have we discussed the effects on foreign trade, due to the fact that national currencies are used *inter*nationally both as units of account and media of exchange *and* as a store of value. However, inflation is still popular with governments as a method of 'forced saving' because inflation operates gradually and is likely to be politically less unpopular than new taxes.

Measuring changes in the price level

In this discussion we have been talking a great deal about 'changes in the price level'. Clearly, we are referring here to some kind of average level of prices. But when we look at the matter closely we shall find that it is extremely difficult to specify accurately what we mean by *the* price level.

Let us consider first a single commodity. Suppose fish costs shs 1.20 per unit in Year 1, and 1.60 in Year 2. We can say categorically that the price of fish has risen by one-third, or 33 per cent, or alternatively that the Year 2 price is 133 per cent of the Year 1 price. The figure of 133 is referred to as a *price relative*, in that it relates the prices in the two years.

Suppose, however, we wished to find the change in the price level of a collection of goods, for example, the goods commonly consumed by an individual. To keep matters simple we can imagine that the individual subsists on only four commodities, fish, rice, beans, and salt. The various prices of the goods over a period of two years and details of his expenditure are given in Table 29.2. If we have prices ruling in several years, we can select one year as a 'base year' and try to calculate an average price for the other years as a percentage of the base-year price level. Let us take Year 1 as the base year in this case.

Table 29.2 *A hypothetical 'basket' of purchases*

	Year 1 Prices	Year 2 Prices	Average monthly purchases in Year 1	
	(shs)	(shs)	volume (units)	value (shs)
Fish, each	1.20	1.60	15	18.00
Rice, per cup	0.80	1.20	12	9.60
Beans, per heap	0.40	0.50	27	10.80
Salt, per ½ kg packet	0.60	0.30	2	1.20
			Total	39.60

We find that while the price of fish has increased by 33 per cent, that of rice has gone up 50 per cent, beans 25 per cent and that of salt has actually fallen by 50 per cent. The price relatives for the four commodities are respectively 133, 150, 125, and 50. To find the *average* price change, we could take a simple average of these relatives, that is,

$$\frac{133+150+125+50}{4}=\frac{458}{4}=114.5$$

We could then say that the price level of these commodities had increased from 100 per cent in Year 1 to 114.5 per cent in Year 2, that is, by 14.5 per cent.

But this would hardly be a good indication of the impact of the change in prices on our consumer. Although, for example, the price of salt fell by half, the consumer will not have benefited much from this, since in Year 1 he was buying only two packets of salt and spending only 1.20s monthly on it! The changes in the prices of rice, beans, and particularly fish are far more important. This suggests that we ought to give these price changes more weight than that of salt. We can do this by calculating what is known as a *weighted average* of price relatives, rather than the simple average calculated above.

Suppose we thought the relative importance of the price changes was given by the ratio 4:3:2:1, so that, for instance, the price change of fish was 'four times' as important as that of salt. We could get an average which reflected this relative importance by counting the first item four times, the second three times, and so on. This would give an average of *ten* items as

follows:

$$\frac{(133+133+133+133)+(150+150+150)+(125+125)+50}{4+3+2+1}$$

$$=\frac{(4\times133)+(3\times150)+(2\times125)+50}{10}=\frac{1282}{10}=128(.2)$$

$$=\frac{\text{sum of the items multiplied by the appropriate weight}}{\text{sum of the weights}}$$

If we use the Greek letter 'Σ' (sigma) to mean 'the sum of ...', and refer to the items as 'Xs' and their weights as 'Ws', we should have a formula for a weighted average:

$$\frac{\Sigma WX}{\Sigma W}$$

These weights however were chosen at random. What weights *ought* to be taken? Clearly the amounts spent by the individual on the various commodities offer a sensible basis. Let us take the expenditure in Year 1, which we selected as base year, as weights. For each commodity P_1Q_1, the expenditure in Year 1, is therefore the weight to be attached to the price relative (P_2/P_1). The weighted average is:

$$\frac{\Sigma(P_1Q_1)(P_2/P_1)}{\Sigma P_1Q_1}$$

In our example in Table 29.2 this equals

$$\frac{18(133)+(9.6)(150)+(10.8)(125)+(1.2)(50)}{18+9.6+10.8+1.2}$$

$$=\frac{5244}{39.6}=132.4$$

This is referred to as an *index number* of price, in that it serves merely to *indicate* the order of magnitude of the price change. The index calculated is referred to as being base-weighted, as the weights refer to base-year values.

Now the numerator in the formula above is the sum of items like $P_1Q_1\times P_2/P_1$ which, cancelling out P_1, is P_2Q_1. The formula thus reduces to:

$$\frac{\Sigma P_2Q_1}{\Sigma P_1Q_1}$$

Here the denominator is the sum of the quantities bought in Year 1 valued at the prices in Year 1, while the numerator is the same quantities valued at Year 2 prices. The formula thus comes down to comparing the cost of a 'basket of goods' typically bought by the individual in the first year with what the *same* basket would cost at second year prices. We can calculate our index number directly, without first working out price relatives. We know ΣP_1Q_1, the total expenditure in Year 1 to be 39.60 shillings, while Table 29.3 gives $\Sigma P_2 Q_1$ to be 52.50 shillings. The ratio is $\dfrac{52.50}{39.60}$ or, as a percentage, 132.6, approximately the same as we obtained previously.

Table 29.3   Cost of buying the Year 1 'basket' at Year 2 prices

Q_1 (units)	P_2 (shs)	P_2Q_1 (shs)
15	1.60	24.00
12	1.20	14.40
27	0.50	13.50
2	0.30	0.60
	Total	52.50

Measuring changes in the value of money

In the previous section we compared the cost of a representative 'basket' of goods at two points of time. Due to rise in the price level the basket becomes more expensive and the individual needs more money to buy it. The 'purchasing power' of money has declined, since for a *given* amount of money the buyer can get fewer goods. In such a case, we can say the *'value of money'* has fallen.

In our example the 'price level' rose by 32.4 per cent, from 100 per cent to 132.4 per cent of the Year 1 level. Hence to continue to buy the same collection of goods our individual would need 132.4 of his money in Year 1. The same money income could only buy the fraction $\dfrac{100}{132.4}$ of the original basket, or 76 per cent, implying a 24 per cent fall in the value of money.

Index numbers may be used to measure various price levels, the general level of retail or wholesale prices, the average price of exports or imports, and price levels of particular groups of commodities. If we attempt to find the change in the level of prices of the *whole range of items* on which people spend their incomes, we are measuring changes in the cost of living of those people, and the resulting index is referred to as a *'cost of living index'*. It is not easy, however, to include all types of expenditure in an index, and more commonly a retail price index is calculated covering the prices of only a selection of goods retailed by traders and for which data are readily available.

Price index numbers in Eastern Africa

What 'cost of living' or 'retail price' index numbers are calculated in East Africa? A brief description of the index numbers compiled by the Statistical Department of the individual governments is usually published in the various *Statistical Abstracts* or *Bulletins* produced regularly in each country. The East African Statistical Departments' quarterly *Economic and Statistical Review* reproduces price index numbers relating to the average expenditure of distinct sets of paid wage and salaried earning households in the three capital cities of Nairobi, Dar es Salaam, and Kampala. On the basis of a household budget survey carried out in 1969, two new indices based on August 1971 = 100 were introduced in Kenya. A 'Middle Income Index of Consumer Prices—Nairobi' uses average weights derived from expenditures by households in the shs 400 to shs 1,400 a month income bracket; while a 'Lower Income Index of Consumer Prices—Nairobi' is based on households below shs 400. Rent, which was formerly excluded from the Nairobi cost of living indices, has now been brought in as a major item of expenditure, and for this reason the index numbers referring to periods before August 1971 are not strictly comparable, although they have been converted to the new base period. For Dar es Salaam there is published a 'Cost of Living Index of Goods and Services consumed by Middle Grade Civil Servants', which uses weights derived from a survey of these workers with a basic salary in the shs 8,000–20,000 annual income bracket carried out in 1963. A 'Retail Price Index of Goods consumed by Wage Earners—Dar es Salaam' is also published, compiled from the prices of 43 articles 'obtained by purchase or quotation in shops and market stalls in the four main African residential areas'. This index has a base of December 1951 = 100, and uses weights obtained from budget studies carried out between 1950 and 1957.

The three Kampala cost of living indices (excluding rent) are also based on household expenditure surveys carried out in the early 1960s. A 'High Income Index' 'measures changes in the cost of maintaining the standard of living prevailing among (civil) servants of all races with a basic salary in 1963, of some shs 27,000 per annum'. The 'Middle Income Index' refers to skilled and semi-skilled workers in Kampala but uses weights obtained from a survey carried out in Jinja in 1964; while the 'Lower Income Index' refers to unskilled workers in Kampala, with commodity weights obtained from a survey in 1964. All three series use January 1961 as a base date with the index number of 100.

Zambia is unusual in Eastern Africa in publishing 'Index Numbers of Consumer Prices' which combine all main urban centres and not just the capital city of Lusaka. 'High' and 'Low' Income Indices are published, as well as a 'Combined Index'. In Malawi the 'Low Income Index' relates specifically to Blantyre households with annual expenditures up to K 600, the average for this range being K 210. The 'High Income Index' refers to households spending more than K 2,000 a year, the average being K 3,719, and uses weights for all the main towns, although the prices are again collected only in Blantyre. These indices, with 1970 = 100, are based on comprehensive *Household Income and Expenditure Survey for Urban Areas and Agricultural Estates, 1968.* We shall refer specifically to some of its findings in describing the general problems of devising consumer price indices.

Problems in the compilation of price indices

1. Relevance of the index

The first requirement is that the index should be relevant, that it should be useful in examining the experience of some group of people. This means that if two groups of people have quite different patterns of expenditure and ways of living, separate indices are required to cover their separate experiences. Thus the Kampala Lower Income Index takes account of the fact that 17 per cent of food expenditure (and $8\frac{1}{2}$ per cent of total expenditure) at the time of the survey in February, 1964 was estimated as being on matoke (plantains), while the corresponding Nairobi Lower Income Index omits this food item. Lower-paid workers in Nairobi would, presumably, be unperturbed if the price of matoke were to increase, say, five-fold overnight, since they do not eat it! On the other hand, the Nairobi Lower Income Index includes a weight of 7 per cent for milk and $5\frac{1}{2}$ per cent for

wheat flour and bread; while the Kampala index assigns a total weight of only 2 per cent for milk and only $1\frac{1}{2}$ per cent for bread, milk and bread supplies being more abundant in Nairobi. Thus the weights used in constructing an index take account of differing tastes and the availability of particular commodities, both of which will affect the expenditure patterns of different groups of consumers.

Apart from tastes and the availability of different goods, the fact that different groups have very different levels of income will have a major effect on their patterns of consumption—even in the same town or geographical area with the same items available to all at a common price. Indeed the calculation of separate price indices for different income groups is the main feature of the index numbers reviewed above for various Eastern African countries. We can see this income effect most clearly when a wide spread of income groups is included in the same expenditure survey for a particular place at a specific point of time. The household budget studies undertaken in Nairobi in 1969, and in Blantyre in 1968, fulfil this requirement, unlike the various studies separated in time or space used in compiling some of the other price indices.

Table 29.4 illustrates the effect of income on the value of the weights assigned to the different items. Since the income gap is much smaller in the case of the Nairobi indices, the difference in weights is much less than in the case of the Blantyre indices which refer to income groups with average annual expenditure of K 210 and K 3,719, respectively. The highly paid civil servants and businessmen in the 'High' income group spend 18 times as much as the 'typical' Blantyre wage earner; whereas in Nairobi the 'Middle' income group were earning and spending

Table 29.4 *Comparison of weights in African urban price indices*

| | Nairobi | | Blantyre | |
	Lower	Middle	Low	High
All items	1,000	1,000	1,000	1,000
Food	522	412	479	230
Drinks and tobacco	43	44	77	65
Clothing and footwear	56	51	176	81
Transport	28	65	18	237
Other	351	428	250	387
of which				
Household goods/services†	92	99	198	139
Domestic help	—	—	16	94
School fees	48	69	—	—
Rent	199	224	—	—

†This item is not strictly comparable as between the two urban areas: it covers fuel, light and water, household operation, and furniture and utensils in the Nairobi indices.

only twice to three times the budget of the 'Lower' income group.

Of the items specified in Table 29.4, the only striking differences between the two Nairobi income groups, were, first, the smaller proportion of expenditure devoted to food, and secondly, the higher expenditure on transport and school fees of the 'Middle' income group. This tendency to spend less on food, a 'necessary' item of expenditure, and proportionately more on 'luxury' (income-elastic) items is very much more marked in the Blantyre weights. Since food accounts for nearly one-half of the Low Income Index, it is very sensitive to price movements of staple foods, but not affected markedly by movements in the cost of running motor cars and other transport or of domestic servants, which have much larger weights on the High Income Index.

Thus price index numbers have to relate to specific groups of people on specific locations and with specific ranges of income. They are correspondingly less efficient index numbers of price changes affecting other groups.

2. The choice of weights

One of the main problems, as is clear already, is the choice of weights. In the first place not all the items being purchased are included in the index, but only a *representative selection* of items. For example, the retail price index of goods consumed by wage earners in Dar es Salaam is compiled from the prices of forty-three articles obtained by purchase or quotation in the shops and market stalls of four main African residential areas. The assumption then is that the prices of items excluded from the index will move in much the same way as the included items. In so far as some items are excluded, the index is said to be *partial*. This is equivalent to giving excluded items zero weight.

The choice of which items to include, and the weight to give them, are determined by sample survey investigations to determine patterns of expenditure. Average patterns of expenditure are thereby established for groups of people with certain ranges of incomes, social class, place of residence, of work, and so on. Most countries now conduct periodic inquiries into spending habits at least of wage-earning families, as we saw above for the Eastern African countries.

Particular problems arise in the choice of weights for cost of living indices in African countries, which do not arise in industrial countries where consumption of home-produced food and other goods is relatively unimportant. If a price index is designed to reflect accurately movements in the prices of all goods and services consumed by specific groups, including this subsistence production, the weights assigned to food, fuel, and dwellings will be larger than those revealed by the analysis of actual cash expenditures alone. Moreover, the difference in the weight assigned to food, especially, if home-grown produce and possibly gifts are included, will be most marked for low income groups than for higher income households which can afford to spend more on non-food items in any case. Thus, for example, cash expenditure on food represented 50 per cent of total cash expenditure of African unskilled workers in Kampala surveyed in February 1964; but the actual weight included in the Lower Income Index for this group for food was 70 per cent, the difference representing this home-produced food. In the 1968 Blantyre survey subsistence food consumption represented 17 per cent of total food consumption for the Low Income group with cash receipts under K 300 per year, making a difference of 4 per cent in the food weight assigned to 'their' Low Price Index. Clearly the actual cost of living for households without access to home-grown food supplies will be affected much more by increases in food prices than similar households with their own gardens. The first group will therefore require a larger increase in money income to maintain their real income than the second group.

A similar problem arises in calculating a weight for the cost of housing. In industrial countries a large proportion of the urban wage-earning households pay cash rents for housing accommodation, and this item of expenditure can be given a price index weight quite easily, as can the housing costs of owner-occupiers who have to pay for repairs and interest charges on mortgage loans. However, in Eastern Africa rented accommodation is in more limited supply: the bulk of rural population live in their own houses which they have built themselves; while the urban population lives in a variety of housing conditions, ranging from subsidized housing for higher-income civil servants and some commercial employees to 'shanty' dwellings for unskilled labourers. Here again two wage earners with the same cash income may experience quite different housing costs, the first being lucky to live in an employer-subsidized (or rent-controlled) flat with modern amenities while the second has to pay the market rent for a share of a small living room in a semi-urban slum location. Until recently, therefore, many of the price indices published were *partial*, excluding a weight for rent altogether. However, with the development of housing estates for rent to specific groups of workers it has become possible, in Nairobi for example, to include an item for rent, although the weight assigned will depend very much on the housing circumstances of the households in the budget survey.

The question of weight for subsistence food and rent naturally interests trade unions, employers, and governments concerned with wage negotiations. Wage earners are anxious that wage increases keep pace with movements in the prices of items actually purchased by them: if they are urban workers who have to purchase all their food and accommodation, they will require a larger weight for these items than, say, better-off workers in Kampala who live in their own homes with gardens outside the city. Employers of estate labour, for example, might like the cost of living index to reflect large weights for housing and food which they supply on a subsidized basis. Since governments are both employers and also responsible for the economy as a whole, they too will wish to contain wage increases by stabilizing the cost of local food and housing using price and rent controls. They may therefore have a special interest in minimizing the weight of items subject to rapid price increases such as imports or heavily taxed goods like drink, tobacco, and petrol. During the 1950s the Kenya Government went as far as to publish what was called a 'Wage Adjustments Index' which deliberately excluded increases since August, 1939 in the taxes levied on those 'noxious' items of consumption, alcohol and tobacco, on the grounds that this expenditure was not really part of consumers' costs of living! Since alcohol and tobacco had a weight of 10 per cent in the old (upper-income) Cost of Living Index, this practice had some effect on the rate of inflation which the government had to compensate for in 'cost of living' salary increases.

3. Changing patterns of expenditure

The most fundamental problem in compiling a meaningful index, however, arises from the need to allow for changes in patterns of expenditure over time. In our base-weighted index the weights always remained the same, relating to base-year data. We can instead construct various types of *variable*-weight indexes, as for instance some average of price relatives with current expenditures as weights. It is easy to see the difficulties of doing this in Eastern Africa. Up-to-date information on household expenditure is rarely available, so that the cost of living indices are based on studies made perhaps decades before, when East Africa was a very different place from what it is now. The Kampala Lower Income Index is based on a survey of unskilled workers made in February 1964, and the Middle Income Index on the Jinja investigation in the same year. The problem here is thus the *loss of relevance* over time.

It may be noted that the change in patterns of expenditure is not independent of the price movements which the index is trying to record. A base-weighted index may be pulled up by sharp rises in prices of just a few commodities, whereas in fact

consumers will tend to avoid these commodities, diverting their consumption elsewhere, and thus be able to dodge part of the effects of these increases in prices.

Over a long period, especially, the specific problem of new goods and of goods of changed quality arises. For example, the first official cost of living index in Britain was based on a sample of 'working class' family budgets in 1904. However, the index did not begin until 1914 and continued with the same base until 1947, by which time real incomes and relative prices had changed markedly: new goods like radios were consumed widely and a great many goods like candles and lamp-oil had almost disappeared. Changes in quality create much the same problem as new goods, as for example the substitution of electricity for candle-light, which may be treated as different goods or as the substitution of a superior form of the same commodity, lighting. Some attempts to take account of any quality improvement in the 'basket of goods' bought must be made in order to assess genuine changes in price.

4. Collection of price data

The collection of information on prices is itself difficult and laborious, more so in African markets. A great deal of produce is sold in 'heaps' rather than by precise weight. Very often the produce is not well sorted into grades, which makes the allowances for quality difference especially difficult to assess. Moreover, prices themselves are often fixed only after a process of bargaining, and even retail stores are prepared to allow discounts to 'tough' customers. Thus there is a great deal of variation in the prices paid for the same articles. Apart from this, seasonal variation in price must be taken into account, and regional variation if the index is used to cover a wide area.

Price data are obtained for most Eastern African consumer price indices in the following way. The government statistician sends out collectors, usually clerks or office messengers, under supervision, who have to bargain for their purchases and who are thought to be 'average' bargainers according to standards of the local market. Actual purchases are made to ensure that the prices are going market prices. Purchases are obtained for each commodity from various retail 'outlet' markets, and the results averaged, to eliminate any possible chance factors. Prices of foodstuffs in some rural markets may be collected by the Ministry of Agriculture, while the Ministry of Labour may also be involved in some cases because it has a special interest in the effect of price movements on *real* wages of workers.

The use of price index numbers

Price index numbers are useful, first, where we are interested in price levels as such, either general price levels, as measured by cost of living indices, or sectional price levels, such as the price of textile goods or engineering products; or secondly in order to 'deflate' value series to estimate real volume changes. Here again we may be interested in aggregate income or in components of income. We started out by saying that a given increase in money income may be 'inflated' by a rise in the price level. 'Deflating a value series' means eliminating the effect of the change in prices by dividing the value series through by a price index. Thus in Table 29.5 the price index indicates that prices went up in Kenya from 100 per cent in 1964 to 130.6 per cent in 1973 and to 147.4 per cent in 1974.

If the current value figure for 1974 of £952 millions is divided by 147.4, we obtain the value of £646 millions for the same year at constant 1964 prices. This shows a 'real' growth in national product of 81.0 per cent, compared with an increase of 166.7 per cent at current money values between 1964 and 1974.

Readers will observe that we have in fact obtained three series of index numbers, relating to 'value' and 'volume' as well as price:

	1964	1974
(1) Value index	100	266.7
(2) Price index	100	147.4
(3) Volume index	100	181.0

The value index is of course straightforward enough; in the case of the national income of Kenya, it is simply the current 1974 money value of aggregate income expressed as a percentage of the current value in 1964. The volume index is more complicated, because we have reduced to a single series a vast collection of goods and services—the nation's 'basket' of fish, rice, clothing, government services, output of capital goods, and so on. Moreover, this is not a constant 'basket' since the structure of this product changes, so that a base-weighted index would be irrelevant very quickly. For this reason the numerous components of expenditure on domestic product have to be deflated separately, and the price index for all goods and services derived by dividing the constant price series of domestic product into the current value series in the table above. This kind of price index number is merely 'implied'. It is called an 'implicit' price index, indicating the 'average price', P, which was mentioned at the beginning of this chapter and which appears whenever we look at the Equation of Exchange $M.V = P.Q$.

Table 29.5 *Kenya's gross domestic product at current and constant prices*

	1964	1973	1974
Gross national product at current market prices (£K millions)	357	815	952
GDP price deflator: implicit price index	100.0	130.6	147.4
Gross national product at constant (1964) market prices (£K millions)	357	624	646

SOURCE: *Statistical Abstract*, 1976, and UN *Yearbook of National Accounts Statistics*, 1975

Questions on Chapter 29

1. Discuss the relation between MV=PT and M/P=kY, and comment on the usefulness of the two algebraic statements.
2. Explain why people may choose to hold money rather than bonds, even though money yields no interest.
3. Discuss the possible effect on the demand for money of a change in the rate of interest.
4. Discuss the relation between the Quantity Theory of Money and the Keynesian Liquidity Preference Theory.
5. What is 'hyperinflation' and how has it generally arisen?
6. Give an account of Wicksell's theory of the 'cumulative process' of inflation. How does inflation arise in this theory, and what makes it cumulative?
7. Compare the Keynesian explanation of inflation with the simple Quantity Theory of Money.
8. Compare the Keynesian explanation of inflation with the modern 'monetarist' view of Friedman.
9. Distinguish between 'excess demand' and 'cost-push' causes of inflation, and explain why policies to control inflation should take account of this distinction.
10. What version of the Quantity Theory of Money, if any, is relevant to contemporary problems of inflation in Eastern Africa?
11. Discuss the possible consequences of different rates of inflation on the economic position of (a) 'small savers', (b) business enterprises, and (c) the government.
12. How is the value of money measured? What are the main problems involved in measuring changes in the volume of money?
13. How are retail price index numbers compiled in Eastern African countries? How relevant are these index numbers in measuring changes in the cost of living of the 'average' household?
14. Explain how household budget surveys are used in compiling cost of living index numbers in your country. What problems arise in interpreting the findings of these surveys?
15. Trace the effects of an expansion in domestic credit created by the banking system on the money supply and on the level of money income in a less developed and open economy.

Notes

[1] In recent years *nominal* rates of interest have risen to much higher levels in most developed monetary systems in line with inflation. But *real* rates of interest, after allowing for inflation, may still be quite low or negative.

[2] Money income transactions may be specified by k.P.Y rather than L(T), as under the Income Version of the Quantity Theory. Changes in the price level, P, as well as real output, Y, will influence the amount of money held for transactions purposes.

[3] Wicksell's *Interest and Prices* was published in 1898.

[4] This evidence is reviewed in R. G. Lipsey, *An Introduction to Positive Economics*, Weidenfeld and Nicolson, various editions.

[5] To be more precise increased spending will raise prices only after the full employment position is reached or as this is approached; before this the supply of output should increase at given prices, also implying an increase in MV.

[6] See E. F. Furness, *Money and Credit in Developing Africa*, Heinemann, 1975, pp. 206–14 for a fuller discussion, and W. T. Newlyn, 'Monetary Analysis and Policy in Financially Dependent Economies' in I. G. Stewart (ed.), *Economic Development and Structural Change*, Edinburgh University Press, 1969, for an application of this model to East Africa. Strictly speaking this 'Polak' model, named after J. J. Polak, a leading economist with the IMF, is not a monetarist theory only since its income is determined by the marginal propensity to import and the main components of aggregate demand (Keynesian characteristics): however, the stable income velocity represents a monetarist approach.

30 International Payments

International trade differs from trade between regions or between individuals within one country partly because national frontiers present barriers to the free movement of goods and factors in the form of protection and other restrictions. Apart from this, an important difference arises out of the fact that different countries normally have different national currencies. Because international trade directly affects a country's national income and because also its national currency is involved, countries are interested in having an accurate record of their international transactions. This accounting record of a country's economic transactions with the rest of the world is known as its *balance of payments*.

The balance of payments

Transactions which make a supply of home currency available to foreigners are put on the 'debit' side of the account. Thus when foreigners supply imports, for example, residents of the home country 'supply' their own currency and 'demand' foreign currency with which to buy the imports. Transactions which create a supply of foreign currency, and a demand for home currency, as for instance when foreigners buy home exports, are listed as 'credits'. The balance of payments is therefore like any balance sheet, with credits and debits, generally given on an annual basis. It follows that *total credits always equal debits*. This means only that a balancing item is always put in to *make* these equal, either on the credit or debit side, which equals the amount of deficit or surplus, and shows the extent to which the country is living within or beyond its current overseas income. We can therefore still talk of a deficit or surplus on current account even though the balance of payments, like any balance sheet, must balance: after all, even the statement of a bankrupt firm does that.

The structure of the balance of payments account

Table 30.1 gives details of Ethiopia's balance of payments for 1971, and in simplified form, for 1972 and 1973. It will be seen firstly that this account, like that of a company, is divided into a Current Account

and a Capital Account. It may be observed further that the net balance on current account is offset by an equivalent sum on capital account. It is not necessary for each account separately to balance: it is necessary that a deficit on one be offset by a credit on the other, and vice versa, in accordance with our statement above. If purchases on current account exceed sales, the extra foreign currency must be found from somewhere, and this can be done by, say, using up foreign exchange reserves or borrowing from abroad. Both these possibilities, it must be noticed, imply a *supply* of foreign currency and are given as *credits* in the capital account, in accordance with our definition.

A distinction is sometimes drawn between 'autonomous' and 'accommodating' items in the capital account. If a country incurs a deficit on current account, part of the extra foreign exchange required can come from voluntary foreign lending, either between governments or between private individuals. Since this lending *is* voluntary, however, there is no reason why it should provide exactly the amount of foreign exchange needed, and it can even *increase* the amount needed if *net* lending by foreigners, after including lending by the home country overseas, is negative. Any deficit which remains after taking into account international lending must be met by a running down of reserves of foreign currency or short-term financial assets. The voluntary lending, *being independent of any other items in the account*, can be described as autonomous, while the change in foreign assets, being necessarily equal and opposite to the remaining deficit, can be described as accommodating that deficit.

In respect of the sale of gold, it is worth noting that countries like Ethiopia which export *newly mined* gold, distinguish between this 'non-monetary gold' and 'monetary gold' which may be used to accommodate 'temporary' deficits or surpluses. The former is really a commodity export, like copper, for example, and not part of foreign exchange reserves. Though it is really part of merchandise trade, it is given separately because of its special significance as one source of 'international money'.

On current account, an important distinction can be drawn between *visible and invisible* trade. The former relates to merchandise transactions, that is,

Table 30.1   *Balance of payments of Ethiopia, 1971–3*

	Ethiopian $ millions				
	1971			1972	1973
	Credit (+)	Debit (−)	Net balance (+ or −)	Net balance (+ or −)	Net balance (+ or −)
A *Visible trade* (1+2)	315.1	394.7	−79.6	+19.3	+123.7
(1) Merchandise (f.o.b.)	314.0	394.7	−80.7	+18.2	+123.2
(2) Non-monetary gold	1.1	—	+1.1	+1.1	+0.5
B *Invisible trade* (3 to 8)	172.0	226.5	−54.5	−40.2	−23.5
(3) Freight and insurance (on 1)	4.0	75.0	−71.0	−66.0	−69.6
(4) Other transportation	56.2	23.1	+33.1	+39.8	+43.9
(5) Travel	19.7	18.3	+1.4	+4.8	+5.8
(6) Government (n.i.e.)	42.7	18.6	+24.1	+29.8	+40.5
(7) Other services (non-factor)	37.7	50.6	−12.9	−4.4	−2.1
(8) Investment income	11.7	40.9	−29.2	−43.8	−42.0
C Trade in goods and services (A+B)	487.1	621.2	−134.1	−20.9	+100.2
D Transfer payments	26.9	4.4	+22.5	+40.6	+53.8
E CURRENT ACCOUNT (C+D)	514.0	625.6	−111.6	+19.7	+154.0
F *Capital Movements* (9–11)			102.6	+75.7	+89.9
(9) Government	102.8	36.8	+66.0	+45.3	+48.8
(10) Private long term	24.2	4.5	+19.7	+29.1	+64.2
(11) Private short term (net)	—	—	+16.9	+1.3	−23.1
G *Monetary movements (net)*			+16.7	−86.0	−218.3
H *Net errors and omissions*			−7.7	−9.4	−25.6
I CAPITAL ACCOUNT (F–H)	—	—	+111.6	−19.7	−154.0

SOURCE: National Bank of Ethiopia, *Quarterly Bulletin*, March 1974

the export and import of physical commodities. Invisible trade relates to services such as the shipping of goods, and the provision of insurance, to interest and profits on foreign investment (payment for the 'service' of lending capital funds), and to tourists' expenditure (either expenditure by nationals overseas or by foreigners in the home country). These items are called 'invisible' not because their values are not known, although in fact accurate information on them is very often difficult to get, but because they involve intangible services which do not pass through Customs warehouses.

The difference between exports and imports of merchandise is termed the *balance of visible trade* and is *not* the same thing as the balance of payments. As it happens, figures for the balance of trade can generally be obtained more quickly and more accurately via the Customs and Excise Department. Since merchandise trade does account for a large proportion of total current payments, though not all, there will be great interest especially in the *change* in the balance of trade from one period to another. A deficit in the balance of visible trade, however, is not

necessarily of any consequence. In 17 out of the 20 years, 1954 to 1973, for example, the United Kingdom had such a deficit, with only small surpluses in three years, and this is the usual situation for Britain to be in. For Britain's earnings through *invisible* exports are in general sufficient to convert a visible deficit into a surplus on current account. In the case of most African countries a surplus on the (visible) balance of trade in goods is required to finance a deficit in invisible transactions in services.

Lastly we may note an item labelled 'net errors and omissions'. This is simply a statistical adjustment made necessary by the fact that many transactions are difficult to record accurately and therefore do not 'add up' exactly. This item ensures that the account is still in balance. It should be noted that an improvement in the statistics may actually increase this figure. Suppose two figures are both underestimated, but one is a credit and the other a debit. To some extent the two underestimates will cancel each other. If the improvement affects one and not the other, the underestimates will no longer cancel, and the residual error will increase. It follows that the size of the residual error does not itself provide a measure of the accuracy or otherwise of the items included in the balance of payments estimates.

Ethiopia's balance of payments

Let us now look more closely at Table 30.1, which shows how the balance of payments of Ethiopia is made up. The actual form in which the various types of transaction are presented under specific headings varies slightly from country to country, but readers in other Eastern African countries should have little difficulty in identifying corresponding transactions in their own country's balance of payments accounts. The figures for merchandise exports and imports are derived from the External Trade Statements or Returns made by the government's Customs and Excise Department. Exports are usually valued 'free on board' (f.o.b.), that is to say, at their value in the exporting port *before* shipment abroad. The figure thus represents the gross receipts accruing to the exporter and excludes payment for shipment overseas which could, of course, be a payment to a foreign shipping line. When we talk about the value of imports we generally refer to the c.i.f. value, covering 'cost, insurance, and freight', that is, including the services of shipping and insuring the goods while in transit, on top of the f.o.b. cost at the ports of origin overseas. In the balance of payments accounts, however, these are normally also shown f.o.b., with freight and insurance charges deducted from the value of merchandise imports, since these are invisible services, shown separately.[1]

In Table 30.1 receipts of a foreign currency are shown as a credit and payments of foreign currency as a debit. It can be seen that in 1971 there was a net deficit of Eth $79.6 millions in visible trade, the value of goods imported exceeding the value of goods exported. Invisible trade was also in deficit to the tune of Eth $54.5 millions, reflecting especially a large payment (B(3)) for foreign-supplied shipping and insurance services, given that Ethiopia lacks her own merchant fleet. In 1971 these services cost $75.0 millions, adding some 20 per cent to the f.o.b. cost of visible imports. Ethiopia's own freight and insurance earnings were a negligible Eth $4.0 millions.

Among other invisibles, item B(4) largely reflects expenditure by foreigners, including tourists, on the national airline, Ethiopian Airways, one of the largest and oldest African-owned international airlines, and was in Ethiopia's favour. Another credit, B(5), represents expenditure by tourists and other visitors to Ethiopia. Expenditure abroad by Ethiopian residents was almost as large, however, almost balancing this out. Government transactions, B(6) (not included elsewhere under other items such as A(1)), was, un-

usually in Eastern Africa, an important foreign currency 'export' for Ethiopia, a reflection of the relatively large number of foreign diplomatic missions and international organizations such as the OAU and ECA based in the country. Their local expenditure was more than twice as large as the foreign expenditure by the Ethiopian government on overseas missions and related services. 'Other services', B(7), includes on the credit side the renting of buildings to foreigners based in Ethiopia and on the debit side services like non-merchandise insurance, private education abroad, and certain forms of entertainment such as the renting of foreign films by cinema houses. Finally, we can note another service which developing countries in Africa have to buy abroad: item B(8) refers to investment income payments to foreign owners of capital invested in Ethiopia. These 'factor' services, in respect of interest on loans raised abroad by the government or by enterprises and in respect of profits earned by foreign companies, are distinguished from other service transactions since they represent part of Ethiopia's domestic product, but have to be deducted to arrive at the national product, as we explained in Chapter 1.

Taking visibles and invisibles together, then, Ethiopia had a net deficit in trade in goods and services of Eth $134.1 millions. Also making up the Current Account are transfer payments. Unlike the other items these are not transactions involving exchange of currency for a good or service and either generating income for the home country or 'using up' the country's income. Transfers are thus 'one-sided' transactions not related to Ethiopia's output although affecting the balance of foreign currency flows. More specifically here the Eth $26.9 millions was the net amount received from overseas aid bodies, while a debit item of Eth $4.4 millions represented net remittances abroad by the private sector. This foreign aid helped to finance the net trade deficit, bringing the deficit on current account down to Eth $111.6 millions. This remaining current deficit was then balanced by an opposite flow on capital account.

Ethiopia usually experiences such a deficit on its balance of trade in goods and services, as do most non-oil-exporting developing countries, the deficit being 'accommodated' by (1) net transfer receipts, item D, (2) long-term capital inflows shown under F (9) and (10), and (3) short-term movements in the foreign exchange assets of its banking system (shown as monetary movements, under G) or in other financial assets (or liabilities) held by the private sector, F (11). Private traders can raise short-term trade credit or bank loans abroad to pay for imports, for a time, instead of paying for imports immediately with foreign exchange derived from the central bank.

Balance of payments statements may distinguish

between *autonomous* transactions, reflected in long-term capital movements, and *induced* balancing flows which simply 'accommodate' the residual surplus or deficit to ensure overall balance in the accounts as a whole. In Table 30.1, F(9) and F(10) can be said to be autonomous in relation to the position for the year, 1971, in that the direction and timing of these flows would not automatically ensure overall balance in the country's external balance sheet.

The figures for 1972 and 1973 show that the deficit in the balance of payments on current account in 1971 had changed to a small surplus of Eth $19.7 millions in 1972 and a much larger surplus of Eth $154.0 millions in 1973. This can be traced especially to the improved balance in merchandise trade, though a reduced deficit on invisibles and a higher level of net transfer payments received also helped. These positive balances on current account were accommodated by a 'debit' on capital account, the Eth $86.0 millions in 1972 and Eth $218.3 millions in 1973 representing acquisitions of foreign exchange assets by the banking system, after allowing also for the other net capital movements *and* errors and omissions in the statistics which produced net credits of Eth $66.3 in 1972 and Eth $64.3 in 1973. Notice that the *increase* in foreign assets is shown by a negative sign (−), as in 1972 or 1973, while a *reduction* in foreign assets (or an increase in liabilities owed to foreigners) is a credit item with a positive sign (+) because it increases the supply of foreign currency.

The significance of the balance of payments

Government officials responsible for the overall management of the economy, and other observers, will be interested in all the individual items appearing in the balance of payments estimates. But above all, interest in these estimates stems from the need to know whether or not the country is 'living within its income'. We have already said that the balance of *visible trade* may be unfavourable and yet the balance on current account in surplus, due to invisible items. But even if there is a deficit on current account *including* these items, this is not necessarily of any significance. The country would then simply be borrowing from abroad an amount equal to the deficit. *What is significant is what the loan is used for and how it is financed.* If the loan is to finance home investment the increase in output eventually resulting from the investment may be sufficient to more than repay the loan with interest. The same will not apply if the deficit is due to excessive consumption of foreign-produced consumer goods. Home investment

will also generally be financed by long-term borrowing: short-term loans on the other hand can only be expected to tide a country over a temporary deficit, since they need to be repaid within a short period. The distinction bears some relation to that between autonomous and accommodating capital changes: a deficit may be 'accommodated' by running down reserves of foreign exchange, or by short-term borrowing abroad. But all these means cannot be sustained indefinitely: reserves of foreign exchange will run out and short-term loans will need to be repaid. It is because this situation cannot be allowed to continue indefinitely that governments are seriously concerned with their balance of payments on current account.

Equilibrium in the balance of payments

Like any account a statement like Table 30.1 of a country's external transactions can be made to balance by the standard system of double-entry bookkeeping. But this does not mean that the country's external transactions are in equilibrium. An equilibrium state is one which can be sustained without adjustment. But we might have external trade balance, i.e. exports equal to imports (X = M), only because of having placed severe restrictions on trade or as a result of accepting heavy unemployment at home in order to keep down demand for imports, neither conditions which we should like to maintain.

And we are not concerned simply with balance on current account, anyway: autonomous capital movements also require foreign exchange. For many developed countries, capital movements are in fact an important source of balance of payments pressure. In this case it would not be enough for *long-term* equilibrium simply to balance the current account: a current account *surplus* would be needed to cover the desired level of net long-term capital investment abroad, including for instance foreign aid commitments. Thus for much of the post-war period the United Kingdom failed to achieve a sufficiently large current account surplus to finance its long-term capital investment abroad, and continued to rely on short-term capital inflows to accommodate periodic deficits. In effect the UK was borrowing 'short' to lend 'long'. Thus rather than simply the balance on current account we need to consider what may be called the *basic balance* on current and long-term capital accounts, *which relates to the long-term equilibrium position*. By paying attention to the basic balance rather than the current account, recognition is given to a country's foreign exchange budget and not just current income transactions. 'Basic balance' is achieved when a country is earning sufficient foreign exchange to do what it wants to do on current and long-term capital accounts without requiring accommodation through short-term borrowing *or* running down exchange reserves (which would eventually threaten confidence in the currency) *or* requiring recourse to undesirable economic policies such as deflating domestic demand or restrictions on trade and capital movements inconsistent with the country's international obligations.

If the basic balance can only be improved by recourse to such measures, then the balance of payments can be said to be in *fundamental disequilibrium*. Although a negative basic balance in a single year is often regarded as *unfavourable*, and a positive basic balance as *favourable*, such temporary imbalances need not indicate long-term disequilibrium unless they persist.

Of course in the very long run equilibrium in the balance of payments may be defined more narrowly as a zero *current* balance. A country cannot indefinitely borrow even long-term capital without repayment, so that at some stage a current account surplus will be needed. However, since it is normal, and desirable, for developing countries to borrow long-term capital from countries with 'favourable' current account surpluses, the zero *basic* balance is a useful indication of equilibrium; and a negative basic balance shows the degree of disequilibrium to be accommodated by short-term borrowing or use of foreign exchange reserves.

The basic balance is not, however, always a good guide to the health of a country's balance of payments. It is often difficult to distinguish clearly between autonomous and accommodating transactions among capital movements, and so many developed countries measure a balance of payments disequilibrium by the size of the movement in the exchange reserves (the so-called 'currency flow' or 'monetary movements'). This indicates the accommodating finance required to match the *overall balance* of payments in all other current and capital transactions.

For developing countries like those in Eastern Africa the basic balance of current transactions and long-term capital movements will normally indicate directly the extent to which the country is using its foreign exchange reserves, since short-term capital movements outside the central bank or other monetary institutions will not be very important.

Table 30.2 shows the Kenyan balance of payments, summarized at three levels: the current account; the balance of current and long-term capital account; and the balance of monetary and short-term capital movements. The first covers real resource transactions affecting national income and expenditure, while the second is the basic balance concept showing how the country's current transactions were financed *without* making calls on foreign currency reserves and other short-term financial assets.

It can be seen that Kenya did not, except in 1971 (row 8), have to rely on monetary or short-term capital credits to obtain the basic balance (row 7) on current and long-term capital account. Over this period, therefore, Kenya may be said to have enjoyed

Table 30.2 Summary of Kenya's balance of payments and foreign exchange reserves, 1969–73

	KE millions				
	1969	1970	1971	1972	1973
(1) Visible imports (c.i.f.)	−121	−152	−196	−186	−219
(2) Visible exports (f.o.b.)	90	102	105	121	165
(3) Visible balance (=1+2)	−31	−50	−91	−65	−54
(4) Invisible balance	28	23	51	41	8
(5) Balance on current account (=3+4)	−3	−27	−40	−24	−47
(6) Long-term capital movements	20	31	15	33	54
(7) Balance on current and long-term capital account (=5+6)	−17	4	−25	9	7
(8) Monetary and short-term capital movements plus errors (net)	−17	−4	+25	−9	−7
(9) Increase in foreign exchange reserves (−)	−21	−19	+21	−9	−10
(10) Foreign exchange reserves held at end of year	65	84	63	72	82

SOURCE: Central Bank of Kenya, *Economic and Financial Review*

a 'healthy' balance of payments. It will be noticed that Kenya was able to finance a deficit on visible trade first, rather unusually for a developing country, by net exports of invisible services and second, by long-term capital inflows. Together these not only sustained the current account deficit but also a rise in the nominal value of the foreign exchange reserves, which almost doubled in value from K£43 millions at the end of 1968 to K£82 millions at the end of 1973. Only in 1971, when a sharp increase in visible imports coincided with a lower, less 'accommodating' level of capital inflow than in the other years, did Kenya have to draw down its foreign exchange reserves.

Foreign exchange systems

So far we have discussed the balance of payments of foreign currencies for a country in terms of balance between payments (arising from imports and capital outflows) and receipts (provided by exports and capital inflows). We have not yet examined the question of what determines a country's foreign exchange rate, the external value of one currency in terms of others. Since the concept of equilibrium in the balance of payments is closely connected with the external value of a country's currency, let us now review the main systems or methods which are used to determine foreign exchange rates.

Exchange rates give the price of one currency in terms of another. Essentially there are two ways of determining an equilibrium price in any market, and the market in foreign currencies is in this respect no different from the market for physical commodities like coffee, or financial securities like government bonds: either price is determined by the free market forces of supply and demand or it is 'fixed' by some monopoly or authority which adjusts supply (and demand) to this price.

For the past century or longer various forms of a fixed exchange rate system have been the rule. 'Floating' or free exchange systems for major trading currencies have operated for relatively short periods, during the 1920s and later 1930s, and more recently since 1971. Moreover, even when major currencies like the US dollar, pound sterling, or French franc have been allowed to float, the extent of their fluctuation has been 'managed' by the various central banks which had foreign exchange stabilization funds available for market intervention—rather like the buffer-stock schemes for primary commodities discussed in Chapter 8.

'Floating' rates in free exchange markets

In a free exchange market the forces of supply and demand are given full sway, and the external value will vary continuously, going up or 'appreciating' when demand for the home currency increases in relation to supply, and going down or 'depreciating' when the demand for *foreign* currencies increases in relation to the supply. Demand for foreign currencies comes from residents of the country who wish to import goods and services from abroad. These will not be consumers, for the most part, but traders buying foreign goods for resale in the home country. People who wish to invest their capital abroad by making long-term investments in physical assets such as factories, land, or houses, or to hold financial assets overseas also represent a 'demand' for foreign currency. Similarly, foreigners wishing to buy the home country's exports or to invest capital will need a supply of the home currency and will offer their own currencies in exchange. It follows that the demand for foreign exchange is a *derived demand*, the currency being needed not for its own sake, generally, but in order to make other purchases. Supply of foreign currency is simply the reverse side of a derived demand for the home currency. *We can define an equilibrium exchange rate as one which equates demand and supply of foreign exchange in a free market.*

Moreover in a free exchange market there is no need to make a distinction between autonomous and accommodating transactions; all can be regarded as autonomous, the accommodating role of foreign exchange or short-term capital movements being performed by fluctuations in the exchange rate itself. Since the market will be cleared in each period of operation, there is no need for official stocks of foreign exchange (except for possible short-run stabilization functions) to accommodate any gap between demand and supply. The balance of payments will be in equilibrium simply because the demand for foreign exchange is equal to the supply.[2]

Figure 30.1 shows how the equilibrium rate of exchange is determined in a free market. For simplicity let 'dollars' represent all foreign currencies and 'shillings' represent the home country's currency. The foreign exchange market is therefore expressed in terms of, say, millions of dollars traded for shillings each day or other time period covered by the transactions of dealers, normally banks and perhaps more specialist dealers in foreign currencies. If the demand for, and supply of, dollars is represented by the curves labelled D and S respectively, the equilibrium rate (the price of dollars in terms of shillings) is seen to be 7 shillings. If the demand curve shifts to the right, the new equilibrium rate where D' intersects S will be 8 shillings, representing a depreciation of the shilling, the home currency. On the other hand, if the supply of dollars offered to the market increases to S', it is the dollar which has

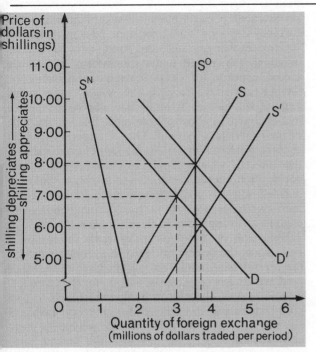

Figure 30.1 *Determination of the equilibrium exchange rate in a freely fluctuating market.*

depreciated; the shilling has *appreciated*, being worth more dollars if now only 6 shillings are needed to buy 1 dollar.

The demand curve for dollars is always downward-sloping, conforming to the normal rule that a fall in price will extend demand. Why is this *always* so? The demand for dollars is derived from the demand for dollar-priced goods (imports) or for foreign assets (capital investment payments abroad). Suppose the price of a dollar falls from 7 shillings to, say, 6 shillings. An imported good costing $1 could now be obtained for 6 shillings instead of 7. There will therefore be the normal substitution effect increasing demand for the imported good compared to a similar home product. The more elastic the home demand for foreign goods, the greater the increase in the volume of foreign purchases and the larger the amount of dollars demanded. Thus a fall in the price of the dollar (the number of shillings needed to buy it) increases the demand for dollars.

Even in the limiting case of a zero substitution effect from a price change, when the demand for foreign goods is completely inelastic (so that the volume of imports remains constant, and with it the amount of dollars), there is likely to be some positive elasticity of demand for investment dollars, since the rate of return on dollar assets will vary inversely with their cost in shillings to investors in the home country.

Turning to the supply curve for dollars, this is derived from the foreign demand for home country goods. Suppose now there is a rise in the price of the dollar from, say, 6 shillings to 8 shillings. The effect on the supply of dollars is somewhat uncertain. Consider a good being sold initially at $1 (= 6 shs). On the one hand, home country exporters could obviously increase shilling prices in the export market (involving price discrimination) to 8 shillings, still charging 1 dollar abroad and presumably selling the same quantity. However exports of manufactured goods from large industrial countries are normally sold abroad at home currency prices determined by domestic costs of production and domestic market demand, these exports usually representing only a small proportion of total output. Thus when the home country's exchange rate depreciates (in this case the shilling price of dollars rises), the home country export is likely to become cheaper in the foreign market. If home producers are still asking 6 shs per unit for the commodity referred to, this will cost foreign buyers only $0.75 instead of $1 since the shilling has depreciated by 25 per cent. This will increase export demand by an amount which depends on the elasticity of foreign demand, so that the effect on the supply of dollars will also depend upon this elasticity.

If, for instance, the foreign demand for the home country's exports has unit elasticity, quantity demanded will increase in the same proportion as the dollar price decreases, so that dollar expenditure, the supply of dollars, is unchanged. This case of constant dollar receipts is shown by the completely inelastic supply curve S^0 in Figure 30.1. It follows that if the foreign elasticity of demand is less than unity, a fall in the dollar price of exports per unit of, say, 25 per cent (from $1 to $0.75 in our example) due to depreciation of the shilling would lead to a *less* than 25 per cent increase in the quantity demanded by foreigners, and an actual *fall* in dollar expenditure or supply of dollars. In this case a rise in the shilling price of dollars leads to a decrease in the number of dollars supplied, so that the supply curve slopes *down* from left to right, as shown by the curve S^N in Figure 30.1.

In practice the foreign elasticity of demand is likely to be quite large, since when home country exports become cheaper they will be substituted not only for domestically produced goods in the importing country but also for some competing imports from other countries. Countries exporting a diversified range of manufactured products to a large number of foreign markets may, therefore, confidently expect the supply of foreign exchange to be reasonably elastic.

Before reaching this conclusion, however, it is necessary to take account of the supply of exports in the home country. Assuming a substantial part of total output goes to the home market, it will be easier to divert more of this production towards the export market if home demand is elastic. The attraction of export markets, following depreciation, will tend to raise home prices, releasing goods for export if home demand is elastic. At some point, of course, if full employment is reached in the export industries, inelastic supply will raise dollar prices more significantly.

Let us now examine how changes in supply and demand affect the equilibrium exchange rate in a free market. An increase in the demand for dollars, represented in Figure 30.1 by a shift from D to D', could be due either to a higher level of import demand *or* to a higher demand for dollars to invest abroad. Increased import demand could be the result of higher domestic incomes, producing a demand for imported consumer goods. Alternatively an increase in home investment may require imports of plant and machinery. Changes in relative prices may encourage substitution of cheaper imports for local substitutes at the given exchange rate: thus domestic inflation induces more imports. Reductions in import taxes may have the same effect. Given the supply curve S, the shift to D' would in a free market raise the shilling price of dollars to 8 shillings, reducing the external value of the shilling. Similar factors operating abroad could increase the supply of dollars, say from S to S', this *appreciation* reducing the shilling price of dollars and *raising* the external value of the shilling.

Fixed exchange rates

Various systems of fixed exchange rates have been operated. Let us consider briefly three types of fixed exchange rate systems: the so-called Gold Standard; the International Monetary Fund system of stabilized exchange rates, sometimes referred to as a 'gold exchange standard'; and the managed exchange rates of Eastern Africa 'pegged' to one of the major currencies but allowed to 'float' with it.

The Gold Standard

Until the outbreak of the First World War in 1914, the major trading nations of the world conducted international trade and payments according to a system which was known as the Gold Standard. Each country had, of course, its own national currency but the price of each currency was fixed in terms of gold, and therefore in relation to each other. There could be no fear of exchange depreciation under this system, short of a nation going 'off' the Gold Standard. The basis of the system was the willingness, at all times, of the central bank in each country to supply gold in exchange for the currency at a fixed rate, if called upon to do so. Each currency was therefore 'as good as gold'. Gold served as an international currency and the foreign exchange market acted simply as a money changer converting one currency into another at constant rates of exchange.

Since exchange rates are 'fixed', how are trade imbalances corrected under this system? If imports exceed exports, for example, and the demand for foreign currency exceeds the supply, the extra amount will be met by an outflow of gold. Countries had of course to allow gold to move freely in and out of their monetary systems. Thus if imports exceeded exports, gold was exported; the loss of gold reduced the domestic money supply; this lowered prices, encouraging domestic consumers to buy more at home and less abroad, and foreign consumers to increase their purchases; exports increased, and imports decreased, to bring trade back into balance.

Even after the development of 'credit money' on a large scale, the system operated in a similar way: for the central bank could not permit large outflows of gold, which was required as backing for the currency, especially since the central bank was obliged to pay gold on demand in exchange for currency. Before a balance of payments deficit could produce an excessive outflow of gold, therefore, the central bank would need to adopt deflationary policies with the equivalent effects outlined above.

The Gold Standard system broke down during the 1914–18 War when free convertibility of currencies was suspended and normal trade and investment between nations were disrupted. Although an attempt was made to return to the Gold Standard during the later 1920s, it collapsed in the economic chaos of the 1929–31 period of financial crises and economic depression. Economists since Keynes tend to view deflation of prices as likely to be associated with serious contraction in output and unemployment, due to its effects on business confidence. As governments have undertaken to use modern economic policies to ensure full employment, they have no longer been willing to leave the operation of the critical international aspect of policy to any mechanism as automatic and independent as the Gold Standard. The Gold Standard system with its associated monetary policy has been called a 'fair-weather' system because of its tendency to break down in difficult periods.

Stabilized exchange rates and the IMF

Instead of having an exchange rate fixed in terms of gold, as under the Gold Standard, or a completely 'free' exchange rate, another possibility is for the monetary authority to undertake to maintain the rate at a fixed or stabilized level, reserving the right to make periodic changes if it has to correct any serious disequilibrium that it cannot put right by other means. In other words the authority may *devalue* the exchange rate, lowering the rate which it undertakes to maintain; or it may, much less commonly, *revalue*, that is, raise the exchange rate. In either case there is a change in the 'par' value of the currency relative to gold, or relative to the major world currency such as the dollar to which the currency may be linked. From 1947 until late 1971 most countries in the world adhered to a system of stabilized exchange rates as members of the *International Monetary Fund* (IMF). This scheme aimed at an orderly system of exchange rates throughout the world. Each member agreed to fix a 'par' or normal value for its currency, and subsequently confine fluctuations to within 1 per cent of this value. Devaluation was to be used only as a last resort to cure a 'fundamental' disequilibrium in the balance of payments: temporary balance of payments problems being tackled by appropriate domestic economic policies. This was greatly facilitated by a credit-pooling arrangement which in fact constituted the 'Fund'. Members subscribed gold and part of their own national currencies into a common pool; each could then draw out prescribed amounts in periods of balance of payments crisis.

This, then, was a system of fixed exchange rates, with only occasional discrete changes in rates. The relative merits of such a system compared to a free market system of 'floating' rates is discussed in full in a later section. We discuss below also how the IMF was established and, in more detail, its scope.

Eastern African 'pegged' rates

The fixed exchange rate systems which evolved after 1914 and were continued under the IMF from 1945 to 1972 resembled the old Gold Standard in that all the major currencies were exchanged against a specific amount of gold. Indeed, until its devaluation in December 1971, the US dollar had been officially 'fixed' since 1933 at the rate of US$35 = 1 fine ounce of gold. As most other currencies were also fixed in relation to gold, or to the dollar, the system has been called a *gold exchange standard*. In Africa, under the colonial Currency Board system and later with the new central banks, the currencies were in effect on a fixed sterling exchange standard' until sterling was devalued in November 1967. In Eastern Africa only Malawi and Mauritius devalued with sterling and subsequently 'floated' in line with the pound. The other countries decided to maintain their rate with the dollar and, with occasional adjustments, have floated with the dollar. To take the example of Kenya, if the US dollar appreciates in the world's foreign exchange markets, so does the Kenya shilling,

and to the same extent unless the central bank of Kenya decides to alter the rate pegged to the dollar. In 1973, for example, the Kenya shilling was revalued upwards against the dollar to avoid depreciating along with the dollar against other currencies in which Kenya dealt widely.

Maintaining fixed exchange rates

Fluctuations in demand for, and supply of, home or foreign currency still occur when the exchange rate has been pegged in this way, for the same reasons as before. If the rate is not allowed to fluctuate, as in the free market case, how is equilibrium maintained? The general principles of maintaining a fixed price in the face of shifts in demand or supply apply to the external value of a national currency fixed by government (or central bank) decree in the same way as they govern the operations of a buffer-stock scheme to stabilize the price of a commodity. As we pointed out in Chapter 8, the buffer-stock method involved the marketing agency (in this case the central bank which manages the country's exchange reserves) in holding stocks (in this case gold or foreign currencies) and making decisions to buy or sell these 'stocks'.

If it fixes the 'price' too low, it is likely to run into problems of excess demand; if the price is set too high, the problem will be of excess supply. If there is excess supply of home currency, for instance, the monetary authorities can sell foreign exchange, creating additional demand for home currency, by running down their exchange reserves. Thus with a fixed exchange rate it is variations in exchange reserves which accommodate excess demand or supply. Usually the market rate is allowed to vary within a restricted band on either side of the official parity value, so that official intervention in the market is only required if the market rate is tending to move outside these limits. The wider this 'band', the less the need to draw upon or add to exchange reserves and the more stable the level of reserves.

The problem of maintaining a fixed parity is illustrated in Figure 30.2. Suppose the central bank decides to maintain an exchange rate of 7 shillings to the US dollar, but to permit a 'band' of free fluctuation within the limits of shs 7.20 and shs 6.80. If the demand curve for dollars, **D**, and the supply curve, **S**, intersect at a 'price' of shs 7.00, then this rate is the equilibrium rate and no official intervention is required. If the demand curve shifts to D^1, the market can establish a new equilibrium at shs 7.10, again without intervention. At the higher shilling price of dollars an extra *st* dollars is demanded and supplied, the supply curve being sufficiently elastic to

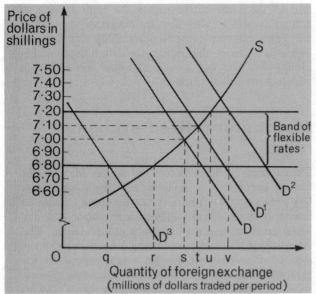

Figure 30.2 *Stabilization of exchange rate using exchange reserves outside a band of free fluctuation.*

prevent the equilibrium price of dollars rising beyond the intervention level of shs 7.20. Had the demand curve for dollars shifted even further, to D^2, however, which would have given a free market rate of shs 7.30, a rate of shs 7.20 could only be maintained if there were sales of *uv* dollars from central bank reserves, to satisfy excess demand. On the other hand, if the demand for dollars shifted to D^3, the central bank would need to take up the excess supply *qr* and add this to reserves to prevent the shilling appreciating beyond its upper limit of shs 6.80. Provided exchange reserves are sufficient to meet any excess demand for dollars which may persist, the official rate can be maintained.

Exchange control and the management of exchange reserves

At this point our analysis links in with our discussion of the balance of payments, which related foreign exchange earnings to foreign exchange requirements. Changes in the exchange rate, by changing the demand for and supply of foreign exchange, can bring foreign payments and earnings into balance. On the other hand a temporary deficit in the balance of payments which cannot be accommodated by a further decline in exchange reserves can equally be covered on the supply side by short-term borrowing abroad, the additional capital inflow shifting the supply curve of dollars, S, to the right. Countries with well-developed financial systems can attract foreign funds to domestic capital markets by raising the level of interest rates, offering international capital a better rate of return. Less developed economies do not usually have this additional option, being unable because of their more rudimentary financial systems to attract much short-term capital by changing interest rates. In the same circumstances they must rely primarily on monetary and fiscal policies to reduce the demand for foreign exchange.

If something is in short supply, its price may be allowed to go up, using the market mechanism, or, alternatively, it may be *rationed*. Many developing countries, especially, operate a system of exchange controls designed to protect exchange reserves specifically by rationing available foreign exchange among persons who wish to make overseas payments for imports or for the purchase of foreign assets. The purpose of all officially imposed rationing schemes is to allocate supply at a price below the free market equilibrium: in the case of foreign currency, the need is to restrict demand within the limits of supply earned by exports or capital receipts. In terms of Figure 30.2, if the free market rate were shs 7.30 and the authorities wished to maintain a maximum rate of shs 7.20, they would be faced with an excess demand for dollars of *uv* at the rate shs 7.20: the amount of foreign exchange O*u* would thus have to be rationed out among applicants hoping to have the amount O*v*. Just as with commodities a 'black market' may arise in foreign exchange when demand exceeds supply at the going rate and a 'free market' rate exceeds this official rate. For anyone wishing to sell foreign exchange unofficially and indeed illegally on the black market will find buyers willing to pay more than the shs 7.20 paid by the banks.

Most developing countries impose exchange controls on private capital movements abroad and give priority in allocation to imports of 'essential' goods. In particular imports of capital goods required by newly established manufacturing industries are given priority, while foreign exchange for the import of luxury consumer goods may be less readily made available.

A fundamental way of managing exchange reserves is, of course, through monetary and fiscal policies to control the level of economic activity in the country. It is at this point that our discussion of measures to protect foreign exchange reserves overlaps with that in previous chapters on the relation between money supply (especially in less developed countries where foreign exchange reserves provide important backing for this supply) and economic activity. Fiscal measures cutting down demand for foreign exchange include the raising of import duties, and even deflating the level of aggregate demand (and with it the demand for imports) by raising a whole range of tax rates, as well as cutting back government expenditure. Deflation, similarly, should reduce money incomes and the demand for imports, and stimulate exports of goods and services. Monetary and fiscal policies are used especially in developed countries for short-term stabilization purposes during the trade cycle: thus if a balance of payments 'crisis' develops, with a large balance of payments deficit, measures can be taken to reduce the level of aggregate spending (though at the risk of increasing unemployment) and thus expenditure on imports.

Devaluation

The alternative to 'managing' exchange reserves in the ways described above in order to maintain a particular official rate, if this rate appears out of line with the long-term balance of supply and demand, is, of course, to change the official rate, that is, to *devalue* the currency.

The effects of devaluation of the currency on the balance of trade and payments, and on exchange reserves, are not straightforward, however. A number of factors will determine the outcome, as we can see from the following illustration.

Suppose Britain has a shortage of dollars and the dollar/sterling exchange rate is US\$2.00 = £1, before a 50 per cent sterling devaluation takes place. The first effect will be that Britons find imports from the United States more expensive. Formerly a Briton paid £3 for an American commodity priced at \$6. After the devaluation £6 will be needed to obtain the \$6 required to buy the good. British imports from the USA will thus be discouraged; however, the size of the reduction in British imports and in payments of foreign exchange will depend *on the domestic elasticity of demand for imports*. The second effect is that American imports of British goods are likely to increase. Originally a British good costing £4 would cost an American \$8: after the devaluation the American could obtain the £4 required to buy the good for only \$4. Again, however, the size of the increased demand for British goods will depend on the *foreign elasticity of demand for domestic exports*.

Some simple algebra might be useful at this point. Let Q_x and Q_m be the volume of exports and imports respectively; P_{sx} and P_{dx} be the sterling price and dollar price of exports; P_{sm} and P_{dm} the sterling price and dollar price of imports; and R the rate of exchange in terms of dollars per pound. Thus $P_{sx}.R = P_{dx}$ (in our example above P_{sx} was £4 and $P_{dx} = £4 \times 2 = \$8$). Earnings of foreign exchange (dollars) are therefore

$$Q_x P_{dx} = Q_x.P_{sx}.R$$

Requirements of foreign exchange, to pay for imports, are $Q_m.P_{dm}$. It follows that the dollar 'deficit', dollar requirements minus dollar earnings, is given by:

$$Q_m.P_{dm} - Q_x.P_{dx}$$

This deficit is reduced by devaluation if the first term decreases and the second term increases. Since $P_{dx} = R.P_{sx}$, P_{dx} decreases if the exchange rate, R, is devalued; in response to this Q_x will increase, *according to the elasticity of demand*. This means for the value $Q_x P_{dx}$ to increase, *the foreign elasticity of demand for domestic exports must be greater than unity*. If it were less than unity, a devaluation would actually *reduce* foreign exchange earnings and a revaluation *upwards* would be needed to increase them.

If the dollar price of American goods, P_{dm}, is taken as constant, since $P_{dm} = RP_{sm}$, a fall in R must mean an increase in P_{sm}, the sterling price. In our example, a 50 per cent devaluation meant that twice as much sterling was needed to get the dollars required to purchase an American good. Since P_{dm} is constant, however, and Q_m decreases in response to the rise in P_{sm}, the value $Q_m P_{dm}$, requirements of foreign exchange, *must* decrease: the only question is how much, as determined by the domestic elasticity of demand for imports. If the domestic elasticity of demand for imports is positive, then the trade deficit can be decreased even if the foreign elasticity of demand for exports is *less* than one; the higher the value of the former, in fact, the lower the latter can be without the devaluation failing to reduce the deficit. It can be proved, in fact, that the deficit will be reduced *if the sum of the two elasticities is greater than one*, leaving supply considerations out of account.

We should however also look at the supply side. Unless British export industries have plenty of excess capacity, increased foreign demand for British exports will eventually bring forth increased supplies, but most likely *at increased prices*. In other words, P_{sx} will not be contant but will increase by an amount determined by the *elasticity of supply of domestic exports*. In our example, the British commodity costing £4 might go up to, say, £5: to Americans the price would be reduced by devaluation from \$8 to \$5, not \$4. This higher price would choke off some of the extra potential American consumption, and dollar earnings would not increase by as much as before.

Suppose, on the other hand, that the supply of American exports to Britain is inelastic: for instance, if America lacks alternative export markets for its commodities, its businessmen may prefer to cut their dollar prices in an effort to maintain export volume. The dollar price of British imports, P_{dm}, would thus fall. If in our example the dollar price of $6 is cut by half to $3, the British price, P_{sm}, will still be £3 after devaluation. The volume imported will be the same but, at a dollar price of $3, dollar requirements will be halved. The effect of devaluation therefore also depends on the *elasticity of supply of domestic imports*.

Summarizing, the effect of devaluation on a trade deficit will depend on:

(a) the foreign elasticity of demand for domestic exports;

(b) the domestic elasticity of demand for imports;

(c) the elasticity of supply of domestic exports;

(d) the elasticity of foreign supply of domestic imports.

Eastern African exchange rates and devaluation

The decision to devalue or revalue may be quite different for primary-producing countries like those in Africa compared to developed countries. We can consider first factors determining the effect on imports, and then those determining the effect on exports.

Devaluation makes imports more expensive to the home consumer compared to home-produced varieties. In Africa, however, there are usually few manufactures which can be produced as new substitutes for imports, reducing substitution possibilities and making for a lower domestic elasticity of demand for imports. In addition imports of capital equipment are made more expensive. This could lead to the adoption of less capital-intensive methods of production: however, there is a good chance that machinery and other capital imports for development schemes will be considered essential items, with the demand again price-inelastic.

Since devaluation makes foreign goods more expensive to home consumers, foreign suppliers could cut 'dollar' prices of domestic imports in order to retain custom. However since the market of individual African countries is relatively small, the supply of imports will generally be perfectly elastic, and devaluation will have little or no effect on the foreign price of imports.

Turning to exports, devaluation makes home exports more competitive, permitting them to be substituted for domestically produced goods in foreign markets and for alternative sources of supply to foreign markets, the substitution possibilities determining the foreign elasticity of demand for home exports. For many primary commodities, however, African countries are *individually* small export producers, selling their exports on competitive international markets in which they are 'price-takers', accepting the world price for their exports and thus facing a perfectly elastic demand for them. In this case devaluation of the home currency does not make home exports cheaper to the foreign consumer, home exports being a small proportion of total world supply, and the dollar price of the exports is unchanged: however since a dollar is now worth more in terms of the home currency, this means that the price of the exported goods in terms of home currency will be raised, providing a stimulus, through the elasticity of supply of domestic exports, for home producers to expand export production. A larger volume of exports at a constant dollar price could then increase the supply of dollars.

Increased foreign demand for home exports could, however, raise home prices for the goods concerned if the elasticity of supply of domestic exports is low. This elasticity is higher, usually, if there are possibilities of diverting supplies from home consumption to foreign consumption, such as exist in industrialized countries with mass consumption of manufactured goods. However developing countries export comparatively few manufactured goods and where they do they are often specialized items for the export market like the assembling of electrical goods, toys, or garment-making in Hong Kong. Sometimes major foodstuffs, such as rice in some Asian countries, are produced for both home and export markets. But most of the agricultural exports of African countries such as cocoa, tea, or coffee are not consumed domestically in significant quantities, so that substitution possibilities are limited. As a result, it is the elasticity of supply of *total* output by African growers that is relevant: as it happens, the evidence is that due to underemployment of family labour in the rural sector in Africa this elasticity is generally high, and response to increased prices and larger markets for African export crops is extremely good.

Primary product markets are not always competitive, however. In many cases, as we have seen, they are regulated by international commodity agreements. If a country has already taken up its full market quota under such agreements for its main exports, then depreciation of the currency could not lead to increased dollar earnings through increased export quantities. In other cases, such as Ghana and Tanzania, with cocoa and sisal respectively, African producers do account for a large proportion of total world trade. In these cases increased production *would* depress the dollar price, and the elasticity of foreign demand for the exports is important. Thus during the 1950s it seemed that no matter how large the volume of Ghana's cocoa exports, export revenue remained stable at around £60 millions, price varying inversely with volume. Foreign elasticity of demand for cocoa thus appeared to have a value of unity. Although in fact Ghana did not vary her exchange rate during this period, this implies that devaluation would have reduced the dollar price of exports (worsened the terms of trade) and not increased the value of dollar earnings.

In July 1967 there was, however, a 30 per cent devaluation of Ghana's New Cedi, designed primarily to stimulate cocoa export production. By that time inflation had raised domestic costs to a level which made it unprofitable to harvest all the existing cocoa trees or to mine gold from the highest-cost mines. Such a situation can arise when a currency is 'overvalued', that is when the foreign exchange rate gives the local currency a higher value than it would be worth in an uncontrolled market. An exporting producer then receives in local currency much less than the real value of the export proceeds that he has produced. At the same time as devaluing the government lowered import duties, reducing the effect of devaluation in raising import prices, so that wage earners would not press for higher wages, thereby putting further pressure on local prices and costs. Quite apart from the need to improve the balance of trade, it was hoped that foreign investors would supply more foreign capital when they could receive 30 per cent more local currency than before for a given 'import' of foreign currency invested.

Until the devaluation of the £ sterling in 1967, the three central banks in East Africa (Kenya, Uganda, and Tanzania) were not faced with the immediate need to consider their own exchange rate. Although these separate and independent banks had succeeded the currency board system with its sterling exchange standard, they continued until 1967 to cooperate (a) in maintaining fixed parities with one another and (b) in maintaining fixed parities with the rest of the world through the retention of a fixed rate with sterling at 20 shillings (East African)=£1 sterling. Other Commonwealth African countries were in a similar situation, except for Ghana which had devalued just before. In November 1967 Britain devalued sterling, to which so many African currencies had been linked, by 14.3 per cent: suddenly these countries had to make a decision on devaluation, whether to follow sterling and devalue, or whether to remain at the previous level, implying an effective revaluation, or appreciation, in relation to sterling. It will be useful to examine the decisions taken by one or two of the countries in order to throw light on the considerations that must be taken into account in making a decision to devalue.

In Eastern Africa only Malawi and Mauritius devalued in line with sterling. In the case of Malawi there was a desire to give a much needed stimulus to Malawi's tea estates, then acutely squeezed between high domestic costs and a low world price for tea. Taking the foreign currency price as given, Malawi devaluation gave local producers more local currency per unit sold: while sterling devaluation meant that if the sterling price of tea in Britain did not go up, Malawian producers would have received less in home currency per unit sold. Unlike most of the other exports from Africa, tea is very much a 'sterling' commodity, exported to Britain as the main market, and produced almost entirely by Sterling Area[3] countries in Asia and Africa. Moreover India, the largest world exporter of tea, had devalued its rupee in 1966 by more than 60 per cent; while Sri Lanka did so with sterling by over 20 per cent, making their own teas cheaper in the British market and through the possibility of substitution putting Malawi in a position of facing an elastic British demand for Malawian tea.

A second factor, also depressing other exports as well as the tea industry, was the rather overvalued exchange rate, as in Ghana's case. A third was Malawi's acute dependence upon British financial assistance to meet its recurrent budget deficit and the bulk of its capital inflow for both public sector development and private investment. Had Malawi not devalued, its receipt of aid expressed in sterling would have been cut in terms of local currency by 17 per cent. Non-devaluation by Malawi could have reduced the return for British private investors who would have had to pay more in sterling to buy assets in Malawi with a given rate of return. Finally it happened that in 1967 the Farmers' Marketing Board which handled all the smallholder export crops, including tobacco, cotton, maize, and groundnuts, had made large trading losses. Given export prices fixed in terms of dollars for these commodities, devaluation provided a benefit to the Board in terms of higher local currency earnings. Without these much large reductions in producer prices fixed by the Board would have been required, with subsequent disincentive effects on production.

Mauritius, which also followed Britain in devaluing, was entirely dependent upon sugar exports the price of which was fixed, like tea, in terms of sterling, in this case under the Commonwealth Sugar Agreement. There was a need to maintain production incentives after the devaluation of sterling, even if actual increases in exported quantities above the given quota were not possible under the Agreement.

By contrast, in countries where the marketing boards were able to withhold a large proportion of the export earnings from peasant producers, devaluation in itself was not required as a stimulus to export production: the marketing boards could achieve this response by reducing their own retained surpluses. This situation was more typical of Nigeria and Uganda. In addition Nigeria was fast developing a new dollar-earning commodity export in the form of petroleum, which did not require the additional export price incentive of devaluation to expand. And, thirdly, Nigeria was concerned about inflation, which would have been boosted by increased import prices following devaluation. In the case of Uganda, in addition to being able to offer adequate incentives to coffee producers through its marketing board, any effort to increase coffee production would have been frustrated by the International Coffee Agreement's restrictions on exports.

To illustrate Tanzania's position we might switch from the 1967 situation to the reasons for the 10 per cent devaluation of the shilling in February 1973, in line with the US dollar, as given by the Governor of the Bank of Tanzania.[4] The Governor listed 'the adverse effects of non-devaluation' as:

(i) lowering of incomes from exports of agricultural commodities;
(ii) increased demand for imported goods;
(iii) increased competition from cheaper imports to the infant Tanzania industries producing import substitutes, and
(iv) generally a worsening of the balance of payments on current account. Furthermore, a cheapening of imported capital goods in this manner has other adverse effects. It often results in the use of more capital-intensive methods of production than are appropriate for a labour surplus country like Tanzania and this makes eradication of unemployment more difficult. Considerations of a similar nature applied to our partners in the Community and they devalued their respective shillings by the same amount as ourselves.

Since 1967 African central banks have left behind the straightforward situation when their currencies were tied to a stable sterling, and have had to cope with a world of floating exchange rates. After the 14.3 per cent devaluation of sterling in November 1967, dollar convertibility into gold was suspended in August 1971, leading shortly, in December, to a 7.9 per cent devaluation of the dollar against gold; the pound became a 'floating' exchange rate in June 1972; and there was a further 10 per cent devaluation of the dollar against gold in February 1973. Thus most African countries have replaced the former fixed parity with sterling by a fixed parity in terms of the US dollar and later in the case of most Eastern African countries a link to Special Drawing Rights at the IMF.[5] Nigeria has tended to link its currency to gold and the stronger German deutschmark, so that it has appreciated against the dollar as well as sterling. Day-to-day stability of their currencies against another major currency, which they use to settle international payments and hold as foreign exchange reserves, has been a major consideration of countries without large foreign exchange markets. Their central banks have to 'police' much more restrictive Exchange Controls than those in developed countries. Many of the arguments against a freely fluctuating exchange rate (discussed in more detail below) apply to Africa if not to Western Europe and America. Constant exchange rate variations may increase the risks and uncertainties of foreign trade; speculation may increase rather than decrease the size of fluctuations, and may be a much easier avenue for illegal transactions to avoid exchange controls or even to embezzle funds.

Overvalued currencies

Both because the external situation is changing, and because the home country's domestic economic position and balance of payments can change quite rapidly, it is not easy to fix an appropriate external rate of exchange. Where the rate does not reflect the long-term equilibrium position of the balance of payments, it may be overvalued or undervalued. Usually, in the case of developing countries especially, a fixed exchange rate overvalues the home currency. As already mentioned, this will tend to discourage exports, by offering export producers less domestic currency than their export proceeds are really worth; and it encourages imports, of both consumer goods and capital equipment, which are made 'too cheap'.

We have already listed the adverse effects of non-devaluation of the Tanzanian shilling in 1967 and discussed the effects of overvalued exchange rates in allocating investment resources earlier in Chapter 15. A country's *exchange rate policy* is clearly, then, an important instrument affecting a wide range of domestic activity as well as the external balance of payments.

(1) Balance of payments effects

If we refer back to Figure 30.2 on page 438 we can see that a policy of stabilizing the exchange rate above its free market equilibrium level involved using exchange reserves to cover the excess demand for foreign currency. This drain of reserves 'accommodates' the imbalance between demand and supply in the foreign exchange market, and if perpetuated measures the disequilibrium in the balance of payments. However since the size of foreign exchange reserves is usually small in relation to total foreign transactions, sooner or later, imports will have to be restricted by tariffs or quotas as well as exchange controls over capital movements. These fiscal and direct measures are aimed at shifting the demand curve to the left: they constitute a form of partial currency devaluation in so far as they raise the home currency price of imports; but do not increase the supply of foreign exchange, unless domestic subsidies or the rationing of domestic purchases of exportables are employed to shift the supply curve to the right. However, since the foreign exchange rate is still not in free market equilibrium, the balance of payments disequilibrium has been 'suppressed' rather than 'corrected'. Eventually further fiscal or monetary measures may be required to constrain demand for foreign exchange.

(2) Domestic income and employment effects

We pointed out above that fixed exchange rate systems can impose more deflationary discipline than freely floating rates. Overvaluation of the exchange rate increases this deflationary pressure. Even without corrective policy measures to reduce directly or indirectly the external deficit, the foreign trade multiplier process will operate automatically to reduce domestic incomes and employment. Since with a balance of trade deficit, import leakages will be greater than export injections, the equilibrium level of national income will fall. In economies like those of Eastern Africa much of the unemployment and greater poverty will be 'disguised' by rural underemployment and attempts by peasants to shift from export activities into production for subsistence or for the local market. Accompanying the adjustment in the balance of payments disequilibrium by the Keynesian multiplier process will be a multiple contraction of the domestic money supply in response to any drain of foreign exchange. Of course the central bank may replace foreign exchange assets by expanding domestic currency backing for the money supply; but as we saw in the Polak model the additional domestic credit created by such a policy will also induce more imports.

(3) The price level and relative price effects

The overvalued exchange rate makes the home currency prices of both exports and imports too cheap in relation to the price of non-traded output. Any switch in expenditure from cheaper imports to local substitutes or the release of resources from local demand to exports must therefore arise by a decline in the relative price of non-traded output. Overvalued currencies therefore impose very high costs in the deflation of domestic demand to increase the competitive advantage of locally marketed output or potential exports. Many countries have, however, maintained overvalued currencies to discipline the domestic price and wage level, with the aim of making exports more competitive or keeping down the domestic price of imported capital goods, producer materials, or essential consumer goods for the modern manufacturing sector.

(4) Terms of trade effects

Associated with the view that an overvalued currency reduces the 'import' of inflation from abroad (even if it means forgoing the 'export' of unemployment by devaluation), is the argument that any devaluation will make a country's terms of trade deteriorate. Thus fears of being cheated or exploited by foreign countries are added to national pride in a high exchange rate.

However, for most small export economies, the foreign currency price of both imports and (most) exports is unaffected since they are 'price-takers'. Only the home currency prices change in proportion to the exchange rate variation, and with them the domestic distribution of real income. Producers of exports and domestic substitutes for imports gain; consumers of imports lose. Of course to reduce a trade deficit a larger volume of exports, or a smaller volume of imports, is required, and the outcome will depend on the relevant elasticities discussed earlier. If the domestic supply of exports is sufficiently elastic, however, the income terms of trade will improve and the barter terms of trade remain unaffected, whether measured in the home or the foreign currencies. Given the tendency for both the income and barter terms of trade to fluctuate widely because of *shifts* in demand and supply, a policy of maintaining an overvalued fixed exchange rate to insulate the economy from imported inflation or unfavourable terms of trade is usually very costly in perpetuating both domestic and external disequilibrium.

Floating versus fixed exchange rates

We have discussed the way in which external equilibrium may be attained in a free foreign exchange market and also under a variety of fixed exchange rate systems. Since the free market adjustment process avoids the need for government intervention and the holding of exchange reserves to support the exchange rate, why do countries adhere to fixed exchange rate systems?

The following arguments have been used to support fixed exchange rate systems, and continue to be advanced against freely floating rates.

(1) Fixed exchange rates impose 'discipline' on governments in pursuit of economic policies. If a country pursued a highly inflationary policy so that its price level rose much faster than that of other countries, it would, with a fixed exchange rate, find its exchange reserves decreasing as imports rose and exports fell: it would then be forced to take corrective action through domestic price and income adjustments to bring inflation under control. With free

exchange rates there is not the same immediate pressure 'to put one's domestic house in order' since external equilibrium can be maintained despite inflation through a steady fall in the external value of the currency.

(2) The instability of exchange rates inherent in floating rates may discourage international trade and investment, since traders and investors will not know exactly how much the currency they expect to earn will be worth. Traders and investors would prefer the greater certainty of contracts expressed in stable values.

(3) Speculative activity by specialized foreign exchange dealers or by traders could be destabilizing. As in the case of agricultural and other commodities, speculators exist who specialize in foreign exchange dealings, trying to buy a currency when it is cheap and resell at a profit when it is dear. If the majority expect a currency to depreciate, and decide to sell it before the price drops, this increased supply can itself *cause* the price to fall: the reverse applies if an increase is expected. A free exchange rate can therefore fluctuate purely as a result of changes in expectations. On the other hand, this need not happen: as in the case of commodity markets speculators may also help to stabilize exchange rates by buying when the rate is low (increasing demand) and selling when the rate is high (increasing supply).

(4) Apart from speculative dealing, other short-term capital movements will affect a floating rate even if a change is not otherwise justified, the basic balance on current and long term capital account being in equilibrium.

(5) As outlined in detail above, if the relevant elasticities of demand and supply are low, exchange rate fluctuations may have to be very large to clear the market, and these wide and frequent changes, apart from the disadvantages just listed, may have adverse domestic effects. A 'dramatic' depreciation in the exchange rate, for example, in raising the domestic price of imported food or raw materials, could set off 'cost-push' inflation which could not easily be reversed when the exchange rate appreciates again subsequently. Exporters could experience wide variations in home currency receipts from exports if these are sold at constant foreign currency prices or in the volume of exports if priced in domestic currency.

Against these arguments, the case for freely floating exchange rates has developed considerable strength since the 1960s, when the major currencies grew increasingly out of line under the IMF system of fixed rates.

(1) Despite what was stated above under (1), the main advantage of a floating rate is the freedom it offers to the individual country to pursue its own independent domestic economic policy. Suppose that because of, say, domestic unemployment, it wishes to pursue a relatively inflationary policy compared to other countries. The rise in domestic prices compared to foreign prices will, as mentioned previously, cause expenditure by both residents and foreigners to switch in favour of foreign goods, increasing imports and decreasing exports. This will cause the supply of home currency on exchange markets to increase and the demand for it to fall. With a floating exchange rate, instead of this leading eventually to a balance of payments 'crisis', the price of home currency will fall, offsetting the effect of high domestic prices. Floating exchange rates thus provide an automatic mechanism to correct balance of payments deficits arising out of the pursuit of independent domestic economic policies.

(2) The criticism that floating rates remove the discipline of the balance of payments provided by fixed rates assumes that there is no other way of avoiding deficits under a fixed rate system than using monetary and fiscal policies to control the domestic economy. But since the 1930s exchange controls and trade restrictions have been widely used to insulate domestic policies of full employment and growth, escaping this discipline. It has been argued that fixed exchange rate systems may offer the worst of both worlds—little monetary discipline and many restrictions on trade and capital movements, limiting the growth of world trade and the provision of foreign aid and investment funds for poor countries.

(3) As shown above, the effect of a devaluation on a balance of payments deficit depends on a rather complicated set of elasticities, the values of which can only be guessed at by the monetary authorities. It is therefore possible to make a substantial error of judgement about the direction and value of the effect of devaluation from a fixed exchange value, and to misjudge the size of the devaluation required, a problem which does not arise under the automatic mechanism of the floating rate.

(4) How far, if at all, the instability of free exchange rates discourages trade and investment is uncertain. In theory traders, and short-term investors at least, can insure themselves against the risk of exchange rate variations by 'covering' their contracts in a *forward exchange market*. Thus a British exporter who is due to receive dollars in three months' time can assure himself of a certain payment in sterling by entering a contract to buy sterling three months forward. In three months' time he hands over his dollars in exchange for sterling, having protected himself against a rise in the 'spot' or current price of sterling relative to the dollar during the period. In practice traders minimize exchange risks by staying in their own currency, especially if they are exporters; alternatively transactions are carried out between

traders in different countries using one of the major world currencies, especially dollars. This is the normal Eastern African practice and is the argument used for Eastern Africa's maintaining an exchange rate pegged to one or other of the major currencies.

(5) In another way fixed exchange rates can lead to speculation. If there have been balance of payments deficits and losses of exchange reserves, so that the currency is considered 'weak' and in danger of being devalued, speculators may decide to sell the currency, hoping to make a profit by buying back larger quantities of the currency for the same foreign exchange after devaluation. If many speculators do this, the sale of home currency resulting could *itself* force the government to devalue. Moreover speculators who do this do not risk losses if they are proved wrong and no change in the rate occurs. This is in contrast to speculation with floating rates: a speculator who sells in anticipation of depreciation of the currency, and finds that the currency has appreciated instead, may find that he has to buy back the currency at a higher price than he sold it. As far as speculation and instability are concerned, the choice appears to be between periodic but intense bursts of speculation against fixed rates, as occurred in the late 1960s, and continuous but lighter speculative activity as part of free market determination of rates.

(6) The adverse effects of speculative capital movements on exchange rates has led to the adoption of various devices to insulate a floating rate from large capital movements, reducing the seriousness of this criticism. Developing countries, we have already noted, impose strict exchange controls, as do many developed countries. Some European countries adopt multiple exchange rate systems with, for example, a stabilized 'trading franc' determined only partly by the foreign exchange demands of exporters and importers and a more freely floating 'investment franc', determined in another market and not supported by official intervention. In Britain an 'investment dollar' carried a large premium well above the rates obtained for the current transactions of traders. This separation of current and capital transactions could mean that, for example, individuals can buy, say, French wine at a rate of exchange of £1 = 10 French francs, but have to buy property in France at the investment rate of £1 = 7 French francs.

(7) Perhaps the greatest criticism of officially fixed exchange rates is, however, the political emotion aroused by devaluation and revaluation. Politicians in nearly all countries point with pride to any upward revaluation of the national currency, and risk dismissal and discontent if they have to devalue. This means that periodic adjustments of fixed exchange rates are usually delayed too long, causing the currency to be overvalued and producing a distortion in

market prices. In particular the money prices of inputs and outputs which use up scarce foreign exchange or could earn foreign exchange understate the true cost or value of the goods. Project planners have then to try to 'correct' for such distortions in calculating the real costs and benefits of development schemes.

Exchange rate policy and purchasing power parities

We have seen that there are advantages and disadvantages in both fixed and freely floating exchange rate systems: under the first, adjustment in the external balance of payments produces deflationary or inflationary disturbances in the domestic economy; under the latter, speculative capital movements or other temporary shifts in demand or supply for a currency may be inconsistent with the long-term equilibrium balance of payments, or the relevant elasticities may be too small to restore equilibrium in external payments. Under both systems, exchange rate variations may be a *necessary* condition to improve the balance of payments, but *insufficient* without other corrective policy measures to adjust domestic demand and switch resources.

If imports constitute a large part of final expenditure and are relatively price-inelastic, exchange rate devaluation (or depreciation), by raising the domestic price of imports, will 'absorb' more money income, releasing resources to improve the foreign trade balance. The resulting improvement in supply of exports allows the high elasticity of foreign demand for exports to be realized in a greater volume of exports. However both the 'income' and 'price' effects of devaluation may need further reinforcement by other fiscal and monetary policies. In particular the government's budgetary position may be crucial, since additional taxation or reduced expenditure are important in determining domestic income levels.

Governments may therefore use a package of policy measures, including the exchange rate, to improve the balance of payments. Is there, however, any long-run equilibrium rate of exchange that will equate the demand for and supply of foreign currency without repeated policy interventions? One explanation advanced is the *Purchasing Power Parity Principle*. In its simplest form this theory states that if the current exchange rate between two countries is out of line with that rate which makes the purchasing power of the two currencies equal, the price differences in the two countries will attract or repel trade and push the exchange rate towards purchasing power parity. If, for example, the current exchange rate between the US$ and £ sterling is US$2.00 =

£1.00, but the general price level in the USA is such that it takes US$3 to buy as much as £1 in Britain, British goods will attract American buyers, while Britons will be discouraged from buying American goods. These reactions transmitted to the foreign exchange market will cause the pound to appreciate to its purchasing power parity rate of US$3.00 = £1.00. While this theory is not a good explanation of *actual* exchange rates in a world of fixed or 'managed' exchange rates, trade restrictions and exchange controls, it does offer a useful guide to the likely direction of *changes* in currency rates, the direction being the same as the changes in the relative purchasing power of different currencies. The principle can be applied to both fixed and floating exchange rate systems, and is particularly relevant to recent movements in floating rates between countries experiencing very rapid inflation and others with more stable domestic price levels.

Functions of the International Monetary Fund

Following an international conference held at Bretton Woods in the USA in 1944, two international financial institutions were established: the International Bank for Reconstruction and Development (IBRD), better known as the 'World Bank', and the International Monetary Fund (IMF).

The first is not so much an international central bank as an international development corporation, since it is concerned with the provision of long-term finance for development projects in less developed countries, that is, with loans for investment. It borrows from member governments and on the international capital markets and re-lends the proceeds at interest rates which are normally well below the levels charged by private commercial financiers. Since 1960 it has had a 'soft loan' affiliate, the International Development Association (IDA) which provides long-term multilateral aid in the form of virtually interest-free loans for as much as 50 years, to the very poorest countries such as India or Malawi, or for social infrastructure. It is financed by subscriptions from the richer members of the World Bank and from surpluses on other income-earning operations of the Bank.

The International Monetary Fund, on the other hand, is an embryo world central bank. However, during its first twenty-two years of operation from 1947 to 1969, it could not 'create' international money in the way that a national central bank can control the supply of its own currency. Gold, and in practice the US dollar (which was always convertible into gold by foreign holders, and therefore 'as good as gold' from their point of view), remained the only 'international money': and over this money base the IMF had no direct control.

At Bretton Woods, Lord Keynes had argued for an effective world central bank with power to issue its own liabilities which would be accepted by national central banks as international cash to supplement gold, the supply of which might not be sufficient to sustain an adequate level of *international liquidity*, necessary to finance world trade at the fullest level of world output. He feared a return to the restrictive international trade practices of the 1930s when deficit countries imposed high tariffs on imports or adopted competitive devaluation of their exchange rates. Both these policies may amount to what are known as 'beggar-my-neighbour' policies since they simply 'export' unemployment to other countries: the imposition of tariffs diverts home demand away from imported goods, affecting the export industries of other countries; devaluation does the same, as well as giving the home country a competitive advantage for its exports in the other country, and in third countries; and both tariffs and devaluation may for these reasons simply lead to retaliation with no lasting benefit to any country.

The Americans at the conference, on the other hand, wished to impose more discipline on countries incurring balance of payments deficits. They considered that temporary 'loans of last resort' from this embryo world bank, to be financed within the limits of the international money (gold and dollars) subscribed by member countries to the IMF, would be sufficient.

Their scheme was adopted, with its three main objectives: (1) international cooperation and codes of conduct; (2) restoration of a stable but adjustable system of fixed exchange rates; and (3) prevention of international monetary crises and economic depression by the temporary redistribution of reserves from surplus to deficit nations through the IMF's pool of international reserves. As already mentioned, each member country had, on joining the Fund, to fix a 'par' value for its currency and confine fluctuations in its exchange rate to within 1 per cent either side of this par value. Devaluation from a fixed rate was to be a last resort to cure a 'fundamental disequilibrium' in the balance of payments. Temporary imbalances were therefore to be tackled mainly by appropriate domestic economic policies, but assisted by temporary 'Drawing Rights' on the pool of gold and national currencies subscribed by members in accordance with their share of world trade.

This modified gold-exchange standard worked from 1947 until 1969. As with the old Gold Standard, monetary discipline in domestic credit creation was required to prevent countries running large and persistent deficits in their balance of payments, even if the discipline was no longer enforced by automatic movements of gold. In practice, and usually with great reluctance, the IMF had to agree to (a) the imposition of exchange controls, which afforded countries some insulation from the discipline of a fixed exchange rate in a world of 'open' economies, and (b) the periodic abandonment of one fixed rate for another, that is, devaluation, or more infrequently, an upward revaluation.

The USA itself was able to escape the discipline of the IMF's fixed exchange system, and also to provide the rest of the world with exchange reserves by running a growing balance of payments deficit during the 1950s and 1960s, because the US dollar was generally acceptable as international money with the usual functions of money, namely, as a *medium of exchange* for clearing international payments, as a *unit of account*, and as an international reserve *asset*. So long as there was no question about the fixed level of the rate of exchange between the US dollar and gold, creditor countries were prepared to hold dollars instead of gold. Thus, during the late 1960s, especially, the major surplus countries, notably Japan and Western Germany, accepted dollar balances instead of gold or goods. By the end of 1972, for example, some 60 per cent of the world's monetary reserves or *international liquidity* comprised holdings of US dollars, compared with 25 per cent in gold.

However, as these dollar holdings increased, the question of the USA's ability to maintain free convertibility into gold became more pressing, and after the devaluation of sterling in 1967, speculative pressure became concentrated against the dollar and in favour of the Japanese, West German, and other European currencies, which were now regarded as *under*valued. The subsequent build-up of these pressures forced the USA to defend its existing par value against other currencies with controls on outward capital movements, while the opposite action was forced on the surplus countries now reluctant to accept more dollars. The result in 1971 was the abandonment of free convertibility of the dollar into gold, and with it the system of fixed exchange rates. Despite an attempt to widen the band within which central banks might allow their currencies to fluctuate to $4\frac{1}{2}$ per cent ($2\frac{1}{4}$ per cent on each side of the IMF par value), by the middle of 1972 a system of floating exchange rates had replaced the IMF fixed rate system.

Special Drawing Rights and the expansion of international liquidity

Thus the international monetary system established

at Bretton Woods continued as long as it did only because the world's major trading nations accepted dollars as international money, judged to be 'as good as gold' because it was convertible into gold. While there was confidence in its exchange value it was in fact better than gold, in that investments in US government securities or bank deposits earned interest, as did the sterling balances used as international money by members of the Sterling Area. Between 1953 and 1972 the percentage of international money (the sum of each country's foreign exchange reserves) consisting of gold declined from 65 per cent to 25 per cent. During the late 1960s, moreover, speculation on an increase in the dollar price of gold (devaluation of the dollar against gold) led to decreased willingness to accept dollars rather than gold. All the new gold being mined was purchased by *private* traders at an increasing free market gold price which eventually became two or three times greater than the agreed price of US$35 per fine ounce at which central banks transferred gold between themselves.

When, in 1971, the USA abandoned convertibility of the dollar into gold, it had gold reserves of only $11,000 million (compared with $25,000 million in 1949), against which there were foreign holdings of dollars amounting to almost five times as much at some $50,000 millions. There was clearly a need to supplement the fixed stock of monetary gold and limit the size of the USA's overseas dollar liabilities with a new kind of international money: something along the lines of the BANCOR or 'paper gold' proposed by Keynes in 1944.

This need had been discussed sporadically during the 1960s, and led to the first issue of 'paper gold' in 1970. This took the form of *Special Drawing Rights* or SDRs which like the existing Drawing Rights were allocated to members of the IMF in accordance with their quota (itself based on their relative importance in world trade, and their original subscription). However, unlike these Drawing Rights on the fund of members' cash deposits of gold and national currencies, the new SDRs represent 'IMF money', created simply by crediting members' accounts in much the same way as national central banks can create deposit liabilities for their customers.

In this case the IMF calculates the likely deficit in international liquidity needed to support world trade for the next five years and fills this deficit with an allocation of SDRs. Since it will be some years before this 'paper gold' is as good as real gold in the eyes of some member countries, each country is obliged to accept SDRs in settlement of international payments only up to an amount equal to three times its own allotment of SDRs, after which it is entitled to demand settlement in gold or other national currencies, like the dollar. Thus by the end of 1972 the third year's allotment of SDRs had brought the total to some 10 per cent of the world's international liquidity. SDRs could represent a much higher proportion of total exchange reserves for some developing countries which had few alternative reserves. In the case of Malawi, for example, SDRs constituted about 15 per cent of all foreign exchange reserves, compared with only 9 per cent for Kenya at the end of 1972. In local currency the SDRs allotted to Kenya amounted to a total of K£6.6 millions at the end of 1972, so that under the IMF rules Kenya could insist on other countries' settling in gold or other currencies once the SDRs it had accumulated reached a figure of around K£20 millions. In the case of Zambia, by the end of 1972 most of the SDRs alloted in the three annual instalments had been used to settle international payments, so that SDRs represented a tiny fraction of total Zambian foreign exchange reserves.

Since 1972 there have been further increases in both the IMF quotas paid by members and SDRs credited against these quotas. Countries with balance of payments surpluses pay relatively more in quota contributions and also receive relatively more SDRs, some of which they may use again to supply foreign aid. Surplus countries will therefore acquire more 'paper gold'; while deficit countries will use up this paper gold first, before deciding to part with real gold. Thus in future 'IMF money' will become *the* international reserve money, relieving the US dollar of this key currency role and gradually replacing real gold itself as a means of international payment and as a reserve asset.

Exchange reserves of African countries

We have seen that for the world as a whole, international liquidity is provided by gold, the new IMF 'paper gold' and, most important of all, the foreign currency liabilities of *other* countries. Exchange reserves are not held for their own sake, but like 'national' money, to settle debts—in this case to 'accommodate' or finance balance of payments deficits. In recent years 85 per cent or more of all international money has been held by developed industrial countries or by the oil-producing countries. Quite apart from the persistent tendency for other, less developed countries to run balance of payments deficits, the primary producers also suffer from greater short-term instability in their balance of payments, arising from variations in export earnings and/or the bunching of import payments with do-

mestic investment outlays. For both these reasons, international financial assistance from the World Bank and the IMF is required. Although there are no hard and fast minimum foreign exchange requirements, most countries regard a level of reserves representing less than two months' import payments as too low; while reserves representing say, more than seven months' imports might be regarded as too high, involving a waste of capital which might be employed more productively in domestic investment than held abroad in foreign bank balances.

African countries look to the World Bank and the regional African Development Bank for long-term foreign exchange assistance towards their development programmes. They look increasingly to the IMF for short-term assistance in overcoming temporary balance of payments difficulties.[6] Like all other members of the IMF, African countries can borrow back the 25 per cent of their quota which they paid in gold, and this automatic drawing right is a first line of access to the IMF, which can be followed up by further drawings in foreign currencies of the balance of the quotas which they subscribed in their own currencies. Normally, however, provision of temporary borrowing facilities at the nominal interest rates charged by the IMF is conditional on agreement between borrower and banker concerning domestic and foreign economic policies. The IMF wants the loan repaid and gives advice on how the borrower may improve its balance of payments and prevent a recurrence of the problem. Such IMF stabilization programmes have been implemented successfully in Ghana and Sierra Leone in the late 1960s, for example; while even developed countries like the United Kingdom can be committed to domestic policies of deflation and restraint which may be politically unpopular at home. Because of its power as an international 'lender of last resort', the IMF can wield considerable influence and encourage the central banks and finance ministers of developing countries to take tough and unpopular measures to restrain domestic spending and stimulate exports. An additional form of IMF accommodation is also available to poorer, primary exporting countries which may experience short-term export instability: they may borrow an *additional* 50 per cent of their quota under what is called the 'compensating financing facility'. Mauritius borrowed US$4 million in 1969 to strengthen confidence in the currency after the foreign exchange reserves of the new Bank of Mauritius declined sharply in 1967 and 1968. In 1971, 1972, and 1973 Zambia drew altogether nearly $60 millions to 'compensate' for a sharp deterioration in foreign exchange reserves.

Questions on Chapter 30

1. If a country's balance of payments is always balanced, why is there so much concern over the balance of payments?
2. Describe the structure of the balance of payments of any Eastern African country, and explain how the surplus or deficit on current account is accommodated.
3. Define and distinguish between the following: the balance of visible trade; the balance of invisible trade; the balance of payments on current account; the terms of trade; and the foreign exchange rate.
4. What is meant by equilibrium in a country's 'balance' of payments? How may equilibrium in the balance of payments be maintained (a) in the short run and (b) in the long run?
5. Compare the main systems which are used to determine foreign exchange rates.
6. What is meant by saying that the demand for foreign exchange is a 'derived demand'? For what main purposes is foreign exchange demanded?
7. Discuss the factors determining the slope of a country's demand and supply curves for foreign exchange.
8. How would equilibrium in a country's balance of payments be restored under the 'Gold Standard'? What disadvantages did the system have?
9. How may fluctuations in a currency's foreign exchange rate be stabilized by official intervention in the foreign exchange market?
10. Explain how variation in the foreign exchange rate may affect a country's balance of payments. On what main factors will the effect depend?
11. In what ways may the response of the balance of payments to devaluation differ as between developed industrial countries and less developed African countries? How have these differences influenced actual devaluation decisions in Africa?
12. What is meant by an 'overvalued currency' and what are the effects of overvaluation?
13. Discuss the advantages and disadvantages of fixed exchange rates compared with floating exchange rates.
14. Why do African countries peg their national currencies to the SDR or another currency instead of letting them float freely?
15. For what reasons might the IMF, rather than the World Bank (IBRD), be considered an embryo 'world bank'?
16. Explain precisely what 'Special Drawing Rights' are, and their functions.

Notes

[1] Thus, for example, the East African Statistical Department, in its *Economic and Statistical Review*, reports merchandise imports on a c.i.f. basis in some of the balance of payments estimates, although the individual countries now produce estimates on an f.o.b. basis.

Other adjustments are made to the valuation of both imports and exports as reported in the Customs figures to allow for certain differences in the coverage and timing of actual payments and receipts of the foreign currency involved. The balance of payments thus measures financial transactions in foreign currency (although valued in terms of the national currency) rather than actual physical movements taking place, which might not involve receipts or payments in the same accounting period. Land-locked countries like Uganda, Zambia, and Malawi have to make quite large 'valuation adjustments' to provide estimates of the value of merchandise at their national borders instead of at the ports where goods are imported or exported or for the valuation of exports (f.o.r.), which means 'free on rail' at their own railheads, which could be hundreds of miles *within* their own national boundaries. 'Coverage adjustments', which may be quite substantial, include international transfers of goods, including capital equipment, which do not involve foreign currency payments, for example, the households effect of migrants, plants temporarily imported by foreign building contractors which remain in their ownership but have been recorded for Customs purposes. Major 'timing adjustments' have to be made in respect of, say, exports in one year which will be paid for wholly or partially in another year. This applies especially to Tanzania's diamonds, Zambia's copper, and to tea, where the final sales figure depends on a market valuation overseas by the buyers or at the time of sale on an international commodity exchange.

[2] However, under a freely fluctuating exchange rate system long-term equilibrium in the balance of payments should be defined as a situation where *normal* demand for foreign exchange is equal to *normal* supply, without recourse to deflationary or restrictive trade policies.

[3] Commonwealth countries (except Canada) and some others had tied their currencies to sterling after Britain abandoned the Gold Standard in 1931 and kept their foreign exchange reserves in sterling rather than gold or US dollars until the Sterling Area broke up, effectively, after the pound sterling was devalued in 1967.

[4] In a speech, 'Why Tanzania Devalued in 1971 and 1973' reproduced in Bank of Tanzania, *Economic and Operations Report*, June 1973, pp. 51–4.

[5] These are explained in a later section.

[6] In addition to these international organizations, there are, of course, various multinational and bilateral aid arrangements, notably the OECD's Development Assistance Groups, the Lomé Convention's (see Chapter 12), the Arab oil producers', and the socialist countries'.

Part VIII Labour and employment

31 Supply and Demand for Labour

In the earlier chapters we discussed the demand by consumers for final commodities (outputs) and the determination of prices in product markets. Let us turn now to the discussion of factor markets and to the demand by producers for factors of production (inputs), particularly labour. As before, in order to throw light on total *market* demand for labour, it is necessary first to examine the separate demands of individual units, in this case productive enterprises or firms.

I. The demand for labour: derived demand

The most fundamental point we can make is that the demand for a factor is a *derived demand*, that is to say, it is derived from the demand for the product it can produce. For example, if there were no demand for sugar, sugar estates would have no demand for sugar workers. And if the demand for sugar increases substantially, the demand for sugar workers will increase, as existing plantations seek to expand output and perhaps as new plantations are set up, also requiring workers.

Output and substitution effects of a change in the wage rate

In the discussion that follows we shall talk in terms of the firm's demand for labour, for convenience. In fact the analysis applies generally to a firm's demand for any factor of production. Clearly a firm's demand for labour, given its output, will depend on its choice of technique. We saw in Chapter 14 that that this will depend on the relative prices of labour and capital: in a cheap labour situation a firm will tend (given adequate choice of technique) to select a labour-intensive method and employ more labour per unit of output. This choice was shown in Figure 14.13, illustrating the least-cost combination of factors. Figure 31.1 is similar to Figure 14.13 and shows that the cheapest method of producing 15 units of output (produced along the equal product curve labelled 15)

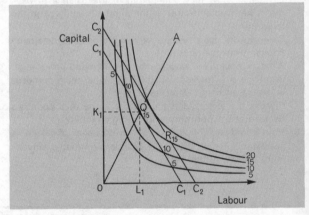

Figure 31.1 Choice of method of production.

is at point Q, since isocost curve C_1C_1 is the lowest isocost curve from which one can reach (*just* reach, at Q, in this case) the 15-unit equal product curve. Thus Q is chosen in preference to points such as R on isocost curve C_2C_2 where output is also 15 units. The method of production at Q is given by the vector OA and the capital–labour ratio OK_1/OL_1.

Our purpose now, however, is to show how a firm's demand for a factor of production depends upon its price. The slope of C_1C_1 in Figure 31.1, and the hiring of OL_1 of labour, assumes given relative prices for labour and capital. If one or both of these changes, the slope of C_1C_1 will change, and the amount of labour hired will change. Suppose, for instance, that the price of labour (the wage rate) falls while the price of capital equipment remains unchanged. In Figure 31.2 assume that the firm makes a given outlay OC on factors of production and initially chooses point Q_1 hiring 10 units of labour. Suppose the wage cut changes the position of the isocost curve from CC_1 to CC_2: he would choose point Q_2 and hire 28 units of labour. A further wage cut and shift of the isocost curve to CC_3 would bring him to Q_3, with 40 units of labour, and so on. In each case the firm will choose the combination given by the point of tangency of the factor price line to an equal product curve, this point indicating the maximum output he can get for his outlay on factors. If we join points like Q_1, Q_2, and Q_3 we have the 'expansion path' which tells us the output obtained, and the method of production used to obtain it, for each successive wage rate. The expansion path Q_1–Q_2–Q_3 is the exact equivalent of the price-consumption curve discussed in Chapter 6.

We can analyse the effect of a fall in the price of labour in terms of income and substitution effects, as in the case of a fall in the price of a commodity. When the wage rate falls the firm is able with the same outlay on factors to obtain more labour with the same capital equipment; or more equipment with the same labour; or more of labour *and* capital. The fall in the wage rate is thus equivalent to an increase in real resources available. More obviously, the same amounts of the factors of production, and therefore of output, are obtainable at reduced cost. In Figure 31.2 when the price line moves from CC_1 to CC_2 the firm reaches a higher equal product curve at Q_2, output increasing from 15 to 25. This extra output could have come about in a different way, however. If instead of the wage cut occurring the firm had been given an extra amount, OD instead of OC, to spend on factors, the price line would be DD, representing the *same* relative prices but an increased outlay on factors: and point R with output also 25 would have been selected.

Thus the second equal product curve (output 25) can be reached at R without any change in relative prices, through increased outlay at constant prices, or it can be reached at Q_2 with the same outlay but a lower wage rate. The difference between the labour hired at Q_2 and at R ($28 - 16 = 12$) is due entirely to the difference in relative prices of the factors and may

be termed the 'substitution effect' of the fall in the wage rate. Since the total increase in labour hired following the wage cut is $28 - 10 = 18$, the difference $18 - 12 = 6$, which is not due to different relative factor prices, must be due to the increased real resources employed. We could call this the *output effect*. This corresponds to the 'income effect' of a change in price in analysis of consumer behaviour. The fall in the price of labour enables the firm to get more factors of production for the same outlay, and thus obtain increased output (though how much extra output it chooses to produce will depend on marginal revenue, as well as costs, as we have seen elsewhere). To sum up, therefore, a fall in the price of the factor increases the amount of labour for two reasons: (a) by encouraging the adoption of more labour-intensive methods—the substitution effect, and (b) by reducing costs and therefore encouraging increased output—the 'output' effect. In general terms we can say in Figure 31.2 that the total effect of the wage cut on labour hired is L_1L_2; the output effect is L_1L_4; and the substitution effect is L_4L_2.

The firm's demand for labour: the marginal productivity theory

We explored the relationship between the equal product diagram and the Law of Diminishing Returns in Chapter 14. Figure 31.3 below is similar to Figure 14.9: here the equal product curves might be taken to relate to the number of bags of cocoa produced annually on a cocoa farm. To find the effect of varying just one input, labour, we can assume that the producer has the fixed amount of capital OK. If we then start from point K on the vertical axis and

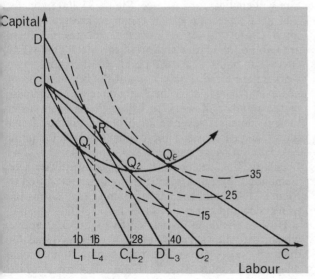

Figure 31.2 *Effect of a wage cut on the firm's demand for labour.*

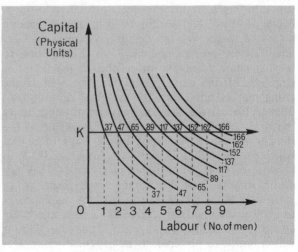

Figure 31.3 *Diminishing returns and the equal product diagram.*

Table 31.1   *Equilibrium employment of labour*

Column 1 Amount of capital (*fixed*)	Column 2 Amount of labour (*variable*)	Column 3 Total physical product (bags of cocoa)	Column 4 Marginal physical product (bags of cocoa)	Column 5 Marginal revenue product (£ per annum)	Column 6 Marginal factor cost (£ per annum)
OK	1	37	—	—	60
OK	2	47	10	30	60
OK	3	65	18	54	60
OK	4	89	24	72	60
OK	5	117	28	84	60
OK	6	137	20	60	60
OK	7	152	15	45	60
OK	8	162	10	30	60
OK	9	166	4	12	60

move outward horizontally in the direction indicated, we shall be applying more labour to the given amount of capital. The number attached to each equal product curve indicates the amount of output in bags of cocoa that it represents. We can thus read off the data scheduled in Table 31.1, columns 1–4, column 4 being derived from column 3 in the usual way. By 'physical' product we mean real product, measured here in bags of cocoa. Let us now suppose our producer is free to hire as much labour as he likes at the rate of £60 per annum and can sell as much cocoa as he likes at the market rate of £3 per bag. How much labour will he hire? Clearly he will continue to hire more labour so long as an extra man can add more to his revenue, through additional cocoa produced and sold, than to his costs, through increased wages. We can define the expression *marginal revenue product of a factor* as the addition to total revenue when one more unit of the factor is employed. If the extra product can be sold at the going market price, then the marginal revenue product will equal the marginal *physical* product times the price of product. Thus the employment of the third man increases output by 18 bags of cocoa, which can be sold at £3 each, bringing an addition to revenue of £54. The *marginal factor cost* is the addition to total cost due to the employment of an extra unit of the factor. In this case the employment of a third man adds another £60 to cost, this being added to the producer's wage-bill. Thus more labour will continue to be hired, if the producer maximizes profits, so long as the marginal revenue product of labour exceeds its marginal factor cost. When these

two are exactly equal, the producer will be hiring just the optimum amount of labour. Thus in Table 31.1, we derive column 5 from column 4 by multiplying through by £3; column 6 shows marginal factor cost to be constant at £60 throughout, that being the wage rate; and the profitable number of workers to hire is six, where marginal revenue product and marginal wage cost are each equal to £60. The data of the last two columns are plotted in Figure 31.4(a), with the equilibrium number of workers given by the intersection of the MRP and MFC curves. If the wage rate changes, the 'best' number of workers to hire will change; for instance, Figure 31.4(a) indicates that at a wage rate of £30, eight workers would be hired. Closer inspection however indicates that there are two points of intersection of the MRP and MFC′ curves, at point S *and* at point R, where only two workers are hired. Point R is not the optimum point however; whereas at point S any increase or decrease in the number of workers will increase costs faster than it increases revenue, or decrease revenue faster than it increases cost,[1] the opposite is true for point R.[2] Thus at wage rates of £84, £60, £45, £30, and £12, 5, 6, 7, 8, and 9 workers respectively would be 'demanded' by the firms. These points are plotted in Figure 31.4(b) and the curve joining them is thus the firm's 'demand curve' for labour.

How is this diagram related to Figure 3.12 above, which also shows the number of workers hired for different wages rates? We repeat part of the same diagram in Figure 31.5. In Figure 31.4 we assumed that the amount of capital equipment was fixed, with only labour variable; in Figure 31.5 the amounts of

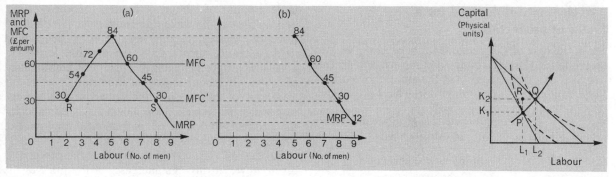

Figure 31.4   (a) Intersection of MRP and MFC curves;
(b) a firm's demand curve for labour.

Figure 31.5   Labour and capital variable.

both factors used can vary. We can, however, 'imagine' the adjustment of capital and labour from P to Q in Figure 31.5 to take place in two parts; first a movement from P to R, increasing capital equipment from OK_1 to OK_2, and then from R to Q, adjusting the labour force from OL_1 to OL_2, with fixed capital OK_2, up to the point where MRP=MFC. Hence points P and Q, and similar points of tangency where the amounts of capital and labour are both optimal, are the points for which MRP=MFC for the labour factor.

The effect of other firms' output plans

The foregoing analysis examined the effect on employment of a change in the wage rate as if it only affected the one firm considered. This is hardly realistic if we are interested in deriving the total market demand for the factor of production. For if for some reason the price of a factor falls, this will affect output plans of *all* the firms in the industry: *all* of them will thus react as we described above. Now if only one firm increases output, this may not have a significant effect on total supply. But if a large number of firms simultaneously do so, total supply may be increased considerably: and if the supply of the product is increased, demand remaining unchanged, the price of the product will fall.

Yet the MRP curve which we drew in Figure 31.4(b) was drawn on the assumption that the price of the product was constant at £3 per bag. Let us reproduce this MRP curve, labelled AB, in Figure 31.6. If the price of cocoa had been only £2 per bag, marginal revenue product would have been just £28 × 2 = £56 for 5 men employed, £40 for 6 men employed, £30 for 7, £20 for 8, and £8 for 9 men employed. This is shown as the line CD, lying below AB. This illustrates clearly what was implied earlier, that *the level of the firm's MRP curve, its demand curve for labour, depends upon the price of the product.*

Suppose now the price of the product was initially

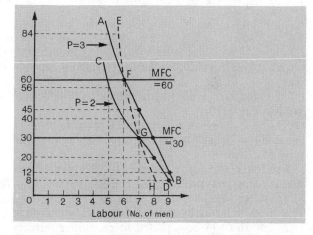

Figure 31.6   The effect of other firms' output plans.

£3 per bag and the wage rate £60 per annum, so that the firm is in 'equilibrium' at F, employing 6 men. The wage rate then falls to £30, inducing firms to increase the supply of the product, but it reduces the price to £2 per bag. This means that simultaneously with the fall in the MFC curve, the MRP curve drops to the level CD. Equilibrium is thus at G on CD, where MFC and MRP are again equal, and 7 men (not 8) are employed. Thus when the wage rate is £60, 6 men are employed, when it is £30, 7 men are employed. F and G are therefore points on the firm's demand curve for the factor. If points E and H are points similarly constructed, then *the line EFGH traces the firm's demand curve for the product, drawn on the assumption of a simultaneous response by other firms in the industry.*

If there were, say, 100 firms in the industry, each in the identical situation depicted in Figure 31.6, we could obtain the total demand curve for the factor by simply adding horizontally the separate demand curves of the individual firms, as we did in the chapter analysing consumers' demands. At a wage rate of £60, 600 workers would be employed, and at £30, 700 workers.

The elasticity of demand for a factor of production

As in the case of the demand for a product, we can calculate the elasticity of demand for a factor. In this case it is the responsiveness of the number of workers hired to a change in the wage rate. We have here:

$$e_D = \frac{\triangle Q/Q}{\triangle W/W} = \frac{\text{Proportionate change in the number of workers hired}}{\text{Proportionate change in the wage rate}}$$

$$= \frac{\dfrac{7-6}{6}}{\dfrac{60-30}{60}} = \frac{1/6}{1/2} = \frac{1}{3}$$

On what does this elasticity depend? Clearly it depends on:

(1) the steepness with which the marginal physical product curve falls;

(2) the rate at which the marginal revenue product curve falls as a result of the decrease in the price of the product.

The latter, of course, depends on the elasticity of demand for the product. It is easy to see why. Suppose we were concerned with farmers supplying vegetables to a nearby town. If farm labourers' wage rates fall, this will be expected to encourage farmers to hire more labourers and thus produce more vegetables—but only if they are in a position to dispose of the extra vegetables! If the urban demand for vegetables is inelastic, prices of vegetables will drop very quickly as employment and output increases, and it will very soon not pay farmers to hire extra workers. Thus the number of workers will not increase very much. The reverse applies for an increase in the price of the factor. If wage rates increase, will this mean a large or small cutting back in the workforce? In part it will depend on the elasticity of demand for vegetables: if producers find it comparatively easy to pass the rise in costs on to consumers then few workers might be laid off; while if any increase in vegetable prices reduces demand drastically, an increase in wage rates might entail a significant reduction in the number of workers employed. We thus have the important proposition that *the elasticity of derived demand for a factor depends partly on the elasticity of demand for the product or products it produces.*

How important this relationship is, however, depends on *whether the factor involved accounts for a small or a large part of the total cost of the product.* Growing vegetables involves the use of a relatively large amount of labour, compared to other factors; hence a rise in the wage rate could raise the cost and price of vegetables quite considerably; this would tend to reduce substantially the demand for vegetables, the output of vegetables, and thus employment of labour. If labour is not an important part of the total cost of the product, the same rise in the wage rate will have less effect on its price, on demand for the product, and thus on output and employment. The same applies for any factor input.

Taking the elasticity of demand for the product as given, however, how far increases in the price of the factor can be passed on to the consumer in the form of higher prices, or vice versa, will depend on *the degree of competition in the product market.* As we examined in detail in Chapter 17, if there is only one or a small number of firms in an industry the firm or firms may have a great deal of power to determine price. The lower the degree of competition the easier it will be simply to raise the price of the product to cover increased wage costs, say, rather than to cut back output and employment.

Finally, we can say that the demand for a particular factor depends on *the possibility of substitution with other factors.* The amount of each factor used depends on the method of production employed, which may be labour-intensive, or capital-intensive, etc. As we stated above, a fall in the relative price of one factor will tend to encourage the adoption of methods involving a more intensive use of that factor. How far this will go will depend on the ease of substitution of one factor for another, as determined by technical considerations. Where factor proportions are fairly rigid, a change in the price of one may have comparatively little effect on the amount of the factor used. In many branches of industry, where operations are extensively mechanized, as for instance cement manufacture, or meat-packing, or cigarette production, it is probable that, for a given size of plant, a labour force may be required of a definite size, only variable within rather narrow limits. In agriculture, factor proportions can certainly be varied much more freely. It is the ease of substitution which determines the 'steepness' of the marginal physical product curve.[3]

We can summarize our discussion by stating again that the demand for a factor is a *derived* demand, derived from the product that it produces. The elasticity of demand for a factor is calculated in the same way as for a product and depends upon:

(1) the elasticity of demand for the product;

(2) the proportion of the total cost of the product spent on the factor in question;

(3) the degree of competition in the product market;

(4) the technical ease of substitution between factors;

(5) the elasticity of supply of substitute factors.

Complementary and substitute factors

As in the case of consumer goods, we can define substitute and complementary factors of production. Some inputs are used together, so that if demand for one increases the amount demanded of the other will also tend to increase. Thus a fall in the wages of bricklayers will reduce the price of houses and increase the demand and output of houses, and this will in turn necessitate the employment of more carpenters to make doors and window frames for the additional houses. A fall in wages of bricklayers might thus in theory increase the demand for carpenters, because bricklayers and carpenters are *complementary* in production. We have already discussed substitutes in production in our references to how capital may be 'substituted' for labour by the adoption of more capital-intensive techniques, and vice versa. It is also possible to calculate a cross-elasticity of demand between factors of production, as with consumer goods, which we can again take as positive in the case of substitutes and negative in the case of complements.

II. The supply of labour

We turn now from the discussion of the demand for labour to factors affecting the supply of labour. Here we can talk about the supply of labour to the whole economy—the size of the national work-force—or the supply of labour to a particular sector, or to a particular occupation or industry. Determinants affecting the size of the *economically active population* or national work-force were discussed in Chapter 3: they were, in addition to the size of the population itself, the age structure, the ratio of men to women, the average working day put in, and the efficiency of quality of the labour effort.

1. The supply of labour to the formal sector

Let us discuss, to begin with, the supply of labour to the *formal sector* of the economy, the characteristics of which sector were discussed in Chapter 4. While the size of the national work-force is fairly rigidly determined by the elements just described above, the formal sector, which forms only a segment of the national economy in a less developed country, can draw on what is a practically unlimited supply of labour from the rural areas.

The famous West Indian economist, Sir Arthur Lewis, produced a well-known model of economic development with unlimited supplies of labour, which we may briefly outline,[4] in a slightly modified form. In this model the important distinction is between a rural sector, where small farmers are working with simple techniques and using very little capital, and a capitalistic formal sector (with either

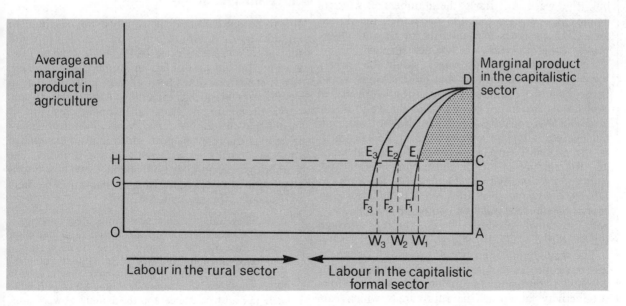

Figure 31.7 *Economic development with unlimited supplies of labour.*

private or state-run enterprises) which uses modern manufacturing techniques, and a great deal of capital per worker, to achieve high productivity. If the total national work-force is equal to OA in Figure 31.7, we can measure labour employed in the rural sector *rightwards* from point O and labour employed in the capitalistic sector *leftwards* from point A. Thus at point W_1 the total work force OA is divided between OW_1 in the rural sector and W_1A in the capitalistic sector.

If there is a plentiful supply of land, the average (and marginal) product of labour in the rural sector can be taken as being constant and, with low productivity, at a low level. The line GB is therefore the average as well as marginal product curve of labour in the rural sector. Lewis assumed that some inducement over and above marginal product in agriculture would be needed to persuade labour to transfer from there to the modern sector, due to the costs of movement and to the higher cost of living in the urban sector. If labour can earn more in this sector than earnings in the rural sector plus this inducement equal to, say, GH, it will move to the modern sector.[5] The line HC therefore represents the supply curve of labour to the capitalistic sector, implying a perfectly elastic supply to this sector, and AC is the wage which needs to be paid to this labour.

The line DE_1F_1 represents the marginal product curve for labour in the modern sector in an initial period, measured from right to left, and total product is given by the area under this curve, ADE_1W_1, when AW_1 workers are employed in the capitalistic sector. Of this total product, ACE_1W_1 constitutes the wage-bill (the wage AC times the number of workers employed, AW_1), so that the remainder, the dotted area CDE_1, accrues to capitalists (or to state enterprises) as net proceeds, or capitalist surplus.

Lewis considered that wages would be largely spent on consumption and that most savings would come from the capitalist surplus. For simplicity of exposition, therefore, he assumed that all of the wage-bill was consumed, and the whole of the capitalist surplus CDE_1 saved *and* invested. Reinvestment of the capitalist surplus increases the capital stock and the amount of labour which can be employed, shifting the average product curve sideways to DE_2F_2 and employment to AW_2. A continuous process of capital accumulation could occur in this way, with marginal product curves shifting through DE_1F_1, DE_2F_2, DE_3F_3, and so on.

The main point of the model is to indicate that the less developed economies have an untapped labour potential consisting of underemployed or low-productivity labour in the rural areas which can, once absorbed into the capitalistic sector, provide output in excess of its own consumption, to provide the savings and capital accumulation necessary for economic growth.

Lewis thought that there was widespread disguised unemployment in the rural areas, with a marginal product of zero (so that labour could be withdrawn from agriculture without any loss of output) and that therefore the unused labour potential was very large. It is not necessary, in fact, for the marginal product of labour in agriculture to be zero for the model to be applicable. So long as the average/marginal product of labour in the rural sector is much lower than in the capitalist sector, and the supply of labour to the latter is elastic, the transfer of labour from one sector to the other can increase output and provide savings necessary for further growth in output and formal employment.

The model is much too simple, and tends to assume lack of capital is the only critical factor limiting expansion. In fact (a) skilled labour, management, and enterprise may be more important than unskilled labour; (b) the capitalist surplus may be spent by capitalists on consumption, or reinvested abroad rather than domestically; and (c) the lack of markets, particularly the 'vicious circle' of a small domestic market, may restrict the incentive to reinvest. Nevertheless, Lewis's model demonstrates the possibilities which exist for capital accumulation and growth based on the absorption of surplus labour if these other constraints can be overcome.

2. The supply of effort: a backward-sloping supply curve for labour?

It is to be expected that the supply curve of labour to an industry or economy 'slopes up' from left to right: that is to say, if the price of labour (the wage rate) goes up, the amount of labour supplied will increase. It has at various times been alleged, however, that in developing countries, including Africa, the supply curve of labour is 'backward-sloping'. By this is meant that the supply curve slopes *down* from left to right over the relevant portion, so that an increase in the wage results in a *decrease* in the amount. The Cambridge economist, Guillebaud, once made this suggestion with reference to sisal plantation workers in Tanzania, for example, stating:[6]

> ... it still appears to be the case with a great majority of African workers that they prefer leisure to money earnings and that they are in that primitive condition ('primitive' from the point of view of a modern monetary economy based on the division of labour) that, at least in the first instance, an increase in money earnings is more likely to lead to a decrease in the amount of work done than an increase in, or even the maintenance of, their supply of effort.

It will be a useful exercise for us to examine this statement and see what meaning, if any, can be given to it.

We should note, first, that with any form of labour anywhere, there must be *some* point at which the amount of labour supplied by an individual ceases to increase, or even decreases, as the wage rate increases. This is because money income is not desired, generally speaking, for its own sake, but for the goods it can buy. And the enjoyment of these goods will be impossible without at least a minimum amount of leisure; as the individual becomes better off he is likely at some point to take at least part of this increased standard of living in the form of *more* leisure—and thus work fewer hours. The point is whether in Africa, and other less developed countries, this point is not arrived at when wage rates are still extremely low, and much lower than in developed countries.

Secondly, we must distinguish one possible explanation of the phenomenon, if in fact it exists. It may be that a portion of the workers recruited by the sisal plantations, to take the case cited, are *'target workers'*: that they have only temporarily left their own homes and peasant farms in order to acquire as quickly as possible certain minimum cash requirements needed for the purchase of certain 'target goods'. They may wish to purchase a piece of land at home; or to buy some 'durable consumer goods' like corrugated iron roofing, bicycles, or radios; or they may be saving to pay bridewealth, perhaps the most expensive item of all.

Figure 31.8 illustrates how long a worker would be willing to work if he were driven by a completely rigid 'target' of money income. Money income earned, in shillings per day, is measured on the horizontal axis, and hours of leisure enjoyed daily, on the vertical axis. There is therefore a limit on this axis of 24 hours, which is the situation if all 24 hours of the day are devoted to leisure. Hours worked can be calculated by deducting the number of leisure hours from 24, that is, by moving vertically *downwards* from point A.

Suppose the wage rate were initially 2s per hour. The 'price of labour' would then be indicated by the line AB, showing that if, for instance, he converted all the 24 hours of leisure potentially available to him into money income, he could obtain 48s per day. Depending, therefore, on how hard he is willing to work and how quickly he wishes to achieve his 'target' he will choose some combination, say, P, on the line AB. Let us suppose that this choice, which gives him 15 hours of leisure (9 hours worked) and 18s earned daily, allows him to accumulate the income he wants in exactly three years.

If the wage rate now increases to 3s per hour this new price of labour will be indicated by the line AB'. If the worker is only interested in achieving his target income, he could do so, for example, by moving to point Q on AB'. He will then earn 18s daily and achieve his target in three years, as before, but will now work only six hours a day instead of nine. The increase in the wage has reduced the amount of labour supplied. Alternatively he might continue to work nine hours a day and work for a period of *two years* only. The effect on the supply of labour is the same: two-thirds of the previous amount is supplied after the increase in the wage rate.

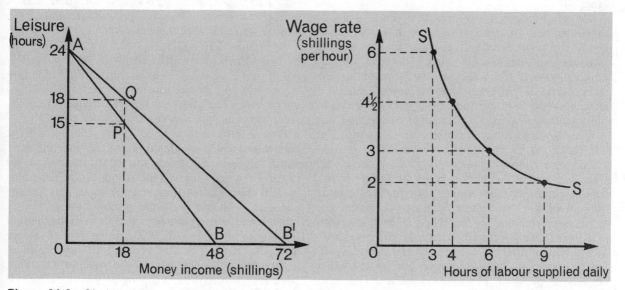

Figure 31.8   *Choice of hours worked with a fixed target of money income.*

Figure 31.9   *A backward-sloping supply curve of labour.*

Extending the analysis, we can see that our worker would work 4 hours a day if the wage rate were 4.50 ($4 \times 4\frac{1}{2} = 18$s), 3 hours a day if it were 6s ($3 \times 6 = 18$s), and so on. Plotting these combinations in Figure 31.9 we obtain SS, which gives the amount of labour supplied as a function of the wage rate. SS is the supply curve of labour and can be seen to slope down from left to right, that is, to be 'backward-sloping' compared to the usual supply curve.

It should be noted, however, that this result need not indicate irrationality on the part of the worker, given his preference for living in his own area on his own land. He is no more irrational than the expatriate in Africa who decides to return to his own country in Europe although he may be paid a rather lower salary there. It is quite compatible, in fact, with the principle of equal net advantage (which we shall expound presently), there being non-pecuniary advantages for the worker obtained from living in his own area.

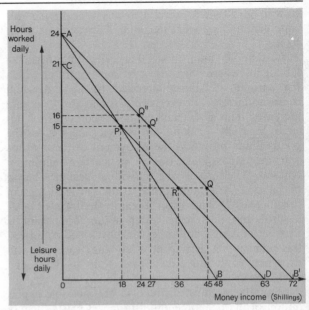

Figure 31.10 *Income and substitution effects of a change in the wage rate.*

Income and substitution effects of a change in the wage rate

This explanation of the backward-sloping supply curve runs in terms of the 'target worker' based on his own farm and more or less temporarily working in a factory or plantation. An alternative interpretation of Guillebaud's and other such statements, however, is that even for *permanent* workers, whether permanent on their own farms or permanent employees, the supply curve of labour is backward-sloping. Let us examine how this could, in theory, arise.

We can distinguish two separate effects of a rise in the wage rate. In the first place it makes an extra hour's work more rewarding, and thus provides an incentive to work more hours. This can be put another way. If the wage rate is 2s per hour the worker loses 2s if he takes an extra hour's leisure; if it is 3s, an extra hour's leisure 'costs' him 3s. A rise in the wage rate increases the 'price' of leisure, and this is likely to cause the amount of leisure demanded to fall, that is, to increase the hours worked.

But there is another factor at work. A rise in the wage rate makes the worker better off in real terms: he can either get more money income for the same amount of work or, which comes to the same, the same money income for less work. In both cases his real income has increased: in one the increased welfare is taken entirely in the form of extra goods (paid for by the extra money income) and in the other entirely in the form of increased leisure. The most likely result, however, is some combination of the two, with more money income *and* more leisure

chosen. This is especially so since most consumer goods, from cinema trips to motor cars, require leisure if they are to be enjoyed. The increase in real income is therefore an incentive to work *less* hard, to consume more leisure. There are therefore two forces operating in opposite directions, the *income effect* due to the rise in real income being positive (more leisure taken) and the *substitution effect* caused by the change in the price of leisure (less leisure taken). The income effect will not be negative, since there is no reason to think that leisure is an 'inferior' good and it is unlikely to be zero. The total effect will depend on the relative importance of these two.

In Figure 31.10 a change in the wage rate from 2s to 3s is shown by a shift in the price line from AB to AB'. Point P on AB shows the combination of leisure (15 hours) and money income per day (18 shillings) which might be chosen when the wage rate is 2s. After the change in the wage rate, some point on AB' will be selected, such as Q, Q', or Q", this point being determined by a combination of income and substitution effects. To isolate the substitution effect, we can draw a price line, CD, through point P, parallel to AB'. The worker thus has the same real income (since at P he has the same combination of money income and leisure) but he is free to exchange leisure for money income along CD at the rate of 3s per hour, instead of 2s. Any change in his choice of leisure must then be due to the substitution effect, since real income is as in the initial situation. We saw in Chapter 6 that the substitution effect is never negative for a decrease in price. In this case, a rise in the price of leisure means a decrease in the amount of leisure consumed, so that the combination chosen would be somewhere along PD. The choice of combination R, for example, would imply that the substitution effect were 6 hours, consumption of leisure decreasing from 15 hours at P to 9 hours.

However, this is purely hypothetical result in the absence of an income effect. The latter is represented by a movement outward from CD to AB′, indicating that more leisure *and* more money income are attainable after the wage rise. If Q is the point selected on AB′, we can compare Q and R to find the income effect. Since the amounts of leisure 'consumed' at R and Q are the same (9 hours), the income effect is zero. No point to the right of Q would be chosen, as this would imply a negative income effect. If Q′ were selected (15 hours' leisure), the income effect would be *plus* six hours. Since the substitution effect is *minus* six hours, the two effects cancel each other out and the total effect is zero: comparing P and Q′, the amount of work done is the same.

If a point is selected to the left of Q′, such as Q″, the amount of labour supplied decreases, implying a backward-sloping supply curve. Comparing P and Q″, the total effect is plus one hour's leisure, resulting from an income effect of *plus* seven hours and a substitution effect of *minus* six hours. A backward-sloping supply curve for labour may result if the income effect is strong, or the substitution effect weak, or both. A 'lazy' man with a marked preference for leisure is likely to exhibit both: (1) he is likely to take a relatively large part of increased real income in the form of increased leisure, rather than other consumer goods, and (2) he is not likely to show much response to the higher reward for work.

The same result might come, not from 'laziness' as such, but from a lack of demand for money income. In the more remote parts of Africa, for example, shops may be infrequent and badly stocked, so that consumer goods which could be purchased with money income are not fully available. Much more important, probably, is that in these remote parts the social structure is such that many 'modern' consumer goods are irrelevant. While a lack of strong demand for income undoubtedly exists and may be a major obstacle to development in the remote regions not open to modernizing influences, there is plenty of evidence of normal economic reactions within the modernized economies. Whether backward-sloping supply curves for labour could be identified, therefore, except as applied to 'target' workers wishing to return to their home regions, is open to serious doubt.

Moreover, a distinction must be made between the *individual's* willingness and opportunity to work and the *market supply* of effort. Over a certain range of

prices an individual's supply curve may be backward-sloping but this does not mean that over time additional workers will not respond positively to changes in rates of remuneration. Thus a rise in the wage rate will attract workers to a particular industry and the total supply of labour can increase, so long as there are some unemployed, even if some individuals now withdraw their labour.

3. The supply of labour: quality

It should be noted that there is another aspect of the supply of labour apart from its quantity: its quality. Because of this there is an important difference between low wages and cheap labour. It is often said that, despite low wages in labour-abundant developing countries, labour is not nearly as cheap as it appears because low wages are to a great extent offset by low productivity. In fact if productivity is very low, *labour costs* may be high, even when wages are low.

There are a number of factors which raise labour costs while at the same time depressing the wage rate of employed labour in developing countries. In the first place workers are often recruited from peasant farming areas, rather than brought up in an urban and industrial atmosphere. Such labour may be less used to taking orders, to punctuality, and to the general regimentation of working life in the factory. Moreover, where workers are unfamiliar with machinery and tools, costs of breakage may be high, particularly where equipment is expensive. However, these problems may apply only to a transitional period after newly recruited labour is employed.

Secondly, there used to be a problem in Africa, and this is still the case in some places, associated with *migrant* labour. Migrants were frequently 'target workers', aiming to earn a specific amount of cash required for a piece of land, for housing improvements, or something of this sort, and then to return to their own areas once the targets were achieved. This produces a high rate of absenteeism and of labour turnover, due to workers returning to the rural areas for short or extended periods. The result is likely to be that employers are less inclined to train labour and, where training is given, part of this will be wasted, this again raising labour costs. To the extent that rural–urban migrants tend to be younger men, the labour force will be more youthful and less experienced than might otherwise have been the case. All the evidence is, however, that there has been considerable stabilization of the urban work-force in many parts of Africa, including Eastern Africa, and that indeed fear of losing jobs which might be very difficult to obtain again has made labour turnover unusually *low* in many urban areas.

Finally, it is clear that the climate in some parts of Africa, in particular its humidity, and the poor health and susceptibility to disease of the labour force, tend to reduce the productivity of African labour in both industry and agriculture.

For the above reasons it has many times in the past been suggested that it might actually pay employers to pay labour *more*: what is referred to as the *economy of high wages*. There is certainly some evidence that, up to a point, the increased standard of living associated with the payment of a higher wage can noticeably increase the productivity of labour in poor countries. As far as the impermanence and instability of African labour are concerned, governments in Africa have in the past tended to fix minimum wages at the level determined by calculation as to the smallest amount that could sustain the male unskilled worker in the town, *but not his family*. The trend in recent years has been towards a minimum wage on which a family could be maintained in the town without the need for additional income to be raised by farming. As a result, a much more permanent urban work-force has evolved, much less subject to instability, and with higher productivity.

4. The supply of labour to different occupations

The wages and salaries of different kinds of worker, in different occupations, vary considerably. The demand for different types of labour will obviously influence the pattern of wages. But before we can attempt to explain this pattern we need also to look at factors affecting the *supply* of workers to different occupations.

If all labour were of equal ability and skill, were completely mobile and did not face any obstacles to their movement, if labour were aware of all employment opportunities, and if there were no non-pecuniary advantages in any occupations, then the wage rate in every occupation would be the same *irrespective* of the demand conditions for different types of worker. For as soon as one occupation offered a higher wage rate to attract more labour, workers (being aware of the differential, and mobile) would switch towards it until the increase in supply, and reductions elsewhere, eliminated the difference. As soon as these conditions do not hold, of course, wage differentials may appear and persist. By examining reasons why these conditions may not hold, therefore, we can throw light on why workers in different occupations receive different remunerations.

Non-pecuniary advantages and disadvantages

We can start by taking into account differences between occupations other than in the ruling wage rate. Before a proper comparison of money incomes can be made it is necessary to take into account the cost of living, which affects the real value of these incomes. Urban workers in Nairobi or other large towns are likely to have higher expenses, in particular for accommodation, than similar workers in rural areas, and will need higher money incomes to be as 'well-paid' as the latter. On the other hand, workers in some occupations may receive income in kind as well as cash earnings: a government employee may be offered subsidized housing on a government-owned housing estate, or other concessions; large employers, in Eastern Africa and elsewhere, often provide good facilities for their employees—free housing perhaps, paid leave, medical services, recreational facilities, schools for children of employees, where these would not otherwise be available, and so on—as a means of attracting and retaining workers.

Secondly, some jobs offer what people consider to be better financial propositions in the long run than others, although these are not included in present cash earnings. Thus some occupations are characterized by periodic unemployment, while others offer good security of tenure. The village schoolteacher is less likely to lose his job than, say, a clerk or supervisor in a private firm. In contrast, workers in the building trade might enjoy high rates of pay for the duration of a specific building project but expect to be 'laid off' on completion of the project. Some jobs carry better chances of advancement: it has been remarked, for example, that in Africa there is always a great demand for jobs as porters or cleaners in garages, even at relatively low rates of pay, among untrained workers who hope to 'pick up' some technical know-how and thereby eventually obtain a more skilled job. Similarly, self-employed small shopkeepers may be willing to remain in this occupation despite very low earnings in the hope that their businesses will some day become highly profitable, even if only a tiny minority ever have these hopes realized.

The conditions so far discussed are only non-pecuniary in the sense that they are not reflected in current cash earnings. Apart from these considerations some jobs have special characteristics which make them more or less attractive. Some are unpleasant, arduous, or even dangerous, as in the case of mining; or they may to some extent damage the worker's self-esteem or social standing, as may be the case with domestic servants. Conversely, jobs may be particularly interesting, such as research posts, or carry social prestige, as in the case of public office, or the professions.

Occupations therefore differ according to the nature of the jobs themselves, the degree of security and prospect of future earnings, and the income in kind offered together with cash earnings. If competition exists the tendency will be to equalize the *net advantage* in all occupations. Labour will then move until there is no net advantage in further movement, taking into account both cash earnings *and* other advantages. In equilibrium, the difference in cash earnings will measure the relative value of the non-monetary advantage or disadvantage of one occupation as compared to another. We may say that this is the outcome of *the principle of equal net advantage.*

Immobility of labour and the cost of movement

Mobility of labour may refer to *geographical mobility*, that is, how easily labour can be persuaded to move from one region to another, or to mobility between occupations; *occupational mobility*. One of the characteristic features of labour in Eastern Africa is its great geographical mobility, both between different parts of the same country and between countries. Mobility between occupations, or lack of it, is more likely to produce differences in wages or salaries. Immobility, in this case, is due especially to the fact that time is needed for the acquisition of skills either through training, or on-the-job experience, or both. Because time is needed to train additional workers in any occupation, an increase in demand for a particular category of worker will tend temporarily to raise wages until the additional supply is forthcoming. This wage difference may be referred to as a *dynamic wage differential*, since it exists in a period of change rather than in a static situation.

The costs of training are related to the time the training takes—a two-year course is more expensive than a one-year course, other things being the same—but not entirely. 'Costs' will depend on the willingness of trainees, or their families, to sacrifice during the period of training savings or income which would otherwise be earned.

Given these costs of training and retraining, how quickly people respond to changed opportunities, and change occupations, depends on various social factors, perhaps on the nature of the society itself. In some countries there will be more social resistance to changing occupations than in others. Occupational mobility may also be related to geographical mobility, as switching occupations may necessitate moving to a new area, if the industry is located elsewhere. Reluctance to move home may therefore increase occupational immobility.

Mobility will depend also on how *specific* or specialized a skill is. If an occupation requires skills which are rather general there will be a larger section of the community who could potentially acquire the skill while presumably people with similar types of skill could learn to modify these as required by this occupation in a relatively short time.

For all these reasons time will generally be required before the supply of workers can adapt to a changed pattern of demand. We can only say that there will be a *tendency* for differences in net advantage to be eliminated by competition, but that the time factor will produce 'dynamic' wage differentials at any given moment.

Ignorance of job opportunities

The mobility of labour in response to wage differentials will also depend on the amount of information about job opportunities available to workers or potential workers. We have already discussed in Chapter 10 how price intelligence affects the efficiency of product markets; and, in the same way, a factor market will be more efficient if, say, buyers and sellers of labour services have adequate knowledge of sources of supply, job vacancies, and different rates of remuneration. In Africa generally where 'news travels fast' about wage employment opportunities, lack of information may not be a serious factor, in itself, in maintaining wage differentials. Nevertheless, it is still quite common for large employers of unskilled labour required in mines, public works, or on plantations to recruit workers using the services of specialized 'middlemen' called labour contractors to communicate offers and conditions of work to people living far away from the places of work. A similar role is performed in developed industrial countries by *Employment* (or *Labour*) *Exchanges* operated by government departments to fill job vacancies with unemployed workers who have 'registered' with them. In Eastern Africa, too, there are Labour Exchanges in the larger towns which perform a similar function, although they do so mainly by being a physical market place where job seekers can congregate in anticipation of work. However, since the number of job seekers usually far exceeds the number of job vacancies, the recorded statistics of 'registered unemployed' at such Exchanges is rarely an adequate guide to the total number of job seekers. Private employment agencies also exist for secretarial and other, more qualified workers; and these are often a more effective source of market intelligence since they charge a fee for their services to employers, and often to job seekers, and thus have to satisfy their clients if they are to stay in business.

Differences in ability

Even if there are no barriers to movement, and all necessary facilities for training are available, net advantages will not be equalized in all occupations if people do not have the same ability to be potential recruits to all occupations. It is fairly obvious that in any country the number of people capable of becoming first-rate scientists, artists, sportsmen, and the like is strictly limited, so that these workers can earn the 'economic rent' of unique or innate ability. However, even lesser skills and ability will not be possessed by all, with the result that manpower tends to be subdivided into separate non-competing groups. Thus great demand for the services of a particular group may raise net advantages considerably above the general level without inducing a further supply of workers. For example, the high earnings of professional footballers and popular ('pop') singers and musicians who frequently enjoy a world-wide market for their services can be explained by the postwar affluence of consumers in developed countries, producing a keen demand for services which are in limited supply; while in Eastern Africa, to take a very different example, the relatively high earnings of long-distance truck drivers reflect in part at least the special innate skills and long experience of a relatively small group of workers.

J. B. Knight[7] has shown how earnings from paid employment in Zambia are largely determined by differences in educational qualifications. In 1965 in the private sector (excluding mining), African employees with university degrees were paid, on average, £1,368, about seven times as much as Africans without any post-primary education earning £197. African employees with 'O'-level qualifications earned £622, over three times as much; while even a Form 2 attainment earned £392, a 100 per cent differential over less educated workers. Table 31.2

Table 31.2 Annual average cash earnings of male employees in Zambia's private sector (excluding mining), 1965

Educational qualification	African employees (£)	Non-African employees (£)
University degree or equivalent	1,368	2,359
Diploma or GCE 'A' level	572	1,992
GCE 'O' level	622	1,589
Form 2 of secondary schooling	392	1,529
Some secondary schooling	359	1,236
Other, primary levels or less	197	Not reported
Average wage or salary	204	1,668

SOURCE: *Manpower Report*, Lusaka, 1966 (quoted by J. B. Knight, op. cit., p. 98)

shows these educational levels and average cash earnings.

Although in 1965 racial differences in earnings still reflected discriminatory practices prevalent in the colonial (and Federation) periods, the 'gap' in earnings between the African graduate at the top of the table and the average African wages is much larger, absolutely as well as relatively, than the corresponding 'gap' for non-Africans. Nevertheless formal educational qualifications produced a differential of 100 per cent between non-African university graduates and those with little or no secondary schooling. Moreover at the lower levels of education the racial differences in earnings reflect not only pure discrimination but also differentials paid as inducements to expatriates with higher supply prices and differences in experience and on-the-job training.

It is not possible, of course, to draw a strict line between inequalities due to differences in ability and differences due to the cost of training and access to education, or long years of experience on the job, particularly when education and training are open only to the fortunate few, as in the case of most underdeveloped countries. How restricted educational facilities have been in East Africa is illustrated in Figure 31.11 which refers to Tanzania, admittedly one of the worst-off countries in respect of educational opportunities at the time of independence. In 1961 only one of every ten pupils in Tanzania could expect to receive a full seven years of primary education (in Figure 31.11 the numbers completing Standard VII were 12,000, compared to 121,000 entering Standard I). Only 1 out of every 76 of the original primary school intake into Standard I might finish Form IV of secondary school, the GCE year. Figure 31.11 shows how minute the chances were in 1961 of a primary school pupil progressing to the top of the educational pyramid and obtaining a university place. There were only about 100 students from Tanzania entering Makerere College, then the only university institution in East Africa, and even fewer graduating, while the number returning from overseas universities was probably barely 100, or only 1 in every 1,200 of the Primary Standard I intake. Even in 1971, ten years later, the annual output of university graduates was less than 1,000 and the intake into Primary I of 190,000 was about 160 times the intake into university, implying that the chance of a new primary school pupil progressing to the top of the system was of the order of 1 in 160. While the fortunate graduates could expect to earn a very high income compared to a primary school leaver, we can see that the *main* reason for their good fortune was not 'innate ability', though ability would be required if a university standard was reached. This is because

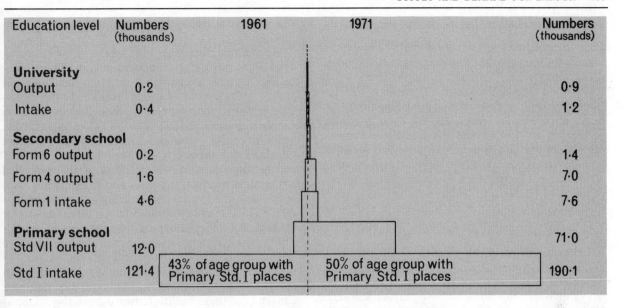

Education level	Numbers (thousands)	1961	1971	Numbers (thousands)
University				
Output	0·2			0·9
Intake	0·4			1·2
Secondary school				
Form 6 output	0·2			1·4
Form 4 output	1·6			7·0
Form 1 intake	4·6			7·6
Primary school				
Std VII output	12·0			71·0
Std I intake	121·4	43% of age group with Primary Std. I places	50% of age group with Primary Std. I places	190·1

Figure 31.11 Enrolment in public-aided primary and secondary schools in mainland Tanzania, 1961 and 1971, and estimated numbers of Tanzanian students at university level institutions (including overseas).

the educational advancement of *most* pupils was extinguished after primary school, not secondary school: in 1961 only 4.6 thousands were entering Form I compared to 121 thousands entering Standard I, so that 26 out of 27, roughly, were not getting the chance to proceed to secondary school, for which *any* child has the potential in ability. This ratio was virtually identical in 1971 indicating that prospects for the primary school entrant remained bleak.

Even so, the primary school entrants were not the least fortunate, since there was still at least one other six-year-old child without a primary school place for each one of the 190,000 enrolled in Standard I.

Institutional obstacles and discriminatory practices

Apart from 'natural' immobility of labour, including differences in innate abilities, movement between occupations may be restricted by artificial obstacles to competition. Wages in an occupation may be maintained at artificially high levels by barriers to entry based on race, tribe, religion, sex, age, or other social characteristics. Many of the 'man-made' obstacles are enforced by the law of the land, as for example the racial barriers in South Africa. Others are enforced by private sanctions and customs. Trade unions, for instance, attempt to keep wages of their members high by restricting entry into the occupation to qualified workers who have undertaken long periods of apprenticeship or other training—or by insisting on strict 'demarcation' of occupations that prevents em-

ployers using other kinds of workers for certain tasks. The various professional bodies representing doctors, lawyers, and accountants are, in fact, as adept as any union of craftsmen or labourers at the practice of restricting entry into their profession: generally because they can obtain state enforcement so that it becomes illegal for unqualified people to practice in, say, the medical or legal professions. In a less formal way, but even more effectively, women may be denied access to particular types of job as business executives, for example, or taxi-drivers, or technicians. The government itself may discriminate in favour of certain groups of workers by reserving certain jobs for its own citizens or, with the highest of motives, enforcing minimum rates of pay and conditions of work in selected occupations which effectively exclude some workers who would have gained employment in favour of those who do.

The economics of discrimination

The effect on employment and wage rates of institutional obstacles raised by trade unions or by the state itself are discussed elsewhere. Here we shall consider the *economic* effects of the two main forms of job discrimination practised in many countries, those based on (a) sex and (b) race, briefly extending this type of analysis to consider (c) the division between formal and informal sectors.

Job discrimination between the sexes

Even in countries which are socially advanced in regard to sex equality women normally experience disadvantages in (1) finding employment in the higher-paid occupations and (2) earning the same rates of pay as men in the same occupation. As a result of both these tendencies, the average earnings of women are lower than the average earnings of male workers. This problem is more serious still in less developed countries like those in Eastern Africa, where females constitute a much smaller proportion of the paid labour force than in industrial countries of northern Europe, the USA or the USSR where they account for a third or more of all wage or salary earners.

Let us look first at the problem arising out of the exclusion of women from higher-paid occupations. There are, of course, some jobs, those involving very heavy manual work, for which women are less suited. However women are frequently excluded from jobs which have become traditionally 'male' occupations on false grounds of 'unsuitability' for 'heavy' jobs (when in fact the tasks are not really too heavy for women) or jobs involving specific skills (such as taxi-driving) or 'responsible' managerial jobs. As a result of such exclusion females seeking paid employment are crowded into a relatively narrow range of lower-productivity jobs which have then become known as 'female' occupations. Examples are domestic service, retailing (as shop assistants), nursing, primary and nursery school teaching, among the tertiary services; textiles and garment-making, in the manufacturing sector; and seasonal jobs in agriculture, such as fruit-picking.

We can therefore regard the labour supply as being divided into two 'non-competing groups': males competing for the higher-paid high-productivity jobs ('men's jobs'), and females restricted to lower-productivity jobs ('women's jobs'). The position is shown in Figure 31.12. The curve D'D represents the demand curve (the marginal revenue product schedule) for labour in various 'high-productivity' occupations. Since labour will first of all be applied at the most productive points, and subsequently seek somewhat less productive and high-paying employments, this curve will decline as more labour is applied, moving rightwards from the origin at O_m. The curve d'd represents the marginal product of labour in low-productivity occupations. Instead of measuring the application of labour in these occupations from left to right, however, we shall for convenience measure this leftward from the origin at O_f, so that the curve d'd slopes down from *right to left*.

To focus on the problem of discrimination, let us assume male and female labour is of equal efficiency and skill, but that while male labour is free to take employment in the high-productivity occupations, female labour is excluded from these and forced to find employment in low-productivity occupations of the type described above. Then the application of male labour is measured rightwards from O_m, up to point S, and that of female labour leftwards from O_f, also up to point S. The curve S'S is simultaneously the supply curve for male labour (viewed from O_m) and the supply curve for female labour (viewed from O_f), indicating the quantities of male labour, O_mS, and female labour, O_fS, available: total labour supply equals O_mSO_f.

The curve d'd not only starts at a lower level than D'D, but declines much more rapidly. This is because we can assume that D'D refers to a wide range of occupations while female labour, subsumed under d'd, is confined to a limited range of jobs, such that the demand for additional labour services falls off rather rapidly. It should be noted that the lower position of d'd compared to D'D is not due to any lower efficiency of female labour but to the fact that male labour can work in more capital-intensive industries and industries in which products are in good demand and fetch high prices.

Supply and demand for male labour intersect at P, yielding the male wage rate W_m; those for female labour intersect at R, yielding the much lower female wage rate W_f. In the absence of discrimination, with females free to obtain employment in any occupation, females would move out of the lower-paid occupations into the higher-paid, continuing to do so

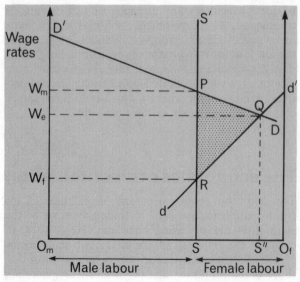

Figure 31.12   *The effects of sex discrimination on wages.*

until wages were equalized between the two sets of occupations and the incentive to move disappeared. Equilibrium would be at point Q with the common wage W_e. Labour equal to O_mS'' would now be employed in the high-productivity occupations and O_fS'' in the formerly low-paid jobs: this labour could be either male or female. Not only would the inequity in wage rates be eliminated by the removal of discrimination, it should be noted, but *national income would also increase*. This is evident from the fact that initially the marginal product of labour in 'female' jobs is SR, while that in 'male' jobs is PS. Shifting a marginal unit of labour from one to the other increases the value of output by PR, and shifting SS'' of labour into the high-productivity occupations increases the value of output by the shaded area PQR.

It should not be supposed from the above analysis that *all* of the difference in pay between male and female labour is due to discrimination. In many cases there may be genuine differences in productivity, as when heavy physical work is involved. This would produce differences in wage rates even *without* discrimination. Thus in Figure 31.13 the outer curve, D_mD_m, represents the marginal productivity of male labour, while the curve D_fD_f represents that of female workers. Employers who can profitably employ OR males at the wage rate W_m will only be prepared to employ the same number of females at the lower wage W_f, lower in proportion to the lower productivity of females. From the units on the vertical axis we see that the diagram implies a unit of female labour produces two-thirds the output of a unit of male labour, so that an employer will be willing to pay the former just two-thirds of the male wage rate or, alternatively, will be willing to pay $1\frac{1}{2}$ units of female labour the same as one unit of male labour. If we take one unit of male labour to represent one 'efficiency unit' and treat $1\frac{1}{2}$ units of female labour as one efficiency unit, we can take D_mD_m as representing the marginal product of efficiency units (demand curve for efficiency units of labour) and add male and female labour to get the total supply of efficiency units, SS. The wage for an efficiency units will be W_e, given by the point of intersection T, male labour obtaining this in full, and female units obtaining two-thirds of it.

A second reason for lower female wage rates, also related to lower productivity, may arise out of a higher rate of sickness, pregnancy, or days taken off to look after children. In addition extra costs may be imposed on employers who have incurred expenditures on training female labour if females retire earlier than males or work less continuously. Differences between males and females in respect of absenteeism and the like are frequently exaggerated or imagined, however.

Thirdly, wage differences may not reflect differences in productivity or costs of employment, but simply result from the superior bargaining power of male workers, who are normally better organized in trade unions. Moreover, if there is an 'excess supply' of female labour in a restricted range of overcrowded occupations, this will further reduce their bargaining position. An additional factor, affecting the supply price of female labour, is that the opportunity-cost of female labour in these paid occupations will be low, being the value obtained from domestic work in the home, or unpaid work on family farms.

Lastly, we should note that the lower productivity of female labour, even the non-availability of *any* qualified female labour in many occupations, may reflect the absence of training facilities open to females, or social obstacles imposed on females who might otherwise have undergone the training required. This factor may be the biggest single reason why the proportion of females in any occupation is often low, and why even these females may not receive the same wage rate. In Africa this has been particularly true, a much smaller proportion of girls in general being offered the opportunity of schooling, particularly secondary schooling, and other kinds of training. In Eastern Africa, where African women have only recently entered regular wage employment in any numbers, the problem is further aggravated by the occupation by males of many jobs which in developed countries are now regarded as largely for women. Domestic service in particular is undertaken by males rather than females, and many clerical posts including those of typists are held by men, sometimes, ironically, as the result of 'localization' of posts once held by non-African women.

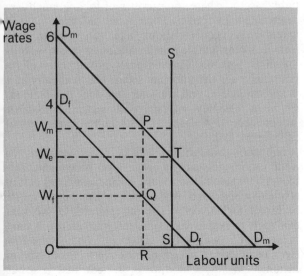

Figure 31.13 *Wage rate differences arising out of productivity differences.*

The above discussion refers only to the position of women *in paid employment*. The exploitation of female labour in the rural sectors of African economies is a major subject in itself, which we cannot treat here.

Job discrimination between racial groups

The economics of racial discrimination in the labour market may be analysed in the same way as discrimination by sex. In South Africa it is the majority of Africans who have been excluded from the better paid jobs held by a white minority of the labour force. Figure 31.12 can be applied to this situation with 'white' labour replacing male labour and 'black' labour replacing female labour, although the amount of black labour, O_fS, will represent a much larger proportion of the total. As in the case of females, blacks are forced to work in inferior jobs, including domestic service, which are oversupplied with labour, while whites gain employment in high-productivity industries, with the assistance of considerable capital per worker, and in the higher grades within industries, to which access is restricted.

Apart from direct discrimination, differences in pay and employment may be affected by the same factors discussed with reference to women. There may be differences in productivity due, for instance, to the poorer health of blacks caused by their lower standard of living. Secondly, there may be differences in costs to employers, due for example to having constantly to train new migrants from the rural sector. In South Africa this factor would generally work in the opposite direction, since white employers are able to spend much less in improving working conditions (including safety in the mines), canteen and social services, and pensions funds, in relation to the 'reserve army' of black labour. Thirdly, black labour is usually less well unionized, this condition being partly the result of political curbs on black union activity in South Africa, as well as the large proportion of short-term migrant labour, the abundant supply of which further reduces the bargaining position of black unionists. Finally, and most important again, there is the restricted access of Africans to training facilities and education, particularly for the highest-paid occupations. Some improvement in the position of Africans in paid employment has occurred in South Africa where, due to expansion of the economy and demand for labour, there has been a shortage of whites for previously reserved occupations, and employers have been forced to train African labour for a wider range of jobs.

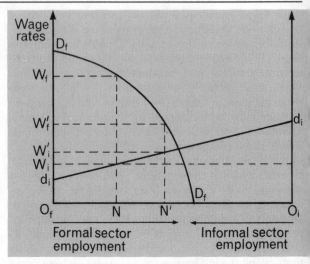

Figure 31.14 *The effects of privileged formal sector employment.*

Wages in the formal and informal sectors

A similar diagram to that above may be used to consider the effects of privileged 'formal sector' employment. In Figure 31.14, D_fD_f, measured from left to right, represents the demand curve for labour (marginal productivity) in the formal sector and d_id_i, measured from right to left, demand for labour in the informal sector. D_fD_f is made to slope down fairly rapidly from left to right, since the demand for labour is likely to be inelastic in the capital-intensive mining sector, in the manufacturing sector where the choice of techniques may be limited, and in the public sector where the number of jobs is much less determined by price. Thus a considerable fall in wages may occur without very large increase in formal sector employment, although some substitution is possible. The marginal productivity of labour curve for the informal sector starts already at a much lower level and continues to slope down steadily in a possibly oversupplied sector. The total labour force, O_fO_i, has to work either in the formal or informal sectors.

Suppose, through the effects of government or trade union pressure, or because of 'benevolent' employers, wages in the formal sector are fixed at the artificially high level W_f. O_fN workers will therefore be hired in this sector, the remaining NO_i workers being left to seek work in the informal sector in paid or self-employment. The latter will obtain the low level of earnings, W_i, and the very wide gap in earnings, W_iW_f, will appear. In contrast a lower formal sector wage such as W_f' would encourage employment and the adoption of more labour-intensive techniques, reduce the pressure on earnings in the informal sector but, most of all, remove the inequality between workers by reducing the earnings gap to the amount $W_i'W_f'$.[8]

The price of labour

We have so far discussed the demand for and supply of labour, and factors affecting: (1) the supply of labour to the formal sector; (2) the supply of effort; (3) the supply of labour in terms of quality; and (4) the supply of labour to different occupations; the last as affected by (i) non-pecuniary advantages and disadvantages, (ii) immobility and the costs of movement and training, (iii) ignorance of job opportunities, (iv) differences in ability, and (v) institutional obstacles and discriminatory practices. Having discussed the factors affecting demand for and supply of labour, we may proceed to consider how the price of labour, the wage rate, and the structure of wages in different occupations are determined.

The most obvious feature of the structure of wages and salaries in Africa is the vast gap between the earnings of the so-called 'educated elite' and the earnings of, say, the unskilled worker or the value of income per head in the country. To give an illustration, a newly graduated schoolteacher in Zambia and in the United Kingdom obtained in 1975 not very different starting salaries, roughly K4,000 and K2,500 per annum respectively: but whereas in the United Kingdom this represented only about the same as the average wage for a male manual worker in manufacturing industry, in Zambia it represented around three times as much. Taking what is perhaps a less fair comparison, teachers' salaries might be

about double the average income in the United Kingdom and in Zambia nearly six times the average income. This gap in earnings is widened if we take into account both non-cash benefits received and taxation. In the United Kingdom welfare services, including such things as schooling, medical services, and child allowances, raise benefits relatively more at the bottom end of the scale, whereas in Zambia subsidized housing or housing loans and medical services, for example, accentuate the advantage of the higher income groups. In addition taxation hits the higher income groups relatively harder in the United Kingdom than in Zambia, making the difference in income after tax relatively smaller in the former.

How can we explain this highly unequal distribution of income? One obvious explanation would be in terms of the marginal productivity theory outlined above. A shortage of one category of manpower implies that its marginal product and therefore its wage will remain high, while, due to the law of diminishing returns, abundance of another category implies a low marginal product and therefore a low wage. This *marginal productivity theory* in its pure form is essentially a supply and demand explanation and assumes a free market for labour. This is true even though it concentrates on elaborating factors operating behind the demand curve, and has often been criticized for neglecting the supply side.

Looking at Figure 31.15(a) we might take this to represent the supply–demand position for unskilled labour. The supply curve has been made highly elastic, since the amount of labour can easily be increased by drawing on the rural sector, where incomes are very low, and since the number of workers in employment is only a small proportion of

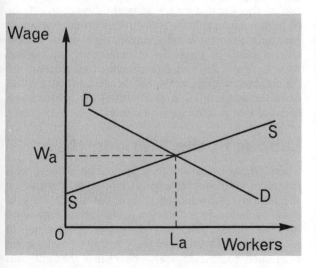
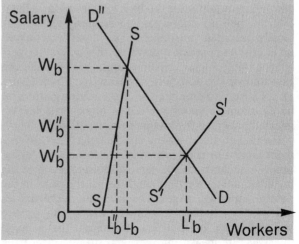

Figure 31.15 *Hypothetical supply and demand positions for skilled and unskilled workers: (a) unskilled workers, (b) skilled workers.*

those in the rural areas. The demand curve has also been made fairly elastic, as it is likely that with very low wage rates employers will not worry much about having 'too much' labour, whereas they will fairly quickly economize on labour if wage rates are raised. Figure 31.15(b) can be taken to represent the supply and demand position for skilled workers taken as a group. The supply curve will be inelastic, supply being determined fairly rigidly by the skilled manpower that the country has been able to train up to this moment of time; and demand will be less elastic, as businesses no doubt require a minimum quota of skilled administrative and technical workers and will not easily be able to economize on them. The resulting disparity in wage levels is illustrated in the diagrams, a low wage W_a resulting, in Figure 31.15(a), for unskilled workers, and a high wage W_b for skilled workers, in Figure 31.15(b).

The foregoing analysis, however convincing, makes the crucial assumption of a free market; that supply of and demand for the various categories of labour operate freely. This is not likely to be the case in reality for a number of reasons. In the first place groups of workers can organize themselves into trade unions, or operate in other ways as a pressure group to raise their wages. It could well be the case that the highly skilled elite can, politically as well as economically, by virtue of their key position, operate as a more effective pressure group compared to the relatively weak unions of unskilled workers. Secondly, the wage structure may be considerably influenced by institutional and historical factors. In the case of ex-colonial territories, existing wage-salary structures tend to inherit the inequality of income distribution which existed when the large proportion of skilled manpower was expatriate and had to be 'induced' by high salaries to serve abroad. Even after independence, so long as expatriates are employed on any important scale the high salaries paid to them tend to 'pull up' those paid to similarly skilled but locally recruited personnel. This is partly to avoid invidious comparisons between the wages of personnel with similar qualifications, but of different race and origin, and partly because there is pressure on local staff to emulate the consumption pattern of its expatriate counterpart. Once higher salaries are granted, downward revision becomes difficult.

Related to this point is the fact that the government is a major employer of labour in Eastern Africa, at any rate, for both the very skilled and much of the unskilled manpower, and tends to 'set the pace' in the determination of wages. The fact that high salaries are paid for skilled manpower within the private sector is not proof that these represent the genuine 'market' rate measuring marginal product, since the private sector is in competition with the public sector for manpower, and must to some extent follow salaries in the latter when the government is a major user of this type of labour.

However even if wages and salaries did measure 'marginal product', this would still not necessarily imply that the wage structure represented a 'fair' distribution of incomes. The marginal productivity theory is simply a statement of the demand for labour which, combined with the supply side, and assuming a free market for such labour, determines its price. With a different supply curve, as for instance $S'S'$ in Figure 31.15(b), the wage or salary would differ. Figure 31.15(b) shows that the wages of skilled manpower would then be W_b', actually lower than W_a, the rate of wages for unskilled workers. The two wage rates are simply those which bring supply and demand into equilibrium.

Moreover we showed in Chapter 8 that if a particular type of labour is in inelastic supply it may earn 'economic rent', that is, more than the minimum for which it would be willing to supply its services. It is likely that the supply of skilled manpower to Eastern African countries is highly inelastic. This was reflected in the original supply curve SS in Figure 31.15(b). This shows that it would be possible to reduce salaries substantially from W_b to W_b'' with only a small reduction in the work-force from L_b to L_b''.

In general we can say that while demand factors and supply factors do affect the 'price' of different kinds of labour it would be unwise to conclude that supply and demand 'determine' the structure of wage and salary earnings in an economy. The market for labour is not a perfect one, as a supply and demand theory requires. As we shall see in the next chapter, institutional factors have a major influence on wages and the distribution of income generally. Secondly, the supply and demand theory is essentially short-run analysis and does not indicate the contributions of labour and capital within the dynamic context of economic growth. Finally, and perhaps most important, it takes as given the ownership of capital and natural resources, and the influence that this carries. As we shall see presently, the Marxian theory questions this assumption and examines the contribution of labour in a more general context.

Labour in the Marxian theory

Marx[9] starts by assuming, following classical theory, that commodities exchange at values determined by the labour time required to produce them. All products exchange in proportion to the labour embodied in their production, and all prices correspond to labour value. This 'labour theory of value', which continued to inspire Marxist socialist thought, was derived in fact from the classical economists such as Ricardo and contrasts with the 'marginal productivity' theory developed by the so-called 'neoclassical' school, economists like Marshall and Pigou, to explain the determination of wages and distribution of income between the various factors of production.

It is important to understand what Marx meant by labour here. He distinguishes between 'abstract labour'—the mere expenditure of human labour—and 'useful labour': the latter indicates that labour is producing a product with use value, a product which has utility. Thus Marx is careful to state that if the thing produced is useless, so is the labour contained in it, and the labour 'does not count' as labour. Hence Marx did not disregard utility, but emphasized costs of production, costs in terms of labour expended. Likewise, although he adopted the labour theory of value, he accepted that the products of nature could yield utility without being due to labour. Things 'could have use value' without having value, this being the case for a good 'whenever its utility to man is not due to labour', as for instance with 'virgin soil or natural meadows'.

From the determination of exchange values of commodities, Marx goes on to assume labour alone produces value. But labour does not receive the full value of what it produces. The wage rate or exchange value of labour as a commodity (i.e. on the market) is also determined by its labour value, that is, by the labour-time required to produce the physical commodities which go to maintain labour. This 'labour value of labour' is the value of the goods necessary to maintain labour's physical fitness: however, since labour is not merely the use of muscle, but of brain and skill as well, subsistence here is defined on the basis of 'a cultural minimum plus the expenses of education and training'.[10] The wage rate is kept at this level through competition in the labour market, particularly a 'reserve army' of unemployed labour, which means in effect a perfectly elastic supply of labour at this wage.

This 'reserve army' differed from the 'disguised unemployed' of present-day developing countries. Whereas earlier 'classical' economists like Malthus held that real wages would be kept down to a subsistence level by population pressure on limited natural resources, by the mid-nineteenth century Marx could observe the existence, off the land, of a growing class of job seekers (the 'industrial proletariat') in disguised or open urban unemployment as the result of technological changes. However just as much as with low average productivity of labour in traditional agriculture, as in the Lewis model, wages were supply-determined.

Labour thus has the special quality of being able to produce more than its own value (subsistence). The difference, profit, or surplus value as Marx called it, is appropriated by the capitalist. This can be visualized,

he says, as the worker spending part of the day producing for himself (the goods to be consumed as wages) and the rest working for the capitalist, the latter receiving more the greater the productivity (i.e. average product) of labour. This surplus value was essentially unearned income or alternatively 'unpaid labour'. While capital might have been used in conjunction with labour to produce the output, capital was merely 'stored' labour, having been produced in the first place by labour. The 'rate of exploitation' of labour was measured by the ratio, s/v, of surplus value (net profit, interest, and rent) to variable capital (the wage-bill). Roughly speaking, this is the ratio of profits to wages in the economy.

We can now see the difference between the Marxian theory and the neoclassical marginal productivity theory outlined above. The neoclassical theory is cast in terms of *three* basic factors of production: land, labour, and capital.[11] But what is capital? Since it has itself to be produced in the first place, it can simply be looked at as stored labour power. This is in contrast with much of the neoclassical analysis which takes the stock of capital as being determined independently of the labour supply.

This storage of labour implies the accumulation of capital, of course, and this is made possible by saving. But in Marxian analysis this saving must come out of surplus value, which is in turn obtained by exploiting labour: by not paying labour the full value of its product. Thus savers or accumulators are those who are in the position of owning capital: bringing us to the question of ownership of the means of production and control over the production process, again something which the neoclassical theory does not explore.

The rate of exploitation in the economy as a whole would perhaps be indicated today by the share of wages in the overall national income, which is what Marx was concerned with, and what the neoclassical theory does not adequately explain. On the other hand, Marx was *not* concerned with *relative* wage rates in different occupations, on which neoclassical theory dwells, and for this reason was not concerned with distinguishing different *kinds* of labour. He assumed labour could, with suitable training, pass easily from one kind of labour to another and could be reduced to a common yardstick. Thus he says that 'skilled labour counts only as simple labour intensified, or rather, a multiplied simple labour, a given quantity of skill being equal to a greater quantity of simple labour'. 'Labour' was thus the aggregate of different kinds of labour and could be defined as 'the means of creating wealth'.

As well as assuming the three 'factors of production', neoclassical theory in effect assumes classes in society already exist—owners of land, and labourers, those who exist by selling their labour power—or are the consequence rather than the cause of income distribution.

To Marx, income distribution was the result of the class structure, the development of which was to be explained. Exploitation of surplus value was *based* on a division between owners of wealth, the concentration of property in the hands of a few (originally under feudalism the land-owning class and later, under capitalism, the small capital-owning class) and a proletariat or working class forced to live by selling their labour power on the market. The class structure is thus the basis of his analysis.

Marx wrote particularly about industrial societies where, in any case, this division between capitalists and labour was most clearly defined and developed. In agricultural societies the ownership of natural resources (land) may be more important than the ownership of a stock of man-made capital. Thus in many developing countries we have elements of feudalism, with the problem of landlords and landowners, rather than capitalists: Ethiopia was in this position until quite recently. Concentration in the ownership of one factor can lead on to concentration in the ownership of the other, however. Thus Marxian theory is relevant to some of the major issues in Africa today, that of class formation, specifically, and, within agriculture, rural stratification, which we discussed in Chapter 10.

There are a number of assumptions in Marx which do not stand up to modern scrutiny: for instance, the payment of a subsistence or minimum wage for labour. Real wages in the capitalist world have been increasing over time and have reached extremely high levels compared to those of Marx's day. Marx did not anticipate the development of effective trade unions. This could, however, be seen as the working class, through bargaining, securing a rather larger proportion of value, simply reducing the rate of exploitation.

Marx's theory of competition in the labour market and an elastic supply of labour at a subsistence wage has obvious relevance to the situation of less developed countries today, with the supply of *foreign-owned* capital often determining the employment opportunities open to labour, accentuating the division between capital and labour. The relation between large multinational companies and less developed countries was examined in Chapter 17.

Marx's analysis has been developed and expanded by modern Marxist economists such as Paul Baran and Paul Sweezy,[13] who have considered the way in which 'surplus value' is created under monopoly capitalism to be crucial to an understanding of the economic system.

Questions on Chapter 31

1. Distinguish between the 'substitution effect' and the 'output effect' on the numbers employed by a firm following a change in the wage rate.
2. Define the 'marginal revenue product' and 'marginal factor cost' of a factor of production. Show how these are derived and how they might determine the equilibrium number of workers employed by a firm.
3. Show how you would derive the total demand curve for a factor in a particular industry.
4. Discuss the factors affecting the elasticity of demand for a factor of production.
5. Discuss the possible effects of a fall in the wages of bricklayers on the demand for carpenters.
6. Outline Lewis's model of economic development with unlimited supplies of labour. Discuss its usefulness and its limitations.
7. Distinguish between the 'income' and 'substitution' effects of a change in the wage rate on the supply of effort. Show how these could *in theory* combine to produce a 'backward-sloping' supply curve for labour.
8. What is meant by the 'economy of high wages'? Discuss reasons why it may exist in parts of Africa.
9. Discuss the 'principle of equal net advantage' and the distribution of non-cash advantages and disadvantages in different occupations.
10. Discuss the role of 'Employment Exchanges' in developed economies. Why are they likely to be less effective in less developed countries?
11. How would you account for differences in the rates of pay earned by workers in different occupations?
12. Why do professional workers earn much more than manual labourers in Eastern Africa? Why can 'uneducated' sportsmen and popular singers earn much more than professional people like lawyers in developed countries?
13. Show how job market discrimination may affect the wages of underprivileged and repressed groups, and how its abolition may actually increase national income.
14. Discuss the ways in which African female labour is exploited in the rural economy.
15. Use a diagram to show the effects on employment and wage differentials of maintaining an artificially high formal sector wage rate.
16. Compare the way in which the level of wages is said to be determined in the neoclassical marginal productivity theory and in Marx's theory.
17. Discuss the relevance of Marx's labour theory of value as an explanation of the distribution of national income between labour and property-owners in less developed countries today.

Notes

[1] Thus employing nine workers (one more) increases costs by £30 but revenue by only £12, while employing six workers instead of seven decreases revenue by £45 and costs by only £30.

[2] The explanation is that equality of MRP and MFC is a necessary but not sufficient condition for 'equilibrium'; sufficiency requires also that MRP is decreasing faster than MFC.

[3] This paragraph talks in terms of the 'substitution effect' only. Strictly speaking the 'output effect' referred to above should also be taken into account.

[4] W. A. Lewis, 'Economic development with unlimited supplies of labour', *Manchester School*, May 1954.

[5] It is now considered dubious whether this inducement to rural labour is necessary, in view of the excessive flow of migrants to the urban areas in Africa and elsewhere in less developed economies.

[6] C. W. Guillebaud, *An Economic Survey of the Sisal Industry of Tanganyika*, revised edition, Nisbet, 1958, p. 64.

[7] J. B. Knight, 'Wages and Zambia's Economic Development' in Charles Elliot (ed.), *Constraints on the Economic Development of Zambia*, OUP, Nairobi, 1971.

[8] Other things remaining the same, lower formal sector wages would increase the earnings of 'capitalists'. Inequality as between wage earners and capitalists could be handled by taxation of the latter's increased earnings.

[9] Karl Marx (1813–83), German socialist, economist, and sociologist, published his *Critique of Political Economy* in 1859 and the first volume of his famous work, *Capital*, in 1867.

[10] See R. Freedman (ed.), *Marx on Economics*, Penguin Books, 1962, p. 43.

[11] A fourth factor, 'entrepreneurship' is also sometimes distinguished.

[12] However, whereas Marx was concerned with the analysis of the *origin* of the nineteenth-century class structure, earlier classical economists from Smith onwards, as well as the later neoclassical economists, concentrated on growth and distribution of factor incomes. Rapid capital accumulation depended on a thrifty capitalist class, as illustrated in the Lewis model; while one of the effects of this capital accumulation would be an improvement in wages as the marginal productivity of labour increased.

[13] Paul A. Baran, *The Political Economy of Growth*, New York, 1957, and Paul M. Sweezy, *The Theory of Capitalist Development*, Dobson, London, 1946, and Baran and Sweezy, *Monopoly Capitalism*, New York, 1966.

32 Wage Bargaining and Incomes Policy in Eastern Africa

The analysis of earnings differentials in Eastern Africa in the previous chapter was largely in terms of supply and demand factors. In particular the highly elastic supply of unskilled labour from the rural areas would keep the wages of unskilled labour down, while the shortage of various specific skills would raise those of skilled workers and create a relatively wide differential in wages between skilled and unskilled workers. Over time, of course, we should expect the increasing availability of skills and educated manpower to bring down the differentials earned in excess of the unskilled rate.

Institutional intervention in the labour market

While these forces of supply and demand determine the framework of bargaining over wages, institutional factors are of fundamental importance in wage determination in Eastern Africa as elsewhere. There are three main forms of institutional interference in the labour market:

(1) government intervention to fix wage rates for specific categories of labour, usually known as *minimum wage legislation*, because minimum rates of pay are legally imposed on employers;

(2) intervention by employers, usually large firms; or governments as employers who, by offering wages above the ruling rates, act as 'wage leaders' for other firms in the same industry and for firms generally employing workers with similar occupational skills;

(3) trade unions of workers who by direct action or pressure on the government (to act for them) effect an increase in wage rates or other improvements in working conditions which have to be borne by employers.

Minimum wage legislation

Historically minimum wage rates for unorganized workers in the industrial or industrializing countries were imposed on employers who might be the largest buyers of labour in mining villages or textile towns; they were designed also to protect the so-called 'sweated labour' of females, juveniles, and immigrant workers in overcrowded 'workshop' industries like garment-making where unions were particularly weak and where wages were depressed by an excess supply of labour.

During the early colonial period in Eastern Africa, right up to 1945, governments showed little interest in urban and formal sector wage levels. With a low level of industrial development there were relatively few formal sector jobs available, and usually an excess supply of unskilled labour which might be recruited. The emphasis was on encouraging the establishment of additional enterprises through the bait of 'cheap labour'. Wage rates in the formal sector and in domestic service, in which many were employed, were extremely low. After the war conditions in the colonies were examined a little more closely and minimum wage regulations were enacted, first for the main towns like Nairobi, Mombasa, and Kisumu in Kenya (in 1946) or Kampala and Jinja in Uganda (in 1949).

Originally the minimum wage level aimed to provide for the simplest needs of a single male worker who was expected to leave any family in the rural area and eventually return there after a period of work. However it was clear by the early 1950s that the African urban labour force was not composed entirely of short-term migrant workers, but was becoming increasingly stabilized as families were brought to the towns. The Carpenter Report on African wages in Kenya therefore proposed in 1954 a 'Family' minimum wage for workers who had resided in urban areas for at least three years in continuous employment. By the mid-1960s most Eastern African countries had moved to a family minimum wage for adult males in the main towns and lower minimum wage rates for rural areas and smaller towns where the cost of living was lower. In addition, Wages Councils or Wage Advisory Boards were set up for specific occupations other than general unskilled labourers, and these councils regulated wages and working conditions in such occupations as retailing, catering, or farm work (where trade unions tend to be more difficult to organize) in consultation with the trade unions and employers' associations involved. By 1968 minimum wage rates for general unskilled workers in Eastern Africa's capital cities ranged from some £60 a year in Blantyre, £90 a year in Dar es Salaam and Kampala, and £105 in Nairobi, to £160 in Lusaka. Compared to average cash earnings in formal sector agriculture and forestry employment (jobs for which usually lower rural minimum wage rates were paid) these urban minimum rates ranged from around 110 or 120 per cent in the first three countries, to about 150 per cent in Nairobi and Lusaka.

Although minimum wage rates were supposed to apply to all employers, in practice, and this is still true today, only large-scale employers adhered close-ly to them. Thus, minimum wage rates have acted as a 'floor' for formal sector workers only: labour employed by urban informal sector employers and by smallholders in the rural areas is hired at rates more directly reflecting market forces.

Let us see how far economic theory can help us to predict the result of legislation passed to impose a minimum wage in an industry. The effects will de-pend first on whether the industry is competitive or monopolistic. In the competitive situation, imposing a minimum wage above the current market rate would increase variable costs of all firms in the industry, shifting the typical cost curve upwards and also shifting the supply curve for the industry, as in Figure 32.1. In the initial situation, with supply equal to demand, all firms will be earning normal profits: an increase in costs will therefore mean that normal profits are no longer earned and total supply will be cut back as a result of some firms leaving the in-dustry. Given the demand position, the reduction in supply will raise the price of the commodity, this process continuing till price has gone up sufficiently to restore normal profits for firms remaining in the industry, despite increased wage costs.

Employment in the industry will be reduced, by the exodus of firms, in some proportion to the re-duction in output. From the analysis of Figure 32.1 it is obvious that the decrease in employment will be determined by two factors, namely, (1) the amount of the vertical shift in the cost curve, *which will depend on the relative importance of labour costs in total costs*, and (2) *the elasticity of demand*, which de-termines how far output has to be reduced in order to raise price to cover increased costs. The elasticity of demand determines the ease with which the in-creased costs can be 'passed on' to the consumer.

We can introduce monopoly either by considering a large firm which has a 'monopoly' in the sale of its product *or* in the buying of labour (that is, in the factor market, as opposed to the product market) *or* both. We have already described a person who is the sole seller of a commodity as a monopolist: it is common to describe a person who is the sole *buyer* of a commodity as a *monopsonist*, meaning a single -buyer. Just as the monopolist has some freedom in fixing the price of the commodity he sells, so the monopsonist will have some freedom in fixing the price of the commodity he buys. In this case the commodity is labour. Thus the supply curve in Figure 32.2 labelled AFC indicates the wage rate that must be paid by the firm to attract different amounts of labour. To obtain more, it has to pay a higher wage rate, and, conversely, by employing fewer workers, the firm can reduce the wage rate. Assuming each worker is paid the same rate, the wage is the cost per unit of labour used or the *average factor cost*. Since in this case the average is increasing, the marginal factor cost curve will lie above it, as in Figure 32.2.

Let us assume to begin with that the employer is a monopsonist in the labour market but a perfect competitor in the market for his product. He might for instance, be selling his product on the world market in competition with producers from other countries. To find how many workers he will employ we can superimpose marginal and average revenue product curves, as in Figure 32.3. As we found in

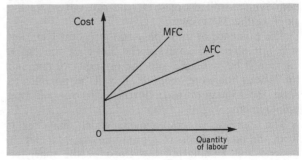

Figure 32.2   *The supply of labour to a monopsonist.*

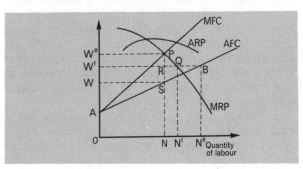

Figure 32.3   *The supply of labour to a monopsonist.*

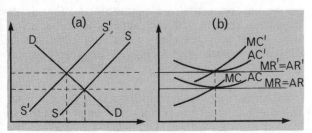

Figure 32.1   *The effect of a minimum wage in a com-petitive situation: (a) market demand and supply, (b) the firm's costs and revenue.*

Chapter 31, the number employed is given by the intersection of the MRP and MFC curves at P, giving ON workers. The wage is read off from the AFC curve to be OW, that being the wage needed to attract ON workers.

Suppose now a minimum wage of OW ' is imposed: the government in effect forbids the employment of labour below this wage rate. The firm cannot now pay less than OW ' but can get up to ON'' workers at this wage. In other words the part AB of the supply curve AFC is now irrelevant and replaced by the completely elastic segment W'B: after point B it resumes its upward slope. Over the segment W'B, average and marginal factor cost are each equal to OW'. Equilibrium is now given by the intersection Q, and ON' workers would be employed. The wage rate has gone up, *and yet employment has actually increased, from ON to ON'*. How can we explain this?

The answer is simply that prior to the minimum wage the monopsonist could reduce the wage rate by offering less employment: the minimum wage prevents this and presents him with a completely elastic supply curve at this wage. If the new *marginal* factor cost (RN) is lower than it was previously (PN) *at the original level of employment ON* and the marginal revenue product is unchanged, employment must increase. The fact that the wage has increased is not relevant, for it is the marginal factor cost that determines employment. Clearly the wage rate could be increased, without any actual decrease in employment, up to the level of OW''; beyond that however employment will decrease at the rate given by the slope of the MRP curve.

The existence of monopoly in the product market will not alter the analysis: the slope of the MRP curve will be increased and the elasticity of demand for labour therefore reduced. It will be possible to raise the minimum wage further without affecting employment.

The increase in employment which may result from the introduction of a minimum wage therefore depends on eliminating the slope of the marginal wage cost curve, that is, on eliminating the monopsony element. *How far the wage can be raised without causing some reduction in the numbers employed depends first on the elasticity of supply of labour* (determining the slope of AFC and MFC curves) *and secondly on the elasticity of demand for labour* (given by the slope of the MRP curve). The factors which in turn determine the elasticity of demand for labour were given in detail in Chapter 31.

In tropical Africa it is relatively common for a small number of large firms to predominate in the labour market in any given region, and therefore to possess some degree of monopsony power. On the other hand, even large employers generally face a comparatively elastic supply of labour drawn from the agricultural sector at a wage determined by the level of income in that sector. This is the main factor operating against effective minimum wage legislation in tropical Africa: urban wages will be primarily determined by the level of productivity and real income in agriculture so long as the largest proportion of the population is employed in this sector.

'Wage leadership' by employers

Quite apart from official regulation or trade union pressure, so-called 'benevolent' employers may themselves raise wages. They may do this either because they consider it will pay them to do so in the long run (the 'economy of high wages') or because of the fear of political pressure or the desire to avoid possible political problems. Thus it may be more profitable for firms to have a stable, well-fed, and contented labour force capable of higher labour productivity. In particular, the relatively high costs of housing and training workers will encourage measures to reduce labour turnover (measured by the length of stay on a job). Employers faced with a shortage of available or potential skilled labour may, by raising the wage paid, 'cream off' the best labour from other employers. In addition, payment of higher wages may secure the loyalty of employees at times of industrial disputes or periods of competition for skilled labour.

In developing countries expatriate companies in particular may fear the threat of nationalization or any other 'punitive' government measure such as increased taxation, removal of tariff protection, or restraints on the repatriation of profits; and thus prefer to pay good wages and earn reputations for being good employers rather than attract unwanted attention as a result of disputes or strikes involving themselves and their employees.

Whether the motive is company profitability or political advantage (also indirectly affecting profitability), the incentive to pursue a 'benevolent' policy will be greatest where wage costs are a small proportion of total costs. We shall see later that this has been important in the Zambian copper industry, for example. A special case of an apparently benevolent policy has been where expatriate and other large businesses appoint African graduates and other members of the educated elite to executive positions, in part as a means of heading off possible political pressures to nationalize or part-nationalize their concerns.

In Africa wage leadership has usually come from two sources: first, from public sector employers (parastatals) together with central and local governments *as employers* and, secondly, from large-scale multinational firms in manufacturing and other even less labour-intensive industries. In Uganda, for example, the central government acted as a wage leader or pace-setter during the 1950s when the urban minimum wage remained well below the supply price of labour from a prosperous peasant farming sector. In effect the government's minimum rates for unskilled labour became the effective urban minimum, followed closely by larger private employers who required similar grades of labour. Since there were also recognized differentials between the unskilled wage rate and other levels of skill, also largely set by government rates of pay, other wage rates also moved in line with minimum rates. In Kenya among the foremost private pace-setters were the multinational petroleum, tobacco, and other manufacturing firms. The oil companies were among the first private employers to recruit African university graduates and other educated workers in close competition with public sector employers.

Collective bargaining: the scope for trade unions to raise wages

Much of our analysis in respect of government legislation for minimum wages applies to the situation where workers attempt to raise their own wages directly, by negotiating through a trade union. Trade unions lack the strong weapon of the law, but can threaten a strike, in which all labour to the employer is withheld, or a 'go-slow', in which part of it is withheld, in each case imposing economic loss on the employer. An important difference in the analysis arises out of the fact that whereas minimum wages legislation leaves employers free to choose how much labour they wish to employ, a trade union can try to persuade employers to grant higher wages *without* at the same time cutting the numbers employed, by threatening to strike and thus to withhold *all* labour if this is not done.

Once labour has been 'unionized', straightforward supply and demand analysis of the labour market is not appropriate. Workers no longer 'sell' their labour as a result of individual bargains with employers but negotiate *collectively* through a trade union for a common wage rate to apply to all workers of a given grade, a process known as 'collective bargaining'. Moreover, on the demand side, when there is more than a single employer, employers tend to respond by forming an employers' association with a common wage policy, this association acting as a single 'buyer' of labour. We then have in the market a single seller of labour facing a single buyer, a situation which may be described as two-sided or 'bilateral monopoly'.

If we call an agreed wage rate a 'solution' or 'equilibrium position', can we predict this solution in a situation of bilateral monopoly in the same way as we predicted the outcome in situations of competition or monopsony? Such an equilibrium wage rate, which 'shows no tendency to change', is only possible if both parties are at least temporarily satisfied with it. To predict the outcome in any situation it would be necessary therefore to predict the outcome of a bargaining process leading up to the achievement of a mutually acceptable 'bargain'. We can say something about the way in which this process will be conducted, even if it is not possible to be precise.

We can, for example, specify the theoretical limits to the bargaining range within which the outcome will fall, before looking at the actual bargaining *process* which determines precisely where, within the range, the final outcome will be. Raising the wage rate without a corresponding fall in numbers employed increases the employer's wage-bill at the expense of profits. This can in theory be done up to the point where the increased wage-bill absorbs all except 'normal' profits. Since beyond this point the firm would be forced out of business, and no employment would be offered at all, this imposes an upper limit. The extent to which monopoly profits can be 'squeezed' in this way depends, of course, on the elasticity of demand for the employer's product. We saw above that in a competitive situation also, the scope for raising wages depends on the elasticity of demand in the product market. Thus whether the product market is monopolized or competitive *the elasticity of demand for the product will have an important effect on the ability of the union to raise the wage.*

The lower limit of the bargaining range is where the union is completely ineffective, which will be either (1) the competitive wage rate which exists when many buyers of labour are competing, or (2) the monopsony wage if there is a single buyer. In case (2), that of monopsony, how far apart the upper and lower limits will be depends on the elasticity of demand for the product of the industry, which measures the degree of monopoly power in the product market, and on the elasticity of supply of labour, which measures the degree of monopsonistic power in the factor market. These limits are similar to those in the analysis of minimum wages above.

The exact position within this range, however, will be a matter of bargaining between the two parties concerned, between the employers and the union. This will depend on the relative bargaining *strengths* of the union and employers, that is to say, the objective factors determining their position, and also their relative bargaining *skills*, their cleverness in making use of their respective advantages. Objective factors consist of all things which affect the ability of one party to inflict economic damage on the other, and the ability of each to withstand such losses. For example, if a trade union is well endowed with financial reserves it can offer to pay members 'strike pay' during a prolonged strike, without having to give up earlier on and to accept a poor offer from employers. Although a firm which enjoys lucrative monopoly profits offers a better 'target' for unions, the holding of a strong monopoly position also improves the ability of the employer to withstand the effects of a strike. This is so because a monopolist firm, whether in the domestic or export market, may be able to hold up supplies without permanently losing its market, whereas in a more competitive situation a competitor may move in to 'capture' the consumer market, which will be regained only with great difficulty, if at all, after consumers have become used to an alternative product.

Quite apart from the actual bargaining advantages held by each side, however, one party may achieve a more favourable outcome at the expense of the other by skilful use of its own advantages, or by overcoming a disadvantageous position. By a show of determination, for example, a union may be able to give the impression that it is able and willing to support a long and costly strike, and thus persuade employers to grant concessions. Or in their turn employers may be able to 'bluff' the trade union into thinking that any sizeable increase in wages will, say, severely reduce the firms' ability to compete effectively in overseas markets and thus cause a curtailment of output and employment, even if this is not in fact the case. Thus bargaining strength and bargaining skill certainly affect the immediate outcome of wage negotiations. What is less clear is how far these are effective in determining the long-run situation in the industry independently of the supply and demand position. However let us examine in more detail the factors which affect the scope for bargaining by trade unions in the situations in which they currently find themselves in tropical Africa, Eastern Africa in particular.

Trade unions and bargaining in Africa

Again we can consider separately determinants of the bargaining range as well as of the relative bargaining strengths affecting the final outcome within the range. Considering first elasticity of supply, we have already mentioned that the highly elastic supply of labour drawn from the agricultural sector generally provides the greatest obstacle to the raising of wages, either through minimum wage legislation or by union pressure. This is perhaps the fundamental weakness in the position of African trade unions. It is of course true that not all parts of Eastern Africa suffer equally from

labour surplus in the agricultural sector, and there are areas in which the problem is one of labour shortage. Nevertheless the high degree of mobility of labour in Africa generally ensures an ample supply of labour to the urban areas at comparatively low wage rates.

In their efforts to monopolize the labour supply, trade unions in Africa are often frustrated by the special characteristics of employment and unemployment in underdeveloped countries. We shall examine these in more detail in the next chapter; at this stage we shall merely emphasize the likelihood of an excess supply of workers actively seeking employment in urban areas. This 'pool' of unemployed labour makes enforcement of minimum wages or negotiated terms of service difficult for trade unions.

We stated in Chapter 23 that a large proportion of manufacturing firms in East Africa are small-scale concerns. These will not be in a monopsonistic position, and therefore able to influence the price of labour. Nevertheless employment tends to be concentrated to a great extent with the small number of large-scale mining, manufacturing, and transport enterprises which exist, with large plantations and farms, and with government and parastatal organizations. Thus the employment market in Eastern Africa is still likely to have considerable monopsonistic elements.

The elasticity of demand for labour probably varies widely from sector to sector. In the distributive trades which are for the most part highly competitive, and where the level of profits tends to be low, demand for labour will probably be elastic. Even where profits are higher in parts of the manufacturing sector, many of the firms are expatriate concerns, for which low wage costs may have been an important inducement for setting up in Eastern Africa at all. With the exception of sisal, many export commodities are sold in competitive world markets, the Eastern African supply forming only a small part of the total. However there are a great many large employers supplying the Eastern African market who may have a degree of monopoly power, always threatened, of course, by the possibility of imports.

Having made these observations regarding the *scope* for trade union activity to raise wages, we can consider factors affecting the bargaining strength and skill of unions in exploiting this scope. Unfortunately, although Eastern African trade unions have not been entirely without good leaders, they have suffered from two main weaknesses: inadequate finance and bad organization.

Factors contributing to the financial weakness of unions and therefore to the difficulty in sustaining lengthy strikes have been:
(1) the lack of strike funds;
(2) the absence of state unemployment benefits to

support dismissed workers, or other forms of 'Welfare State' transfers to relieve poverty;[1]

(3) the reluctance of workers to forgo wages in the short run in order to negotiate higher wage rates to be paid later, this being due to low incomes, which prevent their making any savings to cover such emergencies, and to high rates of time preference;

(4) the reluctance of workers to pay their union dues, due partly to short-sightedness and apathy, and partly to the fact that in some cases a large proportion may be temporary 'migrant' workers who do not expect to be in employment long enough to benefit from union action which they find costly in the short run.

This financial weakness has been reduced somewhat where the 'check-off system' of paying union dues has been adopted. This is a system whereby employers may, with the consent of the employee concerned, regularly deduct union dues from his salary and transfer them to the union. Since the early 1960s it has become quite widespread in Eastern Africa, and obligatory in Tanzania.

Quite apart from the financial handicap, however, union effectiveness has been considerably reduced by weaknesses in organization and leadership.

(1) There has been a scarcity of able trade union personnel, largely due to the fact that the bulk of African urban labour is unskilled, with a minority who have received even a minimum education. The most able leaders have often been drained away into personnel management or other salaried jobs. Poor leadership is evidenced by the incoherent way in which claims are often presented, and by the quite unrealistic wage increases that are commonly demanded. Union accounts have not always been well kept, and cases of misuse have sometimes reduced the confidence of the ordinary 'rank and file' members in union officials and in the union.

(2) Moreover, the high degree of illiteracy among rank and file means a less efficient check on the activities of officials and increases the danger of misappropriation of funds. Illiteracy is also responsible for the common failure to understand the functions of a trade union, leading to apathy and lack of support for union affairs: a common failing among members of cooperatives also, as we have already noted in Chapter 11.

(3) The existence of such apathy is evidenced, for example, by the low proportion of paid-up to total membership, and by the fact that support tends to increase in periods of intense activity by the unions, and to fall off at other times. The full extent of support for the union is thus unclear.

(4) The high proportion of 'migrants' within the work-force results in a constantly changing composition, making organization particularly difficult. This is so especially because such migrants lack a permanent commitment to the industry and therefore to the union. This problem will be less important as the work-force becomes more stable and permanent.

(5) Tribal, racial, and national differences, including differences of language, have seriously aggravated problems of organization, and caused a general lack of cohesiveness. In Uganda, for example, many union officials in the larger unions were until the early 1970s Kenyans.

The development and structure of trade unions in Eastern Africa

Despite these handicaps, trade union development in Eastern Africa was quite impressive after independence and in the few years just prior to this. Previously, in the colonial period, development was not especially encouraged by the authorities, and was quite slow, as indicated in Table 32.1 for Kenya, Tanganyika, and Uganda. In 1954, for example, all registered trade unions in Tanganyika and Uganda together had a membership of only around one thousand. The table shows clearly that early trade union development in East Africa centred upon

Table 32.1 Development of unions in East Africa 1952–62

	1952	1954	1956	1958	1960	1962
Estimated paid-up membership (thousands)						
Kenya	28	33*	17	30	70	187
Tanganyika	1	$\frac{1}{2}$	12	47	95	177
Uganda	$\frac{1}{2}$	$\frac{1}{2}$	$2\frac{1}{2}$	7	21	90
No. of registered trade unions						
Kenya	13	15	21	33	42	52
Tanganyika	3	7	26	26	26	12
Uganda	3	4	10	16	24	40

SOURCE: Annual Labour Department Reports

Kenya, where unions in 1954 had a book membership of 33,000. Obviously historical, social, and political factors, such as the attitude of government, the emergence of outstanding labour leaders, and the inclination of local workers to unionize, have been important in bringing this about. However the stronger and more diversified industrial and commercial sector in the Kenyan economy at the time, strengthened by its position as the commercial and industrial centre for East Africa as a whole, was a fundamental factor.

Table 32.1 shows, however, the rapid development of unions in all three countries in the period immediately leading up to independence, between 1958 and 1962. Union membership in Tanganyika was in a short time, by 1960, even larger than in Kenya, although this was temporary. The high figure of 177,000 members for 1962 was due especially to 108,000 belonging to the Plantation Workers' Union. Plantation labour is generally easier to organize because in such a labour-intensive industry large numbers of workers are concentrated, doing similar work, in a single 'firm' (large sisal or tea estates, for example) and more broadly, in the industry. In some small-scale industries, union activity is handicapped by the difficulty of dealing with a large number of scattered employers who are not easily identified and brought to the bargaining table.

Table 32.2 gives more detailed information on the development of trade unions in Kenya. The last two rows of the table confirm some of the observations made above, such as the low level of activity during the colonial period. Thus in 1956 the total union membership of 17,500 was only 2.9 per cent of the number of reported employees. From 1956 to 1962, however, the number of union members increased ten-fold, and the percentage of reported employees in unions from 3 per cent to 32 per cent. It should be noticed that the reduction in union membership which is observable between 1966 and 1971 is due largely to the effect of the fall in numbers given for the Domestic and Hotel Workers' Union from 134,000 to 17,000, and does not reflect a general trend in trade union growth. The rapid growth of unions in Tanganyika in the same pre-independence period is reflected in the fact that a large 45 per cent of reported formal sector employees were in unions in 1962, compared to the 32 per cent mentioned above for Kenya.

While these figures do indicate considerable trade union development, they are, of course, well short of the proportion unionized in industrial countries, and would be smaller if employees in the *informal* urban *and* rural sectors were taken into account. Thus in Kenya, for example, in 1971 there were a further estimated 476,000 regular or casual wage employees on small farms and settlement schemes outside the scope of unionization.

Before examining Eastern African trade unions more closely, we should make a distinction between the following types of union.

(1) The most simple form of union is the *company union* which embraces the employees of only one firm with one or two establishments. These used to be a feature of the trade union movement in Uganda, for instance, with separate unions for major establishments in tobacco, textiles, cement, electricity, breweries, and so on. Thus in 1961 the Transport and General Workers' Union enjoyed a membership of only 2,600, compared with a national membership of 40,000. The movement in Uganda has remained highly fragmented in contrast with that in Kenya and, especially, in Tanzania. The importance of company unions is to some extent inevitable where the country's industrial development remains embryonic, with each industry comprising only a few establishments and the number of formal sector employees in manufacturing still relatively small.

(2) A second type is the *craft union*, which covers, or attempts to cover, all workers with particular skills, irrespective of the specific company or industry in which they are employed. An example would be the Kenya Electrical Trades Workers' Union, embracing electricians employed in various industries throughout the economy. In some cases, printers for example, where the particular skills are largely employed in one industry, a craft union would in effect be an industrial union, but the two do not necessarily coincide.

A special case of the craft union is the *professional union*, where the skills involved might be deemed as being at a higher level than a simple craft or 'trade'. Examples are 'associations' of medical practitioners (doctors), airline pilots, or schoolteachers. It might be noted here that an association of 'professional civil servants' ought perhaps to be considered not as a professional or craft union but as an industrial union, since the specific feature of these employees is that they are employed in one industry, the public service: whereas the skills involved are either general administrative ones, applicable outside the public sector as well as inside, or diverse, such as when economists, lawyers, or engineers are employed in the civil service. In another sense public sector unions such as those of teachers or clerical civil servants are also company unions, in that they negotiate with a single employer, the government, or a local authority.

(3) As implied above, an *industrial union* caters for the majority of employees within one industry, irrespective of their occupation. Examples in Kenya include the Railway African Union, the Kenyan Motor Engineering and Allied Workers' Union, and the

Kenya Union of Commercial Food and Allied Workers' Union.

(4) A more advanced development is a *general trade union* covering workers who may work in different establishments, occupations, and industries. We describe this as a more advanced development because here the union is taking responsibility for negotiating on behalf of a heterogeneous group of workers over a range of different employing groups, and because this may be said to represent a move towards a general association of *labour* for negotiation with employers or capitalists as a whole. Membership of such unions, such as the Transport and General Workers' Union in Britain, may exceed one million. Examples in Eastern Africa include the National Union of Commercial and Industrial Workers in Zambia, which had 30,000 members in 1971, and the old Tanganyika Commercial and Industrial Workers' Union, which had 22,350 members in 1962.

Generally speaking, the degree of consolidation within the Eastern African trade union movements has been limited, and they remain rather fragmented. Thus in Kenya there were in 1971, excluding the Central Organization of Trade Unions, 34 unions, averaging fewer than 8,000 voting members and having, apart from the four largest unions (Teachers, Civil Servants, Plantation Workers, and Commercial Food and Allied Workers), 30 unions averaging a membership of some 4,600.

The most consolidated trade union movement in Eastern Africa is that in Tanzania. This may be put down in part to economic factors in a country that lacked much large-scale industry (diamond-mining was the exception) at the time of Independence and where in 1962 the 108,000 membership of the Tanganyika Plantation Workers' Union accounted for 60 per cent of the total of 177,000. Political factors have probably been more important, however. In the first place, the independence movement in Tanzania was more unified under the political party, TANU, than most, while workers and unions were closely associated with it. Secondly, the socialist government has since Independence encouraged the growth of a national union of workers who might respond, with peasants, to general exhortations for sacrifice and hard work for the purpose of nation-building.

Thus in Tanzania the National Union of Tanganyika Workers, NUTA, represents a general trade union as well as a *central organization* for the separate unions, as in the case of COTU, the Central Organization of Trade Unions of Kenya, the membership of which comprised, in 1971, 28 individual unions. Thus members would, in Tanzania, pay their dues to NUTA, while in Kenya these would

be paid to the appropriate union, which could in principle decide whether or not to affiliate itself to the central organization. A similar central organization of unions to COTU exists in Britain, the Trades Union Congress (TUC). Like COTU, the TUC may raise general issues affecting labour with the government of the day, including general economic policy as it affects employment and wages, while leaving most of the hard wage bargaining to the individual unions. NUTA may be said to combine the role of a comprehensive general union and a central organization representing labour as a whole.

The last columns in Table 32.2 attempt to classify Kenyan unions into the various categories, company, craft, industrial, and general. Where two or more asterisks occur, it is implied that the union shows characteristics of more than one category. Thus the Kenya Shoe and Leather Workers' Union represents a particular craft, covers the formal sector of the shoe industry, but is dominated by employees of one firm, the Bata Shoe Company. The difficulty of making a strict classification is thus obvious.

The most noticeable feature of union structure in Kenya is the large number of separate unions, reflecting the more diversified economy and the greater relative importance of private sector employment but also, perhaps, a more favourable attitude towards 'free' collective bargaining as a means of achieving wage settlements: this is in contrast with the objective of consolidation mentioned above in Tanzania, where in addition there has been a much stronger incomes policy, with wage claims considered and often decided at the national level. A special feature of collective bargaining and the trade union movement in Kenya is the number of employers' associations. These are referred to officially as employers' trade unions and indicate the existence of bilateral monopoly in the separate sub-markets of the labour market. Thus while the first employees' trade union to be registered in Kenya was the Printing and Kindred Trades Workers' Union of Kenya in 1946, one of the first two employers' trade unions to be registered in 1950 was the Federation of Master Printers of East Africa. The full list of employers' trade unions as at December 1971 is given in Table 32.3. These will be seen in many cases to be the counterpart of an employees' trade union. The Federation of Kenya Employers is the equivalent of a general trade union and was registered a few days after COTU in 1966.

Table 32.4 shows the structure of the trade union movement in Zambia in 1973, and the development of the movement since 1965. This growth has been quite rapid, with an 80 per cent increase in membership between 1965 and 1973, a feature of this growth being the expansion of two general unions, the

Table 32.2 *Trade union growth in Kenya*

Year of registration	Name of trade union
1946	Printing and Kindred Trades Workers' Union of Kenya
1947	Transport and Allied Workers' Union
1948	Tailors and Textiles Workers' Union
1951	Domestic and Hotel Workers' Union
1951	Kenya Pilots Association
1952	East Africa Federation of Building and Construction Workers' Union
1952	Kenya Local Government Workers' Union
1953	Railway African Union (Kenya)
1954	The Dockworkers' Union
1957	Union of Posts and Telecommunications Employees (Kenya)
1958	East African External Telecommunications Workers' Union (Kenya)
1958	East African Posts and Telecommunications Senior Officers' Association (Kenya)
1958	Kenya Electrical Trades Workers' Union
1958	Kenya Petroleum Oil Workers' Union
1958	Kenya Chemical Workers' Union
1958	National East Africa Seamen's Union
1959	Kenya Timber and Furniture Workers' Union
1959	Kenya National Union of Teachers
1959	Kenya Civil Servants' Union
1959	Kenya Engineering Workers' Union
1960	Kenya Motor Engineering and Allied Workers' Union
1960	Kenya Shoe and Leather Workers' Union
1960	Kenya Union of Sugar Plantation Workers
1961	Kenya Quarry and Mine Workers' Union
1961	Senior Civil Servants' Association of Kenya
1961	East African Airways Staff Association
1962	Kenya Union of Journalists
1962	East African Community Union (Kenya)*
1962	Customs Workers' Union (Kenya)
1963	Kenya Plantation and Agricultural Workers' Union *Tea Plantation Workers Union (Reg. 1959)* *General Agricultural Workers' Union (Reg. 1961)* *Sisal and Coffee Plantation Workers' Union (Reg. 1962)*
1963	Kenya Game Hunting and Safari Workers' Union
1965	Kenya National Union of Musicians
1965	Kenya Union of Commercial, Food and Allied Workers *Kenya Distributive and Commercial Workers (Reg. 1952) and other predecessors*
1966	Central Organization of Trade Unions (Kenya)
1968	Kenya Union of National Parks Employees
	Total union membership ('000s)
	Reported employment: all races ('000s)
	Percentage of reported employees in wage employment with trade union membership (%)

SOURCE: *Annual Report of the Registrar-General* for 1966 and 1971; *Annual Report of Labour Department* for earlier years

NOTE: Membership figures are for end of year; union names those on Registrar-General's Register at end of year. Only unions registered as at end of 1971 are listed above, although total membership figures in the bottom row include members of unions de-registered since the year shown in each column.

* Refers to information reported twelve months previously

(E) Refers to the exclusively European membership of the Pilots Association in 1962 and 1966

	Membership (thousands)					Type of union			
	Book	Book	Book	Voting	Voting	Company	Craft	Industrial	General
	1952	1956	1962	1966	1971				
	0.3	0.3	11.2	2.2	2.6		*		
	9.8	1.0	14.2	5.9	8.0				*
	..	..	7.4	4.4	7.3			*	*
	7.2	..	22.9	133.7	17.0			*	*
	..	..	0.2(E)	0.2(E)	0.2		*	*	
	7.5	1.6	8.3	4.2	10.0	*		*	
	..	2.2	11.1	19.7	17.9	*		*	
	—	4.8	6.0	13.9	13.3	*		*	
	—	1.8	3.0	7.6	7.5	*			
	—	—	2.2	2.6	3.6	*			
	—	—	..	0.1	0.4	*			
	—	—	..	0.04	0.1	*			
	—	—	1.0	1.5	2.2		*		
	—	—	1.6	1.7	1.4	*		*	
	—	—	4.7	2.5	3.8			*	
	—	—	..	4.8	0.5			*	
	—	—	2.3	2.9	3.5		*	*	
	—	—	3.6	29.0*	45.1	*		*	
	—	—	11.8	21.5	39.4	*		*	
	—	—	3.5	6.5	4.6		*		
	—	—	—	—	3.8			*	
	—	—	—	—	1.4	*	*	*	
	—	—	—	—	4.4			*	
	—	—	—	—	1.9			*	
	—	—	—	—	1.6	*		*	
	—	—	—	—	0.1	*			
	—	—	—	—	—		*		
	—	—	—	—	1.7	*			
	—	—	—	—	0.6	*			
	—	—	(71.8)	57.0	33.9				*
	—	—	18.1	—	—				
	—	—	27.9	—	—				
	—	—	25.8	—	—				
	—	—	—	0.3	1.1			*	
	—	—	—	0.1	0.1		*		
	—	—	—	13.9	21.3				*
	—	(1.5)	(14.7)	—	—				
	—	—	—	(29 TU)	(28 TU)	—	—	—	—
	—	—	—	—	0.4	*			
	27.6	17.5	201.8	345.5	260.7				
	475.7	596.7	581.3	585.4	691.2				
	5.8	2.9	32.2	59.0	37.7				

`..` indicates 'a small quantity not specified'

National Union of Building, Engineering and General Workers (which might also be considered an industrial union, being centred on the construction industry) and the National Union of Commercial and Industrial Workers, this representing a broadening of the trade union movement in Zambia. More significant than the increase in total membership of the trade union movement is the percentage of formal sector employees who are members: this went up from 35 per cent in 1965 to 50 per cent in 1973.

The movement's structure is not too different from that in Kenya with a central organization, the Zambia Congress of Trade Unions (ZCTU), embracing 17 primary unions. The importance of the Mineworkers' Union of Zambia can be seen from the size of its membership, 47,000, and roughly a quarter of the total in 1973 (more than one-third in 1965) but also from the fact that it was registered in 1957, three years before any other union. It is not difficult to understand why the Mineworkers' Union has dominated trade union activity in Zambia. Mineworkers are comparatively easy to organize, being concentrated in a limited number of sites and companies. Secondly, copper-mining is a capital-intensive and natural resource-intensive activity in which expenditure on wages is small relative to total costs and relative to the value of the product: labour's bargaining power is therefore considerable, strikes being very costly for management, and wage concessions relatively inexpensive. Thirdly, the existence of a European mineworkers' union on the copperbelt, following the Western tradition, provided the example for the formation and recognition of an African mineworkers' union.

Table 32.4 indicates in a similar way to that for Kenya which unions might be classified as company, craft, industrial, and general unions. Compared with Kenya and Tanzania we may note the special importance of one industrial union in mining (none of those in the other countries is very large) and the reduced relative importance of the Plantation and Agricultural Workers' Union, which is only partially explained by the lesser importance of the plantation and large-farm sector in Zambia.

The last column in the table indicates which unions occur within the public and parastatal sector. If we include the University of Zambia Workers' Union as being in effect in the public sector, being financed by government, we see nine out of eighteen unions were established in the public and parastatal sector. Those composed of employees directly employed in the public service (Public Service Workers, Local Authorities Workers, Teachers, and Civil Service Association) accounted for some 44,400 members in 1973, about a quarter of the total; while, as usual in Eastern Africa, workers in the public utilities and other parastatals, in railways, airways, postal services, and electricity, were effectively unionized. It will have been noticed that in Kenya the two largest unions were those of the teachers (45,000 in 1971) and civil servants (39,000). In Uganda and Tanzania, also, these unions have been not only important but have played an especially significant role in the early development of the trade union movement in the country.

Table 32.3 Employers' trade unions in Kenya as at 31 December, 1971

Date of registration	Name of trade union	Voting membership (no.)
12–4–50	Kenya Association of Building and Civil Engineering Contractors	258
8–11–50	Federation of Master Printers of East Africa	65
7–7–59	Motor Trades and Allied Industries Employers' Association	41
1–2–60	Distributive and Allied Trades Association	41
7–4–60	Engineering and Allied Industries Employers' Association	21
2–5–60	Kenya Coffee Growers' Association	209
28–6–60	Timber Industries Employers' Association	34
29–11–60	Kenya Sugar Employers' Union	29
4–8–61	Sisal Employers' Association (Kenya)	28
16–7–62	Kenya Bankers' (Employers) Association	11
7–9–62	Agricultural Employers' Association	476
8–11–65	Mombasa and Coast Tailors (Employers) Association	51
29–1–66	Federation of Kenya Employers	2,298
15–2–66	Kisumu Distributive Employers' Association	42
16–5–66	Association of Local Government Employers	44
	Total	3,648

SOURCE: *Statistical abstract*

Table 32.4   Growth of trade union membership in Zambia

Year of registration	Name of trade union	Membership (thousands) 1965	Membership (thousands) 1973	Type of union Company	Type of union Craft	Type of union Industrial	Type of union General	Public service statal unions
1966	Zambia Congress of Trade Unions (ZCTU)	11†	17†	—	—	—	—	—
	Number of Primary Unions	28	18	—	—	—	—	—
1957	Mineworkers' Union of Zambia	36.6	47.0			*		
1960	National Union of Building, Engineering and General Workers	12.0	33.0			*	*	
1960	National Union of Commercial and Industrial Workers	16.0	30.0				*	
1960	National Union of Public Service Workers	6.0	19.4	*		*		*
1962	Zambia National Union of Teachers	2.1	11.1	*	*			*
1962	National Union of Plantation and Agricultural Workers	4.5	6.8			*	*	
1964	National Union of Postal and Telecommunications Workers	1.1	2.4	*				*
1966	Hotel Catering Workers' Union of Zambia	—	3.2			*		
1967	Zambia Railways Amalgamated Workers' Unions	6.6	7.4	*				*
1967	National Union of Transport and Allied Workers	2.3	5.8			*	*	
1968	Airways and Allied Workers' Union	—	1.1	*				*
1968	University of Zambia Workers' Union	—	0.7	*				*
1969	Civil Servants' Association of Zambia	1.5	1.4	*		*		*
1970	Zambia Union of Financial Institutions	0.4	1.1			*		
1971	Zambia United Local Authorities Workers' Union	6.4	12.5	*		*		*
1971	Zambia Typographical Union	0.2	0.7		*			
1971	Zambia Electricity Workers' Union	—	0.8	*				*
1972	Guards' Union of Zambia	—	0.7	*				
	Total union membership	105.3	187.1					
	Estimated employment in formal sector	298.4	377.6					
	Percentage of formal sector employees in trade unions (%)	35.3	49.5					

SOURCE: *Annual Reports of the Department of Labour and Statistical Year Books*
NOTE: † Denotes *Reports of the Department of Labour and Statistical Year Books*

Table 32.5   Average cash earnings of reported employees by industry and race in Zambia, and degree of unionization by sector

Sector	Average cash earnings (kwacha per employee) African 1954	African 1966	African 1972	Non-African 1954	Non-African 1966	Non-African 1972	Ratio of African to non-African earnings 1954	1966	1972	Unionization (%) 1973
Agriculture	82	190	376	1,606	3,040	4,515	19.6	16.0	12.0	16
Mining	264	934	1,491	4,240	5,598	6,971	16.1	7.1	4.7	90
Manufacturing	152	478	853	2,160	3,556	6,128	14.2	7.4	7.2	(57)[1]
Construction	148	332	674	2,188	3,908	6,479	14.8	11.8	9.6	45
Transport/ Communications	172	688	1,311	2,048	4,462	5,553	11.9	6.5	4.2	73
Commerce	146	488	864	1,500	2,898	5,140	10.3	5.9	5.9	n.a.
Services	154	526	831	1,658	2,736	2,968	10.8	5.2	3.6	67
All sectors	156	480	960	2,474	4,090	5,500	15.9	8.5	5.7	54[2]

SOURCE: *Monthly Digests of Statistics* and *Statistical Year Book*
NOTES: [1] Some employed in commerce
[2] African employees only

The reasons for this are fairly obvious. Educated groups such as teachers and civil servants are not likely to be unaware of their own group interests, and were politically articulate even in the colonial period; they can afford to pay union dues and provide strong union financing; they are easily organized as 'company' unions of employees working for a single employer.

We argued above that a union's strength in the private sector arises out of its capacity to inflict damage on employers through the loss of profits. In the public sector it is the loss which the union can inflict *on the economy* which is its strongest weapon, and its capacity to embarrass the government. This certainly exists in the key public utilities such as railways and electricity supply where a strike will affect not only the finances of the parastatal but also the operations of numerous other industries and cause direct inconvenience to final consumers. Not surprisingly in countries where the railways have been the 'lifelines' of the economies, railway unions have been organized at an early stage. These are also easy to organize as company unions among fairly compact groups of workers.

Before Independence the wage and salary structure in Northern Rhodesia afforded a good example of the effects of racial discrimination discussed in the last chapter. This had been reinforced by the pressure of financially strong unions among the highly paid European workers well organized, for instance, in the Northern Rhodesian Mine Workers' Union and the Rhodesia Railway Workers' Union and able to enforce 'colour bars' against the advancement of African workers to skilled manual jobs. Since Independence Zambianization has rapidly replaced expatriates in mining and the public services, and by 1971 it was the Zambian Mineworkers' and Zambia Railways Unions which were the most effectively organized pacemakers in collective bargaining for African wage earners in non-agricultural jobs.

Just how successful African trade union action has been in Zambia can be gauged from the figures in Table 32.5. Not only have the average cash earnings of African workers advanced rapidly in absolute terms, but the wide race differential between them and non-African employees has narrowed substantially, particularly in the highest-paid industries, mining and transport/communications. The last column in the table shows the degree of unionization in each sector, the percentage of employees who are union members. Unions whose members account for only a small percentage of the total work-force in an industry or occupation will lack bargaining power, since total withdrawal of labour from employers will be difficult to achieve. Hence this percentage offers some measure of union bargaining strength. The degree of unionization is a high 90 per cent in mining: and here we see that while in 1954 the *average* earnings of African mineworkers were only one-sixteenth that of European mine employees, in 1966 the differential had narrowed to one-seventh and by 1972 to less than one-fifth. The lowest degree of unionization was in agriculture, only 16 per cent, and at a higher level but still significantly lower than in mining, construction, at 45 per cent. These are both industries to which there is a highly elastic supply of labour from the rural sector or from the large pool of unskilled rural or urban workers and where tight union organization is the most difficult to achieve. In these sectors the ratio of non-African to African earnings was still 12.0 and 9.6, respectively, in 1972, much higher than in most sectors, where this gap had closed considerably.[2]

Overall the ratio of non-African earnings to African fell from 15.9 in 1954 to 8.5 in 1966, and 5.7 in 1972: the degree of unionization was 54 per cent. This relative increase in African earnings would re-

Table 32.6   *Average annual earnings by main industrial sector of paid employment in Eastern African countries, 1965 (£ sterling)*

	Malawi[1]	Tanzania	Uganda	Kenya	Zambia
(1) Agriculture	53	82	80	61	107
(2) Mining	—	204	184	174	741
(3) Manufacturing	154	176	173	210	421
(4) Construction	93	122	120	207	239
(5) Electricity and water	254	185	—	440	482
(6) Commerce	154	267	300	359	515
(7) Transport and communications	258	214	207	354	502
(8) Services	195	192	211	236	300
National average	117	138	170	274	386

SOURCE: J. B. Knight, 'Wages and Zambia's Economic Development' in C. Elliot (ed.), *Constraints on the Economic Performance of Zambia*, OUP, Nairobi, 1971, p. 108

NOTE: [1] Malawi figures are for 1964 and are added by the authors.

sult partly from training programmes for Africans and increased acquisition of skills, and partly from localization, the breakdown of barriers to African employment, and the reduction in discrimination in pay being given to the two racial categories of worker at the same level of skill.

A less desirable effect of these increases in earnings, however, is that the differential enjoyed by better organized and skilled workers over the average earnings of less organized and less skilled agricultural wage earners has widened. Whereas African mineworkers earned, on average, just over three times the wages of agricultural employees in 1954, they earned about four times as much in 1966 and 1972. Workers in transport and communications have improved their relative position even more, earning on average 88 per cent of the miners' pay in 1972, compared with only 65 per cent in 1954, or 37 per cent more than the national average, against only 10 per cent more in 1954.

Sectoral wage structures in Eastern Africa

What patterns of wage and salary earnings have developed in Eastern Africa as a result of the combination of market and institutional factors described above? Table 32.6 compares the average annual earnings of paid employees in the main industrial sectors of Eastern African countries. Although these intercountry statistics are not strictly comparable in every respect, they all refer to similar categories of formal sector activity, only, and comprise cash incomes received by employees in 1965 when all these countries had currency exchange rates on a par with each other, that is, shs 20 = £1.

Looking at the first row, this indicates that agricultural wages are very low compared to other sectors, varying between one-quarter and one-half of wages in manufacturing, for instance. The most important reason for this is that much of the labour involved is unskilled, and in elastic supply from surrounding rural areas; the cost of living will also be substantially lower in these areas; and agricultural labour is often non-unionized or less effectively unionized.

Row 2 shows that wages are very high in mining, particularly in Zambia. The main factor here is that mining industries in Africa deal with high-priced resources, are capital-intensive and low in labour intensity, and can therefore afford to pay high wages; while the industries were dominated by large expatriate companies perhaps under greater political pressure to act as benevolent employers. In the case of Zambia a special factor was the importance of non-African workers who, in the mid-1960s, were paid about ten times as much as African employees, and

accounted for as much as 10 per cent of all employees, a much larger share than in other Eastern African countries. Thus in 1965, the high average earnings of £741 for mining workers in Zambia were the direct result of paying 7,000 European miners an average of £2,700, about seven times the £41 average pay of the 45,000 African employees in mining. Since the 1960s, of course, racial differentials have diminished, as has the proportion of non-African employees generally in Eastern Africa. As already mentioned, however, the strong unions of white miners on the copperbelt also gave stimulus to African trade unionism, which developed rapidly in the mining industry of Zambia.

Average wages in the construction industry are somewhere between those in agriculture and in manufacturing. As in the case of agriculture, the construction industry employs a large proportion of unskilled workers, frequently drawn from the rural areas and in elastic supply, while the important element of casual labour within the work-force makes for a low degree of union power in the industry.

The high figures for the electricity and water sector reflect partly the high capital and low labour intensities and partly the operation of public sector wage leadership. Those for commerce, transport, and services are perhaps surprisingly high in occupations where unions' organization may be less strong. However these will include a substantial amount of public services where higher wages are enjoyed, while it must be remembered that the figures refer to those in formal sector employment and would exclude many employees earning very low wages in the informal urban sector and in the rural areas.

If we turn now to differences between countries, we may note first the high figure for manufacturing in Zambia, no doubt reflecting the lack of very much small-scale manufacturing enterprise and the dominance of a relatively few large firms. The relatively low level of agricultural wages in Malawi and Kenya is noticeable, despite the size of the large-farm sector, in Kenya particularly. Wages in the construction industry in Malawi were also low in 1964, suggesting that, apart from an economic recession, a longer-term surplus of unskilled labour was depressing wages of this category of worker. The higher wages in the commerce and transportation sector of the Kenyan economy presumably derives from a more developed formal commercial sector, including larger expatriate firms, many operating on an East African basis, while the East African Public Corporations provided substantial employment for more skilled workers in railways, telecommunications, and airways.

Comparing national averages we see that average earnings are lowest in Malawi and Tanzania, somewhat higher in Uganda, and substantially higher in Kenya and especially Zambia. Although, of course, the internal purchasing power of the national currencies differed in 1965, and now, in terms of sterling we can say that £117 could have purchased the annual labour services of the average worker in Malawi, while more than three times as much, £386, would have been required on average to hire a Zambian worker. Despite exporting a great deal of labour to Zambia and other countries in 1964, a large proportion of wage earners in Malawi were engaged in labour-intensive agricultural and processing activities: these produce lower-value primary products and personal services, using less capital and simple techniques, and do not usually pay high wages. Tanzania's wage structure is rather like Malawi's, heavily weighted in 1965 towards estate agriculture and service activities. Because Uganda's agriculture is small-scale, largely outside the coverage of formal employment to which these statistics refer, its weight is lower, producing the higher average figure of £170. Kenya's wage structure presents, as does Zambia's, a wider dispersion of earnings between industries than the other countries, ranging from £61 in agriculture to £440 in electricity and water. Unlike Zambia, Kenya does not have any important mineral industry to pull up the national average earnings figure, but rather a large agricultural wage labour force to push it down. Nevertheless its capital-intensive and skill-intensive secondary industries and services were important enough to produce a figure of average earnings from employment which in 1965 was twice the figures for Tanzania and Malawi. The basic explanation for the high cash earnings of Zambian workers lies in the high productivity of workers in mining, where labour works together with a large amount of capital, advanced technology and a high-valued natural resource, together with the 'pull' effect of these high earnings on the rest of the formal sector wage, and in addition the relative *un*importance of agricultural and informal sector employment, almost all paid employment being in larger-scale enterprises and outside agriculture.

In general we can say that a country's overall wage level reflects the relative importance of various sectors in the national economy. Industries with high labour productivity and wage-inelastic labour demands have high wage rates. If a country's industrial structure is heavily weighted in favour of these highly paid industries then the national average level of wage earnings will be high: however, such industries may also affect wages indirectly by exerting a 'pull' effect on wages elsewhere, particularly for special categories of skilled worker.

A simple model of wage determination with unlimited supplies of unskilled labour from rural areas and an inelastic supply of skilled labour can explain the main differential, between average wage earnings in agriculture and formal sector urban employment. The figures in Table 32.6 generally support this theory of wage determination for all the countries shown. The agricultural–national average ratios for Malawi, Tanzania, and Uganda are respectively 53/117, 82/138, and 80/170, all about one-half. The lower ratios of around one-quarter for Kenya and Zambia no doubt incorporate the effects of the other factors mentioned which raise wages in the urban and industrial sector still further. Let us look in more detail at the way in which market forces and institutional arrangements have determined Zambia's wage structure.

Wage determination in Zambia

Unlike other Eastern African countries (except Mauritius, which is a special case), a large proportion of the working population in Zambia works in the formal sector and outside agriculture altogether. According to the 1969 Population Census, the 'dimensions' of the labour force were as shown in Table 32.7. Table 32.7 brings out the striking fact that the working population aged between 15 and 59 years amounted to only 17 *per cent* of the total population in the country. This reflects, first, the fact (commented upon also in our chapter on Population) that 49 per cent of the population were of working age, between 15 and 60, the remainder being either children or old people, and secondly that, of those of working age, more than half were housewives, students, etc., not seeking paid employment, while there was a substantial pool of unemployed labour, 374,000 people, seeking work. The working population thus comprised 690,000 people, out of a total population of four millions.

Of these 690,000, nearly one-half, 321,000, were in formal employment as employees. Agriculture was not an important source of wage employment, and amounted to only 12 per cent of the total. Only about 50 per cent of the working population in Zambia comprised small farmers in the rural sector and self-employed people generally, a relatively small proportion for Eastern African countries.

Following independence Zambia found itself with an acute shortage of skilled manpower, whether manpower with high-level formal education or skilled technicians. For this reason and because of its inheritance as a constituent part of the former white-dominated Central African Federation, Zambia continued to rely heavily for some time on expatriate white workers for the highest-paid and technically skilled jobs. This increased the gap which would in any case have existed, for the reasons mentioned

Table 32.7 *Dimensions of the Zambian labour force (mid-1969)*

	Male (thousands)	Female (thousands)	Total (thousands)	(%)
Total population	1,987	2,070	4,057	100
Below 15 years	929	930	1,859	46
Aged 60 and over	100	87	187	5
Population of working age, 15–59	958	1,053	2,011	49
of which:				
Housewives, students, others not seeking work	122	732	854	21
Activity unstated	75	18	93	2
Seeking work	199	175	374	9
Working population	562	128	690	17
Working population			690	100
Self-employed, rural sector, etc.	257	112	369	53
Formal sector employees	305	16	321	47
of which:	African	Non-African		
Formal sector employees	291	30	321	100
in Mining	49	6	55	17
Public Sector	117	9	126	39
Other non-primary: private	87	15	102	32
Agriculture, etc.: private	38	—	38	12

SOURCE: *Statistical Year Book, 1971*, Government Printer, Lusaka

earlier, between the wages of skilled and unskilled workers, and between wages in the capital- and skill-intensive mining industry and wages elsewhere. Originally the employment of a relatively large number of European miners in the highly paid skilled jobs had reproduced in Zambia's copper mines the 'colour bar' to African advancement to better-paid jobs which characterizes the South African mining industries. However by the 1960s the African mine-workers had become better organized in their own trade unions and were able to press for improvement of their own conditions and, a factor which produced its own strong upward pull on African wages in the industry, a reduction in racially based wage differentials.

Mining accounted for 17 per cent of formal sector employment and the mining companies thus acted as 'wage leaders' for other private employers in the formal sector. Table 32.7 shows, however, that almost 40 per cent of formal sector employment was actually *in the public sector*, so that mining and public sector employment together dominated the wage structure and wage movements. Localization of an expatriate service, and the influence of expatriate salary scales, were again very important here. The public services were localizing rapidly in the 1960s and offered salary scales which, for example, gave holders of degrees about seven times as much as the average earnings of Zambians with only primary schooling.

The 'pull' effect of wages in the copper industry on wages elsewhere was strong, for a number of reasons. Other employers in manufacturing, transport, con-

struction, and so on often used workers with similar skills: mechanics, drivers, store-keepers and accountants, etc. Secondly the complicated pay scales for different races or skill grades covered a variety of occupations shared with other industries, so that the influence of these factors was transmitted elsewhere. Thirdly the development of 'industrial' unions for *all* workers in an industry, discussed above, allowed in particular unskilled and less scarce general labour employed in factories or public services to share in the 'wage pull' exerted by the shortage of skilled grades. The wages of unskilled workers in the formal sector were also pushed upwards quite rapidly as a result of minimum wage legislation and the efforts of Wage Commissioners, appointed to recommend awards which would improve 'industrial relations', and Wages Councils, established to monitor wages in the less well-organized industries and occupations. These factors to a considerable extent couteracted the effect of the elastic supply of unskilled labour from the rural areas, which supply was supplemented by substantial numbers of immigrant African workers from Rhodesia and Malawi.

Thus a variety of factors, including deliberate government policy, have combined to produce a 'dual' structure of wage earnings in Zambia as between highly paid formal sector employment and the low level of rural earnings. This has undoubtedly been a contributory element in the emergence of a high level of unemployment, shown in Table 32.7 as 374,000 in 1969 compared to a working population of 690,000 in the economically active ages between 15 and 59 years. Rather more than half of this pool of unemployed was stated as being still in rural areas, with the remainder already living in the copperbelt and other main towns.

Incomes policy in Eastern Africa

'Incomes Policy', a term originally employed in advanced industrial countries, may be said to refer to a policy of regulating increases in money wages and other money incomes according to some national guidelines or plan. Governments in such countries have generally been led to adopt incomes policies as a result of the upward pressure of wage claims by the more powerful trade unions, particularly, leading to cost-push inflation in the economy as a whole. The focus of such policies has always been on *wage* restraint, although measures to restrict other incomes, such as dividends and, through price controls, company profits, have been a necessary supplement, if only to ensure acceptance of wage restraint by the major unions. Incomes policy has thus involved intervention by the government in free collective bargaining, generally through persuasion, and some national 'norm' or 'guidelines' for acceptable money wage increases throughout the economy.

Not many years after independence, however, several of the Eastern African countries felt the need for some national wages or incomes policy following increases in urban money wages rates. H. A. Turner, an ILO consultant and Cambridge University Professor of Industrial Relations, made separate visits in the middle and late 1960s to Tanzania, Zambia, and Malawi at the request of their respective governments in order to analyse their wage and employment problems and to report on appropriate incomes policies.

The incomes policies appropriate to less developed countries are, however, likely to be different from those for industrial countries, first because wage structures are quite different and second because the nature of the economies will differ, as well as the nature of the employment problem. In developed countries, with full or near-full employment creating pressures on wages, and the wage-bill constituting as much as two-thirds of national income in most cases, the objective of an incomes policy has been largely the macroeconomic one of controlling cost-push inflation, with the aims of achieving equity between groups of workers and of employment creation clearly subsidiary. But with wages and salaries accounting for a very much smaller proportion of national income in the less developed countries with large traditional agricultural sectors, the main issue there

has not been one of controlling inflation and avoiding balance of payments difficulties, even if wage inflation in the urban sector was one of the factors causing concern in Eastern Africa. Rather than inflation as such, the main issues have been (1) the effect on the distribution of real income between groups, particularly as between urban unskilled workers and rural smallholders; (2) the effect on employment and unemployment; and (3) the effect on savings, investment, and growth.

The structure of less developed countries, with a dominant agricultural sector based largely on smallholders, means that unionized urban wage labour generally represents a small minority rather than a dominant 'working class'. The largest and generally the poorest group of income recipients are likely to be peasant farmers (though the distribution of income among smallholders does, as we have seen, vary widely) and the landless rural poor, who are also the least organized in trade unions or producer pressure groups, together with those in the urban informal sector. Hence successful action to raise wages by powerful trade unions, rather than *de*creasing inequalities, as might be the case in industrial societies, may here widen them, and produce a 'labour aristocracy' and urban elite in the urban formal sector and public service employment. The change in relative rural–urban incomes would come about not simply through the faster rate of increase in urban money wages, but through an adverse change in the rural–urban *terms of trade* affecting rural producers. This may come about first because the real income of agricultural households falls as the price of urban manufactured goods increases, and perhaps as the quantity of public services supplied, particularly to rural families, diminishes as a result of rising wage costs; and secondly because the more politically influential urban groups exert direct and indirect pressure on government to keep down consumer prices (and thus prices paid to farmers) for staple food commodities.

In the Eastern African countries referred to here, interest in an incomes policy also grew out of concern over the slow rate of expansion of employment opportunities over the preceding ten or more years,[3] to which rising wage rates were thought to have contributed. These would also stimulate rural–urban migration, further worsening urban unemployment. Finally, employment would decrease as employers substituted capital (and management) for skilled and unskilled labour. Rural employers could also mechanize some operations, aggravating rural unemployment. Public sector employment would decrease because of financial constraints.

Thirdly, rising money wages, to the extent that this was at the expense of profits, might increase consumption and reduce savings, investment, and growth. A shift from profits to wages would also mean that future employment would grow less rapidly. Higher domestic wage costs could affect growth by reducing profitability where foreign competition was important, in export industries and import-substitute industries, as well as industries in which domestic price controls suppressed price increases.

Turner[4] was asked in 1966 to advise the government of Tanzania on the formulation of a national policy with regard to income and wages. As far as distribution was concerned he found that the rapid increase in wages and substantial improvement in fringe benefits meant that most of the benefit of development since independence had gone to wage earners who, with their families, made up less than one-tenth of the population. Specifically, the average yearly increase in wages from 1960–1 to 1965–6 had been 17 per cent, whereas the average real income per head of smallholders in 1965 was about 7–8 per cent *lower* than in 1960–2. This second result was partly due to low prices for produce obtained on world markets but also, he said, because of a deterioration in the internal terms of trade between rural and urban sectors.

Distribution of income among wage earners within the urban sector was also affected, Turner observed, because of the policy of the national trade union, and the Ministry of Labour, to support relatively large annual wage demands made to the bigger firms and enterprises with the ability to pay, while accepting wage settlements in smaller firms at much lower rates, and even avoidance of payment of prescribed minimum wage levels. This had the double effect of increasing the gap in wages between the formal and 'informal' sectors and, since unskilled workers in large enterprises might earn substantially more than skilled workers in small concerns, reducing the wage differential obtainable by skilled over unskilled manual workers.

Turner also found that 'sharp increases in labour costs have undoubtedly made some contribution to an increase in urban unemployment and to underemployment in rural areas, because they have led employers to reduce their labour forces'. He refers here rather misleadingly to the fact that total wage employment, which had been 400,000 in 1961, would be not much more than 300,000 in 1966. It is misleading here, of course, to suggest that this change was due primarily to increasing wage costs, the main factor being the decline in employment on sisal estates as a result of a severe recession in that industry: but certainly at a time of shrinking employment opportunities aggravation of the problem by over-pricing of labour would have been undesirable.

Finally, Turner detected in Tanzania what he took to be the beginning of an inflationary wage–price spiral, though whether increase in urban wages would be sufficient to produce a general inflation in this sort of open, dependent economy is to be doubted. Nevertheless the government of Tanzania in a White Paper[5] accepted Turner's main findings and recommendations.

Turner's analysis of the Zambian situation, following a visit in late 1969, was very similar.[6] President Kaunda's letter to the ILO requesting the study referred to three aspects of the wage–employment problem:

(1) following 'a sharp increase in living costs after Independence', there was a danger that 'future increases in wages and other incomes [will lead to] an inflationary spiral';

(2) increases in real wages since independence have been unevenly distributed between groups of workers. In particular, the gains from development are not very equitably distributed as between the urban population and the rural population;

(3) employment had not risen as much as was hoped and there was 'a need to ensure that the relation between different kinds of costs should be such that the capital available for development shall be devoted to increasing output and employment and not to unnecessary imports of labour-saving equipment'.

Turner found, first, that inflation existed, with an annual rate of increase in the cost of living of over 7 per cent per annum between 1964 and 1968, for that period well above the inflation rates of neighbouring countries and of Zambia's trading partners. Secondly *real* consumption per employee had risen by 19 per cent over this period, whereas labour efficiency (productivity) had dropped by 21 per cent, implying not only a change in the relative distribution of real income away from other groups, particularly the rural population, towards wage-earners, but a change which was undeserved and accruing to inefficient or 'lazy' workers. Finally, it was diagnosed that the annual rise in employment was petering out, and that an actual *fall* in employment in 1969 was imminent.

A special feature of the Zambian Report was the accent on labour productivity and the 'laziness' or decreasing efficiency of Zambian industrial workers. Turner's statistical analysis has, however, been criticized by a number of economists, including Fry.[7] The latter, calculating an alternative statistical index of labour productivity, estimated that this had *increased* by over 8 per cent during the period rather than decreasing by 21 per cent. Hence Turner had completely overestimated the extent to which real wage increases had diverged from productivity. Fry also disputed the cause of the Zambian inflation, arguing that this had been due much more to the effect of UDI in Rhodesia and the subsequent disruption of trade channels; and that in any case ordinary fiscal policy was a more effective method of dealing with it than a prices and incomes policy. As regards employment, other factors, particularly tax policy and the duty-free importation of capital goods, may have had at least as important an effect.

Fry did, however, find that Turner had significantly underestimated the gains made by Zambian paid workers relative to peasant farmers. Whereas workers had enjoyed rises in real wages of over 40 per cent during 1964–8, the typical farmer had benefited by no more than 3 per cent. Moreover, other evidence[8] suggested that peasant farmers might have suffered a deterioration in the rural–urban terms of trade in this period of nearly 30 per cent, and thus an average fall in real income of over 15 per cent. Fry thus found that the most powerful case for the adoption of a firm incomes policy rested on the income distribution argument.

Subsequent to the ILO Reports, both Tanzania and Zambia adopted incomes policies. Tanzania laid down a 'Wages Plan' which related future increases in urban minimum wages to the level of real incomes in rural areas. It also proposed to reduce urban wage and salary differentials by tapering future pay increases in a way which would give significantly smaller percentage rate additions at higher levels of income. In Zambia it was decided that in future annual wage increases should not exceed 5 per cent and should pay regard to productivity improvements. A Wages and Incomes Board was later established to deal with the interconnected problems of inflation, industrial expansion, greater income equality, and more jobs.

In Malawi the approach adopted after 1966, when minimum wage levels were raised to restore real wage rates for unskilled employees to their pre-Independence level, was to freeze minimum wage rates for the next six years. This policy was directed rather successfully towards all the objectives discussed above, especially the avoidance of open urban unemployment, and to improving rural income levels both absolutely and by keeping down the domestic price level relative to farm prices.

While Kenya did not have the benefit of a visit from Professor Turner, it did receive a much more substantial mission from the ILO in 1972.[9] Its concern however dates from the mid-1960s or earlier, the focus in Kenya, with open urban unemployment developing in Nairobi and rapid rural–urban migration, being on the employment objective rather than the application of controls over wages. Thus, for example, the Special Rural Development Programme initiated in 1966[10] was aimed at expanding rural employment as well as income, and reducing incentives to migrate. The employment objective was emphasized in Kenya by the rather unusual 'Tripartite Agreements' between the government, trade unions, and employers aimed at expanding formal employment in return for a voluntary wage freeze by unions. The 1964 agreement involved government in a contract to expand its labour force by 15 per cent, and employers theirs by 10 per cent. Some 34,000 jobs were supposed to have been created as a result, though how far a permanent net increase in employment was achieved is uncertain. The 1970 agreement involved a 10 per cent increase by both employing parties and was intended to create another 45,000 jobs.

Despite the special importance attached to employment, there was also concern over the income distribution and other implications of a rapid increase in urban wage rates. Thus average urban African earnings rose from £97 per annum in 1960 to £180 in 1966, an annual compound rate of increase of 11 per cent, or 8 per cent in real terms. In contrast, Ghai estimated[11] that the average total income of farmers had risen at about half the rate of unskilled urban workers, while the wage of the latter was given in absolute terms as about twice that of the average peasant household in Kenya. Since one of the objectives of incomes policy was to reduce this differential, and since the level of peasant incomes is the most important determinant of the supply of labour to the formal sector (as outlined in the Lewis model of the previous chapter), Ghai suggested that an appropriate 'norm' for wage rate increases in this sector would be a (moving) average of the increase in average peasant incomes over the preceding 3–4 years, something which would ensure equality, if it were politically acceptable to urban wage earners.

With the ILO Mission of 1972, however, the Kenya government embraced a much more comprehensive, if less specific, incomes policy. Income redistribution in favour of the rural population and the urban informal sector was a stated major objective of the 1974–78 Development Plan. Associated with this aim were tax measures to discourage capital-intensive techniques of production, a programme of labour-intensive rural industry promotion, and limitations of trade unions' freedom to strike in pursuit of wage demands.

Questions on Chapter 32

1. Discuss the main objectives of minimum wage legislation. Explain the effect of imposing a minimum wage rate (a) in a competitive market and (b) under conditions of monopsony.
2. Why may employers offer their workers wages above the ruling rate?
3. How far can economic theory be used to predict the equilibrium wage in a 'bilateral monopoly' situation between union and employer?
4. Why is the bargaining power of trade unions generally more limited in Eastern African countries than in industrial countries?
5. Using additional historical material of your own, write a brief history of trade union development in Eastern Africa, with special reference to a country of your choice.
6. What kinds of trade unions have developed in Eastern Africa, and in what sectors? What factors have determined this development?

7. What evidence is there that the degree of unionization in different sectors of the Zambian economy has affected effectiveness in bargaining?
8. Compare the sectoral wage structure of any two Eastern African countries. How do you account for the wide differentials in average earnings between sectors?
9. Discuss the effects of historical, economic, and institutional factors on the gap between wage rates for skilled and unskilled workers in Eastern Africa.
10. Using the material discussed in this and previous chapters, explain the main dimensions of a country's labour force. How would you expect the structure of the labour force to change with long-term economic development?
11. Compare the main objectives of 'Incomes Policy' in developed countries with its objectives in less developed countries like those of Eastern Africa.
12. How did Professor H. A. Turner analyse the wage and employment problems of Eastern African countries in the mid-1960s?

Notes

[1] As a rule workers 'on strike' are not eligible for unemployment insurance benefit.

[2] It must be realized, however, that these ratios are averages for the whole class of employee working in the sector. The number of European employees in the unskilled category will be less, so that the higher earnings ratios in agriculture and construction will be due in part simply to the higher proportion of unskilled workers employed in those sectors.

[3] The slower rate of growth of employment compared to output is discussed in the next chapter.

[4] H. A. Turner, *Report to the Government of the United Republic of Tanzania on Wages, Incomes and Prices Policy*, Geneva, 1967.

[5] *Wages, Incomes, Rural Development, Investment and Price Policy*, Government Paper No. 4, Dar es Salaam, 1967.

[6] *ILO Report to the Government of Zambia on Incomes, Wages and Princes in Zambia: Policy and Machinery*, ILO, Geneva, 1969.

[7] J. Fry, 'The Turner Report: A Zambian View', *East African Economic Review*, Vol. 2, No. 2, December 1970.

[8] Charles Young, in a paper to the Zambian Economics Club.

[9] *Employment, Incomes and Equality, a Strategy for Increasing Productive Employment in Kenya*, ILO, Geneva, 1972.

[10] This programme is evaluated in I. Livingstone, 'Experimentation in Rural Development: Kenya's Special Rural Development Programme', *Agricultural Administration*, Vol. 3, No. 3, 1976.

[11] Dharam P. Ghai, 'Incomes Policy in Kenya: Need, Criteria and Machinery', *East African Economic Review*, Vol. 4, No. 1, June 1968.

33 Employment and Unemployment

We concluded Chapter 28 by stating that the unemployment and underemployment typical of less developed economies were of a fundamentally different type from those experienced during depressions in advanced capitalist countries. We can now examine different types of unemployment as they occur in developed and less developed countries, and their causes.

Types of unemployment: open and disguised

We may first of all distinguish between 'open' unemployment and 'disguised' or 'hidden' unemployment. *Open involuntary unemployment* occurs when a person is willing to work at the ruling wage rate but is not able to secure a job, and thus obtains no earned income from employment: in the welfare states of advanced societies the unemployed have to rely on unemployment benefit paid by the state as a transfer payment and, in the urban areas of less developed countries which lack social security systems, on the private charity of friends and relatives.

Disguised unemployment occurs when the work available to a given work-force is insufficient to keep it fully employed (on certain assumptions about what constitutes a fully employed worker), so that *some members of the workforce could be withdrawn without loss of output*. If total output or product remains unchanged when labour is withdrawn, or added, it follows that the mark of disguised unemployment is that the marginal product of labour is zero.[1]

It is important to realize that this does *not* mean that there is a specific marginal worker who produces nothing. What it means is that the available work is shared out among the existing work-force, with each worker less than fully employed. Such work-sharing occurs in advanced countries, where it is possible for an initial reduction in the work done by each worker to take place simply by working more slowly or by abandoning what has often been regular 'overtime' working; where trade unions resist redundancies and accept work-sharing (such as a three-day working week) as an alternative to sackings; and where employers wish to hang on to their regular work-force, despite a current shortage of orders and work, in order to retain their availability and loyalty for better times.

Nevertheless disguised unemployment is more typically a rural phenomenon associated with less developed economies, occurring in countries and regions where overpopulation has reduced the amount of land available per family, so that underemployment arises because *each unit of labour lacks sufficient land to keep itself fully occupied*. Overpopulation may generate open unemployment, when some people, the younger ones perhaps, become entirely landless and are forced to migrate to the towns where they become unemployed; or it may lead to disguised unemployment when the land, and thus the amount of work, is shared out among all members of the family. Although, again, nobody is entirely idle in this case, the marginal product of labour is again zero, since it would be possible for output to be maintained even if some members of the family left. While the *marginal* product of labour is zero, however, if the output is shared out among all members of the family, or extended family, each member of the family will enjoy consumption or income equal to the *average* product of labour.

In fact, under a practical definition of disguised unemployment, it would be possible for the marginal product of labour to have a positive, low value rather than actually to equal zero. Professor Joan Robinson, who originally introduced the concept, defined it more widely to cover situations in which workers' full productive capacities were not being completely utilized. She had in mind here the adoption of inferior occupations by industrial workers after losing jobs in their normal occupations or trades.[2]

In the less developed countries of today this situation is a common one, and can be observed in the form of pedlars, shoe-shine boys, surplus domestic servants, and the like, in the urban areas and, especially, of low-paid casual labourers hired at rates within the pocket of even comparatively poor peasant farmers in the rural areas. Disguised unemployment in this sense, of people employed in an unproductive way, is common also in the public sector—in Latin America particularly—as well as in private formal sector employment, where frequently an unnecessarily large number of porters, messengers, clerks, or even highly paid staff are engaged.

A special example of the deployment of labour in inferior occupations—inferior in relation to the qualifications or desired occupations of the candidates—are the widespread cases of university graduates in India and elsewhere who can only find jobs as clerks or unskilled labourers. In Eastern Africa there is a similar problem for secondary school leavers, who can often only find work in 'informal' activities which make no call on their formal educational training.

Types of unemployment: general, structural, and seasonal

We can, secondly, distinguish between three categories of unemployment (whether open or disguised): general, structural, and seasonal or erratic unemployment, these categories being related to different causes of unemployment.

General unemployment is that which is widespread throughout the economy and not confined to particular regions or categories of labour. There are two general explanations of its 'mass' occurrence in advanced capitalist countries, the neoclassical and the Keynesian; while the disguised unemployment and underemployment which are sometimes said to be widespread in less developed economies, though of a different type, may also be classified as general unemployment.

Structural unemployment, unlike general, is that which affects particular regions or categories of labour and results from an imbalance between the supply of a particular group of workers and the demand for their services. Such an imbalance may occur where technological change makes obsolete the product on which a particular industry is based, or new methods of production render labour with particular skills redundant. However, any factor permanently affecting the demand for a product or specific group of workers could create structural unemployment.

A characteristic of this type of unemployment is its regional distribution, since it has in the past been due to the stagnation or decline of old-established industries concentrated geographically, and thus is sometimes referred to as *regional unemployment*. The decline of traditional industries and industrial areas may be caused, on the supply side, by the exhaustion of natural resources. On the demand side, changes in consumer tastes, competition from substitute products, or new producers in other areas may be responsible. Thus the coal industries of Europe and North America have suffered from new sources of fuel and power, especially petroleum; while the cotton industry in Lancashire suffered first from a loss of export markets to new competitors, Japan initially, then India and other developing countries, secondly from synthetic substitutes like nylon and rayon, and finally from cheaper imports generally. Towns and regions specializing in shipbuilding, railway rolling-stock, and more recently even technologically advanced aircraft and spacecraft, have been affected adversely by structural changes of this sort.

Changes in supply and demand can result in unemployment of the affected workers because these are *immobile*, either because they are reluctant to leave a particular region to seek their fortunes elsewhere, or because they cannot easily be retrained in order to enter new occupations. For this last reason, older workers in declining industries are particularly susceptible.

The characteristic of structural unemployment is its long-term nature. When changes in supply and demand are less fundamental, and immobility less great, labour may be left unemployed for much shorter periods. In this case, as a sub-category of structural unemployment, the unemployment may be described as *frictional*, due to 'friction' reducing the speed of adjustment of the price mechanism, in particular relative wages in different labour markets.

Structural unemployment mainly relates to industry and therefore to industrial countries, but less developed countries may also experience unemployment of this type if a mineral is exhausted, or if demand for a primary export falls sharply. Thus the decline in the price of sisal, caused by the advent of artificial fibre (nylon rope and twine), led to a drastic reduction in the work-force on Tanzanian sisal estates from 100,000 in 1964 to around 30,000 in 1967. The difference in the case of less developed countries is that labour is generally more mobile, since mine or plantation workers who have been recruited as migrant labour are able to return to their home areas; and that the resultant unemployment will be less visible, and not open unemployment, workers being able to turn to low-productivity self-employment on small farms.

The unemployment of school leavers or of university graduates in less developed countries may also be described as structural unemployment, in the sense of their being trained for specific 'white-collar' jobs which are in short supply. The difference here is that demand for a given category of manpower is limited to begin with, but the educational machinery over time produces an excess supply of trained people to fill the jobs available.

In less developed countries regional immobility of labour may be caused, not by unwillingness of labour to move, but by obstacles to this movement. The labour force is industrial countries is now fairly homogeneous in respect of its cultural features. Despite some institutional barriers, the labour force is not separated by very many differences of race, religion, caste, tribe, or sex into completely isolated and non-competing groups. There is considerable mobility between different occupations within the paid labour force and between the various levels of skill and responsibility within an occupation. In Africa some of these barriers are greater, particularly the tribal one, which may take the form of favouritism in the offer of jobs and job promotion, or barriers preventing people from overcrowded regions from obtaining jobs or land elsewhere where it is available.

Finally, we may distinguish *seasonal unemployment* and *erratic (casual) unemployment*. Regular seasonal unemployment is caused by annual variations of season which affect agriculture and fisheries, and out-of-door activities such as construction, summer or winter sports, or tourism. Since agricultural employment forms a greater part of total employment in less developed economies, seasonal unemployment is greatest, in absolute and relative terms, in the developing countries. And since a large proportion of this agricultural employment is self-employment on family farms, a large proportion takes the form of disguised unemployment, since workers continue to do minor tasks on their farms during the 'off-peak' seasons.

Apart from seasonal variations in demand for labour caused by variations in the climate, certain occupations such as dock labour or construction work on roads and buildings are affected by erratic variations in demand for their services. Dockworkers are often hired when work on ships is available, being offered 'casual employment' at such times and at other times being unemployed. This casual or erratic employment is becoming less serious in developed countries, partly because mechanization has reduced the number of casual workers, and partly because the terms of service now available to dockers and similar groups guarantee them regular employment (even if this is, in fact, partly disguised unemployment!). Many workers in less developed countries, not covered by trade unions, obtain work on a casual or temporary basis, particularly in local road construction.

Structural 'over-unemployment' in Eastern Africa

A particular form of structural imbalance in the labour market of less developed economies is as-sociated with migration of people to the towns in excess of the towns' capacity to offer jobs, generally resulting in serious and increasing urban unemployment. Professor Bairoch has estimated[3] that in the late 1960s the rate of open unemployment in developing countries was of the order of 16 or 20 per cent of the relevant labour force (four or five times the rate in developed countries), and argues that this is primarily 'structural over-unemployment', as he defines it. In his definition this urban unemployment is 'a high level of structural unemployment resulting from a disequilibrium between supply and demand caused especially by a massive inflow of an active population cast out of a rural environment'. As in the cases of school leaver and graduate unemployment mentioned above, this arises not out of a decline in the number of jobs available, but from an excessive rate of increase in the supply of workers in a particular section of the labour market.

Open unemployment in the urban areas of Eastern Africa has only become a major economic policy problem for the governments since the 1950s: since independence largely. In this respect Eastern Africa (Mauritius apart) is a late arrival to the problem: many parts of Latin America, South Asia, and even North and West Africa have experienced high rates of open unemployment and serious disguised urban unemployment for a much longer time.

Taking developing countries as a whole, the rate of open urban unemployment is estimated to have been about $7\frac{1}{2}$ per cent of the urban paid labour force in the 1960s, or more than twice the rate experienced in the 12 industrial countries of OECD, where it averaged about 3 per cent. Moreover urban unemployment in Africa and elsewhere today appears to be at a much higher rate than the urban unemployment experienced by industrial countries at earlier stages of their growth. Bairoch attributes this contemporary problem for developing countries to one main factor, which he calls 'urban inflation'—the too rapid urbanization of poor countries compared with industrial countries at comparable stages of their economic development. Thus, for example, by 1970 something like 21 per cent of the total populations of developing countries lived in towns, the same proportion which was not reached by Europe (excluding the UK and Russia) until 1890, when their real GNP per head was already about 90 per cent higher than the 1970 level for developing countries. Today's poor countries have become urbanized, moreover, without becoming very industrialized; unlike nineteenth-century Europe. In Europe the percentage of the labour force employed in manufacturing was actually higher than the share of the population living in towns until around 1980; whereas in developing countries the degree of urbanization was higher than the percentage of employment provided by manufacturing by 1940. Even Africa had some 13 per cent of its population living in towns by 1960, but only 7 per cent of its labour force engaged in 'modern' manufacturing. By 1970 over 20 per cent of African people lived in urban areas; but the scope for employing its population in manufacturing had hardly widened beyond the 7 per cent estimated for 1960.

Causes of urban over-unemployment in Eastern Africa

On the 'supply' side, the principal causes of rapid urbanization and urban unemployment can be analysed as:

(a) population growth and rural population pressures;

(b) wide gaps in income level between urban and rural areas;

(c) expansion in formal and inappropriate education.

On the 'demand' side, the supply of capital and other cooperating factors of production has not kept up with this too rapid rate of urbanization, while for various reasons employment opportunities in the formal sector have grown less than in proportion to output. The problem of urban over-unemployment must therefore be tackled by improving the labour-absorptive capacities of urban activities (on the demand side) as well as efforts to reduce the long-term problem of rural–urban migration. We start by looking at each of the supply factors listed above. Migration appears to have occurred as a result of a combination of 'push' and 'pull' factors.

Population growth and migration 'push'

In Chapter 3 we discussed the post-war population explosion, which has affected Eastern Africa along with most other poor countries. Since around 1950 the total population of Eastern Africa has been increasing at an average compound rate of some $2\frac{1}{2}$ per cent, compared with a rate of only 1 per cent in the first half of the century. Since the majority of people still live in the rural areas—over three-quarters in fact—the rural population has been growing almost as fast as the total population and, with it, the proportion in the younger age groups who are most likely to migrate in search of work. Thus the 'push' factor behind the rural–urban drift of job seekers has been the increasing population densities on arable land, leading to more underemployment and, in some regions particularly, open rural unemployment among landless families.

Of course the urban populations have been increasing still faster, at almost twice the total African rate of $2\frac{1}{2}$ per cent; and while this has been mainly due to immigration from rural areas in Eastern Africa, the natural rates of increase amongst the existing urban populations have also been higher than the rural natural increase. Thanks to improvements in medical science, as well as better health facilities, urban birth rates have been higher, and mortality rates lower, than in the more impoverished rural areas. Thus part of the urbanization process has sprung from natural increase and will continue to add to the size of the active population even if the drift from rural areas were to cease. Nevertheless it is still this drift which is responsible for the greater part of urbanization. What factors have lured people to the towns, or have kept them there, despite the growing problem of unemployment?

Wide gaps in income level: urban 'pull'

In addition to the 'push' of population pressure in the rural areas, migration has resulted from the 'pull' or attraction of the urban areas. Some debate has taken place regarding the motives or migrants to the towns as between (1) differences in earning possibilities between town and country; (2) the general attraction and excitement of 'modern' life in the towns; and (3) the search for jobs appropriate to the kinds of formal education received in the schools.

Of these the size of the urban–rural income differential (URID) appears to be the most important. Bairoch has argued that the gap between the real income available to the average townsman and the average rural inhabitant in developing countries today is not only substantial and widening, but is also much bigger than the gap between farm labourers and unskilled urban workers in nineteenth-century Europe. More specifically, he states[5] that the average gap in developing countries between the wages of agricultural labourers and those of unskilled workers in industry can be estimated very roughly as between 80 and 150 per cent. The gap in *average* wages in agriculture and industry he puts at between 100 and 200 per cent, and the gap in real income (taking into account cost of living and other differences) at between 60 and 120 per cent.

These estimates must be treated with extreme caution, as they are not based on accurate measurement; and in particular a distinction needs to be made between urban earnings in the formal sector and in the informal sector, for which the urban–rural income differential will be very much less. However the percentage difference between the GNP per head of the active population in agriculture and other sectors of activity seems to be wider in African countries than in other developing regions. In the early 1960s it was some 940 per cent ($9\frac{1}{2}$ times) larger in Liberia,

460 per cent in Sierra Leone, 230 per cent in the Sudan, and around 150 per cent in Ethiopia. The wage gap between unskilled rural labourers and unskilled urban workers was rather smaller, of course, since non-labour factor incomes are excluded, but was probably at least 100 per cent in most African countries during the later 1960s. In Ethiopia the gap was around 200 per cent, urban unskilled wages being 300 per cent of rural income per worker.

Expansion of formal and inappropriate education

The role of formal education as a major cause of rural–urban drift is clearly apparent in the available statistics and in the research studies of sociologists and economists. In nearly all developing countries the rate of urban unemployment in the 15–24 age group is at least double the rate for all age groups. Table 33.1 shows some comparisons among a selection of developing and developed countries. Although unemployment is also markedly higher among young people in developed countries, the contrast is less striking and the unemployment rate much lower. Unemployment among young people in these countries is usually short-term frictional unemployment among recent school leavers seeking their first job, and nowadays has little to do with migration from rural areas or differences in educational levels compared with older workers. The situation in developing countries is clearly different. While only 4 per cent of 15–24-year-olds were unemployed in Britain (in 1968) nearly 40 per cent of young people in this age group were unemployed in Algeria and Sri Lanka, 22 per cent in Ghana, and 23 per cent in Kinshasa (Zaire). The table shows also that the problem in less developed countries is especially one of unemployment among younger people, the rates in the 15–24 years group generally being about *double* the rates for all ages, 22 per cent in Ghana, for instance, compared to $11\frac{1}{2}$ per cent, for other ages. This compares with 4.1 and 3.7 per cent for Great Britain.

Indications are that it is not simply younger people that are particularly vulnerable to unemployment, as these data suggest, but those with a certain amount of formal education. A recent study of urban unemployment in Ethiopia[6] indicates that the 15–19 years group accounted for as much as 74 per cent of the *registered* unemployed in a two-year period ending mid-1971. Less than 10 per cent of these registered job seekers were placed in jobs during this time, and most of these placements were for machine operators or labourers. Illiterates accounted for less than one-half of the registrations; elementary school leavers represented 37 per cent; secondary school leavers, 13 per cent; and people with higher levels of eduction, 4 per cent. An analysis of job seekers registering with Labour Exchanges in Ethiopia in 1967–71 provides more evidence. Whereas labourers had a 10 per cent chance of a job placement, clerical and sales workers had only a 6.5 per chance. The occupational groups in greatest demand were in fact those requiring higher skills or experience: machine operators had the highest chance of a job, 29 per cent being placed, followed by professional and technical workers with a 21.5 per cent chance of placement.

Other African countries show similar patterns: the typical urban unemployed worker is a young person with *more* than six years' schooling, and it is among these primary school leavers that the unemployment rates are highest, as they compete increasingly in vain for the traditional white-collar clerical and sales jobs now pre-empted by secondary school leavers.

While not all school leaver unemployment is due to migration, movement to the towns by this group accounts for a large proportion. Thus a study of one region in the Ivory Coast[7] showed that among young people only 8 per cent of illiterate males intended to migrate, compared to 42 per cent for literate males, and 61 per cent for those with six years of primary schooling. Corresponding figures among females were 11.55 and 75 per cent. As another indication of migration, Nairobi finds wage employment for one-third of Kenya's paid labour force and contains one-half of the country's urban population. But in 1973 it accounted for less than 5 per cent of primary school enrolment: thus most of Nairobi's workforce had not been to school in Nairobi but had migrated from other areas where they would have obtained their schooling.

Table 33.1 Rates of urban unemployment among young people and for all age groups in selected countries

Country	Year	15–24 years (%)	All ages (%)
Africa			
Algeria	1966	39.3	24.7
Ethiopia*	1970	15.0	8.0
Ghana	1960	21.9	11.6
Zaire (Kinshasa only)	1967	23.0	12.9
Other developing countries			
Colombia	1968	23.1	13.6
India	1961–2	8.0	3.2
Trinidad	1968	26.0	14.0
Sri Lanka	1968	39.0	15.0
Developed countries			
Great Britain	1968	4.1	3.7
Japan	1968	2.0	1.2
West Germany	1968	2.5	1.5

SOURCE: P. Bairoch, op. cit., pp. 57 and 58 (adjusted by authors)
* Authors' estimate

Similarly in Tanzania R. H. Sabot found[8] that there were two and a half times as many migrants with some education as there were among the rural population as a whole (for the over-14 age group). Not only were migration rates markedly higher for educated people, but the migration rate rose with the level of educational attainment. Within the Standard I–IV grades the migration rate was only a little higher than the overall rate; but that for Standard V–VIII grades was five times higher, for Forms I–VI some eleven times higher, and for university graduates as much as twenty-two and a half times.

An economic model of rural–urban migration

Thus rural–urban migration appears to be the result of a 'push' from population pressure and a 'pull' from the incentive of high urban earnings, supplemented by the effect of formal education on the aspirations of young people, again inducing them to seek their fortunes in the town. Focusing again on the urban–rural income differential, two American economists, J. R. Harris and M. P. Todaro, have developed a theoretical model of rural–urban migration, based on their Eastern African research experiences, which relates net urban immigration to the *expected* income gap.[9] They were concerned to explain why people continued to migrate to the towns when there was already substantial urban unemployment. By relating movement to expected earnings, they were able to show that it would still be rational to migrate, even if there was a possibility, or probability, of remaining unemployed. The expected income gap is not simply the difference between an urban wage rate and a rural earnings rate, but the smaller difference between the urban wage rate adjusted for the probability of getting a job and the rural earnings rate, both expressed in real terms.

The key equation in their model is given by the equilibrium condition:

$$W_a = \frac{N_m}{N_u} \cdot \bar{W}_m$$

where W_a is the rural earnings rate, $\bar{W}_m$ is the fixed urban wage rate, determined largely by minimum wage policy, N_m is the number employed (jobs available) in the formal sector, and N_u the total number of people in the urban pool of labour looking for jobs. Assuming that there is a high rate of labour turnover and thus a revolving labour force (so that he has the same chance of employment as anyone else), the probability of a new migrant's obtaining a job is given by the proportion of jobs available to the number of job seekers, that is, by N_m/N_u. If $\frac{N_m}{N_u} = \frac{2}{3}$,

for example, the migrant could assume that over a long period such as a year, say, he might be employed for eight months out of twelve, and unemployed the rest of the time. If the urban wage rate were shs 300 a month, he could *on average* over the year obtain shs 200 per month.

Suppose $\bar{W}_m$ is 50 per cent higher than W_a, so that $\bar{W}_m = \frac{3}{2} W_a$, while four-fifths of the urban pool are employed, so that $\frac{N_m}{N_u} = \frac{4}{5}$, with $N_m = 40{,}000$, say, and $N_u = 50{,}000$ people. The right-hand side of the equation, the *expected* urban wage rate, would be equal to:

$$\frac{4}{5}\left(\frac{3}{2}W_a\right) = \frac{6}{5}W_a$$

Thus the expected urban wage would be 20 per cent or one-fifth, higher than the rural earnings rate. It would therefore pay migrants to continue to come to the urban area, even though we start here with 10,000 unemployed.

If only one-third of the urban work-force were employed, then, with the same income gap, the expected urban wage rate would be only:

$$\frac{1}{3}\left(\frac{3}{2}W_a\right) = \frac{1}{2}W_a$$

or only half the rural earnings rate. In this case the incentive to migrate to the urban area would not be sufficient, and indeed the direction of the migration flow would be reversed.

Assuming the former situation, with the expected urban rate higher than the rural earnings rate, migration would continue, with an elastic supply of would-be migrants, until N_u equalled 60,000, an increase of 10,000 migrants. This would make $\frac{N_m}{N_u} = \frac{4}{6}$, so that the expected urban wage rate would be equal to $\frac{4}{6}\left(\frac{3}{2}W_a\right) = W_a$, exactly equal to the rural earnings rate. There would then be no more incentive for migrants to move, and we should have an equilibrium situation.

A particular interesting feature of the model is its implication that efforts by the government, for example, to increase the number of jobs available, could actually lead to an increase in the number of urban unemployed in an Eastern African country. Since more urban jobs attract more migrants (by increasing the probability of a new migrant's getting a job), the urban unemployment pool fills up again.

If potential candidates relate their chances of obtaining an urban job (and hence their expectations of higher real incomes) to some fairly fixed ratio of urban jobs to the total work-force (including the unemployed and those waiting in informal sector jobs), the open unemployed and informal sector underemployed will also be some constant multiple of the number of jobs. In terms of our numerical example, suppose we are initially in equilibrium with $N_m = 40{,}000$, $N_u = 60{,}000$, and $\bar{W}_m = \frac{3}{2}$, when employment (jobs available) increases to 50,000. The expected urban wage rate will now equal $\frac{50}{60}\bar{W}_m$, or $\frac{5}{6}\left(\frac{3}{2}W_a\right) = \frac{5}{4}W_a$. There is now a positive incentive for further migration to the urban area, which will exist until the urban pool has increased to 75,000, when the expected wage rate will equal $\frac{50}{75}\bar{W}_m = \frac{50}{75}\left(\frac{3}{2}W_a\right) = W_a$. Thus an increase of 10,000 in the number of jobs available will have increased the numbers *unemployed* by 5,000, from 20,000 to 25,000.

Wages and employment growth

We stated above that structural 'over-unemployment' in the towns had arisen out of rural–urban migration, on the supply side, and slow growth of job opportunities, on the demand side. The relatively slow growth in the number of jobs available, despite capital formation and substantial growth in aggregate output, has been a common feature of paid employment in Eastern Africa during the past twenty years or so. Annual rates of growth in real GDP averaging 4 or 5 per cent have been sustained, but the number of workers in formal wage employment has grown much more slowly, so that in terms of the concept which we introduced in Chapter 22 (see page 316) the output-elasticity of employment has been very low. In fact, over the period 1954–64 Robson and Lury calculated that formal wage employment stagnated or actually *declined* in absolute terms in most Eastern African countries, as shown in Table 33.2.

Several factors appear to have contributed to the slow growth in employment, including structural changes in the industrial composition of national output. In particular there was a decline in construction activity, which is highly labour-intensive and has production linkages with other industries like building materials and transport. Total paid employment in Uganda, Zambia, and Malawi, especially, declined sharply in the late 1950s, largely because of a fall in construction.

Table 33.2 *Annual percentage changes in African wage employment and real wages, 1954–64*

	Annual percentage change in	
	Employment (%)	Real wages (%)
Tanzania	−2.6	14.1
Uganda	−0.6	8.2
Zambia	0.0	8.0
Kenya	0.7	3.4
Rhodesia (Zimbabwe)	1.2	3.5
Ghana	6.9	3.0

SOURCE: P. Robson and D. A. Lury (eds.), *The Economies of Africa*, Allen and Unwin, London, 1969, Table 15, p. 62

However, increases in real wages also appear to have been a significant factor restraining the growth in employment, the change in wage employment and in real wages showing a marked negative correlation in Table 33.2. In other words, there appears to have been a statistical association between growth in the number of jobs and the rate of change of real wages.

As Table 33.3 shows, there has been some reversal of the situation since the mid-1960s with wage employment increasing at a faster rate, while rates of increase in real wages have been controlled. The figures this time exclude employment in agriculture. Association with changes in real wages is not clear in respect of all non-agricultural jobs, but appears to exist again for employment in manufacturing. There is thus some support for the argument that rapid increases in real wages retard paid employment opportunities.

It is the combination of high formal sector wage rates and various subsidies to capital which has

Table 33.3 *Annual percentage changes in African wage employment and in real wages in the late 1960s.*

	Annual percentage change in employment in		Non-agricultural real wages (%)
	Manufacturing (%)	All non-agricultural jobs (%)	
Malawi, 1968–74	8.7	9.2	−0.2
Mauritius, 1966–73	10.6	6.7	0.1 (−0.5)
Ghana, 1964–71	7.2	0.8	1.5 (2.5)
Tanzania, 1964–71	5.2	3.8	3.9*
Uganda, 1964–71	6.2	6.0	n.a.
Zambia, 1964–72	4.3	6.4	4.9
Kenya, 1964–72	5.7	4.3	5.7

SOURCE: Authors' estimates from ILO, *Yearbook of Labour Statistics* and national data sources
* 1965–70 wage change
Figures in brackets represent change in real wages for manufacturing.

tended to encourage capital-intensive techniques and low output-elasticity of employment in Eastern African countries. We might mention especially:

(1) for a long time in Eastern Africa imports of machinery and equipment were allowed in duty-free, as a means of encouraging investment;

(2) generous investment and depreciation allowances for tax purposes were made, with the same intention, but also helping firms more the greater the capital-intensity of their method of production, thus discouraging the choice of labour-intensive methods.

To the extent that factor price distortions, by encouraging the adoption of capital-intensive techniques or the choice of capital-intensive industries, reduce the availability of jobs and increase unemployment, such unemployment may also be described as neoclassical unemployment, as discussed presently.

General unemployment: the contrast between developed and less developed countries

We made the distinction above between general, structural, and seasonal unemployment, but discussed only the last two in any detail. Here we shall examine the origins of general unemployment in developed and less developed countries, and show that these are very different in the two cases.

The Keynesian theory of aggregate income and employment outlined in Chapter 28 was developed during the 1930s, a period of widespread unemployment in the developed industrial countries. It attributed the unemployment of labour and other resources to the lack of effective demand. Thus the Keynesian theory made the level of aggregate employment *demand-determined*, and the cure for any pronounced degree of unemployment lay in expanding aggregate money demand so that all involuntarily unemployed labour could be employed to produce more real output. Such unemployment was essentially *short-term* (though Keynes and other Keynesian economists were also concerned about the possibility of long-term or secular stagnation due to lack of effective demand), in that the level of investment, and thus expenditure generally, might be affected by a temporary loss of business confidence lasting a few years only. Another feature of Keynesian unemployment is that *unemployment of labour is associated with unemployed capital*, as plant and machinery become idle during an economic depression due to lack of orders.

Keynes appeared to be more successful in explaining general unemployment than the previous classical and neoclassical economists. For the neoclassical economists, unemployment of any factor, or a 'glut' of goods on the market, was due to price rigidity, in this case *general wage-price rigidity*. If product and factor markets were functioning properly, any 'glut' or excess supply would force suppliers to reduce price towards the equilibrium level. And according to the 'marginal productivity' theory of factor pricing, a fall in wage rates would induce employers to engage more labour. Moreover, since capital and land could also be hired in factor markets, insufficiency of investment could be eliminated by a fall in the rate of interest, making investment more profitable. Keynesian economists rejected this neoclassical view that wage-price flexibility could be relied upon to 'clear' markets at a full employment level of income. It was the levels of output and employment which were flexible, not product and factor prices. 'Organized labour' in trade unions resisted money wage cuts, and since wage incomes provided the largest and most stable portion of aggregate money demand, cuts in money wages would reduce demand and prices, so that real wages might not fall; while at the same time changes in the rate of interest might be ineffective in stimulating investment, particularly during a crisis of business confidence. While Keynesian analysis is widely accepted for advanced capitalist countries, however, its relevance to less developed countries has been seriously questioned and, as we shall see, some elements of the neoclassical analysis are useful in discussing employment problems in the less developed countries.

In contrast to industrial countries, general unemployment in less developed countries is the result of *deficiences on the supply side*, rather than deficiencies of effective demand, the basic problem being the shortage of cooperating factors, especially capital, land, and enterprise, to combine with labour in productive activities. Economists sometimes refer to unemployment in poor countries as being 'classical' unemployment, since its alleviation involves the *longer-run* problem of capital accumulation by *increasing* thrift—quite the opposite of 'Keynesian' unemployment caused by 'too much' thrift!

Shortage of *land*, in overpopulated countries, and regions within countries, may, as we have seen, result in open or disguised unemployment in both rural and (through rural–urban migration) urban areas. A special feature of less developed economies with predominant agricultural sectors is that land shortage is likely to manifest itself in *underemployment*, with each family lacking sufficient land to keep itself fully employed, the size of holding varying in size until an increasing proportion of people are actually landless.

Shortage of *capital* means, in the rural areas, that productivity will be low and that even where land is plentiful and labour fully employed, as in many parts of Africa, family incomes will be low. This means, significantly, that in less developed countries *the problem of unemployment and underemployment is part of a general problem of poverty and low productivity due to lack of the cooperant factors, either capital or land, with which labour can work*. In the urban areas shortage of capital, due to lack of investment in the relatively small modern sector, means fewer jobs available, and thus, as labour migrates, open or disguised unemployment once more.[10]

General underemployment may stem not merely from lack of land or capital, but from lack of markets. In Chapter 19 we outlined the 'vent-for-surplus' theory of international trade which argued that the rapid expansion of agricultural export production which had occurred in many less developed countries following the introduction of cash crops indicated that resources, both land and labour, had previously been idle, for lack of export production possibilities. Varying opportunities from area to area for adding to subsistence food production mean that this factor will underlie unemployment of labour in many cases, occurring either as disguised or open unemployment. As in the case of Keynesian unemployment, lack of demand is the problem, and the supply of output is highly elastic: but whereas the Keynesian problem is short-run, in this case there is a long-term problem of markets.

The extent of disguised unemployment in less developed countries

We have referred extensively to disguised unemployment in less developed countries. Formerly it was thought that such underemployment was widespread and that it implied a great labour potential which, if put to work, might even provide the basis of economic development. Thus Arthur Lewis's model of economic development with unlimited supplies of labour, discussed in Chapter 31, was based on utilizing this apparent reservoir of labour.

In recent years the existence of a vast pool of disguised unemployment has been questioned, on the basis of an increasing number of empirical studies, and it is clearly much less extensive than originally thought. In particular it appears that much apparent unemployment, when people in the rural areas appeared idle, was merely seasonal. People were idle because they were between seasonal labour peaks, having planted, say, and now waiting for harvest. In this situation surplus labour, in the sense of labour with a zero marginal product, does not exist, and withdrawal of workers from the rural sector would reduce *annual* output, since in peak periods less land

could be cleared for planting, say, or the same volume of crops could not be harvested.

Labour potential in the rural areas may still exist, however, even if the marginal product of labour is positive and there is no disguised unemployment in this sense: if labour productivity (average product per worker) in agriculture is low, output could be increased by transferring workers from the low productivity sector to a high productivity 'modern' sector, if this could be expanded. For labour supply to the modern sector to be elastic at a low wage rate it is only necessary for average and marginal product to be low in the supplying sector, not for marginal product to be zero.

Features of employment and unemployment in less developed countries

It will be useful to summarize briefly, using the material of Chapter 28 and this one, the differences we have found in the nature of employment and unemployment in advanced and less developed countries.

(1) Both can have general unemployment and underemployment, but the causes are frequently not the same, short-run demand deficiency in the one case, and long-run supply deficiencies, of land and capital, in the other, being important.

(2) The 'vent-for-surplus' theory implies a further explanation of unemployment and underemployment in less developed countries, also based on demand deficiency, but through a long-term rather than short-term lack of markets.

(3) To the extent that Keynesian multiplier analysis operates on the demand side, this operation differs, with exports rather than investment as the most important element of autonomous demand, and the high propensity to import restricting the domestic effect of the multiplier process rather than excessive saving ('underconsumption').

(4) Employment in the subsistence economy is important in less developed economies or, more exactly, the application of labour to non-monetary activities.

(5) This non-monetary sector is insulated from the effects of multiplier analysis, which is limited to income derived from the market. Rounds of monetary spending cannot be transmitted to unpaid labour. Any income benefits from extra money outlays must involve the sale of products and labour services to the market economy if idle labour or other resources in the non-monetary sector are to be employed more fully.

(6) A substantial part of unemployment may take

the form of underemployment or disguised unemployment. Displacement of labour in the formal sector, whether for Keynesian effective demand reasons or structural reasons, may lead, not to open unemployment, but to low-productivity employment in rural areas or in the informal sector.

(7) For this reason it is difficult to draw a firm line in less developed countries between the problem of employment and the problem of low production and incomes.

(8) Factor price distortions may produce a 'neoclassical' type of unemployment in less developed countries.

(9) Large-scale urban unemployment, which has been termed 'structural over-unemployment', is a special feature of the unemployment problem in less developed countries.

(10) Unemployment of school leavers and in some countries of graduates is a form of structural unemployment to which less developed countries are prone.

(11) A non-homogeneous labour force, and immobility of labour between regions for tribal and other reasons, is another special feature.

(12) Seasonal unemployment and underemployment are much more important in less developed countries, because of the predominance of the agricultural sector.

Remedies for unemployment in less developed countries

The measures appropriate as remedies for unemployment will clearly depend on the type and cause of the unemployment.

Keynesian remedies

Keynesian counter-cyclical remedies are clearly irrelevant to a great extent to the basic causes of unemployment in less developed countries which are *structural* in nature. There *are* elements of cyclical unemployment, nevertheless, associated with fluctuations in export demand, in public investment, and, on the supply side, in variations in the volume and value of domestic agricultural production.

Hence fiscal and monetary policies can be used to reduce the impact of short-term fluctuations in demand. However, the main relevance of Keynesian remedies lies in international measures to stabilize export earnings (cutting out the source of fluctuations) through IMF compensatory financial arrangements and, more fundamentally, to ensure stable and expanding export markets. Since the supply of foreign capital for development projects also fluctuates with economic conditions

abroad, as well as at home, the World Bank and other aid agencies can help to even out any marked fluctuations in private capital flows.

Keynesian measures to manage the domestic components of demand may become more relevant in the future as the supply of cooperating factors for labour increases, thus increasing the elasticity of aggregate supply. A multiplier process will then operate more on real output and less on the price level or on the level of imports. But the scope for domestic demand management will remain limited while exports are such a large component of final demand, and imports constitute the main leakage in the multiplier process.

Classical remedies: control of population growth and accumulation of physical and human capital

The classical remedy for unemployment is growth: via the accumulation of capital, the cooperating factor. This long-term solution is favoured under both capitalist and socialist systems, and socialist planners may in fact favour a much greater sacrifice of present consumption for the sake of achieving expansion. It is, of course, a solution to both unemployment and poverty, but it is not a remedy to immediate and pressing problems of employment in the short run.

Accumulation of capital will be ineffective, as will most other measures in the long term, if it is outpaced by population growth. Particularly where the supply of land is limited, population growth must be kept within limits if the problems of urban unemployment and rural underemployment are not to become unmanageable.

Neoclassical remedies for unemployment

'Neoclassical' solutions for structural unemployment in less developed countries focus on distortions and rigidities in factor and product markets. As we have seen, institutional factors may raise wage rates above the market equilibrium, reducing employment and encouraging the substitution of capital. Almost all the Eastern African countries are now making serious attempts to restrain wage increases in the formal sector through incomes policies and other means. Fiscal policy has recently been altered in Kenya with the imposition of import duty on capital goods and reconsideration of investment allowances. Attempts are being made to encourage the employment of lower-paid workers directly through the choice of the techniques in industry *and* agriculture, and by the encouragement of small-scale industry. The gap between the formal and rural sector of the economy may be bridged by encouraging the development of the informal sector in which 'appropriate' technology is used.

Policies for education and training

Structural unemployment among particular educational levels or sections of the labour force can be reduced or avoided by designing suitable educational policies, as we shall see presently. This will also reduce migration and urban unemployment. Formal education which exaggerates the glamour of urban life and is geared to 'urban' jobs for which there is an excess supply of labour may be modified in favour of education and training which provide preparation for a life of work in the rural areas. Direct measures may also be taken through the provision of welfare services and social amenities in the rural areas in order to reduce rural–urban 'drift.'

Remedies for seasonal unemployment

We have already commented on the magnitude and importance of seasonal unemployment in less developed economies. This may be reduced (1) by measures to reduce labour bottlenecks: for instance mechanization of a particularly labour-intensive operation like clearing new land could permit total acreage to expand, increasing the amount of work required at *other* times of the year; (2) by measures to even out labour requirements over the year, for instance by irrigation, to reduce dependence on seasonal rainfall, by selecting a complementary combination of farm activities, each of which uses maximum labour at different times, or research into crop varieties which can be grown during other parts of the year; (3) by introducing supplementary activities during the slack season, such as handicraft industries, tourism, or communal construction projects.

Planning productive employment in Mauritius

In Mauritius, an island economy with an explosive rate of population growth, as we saw in Chapter 3, the employment problem was considered so acute that the government's Four-Year Plan for 1971–1975[11] was given the title of 'Plan Towards the Creation of Productive Employment', and focused on this problem. In an earlier report to the Government, subsequently published as a book, Professor J. E. Meade had stated, in 1960, that 'the major objective of future economic planning must be to keep unemployment as low as possible'.[12] In addition to the overall problem of unemployment associated with the population—land balance—he identified a structural problem of school leavers (many with inadequate academic, let alone technical, qualifications) arising from (a) a shortage of the type of jobs which school leavers aspired to hold, and (b) a disinclination among young men, especially, to do manual work. One result was, for instance, that seasonal shortages of labour for the sugar industry existed side by side with unemployment calculated, in the late 1950s, to be some 15 per cent of the economically active population.

Meade recommended as a means of maximizing the expansion of employment opportunities for school leavers and others a strong incomes policy aimed at stabilizing labour costs for several years. In the longer run more effective population planning and a more appropriate educational system might make it possible for real wages to rise without endangering the balance between job creation and the growth in job seekers.

The 1971–75 Plan followed closely the broad strategy recommended by Meade in 1960, and set a target for creating 130,000 new jobs between 1969 and 1980, an increase of 67 per cent on the total of 195,000 employed in 1969. Where these additional jobs were expected to be made available is shown in Table 33.4. Out of the 130,000 additional jobs, 110,000 were to be in the following: agriculture (33,000), 'other manufacturing' (42,000), construction (17,000), and services (18,000). Agriculture will provide a sizeable proportion of the increase and must make a major contribution as a predominant economic sector: but it will actually decline in relative importance by 1980, from 39 per cent to about 33 per cent of total employment, reflecting the limitations of land shortage and monoculture based on sugar. The key sector is 'other manufacturing', where employment was expected to increase by 228 per cent in eleven years (doubling its share of the total from 9.4 to 18.6 per cent), supported by construction, where employment was to increase by 130 per cent. This expansion was to be based on small-scale labour-intensive industries, and the plan to adopt a policy of industrialization in an overpopulated island, making the most of the cheap labour available though selection of labour-intensive industries, is in line with Arthur Lewis's recommendations for the West Indies and Ghana, as described in our Chapter 23, Industry in Eastern Africa. Such industries are best able to absorb surplus labour. In the Mauritian Plan, with an emphasis on job creation rather than maximizing the rate of growth of GDP, only small improvements in labour productivity were expected in advance of reaching full employment. A 'trade-off' between productivity increases and job opportunities was thus recognized in the Plan.

The emphasis on construction and public works is also because of the labour intensity of these activities, chosen for this reason despite what would be a low immediate social return on investment, although contributing to the productive capacity of the economy in the long term. Similarly tourism, listed under Services, though having drawbacks as a vehicle for economic development, is highly labour-intensive and, with the obvious potential of Mauritius as a tourist centre, along with other Indian Ocean islands such as the Seychelles, is expected to contribute much of the substantial increase in employment under this head, as well as diversifying export earnings. As we showed earlier, in Table 33.3, Mauritius was already very successful in restraining increases in real wages during the 1960s, with the effect that non-

agricultural jobs increased quite rapidly: by about 60 per cent, in fact, between 1966 and 1973. At the same time, over the six years 1967–73, manufacturing jobs doubled. During the first four years of the period covered in Table 33.4, from 1969 to 1973, employment in manufacturing increased by 83 per cent, well in line with the 228 per cent expansion envisaged over the thirteen years to 1980. Total non-agricultural jobs over the same four years increased by 41 per cent, a cumulative rate again ahead of the 87 per cent expansion (from 112,300 to 209,400) envisaged in the Plan.

Table 33.4 *Creation of productive employment in Mauritius: planned number of jobs by sector*

	Numbers in 1969 (thousands)	(%)	Target for 1980 (thousands)	(%)	Increase (%)
Agriculture, livestock and fishing	76.1	39.0	109.0	33.5	43.2
Mining and quarrying	0.4	0.2	1.0	0.3	—
Sugar and tea manufacture	6.6	3.4	6.6	2.0	—
Other manufacturing	18.4	9.4	60.4	18.6	228.3
Total manufacturing	25.4	12.8	67.0	20.6	168.0
Construction and public works	13.0	6.7	30.0	9.2	130.8
Electricity and water	1.3	0.6	3.0	0.9	—
Transport and communications	13.4	6.9	20.0	6.2	49.2
Trade	19.8	10.2	28.0	8.6	41.4
Services, including education and health	32.0	16.5	50.0	14.5	56.2
Central and local government	13.9	7.1	17.0	5.3	22.3
Total	195.0	100.0	325.0*	100.0	66.3

SOURCE: Mauritius, *Four-Year Plan for Social and Econimic Development, 1971–5, Vol. I: General Analysis and Policies*

* Plus another 18,000 jobs in the *Travail pour Tous* programme—the work-for-all programme to find productive jobs for the unemployed

Questions on Chapter 33

1. Explain the meaning of disguised unemployment, and discuss the forms it takes in rural and urban areas.
2. Compare general and structural unemployment, showing how each of these may arise in developed and less developed countries.
3. Discuss the nature and origin of 'structural over-unemployment' found in the urban areas of less developed countries today.
4. What evidence is there that education contributes to unemployment in developing countries?
5. Use the Harris-Todaro 'model' to show how an increase in the number of urban jobs available could actually *increase* urban unemployment.
6. What kinds of factor price distortions have contributed to unemployment in Eastern Africa?
7. Discuss the special features of employment and unemployment in less developed countries.
8. For what reasons do you consider that the scope for domestic demand management on Keynesian lines will be limited in less developed countries?
9. What kinds of action may be taken to reduce seasonal unemployment in developing countries?
10. Discuss the main features of Mauritius's Plan for the creation of productive employment'.

Notes

[1] It may, however, be low and positive, if labour is employed in inferior occupations, as explained later.

[2] She illustrated its occurrence in London during the depression of the 1930s when unemployed professional people sold matches in the streets. See J. Robinson, *Essays in the Theory of Employment*, Macmillan, London, 1937.

[3] Paul Bairoch, *Urban Unemployment in Developing Countries*, ILO, Geneva, 1973.

[4] ibid., p. 66.

[5] ibid., p. 31.

[6] G. K. Ajaki, 'Urban–Rural Income Differentials in Ethiopia', University of Strathclyde Thesis for MSc, 1972 (unpublished).

[7] Louis Roussell, 'Measuring rural–urban drift in developing countries: a suggested method', *International Labour Review*, Vol. 101, 1970.

[8] R. H. Sabot, *Education, Income Distribution and Rates of Urban Migration in Tanzania*, ERB Paper 72.6, September 1973.

[9] For further details, see J. R. Harris and M. P. Todaro, 'Urban Unemployment in East Africa: an Economic Analysis of Policy Alternatives', *East African Economic Review*, December 1968, and 'Migration, Unemployment and Development: A Two-Sector Model', *American Economic Review*, Vol. 60, 1970.

[10] As we noted earlier, this urban unemployment can also be interpreted as structural, to the extent that such labour might have been successfully employed in the rural areas at some level of income, but for excessive migration.

[11] *Four-Year Plan for Social and Economic Development, 1971–1975*, Mauritius, Government Printer.

[12] J. E. Meade, *The Economic and Social Structure of Mauritius*, Frank Cass & Co., London, 1961, p. 59.

34 Education and Manpower

The economic effects of education

The large majority of people think of education as the sole concern of teachers and educationists, rather than of economists. But we discussed the role of education and technical knowledge as factors in economic development, however briefly, in Chapter 2; and education can be shown to have a number of economic effects.

(1) In the first place, as we shall see presently, education costs money, and has come to absorb an increasing proportion of government budgets in developing countries. This expenditure has, in particular, a high *opportunity-cost*, in that it could have been devoted either to alternative ways of fostering growth, such as private and public saving for capital accumulation, or alternative forms of private or public consumption, such as medical services.

(2) Governments have expanded educational budgets in part because they have seen education as *investment* in human capital and the training of manpower needed for development: it is, therefore, a form of national (and private) investment.

(3) At the same time, even if education did not increase an individual's earning power or potential contribution to the economy, people would still desire education for its own sake, because they enjoy learning and the knowledge obtained: education is therefore a form of *consumption*, yielding direct utility to the recipient just like other consumer goods.

(4) Fourthly, as we have seen already in the previous chapter, education may have important *labour market effects*, accelerating rural–urban migration and increasing the extent of unemployment, with all its associated waste of manpower.

(5) Again, as already analysed, education may, through its effects on the wage and salary structure, affect *income distribution* and equality of opportunity (giving children of rich parents a better chance of remunerative careers) and, by creating a politically influential élite, permit the rich or advantaged groups to reinforce their positions.

(6) Finally, the type of education offered could influence *attitudes*, attitudes to manual or agricultural work, for instance, or interest in business enterprise and risk-taking, again affecting economic growth.

Education as consumption or investment?

Let us show more precisely how expenditure on education can be considered as investment. Fairly obviously, expenditure on school buildings falls in this category since, after the initial sum is spent on the buildings, these can be used for a long time into the future. However current expenditure on teachers' salaries and teaching materials is also investment in that the 'output' produced is the extra productivity which the pupils obtain as a result of their training when they eventually go out to earn their living. Thus investment in an individual may go on for 15 years, at school and college, up to the age of, say, 22 years, and the 'returns' on this are obtained during the period of his working life, say, from 22 to the age of 60. There is thus an initial investment followed by a stream of 'returns'. Moreover this is long-term investment, compared even to most investment in manufacturing, since no returns *at all* may be obtained for as many as 15 years, and returns may still be accruing as long as 50 years after the initial investment! As with other investments, therefore, it is possible in principle to calculate a rate of return, generally in this case a *social* rate of return if we are dealing with public investment and benefits accruing to the society as a whole.

Education may also be considered a consumption good, however, since it may be desired as an end itself: as just mentioned, people enjoy learning. It is this, for instance, which makes them buy a newspaper or a book, instead of buying food. Furthermore the educated person may also enjoy direct utility from the social status which his education brings him, something on which he might place quite a high value. And in addition to providing direct utility, education may permit an individual to enjoy a whole range of additional goods more fully: an illiterate man cannot enjoy newspapers or, to the same level of appreciation, the arts, or even, perhaps, conversation.

Access to education should therefore be included

as an important element of economic welfare, along with other forms of consumption, and be counted as part of the 'standard of living' in a country. Whether a particular expenditure on education is consumption or investment, or both, depends partly on the motive behind it. It is fairly clear that in Eastern Africa the scramble for education, and the willingness by relatively poor people to pay high school fees, is based on a private assessment that education will lead to higher incomes, that is, that it represents a sound investment for the private individual or his children. Very often, though, this is not the foremost objective, and education is desired for its own sake, that is, as a consumption good. There is no reason, of course, why the two objectives should not be fulfilled simultaneously, learning providing both present enjoyment and future earning power.

Sometimes, however, the *intention* may be investment but the effect may simply be consumption. Thus governments may spend a large sum over the years training graduates, who may then be unemployed. The rate of return will then be zero and the expenditure will have to be justified, if at all, by any direct utility it brings as a form of consumption.[1]

The need for educational planning

The need for planning of education should now be self-evident. Because of the long-term nature of investment in education, so that expenditure on a primary school class now can affect the output of secondary school leavers in ten years' time, for instance, it is necessary to plan far ahead if serious shortages or surpluses of manpower or types of manpower are to be avoided. This itself would make it difficult to rely on the price mechanism to produce the correct decisions, since wage structures tend to indicate only *current* shortages or surpluses and not the likely position in ten or even five years' time. But in addition labour markets in less developed countries are notoriously inefficient, so that relative wages do not necessarily reflect the *social* marginal product of labour in any occupation, the benefit to society (as opposed to the individual) from an additional unit of different kinds of labour. This also calls for planning and foresight. We have seen what costs occur to the economy as wasted labour in the form of unemployment, if surpluses are created: while manpower shortages in one industry or occupation could lead to loss of potential output in other industries interdependent with it. And since education is important to individuals as consumption and in order to improve their productive capacities, the issue of equity as between individuals, groups, or regions is a crucial

one, with serious political implications, as politicians in developing countries are well aware: hence planning to minimize inequality of access to education is essential.

Planning is required because of the wide range of choices that must be exercised *within* the educational budget. Thus a choice has to be made regarding the proportion to be spent on primary, secondary, tertiary (college and university) education, requiring an evaluation of the relative rates of return in each category. Other choices may be between spending on school-age children or on adult literacy classes; or on formal education or 'informal' education and training, such as apprenticeships in industry, agricultural extension, or even assistance to small-scale entrepreneurs in the informal sector, and between general and technical education.

Finally, planning is needed to ensure that capital expenditures in education are not out of line with finance likely to be available for recurrent expenditures: thus it is of no use building schools if finance will not be available to pay the salaries of the teachers, and other costs of running the schools!

Educational expansion in Eastern Africa

The increasing emphasis which is being placed on education by developing countries is indicated in Table 34.1. This gives a selection of countries ranked according to their level of income per head in 1967, together with the percentage of GNP (at factor cost) devoted to general government current expenditure

Table 34.1   *Public current expenditures on education as a percentage of GNP*

	Rank of country in terms of GNP per head in 1967	Percentage of GNP devoted to education	
		1954	1967
USA	1	2.4	5.4
Sweden	2	4.3	5.5
France	3	2.0	3.0
UK	4	3.5	4.4
Trinidad	5	2.2	3.0
Ghana	6	3.1	4.3
Sri Lanka	7	2.9	4.8
Uganda	8	2.4	3.3
Nigeria	9	0.8	1.8
India	10	0.8	3.5
Tanzania	11	1.7	2.6

SOURCE: 1954 data from A. Martin and W. A. Lewis, "Patterns of Public Revenue and Expenditure', *The Manchester School*, September 1956

Data compiled from UN *System of National Accounts*, 1969

on education.[2] The table shows that the percentage allocated to education among the developing countries had expanded significantly between 1954 and 1967, in all cases; and secondly that the percentages (not the absolute levels of expenditure) were as high in several of the developing countries by 1967 as in the developed countries. In particular the percentages for the developing countries in 1967 were generally as high as they had been not very long previously, in 1954, in the developed countries.

Turning specifically to Eastern Africa, in most cases the share of central government recurrent expenditures devoted to formal education has risen from 10 per cent or less in the late 1950s, before independence, to approaching or even exceeding 25 per cent by the early 1970s, a decade or so after independence. Kenya, for example, devoted just under 17 per cent of its recurrent budget to education in 1962–3; but nearly 27 per cent a decade later. In Malawi the corresponding shares were $11\frac{1}{2}$ per cent in 1964 and 16 per cent in 1973–4. In Tanzania, on the other hand, where education had been particularly neglected in the colonial period, the big jump came just around independence, and since the mid-1960s the share of education has been constrained by a growing emphasis on universal primary education rather than selective secondary schooling. Thus the corresponding shares were only 17 per cent in 1969, not much more than the 15 per cent of 1961, when the jump from the 8 per cent of 1953, for example, had already taken place.

In tropical Africa as a whole, the expansion in primary school enrolments was very rapid in the 1950s, exceeding an annual growth rate of 9 per cent, or about three times the increase in children of primary school age. From less than 20 per cent in 1950, the attendance rate nearly doubled to 33 per cent with school places by 1960, and exceeded 40 per cent by 1970. Since, on the whole, Eastern Africa has emphasized rural primary schools, the proportion of rural children with access to schooling probably reached 35–40 per cent, also by 1970.

Looking at tropical Africa as a whole, however, it was in the more rapid expansion of secondary school places (each of which is much more expensive to provide), at 11 per cent per annum since 1950, that the main thrust of public expenditure took place. The percentage of children attending these schools rose from 5 per cent in 1950, to 12 per cent by 1960, and then to around 20 per cent by 1970, a percentage that most developed countries did not reach until after 1900.

For Eastern Africa the distribution of educational expansion in the 1960s and early 1970s, as between the primary, secondary, and higher sectors of education, is indicated in Table 34.2. The table shows first of all, that there is considerable variation between countries in the overall rate of educational expansion, the percentage increases (from a higher base, moreover) being highest for Kenya, and relatively low in Malawi and the Sudan: pointing to the choice that exists regarding the total size of the educational budget. Secondly we see that the percentage increases in enrolments differ between primary, secondary, and tertiary sectors, this pointing to the choice which exists in the allocation of the educational budget between the three sectors. Governments have to choose between sending more children to primary school (increasing the proportion of primary school age children in schools) and sending more children to secondary school (increasing the relatively low proportion of primary school leavers given the chance to proceed to secondary school). In making this choice the planners must take into account the relative costs per pupil. During the 1960s, as a general rule a primary school place (usually in a rural school) cost

Table 34.2 *Enrolments at school and higher educational institutions in Eastern African countries*

	Period compared (no. of years)	Primary		Secondary		Higher	
		No. (thousands) enrolments in year (1) (2)	Percentage increase over period	No. (thousands) enrolments in year (1) (2)	Percentage increase over period	No. (thousands) enrolments in year (1) (2)	Percentage increase over period
Kenya	10	1,011 2,788	176	36 196	444	6 22 (26)	266
Zambia	7	378 402	6	14 56	300	1 4	300
Tanzania	10	487 903	85	12 33	175	3 6 (7)	100
Malawi	10	360 537	49	6 14	133	— 2	—
Sudan	8	415 611	47	18 39	117	5 12	140

SOURCE: *Statistical Abstracts*
Notes on Years (1) and (2): Kenya, 1964 and 1974; Zambia, 1964 and 1971; Tanzania, 1961 and 1971; Malawi, 1964 and 1974; Sudan, 1961 and 1969. Figures in brackets include university students studying abroad in later year only.

about £10 a year to finance (perhaps less if there was a fee element), whereas a secondary day school place often had an annual recurrent cost nearer to £100 and a university place, £1,000. Thus the direct recurrent cost of maintaining a university student was about one hundred times greater than that of a primary scholar: governments could choose between putting one secondary school leaver into university or giving 100 children a primary school chance.[3]

Primary versus secondary education

Table 34.2 shows that generally expansion occurred much the fastest in secondary school enrolments and, given the cost per pupil, this absorbed a large share of the education budgets. Choices were not made in the same way by different countries, secondary school enrolments in Kenya increasing the fastest, by 444 per cent, three or four times the increases in Malawi and the Sudan; and Zambia showing the greatest divergence between primary and secondary school expansion, increasing secondary school enrolments by 300 per cent and primary school enrolments by only 6 per cent.

In making this choice governments must consider both efficiency and equity. If there is a shortage of trained manpower while economic returns from more primary school leavers are considered low, economic efficiency might dictate that preference be given to secondary school expansion, whereas on equity grounds it would be preferable to give ten times as many primary pupils a minimum amount of education and at least a chance of proving their ability. Generally it has been assumed that expenditure on primary education has been largely for consumption while that on secondary education is for manpower purposes and made for economic reasons. It has, on the other hand, been argued that economic returns may be higher in primary education, because of the beneficial effects eventually on agriculture, through increased receptiveness to extension advice and responsiveness to change.[4]

Moreover if there is unemployment of secondary school leavers, the economic returns from a *marginal* increase in expenditure on secondary education may be zero, as far as investment in human capital is concerned. There would still, no doubt, be a benefit from the additional secondary schooling received *seen as a consumption good*. But if secondary education were *only* of benefit as consumption then equity would dictate that, as far as public expenditure is concerned (private expenditure on education as consumption might be viewed differently), the expenditure be reallocated to primary education where the benefits would be spread more widely.

Formal versus non-formal education

Government has a further choice to make as between formal education in schools and colleges and non-formal education outside the formal educational system. Learning does not only go on inside schools. It has been said, in fact, that 'what is learnt outside school—on the farm, in the village, in apprenticeship, on the job, in the home and in a multitude of other forms of learning (many not conventionally thought of as education at all)—may add up to a more significant accumulation of knowledge and intellectual development than is acquired in the classroom'.[5] The educational services should therefore be thought of as including agricultural extension, advice to mothers on family planning or home economics, and training of small-scale entrepreneurs in technical skills or book-keeping. This being so, it is better for governments to formulate a 'human resources development programme', which makes explicit the choice between formal and nonformal education rather than simply different types of formal education, within an 'educational plan' confined to formal education.

If there is an excess supply of formally educated manpower so that school and college leavers remain unemployed or have to accept jobs for which their education is largely irrelevant, there will have been a waste of resources through 'misinvestment' in human capital involving the costs of the educational expenditure, the opportunity-costs of earnings forgone while at school, *and* the costs of output lost while the job seekers remain unemployed if they could otherwise have produced a positive marginal product by remaining in agriculture.

Investment in formal education may bring positive *private* returns but zero *social* returns. This occurs because employers, faced with a long line of applicants for a limited number of jobs which all could carry out equally well, may find it convenient to select those with school-leaving certificates simply as a means of making a choice. Thus an increased educational output of certificate holders may simply lead to the substitution of these for other actual or potential job holders without any difference in productivity. Thus 'instead of providing training which prepares people for high-level work, education sometimes has served as little more than a means of rationing the certificates needed to enter the best jobs'.[6] In this situation education has benefited the certificate holder by allowing him to 'jump the queue' and secure a job ahead of others without certificates, but has no social returns in terms of increased output.

Expansion of formal education could actually have

negative effects on informal training through adverse 'demonstration effects' if formal paper qualifications come to be thought of as inherently superior to more 'down-to-earth' knowledge and skills derived from technical courses, apprenticeships, 'on-the-job' training, or even more practical experience. Moreover the hierarchy of formal education, from the secondary schools up to the universities, may produce an influential educated elite (employed in administration, teaching and similar professions) which can perpetuate a wage and salary structure which favours itself rather than less formally qualified workers: reducing the incentives for new entrants to train for practical trades.

Another part of the case 'against' existing formal education is its tendency to encourage rural–urban migration in excess of the urban jobs likely to be available. In 1971 it is stated that in Nigeria about 600,000 persons were leaving school each year, whereas only 10,000–20,000 new wage-earning jobs per year were being created; in Tanzania an average of 250,000 school leavers per year were expected during the period of the 1969–74 Plan, compared with an average expected increase in wage-earning jobs of only 11,000 annually.[7] It follows that the large majority of persons leaving school in African countries such as these cannot expect to enter formal sector wage-employment and must expect to remain in the rural areas, mostly as small farmers. The 'appropriateness' of formal sector education in this context is obviously questionable. The implication for education policy might be: (a) that informal education in the rural areas, including agricultural extension, should be given considerable weight; (b) that, except in countries with an acute shortage of higher level manpower, more weight should be put on primary as compared to secondary education than would otherwise be the case; and (c) that the primary education should have some agricultural flavour, if not emphasis, and should avoid fostering the 'wrong' attitudes towards rural life among primary school pupils.

Finally it should be noted that in addition to the allocation of public expenditure between formal and non-formal education, it is necessary to examine the structure of incentives, which in the past have favoured 'white collar' work as against artisans and skilled manual workers. Changes in monetary and fiscal policy in order to encourage more labour-intensive techniques would also increase the scope and incentives for skilled workers of this type.

Cost-benefit analysis of educational investment

Economists have attempted to apply cost-benefit analysis of the type described in Chapter 15 to two separate questions: (a) to determine the social rate of return on educational spending as a whole, in order to assess its value in terms of output and growth in the economy as compared to alternative forms of spending, and (b) to determine the relative rates of return to different *types* of educational spending, such as primary or secondary education.

In the latter case we need to distinguish between private costs and benefits and social costs and benefits. For a private household, the costs of education comprise two main elements: first, the direct money costs of school fees, extra travel, and possibly boarding expenses, uniforms, and the like and, secondly, the earnings forgone by the pupils (or by apprentices to a trade or profession as the case may be). Of course these earnings forgone can be zero or very low for young schoolchildren or for young people without scarce skills in a labour market with an excess supply of unskilled workers.

On the benefit side, the private household may expect a direct pecuniary or non-pecuniary advantage from their sacrifice: more educated or technically trained workers earn higher money incomes and/or have more pleasant or secure jobs. Economists measure these direct private benefits as the *increment* in lifetime earnings attributed to the extra education. Thus if for instance clerical workers with a General School Certificate earn on average 25 per cent more than clerical workers who completed Standard VII at primary schools, then this 25 per cent increment (measured as shillings per annum over the number of years of working life) is taken as the private benefit from the *extra* spending and other costs due to proceeding beyond Standard VIII up to GCE.

As we saw in the case of Zambia in Table 31.2 (page 462), a person of 'O'-level educational attainment may earn *three times or more* what the primary school leaver earns, suggesting potentially very high private benefits from education. To obtain the present value of the net benefits, of course, the costs have to be deducted and the net benefits discounted in the usual way, using a rate of discount reflecting the private household's rate of time preference. Net benefits should also be discounted for risk since, of course, after spending secondary school fees for four years, the pupil may fail his leaving examination! We should include on the benefit side, in line with our previous discussion, any direct or indirect consumption benefits obtained from the education, including utility received from improved social status. The private individual's willingness to pay for education will depend on the sum of investment and consumption benefits.

Social costs will include private costs but generally exceed them by the amount by which the costs of training are subsidized. School fees will normally cover only a small proportion of the direct money costs of teachers' salaries, rent of school buildings, etc., the rest being paid for by the state out of tax revenue.

Much more difficult to calculate are the social benefits. The benefit to society will be the higher productivity resulting from better educated or trained workers.[8] Generally it has to be assumed that wages measure marginal product, so that the increased productivity due to the extra education or training is measured by the difference in wages which a trainee can secure in the labour market as a result. In the Zambian case mentioned (Table 31.2) the extra £425 which the 'O'-level holder secures compared to the primary school leaver would be taken to measure the extent to which the value of *his* services exceeds those of the primary school leaver.

There are a number of difficulties with this assumption. First, wages only measure the marginal product of labour accurately if there is perfect competition in the labour market. As we have already seen, labour markets in developing countries (and usually in developed countries also) are highly imperfect, because of monopoly, monosony, and various institutional factors affecting wage rates. Secondly the certificate obtained by the secondary school leaver may only permit him to replace another person who lacks this paper qualification but who was doing the job or could potentially do the job just as well. Thus the increase in earnings secured would measure private benefit, but no real social benefit. This is clearly related to the first point, since under perfect competition, wages for people doing a job equally efficiently would be the same. Thirdly, even if the labour market were functioning effectively, wages would tend to measure the immediate or short-term value of different kinds of labour. Educational investment in the present year will only produce outputs a number of years later, when the demand for labour will have altered; and it may be part of a development programme aimed at making major changes in economic structure, so that present marginal productivities are not relevant. Fourthly, there may be external economies or diseconomies, not included in these incremental earnings or retained by the private household. The spread of education may ensure higher standards of social conduct or strengthen local or national democracy. On the other hand the expansion of secondary and higher education may have adverse effects on income distribution or on informal education. These externalities are difficult to quantify, of course, and are invariably omitted in rate-of-return calculations.

Manpower planning

A different approach towards planning educational investment is the method of manpower planning. The approach here is to make a 'demand projection', or forecast of the economy's requirements of different categories of labour in future time periods, and a supply projection for the same categories and periods, comparing them to identify which types of manpower will be in short supply and when. Training programmes can then be adjusted to remove or alleviate shortages of particular categories of labour. To make the demand projection it is necessary first to carry out a current manpower survey to find the numbers of each type of labour actually used presently in each sector.[9] This gives a labour–output ratio or coefficient for each sector, giving the labour requirements (for each type of labour) per unit of output in that sector. This coefficient can be adjusted if there is reason to think that the sector's desired or optimal use of labour is greater or less than its current usage. The growth and sectoral structure of the economy must then be projected into the future, after which, applying the labour coefficients calculated, it is possible to estimate labour requirements per sector and in total for each type of labour. Supply forecasts are made on the basis of current stocks of each type of labour, expected additions to this supply as people leave school or training programmes each year, and expected subtractions as others retire, move elsewhere, or become 'localized'.

Having established where the shortages will occur, and the extra manpower which must be secured, a manpower plan for education and training of new manpower, and also perhaps for the allocation of manpower as it becomes available, may be produced. This plan must aim not only at balancing the stock of labour required with that demanded, but also at *flow balance*, so that when stocks are in equilibrium the annual addition to the work-force from the education 'industry' equals annual withdrawals through retirement or migration.

The manpower planning approach, like rate-of-return analysis, has been criticized. There is, first of all, the assumption of constant labour coefficients. Labour requirements per unit of output in any sector might change for a variety of reasons, including technical progress or changes in factor prices and wage structures. Secondly, there are data problems: data are often lacking with respect to the amounts of labour used in different industries (even comprehensive labour surveys rapidly get out of date), while sectoral output forecasts for the economy are difficult and prone to substantial error. Thirdly, because the manpower plan is not based on an 'optimization' model, it tends to be based on the existing use of manpower, not necessarily the 'optimal' or desirable labour usages. Finally the approach has been said to suffer from 'technological determinism', in that labour requirements are specified as a technical relationship between the expected level of physical output and quantities of labour required. There are no *cost* estimates or attempts to measure rates of return for different types of education and training: the approach is in this respect the exact opposite of the rate-of-return approach which is cast directly in economic terms.

Manpower planning in Eastern Africa

In addition to these general criticisms of the manpower planning approach, specific criticisms have been made of the manpower planning experience in Eastern Africa. A study of 38 African manpower plans prepared in 23 African countries during the period 1959–70, when these newly independent countries were nearly all faced with an acute shortage of indigenous high-level manpower, has been carried out by Jolly and Colclough,[10] to which we can refer.

First, although a fair degree of success in forecasting was achieved, taking into account the difficulties involved, there were some obvious deficiencies. For instance, the plans often neglected to take into account 'repeaters', who stay long in the system before becoming available for employment, and 'drop-outs' who do not qualify at all to take up their allocated positions among high level manpower, both factors affecting the accuracy of estimates. Secondly, and more fundamentally, the plans concentrated on shortages and not surpluses of manpower. During the course of the 1960s, however, shortages of local manpower to fill senior posts in the public sector and in a large part of the private sector have given

way to a growing problem of unemployment facing secondary school leavers, and even university graduates in North and West Africa. More specifically, the plans concentrated on shortages of high level manpower, the skilled and the educated, and especially on the replacement of expatriate manpower by localization of high salaried posts: they gave little attention to the broader problem of unemployment and job creation among the unskilled.

Stemming partly from this focus on localization of expatriate-filled posts, there was a tendency to concentrate on formal education and obtaining people with the right 'paper' qualifications rather than upgrading and providing experience 'on the job'. There was hardly any attempt in the official plans and educational systems to upgrade and retain 'low-level' or even 'intermediate' skilled workers, or to expand employment and raise productivity in the informal sector.

Fourthly, the manpower and educational plans neglected the structure of incentives (and usually also problems of supply) for intermediate and lower skills, especially, ignoring wage differentials among these skill grades as well as the overall differential between intermediate and high level manpower. Although there were exceptions,[11] the public service pay scales mostly favoured formally educated but otherwise vocationally untrained 'white-collar' workers, and offered weak incentives for artisans and skilled manual workers. In general the question of the allocation of the labour force between sectors, occupations, and geographical regions in order to fill more urgent needs, whether through incentives or the compulsory 'direction' of labour, was ignored.

Lastly, the acceptance of existing wage/salary structures, the educational systems themselves, and the narrow approach followed in the manpower plans, have been criticized for producing educated elites and unequal income distributions in most African countries.

Questions on Chapter 34

1. Discuss the economic effects of educational policy.
2. Explain carefully what is meant by 'investment in human capital.'
3. In what sense can education spending be considered to be 'consumption' or 'investment'? Can it be both at the same time?
4. Why is there a need for educational planning?
5. Explain how private and social returns to spending on education may diverge.
6. 'Since all secondary school pupils must first go to primary school, there is no need to choose *between* primary and secondary school education.' Comment on this statement.

What sort of choices were made in Eastern African countries in the 1960s?
7. Discuss the potential importance of non-formal as opposed to formal education in promoting development.
8. How would you estimate the social costs and benefits of a university education?
9. Compare the 'rate-of-return' approach to educational planning and the 'manpower planning' approach.
10. What were the main objectives of manpower plans in African countries during the 1960s, and their main limitations?

Notes

[1] Including any wider social benefits which accrue to a community which contains a larger population of more educated people. This would be an external economy of *consumption*.

[2] The figures are inclusive of public payments to grant-aided educational establishments but exclude private expenditure on education—which can be very important in some poor countries, and is important in the USA for tertiary (college) education.

[3] The non-recurrent or capital cost of a university place was an even larger multiple of the corresponding day school cost, since university and other tertiary education students require residential accommodation and expensive equipment rather than the simple rural classroom.

[4] Schoolchildren may also influence their parents and make *them* more responsive to agricultural advice.

[5] Richard Jolly, 'African Manpower Plans: An Evaluation', *Institute of Development Studies Bulletin*, Vol. 6, No. 3, February 1975, p. 75.

[6] ibid.

[7] Richard Jolly, 'Manpower and Education', in D. Seers and L. Joy, *Development in a Divided World*, Penguin, 1971, Chapter 10, p. 219.

[8] In principle the consumption benefits from education should also be calculated in the cost-benefit calculation. However if we are comparing returns for two kinds of education, it can be assumed that the consumption benefits are similar, and do not affect the comparison.

[9] These manpower surveys were usually confined to 'inventories' of so-called 'high level' and 'intermediate' level manpower, and ignored unskilled or semi-skilled workers.

[10] A. R. Jolly and C. Colclough, 'African Manpower Plans: an Evaluation', *International Labour Review*, August/September 1972, and reprinted in *Employment in Africa: Some Critical Issues*, ILO, 1973.

[11] For example printers who had also a strong craft union to support them; and also various engineering grades employed by the East African Railways, Harbours, and Postal Corporations.

Part IX Public finance and development planning

35 The Structure of Taxation

This last section of this book is devoted to a study of *public finance*, the spending and revenue-raising activities of the state. Nowadays, the government of almost every country absorbs a large proportion of annual output to provide its citizens with *collective goods* on a non-commercial basis, quite apart from owning and running the state enterprises which we have discussed already in Chapter 18. These collective goods and services must be financed somehow, hence the necessity for taxes: taxes being *unilateral transfer payments* levied on taxpayers without involving a direct exchange of goods and services as a 'quid pro quo', as is the case with private goods exchanged in a market by a *bilateral* flow against private expenditures.[1] Apart from their direct public expenditure on goods and services, however, governments also make transfer payments in cash to households and firms, to relieve poverty due to unemployment, sickness, old age, or family size, to alleviate crop failures and other disasters, or to subsidize business operations. Unfortunately, in poor countries, where the need for such social provisions or business stimulus is greatest, the capacity to tax is lowest and the difficulties of raising taxes in the fairest ways are greatest. Let us, therefore, consider the characteristics of a good tax system, before examining the ways in which Eastern African governments finance their 'budgets' or annual expenditure programmes.

General principles of taxation

A good tax system may be judged by the following criteria:

(1) its effect on the supply and allocation of resources;

(2) its effect on the distribution of income and employment;

(3) its effect on the stability and growth of aggregate income and employment;

(4) administrative. efficiency, and convenience to the taxpayers.

Unfortunately a tax which is good in one direction is often poor in another, so that in practice tax systems tend to be a compromise between these economic and social objectives, and incorporate a combination of various forms of taxation.

The supply and allocation of resources

The first criterion involves not only the supply of resources in the economy—labour, enterprise, and capital—but also how they are used. We have already examined, in Chapter 7, how the imposition of a specific tax on a commodity could affect not only its price, but the amount producers were willing to supply. We discuss presently how different types of taxes on income as well as on goods may disturb supply and lead to a reshuffling of existing resources. In poor countries, especially, particular attention has to be paid to the disincentive effects of various taxes on labour's willingness to work, or on the voluntary supply of saving and enterprise.

The principle of equity or fairness

A good tax system should not offend popular notions of fair play or equality of treatment before the law. There should be *horizontal equity* or 'like treatment of equals' with the same level of income and circumstances. This is easier said than achieved, quite apart from deliberate evasion of taxes by payers or discrimination by tax collectors, however, since it is often easier for certain groups to *avoid* taxes legally by claiming allowances or special concessions not available to other groups with the same income. An even more difficult problem is *vertical equity* among people with different levels of income. One approach to this problem is to base taxes on the *benefit principle* so that taxpayers who benefit from a particular service are charged accordingly for its cost, and thus pay a sum of taxes proportionate to the benefits received. Although this benefit principle is applicable to divisible goods like school places or, indirectly, to road facilities financed by vehicle licences and taxes on petrol, it is clearly less equitable in financing indivisible goods like defence or public health where benefits cannot be priced in a market by excluding citizens unwilling or unable to pay. The basis of financing these collective goods must therefore be one of *ability to pay*. This principle might support a notion of vertical equity produced by making taxation proportional to income, so that everyone paid the same percentage of income as taxes. Nowadays, however, the principle of ability to pay or 'equal sacrifice' of income is interpreted to support a system of *progressive* taxation, the theory being that taxpayers with high incomes and much wealth sacrifice less utility than poorer taxpayers. Thus by levying more taxation from the rich than from the poor, the total sacrifice for the community as a whole will be smaller than under a system of proportional taxation.

In most countries today, the criterion of equity in taxation requires the system as a whole to produce a distribution of income after tax which is as equal as possible. Here we refer not to a simple equality of personal or private income after tax: the income which is compared should take account of the benefits arising out of the government's expenditure out of taxation. Secondly, in considering the desirability of a more equal distribution of income, we need to take account of possible adverse economic effects arising out of increased taxes. If there are serious disincentive effects on work and enterprise (though the importance of these is often exaggerated), poor countries, especially, may be restricted in using taxation to move towards a more even distribution of income, and of income-yielding wealth. Taxes may also affect the distribution of income among factors of production and income groups *indirectly*, it should be noted, by changing the relative prices of factors and goods.

Nevertheless, one of the aims of taxation is to effect a redistribution of income and wealth by taxing the rich more heavily than the poor. In this connection an important distinction is made between proportional, progressive, and regressive taxes. If we define the average rate of tax as the value of the amount paid in tax by the taxpayer divided by his income, then we can say that a particular form of tax is *proportional* if the average rate of tax is constant irrespective of the size of the income of the individual on which it is imposed. If the average rate of tax increases with income, the tax is said to be *progressive*, and if it decreases the tax is *regressive*. It must be stressed that in each case we are not re-

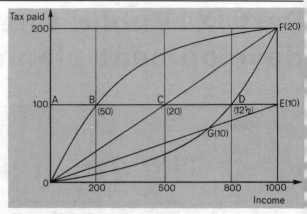

Figure 35.1 *Tax progression.*

ferring to the absolute amount of tax paid, but to the proportion of income paid out in tax.

The definitions may be clarified by reference to Figure 35.1. All the various lines on the diagram plot hypothetical tax liability against income. At C, for instance, income is 500 and tax is 100, or 20 per cent. Since at F income is 1,000 and tax paid 200, still 20 per cent, it is obvious that the line OCF represents a proportional tax, levied at the proportionate rate of 20 per cent. Similarly the line OGE represents a proportional tax, but at the rate of 10 per cent, since at all points along it the ratio of tax paid to total income is the same. The line OGDF represents a progressive tax, the tax ratio increasing from 10 per cent at G to $12\frac{1}{2}$ per cent at D, and 20 per cent at F. The line OBF represents a regressive tax, the tax ratio falling from 50 per cent at B to 20 per cent at F. Thus a proportionate tax may be represented by a straight line through the origin, the slope being determined by the (constant) rate of tax, a progressive tax by a line *increasing* in slope away from the origin, and a regressive tax by a line decreasing in slope away from the origin. The line ABCDE represents a poll tax, liability being at 100 irrespective of income. That this is regressive can be seen from the fact that the tax ratio declines as income increases from 50 per cent at B, to 20 per cent at C, $12\frac{1}{2}$ per cent at D, and 10 per cent at E, the amount of tax paid remaining at 100 throughout.

Income correction for stability and growth

One of the economic functions of government, even in a largely private enterprise economy, is to *stabilize* the level of aggregate income and employment by appropriate policies, including fiscal policy, which means using the government's discretionary powers of taxation and public expenditure to smooth out fluctuations in activities in the private sector. We have already touched on the stabilization aspects of government expenditure in Chapter 28, and will return to the problems of budgetary policy in the next two chapters when we shall also be examining how taxation may foster longer-term growth. It should be clear from our discussion of tax progression, however, that if the bulk of revenue can be derived from a progressive income tax (or a progressive expenditure tax), more taxes will be paid when private income and expenditure are at a high level than at a lower level. Taxation can therefore act as an automatic 'built-in' stabilizer of national income. Below we shall see how taxes on exports can be used to stabilize the economies of countries with a high percentage of private income arising from export production by small farmers who cannot be taxed so easily by alternative methods.

Administrative efficiency

'Certainty', 'convenience', and 'economy' were three of Adam Smith's four *Canons of Taxation*;[2] they are still important elements of an efficient tax system. Payment of taxes should not involve arbitrary demands on taxpayers and should be collected in a convenient form and at a convenient time: in Eastern Africa, in the past at least, various poll taxes, produce cesses, or quasi-official 'taxes' levied by political parties have been uncertain and inconvenient for taxpayers who may not be literate. The costs of collection and administration should be small in relation to the revenue yielded, since real and often scarce administrative resources are involved. Apart from government expenditure on tax assessment and collection, taxpayers employ accountants to avoid taxes legally or resort to evasion which may be resource-using, such as the smuggling of produce in headloads across frontiers to avoid export taxes and to exchange for other goods which will avoid customs and excise taxation. Countries with long land frontiers tend to suffer more from evasion of taxes on foreign-traded goods than countries which can more effectively 'police' ports and harbours. In order to restrict the scope for smuggling, the three partners in the East African Community tend to levy the same excise taxes. Evasion of taxation, whether levied on goods or on incomes, reduces the revenue yielded by a given *tax base*, which is the object that is taxed, whether this is a physical unit like a litre of petrol or the value of taxable income as assessed by the tax authority concerned. Erosion of all the tax bases by evasion or legal avoidance reduces the taxable capacity of the economy as a whole, requiring for the finance of a given level of public expenditure higher rates of tax on the reduced tax bases and involving departures from the principle of horizontal equity.

Furthermore, if evasion of, say, personal income taxation is more widespread among higher income groups liable to progressive income tax than among lower income groups liable to a graduated personal tax (or a poll tax) vertical equity may be reduced rather than increased.[3]

Taxes on income versus taxes on outlay

We can now look a little more closely at the possible effects of taxes on the supply and allocation of resources, in particular one aspect which has caused a great deal of controversy in the past: whether taxes on outlay have worse effects on the allocation of resources than taxes on income. If we consider this specific controversy we can obtain a good idea of the various ways in which taxes affect incentives without going into all of them.

The operation of the 'price mechanism' was described in Chapter 5. If consumer tastes change from, say, maize to millet, demand for maize will fall and that for millet increase. The price of maize will no doubt fall as a result, and that of millet increase. Producers will find millet more profitable to grow than formerly, and maize less so. They will therefore have an incentive to switch over more land and labour to millet production at the expense of maize. Thus resources will be reallocated and the composition of output remoulded to suit the taste of consumers, through profit incentives to producers. The allocation of resources is thus determined automatically to suit consumers by the price mechanism.

This argument does not of course apply to the public sector, and even within the private sector the price mechanism never works perfectly. But we can say that broadly speaking, from the purely economic point of view,[4] the best tax system is one which gives the government the revenue it has decided to raise with the least possible disturbance to the allocation and supply of resources which would exist in the absence of taxes. If the supply and allocation *are* disturbed, it is likely to be for the worse, if the original allocation of good was geared to the proportion dictated by consumer tastes.

While the pattern of consumer demand determines the composition of output in the private sector, consumer demand is in turn determined, as we saw in Chapter 6, by tastes, by the relative prices of different commodities, and by the level of consumer incomes. It follows that both direct *and* indirect taxes will disturb the allocation of resources. For if the government has decided to raise a given amount of revenue and has simply to choose which *way* it ought to raise this sum, the same amount will be deducted from people's disposable income in each case. This reduction in income will affect demand, and therefore disturb the allocation of resources in the same way. Thus far there is nothing to choose between the taxes. But it has often been claimed that a tax on outlay, such as an excise tax, disturbs the allocation of resources *still further*. This is because in addition to reducing incomes it will raise the prices of taxed goods relative to other goods, discourage people from buying them, and thus divert consumption, and productive resources, towards the non-taxed goods.

Let us imagine a peculiar sort of individual who spends all his income on beer, partly factory-made bottled beer and partly local beer. We can represent his opportunities in Figure 35.2 by the budget line APB, before a tax is imposed. Suppose in the tax-free situation he selects P. The imposition of an excise duty on bottled beer will make this more expensive in relation to local beer. With the same amount of money income he might now only be able to buy OC of bottled beer, instead of OA, so that his budget line is now BC, on which his choice might be the combination Q.

The choice of combination Q implies that he spends the money equivalent of Q'T on bottled beer, giving up Q'Q of this in tax. He also buys OT of local beer, paying no tax on this. By choosing combination Q he reveals that he prefers this to all other combinations within the shaded triangle OBC which he *could* have selected instead.

Suppose now that instead of an indirect tax, a direct tax is imposed yielding the government the same amount of revenue. The effect of this is shown by drawing a budget line A'B' through Q parallel to the line AB. Thus irrespective of how the individual distributes his expenditure between bottled beer and local beer he will pay the same in tax. If, for example, he now spent all his income on bottled beer he would pay A'A, equal to the amount Q'Q payable if he selected combination Q. The effect is a straight deduction from income with no change in the relative prices of the two commodities.

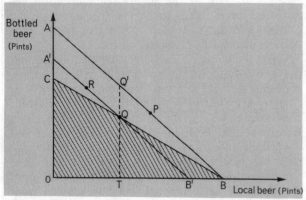

Figure 35.2 *The effect of an indirect tax.*

In this situation the consumer will select a combination somewhere on A'B'. This will not, however, be in the range QB' below Q, since these combinations have already been revealed inferior to Q. His choice will therefore lie in the range A'Q, possibly at Q again, but more likely to the left of Q at, say, R. If he chooses R instead of Q, this would show that he 'prefers' R to Q, and is therefore better off.

It is on this basis that a direct tax is alleged to be less harmful than an indirect tax. With the direct tax, a deduction is made from income, but the consumer is left free to make his choice at the same relative prices. With an indirect tax yielding no more revenue to the government relative prices will be disturbed, inducing the consumer to select a combination which he would not otherwise have chosen. In this case, he buys less of the taxed bottled beer at Q than at R, with a direct tax. This effect has been called the 'excess burden' of indirect taxation. Without yielding the government any more revenue, the taxpayer is forced into a less preferred position.

Further analysis, however, reveals this excess burden to be an illusion. In fact, a consumer's well-being depends not only on the goods and services he obtains, but also on the leisure he enjoys. And most people can secure for themselves more goods and services by sacrificing leisure, that is, by working harder or longer. The fact that they do *not* work suggests that they prefer the extra leisure to the extra goods. We can in fact think of leisure as any other 'commodity' to be enjoyed.

Suppose, for example, an individual is being paid at the rate of 75c ($=\frac{3}{4}$s) per hour. If he works for one hour less, he loses 75c. The 'price' of leisure is therefore 75c. If an income tax of one-third is imposed, his *net* pay per hour will be just 50c. The price of leisure is now only 50c. The effect of imposing or increasing income tax is thus to reduce the 'price' of leisure and to encourage its 'consumption', that is, to discourage work or effort generally. An income tax does therefore disturb the pattern of consumption, but this time it is the consumption of leisure that is directly affected. If we treat leisure like any other consumption good, we can no longer say for certain that an indirect tax will disturb relative prices more than will income tax.

The argument is illustrated in Figure 35.3. Leisure is measured along the horizontal axis, and money income earned on the vertical. Every individual has just 24 hours of time or leisure per day to dispose of. At a wage rate of 75c per hour, he could obtain 18s per day by working 24 hours. The line AB is his budget line, specifying the combinations of leisure and money income which he can obtain at this wage rate. Depending on his relative desire for leisure and income, he might choose some combination P on

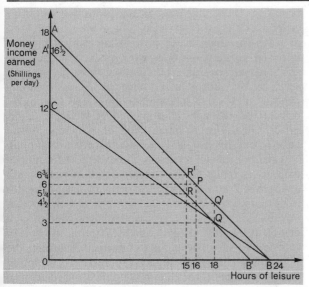

Figure 35.3 *The effect of an income tax on work and leisure.*

AB, choosing 16 hours of leisure, working the other 8 hours at 75c per hour, and receiving 6s in daily income. If a tax of one-third is now imposed, working for 24 hours would only bring him 12s net, and his budget line would be BC. Suppose his choice in the new situation is combination Q, he would work only 6 hours, earning $4\frac{1}{2}$s *before* tax (read from Q' on AB) and 3s after tax, paying tax equal to the difference $1\frac{1}{2}$s.

Suppose instead of an income tax, that a poll tax yielding to the government exactly the same amount, $1\frac{1}{2}$s, could be imposed. This can be represented by moving the budget line inwards to A'B', where A' is at $16\frac{1}{2}$s instead of 18s. Since he has to pay the same amount of tax irrespective of the number of hours he works per day, A'B' is parallel to AB, the rate of exchange between leisure and income being unaffected. The line A'B' also passes through Q, the distance QQ' being again $1\frac{1}{2}$s. His preferred position, R, will be somewhere on A'B', but not in the range QB' beyond Q, since these combinations were previously shown to be inferior to Q. R will therefore fall in the range A'Q, probably to the left of Q.

As drawn in the diagram, R would represent a choice of 15 hours of leisure and 9 hours' work (earning $5\frac{1}{4}$s net of 'poll tax'). The result we get in this case is that the imposition of the poll tax makes the individual *work harder*, for 9 hours instead of 8. This effect must still be present with the income tax, which creates the same loss of income, but *in addition* there is with this tax a 'substitution effect' due to a change in relative prices of leisure and income. Leisure is made relatively 'cheaper', and the fruits of labour more expensive. More leisure is therefore chosen and

only 6 hours worked instead of 9. The total effect is the combined effect of the loss of income (plus 1 hour worked) and the substitution effect (minus 3 hours worked), so that at Q the individual works 2 hours less than at P.

Readers will observe that the analyses of Figure 35.2 and 35.3 are identical in form: there is a substitution effect in the former case towards the non-taxed commodity, local beer, and in the latter towards leisure as the non-taxed commodity. There is no reason to draw a distinction between the two commodities, leisure and beer, for one can be substituted for the other *if preferred*. By sacrificing leisure and working harder extra income can be earned with which to buy beer, and vice versa. Thus both the direct and indirect taxes affect the pattern of consumption and corresponding allocation of resources, the latter presumably for the worse.

We can however note that the consumption of some goods is less *elastic* than others with respect to price: this suggests that if we want to alter consumption as little as possible we should select for taxation those goods which are in inelastic demand. To the extent that the demand for leisure is more price-inelastic than other commodities, therefore, there is a case for preferring direct taxation. Within the category of indirect taxes, we can see that this is why alcohol and tobacco are heavily taxed in most countries: it is not because governments are seriously interested in reducing the habits of smoking and drinking, but because they know that consumers are so reluctant to abandon these habits in the face of price rises. Taxing them becomes an easy way of raising revenue.

Equity versus incentives

The effect of taxation on the willingness to work as just discussed depends on the *marginal* rate of tax, rather than the average as such. If an individual is in doubt as to whether it is worth his while working a little longer or not, it is the rate of tax on the income due to an *extra* hour's work that will concern him. In the case of a poll tax, for example, since the total tax paid is the same irrespective of income, the marginal rate of tax is zero. It is for this reason that there is no substitution effect in favour of leisure in the case of a poll tax.

We defined a progressive tax as one in which the average rate of tax increases with income. It follows that if the average is increasing, the *marginal* rate of tax will be increasing even faster. This compares with a proportional tax in which the average, and therefore the marginal, rates of tax are constant. The progressive tax, which has the greatest redistributive effect on income, will thus also have the greatest disincentive effects on the supply of effort. Moreover the greater the *degree* of progression, the more rapidly will the marginal rate of tax increase, and the more damaging will be the effect on the supply of labour and effort. The two objectives of an egalitarian distribution of income and maximum incentives to work therefore clash head-on.

It is, of course, not only a direct tax which has these disincentive effects. Obviously it makes little difference to the desire to work if proceeds are taxed when they are earned, or when they are spent. For a man who spends all his income, if the amount of tax paid is the same in both cases, it will make *no* difference whether the tax is paid directly or indirectly. As we shall see in a moment, a system of indirect taxes can be made just as progressive as any direct tax system. There is *one* qualification to be made here: an individual may not realize he *is* paying the same amount of tax when it is hidden in the prices of the things he buys than when he finds it missing from his pay envelope. To that extent he may work with more enthusiasm than in the latter case.

So far we have mentioned only the effects of a high marginal rate of tax on the supply of labour. There will, however, be wider effects on incentives. In the first place the supply of 'labour' should be interpreted as the supply of effort in general, including the effort put in by salaried workers and especially by entrepreneurs. Associated with this will be, for example, the specific discouragement of risk-taking by entrepreneurs and investors. If the tax structure is progressive, it means that if a project is much more successful than the average, the government will take a comparatively large chunk of the extra proceeds, while if it falls well short of the average, the firm's tax liability is reduced, but not so much. The effect is as if the government were more willing to share in the proceeds of a good outcome than in the disappointing proceeds or actual losses of a bad outcome.

The preference of investors for the safer 'average' project over riskier ones carrying an equal possibility of a very good or very bad result may thus be increased.

This tendency will apply also in agriculture. Farmers might be encouraged, for instance, to plant safer crops, including subsistence crops for self-consumption, in preference to higher-priced export crops, the prices of which may fluctuate more widely.

Types of taxes

What kinds of taxes are there, and how can we classify them? We may first of all distinguish between taxes on the current *flows* of output, income or expenditure, on the one hand, and taxes on *stocks* of capital assets (or wealth) on the other. This distinc-

tion can have important implications for our four criteria of a good tax system, and so we need to look at ways in which a tax on existing capital may be imposed. Since economic development is closely associated with capital accumulation, most tax systems seek to encourage investment in income-yielding capital; they do not normally therefore levy taxes directly on the capital employed in business enterprises. On the other hand, taxes on personal capital have a long history, since personal wealth is a rough and ready measure of ability to pay and redistributes income by reducing the concentration of wealth in a few hands. The normal method of taxing private wealth is by a once-for-all *estate duty* or *gift tax*, the former payable on the 'estate' or assessed total wealth of a person at the time of death and the latter at the time of transfer. In most developed countries, including the USA, these taxes are highly progressive, exempting small holdings of wealth and concentrating mainly on the 5–10 per cent of the population which usually owns more than half the total private wealth in the country. If, as is usual, the tax at progressive rates is levied on the deceased person's wealth or the total value of the gift rather than on the inheritance or amount received, the amount of tax is greater, the government receiving more revenue than would be the case with taxing recipients at rates applicable to their own wealth. In practice wealthy people can avoid tax by settling parts of their estate on their relatives long before death or by establishing family trusts which, like public corporations, have 'a life of their own' and are not subject to the same 'death duties'. However, some countries have introduced *wealth taxes*, periodic or regular annual taxes on private wealth so that, say, 1 or 2 per cent of a person's capital is liable to be payable as a form of personal tax. These are to be distinguished from a *capital gains tax*, which is a tax on the *increase* in value of an asset, rather than the value itself, which increase is usually deemed to have been realized only when the asset is sold. Quite apart from the greater 'equity' and 'certainty' of the above form of wealth tax (as opposed to estate (death) duties, which many avoid), it has been argued by some economists that an annual tax on wealth will allow capital gains to be taxed as they arise rather than when they are 'realized' on the sale of an asset or when assessed under an estate duty or gift tax. Capital gains arise as the result of an appreciation in the market value of any asset, be it a financial security or real property like land or buildings. Nowadays capital gains, since they increase the purchasing power of their owner, are regarded as a form of personal income by many economists and by tax authorities which levy taxes on them as part of a person's annual taxable income. The uneven occurrence of capital gains due to general price increases, fluctuations in the market value of stocks and shares, or to lucky 'windfalls' like the appreciation of land values due to urban development is said to divert effort and savings into activities which do not earn income. If capital gains or 'paper profits' arise mainly from stock exchange transactions in developed capitalist countries, they can be just as significant in less developed countries through land and property speculation.

In Africa taxes on capital, and capital gains, are as yet relatively unimportant as direct sources of public revenue, although the device of assessing individuals for personal income tax has often been based on their apparent wealth in land, livestock, permanent tree crops, size of dwelling, and other property. In rural areas this wealth assessment has been largely a substitute for a more accurate system of *income* taxation. Provided the tax base is defined fairly widely, there is probably little adverse effect on resource allocation or evasion, unlike taxes and cesses levied on production of specific crops or on expenditures. Specific *property taxes* levied mainly by local authorities on land and buildings, again, are attempts to tax rental income rather than tax the stock of capital itself.

A further distinction can be drawn between *direct* and *indirect* taxes. Whether a tax is 'direct' or 'indirect' does not depend on whether it is collected directly from the ultimate taxpayer; in fact it is often not clear who pays the tax in the end, since as we saw in Chapter 7, the initial *impact* of a tax on a commodity could be shifted so that its ultimate *incidence* is shared between sellers and buyers. In the case of specific taxes on goods it is fairly clear how the tax is shifted: if consumer demand is very price-inelastic the tax is shifted *forward* to the consumer who is prepared to pay the tax through higher prices. If, on the other hand, demand were much more elastic so that the tax resulted in a smaller quantity demanded, then the tax burden might be shifted *backwards*, placing more of the incidence on suppliers. In the limiting cases, illustrated in Figure 7.6 of Chapter 7, if demand is completely inelastic, the tax is borne entirely by consumers; if supply is completely inelastic, the incidence is placed entirely on suppliers. In some cases the impact and incidence of a tax are identical, as we might expect to be the case with a poll tax levied directly on individuals' 'heads' as a fixed amount. But it is less clear who ultimately pays a tax on business profits; does it come out of existing profits or is it shifted forward in higher prices? Or shifted backwards in lower wages or rents? Do wage earners and other persons pay all the income tax levied on them? The incidence is not at all clear and depends on complicated factors requiring detailed study of various tax systems.

For convenience, therefore, the distinction between direct and indirect taxes is drawn on the *basis* of assessment rather than the *point* of assessment: direct taxes get at income directly, that is, the tax is levied as a straight deduction from income or wealth irrespective of the way these are earned or consumed. Taxes or personal incomes, or profits, on capital gains and on wealth, are direct. An indirect tax, in contrast, is one where the taxpayer's liability varies in proportion to the volume or value of particular goods sold or purchased. Thus a *customs duty* is an *in*direct tax on expenditure, the amount paid varying with the volume or value of the commodity imported. *Excise duties* are also indirect taxes, levied this time on specific goods produced and consumed in the country imposing the tax. Cigarettes and beer are favourite targets for excise taxes. The 'indirectness' of these taxes is revealed by the fact that the consumer can avoid paying them by not consuming cigarettes or beer. The same is true of other commodity taxes or general *sales taxes* which may be levied on a wide range of goods and even services, although clearly the wider the coverage of taxes on consumers' expenditure, the smaller the option of refraining from consumption becomes.

Because specific excise taxes on 'conventional necessities' like alcohol and tobacco or so-called *purchase taxes* on 'income-elastic' goods purchased by higher income groups distort the supply and allocation of resources, most European countries have come to rely on a version of a *general* sales tax called the *value-added tax (VAT)*. The tax base here is the 'value added' by all the factors of production employed by firms at each stage of production. VAT thus has a broader base than a tax on profits: it taxes the firm's wages and salary bill as well as profits retained and payments of interest, dividends, and rents, since it is levied at, say, 10 per cent of the gross output minus purchases on non-factor inputs like materials purchased from suppliers. Its effect on a firm's choice of factors of production is neutral, since all bear the same tax rate. It is also 'neutral' in its effect on different types of business unit since there is no incentive for firms to integrate vertically to avoid a turnover tax levied on gross output. It can be applied to all industries and services, although in practice small businesses and certain activities are exempted, or pay a lower rate of tax. Foodstuffs, for example, may be taxed at a zero rate.

Although VAT avoids the distortions of a selective system of excise taxes, and does not discriminate between the use of factors, it tends to be regressive in its incidence. Thus the replacement of an equal yield from company profits tax by VAT involves a larger tax on wages, the incidence of which will fall at least partly on labour. Since the initial impact of the tax is on buyers, the tax will also be shifted more easily to consumers in higher prices. Finally, it falls more heavily on less profitable companies which must pay the same tax rate as successful businesses whose higher profits could be the main revenue source under a direct profits tax.

As the tax on profits, the income of risk capital, is less, it encourages risk-bearing and the use of capital; but since it taxes wage costs it is likely to lead to more capital-intensive techniques—a tendency aggravated still further by the usual practice of exempting purchases of capital goods from VAT. Thus in developing countries with unemployed labour the new bias towards greater capital intensity is a serious disadvantage. Those Eastern African countries which have widened the coverage of their sales taxes have therefore tended to restrict the new taxes to manufactured goods produced mainly by larger firms, which already employ more capital-intensive techniques, and to competing imports of the same type.

Two major sources of tax revenue which are less easy to classify are export taxes and various payroll taxes of social security contributions paid by workers. By our criterion *export duties* are indirect taxes since they are levied on commodities, and liability varies directly with the volume or value of the commodity exported. However, since the local market for most of these dutiable commodities like coffee and cotton is very limited, the producer has little scope for avoiding taxation by domestic sales. Moreover the local market for alternative crop production is usually much less profitable so that he has to 'pay up' the tax on the export crops rather than attempt to switch to the lower-valued domestic crops. In addition, in most African countries there is only a limited range of export crops which can be grown easily by small farmers, so that producers cannot switch to non-taxable exports either. Thus if the full range of export crops is taxed, the bulk of small farmers' cash income is liable to tax. In its *effect*, an export tax is in this context a direct tax. In addition to export taxes, marketing boards may withhold growers' potential income which, as we saw in Chapter 12, constituted a very substantial 'hidden tax' during years of sharply rising export prices.

Although Kenya and Uganda classify export duties as direct taxes, while Tanzania and Zambia show them among indirect taxes in their official statistics, from what has been said it is fairly clear that both the impact and the incidence of most export taxes are borne by the peasant farmer in the primary producing country. Only if the export demand curve for a particular commodity exported by the individual country is inelastic will there be some scope for shifting the tax to buyers in the foreign markets. This is not generally the case with the main export crops from Eastern Africa; the income of the factors engaged in producing the crops or minerals subject to export taxes is normally reduced to the extent of the tax. Such export taxes are therefore *selective* income taxes.

Another kind of 'hidden' tax which constitutes an important source of government revenue in many 'welfare states', including Britain, is *social security contributions* levied on employees and their employers. Similar compulsory schemes have more recently been started in African countries, although their coverage is restricted by the relatively small size of the wage labour force in the formal sector. The rationale of this type of tax is the 'benefit principle': generally only those workers contributing to the national insurance or social security fund benefit from the unemployment or pension payments. Although the social security fund may be established separately from the ordinary government budget, however, the surplus of receipts over payments out of the fund can constitute a major source of public finance. The contributions paid by employees may be graduated with their wage income but usually they are regressive, especially if there is a minimum flat rate contribution and exemption of higher salaried employees with other insurance or pension provisions. In the UK the system is, in fact, a modified *poll tax* on all employed persons, with a limited element of graduated contributions and benefits. Employees' contributions can therefore be regarded as a form of direct income tax; employers' contributions are an indirect tax (on their labour costs) some of which is probably shifted into lower wages and higher prices. Some countries operate a percentage *payroll tax*, taking, say, 10 per cent of the wage-bill directly from employers. As a tax on employment it discriminates against the use of labour, and if it is a flat rate employment tax it discriminates further against employing unskilled workers, since the tax will constitute a larger proportion of their wage costs than the same amount of tax levied on higher-paid workers.

Useful classification of taxes

The main distinctions we have made so far are, first, between taxes on capital (wealth) and taxes on income, output, and expenditure; and second between direct and indirect taxes. A common characteristic of less developed countries is in fact their greater dependence on indirect taxes, particularly if export taxes are included in this category. However since a large proportion of these indirect taxes are actually either customs duties on imports or export taxes, this amounts to greater dependence on *taxes on foreign trade*. Thus government revenue in most poor countries is subject to the same high degree of external dependence as other structural features of the economy, described already in Chapter 4.

Alan R. Roe, when at the University of Dar es Salaam, studied this aspect of external dependence and concluded that 'in the poorest countries the size of the budget would appear to depend not so much on any political or ideological commitment but on the Government's ability to raise revenues which, in a predominantly subsistence economy will depend, in a large part, on the size of the foreign trade sector.'[5] Although this study referred to a period, 1957–60, before independence in Eastern Africa, it is worth illustrating his argument with a few figures: government revenue represented 17 per cent of Kenya's national income, 11 per cent of Tanzania's, but only 5 per cent of Ethiopia's, which he explained by the fact that imports as a percentage of national income were respectively 34 per cent, 26 per cent, and 7 per cent.

The low level of the majority of household incomes, as well as the considerable amount of tax evasion in many countries, also means that in addition to dependence on foreign trade taxes (collected from trading enterprises) we find considerable dependence on direct income taxes on company profits in those countries where large-scale mining is important or where there is a significant large-scale or formal industrial sector.

The predominance of company taxation is seen for instance in the percentage shares of the Zambian government's Recurrent Revenue contributed by mining companies, shown in Table 35.1 for 1970. The distinction in this country between 'indirect' mineral taxes on copper exports or royalties on the volume of production reflects more the method of tax collection than any fundamental constraint on the various tax sources. The figures also indicate the incidence of taxation, since they attribute all taxes on consumption goods and services—customs, excise, licences, etc.—to households.

A further useful classification of taxes is therefore to distinguish the main points of impact (sources of collection) as (1) taxes on foreign trade, (2) taxes on

business enterprises, and (3) taxes on households. The relative importance of these three will reflect the nature of the economy, particularly the dependence on foreign trade, the importance of the industrial or mining sector, and the degree of monetization or level of cash incomes in the economy as a whole.

Features of the Eastern African tax systems

Let us now examine the main features of the tax systems in Eastern African countries, and seek explanations for them. A statistical outline is provided in Table 35.2, showing (1) the main categories of taxation and, in the lower part of the table, (2) the importance of total tax revenue in relation to (a) all central government recurrent revenue and (b) total central government budget expenditure (on both recurrent and development accounts); and as a percentage of GDP at market prices.

Looking at the lower part of the table, we see that, although taxation is not the only source of government revenue, it is usually the most important, accounting for 75 per cent or more of ordinary recurrent revenue in all the Eastern African countries in 1970–1, except in Malawi and the Sudan where at that time foreign aid and the profits of state monopolies were important sources of revenue in the two countries respectively. In addition to taxation, governments earn regular revenue from the sale of goods and services, like official publications or forest products, to take just two examples, from fines, fees, and charges for schools or hospital places, and from interest, dividends, and rent on their loans or investments.

Normally, however, taxation is required to cover the bulk of recurrent expenditure on collective goods, while capital expenditure on development account is financed by borrowing loans or receiving grants. For this reason we see that taxation accounts for a smaller percentage of total government expenditure—between 50 and 60 per cent in most Eastern African countries—than of recurrent budget expenditure, which is financed from ordinary revenue.

It will also be noted from Table 35.2 that taxation tended to represent a smaller share of national income, as measured by GDP at market prices, in the poorer countries, Ethiopia and Malawi, than in countries with a higher income per head, like Zambia, although even in this latter case the 'tax–income ratio' at 24 per cent was still much less than the corresponding ratio of 35–40 per cent common in developed countries. We shall look more closely at the problems of increasing a country's 'taxable capacity' later on in Chapters 36 and 37, after we have seen how Eastern African governments raise their taxes.

Table 35.1 *Share of various taxes in government revenue, Zambia, 1970*

Kind of taxes	Per cent
(a) Taxes paid by mining companies	
Income taxes on profits	18 ⎫
Mineral royalties and copper export tax	30 ⎬ 57
(b) Taxes on other companies' profits	8
(c) Taxes on households	
Income taxes	8 ⎫
Expenditure taxes	19 ⎬ 27
(d) Other revenue	8
Total	100

SOURCE: Zambian Ministry of Planning and Finance, reproduced in Bank of Zambia, *Report and Accounts*, 1973, p. 50

Table 35.2   *Structure and relative importance of central government taxation in Eastern Africa*

Country	Ethiopia	Malawi	Tanzania	Sudan	Uganda	Kenya	Mauritius	Zambia
(1) *Main categories as %*								
of total government taxation:								
Direct taxes on income and wealth	28	41	32	16	19	44	30	61
Poll or graduated personal tax		10	8	—		3	1	—
Income tax on persons		11	} 24	6	} 19	21	} 28	15
Income tax on companies		20		10		20		46
Estate duty	—	—	—	—	—	—	1	—
Export duties	7	—	4	8	23	1	10	10
Import duties	32	34	26	50	24	31	35	9
Other indirect tax	33	25	38	26	34	24	25	20
Excise duties	—	8	15	20	18	16	16	20
Sales tax	—	10	16	—	17	—	—	—
Other licences, etc.	—	6	7	6	—	8	9	1
(2) *Total central government*								
taxation as % of:								
(a) Recurrent budget revenue	84	60	81	62	89	75	76	88
(b) Total budget expenditure	63	35	55	54	65	58	55	49
(c) Gross domestic product	8.5	11	15	17	12	16	17	24

SOURCE: *Statistical Abstract*; IMF *Surveys of African Economies, 1970–1*
NOTE: Data for Zambia refer to year 1971

The importance of indirect taxes versus direct taxes

The most striking feature of Eastern African tax systems revealed in Table 35.2 is the overwhelming importance of indirect taxes, particularly if export duties are included in this category. Only in Zambia were direct taxes on income, at 61 per cent of total tax revenue, more important than indirect taxes; and within the 39 per cent so raised there was an important contribution from the copper export tax and mineral royalties (10 per cent of total taxes) which were effectively direct taxes on mining companies. As we saw on page 521, in the previous year, 1970, these mineral taxes constituted an even larger share of ordinary revenue, 39 per cent (or 42 per cent of total taxes).

If direct taxation of high incomes seems the most effective means of producing an egalitarian tax system, what accounts for the relative unimportance of direct taxes in other Eastern African countries? One of the reasons is the comparative absence of large-scale company businesses such as the mining companies of Zambia, or Sierra Leone in West Africa, together with a reluctance to tax existing companies too heavily while efforts are being made to attract still more overseas capital. It is largely the existence of foreign or at least non-African enterprises in Kenya, and on a much smaller scale in Malawi, which accounts for the figures of 44 per cent and 41 per cent, respectively, from direct taxes. In neither of the cases are mining enterprises important, but large farms and estates are. The existence of a large-scale commercial or industrial sector in Kenya results not only in company profits, which are convenient and economical targets for taxation, but also in a higher yield of personal income taxes from their employees. Thus out of the 44 per cent for Kenya, about 20 per cent is derived from taxation of company income, another 21 per cent is paid by individuals charged on the higher progressive 'income tax', and about 3 per cent comes from a 'graduated personal tax' paid by lower income earners. This regressive tax, a modification of the old 'poll tax', had a low yield and high collection costs. It was eliminated in 1973 when a sales tax was instituted. Out of the 41 per cent raised in direct taxes in Malawi, again 20 per cent came from company profits, 11 per cent from income taxes on individuals, and 10 per cent from Minimum and Graduated Taxes levied on lower income earners.

Although Kenya abandoned the Graduated Personal Tax as a revenue source for both central and local governments at the end of 1973, neighbouring Uganda and Tanzania have not done so. Indeed in Uganda the 'Graduated Tax' is a major source of public finance although it is not included in the central government budget, being assessed, collected, and used by the District Councils which are relatively more important elements of the public sector in Uganda than in many other Eastern African countries.[6] If the Graduated Tax were included in the figures shown in Table 35.2, it would raise the share of taxation obtained from direct income assessment from 19 to 25 per cent, and raise the very low 'tax-income' ratio at the bottom of the Uganda column from the figure of 12 per cent to about 14 per cent, a figure nearer the 15 per cent shown for Tanzania. In the latter case personal tax of a similar minimum 'poll tax' type was an important element of central government revenue, helping to explain how Tanzania was able to rely on direct taxes on income for 32 per cent of tax revenue despite the low level of average personal incomes and the absence of many large-scale corporate businesses in private ownership.

Thus we can attribute part of the variation in the relative importance of direct taxes on incomes to the need to share tax bases between different levels of government, with minimum or simple graduated personal taxes being a suitable tax for assessment by local authorities, including the district officials and traditional chiefs who know more about the personal circumstances of their people than civil servants of the central government.

Another, institutional, reason why direct taxes on personal income are relatively unimportant in Eastern Africa is the separate funding of 'social security' or 'national insurance' contributions collected from paid employees. In the UK the total contributions of employees and employers to national insurance in 1970 added another 17 per cent of central government tax revenue: the employees' contribution represented a kind of poll tax or at best a regressive personal tax, and increased the revenue from direct taxes on income by 17 per cent also. In Table 35.2 these 'taxes' are not included, except in the case of Mauritius where social security contributions brought in 1 per cent of tax revenue in 1970–1. Both Kenya and Zambia have since 1966 operated, respectively, a National Social Security Fund and a National Provident Fund for most regular paid urban workers employed outside the public services.[7]

The smaller role of direct taxes on individuals' incomes in Eastern Africa is generally attributed to the narrow tax base afforded by populations with low levels of income per head (or per household), and the comparatively even distribution of income within the peasant farming sectors. If the exemption limit below which no income tax is paid is fixed at a high level, the majority of the population will be excluded and the tax revenue from a small minority of better-paid salaried workers or businessmen will be low. If, on the other hand, the limit is set at a much lower level, the high costs of collecting small sums from a large number of small income earners may also take up much of the tax yielded, so that net revenue is not increased significantly.

Direct taxation of both persons and companies is made difficult by the widespread lack of systematic accounting in business firms, or often the absence of records of any kind, particularly among small traders or peasant farmers. As a result the costs of collection are greatly increased. Moreover tax evasion is easy if tax relief can be claimed for a large number of dependants or for business expenses which are not recorded in situations where cash transactions are more common than the use of cheques to pay invoices.

Finally among direct taxes levied in Eastern Africa we need to look at the scope for raising revenue from regular or periodic levies on wealth. In Table 35.2 direct taxes on capital (estate duty in the table) constitute less than 1 per cent of tax revenue in all countries except Mauritius where it realized just 1 per cent in 1970–1. Estate duties are the normal method of taxing wealth: regular annual taxes on wealth or taxes on gifts have not featured prominently, despite the very unequal distribution of wealth in most Eastern African countries.

One of the limitations of relying on wealth taxes in Eastern Africa has been the very narrow tax base constituted by the very small number of really wealthy owners of personal assets valued above, say, £100,000, which is the minimum figure for the new annual wealth tax recently introduced in Britain and the value of 'estates' liable to the maximum rate of duty of 25 per cent in Kenya. If wealth taxes are levied on smaller estates in Eastern Africa, important problems of equity and incentive arise. The principle of horizontal equity requires 'like treatment of equals' but this is difficult if evasion or legal tax avoidance makes it harder to put a market value on 'intangible assets' like the goodwill of a business or investments on traditional (customary) land than, say, urban property or financial securities. If 'immobile' fixed assets like farms or factories are easier to tax, investment in productive activities may be discouraged and wealthy people may invest overseas or in non-income earning assets like uncultivated land or jewellery. Despite the difficulties of fair assessment, however, in the interests of vertical equity as well as increasing taxable capacity, the scope for wealth taxes should certainly be given more attention.

The composition of indirect taxes: taxes on foreign trade

Table 35.2 shows that a high proportion of *total* tax revenue—which means an even higher share of *indirect* taxation—is derived from taxes on foreign trade. Excluding export duties, customs duties (import taxes) provided a quarter or more of total tax revenue in all countries listed, with the exception of Zambia, and with the Sudan obtaining as much as one-half of its tax revenue in this way. If we include export duties within the category of indirect taxes, it can be seen that taxes on foreign trade provide more than all other sources of indirect taxation except in Zambia and, perhaps surprisingly, in Tanzania.[8] This reliance on foreign trade taxes reflects the fact that most African countries are still very much 'dependent' economies in the sense of having a high ratio of imports and exports to national income. However, the overwhelming reason for this emphasis on foreign trade taxes is the administrative convenience, in this situation, of taxing goods as they are funnelled into a small number of major assembly points at the ports, where they must in any case be checked for routine customs purposes such as controlling traffic in dangerous products. Since foreign trade taxes are less easily evaded than income taxes or indirect taxes on purely local transactions, even countries with a relatively low ratio of foreign trade to national income, like Ethiopia, have come to rely on customs duties. Export taxes are particularly convenient in countries with a small range of export commodities, like Uganda, Mauritius, or Ethiopia, and the task of assessment and collection is made even simpler if the exports are the responsibility of statutory marketing boards or producer cooperative associations.

There are some disadvantages in taxing foreign trade, however. In the case of import duties they constitute an interference with free trade and international specialization. Other countries may suffer a fall in export income, and retaliate; while domestic consumers of dutiable goods are induced to divert their consumption to less preferred combinations of goods. In Eastern Africa high *general* revenue tariff rates of duty of, say, 25 per cent of the import value of goods have afforded a means of protection for local substitutes, quite apart from the higher specific taxes (or quotas) aimed at more complete exclusion of imports. Where this degree of protection has diverted demand to local substitutes, the import duty receipts have fallen. In cases where import taxes have been raised to 'prohibitive' levels, of course, the revenue has been lost altogether. Thus the government's reliance on, say, substantial customs revenue on imported textiles, sugar and soap—all favourite targets for taxation—have caused serious revenue losses when local production has replaced imports without commensurate local sales or excise tax receipts.

Export duties may also imply decreased international trade, since it is more difficult to impose similar taxes on locally traded goods, resulting in a bias towards production for the local market and against producing for export markets, and therefore against specialization on the basis of comparative advantage. Export duties may therefore have adverse effects on the supply and allocation of resources, militating *against* a more favourable balance in foreign trade. A specific disadvantage of export duties, however, is their equity effects. Since they directly affect only producers in the export sector, and not all income earners, they will offend against the principle of horizontal equity if urban workers and businesses with similar levels of income are not covered adequately by alternative forms of taxation. If, as is quite likely, small cotton growers and other export producers are less well placed in terms of income than workers in other sectors, then the principle of vertical equity is also offended. Thus, for example, a cotton farmer in Uganda in 1970 with an annual income assessed for direct graduated tax at 2,000 shillings might appear to pay only 100 shillings or 5 per cent in tax, an absolute tax burden comparable to that imposed on a typical semi-skilled employee in Kenya's 'modern' sectors in the same year. However, if in the absence of a cotton export duty the Uganda farmer could have earned 2,400 shillings a year, his total tax burden is 500 shillings or a rate of over 20 per cent which could not be reached by a paid employee in the modern sector until he earned (as a married man with four children) over 80,000 shillings in Kenya, or a comparable £5,000 in the UK! Even without further deductions from farmers' potential income in the form of marketing board surpluses, export duties have often reduced their cash income by over 20 per cent; and as we noted in Chapter 12 export duties and marketing surpluses withheld more than one-half of Uganda's cotton and coffee growers' potential income in the early 1950s.

As direct taxes, then, export duties tend to be regressive in an absolute way, taxing small farmers more than richer income earners engaged in non-export activities. They are not even efficient *redistributors* of income, since at best they are proportional, not progressive, taxes: a rich farmer with a large amount of cotton or coffee will pay the same proportion of the value of his crop as a poor farmer. At the same time, however, this proportionality *might* be fairer than import and excise taxes which are often in practice, as we shall see, rather haphazard in their incidence, and even fairer than direct income tax which can also be shifted, legally avoided, or illegally evaded.

Although export duties might be regarded as an alternative foreign trade tax to import duties, and have clearly been adopted as such in Uganda (where the percentage of tax obtained from imports is rather smaller than in other Eastern African countries), they also seem to be imposed instead of direct income taxes. Table 35.2 shows that if we add export duties to direct income taxes, we get much the same percentage of total tax in most countries, the range being 35–45 per cent, the exceptions being Zambia and the Sudan. Export duties are an administratively simple method of taxing the income of small-scale producers and are relatively important when large-scale producers, either agricultural estates or large manufacturing and trading enterprises, are few in number. As we pointed out earlier, export duties have the effect of direct taxes when production is concentrated on a small range of export commodities; and in Uganda (and Ghana), where they are still the most important form of tax, they are also convenient tools for stabilization of private income and expenditure. By contrast most other taxes involve a more complex structure of tax rates and a more expensive machinery for collection. Unlike export duties, other taxes take time to adjust to changing economic circumstances, either because income tax receipts are collected in arrears, being based on the assessment of the previous year's profits or personal income, or because legislative approval is required for rate changes at the time of the annual Budget Debate.

Even with constant rates of tax, export duties can act as an automatic or 'built-in' stabilizer of *private* incomes. A constant proportionate rate of tax means that the *absolute* amount deducted from export producers' incomes is larger when these are high, and smaller when export proceeds are low. The deflationary effect of taxation (if left unspent in the hands of the government) is thus automatically greater when the inflationary pressure from the farmers' high incomes is greater, without any revision of tax rates. This effect is usually improved by applying a sliding-scale tax formula so that the tax *rates* also vary with the average export price. Thus in Uganda the export duty on cotton lint of A.R. quality might be set at 4 cent per lb, or 5 per cent at a price of 80 cents per lb, moving up to, for example, 33 cents or 15 per cent at a price of 220 cents per lb. This degree of progression is normally reinforced by a minimum cut-off price below which no duty is paid, so that farmers can maintain private expenditure when they, and aggregate demand, most need it. We should note, however, that stabilization of income after tax in the private sector means destabilizing tax revenue to the government. If the government can afford such flexibility, it will welcome the opportunity to stabilize private income. However if, as is likely in developing countries, the government would have to reduce the level of public expenditure in the face of lower tax revenue, it is more likely to place stability of public consumption and investment before the less predictable level of private spending.

Indirect taxes on expenditure and production

Turning now to other indirect taxes where the revenue varies with the volume or value of the goods *and services* purchased or sold, we can distinguish a number of headings which appear in the statement of any central government's recurrent revenue. Customs duties levied on imports are usually the most important indirect tax on local expenditure in African countries, and as such have been shown separately in Table 35.2. Excise duties raised on specific goods produced and consumed locally have been the next source of indirect tax revenue in many countries, but for reasons to be explained they are nowadays often supplemented by more general sales taxes covering a wider range of goods.

Then there are various specific consumption taxes, licences, and fees which are usually in effect excise taxes under other names: the most important nowadays are the various taxes on road vehicle users such as specific petrol and diesel consumption taxes and motor vehicle licences. Other favourite targets for licences and taxes, which like driving and vehicle licences involve regulatory as well as revenue objectives, are entertainment (cinemas, television, or radio), dogs or guns, with big game or fishing licences to tax tourists! Other licences and taxes are usually levied on traders or producers extracting natural resources like minerals or timber. Although the impact of trade licences and produce cesses is on the seller, the incidence is usually shifted to the final consumer, making them effectively expenditure taxes.

Specific production taxes on minerals, called 'royalties', tax part of the value added by miners and are thus a tax on income. In Table 35.2 they have been shown under export taxes for Zambia; but for other countries where they are of much less importance, and include royalties on quarrying and timber for local use, they have been included under 'other indirect taxes'.

We need to mention also various taxes on the ownership and use of land and buildings, including private dwellings. These 'rates' on property are levied usually with the rental income from the property as the tax base, and are chargeable on owner-occupied premises as well as property actually rented out, an 'imputed' rent being assessed for owner-occupiers. These taxes are regarded as indirect taxes on (housing) expenditure. Since they are usually local government rather than central government taxes, they do not feature prominently in central budget accounts.

By much the same token, employers' contributions to social security schemes are a payroll tax on one of a producer's factor inputs, labour. This payroll tax is an indirect tax, because it is variable and its incidence is normally passed on like other sales or 'value added' taxes to final buyers. However, it has not been included under other indirect taxes in Table 35.2, because these social security schemes are excluded from the governments' budgets, except for Mauritius.

Let us now see how indirect taxes levied in African countries fit into our criteria for tax systems. In theory a tax system based on customs and excise and other indirect taxes could be made as progressive as desired by careful adjustment of rates, as already mentioned. This would be a matter of taxing the goods that rich people buy more heavily than those less well-to-do people buy. Any desired redistribution could be achieved by varying taxes between each expenditure item in such a way that each successive income group could be found, on examining its actual purchases, to have paid the same amount of tax as it would be paid under any assumed progressive direct tax structure.

What advantages might result from changing the tax base, entirely, from income to expenditure? Professor Nicholas Kaldor, the Cambridge economist, has argued[9] that consumption measures the resources that a person withdraws from the economy for his personal use; that part of his personal income which is not consumed, his saving, adds to the nation's stock of capital; while dis-saving, resulting from consumption in excess of income, depletes productive capacity and ought to be discouraged by a higher rate of tax. Kaldor's proposals were designed with the problems of less developed countries specifically in mind, since high consumption by the rich reduces private capital accumulation, while direct income taxes are often evaded. An expenditure tax on consumption could, in principle, be levied in the same way as an income tax: individuals liable to the tax would have to declare their annual income and the net change in personal assets representing their saving or dis-saving. The residual balance of consumption expenditure would then be taxed at a progressive rate. If, as in India and Sri Lanka where Kaldor's proposals were introduced, this progressive expenditure tax is confined to upper income groups, the administrative costs might not be much greater than those of more conventional income taxes with their special allowances and surcharges on specific types of income like that from investments. If an expenditure tax encouraged more effort, risk-taking, and personal saving in developing countries it could improve the supply and allocation of resources, including the redistribution of aggregate consumption away from items consumed by high income groups. On the other hand, the principle of equity may be offended in two respects. First, whereas direct income tax must be paid, whether income is saved or not, taxes on expenditure can be avoided by abstaining from consumption so that a larger relative tax burden is borne by the lower income groups, who would save very little in any case. Secondly, the greater rate of saving and wealth accumulation by the rich

reduces equity, in that the possession of wealth gives its possessor benefits over and above any income derived from it and as such confers additional taxable capacity or ability to pay. It follows therefore that particular reliance on taxing consumption instead of income might also require a regular wealth tax to reduce the accumulation of wealth in the hands of the very rich.

Attempts to make existing expenditure taxes in Eastern Africa more progressive are also faced with difficulties. Accurate, up-to-date details of how different income groups allocate their expenditure are usually lacking. Moreover when local substitutes are produced, import duties need to be supplemented by appropriate excise taxes in order to achieve a progressive structure. As the range of domestic industry widens, and the number of firms in each industry increases, it becomes increasingly difficult to collect excise duties, which are specific taxes on the volume of goods leaving factories or store-rooms under the scrutiny of officials from the Customs and Excise department. New sales taxes have therefore been introduced to widen the coverage of local goods subject to indirect taxes and make good the loss of customs revenue from local substitution. In 1970–1 Tanganyika obtained 16 per cent of tax revenue from a sales tax (introduced in 1969–70), more than the 15 per cent from the old excise duties; Uganda in the same year derived 17 per cent revenue from a sales tax and 18 per cent from excise duties. Kenya introduced a sales tax in 1972–3 and by 1973–4 obtained 20 per cent of total tax revenue from this new tax levied on both local manufacturers *and* imports, compared with 13 per cent from excise duties (17 per cent in 1970–1). In the search for new tax revenue, Malawi introduced a general sales tax in 1970–1. This 'surtax' was fixed at 5 per cent of the normal ex-factory selling price *including* excise duties for local manufacturers or 5 per cent of the landed cost of equivalent imported manufactures after customs duty and augmented by a 20 per cent margin representing the hypothetical cost of transport to the main consuming centres where locally taxed goods may compete. This 20 per cent margin may be regarded as an attempt to tax at least some service inputs like transporters' and wholesalers' 'value added'. As a local sales tax, it exempts exports, capital goods, and manufactures imported duty-free from some countries, mainly low-income basic consumption goods. In Table 35.2 this surtax brought in 10 per cent of tax revenue, compared with 8 per cent from excise duties.

Despite attempts to widen the indirect tax base with general sales taxes, Finance Ministers (in practice) tend to attack specific targets rather than the whole range of consumer goods. Even countries with very comprehensive tax administrations like Britain in 1970 relied on customs and excise duties for over one-third of total central government tax revenue. Moreover taxes on alcoholic beverages (beer, wines, and spirits), on tobacco, and on petroleum products together accounted for two-thirds of all customs and excise receipts, compared with about one-quarter of these duties received from a more general purchase tax levied on a much wider range of consumer goods. Taxation of alcohol and tobacco together raised over £2,000 millions, about 40 per cent of all customs and excise, almost one-third of all expenditure taxes and 15 per cent of all tax revenue. If developed countries still rely on personal consumption of beverages, tobacco, and private motoring for a large share of tax revenue, we need not be surprised to find a similar or even greater concentration on these items in countries with less developed tax systems. Thus in most Eastern African countries about one-quarter of customs and excise revenue comes from taxing beverages and tobacco; a fifth or a sixth from taxing petroleum products;[10] a similar proportion, often, from textiles and clothing; with sugar as another important revenue source in many cases.[11] For example, Zambia in 1970 obtained as much as 36 per cent of all its customs and excise revenue from various excise taxes on beer and spirits, and another 14 per cent from an excise tax on cigarettes. Thus half the customs and excise revenue and almost half of all indirect tax revenue (excluding mineral duties) came from beverages and tobacco. In the same year in Kenya, when customs and excise accounted for almost 90 per cent of all revenue from expenditure taxes (before the introduction of the sales tax in 1974), 77 per cent of the revenue came from duties on beverages, tobacco, sugar, textiles, and transport equipment, as can be seen from the details

shown in Table 35.3. Of the 14 per cent of expenditure tax revenue raised in addition to customs and excise duties, the 'petrol and diesel tax' and 'licences and fees' under the Traffic account produced more than half.

Indeed, if we group all taxes on road users and from petroleum together, they provide 31 per cent of Kenya's indirect tax revenue, with a similar proportion derived from taxes on drinking and smoking or sugar, also used in local beer-brewing. About three-quarters of all indirect taxation was obtained from these sources or from taxes on textiles and clothing.

The relative weight of these taxes on 'drinking', 'smoking', and road transport would appear even greater if we could compare the amount of duty paid on each item with the value of consumers' expenditure on that item. Although detailed personal expenditure figures are not readily available in many Eastern African countries, a study of the incidence of indirect taxation on different African income groups in Kenya's main towns[12] indicates that, on average, some three-quarters of all indirect taxes paid by these households is levied on the 14 per cent of their expenditure devoted to 'drink and tobacco', clothing, and transport.

It will be seen from Table 35.4 that, for obvious reasons, foodstuffs produced locally and consumed by lower income households in the main are not subject to much indirect taxation, it being estimated at 0.9 per cent, only, of total household expenditure, implying an average food tax rate of 2.8 per cent[13] when divided by the 32.5 per cent expenditure devoted to foodstuffs. On the other hand, although these urban households only devoted 3.8 per cent of their expenditure to 'drink and tobacco' almost 40

Table 35.3 Composition of indirect taxes on expenditure in Kenya, 1970–1

	K£ million	% of customs and excise		% of all indirect taxes		
Beverages (beer, wines, mineral waters, and spirits)	7.2	16.3		30.5		
Cigarettes and tobacco	5.3	12.0				
Sugar	3.2	7.2	77.4			74.5
Textiles and clothing	6.7	15.2		13.0		
Mineral fuels	7.4	16.7		14.4		
Transport equipment	4.4	10.0		8.6		
Other customs and excise duties	10.0	22.6		—		
Total customs and excise	44.2	100.0		—	31.0	
Petrol and diesel tax	2.4			4.7		
Motor vehicle and driving licences	1.7			3.3		
Other indirect taxes	3.1			—	25.5[1]	
Total taxes on expenditure	51.4			100.0		

NOTE: [1] Includes other customs and excise duties

Table 35.4   *Distribution of urban household expenditure and indirect taxes by main consumption category in Kenya, 1968–9*

	(a) Household expenditure (%)	(b) Indirect taxes as % household expenditure total	(c) Tax rate by category (b) ÷ (a) (%)
Foodstuffs	32.5	0.9	2.8
Drink and tobacco	3.8	1.5	39.4
Clothing	5.5	1.0	18.2
Transport	5.0	2.5	50.0
Other items	53.2	0.3	0.6
Total	100.0	6.2	6.2

per cent of this constituted taxation; and, indeed, this tax revenue accounted for about one-quarter of all indirect taxes levied by the government on urban household consumption. Another favourite target was clothing, 18.2 per cent of these purchases constituting taxation; while various taxes on the householders' *own* expenditure on transport produced over 40 per cent of the indirect tax revenue. Since more than half of household expenditure, 53.2 per cent in fact, was subject to a very low tax rate of only 0.6 per cent, the introduction of a more general sales tax from 1974 can be explained as a search for tax revenue from other categories of non-food expenditure, generally regarded as more income-elastic than demand for foodstuffs or even demand for the other highly taxed items like clothing.

We have suggested that reliance on indirect taxation of drink, tobacco, and clothing is very widespread. Table 35.5 provides us with an illustration taken from West Africa where in Ghana detailed surveys of household expenditure have been undertaken for some years. It will be observed that in 1970 Ghana had reduced somewhat the rate of taxation on beverages and tobacco and on clothing, from around 49 per cent in 1960 to 34 per cent, and from 15 per cent to 5 per cent, respectively. Greater reliance was placed by 1970 on general sales taxes. Nevertheless what still stands out is the high rate of tax on drinks and tobacco and on imported foods,

Table 35.5   *Indirect taxes as percentage of consumer expenditure in Ghana*

Category	1960	1970
Food, imported	3.0	16.7
Beverages and tobacco	48.9	34.3
Clothing	15.1	4.9
Other items	11.7	27.6
Total consumer's expenditure	9.1	9.7

considered a 'luxury' in West Africa. If the 34 per cent tax in the retail price of beverages and tobacco in Ghana (and 39 per cent rate in Kenya) appear high, they are still lower than in Britain where the 1970 tax rate was 40 per cent on alcohol and nearly 70 per cent on tobacco!

Yet it is not necessarily the rich who spend the largest proportion of their incomes on drink and tobacco. And, quite apart from the question of vertical equity, it discriminates unfairly against smokers and drinkers as such. There is therefore not a strong case on grounds of either vertical or horizontal equity for this pattern of taxation, and the reason for it clearly lies in the fact that demand for these goods is price-inelastic. Similarly, the taxes on petrol and other items of transport costs like diesel, tyres, and the vehicles themselves, which are substantial in Africa, really form a general tax on all commodities, since the taxation adds a margin to the transport costs for them. Again, demand for all commodities will be highly price-inelastic. These taxes on the transport of goods are more likely to work out as proportional than progressive. On the other hand, indirect taxes on private motoring are usually quite progressive, since most family budget studies show expenditure on transport and travel as an increasing proportion of income.

Reforming the tax structures

Our discussion has centred on the most important taxes actually in operation in Eastern Africa. Even then we have hardly commented on the complex issues surrounding the best form of company tax, which is an important tax, especially in Zambia and Kenya. Nor have we dealt specifically with the various problems of local government finance, with its special reliance on modified forms of the old poll tax, indirect tax revenue from produce cesses, licences, and, especially, the rating of land and property. We have not, moreover, attempted a comprehensive analysis of taxation covering all forms of taxation which *might* be introduced or reformed to yield more revenue, like the various land taxes paid by landowners and tenants in Ethiopia.[14] Before concluding this review of taxation, however, we need to see if the existing tax systems do, in fact, affect the distribution of income in any of the Eastern African countries.

Redistribution of personal income by taxation in Kenya[15]

In this section we look at the ways in which central government taxes on personal income and household expenditure affect the distribution of incomes received by persons. A tax system can redistribute personal income in an *absolute* sense by taking absolutely larger amounts from the better-off than from the poorer members of the population, provided the benefits arising from governments' spending of tax revenue are *not* distributed according to the amount paid in tax. In Africa it is not always certain that the poor derive as much benefit as the rich from public expenditure, but this is a problem to be tackled from the expenditure side of the government budget. In Eastern Africa taxes are used to reduce incomes, not to reallocate them, since there is little or nothing in the way of cash transfers (negative taxes) to assist people in the lowest income groups. By income redistribution, therefore, we normally mean taking *relatively* more from the rich by progressive taxation, since even proportional taxes will not reduce the degree of income inequality, *everybody* being left with, say, 10 per cent less disposable income with a proportional income tax of 10 per cent. How progressive, then, was the tax system of Kenya before budgetary measures in the 1970s abolished the rather regressive Graduated Personal Tax and placed increasing emphasis on a more progressive income tax and general sales tax aimed at a higher income group?

An interesting comparison of the degree of progression was calculated by M. J. Westlake, reproduced in Table 35.6, which shows the percentage of personal income taken in direct taxes from single persons at different income levels in Kenya and the UK. These income levels are expressed as multiples of the average national income per head rather than absolute annual income figures, since a low-income country like Kenya may need to levy some direct tax on persons with an income equal to the national average even though this may only be about 900 shillings (in 1970) or only one-fifteenth of the British average. Alternatively a personal income of only 900 shillings in Britain would be well below any conventional measure of poverty in a high-income country.

The figures in Table 35.6 indicate very little progression in the Kenya direct tax system: it is proportional in the lower income range for single men (and more regressive for married men with children's allowances) and also regressive at the highest income level shown. By contrast in Britain persons with 20 times the national average income pay almost half their income in tax, although of course at this income level of around £14,000 they are earning much more than a Kenyan with 18,000 shillings, which is 20 times the Kenya average national income per head.

Although taxes in Kenya on personal income become progressive again for incomes above 20,000 shillings (and the percentage of income taken in tax becomes greater than in Britain for incomes over about 80,000 shillings), these high income ranges are

Table 35.6 *Comparison of income tax progression in Kenya and the UK*

Income as a ratio of GNP per head	Percentage of income taken in direct tax	
	Kenya 1970–1	UK 1965–6
1	0.0	4.7
2	2.8	20.3
3	2.8	25.3
4	3.1	26.7
5	3.6	27.8
10	10.4	33.2
15	13.0	41.9
20	12.8	48.1

SOURCE: M. J. Westlake, op. cit., p. 8, Table 5 (abbreviated)

of little importance since the vast majority of people earned money incomes well below 4,000 shillings (which was 4–5 times the average national income per head in 1970). More to the point, therefore, was the regressive nature of direct taxation within the relevant income range up to 12,000 shillings covered by the Graduated Personal Tax (GPT), plus the greater apparent evasion of the more progressive income tax by higher income groups. Westlake calculated that, whereas perhaps up to 37 per cent of GPT was evaded, as much as 60 per cent of income tax was evaded, thereby making the effective tax incidence more regressive. As might be expected, the incidence of indirect taxes was also regressive at least as between different income groups in the main towns, the poorest households with monthly incomes below 300 shillings in 1968 paying 8 per cent of the income in indirect taxes, compared with only $4\frac{1}{2}$–5 per cent for those with incomes over 2,000 shillings per month.

Since Westlake's study, the Kenya government has reformed the tax system,[16] replacing GPT (which yielded over £3 millions in its last 'full' year of collection, 1972/3) with a general Sales Tax (which yielded £22 millions in its first 'full' year, 1973/4), and introducing reforms in the rate and structure of the other two major taxes, Income Tax and Import Duties. Let us end by explaining how these reforms are expected to meet the main criteria of a good tax system which we discussed at the beginning of this chapter.

First, *improvement in the supply and allocation of resources* is expected to be obtained by reducing the proportion of tax revenue derived from import duties, levied mainly on final consumption goods, and increasing the share of taxation obtained from both intermediate and final consumption of manufactured goods, whether these are locally produced or imported. Before the introduction of the general Sales Tax in 1973 local production of many final consumption goods was protected by specific as well as 'ad valorem' import duties; whereas local substitution of capital and intermediate goods was not, since import taxes on these goods were much lighter or zero. As a result domestic resources tended to be drawn from production for export or from production of capital and intermediate goods and into local substitution of imported final consumption goods only. By applying the Sales Tax to a wider range of manufactured goods, both imported and locally produced, it is hoped to stimulate local substitution of machinery and materials which now enjoy a higher degree of 'effective protection'. On the other hand, by reducing the general level of import duties on final goods and making them more uniform on an 'ad valorem' basis, many locally produced final consumption goods will have to be more competitive with imports, and thus with prices abroad if, as it is hoped, more of them are to be exported.[17]

Secondly, the tax system has been made more *equitable* by the abolition of Graduated Personal Tax levied on low income groups. By replacing this tax revenue with the Sales Tax applicable only to manufactured goods which are consumed mainly by higher income groups, a regressive direct income tax has been replaced by an indirect tax more progressive in its incidence. Additionally, by reforming the system of dependants' allowances, previously deductible from taxable income (and thus giving higher income groups greater absolute tax relief than lower incomes), and now deductible from the tax itself, the tax relief is the same for all income groups. Since it is

the higher incomes which also earn income from dividends, the 1973 tax reforms included an additional tax on dividends and on all income payments to foreigners.

Thirdly, the tax system has been made more *elastic* with respect to the growth of personal incomes and personal expenditure, since both the direct income tax and the indirect sales tax are more progressive. As we saw, progressive taxes act as 'built-in' stabilizers of private income and consumption, and ensure that the government's revenues can keep pace with its expenditures without the need for frequent changes in rates of tax. Thus the *stabilization* and development aspects of the tax system are improved, as well as its *administrative convenience and efficiency*. Finally, in the East African context especially, the Kenya tax system has become more *efficient* as a result of the reduced chances of evading a sales tax compared with direct taxes on income. Whereas in 1970–1, indirect taxes contributed 56 per cent of tax revenue, by 1973–4 they contributed only 37 per cent.

The progressiveness of the Tanzanian tax structure

In the case of Tanzania, considerable advance appears already to have been made towards achieving a progressive tax structure. Huang, reviewing previous studies of tax structure in less developed countries, finds that most studies conclude that the tax structures are either regressive or at best proportional, as

Table 35.7 The progressiveness of the Tanzanian tax structure, 1971

Types of tax	Income class						All
	0–999	1,000–1,999	2,000–3,999	4,000–7,999	8,000–24,999	25,000+	
	(percentage of income absorbed by tax in each class)						
Total, all taxes	9.6	10.7	13.1	19.8	37.0	49.1	18.8
Individual income	—	—	0.2	3.5	14.5	27.8	4.5
Corporate income	0.9	0.9	1.0	1.2	1.9	2.8	1.2
Total, other taxes	8.7	9.8	11.9	15.1	20.6	18.5	13.1
of which:							
Excise	2.2	2.6	3.8	4.9	5.9	3.8	3.7
Domestic sales	1.4	1.6	1.9	2.5	2.9	2.3	2.0
Import	3.8	4.1	4.6	5.4	7.4	7.8	5.1
Foreign sales	1.1	1.2	1.3	1.6	2.1	2.2	1.5
Other	0.2	0.3	0.5	0.7	2.3	2.4	0.8
Urban, all taxes	16.3	18.7	24.7	30.6	43.1	49.6	39.9
Rural, all taxes	9.5	10.6	12.0	15.3	25.7	47.5	12.9

SOURCE: Y. Huang, op. cit., Table 35.3

NOTE: Assumed consumption patterns based on the 1969 Household Budget Survey; income classes are on a 1969 basis—in 1971 all limits would be about 20% higher; tax rates applied reflect 1971 tax structure

a result, first, of the limited impact of income taxes and, second, of reliance on indirect taxes on consumption.[18] After careful statistical analysis of the Tanzanian situation, however, he found that both direct and indirect taxes, and the system as a whole, are very progressive. His results are summarized in Table 35.7, which shows the percentage of income paid in each kind of tax at different levels of income.

The first row gives the total percentage paid in tax, indicating the progressiveness of the system as a whole: these percentages can be seen to rise throughout, quite rapidly after 4,000 shillings. The second row shows that a significant factor in this overall progressiveness is the tax on individual income. As pointed out in the previous section, it is possible to have very high tax rates at very high levels of income without affecting the effective degree of progressiveness among most of the population: in this case, however, we see that the percentage taken in tax rises quite sharply at incomes as low as shs 8,000 and is mildly progressive even at shs 1,000 per annum.

Lower down the table we see that other taxes, predominantly indirect, are also progressive up to an income of shs 25,000 (although they are regressive over the last two classes), again starting as low as shs 1,000. The percentage taken in tax increases for all categories, excise tax, domestic sales tax, import duties, and foreign sales (export duties), up to shs 25,000. This illustrates the point made earlier, that it *is* possible to choose a set of excise taxes and other taxes which will produce a progressive tax effect: indirect taxes do not *have* to be regressive. Examples of taxed items consumed by the 'rich' in Tanzania are consumer durables for the house, electricity, cinema charges, and, of course, motor vehicles and petrol.

An important feature of Huang's calculation is that he includes, as part of income, income received in kind, such as subsidized housing, and home-produced, non-cash income, such as the own-account consumption of farm families.[19] Since this type of income is proportionately more important among the poorest farm families, and yet is not subject to either direct or indirect tax, this reduces the percentage paid in tax at the bottom end of the income scale and increases the progressiveness of the structure, in respect of direct *and* indirect taxes.

Questions on Chapter 35

1. What criteria would you use to assess a good tax system?
2. Distinguish between 'regressive', 'proportional', and 'progressive' taxes and tax systems.
3. Demonstrate the effect of a specific tax on a commodity on a consumer's demand for an untaxed substitute good. On what factors will this effect depend?
4. Discuss the view that an indirect tax on consumer goods produces an 'excess burden' avoided by a direct tax, yielding the same revenue, on the consumer's income.
5. Compare the effects of (1) a poll tax and (2) a proportional tax on wages (yielding the same revenue) on a worker's willingness to supply effort.
6. In choosing a tax structure it is often said that the objective of equity is in conflict with the objective of preserving incentives. Discuss.
7. Define the following: horizontal and vertical equity in taxation; 'ability-to-pay' and 'benefit' principles of taxation; 'built-in' stabilization; wealth taxes; capital gains tax; property taxes; tax incidence and impact; excise duties; sales taxes; value-added tax; payroll taxes; poll tax; a tax base; taxable capacity.
8. How far do Eastern African tax systems reflect the structure of Eastern African economies?
9. How do you account for the relative unimportance of direct taxation in African tax systems?
10. How easy do you think it would be to extend the use of wealth taxes in African countries?
11. Why are many African countries heavily dependent upon taxes on foreign trade? What disadvantages may export duties have?
12. Discuss the case for a general expenditure tax, both generally and in the specific African context.
13. Why are taxes on smoking, drinking, and motoring so popular with governments? Illustrate your answer with reference to the relative importance of these taxes in any African country.
14. How has Kenya attempted to reform its tax structure to make it more 'equitable' and 'income-elastic'?
15. Discuss the progressiveness exhibited by Tanzania's tax system. What lessons can be drawn by other African countries?

Notes

[1] A *tax* may be distinguished, in principle, therefore, from *fees* and other charges made by governments for goods and services provided on the basis of exclusion (discussed in Chapter 18) such as school fees, although in practice the distinction becomes blurred when the charges include an element of tax or subsidy.

[2] Adam Smith's first canon being equity which has been discussed above. Smith argued that proportional taxes constituted the fairest application of the principle of 'ability to pay'. Although he was writing in 1776 and in the British context, what would now be regarded as a very conservative view of equality of sacrifice has yet to be applied in practice in many countries.

[3] See, for example, M. J. Westlake, 'Tax Evasion, Tax Incidence and the Distribution of Income in Kenya', *Eastern Africa Economic Review*, December 1973.

[4] In other words excluding considerations of equity or administrative convenience. We are also ignoring particular cases where the government wants deliberately to affect the allocation of resources, as where it imposes a protective duty to protect an 'infant' industry.

[5] Alan R. Roe, 'The Government-Revenue Share in Poorer African Countries—A Comment,' *Economic Journal*, June 1968.

[6] For a detailed study of Uganda's Graduated Tax, which includes a standard rate minimum 'poll tax' element, see Kenneth Davey's *Taxing a Peasant Society: The Example of Graduated Taxes in East Africa*, Charles Knight & Co., London, 1974.

[7] Under Kenya's Fund in 1970 some 600,000 employees contributed 5 per cent of their earnings (up to a maximum of 40 shillings a month related to earnings of 800 shillings), while their 21,000 registered employers contributed a further 5 per cent. With annual contributions exceeding K£6 millions, the Fund was a major source of public revenue since the proceeds (net of annual benefits for old age, invalidity or death) are invested in government loans available for development expenditure. Indeed since 1969 the NSSF has been the largest holder of locally issued Public Funded Debt, with over K£30 millions so invested or about one-third of all holdings by 1972. Contributions to this Fund represent, therefore, an increasingly important form of personal taxation available for public investment: since 1970 they have provided about 15 per cent of the public sector's total capital formation. In 1972 they were sufficient to finance 40 per cent of the Kenya government's Development Expenditure; and in effect raised total tax revenue by a useful 6 per cent.

Although Zambia's National Provident Fund is a relatively smaller source of national saving, given the greater scope for taxing mining companies, by 1970–1 it produced contributions of over K14 millions, representing another 5 per cent of tax revenue and raising the proportion of central government revenue obtained from taxes to 93 per cent. As in the Kenya scheme, contributions are based on a 10 per cent payroll 'tax', with half paid by employers and the other 5 per cent by employees subject to a maximum employee contribution of K8 per month. Since wage levels are generally higher in Zambia than in Kenya, the scheme is less progressive. However in both countries, these payroll 'taxes' are more progressive than the old poll taxes or the simple graduated taxes. They are also more 'income-elastic', since the growth of wage bills can be taxed automatically as the numbers in paid employment and average earnings increase. For the bulk of African employees, still earning in 1970 or 1971 well below the monthly wage level of 800 shillings in Kenya or 80 kwacha in Zambia (above which level the maximum contribution of 40 shillings or 8 kwacha would represent a regressive poll tax), this proportional tax constitutes a valuable addition to the personal income tax base. However, as pointed out earlier, the rationale of these social security taxes is the 'benefit principle' so that if wage employment and earnings ceased to expand faster than benefits paid out to retiring workers then governments would be faced with finding alternative sources of tax revenue as well as meeting repayments of these 'compulsory loans'.

[8] In fact Zambia can be said to rely on foreign trade taxes for 51 per cent of tax revenue if direct income tax on mining companies (32 per cent of all taxation in 1971) is added to the 10 per cent from export duties and 9 per cent from customs duties. The low percentage of only 30 per cent from Tanzania reflects partly the limited scope for taxing a larger range of export products and partly greater reliance on a sales tax instead of import duties.

[9] Nicholas Kaldor, *An Expenditure Tax*, Allen & Unwin, London, 1955.

[10] Since the sharp increase in petroleum import prices in 1973–4, tax rates have been increased although the revenue yield has remained fairly constant, the purpose of the tax increase being to *reduce* consumption rather than raise tax revenue.

[11] In addition to customs or excise duties on sugar, some countries like the Sudan receive public revenue from the profits of a state monopoly trading in sugar.

[12] See M. J. Westlake, op. cit., pp. 11–5.

[13] Since 0.6 per cent, or two-thirds of the household's expenditure going on food taxes, represented excise on sugar, the average rate of tax on other foods was only about 1 per cent.

[14] In 1964 the Sudan introduced a Land Rent Income Tax, since previously ownership of land and buildings had proved an attractive tax-free investment. However this tax yielded less than 1 per cent of tax revenue in 1970–1, suggesting a reluctance to increase tax rates, despite the favourable resource and equity effects.

[15] This section draws heavily on the study by M. J. Westlake, op. cit.

[16] A useful summary of the fiscal policy objectives introduced in Kenya's 1973 Budget are contained in Republic of Kenya, *Development Plan, 1974–78, Part I*, Government Printer, Nairobi, 1974, pp. 167–70.

[17] As an additional incentive to the export of manufactures, producers who export a substantial proportion of their output have been given a cash subsidy to compensate for the higher general rate of import duties on their intermediate inputs.

[18] Y. Huang, 'Distribution of the Tax Burden in Tanzania', *Economic Journal*, March 1976.

[19] This consumption in kind was valued at local prices for aggregation purposes.

36 Public Expenditure

Governments are set up, or should be set up, to serve the citizens of a country. A major objective of the government is therefore to promote the economic welfare of citizens by means of appropriate economic policies and, as we saw in Chapter 18 on public enterprise, by direct participation in production.

Activities of the state

More specifically, the activities of the state may be classified as follows:

(1) ensuring internal security and external defence, as well as carrying out general administration;

(2) providing productive infrastructure such as communications, water, and power as a service to industry, agriculture, and other productive sectors;

(3) providing basic social services such as sanitation, medical care, and education;

(4) participating directly in the production and marketing of goods other than so-called 'public goods', either through the establishment of public enterprises or by combining with private business in various ways, by providing finance, or perhaps guaranteeing markets;

(5) influencing or guiding the level and direction of private economic activity by various regulations, by means of monetary and fiscal policies and through the multiplier effects of public spending;

(6) redistributing income and wealth by taxation and via public spending.

As pointed out in Chapter 5 and again in Chapter 18, the extent of the state's involvement in economic affairs will vary with the political ideology prevailing in the country. In fact, however, if we leave out of account the fully collectivist economies of the Soviet type, where most economic enterprise is state-run and private property is severely restricted, the size of the public sector seems to be related less to a country's degree of commitment to socialism or economic equality than to its stage of economic development. We find, for instance, that the most advanced capitalist country, the USA, spends much the same proportion of its national income on collective consumption as Western European countries such as the UK and even Sweden, with its well-known commitment to 'social welfare'. Against this Japan in 1970 devoted only 8 per cent of GDP to government consumption, less than half the share spent in most other industrial countries and below the 16 per cent estimated for many Eastern African countries. Within the developing world very poor 'socialist' countries like India and Tanzania spend a smaller proportion than the slightly richer but more 'mixed' economies of Kenya and Zambia.

On the other hand, if instead of relating only general government current expenditure on consumption goods and services to national income, we take account also of capital formation by governments and public enterprises, the role of the state might be said to be more closely identified with political ideology. Thus in 1970 almost half of all capital formation in Tanzania was within the public sector, compared with only 30 per cent in Kenya. Similarly, among developed countries, the public sector is responsible for about 50 per cent of Britain's annual rate of capital formation, compared with only about 20 per cent in the USA. The reason for the much smaller figure in the USA is, of course, the absence of a wide range of public enterprises: even 'public utilities' like railways, airways, electricity, and telephones are privately owned, let alone 'basic' industries like coal and steel which have been nationalized in Britain.

Categories of state spending

Before we look in more detail at how governments may 'spend' their revenue, we may note three *categories* of spending undertaken by them. We distinguish first between direct purchases of consumption goods and services by public authorities (public consumption) and direct purchases of capital goods by the public sector, including state enterprises (public capital formation). Public capital formation, which involves the direct purchase of plant and machinery and the construction of buildings, roads, dams, and other public works, forms an important part of public expenditure in developing countries and, for obvious reasons, the younger nations of Africa have to spend more of their limited budgets catching up with social overhead capital.

Apart from these two forms of state spending on goods and services, a share of public revenue is allocated to *transfer payments* in the form of pensions

Table 36.1   *Economic and functional classification of Kenya Government expenditure, 1970–1 (K£m)*

	General (Administration, security, defence)	Community (Roads, water, etc.)	Social (Education, health, etc.)	Economic (Agriculture, commerce, industry, etc.)	Public debt (Interest and redemption)	Other (Pensions, unallocable items)	Total (Recurrent and development accounts)	Per cent
Wages and salaries	16.6	2.4	23.7	7.0	—	4.1	53.9	34.4
Other direct purchases	9.8	2.1	5.1	4.4	—	1.7	23.0	14.7
Total public consumption	*26.4*	*4.5*	*28.8*	*11.4*	—	*5.8*	*76.9*	*49.1*
Subsidies	—	—	—	1.2	—	—	1.2	0.8
Public Debt interest	—	—	—	—	7.5	—	7.5	4.8
Transfers: Households	—	—	1.1	—	—	1.9	3.0	1.9
Other private	—	—	—	0.5	—	—	0.5	0.3
Other public	0.1	0.2	7.1	0.8	—	0.8	9.0	5.7
Rest of world	0.1	—	—	—	—	3.6	3.7	2.4
Total transfer payments	*0.2*	*0.2*	*8.2*	*2.5*	*7.5*	*6.3*	*25.1*	*16.0*
TOTAL CURRENT EXPENDITURE	26.7	4.7	37.0	14.0	7.5	12.1	102.0	65.1
(Percentages by function)	*26.2%*	*4.6%*	*36.3%*	*13.7%*	*7.4%*	*11.9%*	*100.0%*	
Gross capital formation	3.6	14.8	5.1	4.5	—	0.8	28.7	18.3
Investments in state enterprises	—	—	—	9.8	—	—	9.8	6.3
Loans to public & private sectors	—	0.2	2.2	3.2	—	—	5.5	3.5
Loan repayments	—	—	—	0.1	10.6	—	10.7	6.8
TOTAL CAPITAL EXPENDITURE	3.6	14.9	7.3	17.6	10.6	0.8	54.7	34.9
(Percentages by function)	*6.6%*	*27.2%*	*13.3%*	*32.1%*	*19.4%*	*1.5%*	*100.0%*	
TOTAL CURRENT & CAPITAL EXPENDITURE	30.4	19.6	44.3	31.5	18.1	12.8	156.7	100.0
(Percentages by function)	*19.4%*	*12.5%*	*28.3%*	*20.1%*	*11.6%*	*8.2%*	*100.0%*	

SOURCE: *Statistical Abstract, 1972*, Table 206, p. 194 (summarized)

and the like which permit *private* consumption, and loans to other sectors which permit additional private capital formation.

Table 36.1 gives a detailed economic and functional classification of Kenya government expenditure in 1970–1. Here we comment only on the division between consumption and capital expenditure, as well as transfer payments. Public consumption was equal to 49 per cent of the total, and public capital expenditure to 35 per cent. Transfer payments accounted for the remaining 16 per cent, although about 10 per cent of the 35 per cent given for capital expenditure actually went on loans and loan repayments rather than direct expenditure on goods and services and thus represents a transfer.

As we saw in Chapter 2, however, the definition of what is 'capital' is rather arbitrary. This applies here to expenditure on teachers or on health workers which is classified by economic statisticians as public consumption but may contribute much more to increasing future output, through 'human capital', than, say, office blocks which are included under public capital formation.

While government can and indeed must make a choice at the margin between more public consumption and more public capital formation, it is important to realize also that spending on capital account and on recurrent account are not entirely independent of each other. Thus governments have sometimes received foreign assistance to build additional hospitals or schools only to find that they lacked the current revenue to pay for doctors, nurses, and teachers so that hospitals, for instance, have remained empty and unstaffed.

In a number of other ways present government expenditure either involves future commitment or reflects past commitments. Hence the government's hands are *partially* tied in framing its annual budget. Thus a percentage of the budget must go on paying pensions and gratuities to former civil servants or, more important, in paying back loans and paying interest on loans raised to finance expenditure in the past, both of which are contractual obligations of the government. Most forms of physical capital need regular maintenance and repair, and eventually replacement.

Composition of the public sector and its contribution to national income

Table 36.1 shows how central government spending generates demand for national output directly through expenditure on public 'consumption' goods and especially services and on capital goods, and indirectly by transfer and loans to other sectors. This is quite apart, of course, from other indirect effects on private spending through the operation of the 'multiplier'. It may be seen from Table 36.1 that a large part of the K£28.8 million of public consumption on education, health, etc., in 1970–1 consisted of wages and salaries for teachers and medical staff, the rest being direct purchases of goods such as school-books or chalk. The proportion of expenditure which is for equipment was much higher in the case of security and defence, it may be noticed. Very largely, however, public consumption expenditure is the government's own wage-bill, although public sector enterprises will contribute gross profits in addition to wage income.

There is an important difference between central government and government as a whole, including *local* government authorities, and also the *public sector* as a whole, which must always be kept in mind. In Eastern Africa as elsewhere, there are large current and capital outlays by these other components of the public sector. Thus in 1971 (not shown in the table), out of total public consumption of K£114.2 millions (equal to 17.8 per cent of GDP at market prices), local authorities were responsible for about one-tenth or K£12.6 millions; the East African Community General Fund Services for another K£5.0 millions; and the various Kenya government parastatal general government functions for another K£8 millions or so, leaving the central government itself purchases of K£88 millions, just 77 per cent of the total.

Likewise, of total gross capital formation of K£162.2 millions estimated for Kenya in 1971, as much as one-third, or K£55.6 millions was in the public sector: the Kenya government itself was responsible for K£31 millions, or 56 per cent; its parastatal bodies 14 per cent (K£7.7 millions); local authorities for 10 per cent (K£5.7 millions); and the East African Community for 20 per cent (K£11.2

millions), almost entirely in respect of its corporations, covering railways, harbours, postal services, and airways.

It follows that when we talk about activities undertaken by 'the state', we must be aware how the latter is defined, and similarly in referring to 'the public sector'. In particular, care must be taken not to use central government expenditure as the only or in some cases the most important source of public investment.

Table 36.2 shows how the contributions of the different components of the public sector in Kenya to gross domestic income (product) at factor cost have varied between 1964 and 1973. We see that the contribution of 'general government' under the central government authority was only K£28.2 millions out of 79.6, or 35 per cent, in 1964 and rather larger at 47 per cent in 1973. The size of the public sector as a whole increased from 24 per cent of the GDP in 1964 to 28 per cent in 1973. This was not a very significant increase, however, and Kenya remains very much a 'mixed economy'. Indeed this increase is related to a fall in the share of non-monetary output from 27 per cent to 21 per cent, rather than to a reduced share of the private sector within the monetary economy: this share actually rose from 49 to 51 per cent.

Within the public sector it was general government activities which expanded more than public enterprises, and the table identifies the main reason for this increased share: the expansion of education as a public good, supplied directly by the central government in particular. Increasing centralization of social services, particularly education, reduced the relative importance of local authorities within government, and within the public sector. Finally, the other 'structural' change over the period was the increasing share of parastatal enterprises set up by the Kenya government, compensated by a declining share of

Table 36.2 *Contribution of the public sector to GDP in Kenya, 1964 and 1973 (K£m)*

	1964					1973			
	General government		Public enterprises	Total	(%)	General government		Public enterprises	Total	(%)
	Educ.	Total				Educ.	Total			
Kenyan Government	3.6	28.2	6.3	34.8	*(43.7)*	37.2	95.9	13.6	109.5	*(54.0)*
Local authorities	7.1	11.1	1.2	12.3	*(15.4)*	2.4	10.7	3.4	14.1	*(7.0)*
Parastatals	0.6	0.7	4.2	4.9	*(6.2)*	2.2	2.3	28.5	30.8	*(15.2)*
E. A. Community	—	2.5	25.1	27.6	*(34.7)*	0.2	4.3	44.0	48.3	*(23.8)*
Total	11.2	42.5	37.1	79.6	*(100)*	42.1	113.2	89.5	202.7	*(100)*
as percentage of		330.1					731.1			
GDP at factor cost	*3.4*	*12.9*	*11.2*	*24.1*		*5.8*	*15.5*	*12.2*	*27.7*	

SOURCE: *Economic Survey, 1974,* Table 1.5, p. 8 (abridged)

wages and profits from public enterprises under the East African Community. The latter contributed two-thirds of all public enterprises income in 1964, against one-half in 1973. This relative change reflects a change from concentration on basic infrastructure such as railways, harbours, and postal services at an earlier stage of economic development to the establishment of a much wider variety of public enterprises in manufacturing and commerce.

Opportunity-costs in the allocation of public expenditure

In the allocation of resources the opportunity-cost of any line of action must be borne in mind. This applies to public expenditure in a number of different ways. The percentages mentioned above for public consumption and public capital expenditure represent one major alternative, between (social) consumption and (public) investment. Within public capital formation, governments need to choose how much to spend on social overhead capital aimed at providing the basis for long-run economic development and how much to spend on directly productive projects with a more immediate pay-off. In the post-war literature on the problems of underdeveloped countries spending on infrastructure was often seen as the basis for development: the provision of adequate transport facilities, electricity supplies, and the training of skilled and semi-skilled labour was seen as a prerequisite of industrial and other expansion, and had to precede the latter. Thus in Uganda, in the early 1950s, it was hoped that the building of the Owen Falls Dam and the provision of cheap electricity would stimulate rapid industrial development in the Jinja area, mainly attracting private enterprise: the necessary response, however, proved lacking. Certainly there *is* interdependence between infrastructural investment and other development projects, and infrastructure is required if general development is to go forward. But there is still scope for choice regarding the level and quality of infrastructural provision at any level of national output, and the rate at which such provision is expanded as output expands.

Related to the choice between public consumption and capital formation, but not identical with it, is the choice between 'social services' such as education, health, housing, and community development, and 'economic services', spending on services related to the development of agriculture, industry, commerce, and other productive sectors. Table 36.1 shows that there is a choice also as regards the proportion of the budget to be devoted to general administration, security, and defence. Defence spending can, of course,

be regarded as infrastructural, 'permitting' other activity to proceed. On the other hand it may, and often does, reflect simply a 'warlike' attitude on the part of a government or a response to a purely imaginary threat, and to that extent represents a form of consumption carried out at the expense of other public consumption on hospitals, say, or education. Kenya spent 26 per cent of total current expenditure by government on general administration, security, and defence, and 19 per cent of its total current and capital expenditure by government; 37 per cent of current expenditure was spent on social services and about 14 per cent on the 'economic services' category. The 4.7 per cent spent on 'community services' such as roads and water supplies was partly for economic and partly for social purposes.

Figure 36.1 illustrates in a similar way the objectives of Tanzania's central government expenditure in 1970–1, the same fiscal year as was analysed in Table 35.2 (page 522) with respect to the structure of taxation. Here the functions of ensuring defence, public order, and general administration, (including regional and district officials paid for by the central government) absorbed under the category of 'general public services' about 27 per cent of the total. Social services cost 25 per cent of the budget, and consisted particularly of spending on education and health. Basic 'community services' such as roads and water supplies accounted for 17 per cent or so. Expenditure on 'economic services' other than roads and water, already covered, formed another 23 per cent share. The remaining 8 per cent of expenditure covered under 'financial obligations' consisted of interest and capital repayments of Public Debt, together with pensions. The diagram illustrates the need to decide what share of the 'pie' each category of spending should get, and the opportunity-cost of expanding one component at the expense of the others.

On what basis does a government choose to devote, say, 14 per cent of its resources to education and just 6 per cent to health, as Tanzania did in 1970–1? Although goods and services produced by public enterprises are sold to consumers in the market (though generally a monopolistic one), the bulk of government activity is not subject to the market test. Thus decisions to spend more, or less, on particular services are essentially political decisions reflecting the distribution of political power or influence within the community. At best, in democratic states, each citizen with a single vote can periodically at election times indicate his desire for a change in the allocation of expenditure,[1] but the level and distribution of expenditure are determined more directly by politicians and civil servants. Specific spending decisions, school, hospitals, and the like are incorporated in the annual Budget, which is a detailed statement of the government's expenditure proposals and revenue requirements for the forthcoming fiscal year. However to the extent that the government needs to please its electorate it must weigh the estimated benefit to its citizens from more of one type of service against the opportunity-cost of another type which needs to be curtailed as a result. We saw in Chapter 15 how cost-benefit analysis may be used to estimate the relative advantage to be obtained from particular public investments, and attempts have been made to use this to estimate the relative

advantage of entire *categories* of spending such as, for instance, on primary or secondary school education. For the most part, though, allocations are determined on rough ideas and subjective valuations of benefit, on estimates of electoral advantage, and as a result of direct political pressures.

Public versus private expenditure

Opportunity-cost is also involved in determining the *level* as well as distribution of public expenditure. Governments will normally attempt to strike a bal-

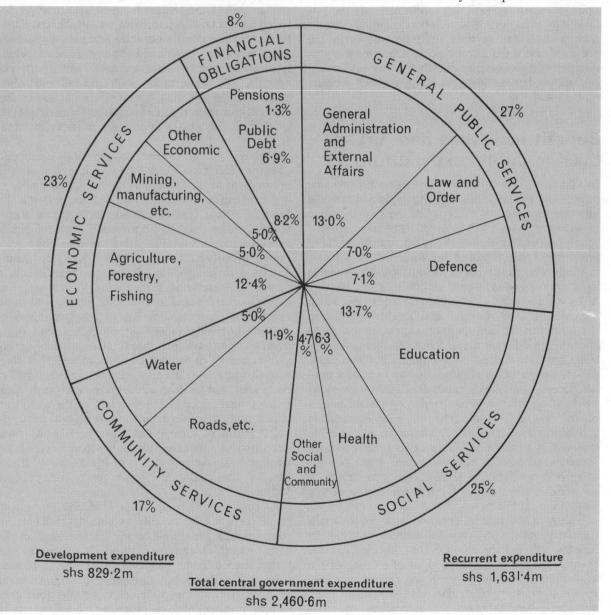

Figure 36.1 Functional classification of Tanzania Government expenditure in 1970–1 (SOURCE: United Republic of Tanzania, The Economic Survey, 1971–72, Table 24).

ance between public consumption and the benefits its citizens derive from the satisfaction of private wants. A rational government can, in principle, solve both aspects of resource allocation at the same time by comparing marginal benefits and marginal costs: the last shilling spent on one particular public good should at least equal (1) the satisfaction from private goods forgone and (2) the satisfaction from alternative public goods forgone.

This is not without problems for the government, however. Citizens in every country of the world grumble simultaneously about the high level of taxation (reducing private expenditure) and the inadequate level of public services (which would require more tax revenue to improve). As in the previous case a democratic government must try to interpret the collective will, that is to say, social preferences, but in the end comes to its own decision on the issue.

Benefit incidence and 'urban bias' in public expenditure

In Chapter 35 we noted the distinction between the impact and incidence of a tax, and explained how the ultimate incidence of a tax would be shifted. But a government raises taxes in order to finance expenditure: in order to estimate the redistributive effects of government intervention, therefore, we should ask, not only who pays what taxes, but *also* who benefits from the consequent public expenditure? As we have just seen, apart from public capital formation which increases the level of output and benefits available in the future, public consumption expenditure may be allocated in different ways. Since the real consumption enjoyed by individuals is composed of two parts, private consumption of goods and services and public consumption of such goods as education provided by the state, this has implications for the distribution of real income: for some types of public expenditure will benefit some groups and classes of people more than others. In addition, public expenditure on transfer payments such as pensions brings direct benefits to specific categories of person. Hence as well as in tax incidence we may be interested in the *benefit incidence* of public expenditure.

Except in the case of pensions and certain other transfer payments and subsidies, public consumption benefits will not be in cash but in kind, as for example the use of a new road, or of a clinic, or the availability of school places. Some expenditure may benefit nobody in particular, such as unwarranted military expenditure on jet aeroplanes or 'conspicuous' consumption in the form of palaces or luxurious public buildings.[2] Other expenditure may

contribute relatively more to the richer classes such as extra spending on secondary schools and universities at the expense of primary education, spending on one or two large, modern hospitals at the expense of large numbers of rural clinics, or spending on piped water supplies in the towns at the expense of distributed water supplies through simple boreholes. Within the farm sector spending may be on subsidies for tractors, fertilizers, and other inputs used by large farms or on subsidies to staple food crops produced by large numbers of small farmers or consumed widely by poorer consumers.

The benefit incidence of public spending as between different *regions* is also important. This is related to the previous point, since some regions are generally much richer than others, and although public expenditure can be used to secure a partial redistribution of benefits, the pattern of such expenditure often aggravates the situation, favouring the already better-off areas and neglecting the poorest and least developed which lack the 'ability to pay': for example, pastoral areas.

Finally, public expenditure in less developed countries has been alleged to favour systematically urban areas at the expense of the rural, thus embodying a significant *urban bias*. As put forward by Lipton,[3] urban bias occurs when the urban sector receives more than its appropriate share of public development and consumption spending than warranted by either (1) *equity*, relative levels of income and need, or (2) *efficiency*, the relative rates of return on marginal spending in the two sectors. In so far as urban workers including civil servants are well-to-do relative to peasants, this relates to such things as modern hospitals, piped water supplies, and other items which have just been mentioned as giving greater benefit to the richer groups in society. Urban bias also relates to the allocation of the development effort between industrial development and rural development, since the former will in the short run create limited employment and benefit a relatively small group of formal sector workers, while rural development—spending on feeder roads, say, or agricultural extension—could benefit a much wider section of the community, and generally a poorer section.

Attempts actually to assess the distribution of public expenditure benefits as between different income groups are usually made on the basis of the very crudest assumptions about the direct impact rather than ultimate incidence. Also, just as various taxes can be described as progressive, proportionate, or regressive, so may different types of public consumption expenditure be progressive or regressive in their effects. Thus expenditures which benefit the poor more than in proportion to their incomes, such as that on education or rural water supplies, contribute to a more progressive overall system, while such items as subsidized housed rents or cheap car loans to well-paid civil servants are regressive in effect.

The growth of public expenditure

At the beginning of this chapter we discussed briefly factors affecting the relative size of public expenditure, such as commitment to socialism and level of economic development. We indicated with examples that as far as public *current* expenditure is concerned relatively rich, capitalist countries might show a larger share in national income than poorer, socialist countries and that therefore the level of development might be more important in actual effect than ideology. In fact Adolph Wagner, a nineteenth-century German economist, formulated a law of ever-expanding state activity, cutting across differences in economic systems and politics. This law, which has come to be known as 'Wagner's Law', attributed the growing share of *total* government activity in 'progressive states' to (1) an expansion in the administrative and protective functions of the state, (2) an expansion in 'cultural and welfare' expenditures, particularly for education, and (3) increasing investment in public expenditures.

There is certainly plenty of historical evidence to support Wagner's Law: general government consumption expenditures in the leading industrial countries of the world when Wagner was writing in the early 1880s (the USA, UK, Germany, and Sweden) constituted about 6 per cent of GNP, compared with about 18 per cent in the 1960s. In the United Kingdom general government expenditure (including transfers) increased from $6\frac{1}{2}$ per cent of GNP in 1890 to 27 per cent by 1970, increasing in real terms more than twelve-fold.[4] In the USA general government expenditure has increased from 10 per cent of GNP in 1929 to about 30 per cent in 1970. To take examples nearer at hand in East Africa, general government expenditure in both Tanzania and Uganda rose from about 12 per cent of GNP in 1954 to approximately $17\frac{1}{2}$ per cent in 1967, an increase of nearly one-half in the degree of public utilization of resources in a matter of 13 years.

The causal factors in this relationship are not straightforward, however. Thus Peacock and Wiseman[5] tested Wagner's Law with British public expenditure data for 1890–1955 and concluded that the expenditures grew because public revenues grew, rather than the other way about: that is, increased public revenue associated with expanding incomes

'permitted' public spending to increase rather than increased desire for items involving public expenditure requiring an increase in revenue. We noted in Chapter 35 the difficulties of less developed countries in raising direct taxes, leading to greater reliance on indirect taxes and lower 'taxable capacity'. This also suggests that over time the expansion of the monetary economy, and within that the formal and industrial sectors, as well as improvements in administrative efficiency, would increase the ability to raise public revenue.

Apart from this long-term growth of public expenditures in line with revenues, Peacock and Wiseman suggested that social disturbances, particularly the two world wars, had by requiring a significant broadening of the tax system to deal with emergencies, produced structural shifts in or 'displacement effects' on revenue and expenditure. In Eastern Africa political changes, notably independence and/or the break-up of federal institutions, may be regarded as displacement effects, shifting central governments on to new and higher plateaux of public spending.[6]

Part of the explanation of Wagner's Law given above is that in fact public consumption follows another 'law' in economics, Engels's Law regarding the income–consumption relationship, discussed in Chapter 6. In this context it would mean that demand for public consumption is 'income-elastic' so that a country can afford to spend a greater proportion of its national income on public goods and transfer payments, e.g. for pensions, as national income increases.

Related to this is the tendency to replace informal rural welfare services and private charity with public welfare provisions. Lewis and Martin[6] refer to the unpaid services of eighteenth-century English squires (landowners who acted as magistrates and often recruited their tenants and employees for military and police service). A similar trend away from traditional rulers and 'Native Authorities' can be traced more recently in both East and West Africa.

Two other factors affecting trends in public expenditure may be mentioned. First, as also pointed out by Martin and Lewis, there are costs associated with urbanization and industrialization such as the costs of building skyscrapers, or motorways to relieve congestion, or of pollution control, requiring an increase in public spending. Another influence is the tendency for the growth in productivity in labour-intensive service industries to lag behind that in manufacturing and even agriculture. Thus if the 'output' of education services is to grow at least as fast as the output of other things, the number of teachers would need to increase more than in proportion to the number of workers in manufacturing or agriculture, thus raising the relative level of public spending on education.

Other factors may operate in the opposite direction, however. Thus even if the *number* of public employees such as schoolteachers increases, their relative wages may fall as wider education and training reduce the economic rent which they obtain for scarce skills. Most important, perhaps, are the greater requirements for social infrastructure at early stages of economic development, as already discussed. This would apply also to public loans to the private sector through development corporations, necessitated by shortage of private capital. Thus, as the economies develop, the need for certain public works may become less pressing and private investment may, in non-socialist economies, take on a larger role.

This may, however, only permit the authorities to substitute more spending on social services and income-redistributing transfers to poorer households. Hence although direct public consumption may increase as a proportion of total public expenditure, it is less certain whether it will increase as a proportion of national income, because of the diverse influences mentioned earlier.

Questions on Chapter 36

1. Why does a government buy goods and services?
2. Distinguish between 'public consumption' and 'public capital formation'. How easy is it to make this distinction? Of what does public consumption mainly consist?
3. Comment as fully as possible on the significant facts revealed in Table 36.1.
4. Discuss the various ways in which opportunity-costs must be considered in deciding the level and allocation of public expenditure.

5. Of what significance is the 'benefit incidence' of public expenditure? How easy is it to estimate this incidence on different groups of people?
6. What is 'urban bias', as defined by Lipton?
7. What is 'Wagner's Law' of ever-expanding state activity, and how valid do you consider it to be? Discuss the various factors affecting the long-run growth of public expenditure.

Notes

[1] In many African countries people often vote for an MP or councillor who they think will be the most effective in pushing for schools, clinics, or water supplies in their own area. They may be more concerned with this than with the political 'complexion' of the central government, and local politics is therefore often of considerable importance.

[2] Building construction is generally considered to be capital formation but if buildings are built of a quality and style which does not contribute to increased output, expenditure on them may be treated as consumption.

[3] Michael Lipton, *Why Poor People Stay Poor, a Study of Urban Bias in World Development*, Temple Smith, 1977.

[4] See G. H. Peters, *Private and Public Finance*, Fontana/Collins, 1971, p. 140.

[5] A. T. Peacock and J. Wiseman, *The Growth of Public Expenditure in the United Kingdom*, Oxford University Press, 1961.

[6] Alison Martin and W. Arthur Lewis, 'Patterns of Public Revenue and Expenditure', *The Manchester School*, September 1956.

37 Development Planning

We have already referred to central, or socialist, planning in Chapter 5, where it was considered as an alternative to the market price mechanism in allocating resources. We need to consider here the meaning, scope, and usefulness of planning in accelerating economic development, specifically in Africa.

Economic planning: its nature and dimensions

Three dimensions to economic planning may be distinguished: *resource allocation, resource accumulation,* and *resource management*. The first dimension or function can be interpreted as state intervention in the price system aimed at the reallocation of the current flow of resources in order to produce a different pattern of output, income distribution, and expenditure. This need not necessarily involve a wider extension of public sector activity if it is confined to such things as price controls and taxation, or various stabilization measures to restore and maintain full employment of these existing resources. Historically, however, it has been associated with socialist policies of wider public ownership, since it was usually held that the state itself would need to own and manage the 'means of production, distribution, and exchange' in order to ensure the successful implementation of plans for increased efficiency, more equitable distribution of income, and full employment. Thus both in the planned economies of Eastern Europe and the socialization programmes of 'Western' socialists, planning and public ownership were intimately connected, with the control over resources or 'resource management' an important element.

We may distinguish in principle between planning related to the efficiency of resource use, or resource allocation, and that related to the accumulation of resources, or growth and development of the economy. In practice these static and dynamic aims overlap, and socialist planning in Soviet Russia after 1917, for example, was just as much or even more geared towards the structural transformation of the economy, through land reforms and the industrialization programme, as it was towards immediate gains in economic efficiency and income distribution.

In economic planning in less developed countries since independence, particularly, the emphasis has been on resource accumulation and *development planning*, focusing on raising the rate of growth and achieving the long-term development of the economy in relatively poor countries.

Three levels of development planning

Development planning has itself a number of different dimensions, and we may distinguish several levels and categories within it. There is first of all *macrolevel planning*, relating its calculations to the economy as a whole. Macroeconomic plans in developing countries have generally been prepared to cover periods of four or five years, and a great many developing countries have had a series of *four-* or *five-year plans* since the war, or since independence. Very often these detailed five-year plans have been presented against a background of 15, 20 or 25-year *perspective plans* which present very tentative outlines of possible development over the long period. Thus in India a 25-year perspective plan exists. Uganda's Second Five-Year Plan, 1966–71[1], covered the first part of a 15-year perspective programme from mid-1966 to mid-1981, and similarly the Tanganyika Five-Year Plan for Economic and Social Development, 1 July 1964–30 June 1969, was accompanied by projections for a 15-year period up to 1980. The details of such perspective plans are not always published, since they involve so much guesswork. Nevertheless, by providing a clear statement of the direction in which the planners expect the economy to move in the long run, they may provide a useful background for current medium-term plans. As we shall see later, planning ahead for even five years has proved difficult, and countries have found it necessary to be more flexible than that, using medium-term plans in turn as guidelines for *annual plans*, mainly focused on proposed public expenditures for the coming year, still relating to the economy as a whole.

While all these are macrolevel or economy-wide plans, there is in addition *secondary-level planning*. Here we may distinguish first *sectoral planning*, which refers to detailed planning of a specific sector. Agricultural planning thus refers to a comprehensive set of policies for the development of the agricultural sector. On the industrial side, the main task of industrial sector planning might be the devising of a specific industrial *strategy*, together with the selection of particular industrial projects. Also at the secondary level we have *regional or area planning* where the focus of attention is a particular region or area within the country. This is discussed in more detail presently. There is, finally, *tertiary level planning*, which refers to the identification of possible projects, appraisal of these projects, generally in cost-benefit terms, and their implementation, or execution. This project planning or *project analysis* was discussed in Chapter 15. This classification of types of planning is summarized in Figure 37.1.

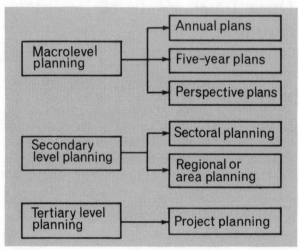

Figure 37.1   *The three levels of planning.*

The ingredients of development planning

The term 'Development Plan' has in practice been used, however, to describe a wide range of documents or even just verbal statements of a government's longer-term objectives. In particular some of these published documents may comprise statements of proposed public expenditure over some future time period, together with a brief economic survey or review of government policy, certainly not amounting to a comprehensive socialist plan of the Soviet type. It is useful therefore to have a checklist of the elements which may appear in a Development Plan: actual plans will combine only some of the elements, or accord different emphasis to these components.

(1) Economic plans may be either *comprehensive* or *partial*. In contrast with, for instance, the earlier public sector capital expenditure programmes of colonial planning in Africa, a comprehensive plan looks at the economy as a whole, the private as well as the public sector. The plan is comprehensive in that, although the public expenditure programme will probably be the basis of the plan, it is fitted into the framework of the expected overall development of the economy, and is likely to incorporate policies designed to influence the private sector in a given direction. Partial planning, as the name suggests, covers only a part of the national economy, such as the public sector, agricultural sector, or foreign sector. Unfortunately, with limited statistical information, and limited planning personnel, partial planning may be as much as can be accomplished in some developing countries.

(2) This implies an element of *macroeconomic forecasting*, making projections of the expected movements of the economy. The perspective plans mentioned above are more than anything else long-term forecasts of the possible development of the economy in the light of external factors and internally adopted policies. But quite apart from these, and medium-term plans, even an annual budget for public expenditure requires forecasts of what revenue is likely to be available as a result of the growth of output and taxable incomes. The forecasts made are often presented in the form of *plan targets* for the expansion of output in different sectors, where achievement in some sense is made to imply success and under-achievement in some sense failure. Targets, even more than forecasts, require the plan to be *time-specific* in that targets must be achieved within a given time period. It could be said, perhaps, that without the time element, the plan would reduce to a (possibly comprehensive) set of policies rather than a 'Plan': though as we shall see this is not necessarily a bad thing.

(3) The most thorough-going Development Plan will not simply be comprehensive in forecasting or planning the development of the whole economy but will be *detailed* as regards sectors and/or regions. It is possible to have worked out very detailed policies for each sector, or only very general policies, in other words to have more or less advanced sectoral planning. Regional planning gives planning an important *spatial* dimension in that it involves specifying the *location* of a new public expenditure or new economic activity, and the spatial distribution of income and welfare resulting from this and existing activity. Actual development plans in Africa vary in terms of both sectoral detail and regional planning element.

(4) Macroeconomic planning should also be based on the *micro*economic evaluation of projects, our tertiary level above. Again the amount of detailed economic analysis of public sector projects, let alone

any private investment proposals, depends on the availability of project planners in the government, so that it is too much to say that all possibilities and alternatives are always closely evaluated. Indeed how 'good' or 'bad' a plan turns out may well be a matter of how much basic groundwork has been carried out in identifying good projects, appraising the alternatives, and of course implementing them in an efficient way. Many of the earlier Development Plans in newly independent countries have been ineffective because they were drawn up without proper appraisal of projects—indeed in some cases the main projects to be included in sector programmes making up the overall plan were not even identified. As we discussed in Chapter 15, evaluation of projects from the point of view of *society* advantage is in developing countries at least likely to require the calculation of appropriate shadow prices for factors and social prices for goods, rather than market prices, and the assessment of possible external economies.

(5) However, if 'Plans need projects', projects also require a plan it is necessary for all major investment decisions to be consistent, one with the other. An important requirement of a systematic Development Plan is that all its proposals and projections should be *internally consistent*. In particular it is necessary that (a) planned investment should be balanced by the expected supply of finance from domestic saving and external sources; (b) the amount of skilled manpower and other scarce inputs required by the new level of activity should not exceed the expected supply; (c) the demand for output should roughly equal expected supplies in all industries; and (d) expected foreign exchange requirements for imports of consumer and capital goods should not exceed expected receipts from exports and net capital inflow.

(6) A macroeconomic plan is generally based on some sort of *planning model*. Since the main objective of most development plans is to raise the level of *aggregate* output (GDP), the most commonly used development model is an *aggregative* growth model specifying the relation between saving and investment on the one hand, and a target growth rate for GDP on the other. Alternatively a *dis*aggregated approach may be employed using, for instance, a *multi-sector* or *inter-industry model* based on an 'input–output table' which specifies the linkages or transaction flows between sectors or industries. The nature of these models is discussed in more detail presently.

(7) Underlying macroeconomic planning, with its more or less sophisticated theoretical basis, however, is the basic *resource allocation function* mentioned at the outset.

(a) This still involves first and foremost a set of *public expenditure proposals*. In a five-year Development Plan these will not be the only element, as in a partial plan for the public sector, or limited to one year ahead, as in the case of the annual budget exercise. They will, however, involve the same choices already discussed for public expenditure of public and private consumption, directly productive investment versus social infrastructure investment, economic services versus social services, etc.

(b) Corresponding to these expenditure proposals, there will need to be some calculation and *statement of proposed financial sources*, more narrowly to cover public spending and in a comprehensive plan more widely to support consumption and investment in the economy as a whole.

(c) Comprehensive development plans, however, also aim to influence the private sector, which they can do in several ways. They can, of course, give concrete aid to the private sector, for example by making public loans available directly or indirectly for private investment projects. However, simply by setting out within the plan what the government hopes to provide in terms of infrastructure, skilled manpower, and new projects, and what the private sector is expected to do, businessmen may be given confidence to carry out the higher level of private investment required by the plan. Planning with a large private sector is known as *indicative planning*, since it indicates possible development targets for private enterprises to aim at and forecasts the possible expansion of both public and private sectors. Although indicative planning may appear a contradiction in terms, France, in particular, has made considerable use of this approach since the 1950s, aided no doubt by the sharp 'teeth' provided to the government planners by the close control of the capital market by the central bank and other public bodies.

(8) As we might have said at the beginning, a plan ought to make explicit—many plans do not, in fact—a set of *objectives or guiding principles*: what emphasis is to be placed on such objectives as growth of output, income distribution (between social classes and between regions), employment creation, and in particular the trade-off between any two objectives, the sacrifice of output growth tolerable for the sake of distribution objectives, or efficiency versus employment objectives, or short-term growth versus long-run economic transformation.

The relative weights to be placed on these different objectives are also relevant, it should be stressed here, for project appraisal, since apart from their contributions to output, projects have different effects on employment, income distribution, and on long-term growth, and, related to income distribution, may be located in different regions.

(9) In settling on objectives, the planners must also weigh the relative welfare of the present generation with that of future generations in deciding what proportion of income to invest and what sacrifice to impose in terms of current consumption on the present generation. A basic decision of any plan is in fact what proportion to invest, as we discussed in Chapter 5. It is worth elaborating here on that discussion.

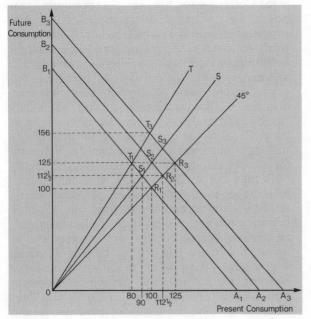

Figure 37.2   *The opportunity-cost of investment and growth.*

Let us suppose that in Figure 37.2 A_1B_1 is a transformation curve showing the investment opportunities for an economy. For simplicity we shall assume here that A_1B_1 is a straight line (in the analysis of Chapter 5 the assumption of decreasing returns resulted in a curved transformation curve). The slope of A_1B_1 is greater than 1: the sacrifice of 1 unit of present consumption permits more than 1 additional unit of future consumption, due to the productivity of capital. To be precise, the slope is 1·25, implying that the investment of 1 unit brings a gross return of $1\frac{1}{4}$ units of future consumption. Even in a mixed economy the government can restrict present consumption to any chosen level, determining total 'savings' through taxation or other methods of 'forced' savings. We can assume that the government selects some combination of present and future consumption for the economy, represented by some point along A_1B_1. A choice of R_1, on the 45° line from the origin, would mean that the country's capacity to produce was being kept constant, so that expected future consumption is the same as present

consumption: in other words it would imply zero net investment. If this choice were made, no growth (expansion of productive capacity) would take place, and the transformation curve marking the production boundary would remain where it was.

A choice of point S_1 on the other hand, would mean reducing present consumption from 100 to 90 units, and a net investment of 10 units. This would increase expected future consumption by $12\frac{1}{2}$ units to $112\frac{1}{2}$, implying an average rate of return of 25 per cent. This net investment will result in an increased capacity to produce, so that the transformation curve would move outwards to the position A_2B_2. The exact position of A_2B_2 is given by the point R_2, which shows that if in the *future* period there is zero net investment, consumption will remain at the level $112\frac{1}{2}$ for subsequent periods. If, as is more likely, the same proportion is allocated to net investment, the point S_2 would be selected, and the transformation curve would again move outwards. If instead of S_1 the point T_1 on A_1B_1 had been selected, investing 20 units instead of 10, this would give an income of 125 in the second period, and the transformation curve would then have been A_3B_3, passing through R_3 instead of R_2. If the same proportion were again invested, point T_3 would be selected (implying net investment of 20 per cent of 125, that is, of 25 units).

The diagram illustrates the fact that positive net investment can progressively increase national income, but that it requires a sacrifice of present consumption. The higher the proportion sacrificed, the higher the rate of growth of national income: the transformation curve is pushed outwards faster if the proportion invested is 20 per cent, say, as along the line OT, than if it is 10 per cent, as along the line OS.

Figure 37.2 is an extension of the simple two-period analysis of Chapter 5; it is not very suitable, however, for discussing rates of growth, since growth is a continuous process. In Figure 37.3 we assume that a higher rate of investment results in a higher rate of *growth* of income, rather than a higher *level* of income at some fixed future date. Suppose income is initially 100 units, and that by saving and investing 10 per cent of this, income can be made to grow at the rate of $2\frac{1}{2}$ per cent per annum, and that investment of 20 per cent results in a 5 per cent growth rate. The path of income is shown by the line AC in the first case, and AB in the second. Consumption starts at 90 units in the first case, and grows along DE at $2\frac{1}{2}$ per cent, the same rate as income, a constant proportion of the latter being deducted for investment. In the second case consumption starts at 80 units, more being sacrificed for investment, but grows at the rate of 5 per cent along FG.

The line AC shows that at the modest rate of growth of $2\frac{1}{2}$ per cent per annum national income can nevertheless be doubled within the space of 28

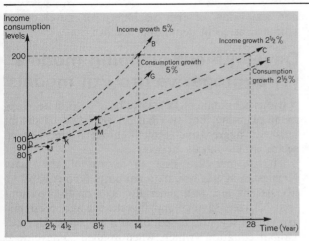

Figure 37.3 *Alternative growth rates for income and consumption.*

years, to 200 units. A 5 per cent rate achieves the same target in half the time, 14 years. What is important for consumers' welfare, however, is the level of consumption. The sacrifice of consumption involved in achieving the higher rate of growth is as follows: initially 20 units of consumption are given up, instead of 10; moving up FG, the level of consumption enjoyed immediately at D is not reached for $2\frac{1}{2}$ years, at point J; consumers are still worse off than with the lower rate of investment, however, since this lower rate also increases income and consumption. Not until point K is reached, $4\frac{1}{2}$ years from the initial moment, are the current levels of consumption the same; even then more time must elapse before the extra consumption derived along KL balances the lower consumption in the first $4\frac{1}{2}$ years along FK. This happens when the two triangles DFK and KLM are equal in area, after $8\frac{1}{2}$ years. After $8\frac{1}{2}$ years, there is a clear gain in terms of both current levels of consumption and aggregate consumption over the full period: whether this is sufficient to compensate for the sacrifice made in the early period is entirely dependent, however, upon the society's rate of time preference.

Table 37.1 shows the considerable difference in savings and investment rates between the advanced

Table 37.1 *Savings and investment ratios, 1960–7 (per cent)*

Ratio to GNP	Industrial countries (non-Soviet)	LDCs (excl. China)	of which		
			Latin America	South Asia	Africa
S/Y	21.7	15.0	16.3	11.3	13.1
I/Y	21.2	17.8	17.7	13.9	16.7

SOURCE: Pearson Report

industrial countries and the less developed countries. It might be considered desirable for the less developed countries to be saving and investing a *higher* proportion of their incomes in an effort to achieve higher rates of growth and thus catch up with the developed countries. But while the industrial countries were saving nearly 22 per cent of GNP in this period 1960–7, African countries saved only 13 per cent, though foreign assistance permitted the investment ratio to be raised to the somewhat higher ratio of 16.7. Less developed countries thus clearly have *difficulty* in raising their rates of national saving and investment, but their much lower rates compared to industrial countries are obviously an important reason for their lower rates of per capita income growth. The choice of investment rate is therefore of major significance.

(10) Once the main objectives of the planners have been specified, the next step is to decide on the *broad development strategy* or combination of strategies to be used in order to achieve those ends. The kinds of choices and alternatives available have already been discussed in some detail in Chapter 22 on 'issues' in industrialization: there is the relative emphasis on rural development as compared to industrialization; capital goods industries versus consumer goods industries; large-scale versus small-scale industry; import-substituting industry versus export-promoting industry; choice of techniques; location policy, perhaps dispersal of industry through newly designated growth poles, infrastructural investment versus directly productive investment, and so on. The decision regarding the planned rate of saving and investment for the economy is closely related to the choice of strategy since, for instance, a strategy for the rapid structural transformation of the economy would require a high rate of saving and sacrifice of present consumption.

(11) A Development Plan generally implies the setting up of additional institutional machinery. Whereas the 'Development Programmes' and capital expenditure plans for public investment undertaken in the immediate post-war period before independence in African countries, for instance, tended to be an extension of the annual Budget, prepared by the Ministry of Finance, the later and more comprehensive plans have been generated by more specialist economic planning staffs often located in a separate Planning Office or Ministry of Planning. Indeed, the employment of professional economists by African governments since independence has been closely associated with the preparation of Development Plans and the need to coordinate the activities of the main 'operational' Ministries such as Agriculture, Commerce and Industry, Transport, and Education with 'central' Ministries of Finance and Planning. In

many cases 'planning units' employing economists have been established within 'operational' Ministries such as Education and Health.

As far as administrative machinery for development planning is concerned, however, the most interesting issues have come with the more recent emphasis on regional planning and rural development planning, leading to the opening up of the new field of *development administration*. Development administration relates to the most appropriate organizational structures, administrative machinery, and systems of decision-making for fostering development, recognizing the fact that in less developed countries professional staff within both central and local government authorities are also concerned with the execution of development projects and programmes as distinct from the usual civil service activities.

Development planning versus socialist planning

The above constitute the main elements of a 'Development Plan' as generally interpreted in developing countries. As was discussed in Chapter 5, the extent to which planning is *socialist* depends primarily on the proportion of resources owned and controlled by the state, and the extent of other forms of participation by the state in direct economic activity. But a Development Plan may be comprehensive, with consistent macroeconomic forecasting and even target-setting, without envisaging a great deal of government intervention in the economy. In Eastern Africa, for instance, recent development plans give government a key role in promoting new ventures, particularly in the fields of manufacturing, transportation, and energy, but for the most part have left African land and smaller enterprises, as well as established industry and commerce, in private hands. They therefore envisage mixed economies of some kind, even if the extent of reliance on private enterprise has varied very much, as for example between Kenya and Tanzania.

It remains true, of course, that the formulation and acceptance of a Development Plan does facilitate the extension of socialized planning. Plans also tend to become more socialistic, in the sense of extending state control over the economy, as plans have broadened out from the macroeconomic level, where forecasting and consistency calculations based on model-building need not imply state control, into sectoral and regional planning at the secondary level, and project analysis at the tertiary level. These have in particular led to considerable increases in the number of technical and economic planners employed,

and extension of the machinery of development administration in depth and breadth.

Development planning models: (1) aggregative growth models

Various economic models have been used in development planning, but two basic types may be distinguished: aggregative growth models, and multi-sector input–output models.

The former are cast in terms of the main Keynesian aggregates, national output, consumption, investment, etc., and generally focus on the relationship between savings and investment and economic growth. They are based on the so-called Harrod-Domar equation[2] which, when applied to developed countries prone to problems of effective demand, showed the rate of growth required to stimulate sufficient investment to absorb savings as incomes expand. Applied to less developed countries, where the problem was seen to be shortage of savings rather than deficiency of demand, the same equation could be used to give the level of saving required to achieve any particular rate of economic growth, assuming a given capital–output ratio.

If we assume that the level of investment cannot exceed the level of desired savings and if the shortage of capital is the only constraint holding back investment, so that it therefore equals savings, then we have:

$$I_d = S_d \qquad (37.1)$$

We write S_d to refer to *desired* savings, which we can take to be a given proportion, s, of national income, Y, so that:

$$S_d = sY \qquad (37.2)$$

Suppose that expansion of output requires expansion of the capital stock in direct proportion, and that businessmen, whether they are industrialists or peasant farmers, want to keep the amount of capital equipment they have in line with, i.e. proportional to, their current level of output.[3] Thus if planned output increases by an amount $\triangle Y$, and C_d is the desired capital–output ratio, they would wish to increase the capital stock by an amount $C_d \triangle Y$. This increase in capital is over and above maintenance of existing capital, and is therefore desired *net* investment. Hence we can write:

$$I_d = C_d \triangle Y \qquad (37.3)$$

If G is the rate of growth of income and output, given as a percentage by $\dfrac{\triangle Y}{Y}$, then:

$$\triangle Y = G.Y \qquad (37.4)$$

Substituting equations 37.2, 37.3 and 37.4 into equation 37.1, we have:

$$C_d.G.Y = sY \qquad (37.5)$$

which, cancelling the Ys, gives:

$$G = \frac{s}{C_d} \ or \ G.C_d = s \qquad (37.6)$$

This tells us that the rate of growth of income which a country can attain depends first on the propensity to save (the saving ratio) and secondly on the capital–output ratio—how much capital is needed to produce one more unit of output. *According to this equation, therefore, if countries can either save more, or supplement savings by foreign aid, or economize their use of savings by adoption of less capital-intensive techniques, they can increase their rate of growth. Or, if the targeted rate of growth is fixed at G, and the capital–output ratio is given, the equation gives the savings rate that must be obtained.* For example, if a 5 per cent growth rate is required, and three dollars' worth of additional capital stock is required to raise annual income by one dollar ($C_d = 3$), then $s = G.C_d = 5.3 = 15$: the required saving rate is 15 per cent.

The argument can be put in an alternative way: the more a country can save and invest, the faster it can grow. If saving is the only constraint on investment, and all savings are invested, then we have:

$$I = S = sY \qquad (37.7)$$

If the capital–output ratio is C, then an increment of output ΔY requires a net investment of $I = C\Delta Y$. If an investment of I produces output $C\Delta Y$, then the productivity of investment, output per unit invested, is:

$$\frac{\Delta Y}{I} = \frac{1}{C} \qquad (37.8)$$

The increase in national output or income is investment ($= sY$) times the productivity of investment $\left(= \frac{1}{C} \right)$, so that:

$$\Delta Y = s.Y.\left(\frac{1}{C} \right) \qquad (37.9)$$

The rate of growth of income can be obtained by dividing both sides by Y, giving, as before:

$$G = \frac{\Delta Y}{Y} = \frac{s}{C} \qquad (37.10)$$

Strictly speaking C is not the average, but the *incremental capital–output ratio*, often referred to by development economists as ICOR. It is quite likely that new investment will be in different kinds of enterprises, for example industrial rather than agri-cultural, from those already most important in the economy. The incremental ratio is relevant here, since we are talking about increases in the level of output. It is in fact likely to be *lower* than the average ratio in less developed countries since increases in output generally do not require proportionately greater amounts of social overhead capital such as roads.

We should be aware of the limitations of the equation we have derived.

(1) The assumption underlying it is that the rate of growth of income depends entirely on the availability of capital for development. As we suggested in our elementary discussion of the factors in economic development, in Chapter 2, capital is a major, but not necessarily the only, constraint on development. It is probably true to say that the assumption is more applicable once the process of development is in full swing than in the early stages when the economy is beset by a multitude of 'vicious circles' and other problems.

(2) In the second place, the aggregative approach implied by the equation may be questioned. The capital–output ratio is an average value relating to the whole of economic production and, obviously, the ratio may be very different in different industries — and much lower in agriculture than in manufacturing industry or mining. In an economy dependent on a small number of export industries which may change periodically in relative importance, especially, and in an economy attempting to diversify its structure of production, the overall capital—output ratio may change considerably, and not necessarily in any systematic way.

(3) Finally, it should be noted that s and G are not independent of each other, since savings are not all supplied voluntarily but are partly obtained through taxation. Heavier taxes are likely to have disincentive effects on investment and therefore on the rate of growth of output.

Development planning models: (2) input–output models

Aggregative growth models, however, are cast only in terms of the main aggregates, national output, savings, investment, etc. To forecast what will happen to individual sectors or particular industries, or to find the desirable rate of expansion of individual sectors and industries, it is necessary to disaggregate overall growth targets. In particular, since any one industry is likely to supply others with inputs and to use inputs produced by other industries, it is necessary to ensure *consistency* between projected rates of expansion for different industries. *Input–output* analysis is therefore commonly advocated as a planning tool. Input–output analysis was developed originally to trace the inter-industry transactions in more developed industrial economies where there are backward and forward linkages between a large number of domestic industries. Its purpose is to estimate the additional inputs required when one or more industries expand to meet changes in final demands such as consumption, capital formation, or exports. First we need to explain the layout of an input–output table, which we can do by examining an abridged version of a table which was actually used for development planning in Zambia.[4]

The layout of an input–output table

Table 37.2 is divided into four segments or quadrants. All the entries represent values, given in million kwachas. The top left-hand quadrant shows the inter-industry transactions, with the sectors supplying inputs (origin of output) given on the left-hand side and sectors receiving inputs, (uses of output) along the top. Thus the transport sector (7) supplies K22 million of transport services in all, 3 to metal mining (3), 2 to manufacturing (4), 10 to the distribution sector (8), and 7 to 'other services' (10). Similarly,

looking at column (5), the construction industry purchases K29 million of intermediate inputs in all, 13 from manufacturing, 6 from construction itself, 7 from distribution and 3 from 'other services'. Each sector appears twice, as a producer of outputs and as a user of inputs.

The upper *right*-hand quadrant shows the value of outputs from each of the same sectors for final demand, that is, the value of goods or services supplied to consumers, to government, for investment, and for export to consumers abroad. The manufacturing sector satisfies final demands to the extent of K75 million, 59 for consumers, 5 for government, 7 for investment (of which 4 is addition to stocks), and 4 for export. The total value of output in each sector is given in the final column, the manufacturing sector producing K116 million of goods altogether, 41 as intermediate inputs and 75 for final use.

The lower left-hand quadrant analyses the so-called 'primary inputs' purchased by industrial sectors, purchases *other* than from other industries in the economy. Thus looking at column (4), the manufacturing sector purchases labour, spending K20 million on wages and salaries, 'purchases' capital and entrepreneurial services, paying out K22

Table 37.2 *An input–output analysis of the Zambian economy in 1965 (in kwacha, millions)*

Uses of output → / Origin of output ↓	(1)	(2)	(3)	(4)	(5)	(6)	(7)	(8)	(9)	(10)	(1)—(10)	Consumption Private (C)
(1) Subsistence agriculture	—	—	—	—	—	—	—	—	—	—	—	38
(2) Commercial agriculture	—	—	..	10	—	—	—	—	—	—	10	4
(3) Metal mining	—	—	4	—	—	—	—	—	—	—	4	—
(4) Manufacturing	—	1	18	4	13	—	2	2	..	1	41	59
(5) Construction	—	..	15	1	6	—	..	..	..	4	26	—
(6) Electricity & water	—	..	14	1	..	1	..	1	..	..	17	3
(7) Transport & communications	—	..	3	2	..	..	..	10	..	7	22	5
(8) Distribution	—	1	9	9	7	..	2	9	1	5	43	60
(9) Government services, education & health	—	—	—	—	—	—	—	—	—	—	—	9
(10) Other services	—	1	2	7	3	1	3	8	1	15	41	31
(1)–(10) Total intermediate inputs	—	3	65	34	29	2	7	30	2	32	204	209
Imports, c.i.f.	—	5	37	32	20	10	6	4	1	11	126	79
Wages & salaries	—	8	77	20	22	2	18	25	54	19	245	—
Gross profits	38	8	131	22	17	8	15	47	..	15	301	—
Net indirect taxes	—	−1	65	8	2	..	..	9	—	3	86	12
Primary inputs	38	20	310	82	61	20	39	85	55	48	758	91
TOTAL OUTPUT	38	23	375	116	90	22	46	115	57	80	962	300
GDP at market prices	38	15	273	50	41	11	33	81	54	37	632	12

SOURCE: Zambia Central Statistical Office, op. cit. (abridged version by authors of this text)
NOTE: A cell entry of — means zero transaction recorded; ... small entry of less than K0.5.

million as gross profits (this includes depreciation, interest, and rents as well as net profits of enterprises), spends K32 million on imports, and pays K8 million as indirect taxes, a total of K82 million on primary inputs. Reading across the first row gives the value of imports for all industrial purposes (not counting investment) as K126 millions.

The lower right-hand quadrant shows any *direct* purchases of imports and indirect taxes (like customs duties) paid by final users which have not been routed through industrial sectors.[5]

The bottom row of this quadrant, under Total Output, in fact gives exactly the same components, *but including imports*, which are the final demands for GDP at market prices: C, G, I, and X. Thus consumption expenditure is K300 million, of which 209 is spent on domestic output, 79 on imported goods and 12 paid in indirect taxes. The input–output table is thus simply a set of accounts for the economy, in which all transactions are recorded, in their various categories. We should, therefore, be able to derive from it GDP at market prices.

We can do this in either of two ways: if we deduct total imports from total final demands, we obtain C + G + I + X (K905m) − M (K258m) = K647m; or we

can sum the total of value added by the wage-bill (K245m) and gross profits (K301m), *plus*, to obtain GDP at market prices, net indirect taxes (K86 + 15 = 101m), giving the identical figure of K647m shown in italics at the right-hand corner of the table.

The use of an input–output table for the description of economic structure

Just as the accounts of a business enterprise are revealing of its mode of operations, so an input–output table which represents a more detailed breakdown of national income accounts gives a revealing picture of the structure of an economy and the relationship between its various sectors. As just mentioned, Table 37.2 is an abridged version of the official Zambian Input–Output Table for 1965 which in fact detailed some 40 industry groups by rows and columns, instead of the 10×10 matrix shown above. Although this condensed table leaves out data on 20 subsectors of manufacturing[6] and quarrying, and also consolidates transport and service industries somewhat, nevertheless it illustrates the main features of the Zambian economy, showing us in fact the development problem still facing planners in Zambia.

Zambia in 1965 was typical of less developed, open economies in having few inter-industry linkages. Understandably, since nearly two-thirds (38 out of 61) of the value of agricultural output was estimated to be subsistence production for direct final consumption on the farms (indicated as 38 supplied to final consumers), there are no linkages in row (1) and column (1). However, unlike other Eastern African countries, commercial agriculture was relatively unimportant both as a source of cash income by exports (K8m out of 368) and in supplying consumers (K4m out of 209 consumers' expenditure). Row (2) shows some forward linkages with Manufacturing in column (4), through the processing of livestock and grains. Commercial agriculture itself purchased few domestic intermediate inputs, however, relying on imports (mainly fertilizers) and contributing relatively little to factor incomes. The negative indirect taxes of (− 1) in column (2) reflected a small subsidy to agriculture, showing that, unlike its neighbours, Zambia was in the mid-1960s without an agricultural foundation for broad-based development.

The large figure of 338 in row (3) dominates the table, and reflects the dominance of copper-mining in the Zambian economy: these copper exports (K346m including stocks of inventories for future export) compare with total Zambian exports of K368m.

| | Final demands (B) | | | Total | Total |
| sumption overnment | Investment | | Exports | | outputs |
(G)	(GFCF)	(Stocks)	(X)		(A)+(B)
—	—	—	—	38	38
—	—	1	8	13	23
—	25	8	338	371	375
5	3	4	4	75	116
5	59	..	—	64	90
2	—	—	..	5	22
6	1	—	12	24	46
3	6	3	..	72	115
48	—	—	—	57	57
1	1	—	6	39	80
70	95	16	368	758	962
13	24	16	..	132	258
—	—	—	—	—	245
—	—	—	—	—	301
..	1	2	—	15	101
13	25	18	..	147	905
83	120	33	368	906	1,867
..	1	2	—	15	647

From column (3) we see that the copper industry accounted for K77m out of 245m of wages and salaries, K131m out of 301m of gross profits in the economy, and provided government with 65 per cent (65m out of 101m) of its indirect taxes (quite apart from direct taxes on profits and wages). At the same time the *dis*advantage of dependence on copper is apparent: its linkages with other sectors are relatively unimportant. Its only intermediate sales are processing within the sector itself (K4m), while the relatively large fixed capital formation demand (for developing mines and facilities) is undertaken within the industry. It is a more important intermediate *user* of other sectors' output, as shown in column (3): it purchases a range of manufactured goods like engineering and metal goods, and is the largest industrial consumer of the Construction, Electricity/Water, and Distribution sectors. But these values are still not large in relation to that for copper output and exports. Its prominent position in the Zambian economy in 1965 thus offered both a reason for pursuing a development policy of diversification and a means of financing the investment required in secondary industries and commercial agriculture. Row and column (4) show that manufacturing, though a relatively small contributor to domestic output and income, offered more linkages in relation to value. Apart from a backward linkage with commercial agriculture, the linkage construction was important, indicating the close connection between the rate of domestic capital formation and the demand for manufactured building materials like cement, clay (bricks and tiles), and metal products. Row (5) shows something like 65 per cent of Construction output (59m out of 90m) going into gross domestic fixed capital formation.

Assumptions of input–output analysis

We move from consideration of a set of accounts to input–output *analysis* by assuming that the relationships given in the table are stable and technologically determined. It will be recalled that all industries are viewed both as producers of *output* and users of *inputs*. If, using column (4) in the table, for example, we assume 116 units of manufacturing output will *always* require inputs of 10 units from commercial agriculture, 4 from manufacturing itself, 1 from construction, and 1 from electricity and water, etc., we may divide throughout by 116 to find the value of intermediate inputs required from e.g. agriculture in order to produce 1 unit of manufacturing output as $\frac{10}{116} = 0.086$ units. The same holds for primary inputs such as labour (wages and salaries), where $\frac{20}{116} =$

0.172 units of labour are required for 1 unit of manufacturing output. This defines a 'Manufacturing' 'process' or 'activity', relating the amount of each input required to produce 1 unit of 'Manufacturing' output. For each process fixed technical coefficients are assumed, while it is assumed that just one process exists for each defined industry or sector.[7]

The assumption of fixed technical coefficients for each process implies two things:

(1) constant returns to scale. For instance, to double the output produced we must double the amounts of *all* the inputs used. In the example *two* units of manufacturing output will require $2 \times 0.086 = 0.172$ of intermediate inputs from agriculture and $2 \times 0.172 = 0.344$ units of labour, etc.;

(2) no substitution among inputs is possible—the level of output uniquely determines the level of each input required. Two units of manufacturing output requires 0.344 units of labour with no possibility of substituting capital for labour by adopting a more capital-intensive technique.[8]

Uses of input–output analysis

(1) We have already seen how an input–output table can be used to provide a useful *description* of the industrial and general economic structure of an economy.

(2) A second use is in ensuring *consistency* in macroeconomic plans and projections. Given fixed technical coefficients a planned change in the demand for the products of any *one* industry will require appropriate changes in production elsewhere, which changes may themselves require further changes in the first activity. The repercussions can thus be traced throughout the whole economy, including effects on the labour market, on foreign trade, and on government finances. Clearly the changes in one industry have to be consistent with the calculated changes in the others. Input–output analysis can be used to produce a comprehensive development plan with mutually consistent production levels, resource requirements, and resource availabilities.

(3) The main use in development planning is, of course, for making forecasts or positive *projections of output*. The input–output table can in fact be seen as a set of equations. The basic structure of Table 37.2 can be schematized and abbreviated as in Table 37.3 below. Reading across the first three rows of this table, we obtain the three equations:

$$x_{11} + x_{12} + x_{13} + Y_1 = X_1$$
$$x_{21} + x_{22} + x_{23} + Y_2 = X_2$$
$$x_{31} + x_{32} + x_{33} + Y_3 = X_3$$

which simply state that in the case of sector (1) all

output produced (X_1) is either consumed by other industries as intermediate inputs (x_{11} to x_{13}) or supplied to final demand (Y_1), and similarly for the other two sectors. In these equations the suffixes indicate the sectors involved, so that for instance x_{32} is the amount of output supplied by sector (3) to sector (2). More generally x_{ij} would be output supplied by sector (i) to sector (j). The equations can be written more briefly as:

$$\sum_{j=1}^{3} x_{ij} + Y_i = X_i \quad (i = 1, 2, 3)$$

They can also be expressed in terms of fixed input–output coefficients. Thus x_{11} must be in fixed ratio to X_1. If this ratio is written as a_{11}, then $a_{11} = \dfrac{x_{11}}{X_1}$ or $x_{11} = a_{11}X_1$. More generally we have $x_{ij} = a_{ij}X_i$. If we substitute for the x_{ij} in the previous equation, this gives:

$$\sum_{j=1}^{3} a_{ij}X_i + Y_i = X_i \quad (i = 1, 2, 3)$$

From this we obtain:

$$Y_i = X_i - \sum_{j=1}^{3} a_{ij}X_i \quad (i = 1, 2, 3)$$

which are three equations relating final demands to required total outputs, assuming fixed input–output coefficients. Since the equations hold, in equilibrium, whatever the level of the Y_i, they will hold also for increases in Y_i from say Y_i to Y_i'. If the increases are:

$$\Delta Y_i = Y_i' - Y$$

these can be expressed in terms of the corresponding increases in total output, X_i, as:

$$\Delta Y_i = \Delta X_i - \sum_{j=1}^{3} a_{ij}\Delta X_i \quad (i = 1, 2, 3)$$

This says that the increases in final demands will equal the increases in total outputs less the required increases in intermediate output. Given these equations, which can be reformulated in terms of matrix algebra, it is possible by comparatively simple computational methods to calculate total and intermediate outputs for any set or 'vector' of final demands, or the *change* in sectoral outputs and inputs required by any given vector of *changes* in final demands.

(4) The same basic analysis can be extended for other purposes such as the making of *employment projections*. The row for 'wages and salaries' in Table 37.2 can be converted into numbers employed in each sector, N_i, by dividing by the appropriate wage rate for the sector. If this is divided by the total

output for the sector, we get the labour coefficient:

$$n_i = \frac{N_i}{X_i} \quad (i = 1, 2, \dots n)$$

where N_i is the level of employment in sector i and X_i the total output of sector i, for n sectors. These labour coefficients, as in the case of the a_{ij}, are assumed fixed. *Total* employment in the economy is therefore:

$$N_T = \sum_{i=1}^{n} n_iX_i$$

Since the n_i are constants, the same relationship will hold for *changes* in output and employment, so that:

$$\Delta N_T = \sum_{i=1}^{n} n_i\Delta X_i$$

Since the ΔX_i are a function of the changes in final demands ΔY_i, we can obtain ΔN_T as a direct function of the ΔY_i and predict the change in total employment resulting from any given vector or set of changes in final demand. By splitting employment into demand for different categories of labour, the analysis can be used for *manpower planning*, determining the quantities required of different types and levels of labour for different projections of output mix.

The same sort of analysis can be used to make balance of payments projections and to ensure compatibility of output projections with balance of payments equilibrium. This can be done in a similar way to that for labour, the row for 'imports' being used, instead of that for 'wages and salaries'.

(5) In Chapter 13 we analysed the individual firm's choice of products, showing how linear programming solved the problem of finding an optimum solution. Similar programming techniques of *optimization* can be employed by macroeconomic planners to find the best combination of final products in the economy as a whole. If the main planning objective is to maximize net output (national income), the planners can test

Table 37.3   *A schematized input–output table*

Use of output / Origin of output	Intermediate demands of industrial sectors			Final demand	Total outputs
	(1)	(2)	(3)		
(1)	x_{11}	x_{12}	x_{13}	Y_1	X_1
(2)	x_{21}	x_{22}	x_{23}	Y_2	X_2
(3)	x_{31}	x_{32}	x_{33}	Y_3	X_3
Imports	m_1	m_2	m_3	m_4	M
Wages	w_1	w_2	w_3	—	W
Profits	p_1	p_2	p_3	—	P
Total inputs	X_1	X_2	X_3		

various alternative solutions against the *real* constraints in the economy.[9]

Limitations of input–output analysis

The strict assumptions of given processes and fixed input–output coefficients, however, limit the usefulness of the analysis generally, and in particular for less developed countries. Factor combinations and choice of technique cannot vary, despite possible changes in relative factor prices, and in addition a fixed pattern of consumption demands is assumed, despite the possibility of changes in relative product prices and the effect of different income-elasticities. The assumption of fixed coefficients will be more realistic for narrowly specified processes, that is, in a highly disaggregated model with a large number of separate industries: but such a model needs more data, which are less likely to be available in a less developed country. The assumption of constant returns to scale is also less appropriate in a less developed country where there is generally considerable undercapacity working, due to small markets, and increases in aggregate output permit fuller utilization of social overhead capacity such as roads and power.

Secondly, a good deal of up-to-date statistical information is required for input–output analysis, whereas there is an absence of detailed records of business transactions in developing countries, and only periodic censuses of production. More specifically developing countries usually do not have up-to-date output tables, so that coefficients have to be derived from actual inter-industry transactions at least three to five years prior to their use in the planning exercise,[10] making their use for projections even more risky. Moreover, since the main aim of planning is likely to be the transformation of the economy, and the alteration of its present industrial structure, the use of unadjusted pre-plan technical coefficients is obviously problematic. Some way of adjusting for planned changes is thus required, and though reference can be made to coefficients in other countries at different stages of development, this is not easy.

This is related to the fact, thirdly, that in a less developed country many or most of the 'cells' or boxes in the input–output matrix will be empty, and the aim will be to fill in some of the blanks by establishing new industries. The large number of empty cells (or cells with low values) will be due, as we have seen, to the lack of linkages between industries at an early stage of industrial development, the fact that direct imports constitute a large part of intermediate inputs and of final demand for manufactures, the importance of direct exports of primary products (agricultural and mineral), and the large portion of farm production going directly to meet final consumer demand as 'subsistence' output.

For all these reasons it is to be doubted whether input–output analysis is sufficiently useful in the context of a great many developing countries to warrant statisticians' and planners' expenditure of effort on it. Judicious use of input–output calculations can, however, be a useful aid to planning, particularly for the purpose of applying consistency tests.

The usefulness of development planning

Is development planning worthwhile? Most economists would say that it is: they differ very greatly, however, in their optimism regarding the extent of the benefits to be obtained from such large-scale planning exercises. The benefits stem especially from:

(1) a better evaluation of projects: projects can be seen against a background of anticipated development of the economy as a whole, and of more explicit government policies regarding development; while it is hoped that the establishment of a Planning Office provides the machinery for forcing Ministries to defend projects which they are sponsoring, with the Office in a position to present the final bundle of projects from the full list of alternatives put forward;

(2) the long-term view required by some decisions: for example, planned industrial development may be dependent upon an increased supply of skilled manpower such as engineers, accountants or technicians of different kinds; to provide for this, additional colleges may need to be built or old ones expanded, and staff found for them, which will take a great many years;

(3) the complementary nature of investment decisions: the viability, or worthwhileness, of one project may be conditional upon another project being undertaken. Thus the development of a fishing industry on an inland lake may require the setting-up of a fish-processing plant, as well as special transportation facilities connecting the lake with the major market, or a new garment factory may require increased production of textiles;

(4) the necessity for overall balance in the economy: apart from specific complementary of projects, there is the problem of general complementarity in the sense of the need for general balance in the economy. For example, foreign exchange earnings should be sufficient to cover requirements;

(5) the possibility of using the plan to stimulate effort by the people: by demonstrating possible achievements businessmen may be persuaded to invest with greater confidence, workers to put in greater

efforts towards the fulfilment of plan targets, and consumers to make greater sacrifices to permit the necessary domestic savings to be raised. A plan may thus have an important psychological or attitudinal effect;

(6) the presentation of a case for additional foreign aid: foreign governments and international organizations making grants or loans need to be satisfied that the finance they provide will be put to good use. At the same time private investment will be encouraged by a realistic plan showing the extent of economic growth that is expected to be attained, and by a clear statement of the policies to be pursued in attaining it, assuming expected growth sufficiently great and policies not antagonistic towards private capital;

(7) the achievement of distributional objectives, including regional income distribution and the regional distribution of new economic activity.

The limitations of development planning

Appreciation of the necessity of development planning entails awareness of its limitations.

(1) One of the most basic limitations is the lack of sufficiently accurate or detailed information on the economy as a whole and regarding possible projects. The usefulness of the sophisticated mathematical exercise underlying modern development plans is entirely dependent upon the quality of the statistics 'fed into' the calculations. At the same time failure to meet planned targets is not itself sufficient to condemn attempts at planning: uncertainty is a fact of economic life, and while planning might be expected to reduce uncertainties by avoiding the worst bottlenecks, it cannot be expected to eliminate them altogether.

(2) Development Plans, it has been said, have a 'propensity to dazzle'. But the fact that a plan is comprehensive and mathematically consistent does not in itself ensure that it can be achieved. Consistency can be obtained for *any* hypothetical target rate of economic growth. To make supply of finance consistent with projected requirements, for example, any level of foreign aid could be specified in the plan: this does not ensure that the level of foreign aid specified can be obtained.

(3) As a leading authority has stated, 'the commonest error in development planning is to project an impossibly high rate of growth'.[11] Failure to achieve the target in this case will no doubt be due to the failure of one or more sectors to develop as planned, and this will in turn imply that consistency with other sectors has been lost, resulting in the imbalances that the plan was partly designed to avoid. Moreover, failure to achieve targets may jeopardize future planning by producing a loss of faith by the public.

(4) As we have pointed out, the success of a development programme rests ultimately on the availability of productive projects, which determine the immediate scope for development. The existence of a plan does not produce such projects. Indeed planning is most urgently needed when there is an ample supply of projects among which to choose, rather than at a very early stage of development when the first necessity is to identify worthwhile projects.

(5) The existence of a large private sector means that a large part of the economy is not directly controlled by the Planning Authority. Doubts may be raised about the efficacy of 'indicative planning' and the possibility of influencing the private sector through consultation or exhortation.

(6) Apart from the existence of a private sector, the economy lies outside the control of government in certain other respects. In the first place developing countries are often 'dependent' economies in that (a) they rely heavily on the export of a few commodities, frequently sold on a perfectly competitive world market, (b) they rely to an important extent on foreign enterprise and capital, which is 'mobile' in that it can transfer its resources elsewhere, and (c) substantial foreign aid is required to support a sufficiently ambitious programme. The uncertainty regarding the amount of foreign aid that is likely to be available makes it extremely difficult to plan. Moreover, there is an obvious tendency for the Planning Authorities and Ministries in such a situation to 'cram' the plan with projects in the hope of obtaining finance for them even if they do not anticipate that the full amount of aid they would like will be granted. There is therefore a conflict between producing a realistic plan likely to be closely fulfilled, and using the plan as a means of obtaining the maximum amount of foreign aid. Another factor is that the local market may be insufficient to support new industries so that the country is, as in the East African case, dependent jointly with its neighbours upon a Common Market. This really requires that the separate development plans of the adjoining countries be made consistent with each other, something which is most difficult to achieve in the absence of any supranational planning machinery, as is usually the case.

(7) A development plan is complementary to and not a substitute for good and appropriate *policies*. If for example, inappropriate prices are fixed for the nation's main food crops and export crops, this could in a predominantly agricultural economy have major effects, short-term and long-term, on output and

economic welfare. Yet many African countries have had suspect pricing policies, as we saw in Chapter 12, which would have been relatively easy to remedy, while producing relatively sophisticated development plans. In many fields, the most appropriate policies cannot be devised until a considerable amount of *research* is undertaken. Thus if research were being carried out in each sector of the economy, leading to the specificiation of appropriate policies for each sector, the function of the development plan would simply be to bring these policies together and integrate them. Very often, however, when a five-yearly planning exercise is being carried out, the necessary prior research has not been initiated or completed by the various Ministries and other agencies, so that only sketchy and general policy statements are available for incorporation into the plan. Thus research and planning should go together.[12]

(8) The most crucial limitation of all may be not in the quality of the 'paper' plan itself, the plan document, but in the absence of adequate machinery with which to implement it. The great weakness of many plans in Africa and elsewhere has been the failure to translate the plan on paper into operational planning. In some cases there has been a tendency to believe that the adoption of the plan document will itself result in the achievement of its objectives. A particular weakness of many plans is the absence of the appropriate machinery at the local and regional level, as well as inadequate communication between central and local authorities and agencies. Just because the country is underdeveloped, administration tends to be weak. A major problem in some countries has been widespread corruption, against which constant vigilance is required.

(9) In part related to this last point, affecting the execution of Development Plans, has been the question of political commitment or 'political will' to execute the plan. Crucial elements in the plan may be unpalatable to particular classes or groups, regional or tribal, within the country, who have vested interests in the status quo or are affected by policies proposed in the plan. Thus industrialists with political influence might resist a change away from protective import-substituting policies, urban trade unions may resist the imposition of a strong incomes policy, richer regions may object to regional development policies designed to permit backward regions to 'catch up', and the population as a whole may not be persuaded that it needs to make a sustained sacrifice of present consumption for the sake of future growth as envisaged, perhaps, by the plan.

It should be stressed here that it is one thing for a set of apparently desirable policies to be put together by professional planners and economists, and quite a different matter for them to gain the full backing of the government and politicians, who often directly represent the vested interests and class alignments of the economy,[13] and certainly cannot afford to ignore them. Without political backing, the plan will remain a 'paper plan'. It follows that existing political conditions are a major determinant of possible success in development planning. Planning is both an economic and a *political* exercise.

The 'crisis' in planning

After years of enthusiasm in which eventually a large proportion of developing countries were engaged, following independence, in preparing successive four- or five-year Development Plans, a considerable amount of disillusionment has set in, particularly with medium-term plans and massive plan documents. An early critic was Albert Waterston who stated that:

> An examination of postwar planning history reveals that there have been many more failures than successes in the implementation of development plans.[14]

In similar vein, Sir Arthur Lewis said that:

> Making Development Plans is the most popular activity of the governments of under-developed countries, since the war, and it is almost always their biggest failure.[15]

Later, Faber, Seers, and others talked about the 'crisis' in planning.[16]

Lewis in particular attributed the failure to the acute shortage of competent and incorruptible administrators to carry out all the tasks of state intervention involved, in contrast with their relatively abundant supply in developed countries, including Russia after 1917. Waterston and others have referred to the gap between the professional economists in the Planning Office, often mainly expatriate until recently, concerned with writing paper plans and constructing economic models to ensure internal consistency, and the executive branches of the public sector, executive civil servants and parastatal managers in the Ministries and regions concerned with day-to-day management of the economy as well as physical implementation of investment projects. In these circumstances the planners and 'their' plan can get ignored, while continuous planning of the economy evolves out of the policy decisions and activities of officials and politicians at all levels. A further factor is that, as already mentioned, the development of the economy is likely to be so conditioned by unpredictable factors that five-year plan documents prove to be excessively rigid as the assumptions on which they were based change. As a result of all these factors, governments in several countries, notably Tanzania, are beginning to de-emphasize 'discontinuous' planning at five-year intervals in favour of *continuous* planning more closely tied to the available machinery of development administration in the country.

Regional and district planning

Turning our attention now towards 'secondary level' planning, we have already made the distinction here between sectoral planning and regional (or district) planning. The former is naturally related to *Ministries*, for instance Ministry of Agriculture officials at different levels in the case of agricultural planning, and is based on a hierarchical system emanating from the central Ministry, communicating to officers of the Ministry in the field. It is characterized, in other words, by a vertical organization. In contrast, regional planning is a form of *area* planning, of which the essential feature is the introduction of a spatial element. This generally involves specialist officers in *different* Ministries cooperating on a local area basis across departmental boundaries, and it is characterized by a horizontal organization.

These two aspects, (1) the *area focus* and *spatial element* and (2), the *horizontal organization*, are also points of contrast between national macroeconomic planning and regional planning. As far as the second is concerned, regional planning is distinguished particularly, (3) by the deliberate establishment of *planning machinery at the local level*. In turn this is associated for obvious reasons, (4), with a greater emphasis on on-the-ground *implementation* of plans, as compared to plan formulation. As we have already noted, some five-year national plans have been drafted in a relatively short time by expatriate economists and planners who have not been concerned with the implementation of the plan document and who have seldom remained in the country during the period of implementation. Related again to this, regional planning can be characterized, (5), as a much more *continuous process* as compared to the discontinuous process of macroeconomic plan preparation. A greater emphasis on implementation is inevitable, of course, given that regional planning is one stage nearer to the tertiary level of project planning: but this means not only responsibility for overseeing the implementation of projects but also, (6), responsibility for *project identification*, that is, for identifying projects at the local and regional level to be passed up through the three levels of planning for final approval and incorporation in the macro-plan. This is not to say, of course, that all responsibility for project identification is with local officials rather than central Ministry officials and planners, who in fact will generally identify larger-scale projects in different parts of the country. However, more broadly than simply project identification, (7), regional plans generally attempt more comprehensive *resource assessment*, this being related, (8), to a comprehensive, integrated view of the area's development possibilities. These aspects are discussed further in the next section on 'integrated rural development', which in less developed countries may be an integral part of regional planning.

Regional planning and national planning are interdependent in several respects. Regional plans 'feed' projects and local area programmes into the national plan, as we have just described, but are also dependent on certain decisions and policies which can only be determined centrally. For instance, local agricultural crop priorities must depend on national pricing policies and crop priorities, as prices for major export crops and staple food crops are generally fixed centrally. Local possibilities for industrial development depend especially on what 'national' industries have been allocated to the region, which industries may provide stimulus to other linked activities.

Secondly, the development of regional planning is generally conditional on national plan objectives, particularly the extent to which these emphasize distributional aims as between individuals and regions. Just as in industrialized countries regional planning has emerged especially as a response to problems of welfare and employment in declining or 'lagging' regions, so in less developed countries those countries which have made the greatest efforts in regional planning have been those most concerned with emerging regional income inequalities and regional differences in growth and development.

The administrative unit for this sort of planning is not always the 'region', which is often considered to be too large a unit. Thus Kenya has decided to focus on the District as a more convenient unit and adopt 'District Development Planning', just as Uganda attempted to do in its Second Plan. In general neither regional nor District development planning have been carried very far in African countries up to the present time, and such planning is still at the experimental stage. Tanzania is one country that has made considerable efforts in this direction, as we shall see presently.

Integrated rural development planning

A discussion of development planning in less developed countries would today not be complete without reference to the concept of 'integrated rural development planning'.

This type of planning exercise involves a number of elements. First, it involves planning for a specific geographical *area*, rather than simply planning projects (project appraisal) or planning particular sectors (sectoral planning) cutting across several or all geographical areas within the country. Secondly, and related to this area focus, it may incorporate a diagnosis and *analysis* of the area's development problem(s) and prospects. This generally leads, thirdly, to a component of *physical planning* involving spatial treatment, the identification of ecological and economic zones and sub-areas, the geographical location of recommended activities and, in particular, as a basis for this, resources assessment throughout the area or region. Finally, the last component of an area plan, as already discussed under regional planning, may be found where specific institutions, planning machinery, or techniques of implementation are proposed, and where provision is made for a continuous process of planning at the local area level. These may be supported by specific manpower proposals to permit implementation.

Rural development plans are often described as being 'integrated' when in fact 'comprehensive' would be a much more appropriate and consistent description. Such plans for particular areas may be comprehensive, in the sense of providing complete coverage, in a number of ways: the plans usually cover the whole area, from a spatial point of view; and they may aim to cover all productive activities (all crop possibilities, for example, but also non-agricultural rural activities), as well as productive and social infrastructure, being in effect *multi-sectoral* within the boundaries of the area concerned.

The focus on comprehensive resource assessment does mean that the 'plan' may not be phased in the strict manner of a national four or five-year plan, in which only those projects which are proposed for implementation during the limited plan period are included. In an area development plan the time scale for exploitation of the resources identified may be considered to be an independent matter, and left open. The plan may therefore be comprehensive in covering the entire resource base and not simply projects for immediate implementation.

The multi-sectoral nature of the plan, and the ingredient of comprehensive resource assessment, generally mean that plan formulation has to be a multi-disciplinary exercise—involving not only general and agricultural economists but engineers, agronomists, soil scientists, and others—and plan implementation must involve a multi-agency effort.

A final element of comprehensiveness occurs where one objective is to secure external funding for the area or regional plan, where it is considered that the building-up of a complete picture of possible development in the area increases its attractiveness for donors. In Tanzania, where increasing emphasis has been placed since the mid-1970s on regional

planning, potential bilateral and multilateral donors, such as the German Federal Republic and the World Bank, respectively, have been encouraged to assist directly in the formulation of regional plans, and later in their implementation and *funding*.

Plans may be comprehensive in the above senses without being 'integrated'. The point of having an 'integrated' plan would exist if there were some advantage in *combining* several activities or components: if there were incomplete divisibility in the sense that particular activities could not just as well be carried out independently of each other. However an area plan which is comprehensive as described above could still be quite divisible, with separate segments capable of being implemented largely independently of the others.

The closest form of interdependence is where two projects depend directly on each other, as when, say, the exploitation of iron ore requires the exploitation of an adjacent source of coal. Somewhat weaker interdependence exists between the production base as a whole and supporting productive infrastructure. There is generally a wide choice available here as to the degree of infrastructural support which needs to be provided. For example, the expansion of agricultural production may depend on the provision of additional 'feeder' roads to facilitate the marketing of the produce. But there may be considerable choice regarding the degree of improvement in communications required. Finally, integrated plans usually include provision for additional social services such as health and education, if only to maintain the level of social service expenditure per head if population is expected to expand along with the expansion of production: and indeed the goal of increasing the level of economic welfare in an area would require increasing expenditure on social services *more* than in proportion to population. But this interdependence between production plans and supporting *social* infrastructure will be even less strong, since the extra social spending is something which is desirable rather than a required condition of increased output.

It follows from our definitions that national macroeconomic plans are 'integrated' to an important extent, in that components of the plan are highly interdependent: public sector plans will depend on adequate government revenue being raised from taxation, this in turn depending on expansion of the private sector; consumption and investment plans will depend on the availability of foreign exchange, and therefore on the accuracy of foreign earnings projections, and so on. This is most obvious in a multi-sector plan based upon input–output analysis, but applies also to one based on a simple aggregate growth model incorporating the main aggregates, C, I, G, X, and M. An area rural development plan may be less integrated, in fact, if the area is small and fairly homogeneous, such as an area specializing in the production of coffee for export. Here the main activity of coffee growing would depend much more on external factors, particularly the coffee price, than on other activities in the area.

However, with the increasing emphasis on rural development in the programmes of most developing countries, there has been more and more stress on 'integrated rural development planning' with perhaps more stress on a comprehensive approach to the development of an area than on genuinely interdependent activities. Integrated rural development planning may be pursued in any *area* planning exercise, either regional or district level planning as discussed above, or, frequently, when a large river basin development study is being carried out or a large-scale irrigation scheme of the Gezira or Volta River type. A well-known example of this approach to rural development which met with partial success is Kenya's Special Rural Development Programme.[17]

The evolution of development planning in Eastern Africa

Development planning in most African countries has evolved over the post-war period from what were essentially public sector programmes for capital expenditure. The original Ten-Year Development Programmes initiated by the British Colonial Office at the end of the war in 1945 were of this type: they aimed at providing especially the social overheads of development, the basic infrastructure for both private sector activity and public services. The need to insulate capital expenditure from year-to-year fluctuations in ordinary recurrent revenue was an important element in separating the so-called Development Account Expenditure from the ordinary recurrent budget. In Uganda, Ghana, and Nigeria, the increasing availability of Marketing Board funds and export tax receipts in the 1950s allowed the capital expenditure to extend into various large-scale projects. In countries such as Kenya without large current revenue surpluses derived from peasant agriculture the financing of development projects was more difficult. The most important feature of such pre-independence programmes, however, was their *limited scale*, reflecting dependence on the willingness of a single colonial power to expend funds, compared to the later macroeconomic plans of post-independence countries, reflecting the necessarily greater political commitment of national governments and their access to a wider range of sources of overseas aid. Apart from other colonial policies obstructing development, limited spending during colonial times on educational provision, capital and recurrent, left most African countries seriously deficient in trained manpower of all kinds, at the time of independence.

Early application of planning in Uganda

Despite this, development planning in Uganda, especially, was quite 'comprehensive' at an early postwar stage. Comprehensive planning in Eastern Africa might be said to have begun with Uganda's Ten-Year Development Plan, 1946–56, drawn up by Professor E. B. Worthington, a biologist, and enthusiastically supported by the then Governor Sir John Hall. A major advantage, as already suggested, was the existence of financial surpluses which could be 'creamed off' through the Marketing Boards, from high-priced export crops grown by peasants. Uganda had in fact, until the late 1950s, one of the highest savings ratios ever recorded for a poor country. Thus finance was, for a limited period, not the main constraint on development, and was available without substantial foreign aid transfers. Under the strong personal influence of Sir John Hall, moreover, the decision was taken to emphasize expenditure on economic services and economic development, rather than social services (which services, particularly education, received more emphasis under the next Governor, Sir Andrew Cohen). In particular, relatively 'radical' decisions were taken in the early 1950s to invest in the massive Owen Falls hydro-electricity scheme at Jinja, to go for industrialization, based on this, through an expanding industrial complex at Jinja, and, although relying mainly on private investment, to establish at an early stage a National Development Corporation, the UDC, to act as a vehicle for investment in industry (and commercial agriculture) as we described in Chapter 18. This deliberate policy was adopted well ahead of Kenya, though the geographical advantages of Kenya and the landlocked nature of the Ugandan economy nevertheless later biased industrial development in East Africa heavily in favour of the former.

The subsequent First Five-Year Development Plan, 1961–2 to 1965–6, and the Second Five Year Plan, 1966–71,[18] were both well-constructed, comprehensive macroeconomic development plans, attempting to plan total resources with detailed output targets and investment requirements, without having a great deal of impact on the economy. In part, this may be put down to the negative effect on the economy of external factors, particularly affecting coffee revenues, but also, perhaps, to the heavy involvement of expatriate planners in the exercise, and the failure to secure participation in the development effort at the regional and district level, a fault of many development plans, already commented upon above.

From macroeconomic to decentralized planning in Tanzania

Tanzania's planning experience is interesting from two particular points of view. First, although it produced two fairly standard comprehensive plans following independence, the most fundamental decisions of development policy were taken right *outside* the framework of the Five-Year Plans. Secondly, and only partly within the context of these plans, Tanzania is perhaps the country which has gone furthest so far in Africa in developing a decentralized system of regional planning. Both aspects have reduced the importance of the large Five-Year Plan document as the focus of planning activity in Tanzania.

Tanzania's first Five-Year Plan

The First Plan was a comprehensive macroeconomic plan, putting forward a consistent set of objectives and spelling out the corresponding financial, manpower organization, and policy measures necessary for its implementation as the first phase of a longer-term perspective plan to meet specified targets by 1980.[19] The planners diagnosed Tanzania's economic backwardness as stemming from 'structural deficiencies in economic and social fields rather than any real lack of potential within either of them', and adopted a strategy of 'structural transformation'. Apart from this strategy, the main features of the plan might be said to have been the relatively high-targeted rates of growth; the emphasis on industrial development; and, in order to achieve these, a substantially increased rate of aggregate investment and dependence for finance of the plan on outside sources.

Table 37.4 illustrates the extent of structural transformation anticipated. This shows that in addition to

setting a high overall rate of growth of GDP of 6.7 per cent, the First Plan envisaged a great reduction in the relative size of the subsistence sector, from about one-third of GDP in 1960–2 to only 14 per cent by 1980, a decline of more than one-half in less than 20 years. The statistical problem associated with estimates of subsistence output renders such comparisons very difficult. Nevertheless, the planned targets for monetization of the economy for 1970 and 1980 were very ambitious.[20] Primary production (subsistence plus monetized rural output plus mining) was planned to fall from 60 per cent of GDP in 1960–2 to 50 per cent, and 39 per cent by 1980.[21]

At the same time, manufacturing was planned to grow at an annual rate of nearly 15 per cent to 1970 and thereafter at 13 per cent, twice the overall average for GDP as a whole. Thus the planned contribution of all secondary industry was to increase from 13 to 19 per cent of GDP by 1970 and then to as much as 27 per cent by 1980. Investment plans were made accordingly, 20 per cent of proposed capital formation being for secondary industry (and 17 per cent for housing and township development) compared to only 10 per cent for agriculture.

In the event, as can be seen from the fourth column of Table 37.4, the share of secondary activities increased only marginally from 13 per cent in 1960–2 to 15 per cent in 1970. Subsistence output was still estimated at 29 per cent, only a slight reduction from 32 per cent. Rapid structural transformation in countries such as Tanzania was clearly much more difficult to achieve than the planners envisaged.

Indeed, within the first two years of the First Plan, it became necessary to reappraise both its targets and machinery of implementation. Within a year of its publication, by early 1965 according to one source, it was evident that the plan was not being followed, and could not be followed, as a guide to action. Most planning activity stopped and did not resume until

Table 37.4   *Planned change in the structure of Tanzania's GDP*

Sectoral contribution to GDP (per cent)	(1) 1960–2	(2) First Plan 1970	(3) targets 1980	(4) 1970	(5) Second Plan 1973–4	(6) targets 1968–9/73–4 Growth rate
	(actual)	(planned)	(planned)	(actual)	(planned)	(planned)
Subsistence	32	22	14	29	22	3
Other rural & mining	28	28	25	20	26	7
Secondary	13	19	27	15	15	12
Tertiary	27	31	34	36	37	6.5
Total GDP	100	100	100	100	100	6.5

SOURCES: *Five-Year Development Plan, 1964–1969*, Vol. I, p. 11; *Second Five-Year Plan, 1969–74*, Vol. I, p. 203, and *Economic Survey, 1971–72*, p. 6

1966.[22] In 1968, Helleiner observed that the plan had had relatively little influence on investment allocations or on the rate of economic progress.[23] Taking an example, he showed that in the 1967-8 estimates of development expenditure for the Ministry of Agriculture and Cooperatives, 49 per cent of the total expenditure in Group A (those for which funds were available), and 68 per cent of those in Group B, were listed under headings 'not even appearing *at all*' in the Development Plan. And yet according to Helleiner 'the Tanzanian plan was a model of everything that it was believed by planners and economists at the time a development plan should be. It was comprehensive in its coverage, it included a longer-term perspective, and it was reasonably specific about its targets.'[24]

The reasons for the failure of the plan, and for the failure of earlier attempts at comprehensive planning in less developed countries, have been analysed by E. Bevan Waide.[25] First, there may be external economic factors outside the control of national planners: in Tanzania's case in 1964-5 the expected growth in export earnings was retarded by a fall in prices for cotton, coffee, and sisal, the three main exports, *and* by a drought which adversely affected the volume of output.

Secondly, the inflow of private investment capital and official aid from overseas failed to match its planned contribution to total capital formation. It was anticipated in the plan that about 80 per cent of Tanzanian central government and government enterprise investment was to be financed from abroad, and just over half of the country's total investment to be financed from overseas.[26] This was much too optimistic. In the event, foreign-financed investment amounted to only 25 per cent rather than 50 per cent of total Tanzanian investment.

Thirdly, there was the already discussed gap in communication between the planners who produced the plan document and the officials who were charged with implementing the plan and the mass of the people who participate in it. The plan had been drawn up, in fact, by a team of French planners, who then departed: while British and West German technical assistance experts were also withdrawn in 1965-6 following political disputes between the donors and Tanzania. Although Tanzania had made more use than most countries hitherto of its political party, TANU, as an extension agent for development, it was stated subsequently that TANU 'did not provide a body of detailed proposals and did not develop a prior set of firm socio-political ideological commitments', so that there was 'a dangerously low level of national consciousness of the plan and of its relevance to national aspirations, for example in the lower ranks of the civil service, the party, and the party-related mass movements.'[27] This situation had changed to a considerable extent during the time of preparation of the Second Plan, and most developments in planning since that time have involved a substantially increased degree of participation.

As can be seen from the last three columns of Table 37.4, the industrialization goals of the Second Five-Year Plan[28] were more modest, the targeted growth rate for secondary industry only just exceeding that for GDP and its share of GDP in 1973-4 remaining at 15 per cent. The plan's emphasis on rural development is reflected in a relatively ambitious growth rate (for a large monetary sector) of 7 per cent and a share of GDP increasing to 26 per cent.

Development choices made outside the plan

The most fundamental decisions made in Tanzania in respect of the economy and of development strategy were, however, not made within the framework of either of these two macroeconomic plans. The most crucial was the Arusha Declaration of 1967 which laid down a definite commitment to a policy of 'Socialism and Self-Reliance', and it is this rather than the Development Plan which provided the framework for subsequent development though the Second Plan did, of course, reflect the Declaration. From its statement of the need to control the 'commanding heights of the economy' followed the subsequent extension of public control, including the nationalization of the banking system, the expansion of industry under a national development corporation, the state take-over of sisal estates, and the control of the import trade, wholesale trade, and sections of the retail trade.

A second major feature of Tanzanian development policy, related to the above, and also initiated outside a specific Development Plan, was that of rural socialism in the form of ujamaa villages, described earlier in Chapter 10.

The third major aspect, that of regional planning and regional emphasis, was a significant feature of the Second Five-Year Plan, 1969-74. It was, however, carried very much further in a decision of 1971-2, midway through this plan, to decentralize the entire system of government and to transfer a substantial amount of power and delegate decision-making to the Regions. Regional plans for particular regions have since been prepared within this new structure of administrative responsibility.

Regional planning in Tanzania

There are a number of reasons why Tanzania appears to have shown a much greater awareness of the necessity for regional planning than other African countries. First of all, the problems of regional development appeared here in a starker form. The country is vast in size, roughly equal for example to the combined area of France, Belgium, and Italy. The sheer size of Tanzania would make it difficult to treat the country as a single unit: but, secondly, the underdeveloped transportation system at the time of independence further divided the country. Moreover the different regions of Tanzania vary enormously in factor endowment—in climate and soils, water supply, density of population, and suitability for cash crops—so that economic problems and solutions, and development possibilities, vary widely from region to region. Another possible factor was that the general lack of development at the time of independence made it easier, starting as it were from scratch, to view all the regions together. A more important factor, however, was the strongly socialist philosophy of the government with regional planning stemming in large part from egalitarian objectives. This has been reinforced by the related focus on rural development as means of laying the foundation for a subsequent 'leap forward'.

We cannot describe Tanzanian policies in respect of regional development in full here.[29] The First Five-Year Plan was virtually devoid of regional goals and concentrated almost entirely on macroeconomic and sectoral objectives. The elements of regional policy listed below are illustrative, however, of the efforts made since:

(1) As long ago as 1967 a Regional Development Fund was established, amounting to one million shillings per annum for each Region, to be spent largely at the discretion of the regional authorities. While the finance involved was not large, this did represent an attempt to draw regional authorities further into the planning process and was a first step towards the subsequent decentralization of government.

(2) A second interesting step was the appointment in 1968 of Regional Economic Secretaries—trained (though junior) economists—to the Regions with a view to coordinating decision-making at the regional level and providing some economic advice. The significant point here is that the Secretaries were officers of the central planning ministry, the Ministry of Economic Affairs and Development Planning. The fact that they were therefore in some sense agents of the planning ministry in the regions indicates that this was a distinct move in the direction of regional planning and towards introducing a spatial element into the national macroeconomic plan.

(3) Apart from the general emphasis on rural development already mentioned, there was the specific attempt to develop non-agricultural activities in the regions. The National Small Industries Corporation (discussed in Chapter 23) was established in 1968 to develop rural industries and in 1971 the decision was taken to establish District Development Corporations in every district of Tanzania to initiate projects and act as catalysts for investment at the local level in much the same way as the National Development Corporation (NDC) was expected to do at the national level. These have not, in fact, proved very successful but remain in existence and are indicative of a desire to bring development planning down to the local level.

(4) Two strategic decisions made in respect of infrastructural investment have considerable significance for regional development in the long term. The first of these, incorporated in the Second Plan, involved the building of a tarmacadam road, the Tanzam Highway, and railway, the TAZARA, from Dar es Salaam through Southern Tanzania to Zambia. These two will serve to integrate the southern part of the country, previously difficult to reach during the rains, with the rest. The second decision, taken later, was to shift the Tanzanian capital from the main town and port at the coast, Dar es Salaam, to Dodoma, centrally situated in Tanzania, but located within a relatively undeveloped part of the country.

(5) A particular feature of the Second Five-Year Plan were the proposals for urban development and industrial location. Eight towns were selected, in addition to Dar es Salaam, for development as 'growth poles': Arusha/Moshi[30] and Mwanza (which were already growing fast, without assistance), Tanga (which was stagnant as a result of a decline in the surrounding sisal estates, but which had a substantial population and established urban and port facilities), Mbeya and Mtwara (as part of an attempt to develop the high potential of the south), and Morogoro, Dodoma, and Tabora (to develop the 'empty' centre of the country). The concept of growth poles was discussed in Chapter 22. A strong industrial location policy would allocate major new enterprises among the proposed centres to offer linkages for further industrial development and provide stimulus to agricultural development in the surrounding area. The size of the planned redirection of industry and urban growth was considerable. Dar es Salaam's growth was to be cut from 11 per cent to 7 per cent over the plan period, and to under 6 per cent by 1974. Mbeya and Tanga were planned to grow at double their previous rates, 12 and 10 per cent respectively over the period 1970–4, compared to 6 and 5 per cent for 1967–70. Projections for Dodoma were overtaken by the later decision to make it the capital.

(6) A significant step taken in the Second Plan was the publication of a third, regional volume. The regions had not each themselves produced a regional component of the overall plan, since they would have

lacked the necessary organization structure and man-power at the time. Hence the national plan was not based on individual regional plans, but rather the reverse: the regional volume merely decomposed the national plan into regional parts, providing an assembly of proposed regional expenditures taken from the first volume. Nevertheless, the publication of a specific regional volume is itself of some significance. The publication of data and proposals on a regional basis provides a useful guide to workers in the region and makes a political contribution in permitting people in the region to feel that a specific 'piece' of the plan belongs to them. Most important, the volume presented in tabular form a number of indicators of welfare permitting regional comparisons: regional income estimates, school enrolment figures, population-to-doctor and population-to-hospital bed ratios, and so on, as well as regional comparisons of investment and recurrent expenditures per head of population. The mere publication of such data increases the pressures on government to correct divergences and to prevent their widening.

(7) As already mentioned the decision to decentralize the system of government, taken in 1971–2, was of fundamental importance for regional planning and development planning generally in Tanzania. At the same time as the central planning ministry, the Ministry of Economic Affairs and Development Planning, was re-absorbed into the Ministry of Finance, the Prime Minister's Office, located in Dodoma, was placed at the apex of a regional system of government in which the powers and influence of Regional Commissioners were considerably strengthened, and they were made responsible for the coordination of regional planning efforts. Subsequently a number of regions have produced separate regional plans. That for Iringa Region, for example, appeared in two substantial volumes, each as large as many national plans.[31]

Development policies in Malawi

While Tanzania illustrates the case of a country changing its emphasis from centralized comprehensive macroeconomic plans to decentralized planning and implementation, Malawi is a smaller country which never emphasized comprehensive planning, but always concentrated on projects and policies.

In 1962 Malawi's development priorities were 'read' as being (a) to develop basic social infrastructure of transport facilities, (b) to develop secondary and tertiary education, to fill an enormous gap in trained manpower and permit localization after independence, and (c) to improve the low level of productivity in peasant agriculture. The three-year Development Plan, 1962–5, drawn up before the end of Federation in 1963, was basically a public sector plan, supported by some macroeconomic analysis of the economy and its development needs and prospects. The figure of £19 millions allocated for public investment expenditure was calculated in part with reference to the cross-country study of public expenditure patterns made by A. Martin and W. Arthur Lewis.[32] We can make use, as a general illustrative example, of the calculation made for the planned target for per capita income growth of 3.7 per cent. The growth rate for national income, G_Y, was calculated with a capital–output ratio of 2.5 and savings ratio of just under 15 per cent to be:

$$G_Y = \frac{s}{C} = \frac{14.7}{2.5} = 5.9\%$$

Growth of income *per head*, $G_{Y/P}$, is the difference between this and annual population increase, G_P, so that:

$$G_{Y/P} = G_Y - G_P = 5.9 - 2.2 = 3.7\%$$

This required investment ratio meant a gross capital formation over the three years of some £33 millions, including £9 millions by the private sector. In the event, dissolution of Federation at the end of 1963 and the need to use more foreign aid to maintain recurrent budget expenditure meant (a) a lower rate of development spending in the three years than planned; and (b) a recasting of development priorities in a new development programme.

A new Development Plan for 1965–9 was therefore drafted, and had the same objectives of (1) improving the internal road system and (2) expanding post-primary education facilities, but was based on (3) expanding agricultural production, both for exports and to feed a comparatively densely population nation, expanding at around $2\frac{1}{2}$ per cent per annum, and (4) stimulating industrial development by the private parastatal sector through the establishment of a development corporation. The plan centred on an ambitious public sector investment programme comprising a large 'shopping list' of projects, almost all for external aid, amounting to £44 millions. This involved raising the annual rate of Development Account spending from a little under £3 millions during the $2\frac{1}{2}$ years from mid-1962 to end-1964 to an annual rate averaging nearly £9 millions. The difficulty was likely to be, first, the availability of finance, hardly discussed in the document, and secondly the country's 'absorptive capacity' to administer and implement the physical construction and project management involved.

Since the United Kingdom was at that time Malawi's main aid donor, having undertaken to finance by annual grants the Recurrent Budget deficit as well as to provide aid on Development Account, it sent an Economic Mission in mid-1965 to scrutinize the new plan. Its report, the *Report of an Economic Mission to Malawi, July–August, 1965*, was a Development Plan document produced by a team which included four experienced economists. It envisaged a four-year investment programme by the central government of £30 millions for 1966–9, somewhat lower than that in the Development Plan. There was also a conflict of objectives, the Mission regarding certain major infrastructural projects, particularly the proposed new capital at Lilongwe, as carrying a much lower economic priority in view of financial constraints at the time.

Following the Mission, the government established a new Ministry of Development and Planning to compile a three-year 'rolling' Development Programme, 1968–70. This is an interesting example of this more flexible approach to planning which was coming into vogue about that time. In this case the first year of the rolling programme contained firm figures of Expenditure Estimates on Development Account approved by Parliament and available as monies voted to spending Ministries, with the second and later years of the programme giving preliminary indications of further expenditure on the same and additional projects. Such a programme rolls forward so that as the first year, say, 1968, comes to an end an additional plan year, 1971, is added, in continuous fashion. This procedure has been followed in Malawi since 1968. It reconciles the need to plan for the most distant future, and obtain the necessary finance, with the budgetary discipline of only including in the current year expenditure for which finance is assured. Of course, few major projects can be completed in one fiscal year, and the Development Account Estimates will show each year its total estimated cost as well as its phasing within the three years. But the procedure is very flexible in that new projects can more easily be included in the plan.

Since 1965 Malawi has in fact not published a conventional Development Plan document. It has been the government's view that a pragmatic and practical approach to both project planning and policy formulation might be inhibited by documents which are liable to be out of date by the time they are published. During the late 1960s, therefore, economic planning in Malawi followed a partial, sector-by-sector approach. Individual Ministries and public corporations prepared sector or enterprise plans, and selected projects for inclusion, which could then be evaluated in terms of costs and benefits. Development planning was thus largely concerned with the priority listing of projects.

The main macroeconomic aggregates like income, investment, and exports were, of course, also calculated for periods of three to four years, this against the background of a ten-year perspective period. This was published in 1971 as the *Statement of Development Policies, 1971–80*, the title deliberately emphasizing *policies* rather than *plans*. Although not detailed in the document the plan involved various consistency tests. Given specified sources of national and external saving, possible rates of investment and income growth were projected, using the usual Harrod–Domar type of calculation. Overall consistency between the main components of aggregate demand and the output of the main sectors was provided by checking against very simplified input–output tables for main sectors only for certain years covered by the development period to 1980. The emphasis was still largely on project and sectoral plans, and the *Statement of Development Policies* constituted an example of 'planning up' from project and sector level to a comprehensive macroeconomic plan.[33]

An input–output approach to planning in Zambia

Dudley Seers pioneered the use of a *modified* input–output system when advising the government of Zambia in drawing up its First National Four-Year Development Plan, 1966–70.[34] Zambia had previously had a public sector Development Programme, 1947–56, continued into the Federation period in a new plan for 1957–61 and another for 1961–5, which included a rural development programme. These plans were, however, all influenced by the desire to develop the copper-mining industry, which could yield substantial profits, and to encourage large-scale European farming and commerce. A Transitional Development Plan was evolved to cover the period January 1965 to June 1966, before the First National Development Plan was initiated. But it is this plan, and specifically its relatively 'sophisticated' input–output approach, which is particularly interesting.

Dudley Seers modified the normal layout of the input–output table to suit the special features and development needs of Zambia. These were (1) the dominant position of the copper-mining industry in all its aspects (as discussed earlier); (2) the need to separate African and non-African sources of income by industry, together with the consumption expenditures of the two groups, separate identification of these being particularly important for planning in the transition following independence; and (3) concern with fiscal and balance of payments implications of expanding investment, particularly in a country like Zambia, dependent on world copper prices for export proceeds and dependent on imported supplies of most goods. Seers and his UN Economic Mission produced projections to 1970 in the form of quite detailed input–output tables in a matter of four months in 1963. But their work was a prominent and original feature of the First National Development Plan, 1966–70, and the plan was able to specify a number of major objectives which had already been tested against Seers's input–output projections.

The main *strategy* in the plan was diversification, to reduce dependence on copper, this to be achieved by establishing import-replacing manufacture of consumer goods.[35] The plan envisaged a further expansion of mining output (and export earnings) but only of some 15 per cent over the four years. On the other hand, commercial farming and manufacturing were to double, as was construction, while 'government services' were to grow by about 50 per cent.[36] The overall growth of GDP was to be an ambitious 37 per cent, or nearly 8 per cent per annum. The aim was that the mining sector would decline from some 43 per cent of GDP in 1965 to about 36 per cent in 1970. Diversification of the economy away from min-

ing remains the greatest need in Zambia.

Another problem in Zambia, associated with the dominance of copper and the highly capital-intensive nature of this industry, as well as with the limited development of commercial and smallholder agriculture, is the restricted level of formal sector employment available. A particular *target* in the plan was therefore the creation of an additional 100,000 paid jobs, an increase of 40 per cent over 1965. Under the stimulus of a doubling in the level of gross fixed capital formation between 1965 and 1970, construction output would also double, providing the largest scope for paid employment outside the service sectors: 27,000 extra jobs were expected in construction by 1970, a rise of 75 per cent on 1965.

The Second National Development Plan 1972–6, published at the end of 1971,[37] includes an evaluation of the First Plan, which appears to have achieved many of its targets. Wage employment increased by 77,000 jobs, from 313,000 in June 1966, to 390,000 in December 1970, not so far short of the ambitious target of 407,000.

Questions on Chapter 36

1. Discuss the main levels of development planning and types of Development Plan. How are they related?
2. What are the most important elements in a Development Plan?
3. Distinguish between Annual Plans and Government Budgets; partial plans and comprehensive plans, indicative planning and socialist planning.
4. 'To plan is to choose.' What are the main strategic choices involved in comprehensive development plans?
5. Discuss the use of the Harrod–Domar equation in development planning. What assumptions limit its usefulness?
6. What is meant by saying that an input output table represents a set of accounts for transactions in an economy? How is it related to national income accounts? Discuss with reference to a hypothetical table.
7. Discuss the main purposes of input–output analysis as a planning technique.
8. What are the main assumptions of input output analysis? How realistic are these in the context of underdeveloped

countries? What other limitations exist on its use?
9. What do you think will be the main differences in appearance in an input–output table for an industrialized country and for a country in the early stages of industrialization?
10. Discuss the use and limitations of National Development Plans.
11. What led to the 'crisis' in planning? How have attitudes to four- or five-year plan documents altered?
12. What are the distinguishing features of regional and district planning in the context of less developed countries?
13. '"Integrated" rural development plans are often better described as comprehensive rather than integrated.' Discuss.
14. 'Plans are less important than policies.' Discuss, with special reference to the Eastern African experience.
15. Discuss the evolution of development planning in Tanzania since independence.
16. Compare post-war development planning in Tanzania and Malawi.

Notes

[1] *Work for Progress, Uganda's Second Five-Year Plan, 1966–1971*, Government Printer, Entebbe, 1966.

[2] The British economist, Roy Harrod, and American economist, Evsey D. Domar, produced similar models at about the same time and are jointly credited with this important extension of the static Keynesian model.

[3] This assumes that businessmen's requirements are closely determined by technological considerations. In practice they might not always want to expand capacity in proportion to output. For example if they thought that an increase in demand and output might prove to be only temporary, they might prefer to 'manage' with the equipment they have already, rather than to expand capacity.

[4] Republic of Zambia, *National Accounts, 1964–65 and Input–Output Table, 1965*. Central Statistical Office, Lusaka, November, 1966. The table is discussed again presently in the section on development planning in Zambia.

[5] Some versions of an input–output table show this quadrant as an empty 'box' if there are no such direct imports and duties; while others may show direct sales of factor services like domestic servants working in households or civil servants working for the government as additional elements of final demand.

[6] In fact most of the cells are empty for inter-manufacturing transactions, and also for the transactions between manufacturing and service activities.

[7] However a sector may be defined narrowly or broadly according to the degree of disaggregation. Thus we may define a broad 'engineering industry' or a number of different types of engineering industry each represented as a separate process.

[8] However an extension of the input–output approach, activity analysis, applies linear programming to select optimum combinations of activities or processes, including alternative processes or techniques for a particular industry.

[9] See W. A. Lewis, *Development Planning*, Allen & Unwin, 1966, pp. 94–210; M. P. Todaro, *Development Planning: Models and Methods*, Oxford University Press, Nairobi, 1971, pp. 87–101, and B. Van Arkadie and C. R. Frank, *Economic Accounting and Development Planning*, Oxford University Press, Nairobi, 1966.

[10] Dudley Seers, who used a 1965 input–output table in helping to prepare projections for Zambia's First National Four-Year Development Plan (as we discuss in a later section) did not, in 1963, have the data reproduced in Table 37.2, but worked with data for 1961 which he projected for 1965 at 1961 prices and then for 1970, introducing estimated wage and price changes between 1961 and 1965.

[11] Lewis, op. cit., p. 150.

[12] See I. Livingstone, 'The Relation Between Research and Planning in Development,' *Uganda Economic Journal*, Vol. 1, No. 1, December 1971.

[13] Here we should not forget the 'military class' in a number of countries.

[14] Albert Waterston, *Development Planning: Lessons of Experience*, Johns Hopkins University Press, 1965, p. 293.

[15] W. Arthur Lewis, Aggrey-Guggisberg Lecture, University of Ghana, 1968.

[16] Mike Faber and Dudley Seers (eds), *The Crisis in Planning*, Chatto & Windus, 1972, 2 vols.

[17] For a description and assessment, see I. Livingstone, 'Experimentation in Rural Development: Kenya's Special Rural Development Programme', *Agricultural Administration*, Vol. 3, No. 3, July 1976.

[18] *Work for Progress, Uganda's Second Five-Year Plan, 1966–1971*, Government Printer, Entebbe, 1966.

[19] The United Republic of Tanganyika and Zanzibar, *Tanganyika Five-Year Plan for Economic and Social Development, 1st July, 1964–30th June, 1969*.

[20] They assumed that the population increase would only be 2.1 per cent per annum between 1962 and 1970, and 2.3 per cent from 1970 to 1980, so that the resources required for 'own-consumption' would not need to expand very much. Subsistence output was projected to grow at the same rate as population until 1970 and at a slower 2 per cent rate from then until 1980.

[21] Some of this fall would be involuntary, however, as diamond deposits in Central Tanzania were expected to become depleted and output diminish over time.

[22] E. Bevan Waide, 'Planning and Annual Planning', in *Planning in Tanzania* (A. H. Rweyemamu and B. U. Mwansaru, eds), East African Literature Bureau, 1974.

[23] G. K. Helleiner, 'Socialism, Self-Reliance and the Second Plan', *ERB Paper* 68.9, Economic Research Bureau, Dar es Salaam, April 1968, p. 3.

[24] G. K. Helleiner, op. cit., p. 4.

[25] E. Bevan Waide, op. cit.

[26] Helleiner points out that this to some extent exaggerates Tanzania's planned dependence on foreign finance. The foreign share of *total* expenditure (capital *and* recurrent) by central government was planned to be only 27 per cent, about average for development plans around that time.

[27] United Republic of Tanzania, *Tanzania Second Year-Plan for Economic and Social Development, 1st July, 1969–30th June, 1974*.

[28] R. H. Green, 'Four African Development Plans, Ghana, Kenya, Nigeria and Tanzania', *Journal of Modern African Studies*, Vol. 3, No. 2, 1965, pp. 252–4.

[29] For more detail, see R. G. Saylor and I. Livingstone, 'Regional Planning in Tanzania', in *African Review*, Vol. 1, No. 2, 1971, pp. 53–75.

[30] Arusha and Moshi are separated by about 40 miles of fast tarmac road and may be treated as one industrial centre.

[31] *Iringa Region Tanzania—Integrated Rural Development Proposals for the Third Five-Year Plan, 1976–81*, Vols I and II, Tanzania Rural Development Bank Project URT/71/004, FAO, 1976.

[32] These patterns were discussed in the last chapter.

[33] This 'planning up' is to be distinguished, however, from 'planning up' from a spatially decentralized system of regional or district planning which has always been comparatively neglected in Malawi.

[34] See Dudley Seers, 'The Use of a Modified Input–Output System for an Economic Programme in Zambia', in Irma Adelman and Erik Thorbecke (eds), *The Theory and Design of Economic Development*, Johns Hopkins University Press, Baltimore, 1966.

[35] For a useful summary of the aims of this Plan, see *Zambia's Plan at Work 1966–70*, Office of National Development and Planning.

[36] We refer here to the sectors in the input–output table.

[37] *Second National Development Plan, January, 1972–December 1976*, Ministry of Development Planning and National Guidance, Lusaka, December 1971.

Index

Only the more significant references to persons, organizations and countries have been indexed (the latter as subheadings under the relevant topic). East Africa and Eastern Africa have been abbreviated E.A. Organizations have been entered under the full version of their names followed by the abbreviated form (in brackets).